POLITICAL

SYSTEMS

of the WORLD

POLITICAL

SYSTEMS

---

of the WORLD

J DENIS DERBYSHIRE
IAN DERBYSHIRE

St. Martin's Press
New York

First edition published 1989 by W & R Chambers
Second edition (revised and expanded) published in the
United Kingdom 1996 by Helicon Publishing Ltd

© J Denis Derbyshire & Ian Derbyshire 1996

Maps copyright © Helicon Publishing Ltd 1996

St. Martin's Press, Scholarly and Reference Division,
175 Fifth Avenue, New York, N.Y. 10010

First published in the United States of America in 1996

Printed in the United Kingdom

Library of Congress Cataloging-in-Publication Data applied for.

ISBN: 0-312-16172-2

Papers used in this book are natural recyclable products made
from wood grown in sustainable forests. The manfacturing
processes of both raw materials and paper conform to the
environmental regulations of the country of origin.

Managing Editor
Denise Dresner

Project Editor
Shereen Karmali

Text Editor
Edith Summerhayes

Proofreaders
Avril Cridlan
Kate O'Leary
Catherine Thompson

Design/make-up
Roger Walker/Graham Harmer

Contents

Part II: Political Systems of the World's Nation-states

Part III: Towards One World

Chapter 8 The Relics of Empire – Colonies, Dependencies and Semi-Sovereign States

Chapter 9 The World Grows Smaller: International Cooperation

Preface

There are 192 sovereign nations in the world today, each with its own unique ethnic and social composition and its own unique history. The interplay of these, and other factors, has created, in turn, a unique system of government.

In this book we describe these systems and try to relate them to the social and economic influences which, over the years, have fashioned them. At the same time, we have identified particular features which are common to all, or most, countries and have classified them in an attempt to make objective comparisons.

In our classification we have sought to distinguish between those nations whose citizens have a completely free choice of which people should control the levers of political power and those where that choice is limited. The first we have called multiparty, or pluralistic, states and the second one-party, or monistic. This is an important distinction but it is not the only criterion for deciding whether or not a political system can be said to be democratic.

When the first edition of this book was written, some six years ago, there were 165 independent, sovereign states. Of these, 83, or just under half, could be classified as truly democratic. By 1995 the number had grown to 145, or some three-quarters, of the total.

As we said in our first study of the international political scene, the accession to power in the Soviet Union of Mikhail Gorbachev, in 1985, had the effect of casting a stone into the apparently static pond of Eastern European politics and we predicted that its ripples would spread to other regions. That prediction has come to pass, within a shorter time than we envisaged, and now one-party, monistic states are very much in a minority in most regions of the world. However, reconstructed communist parties have returned to power in several of the recently democratized states in Eastern Europe, with Lech Wałesa, so instrumental in the downfall of communism, being replaced as Polish president in November 1995 by the communist leader, Alexander Kwasniewski.

In the pages that follow we have tried to provide a better understanding of political institutions and events in the contemporary world and have addressed ourselves not just to academics and professional observers of the political landscape but also to the more general reader who is looking for a serious, but not over-technical, account of global politics.

When we embarked on this task we believed that our approach was new in a number of ways. First, we have considered all the contemporary states and not just the well-known and obvious. Second, we have attempted to identify connections between a country's political system and its historical, social, and economic background. Third, we have looked in some detail at the dynamics of political systems, including the activities of parties and similar groupings, as well as the formal institutions that states have created. Fourth, partly to make the material more manageable, but also to provide a better understanding of geographical and demographic influences, we have adopted a regional approach to our exposition of political systems. Finally, we have looked at examples of how sovereign states, either by choice or necessity, have found it increasingly profitable to co-operate with each other rather than just compete. Six years later, we believe that this approach is still unique and has been justified by recent events.

Although the task has been enjoyable, there have been inevitable frustrations resulting from the almost impossible task of ensuring that the information about each state is still valid in a world where change tends to be the rule rather than the exception.

'To understand others is a certain way of understanding ourselves' might well be the motto for this book. If we have succeeded in this task of creating a better understanding of politics throughout the world we will be well content.

Acknowledgments

We would like to record our appreciation for the encouragement and support we have received from our publishers, Helicon. To Michael Upshall and Denise Dresner, for their faith in us and our project, and to Shereen Karmali and Edith Summerhayes, for keeping us to our task and ensuring the accuracy of our work. Having said this, we accept that any consequential errors or omissions are ours. Finally, nearer home, we are particularly grateful to Joyce for her patient encouragement and support.

JDD and IDD
January 1996

Tables

Regional maps

1

The Comparative Approach

CHAPTER 1

Understanding Political Systems

1.1 Political animal

The Greek philosopher, Aristotle (384–322 BC), said that man was by nature a political animal. He argued that it was within man's natural development to live in some sort of ordered society under a system of government. In the times in which he lived the kind of community he saw as natural was the comparatively small city-state of ancient Greece, with thousands, rather than millions, of citizens able to practise direct democracy.

In the world of today there are few communities that resemble those small early communities. The Most Serene Republic of San Marino in Italy is probably the best example. It is the sole city-state which survived after the unification of Italy in the 19th century and has the distinction of being the world's oldest republic, its independence recognized and its protection guaranteed by Italy. Because of its small population, about 24,000, San Marino is able to enjoy a uniquely intimate kind of government.

The majority of countries have considerably larger populations, of course, and their governments are more remote from the average citizen. Nevertheless, Aristotle's belief that mankind achieves natural fulfilment by living in a political community seems to have been borne out by subsequent events, as this account of the political systems of the world will try to show.

1.2 What is a political system?

So that we can better understand the nature of a political system, it will be helpful if we first attempt to define certain words which are frequently used in everyday speech but whose meanings are not always clear.

We use the word 'government' in a variety of ways. In a general sense we use it to mean an orderly way of running a community's affairs and it is possible to distinguish between local government, perhaps regional government, and national government. The absence of government is anarchy, with everyone looking after himself or herself: the law of the jungle. In a more specific sense we speak of 'the government' as a body of people who have power to make us behave in certain ways. Because they are the government they have authority as well as power. In other words, their power is legitimate. We will not concern ourselves for the moment about how this power is achieved. That is something we shall discover as we look at each country more closely.

Another word frequently used in this context is 'state'. Often we see state as synonymous with government, with the two words being interchangeable. To some extent this is quite valid: a government department might also be called a department of state. The word should be used a little more precisely, however. Governments come and go, as we all know, but the state may be said to be permanent, comprising the whole apparatus by which a community is governed: the armed forces, the police, the civil service, the judicial system, and so on. This emphasizes elements included in the classic definition of a state by the German sociologist, Max Weber (1864–1920), most importantly the monopoly of the application of legitimate physical violence within a specific territory and the enforcement of a system of rules.

The word can also be used to describe a country which has an independent, internationally recognized, government, such as the state of Israel or the state of Egypt. What then should we say of the United States of America? Is this another use of the word state? No, the word is applicable to nations or parts of nations. It just happens that the contemporary world consists largely of nation-states and the United States is simply a nation-state comprising 50 subnational states. We will look at the concept of the nation-state more closely a little later.

Within the same broad context we speak of 'politicians'. They are the people who achieve, or hope to achieve, power and, in simple terms, run the government. How do they fit into the scheme of things? Civil servants, members of the armed forces, judges, and similar public servants are the permanent personnel of the state while the politicians provide the temporary element. Politicians are the people who occupy positions of power as long as they have the support of the community, or they may be the people who aspire to power but are temporarily out of office. Exactly how politicians achieve power need not concern us at the moment; this will become evident as our study proceeds. We will see that power is obtained sometimes on the basis of consent, the democratic approach, and sometimes on the basis of force, the autocratic approach.

Both the words government and state are rather static terms but if we add to them the political dimension, provided by politicians and their activities, we have something much more dynamic: a 'political system'.

A political system can probably best be understood in demand-response terms. In the majority of countries politicians are elected to positions of power and authority, the ballot box giving the ordinary citizen an opportunity to make his or her demands known. Politicians will try to anticipate these demands by offering a prospectus of what they will provide if elected – a manifesto of promises – and the elector can then choose between different manifestoes on offer. Once a political party has been elected to office it will be judged by its performance and the electorate's response to that performance will again be demonstrated through the ballot box when elections come round again.

A country's political system, then, is more than its institutions and more than the formal processes of government. It includes the dynamic interplay of people's ideas and interests: the whole process of demand and response which politics represents. Even if a government is highly authoritarian, giving little room for the political process to work, there will always be at least an undercurrent of activity which expresses the true aspirations of the people, however subordinated they may be by those with power and authority.

1.3 The advantages of comparing systems

The comparative approach is a particularly advantageous way of arriving at a better understanding of political systems. Not just systems in general, but also a specific one about which you may consider yourself to be very knowledgeable.

First, the comparative approach forces you to stand back and look objectively at a particular system. It should be no surprise that some of the best studies of the American and British systems of government, for instance, have been made by people whose personal experience has been gained in a different political environment.

Second, the comparative approach alerts you to similarities in institutions and processes which make your own system more understandable.

Third, the experience of one country can be used to anticipate the effects of change in the political system of another. For example, a knowledge of the voting system in Ireland, where a form of proportional representation operates, will enable some sort of prediction to be made of the likely impact if it were introduced into the United Kingdom.

Finally, and this is probably the greatest advantage of all, a wider understanding of how countries with different histories, different ethnic compositions, different social problems, and different philosophical backgrounds have approached the basic problem of creating and sustaining satisfactory institutions and processes of government is an excellent way of stimulating interest in the political process and a greater degree of participation. It is surely a sad reflection on the state of contemporary democracies that, at best, fewer than 5% of their populations can be classed as being 'regularly' active in a political sense.

1.4 The nation-state

The comparisons of political systems which will be made are based on the concept of the nation-state or sovereign state, defined, following Lane and Ersson, as 'a state that recognizes no higher decision-making power outside itself'. Table 1 lists, in order of formation, those nation-states which will be considered. Although today it is seen as the 'natural' political unit for most areas of the world, the nation-state is a comparatively new concept. The nation-state, or 'stato', of the Weberian type, characterized by the monopoly of the legitimate use of force within a specified territory and the concentration of power in an impersonal administrative organization, is essentially an early modern and modern phenomenon, a product of the Renaissance and succeeding periods. Prior to this, personalized 'segmentary states' predominated. Here authority was layered and shared between local and central, or imperial, rulers, and clear territorial specification of boundaries was lacking. Nevertheless, in this earlier period substantial, quasi-national political units were established in a number of countries in Europe, Asia, and North Africa and this has been taken as the date of state formation for 11 countries.

As Table 2 shows, no less than 141 of the 192 states which will be examined in Part II of this volume are products of the present century: 98 being post-1959 creations. In the Middle East and Africa only three of the 66 were in existence before 1910 and even in Europe, where a majority of 'old' states might be expected, more than half of them achieved full, independent nationhood after World War I.

Before the 20th century most of the world's inhabitants were, in one way or another, in the thrall of the established Western European powers and if a datum point of, say, 1800 is taken, only 22 of today's 192 states existed in a form that might be readily recognizable in 1996. Between 1800 and 1850 the world witnessed its first significant wave of nation-state formation. Twenty-three states originated during this period, including 18 in Central and Southern America, which had been liberated from Spanish colonial control. The second, and, numerically, the most important wave of state-building occurred between 1944 and 1984. During this period, 97, or half of the contemporary world's nation-states, were established. This was made possible by European decolonization in Africa, Asia, the Middle East, the Caribbean, and Oceania. The final, and certainly the most dramatic, wave of state formation occurred between 1990 and 1994. Twenty-five new sovereign states came into existence. The great majority were situated in Central and Eastern Europe and Central Asia and their formation was the direct result of the dissolution, in 1991, of the formal and 'informal' empire of the Soviet Union and the collapse of the Yugoslav socialist federation. In addition, in Oceania and Western Europe a number of former 'Trust Territory' colonies and semi-sovereign micro-states have become fully fledged sovereign states since the first edition of this book was published. However, two states have disappeared, as a consequence of the unification of both Germany and Yemen.

Table 3 sets out the average age of states in the regions of the world. The youngest states, on average half a century old, are to be found in Oceania, Africa, and Central and Eastern

Nation states of the world | **Table 1**

Country	Region	Year of state formation	Country	Region	Year of state formation
China	Asia	2nd century/ 1368/1949	Romania	C, E, & S Europe	1881
			Cuba	C America & Caribbean	1899
San Marino	N & W Europe	301	Australia	Oceania	1901
Japan	Asia	5th century/1603	Panama	C America & Caribbean	1903
France	N & W Europe	741	Norway	N & W Europe	1905
Denmark	N & W Europe	940/1849	Bhutan	Asia	1907
Ethiopia	C & S Africa	11th century	Bulgaria	C, E, & S Europe	1908
Portugal	N & W Europe	1128	South Africa	C & S Africa	1910
Andorra	N & W Europe	1278	Albania	C, E, & S Europe	1912
Monaco	N & W Europe	1297	Finland	N & W Europe	1917
Liechtenstein	N & W Europe	1342	Austria	N & W Europe	1918
Thailand	Asia	1350	Estonia	C, E, & S Europe	1918/1991
Vatican City State*	N & W Europe	1377/1929	Hungary	C, E, & S Europe	1918
Spain	N & W Europe	1492	Poland	C, E, & S Europe	1918
Iran	M East & N Africa	1499	Ukraine	C, E, & S Europe	1918/1991
Sweden	N & W Europe	1523	Yugoslavia	C, E, & S Europe	1918/1992
Russia	C, E, & S Europe	1547/1917/1991	Lithuania	C, E, & S Europe	1919/1991
Netherlands	N & W Europe	1648	Latvia	C, E, & S Europe	1920/1991
Switzerland*	N & W Europe	1648	Mongolia	Asia	1921
United Kingdom	N & W Europe	1707	Egypt	M East & N Africa	1922
Afghanistan	Asia	1747	Turkey	C, E, & S Europe	1923
Nepal	Asia	1768	Iraq	M East & N Africa	1932
United States	N America	1776	Saudi Arabia	M East & N Africa	1932
Haiti	C America & Caribbean	1804	Ireland	N & W Europe	1937
Paraguay	S America	1811	Iceland	N & W Europe	1944
Argentina	S America	1816	Lebanon	M East & N Africa	1944
Chile	S America	1818	Jordan	M East & N Africa	1946
Costa Rica	C America & Caribbean	1821	Philippines	Oceania	1946
Mexico	C America & Caribbean	1821	Syria	M East & N Africa	1946
Brazil	S America	1822	India	Asia	1947
Peru	S America	1824	Pakistan	Asia	1947
Bolivia	S America	1825	Korea, North	Asia	1948
Uruguay	S America	1825	Korea, South	Asia	1948
Greece	C, E, & S Europe	1829	Myanmar	Asia	1948
Belgium	N & W Europe	1830	Sri Lanka	Asia	1948
Colombia	S America	1830	Indonesia	Asia	1949
Ecuador	S America	1830	Taiwan*	Asia	1949
El Salvador	C America & Caribbean	1830	Libya	M East & N Africa	1951
Venezuela	S America	1830	Oman	M East & N Africa	1951
Tonga*	Oceania	1831/1970	Cambodia	Asia	1953
Honduras	C America & Caribbean	1838	Laos	Asia	1954
Nicaragua	C America & Caribbean	1838	Vietnam	Asia	1954
Guatemala	C America & Caribbean	1839	Morocco	M East & N Africa	1956
Dominican Republic	C America & Caribbean	1844	Sudan	C & S Africa	1956
			Tunisia	M East & N Africa	1956
Liberia	C & S Africa	1847	Ghana	C & S Africa	1957
Luxembourg	N & W Europe	1848	Malaysia	Asia	1957
New Zealand	Oceania	1853	Guinea	C & S Africa	1958
Italy	N & W Europe	1861	Israel	M East & N Africa	1958
Canada	N America	1867			
Germany	N & W Europe	1871/1949/1990			*continued*

Nation states of the world (continued) — Table 1

Country	Region	Year of state formation
Benin	C & S Africa	1960
Burkina Faso	C & S Africa	1960
Cameroon	C & S Africa	1960
Central African Republic	C & S Africa	1960
Chad	C & S Africa	1960
Congo	C & S Africa	1960
Côte d'Ivoire	C & S Africa	1960
Cyprus	C, E & S Europe	1960
Gabon	C & S Africa	1960
Madagascar	C & S Africa	1960
Mali	C & S Africa	1960
Mauritania	C & S Africa	1960
Niger	C & S Africa	1960
Nigeria	C & S Africa	1960
Senegal	C & S Africa	1960
Somalia	C & S Africa	1960
Togo	C & S Africa	1960
Zaire	C & S Africa	1960
Kuwait	M East & N Africa	1961
Sierra Leone	C & S Africa	1961
Tanzania	C & S Africa	1961
Algeria	M East & N Africa	1962
Burundi	C & S Africa	1962
Jamaica	C America & Caribbean	1962
Rwanda	C & S Africa	1962
Trinidad & Tobago	C America & Caribbean	1962
Uganda	C & S Africa	1962
Western Samoa	Oceania	1962
Kenya	C & S Africa	1963
Malawi	C & S Africa	1964
Malta	N & W Europe	1964
Zambia	C & S Africa	1964
Gambia	C & S Africa	1965
Maldives	Asia	1965
Singapore	Asia	1965
Barbados	C America & Caribbean	1966
Botswana	C & S Africa	1966
Guyana	S America	1966
Lesotho	C & S Africa	1966
Equatorial Guinea	C & S Africa	1968
Mauritius	C & S Africa	1968
Nauru*	Oceania	1968
Swaziland	C & S Africa	1968
Fiji	Oceania	1970
Bahrain	M East & N Africa	1971
Bangladesh	Asia	1971
Qatar	M East & N Africa	1971
Bahamas	C America & Caribbean	1973
United Arab Emirates	M East & N Africa	1971
Grenada	C America & Caribbean	1974
Guinea-Bissau	C & S Africa	1974
Angola	C & S Africa	1975
Cape Verde	C & S Africa	1975
Comoros	C & S Africa	1975
Mozambique	C & S Africa	1975
Papua New Guinea	Oceania	1975
São Tomé	C & S Africa	1975
Surinam	S America	1975
Seychelles	C & S Africa	1976
Djibouti	C & S Africa	1977
Dominica	C America & Caribbean	1978
Solomon Islands	Oceania	1978
Tuvalu*	Oceania	1978
Kiribati*	Oceania	1979
St Lucia	C America & Caribbean	1979
St Vincent & the Grenadines	C America & Caribbean	1979
Vanuatu	Oceania	1980
Zimbabwe	C & S Africa	1980
Antigua	C America & Caribbean	1981
Belize	C America & Caribbean	1981
St Kitts-Nevis	C America & Caribbean	1983
Brunei	Asia	1984
Micronesia	Oceania	1986
Marshall Islands	Oceania	1990
Namibia	C & S Africa	1990
Yemen	M East & N Africa	1990
Armenia	C, E, & S Europe	1991
Azerbaijan	C, E, & S Europe	1991
Belarus	C, E, & S Europe	1991
Croatia	C, E, & S Europe	1991
Georgia	C, E, & S Europe	1991
Kazakhstan	Asia	1991
Kyrgyzstan	Asia	1991
Moldova	C, E, & S Europe	1991
Slovenia	C, E, & S Europe	1991
Tajikistan	Asia	1991
Turkmenistan	Asia	1991
Uzbekistan	Asia	1991
Bosnia-Herzegovina	C, E, & S Europe	1992
Macedonia	C, E, & S Europe	1992
Czech Republic	C, E, & S Europe	1993
Eritrea	C & S Africa	1993
Slovakia	C, E, & S Europe	1993
Belau	Oceania	1994

* Not members of the UN

The historical and regional pattern of nation state formation — Table 2

Number of states formed

Period	Asia	Central America & Caribbean	Central, Eastern, & Southern Europe	Central & Southern Africa	Middle East & North Africa	North America	Northern & Western Europe	Oceania	South America	Total
Pre AD 1000	0	0	0	0	0	0	3	0	0	3
1000–1599	2	0	1	1	1	0	7	0	0	12
1600–1799	3	0	0	0	0	1	3	0	0	7
1800–1899	0	9	2	1	0	1	4	2	10	29
1900–1950	10	1	6	1	6	0	5	2	0	31
1951–1975	7	5	0	40	10	0	2	4	2	70
1976–1995	6	6	15	5	1	0	0	7	0	40
Total	28	21	24	48	18	2	24	15	12	192

Europe. Though formerly known as the 'New World', the states of the Americas are, on average, now more than a century and a half old. However, it is Northern and Western Europe, the birthplace of the Weberian 'modern state', which contains the oldest group of nation-states of the world, with an average antiquity of four centuries.

A nation may be described as a group of people, often from different backgrounds, and sometimes from different races, who have come to live together and have adopted a common identity. The unity of a nation is usually reinforced by a common language and sometimes a common religion. A state is the name given to the whole apparatus of government which a nation creates as the machine for operating its political system.

The nation-state is then enshrined and perpetuated by the adoption of symbols such as a national flag and a national anthem. The human apex of the nation-state is the individual designated as head of state, in the person of a king, queen, or president. Sometimes the head of state is little more than a symbol of national unity, with few or no political powers. Sometimes the roles of head of state and head of government are combined but, in such cases, an attempt is usually made to differentiate between the two roles. In the United States, for example, the office of president generally attracts the respect of most citizens regardless of the personality or political views of the holder.

The nation-state manifests itself in a wide variety of different forms, ranging from the democratic to the highly authoritarian. It is this rich variety which provides the material for what will follow.

1.5 The plan of the book

The first part of the book concentrates on the comparative approach, looking first at the various constitutional forms which can be adopted for political systems and then at the philosophies or ideologies which underlie the constitutional structures. Then executives, heads of state, and heads of

Average ages of nation states — Table 3

Region	Number of states	Average age (years)	Standard deviation
Asia	28	106	170
Central America & Caribbean	21	83	69
Central, Eastern, & Southern Europe	24	52	94
Central & Southern Africa	48	52	132
Middle East & North Africa	18	66	106
North America	2	174	46
Northern & Western Europe	24	438	430
Oceania	15	42	49
South America	12	147	55

government, and assemblies, or parliaments, in different countries are compared. Then, moving on to the more dynamic elements of political systems, voting methods and parties are examined.

The second part is designed to show political systems in action, giving a factual account of the political institutions and processes of each country and an objective summary of how they currently operate. One hundred and ninety-two states are covered. They include the current 185 full members of the United Nations, plus the seven independent states of Kiribati, Nauru, Switzerland, Taiwan, Tonga, Tuvalu, and the Vatican City.

The seven non-UN states have been added because all have full national sovereignties and their presence outside the United Nations organization has no useful bearing on the subject matter of our present examination of political systems. Switzerland, for example, has chosen, on the basis of its long history of neutrality, not to be a UN member and Taiwan was a member, under the title of the Republic of China, from 1945 to 1971, when the People's Republic of China received full international recognition. The four South Pacific states of Kiribati, Nauru, Tonga, and Tuvalu have determined on a neutralist course and have not applied for direct UN representation. The Vatican City, as a purely theocratic state, has jealously retained its political neutrality.

The states in Table 1 that are not current members of the United Nations are denoted by asterisks. The dates indicate the year of each country's inception as a nation-state. This date will normally be the year of release from colonial control or in which its first constitution was adopted, which may or may not be the one currently in force. In the case of a minority of countries, particularly those with dates prior to the 19th century, the inception of nationhood will predate the adoption of the first constitution or a codified constitution may never have been adopted.

The 192 states have been grouped into nine geographical regions: Asia; Central America and the Caribbean; Central, Eastern, and Southern Europe; Central and Southern Africa; the Middle East and North Africa; North America; Northern and Western Europe; Oceania; and South America. This classification has been chosen in preference to one based purely on philosophical values, such as liberal-democratic, totalitarian, and so on. Such an approach is superficially attractive but fraught with difficulties. It is, inevitably, subjective and can have the effect of distorting the profile of a political system so as to force it into one of the chosen categories. On the other hand there are, apart from convenience, some good reasons for adopting the regional approach.

First, there is an undoubted link, as will be demonstrated, between a country's geography and history and the political system it develops. A look at the continent of America, and its associated islands, will illustrate this point.

The whole of North America was at one time a British colony. The fact that Canada, which retained its connection with Britain, also retained aspects of the British constitution in its political system is understandable. Equally understandable is the recognition that the United States, which broke its link with Britain 200 years ago, chose to develop a different system, which looks more guardedly at the dangers of unfettered executive power and seeks to control and restrain it. The US constitution, therefore, reflects other influences, such as the political climate in 18th-century France.

The geography and social composition of North America have also had effects on the political systems of both Canada and the United States, resulting in federal structures of government which take into account the size and diversities of both countries.

Moving south down the continent, the fact that much of Central and South America were once part of a Spanish empire whereas the islands of the Caribbean came under British and French influence is, again, reflected in their political systems.

Second, there is a discernible link between a country's ethnic characteristics and the political system it develops and these characteristics tend to be regionalized in many cases. For example, it is not surprising that the majority of Islamic states are to be found in the Middle East, North Africa, and West Asia.

One somewhat artificial region which has been used for classification purposes is Oceania. Where exactly are its boundaries? Indeed, can it be said to exist at all? For the purposes of this book it is regarded as including Australasia and those island territories in the Pacific which do not fit easily into any other of the regional groupings which have been chosen.

The arbitrary nature of the classification is freely admitted and no apologies are offered. Without such an approach much of the material would have been less manageable and, in any event, for the majority of states alternative groupings would not have brought out so clearly the influences of history, geography, and social development.

The third part of the book deals with residual territories in the world which cannot be viewed as fully fledged independent states. Into this category fall the 42 overseas colonies and external dependent territories that still exist in the world of today.

This final part also looks beyond nation-states and their dependencies to regional and global groupings. Here it is recognized that the accelerated improvements in communications of all kinds, and the growing economic interdependence of countries, will, inevitably, cause the world to shrink in political as well as physical terms and, as a result, seems likely to lead to a diminution in absolute levels of national sovereignty.

Recommended reading

Almond, G A, Powell, G B and Mundt, R J *Comparative Politics: A Theoretical Framework*, Harper Collins, 1993

Anderson, J (ed.) *The Rise of the Modern State*, Humanities Press, 1986

Blondel, J *Comparative Government: An Introduction*, 2nd edn., Prentice Hall–Harvester Wheatsheaf, 1995

Charlton, R *Comparative Government*, Longman, 1986, Chap. 1

Chilcote, R H *Theories of Comparative Politics: The Search for a Paradigm Reconsidered*, Westview Press, 1994

Crick, B *In Defence of Politics*, 2nd edn., Penguin, 1982

Dogan, M and Kazancigil, A *Comparing Nations*, Basil Blackwell, 1994

Evans, P B, Rueschemeyer, D and Skocpol, T (eds) *Bringing the State Back In*, Cambridge University Press, 1985

Hague, R, Harrop, M and Breslin, R *Comparative Government and Politics: An Introduction*, 3rd edn., Macmillan, 1992, Chaps 1–3

Harding, N (ed.) *The State in Socialist Society*, Macmillan, 1984

Hobsbawm, E J *Nations and Nationalism since 1970*, Cambridge University Press, 1990

Kellas, J *The Politics of Nationalism and Ethnicity*, Macmillan, 1991

Keman, H (ed.) *Comparative Politics: New Directions in Theories and Methods*, Free University Press, 1993

King, R *The State in Modern Society: New Directions in Political Sociology*, Macmillan, 1986

Lane, J-E and Ersson, S *Comparative Politics: An Introduction and New Approach*, Polity Press, 1994

Leftwich, A (ed.) *What is Politics?*, Basil Blackwell, 1984

Lukes, S (ed.) *Power*, Basil Blackwell, 1986

Macridis, R C and Burg, S L *Introduction to Comparative Politics: Regimes and Changes*, 2nd edn., Harper Collins, 1991

Roberts, G K *An Introduction to Comparative Politics*, Edward Arnold, 1986, Chap. 1

Smith, A D (ed.) *Ethnicity and Nationalism*, Brill, 1992

Wiarda, H J (ed.) *New Directions in Comparative Politics*, Westview Press, 1991

CHAPTER 2

Constitutions

2.1 What a constitution is

A constitution can be regarded in two ways. First, it is a general statement of how a country is governed. For example, the US constitution could be described as republican, federal, and presidential, whereas that of the United Kingdom would be monarchical, unitary, and parliamentary. For someone familiar with 'constitutional language' but who knew nothing about the political systems of the United States and the United Kingdom these two statements would say something, but not much.

On the other hand, for someone completely unversed in constitutional and political terminology the two descriptions would do little or nothing to advance a knowledge of the two countries. 'Republican', 'monarchical', 'federal', 'unitary', 'presidential', and 'parliamentary' are all words which are intended to have precise meanings within the context of an exposition of a political system.

In an even more general sense a constitution may be said to be 'liberal' or 'authoritarian', using two contrasting words which can be found in any nontechnical dictionary. These distinctions would probably conjure up a picture of two political systems that a layman would understand. If you had the choice, which would you prefer: liberal or authoritarian? Most people would choose the former, if only because it had a more 'comfortable' sound. But if one constitution was said to be more liberal than another or more authoritarian than another difficulties would immediately be created.

To use the word constitution in a general sense, therefore, is not particularly helpful. It is rather like saying that France has better weather than Britain. What parts of France and Britain? What times of the year? Is the weather consistent, year in and year out? Obviously, more questions are raised than answered.

In a more specific sense, a constitution is a document or set of documents describing the framework of a political system. It stipulates where power lies within a state, what the institutions of government are, how they are constructed and how they are intended to operate. In doing so, it provides what might be said to be a set of rules for politicians in a particular country to follow. What offices they can hold, how they get to office, what they can do and not do in office, how laws are made, how they are enforced, how disputes between citizens and the state are resolved.

2.2 What a constitution is not

A constitution falls far short of being an accurate description of a political system. For example, it is unlikely to even mention political parties or any other forms of organized interests. It will say how power is distributed but not how it is used.

There are several possible analogies which could be used to point out differences between a constitution and a political system but the most accurate is probably a theatrical one. A constitution can be said to be the text of a play whereas the political system is its enactment. Often a constitution even falls short of being a complete text and is rather more a plot with a cast of characters. There are two missing elements which are needed if a constitution is to become alive and translated from a written text into a live production.

The first is political activity or the interplay of power. In other words, how a head of government arrives at a position of power, how that power is used, how he/she and his/her supporters try to retain power, and how their opponents try to divest them of it. This is where the activities of parties and interest groups are all important.

The second missing element is what are called constitutional conventions. These are the understandings which politicians accept as being the unwritten rules of how a constitution should work in practice. Conventions bring flexibility and reality into the political process. They allow a constitution to remain firm in its fundamentals but flexible enough to adapt to changing political circumstances.

The use of the word convention is, perhaps, unfortunate because it can have a very different meaning, particularly in the United States where it is the name given to conferences or rallies of political parties. The combined term, constitutional convention, refers, in addition, in the United States to a special meeting of state government representatives, called at the request of two-thirds of state legislatures, to draft new amendments to the constitution. A better approach would be to speak of conventional behaviour, in other words customary practices which politicians adopt because experience has shown that they make the governmental process work more smoothly. This conventional behaviour acts as a lubricant to the political system.

A constitutional convention begins life as an attempt to solve a problem or potential problem. If it is successful then it may be accepted by politicians as an agreed way of approaching a similar problem in the future. If it works successfully on a number of occasions there will be tacit agreement that it has achieved the status of a constitutional convention. It may even be written into a constitution as a formal amendment so that there will be no confusion about whether or not this, originally conventional, procedure should always be followed.

In the United Kingdom there is no legislation which says that the prime minister must be a member of the House of Commons but, although in the second half of the 19th century no fewer than six of the 12 governments were headed by peers, there has been no prime minister sitting in the House of Lords since 1895. A constitutional convention has established this practice. A similar convention ensures that government ministers must be members of one or other of the Houses of Parliament.

To recapitulate, a constitution provides the framework for a political system. It does not give a full, or even accurate, picture of how the system works in practice.

Post-1989 constitutions (69)						Table 4
State	Year	Region		State	Year	Region
Albania	1991	C, E, & S Europe		Mauritania	1991	C & S Africa
Andorra	1993	N & W Europe		Moldova	1994	C, E, & S Europe
Angola	1991	C & S Africa		Mongolia	1992	Asia
Armenia	1995	C, E, & S Europe		Mozambique	1990	C & S Africa
Azerbaijan	1995	C, E, & S Europe		Namibia	1990	C & S Africa
Belarus	1994	C, E, & S Europe		Nepal	1990	Asia
Belau	1992	Oceania		Niger	1992	C & S Africa
Benin	1990	C & S Africa		Paraguay	1992	S America
Bosnia-Herzegovina	1994	C, E, & S Europe		Peru	1993	S America
Bulgaria	1991	C, E, & S Europe		Poland	1992	C, E, & S Europe
Burkina Faso	1991	C & S Africa		Romania	1991	C, E, & S Europe
Burundi	1992	C & S Africa		Russian Federation	1993	C, E, & S Europe
Cambodia	1993	Asia		São Tomé & Principe	1990	C & S Africa
Cape Verde	1992	C & S Africa		Seychelles	1993	C & S Africa
Central African Republic	1995	C & S Africa		Sierra Leone	1991	C & S Africa
Chad	1993	C & S Africa		Slovakia	1992	C, E, & S Europe
Colombia	1991	S America		Slovenia	1991	C, E, & S Europe
Comoros	1992	C & S Africa		South Africa	1993	C & S Africa
Congo	1992	C & S Africa		Tajikistan	1994	Asia
Croatia	1990	C, E, & S Europe		Thailand	1991/1995	Asia
Czech Republic	1992	C, E, & S Europe		Togo	1993	C & S Africa
Djibouti	1992	C & S Africa		Turkmenistan	1992	Asia
Equatorial Guinea	1991	C & S Africa		Uganda	1995	C & S Africa
Eritrea	1993	C & S Africa		Ukraine	1992	C, E, & S Europe
Estonia	1992	C, E, & S Europe		Uzbekistan	1992	Asia
Ethiopia	1993	C & S Africa		Vietnam	1992	Asia
Fiji	1990	Oceania		Yemen	1991	ME & N Africa
Gabon	1991	C & S Africa		Yugoslavia	1992	C, E, & S Europe
Georgia	1995	C, E, & S Europe		Zambia	1991	C & S Africa
Ghana	1992	C & S Africa				
Guinea	1991	C & S Africa		**Post-1989 constitutions by region**		
Kazakhstan	1995	Asia		Northern and Western Europe		1
Kyrgyzstan	1994	Asia		Central, Eastern, and Southern Europe		20
Laos	1991	Asia		Middle East and North Africa		1
Lesotho	1993	C & S Africa		Central and Southern Africa		31
Lithuania	1992	C, E, & S Europe		North America		0
Macedonia	1991	C, E, & S Europe		Central America and the Caribbean		0
Madagascar	1992	C & S Africa		South America		3
Malawi	1994	C & S Africa		Asia		11
Mali	1992	C & S Africa		Oceania		2

If it adapts readily it is said to be flexible and if it does not it is rigid.

Perhaps understandably, an unwritten constitution suggests great flexibility. After all, there is no formal, legalistic procedure for making a change. If the political will is there then a change will take place, probably by introducing a new constitutional convention or usage, or discarding an old one. The assumption that a codified constitution is less flexible than an uncodified one is often misleading. When a usage can be changed or discarded without any technical obstacles it seems reasonable to conclude that the politicians who might make a change will approach a proposal very warily.

If a change has to go through some elaborate, formal procedure, such as in the United States, where an amendment to the constitution has to be proposed by a two-thirds vote of both houses of Congress and then ratified by the legislatures of three-quarters, or 38, of the 50 states of the Union, it seems reasonable to assume that a lightly or poorly conceived change will get a thorough consideration before it is finally accepted. Thus there have been only 27 amendments to the US constitution (1789), ten of which, the so-called 'Bill of Rights', were passed in 1791. The most notable proposed change which failed at the second ratification hurdle was the proposed Equal Rights Amendment. This sailed through Congress in 1971–72, but was approved by only 35, or 70%, of the states in the Union. In other states such as Japan and South Korea, constitutional amendments need to be first passed by a two-thirds vote of all members in parliament and then approved in a national referendum, while in Bulgaria they must be carried in the National Assembly by a three-quarters majority at least three times, on different days.

In a nation where such a weighty, formal procedure is absent the onus is placed on proposers of change to be absolutely certain in their own minds that there will no lasting, damaging consequences. Confronted with this responsibility, it is understandable that, in more cases than not, the status quo will be retained and the change cautiously avoided.

This is especially the case in liberal democracies, where constitutional government, government in accordance with formal rules, is most deeply embedded in the public and political psyche. An exception has been France, which has framed 17 constitutions since 1789. Its current Fifth Republic constitution dates back to 1958. It can be amended by the two chambers of parliament meeting together in a special session and the changes attracting 60% support, or by the amendment bill being passed separately by each house of parliament and then approved in a national referendum. Similarly in India, where minor amendments require only the majority support of both chambers of parliament, there have been more than 70 amendments to the constitution since it was first adopted in 1950. This represents almost two amendments a year.

In newer, emergent, or one-party, regimes the process of constitution redrafting has been more frequent, with fresh codes being introduced to meet the changed circumstances of the day. The Latin American states, independent since the early 19th century, have been particularly prominent in this respect. Venezuela, for example, has had 26 constitutions, though the present one dates back more than 30 years. The Dominican Republic has had 25; Haiti more than 20; Colombia and Ecuador 17 apiece; El Salvador and Bolivia 16 apiece; Honduras 12; and Brazil 7. Asian and African states subject to frequent military coups are also notable for the number of their constitutions. The most extreme case is Thailand, which has had 15 constitutions since the establishment in 1932 of a constitutional monarchy. Similarly, in communist regimes new constitutions were regularly framed as a means of giving recognition to the advancing stages of 'socialist development' that had been attained. The Soviet Union had five such documents, in 1918, 1922, 1936, 1977, and 1989, after the revolution of 1917. Yugoslavia had a similar number after the federal republic was first established in 1945, while Czechoslovakia and Romania each had three.

2.6 Separation or fusion of powers

We have already said that the main area of concern of a codified constitution will be the three main institutions of government: the legislature, the executive, and the judiciary. A comparison of constitutions could attempt to discover whether these institutions are kept separate or are fused.

The best known proponent of the doctrine of the separation of powers was the French philosopher, Baron Montesquieu (1689–1755), who set out the theory in *De l'Esprit des lois* (1748). He argued that by keeping the three institutions separate and balanced the possibility of one of them, and particularly the executive, accruing undue power, and then exploiting it to the detriment of the citizenship, would be avoided.

His views made a considerable impact and were clearly taken into account by the framers of the United States constitution. As one of them, James Madison (1751–1836), said: 'the accumulation of all powers, legislative, executive and judiciary, in the same hands ... may justly be pronounced the very definition of tyranny'. Oddly enough, Montesquieu cited England as a country enjoying relatively great liberty because the powers of government were distributed between the legislative, executive, and judicial institutions and had the effect of balancing each other. In reality, as will be seen later, a political system based on a parliamentary executive, as in the United Kingdom, creates a fusion, rather than a separation, of the legislative and executive functions.

The concept of a separation or balancing of powers is still a useful test of the degree of freedom from autocratic rule within a political system but, on its own, is an insufficient, and sometimes unreliable, criterion.

2.7 Unitary or federal states

A constitution invariably seeks to clarify the relationship between the government with the responsibility for the whole of a state's territory and that concerned with only part of it. In other words, central government and localized government.

Democratic government is believed to have begun in the city-states of ancient Greece, and particularly the city of Athens, which, with a total population of less than 50,000, was able to practise direct and universal participation in government. In fact the very word democracy (*demokratia*), roughly meaning rule (*kratos*) by the people (*demos*), is derived from ancient Greece. In that situation democracy was direct, involving the active and personal participation of all adult 'full citizens' at some time in their lives in government, by accepting office on a rota basis. Citizens' assemblies met around 40 times a year, being attended by around 5,000 people, while morning councils met even more frequently. There are still vestiges of direct democracy in those contemporary states which make use of juries in their judicial systems and more generally, as is noted in Chapter 6, in the increasing resort to regular referenda and 'citizens' initiatives' in a number of West European nations and US states.

Today, of course, there are few, and no major, states small enough to enjoy direct democracy. The unusual, and almost unique, example of the tiny Most Serene Republic of San Marino in Italy has already been noted. Elements of direct democracy also survive in several of the smaller cantons (states) in the Swiss Confederation, with the electorate, numbering, at most, 10,000, meeting in a public place on one day each year to select officials and vote on issues. This tradition of direct Swiss democracy via the annual Landsgemeinde, or sovereign citizens' assembly, is more than seven centuries old, originating in 1294 in the German-speaking canton of Schwyz. These cases are, of course, anachronisms and, although there are suggestions that computerization may, in the future, open up the possibility of a new direct participatory democracy via the Internet, the vast majority of states which claim to be democratic do so on the basis of representative, rather than direct, democracy.

Putting exceptions such as San Marino and the Swiss cantons aside, all modern states find it necessary to have institutions to administer the needs of particular localities as well as the whole population. The larger the area the more obvious the need to cater for local, or regional, as well as national interests. The extent to which power is devolved by the government in the centre to the localities and the nature of the power devolved indicate whether or not a genuinely federal system is operating.

A nation-state is one which claims sovereignty over the whole of its territory. In other words, everyone within its boundaries is subject to its laws. If a government decides to divide its sovereignty within its boundaries and pass some of it to local bodies it means the devolution of some of its law-making powers. If the central government retains the right to override these devolved powers at any time then the state cannot be said to be truly federal.

If a federal system is adopted the respective legislative powers of the governments in the centre and the localities must be clearly defined and the local governments must be protected against the erosion of those powers by central government. This can only be done successfully through the medium of a written, codified constitution. Because circumstances change, there must be provision for this distribution of legislative power to be reviewed. In a truly federal system that review cannot be undertaken arbitrarily by the central government and the process must involve the localities, either by giving them 'blocking' powers with respect to proposed constitutional amendments in their areas of concern or

through the adjudicatory medium of an impartial Constitutional Court.

The supreme example of a genuinely federal system of government is found in the United States constitution. Section 8 of Article I sets out the powers of the central legislature, Congress, and, by implication, leaves the residue of powers to the state legislatures. Article V prescribes how the constitution can be amended, such amendments requiring the approval of three-quarters of the state legislatures, and Article III the adjudicatory authority of the Supreme Court.

This form of devolution is effected by prescribing the legislative powers of the centre and leaving the residue with the localities. An alternative method is to prescribe the powers of the localities and leave the residue to the centre. Virtually all the world's federal systems adopt the former approach although the Canadian constitution comes nearer to the latter, defining precisely the powers of both the federal and state governments.

When executive, rather than legislative, powers are decentralized a state is said to have a unitary constitution and of the 192 states in Table 1 the great majority are unitary, only 24 having federal structures. As with most other aspects of political systems, history, geography, and culture are the strongest factors behind the choice of a federal system of government. Of particular importance, not surprisingly, is country size, with seven of the eight largest nations in the world, and five of the seven most populous, having federal structures. Moreover, the one exception within this grouping, China, has established five 'autonomous regions', for its non-Han minority border communities, which are of quasi-federal nature. It is for this reason that, despite their small numbers, more than 2 billion people, constituting 38% of the world's population, live in states with federal constitutions and these 24 states comprise half the world's land area. There are federal states in all nine regions of the world, but the largest number are to be found in the Americas (7), Europe (7) and Africa (5). The broad range of factors that have determined the existence of federal structures in these and the remaining five states are presented in Table 6, together with a brief exposition of the types of federal system in operation.

Table 6 excludes Somalia where, in 1993, an agreement was reached to establish a federal system of government, based on 18 autonomous regions. However, the country has been beset by civil war since the late 1980s. This has prevented the agreement from being made effective. Indeed, one large region, Somaliland in the northwest, has been a self-declared 'independent state' since May 1991. There have been recent proposals to establish a federation in Sri Lanka, while South Africa is another possible candidate for a federal system.

As Table 6 suggests, federalism is stronger in some countries than others, the most vigorous being Australia, Canada, Switzerland, and the United States, with India and Germany following closely behind. In Germany a strong federal system was actively sponsored by the occupying powers after the end of World War II because of fears of a resurgence of a powerful and belligerent nationalistic central government. The weakest examples of federal systems are probably the Comoros, where most legislative power is retained by the Federal Assembly, and Austria. The Mexican, Russian,

Federal states in the contemporary world *	**Table 6**

Chief determinants of federalism and its form

Argentina (S America) pop. 32.5 m (WR 31) area 2.767 m sq km (WR 8)
Historical, cultural, and geographical
Early history was dominated by a conflict between town and country, particularly the European-style sophistication of Buenos Aires and the rough, basic style of the gaucho. An attempt to impose a unitary system in 1829 failed. There are today 22 provinces, each with its own legislature, governor, and constitution. The five-member Supreme Court adjudges federal-state constitutional conflicts.

Australia (Oceania) pop. 17.8 m (WR 50) area 7.687 m sq km (WR 6)
Geographical and historical
The size of the country and distribution of the population have created distinctive, separate communities. For example, both Darwin, in the north, and Perth, in the west, are more than 3,000 km from the capital, Canberra, whereas the two largest cities, Sydney and Melbourne, are, respectively, less than 300 and 500 km away. Historically, throughout the 19th century the country was divided into six distinct colonies, founded separately, governed separately, and bounded by largely uninhabited land. Not until 1901 did the colonies unite in the Commonwealth of Australia. The six states have their own legislatures and constitutions, with, still today, 60% of the nation's population residing in their capitals. They receive the bulk of their funds from the centre, which has authority to levy income tax, in the form of annually negotiated grants. Federal-state conflicts are ruled upon by the seven-member Australian High Court.

Austria (N & W Europe) pop. 7.8 m (WR 85) area 0.084 m sq km (WR 112)
Partly historical and partly artificial
A weak federal system which had operated between the two world wars was revived, under United States influence, in 1945. There are nine states (*Länder*), each with its own legislature. The policy-framing powers residing with the state governments are, however, limited to the spheres of regional planning, agriculture, hospitals, and electricity. Federal-state disputes are adjudged by the 14-member Constitutional Court.

Belgium (N & W Europe) pop. 10.066 m (WR 73) area 0.031 m sq km (WR 136)
Cultural and linguistic
The northern people are mainly Flemings, of Teutonic stock, speaking Flemish, while those of the south are chiefly Walloons, of Latin stock, speaking French, while the capital, Brussels, has a mixed, cosmopolitan population. From 1980 northern Flanders and southern Wallonia had regional 'sub-governments' then in 1993 the constitution was amended to create a federation of three, mainly autonomous, regions, Brussels, Flanders, and Wallonia.

Bosnia-Herzegovina (C, E, & S Europe) pop. 4.5 m (WR 109) area 0.051 m sq km (WR 124)
Historical, ethnic, and cultural
The state is one of the remaining pieces of the former multi-ethnic federal Yugoslavia. Following the refusal of the Serbs to accept Muslim–Croat–Serb power-sharing, the Muslim and Croat leaders agreed in 1994 to form a federation of eight cantons, each with a significant degree of local autonomy. A new Muslim–Croat and Serb federation was agreed in 1995.

Brazil (S America) pop. 156.360 m (WR 5) area 8.512 m sq km (WR 5)
Geographical and cultural
The size of the country and distribution of the population favoured federalism. The land mass is greater than continental United States, minus Alaska. Each of the 26 states has a single chamber assembly, elected governor, and constitution. In addition, Brasília is a federal district. There is a 16-member Supreme Court to decide on federal-state conflicts. The body is viewed, however, as strongly susceptible to presidential influence. The new constitution, adopted in 1988, enhanced states' powers and their tax raising capabilities *vis-à-vis* the federal government, so that half of the federal tax take is now devolved further down the line. This strengthened what was previously a comparatively weak federal system.

Canada (N America) pop. 27.8 m (WR 33) area 9.971 m sq km (WR 2)
Geographical, historical, and cultural
The size of the country and the wide cultural mix created strong regional differences. Historically, the nation was created by the confederation of four British colonies in 1867. Six other former colonies joined the Dominion between 1870 and 1949. The 10 resulting provinces have their own assemblies and elected premiers. They can frame their own civil laws and have control of education policy. The nine-member Supreme Court rules on federal-state constitutional disputes.

* In brackets are the world rankings (WR) of these states in terms of population and area

continued

| **Federal states in the contemporary world (continued)** | **Table 6** |

The Comoros (C & S Africa) pop. 0.6 m (WR 155) area 0.002 m sq km (WR 167)
Geographical and historical
This state is a group of three islands which came together. Each island has its own elected governor and island assembly, with partial administrative and legislative autonomy.

Ethiopia (C & S Africa) pop. 51.3 m (WR 23) area 1.106 m sq km (WR 27)
Historical, cultural, and ethnic
In recognition of the country's ethnic and cultural diversity, in 1952 it became a federation but returned to unitary status in 1962. With the secession of Eritrea, and the acceptance that other regions might seek similar independence, in 1994 the country returned to federalism, based on nine ethnically distinct states, each with a significant degree of autonomy. In making the change, the constitution unusually gave any state the right to secede through a popular referendum.

Germany (N & W Europe) pop. 80.6 m (WR 12) area 0.357 m sq km (WR 61)
Historical and partly artificial
The Weimar Republic, carrying on earlier German Empire traditions, had a weak form of federalism which was destroyed by the Hitler regime. Under United States influence it was revived in 1945, as a means of providing a check against the possible future abuse of central authority. With unification of the West and East, in 1990, the federal structure was retained. There are 16 states (*Länder*), each with its own constitution, elected assembly and government headed by a minister-president, and substantial-sized civil service. The states have original powers in education, police, and local government matters and substantial local tax-raising powers, and receive assigned shares of federal revenue accruing from value added tax (VAT) and income tax. They are responsible for carrying out the administration of federal matters and account for a half of total government spending in the federal republic. Federal-state disputes are policed by an independent 16-member Federal Constitutional Court. In practice, however, German federalism is largely consensual in character, based around the striking of pragmatic committee-room deals between senior federal and state politicians and civil servants. For this reason, the term 'bureaucratic federalism' is frequently employed to describe the German federal system.

India (Asia) pop. 896.6 m (WR 2) area 3.287 m sq km (WR 7)
Geographical, historical, and cultural
The land mass makes it the second largest state in Asia and historically the country was apportioned during the British period into separate provinces, with specified areas of legislative and fiscal autonomy, and princely states, each owing separate allegiance to the Crown. Today there are 25 self-governing states, organized primarily on language lines, and seven 'Union territories'. Each state has its own elected assembly, council of ministers, and chief minister. There is also a figurehead governor appointed by the federal president. The states have primary control over health, agriculture, education, police, and local government. Overall, however, although relatively strong in comparative terms, particularly when non-Congress parties control state assemblies, Indian federalism remains weighted towards the federal government, which has sole control of income tax, the states relying on land and sale taxes and federal grants for their revenue. The government at the centre also has the power to impose direct 'President's Rule' in any state during a period of turmoil. A substantially independent 18-member Supreme Court adjudges federal-state constitutional conflicts.

Malaysia (Asia) pop. 19.2 m (WR 47) area 0.330 m sq km (WR 64)
Historical and cultural
The country is a federation of 11 separate states and two British colonies which were brought together into a federation between 1963 and 1965. Each state has its own constitution, elected assembly, led by a chief minister and cabinet, and head of state. The states, however, have only limited original powers in the spheres of land and natural-resource management and are reliant upon the federal government for almost all of their funds. Federal-state constitutional disputes are ruled upon by a traditionally independent Supreme Court. This has, however, been subject to mounting central political pressure, exerted by the prime minister and monarch, during recent years.

Mexico (C America & Caribbean) pop. 90.0 m (WR 11) area 1.958 m sq km (WR 14)
Geographical and partly imitative
The size of the country made a federal system sensible in geographical terms and also the United States constitution was seen as an attractive model to copy. The 31 states have their own elected Chamber of Deputies, governors, and constitutions. In most states most powers reside with the governor who is pre-selected by the dominant Institutional Revolutionary Party's (PRI) inner-council. For this reason, Mexico remains, in practical terms, a significantly centralized state. For similar reasons, the Supreme Court is subject to effective PRI control.

continued

Micronesia, Federated States of (Oceania) pop. 0.102 m (WR 176) area 0.0007 m sq km (WR 172)
Geographical and historical
The dispersed nature of the state, consisting of hundreds of islands, mostly uninhabited, scattered across the South Pacific, meant a political federation was inevitable. The federation consists of four states, each with its own constitution, providing for a governor and legislature. Each state enjoys considerable freedom under a federal executive president who coordinates and directs policy.

Nigeria (C & S Africa) pop. 119.3 m (WR 10) area 0.924 m sq km (WR 31)
Geographical, historical, and cultural
The recognition of tribal and religious differences, particularly between the north and south east, which culminated in civil war between 1967 and 1970, has been made in a federal system. Prior to independence, Nigeria was divided, in accordance with the 1946 'Richards constitution', into three semi-autonomous regions. These became four in 1963, 12 in 1967, 19 in 1979, 21 in 1987, and 30 in 1991. At present, each state is under the control of a military governor appointed by the central Armed Forces Ruling Council.

Pakistan (Asia) pop. 128.1 m (WR 7) area 0.804 m sq km (WR 34)
Historical and cultural
The absorption of 12 princely states into independent Pakistan in 1948 was achieved by recognizing their earlier history and creating a federal structure of four provinces. These provinces exhibit strong cultural and ethnic distinctions and rivalries. They are administered by centrally appointed governors and local governments drawn from elected provincial assemblies.

Russian Federation (C, E, & S Europe) pop. 149.2 m (WR 6) area 17.075 m sq km (WR 1)
Historical, geographical, and cultural
The federal system was established by the Soviet Union in 1922, allowing national minorities to be recognized while maintaining the unity of the state through the party machine. The Russian Federation now includes 21 republics. Sixteen of them were autonomous republics during the communist period, four were formerly autonomous regions (*oblasts*), while the last, the Ingushetia republic, was newly created in 1992. The unit called Russia comprises those parts of the Russian Federation that are not included within any of the other 21 republics and, with five-sixths of the Federation's total population, is divided into 68 administrative regions (*oblasts* and *krais*) and autonomous territories and districts, which have considerable devolved authority. The republics have, in theory, a free hand in the welfare and social spheres, as well as the right of secession but this freedom is sometimes overridden in practice.

St Christopher (St Kitts) – Nevis (C America & Caribbean) pop. 0.044 m (WR 185) area 0.0003 m sq km (WR 185)
Geographical and historical
The state is a unique union of two islands which are the residue of what was to have been a wider West Indies federation. Nevis Island, with its own elected assembly, prime minister, and cabinet, retains the option to secede.

Sudan (C & S Africa) pop. 27.4 m (WR 34) area 2.506 m sq km (WR 10)
Geographical and cultural
In recognition of the country's geographical and cultural diversity, in 1994 a federation of 26 states was created, each with its own governor, assisted by state ministers, appointed by the federal president. However, with the military still powerful, the durability of this constitutional arrangement must be in doubt.

Switzerland (N & W Europe) pop. 6.9 m (WR 90) area 0.041 m sq km (WR 131)
Historical and cultural
The state is a federation of 26 cantons (including six half-cantons), or political units, dating back to the late 13th century. The cantons also reflect the cultural diversity of a country divided between German-, French-, Italian-, and Romansch-speaking communities and between Catholic majority and Protestant majority areas. Each canton has its own constitution, legislative assembly, and government, with substantial powers in socio-economic spheres such as education, environmental issues, tourism, transport, and police affairs. Cantons also have protected sources of finance and the ability, through the successful use of referenda, to effectively veto federal policies.

United Arab Emirates (Middle East & N Africa) pop. 1.7 m (WR 140) area 0.078 m sq km (WR 114)
Historical
This is a loose federation of seven sheikhdoms which were under British protection between 1892 and 1971. Each sheikh is an hereditary and absolute ruler in his own emirate.

continued

Federal states in the contemporary world (continued)	*Table 6*

United States (N America) pop. 257.8 m (WR 3) area 9.373 m sq km (WR 4)
Historical and geographical
The federal system resulted from the voluntary coming together of the original 13 British colonies after the War of Independence (1776–83). The state developed by expanding its federal membership and the structure also usefully recognizes the geographical and cultural diversity of the country. Each of the 50 states that presently exist has its own constitution, assembly, elected governor, and supreme court. The federal government has responsibility for defence and foreign affairs and the authority to coordinate 'inter-state concerns'. A liberal interpretation of what the latter phrase might constitute has resulted in a steady expansion in federal government interests. State governments remain, however, influential bodies, framing much of their own civil and criminal law; being substantially involved in health, educational, and welfare affairs; and raising more than three-quarters of their funds from state property, sales and, in some cases, local income taxes. Federal-state constitutional disputes are adjudged by the independent nine-member Supreme Court.

Venezuela (S America) pop. 20.6 m (WR 44) area 0.912 m sq km (WR 32)
Historical, cultural, and imitative
The federal system recognizes the historical and cultural differences in the country but also reflects admiration for the US model, the country having been called the United States of Venezuela until 1953. It is divided into 20 states (*estados*), each with its own elected assembly and executive governor. Since, however, the governor is appointed by the federal president and the states are heavily dependent upon the centre for revenue resources, the federal system remains weak in practice. The adjudicatory supreme court is heavily susceptible to political influence.

Yugoslavia (C, E, & S Europe) pop. 10.6 m (WR 66) area 0.102 m sq km (WR 104)
Historical and cultural
Formerly a socialist federation of six republics, following the breakaway of Slovenia, Croatia, Bosnia-Herzegovina, and Macedonia in 1991–92, a new constitution was adopted in 1992 for the 'rump federation' of the republics of Serbia and Montenegro, the federal structure recognizing the historical independence of the different national minorities and religious groupings. The present federal republic consists of the two republics of Montenegro and Serbia and, within Serbia, the autonomous provinces of Vojvodina and Kosovo-Metohija. Each republic and autonomous province has its own elected assembly, although the Kosovo assembly was dissolved in 1990 by the government of the republic of Serbia. Within each republic and province there are locally elected councils. There is a Constitutional Court to adjudge federal-state disputes.

Venezuelan, and Malaysian federal systems are also weak in practice as a result of the *de facto* control exerted over state/regional associates by the federal party leadership and machine.

Federal systems have been established in some states, notably Belgium, Bosnia, Ethiopia, Nigeria, Sudan, and Yugoslavia, to accommodate the political aspirations of regionally based ethnic communities which would otherwise seek secession from the state. In practice, the federal solution has not always proved sufficient to assuage secessionist movements. As a consequence the federal unions of the USSR, greater Yugoslavia, and Czechoslovakia collapsed between 1991–92 and Cameroon abandoned its federal structure in 1972. Meanwhile, Bosnia, Canada, Ethiopia, India, Mexico, Pakistan, the Russian Federation, Sudan, and Yugoslavia all currently face regionally based secessionist and 'home rule' movements of varying strengths.

Other states which are not strictly federal but have 'highly decentralized' forms of government, are identified in Table 7. During the past two decades there has been a general trend towards political decentralization, entailing the establishment of elected regional governments with enhanced responsibilities and sources of finance. This has been particularly apparent in Western Europe in France, Italy, and, to the greatest degree, Spain. As a consequence the distinction between 'weak federal' states such as Austria and 'strongly decentralized' states such as Spain is now quite narrow. Indeed, it is noted by Daniel Elazar, who has compiled a handbook of federal and federal-style states, that: 'Nearly 80 per cent of the world's population now live within polities that either are formally federal or that utilize federal arrangements in some way, while only 20 per cent live in polities that can be denominated as outside of any federal arrangements'.

2.8 The distribution of power

Whatever safeguards may be written into a constitution, political realities will ultimately determine the distribution of power between the centre and the localities and the most significant reality is, invariably, a financial one.

In Australia, for example, the states are dependent on the federal government for about 60% of their revenue and even in the United States, where the clearest distinction between central and local power is made, the states rely on indirect sales taxes which are much less buoyant and stable than the direct income tax which forms the bulk of federal government revenue.

At the other extreme, in a unitary state such as the United Kingdom local authorities are entirely the creatures of parliament, which is controlled by the party in power, and dependent on central government not only for the bulk of

Unitary states with decentralized features	Table 7

State	Form of decentralization
Belau	16 states, each with an elected legislature and governor
Bolivia	9 departments with appointed prefects
Burkina Faso	25 provinces
Burma	14 states and divisions
China	21 provinces and five 'autonomous regions', including Tibet (see Part 3)
Denmark	mainland, Faroe Islands and Greenland (see Part 3) are administered separately and all are represented in the single chamber Folketing
Dominican Republic	31 provinces
Ecuador	21 provinces
Finland	Åland Islands are a self-governing province
France	22 elected regional councils, influential in the economic planning process, and 96 department councils. Corsica (see Part 3) has its own assembly
Georgia	2 autonomous republics: Abkhazia and Adzharia
Haiti	9 departments
Indonesia	24 provinces, a metropolitan district and two autonomous districts, each with a governor
Israel	since 1993, Palestinians living in the occupied territories of Gaza and the West Bank of the Jordan have enjoyed partial autonomy
Italy	20 regions with elected councils; five enjoy a 'special status'
Kiribati	elected councils on each inhabited island, enjoying considerable autonomy
Moldova	the Gagauz and Dnestr regions have special autonomous status
Netherlands	11 provinces with appointed governors and elected councils
Papua New Guinea	20 provinces with consultative assemblies
Philippines	12 regions and 75 provinces. Muslim Mindanao is an autonomous region
Portugal	the Azores and Madeira (see Part 3) are autonomous regions, each with an elected regional assembly and an appointed chair
San Marino	9 partially self-governing 'castles'
São Tomé e Príncipe	Príncipe has internal autonomy
Senegal	10 regions with appointed governors and elected assemblies
Solomon Islands	7 provincial assemblies
South Africa	4 provinces with appointed administrators and elected councils. Constitutional amendments in March 1994 extended the legislative powers of the provincial legislatures
Spain	17 regional autonomous communities with elected parliaments and governments. Each has the constitutional right to self-rule
Sri Lanka	8 elected provincial councils
Tanzania	Zanzibar has its own constitution and House of Representatives. The state constitution prescribes that when the president comes from the mainland the vice president must come from Zanzibar, and vice versa. There are 25 regional commissioners
Trinidad & Tobago	Tobago Island has its own House of Assembly, with full self-government since 1987
Tuvalu	each inhabited atoll has its own elected Island Council
Ukraine	the Crimea has been afforded a special status
United Kingdom	Channel Islands and their dependencies (see Part 3) have their own assemblies and laws. The Isle of Man (see Part 3) has its own lieutenant-governor and legislative council
Vanuatu	6 elected regional councils
Zambia	each of the 9 provinces is represented on the president's advisory body, the House of Chiefs

their income but for their very existence. The abolition, in 1986, of a whole tier of local government, the metropolitan county councils, including the Greater London Council (GLC), is evidence of the disproportionate distribution of power in the United Kingdom.

2.9 The role of the judiciary

Most constitutions speak, directly or indirectly, about the supremacy of law. This is generally seen as the guarantee of

personal liberty and the chief protection against the overweening power of the state. Clearly the law of the land is the law enacted and whether or not the laws which are passed are fair is a matter which the political system, as a dynamic entity, must determine.

However, once a law has been enacted it is the role of the judiciary to ensure that it is fairly enforced and in practice this means more than just adjudicating in disputes between individuals and groups or between them and the state. It also involves interpreting the law. Since it is virtually impossible to construct a law which is completely unequivocal, the task of judicial interpretation is a continual process and of considerable importance. To have an independent and unbiased judiciary is, therefore, vital if personal liberty is to be protected.

Judges are generally guaranteed their independence in a constitution by a provision which ensures their continuance in office during 'good behaviour'. Although independence and security of tenure usually apply to judges in the higher courts, in lower courts this is not always true. In many US states, for example, members of the state judiciary are elected and may be dismissed by the people who elected them. A notable recent example is the California voters' sacking of Chief Justice Rose Bird in November 1986 for alleged 'liberalism' in her conduct of affairs. This makes judicial office holders responsive to public opinion, but is not always the best prescription for justice. In most one-party states, as well as in many Latin American countries, it is the party which chooses the judges for election by the assembly, another process clearly open to abuse.

In the United Kingdom the judiciary is appointed by the government of the day and although the lord chancellor, as the head of the judiciary, provides advice, to ensure the quality of the appointees and, in theory at least, to avoid political bias, it should not be forgotten that lord chancellors are politicians and leading members of the government. In the United States, Supreme Court judges are appointed, subject to Senate approval, which in recent years has by no means been automatic, by the president and, inevitably, subject to some political influence. Nor is it possible to say that any judge, however qualified and experienced, can be completely free from the bias which stems from his own social background and political inclinations.

A constitution can, therefore, go some way towards ensuring an independent judiciary but it can never guarantee complete impartiality. In practice most constitutions go little further than setting out the structure of the judicial system, with a few adding something a little more specific. The constitution of the Republic of Algeria states: 'Judges obey only the law. They defend the socialist revolution', and in Cameroon and Gabon the president is given the task of ensuring the independence of the judiciary.

An important role of judges is, of course, to protect the constitution itself and even in a state, such as the United Kingdom, which has no codified constitution, they are required and expected to uphold the rule of law. In federal states, as has been noted, the judiciary's task of upholding the constitution is particularly significant in that they have to interpret as well as enforce, so as to preserve the intended balance between the centre and the localities. In quasi-federal Spain there is a Constitutional Court with this specific task, as there is in Italy and, though the body is somewhat less influential, in France also. The similar apical judicial bodies which exist in fully federal states are set out in Table 6.

2.10 Religion and the state

Some states have adopted a particular belief as the national religion and enshrined this in their constitutions. Table 8 sets out the current established or state religions. In all, 51 states

fall into this category, almost half of which have Islam as the state religion. Fourteen of the states where Islam is established as the state religion are situated in the Middle East and North Africa, six in Asia and five in Central and Southern Africa. Roman Catholicism is the second most widely officially established religion, with a strong regional bias towards Central and South America.

2.11 Unusual constitutional features

Some constitutions contain unusual or unique provisions, most of them being products of the country's history, geography, or social structure.

The Mexican constitution, reflecting the country's history of exploitation by the wealthy and powerful, places restrictions on the activities of the Church, large landowners and foreign organizations. Following a record of unequal educational opportunities, the constitution also stresses the importance attached to state education. In similar vein, the 1992 constitution of Paraguay provides for agrarian reform in its Chapter 6, but also guarantees the autonomy of the army.

State or established religions	*Table 8*

Islam (25)
Afghanistan, Algeria, Bahrain, Bangladesh, Brunei, The Comoros, Egypt, Iran, Iraq, Jordan, Kuwait, Malaysia, The Maldives, Mauritania, Mauritius, Morocco, Oman, Pakistan, Qatar, Saudi Arabia, Somalia, Sudan, Tunisia, United Arab Emirates, Yemen

Roman Catholicism (12)
Argentina*, Colombia*, Costa Rica, Dominican Republic, Haiti, Malta, Panama*, Paraguay**, Peru**, Seychelles*, Vatican City State, Venezuela*

Evangelical Lutheran/Protestant Church (6)
Denmark, England & Scotland, Iceland, Norway, Sweden, Tuvalu

Greek Orthodox Church (1)
Greece

Judaism (1)
Israel

Buddhism (4)
Bhutan, Cambodia, Sri Lanka, Thailand

Hinduism (1)
Nepal

Pancasila (1)†
Indonesia

---
* Quasi-state religion
** Roman Catholicism is the official religion, although the constitution guarantees religious freedom
† A national secular-state ideology, stressing unity and social justice, which is a compulsory belief for all social organizations

Because of the small size of the country, the constitution of Nauru permits the president, who combines the roles of head of state and head of government, to take on additional personal portfolios in a cabinet of only five or six.

To ensure a balance between the religious communities, the Lebanese constitution prescribes that if the president is a Christian the prime minister must be a Muslim, and vice versa.

The constitution of Liberia includes a provision for monitoring and ensuring the maintenance of a one-party state, while the constitution of Mongolia specifically permits the imposition of forced labour.

The different geographical bases required of the president and vice president by the Tanzanian constitution has already been mentioned.

Finally, the newest Brazilian constitution, whose 245 articles and 70 clauses took 19 months to be scrutinized and approved by the federal Congress, contains the most detailed statement of specific social and economic rights currently in force in a noncommunist regime. These include a prescribed 44 hours for the working week and stipulated rights to five days of paternity leave and extended maternity leave. In addition, the new constitution, in its economic chapter, restricts the future levying of real interest rates to a maximum level of 12.5% above inflation.

In terms of length, currently two of the world's longest constitutions are those of India (1950), which contains 397 articles and nine schedules, and Colombia (1991), which has 380 articles.

2.12 How important are constitutions?

Are constitutions merely statements of a grand design and, as such, removed from the realities of the political process? In the final analysis surely naked, military power must prevail? The answers to these questions, based on recent experience, must be yes and no.

In liberal democratic countries with long established codified constitutions, such as the United States, there can be no doubt about their supreme significance. The content and importance of the American constitution are made clear to every school child and the newest immigrants will cherish the freedoms it proclaims. Specific provisions are frequently quoted in contemporary life. Both Rear Admiral John Poindexter and Lieutenant-Colonel Oliver North pleaded the fifth amendment, the right to remain silent in a criminal case, when required to testify at the 1986 'Irangate' hearings. Since the Watergate affair all Americans must be aware of the impeachment powers contained in Articles I–II of the constitution.

Even in a country such as the United Kingdom, with an uncodified constitution, constitutional controversies arise over such matters as the powers of the House of Lords, devolution, parliamentary sovereignty vis-à-vis the European Union, electoral reform, and the possibility of introducing a Bill of Rights.

Admittedly, given the necessary political will and military might, any constitution can be suspended or annulled and at the present time there are about ten which fall into this category. Nevertheless, the aura of legitimacy which, accurately or not, a constitution brings is almost universally sought, even by clearly despotic regimes.

Recommended reading

Banting, K and Simeon, R (eds) *The Politics of Constitutional Change in Industrial Nations: Redesigning the State*, Macmillan, 1985

Bogdanor, V (ed.) *Constitutions in Democratic Politics*, Gower, 1988

Burgess, M (ed.) *Federalism and Federation in Western Europe*, Croom Helm, 1985

Burgess, M and Gagnon, A-G *Comparative Federalism and Federation: Competing Traditions and Future Directions*, Harvester Wheatsheaf, 1993

Duchacek, I *Comparative Federalism: The Territorial Dimension of Politics*, Rinehart & Winston, 1970

Duchacek, I *Power Maps: The Comparative Politics of Constitutions*, ABC Clio, 1973

Dunn, J (ed.) *Democracy: The Unfinished Journey, 508 BC to AD 1993*, Oxford University Press, 1992

Elazar, D J (ed.) *Federal Systems of the World: A Handbook of Federal, Confederal and Autonomy Arrangements*, 2nd edn., Longman, 1994

Finer, S *Five Constitutions*, Harvester Press, 1979

Finley, M I *Politics in the Ancient World*, Cambridge University Press, 1994

Griffith, J *The Politics of the Judiciary*, Fontana, 1977

Hicks, U K *Federalism: Failure and Success, A Comparative Study*, Macmillan, 1978

Hodder-Williams, R *The Politics of the US Supreme Court*, Allen & Unwin, 1980

Reagan, M and Sanzone, J *The New Federalism*, 2nd edn., Oxford University Press, 1982

Simons, B W (ed.) *The Constitutions of the Communist World*, Sijthoff & Noordhoff, 1980

Unger, A L *Constitutional Development in the USSR: A Guide to the Soviet Constitutions*, Methuen, 1981

CHAPTER 3

The Ideological Bases

3.1 The nature of ideology

We are now entering the treacherous world of ideologies where we are as likely to be misled as informed. Nevertheless, it is an area which must be explored if we are to make distinctions between political systems which get beneath the layers of institutions to the cultures and attitudes which have shaped them.

It is not particularly important to the ordinary citizen that there is a two-chamber assembly or that the head of state is a king or a president. Whether the economy is planned from the centre or left to market forces, or whether there is a choice of political parties to support or only one: these things are important.

Identifying the ideology on which a political system is based, or influenced by, will help us penetrate the façade of institutions and slogans, but we must first clarify what we mean by ideology.

It is generally recognized that the political system of the Soviet Union had its theoretical beginning in the writings of Karl Marx (1818–83) and Friedrich Engels (1820–95), subsequently developed and adapted by Vladimir Ilyich Lenin (1870–1924), and that the current regime in Iran is motivated by the religion of Islam, through its Shi'ite branch, but what about the system in the United Kingdom? Is it not too evolutionary and pragmatic to have any substantial theoretical or philosophical basis?

It depends on how we construe ideology. 'Ideology' is a much abused, and overused, word. In recent years it has, more often than not, been associated with zealots and fanatics. The spread of international terrorism has built up a picture of ruthless groups imbued with a single-mindedness which rejects customary morality so as to advance the aims of some particular ideology. An ideology has too often come to mean blind faith and irrationality. This is too narrow an interpretation, and indeed a distortion, of the word.

The definition which will be used for our purposes is one which might be found in any good, general dictionary. An ideology is a body of ideas which reflects the beliefs and values of a nation and its political system. Such a definition is wide enough to encompass a variety of political cultures, from the mature, rational attitudes to be found in many states

in what we call the West to the more inspirational, and often emotive, ideas found in countries with less experienced political systems.

Ideologies can be individually or socially inspired. More often than not they are both. Politicians are essentially doers rather than thinkers, even though some of them would have the public believe they are both. They adopt and use philosophies as a platform for political action.

But why and how does a philosophy eventually become so much a part of the beliefs and values of a country that it can be said to be the ideology on which its political system is based? Initially, it usually results from a revolution of one kind or another and then proceeds through a process of what might be called evolutionary absorption.

For example, the 'ancien régime' of 17th- and 18th-century France was ended abruptly by the Revolution of 1789. Opposition to the profligacy and inequity of the absolute monarchy, allied to the democratic message of the 'Enlightenment' philosophers and writers such as Jean-Jacques Rousseau (1712–78), brought about the dramatic change. Then, over a much longer period, the forces which had initially impelled the revolution were modified and absorbed into the French psyche so as to become the ideology which now underlies its political system.

Other writers, such as John Stuart Mill (1806–73) in England, expanded and amended Rousseau's concept of liberal democracy into a more practical idea of representative government, while in other countries French and British experience was adapted to suit differing social and political needs. Thus, liberal democracy became the ideology of a wide family of nations.

The inequities of the Tsarist regime in Russia also ended abruptly in the Revolution of 1917, with, again, practical discontent allying itself with theoretical justification through the writings of Marx and Engels and the 'praxis' of Lenin. The communist ideology of the Soviet Union was, over the years, adopted and modified by another, mixed family of nations. Then, in the later 1980s, the inequities and inefficiency of the Soviet style of communism, with its emphasis on the command economy and the repression of individual thought, became apparent and produced another revolution, not entirely bloodless, but less violent than many might have anticipated.

In attempting to identify different ideologies and relate them to individual nation-states we realize that the choices are necessarily somewhat arbitrary and, indeed, a purist might well argue that each nation has its own unique ideology and that any classification is misleading. We reject this argument because we believe that, if accepted, the very notion of comparative politics would be questionable and a study such as this would have to be abandoned. Thus, accepting the arbitrary nature of the choice, an eightfold grouping is offered, in the belief that any classification is preferable to none at all. At the same time, some of the deficiencies in the process should be noted.

The first is that the ideology associated with particular countries is, inevitably, a 'broad brush' description of something more subtle and complicated than the simple 'label' would suggest. The second defect is that a static situation has been assumed. This may be acceptable as far as long-established states, with stable political systems, are concerned, but less so for newer states whose systems are still in a state of flux. Where such conditions are believed to exist an appropriate caveat will be added, with several countries, notably Afghanistan, Bosnia-Herzegovina, Liberia, and Somalia, currently in a state of transition.

With the foregoing reservations, the following ideologies will be identified and used:

1   Liberal democracy
2   Emergent democracy
3   Communism
4   Nationalistic socialism
5   Authoritarian nationalism
6   Military authoritarianism
7   Islamic nationalism
8   Absolutism.

Tables 9 and 10 provide an overview of the regional distribution of regime types, the relative demographic and economic importance of each regime, and related socio-economic characteristics.

A possible ninth new ideology, that of political Populism, appears also to be emerging during the 1990s. It is characterized by an emphasis on charismatic individual leadership, rather than politics based around party machines; skilful use of the television media; direct appeals to the populace via frequent referenda; anti-establishment rhetoric; mobilization on ethnic or nationalist lines; and, in the economic and social spheres, the offering of 'simple solutions to complicated problems'. Populism's roots lie in the Midwest-based People's Party, formed by agrarian interests, which was a force in US politics during the 1890s. A century later, its standard bearers have included: the maverick billionaire H Ross Perot, who contested the US presidential election of 1992 as an independent; the Reform Party in Canada; the media tycoon Silvio Berlusconi, who briefly became prime minister in Italy in 1994; the ultra-nationalist xenophobe Vladimir Zhirinovsky, whose Liberal Democrats attracted nearly a quarter of the national vote in Russia's December 1993 parliamentary elections; and Alexander Lukashenko, who was elected President of Belarus in July 1994. Populism has begun to put down roots most firmly in those states recently freed from communist monism which are finding the transition to a competitive market economy and multiparty liberal democracy particularly painful and difficult. However, it is currently not sufficiently established as an ideological base to merit inclusion in this volume as a ninth category.

3.2 Liberal democracy

Liberal democracy is a product of two concepts: the right to representative government and the right to enjoy individual freedom. The term 'liberal' is derived from the first concept and 'democracy' from the second. The tests for a political system claiming to be based on this philosophy would, therefore, seem to be the extent to which the government truly represents the mass of the people and the extent to which rights which individuals claim to have are protected.

In practice the essential features of a liberal democratic system can be identified as:

1   Representative institutions based on majority rule, through free elections and a choice of political parties.
2   Limitations on the power of government, implying a pluralistic society in which the state is not all-embracing and exists alongside other, sometimes competing, interests.
3   Accountability of the government to the electorate.
4   Freedom of expression, assembly, and the person, guaranteed by an independent judiciary.
5   A skilled and impartial permanent public service responsible to the government of the day and, through it, to the electorate.

Of the 192 states under examination 73 have been identified as having political systems founded on liberal democracy and they are listed in Table 11. They embrace 2.3 billion people, a figure which corresponds to 41% of the world's total population. The oldest and most stable liberal democracies are to be found in Northern and Western Europe but by no means all, or even a majority, because, although its roots are European, it is an ideology which has been successfully exported to all parts of the world. Thus, there are 28 liberal democracies in the Americas and 12 in Oceania. There is, however, a tendency, which is apparent from the national income data provided in Table 11, for this type of political system to flourish best in high-income, 'First World', states. Thus, liberal democracies are found in 26 of the world's 'Top 30' countries in terms of per-capita incomes, but in only two of the 'Bottom 50'. Similarly, while 18 of the 20 most urbanized states in the world are liberal democracies none of the top 30 states in terms of the proportion of the labour force employed in agriculture fall into this category. The 73 states with liberal democracies account for a staggering 86% of world GDP and, as Table 10 shows, have high levels of literacy and urbanization and low proportionate levels of government defence expenditure.

In compiling this list of liberal democratic states, the following seven markers have been looked for:

1   Evidence of constitutional government.
2   Evidence of free elections for assemblies and executives.

Political regimes — *Table 9*

Regional distribution

Regime	Asia	Central America & Caribbean	Central, Eastern, & Southern Europe	Central & Southern Africa	Region Middle East & North Africa	North America	Northern & Western Europe	Oceania	South America	Total
Lib-dem	5	17	3	2	2	2	21	12	9	73
Em-dem	9	3	20	30	4	0	1	2	3	72
Communist	4	1	0	0	0	0	0	0	0	5
Nat-soc	0	0	0	4	4	0	0	0	0	8
Auth-nat	6	0	2	5	0	0	0	0	0	13
Military	1	0	0	6	0	0	0	0	0	7
Islam-nat	1	0	0	0	1	0	0	0	0	2
Absolutist	2	0	0	1	7	0	1	1	0	12
Total	28	21	25	48	18	2	23	15	12	192

Combined area, population, and GDP (c. 1992)

Regime	(million sq km) Area	(m) Population	(US $'000 m) GDP	% Shares of world total Area	Population	GDP
Lib-dem	56.7	2,295	19,815	42.6	41.1	86.1
Em-dem	40.5	1,173	1,842	30.6	21.0	8.0
Communist	10.4	1,315	568	7.8	23.6	2.4
Nat-soc	6.4	117	145	4.8	2.1	0.6
Auth-nat	9.0	355	228	6.8	6.4	1.0
Military	4.9	209	61	3.7	3.7	0.3
Islam-nat	2.3	84	135	1.7	1.5	0.6
Absolutist	2.7	30	227	2.0	0.5	1.0
Total	133.0	5,578	23,021	100.0	100.0	100.0

Key:
Lib-dem   Liberal democratic
Em-dem   Emergent democratic
Nat-soc   Nationalistic socialist
Auth-nat   Authoritarian nationalist
Islam-nat   Islamic nationalist
GDP   Gross domestic product

3 The active presence of more than one political party.
4 Evidence of checks and balances between the three elements of government: executive, legislative, and judicial.
5 Evidence of an independent judiciary.
6 Evidence of the protection of personal liberties through constitutional or other legal guarantees.
7 Evidence of stability in liberal democratic government.

Our test of stability is necessarily arbitrary. We have included those states where liberal democratic systems have been in place for at least a decade, that is since 1986.

The states that are included in Table 11 include the seven markers listed above to varying degrees. An indicator of this is the 'Human Rights Rating', compiled by Charles Humana, which is displayed in Table 11. It is a composite measure which embraces various aspects of political and social liberties as in 1991. As a useful rule-of-thumb, a 'Human Rights Rating' of 70% or more is indicative of a political system that displays all seven features noted above. States with ratings below this tend to fail most commonly in markers 3 and 4, being characterized by effective dominance of the political system by one ruling party, although opposition parties are officially allowed to function.

Socioeconomic characteristics of political regimes (country averages c. 1991–92)						Table 10
Regime	US$ per capita GDP	Level of urbanization (%)	Labour force in agriculture (%)	Adult literacy rate (%)	Human rights rating (%)	Govt. defence spending (% of GDP)
Lib-dem	8,473	62	21	88	80	2.0
Em-dem	1,488	44	46	66	63	3.8
Communist	810	40	50	87	25	9.4
Nat-soc	1,503	51	45	57	45	6.0
Auth-nat	680	33	50	79	43	3.1
Military	297	32	68	39	38	5.2
Islam-nat	1,195	39	50	39	25	6.5
Absolutist	8,234	59	28	66	44	8.1

Key:

Lib-dem	Liberal democratic	Nat-soc	Nationalistic socialist	Islam-nat	Islamic nationalist
Em-dem	Emergent democratic	Auth-nat	Authoritarian nationalist	GDP	Gross domestic product

Two such classic examples are Mexico and Singapore, which, respectively, had 'Human Rights Ratings' of just 64% and 60% in 1991. In both these states, effective opposition movements are particularly weak, being hampered by alleged pro-government ballot-rigging in the first and by increasing direct harassment in the second. Despite this, however, in comparative terms, the degree of liberal freedom which is tolerated in these two countries remains tolerably high. Moreover, the longevity and stability of the PRI and PAP party regimes in place render alternative classification in the emergent democracy category inappropriate. A more accurate descriptive term for these two countries would, however, be 'restricted' or 'partial' liberal democracies. In Malaysia, where the UMNO has been in power since independence and also controls the legislatures of all but one of the federation's 13 states, the term liberal democracy is also somewhat 'restricted'. Similarly dominance by one party is a prominent feature of the political system of Egypt.

Table 12 sets out the average ages of liberal democratic regimes by regions of the world. This has been computed by calculating, for each state, how many years its liberal democratic regime had been functioning without interruption up to 1995 and then producing regional means. It shows North America, with two well entrenched liberal democratic political systems in Canada and the United States, to have the highest overall regional average, at 174 years, followed by Northern and Western Europe, at 88 years. Within Northern and Western Europe there are states such as San Marino and the United Kingdom with liberal democratic regimes which are even older than those of North America. However, the period of Nazi German occupation of France, the Benelux countries and parts of Scandinavia, has meant that in many states in this region there has been uninterrupted liberal democracy for only half a century.

The world regions with the youngest liberal democracies are revealed to be Central, Eastern, and Southern Europe, South America, Central America and the Caribbean, and Africa. Many of the liberal democracies in these regions remain very much 'on trial'. In Central and South America,

such has been the periodicity of lurches between liberty and military coercion in Argentina, Bolivia, Brazil, Ecuador, El Salvador, Guatemala, Honduras, Peru, and Uruguay that the term 'Latin Americanization' has been coined by political scientists. Indeed, as recently as May 1993 an attempt was made by President Jorge Serrano in Guatemala to revert to type and establish dictatorial rule. However, on this occasion, military support was not forthcoming and Serrano was deposed.

The average ages, in 1995, of other regime types were: absolutist, 93 years; communist, 40 years; nationalistic socialist, 21 years; authoritarian nationalist, 11 years; Islamic nationalist, 9 years; military authoritarian, 7 years; and emergent democratic, 4 years.

3.3 Emergent democracy

The states identified as emergent democracies bear many of the characteristics of liberal democracies except evidence of stability in their political systems, the majority having experienced at least one nondemocratic coup or change of government at some time or other during the past decade. Some have enjoyed stable liberal democratic government for extensive periods only to revert to militaristic or other autocratic rule. Others have emerged from a prolonged spell of autocracy in relatively recent years and it is still too early to judge how permanent the new regime will be.

Two of the most firmly established emergent democracies are those of South Korea and the Philippines in Asia and Oceania, which are now almost a decade old and exhibit improving human rights ratings. Also qualitatively high are the liberal democracies of the Central European states of the Czech Republic, Estonia, Hungary, Latvia, Lithuania, Poland, and Slovenia, drawing upon democratic traditions that had been frozen during half a century of communist control. Several of these states are candidates for entry into the European Union within the foreseeable future.

By contrast, the roots of democratic and civil freedoms have barely been planted in more recently emergent

Liberal democratic systems (73) | Table 11

Region/country	Year established	c. 1992 Per capita GDP (US$)	World ranking	c. 1991 Human rights rating (%)	World ranking
Asia (5)					
India	1947	290	166	54	69
Japan	1946	30,000	4	82	33
Malaysia	1957	3,050	51	61	59
Singapore	1965	13,800	27	60	60
Sri Lanka	1948	550	139	47	82
Central America & Caribbean (17)					
Antigua	1981	2,340	67	n/a	
Bahamas	1973	11,320	31	n/a	
Barbados	1966	6,350	42	n/a	
Belize	1981	1,720	83	n/a	
Costa Rica	1948	1,780	81	90	21
Dominica	1978	1,680	84	n/a	
Dominican Republic	1966	790	124	78	38
El Salvador	1983	1,125	105	53	72
Grenada	1984	1,900	75	n/a	
Guatemala	1985	910	115	62	57
Honduras	1982	580	136	65	53
Jamaica	1962	1,260	100	72	43
Mexico	1917	3,750	50	64	56
St Kitts	1983	4,100	48	n/a	
St Lucia	1979	2,900	56	n/a	
St Vincent	1979	1,750	82	n/a	
Trinidad & Tobago	1962	3,770	49	84	29
Central, Eastern, & Southern Europe (3)					
Cyprus	1960	8,000	35	n/a	
Greece	1974	7,184	41	87	26
Turkey	1982	1,954	74	44	85
Central & Southern Africa (2)					
Botswana	1966	2,790	58	79	37
Mauritius	1968	2,700	61	n/a	
Middle East & North Africa (2)					
Egypt	1971	630	133	50	75
Israel	1958	13,233	28	76	39
North America (2)					
Canada	1867	20,320	17	94	15
United States	1776	23,500	7	90	21
Northern & Western Europe (21)					
Austria	1945	22,000	11	95	14
Belgium	1945	20,000	18	96	12
Finland	1917	18,000	21	99	1
France	1946	22,700	9	94	15
Germany	1949	22,500	10	98	4
Iceland	1944	20,516	15	n/a	

continued

Liberal democratic systems (73) continued					Table 11
Region/country	Year established	c. 1992 Per capita GDP (US$)	World ranking	c. 1991 Human rights rating (%)	World ranking
Denmark	1945	25,927	5	98	4
Ireland	1937	12,104	29	94	15
Italy	1946	20,513	16	90	21
Liechtenstein	1921	35,500	2	n/a	
Luxembourg	1944	32,500	3	n/a	
Malta	1974	7,900	37	n/a	
Monaco	1911	22,000	11	99	1
Netherlands	1945	20,593	14	98	4
Norway	1945	24,000	6	97	9
Portugal	1976	7,451	40	92	19
San Marino	1600	9,091	32	n/a	
Spain	1978	14,022	26	87	26
Sweden	1809	23,000	8	98	4
Switzerland	1874	36,231	1	96	12
United Kingdom	1689	17,760	22	93	18
Oceania (12)					
Australia	1901	17,065	23	91	20
Belau	1981	n/a		n/a	
Kiribati	1979	720	129	n/a	
Marshall Islands	1979	1,530	88	n/a	
Micronesia	1979	1,570	87	n/a	
Nauru	1968	9,000	33	n/a	
New Zealand	1853	12,060	30	98	4
Papua New Guinea	1975	975	111	70	47
Solomon Islands	1978	630	133	n/a	
Tuvalu	1978	560	138	n/a	
Vanuatu	1980	1,210	101	n/a	
Western Samoa	1962	945	113	n/a	
South America (9)					
Argentina	1983	6,051	43	84	28
Bolivia	1982	770	126	71	45
Brazil	1985	2,759	59	69	49
Colombia	1957	1,134	104	60	60
Ecuador	1979	1,170	103	83	30
Guyana	1966	330	159	n/a	
Peru	1980	1,490	93	54	69
Uruguay	1985	2,620	63	90	21
Venezuela	1961	2,560	65	75	40

regimes, notably those in parts of Central and Eastern Europe and sub-Saharan Africa. In Central, Eastern, and Southern Europe, there are several states, notably Albania, Belarus, Georgia, Macedonia, Romania, and Yugoslavia, which currently stand midway between the emergent democratic and authoritarian nationalist categories, while Bosnia-Herzegovina has been in an anarchic condition, crippled by civil war. In Africa, which was dominated when the first edition of this book was published by one-party nationalistic socialist and authoritarian nationalist regimes, there has been a wave of apparent democratization from the early 1990s. Encouraged by changes in Central and Eastern Europe and by the prompting by Western donors of economic aid, the formation of opposition parties has been tolerated in the states shown in Table 13 and multiparty elections have been held. However, in some of the states, for example Cameroon, Congo, Djibouti, Equatorial Guinea, Gabon, and Mauritania, there have still been charges of

Age of liberal democratic regimes Table 12	
The average age of liberal democratic regimes by world regions	
(Average years since regime established: as at 1995)	
North America	174
Central & Southern Africa	28
Northern & Western Europe	88
Central America & the Caribbean	24
Asia	42
South America	20
Oceania	36
Central, Eastern, & Southern Europe	23
Middle East & North Africa	31
World average	*52*

election-rigging and intimidation of opposition candidates in what could be viewed as 'façade elections'. Changes of government have occurred in Benin, Cape Verde, Mali, São Tomé, South Africa, and Zambia. However, in some countries there is still a close identification of the ruling party with the state and the real test of multiparty democracy will come when this ruling party is defeated at the polls and expected to relinquish power.

Several African, Asian, and South European states, notably Angola, Cambodia, Georgia, Mozambique, and Yemen, still face the problem of continuing insurgencies by rebel groups and ethnic fragmentation is acute in some countries. For this reason, the armed forces, in these and several Asian and American states, remain influential background watchdog arbiters who might be tempted to reassert direct control in the near future if the democratization process moves ahead in a direction which sharply conflicts with their own interests. Indeed, there have been recent attempted coups in Cape Verde, Chad, the Comoros, Equatorial Guinea, and São Tomé. At present many states in Central and Southern Africa are situated, most accurately, at various positions on a continuum between the emergent democratic and the nationalistic socialist and authoritarian nationalist ideological categories. However, the existence of multiparty politics, despite its fragile, nascent form, has resulted in the tentative inclusion of these states in this ideological category.

Despite these clear variations in degrees of 'democratization', all the states categorized as emergent democracies might usefully be described as liberal democracies on trial and the 72 so identified are listed in Table 13. The dates of origin of the current regimes are also shown. The states included embrace nearly 1.2 billion people, or 21% of the world's population. Thirty-three are middle-high income states, situated predominantly in Central and Eastern Europe and Southeast Asia. However, the overall share of emergent democracies in world GDP is only 8% and, as Table 10 shows, the average per-capita income in emergent democracies was only $1,488 in 1992.

3.4 Communism

As an ideology communism stems from the writings of Marx and Engels which were subsequently taken up by Vladimir Ilyich Lenin and his associates and adapted to meet the needs of early 20th-century Russia. According to Marx, communism is an ideal which is eventually reached when all private property and class distinctions have been abolished and the state has become redundant and 'withered away'. In these terms, the nations which are commonly referred to as communist can hardly be said to be 'without states'. Indeed, they possess some of the most elaborate structures of state institutions in the world.

Nor were the origins of the Soviet Union, which used to be the 'model' for all communist systems, congruent with the classic texts of Marx and Engels. According to these, anti-capitalist revolutions should have first taken place in Western Europe, the most developed region of the world, where the industrial proletariat (working class) were expected to rise up in revolt against mounting exploitation by the bourgeoisie (industrial/business middle class). This would then have led on to an intermediate 'socialist' phase in which the state remained in place, serving as the instrument of the working classes in a 'revolutionary dictatorship', and in which inequalities continued to be tolerated, with each producer being remunerated in accordance with work done. Later, as affluence increased, a final, 'higher' phase of full communism would be achieved, no longer requiring the apparatus of government for its sustenance, in which all labour divisions would be ended and each worker would be able to receive 'according to his needs'.

In reality, however, revolution occurred first in underdeveloped Russia, in October 1917. This revolution was, moreover, far from a spontaneous uprising of industrial workers. Instead, it was a wartime 'coup', stimulated and led by Lenin, a member of the white-collar intelligentsia, with most of its 'revolutionary troops' drawn from peasant stock. Theoretical justification for this was provided by Lenin's theory of 'Imperialism: The Highest Stage of Capitalism', with the 'vanguard' position it ascribed to disciplined communist parties, fomenting revolution at the periphery so as to sever the links which bound together the global capitalist system and thus precipitating a final revolutionary cataclysm in the advanced West. This subsequent revolution failed to take place, however, leaving the Soviet Union to protect and 'build socialism' alone during the interwar period. Only after the end of World War II did significant new communist regimes become established. As in the Soviet case, however, they were to be found in the backward 'Second and Third Worlds' of Eastern Europe and Asia, having been imposed either by military force, where, as a consequence, they suffered from a lack of popular legitimacy, or following guerrilla-based, anticolonial liberation struggles.

Today, the followers of Marx and Lenin reluctantly agree that the ideal of communism has not been reached and that the intermediate condition of socialism remained a truer description of the Soviet system and those of its imitators. In no country did the state 'wither away'. Instead, the communist party remained firmly in charge, dominating state institutions, having assumed its prescribed role as the 'vanguard

Emergent democratic systems (72)   Table 13

Region/country	Year established	c. 1992 Per capita GDP (US$)	World ranking	c. 1991 Human rights rating (%)	World ranking
Asia *(9)*					
Bangladesh	1990	220	172	59	63
Cambodia	1993	200	175	33	90
Korea, South	1988	7,500	39	59	63
Kyrgyzstan	1991	840	119	n/a	
Mongolia	1990	400	149	n/a	
Nepal	1991	170	183	69	49
Pakistan	1988	420	147	42	86
Taiwan	1991	9,000	33	n/a	
Thailand	1992	2,040	73	62	57
Central America & Caribbean *(3)*					
Haiti	1994	360	154	n/a	
Nicaragua	1990	360	154	75	40
Panama	1989	2,400	66	81	35
Central, Eastern, & Southern Europe *(20)*					
Albania	1991	1,125	105	n/a	
Belarus	1991	2,925	55	n/a	
Bosnia-Herzegovina	1990	n/a		n/a	
Bulgaria	1990	1,500	91	83	30
Croatia	1990	1,530	88	n/a	
Czech Republic	1989	2,815	57	97	9
Estonia	1990	3,000	53	n/a	
Georgia	1992	850	118	n/a	
Hungary	1989	3,050	51	97	9
Latvia	1990	2,050	72	n/a	
Lithuania	1990	1,850	77	n/a	
Macedonia	1990	800	121	n/a	
Moldova	1990	1,280	98	n/a	
Poland	1989	2,180	69	83	30
Romania	1989	1,045	108	82	33
Russia	1990	2,600	64	54	69
Slovakia	1990	2,080	71	n/a	
Slovenia	1990	5,330	47	n/a	
Ukraine	1990	1,820	79	n/a	
Yugoslavia	1990	1,500	91	55	68
Central & Southern Africa *(30)*					
Angola	1994	610	135	27	97
Benin	1991	410	148	90	21
Burkina Faso	1991	290	166	n/a	
Cameroon	1991	820	120	56	66

continued

Emergent democratic systems (72) (continued)   Table 13

Region/country	Year established	c. 1992 Per capita GDP (US$)	World ranking	c. 1991 Human rights rating (%)	World ranking
Cape Verde	1991	780	125	n/a	
Central African Republic	1995	390	150	n/a	
Chad	1993	190	177	n/a	
Comoros	1992	460	144	n/a	
Congo	1992	940	114	n/a	
Côte d'Ivoire	1990	674	131	75	40
Djibouti	1992	730	127	n/a	
Equatorial Guinea	1993	330	159	n/a	
Ethiopia	1993	120	187	13	106
Gabon	1990	3,000	53	n/a	
Ghana	1992	390	150	53	72
Guinea	1993	430	145	n/a	
Guinea-Bissau	1993	180	179	n/a	
Lesotho	1993	547	140	n/a	
Madagascar	1992	230	171	n/a	
Malawi	1994	180	179	33	90
Mali	1992	270	169	n/a	
Mauritania	1991	500	142	n/a	
Mozambique	1994	80	189	53	72
Namibia	1990	1,030	110	n/a	
Niger	1992	290	166	n/a	
São Tomé	1990	340	158	n/a	
Seychelles	1991	5,500	46	n/a	
South Africa	1993	2,666	62	50	75
Togo	1993	390	150	48	80
Zambia	1991	330	159	57	65
Middle East & North Africa (4)					
Lebanon	1990	1,370	95	n/a	
Morocco	1992	1,036	109	56	66
Tunisia	1994	1,404	94	60	60
Yemen	1993	540	141	49	77
Northern & Western Europe (1)					
Andorra	1993	21,150	13	99	1
Oceania (2)					
Fiji	1990	1,650	85	n/a	
Philippines	1986	800	121	72	43
South America (3)					
Chile	1990	2,725	60	80	36
Paraguay	1993	1,530	88	70	47
Surinam	1991	1,210	101	n/a	

of the proletariat', so as to protect socialist society before the advent of true communism. The accession of Mikhail Gorbachev to the leadership of the Communist Party in the Soviet Union in 1985 resulted in the effective abandonment of striving for achievement of this theoretical ideal. Instead, through his 'perestroika' (economic restructuring), 'glasnost' (openness), and 'demokratsiya' (democratization) initiatives, an attempt was made to build an economically successful and democratically accountable 'socialist democracy', very much on the lines of Western social democracy. This attempt failed, with the unbottled ethnic and nationalist tensions within the Soviet Union and its satellites and the tremendous economic hardship caused by the transition from a planned to a capitalist economy, resulting in the collapse of the Soviet bloc between 1989 and 1991.

In Asia, legitimate, purportedly communist regimes have survived in China, North Korea, and Indo-China and, in the Caribbean, Castro's Cuba also remains a defiant outpost. However, these states, which have been distinguished by the charismatic leadership of their 'liberation leaders' and a powerful role for the armed forces, have all followed 'paths to socialism' which have diverged significantly from the Soviet model. In China, in particular, since 1978, under the leadership of Deng Xiaoping, there has been emphasis on market-centred economic reform, while tight political controls have been maintained in almost an authoritarian nationalist manner. During recent years the market has also been embraced in Laos, Vietnam, and Cuba.

The five states which can still currently be described as 'communist', since one-party control is maintained by a party which subscribes to the ideology of communism, in Marxist terms, are set out in Table 14. They account for a disproportionate share of the world's population, 24%, but only a fraction, 2.4%, of its GDP. Human rights ratings in all five states are abysmally low, but levels of government defence expenditure are exceptionally high, ranging from 3.7% in Cuba (WR: 58) to a crippling 25.2% in North Korea (WR: 2). Literacy rates are high.

Four distinguishing features characterize such communist states:

1 Marxism–Leninism (in the case of China, Maoism–Dengism) has been adopted as the official ideology, source of legitimacy, and vocabulary of political affairs.
2 The bulk of economic activity is under state ownership and subject to administrative (central) planning.
3 One party, the Communist Party, dominates the political scene and is tightly controlled from above in accordance with the Leninist precept of 'democratic centralism'.
4 The influence of the Communist Party, constitutionally ascribed a 'leading role' in the nation's affairs, is all-pervasive, controlling state organs, trade unions, the media, the judiciary, and industrial and agricultural enterprises through both supervision and direct membership.

Communist parties, able to attract a significant share of the national vote and even win shares in power, operate with success in several emergent democratic states in Central and Eastern Europe. However, they accept the tenets of multi-party liberal democracy. This is not the case with restyled former communist parties and their leaders who continue to control the states of Azerbaijan, Kazakhstan, Tajikistan, Turkmenistan, and Uzbekistan in the former Soviet-controlled regions of the Caucasus and Central Asia. Communism has been officially abandoned in these states, so they have been categorized in this volume as authoritarian nationalist states. However, a 'return to type' may occur in future years in several of them.

3.5 Nationalistic socialism

Countries which have been placed in this category display many of the attributes of a communist state but in a less developed and structured form. A key feature is the existence of one political party of avowed socialist orientation, but whose role, in practice, has been more that of a promoter of nationalism and an opponent of imperialism than of a 'guardian of the proletariat' and radical transformer of the country's economic structure. Private farming and petty manufacturing have, for example, remained predominant in these states.

In many countries subscribing to nationalistic socialism the presence of a 'charismatic leader' has been a distinctive characteristic. Muammar al-Kadhafi of Libya, Robert Mugabe of Zimbabwe, Julius Nyerere of Tanzania, Issaias Afwerki of Eritrea, Saddam Hussein of Iraq, and Hafez al-Assad of Syria are obvious examples, the former two having established their reputations as a guerrilla or political leader during their nations' independence struggles. In addition, a significant number of the states included in Table 15, Eritrea, Iraq, Libya, and Syria being the most prominent examples, have been involved, in recent years, in militarized border disputes with their neighbours. This has served to enhance the nationalist standing and inclination of their leaderships and has also resulted in the states being burdened by high levels of defence expenditure, equivalent to as much as 15% of GDP in Iraq (WR: 3).

The eight states identified as having nationalistic socialist regimes and set out in Table 15 embrace 117 million people, or just over 2% of the world's total population. They are concentrated in the Middle East and Africa. Indeed, it has been seriously argued that in Africa, with many societies divided vertically along tribal, regional, ethnic, and religious lines, rather than horizontally by social class, multiparty democracy can be a recipe for chaos and that one-party regimes are able to bring greater stability.

In terms of civil rights restrictions, the overall ratings recorded by most nationalistic socialist regimes are disappointingly low. Four regimes, however, those of Algeria, Senegal, Tanzania, and Zimbabwe, despite the monism of their political structures, stand out as significantly more 'liberal', exceeding the rating registered by several emergent democratic nations. In all four states multiparty political systems have been recently restored. However, such is the long-standing de facto dominance exerted by the ruling party in each state, and the military in Algeria, that it has been sensible to include these regimes in the nationalistic socialist category in preference to that of emergent democracy.

Communist systems (5)					Table 14
Region/country	Year established	c. 1992 Per capita GDP (US$)	World ranking	c. 1991 Human rights rating (%)	World ranking
Asia (4)					
China	1949	430	145	21	101
Korea, North	1948	1,285	97	20	102
Laos	1975	270	169	n/a	
Vietnam	1945*/1976**	180	179	27	97
Central America & Caribbean (1)					
Cuba	1959	1,886	76	30	93

* North
** South

3.6 Authoritarian nationalism

In its starkest form nationalism is a belief that people of the same racial stock are so unique that only they have the right to be regarded as members of a nation. This extreme kind of nationalism is so intolerant of other races and creeds that, at best, they are disenfranchised and, at worst, eliminated. Nazi Germany exhibited this attitude in its most brutal form and until quite recently the formerly white-dominated regime in South Africa pursued its own version of the 'final solution' through the operation of the system of apartheid.

Fortunately, although atrocities of 'ethnic cleansing' have been committed during the 1990s in Bosnia-Herzegovina, Burundi, and Rwanda, extreme examples of this kind are rare. Most present-day exponents of nationalism use it as a device to claim the loyalty and obedience of members of the public. Even liberal democratic states are guilty of nationalistic tendencies, though they may disguise the fact under the banner of patriotism. The national flag and the national anthem are manifestations of nationalism under the guise of patriotism and even sport has succumbed to its temptations.

A state which subscribes to the ideology of authoritarian nationalism displays the following three features:

1 Restrictions on the activities of all political parties, or a limitation to one which gives undivided and uncritical support to the state.
2 An authoritarian charismatic personal or collective executive.
3 Either the absence of an assembly to balance the power of the executive or the presence of an assembly which is essentially the servant of the executive.

For many states adherence to authoritarian nationalism will be a stage in the progression of independence from the rule of a colonial power to emergent democracy and, eventually, to a full, pluralistic democracy. Given a much longer time span, it is conceivable that all states will eventually abandon nationalistic tendencies and move towards regional, and even global, groupings. These developments are examined in Part 3.

The 13 countries identified as proponents of authoritarian nationalism are listed in Table 16. Within this grouping it must be stressed, however, that there exist considerable differences

Nationalistic socialist systems (8)					Table 15
Region/country	Year established	c. 1992 Per capita GDP (US$)	World ranking	c. 1991 Human rights rating (%)	World ranking
Central & Southern Africa (4)					
Eritrea	1993	115	188	n/a	
Senegal	1960	710	130	71	45
Tanzania	1961	130	186	41	87
Zimbabwe	1980	570	137	65	53
Middle East & North Africa (4)					
Algeria	1976	1,832	78	66	52
Iraq	1970	2,104	70	17	104
Libya	1977	5,551	45	24	99
Syria	1971	1,070	107	30	93

between both the policy outlooks and the degree of illiberalism of the regimes in power. For example, those in former Soviet-controlled Central Asia and the Caucasus region are, as noted, successors to powerful state-dominated communist regimes, while that in Indonesia is a military-backed regime which has successfully pursued a programme of capitalistic economic modernization. Those in Africa are found in states where tribal-based ethnic divisions are especially acute, leading to recent civil wars in Burundi and Rwanda.

Despite these clear variations, two elements remain common to all 13 states:

1   The existence of *de facto* one-party dominance.
2   Policy orientations which fall short of being fully socialist.

The second characteristic serves to distinguish these states from those included in the nationalistic socialist category above, thus making their inclusion in this group defensible.

The 13 states identified embrace 355 million people, or just over 6% of the global population. There is an even division between locations in Central and Southern Africa and Asia. The single most important authoritarian nationalist regime in demographic terms, accounting for 55% of the combined population total, is Indonesia. Here the Golkar Party, the dominant of the three political parties which are permitted to operate, controls affairs in a relatively sophisticated manner, ruling conjointly with the military in accordance with its own unique, Pancasila philosophy. Authoritarian nationalist regimes have also been established for more than two decades in Kenya, the Maldives, and Zaire.

3.7 Military authoritarianism

Military authoritarianism is a form of authoritarian nationalism whereby military leaders take it upon themselves to impose a government on the people, claiming, invariably, that it is for the public good. History is littered with examples of regimes when 'men of action' have felt it necessary to use their military strength to overthrow and replace civilian administrations. In some cases the transition is short-lived, in others military rule has become a quasi-permanent feature.

The characteristics of a state accepting authoritarian nationalism will be found also in this category with, of course, a military regime always in control. Sometimes a state based on military authoritarianism will try to disguise itself by using a civilian administration as a façade, fronting the military power behind. Panama, during the 1980s, provided an example of this. The military remain influential in a number of emergent democratic, nationalistic socialist and authoritarian nationalist states, notably Algeria, Angola, Bosnia, Burundi, Chile, Ghana, Guinea, Guinea-Bissau, Indonesia, Iraq, Mozambique, Pakistan, Paraguay, Rwanda, São Tomé, and Thailand, as well as in 'liberal democratic' Peru.

In Ghana the charismatic Flight-Lieutenant Jerry Rawlings, who twice seized power as a populist military leader in 1978 and 1981, succeeded in effecting the transition from military ruler to popularly elected president in a multiparty, emergent democratic state in 1992. In Indonesia, T N J Suharto, who assumed power in a coup in 1965, has been

president since 1967, being re-elected at regular five-yearly intervals. The 'presidential path' was also pursued, with varying success, by General Alfredo Stroessner in Paraguay (1954–89), General Zia ul-Haq in Pakistan (1977–88), and Lieutenant-General Hossain Mohammad Ershad in Bangladesh (1982–90). In most other cases military leaders, aware of their lack of legitimacy, have sought to 'return to barracks' and hand over power to civilian leaders once the circumstances that precipitated a coup have been resolved. However, after a country's armed forces have entered the political arena once, they appear to be less inhibited from re-entering again to 'correct' the political process. This has certainly been the experience of Pakistan, Thailand, and the states included in Table 17.

The seven states subscribing to military authoritarianism and listed in Table 17 embrace 209 million people, or 4% of the global total. Six-sevenths are located in Central and Southern Africa and the states are located in the world's bottom quartile in terms of per-capita GDP. Literacy rates and urbanization levels are also low, as Table 10 reveals, with a high proportion of the labour force still engaged in agricultural activities. There are no military regimes currently in Europe, Oceania, and the Americas and in recent decades only two military states have been established in Europe and Oceania: in Greece between 1967–73 and in Fiji between 1987–90. Periods of military junta rule have, however, been common in Central and South America during the course of this century.

The average age of the world's seven current military regimes is less than seven years. This reflects the necessarily transient character of this illegitimate regime type. The longest entrenched military-based regime is in Somalia, dating back to 1969, although it has a presidential façade. However, in Myanmar the military first effectively came to power in 1962, while in Nigeria there has been only a brief period of civilian rule since 1983. In Liberia power has been shared since August 1995 by a transitional council composed of rebel warlord leaders, pending elections promised in August 1996. In Sudan the military regime adheres to Muslim fundamentalist principles and has waged campaigns against the Christian and animist population in the country's south.

3.8 Islamic nationalism

As Table 18 shows, there are two countries with Islamic nationalist political regimes, Afghanistan and Iran. In these states the political process is completely dominated by fundamentalist Islam, a religious ideology that fulfils a political function similar to that performed by Marxism–Leninism in a communist regime. Sharia law is enforced, Islamic spiritual leaders (ayatollahs and mullahs) provide strategic guidance, and the policies of the (Islamic) political parties are framed in accordance with the Koran and Sharia, with religious scholars occupying prominent positions. In Iran an Islamic state was established in 1979 after a popular revolution, inspired by the exiled Ayatollah Khomeini, succeeded in overthrowing the Western-backed Muhammad Reza Shah Pahlavi. The background to this revolution was the disenchantment of young people, especially students, with the

Authoritarian nationalist systems (13)					Table 16
Country/region	Year established	c. 1992 Per capita GDP (US$)	World ranking	c. 1991 Human rights rating (%)	World ranking
Asia (6)					
Indonesia	1966	730	127	34	89
Kazakhstan	1991	1,800	80	n/a	
Maldives	1968	650	132	n/a	
Tajikistan	1991	480	143	n/a	
Turkmenistan	1991	1,270	99	n/a	
Uzbekistan	1991	950	112	n/a	
Central, Eastern, & Southern Europe (2)					
Armenia	1990	900	116	n/a	
Azerbaijan	1993	800	121	n/a	
Central & Southern Africa (5)					
Burundi	1994	210	174	n/a	
Kenya	1969	327	163	46	83
Rwanda	1994	320	165	48	80
Uganda	1986	190	177	46	83
Zaire	1965	214	173	40	88

widening gap between rich and poor that had been created by the Shah's economic modernization drive and their desire to recreate a Golden Age of Islam through a return to traditional Islamic values. In Afghanistan, Islam was established by force after a 13-year guerrilla war by the mujaheddin ('holy warriors') against a Russian-backed communist regime. Nationalism in both states is thus intimately linked with defence of Islamic faith against 'corrupting' outside religions and ideologies, specifically Western materialism and atheistic communism. There have also been attempts to extend the jihad (Islamic holy war) and export fundamentalist Islam to neighbouring states, notably Iraq and Tajikistan.

The combined population of the two states with Islamic nationalist regimes is 84 million and, as Table 10 shows, human rights ratings and literacy and urbanization levels are comparatively low. Since 1989 and the death of Ayatollah Khomeini, the Islamic revolution in Iran has entered a less militant phase. The country's economy was greatly weakened by a 1980–88 war with neighbouring Iraq. This persuaded Hoshemi Rafsanjani, the president from 1989, to rule pragmatically. In Afghanistan, since toppling the socialist regime of Najibullah Ahmadzai in 1992, the mujaheddin has been riven by regional and ideological-based factional rivalries. As a consequence, the civil war has continued.

In 23 other countries in the world Islam is similarly the state religion (see Table 8). Although Sharia law is followed by many of these states, the party political processes have not yet been so thoroughly permeated by the ideology of Islam as to merit application of the classification 'Islamic nationalist'. However, in Sudan, under the military's patronage, fundamentalist Islam has grown greatly in influence during recent years and Islamic militants were involved in 1995 in virtual civil wars in Algeria, Tajikistan and Kashmir, within India.

3.9 Absolutism

Absolutism is an ideology which can be traced back to *The Leviathan* written by Thomas Hobbes (1588–1679) soon after the mid-17th-century English Civil War (1642–52), in support of the English monarchy as the guarantor of stability and order. The ideology had even earlier roots in the medieval European doctrine of 'The Divine Right of Kings'. It argues that no limits whatsoever should be placed on the activities of a legitimate government, which will usually be in the form of an absolute monarch. Legitimacy is often claimed through the accident of birth, although it is convenient to forget that at some stage in history that legitimacy must have been acquired by force.

For a nation in an early stage of economic and social development, or one threatened by external forces, absolutism is an attractive ideology to accept, offering a guarantee of stability and order. For some countries it may only represent a stage in their development, to be superseded by a republican form of government or by a constitutional monarchy. For others it has become a permanent condition.

The characteristics of a state based on absolutism are:

1. The absence of any constitutional form of government, or a popular assembly or judiciary to counter executive power.
2. The denial of the right to form political parties or other forms of organized interests.
3. Governing systems based on clientism or neo-patrimonialism.

The 12 states adhering to absolutism, or a 'traditional regime', are listed in Table 19 and comprise an assortment of monarchies (Bhutan, Jordan, Saudi Arabia, Swaziland, and

Military authoritarian systems (7)　　　　　　　　　　　　　　　　　　　**Table 17**

Region/country	Year established	c. 1992 Per capita GDP (US$)	World ranking	c. 1991 Human rights rating (%)	World ranking
Asia (1)					
Myanmar	1988	385	153	17	104
Central & Southern Africa (6)					
Gambia	1994	350	157	n/a	
Liberia	1994	353	156	n/a	
Nigeria	1993	323	164	49	77
Sierra Leone	1992	150	184	67	51
Somalia	1969	150	184	n/a	
Sudan	1989	330	159	18	103

Islamic nationalist systems (2)　　　　　　　　　　　　　　　　　　　　**Table 18**

Region/country	Year established	c. 1992 Per capita GDP (US$)	World ranking	c. 1991 Human rights rating (%)	World ranking
Asia (1)					
Afghanistan	1992	200	175	28	96
Middle East & North Africa (1)					
Iran	1979	2,189	68	22	100

Tonga), sultanates (Brunei and Oman), and sheikhdoms and emirates (Bahrain, Kuwait, Qatar, and the United Arab Emirates), in addition to the papacy of Rome. In Bhutan there has been growing popular pressure for democratization and the monarchies in Jordan and Tonga, although absolute in the final analysis, do have vestiges of constitutional checks and balances. One other state, Morocco, is also characterized by monarchical rule, but within a more fully developed and party-based constitutional structure. For this reason it has been assigned, instead, to the emergent democracy category. Nepal was also an absolute state until widespread prodemocracy demonstrations in 1990 resulted in the establishment of a constitutional monarchy on the parliamentary executive model.

The 12 absolutist regimes included in Table 19 embrace a population of 30 million, corresponding to less than 1% of the world total. Seven are located in the Middle East, in which region it constitutes the predominant political type. It should also be noted that seven of these absolutist states, including six in the Middle East, are, as a consequence of their mineral oil wealth, among the world's 'Top 50' nations in terms of per-capita national income. This has meant that, although Bhutan and Swaziland are low-income states, the average per-capita income for absolutist states was $8,234 in c. 1992. As Table 10 shows, urbanization rates are also quite high, while levels of government defence spending are very high. Significantly, all the absolute states, except Swaziland, have an established religion.

3.10 The changing balance of ideologies

In 1989, when the first edition of this book was written, slightly more than half, 83 out of 164, of the nation-states of the world had regimes which could be classified as either liberal democratic or emergent democratic. Nearly a quarter, or 37 states, had effectively one-party socialist regimes, categorized either as communist or nationalistic socialist. This state type was particularly common in Central and Eastern Europe and Africa. The remaining sovereign states in the world had predominantly rightwing authoritarian nationalist, military, and absolutist regimes.

Six years on, as Table 20 demonstrates, the world political map has been radically transformed. With the collapse of the Soviet Union's communist empire and the adoption of multiparty democracy in much of Africa, the number of states with liberal democratic and emergent democratic political systems has increased to 145, equivalent to three-quarters of the world's total. Pluralist democracy predominates in Europe and the Americas, in particular, but has also put down new roots in Asia and Africa. Only 13 of the world's 192 states now have avowedly socialist regimes of a communist or nationalistic socialist type but, while the number of military regimes has also fallen sharply, there are still 25 absolutist and authoritarian nationalist states.

The onward march of pluralist liberal democracy, allied to

Absolutist systems (12) — Table 19

Region/country	Year established	c. 1992 Per capita GDP (US$)	World ranking	c. 1991 Human rights rating (%)	World ranking
Asia (2)					
Bhutan	1907	180	179	n/a	
Brunei	1984	14,500	25	n/a	
Central & Southern Africa (1)					
Swaziland	1968	900	116	n/a	
Middle East & North Africa (7)					
Bahrain	1971	7,870	38	n/a	
Jordan	1952	1,640	86	65	53
Kuwait	1961	20,000	18	33	90
Oman	1951	5,600	44	49	77
Qatar	1971	15,140	24	n/a	
Saudi Arabia	1932	7,942	36	29	95
United Arab Emirates	1971	19,300	20	n/a	
Northern & Western Europe (1)					
Vatican City State	1377	n/a	n/a	n/a	
Oceania (1)					
Tonga	1875	1,350	96	n/a	

World political regimes in 1989 and 1995 — Table 20

Year	Lib-dem	Em-dem	Communism	Nat-soc	Auth-nat	Military	Islam-nat	Absolutist
			Number of states by regime type					
1989	50	33	16	21	16	16	0	12
1995	73	72	5	8	13	7	2	12
Change	+23	+39	−11	−13	−3	−9	+2	−

Key:
Lib-dem   Liberal democratic
Em-dem   Emergent democratic
Nat-soc   Nationalistic socialist
Auth-nat   Authoritarian nationalist
Islam-nat   Islamic nationalist

a capitalist mixed economy, has been presented by some writers, notably Francis Fukuyama, as an inexorable process. Communism, criticized now as a 'grand oversimplification', and socialism are viewed as failed experiments, while the increasing competitive pressures of the global economy and popular demands for individual liberties are seen as key elements which will force a convergence in political types.

However, the annual reports of such human-rights monitoring bodies as Amnesty International and Freedom House show that, in 1994, in more than 60 countries prisoners of conscience were held, political killings sanctioned, and people were held in detention without charge or trial. Clearly many states are far from being pluralist entities and are guided by different ideological impulses. In addition, history shows that waves of democratization have been followed later by periods of reversion. Nationalism, mobilizing citizens on ethnic lines, remains a potent political force despite the continued development of regional political groupings. Populism, as noted earlier, is also emerging as a new ideology, while the limitations of free-market capitalism, which produces 'losers' as well as 'winners', mean that democratic socialism, with its recognition of, and compensation for, natural, individual inequalities, will remain a relevant and popular political ideology.

Recommended reading

Beetham, D (ed.) *Defining and Measuring Democracy*, Sage, 1994

Brown, A (ed.) *Political Culture and Communist States*, Macmillan, 1984

Brzezinski, Z *The Grand Failure: The Birth and Death of Communism in the Twentieth Century*, Macdonald, 1989

Cammack, P, Pool, D and Tordoff, W *Third World Politics: A Comparative Introduction*, 2nd edn., Macmillan, 1993, Chap. 2

Clapham, C *Third World Politics: An Introduction*, Croom Helm, 1985, Chap. 3

Decalo, S *Coups and Army Rule in Africa*, Yale University Press, 1986

Deutsch, K W, Dominguez, J I and Heclo, H *Comparative Government: Politics of Industrialized and Developing Nations*, Houghton Mifflin, 1981

Dunleavy, P and O'Leary, B *Theories of the State: The Politics of Liberal Democracy*, Macmillan, 1987

Eatwell, R and Wright, A *Contemporary Political Ideologies*, Pinter, 1993

Ferdinand, P *Communist Regimes in Comparative Perspective*, Harvester Wheatsheaf, 1991

Finer, S E *Comparative Government: An Introduction to the Study of Politics*, Penguin, 1970

Finer, S E *The Man on Horseback: The Role of the Military in Politics*, 2nd edn., Penguin, 1976

Fukuyama, F *The End of History and the Last Man*, Penguin, 1992

Furtak, R *The Political Systems of the Socialist States: An Introduction to Marxist–Leninist Regimes*, Harvester Press, 1986

Ghayasuddin, M (ed.) *The Impact of Nationalism on the Muslim World*, The Open Press, 1986

Harrop, H (ed.) *Power and Policy in Liberal Democracies*, Cambridge University Press, 1992

Hiro, D *Islamic Fundamentalism*, Paladin, 1988

Huntington, S P *The Third Wave: Democratization in the Late Twentieth Century*, University of Oklahoma Press, 1991

Kamrava, M *Politics and Society in the Third World*, Routledge, 1993

Szporlouk, R *Communism and Nationalism: Karl Marx versus Friedrich List*, Oxford University Press, 1988

Wesson, R (ed.) *Democracy: A Worldwide Survey*, Praeger, 1987

White, S, Garner, J and Schopflin, G *Communist Political Systems: An Introduction*, 2nd edn., Macmillan, 1987, Chaps 1 and 2

CHAPTER 4

Executives

4.1 Political executives

It is usual to make a distinction between the political executive and the nonpolitical, or permanent, executive. The latter is the salaried civil service which normally remains in office to work for whichever politicians happen to be in power. They, in turn, constitute the political executive and, as such, provide the leadership for both the political system and the state.

The modern political executive can be personal or collective and is found in a variety of forms including president, prime minister and party chairman or secretary-general. Whatever the contemporary form and title, each is a direct descendant of the personal autocrat or absolute monarch, at one time universal.

States with more than one operating political party have been identified as liberal democracies or emergent democracies. With only a few exceptions, their executives are either presidents or prime ministers. We shall refer to them, respectively, as presidential or parliamentary executives. In the exceptions, a dual executive, usually of a president and a prime minister, operates.

One-party states have been subdivided into communist, nationalistic socialist, authoritarian nationalist, and military authoritarian. In these cases the most common form of executive is, again, presidential, although in those we have identified as communist the executive assumes a distinctive form, partly collective and partly personal as, at the apex of power, the state and party machines merge.

Finally, there are the few surviving absolutist states, where political parties have no role to play, and the executives are individuals exercising virtually unbridled power in very much the same way as the original precursors of what we now call democratic governments.

Table 21 shows the current distribution of political executives in the 192 states under consideration.

4.2 The parliamentary executive

This is the second most common form of political executive in the world today, 55 states having adopted it, embracing almost a third of the global population. Thirty-one of them are constitutional monarchies and 24 republics. It is some-times referred to as the 'Westminster model' because it originated, and is found in its clearest form, in the United Kingdom. It is not coincidental that of the 55 nations with parliamentary political executives 28, including the United Kingdom, were formerly part of the British Empire and are now independent members of the Commonwealth. It is useful, therefore, to examine the UK system, even though the executives of other countries have been adapted from the original example to suit particular needs. All parliamentary executives are found in multiparty liberal (44) or emergent democracies (11), with 18 of the total being in Northern and Western Europe, 11 in the Caribbean region and eight in Oceania. Almost half, 47%, are located in island states and, as Table 21 shows, although India, the world's second most populous nation has a parliamentary executive, there is a general bias towards this executive type being found most commonly among the smaller states of the world. Thus two-thirds of the states with parliamentary executives have populations below 10 million and areas less than 100,000 square kilometres. The full list, showing geographical distributions, is given in Table 22.

The parliamentary executive displays three essential features:

1 The role of head of state is separate from that of head of government and is distant from party politics, serving mainly as the patriotic and ceremonial focus of the nation. The head of state can be a president, as in Germany or India, or a monarch, as in the Netherlands or the United Kingdom. In the majority of Commonwealth countries with parliamentary executives, the head of state is still the British monarch, represented by a resident governor general.
2 The executive is drawn from the assembly and directly responsible to it, and its security of tenure is dependent on the support of the assembly, or parliament. In other words, a 'no-confidence' vote in parliament can bring down the government, resulting in a change of executive or a general election. It is in such circumstances that the nonpolitical head of state may become temporarily involved in politics by either inviting the leader of a party in opposition to form a new government, or by dissolving parliament and initiating elections.

World distribution of executive systems

Table 21

By region

Region	Parliamentary	Limited presidential	Dual	Communist	Unlimited presidential	Military	Absolute	Total
Asia	8	4	2	4	7	1	2	28
Central America & Caribbean	11	8	1	1	0	0	0	21
Central, Eastern, & Southern Europe	6	13	4	0	2	0	0	25
Central & Southern Africa	2	30	0	0	9	6	1	48
Middle East & North Africa	1	3	2	0	5	0	7	18
North America	1	1	0	0	0	0	0	2
Northern & Western Europe	18	2	3	0	0	0	1	23
Oceania	8	6	0	0	0	0	1	15
South America	0	12	0	0	0	0	0	12
Total	55	78	12	5	23	7	12	192

By population and land area c. 1992–94

Executive type	Number of states	('000 sq km) Area	% of world area	(m) Population	% of world population
Parliamentary	55	27,932	21.0	1,829	32.8
Limited presidential	78	67,424	50.7	1,486	26.6
Dual	12	1,926	1.4	154	2.8
Communist	5	10,369	7.8	1,315	23.6
Unlimited presidential	23	17,744	13.3	556	10.0
Military	7	4,925	3.7	209	3.7
Absolute	12	2,726	2.0	30	0.5
Sub-total	192	133,047	100.0	5,578	100.0
Colonies & dependent territories*	39	2,387	–	13	–
Total	231	135,434	–	5,591	–

* Excludes Corsica, Western Sahara, and Tibet, whose area and population are included in the totals for France, Morocco, and China, within the dual and communist executive categories

By state population size c. 1992–94

(m) State pop. size	Parliamentary	Limited presidential	Dual	Communist	Unlimited presidential	Military	Absolute	Total
< 0.1	9	5	0	0	0	0	1	15
0.1 – < 1	12	9	0	0	1	1	5	28
1 – < 10	16	34	8	1	9	3	5	76
10 – < 20	6	13	2	1	5	0	1	28
20 – < 50	3	9	1	1	6	2	0	22
50 – < 100	5	5	1	1	1	0	0	13
100 – < 200	3	2	0	0	1	1	0	7
200 – < 500	0	1	0	0	0	0	0	1
500 – 1,250	1	0	0	1	0	0	0	2
Total	55	78	12	5	23	7	12	192

continued

| World distribution of executive systems (continued) | | | | | | | Table 21 |

By state areal sizes

('000 sq km)

State areal size	Parliamentary	Limited presidential	Dual	Communist	Unlimited presidential	Military	Absolute	Total
< 1	14	7	0	0	1	0	3	25
1 – < 10	4	3	0	0	0	0	1	8
10 – < 100	16	17	8	4	5	3	6	59
100 – < 500	14	24	3	0	8	0	1	50
500 – < 1,000	4	11	1	0	3	3	0	22
1,000 – < 5,000	1	13	0	0	6	1	1	22
5,000 – < 10,000	2	2	0	1	0	0	0	5
10,000 – 20,000	0	1	0	0	0	0	0	1
Total	55	78	12	5	23	7	12	192

A particular characteristic of the 'Westminster model' is that it is, historically, based on the concept of a two-party system. The House of Commons, for example, is physically constructed to accommodate two opposing parties, the government party sitting on benches to the right of the chairperson of the House, or speaker, and the opposition party to the left. Also, the leader of the opposition is acknowledged formally in legislation, provided with suitable office accommodation, and paid a salary out of public funds. This practice is followed in several Commonwealth states, most notably Australia and New Zealand, but is not an essential feature of a parliamentary executive. Indeed, the majority of European states, including Germany, Austria, Belgium, Denmark, Ireland, Italy, the Netherlands, and Norway, have a wide range of parties and governments are frequently, and in some cases invariably, formed by coalitions of these parties. The term, 'consensus democracy', or consociationalism, has been coined to describe this political model. Conversely, in a number of Asian states with parliamentary executive systems, for example, Malaysia, Singapore and, until recently, India and Japan, effective one-party electoral dominance has been the norm, although opposition parties do operate.

3 The leader of the party, or coalition of parties, commanding the support of parliament is called upon by the head of state, monarch or president, to become prime minister and form a government. The prime minister then chooses a cabinet, drawn from parliament, and they, with other noncabinet ministers, form the government.

The fact that the parliamentary executive is drawn from and responsible to the assembly makes it, in theory at least, particularly accountable. In reality much depends upon the state of the parties in parliament. A British prime minister, for example, enjoying a clear parliamentary majority, usually has greater executive power and discretion than a US president, subject to the checks and balances of a constitution which gives significant power and authority to an independent Congress. In countries where coalition governments are the norm prime ministerial authority is invariably weaker,

with power diffused among ministers drawn from a variety of parties. Special arrangements have been devised in a number of such cases, however, to buttress the chief executive's authority. The most notable example is Germany in which, under the terms of the Basic Law (constitution) of 1949, members of the assembly can only force the replacement of the chancellor (prime minister) through a 'constructive vote of no confidence', by which a majority of members vote positively in favour of a proposed successor.

Four of the newly democratized states of former Soviet-controlled Central and Eastern Europe, Bulgaria, Hungary, Latvia, and Slovakia, now have vigorously functioning parliamentary executives. A further four, the Czech Republic, Estonia, Lithuania, and Slovenia, have executives which have been categorized as 'dual', but are substantially parliamentary in nature. The remaining 19 states in this region and in ex-Soviet Central Asia have presidential executives, both limited (13) and unlimited (6).

An analysis of the data in Table 22 reveals that 43, or 78%, of the heads of the parliamentary executives in the world, either prime ministers or chancellors, had, in 1996, been in office for fewer than five years. This reflects the effective functioning of multiparty politics in these liberal and emergent democracies. However, 8 prime ministers and chancellors had been in power for more than seven years, securing re-election several times. These included Helmut Kohl in Germany (1982), Mahathir bin Mohamad in Malaysia (1981), and Felipe González in Spain (1982).

4.3 The limited presidential executive

The limited presidency is the most common form of political executive in the world today, 78 states having adopted it, embracing 27% of the global population, and half the world's land area. It should be noted, however, that 53 of the countries listed in Table 23 are emergent democracies which have only very recently adopted this type of executive, having moved from unlimited presidential, military, or communist executive systems. Their ability to sustain this form of

States with parliamentary executives (55) — Table 22

Region/country	Republic (R) or monarchy (M)	Member of Commonwealth	Year established	Year current head of state came to power	Year current prime minister came to power
Asia (8)					
Bangladesh	R	Y	1991	1991	1991
India	R	Y	1947	1992	1991
Japan	M	N	1946	1989	1996
Malaysia	M	Y	1957	1994	1981
Nepal	M	N	1991	1972	1995
Pakistan	R	Y	1988	1993	1993
Singapore	R	Y	1965	1993	1990
Thailand	M	N	1992	1946	1995
Central America & Caribbean (11)					
Antigua	M	Y	1981	1981	1994
Bahamas	M	Y	1973	1973	1992
Barbados	M	Y	1966	1966	1994
Belize	M	Y	1981	1981	1993
Dominica	R	Y	1978	1983	1995
Grenada	M	Y	1974	1974	1995
Jamaica	M	Y	1962	1962	1992
St Kitts	M	Y	1983	1983	1980
St Lucia	M	Y	1979	1979	1982
St Vincent	M	Y	1979	1979	1984
Trinidad & Tobago	R	Y	1962	1987	1995
Central, Eastern, & Southern Europe (6)					
Bulgaria	R	N	1990	1990	1995
Greece	R	N	1974	1995	1993
Hungary	R	N	1989	1990	1994
Latvia	R	N	1990	1993	1995
Slovakia	R	N	1990	1993	1994
Turkey	R	N	1982	1993	1993
Central & Southern Africa (2)					
Lesotho	M	Y	1993	1995	1993
Mauritius	R	Y	1968	1992	1995
Middle East & North Africa (1)					
Israel	R	N	1948	1993	1995
North America (1)					
Canada	M	Y	1867	1952	1993
Northern & Western Europe (18)					
Andorra	M	N	1993	1995	1994
Austria	R	N	1918	1986	1986
Belgium	M	N	1831	1951	1992
Denmark	M	N	1849	1972	1993
Germany	R	N	1949	1994	1982
Iceland	R	N	1944	1970	1991
Ireland	R	N	1937	1990	1994
Italy	R	N	1948	1992	1995

continued

States with parliamentary executives (55) (continued)					Table 22
Region/country	Republic (R) or monarchy (M)	Member of Commonwealth	Year established	Year current head of state came to power	Year current prime minister came to power
Liechtenstein	M	N	1921	1984	1993
Luxembourg	M	N	1868	1964	1995
Malta	R	Y	1974	1994	1987
Monaco	M	N	1911	1949	1994
Netherlands	M	N	1814	1980	1994
Norway	M	N	1814	1991	1990
San Marino	R	N	1600	rotating	rotating
Spain	M	N	1978	1975	1982
Sweden	M	N	1809	1973	1996
United Kingdom	M	Y	1689	1952	1990
Oceania (8)					
Australia	M	Y	1901	1952	1991
Fiji	R	N	1987	1994	1992
New Zealand	M	Y	1853	1952	1990
Papua New Guinea	M	Y	1975	1975	1994
Solomon Islands	M	Y	1978	1978	1994
Tuvalu	M	Y	1978	1978	1993
Vanuatu	R	Y	1980	1994	1995
Western Samoa	R	Y	1962	1962	1988

democratic government must, therefore, be viewed with caution. Nevertheless, it is significant that it has been the presidential, rather than the parliamentary, which has been the most popular executive type adopted by newly democratized states. This is shown by the fact that between 1988 and 1996 the number of states with parliamentary executives advanced by a quarter, from 43 to 55, while the number with limited presidential executives more than doubled, from 35 to 78. One region which has provided an exception to this trend has been South Asia where, since 1988, Pakistan and, later, Bangladesh moved from presidential to parliamentary executives, with Sri Lanka promising to follow suit.

Derived from the Latin *praesidens*, the term president has a classical meaning of one who superintends, rules, or directs. In the modern world it is used to signify the head of state in a republic. It includes the ceremonial, and often indirectly elected, heads of state of the 24 republics which have parliamentary executives; the autocratic executive heads of state of nationalistic socialist and authoritarian nationalist regimes, who are designated here as 'unlimited presidents'; and the popularly elected, usually directly, although sometimes indirectly, heads of state and government in liberal and emergent democracies, referred to here as 'limited presidents'.

The clearest, though also the most extreme, example of the limited presidential model is provided by the United States and, although there are practical differences between individual systems, many of the features found in the United States are replicated elsewhere. Like parliamentary executives, all limited presidential executives occur in multiparty

liberal (25) or emergent democracies (53). The full list, with geographical distributions, is given in Table 23.

A general point which emerges from this table is the predilection for this system of executive in the mainland countries of the Americas. Of the 21 states in this broad region, only two, Belize and Canada, have differing executive systems. The two former British colonies, Belize and Canada, have parliamentary executives. For the remaining states of the region, which secured independence from the early 19th century onwards, the influence of United States' political and constitutional conventions and republican ideals is clear. In addition, limited presidential systems are particularly common in the larger states of the world. This is shown by an analysis of the data in Table 21. Two-thirds of states with limited presidential executives have areas in excess of 100,000 square kilometres and 38% have populations greater than 10 million.

As already noted, the limited presidential executive form of government has been a popular model to be adopted in recent years by newly emergent or re-established democracies in the Americas, Oceania, and Asia, the most prominent recently being Argentina, Brazil, the Philippines, South Korea, and Taiwan, as well as in Africa and Central and Eastern Europe. One factor influencing its adoption by such states is its attractive image as a modern form of government for democratic republics. In contrast, as noted above, parliamentary systems are found most commonly in older states, often where there is a hereditary, ceremonial head of state. Another important factor is the perceived need, in newly emergent democracies, for the head of state to act as a strong and charismatic unifying force, exemplified, for example, by Corazon Aquino in the Philippines between 1986 and 1992, Lech Wałesa in Poland 1990–1995, and Nelson Mandela in South Africa from 1994. As a consequence, these states have opted for a directly elected presidential executive, enjoying a clear national mandate, in preference to an indirectly elected parliamentary executive.

There are four key features present in a limited presidential executive:

1 Presidents are elected for a fixed term to perform the dual role of head of state and head of government. As head of state they occupy a mainly ceremonial position and are the focus of popular patriotism. As head of government they lead the executive branch of government, and are usually head of the armed forces and the state civil service. Also, as head of government, they are in charge of foreign affairs and are the main initiator of legislation.

2 Presidents' tenure are secure unless they commit a grave unconstitutional act. The US president, for example, cannot be removed by Congress except by impeachment.

3 Presidents govern with an advisory cabinet of nonelected departmental secretaries, whom they choose and appoint and who are fully responsible to them.

4 Presidential powers are limited by the need for the approval of the assembly for certain executive actions. Under the US constitution, for example, Congress has sole legislative powers and the president's veto of Acts of Congress can be overridden by a two-thirds vote. Although presidents are expected to provide national leadership, their ability to do so is constrained by their ability to carry Congress with them. The US Senate, in particular, has strong counterbalancing powers whereby presidents can only make key federal appointments, judicial and cabinet, with Senate approval. Foreign treaties require a two-thirds majority of the chamber before coming into effect.

It is this balanced relationship between the president of the United States and Congress, as well as the clear statement of their respective roles written into the constitution, which make the presidency, although powerful, a limited form of executive and it is these features which are found in the other 77 states whose political executives fall into this category. The degrees of emphasis differ, however, as do the arrangements for the election of presidents, the restrictions on their length and terms of office, and the presence or absence of a separately elected prime minister, in the legislature.

In Albania, Botswana, Guinea-Bissau, Guyana, the Marshall Islands, Micronesia, Nauru, South Africa, Surinam, and Switzerland, for example, the presidential executive operates in many ways like a parliamentary one, being chosen by the legislature. In Switzerland the presidency is collective or collegial, comprising all seven members of the Federal Council (Bundesrat), one of whom is selected annually to assume the formal title of President of the Swiss Confederation (Bundespräsident).

In general, it would be true to say that few states with limited presidential executives approach the high degree of dispersal of power that exists in the United States. Arguably, those in South America and the Philippines come closest. As a consequence, the effective authority of most of the presidents included in Table 23 significantly exceeds that of the US chief executive. In a number of emergent democracies, the most prominent examples being Egypt, Guyana, Mexico, and a number of African states, true competition from opposition parties remains circumscribed, further enhancing presidential authority. There are also some states, notably Angola, Chile, Ethiopia, Ghana, Mozambique, Peru, and Taiwan, where the military remains an influential force. In such cases, the presidential system can be viewed as only partially limited.

An analysis of Table 23 reveals that 45, or 58%, of the heads of limited presidential executives had, in 1996, been in office for fewer than five years. Fourteen, or 18%, had been in power for at least a decade and two, the presidents of Gabon and Togo, had been in office since the mid-1960s. However, the latter had originally been presidents in one-party states which had only recently become multiparty. In liberal democratic states in 1996, only four presidents, those of Botswana, the Dominican Republic, Egypt, and the Marshall Islands, had been in power for more than nine years. The imposition of term limits, preventing a president from serving more than a stipulated number of, often consecutive, terms, has been an important factor in restricting presidential tenures in many other liberal and emergent democratic states. In seven states, Brazil, Colombia, Guatemala, South Korea, Paraguay, the Philippines, and Switzerland, presidents are restricted to one term in office. In 21 states, which include Albania, Argentina, Georgia, Peru, Poland, Russia, the United States, and Venezuela, the limit is set at two terms. In three states, Angola, Mozambique, and the Seychelles, there is a three-term limit. In contrast, in parliamentary executive systems no formal term limits are imposed although in Japan they have been operated informally for much of the postwar period by the ruling Liberal Democratic Party, which has regularly changed its leader biennially.

Finally, in some states with a limited presidential executive a relatively high minimum age limit is set for candidates, in an effort to ensure that politicians of experience and judgement are elected. In the United States for example, a minimum age of 35 years is stipulated, five years higher than that required for a senator. A similar minimum age has been set in Brazil and Poland, while in the Philippines and Mongolia the respective minimum ages are 40 and 45 years.

4.4 The dual executive

The dual executive is found in four liberal and eight emergent democracies, the most notable example being France. There are significant differences between the 12 cases, however, and, although the French system is usually cited as the model, it should not be assumed that the others contain all, or even most, of the French features. In the Czech Republic, Estonia, Finland, France, Haiti, Lebanon, Lithuania, Portugal, Slovenia, and Sri Lanka the executive consists of a working partnership between the president and the prime minister while in Cambodia and Morocco the partnership is between the monarch and the prime minister. In Haiti, until

States with limited presidential executives (78) — Table 23

Region/country	Year established	Year current head of state came to power	Region/country	Year established	Year current head of state came to power
Asia (4)			Ghana	1992	1981
Korea, South	1987	1993	Guinea	1991	1984
Kyrgyzstan	1990	1990	Guinea-Bissau	1992	1980
Mongolia	1990	1990	Madagascar	1992	1993
Taiwan	1987	1988	Malawi	1994	1994
			Mali	1992	1992
Central America & Caribbean (8)			Mauritania	1991	1984
Costa Rica	1821	1994	Mozambique	1990	1986
Dominican Republic	1962	1986	Namibia	1990	1990
El Salvador	1982	1994	Niger	1992	1993
Guatemala	1975	1996	São Tomé	1990	1991
Honduras	1982	1993	Seychelles	1991	1977
Mexico	1917	1994	South Africa	1993	1994
Nicaragua	1979	1990	Togo	1993	1967
Panama	1989	1994	Zambia	1991	1991
Central, Eastern, & Southern Europe (13)			**Middle East & North Africa** (3)		
Albania	1991	1992	Egypt	1971	1981
Belarus	1991	1994	Tunisia	1988	1987
Bosnia-Herzegovina	1990	1990	Yemen	1990	1990
Croatia	1990	1990			
Cyprus	1960	1993	**North America** (1)		
Georgia	1992	1992	United States	1776	1993
Macedonia	1991	1991			
Moldova	1990	1990	**Northern & Western Europe** (1)		
Poland	1989	1995	Switzerland	1874	1995
Romania	1989	1989			
Russia	1990	1990	**Oceania** (6)		
Ukraine	1990	1994	Belau	1981	1992
Yugoslavia	1990	1993	Kiribati	1979	1994
			Marshall Islands	1979	1979
Central & Southern Africa (30)			Micronesia	1979	1991
Angola	1991	1979	Nauru	1968	1995
Benin	1990	1991	Philippines	1987	1992
Botswana	1966	1980			
Burkina Faso	1991	1987	**South America** (12)		
Cameroon	1991	1982	Argentina	1983	1989
Cape Verde	1992	1991	Bolivia	1982	1993
Central African Republic	1995	1993	Brazil	1985	1995
Chad	1992	1990	Chile	1990	1994
Comoros	1992	1990	Colombia	1978	1994
Congo	1992	1992	Ecuador	1979	1992
Côte d'Ivoire	1990	1993	Guyana	1966	1992
Djibouti	1992	1977	Paraguay	1989	1993
Equatorial Guinea	1991	1979	Peru	1978	1990
Ethiopia	1993	1991	Surinam	1988	1991
Gabon	1991	1967	Uruguay	1985	1995
			Venezuela	1961	1994

recently, the military also retained significant influence. The full list is given in Table 24.

Although not really a 'model' of the other systems, a description of how the dual executive operates in France will be helpful to an understanding of the variations which are found in other countries.

The constitution for the French Fifth Republic was framed in the short time span of three months, during the summer of 1958, while the new administration of Charles de Gaulle was settling into office. Conscious of the recent history of instability in French governments, its authors tried to combine elements of the United States and British constitutions,

States with dual executives (12)			Table 24
Country/region	Year established	Year current head of state came to power	Year current prime minister came to power
Asia (2)			
Cambodia	1993	1991	1993
Sri Lanka	1978	1994	1994
Central America & Caribbean (1)			
Haiti	1987	1996	1996
Central Eastern & Southern Europe (4)			
Czech Republic	1989	1989	1992
Estonia	1990	1992	1995
Lithuania	1990	1993	1993
Slovenia	1990	1990	1992
Middle East & North Africa (2)			
Lebanon	1926	1989	1992
Morocco	1992	1961	1994
Northern & Western Europe (3)			
Finland	1917	1994	1995
France	1958	1995	1995
Portugal	1976	1996	1996

while, at the same time, seeking to strengthen the executive and encourage greater party discipline and stability. To these ends, provision was made for a two-headed executive of a president, to be elected by an electoral college for a seven-year term, and a prime minister, chosen by the president but responsible to the National Assembly.

Under the terms of the constitution the president has considerable powers, including, as well as the appointment of the prime minister, control of the armed forces, the right to preside over cabinet and Defence Council meetings, the right to dissolve the Assembly once a year, and powers to negotiate treaties, countersign legislation approved by the Assembly, and appoint ambassadors.

Nevertheless, the constitution made provision (Articles 20 and 21) for the prime minister and Council of Ministers to wield ultimate power while the president was expected to remain aloof from day-to-day government and act as a mediator and conciliator, who ensured that the different factions, in whatever coalition was formed on the basis of Assembly support, worked successfully together.

The respective roles of president and prime minister were altered when, in October 1962, President de Gaulle forced through, by referendum, a change in the constitution making the president directly elected by the people. This gave him a justifiable claim of popular support and he and his immediate successors used this to dominate policy-making so that the prime minister became, in effect, the political servant of the president, who governed in the style of the US presidency, but without the Congressional checks and balances which limit it.

As long as the French president was able to appoint a prime minister amenable to his directions and acceptable to the National Assembly the unbalanced twin executive worked. In 1986, however, following Assembly elections which swept to power the opposition conservative coalition, President Mitterrand was forced to appoint a prime minister, Jacques Chirac, whose political stance was well to the right of his. An experiment of 'cohabitation' thus began, in which the prime minister assumed the upper hand. This lasted, at times uneasily, until the presidential and Assembly elections of April–June 1988, which were won by President Mitterrand and his Socialist Party. This restored the status quo until there was a further period of 'cohabitation' between 1993 and 1995, with Edouard Balladur as prime minister. The periods of 'cohabitation' proved that the constitution was sufficiently flexible to allow a president and prime minister from different parts of the political spectrum to work together, if need be, for an interim period, with reasonable success.

The dual executive in Lebanon closely resembles that of France but the relationship between the president and prime minister is as much conditioned by religious as political factors. With the object of maintaining religious harmony, the president is always, by tradition, a Christian and the prime minister a Muslim. The president is elected for a six-year, nonrenewable, term by the National Assembly.

In Finland, the dual executive is also very similar to that of France, with the president, who is popularly elected for a renewable six-year term, having responsibility for foreign affairs, the dissolution of the Eduskunta (parliament), the formation and dismissal of governments, and the appointment of senior civil servants. The president also has substantial veto powers over legislation passed by the Eduskunta and more limited decree powers. The multiparty, coalition nature of Finnish politics has served to enhance the effective role of the president, as, until 1991, did the sensitivity and importance of foreign relations with Finland's neighbour, the Soviet Union. This was particularly the case 1956–81 when Urho Kekkonen, of the Centre Party of Finland (KP), was president and used the office to ensure the continuance in power of centre-left parliamentary coalitions, and to promote a foreign policy of 'active neutrality', despite a dwindling in electoral support. In recent years, however, there have been proposals to significantly reduce presidential powers in the legislative and executive spheres.

The Portuguese variant of the dual executive has been evolving since the adoption of a new constitution in 1976. To effect a smooth transition to civilian government after a long period of dictatorship and military rule, the role of the president was cast as a 'watchdog' for the army, to ensure that its interests were not neglected by a civilian prime minister. The relationship between the two parts of the executive depended as much on personalities as constitutional rules. The revised constitution of 1982 reduced the powers of the presidency and four years later the first civilian for 60 years was elected to that office. Political power is now weighted towards the prime minister but he does not yet head a genuine parliamentary executive.

The Sri Lankan constitution of 1978 is based loosely on the French model and provides for a directly elected president and a prime minister, drawn from the assembly, who is appointed by the president and acts as his or her 'parliamentary manager'. The president has considerably more powers than the prime minister and can hold several portfolios. Sri Lanka thus represents a weak form of dual executive, compared with the French version, yet falls short of being a full presidential executive, as in the United States. In 1994 Chandrika Bandaranaike Kumaratunga was popularly elected president and appointed her mother, Sirimavo Bandaranaike, prime minister, creating a unique family 'dual executive'. It is intended to re-establish a parliamentary form of executive in Sri Lanka.

In Morocco the executive partnership is between the monarch and the prime minister but, until the constitutional reforms of 1992, it was a very one-sided affair, with the king holding a near monopoly of power.

In newly democratized Cambodia, the dual executive also takes the form of power-sharing between a monarch and a prime minister, with father and son, King Norodom Sihanouk and Prince Norodom Ranariddh, currently occupying these respective positions.

In the four states of the Czech Republic, Estonia, Lithuania, and Slovenia in Central Europe the executive types are substantially parliamentary, but the directly elected presidents currently retain sufficient authority for the designation 'dual executive' to be applied. In the Czech Republic the position of president is now chiefly ceremonial, but the current incumbent, Vaclav Havel, as leader of the freedom struggle, retains charismatic and moral authority.

A limit of two terms has been set for the presidents of six states with dual executives: the Czech Republic, Estonia, Lithuania, Portugal, Slovenia, and Sri Lanka. In Estonia and Lithuania candidates for the presidency must be at least 40 years old.

The dual executives of the 12 states shown in Table 24 demonstrate the variety of ways in which a constitution can be adapted to suit the circumstances of a particular political environment at a particular time.

4.5 The communist executive

Until recently the Soviet Union provided the 'classic' example of a communist political executive, with its interlocking web of party and state personnel and interests, culminating in a concentration of power at the apex of the political system. Now, however, the Soviet Union has been dissolved and emergent democratic Russia has a limited presidential form of political executive. It is in socialist China where the dominant model of the communist political executive is today best located.

In a communist system it is the party which determines policy objectives and it is the state apparatus which implements them. Whereas in a liberal democratic country, such as the United States, the constitution determines the distribution and exercise of power, in a communist country the constitution is subservient to the needs of the state, as interpreted by the party. In fact, constitutions are fairly frequently changed to meet party requirements.

In a communist state there is a directly or indirectly elected National Assembly, Supreme Soviet ('soviet' means elected council), or People's Congress, which is, constitutionally, but not in reality, the supreme body of state power. In China the National People's Congress comprises nearly 3,000 members, but meets only briefly for several weeks each year, devolving its powers to a smaller, approximately 150-member permanent Standing Committee, and electing from its membership a Council of Ministers (COM) or state council, as the equivalent of a formal government. The COM, with around 40 members, is headed by a chairman who is the equivalent of a prime minister. There is also a state president, who is elected by the legislature.

The state machinery of the COM, its chairman, and the state president are the external, constitutional, manifestations of political power but the real power in a communist state lies within the Communist Party, which ensures its hold on policy-making through its membership of the state institutions and the policy of 'nomenklatura'. This means that key posts throughout society and government, including positions in the legislature, are reserved for persons of 'sound' judgement who have been vetted and approved by the party's apparatus.

In China it is in the approximately 200-member Central Committee of the Communist Party where true authority can first be perceived and it is in the Politburo, a 12–20-member cabinet body which is 'elected' by the Central Committee and meets weekly, and the smaller Secretariat, its administrative and policy-formulating wing, where ultimate power lies. Leading members of these bodies, at the apex of the party, also hold key positions, including those of prime minister and state president. Indeed, it is usual for the general-secretary of the Party, who is the country's effective political leader, to take a major state position as a formal insignia of office. Thus the Chinese Communist Party's general-secretary, Jiang Zemin, is also state president. However, his real power derives from his position as head of the Party.

In China, where the People's Liberation Army (PLA) played a key role in the 'liberation struggle' during the 1940s and which crushed a popular prodemocracy movement in 1989, the armed forces retain significant behind-the-scenes political influence. They are also influential in Vietnam, North Korea, and Cuba.

The distribution of states with communist, or, as they should more correctly be termed, socialist, executives and their date of establishment are set out in Table 25. They are found exclusively in Asia and the Caribbean. In Cuba, a personalized, plebiscitarian form of leadership prevails, with Fidel Castro, the leader of the 'communist revolution' providing charismatic leadership. In North Korea, a 'socialist dynasty' is in place, with the 'Great Leader' Kim Jong Il succeeding his father, Kim Il Sung, the self-designated 'Sun of Mankind', on the latter's death in 1994. In both China and Vietnam significant parts of the economy have been opened to market forces and private initiative. Still, however, in all cases, control of the state, including large parts of the economy, through the party, is the dominant, and clearly recognizable, characteristic. It is this, more than anything else, that distinguishes communist from other one-party states. Despite the small number (5) of states falling into this executive category, they embrace, in total, nearly a quarter of the world's population.

4.6 The unlimited presidential executive

The term 'unlimited' is used to describe the executive presidency in one-party, noncommunist states, but in politics, of course, nothing is really unlimited. Even the seemingly all-powerful military dictator can be, and is at times, overthrown. Nevertheless, the 23 states, which have been classified as nationalistic socialist, authoritarian nationalist, and Islamic nationalist, have considerably fewer limitations on their political executives than those in their liberal and emergent democratic counterparts. These states comprise a tenth of the world's population.

As in communist systems, the party is the ultimate source of power but, unlike some communist states, a strong, and sometimes charismatic, leader often predominates and the objectives of the party, even in socialist states, are subordinated to national interests. Most of the countries with this type of executive have comparatively short histories of release from rule by a colonial power and have felt the need to assert their independence. Many, also, have tribal, ethnic, or regional differences which require strong leadership if all social groups are to cohere into a single state. More than 60% of countries with unlimited presidential executives are to be found located in Africa and the adjoining Middle East.

Despite this regional concentration, these states display considerable variations in their political systems and it is something of a distortion to group them together in this way. Some have, for example, histories of instability and their current leaders have reached the top through a bloody or bloodless military coup. This has been the experience of Algeria, Azerbaijan, Indonesia, Iraq, Libya, Syria, Togo, and South Yemen, when it was a separate state, for example. Some, such as Afghanistan, Burundi, Eritrea, Iraq, Rwanda, and Tajikistan, have been racked by recent wars and border insurgency. In contrast, other states, such as Kazakhstan, the Maldives, Senegal, and Tanzania, have strong records of political stability.

Nevertheless, their political executives have certain features in common, including a much greater authoritarianism than is found in liberal and emergent democratic states. This results mainly from the absence of competition and choice which an effectively functioning multiparty political system clearly provides. They have no opposition party 'waiting in the wings' to take over should the electorate express a wish for a change. Many unlimited executive states do now formally tolerate opposition groupings but elections are so heavily stacked in the governing party's favour, through its control of the media and state sector resources, and through resort to electoral chicanery, that there is little or no possibility of its being defeated.

The importance of the political leader in such states cannot be overstressed. Some have been in office for much longer periods than their counterparts in liberal democratic states could ever hope for. This longevity is illustrated in Table 26. The average tenure of an unlimited president was,

States with communist executives (5)			Table 25
Region/country	Year established	Year current head of state came to power	Year current prime minister came to power
Asia (4)			
China	1949	1993	1987
Korea, North	1948	1994	1992
Laos	1975	1992	1991
Vietnam	1945	1992	1991
Central America & Caribbean (1)			
Cuba	1959	1959	1959

Presidential executives (23)		Table 26
States with unlimited presidential executives		
Region/country	Year established	Year current head of state came to power
Asia (7)		
Afghanistan	1992	1992
Indonesia	1967	1967
Kazakhstan	1990	1990
Maldives	1968	1978
Tajikistan	1991	1992
Turkmenistan	1990	1990
Uzbekistan	1990	1990
Central, Eastern, & Southern Europe (2)		
Armenia	1990	1990
Azerbaijan	1993	1993
Central & South Africa (9)		
Burundi	1992	1994
Eritrea	1993	1993
Kenya	1969	1978
Rwanda	1978	1994
Senegal	1963	1981
Tanzania	1961	1995
Uganda	1986	1986
Zaire	1965	1965
Zimbabwe	1980	1980
Middle East & North Africa (5)		
Algeria	1976	1994
Iran	1979	1989
Iraq	1970	1979
Libya	1969	1969
Syria	1971	1971

have been anarchic since the overthrow of the former Soviet-installed administration and the real political controllers appear to be regionally-based warlords and Islamic muja-heddin forces.

To people accustomed to life in liberal democratic political systems the concept of one-party government and strong personal leadership may seem repressive and undemocratic. It would be unwise, however, to make such a sweeping judgement. A country's political system is, inevitably, the product of its history, culture, and resource base and the majority of the states with unlimited presidential executives are still on a 'learning curve' in their political development. Indeed some systems are so volatile that there are fundamental changes currently taking place or likely to become evident in the foreseeable future. In other cases, particularly across black Africa, the system of one-party monopoly is still firmly embedded in some states, drawing its sustenance from older tribal political traditions, with their inclusive decision-making processes, and from the argument that open democracy, with its costly campaigns and interparty quarrels, is an indulgence that cannot yet be afforded.

4.7 The military executive

Of the seven states listed in Table 27 as having military executives six are in Central and Southern Africa and one is in Asia. Many share a common feature, a long record of military conflicts and coups. For good or ill, in each case the army has established order, though often at the expense of the loss of civil liberties.

Some countries have seen the pendulum swing from civilian to military rule with bewildering frequency. Burkina Faso, for example, has experienced no less than six coups in 30 years and Thailand 17 since its absolute monarchy was abolished in 1932. In Latin America, unusually without a military executive in 1995, and Central and Southern Africa as a whole, three-quarters of the 68 states have endured at least one military coup since 1960.

Some have suffered long periods of genuinely despotic rule. Jean-Bedel Bokassa, of the Central African Republic, who was in power between 1965 and 1979, almost brought his nation to economic ruin through his personal excesses, which included an elaborate ceremony to crown him emperor. The Duvalier family ruled Haiti between 1957 and 1986 like gang bosses with their own private armies. In Burundi, in Central Africa, military rule has been ruthlessly used to sustain tribal despotism, in particular the economic and political pre-eminence of the minority Tutsis over the majority Hutu community.

In contrast, some military rulers have brought great political stability. General Alfredo Stroessner of Paraguay enjoyed absolute power, without any real challenge, for 35 years, from 1954 to 1989, by dealing swiftly and harshly with dissidents and astutely allowing potential rivals to share in the spoils of office, while in Indonesia the now civilian ruler, Suharto, has been at the helm since 1967 and has promoted economic development.

The policies pursued by some military regimes, most especially those in South America, have been strongly

in 1995, 11 years. Eight, or 35%, had been in office for 15 years or more, with several having become virtual legends. Marshal Mobuto has dominated politics in Zaire since 1965, President Suharto in Indonesia since 1967, Muammar al-Kadhafi in Libya since 1969, and Hafez al-Assad in Syria since 1971. Meanwhile, in the former Soviet states of Central Asia powerful new personality cults have been established in Turkmenistan and Uzbekistan, suggesting that Presidents Niyazov, the officially styled 'leader of the Turkmen', and Karimov intend to remain in power for a considerable period. However, a limit of two or three presidential terms is officially in place in Burundi, Senegal, Tanzania, and Uzbekistan.

In Iran, on the other hand, the focus of leadership in recent years has tended to shift from one individual to another, as different factions have wrestled for power. Until his death in 1989, the religious leader Ayatollah Khomeini, a revered, charismatic figure, seemed to have the strongest voice, but, at times, the pragmatic Speaker of the Assembly, Hojatoleslam Ali Akbar Rafsanjani, was more influential and in 1989 he was elected president. In Afghanistan political conditions

States with military executives (7)   Table 27

Region/country	Year first established	Most recent coup	Year current head of state came to power
Asia (1)			
Myanmar	1962	1988	1992
Central & Southern Africa (6)			
Gambia	1994	1994	1994
Liberia	1980	1994	1994
Nigeria	1966	1993	1993
Sierra Leone	1992	1992	1992
Somalia	1969	1991	1991
Sudan	1969	1989	1989

States with absolute executives (12)   Table 28

Region/country	Year established	Year current head of state came to power	Written constitution
Asia (2)			
Bhutan	1907	1972	N
Brunei	1984	1968	Y
Central & Southern Africa (1)			
Swaziland	1968	1986	Y
Middle East & North Africa (7)			
Bahrain	1971	1961	Y
Jordan	1946	1952	Y
Kuwait	1961	1977	Y
Oman	1951	1970	N
Qatar	1971	1972	Y
Saudi Arabia	1932	1982	N
United Arab Emirates	1971	1971	Y
Northern & Western Europe (1)			
Vatican City State	1377	1978	N
Oceania (1)			
Tonga	1875	1965	Y

reactionary and conservative, designed to protect the interests of narrow business elites and stifle popular social movements. Others, often drawing their leaders and in-service support from the middle officer ranks, have pursued radical economic and social policies. These reformist regimes, usually having been prompted to seize power because of the corrupt excesses of preceding civilian administrations, have also tended to follow puritanical governing styles. The most notable contemporary examples are the populist regimes of Flight-Lieutenant Jerry Rawlings in Ghana and Captains Thomas Sankara (1983–87) and Blaise Compaore (1987–) in Burkina Faso. Both Rawlings and Compaore are elected civilian presidents.

The identification of the seven military states has been comparatively straightforward but, inevitably, a little arbitrary. In at least a further 35 states classified under other categories the military remains an influential background political force. These include 18 countries identified as limited presidential executives: Angola, Burkina Faso, Chile, Egypt, Ethiopia, Ghana, Guatemala, Guinea, Guinea-Bissau, South Korea, Mozambique, Pakistan, Paraguay, Peru, Sudan, Surinam, Taiwan, and Yemen. Fiji, Pakistan, and Thailand, which have been classified as parliamentary executives, are other examples of states with a military presence in the background. The armed forces are also influential in the remaining communist states of Asia and the Caribbean and in the unlimited presidential executives of Afghanistan, Algeria, Azerbaijan, Burundi, Indonesia, Iraq, Libya, Rwanda, and Syria.

Table 27 gives the dates when the military came to power in the seven states classified as full military executives. In Gambia the military takeover was particularly recent, coming in 1994 after Dawda Jawara had been a civilian president since 1970. In Sierra Leone the military formally came to power in 1992, but had been influential behind the political scene for decades. The other five states had been dominated by the military even more strongly for several decades, although there had been brief periods of civilian rule, until the most recent coups.

4.8 The absolute executive

With the exception of the Vatican City State, all the states listed in Table 28 as having absolute executives are monarchies of one kind or another. Bahrain, Brunei, Jordan, Kuwait, Oman, Qatar, and Saudi Arabia are all Arab monarchies, sultanates, sheikhdoms, or emirates and the United Arab Emirates is a federation of no less than seven emirates. Bhutan, Swaziland, and Tonga are hereditary monarchies.

Another factor that all the states except the Vatican City State have in common is a history of association with Britain, through either a treaty of protection or trade, or both. In ten of them political parties do not operate at all. In Swaziland there is one party subservient to the ruling regime. Only in Jordan, where the ban imposed on political parties in 1976 was lifted in 1991, have multiparty elections recently been held.

Unlike the military states, the absolute executives have not been imposed following a coup. They have usually been part of the social and political lives of the respective communities for many years, surviving during the colonial period as largely autonomous entities, and the rule, though autocratic, has usually been paternalistic. As such, they could alternatively be designated 'traditional executives'.

The Kingdom of Jordan shows clear evidence of constitutionality, with a written constitutional code and two-chamber assembly, but true democracy has had a fluctuating existence, political activity being banned in 1963, restored in 1971, rebanned in 1976 and restored in 1991. Despite the holding of multiparty elections in 1993, Jordan has not democratized to the extent of Nepal, which had an absolutist system until 1990, and ultimate power remains with the king.

The one universal, and most certain, characteristic of an absolutist regime is that of government by personal, or, in the case of Saudi Arabia, family decree, rather than by collective discussion and agreement, and it is this which attracts the description of absolute executive. Seven of the absolutist states are oil-rich and enjoy high per-capita incomes. As a consequence, as Table 10 above shows, the absolutist states enjoyed average per-capita incomes, in 1992, in the region of $8,234 and high levels of urbanization. A trade-off between political liberty and economic affluence of citizens is evident in states such as Brunei, Kuwait, Oman, Qatar, Saudi Arabia, and the United Arab Emirates.

Recommended reading

Baynham, R (ed.) *Military Power in Black Politics*, Croom Helm, 1986

Blondel, J *World Leaders: Heads of Government in the Postwar Period*, Sage Publications, 1980

Blondel, J *The Organization of Governments: A Comparative Analysis of Government Structures*, Sage Publications, 1982

Carter, S and McCauley, M (eds) *Leadership and Succession in the Soviet Union, Eastern Europe and China*, Macmillan, 1986

Clapham, C and Philip, G (eds) *The Political Dilemmas of Military Rule*, Croom Helm, 1985

Jackson, R and Rosberg, C *Personal Rule in Black Africa: Prince, Autocrat, Prophet, Tyrant*, University of California Press, 1982

James, S *British Cabinet Government*, Routledge, 1991

Kellerman, B *The Political Presidency: Practice of Leadership*, Oxford University Press, 1984

King, A (ed.) *Both Ends of the Avenue: The Presidency, the Executive Branch and Congress in the 1980s*, American Enterprise Institute, 1983

King, A (ed.) *The British Prime Minister*, 2nd edn., Macmillan, 1985

Lijphart, A (ed.) *Parliamentary versus Presidential Government*, Oxford University Press, 1992

Lowenhardt, J *The Soviet Politburo*, Canongate, 1982

Neustadt, R E *Presidential Power and the Modern Presidents: The Politics of Leadership from Roosevelt to Reagan*, Free Press, 1990

O'Brien, P and Cammack, P (eds) *Generals in Retreat: The Crisis of Military Rule in Latin America*, Manchester University Press, 1985

Paterson, W E and Southern, D *Governing Germany*, Basil Blackwell, 1991

Rose, R and Suleiman, E (eds) *Presidents and Prime Ministers*, American Enterprise Institute, 1980

Shugart, M S and Carey, J M *Presidents and Assemblies: Constitutional Design and Electoral Dynamics*, Cambridge University Press, 1992

Smith, G B *Soviet Politics: Continuity and Contradiction*, Macmillan, 1988, Chap. 5

Weller, P *First Among Equals: Prime Ministers in Westminster Systems*, Allen & Unwin, 1985

White, S, Batt, J and Lewis, P G (eds) *Developments in East European Politics*, Macmillan, 1993

Wright, V *The Government and Politics of France*, 3rd edn., Hutchinson, 1989

CHAPTER 5

Assemblies

5.1 The nature of assemblies

Although in formal, constitutional terms the three arms of government are described as the executive, the judiciary, and the legislature, the term 'assembly' has been deliberately preferred for the third arm because the role of the vast majority of legislatures in the world today is deliberative and policy-influencing, rather than law-making. Indeed the old term 'parliament', or *parlement*, which is still used in some political systems and is associated with the French verb *parler*, to talk, best identifies the chamber as an 'arena' for debate.

Assemblies do, of course, play a major role in the law-making process but they now mostly legitimize policies presented to them by the executive, rather than initiate them themselves. In doing so, they usually also have a modifying, revising function, based on the concept that assembly members are more likely to have an understanding of what is practical and acceptable to the electorate than politicians in government who, inevitably, become insulated in their positions of power from the real world outside.

Popularly elected assemblies have always epitomized democracy and it is not surprising, therefore, that even the most autocratic rulers have sought to make their regimes 'respectable' by establishing a façade of democratization through puppet assemblies.

The 19th century was the 'golden age' of assemblies as independent law-making bodies, or, as the American political scientist Nelson Polsby has termed them, 'transformative legislatures'. The classic example was the Parliament in London where individual members had a genuine role to play before they were to become overwhelmed by the tyranny of the party system and the burgeoning, and increasingly specialist, scope of legislative affairs. Since that time the balance of power has shifted inexorably towards the executive until we are left with but a few shining examples of assemblies which can, and do, wield real political power. The most notable 'transformative legislature' today is undoubtedly the US Congress. Its position is buttressed by the clear separation of powers that is provided for by the US constitution, the weakness of party discipline, the powerful standing committee structure, and by the large private offices and staff support with which individual members of the House of Rep-

resentatives and Senate are provided. It is closely followed by the Riksdag of Sweden, with the States-General in the Netherlands, the Parlamento, comprising the Camera dei Deputati and Senato, in Italy and the Legislative Assembly in Costa Rica also being influential bodies. Assemblies elsewhere are mostly pale shadows of these and can be categorized as 'arena legislatures', being 'settings for the interplay of significant political forces' as executive actions are debated and scrutinized.

Despite the relative decline in importance of assemblies, they still operate in the vast majority of states and are found within a wide range of ideologies and work alongside all types of political executive. Table 29 gives the basic facts about them, showing that at the present time only seven of the 192 states under consideration do not have active assemblies as a normal feature of their political structures. These nations, Bahrain, Brunei, Oman, Qatar, Saudi Arabia, the United Arab Emirates, and the Vatican City State, are all absolutist states and, with the exception of Bahrain between 1973 and 1975, have never had popularly elected assemblies. However, in five of them, Bahrain, Oman (from 1991), Saudi Arabia (from 1993), the United Arab Emirates, and the Vatican City State, there are appointed consultative councils which provide advice to the political executive. In a number of other states, specifically those with military regimes or which are experiencing civil war, the assemblies described in Table 29 are, in most cases, currently in abeyance. For example, in Myanmar the 485-member Constituent Assembly, which was popularly elected in May 1990 and is dominated by opponents of the military regime, has not been allowed to convene. Instead, its place has been taken by an appointed State Law and Order Restoration Council.

The contemporary scene, therefore, reveals little diminution in the number of assemblies. However, there has been a deterioration in their power and influence, particularly vis-à-vis the political executive. Undoubtedly, the major reason for this decline is the increase in party strength and discipline. Another important factor has been the increasing volume of government business. This has persuaded the executive, anxious to curtail the length of debate and analysis and prevent the tabling of numerous amendments, to impose 'guillotine' and 'block vote' motions in states such as France and the United Kingdom.

The political systems with parliamentary executives, drawn from and responsible to their assemblies, have, in many cases, seen the virtual disappearance of the independent politician and the rise of strong, highly disciplined, parties, demanding unfailing allegiance from their members and consistent support in the voting lobbies. The UK parliament, and particularly the House of Commons, provides clear evidence of this trend, which in Britain has been reinforced by the simple plurality electoral system. This method of voting, almost presupposing the existence of a two-party regime, meant that the arrival of a significant third party in 1981 guaranteed parliamentary domination by whichever party gained 40% or more of the popular vote. In the UK elections of 1979, 1983, 1987, and 1992, for example, the Conservatives' share of the national vote was, respectively, 43.9%, 42.4%, 42.3%, and 41.9%. Similar trends have been noted in the case of the Australian House of Representatives. Here the alternative vote majoritarian system is in force.

In one-party states, assemblies have, traditionally, always been more subservient, providing a comforting democratic gloss of legitimacy to policy decisions taken behind the closed doors of party caucuses. In communist states, the sheer size of 'parliamentary' bodies such as the National People's Congress (c. 3,000 members) in China, and the fact that they meet in plenary session for, at most, only 10–14 days a year have been significant factors behind such impotence. The most important reason for their relative powerlessness, however, has been the rigid control over agenda and placements exerted by the party leadership above, buttressed by the principle of 'democratic centralism'. Similar tight leadership control is exerted in noncommunist, one-party states.

The political systems where assemblies still retain a degree of virility are those with limited presidential executives, those where party structures are weak or absent, and the parliamentary executive states with voting systems which encourage a multiplicity of parties and 'consociational' politics.

In a limited presidential executive state, the constitution places clear restraints on the powers of the executive and protects the assembly in its counterbalancing role. This is evident in its purest and most extreme form in the United States, where it is enhanced by the notorious weakness of party structures, with more than half of the votes taken in Congress being bipartisan, in which a majority from both the two dominant parties vote together on an issue. It is also the case, though to lesser degrees, in Brazil, Colombia, Costa Rica, the Dominican Republic, the Philippines, and Venezuela. These are all countries where efforts have been made to copy the 'US model'.

In parliamentary states with electoral systems which stimulate party multiplicity, coalition executives are the norm and accountabilty to the assembly becomes a reality. Several Northern and West European countries fall into this category, most notably Italy, which has had more than 50 governments since World War II. Others include Belgium, Denmark, and the Netherlands.

In the region we have called Oceania, the political system of Papua New Guinea, where more than six minor political parties effectively function, is an even more notable example of assembly atomization, with votes of no confidence being frequently registered against incumbent administrations, as members shift fluidly in and out of coalition groups. To redress this problem, the constitution has been recently amended to prevent no-confidence votes being held during the first 18 months of a government's life. In Belau, Micronesia, Nauru, and Tuvalu the absence of formal parties enhances the authority and bargaining power of individual legislators.

5.2 Assembly functions

Whatever degree of virility or supineness they display, what are the functions of contemporary assemblies?

First, they have the obvious task of legitimizing policies, in other words turning political decisions into law. Although, at worst, this may mean little more than 'rubber stamping' the actions of the executive, it is a basic function of an assembly and the foundation of what states which claim to be democratic call the 'rule of law'.

Second, they are required to act as the people's representatives and, as such, carry their views to the executives. This is what representative democracy is supposed to be about, but if it is to be effective then the assembly must be able to influence the executive. This brings us back to the question of an assembly's virility.

Third, they are expected to be a 'talking shop': the national debating arena. This is the role for which assemblies in liberal and emergent democracies are best equipped and which they generally best perform. In one-party states it is the party, through whatever closed institutions it devises, which predominantly fulfils this function. However, in one-party states which may be going through a transitional period, as is the case in several contemporary communist regimes, or are riven with internal factions, as, for example, in contemporary Iran, assembly debates can be surprisingly lively and relatively open.

Fourth, in liberal and emergent democracies assemblies perform the vital 'reactive' role of supervising and scrutinizing the actions of the political executive and bureaucracy, calling attention to abuses of authority and inefficiencies, and suggesting improvements to legislative packages presented to them. This may be done by the regular questioning of government leaders and ministers by opposition deputies, on the British 'Question Time' model, or by the work of standing and ad hoc scrutiny and investigative committees.

5.3 Comparing assemblies

Table 29 overleaf provides a variety of data with which to compare assemblies in different states but if it is to be used effectively some criteria need to be established.

For example, is it important that some assemblies are unicameral, with one chamber, and others, bicameral, with two? Why, in two-chamber assemblies, are the 'upper' chambers usually less powerful than the 'lower'? Is it important that membership of some chambers is on the basis of election and others by appointment? Does the duration of the term of office of assembly members have any real significance?

Before these questions can be answered sensibly they must be qualified in some way.

Assemblies of the world
Table 29

Region/country	Name of lower house	No. of lower house members	Lower house term (years)	Lower house electoral system
Asia				
Afghanistan	Shura	51	trans	indirect
Bangladesh	Parliament	330	5	SP
Bhutan	National Assembly	150	3	mixed–E/A
Brunei	–	n/a	n/a	n/a
Cambodia	National Assembly	120	5	SP
China	National People's Congress	2,970	5	indirect
India	Lok Sabha	545	5	SP
Indonesia	House of Representatives	500	5	PR–PL
Japan	House of Representatives	511	4	PR–AMS
Kazakhstan	Majlis	67	4	SB
Korea, North	Supreme People's Assembly	687	4	SP
Korea, South	National Assembly	299	4	PR–AMS
Kyrgyzstan	People's Assembly	70	5	SB
Laos	National Assembly	85	5	SP
Malaysia	House of Representatives	192	5	SP
Maldives	Majlis	48	5	mixed–E/A
Mongolia	People's Great Hural	76	4	SB
Myanmar	Constituent Assembly (susp)	485	trans	SP
Nepal	House of Representatives	205	5	SP
Pakistan	National Assembly	217	5	SP
Singapore	Parliament	81	5	SP
Sri Lanka	National State Assembly	225	6	PR–PL
Taiwan	Legislative Yuan	164	3	PR–AMS
Tajikistan	Supreme Soviet	181	4	SB
Thailand	House of Representatives	391	4	SP
Turkmenistan	Majlis	50	5	SB
Uzbekistan	Supreme Assembly	250	5	SB
Vietnam	National Assembly	395	5	SB
Central America & Caribbean				
Antigua	House of Representatives	17	5	SP
Bahamas	House of Assembly	49	5	SP
Barbados	House of Assembly	28	5	SP
Belize	House of Representatives	29	5	SP
Costa Rica	Assembly	57	4	PR–PL
Cuba	National Assembly	589	5	SP
Dominica	Assembly	30	5	mixed–E/A
Dominican Republic	Chamber of Deputies	120	4	PR–PL
El Salvador	National Assembly	84	3	SP
Grenada	House of Representatives	15	5	SP
Guatemala	National Congress	80	5	PR–AMS
Haiti	Chamber of Deputies	83	5	SB
Honduras	National Assembly	128	4	PR–PL
Jamaica	House of Representatives	60	5	SP
Mexico	Chamber of Deputies	500	3	PR–AMS
Nicaragua	National Assembly	90	5	PR–PL
Panama	Legislative Assembly	72	5	SP

continued

Assemblies of the world (continued)				Table 29
Region/	Name of lower house	No. of lower house members	Lower house term (years)	Lower house electoral system
St Kitts	National Assembly	14	5	SP
St Lucia	House of Assembly	17	5	SP
St Vincent	House of Assembly	21	5	SP
Trinidad & Tobago	House of Representatives	36	5	SP
Central, Eastern, & Southern Europe				
Albania	People's Assembly	140	4	PR–AMS
Armenia	Supreme Council	190	4	PR–AMS
Azerbaijan	National Assembly	125	4	PR–AMS
Belarus	Sejm	260	4	SB
Bosnia–Herzegovina	Chamber of Citizens	130	trans	SB
Bulgaria	National Assembly (Duma)	240	5	PR–PL
Croatia	Chamber of Deputies	80	4	PR–PL
Cyprus	House of Representatives	80	5	SP
Czech Republic	Chamber of Deputies	200	4	PR–PL
Estonia	Parliament	101	4	PR–PL
Georgia	Supreme Soviet	235	4	PR–AMS
Greece	Parliament	300	4	PR–PL
Hungary	National Assembly	386	4	PR–AMS
Latvia	Parliament (Saeima)	100	3	PR–PL
Lithuania	Parliament (Seimas)	141	4	PR–AMS
Macedonia	National Assembly	120	4	SB
Moldova	Parliament	104	4	PR–PL
Poland	National Assembly	460	4	PR–PL
Romania	Chamber of Deputies	341	4	PR–PL
Russia	State Duma	550	2	PR–AMS
Slovakia	National Council	150	4	PR–PL
Slovenia	National Assembly	90	4	PR–AMS
Turkey	National Assembly	450	5	PR–PL
Ukraine	Supreme Council	450	4	SB
Yugoslavia	Chamber of Citizens	138	4	PR–AMS
Central & Southern Africa				
Angola	National Assembly	223	4	PR–PL
Benin	National Assembly	64	5	SP
Botswana	National Assembly	46	5	SP
Burkina Faso	Assembly of People's Deputies	107	5	SP
Burundi	National Assembly	81	5	SP
Cameroon	National Assembly	180	5	SP
Cape Verde	National Assembly	79	5	SP
Central African Republic	National Assembly	85	5	SB
Chad	Higher transitional Council	57	trans	SP
Comoros	Federal Assembly	42	4	SB
Congo	National Assembly	125	5	SB
Côte d'Ivoire	National Assembly	175	5	SB
Djibouti	Chamber of Deputies	65	5	SP
Equatorial Guinea	House of Representatives	80	5	SP
Eritrea	Parliament	150	4	mixed–E/A
Ethiopia	National Assembly	548	trans	mixed–E/A
Gabon	National Assembly	120	5	SB

continued

Assemblies of the world (continued) — Table 29

Region/country	Name of lower house	No. of lower house members	Lower house term (years)	Lower house electoral system
Gambia	House of Representatives	50	5	SP
Ghana	Parliament	200	4	SP
Guinea	Trans Committee of National Recovery	114	5	SP
Guinea–Bissau	National People's Assembly	100	4	SB
Kenya	National Assembly	202	5	SP
Lesotho	National Assembly	65	5	SP
Liberia	House of Representatives	64	6	SP
Madagascar	National Assembly	138	5	SP
Malawi	National Assembly	177	5	mixed–E/A
Mali	National Assembly	129	5	SB
Mauritania	National Assembly	79	5	SB
Mauritius	National Assembly	71	5	SP
Mozambique	Assembly of Representatives	250	5	SP
Namibia	National Assembly	72	5	SP
Niger	National Assembly	83	5	SP
Nigeria	House of Representatives (susp)	593	trans	SP
Rwanda	National Development Council	70	5	SP
São Tomé	National Assembly	55	4	SP
Senegal	National Assembly	120	5	PR–AMS
Seychelles	National Assembly	33	5	PR–AMS
Sierra Leone	House of Representatives (susp)	124	5	SP
Somalia	transitional National Council	74	5	mixed–E/A
South Africa	National Assembly	400	trans	PR–PL
Sudan	transitional National Assembly	300	trans	A
Swaziland	National Assembly	65	4	mixed–E/A
Tanzania	National Assembly	291	5	mixed–E/A
Togo	National Assembly	81	5	SB
Uganda	National Resistance Council	278	trans	mixed–E/A
Zaire	High Council of the Republic	730	trans	trans
Zambia	National Assembly	150	5	SP
Zimbabwe	House of Assembly	150	6	mixed–E/A
Middle East & North Africa				
Algeria	National People's Assembly	430	5	SB
Bahrain	**	n/a	n/a	n/a
Egypt	People's Assembly	454	5	mixed–E/A
Iran	Majlis	270	4	SB
Iraq	National Assembly	250	4	PR–PL
Israel	Knesset	120	4	PR–PL
Jordan	House of Representatives	80	4	SP
Kuwait	National Assembly	50	4	SP
Lebanon	National Assembly	128	6	PR–PL
Libya	General People's Congress	1,112	1	SP
Morocco	Chamber of Representatives	333	6	SP
Oman	**	n/a	n/a	n/a
Qatar	**	n/a	n/a	n/a
Saudi Arabia	**	n/a	n/a	n/a
Syria	Majlis	250	4	SP
Tunisia	National Assembly	163	5	PR/AMS
United Arab Emirates	**	n/a	n/a	n/a
Yemen	House of Representatives	301	5	SP

continued

Assemblies of the world (continued)				Table 29
Region/country	Name of lower house	No. of lower house members	Lower house term (years)	Lower house electoral system
North America				
Canada	House of Commons	295	5	SP
United States	House of Representatives	435	2	SP
Northern & Western Europe				
Andorra	General Council	28	4	PR–AMS
Austria	Nationalrat	183	4	PR–PL
Belgium	Chamber of Representatives	150	4	PR–PL
Denmark	Folketing	179	4	PR–PL
Finland	Eduskunta	200	4	PR–PL
France	National Assembly	577	5	SB
Germany	Federal Assembly	672	4	PR–AMS
Iceland	Althing	63	4	PR–PL
Ireland	Dáil	166	5	PR–STV
Italy	Chamber of Deputies	630	5	PR–AMS
Liechtenstein	Landtag	25	4	PR–LV
Luxembourg	Chamber of Deputies	60	5	PR–PL
Malta	House of Representatives	65	5	PR–STV
Monaco	National Council	18	5	SB
Netherlands	Second Chamber	150	4	PR–PL
Norway	Odelsting	124	4	PR–PL
Portugal	Assembly	230	4	PR–PL
San Marino	Council	60	5	PR–LV
Spain	Congress of Deputies	350	4	PR–PL
Sweden	Riksdag	349	3	PR–PL
Switzerland	Nationalrat	200	4	PR–PL
United Kingdom	House of Commons	651	5	SP
Vatican City State	**	n/a	n/a	n/a
Oceania				
Australia	House of Representatives	147	3	AV
Belau	House of Delegates	16	4	SP
Fiji	House of Representatives	70	5	SP
Kiribati	Maneaba	41	4	SB
Marshall Islands	Nitijela	33	4	SP
Micronesia	National Congress	14	4/2	SP
Nauru	Parliament	18	3	SP
New Zealand	House of Representatives	120	3	PR–AMS
Papua New Guinea	Parliament	109	5	SP
Philippines	House of Representatives	204	3	SP
Solomon Islands	Parliament	47	4	SP
Tonga	Legislative Assembly	30	3	mixed–E/A
Tuvalu	Parliament	12	4	SP
Vanuatu	Parliament	49	4	PR–PL
Western Samoa	Assembly	49	5	SP
South America				
Argentina	Chamber of Deputies	257	4	SP
Bolivia	Chamber of Deputies	130	4	SP
Brazil	Chamber of Deputies	517	4	PR–PL
Chile	Chamber of Deputies	120	4	SP

continued

Assemblies of the world (continued)				Table 29
Region/country	Name of lower house	No. of lower house members	Lower house term (years)	Lower house electoral system
Chile	Chamber of Deputies	120	4	SP
Colombia	House of Representatives	163	4	SP
Ecuador	Chamber of Representatives	77	4	PR–PL
Guyana	National Assembly	65	5	PR–PL
Paraguay	Chamber of Deputies	80	5	PR–PL
Peru	National Congress	120	5	PR–PL
Surinam	National Assembly	51	5	SP
Uruguay	Chamber of Deputies	99	5	PR–PL
Venezuela	Chamber of Deputies	205	5	PR–PL

Key:

**	Appointed consultative councils exist	PL	party list
A	appointed	PR	proportional representation
AMS	additional member system	SB	second ballot
AV	alternative vote	SP	simple plurality
E	elected	STV	single transferable vote
I	indirect	susp	suspended
LV	limited vote	trans	transitional

The relationship between assemblies and political executives is arguably the most important basis of comparison because if democratic, rather than autocratic, government is to be achieved then there must be some limits on executive power and in most political systems the only representative body likely to be able to impose such limits is a popular assembly.

As the bases for objective comparisons, we will, therefore, look at single and two-chamber assemblies, and, where there are two, the relationships between them; the membership of assemblies and the criteria for membership; and the relationships between assemblies and executives.

5.4 One chamber or two?

First, the question of one or two chambers. There is a clear link between federalism and two-chamber assemblies. Of the 24 federal states listed in table 6 above, 19, or 79%, have two-chamber assemblies, compared with only 44 of the 168 unitary states, or just over 25%. In the majority of cases the reason for the link will be obvious and this is illustrated in Table 30. In this table the generic term 'second chamber' or 'upper house' has, for convenience, been used, but this can be slightly misleading. As we will see later, the so-called 'upper house' is often the weaker of the two and in the Netherlands what is listed in Table 30 as the 'second chamber' is in fact known as the 'first chamber' of the bicameral States-General.

It is interesting to observe that one state, Norway, ostensibly has a single-chamber assembly, the Storting, but, after the general election, this divides into two. A quarter of the 165-member Storting becomes an upper house, the Lagting, and the remaining three-quarters the lower house, the Odelsting. Legislation must start in the Odelsting and then be passed by the Lagting. If there is a conflict of view between the two Houses they can consider legislation jointly, as a combined Storting, and approve it by a two-thirds majority. A similar division operated in Iceland until 1991, when a unicameral parliament, the Althing, was established.

A regional pattern is also evident in the distribution of second chambers. They are most commonly found in the Americas, where, influenced by the US and, in the Caribbean, UK constitutional models, 21, or 60%, of the states in the region have bicameral legislatures. In Central, Eastern, Northern, Southern, and Western Europe two-chamber parliaments are also relatively common, featuring in 19, or 40%, of the region's states. In contrast, although seven states established a second chamber during the course of the late 1980s, they are rare in Africa and the Middle East, being found in only 11, or 17%, of the states. In Asia 29% of states have bicameral legislatures and in Oceania 27%.

Overall, the number of countries with bicameral parliaments has advanced from 50 to 63 since the first edition of this book appeared in 1990. Three states, Afghanistan, Peru, and Zimbabwe, have reverted to unicameral structures, while 16 countries have moved in the other direction, establishing a second chamber. These are Bosnia-Herzegovina, the Central African Republic, the Comoros, the Congo, Croatia, Haiti, Kazakhstan, Kyrgyzstan, Lesotho, Madagascar, Mauritania, Nepal, Nigeria, Romania, Slovenia, and South Africa. In addition, there are several African states, not shown in Table 30, which have ad hoc, purely advisory, additional chambers. These are Botswana, Ghana, Namibia, and Zambia.

In making an initial comparison between countries with one- or two-chamber assemblies, Table 30 is relevant, indicating whether the state is unitary or federal, whether members are elected or appointed on a national or regional basis, and whether or not a representative or appointee is required to reside in the constituency he or she represents.

Of the 19 federal states with bicameral assemblies, 17, or 89%, have second chambers which are representative in a regionally or locally biased manner, whereas only 10 out of 43, or 23%, unitary states have similar regionally or locally representative bases. Twenty-six unitary states, or 60%, have national representative bases. There are nine states where the representation is part-national and part-regional and two federal and seven unitary states fall into this category.

This pattern illustrates one of the chief reasons for having a second chamber: to help resolve regional differences in countries which are geographically large and/or, socially and culturally diverse. Regional interests, which might object to a centralized government and dominance by large state or metropolitan interests, are to some extent pacified by the knowledge that they are formally represented at the centre by a 'local' politician. Indeed, in a number of countries, such as Australia, Germany, and the United States, a feature of the second chamber is the way in which smaller states within the federal system are deliberately over-represented to reduce the threat of 'tyranny by the majority'. In the United States for example, where each state, regardless of size or population, returns two Senators, theoretically a coalition of senators from the Union's 26 smallest states, comprising less than a sixth of the country's population, could secure a majority to block legislation. Similarly in Australia, New South Wales, with a population of 6 million sends the same number of senators, 12, to the senate as tiny Tasmania, with a population of less than half a million.

Incidentally, it is interesting to note that, whereas the majority of countries recognize regional aspirations through second chamber representation, Uruguay seeks to achieve this in a reverse way, by having national representation in the second chamber and regional representation in the first.

A minority of constitutions carry this regional representation a stage further by requiring politicians to reside in the region they represent. Argentina, Canada, and the United States have adopted this rule.

The relationship between first and second chambers in terms of political power and authority is another interesting basis of comparison. It is not easy to make clear distinctions and, inevitably, a certain amount of subjectivity will creep in. Table 30 attempts this comparison, using criteria such as the ability to veto legislation, the respective controls of financial legislation, and the extent to which a chamber has powers to interrogate the executive and curb its powers. On the basis of such criteria, it will be seen, in Table 30, that the majority of second chambers are weaker, or enjoy parity, with first chambers and only two, the United States and Philippines' Senates, it can be argued, are stronger.

Typically, lower houses have primacy in finance matters, while upper chambers have only limited delaying powers. This is certainly the case in the United Kingdom, where the House of Lords has the authority to amend legislation and delay nonfinancial bills by one year, but may not examine, let alone reject, financial bills or, as accepted by the 'Salisbury doctrine', measures which appeared in a successful party's election manifesto. In Austria, the Netherlands, Spain, and Thailand all bills must commence their passage in the lower house. In Poland, the Senate has the power of veto in specified areas, but this can be overridden by a two-thirds vote in the lower chamber, the Sejm. In Germany, all legislation relating to *Länder* (states) responsibilities require the approval of the Bundesrat upper house and constitutional amendments require two-thirds majorities in both chambers. On other matters, the Bundesrat may suggest amendments to legislation approved by the Bundestag, the lower chamber, send disputed items to a joint Bundestag–Bundesrat 'conciliation committee', and can block items of which it disapproves, but only temporarily, until a countervailing 50% or 66% Bundestag vote is passed. In other states, such as France, India, and Malaysia, where the Senate's delaying powers are restricted to just one month for money bills and one year for other bills, there are similar constitutional provisions to ensure primacy for the lower chamber.

This imbalance in influence is understandable. It is attributable to the greater popular legitimacy that is enjoyed by lower chambers, which are usually directly elected, and for comparatively short terms, whereas many upper chambers are either elected indirectly or comprise appointees. In addition, in parliamentary regimes, it is in the lower chamber that the executive, the prime minister and cabinet, sit and from which they are predominantly drawn.

The exceptions to this are, significantly, to be found in limited presidential states. In the United States, the lower chamber, the biennially elected House of Representatives, also has primacy in financial matters; all revenue raising and general appropriation bills originate there. However, the upper-chamber Senate, whose members serve six-year terms, has effective veto power over lower-house measures and has additional competence in three areas. Its approval is required for key federal judicial, diplomatic, and presidential cabinet appointments; it ratifies foreign treaties; and it acts as the jury when a president is impeached. For these reasons, it can be viewed as the most powerful chamber of Congress. In the Philippines, as in the United States, the approval of both chambers is required for the passage of legislation, with special joint 'conference sessions' being convened to iron out differences when they arise. Similarly, the Senate has special authority over foreign affairs, two-thirds approval from it being required for the ratification of all treaties and agreements.

5.5 Membership and nomenclature of assemblies

Table 29 above shows that, in the vast majority of states, assembly membership is on the basis of election. It would be surprising if it were otherwise since the main purpose of having an assembly is to ensure, or at least suggest, that the ordinary person has an opportunity to be represented by a politician who has been freely chosen. How this is done and whether or not it is done successfully will be examined in the next chapter.

There are a few first chambers or single chambers where a combination of election and appointment is used. In the vast majority of such cases the nonelected members are executive appointees, giving a president or monarch the opportunity of placing his or her own people. Occasionally appointments are made to try to ensure a particular distribu-

Second chambers or upper houses — Table 30

Region/country	Federal (F) or unitary (U)	Name of upper chamber	Members	Relative term (years)	Relative powers to lower house	Basis of representation	Upper house electoral system
Asia (8)							
India	F	Council of States	245	6/5	<	regional	I
Japan	U	House of Councillors	252	6/4	<	national & local	D–PR/LV
Kazakhstan	U	Senate	***	–	–	–	SP
Kyrgyzstan	U	Legislative Assembly	35	5/5	<	national	D–SB
Malaysia	F	Senate	70	6/5	<	mixed	mixed–E/A
Nepal	U	National Council	60	6/5	<	national & local	mixed–I/A
Pakistan	F	Senate	87	6/5	<	regional	I
Thailand	U	Senate	270	6/4	=	national	A
Central America & Caribbean (11)							
Antigua	U	Senate	17	5/5	<	national	A
Bahamas	U	Senate	16	5/5	<	national	A
Barbados	U	Senate	21	5/5	<	national	A
Belize	U	Senate	8	5/5	<	national	A
Dominican Republic	U	Senate	30	4/4	=	regional	D–SB
Grenada	U	Senate	13	5/5	<	national	A
Haiti	U	Senate	27	5/5	<	national	D–B
Jamaica	U	Senate	21	5/5	<	national	A
Mexico	F	Senate	64	6/3	=	regional	D–AMS
St Lucia	U	Senate	11	5/5	<	national	A
Trinidad & Tobago	U	Senate	31	5/5	<	national	A
Central, Eastern, & Southern Europe (8)							
Bosnia–Herzegovina	F	Chamber of Communes	110	trans	<	local	D–SB
Croatia	U	Chamber of Districts	63	4/4	<	regional & local	D–PR
Czech Republic	U	Senate	81	6/4	<	national	D
Poland	U	Senate	100	4/4	<	regional	D
Romania	U	Senate	143	4/4	<	national	D–PR
Russia	F	Federation Council	178	4/2	<	regional	D–SP
Slovenia	U	National Council	40	5/4	<	national	mixed–E/I
Yugoslavia	F	Chamber of the Republics	40	4/4	=	regional	I
Central & Southern Africa (10)							
Central African Republic	U	Economic & Regional Council	–	5/5	<	regional	mixed–I/A
Comoros	F	Senate	15	6/4	<	regional	I
Congo	U	Senate	60	6/5	<	national	D–SB
Lesotho	U	Senate	–	–/5	<	national	H/A
Liberia	U	Senate	26	6/6	=	national	D–SP
Madagascar	U	Senate	–	5/5	<	national	mixed–I/A
Mauritania	U	Senate	56	6/5	<	local	I
Nigeria	F	Senate	91	trans	<	regional	D–SP
South Africa	U	Senate	90	trans	<	regional	I
Swaziland	U	Senate	30	4/4	=	mixed	mixed–E/A
Middle East & North Africa (1)							
Jordan	U	Senate	40	8/4	=	national	A
North America (2)							
Canada	F	Senate	104	life*/5	<	regional	A
United States	F	Senate	100	6/2	>	regional	D–SP

continued

Region/country	Federal (F) or unitary (U)	Name of upper chamber	Members	Relative term (years)	Relative powers to lower house	Basis of representation	Upper house electoral system
Northern & Western Europe (11)							
Austria	F	Bundesrat	64	varies/4	<	regional	I
Belgium	F	Senate	71	4/4	=	mixed	mixed–E/A
France	U	Senate	321	9/5	<	mixed	I
Germany	F	Federal Council	68	**/4	<	regional	I
Ireland	U	Seanad	60	5/5	<	national	mixed–E/A
Italy	U	Senate	315	5/5	=	regional	I
Netherlands	U	First Chamber	75	6/4	<	regional	I
Norway	U	Lagting	41	4/4	=	national	I
Spain	U	Senate	256	4/4	<	mixed	mixed–E/I
Switzerland	F	Standerat	46	4/4	=	local	I
United Kingdom	U	House of Lords	1220	life/5	<	national	H/A
Oceania (4)							
Australia	F	Senate	76	6/3	<	regional	D–PR/STV
Belau	U	Senate	14	4/4	=	regional	D–SP
Fiji	U	Senate	22	6/5	<	mixed	A
Philippines	U	Senate	24	6/3	>	national	D–SP
South America (8)							
Argentina	F	Senate	69	9/4	<	regional	I
Bolivia	U	Senate	27	4/4	=	regional	D–SP
Brazil	F	Senate	81	8/4	=	regional	D–PR
Chile	U	Senate	47	8/4	=	regional	mixed–E/A
Colombia	U	Senate	102	4/4	=	national	D–SP
Paraguay	U	Senate	45	5/5	<	national	D–PR
Uruguay	U	Senate	30	5/5	=	national	D–PR
Venezuela	F	Senate	49	5/5	=	national	mixed–E/A

Key:

*	Retire at age 75		H	hereditary
**	Depends on terms of state governments		I	indirect
***	Formed December 1995;		LV	limited vote
	current composition uncertain		PR	proportional representation
A	appointed		SB	second ballot
AMS	additional member system		SP	simple plurality
D	direct		STV	single transferable vote
E	elected		trans	transitional

tion of membership. In Tanzania, for example, a complicated mixture of election and appointment makes provision for regional, female, and party representation as well as presidential nominees. Similarly, in Bangladesh a set quota of National Assembly seats, 30, are reserved for women appointees. In Pakistan, ten National Assembly seats are reserved for Christians, Hindus, Parsis, and other minorities. In India, two Lok Sabha seats are allocated for the Anglo-Indian community and in Romania 13 Chamber of Deputies' seats are set aside for representatives of national minorities. In Singapore the Group Representation Constituency (GRC) rules ensure that at least 13 members of Parliament are of non-Chinese racial origin and in Zimbabwe, 10 House of Assembly seats are filled by traditional chiefs. In Venezuela, former state presidents automatically become life members of the Senate.

In the majority of one-party states assembly representatives, whether elected or appointed, are initially selected by the party. In communist systems there is an interweaving of party and state membership, with the party nominees, because of their greater experience and 'professionalism', dominating proceedings. The nonparty deputies are selected as exemplary representatives of the full cross section of society by sex, age, ethnic, and occupational groups. They serve their constituents as mandated delegates on a part-time basis, being given only minor 'out-of-pocket' expenses for the five to ten days spent each year at the national assembly.

Of the 62 states with second chambers, members are directly elected in 23, indirectly elected in 15, wholly appointed or placed by hereditary right in 14, and part-elected and part-appointed in 10. Appointed or hereditary second chambers are typically found in countries in the

Caribbean and Commonwealth, influenced by the model of the British House of Lords, although in Canada there is compulsory retirement at the age of 75. In some of the small states, with a parliamentary executive fashioned on the 'Westminster model', the mixture of election and appointment is constructed so as to reflect the political balance in the first chamber. In Antigua, the Bahamas, Barbados, Belize, Grenada, St Lucia, and Trinidad and Tobago, for example, the prime minister and the official leader of the opposition are entitled to nominate members.

In states with political systems modelled on the United States, most notably those in Latin America, but also the new states of Central and Eastern Europe, direct popular election of the second chamber predominates.

In Northern and Western Europe and South Asia, by contrast, members of second chambers are predominantly elected indirectly, in the majority of cases by regional assemblies. Austria, Belgium, France, Germany, India, Ireland, the Netherlands, Pakistan, and Yugoslavia all provide examples of indirectly elected second chambers. In Germany, the composition of the upper chamber, the Bundesrat, is unusual in that its members are not only appointed by the members of the 16 *Länder* (states), but are themselves members of their own state governments, delegations being made or renewed after each state election. As a consequence, state governments are able to participate directly in the federal parliamentary process. In India the Rajya Sabha is elected by members of state legislative assemblies, using the single transferable vote. In Malaysia a two-term limit is applied to upper-house deputies.

In several African, Central American, and Asian states there are specific literacy requirements for candidates for legislatures. This is the case in Botswana, Cameroon, Costa Rica, Gambia, Kenya, Malawi, the Philippines, and Singapore. The most popular term of membership for first or single chambers is five years, closely followed by four years. The shorter term is found most commonly in Europe and Oceania, where liberal and emergent democratic regimes predominate, while five-year terms are common in Africa and Central America and the Caribbean. The complete analysis is given in Table 31.

The popularity of a five-year term is understandable. A newly elected government, with a policy package it wished to implement, would probably spend at least the first two years framing the necessary legislation and ensuring its passage through the legislative machine. If a proposal was thought to be beneficial in the long term, but unpopular in a short time span, then a reasonable period would be needed for the public to appreciate its benefits. That would be the government's view. On the other hand, immediately popular proposals might be innately flawed and these defects might only reveal themselves over time. A five-year term of office would give the electorate time to assess a government's performance before it submitted itself again for election. That would be the opposition's view.

Politicians in states with first chambers with limited lives of two or three years, such as the United States, Australia, New Zealand, and Sweden, have expressed reservations from time to time about the shortness of the term and some of the practical consequences. Short-term assemblies tend to make governments cautious in their policy proposals,

Assembly: terms of membership			Table 31	
Term (years)	First or single chamber number	%	Second chamber number	%
1	1	1	0	0
2	2	1	0	0
3	11	6	0	0
4	68	37	14	22
5	88	48	18	29
6	5	3	17	27
7	0	0	0	0
8	0	0	3	5
9	0	0	2	3
life	0	0	2*	3
varies	0	0	2	3
transitional	10	5	5	8
Total	185	100	63	100

* With a retirement age of 75 in Canada

fearing a loss of public support with insufficient time to prove that short-term unpopularity can be replaced by long-term satisfaction.

It should be remembered, however, that assemblies in states with parliamentary executives rarely run their full terms. They may end because the government loses assembly support or, as frequently happens, it, or a coalition partner, seeks a dissolution at what it considers to be the most propitious time to ensure electoral success.

In states with limited presidential executives, assembly terms are, invariably, of a fixed duration. This is of potential value to opposition parties, removing the incumbent administration's control over the election timetable and thus subjecting all members equally to the whims of random external forces. It also serves, however, to institutionalize electioneering, sometimes to an unhealthy degree. This is most clearly seen in the case of the US House of Representatives, whose members, facing biennial elections, find themselves condemned to a nonstop cycle of campaigning and fundraising. Fixed-term assemblies are also the norm in two Scandinavian countries with parliamentary executives, Norway and Sweden, and also in Switzerland. In Germany, the term is not formally fixed, but early dissolution for opportunistic reasons is resisted by the Federal Constitutional Court.

As Table 31 shows, the terms of second chambers are invariably longer than those of lower houses, and are never shorter. The most common term for the upper house is, again, five years, but in 17 states it is six years and in five states it is either eight or nine years.

Second chambers with terms of six years or more often stagger those of individual members, with half or a third submitting themselves for election at a time. This serves to 'keep fresh' the accountability of the assembly, but can create problems for a new administration assuming office following a sudden election swing in the lower chamber. The states falling into this staggered category are:

Nine-year term with a third retiring every three years:
Argentina and France

Eight-year term with a third and two-thirds retiring
alternately every four years: Brazil

Eight-year term with half retiring every four years: Jordan

Six-year term with half retiring every three years: Japan, the
Netherlands, and the Philippines

Six-year term with a third retiring every two years: United
States, India, and Pakistan.

Additionally, constitutions invariably specify qualifications for candidates in assembly elections, including a minimum age. Most states with two-chamber assemblies stipulate a more mature entry age for members of the second chamber. In Romania and Venezuela, for example, the minimum ages are 21 years for the Chamber of Deputies and 30 years for the Senate. In Argentina, India, Japan, Pakistan, the United States, and Uruguay, they are 25 years for the lower house and 30 years for the upper chamber. In the Philippines and Thailand, the figures are 25 years for the House of Representatives and 35 years for the Senate. In Brazil, the ages are 21 for the Chamber of Deputies and 35 for the Senate; in France, 23 years for the National Assembly and 35 years for the Senate; and in Italy, 25 years for the Camera dei Deputati and 40 years for the Senato.

This requirement of greater maturity, frequently combined with a longer term of office than in the first chamber, tends to add to the authority of second chamber members, who have often already had sufficiently long political careers to qualify them for the description of 'elder statesmen'.

Finally, influenced by the US model, by far the most popular name adopted for the upper chamber has been the Senate. It is used in 47, or 75%, of the states with second chambers. For lower chambers, there is a wider variety of nomenclature. The most popular designation is National Assembly, used in 66, or more than a third of states with lower chambers. A further 20 states have lower houses described variously as the People's Assembly, House of Assembly, Legislative Assembly, or, simply, the Assembly.

In 27 states, including the United States, the lower chamber is called the House (or Chamber) of Representatives; in 19 states, including 11 in Central and South America, the Chamber of Deputies; and in 14 states, many of which are in the Commonwealth, the name which has been adopted is Parliament. It should be noted, however, that in the United Kingdom the term Parliament encompasses the monarch, the House of Commons and the House of Lords, and not just the lower chamber.

5.6 Assembly size

In Table 32 the size distribution of contemporary world assemblies, lower and upper chambers, is set out and in Table 33 the general population per lower-house member has been calculated for each state with an assembly.

From Table 32 it emerges that 69% of the world's lower chambers have memberships of 200 or less, with the median size being around 150. In addition, it is apparent that upper houses of bicameral legislatures are almost uniformly smaller than their lower-house counterparts, being, on average, half the size. As a consequence, 75% of upper chambers have memberships of 100 or less, the median figure being around 60.

From Table 33 it emerges, not surprisingly, that a state's population size is the principal determinant both of the membership size of its assembly and of the resultant member:population ratio. Thus, the larger, in demographic terms, the state, the larger, on average, the size of its assembly and, notwithstanding this, the higher its member:population ratio. For this reason, India, the second most populous country in the world, appears at the bottom of the Table 33 ratio listings, with each of its deputies representing 1.6 million people, followed by the United States, the world's fourth most populous state. Conversely, tiny, usually island, states, such as Nauru, Tuvalu, Belau, the Marshall Islands, and Kiribati, are to be found clustering at the head of the listings, having small assemblies, with memberships substantially fewer than 50,

Size distribution of contemporary world assemblies				Table 32
Membership size	Lower chambers	Upper chambers	Lower chambers (%)	Upper chambers (%)
10 or below	0	1	0	2
11–50	30	26	16	44
51–100	47	20	25	31
101–200	52	5	28	10
201–300	23	4	12	6
301–400	10	2	5	3
401–500	9	0	5	0
501–750	13	0	7	0
751–1,000	0	0	0	0
1,001–3,000	2	1	1	2
n/a	0	4	0	6
Total	186	63	99	104

Population per lower house member (c. 1995)   Table 33

Country	Region	'000 pop. per lower house member	Country	Region	'000 pop. per lower house member
San Marino	N & W Europe	0.38	Lebanon	Middle East & N Africa	22.66
Nauru	Oceania	0.56	Eritrea	C & S Africa	23.33
Tuvalu	Oceania	0.75	Georgia	C, E, & S Europe	23.40
Monaco	N & W Europe	0.78	Albania	C, E, & S Europe	23.57
Belau	Oceania	1.00	Sweden	N & W Europe	24.93
Liechtenstein	N & W Europe	1.16	Finland	N & W Europe	25.30
Marshall Islands	Oceania	1.48	Lithuania	C, E, & S Europe	26.95
Kiribati	Oceania	1.83	Latvia	C, E, & S Europe	27.00
Andorra	N & W Europe	2.07	Hungary	C, E, & S Europe	27.20
Seychelles	C & S Africa	2.09	Mauritania	C & S Africa	27.85
São Tomé	C & S Africa	2.20	Denmark	N & W Europe	29.05
Dominica	C America & Caribbean	2.40	New Zealand	Oceania	29.17
St Kitts	C America & Caribbean	3.14	Lesotho	C & S Africa	29.23
Vanuatu	Oceania	3.27	Botswana	C & S Africa	30.43
Tonga	Oceania	3.37	Uruguay	S America	31.31
Western Samoa	Oceania	3.33	Tajikistan	Asia	31.49
Antigua	C America & Caribbean	4.65	Mongolia	Asia	31.58
Maldives	Asia	4.65	Korea, North	Asia	33.62
Iceland	N & W Europe	4.76	Greece	C, E, & S Europe	34.00
Libya	Middle East & N Africa	4.95	Switzerland	N & W Europe	34.50
Equatorial Guinea	C & S Africa	5.00	Bosnia-Herzegovina	C, E, & S Europe	34.62
Cape Verde	C & S Africa	5.06	Norway	N & W Europe	34.68
St Vincent	C America & Caribbean	5.57	Slovakia	C, E, & S Europe	35.33
Grenada	C America & Caribbean	6.07	Croatia	C, E, & S Europe	61.25
Bahamas	C America & Caribbean	6.12	Singapore	Asia	35.80
Malta	N & W Europe	6.15	Kuwait	Middle East & N Africa	36.00
Luxembourg	N & W Europe	6.67	Panama	C America & Caribbean	36.11
Belize	C America & Caribbean	6.90	Trinidad & Tobago	C America & Caribbean	36.11
Micronesia	Oceania	7.29	Sierra Leone	C & S Africa	36.29
Djibouti	C & S Africa	7.69	Bulgaria	C, E, & S Europe	37.08
Surinam	S America	7.84	Papua New Guinea	Oceania	37.61
Solomon Islands	Oceania	8.09	Central African Republic	C & S Africa	38.82
Cyprus	C, E, & S Europe	9.06			
St Lucia	C America & Caribbean	9.18	Belarus	C, E, & S Europe	39.62
Barbados	C America & Caribbean	9.29	Jamaica	C America & Caribbean	41.67
Fiji	Oceania	10.00	Moldova	C, E, & S Europe	42.31
Guinea-Bissau	C & S Africa	10.00	Austria	N & W Europe	42.62
Bhutan	Asia	10.67	Portugal	N & W Europe	43.04
Gabon	C & S Africa	10.83	Yemen	Middle East & N Africa	43.19
Guyana	S America	12.31	Honduras	C America & Caribbean	43.75
Swaziland	C & S Africa	12.31	Liberia	C & S Africa	43.75
Comoros	C & S Africa	14.29	Israel	Middle East & N Africa	45.00
Mauritius	C & S Africa	15.49	Nicaragua	C America & Caribbean	45.56
Estonia	C, E, & S Europe	15.84	Angola	C & S Africa	46.19
Macedonia	C, E, & S Europe	16.67	Belgium	N & W Europe	67.12
Gambia	C & S Africa	18.00	Togo	C & S Africa	48.15
Cuba	C America & Caribbean	18.51	Czech Republic	C, E, & S Europe	52.00
Armenia	C, E, & S Europe	18.95	Tunisia	Middle East & N Africa	52.76
Congo	C & S Africa	19.20	Laos	Asia	54.11
Ireland	N & W Europe	21.08	Jordan	Middle East & N Africa	55.00
Namibia	C & S Africa	22.22	Syria	Middle East & N Africa	55.20
Slovenia	C, E, & S Europe	22.22	Paraguay	S America	57.50

continued

Population per lower house member (c. 1995) (continued)			Table 33		
Country	Region	'000 pop. per lower house member	Country	Region	'000 pop. per lower house member
Costa Rica	C America & Caribbean	57.89	Netherlands	N & W Europe	102.00
Bolivia	S America	59.23	Malaysia	Asia	100.00
Zambia	C & S Africa	59.33	South Africa	C & S Africa	102.00
Malawi	C & S Africa	60.45	Niger	C & S Africa	102.41
Mozambique	C & S Africa	61.20	Nepal	Asia	102.93
Algeria	Middle East & N Africa	63.02	Chad	C & S Africa	105.26
Dominican Republic	C America & Caribbean	63.33	Rwanda	C & S Africa	111.43
El Salvador	C America & Caribbean	65.48	Spain	N & W Europe	112.00
Kyrgyzstan	Asia	65.71	Ukraine	C, E, & S Europe	116.00
Senegal	C & S Africa	65.83	Germany	N & W Europe	119.94
Romania	C, E, & S Europe	68.62	Australia	Oceania	121.09
Cameroon	C & S Africa	69.44	Egypt	Middle East & N Africa	123.57
Zimbabwe	C & S Africa	72.67	Argentina	S America	126.46
Burundi	C & S Africa	74.07	Somalia	C & S Africa	128.38
Cambodia	Asia	75.00	Kenya	C & S Africa	129.21
Côte d'Ivoire	C & S Africa	76.57	Taiwan	Asia	128.05
Yugoslavia	C, E, & S Europe	76.81	Turkey	C, E, & S Europe	108.36
Mali	C & S Africa	78.29	Chile	S America	115.00
Sri Lanka	Asia	79.56	Thailand	Asia	145.52
Iraq	Middle East & N Africa	79.60	Azerbaijan	C, E, & S Europe	58.40
Benin	C & S Africa	79.69	Ecuador	S America	146.75
Turkmenistan	Asia	80.00	Korea, South	Asia	148.83
Morocco	Middle East & N Africa	81.08	Uganda	C & S Africa	69.06
Ghana	C & S Africa	82.00	Vietnam	Asia	179.49
Poland	C, E, & S Europe	83.70	Mexico	C America & Caribbean	180.00
Guatemala	C America & Caribbean	125.00	Peru	S America	190.83
Uzbekistan	Asia	87.60	Nigeria	C & S Africa	201.18
United Kingdom	N & W Europe	88.79	Colombia	S America	204.91
Haiti	C America & Caribbean	83.13	Iran	Middle East & N Africa	234.07
Sudan	C & S Africa	91.33	Japan	Asia	244.62
Burkina Faso	C & S Africa	91.59	Brazil	S America	302.90
Italy	N & W Europe	91.75	Philippines	Oceania	325.98
Myanmar	Asia	91.96	Russia	C, E, & S Europe	331.56
Ethiopia	C & S Africa	93.61	Bangladesh	Asia	370.30
Zaire	C & S Africa	56.44	Indonesia	Asia	389.20
Madagascar	C & S Africa	96.38	Afghanistan	Asia	401.96
Kazakhstan	Asia	256.72	China	Asia	405.79
Canada	N America	94.24	Guinea	C & S Africa	420.00
Tanzania	C & S Africa	98.97	Pakistan	Asia	590.32
France	N & W Europe	99.48	United States	N America	592.64
Venezuela	S America	100.49	India	Asia	1645.14

yet, despite this, still registering unusually low member:population ratios, with each deputy representing fewer than 2,000 people. In contrast, in the economically developed and densely peopled states of Northern and Western Europe assembly members typically represent between 20,000 and 120,000 people.

There are two notable exceptions to this general, regular pattern.

First, communist or nationalistic socialist states usually have assemblies far larger than equivalent sized liberal or emergent democracies, or one-party, nonsocialist states. As a

natural corollary, their resulting member:population ratios are lower than might be expected. China, with its 2,970-member National People's Congress; Libya, with its 1,112-member General People's Congress; and North Korea, with its 687-member Supreme People's Assembly are the most prominent examples. The rationale behind the election of these 'jumbo-assemblies' would, in theory, appear to be a desire to broaden the participation base. In practice, however, as has been noted earlier, these assemblies meet in plenary session for less than two weeks a year. They delegate their authority to smaller standing committees and general secretariats, which variously comprise between 40 to 160 members, a figure substantially below the membership average for the permanent assemblies in liberal or emergent democracies.

In two other countries, Indonesia and Taiwan, large quasi-legislatures are found, with respective memberships of 1,000 and 405, and with powers to amend their constitutions and (in Taiwan until 1996) to appoint the state presidents. These are, however, only ad hoc bodies, meeting at five- and six-year intervals, unless specially summoned. In the interim periods, they delegate effective authority to smaller, regular, national assemblies below them. For this reason, they have not been treated as full assemblies in this chapter, being excluded from the listings in Table 29 and from the calculations made for Table 33. A smaller supervisory 'super legislature', twice the size of the regular 50-member legislature, also exists in Turkmenistan, being convened to debate important political and economic issues.

The second, and more specific, anomaly which emerges when Tables 32 and 33 are studied, in conjunction with Tables 29 and 30, is found in the United Kingdom. The United Kingdom has, after Germany, the second largest lower house, with 651 members, of all the world's liberal democracies and, for this reason, has a comparatively low member:population ratio for its total population size. Furthermore, it is the only country in the world having an upper chamber with a larger membership than its lower. This results from the anachronistic combination of hereditary succession and government appointment that is still used to fill the House of Lords, as well as the fact that in earlier years it was the pre-eminent chamber. Today, the House of Lords comprises roughly 800 hereditary peers and 400 life peers, including the law lords and the 'lords spiritual', and 1,038 members have voting rights. However, in practice its active membership is less than 400. Indeed, 300 hereditary peers have never even visited the chamber to take the oath of membership.

5.7 Assembly–executive relationships

There are three possible bases on which to examine the assembly–executive relationship. First, the extent to which an assembly can initiate legislation. Second, the extent to which an assembly can influence policy-making. Third, the extent of an assembly's ability to criticize the executive, block its policies, and even dismiss it.

The vast majority of contemporary assemblies are not significant initiators of legislation. They are, as has already been said, mainly amenders and approvers. For this reason they have frequently been categorized as 'reactive' chambers. There are, however, some notable exceptions which stand out as examples of 'active' legislatures. Nonadversarial Sweden, where assembly members are mainly grouped in constituency, rather than party, blocks, is one. So, to an even greater extent, is the United States.

In Sweden private members' proposals (*motioner*) are ten times as numerous in the Riksdag as government bills (*propositioner*), although the bulk of the former are amendments or party alternatives to government bills, designed to spark off new discussion and inquiries.

In the US Congress thousands of bills and resolutions are introduced each year by senators and representatives, several hundred of which ultimately become law. Even here, however, the key legislative measures are those proposed in January by the president in his annual 'State of the Union' address to both chambers and which are subsequently adopted by party supporters within Congress under the promptings of the White House liaison staff.

The ability of assemblies to influence policy-making is also slight, Sweden, again, being somewhat unusual in this respect. An assembly in a state with a parliamentary executive is, in theory, in a strong position to make policy since the executive is drawn from it and responsible to it. In practice, however, an assembly member who has joined the executive to a great extent loses his or her allegiance to the assembly and becomes, psychologically but not physically, separate from it. The obvious example is the distinction between a front-bench, government, member of the UK House of Commons and a back-bencher.

So we are left with the third base on which to examine the assembly–executive relationship: the ability to criticize, block policies and, *in extremis*, to dismiss an executive.

Most assemblies in parliamentary executive systems have built-in mechanisms for regular questioning of ministers. The UK House of Commons has an hour set aside for this four days a week, and on two of these days 15 minutes are set aside for questions specifically addressed to the prime minister. Although probably the most popular event of the parliamentary week in Britain, as far as the media and public are concerned, there is little evidence that Question Time in the House of Commons is anything more than an opportunity for rival parties to score points against each other. In Germany and Finland 'interpellation' seems more successful, the oral questioning of a minister often being accompanied by a snap vote.

Most assemblies in limited presidential and parliamentary executive systems have strong committee structures, partly to expedite the legislative process and partly to oversee the actions of the executive. The US Congress undoubtedly has the strongest committees of any contemporary assembly in the world. The power and authority of these committees, well provisioned with research staff and armed with extensive rights to subpoena staff from the executive, have been dramatically highlighted in recent years through the wide publicity given to the Watergate, Irangate, and Whitewater hearings. The fact that sessions of the congressional committees can receive nationwide television coverage has increased public awareness and enhanced their influence.

By comparison, assembly committees in other states seem weak. In the United Kingdom, as the result of the composition of the House of Commons and the disciplined party system, standing committees which consider government legislation are government-dominated, introducing only minor amendments to bills presented. Even weaker are the investigative select committees which were introduced into the chamber in 1979 to 'shadow' the work of government departments. Although producing informative reports, with the exception of the longer established Public Accounts Committee, their impact as parliamentary watchdogs has not been great. Their counterparts in Canada and France have been only marginally more successful.

Stronger committee systems operate in Germany, Italy, and Japan, all three having constitutions partly modelled on that of the United States. These committees are primarily concerned with legislation but, from time to time, ad hoc investigative committees have been influential. In Japan, in 1976, an assembly committee vigorously investigated the Lockheed bribes scandal, its work eventually resulting in the arrest and trial of the former prime minister, Tanaka. More recently in Germany, where the Bundestag is obliged to set up an investigation committee upon the motion of one-quarter of its members, a committee successfully probed the 'Flick scandal', which was concerned with illegal party financing.

In one-party states, assemblies are inevitably subservient to the party, and hence the executive, although functional 'Specialized Committees' operate in such bodies as China's National People's Congress to discuss and draft bills and resolutions.

In states with parliamentary executives, the ultimate sanction of assembly members is to dismiss the executive, the prime minister and government, through voting against it in a no-confidence motion. This has occurred frequently in postwar Italy and, as noted above, in Papua New Guinea. In other parliamentary states the government's defeat is difficult to achieve as a result of special constitutional rules. Thus in Germany, as noted in Chapter 4, there is the requirement for a 'constructive vote of no-confidence', in which deputies vote for an agreed successor. In France a 'no-confidence' vote can only be carried against the government if it attracts the support of more than half of the National Assembly's total membership and not just a majority of those voting. If such a motion fails, Assembly members are debarred from calling another such motion during the same parliamentary session. In limited presidential executives, the ability to remove the executive is even more restricted, being limited to the protracted process of impeachment or, as in the cases of Venezuela in 1993, Brazil in 1992, and the United States in 1974, the threat of impeachment.

Thus, on balance, it must be said that, with some rare exceptions, contemporary assemblies have shown little sign of keeping up with, let alone overtaking, the increasing power and authority of executives of all types.

5.8 The representation of interests

The representation of interests is one activity that assemblies usually do well, especially in liberal democratic and emergent democratic states. This representation falls into three broad categories: constituency representation, party representation, and specific group representation.

Constituency representation is a traditional function of all assemblies. In the US Congress it has been developed to a high degree and is reinforced by the residential factor in both the House of Representatives and the Senate. Some congressmen have devoted virtually their entire political careers to the economic advancement of the constituencies they represent, knowing that this is the surest route to re-election. As a consequence, until the November 1994 'anti-incumbent' Congressional elections, 'return rates' were as high as 90% for representatives and 75% for senators. This has led to calls

for the imposition of 'term limits' on assembly membership, as are imposed in several US state legislatures and in the Philippines, where they are set at two consecutive terms for Senators and three for members of the House of Representatives.

Similar, but less well-developed, examples of strong constituency representation can be found in assemblies in other parts of the world, including Kenya, the Philippines, South Korea, France, and the United Kingdom. In the British House of Commons, for example, it is not unknown for a member to ignore a major policy line of his party in order to support his constituency. Some UK Labour Party MPs have in recent years been confronted with 'dilemmas of conscience' in trying to follow a non-nuclear power policy when their constituents have been dependent on nuclear generation for their livelihoods.

Party representation has been the fastest growing activity in most assemblies in recent years. The last independent MP in the UK House of Commons disappeared in the 1960s and there is now only a minority of assemblies that accommodate them. Belau, Kiribati, the Maldives, Micronesia, Monaco, Nauru, and Tuvalu seem to be the few contemporary states where assembly elections are contested exclusively by politicians standing as independents. However, in some of the recently liberated and democratizing states of the former Soviet Union, for example Kyrgyzstan, Ukraine, and Uzbekistan, where party structures are currently weak, the majority of candidates and deputies are independents.

The representation of group interests is another growing activity of assembly members, particularly in liberal democratic countries. In the UK House of Commons many Labour members are sponsored by trade unions and some Conservatives are paid by a variety of interests to present their points of view. In an effort to bring this activity into the open, the House of Commons has produced a Register of MPs' Interests and members are requested to register their interests as well as declare them during the course of debates. The recommendations of the Nolan Committee in 1995 led to a further tightening of these rules. In the United States, with the growing influence of Political Action Committees, which provide a quarter of the funds used in contesting congressional elections, the influence of single-issue ideological interest groups is substantially stronger.

Recommended reading

Adonis, A *Parliament Today*, Manchester University Press, 1990

Arter, D *The Nordic Parliaments: A Comparative Analysis*, Hurst, 1984

Bailey, C J *The US Congress*, Basil Blackwell, 1989

Beamish, D R and Shell, D (eds) *The House of Lords at Work*, Oxford University Press, 1993

Blondel, J *Comparative Legislatures*, Prentice-Hall, 1973

Copeland, G W and Patterson, S C *Parliaments in the Modern World: Changing Institutions*, University of Michigan Press, 1994

Damgaard, E (ed.) *Parliamentary Change in the Nordic Countries*, Scandinavian University Press, 1992

Drewry, G *The New Select Committees: A Study of the 1979 Reforms*, 2nd edn., Oxford University Press, 1989

Goodwin, Jr, G 'The New Congress' in P J Davies and F A Waldstein (eds) *Political Issues in America Today*, Manchester University Press, 1987 (pp. 27–40)

Inter-Parliamentary Union, *Parliaments of the World: A Reference Companion*, 2nd edn., Gower, 1986 (2 vols)

Judge, D (ed.) *The Politics of Parliamentary Reform*, Heinemann, 1983

Kim, C *et al. The Legislative Connection: The Politics of Representation in Kenya, Korea and Turkey*, Duke University Press, 1984

Laundy, P *Parliaments in the Modern World*, Gower, 1989

Mann, T E and Ornstein, N J (eds) *The New Congress*, American Enterprise Institute, 1981

Mezey, M L *Comparative Legislatures*, Duke University Press, 1979

Nelson, D and White, S (eds) *Communist Legislatures in Comparative Perspective*, Macmillan, 1982

Norton, P (ed.) *Parliament in the 1980s*, Basil Blackwell, 1985

Norton, P (ed.) *Parliaments in Western Europe*, Frank Cass, 1990

Norton, P (ed.) *Legislatures*, Oxford University Press, 1990

Sundquist, J L *The Decline and Resurgence of Congress*, The Brookings Institution, 1981

Vanneman, P *The Supreme Soviet: Politics and the Legislative Process in the Soviet Political System*, Duke University Press, 1977

CHAPTER 6

Elections and Voters

6.1 The importance of elections

The majority of contemporary states claim to be democratic and seek to prove their democratic credentials under the banner of representation. The right to vote is almost the only universal right in the world today. Of the 192 states we are examining only six, Brunei, Oman, Qatar, Saudi Arabia, the United Arab Emirates, and the Vatican City State, do not have, and never have had, any institutions which can, even in the loosest sense, be described as popularly representative. A further nine states, comprising Afghanistan, Bahrain, and those states with military executives, have 'suspended' legislatures and thus no currently functioning electoral systems. Among the other 177 there are wide differences in kinds and degrees of representation.

The first, and obvious, difference is between multiparty and one-party political systems. It is reasonable to assume that an election in a multiparty state means a choice of policies as well as representatives, whereas in a one-party system a representative may be changed but the basic policy thrust, as derived from the party, remains the same.

Why then do one-party states bother to go through the charade of elections? First, most of them, indeed probably all of them, would claim that the elections were not a charade. They might well argue that the reality of choice is no greater in a multiparty system than in their own. They might, with some justification, select one of the world's oldest democracies, the United Kingdom, and point out that no government in the postwar period has been elected by a clear majority of the people voting. They might also compare turnouts of less than 80% in general elections in the United Kingdom and little more than 50% in US presidential elections with turnouts well in excess of 90% in most communist, one-party states.

The politician in a liberal democratic state, while conceding these points, would probably argue that, nonetheless, a choice between parties was a substantially greater choice even though, through ignorance or apathy, some people failed to exercise it. He or she would say that the opportunity of voting for a complete change of policy, and even philosophy, was a vital element in a democratic political system and that without it genuine choice was limited.

Leaving aside such arguments, it is clear that in one-party states the voter knows that whatever decision he or she takes in the polling booth the party in power will not change, so the earlier question must be repeated: why are elections held?

The main reason is to demonstrate popular support for the regime. The important work of selecting the candidate has already been done, within the party machine. The election just legitimizes the 'behind-the-scenes' decisions. In some one-party states the question asked is simply 'Yes or No?'. There is only one candidate and therefore choice is given only in a negative form. In other states a choice of candidate may be given. The former communist states of East Germany, Hungary, Poland, Romania, and Yugoslavia offered candidate choice for some years and the practice was later adopted in the Soviet Union, before its demise. In the contemporary communist states of China, Laos, and Vietnam there is candidate choice. In one-party, noncommunist states candidate choice is fairly common.

Although in one-party states the election would appear to make the candidate choice legitimate, the practice is invariably unnecessary on constitutional or practical grounds. The party decision, once taken, is inviolate. The size of the turnout in each constituency will, however, be of interest to party officials because it will indicate the degree of activity, or apathy, in different areas. It will enable them to gauge the work being done by individual candidates and provide public 'feedback' on sensitive issues, allowing them to take steps to improve local morale and efficiency and, if pressed, introduce measures to deal with grass-roots grievances. This is particularly relevant in communist states.

In noncommunist, one-party, and dominant-party states elections may be important on more personal grounds. In some countries, where candidates are fighting each other within the one party, success will often depend on which politician, in the eyes of the voter, offers the best deal. In Kenya, for example, where the Kenyan African National Union (KANU) is the dominant party, there is usually a large (40–50%) turnover of parliamentary representatives as the record of one politician is judged unsatisfactory in terms of what he or she has 'delivered' by way of state money for some local development and so is replaced by another who appears to offer more. This is a variant of what is described in congressional elections in the United States as 'pork barrel' politics: the ability to 'bring home the bacon'.

In multiparty political systems elections are much more significant. Not only do they provide the nonpolitically active public, who invariably comprise more than 95% of the population in most liberal-democratic societies, with an opportunity to participate in the political process, but they actually determine who will wield power. This is why in liberal and emergent democracies so much attention is paid to voting qualifications and voting methods.

6.2 Voting qualifications

The great majority of constitutions refer to voting on the basis of universal adult suffrage which, in simple terms, means the right of all adults to cast their vote. For some countries this is a comparatively recently acquired right. In Western Samoa, for example, until 1990 the franchise was restricted to the holders of *matai* titles, that is to elected clan chiefs. Furthermore, it is a right which varies in detail from state to state.

The age of majority varies and, although 18 is the most common, being the rule in two-thirds of states, in Mongolia it is set as high as 25 years. In more than 20 states the age of voting majority is 21 years. These comprise predominantly a mixture of African, Asian, and South American states, including Gambia, the Ivory Coast, Malaysia, and Singapore, but also such European states as Spain and Turkey. In another ten states, including Austria, Japan, South Korea, and Switzerland, the minimum voting age has been set at either 19 or 20 years. In contrast, in Guinea-Bissau and, in presidential elections in Iran, it is as low as 15, while in Brazil, Cuba, and Nicaragua it is set at 16 years, and in Indonesia and North Korea at the age of 17.

In some Latin American states, Bolivia and Colombia being two examples, the franchise is extended to married persons at an earlier age, 18, than to those who are single, 21, while in Italy the voting age is set at 18 years for the lower house of parliament, but at 25 years for the Senate. Under some constitutions, as in Tonga, literacy is also a necessary qualification, whereas in countries such as India, Honduras, and Madagascar, where the level of literacy is low, there is often provision for people to vote on the basis of party symbols rather than names. In Papua New Guinea, illiterate voters are allowed to cast 'whispering votes' to electoral officers.

Women were the last group in most countries to acquire the right to vote. In New Zealand they were given the franchise as early as 1893, long before it was a fully independent state. In a further 15 states, situated in Europe, North America, and Oceania, the franchise was extended to women between 1900 and 1920. These are: Australia, Austria, Canada, Czechoslovakia, Denmark, Finland, Germany, Iceland, Luxembourg, the Netherlands, Norway, Poland, Russia (the Soviet Union), Sweden, and the United States. In another 20 states, in Africa, the Americas, Asia, and Europe, women were granted the vote between 1921 and 1945. These are: Brazil, Cuba, the Dominican Republic, Ecuador, France, Hungary, Indonesia, Ireland, Italy, Jamaica, Japan, Mongolia, Myanmar, the Philippines, South Africa, Sri Lanka, Thailand, Turkey, the United Kingdom, and Uruguay. In the remaining nations of the world, the female franchise is a postwar phenomenon. It was acquired in Switzerland as late as 1971, in Jordan in 1982, and in Liechtenstein in 1984, while in Kuwait the franchise remains restricted to adult males who are required, in addition, to fulfil strict residency requirements.

Until 1994, South Africa remained the one country in the world where a significant proportion of the population were excluded from electoral participation on racial–ethnic grounds. Between 1909 and 1936, a portion of the black and coloured community of Cape Province did enjoy the right to vote. Thereafter, however, the introduction of a series of new laws served to effectively eliminate black suffrage. This was formally acknowledged in 1959, the official date of complete disenfranchisement for blacks. In 1984 voting rights were restored to coloureds, who comprise 11% of the population, and Indians, who constitute another 3%, for elections to their own assemblies. However, the black community, who comprise more than 68% of the country's total population, were, until 1994, excluded from a political process which was effectively controlled by the 18% white minority.

However, ethnic exclusion persists in several of the newly democratized states of Central and Eastern Europe, where recent citizenship and electoral laws have been framed in such a way as to exclude certain minorities. For example, in Estonia, the voting qualification for the elections of 1992 was restricted to Estonians, or their descendants, who had been citizens of the country between 1918 and 1940. This disenfranchised 38% of the population, predominantly ethnic Russian immigrants. In neighbouring Latvia, many Russian speakers have been similarly disenfranchised by the 1992 citizenship law.

6.3 Voting systems

Elections are usually held to choose either executives or assemblies, or both. In multiparty states where the executive, usually the president, is separate from, and usually limited by, the assembly, the two elections are quite separate, except in the minority of states where the President is chosen by the assembly. The elections may take place at the same time but there are two distinct sets of choices. In parliamentary systems where the executive is drawn from and responsible to the assembly, the assembly determines which party will form the executive and thus only assembly elections are necessary. In one-party states the executive is usually chosen by the party and then 'legitimized' either by the assembly or through a separate election.

The election of political executives is generally a fairly straightforward process and Table 34 sets out the methods employed in the countries of the world. However, considerable ingenuity has been shown by some multiparty states in devising methods of electing assemblies to try to ensure as close a correlation as possible between the number of votes cast for a particular party and the number of seats that party wins.

6.3.1 Simple plurality (SP)

The most frequently used voting system is the simplest and easiest to understand, the simple plurality (SP), or winner-

Electoral systems | Table 34

Region/country	Form of political executive choice	Upper house electoral system	Lower house electoral system
Asia			
Afghanistan	college	n/a	I
Bangladesh	assembly	n/a	SP
Bhutan	hereditary	n/a	mixed–E/A
Brunei	hereditary	n/a	n/a
Cambodia	college & assembly	n/a	SP
China	party	n/a	I
India	assembly	I	SP
Indonesia	college	n/a	PR–PL
Japan	assembly	D–PR/LV	PR–AMS
Kazakhstan	direct	SP	SP
Korea, North	party	n/a	SP
Korea, South	direct	n/a	PR–AMS
Kyrgyzstan	direct	D–SB	SB
Laos	party	n/a	SP
Malaysia	assembly	mixed–E/A	SP
Maldives	direct	n/a	mixed–E/A
Mongolia	direct	n/a	SB
Myanmar	military	n/a	SP
Nepal	assembly	mixed–I/A	SP
Pakistan	assembly	I	SP
Singapore	assembly	n/a	SP
Sri Lanka	direct & assembly	n/a	PR–PL
Taiwan	direct	n/a	PR–AMS
Tajikistan	direct	n/a	SB
Thailand	assembly	A	SP
Turkmenistan	direct	n/a	SB
Uzbekistan	direct	n/a	SB
Vietnam	party	n/a	SB
Central America & Caribbean			
Antigua	assembly	A	SP
Bahamas	assembly	A	SP
Barbados	assembly	A	SP
Belize	assembly	A	SP
Costa Rica	direct	n/a	PR–PL
Cuba	party	n/a	SP
Dominica	assembly	n/a	mixed–E/A
Dominican Republic	direct	D–SP	PR–PL
El Salvador	direct	n/a	SP
Grenada	assembly	A	SP
Guatemala	direct	n/a	PR–AMS
Haiti	direct	D–SB	SB
Honduras	direct	n/a	PR–PL
Jamaica	assembly	A	SP
Mexico	direct	D–AMS	PR–AMS
Nicaragua	direct	n/a	PR–PL
Panama	direct	n/a	SP
St Kitts–Nevis	assembly	n/a	SP
St Lucia	assembly	A	SP
St Vincent	assembly	n/a	SP
Trinidad & Tobago	assembly	A	SP
Central, Eastern, & Southern Europe			
Albania	assembly	n/a	PR–AMS
Armenia	direct	n/a	PR–AMS

continued

Electoral systems (continued)			Table 34
Region/country	Form of political executive choice	Upper house electoral system	Lower house electoral system
Azerbaijan	direct	n/a	PR–AMS
Belarus	direct	n/a	SB
Bosnia–Herzegovina	direct	D–SB	SB
Bulgaria	assembly	n/a	PR–PL
Croatia	direct	D–PR	PR–PL
Cyprus	direct	n/a	SP
Czech Republic	college & assembly	D	PR–PL
Estonia	college & assembly	n/a	PR–PL
Georgia	direct	n/a	PR–AMS
Greece	assembly	n/a	PR–PL
Hungary	assembly	n/a	PR–AMS
Latvia	assembly	n/a	PR–PL
Lithuania	direct & assembly	n/a	PR–AMS
Macedonia	direct	n/a	SB
Moldova	direct	n/a	PR–PL
Poland	direct	D	PR–PL
Romania	direct	D–PR	PR–PL
Russia	direct	D–SP	PR–AMS
Slovakia	assembly	n/a	PR–PL
Slovenia	direct & assembly	mixed–E/I	PR–AMS
Turkey	assembly	n/a	PR–PL
Ukraine	direct	n/a	SB
Yugoslavia	college	I	PR–AMS
Central & Southern Africa			
Angola	direct	n/a	PR–PL
Benin	direct	n/a	SP
Botswana	assembly	n/a	SP
Burkina Faso	direct	n/a	SP
Burundi	direct	n/a	SP
Cameroon	direct	n/a	SP
Cape Verde	direct	n/a	SP
Central African Republic	direct	mixed–I/A	SB
Chad	direct	n/a	SP
Comoros	direct	I	SB
Congo	direct	D–SB	SB
Côte d'Ivoire	direct	n/a	SP
Djibouti	direct	n/a	SP
Equatorial Guinea	direct	n/a	SP
Eritrea	direct	n/a	mixed–E/A
Ethiopia	college/transitional	n/a	mixed–E/A
Gabon	direct	n/a	SB
Gambia	military	n/a	SP
Ghana	direct	n/a	SP
Guinea	direct	n/a	SP
Guinea–Bissau	assembly	n/a	SP
Kenya	direct	n/a	SP
Lesotho	assembly	H/A	SP
Liberia	military	D–SP	SP
Madagascar	direct	mixed–I/A	SP
Malawi	direct	n/a	mixed–E/A
Mali	direct	n/a	SB
Mauritania	direct	I	SB
Mauritius	assembly	n/a	SP
Mozambique	direct	n/a	SP
Namibia	direct	n/a	SP

continued

Electoral systems (continued) — Table 34

Country/region	Form of political executive choice	Upper house electoral system	Lower house electoral system
Niger	direct	n/a	SP
Nigeria	military	D–SP	SP
Rwanda	direct	n/a	SP
São Tomé	direct	n/a	SP
Senegal	direct	n/a	PR–AMS
Seychelles	direct	n/a	PR–AMS
Sierra Leone	military	n/a	SP
Somalia	military	n/a	mixed–E/A
South Africa	assembly	I	PR–PL
Sudan	military	n/a	A
Swaziland	hereditary	mixed–E/A	mixed–E/A
Tanzania	direct	n/a	mixed–E/A
Togo	direct	n/a	SB
Uganda	direct	n/a	mixed–E/A
Zaire	direct	n/a	trans
Zambia	direct	n/a	SP
Zimbabwe	assembly	n/a	mixed–E/A
Middle East & North Africa			
Algeria	direct	n/a	SB
Bahrain	hereditary	n/a	n/a
Egypt	direct	n/a	mixed–E/A
Iran	direct	n/a	SB
Iraq	party	n/a	PR–PL
Israel	assembly	n/a	PR–PL
Jordan	hereditary	A	SP
Kuwait	hereditary	n/a	SP
Lebanon	assembly	n/a	PR–PL
Libya	college	n/a	SP
Morocco	hereditary & assembly	n/a	SP
Oman	hereditary	n/a	n/a
Qatar	hereditary	n/a	n/a
Saudi Arabia	hereditary	n/a	n/a
Syria	direct	n/a	SP
Tunisia	direct	n/a	SP
United Arab Emirates	hereditary	n/a	n/a
Yemen	direct	n/a	SP
North America			
Canada	assembly	A	SP
United States	direct	D–SP	SP
Northern & Western Europe			
Andorra	assembly	n/a	PR–AMS
Austria	assembly	I	PR–PL
Belgium	assembly	mixed–E/A	PR–PL
Denmark	assembly	n/a	PR–PL
Finland	direct & assembly	n/a	PR–PL
France	direct & assembly	I	SB
Germany	assembly	I	PR–AMS
Iceland	assembly	n/a	PR–PL
Ireland	assembly	mixed–E/A	PR–STV
Italy	assembly	I	PR–AMS
Liechtenstein	assembly	n/a	PR–LV
Luxembourg	assembly	n/a	PR–PL
Malta	assembly	n/a	PR–ST
Monaco	assembly	n/a	SB

continued

Electoral systems (continued) | Table 34

Region/country	Form of political executive choice	Upper house electoral system	Lower house electoral system
Netherlands	assembly	I	PR–PL
Norway	assembly	I	PR–PL
Portugal	direct & assembly	n/a	PR–PL
San Marino	assembly	n/a	PR–LV
Spain	assembly	mixed–E/I	PR–PL
Sweden	assembly	n/a	PR–PL
Switzerland	assembly	I	PR–PL
United Kingdom	assembly	H/A	SP
Vatican City State	college	n/a	n/a
Oceania			
Australia	assembly	D–PR/STV	AV
Belau	direct	D–SP	SP
Fiji	assembly	A	SP
Kiribati	direct	n/a	SB
Marshall Islands	assembly	n/a	SP
Micronesia	assembly	n/a	SP
Nauru	assembly	n/a	SP
New Zealand	assembly	n/a	PR–AMS
Papua New Guinea	assembly	n/a	SP
Philippines	direct	D–SP	SP
Solomon Islands	assembly	n/a	SP
Tonga	hereditary	n/a	mixed–E/A
Tuvalu	assembly	n/a	SP
Vanuatu	assembly	n/a	PR–PL
Western Samoa	assembly	n/a	SP
South America			
Argentina	direct	I	SP
Bolivia	direct	D–SP	SP
Brazil	direct	D–PR	PR–PL
Chile	direct	mixed–E/A	SP
Colombia	direct	D–SP	SP
Ecuador	direct	n/a	PR–PL
Guyana	assembly	n/a	PR–PL
Paraguay	direct	D–PR	PR–PL
Peru	direct	n/a	PR–PL
Surinam	assembly	n/a	SP
Uruguay	direct	D–PR	PR–PL
Venezuela	direct	mixed–E/A	PR–PL

Key:

A	appointed	H	hereditary	SB	second ballot
AMS	additional member system	I	indirect	SP	simple plurality
AV	alternative vote	LV	limited vote	STV	single transferable vote
D	direct	PL	party list	trans	transitional
E	elected	PR	proportional representation		

takes-all 'first-past-the-post' (FPTP), method. It is used for assembly elections in the world's two largest liberal democracies, the United States and India, as well as in the United Kingdom and most of the former British colonies which, after independence, retained a 'Westminster model' constitution.

This voting system does not, however, make any pretence of trying to equate the number of seats won with the number of votes cast. Consequently, in countries with two major parties, such as the United Kingdom, third or fourth parties tend to win disproportionately fewer seats than votes. This is clearly demonstrated in Table 35. On two occasions, the party which won the largest number of UK votes actually won fewer seats than the second party. This happened in the cases of the Labour Party in 1951 and the Conservative Party in February 1974. At the April 1992 UK general election it took around 42,000 votes to elect each Conservative and Labour Member of Parliament, but 210,000 votes for each Scottish National Party MP and 300,000 votes for each Social and Liberal Democrat MP.

In countries where numerous minor parties, usually regionally or occupationally based, but only one significant national party operate, the larger grouping is usually able consistently to hold power, despite capturing a relatively low share of the total vote. This has been apparent in India, where the Congress Party is the predominant force. It has been in power for all but five years since independence was achieved in 1947, despite never having secured more than 49% of the national vote. In countries where there are strong, localized, ethnic concentrations, such as Northern Ireland and parts of Scotland and Wales, the SP system can, however, on occasions be of potential advantage to smaller parties. In the Philippines, where SP is used for presidential elections, as well as assembly contests, a consequence in May 1992, when seven candidates contested the presidency, was that Fidel Ramos was elected on the basis of only a 23.6% share of the popular vote and thus had a weak national mandate. Similarly, in Panama, Ernesto Perez was elected president in May 1994 with barely a third of the national vote.

As Tables 34 and 36 show, the SP system is currently employed by 87 states for lower-chamber assembly elections, 63 being either liberal or emergent democracies. The remainder are one-party or dominant-party states. In Cameroon, a 'slate-system' variant of SP operates. Here, the party which gains the majority of votes secures all the available assembly seats.

Simple plurality is used by a significant proportion, 43%, of emergent democratic states. However, 19 of these 31 states are situated in sub-Saharan Africa and have particularly weakly developed pluralist political systems. In contrast, many of the recently democratized states of Central and Eastern Europe, whose prospects for future transition into the liberal democratic regime category appear more promising, have chosen to employ proportional or absolute majority electoral systems. This is because they view these systems as more modern and likely to produce assemblies more representative of voters' wishes. There are statistical grounds for this belief. For 25 states in the developed world, comprising countries in Northern and Western Europe, North America, Oceania, and Japan, 'indexes of proportionality' have been calculated on the basis of the degree to which a party's share of the national vote is reflected by its representation in the legislature. For the four states with the SP system this index, at the most recent elections, was 87%, ranging from 79% in the United Kingdom to 94% in the United States, where only two significant parties operate. For the 18 states with proportional systems, the index averaged 94%, ranging from 87% in Spain to 100% in Malta.

In New Zealand, despite a classic two-party system, the SP voting method has now been abandoned on the grounds of its unfairness towards minority parties and communities, notably indigenous Maoris. In a referendum held in September 1992 voters approved its replacement, from 1996, by a mixed-member proportional system on the German model, with four seats set aside specifically for the Maori community. However, in Italy, where postwar politics have been characterized by the chronic instability and weakness of party governments, a party list-based system of proportional representation (PR) was replaced in 1994 by a predominantly SP-based system, with single-member constituencies.

The attractions of SP were both its perceived ability, on the UK model, to produce strong party executive government on the basis of a relatively low share of the national vote and also the direct link its single-member constituency gives between voters and assembly deputies.

The alternatives to the SP system fall into two broad categories, the absolute majority (see 6.3.2 and 6.3.3) and the proportional systems (see 6.3.4 to 6.3.7). Within each of these two groups there are variations, sometimes of detail and sometimes of substance.

6.3.2 The alternative vote (AV)

The alternative vote (AV) is not theoretically a form of proportional representation (PR) in that it cannot guarantee a close relationship between votes and seats and, indeed, can sometimes produce surprising results. It does, however, go some way towards making the voting system fairer and is relatively simple and easy to understand.

It uses single-member constituencies, the voter choosing a candidate by marking '1' against a preferred choice on the ballot paper. If desired, the elector can also mark '2' against a second choice and so on, but this is not compulsory. First preference votes are then counted and any one candidate who collects more than 50% of all the votes cast is automatically elected. If no candidate achieves more than 50% the candidate with the least number of first-choice votes is eliminated and the second preferences of those who made this candidate their first choice are distributed among the other candidates. This process continues until one candidate emerges with 50+%.

The main objection to AV is that it tends to help compromise candidates and its results can sometimes be quite unpredictable, with the successful candidate being someone whom very few people positively want. At present, only Australia employs this voting system. It was first introduced in 1919 and applies to its lower chamber, the House of Representatives. It has had little perceptible impact on the party system, which remains firmly set in a two–three party mould and the index of proportionality, at 87%, shows little difference from that registered in states with SP systems.

6.3.3 The second ballot (SB)

The second ballot (SB) is similar in some respects to AV. A simple majority election is held and if no one gets more than 50% of the total vote, the candidate with the least votes is eliminated and a second election is held, usually within the next week to ten days. The rules concerning who can participate in the 'run-off' contest vary considerably. In France, where the system is used for National Assembly elections, candidates who have received support from at least 12.5% of the registered electorate are entitled to compete in the following week's second ballot. The candidate who achieves a plurality in this second contest is the one who is elected. For French presidential elections, only the top two candidates go forward to the 'run-off' ballot. This is designed to ensure that a president is elected with a majority of the national vote and thus a clear popular mandate. However, in the May 1995 French presidential election, for the first time ever, a president was elected with only a plurality of the vote, Jacques

Parties' share of House of Commons in UK general elections: 1945–92*　　　Table 35

By votes

General election year	Conservative share (%)	Labour share (%)	Lib/Alliance† share (%)	Total votes (m)	Voter turnout (%)
1945	40	48	9	24.1	73
1950	43	46	9	28.8	84
1951	48	49	2	28.6	82
1955	50	46	3	26.8	77
1959	49	44	6	27.9	79
1964	43	44	11	27.7	77
1966	42	48	8	27.3	76
1970	46	43	7	28.3	72
1974 Feb	38	37	19	31.3	78
1974 Oct	36	39	18	29.2	73
1979	44	37	14	31.2	76
1983	42	28	25	30.7	73
1987	42	31	23	32.6	75
1992	42	34	18	33.6	78

By seats

General election year	Conservative share (%)	Labour share (%)	Lib/Alliance† share (%)	Total seats (number)	Voter turnout (%)
1945	33	61	2	640	73
1950	48	50	1	625	84
1951	51	47	1	625	82
1955	55	44	1	630	77
1959	58	41	1	630	79
1964	48	50	1	630	77
1966	40	58	2	630	76
1970	52	46	1	630	72
1974 Feb	47	47	2	635	78
1974 Oct	44	50	2	635	73
1979	53	42	2	635	76
1983	61	32	4	650	73
1987	59	35	3	650	75
1992	52	42	3	651	78

*Source: J D Derbyshire and I D Derbyshire Politics in Britain: From Callaghan to Thatcher, W & R Chambers, 1990, Table 4, p. 6 (updated)

† The Alliance fought its first general election in 1983

Chirac attracting 49.5% of the second ballot votes cast, with 6% of ballot papers left blank.

In terms of achieving better proportionality, the SB system generally fares worse than AV and even SP, with an 'index of proportionality' of only 81% in recent French National Assembly elections. In addition, it is more costly to operate. The reason for its adoption by the framers of France's Fifth Republic constitution was their concern to encourage the emergence of more streamlined and disciplined party groupings, following the 'immobilisme' of the Fourth Republic,

whose assembly had contained representatives from more than a dozen competing parties, elected by the party list system of proportional representation (PR). This has certainly occurred to a substantial extent, with parties of the right of centre and left of centre frequently entering into coalition or agreed 'stand-down' pacts for second ballot contests, and the first ballot being used as an effective intracoalition primary contest.

Twenty-six countries currently use the SB system for their lower chamber elections, including 19 liberal democratic

World election systems: summary table		Table 36

Direct voting systems for lower chambers

All states

Voting system	Number of states	As % of total states
Simple plurality	87	48
Party list PR	42	23
Second ballot	26	14
Additional member PR	21	12
Single transferable vote	2	1
Limited vote	2	1
Alternative vote	1	1
Total	181	100

Liberal-democratic and emergent-democratic states

	Liberal democratic		Emergent democratic	
Voting system	No. of states	% of states	No. of states	% of states
Simple plurality	32	44	31	43
Party list PR	26	36	14	19
Second ballot	4	5	15	21
Additional member PR	6	8	12	17
Single transferable vote	2	3	0	0
Limited vote	2	3	0	0
Alternative vote	1	1	0	0
Total	73	100	72	100

and emergent democratic states. SB is also used by several other states, including Belarus, Bulgaria, Cyprus, Ecuador, El Salvador, Guatemala, Peru, and Ukraine for presidential contests, by Albania, Armenia, Azerbaijan, Georgia, Hungary, and Lithuania as part of an additional member (AM) system (see 6.3.5), and for governorship contests in some southern states of the United States. In Peru the system is unusual since the minimum proportion of the vote required for a first-round candidate to win on a plurality basis is 36%. If this is not achieved, there is a second ballot.

In several democratizing former communist states in Central and Eastern Europe, including Belarus, Macedonia, and Ukraine, the SB system is used in conjunction with the requirement that voter turnout must be at least 50%. If this is not achieved there is provision for an unlimited number of repeat elections. Thus in Ukraine in 1994 there were five rounds of voting in the parliamentary elections, after which 45 seats in the 450-member Supreme Council still remained unfilled. In Belarus, the first two rounds of voting in the parliamentary elections in May 1995 resulted in only 119 deputies being returned. This left the 260-member Supreme Council inquorate and further elections had to be held in the autumn of 1995.

Compared with the SP system, both the SB and AV systems have had a tendency to promote tactical alliances between minor parties or major and minor parties, improving their chances of success.

Majority voting systems (6.3.2 and 6.3.3) are concerned principally with returning effective governments, usually of a single party, even though they do not always achieve this. In contrast, proportional electoral systems (6.3.4 to 6.3.7) place their chief priority on the principle of representation, seeking to effect the return of assemblies which, in party, social, gender, and ethnic composition, closely mirror the profile and wishes of the electorate. Four principal variants of proportional representation are currently to be found in operation, as detailed below.

6.3.4 The party list (PL)

Party list (PL) systems are, potentially, the most truly representative form of proportional representation (PR), being designed to return members reflecting the broadest possible spectrum of public opinion. To achieve this, unlike absolute majority systems, they are, of necessity, based on large multi-member constituencies of, usually, regional but sometimes, as in the cases of Israel and the Netherlands, a national character.

The first stage in the complicated operation of the PL system is the production of lists of candidates by each of the political parties fighting the election. Each list shows names in descending order of preference, as chosen by the party. In many cases, an elector merely votes for the party of his or her choice and seats are then allocated to each party according to the total proportion of votes received. Thus a party winning 30% of the votes would be entitled to 30% of the seats and enough names would be taken from the party's list to fill those seats.

Like the AV, the PL system cannot always guarantee full proportional representation. In general, however, it has been calculated that it results in a correspondence between parties' shares of the national vote and assembly seats of around 94%. This 'index of proportionality' is more than seven points higher than that recorded for plurality and majoritarian SP, AV, and SB systems.

In some versions of the list system, such as the inflexible 'closed list', used in Israel and Spain, the voter is given no choice of candidate and simply votes for the party. This can make an election very impersonal and has been criticized for transferring too much influence to party machines. Other versions, however, allow voters to indicate a preference for an individual as well as a party. Varying examples of these are the 'flexible list' system, used in Belgium, the 'open list' system of Finland, and, the most liberal of all, the 'free list', or *panachage* ('mix-in') system of Luxembourg and Switzerland, which allows voters to choose specific individuals from across the lists.

List systems can be 'doctored' by stipulating a 'cut-off' point of percentage votes to be won below which very small parties get no representation at all. If this is not done then virtually any party, whatever its size, will have a chance of winning at least one seat and an assembly could be peppered with 'one-off' representatives. The nature and size of the 'cut-off' threshold can vary considerably. In Denmark it is as low as 2% of the vote; in Bulgaria, Moldova, and Sweden, 4%; in the Czech Republic, Estonia, Germany, Hungary, Latvia, and Slovakia, 5%; and in Sri Lanka, 12.5%. In Poland, where, following its release from communism, firm party structures are only slowly being established, no cut-off threshold was applied to the 1991 general election. As a consequence, 29 parties secured representation in the Sejm, with the highest share of the national vote attracted by a single party being only 12%, and a period of weak, shifting coalition governments ensued. The electoral law was thus changed for the 1993 parliamentary elections, with a 5% national threshold applied to individual parties and 8% to alliances. The new electoral arrangements ensured that only six parties and alliances secured representation, yet still the most popular party could only attract 20% of the vote. In Bulgaria, Moldova, and Estonia the 4% thresholds in force proved effective in excluding, respectively, 50, 30, and 15 minor parties from parliament in the recent 1993 and 1994 general elections.

Currently, 42 states employ list systems. Twenty-six are liberal democracies, 14 are emergent democracies, and two, Indonesia and Iraq, have authoritarian regimes; 23 are situated in Europe and 11 in Latin America (see Table 42 in Part II). To allocate the seats a variety of electoral quotas and apportionment systems are used. These include: the 'highest average' system, d'Hondt version, used in Belgium, the Netherlands, Portugal, and Spain; the more complex 'highest average' system, Saint-Lague version, used in Denmark, which is more favourable to minor parties; and the Hagenbach-Bischoff quota, used in Greece, in which the number of votes is divided by the number of seats plus one.

On the whole, list systems have tended to favour the development of multiparty coalition politics. In the Netherlands, for example, where the purest possible form of list system is to be found, no 'cut-off' limits being imposed, a dozen or so parties frequently secure representation in the 'second chamber', although the three principal parties, the Labour Party (PvdA), the Christian Democratic Appeal (CDA), and the People's Party for Freedom and Democracy (VVD), invariably capture around 80–85% of the total vote and assembly seats. Included in the ranks of the minor parties are Calvinist and Evangelical religious groupings, as well as peace, communist, and ecological organizations.

In Switzerland, Belgium, Finland, Denmark, Sweden, and Iceland, where almost similarly liberal 'cut-off' restrictions are in operation, in recent lower chamber elections 12, 9, 9, 8, 7, and 5 parties respectively won seats. However, the consociational character of politics in these states has meant that the consequent coalition administrations have governed with a measure of stability and success.

The absence of a suitable cut-off point for elections to the Knesset in Israel has recently resulted in 'hung' assemblies, in which ten parties have secured assembly representation. As a consequence, minor parties have been given a disproportionately larger influence over the composition of the government than their voting strengths would normally merit. However, in Portugal and Spain, despite list systems being in place, the assemblies have been dominated by a few major parties, with left-of-centre governments continually in power from the early 1980s.

In some countries, tighter 'cut-off' variants of the list system have been used so as to favour the larger parties. The most prominent example is Turkey, where parties need 10% of the national vote to secure entry to parliament and 25% or 33% respectively of the vote in three- or four-member constituencies. In addition, bonus seats are given to the party achieving the most votes. This 'up-loaded' system is designed partly to exclude small religious extremist parties from the National Assembly but also as a means of discouraging a coalition government. It had the consequence in the November 1987 general election of giving the incumbent Motherland Party (ANAP) 65% of Grand National Assembly (GNA) seats with only a 36% share of the popular vote.

In less democratic countries, even cruder forms of 'up-loading' are to be found. In Paraguay, for example, before truly multiparty politics were tolerated in 1993, congressional elections were fought on single national party lists, and the party which received most votes was automatically awarded two-thirds of the assembly seats. This approach can be termed a form of 'disproportionate representation'.

An important consequence of the operation of PL systems is the effect on female representation. A clear feature of its working in Northern and Western Europe has been to promote the return of substantially higher proportions of female members than has been the case in elections based on majoritarian systems, operating in similar socio-cultural conditions. Thus, at the present time, in the assemblies of the Scan-dinavian countries where a PL system is used, women comprise around a third of their memberships. This is comparable to the level of female parliamentary representation in communist Cuba and higher than that, 21%, in communist China. In Iceland an all-female political party, the Women's Alliance Movement, has held seats in the Althing since 1983. Elsewhere in continental Europe the proportionate figure for female assembly representation invariably exceeds 10%. In comparison, in the SP and SB legislatures of France, the United Kingdom, and United States the figure stands at barely 6%, while in Japan only 2% of deputies are female.

Another useful aspect of list systems is that there is no necessity for by-elections when members retire or depart. Candidates ranking next on the party's previous list are automatically drafted in to fill vacancies as they arise. There are some exceptions to this, however, Greece being one.

By-elections are also avoided in France, where the SB operates, since all candidates must fight with a running-mate (*suppléant*) who will take their place if they resign to assume ministerial office, retire, or die in office.

6.3.5 The additional member (AM)

The additional member (AM) system makes use of party lists but also allows the elector to vote for a candidate, two votes being cast, one for the candidate and one for the party. Half the assembly is then elected on an SP basis, or, as in Albania, Georgia, and Hungary, via the SB system, and the other half, using the party lists, is chosen so that the membership of the chamber accurately reflects the national vote. The party lists, therefore, are used to correct any unfairness in the SP system.

The main advantage of the additional member system, also known as the mixed member system, is that it uses single-member constituencies and so keeps the link between the candidate and the elector. At the same time, however, a high level of 'proportionality', comparable with the 'best' list systems, is achieved.

The AM system in its purest form is used in elections to Germany's Bundestag. Here lists operate at the state (*Land*) level, but to qualify for assembly representation on the second list ballot (*Zweitstimme*) parties need to secure either at least 5% of the national vote or win three single-member constituency seats. If a party wins more constituency (*Erststimme*) seats than it appears 'entitled' to on a statewide percentage basis, it is allowed to retain these excess, or *Überhangmandate*, seats and the size of the Bundestag is increased accordingly. The 1994 general election resulted in 16 'excess seats'.

Forms of AM systems operate in 20 other states, five of which are liberal democratic and 12 are emergent democratic, including seven of the recently democratized states of Central and Eastern Europe. The exceptions are Senegal, where the system was introduced in 1973 with the assistance of German political consultants, Armenia, and Azerbaijan. In most countries with AM systems, the system is not fully proportional. Instead, single-member constituencies predominate, but there is a leavening of proportionality via the supplementary national list. In Georgia 64% of the assembly is filled on a proportional basis; in Senegal 58%; in Japan and Mexico 40%; in the Seychelles a third of the National Assembly; in Albania, 29% of the People's Assembly; in Italy, a quarter of the Chamber of Deputies; and in Armenia, Azerbaijan, and South Korea only a fifth of the National Assembly; in Guatemala 15% of the Congress; and in Tunisia only 12% of the National Assembly. The Upper Chamber of the Japanese Diet has also been elected by a variant of the AM system since 1982, with 40% of its seats filled by national level PR.

In Russia, the 450-member State Duma is elected on the basis of a pure AM system, 225 seats being drawn from national party lists, with a 5% cut-off threshold imposed for qualification. However, it has been argued that, in a fledgling democracy where party organizations and identities are underdeveloped, the system of national lists accords disproportionate influence to extremist parties. Thus, in December 1993 Vladimir Zhirinovsky's populist-xenophobic Liberal Democratic Party of Russia (LDPR) won only 11 constituency seats directly but, with 23% of national support, qualified for 59 party list seats. As a consequence, President Yeltsin recommended increasing the proportion of Duma members who are directly elected from single-member constituencies, and are thus believed to be more accountable to the electorate, to two-thirds in future elections.

6.3.6 The single transferable vote (STV)

The single transferable vote (STV) is, in many respects, theoretically the best method of ensuring proportional representation, eliminating the problem of wasted votes that is inherent in majoritarian systems. Indeed, it is the electoral system favoured by the UK Electoral Reform Society. It uses multimember constituencies which may be large but which can be small enough to elect three representatives. All the candidates are listed on the ballot form, usually in alphabetical order, and the elector states an order of preference, from 1 downwards. All the votes cast are counted and the 'electoral quota' is calculated, in other words, the minimum number of votes needed to be elected.

The calculation would work as follows:

$$\frac{(\text{total number of votes})}{(\text{number of seats} + 1)} + 1 = \text{electoral quota}$$

(Droop formula)

Thus, in a three-member constituency with a total of 120,000 votes cast, the quota would be:

$$\frac{(120,000)}{(3 + 1)} + 1 = 30,001$$

and any candidate with 30,001 or more first-preference votes would automatically be elected.

For example, there might be 12 candidates for the three seats and only one who obtained more than the 30,000 quota, in fact 31,001, or 1,000 more than was needed. All the second preferences of voters who made the top candidate their first choice would be counted and their percentage distribution among the other candidates calculated. The 1,000 'surplus' votes would then be redistributed on this percentage basis. If this redistribution brought another candidate up to the 30,001 quota he or she would be elected and the process would continue until all three seats were filled. If all the surplus second-preference votes were used up and there were still seats to be filled then the bottom candidates would be progressively eliminated, with their second preferences redistributed among the other candidates on a proportionate basis.

The STV requires multimember constituencies, but they are often smaller than those used in some varieties of the party list system. The STV is also usually more 'personalized' than the list system, theoretically giving electors the power to choose not only between parties but also between different candidates standing for the same party. Despite this, high degrees of proportionality, in terms of the correlation between parties' shares of the national vote and assembly seats, ranging from 95% to 100%, have been achieved.

Described as the 'Anglo-Saxon version of PR', the STV is currently used for lower chamber elections in both Ireland (since 1922) and Malta (since 1921). It is also used for elections to Australia's and Ireland's Senate and to the lower House of the Assembly in the state of Tasmania (since 1907), as well as for Sri Lankan presidential elections, local government elections in Northern Ireland, and by state assemblies in India when choosing members for the federal upper house, the Rajya Sabha.

6.3.7 The limited vote (LV)

The final PR variant, the limited vote (LV), is currently used in four states, in Liechtenstein and San Marino, for lower chamber elections, and in Japan and Spain, for upper house contests. In Japan it is used to fill 152 of the House of Councillors' 252 seats. It was formerly employed in Spain and Portugal in the 19th and early 20th centuries and in 13 UK parliament constituencies between 1868 and 1880. Under this system, multimember constituencies are used, each returning between three to five members, but electors are allowed only one, nontransferable, vote. The three to five candidates winning most votes in each constituency are then subsequently returned on a simple plurality basis.

The use of multimember constituencies means that minor parties, through restricting themselves to one candidature per constituency, can win seats on relatively low shares, about 15–30%, depending on the size of the constituency, of the total vote. In this respect, the LV system, which is really only 'semi-proportional', differs significantly from the SP, with its single-member constituencies. The LV system, while being of some assistance to minor parties, has been criticized for encouraging faction-based and increasingly corrupt 'money politics' in Japan, where it was also used for lower assembly elections up to 1994. The critics argued that it led to backroom deals between the leaders of the main factions of the dominant Liberal Democratic Party (LDP) so as to ensure that the party captured all three to five seats in the multimember constituencies. Consequently, under the terms of the electoral reform act of December 1994, Japan has now adopted an AM system.

6.4 Election turnouts

The size of the election turnout provides some information about popular participation in the political process but it can also be misleading.

Turnouts in the United Kingdom parliamentary general elections of 1979, 1983, 1987, and 1992 were 76.2%, 72.7%, 75.4%, and 77.7% respectively. These figures compare favourably with those for UK local government elections and for elections to the European Parliament, which have averaged around 35%. German Bundestag election turnouts

varied between 78–91% between 1976–94, showing a generally declining tendency. In France, National Assembly election turnouts have invariably ranged between 65–83% during the last two decades, while presidential election figures have averaged around 80%. In the Scandinavian and North European countries of Denmark, Iceland, the Netherlands, Norway, and Sweden, parliamentary election turnouts of between 80–90% are the norm.

In general, then, in the liberal democracies of Northern and Western Europe turnouts for elections to national assemblies currently cluster within a range band of between 70–90%. Only Switzerland diverges, with general election turnouts averaging 50% or lower. Elsewhere in the developed world, recent general election turnouts have ranged between 67–86% in Japan, South Korea, and New Zealand. In all the countries for which turnout figures have been quoted voting is not compulsory. The state, however, shoulders the burden of responsibility for registering electors and compiling the electoral roll in advance of polling day.

In contrast, in the United States the burden of registration falls upon individual citizens, with parties being employed as a private backup mobilizing force. At the present, however, fewer than 70% of the US population of voting age are registered, including only 40% of Hispanics and 50% of those in the lowest socio-economic category. For this reason, US national election turnouts are, by comparative standards, unusually low, standing at barely 53% of the adult population, though 80% of those registered, for presidential elections between 1980 and 1994, and at around 40% for midterm congressional and governorship elections.

Low electoral participation is also, not surprisingly, a feature of many of the world's poorer liberal and emergent democracies. In India, Nepal, Pakistan, and Botswana, for example, turnouts have averaged between 40–60% for recent assembly elections. In Mexico, the figures have been around 50% for presidential and Chamber of Deputies elections, and in Colombia and Equatorial Guinea, below 40% for assembly elections.

There are, however, some notable exceptions. In Sri Lanka and the Bahamas, for example, parliamentary election turnouts have sometimes exceeded 85%, although they have fallen to around 60% now in Sri Lanka. In Gambia, Honduras, Morocco, and Vanuatu recent turnouts have been around 80%; in Costa Rica, Dominica, and Surinam, 75%; in Barbados and Malaysia, 70%; and in Papua New Guinea, despite the remoteness of many polling stations, above 65%. In Lebanon, the archaic requirement that electors must cast their ballot in their ancestral villages or towns serves to depress turnouts to a level of 50–55%. In Cambodia, the turnout reached 90% in the May 1993 UN-supervised general election, held after two decades of civil war.

In communist states, turnouts for elections at all levels are invariably high, usually exceeding 95% and sometimes getting as near to a 100% response as is physically feasible. In the Laos National Assembly elections of December 1992, for example, 99.3% of eligible voters participated, according to official figures, while turnout was recorded at 99% for North Korea's Supreme People's Assembly elections of April 1990. This does not, however, necessarily denote great popular enthusiasm for the party or the electoral process. For such ritualized contests, the local party machine usually puts considerable effort into securing high turnouts, with up to a quarter of the adult population, party members, local state and work council representatives, and 'reputable citizens', being brought into action as campaign workers. Special transport is laid on for the housebound and ballot boxes are posted at every workplace and housing complex, as well as being carried out to those living in remote areas.

Faced with this huge mobilization and publicity drive, the average citizen who is not a party member may well feel that for the small cost of casting a vote there may be some potential advantage in openly showing support for the official candidate. Only rarely, as was the case in the Polish local elections of 1984, do citizens 'rebel' and stay at home. On this occasion, the official turnout slumped to 75%, although government opponents suggested the true figure was closer to 60%.

High electoral turnouts are also invariably the case in one-party nationalistic socialist and authoritarian nationalist regimes. In Indonesia, for example, turnouts are put at over 90%. However, in Syria they have been as low as 45%.

In former communist states which remain under autocratic leadership, for example Azerbaijan, Turkmenistan, and Uzbekistan, turnouts in excess of 90% have been recorded for recent national elections and referenda. In many other democratizing excommunist states, for example Bulgaria, Hungary, Latvia, Macedonia, Mongolia, Slovakia, Slovenia, and Ukraine, recent general and presidential election turnouts have ranged between 70–95%. This suggests a transfer of civic responsibility between regime types. However, in Russia, where election turnouts of 99.9% were the norm during the communist era, only 55% of the electorate participated in the December 1993 Federal Assembly elections according to official returns, while unofficial observers claimed that turnout may actually have been as low as 46%.

In 30 countries voting is compulsory. Half of these states are situated in Latin America, including Argentina, Brazil, where election days are also public holidays, the Dominican Republic, and Peru, but seven are also in Europe and Oceania, including Australia, Belgium, Greece, Italy, Luxembourg, and Turkey. This compulsion may be real, in the sense of running the risk of being fined for not voting, but in most cases the offenders are rarely, if ever, prosecuted. Some constitutions, including those in most of the communist states, specify that voting is a 'civic' or 'socialist duty' but stop short of compulsion. In addition, in some South American states, the 'constitutional duty' is relaxed for more elderly citizens, who may find it difficult to travel to the ballot booths. Thus in Brazil, voting is optional for those aged 16–17 years, 70 and over and for illiterates. In Paraguay it is compulsory up to the age of 60 and in Peru up to the age of 70. In a further variant, in New Zealand and Senegal voter registration is compulsory but the actual voting is not.

Whether or not the requirement is enforced, there is evidence that turnouts in countries which formally make voting compulsory are generally perceptibly higher than in those which do not. Turnouts of 85–95% are, for example, the norm in Australia, Belgium, and Italy, and for the latter two states these participation levels are also maintained in European Parliament elections. However, lower turnouts of 80%, and sometimes substantially less, have been recorded in the Dominican Republic, Greece, and Peru, while blank and null ballots are quite common in Brazil. In contrast, in Malta, where voting is not compulsory, general election turnouts of 95% or more are the norm.

6.5 Election-rigging: methods and extent

One hundred and seventy-seven countries are shown in Table 34 above as currently holding regular national assembly elections. However, a significant proportion of these polls are either uncompetitive, involving no candidate or party choice, or of a 'façade' nature, involving outward shows of open debate and candidate pluralism but with outcomes that are ultimately rigged by the incumbent regime.

To be truly free and democratic, election contests need to satisfy seven basic criteria:

1   Voting rights: all adults, regardless of race or religion, should enjoy the right to vote.
2   Voting practices: the ballot should be cast freely and secretly, without intimidation or subsequent redress.
3   Election timetable: elections should be held regularly, within prescribed time limits and in accordance with constitutional rules.
4   Candidature rules: all sections of the community should be free to put forward candidates, form political parties, and openly campaign.
5   Campaign period: the campaign period should be of sufficient length to enable all parties and candidates to get their messages across. There should be reasonable equity in media access and coverage. Voter bribery by candidates and parties should be disallowed and maximum limits placed on campaign spending.
6   Election supervision: the campaign and vote counting should be supervised by an impartial administration, with an independent body available to adjudicate in electoral disputes.
7   Power transfer: all parties and candidates should accept the adjudged results, handing over power to the successful party or parties within a prescribed timetable.

At present, these conditions are approached only by the 145 countries which we have designated in Chapter 3 as liberal democracies or emergent democracies. Communist and other one-party states fall short of the important plurality of condition 4 above, while authoritarian regimes, which allow semblances of candidature pluralism, invariably breach conditions 2, 5, and 6. Even many liberal and emergent democracies, totalling up to half, fall substantially short of meeting these conditions and can thus be viewed as holding only partially democratic elections.

This is true of the four liberal democratic states of Mexico, Singapore, Egypt, and Malaysia which hold what have been termed 'dominant-party elections'. In these contests, restrictions are placed on the free operation of opposition parties and the holding of public rallies, media coverage is slanted slavishly in the ruling party's favour, and state resources are employed to intimidate and sometimes effectively bribe voters.

In Mexico, the ruling Institutional Revolutionary Party (PRI), which has monopolized power at both federal and state levels for almost six decades since its inception in 1929, has succeeded in winning elections by building up an extensive rural and urban corporate client network. In return for pledging electoral support, the party has ensured a steady flow of contracts, pay rises, and assured employment to its local political bosses (*caciques*). In recent years, however, as economic modernization has progressively weakened the links binding together this system of traditionalist patronage, the PRI has been forced to resort to cruder ballot-rigging as a means of ensuring its continued electoral dominance. For example, in the 1986 Chihuahua governorship election, with the help of the government-appointed Federal Election Commission, it set about falsifying the electoral rolls in areas of PRI strength and restricting polling station access elsewhere. The actual count was also rigged by impersonations and the crude stuffing of ballot boxes. In the July 1988 presidential and congressional elections, faced with a strong challenge by Cuauhtemoc Cardenas of the National Democratic Front (FDN), these practices continued. As counting got underway, the Electoral Commission's computer mysteriously broke down. It was a week later before official returns were published, giving the PRI's presidential candidate 50.7% of the national vote. Condition 7 of a fully democratic electoral system had clearly been breached. There were claims of fraudulent practices again in 1994 in a number of state election contests, notably in the southern state of Chiapas, where Zapatista rebels were based, and nearby Tabasco, and in 1995 it was finally agreed by the government that impartial observers should re-examine these results.

In Singapore, the dominant People's Action Party (PAP) has so far eschewed such crude methods of ballot-rigging. Instead, it has maintained its electoral dominance by infringing democratic election requirements 2 and 5. First, both prior and during election campaigns, opposition candidates have been mercilessly hounded by the state, falling prey, for example, to trumped-up fraud and tax evasion charges. Second, and more generally, the electorate has been intimidated by fears that any votes cast against the government party might be traced, with adverse employment and financial consequences. By these means, and aided, it must be noted, by successful management of the economy, the PAP has invariably been able to secure well over 70% of the popular vote in parliamentary elections. In elections in August 1991 the PAP's share of the national vote fell somewhat to 61%, nevertheless, it succeeded in capturing 77 of the 81 available assembly seats.

In Egypt, the National Democratic Party (NDP) has been the dominant force for nearly two decades and its restrictive actions prompted most of the opposition parties to boycott the general election of December 1990, when the NDP attracted 80% of the national vote.

In Malaysia, the United Malays National Organization (UMNO) has been in power continuously since independence, as part of a 14-party National Front coalition. The Front's dominance, attracting 63% of the vote and a record assembly majority at the most recent April 1995 general election, can be ascribed, as in Singapore, partly to its success in promoting rapid economic development, but also partly because of the ability of the National Front to act as a 'catch-all' force, with wings orientated to a range of ethnic communities. However, the party coalition also enjoys strong backing from the state machine, media coverage being biased in its favour and public rallies being outlawed.

For both Mexico and Singapore the striking feature of the past decade has been the marked and steady decline in dominant party support, even on the manipulated official returns. It remains an open question, however, whether official totals, particularly in Mexico where the psychological 50% mark is being rapidly approached, will be permitted to fall much further in future contests and whether a peaceful change of party regime would be accepted.

Ten other countries which have been classified in Chapter 3 as liberal democracies have only partially democratic elections. These comprise chiefly the majority of the mainland states of Central and South America, where election contests have been marred by civil violence and where the military still remains a lingering background influence. In addition, in Western Samoa, vote buying, both with cash and goods, and impersonation have been past features of electoral contests. Indeed, in the February 1982 elections the Human Rights Protection Party (HRPP) led by Prime Minister Va'ai Kolone, was removed from office by the Supreme Court on these grounds.

The remaining liberal democracies, numbering more than 59 and situated chiefly in Northern and Western Europe, the Caribbean, North America, and Oceania, substantially meet all seven of the 'free-election' criteria. In addition, the majority of them have experienced electorally induced changes of government at some stage or other during the past two decades: a useful, though by no means essential, indicator of election fairness. These states can be said to hold basically democratic elections. Within these states, however, there are gradations of openness, related to variations in election campaign regulations, violating condition 5, in such areas as media access and spending ceilings.

To these 59-odd liberal democracies which conduct substantially democratic elections can be added, from the evidence of recent polls, 25 rapidly progressing emergent democracies situated in Central and Eastern Europe (Albania, Belarus, Bulgaria, Croatia, the Czech Republic, Estonia, Hungary, Latvia, Lithuania, Moldova, Poland, Romania, Russia, Slovakia, Slovenia, and Ukraine), Asia (South Korea, Kyrgyzstan, Nepal, Pakistan, Taiwan, and Thailand), Africa (South Africa), Western Europe (Andorra), and Oceania (the Philippines).

In South Africa, in April 1994, democratic use of the ballot, in the country's first ever all-race elections, brought about peacefully one of the most dramatic transfers of power and changes of regime in recent history. This *uhuru* (liberation) election has been accepted as having been 'substantially free and fair', although there were localized cases of intimidation and ballot-box fraud. However, the final result was politically neat. The African National Congress (ANC), orientated towards the black majority community, attracted 63% of the vote. This was just short of the two-thirds majority that would have enabled it to write a permanent constitution by itself. However, the old ruling National Party and the Zulu-orientated Inkatha, by securing 20.4% and 10.5% of the vote respectively, received sufficient support to qualify for four and two cabinet seats. This raised suspicions that there may have been some fine-tuning adjustment, the product of behind-closed-doors bargaining by party chiefs, to ensure a politically satisfactory result.

In the remaining 47 emergent democracies, election contests continue to be marred by combinations of vote-counting frauds, dominant-party candidate list-rigging, and bribery, as well as voter intimidation by both government and opposition groups. In Equatorial Guinea, for example, multiparty and supposedly democratic elections were held for the first time in November 1993, but there was no electoral roll, a media blackout was imposed, and some opposition leaders were prevented from campaigning. Similar accusations of ballot-rigging attached themselves to the multiparty elections in Burkina Faso, Cameroon, and Mauritania in 1992 and the presidential election in Togo in 1993.

A recent prominent example of electoral fraud was the Bangladesh Jatiya Sangsad election of March 1988, which was boycotted by the opposition. It was reported that one villager, Shawkat Ali, from near Dhaka, complained, typically, 'I went to cast my vote, but found that someone else had already done it'.

Vote buying has also been a conspicuous feature of recent elections in Thailand, although contests have become progressively fairer. In the July 1988 assembly elections, despite the imposition of official spending limits of 350,000 baht (US$15,000) per candidate, well over 3 billion baht (US$120 million) were distributed to voters by the 3,606 candidates standing. In the poor northeast 100 baht (US$4.5) packages were openly on offer for each vote pledged, plus 10,000 baht bounties for entire villages which successfully elected candidates. Altogether, it has been estimated that this election resulted in an expenditure expansion equivalent to 0.5% of Thailand's GDP. In the 1995 election parties concentrated on the more efficient practice of 'buying' amenable MPs once they had been elected, with the going rate for a deputy who was willing to switch parties being estimated at 10 million baht (US$400,000).

Physical violence and intimidation, both during the campaign and on election day, have been a recurrent feature of contests in South and Central America and also in the Philippines. There, 905 were killed during the 1971 local elections. The death toll in the May 1995 congressional elections, put at 80, was thus a significant improvement. In the Congo, a month-long curfew had to be imposed in 1993, after violent unrest had followed disputed legislative elections. Meanwhile, in areas of ethnic unrest, such as the Kosovo and Sandzak regions of Serbia, Chechnya, and Tatarstan in Russia, and Karachi in Pakistan, poll boycotts have been successfully organized at recent elections by opponents of the regime.

Of the 84 liberal and emergent democracies which, on the broadest count, can be viewed as holding substantially democratic elections 27% are in Northern and Western Europe; 21% in Central, Eastern, and Southern Europe; 14% in Oceania; 12% in the Caribbean; and 11% in Asia. Of the remaining 93 countries holding regular assembly elections, five are communist states. Here, election contests are subject to rigid 'democratic-centralist' control. A further 21, situated

chiefly in Africa, the Middle East, and Asia, are nationalistic socialist or authoritarian nationalist states, in which opposition activity is either outlawed or strictly controlled. This leaves 57 countries, 30% of the world total, in which elections are at present of a 'façade' nature. In these states, despite outward semblances of candidature pluralism, the results are effectively rigged to the incumbent regime's advantage. Control of the media, the electoral commission, and the vote-counting process are the principal means of achieving this, following the cynical maxim, 'He who counts, elects'.

Also of importance is the imposition of severe constraints, and frequently outright bans, by the ruling regime on the candidature and campaign activity of opposition members. All such features were prominent in the February 1988 presidential and assembly elections in Paraguay, which returned General Alfredo Stroessner and his ruling Colorado Party with a 90% share of the vote, the remaining 10% being apportioned between legalized opposition candidates. A turnout of 93% was officially claimed, but the opposition-formed Committee for Free Elections estimated the true figure to be below 50% in many areas. The stuffing of ballot boxes and the impersonation of dead electors were practices which were frequently alleged. Not surprisingly, such loaded contests are often succeeded by frustrated eruptions of opposition, leading to street violence, and in 1989 General Stroessner was deposed in a coup and by 1993 a multiparty emergent democracy had been established.

In Senegal, where the prepared result for the February 1988 presidential election was announced almost as soon as voting stopped, riots erupted in the streets of Dakar and Thies, prompting the government to arrest opposition leaders and declare a state of emergency which lasted for two months. In the Philippines, in February 1986, stronger and better coordinated public opposition to flagrant ballot-rigging succeeded in bringing down the regime of Ferdinand Marcos.

Condition 3 of the basic democratic election criteria, adherence to the election timetable prescribed by the constitution, has been breached in Guyana and the Central African Republic (CAR) during recent years. In Guyana, elections were due to be held in December 1991, but were postponed until October 1992. In the CAR, President Kolingba suspended the second round of presidential elections in 1992 and 1993 after he had failed to finish in the leading position in the first round. Condition 7, acceptance of the verdict of the ballot box, was breached in 1990 by Myanmar's military junta, in September 1992 by the opposition leader in Angola, Dr Jonas Savimbi, and, in June 1993, by Nigeria's military leadership.

6.6 Direct democracy: the growing use of referenda

While regular elections are held to choose legislatures and political executives, more direct legitimizing appeals to the electorate are made, in both democracies and authoritarian regimes, in the form of referenda and citizens' initiatives. Indeed, during recent decades resort to such direct appeals has been increasing, particularly in Western democracies. This has been a consequence of the weakening of voter identification with and allegiance to political parties and the increasing popularity of issue voting and citizens' lobbies. In short, there has been some shift from representative, or 'delegated', democracy towards direct democracy.

A crucial distinction exists between a referendum and an initiative. The former, which is much more common, is a ballot held at the government or parliament's request. It concerns a proposed change in the constitutional framework or policy or a significant and contentious measure which has already been passed by the legislature, but on which electors are now called to pass judgement. It is thus essentially a legitimatizing device, although, on occasions, such plebiscites may also be called by populist executives as a means of using the 'popular will' to overcome the opposition of other elected political forces, usually in the legislature. An initiative is, in contrast, a bottom-up grass-roots device. It is an arrangement, permitted in a limited number of states, by which an individual or group may draft a proposed law or constitutional amendment. Subject to the proposition attracting a certain stipulated measure of initial backing, it is then referred directly to the electorate for approval or rejection.

The citizen's initiative is the ultimate 'populist' instrument of direct democracy. However, its use is very limited in the contemporary world since it is believed that voters are too malleable and short-sighted to be trusted to take sensible decisions. In practice, it is restricted to Switzerland, Liechtenstein, US states, Italy, and the Slovak Republic, although in the UK it is advocated as a policy proposal by the opposition Liberal Democratic Party.

In Switzerland, which is characterized by strong ethnic and religious divisions but where politics are consociational, the first direct vote of citizens on policy occurred in 1294, in the canton of Schwyz, and the first nationwide referendum was held in 1802. Today, proposals for constitutional change must go to a binding national vote if at least 100,000 sign a petition and federal laws, decrees, and long-term treaties must be voted on if at least 50,000 people (corresponding to 0.7% of the population) demand a referendum. During recent decades, between four and five initiatives have been submitted per annum. More than a third of parliamentary measures considered in this way by voters in Switzerland are rejected.

Within the United States, the constitutions of 23 states permit the calling of initiatives and more than 1,750 statutory and constitutional initiatives have been proposed at state level this century. Forty per cent of these have been approved. Six westerly states, Oregon, California, North Dakota, Colorado, Arizona, and Washington, have been responsible for nearly two-thirds of the initiatives, some of which, notably the tax-cutting Proposition 13 in California in 1978, have had far-reaching national impacts.

In Italy, voters can trigger a referendum either on a constitutional law, which has not been passed by both houses of parliament with a two-thirds majority, or to veto any nonfinancial law passed by the legislature if at least 500,000 (0.9% of the population) sign a petition. For the result of the referendum to be binding, turnout must exceed 50%.

In the Slovak Republic, a national referendum must be held if at least 350,000 citizens (7% of the population) sign a petition, but again, for the result to be valid, turnout must exceed 50% of the electorate.

Unlike the initiative, the national referendum is a common constitutional device which, at some stage this century, has been used by almost every nation-state in the world. Prominent exceptions have been Argentina, the Federal Republic of Germany, India, Indonesia, Israel, Japan, Mexico, the Netherlands, and the United States. As Table 37 shows, resort to referenda has increased during recent decades and more than 500 have been held worldwide during the postwar era. Switzerland, with 279 referenda between 1941 and 1993, has been responsible for the largest number, followed by Liechtenstein (more than 50), Italy (29), Australia (24), Egypt (19), Ireland (17), Denmark (13), France (12), the Philippines (11), New Zealand (9), and Uruguay (9).

There are two broad purposes for which referenda are held: to sanction a significant change in a country's constitutional arrangements and to approve a fundamental change in policy.

Constitutional-related referenda have been by far the most common, particularly in those states, the majority, where the calling of referenda has been infrequent. Eight categories of constitutional referenda can be identified.

1   Changes in the status of a state: a referendum may be held to approve independence or unification. This occurred in Slovenia in December 1990; the three Baltic states of Estonia, Latvia, and Lithuania in February–March 1991; Armenia and Georgia in March 1991; North and South Yemen and Croatia in May 1991; Macedonia in September 1991; Turkmenistan in October 1991; Azerbaijan, Uzbekistan, and Ukraine in December 1991; Bosnia-Herzegovina in March 1992; Eritrea in April 1993; and Belau in November 1993. It may also result, however, in a vote to reject independence, as occurred in the British colony of Bermuda in August 1995 and in the Canadian province of Québec in 1980 and 1995, or to oppose unification with an adjoining state, as happened in Moldova in March 1994. However, German unification, in 1990, and the 'velvet divorce' of the Czech and Slovak republics, in 1992–93, took place without national plebiscites, the approval of preceding parliamentary elections deemed sufficient.

2   Alterations in a state's internal structure: a referendum may be held to approve the shift from a unitary to a federal structure, as occurred in Belgium in 1993, or to approve or reject, as occurred in Scotland and Wales in 1979, the devolution of greater power to constituent regions. In the USSR, an all-Union referendum was held in March 1991 on the preservation of the Soviet Union. This resulted in a large, 75%, 'Yes' vote, but concurrent votes for independence were held in several constituent republics and within nine months the Union had been dissolved.

3   Membership of a regional or international grouping: a referendum has commonly been held by countries prior to entry into the European Union, on continuance of membership (as occurred in the United Kingdom in June 1975), and on fundamental developments in the organization of the Union, notably the 1991 Maastricht

Nationwide referenda held in the world since 1941*						Table 37
Period	Switzerland	Rest of Europe	Africa & Near East	Asia	North & South America	Australia & New Zealand	Total
1941–60	53	21	9	6	6	16	111
1961–80	117	32	54	18	12	21	254
1981–93	109	52	29	6	16	6	218
Total	279	105	92	30	34	43	583

* Source: D Butler & A Ranney (Eds) Referendums Around the World, *Macmillan 1994, Table 1–1, p. 5*

Treaty. In the case of Denmark, a referendum held in June 1992 resulted in initial rejection, by 51%, of the Maastricht Treaty, but a year later, in May 1993, there was approval by a 57% majority. In Norway, voters have rejected twice, in 1972 and 1994, proposed membership of the European Community/Union. In Spain, a referendum was held in March 1986 to approve continued membership of the NATO defence organization.

4   Approval or rejection of a new constitution: this has been the most common reason for the holding of referenda. It is a requirement in a number of states and explains why, with so many constitutions recently being framed (see Chapter 2), there has been an upsurge in resort to referenda. Examples of referenda held to approve constitutions include Algeria in 1989, Ghana in 1992, Andorra, Peru, and Russia in 1993, and Armenia and Kazakhstan in 1995. In Albania, in November 1994, voters rejected a government-framed new constitution.

5   Approval of a fundamental change of regime: in recent years referenda have been used for this purpose in Africa, to replace one-party systems with multiparty democracies, such as Zambia in 1990, Mauritania and Sierra Leone in 1991, Congo in 1992, and Malawi in 1993. There was also a whites-only referendum in South Africa, in March 1992, to establish constitutional equality for all races.

6   Approval of a change in executive type or powers: in Bangladesh, in September 1991, the public approved, by national plebiscite, reversion from a limited presidential to a parliamentary system, while in Brazil, in April 1993, retention of the limited presidential system was supported. In Russia, in December 1993, and in Belarus, in May 1995, a strengthening of presidential powers was approved by national referendum.

7   Approval of a change in the electoral system: in New Zealand, in November 1993, voters backed, in a national referendum, a change from the first-past-the-post system to proportional representation. In Italy, in 1993–94, voters chose to repeal the system of proportional representation, and also to end the state financing of political parties.

8   Approval of an extension of the executive's term: in the authoritarian-nationalist states of Kazakhstan, Turkmenistan, and Uzbekistan in Central Asia referenda were held in 1994–95 to confirm the continuance in

office, for periods of between five and eight years, of the executive presidents. They have also been held at regular intervals in Egypt, most recently in October 1993. Taking the place of formal election contests, they have provided a veneer of legitimacy. However, turnouts and approval rates have been so unbelievably high, officially put at 99.3% and 99.6% respectively in Uzbekistan in March 1995, that they cannot be viewed as truly democratic.

The holding of referenda on policy issues has been most typical in states, such as Switzerland, Italy, Ireland, Denmark, and Uruguay, where the device is most deeply entrenched. Policy referenda have also been promised in France by Jacques Chirac, who became president in May 1995. In Ireland, such referenda have focused on contentious social issues, notably divorce, adoption, and abortion. In Italy, the range of issues has been considerably wider, embracing nuclear and environmental laws, the depenalization of drugs, wage indexing, the abolition of specific government ministries, and, in June 1995, trade union and media control issues. In Uruguay, recent referenda have been held on the indexation of pensions, which was approved, and privatization, which was rejected.

The experience of referenda has shown that, in general, turnouts have been significantly lower than in assembly or presidential elections. The differential has been as much as 30% in New Zealand and Austria, and between 10–20% in Denmark, the United Kingdom, Ireland, Switzerland, Italy, and Sweden. This suggests an element of 'democratic exhaustion' or apathy. Indeed, in Guatemala turnout dipped to as low as 16% for a referendum in 1994 which was called by the president on proposals to decentralize government spending and bring forward assembly elections. In France, the November 1988 referendum held on the somewhat tangential issue of a new statute for the overseas colony of New Caledonia resulted in a turnout of only 37%, less than half the norm for a French plebiscite.

An analysis of referenda results shows that normally decisions are quite clear cut. There have been relatively few 'Yes' votes in the range of 49–51% and the verdicts of most referenda have been uncontroversial and, on balance, conservative. For example, 36 out of 42 proposals by referendum to change the Australian constitution have been rejected, devolution was not approved in the United Kingdom in 1979 and secession from the Canadian federation was rejected by Québec in 1995. A notable exception was Italy during

1993–94. Here voters, sickened by the Tangentopoli ('kick-back city') political corruption scandal, approved a draft of radical referenda proposals to change the electoral system and constitutional framework.

Recommended reading

Bogdanor, V *What is Proportional Representation? A Guide to the Issues*, Martin Robertson, 1984

Bogdanor, V and Butler, D (eds) *Democracy and Elections: Electoral Systems and their Consequences*, Cambridge University Press, 1983

Butler, D and Kavanagh, D *The British General Election of 1992*, Macmillan, 1992

Butler, D and Ranney, A (eds) *Referendums Around the World: The Growing Use of Direct Democracy*, Macmillan, 1994

Butler, D and Ranney, A (eds) *Electioneering: A Comparative Study of Continuity and Change*, Clarendon Press, 1992

Crewe, I and Denver, D (eds) *Electoral Change in Western Democracies*, Croom Helm, 1985

Dalton, R, Flanagan, S and Beck, P (eds) *Electoral Change in Advanced Industrial Societies*, Princeton University Press, 1984

World Atlas of Elections, Economist Publications, 1986

Furtak, R K (ed.) *Elections in Socialist States*, Harvester Wheatsheaf, 1990

Grofman, B and Lijphart, A (eds) *Electoral Laws and their Political Consequences*, Agathon, 1986

Harrop, M and Miller, W *Elections and Voters: A Comparative Introduction*, Macmillan, 1987

Hermet, G, Rose, R and Rouquie, A A (eds) *Elections without Choice*, Macmillan, 1978

Lijphart, A *Electoral Systems and Party Systems: A Study of Twenty-seven Democracies*, Oxford University Press, 1994

Mackie, T T and Rose, R (eds) *International Almanac of Electoral History*, 3rd edn., Macmillan, 1991

Reeve, A and Ware, A *Electoral Systems: A Comparative and Theoretical Introduction*, Routledge, 1992

Reynolds, A (ed.) *Election '94 South Africa*, James Currey, 1994

Sartori, G *Comparative Constitutional Engineering: An Inquiry into Structures, Incentives and Outcomes*, Macmillan, 1994

Weiner, M and Ozbudun, E (eds) *Competitive Elections in Developing Countries*, Duke University Press, 1987

CHAPTER 7

Political Parties

7.1 The mobilization of sectional interests

Everyone has an interest in something, even if it amounts to little more than pure self-interest or self-preservation. Millions of people are regular television watchers and if someone sought to deprive them of this pleasure it is certain that they would immediately be up in arms. Some people attach great value to personal privacy and will resist any intrusion, particularly by a public body. Others are more concerned about what they see as the rights of others. Often they feel a duty to protect the seemingly defenceless, especially in the animal kingdom.

Whereas interests are shared by thousands, or even millions, of people, only a relative few will take the trouble to mobilize them into a source of influence and power. These are the organizers of interests: the active members of 'interest groups'.

An interest group is, therefore, an association of people who come together, or are brought together, to represent, promote, and defend a particular interest or set of interests. There are numerous examples to choose from.

Some are chiefly promotional, seeking to bring attention to the needs of particular people, such as unmarried mothers or the disabled. Others are mainly defensive, such as the environmental groups, anxious to protect natural conditions and phenomena. All are representational in one way or another but some, such as the labour unions and professional organizations, are particularly strong in this respect.

A distinction can be made between groups which are concerned with limited, specific interests and those which aim to promote and defend a much wider cross section. These wider interest groups are often referred to as 'cause groups'. They fight for a particular cause, irrespective of whether or not the people they seek to help have direct contact with them, or even know of their existence. They are usually impelled by higher motives than self-interest and could well be called conscience groups.

Cause groups usually ignore national boundaries and can be found throughout the world. Greenpeace, Amnesty International, Oxfam, and Christian Aid are all well-known examples.

7.2 Pressure groups

Sometimes interest groups are referred to as 'pressure groups' as if the two terms are synonymous. This is not strictly the case.

A pressure group is a group representing an interest which seeks to achieve its aims by putting pressure on government. It will use a wide range of tactics to try to influence public opinion but it knows that ultimately the pressure must be on the government in whichever country it operates.

International cause groups will usually exert pressure on governments indirectly, knowing that they are unlikely to gain direct access to national seats of power. They make their case to the public at large, utilizing the mass media, hoping that popular opinion in each country will apply the necessary pressure to produce action.

7.3 Monism, pluralism, and corporatism

A monistic state may be said to be one in which interest group activity is frowned upon, discouraged, or even banned. This contrasts with a pluralistic state where independently organized groups freely operate and act as intermediaries between the public and the government.

Communist regimes and most other one-party states are essentially monistic, mainly because they find it difficult to 'manage' an organization which is outside the established political system. Because it is outside, its actions are unpredictable and unpredictability is seen as a threat to the settled order of things. A good example of this is the protracted opposition, between 1980–89, of the Polish communist government to the independent labour union, Solidarity.

Churches in one-party states produce similar problems. The activities of religious organizations extend beyond national interests, as defined by the ruling regime, and, again, tend to produce unpredictable behaviour. There are, however, states where a religion has been absorbed into the political system so as to become not only acceptable but the main driving force. Iran provides a striking example of this kind of theocratic state.

Some secular one-party states have accepted that interest activity cannot be ignored but can be managed if absorbed into the political system. Thus the pressures, which in a pluralistic system express themselves in a wide variety of outlets, are channelled into the state machine. As the state institutions are invariably controlled by party activists, interests become easily controllable too.

In stark contrast, pressure groups flourish in pluralistic systems, even though the most liberally inclined governments may find them an inconvenience. The United States is an example of a country where interest groups are particularly virile. Over the years their activities have become increasingly evident and their methods more sophisticated so that members of Congress, state governments, and even the presidency, ignore them at their peril.

In some parts of the world the pluralistic state has become the corporate state in which a limited number of powerful interest groups, industrial, financial, and labour, dominate the political scene, the government choosing, or being forced, to negotiate with them before making a major policy decision.

In Austria, for example, political decisions are often arrived at, with the government's blessing, following discussions between strong chambers of commerce and labour unions. Once agreement between these powerful bodies has been reached the government takes over the task of legitimizing and implementing what has been agreed.

The so-called 'social contract' in the United Kingdom in the mid-1970s, between the Labour governments of Harold Wilson and James Callaghan and the Trades Union Congress, whereby the unions accepted a policy of wage restraint in return for the government's promise to follow an agreed social welfare programme, was another strong example of corporatism in a liberal democratic state.

It can be argued that pluralism extends and enhances democracy, because it encourages people who would not normally involve themselves in politics to contribute to the policy-making process. Corporatism, on the other hand, can be said to be antidemocratic in that it increases the power of those sections of the community who organize themselves in the pursuit of self-interest.

Furthermore, corporatism is often associated with the fascist regimes of the 1930s when, in Italy in particular, the government incorporated interest groups representing capital and labour into the state machinery.

The dividing line between thriving pluralism and corporatism is not always easy to discern and sometimes, as in the United Kingdom in the 1970s, an essentially pluralistic state may become temporarily corporatist and then, with a change of government, revert. There is evidence of corporatism in some Central and South American countries. Here powerful groups representing capital and labour wield enormous power and influence, and both the church and the military are involved in major policy decisions. Indeed, those states where the military has seized executive power may be said to have taken corporatism to its ultimate limits.

In economically undeveloped areas of the world it is probably misleading to discuss interest group activity in the form of monism, pluralism, or corporatism. Here groups are considerably less well organized and less sophisticated and sometimes represent little more than an updating and extension of old tribal allegiances.

7.4 Pressure groups and political parties

A 'political party' can best be described as an association of people who hold similar views about what should be a community's social and economic priorities and come together to establish these priorities by gaining control of the machinery of government. It is this wish to govern which distinguishes a party from an interest group, but there are other important differences.

First, an interest group is concerned with a clearly defined range of interests whereas a political party is prepared to take on board a virtually unlimited number. Second, each interest group tends to play a distinctive and individualistic role while the agenda of one political party may be similar to that of another, the differences between them being based on alternative solutions to the same problems. The third difference has already been identified. An interest group aims to influence the government while a party is, or wants to be, the government.

Occasionally an interest group will step over the dividing line and become a party itself. Small political parties with narrowly defined aims, making them little removed from interest groups, have been organized in several countries. Some have been short-lived, some have survived for considerable periods with minimal memberships and funds, and a few have achieved enough popular support to make them formidable political organizations.

In Denmark there is the Single Tax Party (Denmark's Retsforbund) advocating the theories of the 19th-century US economist Henry George (1839–97). Even on such a narrow base it has managed from time to time to win seats in the Folketing. The conservative, antibureaucracy Finnish Rural Party represents the interests of the lower middle class, including small farmers and small enterprises, in Finland and with a membership of about 25,000 has won assembly seats but not a position in government. In several recently democratized states in Central and Eastern Europe farmer-orientated Agrarian Parties have also had success in recent assembly elections, notably the Polish Peasant Party, which provided the country's prime minister between 1993–95, the Latvian Peasant's Union, which has provided the country's president since 1993, the Agrarian Party and Bulgarian National Agrarian Union in Bulgaria, the Agrarian Party in the Czech Republic, and the Independent Smallholders' Party in Hungary. In France Génération Ecologie and Les Verts (The Greens) speak for ecological and environmental interests and the National Restoration (estd 1947) and New Royalist Action parties, although attracting little support, aim for the return of the monarchy. In the Federal Republic of Germany the Five Per Cent Block was established in the mid-1970s, with a membership of barely a hundred, as a political movement to oppose the 5% clause which denies parliamentary representation to parties failing to gain 5% of the national vote. In contrast, Die Grünen (the Greens), with a large and growing membership, has emerged from among a

Principal political parties of the world | Table 38

Region/country	Number of parties regularly operating	Number of parties with >10% of assembly seats	Leading parties	Orientation
Asia				
Afghanistan	24	–	electoral process is currently in abeyance	
Bangladesh	22	3	Bangladesh National Party*	right of centre
			Awami League*	centre left
			Jatiya Dal	Islamic nationalist
Bhutan	–	–	no parties permitted	
Brunei	–	–	no parties permitted	
Cambodia	21	2	FUNCINPEC*	right-of-centre nationalist
			Cambodian People's Party*	reform communist
China	9	1	Chinese Communist Party*	communist
India	23	3	Congress Party*	centrist
			Bharatiya Janata Party*	Hindu nationalist
			Janata Dal	centre left
Indonesia	3	3	Golkar*	right of centre
			Indonesian Democratic Party	nationalist
			United Development Party	Islamic
Japan	12**	3	Liberal Democratic Party*	right of centre
			Social Democratic Party	left of centre
			Shinseito	centrist
Kazakhstan	8	1	Congress of People's Unity*	moderate nationalist
Korea, North	3	1	Korean Workers' Party*	communist
Korea, South	6	3	Democratic Liberal Party*	right of centre
			Democratic Party*	centre left
			United People's Party	centre right
Kyrgyzstan	12	–	independents dominate the assembly	
Laos	1	1	Lao People's Revolutionary Party*	communist
Malaysia	42	1***	UMNO/National Front*	centre right
Maldives	–	–	no political parties operate	
Mongolia	10	1	Mongolian People's Revolutionary Party*	reform communist
Myanmar	7	1	National League for Democracy*	centrist
Nepal	12	2	United Nepal Communist Party*	reform communist
			Nepali Congress Party*	left of centre
Pakistan	29	2	Pakistan People's Party*	centre left
			Pakistan Muslim League–Nawaz*	right of centre
Singapore	13	1	People's Action Party*	right of centre
Sri Lanka	25	2	Sri Lanka Freedom Party*	left of centre
			United National Party*	right of centre
Taiwan	10†	2	Kuomintang*	right-wing nationalist
			Democratic Progressive Party*	centrist
Tajikistan	4	2	Communist Party of Tajikistan*	reform communist
			People's Party of Tajikistan*	left of centre
Thailand	22	4	Thai Nation*	right of centre
			Democratic Party*	centrist
			New Aspiration Party	centrist
			Chart Pattana	right of centre
Turkmenistan	3	2	Democratic Party of Turkmenistan*	reform communist
			United Progressive Party (UPP)*	centrist
Uzbekistan	6	2	People's Democratic Party*	reform communist
			Free National Movement	centre left
Vietnam	1	1	Communist Party of Vietnam*	communist

continued

Region/country	Number of parties regularly operating	Number of parties with >10% of assembly seats	Leading parties	Orientation
Central America & Caribbean				
Antigua & Barbuda	5	1	Antigua Labour Party (ALP)*	left of centre
Bahamas	4	1	Progressive Liberal Party (PLP)*	centrist
Barbados	5	2	Barbados Labour Party (BLP)*	left of centre
			Democratic Labour Party	left of centre
Belize	3	2	People's United Party (PUP)*	left of centre
			United Democratic Party (UDP)*	right of centre
Costa Rica	20	2	National Liberation Party (PLN)*	left of centre
			Christian Social Unity Party (PUSC)*	Christian centrist
Cuba	1	1	Cuban Communist Party (PCC)	communist
Dominica	4	3	Dominican United Workers' Party (DUWP)*	left of centre
			Dominica Freedom Party (DFP)	centrist
			Labour Party of Dominica (LDP)	left of centre
Dominican Republic	21	3	Dominican Revolutionary Party (PRD)*	left of centre
			Social Christian Revolutionary Party (PRSC)*	independent socialist
			Dominican Liberation Party (PLD)	nationalist
El Salvador	11	3	Christian Democratic Party (PDC)*	left of centre
			Nationalist Republican Alliance (ARENA)*	right wing
			Farabundo Marti National Liberation Front (FMLN)*	left wing
Grenada	8	3	New National Party (NNP)*	centrist
			National Democratic Congress (NDC)*	centrist
			Grenada United Labour Party (GULP)	left-of-centre nationalist
Guatemala	11	6	Guatemalian Christian Democratic Party (PDCG)*	Christian centre-left
			Guatemalan Republican Front (FRG)*	right wing
			National Advancement Party (PAN)*	right of centre
			Centre Party (UCN)	centrist
Haiti	25	2	Lavalas coalition*	left of centre
Honduras	11	2	Liberal Party of Honduras (PLH)*	centre right
			National Party of Honduras (PNH)*	traditional right-wing
Jamaica	4	2	People's National Party (PNP)*	left of centre
			Jamaica Labour Party (JLP)	moderate centrist
Mexico	21	3	Institutional Revolutionary Party (PRI)*	moderate left-wing
			National Action Party (PAN)*	centre right
			Democratic Revolutionary Party (PRD)	centre left
Nicaragua	22	2	National Opposition Alliance (APO)*	broad based
			Sandinista National Liberation Front (FSLN)	left wing
Panama	13	2	Democratic Revolutionary Party (PRD)*	right wing
			Arnulfista Party (PA)	left of centre
St Kitts–Nevis	5	2	St Kitts–Nevis Labour Party*	left of centre
			Concerned Citizens' Movement (CCM)	centrist
Saint Lucia	3	2	United Workers' Party (UWP)*	left of centre
			St Lucia Labour Party (SLP)	left of centre
St Vincent & the Grenadines	4	2	New Democratic Party (NDP)*	right of centre
			Unity Labour Party (ULP)	left of centre
Trinidad & Tobago	7	2	United National Congress (UNC)*	left of centre
			People's National Movement (PNM)*	centrist

continued

Principal political parties of the world (continued)
Table 38

Region/country	Number of parties regularly operating	Number of parties with >10% of assembly seats	Leading parties	Orientation
Central, Eastern, & Southern Europe				
Albania	25	2	Democratic Party*	centrist
			Socialist Party of Albania*	left of centre
Armenia	13	1	Armenian Pan-National Movement (APM)	nationalist
Azerbaijan	6	2	New Azerbaijan*	left of centre
Belarus	7	2	Belarus Communist Party*	reform communist
			Peasants' Party*	left of centre
Bosnia-Herzegovina	6	3	Party of Democratic Action*	Muslim nationalist
			Serbian Democratic Party*	Serbian nationalist
			Croatian Christian Democratic	Croat Union nationalist
Bulgaria	58††	2	Bulgarian Socialist Party*	reform communist
			Union of Democratic Forces*	right of centre
Croatia	15	4	Christian Democratic Union*	right-wing nationalist
			Croatian Social Liberal Party	centrist
			Joint List*	centre right
			Social Democratic Party	reform communist
Cyprus	7	3	Democratic Rally (DISY)*	centrist
			Democratic Rally (DIKO)	federalist, centre left
			Progressive Party of the Working People (AKEL) *	left wing
Czech Republic	12	2	Civic Democratic Party*	right of centre
			Communist Party	reform communist
Estonia	11	3	Coalition Party*	left of centre
			Estonian Reform Party	right of centre
			Centre Party	moderate nationalist
Georgia	30	1	Citizens' Union of Georgia (CUG)*	centrist
Greece	15	2	Pan-Hellenic Socialist Movement (PASOK)*	nationalist socialist
			New Democracy*	centre right
Hungary	50	2	Hungarian Socialist Party*	reform socialist
			Alliance of Free Democrats	centrist
Latvia	23	4	Latvian Way*	centre right
			Latvian National and Conservative Party	far right
			Harmony for Latvia	centre left
			Latvian Peasants' Union	centre right
Lithuania	8	3	Democratic Labour Party*	reform socialist
			Homeland Union/Sajudis*	right-wing nationalist
			Christian Democratic Party	centre right
Macedonia	8	2	Social Democratic Alliance*	reform communist
			Liberal Party*	centrist
Moldova	30	3	Agrarian Democratic Party*	nationalist centrist
			Socialist Party*	reform socialist
			Peasants and Intellectuals	pro-Romanian
Poland	28†††	3	Democratic Left Alliance*	reform socialist
			Polish Peasant Party*	centre left
			Freedom Union	centrist
Romania	23‡	3	Social Democracy Party*	centre left
			Democratic Convention*	centre right
			National Salvation Front	centrist
Russia	20	4	Russia's Choice*	centre right
			Liberal Democratic Party	right-wing nationalist

continued

Principal political parties of the world (continued)   Table 38

Region/country	Number of parties regularly operating	Number of parties with >10% of assembly seats	Leading parties	Orientation
Russian continued			Communist Party	communist
			Agrarian Party	centre left
Slovakia	12	4	Movement for a Democratic Slovakia*	centre-left nationalist
			Party of the Democratic Left	reform communist
			Hungarian Coalition	Hungarian orientated
			Christian Democratic Movement	right of centre
Slovenia	25	5	Liberal Democrats*	centrist
			Christian Democrats	right of centre
			Social Democrats	left of centre
			Slovenian Nationalist Party	right-wing nationalist
			Slovenian People's Party	right of centre
Turkey	15	4	Motherland Party*	nationalist Islamic right-of-centre
			Social Democratic Populist Party*	left of centre
			True Path Party	centre right
Ukraine	15	1	Ukrainian Communist Party	reform communist
Yugoslavia	22	4	Serbian Socialist Party*	reform communist
			Serbian Radical Party*	far-right nationalist
			Montenegrin Social Democratic Party	reform communist
			People's Assembly Party	centre right
Central and Southern Africa				
Angola	38	2	Popular Movement for the Liberation of Angola Angola–Workers' Party (MLPA–PT)*	Marxist–Leninist
			Union for the Total Independence of Angola (UNITA)*	nationalist centrist
Benin	34	6	Union for the Triumph of Democratic Renewal (UTDR)	left of centre
			National Party for Democracy and Development (PNDD)	left of centre
			Party of Democratic Renewal (PRD)	left of centre
			Social Democratic Party (PSD)	left of centre
			National Union for Solidarity and Progress (USP)	left of centre
			National Democratic Rally (RND)	left of centre
Botswana	7	2	Botswana Democratic Party (BDP)*	centrist
			Botswana National Front (BNF)*	left of centre
Burkina Faso	62	5	Organisation for Popular Democracy Workers' Movement (ODP-MT)*	centre left
			Movement for Democratic Progress (MDP)	centre left
			Union of Burkina Democrats and Patriots (UDPB)	centre right
			Union of Social Democrats (USD)	centre left
			National Convention of Progressive Patriots–Socialist Party (NPP–PSD)	left of centre
Burundi	9	2	Union for National Progress (UPRONA)*	African socialist
			Front for Burundian Democracy (Frodebu)*	left of centre
Cameroon	71	2	Cameroon People's Democratic Movement (RDPC)*	left-of-centre nationalist
			National Union for Democracy and Progress (UNDP)*	centrist

continued

Principal political parties of the world (continued) | **Table 38**

Region/country	Number of parties regularly operating	Number of parties with >10% of assembly seats	Leading parties	Orientation
Cape Verde	5	2	African Party for the Independence of Cape Verde (PAICV)*	African nationalist
			Movement for Democracy (MPD)*	centrist
Central African Republic	15	2	Central African People's Labour Party (MLPC)*	left of centre
			Central African Democratic Rally (RDC)	right of centre
Chad	14	1	Patriotic Salvation Movement (MPS)*	centrist
Comoros	20	2	National Union for Democracy in the Comoros (UNDC)*	Islamic nationalist
			Rally for Democracy and Renewal (RDR)*	left of centre
Congo	28	3	Pan-African Union for Social Democracy (UPADS)*	left of centre
			Congolese Movement for Democracy and Integral Development (MCDDI)*	left of centre
			Congolese Labour Party (PCT)	left-wing
Cote d'Ivoire	37	1	Democratic Party of the Cote d'Ivoire (PDCI)*	nationalist-enterprise
Djbouti	5	1	People's Progress Party (RPP)*	nationalist
Equatorial Guinea	20	1	Democratic Party of Equatorial Guinea*	nationalist
Eritrea	6	1	People's Front for Democracy and Justice (PFDJ)*	left of centre
Ethiopia	20	1	Ethiopian People's Revolutionary Democratic Front (EPRDF)	left of centre
Gabon	14	3	Gabonese Democratic Party (PDG)*	nationalist
			National Rally for Woodcutters (RNB)	left of centre
			Gabonese Progress Party (PGP)	left of centre
Gambia	5	2	People's Progressive Party (PPP)*	centrist
			National Convention Party (NCP)	left of centre
Ghana	11	1	National Democratic Congress (NDC)*	centrist
Guinea	42	2	Party of Unity and Progress (PUP)*	centrist
			Rally of the Guinean People (RPG)	left of centre
Guinea-Bissau	11	3	African Party for the Independence of Portuguese Guinea and Cape Verde (PAIGC)*	socialist
			Guinea-Bissau Resistance Party–Bafata Movement (PRGB–MB)	centrist
			Party for Social Renovation (PRS)	left of centre
Kenya	13	4	Kenya African National Union (KANU)*	centrist
			Forum for the Restoration of Democracy–Kenya (FORD–Kenya)	left of centre
			Forum for the Restoration of Democracy–Asili (FORD–Asili)	left of centre
			Democratic Party (DP)	left of centre
Lesotho	10	1	Basotho Congress Party (BCP)*	left of centre
Liberia	13	2	National Democratic Party of Liberia (NDPL)*	left of centre
			National Patriotic Front of Liberia (NPFL)	left of centre
Madagascar	16	2	National front for the Defence of the Malgasy Socialist Revolution (FNDR)*	nationalist socialist
			Comite des Forces Vives*	left of centre
Malawi	8	3	Malawi Congress Party (MCP)*	right wing
			United Democratic Front (UDF)*	left of centre
			Alliance for Democracy (AFORD)	left of centre
Mali	10	1	Alliance for Democracy in Mali (ADEMA)*	left of centre

continued

Principal political parties of the world (continued)

Table 38

Region/country	Number of parties regularly operating	Number of parties with >10% of assembly seats	Leading parties	Orientation
Mauritania	9	1	Democratic and Social Republican Party (PRDS)*	left of centre
Mauritius	10	2	Mauritian Militant Movement (MMM)*	left wing
			Mauritius Labour Party (MLP)*	centre left
Mozambique	14	2	National Front for the Liberation of Mozambique (Frelimo)*	left of centre – free market
			Mozambique National Resistance (MNR–Renamo)*	right of centre
Namibia	7	2	South-West African Peoples Organization (SWAPO)*	left of centre
			Democratic Turnhalle Alliance (DTA)*	centrist
Niger	18	4	National Movement for a Development Society–Nassara (MNSD–Nassara)*	left of centre
			Social Democratic Convention–Rahama (CDS–Rahama)*	left of centre
			Niger Alliance for Democracy and Progress (ANDP)	left of centre
			Niger Party for Democracy and Socialism–Tarayya (PNDS–Tarayya)	left of centre
Nigeria	2	2	Social Democratic Party (SDP)*	left of centre
			National Republican Convention (NRC)*	right of centre
Rwanda	15	1	National Revolutionary Democratic Movement (MRND)*	left wing
São Tomé	6	3	Movement for the Liberation of São Tomé e Príncipe (MLSTP–PSD)*	nationalist socialist
			Democratic Convergence Party–Reflection Group (PCD–GR)*	left of centre
			Independent Democratic Action (ADI)	centrist
Senegal	16	2	Senegalese Socialist Party (PS)*	left of centre
			Senegalese Democratic Party (PDS)*	centrist
Seychelles	9	2	Seychelles People's Progressive Front (SPPF)*	socialist
			Democratic Party (DP)	centre left
Sierra Leone	12	1	All People's Congress (APC)*	socialist
Somalia	17	3	Somali Revolutionary Socialist Party (SRSP)*	socialist
South Africa	33	3	African National Congress of South Africa (ANC)*	left of centre
			National Party of South Africa (NP)*	right of centre
			Inkatha Freedom Party (IFP)	centrist
Sudan	16	1	National Islamic Front (NIF)	Islamic nationalist
Swaziland	6	–	–	–
Tanzania	13	1	Revolutionary Party of Tanzania (CCM)*	African socialist
Togo	15	2	Rally of the Togolese People (RPT)*	nationalist socialist
			Action Committee for Renewal (CAR)*	left of centre
Uganda	17	5	National Resistance Movement (NRM)	centre left
			Democratic Party (DP)	centre left
			Conservative Party (CP)	centre right
			Uganda People's Congress (UPC)	left of centre
			Uganda Freedom Movement (UFM)	centrist
Zaire	9‡‡	1	Popular Movement of the Revolution (MPR)*	African socialist

continued

Principal political parties of the world (continued)   Table 38

Region/country	Number of parties regularly operating	Number of parties with >10% of assembly seats	Leading parties	Orientation
Zambia	12	2	Movement for Multiparty Democracy (MMD)*	left of centre
			United National Independence Party (UNIP)	African socialist
Zimbabwe	15	1	Zimbabwe African National Union–Patriotic Front (ZANU–PF)*	African socialist
Middle East and North Africa				
Algeria	59	2	National Liberartion Front (FLN)*	socialist-Islamic
			Front Islamique du Salut (FIS)*	Islamic fundamentalist
Bahrain			no parties	
Egypt	12	1	National Democratic Party (NDP)*	centre left
Iran	1	–	–	–
Iraq	1	1	Ba'ath Arab Socialist Party*	nationalist socialist
Israel	28	3	Israel Labour Party *	left of centre
			Likud (Consolidation Party)*	right of centre
			Meretz Party	left Zionist
Jordan	10	1	Islamic Action Front*	Islamic nationalist
Kuwait			no parties	
Lebanon	21	5	Phalangist Party	Christian radical nationalist
			Progressive Socialist Party (PSP)	Muslim moderate socialist
			National Liberal Party (NLP)	centre left
			Amal	shia
			Hizbollah	Islamic fundamentalist
Libya	1	1	Arab Socialist Union (ASU)*	left wing
Morocco	11	5	Constitutional Union (UC)	right wing
			National Rally of Independents (RNI)	royalist
			Popular Movement (MP)	centrist
			Independence Party (Istiqlal)	nationalist centrist
			Socialist Union of Popular Forces (USFP)	progressive socialist
Oman			no parties	
Qatar			no parties	
Saudi Arabia			no parties	
Syria	6	1	National Progressive Front*:	Arab socialist
			Ba'ath Arab Socialist Party	
			Arab Socialist Party (ASP)	Arab socialist
			Arab Socialist Union (ASU)	Arab socialist
			Socialist Union Movement (SUM)	Arab socialist
			Syrian Communist Party (SCP)	Arab socialist
Tunisia	10	1	Constitutional Democratic Rally (RDC)*	nationalist socialist
United Arab Emirates			no parties	
Yemen	30	3	General People's Congress (GPC)*	left of centre
			Yemen Reform Group (Al-Islah)*	right of centre
			Yemen Socialist Party (YSP)	left wing
North America				
Canada	7	3	Liberal Party of Canada*	centre left
			Bloc Quebecois	separatist
			Reform Party	right-wing populist
United States	13	2	Republican Party*	right of centre
			Democratic Party*	centre left

continued

Principal political parties of the world (continued)   *Table 38*

Region/country	Number of parties regularly operating	Number of parties with >10% of assembly seats	Leading parties	Orientation
Northern and Western Europe				
Andorra	5	3	National Democratic Grouping (AND)*	centrist
			New Democracy (ND)	centrist
			Liberal Union (UL)	centre right
Austria	13	3	Socialist Party of Austria (SPÖ)*	left of centre
			Austrian People's Party (ÖVP)*	centrist
			Freedom Party of Austria (FPÖ)*	moderate right-wing
Belgium	20	5	Christian People's Party (CVP)	Christian centre left, Dutch-speaking
			Socialist Party (SP)	left of centre, Dutch-speaking
			Flemish Liberals and Democrats (VLD)	left of centre, French-speaking
			Socialist Party (PS)	left of centre, French-speaking
			Liberal Reform Party (PRL)	centrist, French-speaking
Denmark	15	3	Social Democratic Party (SD)*	left of centre
			Liberal Party (V)*	centre left
			Conservative People's Party (KF)	centrist, free enterprise
Finland	9	4	Finnish Social Democratic Party (SSDP)*	left of centre
			Finnish Centre Party (KESK)*	centrist
			National Coalition Party (KOK)	right of centre
			Left-Wing Alliance (VL)	left of centre
France	25	3	Rally for the Republic*	right of centre
			Union for French Democracy*	centre right
			Socialist Party	left of centre
Germany	13	2	Christian Democratic Union*	right of centre
			Social Democratic Party*	left of centre
Iceland	7	4	Independence Party (IP)*	right of centre
			Progressive Party (PP)*	radical socialist
			People's Alliance (PA)	left of centre
			Social Democratic Party (SDP)	left of centre
Ireland	14	3	Fianna Fáil (FF)*	centre right
			Fine Gael (FG)*	centre left
			Labour Party*	left of centre
			Progressive Democrats (PD)	radical centre left
Italy	18	2	Freedom Alliance	right of centre
			Progressive Alliance	left of centre
Liechtentstein	3	2	Patriotic Union (VU)	right of centre
			Progressive Citizens' Party (FBP)	right of centre
Luxembourg	7	3	Christian Social Party (PCS)*	Christian left of centre
			Luxembourg Socialist Workers' Party (POSL)*	moderate socialist
			Democratic Party (PD)*	centre left
Malta	5	2	Malta Labour Party (MLP)*	left of centre
			Nationalist Party (PN)*	Christian centrist
Monaco			no parties	
Netherlands	19	4	Christian Democratic Appeal (CDA)*	Christian right of centre
			Labour Party (PvdA)*	left of centre
			People's Party for Freedom and Democracy (VVD)*	centrist
			Democrats '66*	environmental centrist

continued

Region/country	Number of parties regularly operating	Number of parties with >10% of assembly seats	Leading parties	Orientation
Principal political parties of the world (continued)				**Table 38**
Norway	14	4	Norwegian Labour Party (DNA)*	left of centre
			Conservative Party	progressive right-of-centre
			Centre Party (SP)	left of centre
Portugal	19	4	Social Democratic Party (PSD)*	centre right
			Socialist Party (PS)*	centre left
			People's Party (PP)	right wing
			United Democratic Coalition	left wing
San Marino	7	3	Christian Democratic Party (PDCS)*	Christian centrist
			Socialist Party (PS)*	left of centre
			Progressive Democratic Party PDP)	moderate left-wing
Spain	21	2	Spanish Socialist Workers' Party (PSOE)*	left of centre
			Popular Party (PP)*	right of centre
Sweden	9	2	Swedish Social Democratic Labour Party (SAP)*	left of centre
			Moderate Party (M)*	right of centre
Switzerland	22	4	Christian Democratic People's Party of Switzerland (CVP–PDC)	Christian centrist
			Radical Democratic Party of Switzerland (FDP–PRD)*	radical centre-left
			Swiss Social Democratic Party (SP-PS)*	centre left
			Swiss People's Party (SVP–UDC)	centrist
United Kingdom	20	3	Conservative and Unionist Party*	right of centre
			Labour Party*	left of centre
			Liberal Democrats	centre left
Oceania				
Australia	11	3	Australian Labour Party*	left of centre
			Liberal Party	centre right
			National Party	centrist non-metropolitan
Belau	–		no political parties	
Fiji	6	3	Fijian Political Party*	Melanesian right-of-centre
			National Federation Party*	Indian left-of-centre
			Fijian Labour Party	Indian left-of-centre
Kiribati	2	2	Maneaban Te Mauri*	centre right
			National Progressive Party	centre left
Marshall Islands	–	–	no formal political parties	
Micronesia	–	–	no political parties	
Nauru	–	–	no political parties	
New Zealand	10	2	Labour Party*	left of centre
			National Party*	centre right
Papua New Guinea	10	3	Pangu Pati*	nationalist
			People's Democratic Movement	centrist
			People's Action Party	centrist
Philippines	24	2	Lakas/Christian Democrats*	centre right
			Laban/Liberal Democrats*	centrist
Solomon Islands	7	3	Group for National Unity*	nationalist
			People's Alliance Party	centre left
			National Action Party	centrist
Tonga	1	1	People's Party	centrist
Tuvalu	–	–	no political parties	

continued

Region/country	Number of parties regularly operating	Number of parties with >10% of assembly seats	Leading parties	Orientation
Vanuatu	11	3	Union of Moderate Parties*	centre right
			Vanuaaku Parti*	left of centre
			National United Party*	centre right
Western Samoa	3	2	Human Rights Protection Party*	centrist
			Samoan National Development Party*	centre right
South America				
Argentina	35	3	Radical Civic Union Party (UCR)*	centrist
			Justicalist Party (PJ)	right wing
			Front for a Country in Solidarity (Frepaso)	centre left
Bolivia	27	4	National Revolutionary Movement (MNR)*	centrist nationalist
			Nationalist Democratic Action Party (ADN)	right wing nationalist
			Movement of the Revolutionary Left (MIR)	left wing nationalist
			Solidarity and Civic Union (UCS)	populist, free enterprise
Brazil	20	5	Social Democratic Party (PSDB)*	left of centre
			Party of the Brazilian Democratic Movement (PMDB)*	centre left
			Brazilian Progressive Party (PPB)	centrist
			Liberal Front Party (PFL)	centre right
			Workers' Party (PT)	left of centre
Chile	30	4	Christian Democratic Party (PDC)*	centrist
			Socialist Party (PS)*	left wing
			Party of National Renewal (RN)	right wing
			Independent Democratic Union (UDI)	right wing
Colombia	20	2	Liberal Party (PL)*	centrist
			Conservative Party (PSC)*	right of centre
Ecuador	18	3	Social Christian Party (PSC)*	Christian socialist
			Ecuadorean Roldosist Party (PRE)	centre left populist
			Republican Unity Party (PUR)	right of centre
Guyana	14	2	People's National Congress (PNC)*	centrist
			People's Progressive Party (PPP)*	left wing
Paraguay	11	3	National Republican Association–Colorado Party (ANR–PC)*	right of centre
			Authentic Radical Liberal Party (PLRA)*	centrist
			National Encounter (EN)	right wing
Peru	30	3	Cambio 90*	centrist
			New Majority (NM)*	centrist
			Union for Peru (UPP)	centrist
Surinam	15	3	New Front (NF)*	left of centre
			National Democratic Party (NDP)	left wing
			Democratic Alternative 1991 (DA '91)	left of centre
Uruguay	26	3	Colorado Party (PC)*	progressive centre-left
			National (Blanco) Party (PN)*	traditional right-of-centre
			Progressive Encounter (EP)*	left wing
Venezuela	20	4	Democratic Action (AD)*	left of centre
			Christian Social Party (COPEI)*	Christian centre-right
			Movement to Socialism (MAS)*	left of centre
			Radical Cause (LCR)	left wing

Key

*	Parties with >20% of assembly seats after the most recent elections	†	More than 70 parties are registered in Taiwan
		††	More than 80 parties are registered in Bulgaria
**	More than 10,000 political parties are registered in Japan	†††	More than 130 parties are registered in Poland
***	The National Front is a coalition of 14 parties, dominated by UMNO	‡	More than 90 parties are registered in Romania
		‡‡	Over 130 parties exist in Zaire

Principal political parties of the world (continued)　　Table 38

number of ecology parties to become a significant political force. In the October 1994 general election it captured 7.3% of the national vote and 49 Bundestag seats and by 1995, with representation in most state assemblies and partners in coalition governments in several, had effectively supplanted the Free Democrats as Germany's third main party.

Women's interests are being increasingly represented throughout the world by parties which have grown from nonpolitical groups. In Belgium, for example, there is the Unified Feminist Party, in Iceland the Women's Alliance (estd 1983), and in Germany the German Women's Movement. In Norway, the Pensioners' Party, and in Germany, Die Grauen (the Greys), have also contested recent elections, representing the interests of older citizens. Parties based on specific religious aims are also found. In Israel the National Religious Party advocates the unity of the Jewish people in faith in Israel and throughout the world, and the Netherlands Roman Catholic Party presses for adherence to Catholic principles on subjects such as abortion, euthanasia, and sexuality.

Whereas interest groups, in one form or another, have existed since the beginnings of civilized life, political parties are relatively new, being products of the 18th century onwards. Their predecessors were cliques and factions, based usually on personal or family power. The modern party displays three essential features: a permanent structure and organization; an authority to represent people, whether or not they are members of the party, based on open elections; and, of course, an intention to form a government or participate in government.

Table 38 lists the leading parties in the contemporary world and their political orientations. The number of active parties in each state, as shown in column 2, is something of an approximation in some cases because the emergence and disappearance of minor groupings is often a notable feature of some political systems.

7.5 Parties in liberal and emergent democracies

It is possible to distinguish six different bases of party formation and support in the states we have defined as liberal or emergent democracies. They are: social class, economic status, religion, regional differences, ethnicity, and philosophical leanings. All parties are based on at least one of these factors, some on most, or all.

The United Kingdom provides a clear example of class-based parties, although the divisions are not as stark in contemporary society as they were earlier in the century. The creation of the Labour Party, known originally as the Labour Representation Committee, in 1900, to represent the working classes, provided a striking contrast to the Conservative Party, which sought to protect and promote the interests of the middle and upper classes. Before the advent of the Labour Party Britain's two-party political system had been based on a division between the Conservatives, representing landed interests, and the Liberals, representing urban industrialists.

Class-based parties are not as marked in most other countries. The Labor Party of Australia and the New Zealand

Political party membership					Table 39
Political party membership as a proportion of state populations in communist and liberal democratic states, c. 1990					
	Communist states			*Liberal democratic states* *	
State	*Ruling party membership (m)*	*% of total population*	State	*Combined party membership (m)*	*% of total population*
N Korea	3.000	14.6	Austria	1.300	17.2
Cuba	0.524	5.1	Norway	0.500	12.0
China	44.000	4.2	Barbados	0.025	9.9
Vietnam	1.75	2.8	Italy	4.500	7.9
Laos	0.042	1.0	Belgium	0.700	7.1
			Belize	0.010	6.0
			Denmark	0.300	5.9
			Switzerland	0.370	5.7
			Ireland	0.150	4.2
			Japan	4.350	3.6
			Germany (FRG)	2.030	3.3
			United Kingdom	1.800	3.2
			France	1.700	3.1
			Netherlands	0.400	2.8
			Australia	0.420	2.7
			Sri Lanka	0.200	1.3

* This is a selective sample as accurate data are lacking for other liberal democratic states

Labour Party, although similar in origin to their counterpart in the United Kingdom, reflect the greater social openness in those two countries.

Ironically, communist parties in liberal democratic states have tended to be homes for left-wing, middle class intellectuals rather than for the proletariat and have seldom won sufficient popular support to control the levers of political power. This has been increasingly true of the two most significant of such bodies in Western Europe, the Italian Communist Party (PCI) and French Communist Party (PCF). In 1991, the PCI, formed originally in 1921, split into two new parties, the social-democratic Democratic Party of the Left (PDS) and the traditionalist Communist Re-establishment Party (PRC).

Economic status has largely replaced, or is replacing, class as an indicator of social position in most liberal democracies. In Italy, for example, class divisions are not clearly defined and economic status is becoming a dominant feature of party support. In the Federal Republic of Germany the postwar rise of a non-unionized working class and a new middle class provide further evidence of the importance of economic, rather than social, factors as a basis for party allegiance.

Religion still provides a widely occurring foundation for political parties in contemporary liberal and emergent democracies. Parties in Italy, Austria, Germany, France, and most other Western European states display this characteristic to varying degrees, having their roots in sides taken during earlier secular–clerical battles. In the United Kingdom economic disparities in Northern Ireland have been underlined by religious divisions.

Regional differences are, arguably, the most common foundation for party support. In the United States, for example, clearly distinguishable parties might well disappear if they were not supported on regional bases. In the Netherlands and Belgium regional variations, accentuated by linguistic differences, have multiplied the party groupings. In Belgium each of the four principal parties, Christian Democrat, Socialist, Liberal, and Green, is currently divided into autonomous, and often antagonistic, Flemish and French wings. In the United Kingdom, nationalist parties operate in Scotland and Wales, and regional parties in Northern Ireland, while support for the two main parties, the Conservatives and Labour, also varies greatly regionally. In Italy, the Lombard League/Northern League, based in northern Italy, has established itself as an influential force with substantial national bargaining power, as have the Catalonia-based Democratic Convergence in Spain, and southern-based Telugu Desam and AIADMK in India.

Ethnic-based parties are a feature of a number of the recently democratized states of Central and Eastern Europe. They include: in Albania, the Greek Albanian-orientated Human Rights Union (EAD); in Bosnia-Herzegovina, the Serb-orientated Serbian Renaissance Movement (SPO) and Croat-orientated Croatian Christian Democratic Union (HDZ); in Bulgaria, the minority Turkish community-orientated Movement for Rights and Freedoms (MRF); in Croatia, the Serb-orientated Serbian National Party (SNS); in the Czech Republic, the Moravian and Silesian communities-orientated Movement for Autonomous Democracy of Moravia and Silesia (MADMS); in Estonia, the ethnic Russ-

ian-orientated Our Home is Estonia party; in Macedonia, the ethnic Albanian-orientated Party for Democratic Prosperity (PDP); in Moldova, the Gagauz community-orientated Gagauz People's Movement; in Romania, the ethnic Hungarian-orientated Hungarian Democratic Union of Romania (HDUR); in the Slovak Republic, the ethnic Hungarian-orientated Hungarian Coalition; and in Yugoslavia, the ethnic Hungarian and Albanian-orientated Democratic Community of Vojvodina Hungarians (DZVM) and the Democratic Party of Albanians (DPA).

Philosophy has not provided a reliable basis for mass party support in liberal democratic states in recent years. Indeed, surveys suggest that the great majority of contemporary electors not only care little for social and political theory but have no clear understanding of the philosophical stance of the parties for which they vote. The 'thinking elector' is certainly in a minority throughout the world and the chances of representation by a party which accurately mirrors the views of this kind of voter are very much determined by the vagaries of the electoral system, as we shall see later in this chapter. The new 'postindustrial' ecological parties, which have made notable progress in Northern and Western European states during recent decades, as a result of proportional representation, are examples of this process. They contrast significantly with the eclectic 'catch-all' nature of most major liberal democratic parties.

The internal discipline of parties varies greatly within liberal and emergent democratic states. The parties of the United Kingdom, where a vigorous 'whipping' system is in place to ensure that Members of Parliament vote according to the 'party line', and Germany are particularly cohesive and disciplined. In Japan, in contrast, control within parties is effectively devolved to the leaders of patronage and personality-based factions. In the United States, congressmen and senators operate in the main as 'freelancers', voting according to personal convictions and constituency interests.

7.6 Parties in communist states

The all-pervading influence of the party provides the sharpest contrast between communist one-party and multiparty states. It is the ultimate source of power and permeates all aspects of the political system and the state institutions.

In contrast to parties in most Western democracies, membership of the party in communist states is a privileged and elitist acquisition. Whereas parties in liberal democracies actively compete with each other to increase their memberships, communist parties are highly cautious and selective about the people who are eventually admitted into full membership. In China, for example, aspirants are initially inducted into the Young Pioneers, a body for children between the ages of 7 and 14 which operates in schools, and then into the party's 'youth' wing for 15–25-year-olds, the Chinese Communist Youth League. Years later, when old enough for consideration for full-party membership, they must be nominated by two full party workers. Then, if accepted, they are required to serve a probationary period, under the title of 'candidate member', and which includes dutiful study of the teachings of Marx, Lenin, Mao Zedong, and Deng Xiaoping.

Despite these hurdles to be surmounted, party membership, with its associated economic and social advantages, is highly sought after in communist states. For this reason, party membership as a proportion of the total population is invariably at a higher level in communist than liberal democratic states, as Table 39 shows.

Parties in communist states have clear ideological bases. Indeed, one of the main purposes, if not the main purpose, of the party is to preserve and project the ideology. This is done by the presence of party representatives throughout the political and social systems, including the media and workplaces.

This all-pervasiveness must be clearly recognized if the political systems of communist states are to be properly understood. Using China as the salient example, it can be seen that any position of reasonable seniority within the state must be 'confirmed' by the party; the more important the post the higher the echelon of approval. The most senior posts of all are closely controlled by the secretariat of the Central Committee of the party. From its earliest days the Chinese Communist Party (CCP) set out to be an elite 'vanguard' organization, comprising the country's 'best citizens', and, although the membership net has been cast more widely since the 1950s, almost tripling between 1961–92, it has never deviated from that original aim. The stress on loyal adherence to the official line has meant that there have been periodic 'purges' of 'disloyal' elements.

Other communist states, and some nationalistic socialist states, have similarly developed and promoted the party as the custodian of the nation's political future and the 'vanguard of the proletariat'. As Table 39 above reveals, however, there are significant variations in membership 'densities' between the 'mass party' of North Korea and the elitist cadres of Vietnam and Laos.

7.7 The party in noncommunist, one-party states

Most contemporary noncommunist, one-party states are found in what has become fashionable to describe as the 'Third World', even though this description can be a little ambiguous.

In these states the party, in addition to acting as a political recruitment, socialization, and resource distribution agency, usually performs two main functions: the promotion of nationalism and patriotism and the maintenance of a certain stable economic and social order. Support for nationalism invariably receives a high priority, the dominant parties usually being those which had spearheaded the independence movement, and the economic and social order is that which is determined by the ruling elite within the party.

Additionally, the noncommunist single party often tends to support and sustain the strong, charismatic leader. Most of the black African states display this characteristic, although it should be noted that the dominance of a strong leader is not always confined to one-party states. The constitution of the French Fifth Republic was originally designed with Charles de Gaulle in mind and the party which supported him not only made his continuance in office its main aim but assumed his name as the popular description of the political move-

ment. Other states, particularly in South America, have spawned strong, autocratic leaders within a highly factionalized, multiparty system.

Compared with parties in liberal and emergent democracies and communist states, those in noncommunist one-party countries are, with notable exceptions in black Africa, such as Tanzania and Zimbabwe, relatively weak organizations and very much the instruments of those nations' political leaders. Some countries, although in theory one-party states, might better be regarded as having no parties at all. The reason for the comparative docility of party politics in these states stems mainly from history and social organization. Modern political parties are not a 'natural' development in most so-called Third World states and many years may elapse before the economic and social environments can sustain a 'sophisticated' multiparty system. Social organization, sometimes based on tribal loyalties or strong regional differences, has also favoured allegiance to the strong, personal leader rather than the 'anonymous' party.

7.8 Parties in militaristic and absolutist states

In states controlled by the military or absolute rulers political parties either do not exist or, if they do, are puppets of the ruling elite and façades for what is little more than autocratic, personal government.

Absolutist states such as those in the Arab world have never experienced what might be described as popular political activity, with representative institutions. Most of the countries which are contemporaneously under the sway of military rulers have, in contrast, previously enjoyed some form of democratic government so that their present condition may be a temporary aberration. There is evidence that military rulers find it difficult to sustain their leadership for protracted periods without creating a single party and building it into the framework of the state or reverting to a multiparty political system.

In Bangladesh, the Jana Dal (People's Party) was formed in 1983 by Lieutenant-General Hossain Mohammad Ershad to support his presidential candidature. Now known as the Jatiya (National) Front, the party has subsequently established itself as a civilian force. In Indonesia, the Joint Secretariat of Functional Groups (Golkar Party), which had been created in 1964 as a loose alliance of anticommunist sectional interest groups, was transformed into a civilian ruling front for the military when, in 1968, it was brought under government control by General Suharto. Similarly, in Ghana, Flight-Lieutenant Jerry Rawlings formed the National Democratic Congress (NDC) in 1992 to successfully support his campaign for the presidency and the NDC also won an overwhelming majority in legislative elections held in December 1992.

7.9 Political parties and electoral systems

Is there a direct connection between a country's electoral system and the structure and numbers of its political parties?

Voting and party systems in liberal democracies | Table 40

States with majoritarian voting systems		States with some form of party system proportional representation	
Antigua and Barbuda (SP)	two-party		
Argentina (SP)	two-party		
Australia (AV)	two-party		
		Austria (PL)	multi-party
Bahamas (SP)	two-party		
Barbados (SP)	two-party		
Belau (SP)	no parties		
		Belgium (PL)	multi-party
Belize (SP)	two-party		
Bolivia (SP)	multi-party		
Botswana (SP)	two-party		
		Brazil (PL)	multi-party
Canada (SP)	multi-party		
Colombia (SP)	multi-party		
		Costa Rica (PL)	two-party
Cyprus (SP)	multi-party		
		Denmark (PL)	multi-party
Dominica (SP)	multi-party		
		Dominican Republic (PL)	multi-party
		Ecuador (PL)	multi-party
Egypt (SB)	dominant party		
El Salvador (SP)	multi-party		
		Finland (PL)	multi-party
France (SB)	two-party*		
		Germany (AMS)	multi-party
		Greece (PL)	multi-party
Grenada (SP)	multi-party		
		Guatemala (AMS)	multi-party
		Guyana (PL)	two-party
		Honduras (PL)	two-party
		Iceland (PL)	multi-party
India (SP)	multi-party		
		Ireland (STV)	multi-party
		Israel (PL)	multi-party
		Italy (AMS)	multi-party
Jamaica (SP)	two-party		
		Japan (AMS)	multi-party
Kiribati (SB)	two-party		
		Liechtenstein (LV)	multi-party
		Luxembourg (PL)	multi-party
Malaysia (SP)	dominant party		
		Malta (STV)	two-party
Marshall Islands (SP)	no parties		
Mauritius (SP)	multi-party		
		Mexico (AMS)	dominant party
Micronesia (SP)	no parties		
Monaco (SB)	no parties		
Nauru (SP)	no parties		
		Netherlands (PL)	multi-party
		New Zealand (AMS)	multi-party
		Norway (PL)	multi-party
Papua New Guinea (SP)	multi-party		
		Peru (PL)	two-party
		Portugal (PL)	multi-party

continued

Voting and party systems in liberal democracies (continued)		Table 40	
States with majoritarian voting systems		**States with some form of party system proportional representation**	
St Kitts–Nevis (SP)	multi-party		
St Lucia (SP)	two-party		
St Vincent & the Grenadines (SP)	two-party		
		San Marino (LV)	multi-party
Singapore (SP)	dominant party		
Solomon Islands (SP)	multi-party		
		Spain (PL)	multi-party
		Sri Lanka (PL)	two-party
		Sweden (PL)	multi-party
		Switzerland (PL)	multi-party
Trinidad & Tobago (SP)	multi-party		
		Turkey (PL)	multi-party
Tuvalu (SP)	no parties		
United Kingdom (SP)	two-party		
United States of America (SP)	two-party		
		Uruguay (PL)	multi-party
		Vanuatu (PL)	multi-party
		Venezuela (PL)	multi-party
Western Samoa (SP)	two-party		

Key:

* Two-party blocs		LV	limited vote	SP	simple plurality
AMS	additional member system	PL	party list	STV	single transferable vote
AV	alternative vote	SB	second ballot		

Writers tend to be ambivalent, suggesting a 'chicken and egg' situation. Some argue that the kinds of parties in a particular country simply reflect its social and economic structure while others attribute much greater influence to the methods of voting available to electors. What is the evidence?

Of the 73 countries identified in Table 11 as liberal democracies, 37 employ majoritarian voting systems of an alternative vote, simple plurality, or second ballot type. The remaining 36 have some variety of proportional representation. An analysis of the respective party systems reveals the pattern set out in Table 40 below.

Of the 37 liberal democratic countries with majoritarian voting methods, 15, 41%, have effectively a two-party system operating, 3, 8%, have a 'dominant-party system', in which one party usually dominates electoral contests, and 6, 16%, have a system in which parties as such do not operate, candidates fighting for assembly seats as independents. Only 13, 35%, majoritarian voting countries have political systems of a multiparty nature, with three or more parties regularly exchanging or sharing power. Conversely, of the 36 liberal democratic states employing some kind of proportional representation 29, 81%, have multiparty systems and only 6, 17%, have effectively two parties operating. In the remaining country a 'dominant-party system' is in force. Although the evidence is not conclusive, a link between electoral systems and party systems seems more than a possibility.

The classic examples of two-party competition, in which minor parties are virtually nonexistent, are to be found in the small island states of the Caribbean and Oceania. In these regions 13, 54% of the 24 liberal democratic systems where political parties are found operate in this way. The smallness of their populations, which in the majority of cases average between 100,000–300,000, and of their assemblies, varying between 11 and 49 elected members, are important explanatory factors. The personalized style of politics and party formation in these regions has had the effect of creating polarization, as have their simple plurality voting systems.

The textbook example of a two-party system is, however, the United Kingdom. Here the simple plurality voting system has played, arguably, a paramount role in fostering polarization. The two major parties, Conservative and Labour, have shared power exclusively for more than 60 years because the electoral system has made it extremely difficult for third or fourth parties to secure enough parliamentary seats to break the monopoly. The advent of a strong challenge from 1981 onwards, first in the form of the Liberal–SDP Alliance and then the Liberal Democrats, on the centre left of the political spectrum, has benefited the centre-right Conservatives, giving them clear majorities in three successive general elections and making some sort of electoral pact between the opposition parties the only likely way of ending the Conservative hegemony.

Canada is only a partial exception to the rule of simple plurality voting producing a two-party system because, although the seats in the House of Commons have been shared in recent years by three parties, for most of the present century the Liberals and Progressive Conservatives have dominated Canadian politics. Similarly, in France and

Mauritius, two other majoritarian electoral states which currently have multiparty systems, the assemblies are invariably dominated by two principal party groupings, with minor 'half parties' holding a much smaller number of seats, though sometimes the balance of power. Only in one majoritarian state, Papua New Guinea, does a full-blown multiparty system operate.

The tendency for majoritarian voting systems to foster restricted party systems thus appears to be strong. In the cases of Canada, the United States, and the United Kingdom the size, social complexity, and regional differentiation of the countries are such that it seems almost certain that if proportional voting systems were in place a multiplicity of party groupings would emerge, although a core of three or four major parties would still be likely to predominate. In the case of France firm evidence exists from the Fourth Republic period and, briefly, from the National Assembly election of 1986, when party list systems were in operation, that the second ballot majoritarian method has served to restrict party development.

The evidence presented in Table 40 also shows, however, that proportional voting systems do not always result in a multiplicity of parties vying for, or sharing, power. The fact that small parties are not disadvantaged by the voting system will not necessarily guarantee them better access to government, as the experiences of Costa Rica, Guyana, Honduras, and Malta reveal. Historical and social factors can sometimes result in domination by two parties, however open the political system might be. In many other states with proportional representation systems, although a multiplicity of parties may have assembly representation, it is usual for three or four major parties to hold a majority of seats.

7.10 Parties and the legal environment

The majority of one-party states have the party's monopoly enshrined within the constitution. In some ostensibly multiparty states legal controls will sometimes favour the dominant government party, making life for opposition groups difficult. Singapore provides evidence of this. In genuine multiparty states the legal environment can range from positive encouragement at one extreme to minimum restraints on fraudulent practices at the other.

Austria provides probably the clearest example of positive support for political parties, the Party Law stating: '... the existence and diversity of political parties is an essential component of the democratic order of the Republic of Austria.' Here the state gives generous financial support. Each party with at least five members in the National Council receives a lump sum and then additional finance is provided on the basis of the number of votes won in the previous federal election. Parties which do not win seats but obtain at least 1% of the popular vote are not overlooked, receiving pro rata support according to votes obtained.

Similarly in Germany, under the law of July 1967, which operates at both the federal and state levels, parties are described as a 'constitutionally necessary element of a free democratic order', with state subsidies of DM5 (US$3) per eligible voter being provided to all political parties which secure 0.5% or more of the popular poll in federal elections, with additional subsidies being granted to parties with more than 2% of the vote. By the mid-1990s, Germany's larger parties secured more than a third of their total funding from the state and smaller parties more than half, while state, federal, and Euro-election campaign spending exceeded 1 billion Deutschmarks per election cycle.

Several other states give finance to help cover election and other party expenses in varying degrees. They include Brazil, Colombia, Costa Rica, Denmark, Ecuador, France (from 1988), Hungary, Israel, Italy (to 1994), Japan, the Netherlands, Norway, Portugal, Spain, Sweden, Turkey, Venezuela, and the United States, for presidential elections only. The amount of the grant usually depends on the size of the vote obtained at the last election, but in Denmark on the size of the party. As a quid pro quo, upper spending limit restrictions are often imposed on election contests. In many countries free time is made available to parties on the state radio and television networks. In the United Kingdom, although there are no state funds for elections, the official opposition party, once elected, is given finance, its leader and a limited number of its parliamentary managers receiving state salaries.

Many states require parties to register and sometimes the conditions of registration can be severe, making it difficult for small or new parties to obtain a foothold on the political ladder. Argentina, Brazil, India (where strict regulations were introduced in 1985 to discourage inter-election changes of deputy allegiance, known as 'floor-crossing'), Malaysia, Mexico, the Philippines, Thailand, and Venezuela are among the countries requiring evidence of popular support as a condition of registration. In Indonesia the number of parties permitted to operate has been restricted to three since 1975.

At the other extreme, there are states where control is at a very minimum. They include Belgium, where one party fought an election under the banner of 'Snow White and the Seven Dwarfs'; Poland, where the Polish Beer Lovers' Party secured parliamentary representation in October 1991, with 3.3% of the national vote, before becoming split between 'Small Beer' and 'Large Beer' factions; Bolivia, whose elections are generally subject to widespread fraud; Honduras; New Zealand; Sri Lanka; Switzerland; and the United Kingdom, where 'oddball parties', such as The Monster Raving Loony Party, are allowed to contest elections provided they are prepared to sacrifice a deposit of £500 if their vote count falls below 5%. In Japan, where more than 10,000 parties are registered, the July 1995 upper house elections were contested by a drivers' party, campaigning for the abolition of car taxes and regulations, a gay rights' party, and a UFO party, which believes that Japan should prepare to receive aliens coming to Earth.

Recommended reading

Ball, A and Millward, F *Pressure Politics in Industrial Societies: A Comparative Introduction*, Macmillan, 1986

Bell, D S (ed.) *Contemporary French Political Parties*, Croom Helm, 1982

Coggins, J and Lewis, D S (eds) *Political Parties of the Americas and the Caribbean*, Longman, 1992

Daalder, H and Mair, P (eds) *Western European Party Systems*, Sage Publications, 1983

Day, A J and Degenhardt, H W (eds) *Political Parties of the World: A Keesings Reference Publication*, 2nd edn., Longman, 1987

East, R and Joseph, T (eds) *Political Parties of Africa and the Middle East*, Longman, 1993

East, R (ed.) *Communist and Marxist Parties of the World*, 2nd edn., Longman, 1990

Epstein, L *Political Parties in the American Mold*, University of Wisconsin Press, 1986

Hill, R J and Frank, P *The Soviet Communist Party*, 2nd edn., Allen & Unwin, 1983

Ingle, S *British Party Politics*, Basil Blackwell, 1989

Lawson, K *The Comparative Study of Political Parties*, St Martin's Press, 1976

McDonald, R and Ruhl, J M *Party Politics and Elections in Latin America*, Westview Press, 1989

Merkl, P H (ed.) *Western European Party Systems*, Free Press, 1980

Sagar, D J and Lewis, D S (eds) *Political Parties of Asia and the Pacific*, Longman, 1992

Sartori, G *Parties and Party Systems*, Cambridge University Press, 1976

Seldon, A (ed.) *The Conservative Party in the Twentieth Century*, Oxford University Press, 1993

Solomon, S G (ed.) *Pluralism in the Soviet Union*, Macmillan, 1983

Stammen, T *Political Parties in Europe*, John Martin Publishing, 1980

Szajkowski, B (ed.) *New Political Parties of Eastern Europe and the Soviet Union*, Longman, 1991

Thomas, A and Paterson, W (eds) *The Future of Social Democracy*, Oxford University Press, 1986

Von Beyme, K *Political Parties in Western Democracies*, Gower, 1985

Ware, A (ed.) *Political Parties: Electoral Change and Structural Response*, Basil Blackwell, 1987

Wattenberg, M P *The Decline of American Political Parties, 1952–1980*, Harvard University Press, 1984

Wilson, G K *Interest Groups in the United States*, Clarendon Press, 1981

2

Political Systems of the World's Nation-states

Introduction

Having considered the various ingredients of a political system and suggested bases for comparing one with another, it is now time to look at the circumstances of individual states as they are found in the world today. In the ensuing pages 192 independent nations will be examined and, as has already been intimated, for comparative purposes they will be grouped into nine regions: Asia; Central America and the Caribbean; Central, Eastern, and Southern Europe; Central and Southern Africa; the Middle East and North Africa; North America; Northern and Western Europe; Oceania; and South America.

Much of the information in Tables 1 to 40 has been extracted from a world database. It has been summarized for each country within a region and additional data have been included, so as to produce a social, economic, and political profile for each state. This profile is set out in Part II at the start of each country entry. Summaries of this information, showing how particular features of political systems are distributed globally, on a regional basis, are given in Tables 2, 9, and 21, and in Tables 41 to 49 below.

Even though a sovereign nation comes into existence at a particular point in time, it is not created in a vacuum, or some sterile laboratory. It is essentially the product of history and so the political development of each country is also outlined in Part II, with particular emphasis on the period since World War II, or since independence was achieved if this was later.

General note

In the references to income type in Table 48 and elsewhere in this volume, the designation 'High Income' indicates a per-capita national income in c. 1992 in excess of US$7,000, 'Middle Income' between US$1,000 and 7,000, and 'Low Income' less than US$1,000. The quality of the per-capita income data is good for the more developed nations and those states characterized by political and economic stability. However, unfortunately for many Third World nations, for countries gripped by the scourges of civil war or hyperinflation, and for the recently democratized states of Central and Eastern Europe, undergoing a transition from a

---

Regional distribution of states Table 41

Regional distribution of states by political structure and number of assembly chambers

	Political structure		Number of assembly chambers			
Region	Unitary	Federal	None	One	Two	State total
Asia	25	3	1	20	7	28
Central America & Caribbean	19	2	–	10	11	21
Central, Eastern, & Southern Europe	22	3	–	17	8	25
Central & Southern Africa	43	5*	–	38	10	48
Middle East & North Africa	17	1	5	12	1	18
North America	–	2	–	–	2	2
Northern & Western Europe	19	4	1	11	11	23
Oceania	13	2	–	11	4	15
South America	9	3	–	4	8	12
Total	167	25	7	123	62	192

* Includes the federal system in Somalia, which is non-functioning due to civil war

command economy to a market economy, the per-capita income figures are unreliable. Widely differing estimates are provided for a number of states by such sources as Keesings, Europa, *The Economist*, and the United Nations, influenced by the basis of their construction. The best available compromise figures have been used, but it should be noted that there is a general tendency for such monetary-based estimates to understate the 'real' per-capita incomes in Third World states, which will appear higher if based on

'Purchasing-Power Parity'. It is interesting to note that a comparison with per-capita income figures displayed in the first edition of this volume shows that between c. 1985 and 1992 regional incomes advanced by 114% in Asia, 92% in South America, 67% in Central America and the Caribbean, 63% in Oceania, and 41% in North America. However, regional incomes increased by just 16% in Africa and the Middle East and declined by more than 40% in Central and Eastern Europe.

Regional distribution of states by voting systems — Table 42

Region	Voting system used for lower house elections										
	None	Apptd. & indirect	E/A mixed	SP	AV	SB	PR-PL	PR-AMS	STV	LV	State total
Asia	1	2	2	11	–	7	2	3	–	–	28
Central America & Caribbean	–	–	1	13	–	1	4	2	–	–	21
Central, Eastern, & Southern Europe	–	–	–	1	–	4	11	8	–	–	25
Central & Southern Africa	–	1	8	26	–	8	2	2	–	–	47*
Middle East & North Africa	5	–	1	5	–	3	3	–	–	–	18
North America	–	–	–	2	–	–	–	–	–	–	2
Northern & Western Europe	1	–	–	1	–	2	12	2	2	2	23
Oceania	–	–	1	10	1	1	1	1	–	–	15
South America	–	–	–	5	–	–	7	–	–	–	12
Total	7	3	13	74	1	26	42	21	2	2	191

* The voting system is in a transitional state in one country.

Key:
A	appointed	LV	limited vote	SP	simple plurality
AMS	additional member system	PL	party list	STV	single transferable vote
AV	alternative vote	PR	proportional representation	trans	transitional
E	elected	SB	second ballot		

Social and economic data for sovereign states — Table 43

Summary of social and economic data for sovereign states by regions of the world (c. 1992–94)

Region	Area sq km (m)	As % of world total	Population (m)	As % of world total	Population density per sq km	In relation to world mean+
Asia	25.075	18.8	3,085.8	55.3	123	292
Central America & Caribbean	2.692	2.0	151.6	2.7	56	133
Central, Eastern, & Southern Europe	20.350	15.3	435.4	7.8	21	50
Central & Southern Africa	24.259	18.2	577.5	10.4	24	57
Middle East & North Africa	11.275	8.5	269.6	4.8	24	57
North America	19.343	14.5	285.6	5.1	15	36
Northern & Western Europe	3.568	2.7	370.8	6.7	104	248
Oceania	8.781	6.6	93.7	1.7	11	26
South America	17.703	13.3	307.7	5.5	17	40
World total*	133.047	100.0	5,577.7	100.0	42	100

* Excluding colonies and dependencies   + World mean = 100

Regional distribution of states by area — Table 44

Region	Size of state: sq km						
	Below 1,000	1,000 – 10,000	>10,000 – 100,000	>100,000 – 500,000	>500,000 – 1,000,000	Over 1,000,000	State total
Asia	2	1	4	12	4	5	28
Central America & Caribbean	7	1	8	4	–	1	21
Central, Eastern, & Southern Europe	–	1	15	6	2	1	25
Central & Southern Africa	2	3	12	12	10	9	48
Middle East & North Africa	1	–	6	5	2	4	18
North America	–	–	–	–	–	2	2
Northern & Western Europe	6	1	7	7	2	–	23
Oceania	7	1	3	3	–	1	15
South America	–	–	–	5	2	5	12
Total	25	8	55	54	22	28	192

Regional distribution of states by population size (c. 1994) — Table 45

Region	State population size						
	Below 0.5 m	0.5–1 m	>1–10 m	>10–20 m	>20–50 m	>50–100 m	Over 100 m	State total
Asia	2	–	8	3	7	2	6	28
Central America & Caribbean	9	–	10	1	–	1	–	21
Central, Eastern, & Southern Europe	–	1	14	5	2	2	1	25
Central & Southern Africa	4	5	22	10	5	1	1	48
Middle East & North Africa	–	2	8	4	2	2	–	18
North America	–	–	–	–	1	–	1	2
Northern & Western Europe	8	–	8	2	1	4	–	23
Oceania	10	1	2	1	–	1	–	15
South America	1	1	3	2	4	–	1	12
Total	34	10	75	28	22	13	10	192

Regional distribution of states by population density (c. 1994) — Table 46

Region	State population density: per sq km						
	10 and below	11–50	51–100	101–250	251–500	Over 500	State total
Asia	3	7	3	7	4	4	28
Central America & Caribbean	1	5	4	6	4	1	21
Central, Eastern, & Southern Europe	1	3	12	9	–	–	25
Central & Southern Africa	10	22	8	4	3	1	48
Middle East & North Africa	3	7	4	1	2	1	18
North America	1	1	–	–	–	–	2
Northern & Western Europe	1	4	2	10	3	3	23
Oceania	2	5	2	3	3	–	15
South America	3	9	–	–	–	–	12
Total	25	63	35	40	19	10	192

Regional distribution of states by urbanization and adult literacy levels (c. 1992)   Table 47

Region	Urbanization levels* (as % of total population)			Adult literacy levels** (as % of adult population)			
	40% and under	41– 70%	Over 70%	40% and under	41– 70%	71– 90%	Over 90%
Asia	18	6	3	5	1	11	11
Central America & Caribbean	3	15	3	1	5	6	9
Central, Eastern, & Southern Europe	2	18	3	–	–	3	22
Central & Southern Africa	34	12	1	22	20	5	–
Middle East & North Africa	2	7	9	2	12	3	1
North America	–	–	2	–	–	–	2
Northern & Western Europe	1	5	17	–	–	2	21
Oceania	8	1	2	–	3	2	9
South America	1	4	7	–	2	6	4
Total	69	68	47	30	43	38	79

* Data are unavailable for four states in Oceania, two in Central, Eastern, and Southern Europe, one in Asia,
and one in Central and Southern Africa
** Data are unavailable for one state in Oceania and one in Central and Southern Africa

Regional distribution of states by shares of world GDP and income type (c. 1992)   Table 48

Region	GDP ($1,000 m)	Share of world total (%)	Average per capita GDP ($)	State distribution by income type			
				High	Middle	Low	State total
Asia	5,579	24.2	1,808	5	5	18	28
Central America & Caribbean	418	1.8	2,757	1	15	5	21
Central, Eastern, & Southern Europe	976	4.2	2,241	2	18	5	25
Central & Southern Africa	269	1.2	466	–	6	42	48
Middle East & North Africa	636	2.8	2,359	6	10	2	18
North America	6,486	28.2	22,710	2	–	–	2
Northern & Western Europe	7,437	32.3	20,059	23	–	–	23
Oceania	399	1.7	4,255	3	6	6	15
South America	821	3.6	2,668	–	10	2	12
Total	23,021	100.0	6,591	42	70	80	192

Key: GDP   Gross domestic product

Regional distribution of states by human rights rating (c. 1992)   Table 49

Region	N/a	30% and below	31– 50%	51– 70%	71– 90%	Over 90%	State total
Asia	11	5	4	7	1	–	28
Central America & Caribbean	10	1	–	4	6	–	21
Central, Eastern, & Southern Europe	16	–	1	2	4	2	25
Central & Southern Africa	26	3	9	6	4	–	48
Middle East & North Africa	4	5	4	4	1	–	18
North America	–	–	–	–	–	2	2
Northern & Western Europe	6	–	–	–	2	15	23
Oceania	11	–	–	1	1	2	15
South America	2	–	–	4	6	–	12
Total	86	14	18	28	25	21	192

Asia

The region of Asia, covering almost a fifth of the world's surface, is the largest global block in both areal and demographic terms, incorporating more than half the world's population and six of its ten most populous nations. Within the region there are 28 states. Twenty-one are continental in situation, occupying the southeastern, sub-Turkestan and sub-Siberian portion of the vast Euro-Asian land mass. The remaining seven are either offshore archipelagos or islands.

The region constitutes the world's most thickly peopled block, boasting an average population density three times the world norm. It is also the world's second poorest in terms of per-capita GDP, with a regional income, at $1,807 in c. 1992, less than half the global average. Indeed, 13 of the region's 28 countries occupy the bottom quartile of world states in terms of national incomes per capita. A further seven are located in the third quartile, while only five, mineral-rich Brunei, the city-state entrepôt of Singapore, industrialized Japan, and the fast industrializing 'little dragons', South Korea and Taiwan, are to be found in the first quartile of high-income nations.

The explanation for this poverty is the continued dominance of rural activities, the agricultural sector still providing employment for more than half the national labour force in 11 of the region's states, including six of its ten most populous. Prior to World War II, only one state, Japan, was substantially industrialized. Since the war it has grown to become the world's economic power house, contributing almost a sixth of global GDP. Within the Asian region, its dominance is even more marked and, enjoying the fourth highest per-capita GDP in the world, accounts for two-thirds of the region's GDP, but only 4% of its population. Japan also provides more than $8 billion in foreign direct investment capital. China and India, in contrast, while accounting for 68% of Asia's population can claim barely a seventh of its GDP.

During recent decades, three other Asian countries, South Korea, Singapore, and Taiwan, have industrialized rapidly, in an export-led manner, gaining the acronym NICs or 'newly industrializing countries'. South Korea, the most successful of these 'little dragons', is now one of the world's ten largest trading nations and is set to join the OECD. Three other states, Indonesia, Malaysia, and Thailand, have followed at a quickening pace. The demographic giant, China, has also enjoyed an economic awakening since the early 1980s, as, more recently, have Vietnam, Laos, Cambodia, and Myanmar, following their embrace of the market. This has made the Pacific part of the Asian region currently the world's most dynamic area.

The successful growth of these NICs has resulted from a unique blend of free-market economics and selective state support. The industriousness, docility, and high educational levels of the work forces in these countries, combined with the inbred sense of frugality of the general population, have also provided ideal conditions. These national traits are underpinned by ancient Confucianist value systems, which have helped to sustain paternalistic, authoritarian political systems, characterized by strict state censorship, enforced conformity, and, in several states, the military retaining a background political role. Recently, however, as affluence has spread, there have been growing signs of internal pressure for greater political pluralism.

Further to the west, in the Indian Ocean region, industrial growth has been less impressive. Here, popular literacy and educational levels have traditionally been lower, literacy rates of 35% or lower being recorded for contemporary Afghanistan, Bangladesh, Bhutan, Nepal, and Pakistan. Islamic and Hindu cultural traditions have also proved to be less conducive than Confucianism to the growth process. Since the 1970s, however, with the spread of new 'green revolution' seeds and production technology, notable, peasant-based, agricultural advances have been seen in a number of the states, most notably in the Punjab regions of India and Pakistan. These have enabled the rapidly expanding populations of these countries, currently increasing at an annual rate of between 2% and 3%, to be fed without a fall in general living standards.

The Asian region is, historically and culturally, one of the richest in the world. It has served as the cradle for such ancient and impressive civilizations as the Harappan or Indus Valley, from c. 2500 to c. 1600 BC, the Xia, from c. 2220 to c. 1700 BC, the Shang, from c. 1500 to c. 1066 BC, the Zhou, from 1122 to 249 BC, the Mauryan, from 321 to 184 BC, the Han, from 206 BC to AD 220, the Gupta, from c. 300 to 500 AD, the Tang, from 618 to 907 AD, the Khmer, from the 6th to the 15th centuries, and the Ming, from 1368 to 1644. For this reason, an unusually high number, amounting to five, or 18%, of the region's contemporary states date their founding to periods prior to the 19th century. This figure is based on territorial affinity. At least five other countries, Cambodia, India, the Koreas, and Vietnam, which were the sites of ancient or medieval kingdoms of national proportions, might also be included in this category if a looser definition were to be used.

The two dominant civilizations in the region have been the Indian and Chinese, each having originated distinctive religious and moral–philosophical systems which were later diffused throughout Asia by their followers.

The five most important religions or moral systems which are indigenous to the Asian region and have retained their importance are Hinduism, Buddhism, Confucianism, Daoism, and Shintoism. The first two originated in India, the second two in China, and the fifth in Japan. Their distribution across the region is clearly defined today. Hinduism, which is a nonproselytizing faith, is predominant only in India and Nepal, although it is a minority religion in neighbouring Bangladesh, Bhutan, and Sri Lanka. Shintoism, which is a unique, national religion, is, similarly, restricted to Japan. In contrast, Buddhism, although it originated in India around 500 BC, and gained popularity during the Mauryan era, has been widely diffused across Asia. Today, it constitutes the dominant faith in Bhutan, Cambodia, Laos, Mongolia, Myanmar, and Sri Lanka. Mixed with Confucianism and Daoism, it also predominates in China, North Korea, South Korea, Singapore, Thailand, and Vietnam and is an important minority faith in Brunei and Malaysia. It is the state religion in four states in the region.

To these indigenous religions there were added, from early medieval times, the outside faiths of Islam and Christianity. Islam was spread by land to Afghanistan and Pakistan in

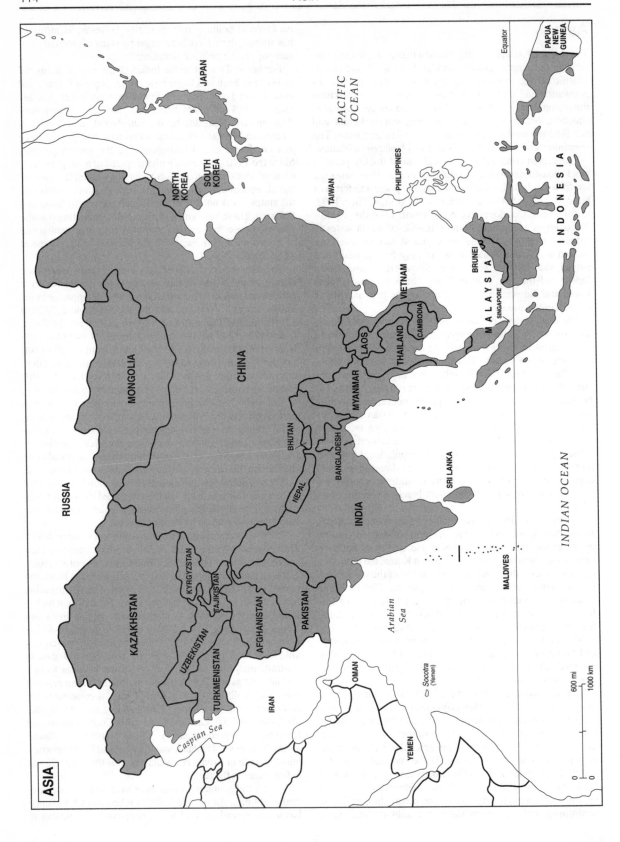

ASIA

West Asia and to Kazakhstan, Kyrgyzstan, Tajikistan, Turkmenistan, and Uzbekistan in Central Asia, although it was suppressed during the Soviet period, and by sea, further east, to Bangladesh, Brunei, Indonesia, Malaysia, and the Maldives. Christianity, however, made only a tangential impact on the region. Today, therefore, even in its areas of highest support, such as South Korea, where a quarter of the population are Christians, Indonesia, 10%, and Malaysia, 7%, it remains a minority religion. In contrast, Islam, which was a proselytizing faith in a number of important medieval and early modern kingdoms and is a state religion in six contemporary nations, has had a marked regional impact. Not only is it today the predominant religion in the 12 countries noted above, but more than two-thirds of the world's Muslim population now reside within the Asian region. Indonesia, with 160 million, Bangladesh, 125 million, Pakistan, 116 million, and India, 100 million, possess the four largest national Islamic communities in the world.

With the exception of the Muslim incursions during the medieval period noted above, Asia, although open to trading contacts, remained substantially free from external territorial conquest and colonization until the later 16th century, when the Dutch established settlements in some coastal areas of Indonesia. This served to reinforce the cultural distinctiveness of the region. Thereafter, however, particularly following the British conquest of the Indian subcontinent, European influence spread rapidly.

The height of the colonization process was attained in the late 19th and early 20th centuries, when four zones of imperial control were established: a 'Russian zone' in Central Asia, in the northwest; a 'British zone' in the southwest; a more tightly controlled 'French zone' in the central region; and a smaller, though intensively colonized, 'Japanese zone' to the east.

The Russian zone was carved out between the 1840s and 1870s and was directly connected, by land, to the empire's Muscovy core. It began as a military occupation designed to stabilize a disturbed frontier region, but developed into a full colonization, involving the immigration of ethnic Russian settlers. It was to continue under Soviet rule, the expansion culminating in the invasion of Afghanistan in 1979, before the Soviet empire collapsed in 1991. The British zone extended from Pakistan to Malaysia and was characterized by a substantial measure of 'indirect rule'. The French zone was mainly in Indo-China, and that of the Japanese in Formosa, now Taiwan, and Korea, although it was later extended, briefly, between 1942 and 1945, to incorporate much of East Asia.

Compared with the equivalent process in Africa, the European colonization of Asia began at an early date but also, with the exception of Russian/Soviet-controlled Central Asia, ended sooner. The Japanese colonial empire was dismembered in 1945, much of the British between 1947 and 1957 and the French in 1954. The strength of indigenous nationalist resistance was an important factor behind this early decolonization. It was also important in explaining the failure of the European powers to impose direct control over China and Japan. Five other, more peripheral countries, Afghanistan, Bhutan, Mongolia, Nepal, and Thailand, also escaped direct colonization.

Despite its relative brevity, the experience of colonial rule has left a perceptible, though varied, in both a positive and negative sense, political imprint on the states of the Asian region. Additional, and in many respects more important, political conditioning factors have been economic structures and conditions and ethnic patterns and rivalries.

The influence of economic factors is most clearly seen in the four states of Cambodia, China, Laos, and Vietnam. In these countries rural overpopulation and distress provided the material conditions which made possible, and successful, the peasant revolutions of the later 1940s, the 1950s, and the 1960s, particularly as they were linked to anticolonial nationalism and communist ideology.

Ethnic rivalries have also been potent political forces, with many of the states experiencing conflict on their frontiers, where ethnic, often tribal, minority communities predominate, all deeply opposed to the imposition of cultural and political hegemony by the majority community. In Indonesia, Myanmar, and Thailand, such minority-versus-majority hostility has sustained persistent peasant guerrilla insurgencies in border zones and has been used to justify a key, unifying political role for the military. In India, similar secessionist movements abound in the northeastern hill zone and in Kashmir, while in the economically successful, Sikh-dominated, Punjab and in culturally resilient Tibet different autonomy movements are found. More generalized, regionally based, ethnic rivalries are also prevalent in contemporary Afghanistan, Pakistan, Tajikistan, and other parts of ex-Soviet Central Asia, impacting adversely on party politics, while in Malaysia, Nepal, and Sri Lanka tensions between the indigenous majority and immigrant minority communities have heightened during recent years.

As a result of these ethnic rivalries, as well as the continuing or simmering state conflicts in Afghanistan, Cambodia, the Koreas, Laos, Myanmar, Sri Lanka, Tajikistan, and Vietnam, contemporary levels of military mobilization and defence expenditure are relatively high in Asia. More than half of the countries in the region appear among the upper half of world states in ratios of soldiers per 1,000 inhabitants, with four, North Korea, Singapore, Taiwan, and Mongolia, in the top ten. Consequently, defence spending as a proportion of GDP is high in all four countries, accounting for a quarter of GDP in North Korea, as well as in Myanmar, Afghanistan, Laos, Brunei, Pakistan, China, Sri Lanka, Malaysia, Tajikistan, Vietnam, and South Korea, ranging between 4% and 11% of GDP. Indeed, it was estimated that in 1991 the countries of Asia annually spent $85 billion on defence, equivalent to a quarter of such global spending, excluding the United States and USSR. In 1982 the equivalent share was just 15%. One of the region's states, China, is declared a nuclear power, while India, Pakistan, and, apparently, North Korea have a nuclear capability.

The range of political and executive types of the states in the region is unusually broad, all categories, with the exception of nationalistic socialist, being represented, as shown in Table 50. This reflects, at least in part, Asia's diversity in historical experiences and varieties of economies and religions. Fourteen, or half, of the countries fall into the categories of either liberal or emergent democracies, while a further four have communist systems. The liberal democracies are predominantly parliamentary in character and are to be found among either the high- or middle-income states, or among parts of what was once British India, where they had been accustomed to democratic structures for at least a century. It is perhaps significant that the emergent democracies are to be found, predominantly, among either NICs or the other remaining parts of British India. By contrast, all the four communist states are low-income countries, being among the dozen poorest states in the region.

Since 1990 the number of states in Asia with multiparty systems has grown significantly and this trend seems likely to continue. However, in several states which are apparently pluralist, notably Indonesia, Malaysia, and Singapore, but also in South Korea and Taiwan and several of the ex-Soviet Central Asian states, *de facto* one-party dominance exists. In terms of voting systems, the simple plurality type predominates, although the majoritarian second ballot system is also quite common. Finally, only three of the region's states, India, Pakistan, and Malaysia, have federal structures. This number is surprisingly small, the absence of federalism being especially notable in the cases of Afghanistan, China, Indonesia, Myanmar, and Sri Lanka.

Asia: social, economic, and political data

Country	Area (sq km)	c. 1992–94 Population (m)	c. 1992–94 Pop. density per sq km	c. 1992 Adult literacy rate (%)	World ranking	Income type	c. 1991 Human rights rating (%)
Afghanistan	652,225	20.500	31	29	175	low	28
Bangladesh	143,998	122.200	849	35	168	low	59
Bhutan	46,500	1.600	34	18	186	low	n/a
Brunei	5,765	0.300	52	87	89	high	n/a
Cambodia	181,035	9.000	50	86	92	low	33
China	9,571,300	1,205.200	126	76	111	low	21
India	3,287,263	896.600	273	50	149	low	54
Indonesia	1,904,569	194.600	102	82	99	low	34
Japan	371,815	125.000	336	100	1	high	82
Kazakhstan	2,717,300	17.200	6	97	44	middle	n/a
Korea, North	120,538	23.100	192	90	80	middle	20
Korea, South	98,222	44.500	453	96	52	high	59
Kyrgyzstan	198,500	4.600	23	97	44	low	n/a
Laos	236,800	4.600	19	84	97	low	n/a
Malaysia	329,758	19.200	58	78	110	middle	61
Maldives	298	0.223	748	98	34	low	n/a
Mongolia	1,565,000	2.400	2	93	70	low	n/a
Myanmar	676,552	44.600	66	81	102	low	17
Nepal	141,181	21.100	149	26	181	low	69
Pakistan	803,943	128.100	159	35	169	low	42
Singapore	623	2.900	4,654	91	77	high	60
Sri Lanka	64,453	17.900	278	88	84	low	47
Taiwan	36,000	21.000	583	93	70	high	n/a
Tajikistan	143,100	5.700	40	97	44	low	n/a
Thailand	513,115	56.900	111	93	70	middle	62
Turkmenistan	488,100	4.000	8	98	34	middle	n/a
Uzbekistan	447,400	21.900	49	85	94	low	n/a
Vietnam	329,566	70.900	215	88	84	low	27
Total/average/range	25,074,919	3,085.823	123	18–100			17–82

Key:

*	Though dominated by one party	F	federal	SB	second ballot
A	appointed	I	indirect	SP	simple plurality
AMS	additional member system	PL	party list	U	unitary
E	elected	PR	proportional representation		

Recommended reading

Baxter, C, Malik, Y K, Kennedy, C H and Oberst, R C (eds) *Government and Politics in South Asia*, 2nd edn., Boulder, 1993

Curtis, G L *The Japanese Way of Politics*, Columbia University Press, 1988

Derbyshire, I *Politics in China: From Mao towards the Post-Deng Era*, W & R Chambers, 1990

Diamond, L, Linz, J and Lipset, S M (eds) *Democracy in Developing Countries*, Vol. 3: *Asia*, Boulder, 1988

Hardgrave, R L and Kochanek, S A *India: Government and Politics in a Developing Nation*, 5th edn., Harcourt Brace Jovanovich, 1993

Table 50

World ranking	Date of state formation	State structure	State type	Executive type	Number of assembly chambers	Party structure	Lower house electoral system
96	1747	U	Islam-Nat	Unlim-pres	1	multi	I
63	1971	U	Em-dem	Parliamentary	1	multi	SP
	1907	U	Absolutist	Absolutist	1	none	mixed-E/A
	1984	U	Absolutist	Absolutist	none	none	n/a
90	1953	U	Em-dem	Dual	1	multi	SP
101	2nd C/1949	U	Communist	Communist	1	one	I
69	1947	F	Lib-dem	Parliamentary	2	multi	SP
89	1949	U	Auth-nat	Unlim-pres	1	multi*	PR-PL
33	5th C	U	Lib-dem	Parliamentary	2	multi	PR-AMS
	1991	U	Auth-nat	Unlim-pres	2	multi	SB
102	1948	U	Communist	Communist	1	one	SP
63	1948	U	Em-dem	Lim-pres	1	multi	PR-AMS
	1991	U	Em-dem	Lim-pres	2	multi	SB
	1954	U	Communist	Communist	1	one	SP
59	1957	F	Lib-dem	Parliamentary	2	multi*	SP
	1965	U	Auth-nat	Unlim-pres	1	none	mixed-E/A
	1921	U	Em-dem	Lim-pres	1	multi	SB
104	1948	U	Military	Military	n/a	multi	SP
49	1768	U	Em-dem	Parliamentary	2	multi	SP
86	1947	F	Em-dem	Parliamentary	2	multi	SP
60	1965	U	Lib-dem	Parliamentary	1	multi*	SP
82	1948	U	Lib-dem	Dual	1	multi	PR-PL
	1949	U	Em-dem	Lim-pres	1	multi	PR-AMS
	1991	U	Auth-nat	Unlim-pres	1	multi*	SB
57	1350	U	Em-dem	Parliamentary	2	multi	SP
	1991	U	Auth-nat	Unlim-pres	1	one	SB
	1991	U	Auth-nat	Unlim-pres	1	one	SB
97	1954	U	Communist	Communist	1	one	SB

Lib-dem	Liberal democratic	Auth-nat	Authoritarian nationalist
Em-dem	Emergent democratic	Islam-nat	Islamic nationalist

Unlim-pres	Unlimited presidential
Lim-pres	Limited presidential

AFGHANISTAN

Republic of Afghanistan
Jamhuria Afghanistan

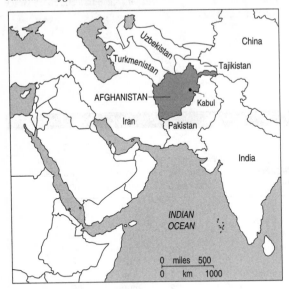

Capital: Kabul

Social and economic data
Area: 652,225 km²
Population: 20,500,000*
Pop. density per km²: 31*
Urban population: 19%**
Literacy rate: 29%**
GDP: $3,800 million**; per-capita GDP: $200**
Government defence spending (% of GDP): 8.7%***
Currency: afghani
Economy type: low income
Labour force in agriculture: 63%**

*1994
**1992
***1985

Ethnic composition
Pathans, or Pushtuns, comprise the largest ethnic group, 54% of the total population, followed by the northern concentrated Tajiks, 27%, and the Uzbeks, 8%, and Hazaras, 7%. Pushtu and Dari, or Persian, constitute the official languages, spoken by 52% and 30% of the population respectively.

Religions
Seventy-five per cent of the population adheres to Islam of the Sunni sect and 24% to the Shia. Effectively, Islam is the state religion.

Political features
State type: Islamic nationalist
Date of state formation: 1747
Political structure: unitary
Executive: military/unlimited presidential
Assembly: two-chamber*

Party structure: multiparty
Human rights rating: 28%
International affiliations: AsDB, CP, ECO, ESCAP, G-77, IAEA, IBRD, IMF, IsDB, LORCS, NAM, OIC, UN

* In theory, though currently there is a single-chamber 'assembly'

Local and regional government
The country is divided into 30 provinces (*wilayat*), each of which is, in theory, administered by an appointed governor. There are plans for the future establishment of elected local committees and councils at the provincial level, as well as in cities, districts, subdistricts and villages.

Head of state
President Burhanuddin Rabbani, since 1992

Head of government
Prime Minister Arsala Rahmani, since 1994

Political leaders since 1970
1933–73 King Zahir Shah, 1973–78 General Daud Khan, 1978–79 Nur Mohammad Taraki (PDPA: Khalq)*, 1979 Hafizullah Amin (PDPA: Khalq)*, 1979–86 Babrak Karmal (PDPA: Parcham)*, 1986–92 Dr Najibullah Ahmadzai (PDPA: Parcham)*, 1992 Sibghatullah Mojaddedi (National Liberation Front), 1992–   Burhanuddin Rabbani (Jamiat-i Islami)

* Communist Party leaders

Political system
Since the downfall of the Najibullah regime in April 1992, Afghanistan has been ruled by a 51-member Leadership Council (Shura), representing the fractious mujaheddin ('Islamic holy warrior') factions and headed since December 1992 by a state president, Burhanuddin Rabbani. The president was elected by a Constituent Assembly for a two-year term, but this was subsequently extended. There is also a prime minister and a 16-member mujaheddin coalition cabinet. The new administration has abolished the political structure of the former regime, including all laws and resolutions contrary to the Sharia (Islamic law). Since May 1993, two commissions have been established to administer the defence and interior ministries.

Previously, under its November 1987 constitution, Afghanistan had a presidential political system. At its apex stood the Loya Jirga (Grand National Assembly), an ad hoc body which comprised members of an elected Meli Shura (National Assembly), the Council of Ministers, the Supreme Court, and the Council of the Constitution. Its task was to elect an executive state president, who, serving a seven-year term, appointed a prime minister and was empowered to approve the laws and resolutions of the Meli Shura. The latter was a two-chamber body, consisting of a 234-member lower house, the Council of Representatives (Wolosi Jirga), and a 128-member upper house, the Council of Elders (Meshrano Jirga). This 'limited presidential' system was suspended following the Soviet troop withdrawal in February 1989 when a new emergency regime was established.

Political parties

In the wake of the April 1978 communist coup, Afghanistan became a one-party state, dominated and controlled by the People's Democratic Party of Afghanistan (Jamiyat-e Demokrati Khalq-e Afghanistan: PDPA). Organized on Leninist 'democratic centralist' lines, the PDPA was governed from above by a 15–20-member Politburo and operated more broadly under the guise of the National Fatherland Front. Party monism was ended in July and November 1987 by the passage of new constitutional laws which permitted the formation of additional political parties.

Currently, the key political forces are the various mujaheddin groupings, which developed in opposition to the former communist regime. The most important are the Sunni fundamentalist, Pashtun-orientated, anti-Western Hesb-i Islami (Islamic Party), whose two factions are led by the 'hardline' former prime minister, Gulbuddin Hekmatyar (b. 1949), and Maulavi Younis Khalis; the more restrained, Sunni fundamentalist, Tajik-controlled Jamiat-i Islami (Islamic Society: estd. 1970), led by the current head of state, Professor Burhanuddin Rabbani; the Movement for Islamic Revolution (Harakat-i-Inqilab-i-Islami), led by Muhammad Nabi Muhammadi and Nasrullah Mansur; the traditionalist National Islamic Front (Mahaz-i-Melli-i-Islami), led by Pir Sayyed Ahmed Gailani; the Saudi Arabian-backed Islamic Unity (Ittehad-i-Islami), led by Professor Abd Ar-Rasul Sayef and Ahmad Shah; and the moderate Afghan National Liberation Front (Jebha-i-Najat-i-Melli), led by Professor Imam Sibghatullah Mojaddedi. Unity between the groupings is notoriously strained, although a loose, seven-party, mujaheddin alliance has been in operation since May 1985. From September 1994, these traditional mujaheddin factions came under military challenge from the Talibaan, a 25,000-member army of former Muslim religious students which sought to bring an end to the internecine quarrels of the mujaheddin and create a united Islamic state. The Talibaan were predominantly Sunni Muslim Pushtuns from southern Afghanistan and it was alleged that they were in receipt of military aid from the Pakistan Inter-Services Intelligence (PSA).

The most important Shia mujaheddin factions are the pro-Rabbani Islamic Movement of Afghanistan (Harakat-i-Islami Afghanistan) and the pro-Iranian and Hekmatyar-allied Islamic Unity Party of Afghanistan (Hesb-i-Wahdat-i-Afghanistan), led until his murder in 1995 by Abdul Ali Mazari.

The formerly dominant, communist PDPA has been known since June 1990 as the Homeland Party (Hesb-i-Watan). It was founded, illegally, in 1965 by Nur Mohammad Taraki. Two years later, because of disputes over strategy, it split into two wings, the rural-based, Pushtu-speaking Khalq (Masses or People's) group, led by Taraki, and the urban-based, Dari-speaking Parcham (Banner or Flag) group, led by Babrak Karmal. After the overthrow of the monarchy, in 1973, factional differences widened when the Parcham group accepted Soviet Union orders to cooperate with the new Daud Khan regime, as part of a more moderate coalition strategy, while the Khalq wing rejected them, preferring a policy of radical class struggle. Unity, under Khalq leadership, was restored in July 1977, but rivalries swiftly re-emerged and intensified in 1979 following the ousting of Taraki as party leader and president of the republic. From December 1979 and the Soviet

Union's installation of Babrak Karmal as PDPA leader, the Parcham group came to dominate the party.

Latest elections

Elections to the National Assembly were last held in April 1988 and were contested by candidates put forward under the umbrella of the PDPA-run National Front of Afghanistan, which included within its ranks representatives from the communist-leaning political parties noted above, as well as from the armed forces, peasants' cooperatives, the Council of Afghan Women, and the Central Council of Nomads. Only 184 Council of Representatives seats were actually contested, the remainder being reserved so as to tempt moderate mujaheddin elements to join the political process at a later date. Fifty-one Senate seats were subject to election, with a further 45 senators being appointed by the president. Some 1.55 million voters were said to have participated, the majority of members returned being non-PDPA members.

The last presidential election was on 30 December 1992, when the Constituent Assembly (formerly the National Assembly) elected Burhanuddin Rabbani as state president. This decision was re-ratified by an accord signed by nine mujaheddin factions on 7 March 1993.

Political history

Under the leadership of Ahmed Shah Durrani (1724–73), Afghanistan became an independent emirate in 1747 and, although defeated by Britain in the 'Afghan wars', of 1838–42 and 1878–80 and subjected to a partial loss of autonomy, after the third Anglo-Afghan war of 1919 Afghanistan was re-established, in 1922, as a fully independent, neutral monarchy. Mohammad Nadir Shah (1880–1933), who played a prominent role in the 1919 Afghan war, became king in 1929, with British diplomatic support, but was assassinated in 1933 after his modernizing reforms had alienated the influential Muslim clergy.

During the 1950s, Lieutenant General Sardar Mohammad Daud Khan, the cousin of King Mohammed Zahir Shah (b. 1914), who had ruled between 1933 and 1973, became prime minister and introduced a major programme of social and economic modernization, drawing economic aid from the Soviet Union. Opposition to the authoritarian nature of Daud's rule, however, forced his resignation, in 1963, and a new constitution was adopted. Under it the king became a constitutional monarch and political parties were outlawed.

Following a serious famine in 1972, the monarchy was overthrown in a military coup, on 17 July 1973, and King Zahir Shah fled to exile in Rome. A republic was declared, with Lieutenant General Daud Khan back at the head of the government. He received Soviet backing for this coup, but, once in power, tried to shift towards a more moderate policy programme, building up broader national support among minority tribes, and reducing Afghanistan's dependence on Russia. He began to develop close ties with the nonaligned, Middle East oil states, where large numbers of Afghans were then employed.

A new presidential constitution was adopted in 1977, but the government was undermined by fundamentalist Muslim insurgents, funded by Libya, Iran, and Pakistan. On 27 April 1978, President Daud was assassinated in a military coup, known, from its date, as the 'Saur Revolution', and Nur

Mohammad Taraki, the imprisoned leader of the radical Khalq (Masses) faction of the banned Communist People's Democratic Party of Afghanistan (PDPA), took charge, as president of a Revolutionary Council. A new one-party regime was established, a Treaty of Friendship and Mutual Defence signed with the Soviet Union, in 1978, and major social and land reforms were introduced.

These radical policy initiatives, which were designed to mobilize the landless poor and weaken support for traditional social and economic structures and leaders, were opposed, however, by conservative Muslims. Thousands of refugees fled to Iran and Pakistan and there was a major uprising in the Herat region. The internal situation deteriorated rapidly and, following an intra-PDPA power struggle, Taraki was ousted and murdered, in September 1979. He was replaced, as president of the Revolutionary Council, by the prime minister, and foreign minister, Hafizullah Amin.

Internal unrest continued, however, and the Soviet Union was persuaded to organize a further coup, in December 1979. Hafizullah Amin was executed and Babrak Karmal (b. 1929), the exiled leader of the more gradualist Parcham (Banner) faction of the PDPA, installed in power, with the backing of 40,000 Soviet troops who invaded the country the day after Christmas.

The 'Soviet invasion' of December 1979 was condemned by many United Nations members and resulted in the American Carter administration implementing a programme of economic and diplomatic sanctions against the Soviet Union, bringing about a serious deterioration in East–West relations. Despite these Western actions, however, Soviet forces remained in Afghanistan, with Red Army troop numbers increasing to more than 120,000 in 1985, as Muslim guerrilla resistance, by the mujaheddin, or 'holy warriors', continued. The guerrillas were now being aided indirectly by the United States, China, and Pakistan. A war of attrition developed, with the Soviets launching regular land and air offensives, but failing to gain full control of many rural areas. Faced with mounting troop casualties, which already exceeded 9,000, and a debilitating drain on economic resources, the new reformist Soviet administration of Mikhail Gorbachev, in 1986, began to take steps to seek a compromise settlement. In May 1986 Babrak Karmal was replaced as PDPA leader by the Pushtun former KHAD secret police chief, Dr Najibullah Ahmadzai (b. 1947), and a number of noncommunist politicians were introduced into the new government. Greater toleration of the practices of Islam was also seen and in October 1986, 8,000 Soviet troops were withdrawn, as an initial goodwill gesture. This withdrawal was followed, in January 1987, by an announcement from the Afghan government that there would be a unilateral six-month cease-fire, to allow discussions to take place about the formation of a possible 'coalition government of national unity', which would remain friendly towards the Soviet Union.

However, the Afghan guerrillas, who were divided along tribal and ideological lines into seven groupings, rejected this initiative, determined to effect a full Soviet withdrawal and a replacement of the communist government.

Additional unilateral extensions of the cease-fire by the Afghan government were made in July and November 1987, with, in the latter month, the ratification of a new multiparty constitution, to further the 'national reconciliation' initiative. In Geneva progress was also made in UN-sponsored talks between Afghan and Pakistan representatives about resolving the 'Afghan crisis'. This was followed in February 1988 by an announcement from the Soviet leader, Mikhail Gorbachev, of a phased nine-month plan for Soviet troop withdrawals, beginning in May 1988 and ending in February 1989.

This pull-out started, as planned, in May 1988, being preceded, in April, by the signing in Geneva of an agreement between the Afghan and Pakistan governments which provided for noninterference in each other's internal affairs and the voluntary return of refugees. The United States and Soviet Union were to guarantee the accord. This agreement promised to bring to an end a decade of direct Soviet interference in the internal affairs of Afghanistan, an involvement which had served to ignite a bitter civil war, resulting, according to official Soviet sources, in the loss of 15,000 Red Army troops and 70,000 Afghan security forces personnel, as well as, according to Western estimates, the lives of more than 1 million Afghans and the uprooting, as refugees, of a further 5 million.

After the Soviet troop withdrawal took place, on 15 February 1989, a 'state of emergency' was imposed by the Najibullah regime, with a new Supreme Council for the Defence of the Homeland (SCDH) being established and in June 1990 the PDPA was renamed the Homeland Party. In February 1989 the mujaheddin met in Peshawar, Pakistan, and elected an Afghan Interim Government (AIG) in exile, with a prominent moderate, Professor Sibghatullah Mojaddedi, as its president, and a Wahabi fundamentalist, Abd Ar-Rasul Sayef, as prime minister. However, the AIG did not receive international recognition.

Between 1990–92 the civil war intensified, with the mujaheddin establishing control over 90% of the Afghan countryside. However, the Najibullah regime retained charge of the key cities and garrisons, except Khost, near the Pakistan border, which fell to the mujaheddin in April 1991. In May 1991 the Najibullah government accepted a comprehensive peace plan brokered by the UN's secretary-general, Javier Pérez de Cuéllar (b. 1920). This provided for an immediate cease-fire, the formation of a broad-based interim government, and a multiparty general election to be held after two years. The plan was rejected by the AIG's prime minister and by Gulbuddin Hekmatyar, leader of the fundamentalist Hesb-i Islami, who refused to countenance including representatives from the Najibullah regime in a transitional government.

From January 1992, Pakistan, the United States, and the Soviet Union halted all supplies of weapons to the contending parties. This contributed to the eventual collapse of the Najibullah regime in April 1992, following the defection of government troops to the mujaheddin troops of the Tajik commander, Ahmad Shah Massoud. Kabul was captured by the mujaheddin and Najibullah placed under UN protection, pending trial by an Islamic court. Sibghatullah Mojaddedi formally took over as interim head of state for a two-month period, being replaced by Burhanuddin Rabbani (b. 1943) in June 1992, with Massoud as defence minister. By August 1992 more than 1 million Afghan refugees had returned to their homes. However, the new administration failed to restore order in Kabul and surrounding areas as a new ethnic and sect-based civil war broke out between contending mujaheddin factions. The chief conflict was between Hekmatyar, with his support base in the traditionally dominant Pathan south, and the northern (Tajik)-based government of Rabbani and Massoud, backed by the 70,000-strong Uzbek militia commanded by General Abdul Rashid Dostam, whose defection and subsequent alliance with Massoud had been crucial in bringing down the Najibullah regime. There was also conflict between pro-Iranian Shia and Saudi Arabian-backed Sunni Muslim groups.

Following heavy fighting between Hekmatyar's Hesbi-i Islami and Rabbani's Jamiat-i Islami, claiming several thousand lives, a temporary cease-fire was agreed in March 1993 and a peace accord in May 1993, with Hekmatyar being appointed prime minister. During the remainder of 1993, Rabbani, based in Kabul, and Hekmatyar, in Charasiab, 25 kilometres to the south, engaged in a power struggle. This soon descended, from January 1994, into another wave of bloody civil war, with Hekmatyar securing military support from General Abdul Rashid Dostam. This fighting claimed at least 3,000 more lives, caused tremendous damage to an already ravaged economy, and led to the flight of a further 1 million refugees to camps in Pakistan. Hekmatyar was officially replaced as prime minister by Arsala Rahmani in November 1994 and was forced to flee his Charasiab headquarters in January 1995, after being surprisingly defeated by the forces of the predominantly Pathan Talibaan (Islamic theology students) army, which, possibly with Pakistani support, had launched an offensive seeking to disarm all the warring mujaheddin groups, eradicate the booming drugs trade, and establish a united and patriarchal Islamic state. The popular Talibaan were repulsed from Kabul in March 1995 by Rabbani government forces, but in September 1995 Herat, the country's second city, fell to the student army and in November 1995 a further assault on Kabul seemed imminent. Rabbani, who controlled only ten of the country's 30 provinces, but was backed by India and Iran, was involved in negotiations with a UN peace envoy, Mahmoud Mestiri, to transfer power to an interim, cross-faction mujaheddin council, but was reluctant to step down as head of state. Since the Soviet troop withdrawal, more than 20,000 Afghans have died in the continuing civil war, and 750,000 have fled the Kabul area, chiefly to refugee camps near Jalalabad. In June 1995 agreement was reached with Iran for the gradual repatriation of 0.9 million of the 1.6 million Afghan refugees still in Iran.

BANGLADESH

People's Republic of Bangladesh
Gana Praja Tantri Bangla Desh

Capital: Dhaka (known before 1984 as Dacca)

Social and economic data
Area: 143,998 km^2
Population: 122,200.000*
Pop. density per km^2: 849*
Urban population: 18%**
Literacy rate: 35%**
GDP: $24,900 million*; per-capita GDP: $220**

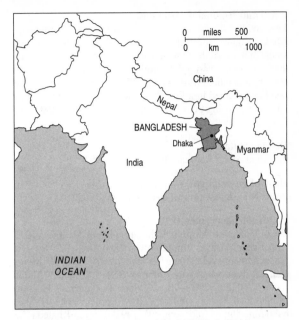

Government defence spending (% of GDP): 1.5%**
Currency: taka
Economy type: low income
Labour force in agriculture: 64%**

*1994
**1992

Ethnic composition
Ninety-eight per cent of the population is of Bengali ethnic stock, half a million are Bihari, and around 1 million belong to 'tribal' communities. In the Chittagong Hill Tracts a Chakma separatist organization, the Shanti Bahini (Peace Force) is active and its insurgency led to many Chakmas fleeing to India during the early 1980s. More than 50,000 returned in 1994. Bengali is the official language, with English also being widely spoken.

Religions
Eighty-seven per cent of the population is Muslim, adhering predominantly to the Sunni sect, though influenced by local Hindu practices, and 12% is Hindu. Following a 1977 amendment to the 1972 constitution, Islam was made a 'guiding principle' of the political system. In 1988, with the passage of the Constitution Eighth Amendment Bill, it was declared the official state religion.

Political features
State type: emergent democratic
Date of state formation: 1971
Political structure: unitary
Executive: parliamentary
Assembly: one-chamber
Party structure: multiparty
Human rights rating: 59%
International affiliations: AsDB, CW, CP, ESCAP, G-77, IAEA, IBRD, ICFTU, IMF, IsDB, LORCS, NAM, OIC, SAARC, UN, WTO

Local and regional government

The country is divided into four divisions (Chittagong, Dhaka, Khulna, and Rajshahi) and 64 districts, with elected local councils. At the base of the local government hierarchy, there are more than 4,400 rural councils (*parishads*), each serving a population of roughly 20,000. These councils are popularly elected in a fiercely contested manner, more than 150 people losing their lives during the February 1988 contests.

Head of state

President Abdur Rahman Biswas, since 1991

Head of government

Prime Minister Begum Khaleda Zia, since 1991

Political leaders since 1970

1971–75 Sheikh Mujibur Rahman (Awami League), 1975 Khandakar Mushtaq Ahmed (Awami League), 1975–76 Abu Sadat Mohammad Sayem (independent), 1976–80 Major General Ziaur Rahman (military/BNP), 1980–82 Abdus Sattar (BNP), 1982–90 Lieutenant General Hossain Mohammad Ershad (military/Jatiya Front), 1990–91 Shehabuddin Ahmed (independent), 1991– Begum Khaleda Zia (BNP)

Political system

Under the terms of the constitutional amendment of September 1991, the 1972 parliamentary constitution has been restored. There is a single-chamber assembly, or parliament (Jatiya Sangsad), which is composed of 300 members, directly elected for five-year terms from single-member constituencies and an additional 30 female members appointed by the assembly itself. From this body, a prime minister and cabinet are drawn. The prime minister may also hold other ministerial portfolios, such as defence and establishment. The Jatiya Sangsad elects, for a five-year term, a president to serve as a ceremonial head of state.

Political parties

The present ruling party is the Bangladesh National Party (BNP: Bangladesh Jatiyatabadi Dal), led by Begum Khaleda Zia, the widow of Major General Ziaur Rahman. It was formed in 1978 by a merger of parties, including the Nationalist Democratic Party, which supported Major General Ziaur Rahman. The party is a right-of-centre grouping which has traditionally been anti-Indian and pro-Islamic in policy outlook.

The principal parliamentary opposition party is the Awami League (AL), led by Sheikha Hasina Wazed, the daughter of Sheikh Mujibur Rahman. It was originally formed in 1949 and currently claims a membership of around 1 million, boasting the best national organizational structure of any political party in Bangladesh. It is pro-Indian in international outlook and campaigns for a secular, moderately socialist, mixed-economy state. In August 1993 dissidents within the AL broke away to form the Gano, or People's, Forum, led by Kamal Hossain.

The third major force in parliament is the Jatiya Dal (JD: National Party). It was originally formed as a civilian political vehicle for Lieutenant General Ershad, the then president,

in November 1983, under the designation Jana Dal (People's Party). The party is nationalist in outlook and committed to Islamic ideals. It split in September 1993, with dissidents forming the Jatiya Party (Nationalist), with Ershad as its leader.

Around 20 other minor parties are currently active. The four most important are the Islamic fundamentalist, Jamaat-e-Islami Bangladesh, which was established in 1941; the formerly Moscow-linked Bangladesh Communist Party (BCP), which was formed in 1948 and which split, during 1993, into Marxist and reformist wings, and which joined the new eight-party Left Democratic Front in 1994; the National Democratic Alliance, a right-wing, ten-party coalition led by Khandakar Mushtaq Ahmed, who briefly held power in 1975; and the pro-Beijing, National Awami Party-Bhashani (NAP), which dates from 1957. Factionalism, leading to frequent party splits and realignments, is endemic in Bangladeshi politics.

Latest elections

In the most recent Jatiya Sangsad elections, which were held on 27 February 1991, the BNP captured 140 of the 300 elective seats. The Awami League won 88 seats, the Jatiya Dal, 35, the Jamaat-e-Islami Bangladesh, 18, and the BCP and other small parties allied to the AL, 12.

Political history

Contemporary Bangladesh, a vast, low-lying, deltaic plain where the great Ganges, Brahmaputra, and Meghna rivers unite to flow into the Bay of Bengal, formerly consisted of the jute-growing East Bengal province and Sylhet district of Assam in British India. Being predominantly Muslim, it was formed into the eastern province of Pakistan when India was partitioned in August 1947. It differed substantially in culture, language, and geography from the western provinces of Pakistan, 1,610 kilometres away, and with a larger population, resented the political and military dominance exerted by West Pakistan during the 1950s and 1960s.

An independence movement developed after 1954, under the leadership of the Awami League (AL), headed by Sheikh Mujibur Rahman (1920–75). This gained strength because of the indifference shown by West Pakistan in 1970, when severe cyclones caused the deaths of half a million people in floods in East Pakistan.

In the first general elections held in Pakistan in December 1970 the AL gained an overwhelming victory in the East and an overall majority in the all-Pakistan National Assembly. Talks on redrafting the constitution broke down, leading to East Pakistan's declaration of secession and the establishment of a Bangladesh ('Bengal Nation') government in exile, in Calcutta, in April 1971. Civil war ensued, resulting in the flight of 10 million East Pakistani refugees to India. There was an administrative breakdown in East Pakistan and an outbreak of famine and cholera. On 16 December 1971 the West Pakistani troops in East Pakistan surrendered to the Bangladesh forces, who had been, briefly, helped by Indian troops. A republic of Bangladesh was proclaimed and it had gained broad international recognition by 1972.

Sheikh Mujibur Rahman became the nation's first prime minister, under a secular, parliamentary constitution, which was adopted in November 1972. He proceeded to introduce a socialist economic programme of nationalization, but became increasingly intolerant of opposition. He established an emergency, one-party, presidential system of government in January 1975.

On 15 August 1975 Sheikh Mujibur Rahman, and his wife and close relatives, were assassinated in a military coup. Power was held for three months by Khandakar Mushtaq Ahmed of the Awami League, before a further military coup in November 1975 established as president and chief martial law administrator the nonpolitical chief justice, Abu Sadat Mohammad Sayem.

Two years later, in November 1976, the army chief of staff, Major General Ziaur Rahman (1935–81), became chief martial law administrator, before assuming the presidency, in April 1977. He adopted an Islamic constitution, which was approved in a May 1977 national referendum. In June 1978 he achieved victory by a 4:1 majority in a direct presidential election and released political prisoners and relaxed press censorship in readiness for parliamentary elections in February 1979.

Major General Zia's newly formed Bangladeshi Nationalist Party (BNP) won a parliamentary majority and, with a civilian government installed, martial law and the state of emergency were lifted between April and November 1979. The new administration was rapidly undermined, however, by charges of corruption and by a guerrilla secessionist movement among Chittagong hill tribesmen in 1980. On 30 May 1981 Major General Zia was assassinated during an attempted coup, forcing Vice President Justice Abdus Sattar to assume power as an interim leader.

With internal disorder increasing, the civilian administration of Sattar was overthrown, on 24 March 1982, in a coup led by army chief of staff, Lieutenant General Hossain Mohammad Ershad (b. 1930). Martial law was reimposed and political activities banned. Under Lieutenant General Ershad, because of the adoption of more market-orientated policies and the introduction of a major 'food for work' rural programme, economic conditions improved. Agitation for a return to democratic government gained strength, however, from September 1983, when a broad opposition party coalition, the Movement for the Restoration of Democracy (MRD), was formed.

Lieutenant General Ershad promised to hold presidential and parliamentary elections in 1984, but these were cancelled after an opposition threat of a boycott and campaign of civil disobedience if martial law was not first lifted. In January 1986 the ban on political activities was removed and parliamentary elections were held in May 1986. The AL agreed to participate, but the BNP, together with many other opposition parties, boycotted the poll.

After an election campaign marked by violence, widespread abstentions, and claims of ballot-rigging, and the rerunning of 37 constituency contests, Lieutenant General Ershad and his Jatiya Dal (JD) party gained a two-thirds majority, giving him the constitutional right to pass a law granting retrospective immunity for any otherwise illegal acts.

In October 1986 Ershad, who had formally stepped down as army chief of staff in August and had been elected chairman of the JD a month later, was re-elected president in a direct election and in November 1986 martial law was lifted and the 1972 constitution restored. Both the AL and BNP had boycotted the presidential contest.

During 1987, opposition groups stepped up their campaign against the Ershad government, calling for the president's resignation and the holding of new free elections. A wave of violent strikes and demonstrations was launched by trade unions and students. The administration's attempt to pass a law which would enable army representatives to participate in district councils heightened the political temperature during the summer and autumn months, just at a time when the country was devastated by the worst floods for 40 years, which claimed at least 1,500 lives.

With the economy rapidly deteriorating and faced by a threat of a general strike, President Ershad proclaimed a state of emergency, on 27 November 1987, and banned all antigovernment protests for 120 days. Political activity and civil rights were suspended and the opposition leaders Sheikha Hasina Wazed (AL) and Begum Khalida Zia (BNP) were placed under temporary house arrest. General urban curfews were also imposed. A month later, with the threat of the mass resignation of the AL's 73 members, parliament was dissolved and new elections were called for March 1988.

The elections were again boycotted by the AL and BNP and, again, there was evidence of flagrant ballot-rigging. In these conditions, the JD gained a sweeping victory, with only a minority of the electorate voting. The president put together a new cabinet, with Moudud Ahmed as prime minister, lifted the state of emergency in April 1988, and intimated that in the forthcoming parliamentary session a bill would be introduced to establish Islam as the state religion. This eighth amendment was duly passed by the Jatiya Sangsad in June 1988.

Extra-parliamentary opposition to the Ershad regime remained strong, however, and to compound the government's difficulties, the country received its heaviest monsoon downpour for 70 years in September 1988. The resulting floods left 30 million homeless, claimed thousands of lives and caused huge infrastructural damage. Ershad was eventually forced to resign on 4 December 1990 after two months of mass popular protests in Dhaka and other cities. He was subsequently charged with and later, in 1992 and 1993, found guilty of corruption and sentenced to imprisonment. Shehabuddin Ahmed, the country's chief justice, took over as interim president. Immediately, the state of emergency was lifted and the Special Powers Act, which had allowed the government to detain persons without trial and summarily close down newspapers, was annulled.

In free, multiparty elections held in February 1991, the BNP, helped by a high turnout of women and young adults in towns, emerged as the dominant force. It captured 140 of the 300 elective seats, while the AL polled less strongly than had been anticipated. Begum Khaleda Zia (b. 1945) duly became the nation's first female prime minister in March 1991. At first she headed a coalition government, with initial support from the Jamaat-e-Islami, until the BNP achieved a narrow absolute majority of seats after by-elections held in September 1991. The Zia administration introduced an outward-looking and deregulationary 'new industrial policy', with the aim of boosting private enterprise, in part via privatization, and encouraging foreign investment, and in September 1991 reversion to a parliamentary system of government was approved by a national referendum. A month later, the Jatiya Sangsad elected its speaker and the BNP nominee, Abdur Rahman Biswas, to become the new ceremonial state president.

In April 1991 the nation was rocked by its worst ever cyclone, which killed an estimated 139,000 people, rendered up to 10 million homeless, and resulted in economic losses of $3 billion. Throughout the period between 1992 and 1995 the Zia administration faced sporadic, and sometimes violent, national strikes and political protests. Orchestrated by opposition forces, who demanded the resignation of Zia and the calling of fresh elections, they intensified from May 1994 when the opposition claimed that the BNP had resorted to fraud in recent by-elections. An opposition boycott of parliament was effected, despite the Dhaka High Court declaring this act to be unconstitutional, and general strikes were held in Dhaka and other main towns in March 1995.

In foreign affairs, Bangladesh has remained a member of the Commonwealth since 1972 and, although heavily dependent on foreign economic aid, has pursued a broad policy of nonalignment. Its relations with India deteriorated after 1975, as a result of disputes over the sharing of Ganges water and the annual influx of 200,000 Bangladeshi refugees to Assam and West Bengal, which has prompted India to threaten to construct a barbed wire frontier fence.

BHUTAN

Kingdom of Bhutan
Druk Yul (Realm of the Dragon)

Capital: Thimbu

Social and economic data
Area: 46,500 km^2
Population: 1,600,000*+
Pop. density per km^2: 34*
Urban population: 5%**
Literacy rate: 18%**
GDP: $280 million**; per-capita GDP: $180**
Government defence spending (% of GDP): N/A
Currency: ngultrum
Economy type: low income
Labour force in agriculture: 90%**

*1994
**1992
+This is a UN estimate. The Bhutanese government claims the 'official overall population' to be as little as 600,000–850,000 million.

Ethnic composition
Fifty-four per cent of the population is of Bhotia ethnic stock, residing principally in the east and north; 32% are descendants of Tibetan immigrants; while a substantial Nepali minority lives in the south, being prohibited from moving into the Bhotia-dominated north. Dzongkha, which is very

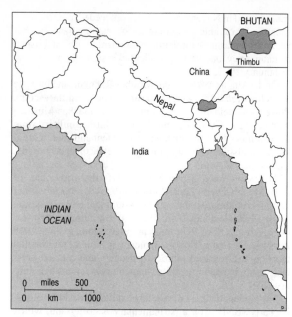

similar to Tibetan, is the official language and is spoken by 70% of the population. Nepali is the main language for 30% of the population.

Religions
The principal, and state, religion is Mahayana Buddhism, or Lamaism, which was introduced during the 8th century AD. Seventy per cent of the population adheres to it. Twenty-five per cent of the population is Hindu, principally the ethnic Nepalese of the southern districts. The country's 5,000 Buddhist monks play an influential role in national and local political affairs, with their head abbot, the Je Khempo, occupying a prominent position in the Royal Advisory Council.

Political features
State type: absolutist
Date of state formation: 1907
Political structure: unitary
Executive: absolute
Assembly: one-chamber
Party structure: no parties permitted
Human rights rating: N/A
International affiliations: AsDB, CP, ESCAP, G-77, IBRD, IMF, NAM, SAARC, UN

Local and regional government
The country is divided into 20 districts (*dzongkhags*), each headed by an administrative and law and order officer (*dzongda*), and a judicial officer (*thrimpon*), both appointed by the Royal Civil Service Commission, which was established in 1982. Seven districts are further subdivided into subdistricts (*dungkhags*), with 'village blocks' (*gewog*) below. Village-level elections are held every three years, with each family being granted one vote.

Head of state and head of government
King Jigme Singye Wangchuk, since 1972

Political leaders since 1970

1952–72 King Jigme Dorji Wangchuk, 1972–   King Jigme Singye Wangchuk

Political system

Bhutan is governed by a hereditary executive monarch and lacks a formal constitution. Since 1953, the king, who is called Druk Gyalpo (Dragon King), or 'precious ruler', has worked with an elected legislature, the National Assembly (Tshogdu) and, since 1965, with a partially elected Royal Advisory Council (RAC: Lodoi Tsokde), with which he shares power. Written rules govern the methods of electing members of the Royal Advisory Council and Tshogdu and define their duties and powers, thus giving the political system elements of a constitutional monarchy.

The National Assembly meets twice a year, in the spring and autumn, for sessions of 10 to 14 days, to enact laws and serve as a debating forum. It currently comprises 150 members, 105 elected by 'direct popular consensus' in villages, ten representing regional monastic bodies, and the remaining 35 being officials, ministers, and members of the RAC. Every three years, the Tshogdu is required to pass a vote of confidence in the king by a two-thirds majority. Theoretically, the National Assembly also enjoys the power to remove the monarch and replace him with another member of the royal family. Also, its bills cannot be vetoed by the king.

The Royal Advisory Council, as its name suggests, has the primary function of providing political advice to the monarch. It also supervises all administrative matters, serving essentially as the *de facto* standing committee of the Tshogdu. It consists of ten members. Two of them are nominees of the king, one of whom acts as chairperson, two are Buddhist monks, and six are 'people's representatives'. These representatives are endorsed by village assemblies, *dzongdas*, and the National Assembly. Members serve for renewable five-year terms. Today the RAC is the originator of most legislation.

Executive administration is the responsibility of an eight-member Council of Ministers (COM: Lhengye Shungtsog), headed by the king. It includes prominent additional members of the royal family. Like the RAC, this body is responsible to the Tshogdu. In practice, however, the king remains the dominant political force.

Political parties

There are no legal political parties within Bhutan. However, illegal parties, mainly ethnic Nepali, include the Bhutan People's Party, formed in 1990 as a successor to the People's Forum for Human Rights (estd. 1989), the United Liberation People's Front (estd. 1990), and the Bhutan National Democratic Party (estd. 1992).

Latest elections

The Tshogdu's directly elected representatives serve three-year terms in individual constituencies at varying dates, depending on the expiry of their terms.

Political history

Formerly ruled by Tibet during the 16th century and China from 1720, Bhutan was invaded by Britain in 1865, and a trade agreement was signed, under which an annual subsidy was paid to Bhutan in 'return for its good behaviour'. The country was thus never formally subjected to direct colonial rule. In December 1907 Bhutan's first hereditary monarch was installed and three years later, under the Anglo-Bhutanese (Punakha) Treaty, foreign relations were placed under the control of the British Government of India.

Soon after India achieved independence in 1947, an Indo-Bhutan Treaty of Perpetual Peace and Friendship was signed, in August 1949, under which Bhutan agreed to seek Indian advice on foreign relations but not necessarily to accept it. Although no formal defence treaty was signed, India has made it clear that it would regard an attack on Bhutan as an act of agression against itself. India also returned to Bhutan, in 1949, territory that had been annexed by British India in 1865.

In 1952 King Jigme Dorji Wangchuk was installed and in the following year a National Assembly was established. In 1959, after the annexation of Tibet by communist China, Bhutan gave asylum to some 4,000 Tibetan refugees, but in June 1979, concerned with their alleged subversive activities, the Tshogdu gave the refugees until the end of the year to take up Bhutanese citizenship or return to Tibet. Most took up citizenship and the rest were accepted by India.

During the reign of King Jigme Dorji Wangchuk, between 1952 and 1972, a series of progressive social, economic, and political reforms was gradually introduced, in an effort to modernize what remained a backward, traditionalist nation. These reforms included the abolition of slavery, in 1958, and the caste system; the emancipation of women; the establishment of a secular school system; and the introduction of an extensive programme of land reform and long-term economic planning. In the political sphere, as part of a democratization process, the king appointed his first cabinet, in May 1968, and in the same year renounced his right of veto and gave the Tshogdu the authority to select and remove the monarch.

The king died in July 1972 and was succeeded by his young, Western-educated, son, Jigme Singye Wangchuk. The new king, while maintaining close links with India, which had provided much of the finance for the country's post-1961 five-year economic plans, proceeded to pursue a somewhat more independent and outward-looking course in external relations than his father had done. Bhutan joined the Non-Aligned Movement in 1973, entered into border negotiations with China, and became a founder member of the South Asian Association for Regional Cooperation (SAARC) organization. In May 1985 it increased its political involvement in the region by hosting the first meeting of SAARC foreign ministers. In the economic sphere, a programme of privatization got underway from 1992.

Since 1988 Bhutan's Buddhist Dzongkha/Drukpa ethnic minority, headed by the king, has sought to impose its language, religious customs, and national dress on the majority community, which, though divided, is predominantly Hindu-Nepali, particularly in the south where there are many recent immigrants. The Nepalese language and customs have been suppressed and hundreds of thousands of non-Bhutanese have been deported as part of an 'ethnic cleansing' process which has led to the establishment of large refugee camps in eastern Nepal. Influenced also by the democratization movement in Nepal, interethnic tensions have increased greatly. Political parties have been formed illegally by the Nepalese and in September 1990 several hundred people were reportedly killed during security crackdowns against prodemocracy demonstrations. In November 1993 Tek Nath Rizal, founder of the banned Bhutan People's Party, was sentenced to life imprisonment for 'antinational activities'.

BRUNEI

Sultanate of Brunei (State of Brunei Darussalam)
Negara Brunei Darussalam

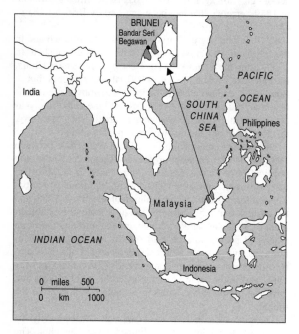

Capital: Bandar Seri Begawan (formerly Brunei town)

Social and economic data
Area: 5,765 km²
Population: 300,000*
Pop. density per km²: 52*
Urban population: 58%**
Literacy rate: 87%**
GDP: $4,070 million**; per-capita GDP: $14,500**
Government defence spending (% of GDP): 7%**
Currency: Brunei dollar
Economy type: high income
Labour force in agriculture: 5%

*1993
**1992

Ethnic composition
Sixty-eight per cent of the population are indigenous Malays, predominating in government service and agriculture, and more than 20% are Chinese, predominating in the commercial sphere. Malay is the principal and official language, but

Chinese, chiefly the Hokkien dialect, is spoken by a quarter of the population and English is also widely spoken.

Religions
Sixty-six per cent of the population, mainly the ethnic Malays, adhere to Islam, of the Sunni sect. Ten per cent of the people, chiefly Eurasians, are Christians and 14%, largely ethnic Chinese, are Buddhists. Islam is the official state religion, and the sultan is its national head.

Political features
State type: absolutist
Date of state formation: 1984
Political structure: unitary
Executive: absolute
Assembly: none
Party structure: no parties permitted
Human rights rating: N/A
International affiliations: APEC, ASEAN, CW, ESCAP, G-77, IsDB, NAM, OIC, UN, WTO

Local and regional government
The state is divided into four administrative districts: Brunei-Muara, Tutong, Belait, and Temburong. Each is governed by a district officer (Malay) responsible to the prime minister (sultan) and home affairs minister. There are also four municipalities.

Head of state and head of government
Sultan Sir Muda Hassanal Bolkiah Mu'izzaddin Waddaulah, since 1968

Political leaders since 1970
1968– Sultan Sir Muda Hassanal Bolkiah Mu'izzaddin Waddaulah

Political system
The September 1959 constitution gives supreme executive authority to the sultan, advised by four Constitutional Councils: the Religious Council, the Privy Council, the Council of Cabinet Ministers, and the Council of Succession. The Council of Cabinet Ministers (CCM) is the most important and has around 11 members. The sultan heads it, acting as both prime minister and minister of defence. Since 1962 he has ruled by decree. Two princes, Mohamed Bolkiah and Jefri Bolkiah, serve as foreign affairs and finance ministers respectively. The most important of the sultan's advisers is the internal affairs minister, Pehin Dato Haji Isa, who functions, in many respects, as a chief minister (*mentri besar*).

Political parties
Currently, there are no registered political parties in Brunei. Two political parties were formed in 1985–86: the Brunei National Democratic Party (BNDP: Partai Kebang-Saan Demokratik Brunei), an Islamic and liberal nationalist grouping with 1,500 members and led by Haji Abdul Latif Chuchu; and the Brunei National United Party (BNUP: Partai Perpaduan Kebang-Saan Brunei), a multi-ethnic splinter group, formed by ex-BNDP members and led by Awang Hatta Haji Zainal Abiddin. However, in 1988 both the BNDP and BNUP were dissolved by government order.

The opposition Brunei People's Party (BPP: Parti Ra'ayat Brunei) operates in exile. The party was formed in 1959 and won all elective seats to the Legislative Council in 1962, before staging a revolt against the government. As a result, it was banned, in December 1962.

Latest elections
There have been no elections since March 1965. Prior to this, a tiered system of indirect elections from district councils to a 21-member Legislative Council, ten of whom were elected, was in operation.

Political history
Brunei was an independent Islamic monarchy from the 15th century, ruling North Borneo, a region which includes contemporary Sabah and Sarawak states which today form part of Malaysia, between the 16th and 19th centuries. However, during the mid-19th century its authority waned, and it lost control of Sarawak in 1841, before eventually becoming a British protectorate in 1888. Under an agreement of 1906, a British resident was appointed as adviser to the sultan, turning the country into a British dependency.

During World War II, Brunei was occupied by the Japanese, from December 1941, but reverted to its former status after Japan's capitulation in September 1945. In 1950, after the death of his father, Sir Muda Omar Ali Saiffuddin Saadul Khairi Waddien, popularly known as Sir Omar, became the new, 28th, sultan. His authority was increased in September 1959 when a written constitution was promulgated making Britain responsible for the country's defence and external affairs, but returning substantial control over internal affairs to the sultan.

In December 1962 a proposal that Brunei should join the Federation of Malaysia (FOM), which was established in 1963, was opposed by a widespread revolution, organized by the Brunei People's Party (BPP), linked to the North Borneo Liberation Army. The revolt, after more than a week of fighting, was put down with the help of British forces from Singapore. A state of emergency was imposed, the BPP was banned, and the sultan began to rule by decree. In 1963 the idea of joining the FOM was abandoned.

In October 1967 the sultan, Sir Omar, refusing to accede to British demands for more representative government, abdicated in favour of his son, Hassanal Bolkiah (b. 1946). He remained, however, as chief adviser. Four years later, in November 1971, Brunei was given full internal self-government. In December 1975 a UN General Assembly resolution called for the withdrawal of Britain and on 1 January 1984 full independence was achieved.

The sultan became prime minister, minister of finance, and minister of home affairs, presiding over a cabinet of six, three of whom were close blood relatives. Britain agreed to maintain a small force of Gurkha troops, paid for by the sultan, to protect the oil and gas fields, which had been developed during the postwar period. These had made Brunei the wealthiest nation, per capita, in Asia and provided funds for social and welfare spending. The sultan, with an estimated wealth in excess of $25 billion, is believed to be the world's richest individual. He owns the Dorchester and Beverly Hills hotels in London and Los Angeles, a private airfleet, and has built, at the cost of $40 million, the world's largest palace.

The 1975 UN resolution had also called for political liberalization, including the return of political exiles and the holding of a general election. Progress in this direction has, however, been slow. In May 1985 the royal family cautiously allowed the formation of a political party, the Brunei National Democratic Party (BNDP), dominated by loyal businessmen. However, ethnic Chinese and government employees, who constitute 40% of the workforce, were forbidden to join. A second grouping, the Brunei National United Party (BNUP), which included ethnic Chinese, was tolerated in February 1986.

Since the death of Sir Omar in September 1986 the pace of political and economic modernization has accelerated. In particular, in the new government, which was formed in October 1986, key portfolios were assigned to nonroyal commoners and aristocrats. However, severe restrictions are still imposed on the operation of 'radical' opposition groupings, with the BNDP and BNUP being banned in 1988. In addition, a conservative, nationalist socio-economic policy has been pursued in recent years, in which preferential treatment has been given to native Malays (*bumiputras*, or 'sons of the soil') in the commercial sphere, at the expense of traditional Chinese, many of whom have emigrated since 1984. Also, an Islamic state is in the process of being constructed, with Melayu Islam Beraja (Malay Islam Monarchy) being promoted as the state ideology.

In its external relations since independence, Brunei has maintained close links with Western nations, particularly the United States and Britain, but has also joined ASEAN, and has begun to cultivate warm relations with neighbouring Singapore and Malaysia. In September 1991 it applied for membership of the Non-Aligned Movement. In the economic sphere, there have been attempts at diversification, away from overdependence on oil, the aim being to establish Brunei as a new centre for international finance and banking. Much of the interior of the country still remains, however, underdeveloped: 70% of it is covered by dense tropical jungle.

CAMBODIA (KAMPUCHEA)

The State of Cambodia (SOC)
Roat Kampuchea

Capital: Phnom Penh

Social and economic data
Area: 181,035 km^2
Population: 9,000,000*
*Pop. density per km^2: 50**
Urban population: 12%**
Literacy rate: 86%**
GDP: $1,750 million**; per-capita GDP: $200**
Government defence spending (% of GDP): 2.3%**
Currency: riel
Economy type: low income
Labour force in agriculture: 68%**

*1994
**1992

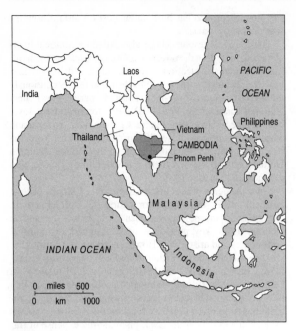

Ethnic composition

Khmers constitute 91% of the population, Vietnamese 4%, and Chinese 3%. The official language is Khmer, but French is also widely spoken.

Religions

The traditional religion is Theravada Buddhism, adhered to by 90% of the population. All religious activity was banned in 1975, but Buddhism was reinstated as the national religion following a constitutional amendment in April 1989. There are now more than 20,000 Buddhist priests (*bonzes*), the same number as in 1975, and 2,800 monasteries. Prior to the communist takeover in 1975, 1.4% of the population, predominantly the Malayo-Polynesian-speaking Cham, also followed Islam. Its worship was banned in 1975, but relegalized in 1989. There are 14,000 Roman Catholics.

Political features

State type: emergent democratic
Date of state formation: 1953
Political structure: unitary
Executive: dual
Assembly: one-chamber
Party structure: multiparty
Human rights rating: 33%
International affiliations: AsDB, CP, ESCAP, G-77, IAEA, IBRD, IMF, LORCS, NAM, UN

Local and regional government

The country is divided into 21 provinces (*khet*), 122 districts (*srok*), 1,325 subdistricts (*khum*), and 9,386 villages (*phum*), in addition to two municipalities (*krung*), Phnom Penh and Kompong Som, which are themselves subdivided into wards (*sangkat*) and groups (*krom*).

Head of state

King Norodom Sihanouk, since 1991*

* Became king in 1993

Head of government

First Prime Minister Prince Norodom Ranariddh, since 1993*

*Shares authority with co-premier Hun Sen

Political leaders since 1970

1970–75 Lieutenant General Lon Nol, 1975–76 Prince Sihanouk, 1976–79 Pol Pot (Khmer Rouge)*, 1979–81 Pen Sovann (CPK)*, 1981–91 Heng Samrin (KPRP)*, 1991– Prince Norodom Sihanouk (FUNCINPEC)**, 1991– Hun Sen (CPP)***, 1993– Prince Norodom Ranariddh (FUNCINPEC)***

*Communist Party leader
**Executive head of state
***Prime minister

Political system

Under the terms of the constitution of September 1993, Cambodia has a pluralistic, liberal-democratic political system based around a limited monarchy. The monarch, Prince Norodom Sihanouk, was elected in September 1993 by a seven-member Throne Council, comprising the two co-chairs of the Provisional National Government of Cambodia (PNGC), three members of the Constituent Assembly, and two Buddhist monks. He acts in consultation with ministers and senior civil servants and is said to 'reign but not rule'. He may only declare a state of emergency with the approval of the prime minister and cabinet. However, so great is the stature and moral authority of the current monarch that the executive system is best described as dual.

The legislature, the National Assembly, comprises 120 members, who are directly elected for five-year terms. From the dominant party or coalition in the Assembly is drawn a prime minister and cabinet, designated the Royal Government of Cambodia (RGC). Currently control of the 22-member cabinet is shared by two co-premiers, drawn from the monarchist FUNCINPEC and excommunist CPP.

Political parties

There are four main political parties in Cambodia: the 'Sihanoukists', the Buddhist Liberal Democratic Party (BLDP), the Cambodian People's Party (CPP), and the Khmer Rouge.

The currently dominant 'Sihanoukists', supporters of King Norodom Sihanouk, are organized in the United National Front for an Independent, Neutral, Peaceful and Cooperative Cambodia (FUNCINPEC), a right-of-centre nationalist force which originated as the military wing of Sihanouk's National Army of Independent Cambodia (ANS). The party enjoys particularly strong peasant support. The ANS transformed itself into a political party to contest the 1993 general election, with Prince Norodom Ranariddh, the son of the king, being elected its president in February 1992.

The BLDP was established in 1992 to contest the 1993 elections by Son Sann, a former prime minister, as a successor to the Khmer People's National Liberation Front (KPNLF), which was formed in France in 1979. It is a republican, anticommunist and elite-orientated party. Led since 1995 by Ieng Muli, it is a member of the ruling coalition government.

The CPP, formerly known as the Kampuchean People's Revolutionary Party (KPRP), dominated Cambodian affairs between 1979 and 1991. As the KPRP, it was formed in January 1979 by 66 exiled Kampuchean communists, at an ad hoc congress called under Vietnamese auspices to 'reorganize the party'. Half of them were ex-Khmer Viet Minh and half ex-Khmer Rouge. The KPRP's roots go back to 1951 when a Cambodian wing broke away from the existing Communist Party of Indo-China, which had been established in 1930 by Ho Chi Minh, to form the Khmer (Cambodian) People's Revolutionary Party. This soon divided into two factions: a pro-Vietnamese grouping, the Khmers Vietminh, which favoured collaboration with the Cambodian head of state, Prince Norodom Sihanouk; and an anti-Sihanouk grouping, led by the Paris-trained Marxist, Pol Pot (Saloth Sar; b.1926).

The second faction became dominant in 1960 and proceeded to rename the party the Communist Party of Kampuchea (CPK) and pursue a new pro-Chinese and anti-Soviet course. Organizing itself among the peasantry, Pol Pot's CPK, popularly known as the Khmer Rouge, engaged in a guerrilla struggle against, first, the Sihanouk and, then, the Lon Nol, governments during the later 1960s and early 1970s. As a result, it emerged as the governing force in Cambodia between 1975 and 1979. Its ruthless policies, however, alienated some people in the party's ranks, resulting in the defection of a number of leading figures, including Heng Samrin (b. 1934) and Hun Sen (b. 1950), who formed the new pro-Vietnamese and pro-Soviet KPRP. The designation KPRP was officially adopted in 1981, superseding the title CPK.

The current CPP, though still organized on hierarchical 'democratic centralist' lines, is a reform-socialist body. At an extraordinary Congress held in Phnom Penh in 1991, it formally abandoned its Marxist–Leninist ideology and endorsed multiparty democracy, a free-market economy and the protection of human rights, and upheld Buddhism as the state religion. Chea Sim replaced Heng Samrin as party chairperson, Heng becoming 'honorary president', while the moderate prime minister, Hun Sen, was elected vice chairperson.

The Khmer Rouge, known as the Cambodian National Unity Party (CNUP), is the successor to Pol Pot's CPK, which was dissolved in 1981. The new group is led by Khieu Samphan, although Pol Pot remains an influential background figure.

Seventeen other minor parties contested, unsuccessfully, the May 1993 Constituent Assembly elections.

Latest elections

The most recent national elections were held, for a Constituent Assembly, between 23–28 May 1993. The nationalist and monarchist FUNCINPEC secured a narrow victory over the former communist CPP, winning 58 and 51 of the 120 contested seats and 42% and 37% of the popular vote respectively. Son Sann's BLDP captured ten seats and the National Liberation Movement of Kampuchea, one seat. The elections were supervised by the UN Transitional Authority in Cambodia (UNTAC). Despite intimidation by the Khmers Rouges, whose CNUP boycotted the contest, polling was relatively peaceful and turnout reached 90%.

Political history

Cambodia originally constituted part of the Kingdom of Fou-Nan, before being conquered by the Khmers during the 6th century. It became the heartland for the sophisticated and extensive Khmer Empire between the 6th–15th centuries, whose capital was established at Angkor in northwest Cambodia. The region subsequently came within the jurisdiction of neighbouring Siam (Thailand) and Champa (Vietnam), but still retained a measure of independence. In 1863 it became a French protectorate but its traditional political and social structures were left largely intact.

From 1887 it formed part of the French Indo-China Union, but during World War II it was occupied by Japan. France regained control of what was then known as the Kingdom of Cambodia, and promulgated a constitution which established a modern parliamentary system. However, in the face of a rural-based guerrilla independence movement that was growing in strength, the country was granted semi-autonomy within the French Union in November 1949, and full independence in November 1953.

Prince Norodom Sihanouk (b. 1922), who had been elected king in 1941, abdicated in favour of his parents in March 1955 and became prime minister, as leader of the Popular Socialist Community mass movement, which swept to power, winning all available seats, in the parliamentary elections of 1955, 1958, 1962, and 1966. In June 1960, following the death of his father, Sihanouk was elected head of state.

During the Vietnam War (1954–75), Sihanouk, although critical of the United States' military involvement in Indo-China, sought to maintain Cambodia's neutrality from the surrounding struggle. This became increasingly difficult during the later 1960s. Domestically the Sihanouk regime had to face a mounting communist insurgency, led by the Khmer Rouge.

With the economy deteriorating, Sihanouk was overthrown in March 1970, while absent abroad, in a bloodless right-wing coup, led by the pro-American prime minister, Lieutenant General, later Marshal, Lon Nol. He continued to serve as prime minister, between 1971 and 1972, before becoming president of what was termed, from October 1970, the new Khmer Republic. The political system had been reconstituted on presidential executive lines, following the promulgation, in April 1972, of a constitution modelled on that of France's Fifth (Gaullist) Republic. Lon Nol's regime was opposed, however, by the exiled Prince Sihanouk, now head of the exiled, Beijing-based, Royal Government of National Union of Cambodia (GRUNC), and by the communist Khmer Rouge, backed by North Vietnam and China. The two joined together to form the National United Front of Cambodia (FUNC).

A bitter civil war developed and, despite receiving substantial military aid from the United States during its early stages, the Lon Nol government lost control of rural, and then urban, areas and was toppled in April 1975. The country was renamed Kampuchea and Prince Sihanouk was appointed head of state.

The Khmer Rouge proceeded to ruthlessly introduce an extreme Maoist communist programme, involving the abolition of money and markets, the forced removal of urban groups into the countryside, and agricultural collectivization, at a breakneck speed. This resulted in the death of a, variously estimated, 1–3 million people from famine, disease, and maltreatment. 'Reactionary' political opponents were also summarily executed. A new constitution was promulgated in January 1976, which renamed the state 'Democratic Kampuchea', removed Prince Sihanouk from power, appointed Khieu Samphan, the former deputy prime minister, as president and placed the CPK, led by its notorious guerrilla leader, Pol Pot, in effective political control.

The new Khmer Rouge regime severed all Western contacts and developed close 'clientist' links with China. As a consequence, it fell out with its former sponsors, Vietnam and the Soviet Union, prompting Vietnam to launch raids into the country during 1977–78, culminating in a full-scale invasion, in December 1978. The Vietnamese successfully overthrew Pol Pot, who enjoyed little popular support, in January 1979, and put into power a pro-Vietnamese puppet government, led by Heng Samrin, a commander of the Khmer Rouge fourth division until 1978. He was now head of the Kampuchean National United Front for National Salvation (KNUFNS), which had been newly constituted in December 1978, and was later renamed KUFNCD, in 1981. It was an amalgam of anti-Pol Pot Kampuchean communists. A new People's Republic of Kampuchea was proclaimed.

Initially, Heng Samrin ruled as president of an emergency People's Revolutionary Council, sharing effective power with the CPK (later KPRP) general secretary, Pen Sovann, an ex-Khmer Viet Minh who had lived in Vietnam between 1954 and 1979. In December 1981, however, Sovann, who was viewed by Vietnam as too gradualist in his approach, pro-Soviet in his outlook, and autocratic in his governing style, was stripped of all his party and state posts and Heng became the new KPRP leader and controlling personality. During the same year a constitution was framed and a National Assembly elected, in an effort to legitimize the regime.

During its first year in power the Heng government was faced with fierce guerrilla resistance by Pol Pot forces, based in jungle hideouts in the west of the country, near the border with Thailand, resulting in the flight of more than 300,000 Cambodians to border refugee camps in Thailand. This resistance movement broadened in June 1982, with the formation, in Kuala Lumpur, in Malaysia, of a broad anti-Vietnamese coalition and Democratic Kampuchea government in exile. This comprised Prince Sihanouk, then living in North Korea, as president, Khieu Samphan, the political leader of the Khmer Rouge, as vice president and Sonn Sann, an ex-premier and contemporary leader of the noncommunist KPNLF, as prime minister. The coalition received sympathetic support from the countries of ASEAN, Indonesia, Malaysia, the Philippines, Singapore, and Thailand, as well as from China, and was officially recognized by both the United States and United Nations as the legitimate government of the country. Militarily, however, the coalition was weak. Its 60,000 troops, 60% of whom were Khmers Rouges, were outnumbered by the 170,000 Vietnamese supporting the Heng Samrin government, and its base camps were repeatedly overrun during the annual dry season, December–April, offensives. The cumulative cost to Vietnam was more than 30,000 of its soldiers' lives.

The Heng Samrin administration at first pursued a relatively liberal policy programme, dismantling the Khmer Rouge-established commune structure and adopting a relaxed attitude towards the Buddhist religion, in an effort to secure popular support. Soon, however, these policies were reversed, communes were re-established and a 'Vietnamization' of the country was launched, with more than 500,000 Vietnamese emigrating to southeastern Kampuchea. From 1985, however, following the installation as prime minister of Hun Sen, and under pressure from the reformist new administration of Mikhail Gorbachev in the Soviet Union, a more flexible and pragmatic, mixed economy, policy approach was pursued and indigenous Khmers were inducted into the regime and a Khmer cultural revival encouraged.

Hopes of a political settlement to the 'Cambodian issue' also began to improve from 1985, helped by the retirement of the reviled Pol Pot as Khmer Rouge military leader in August 1985, and by the beginning of a phased withdrawal of Vietnamese troops. The reconciliation process moved a step further in December 1987 and January 1988, when Hun Sen and Prince Norodom Sihanouk met for a series of talks near Paris. These events were followed, in June 1988, by the withdrawal of 50,000, or half, of the remaining Vietnamese troops within Cambodia, including the high command. The remainder were pulled out in September 1989. Two years of tortuous negotiations followed between the Cambodian government and the resistance coalition. Major concessions were proffered by the Heng Samrin regime, including a promise to liberalize the economy, re-establish Buddhism as the state religion, and alter the country's official designation from the PRK to the ideologically neutral State of Cambodia (SOC).

A breakthrough was eventually achieved on 23 October 1991, when the country's four warring factions, and 18 interested countries, signed a peace agreement in Paris to end the 13-year-old civil war. Under its terms, a 22,000-strong civilian and military UN Transitional Authority in Cambodia (UNTAC) was established to administer the country in conjunction with an all-party Supreme National Council (SNC) until a new legislature was elected in 1993. The UNTAC's task was to enforce a cease-fire, oversee the demobilization of 70% of each contending faction's armed forces, maintain law and order, run the main ministries, and organize free and fair elections. Meanwhile, the SNC represented the country externally, occupying Cambodia's UN seat, and concentrated on reviving the moribund economy and organizing the resettlement of 200,000 internally displaced citizens and 380,000 Cambodians living in border refugee camps. The latter was completed by March 1993.

Prince Norodom Sihanouk returned to Phnom Penh on 23 November 1991 and resumed residence in his renovated former royal palace as the SOC's legitimate head of state. He worked alongside Hun Sen, who remained as prime minister. The Khmer Rouge also returned, but its leader, Khieu Samphan, was forced to swiftly fly back to Thailand, after being attacked by a lynching mob. In January 1992 hundreds of political prisoners were released and freedom of speech and party formation was restored and in March 1993 the head of UNTAC, the Japanese diplomat, Yasushi Akashi, took up the reins in Phnom Penh.

During 1992 there was mounting concern over cease-fire violations and, in particular, the Khmers Rouges' refusal to disarm in accordance with the UN plan. Nevertheless, national elections to a new Constituent Assembly were successfully held in May 1993, resulting in a narrow victory for Prince Norodom Sihanouk's FUNCINPEC.

In July 1993 a Provisional National Government of Cambodia (PNGC) was formed, which was a coalition embracing all four parties which had secured the election of deputies in the general election. At its heart was an alliance between FUNCINPEC and the excommunist CPP, with Prince Norodom Sihanouk's son, Prince Norodom Ranariddh, being appointed first prime minister and the outgoing premier, Hun Sen, second prime minister. The Constituent Assembly promulgated a new liberal-democratic pluralistic constitution in September 1993, which provided for a limited monarchy sharing power with parliament. The Constituent Assembly became automatically transformed into a National Assembly with full legislative powers and a Throne Council elected Norodom Sihanouk as king in October 1993. In the same month, the PNGC was renamed the Royal Government of Cambodia (RGC).

During 1994 the RGC foiled an attempted coup by Norodom Chakrapong, a son of King Norodom Sihanouk, and General Sin Song, both members of the CPP, and launched offensives against the Khmers Rouges, who controlled parts of the countryside in the west and north, adjoining Thailand. The Khmers Rouges, now officially outlawed, responded by announcing, in July 1994, the formation of a 'provisional government of national union and national salvation' based in the northern province of Prey Vihear. However, the Khmers Rouges had been reduced to a hard core of between 5,000 and 10,000 troops, after an estimated 7,000 of its fighters, responding to a government amnesty, had surrendered during 1994. The continuing civil war, combined with a serious failure of the rice crop in 1994, caused hardship in rural areas, despite annual GDP growth averaging 5% between 1993–95 and significant foreign aid inflows being received. In addition, there was Western concern during 1995 that the FUNCINPEC regime was becoming increasingly authoritarian. This was evidenced by attempts to curb opposition voices in the press, with a Press Law being passed in July 1995, and by the expulsion from parliament and FUNCINPEC, in June 1995, of Sam Rainsy, finance minister until October 1994, who had accused leading members of the government of corruption. Rainsy subsequently formed the Khmer Nation Party, in November 1995, but it was swiftly banned.

CHINA

People's Republic of China
Zhonghua Renmin Gonghe Guo

Capital: Beijing (Peking)

Social and economic data
Area: 9,571,300 km²+
Population: 1,205,200,000*
Pop. density per km²: 126*

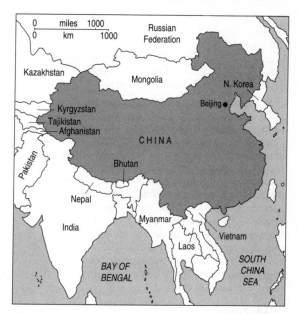

Urban population: 28%**
Literacy rate: 76%**
GDP: $506,000 million**; per-capita GDP: $430**
Government defence spending (% of GDP): 5.4%**
Currency: yuan or renminbi (people's currency)
Economy type: low income
Labour force in agriculture: 60%**

+Two-thirds mountain or desert, with only 15% of the country's area being arable
*1994
**1992

Ethnic composition
Ninety-four per cent of the population are Han Chinese, the remainder being Zhuang, Uygur, Hui (Muslims), Yi, Tibetan, Miao, Manchu, Mongol, Buyi, or Korean. There are numerous lesser nationalities, in 55 groups, numbering around 70 million. The national minorities mainly reside in border regions. The principal language is Northern Chinese (Mandarin), with local dialects spoken in the south and southeast, notably Cantonese and Wu. The Tibetans, Uygurs, Mongols, and other minorities have their own languages.

Religions
Confucianism and Daoism (Taoism), practised by around 20% of the population, and Buddhism, by 15%, are the principal traditional religions, with Muslim, 20 million, and Christian, 10 million, minorities. The Uygur (Wei Wuer) and Hui peoples are the main followers of Islam, which was introduced into China in AD 651. The Christians, evenly divided between Roman Catholics and Protestants, chiefly live on the coast.

Political features
State type: communist
Date of state formation: 2nd century BC (1949*)
Political structure: unitary
Executive: communist

Assembly: one-chamber
Party structure: one-party
Human rights rating: 21%
International affiliations: AfDB, APEC, AsDB, ESCAP, IAEA, IBRD, IMF, IWC, LORCS, NAM (observer), UN Security Council (permanent member)

*Present boundaries and communist regime

Local and regional government
Below the 22 provinces (*sheng*), there are three municipalities, Beijing, Shanghai, and Tianjin, and five autonomous regions, Xizang (Tibet), Nei Monggol (Inner Mongolia), Xinjiang Uygur, Ningxia Hui, and Guangxi Zhuang. Within these are 286 municipalities, 552 rural districts, under city administration, and 2,080 rural counties (*xian*). Local People's Congresses and People's Governments operate at the township and county levels. Multiple, CCP-approved, candidacies were the norm in recent elections. Members are elected directly for three-year terms at the county level and below, and indirectly, by council members, for five-year terms to congresses above.

Head of state
President Jiang Zemin, since 1993

Head of government
Prime Minister Li Peng, since 1987

Political leaders since 1970*
1949–76 Mao Zedong (CCP), 1976–81 Hua Guofeng (CCP), 1981–87 Hu Yaobang (CCP), 1987–89 Zhao Ziyang (CCP), 1989– Jiang Zemin (CCP), [1978– Deng Xiaoping (CCP)]**

*Communist Party leaders
**Paramount national leader

Political system
Under its current constitution, the fourth since 1949, which was adopted in December 1982, superseding earlier 1954, 1975, and 1978 documents, China, despite its size, is a unitary state. The nation is divided, for administrative purposes, into 22 provinces, five autonomous regions, including Tibet (Xizang), and three municipalities, Beijing, Shanghai, and Tianjin. Each enjoys policy-making discretion in a number of defined areas, exercised by elected Local People's Congresses and Governments.

Ultimate authority resides, however, in a single-chamber assembly, the National People's Congress (Quanghuo Renmin Diabiao Dahui: NPC). The NPC is composed of 2,970 members, indirectly elected every five years through a tiered system of Local People's Congresses. At their lower levels, members of Local People's Congresses are directly elected through universal adult suffrage in constituency contests which involve a measure of competition.

The NPC, which is described in the 1982 constitution as the 'highest organ of state power', meets in full session once a year, for two weeks, electing a permanent, 155-member Standing Committee to assume its functions between sittings. This Standing Committee is dominated by an inner body comprising a chairperson, Qiao Shi since 1993, and 16 vice chairperson. Meeting in session at least once every fortnight, the Standing Committee directs the work of the NPC's six functional 'Specialized Committees': finance and economic affairs; nationalities; education, science, culture and public health; foreign affairs; legal affairs; and overseas Chinese affairs. It also drafts bills and resolutions. It operates as a 'substitute parliament', interpreting the constitution and current laws, issuing decrees, overseeing the work of lower level governments and appointing and dismissing ministers and officials.

In addition, for a five-year term, the NPC elects a state president and vice president, a State Central Military Commission, to supervise the work of the army, and leading members of the judiciary. The functions of the state president, who must be at least 45 years of age and who is restricted to two terms in office, are primarily ceremonial.

Executive administration is carried out by a State Council or national cabinet of approximately 45 members, which is headed by a prime minister and which includes vice premiers, departmental ministers, state commission chiefs, and the auditor-general, secretary-general and governor of the Bank of China. The State Council is 'appointed' by and accountable to the NPC and its Standing Committee. It has the task of directing and overseeing the work of government departments, commissions and local bodies, enacting administrative regulations, drawing up and implementing the economic plan and annual budget, and submitting drafts to the NPC's Standing Committee. A 13-member inner cabinet, consisting of the prime minister, four vice premiers and eight state councillors, meets regularly to decide on day-to-day matters. Membership of this body is limited to two five-year terms.

The directing force in the People's Republic of China is, however, the Chinese Communist Party (CCP), headed by its general secretary, Jiang Zemin. The CCP is controlled by a governing Politburo of some 20 members, which has a seven-member inner Standing Committee, including in its ranks the state president, prime minister, vice premier (Zhu Rongji), chairperson of the NPC Standing Committee, and chairperson of the CPPCC.

During recent years there has been both increased democratization and decentralization in the governmental process. The members of the new NPC's Standing Committee, for example, were elected in a purportedly competitive manner, in March 1988. Votes registered against candidates were recorded for the first time, and NPC deputies were allowed to play a more prominent and independent role in policy discussions. Since 1993 voting in the NPC has been secret. Additionally, an effort has been made to more clearly demarcate party and state spheres of responsibility, with the day-to-day interference of local party committees over state decision-taking being substantially reduced.

Also, as part of a revivified, broad front, policy formulating process, the Chinese People's Political Consultative Conference (CPPCC) has been reactivated since 1978. The CPPCC is a broadly based appointed body which originally operated between 1949 and 1954. Chaired since 1993 by CCP Politburo member Li Ruihuan, it includes intellectuals, overseas Chinese, and 'democratic party' representatives. It now convenes concurrently with the NPC so as to provide an additional advisory voice.

Despite these substantive structural changes, ultimate power in the Chinese polity continues to reside at the uppermost level of the factionalized CCP. The party machine continues to vet nominations in state election contests and control state appointments, according to the 'nomenklatura' principle.

Political parties

The ruling Chinese Communist Party (CCP: Zhongguo Gongchan Dang) was founded in July 1921 at the French concession of Shanghai by a group of intellectuals, led by Chen Duxiu, who was its leader between 1921 and 1927, and Li Lisan, leader from 1927 to 1930. They had been strongly influenced by the 1917 Russian Revolution and by the theoretical writings of Marx, Engels, and Lenin. Soon afterwards, in June 1922, a separate overseas branch, the Young Communist Party (YCP), was formed in Paris by a group of Chinese students, including Zhou Enlai and Deng Xiaoping, who had been sent abroad on a 'work and study' scheme.

The Shanghai-based CCP worked closely with the Moscow-based Communist International (Comintern), seeking to foment urban worker revolutions in the country's seaboard cities during the early 1920s. These proved, however, to be unsuccessful. The party, following Comintern orders, also allied itself closely, during the mid-1920s, with the larger and more popular nationalist (Kuomintang: KMT) movement, led successively by Dr Sun Yat-sen and General Chiang Kai-shek. They were duped, however, by the anticommunist Chiang, in April 1927, when the CCP's Shanghai cell was brutally purged, and its few surviving members were forced underground.

Following the failure of the urban revolution approach, the party's rural wing, led by the charismatic self-taught Marxist, Mao Zedong, gained the ascendancy. Mao, who had been a founder member of the CCP in Shanghai, in 1921, began to construct a unique Third World brand of communism, based on an alliance with the peasantry and the use of antigovernment guerrilla tactics. He established a rural soviet, or 'workers' republic', in Jiangxi province during the late 1920s and early 1930s and assumed leadership of the 0.3 million-member CCP, with the support of Zhou Enlai's pragmatic 'Paris wing', at the Zunyi conference of May 1935. All this happened in the midst of the 'Long March' of 1934–35. The Maoist brand of rural-based revolution was further refined during the party's period at Yanan, from 1936, and eventually proved successful in overcoming Chiang Kai-shek's KMT forces, in 1948–49.

In the new People's Republic of China, politics after 1949 were to be characterized by periodic struggles between the different personality- and policy-based factions that had been apparent within the CCP since the later 1920s. At the head of the party's 'orthodox', pro-Soviet, faction stood Liu Shaoqi, gaining the ascendancy during the early 1950s and between 1962 and 1965, and pursuing an urban-industrial-orientated and incentives-based development strategy. In stark opposition stood Mao Zedong, predominant between 1957 and 1961 and between 1966 and 1973. He sought to establish a unique 'Sinified' model of socialism, based on parallel progress in both the rural and urban spheres, the maintenance of close and regular contact between party members and the general population, which he called the 'mass line', and on ideological, as well as economic, transformation.

Finally, and in some respects intermediate between the 'right' and 'left' factions, stood the eclectic Paris 'work-study' wing, led initially by the adroit Zhou Enlai, and subsequently by the more innovative and risk-taking Deng Xiaoping. This wing, apart from a break between 1976 and 1978, has generally dominated policy-making in the People's Republic since 1973, seeking to build a new 'socialism with Chinese characteristics', in which market mechanisms are given a prominent role.

The present CCP is organized, parallel to the state government hierachy, on pyramidal lines, based on a hierarchy of elected congresses and committees which function from the village and factory, or 'basic', level upwards and follow orders from above, in accordance with the tenets of Leninist 'democratic centralism'. A quinquennial, 2,000-member, National Party Congress, the most recent (14th) being held in October 1992, elects a Central Committee of approximately 319 members.

This Committee, 189 of whose members have full voting powers, meets at least once a year and 'elects' a smaller Politburo of some 20 members and a five-member Secretariat. The two bodies exercise ultimate day-to-day control over the party and frame longer-term state and party policy goals.

The Politburo convenes weekly and is the single most significant political body in China. It is dominated by an inner Standing Committee, headed by the CCP's general secretary. Following rule changes, which were adopted at the 13th National Party Congress in October–November 1987, the Standing Committee has formally been given power to nominate the members of the Secretariat. More generally, in recent years competitive inner party democracy and discussion have been encouraged, particularly at the lower levels.

Other senior CCP bodies include the Central Military Commission (CMC), which, headed by Jiang Zemin, maintains party control over the armed forces.

In 1992 membership of the CCP stood at 50 million, a figure which corresponded to 4.4% of the total population. This constituted an advance of 79% on the 1973 total of 28 million and of 194% on the 1961 figure of 17 million. Throughout this period, however, there have been recurrent purges of both 'ultra-Maoist' and 'ultra-rightist' elements.

Over the past few years the stress of the Deng administration has been on the recruitment of well qualified and educated technocrats, able to manage effectively at the local level, as more and more governmental responsibilities are decentralized. However, despite this recruitment bias, fewer than 5% of party members can currently boast a higher education, while more than 50% are illiterate or have been educated only to primary school level.

Closely linked to the CCP is the Young Communist League (YCL), a youth wing for citizens aged between 15 and 25. This has a membership of 56 million. Eight minor 'democratic parties' are now allowed to operate. They include the China Association for Promoting Democracy, which was established in 1945, the China Democratic League, dating from 1941, the China Democratic National Construction Association, which was formed in 1945, the China Zhi Gong Dang, founded in 1925, the Chinese Peasants' and Workers'

Democratic Party, which was established in 1947, the Kuom-intang Revolutionary Committee, dating from 1948, the Jiu San (3rd September) Society, which originated in 1946, and the Taiwan Democratic Self-Government League, which dates from 1947. Orientated primarily towards bourgeois and intelligentsia groups, these bodies work in alliance with the CCP and are accorded representation in the NPC and on its Standing Committee.

Latest elections

The most recent NPC elections were held in January–March 1993, taking the form, as usual, of indirect elections by provincial, municipal, and autonomous region level People's Congress and PLA units. There was an element of competition in some constituencies, with more candidates standing than the number of seats available.

Political history

Chinese civilization is believed to date from the Xia dynasty era, 2200–1700 BC, during which period a relatively sophisticated bronze age state, utilizing irrigation and the written word, was established, in the Shaanxi-Henan region of central China. During the Zhou (Chou) dynasty, 1122–249 BC, the great philosophers Confucius (551–479 BC) and Lao Zi (6th century BC) lived. Lao Zi was the founder of Taoism and formulated a distinctive, new cultural–ethical system. Later, during the Qin, 221–207 BC, and Han, 206 BC–220 AD, dynasties, the country's warring states were finally unified and brought under central direction. Buddhism was introduced from India in AD 67 and flourished during the Sui and Tang dynasties, between the 6th and 8th centuries AD.

A Confucianist-educated 'mandarin' bureaucracy was placed in charge of state affairs, with its members, from the Tang dynasty, 618–907 AD, onwards, being recruited through a competitive and open system of public examinations. This scholar gentry elite, in conjunction with a 'divine' emperor and powerful regional potentates, provided a stable political framework within which impressive technical and economic advances were achieved. Thus, during the Song, 960–1279, Ming, 1368–1644, and, early Manchu Qing, 1644–1911, dynasties, China became established at the forefront of world civilization.

During the early Qing era, Chinese sovereignty was extended over the three northeastern provinces of Heilongjiang, Jilin, and Liaoning, commonly designated together as Manchuria, as well as the western provinces of Xinjiang, Xizang (Tibet), Qinghai, and Nei Monggol (Inner Mongolia). This represented the apogee of the Imperial system. Thereafter, during the later Qing period, mounting economic difficulties, resulting from overpopulation, technological stagnation, and the growing seaboard intrusion of the expansionary European powers and Japan, began to dissever the fragile bonds which had held together the Manchu polity.

In the wake of China's ignominious defeat at the hands of Japan in 1895 and the territorial concessions which were thereafter granted to foreign powers, popular nationalist sentiment grew, culminating in the antiforeigner Boxer Rebellion of 1900. A decade later, in 1911–12, regional gentry and Western-trained New Model Army leaders combined to overthrow the infant Manchu emperor Pu-Yi (1906–67), in a 'Republican Revolution'. A parliamentary regime, headed by the Western-educated, Cantonese 'Christian socialist', Dr Sun Yat-Sen (1866–1925), was, at first, established. This was replaced, in 1912, by the presidentialist rule of the northern-based military commander, Yuan Shikai (1859–1916). However, following Yuan's death in 1916, the new republican political system began to be torn apart, and power was increasingly devolved to regional military commanders. Eventually, internal civil war broke out between militarists and Dr Sun's Republicans (Nationalist Party: KMT), with the newly formed Chinese Communist Party (CCP) joining the fray in tactical alliance with the KMT. There began a destructive decade, which became known as the 'Warlord Period', 1916–26.

In northern and central China order was restored in 1928 by the Japanese-trained KMT leader, General Chiang Kai-shek (1887–1975), who had moved decisively both against his erstwhile CCP allies, in the Shanghai putsch of April 1927, and against the warlords of central and northern China, in the 'northern expedition' of 1926–28.

Chiang Kai-shek proceeded to establish a rightist, quasi-fascist, regime, founded on a close alliance with landlord, business, and industrialist elite groups, the propagation of populist nationalism, the building-up of a modern, substantial, German-trained army, and new infrastructural, predominantly railway, investment. The nationalist regime faced, however, internal guerrilla opposition from the remnant forces of the CCP, now led by the Hunanese 'middle peasant', Mao Zedong (Mao Tse-tung; 1893–1976). Mao's forces moved north along a 6,000-mile zigzag course from Jiangxi province to isolated Shaanxi, in the 'Long March' of 1934–35, to establish a firm rural base at Yanan.

In addition, Chiang's regime faced the external threat of Japan, which forcibly annexed Manchuria (Dongbei) in September 1931, before attacking Beijing and invading northern China in 1937. To meet this challenge, a KMT–CCP truce was eventually declared and an anti-Japanese pact signed. However, the Chinese forces were rapidly overwhelmed by the Japanese, the KMT being forced into refuge in the remote western province of Sichuan, while the CCP retired to rural fastnesses in the north and centre of the country, from where they harassed the urban-based Japanese in classic guerrilla fashion.

During the war years the CCP established themselves as popular 'freedom fighters' against a brutal Japanese regime, building up substantial support by their just treatment of the local population and the implementation of populist land reform programmes in the areas ('soviets') under their charge. By the early 1940s much of the hinterland of north central China was effectively controlled by the CCP. This left the communists in a strong position when the Japanese finally withdrew, in August 1945.

A civil war between Chiang Kai-shek's US-backed KMT forces and the CCP's Red Army (People's Liberation Army: PLA) ensued between 1946 and 1949. Using mobile tactics, the PLA, led by Zhu De (Chu Teh; 1886–1976), emerged triumphant, cutting Chiang's supply lines before decisively defeating his 550,000-strong army at the battle of Huai-Hai, in December 1948. Chiang Kai-shek and his nationalist supporters thereafter retreated to the island province of Taiwan, establishing a KMT regime which they claimed to still be the legitimate government of all China. In reality, however, *de facto* power on the mainland passed to the communists, where a new People's Republic of China (PRC) was proclaimed by Mao Zedong in Beijing on 1 October 1949.

The early years of the new CCP regime were, following more than a decade of constant warfare, consumed with the task of economic and political reconstruction. A centralized Soviet-style constitution was adopted, in September 1954; leading 'commanding-height' industries were nationalized; a system of quinquennial central planning was instituted, from 1953; a programme of moderate, anti-gentry land reform was introduced; and a major party recruitment drive was launched. This increased CCP membership from 4.5 million to 10.8 million between 1949 and 1956.

The general tone of the early 'post-liberation' years was one of consensual, 'united-front' cooperation, with small-scale private enterprise being tolerated and the cooperation of white collar intelligentsia and technocrat groups sought. Less tolerance was, however, shown towards the traditionally pro-KMT landed elite. In addition to being dispossessed of their holdings, members of this group were, between 1949 and 1953, publicly tried and forced to repent for past misdeeds. Two to four million of those who refused were publicly executed.

During its first decade in power, the CCP administration maintained close links with the Soviet Union, which provided the country with substantial economic and technical aid. A compelling factor behind this close relationship was the active hostility which the infant CCP regime faced from the United States. Thus, during the Korean War of 1950–53, the PLA clashed with American forces, fighting under the United Nations' flag, to defend the neighbouring North Korean communist regime. As a result, in 1954, the United States effected a Mutual Security Treaty with the Taiwan-based KMT, recognizing it as the legitimate government of China.

Reflecting these close Soviet ties, the CCP leadership, in its first five-year plan of 1953–57, embarked on a heavy industrialization, and material incentives-based, development strategy, which was substantially modelled on the USSR's Stalinist prototype. Concern grew, however, with the widening of social, regional, and sectoral income and growth differentials which resulted from the implementation of this plan. In 1958, under the charismatic leadership of state president and CCP chairman, Mao Zedong, China suddenly shifted course, instituting a radical new policy programme, which Mao called the 'Great Leap Forward'.

Founded on the slogan, 'walking on two legs', this new programme sought to achieve rapid and simultaneous growth in both food and manufacturing output, by the collectivization of land and the formation of large new, self-sufficient, agricultural and industrial communes. As well as functioning as cooperative production units, these communes were designed to act as residential units for political and ideological indoctrination, the aim being to remould attitudes and create a new breed of 'complete communists'. This new generation would serve as the progenitors of a new, classless and egalitarian 'true communist' society.

In practice, despite its lofty goals, the 'Great Leap' experiment proved to be over-ambitious and was impossible to coordinate. It was, moreover, strongly opposed by ordinary peasants who were used to more individualistic forms of farming and living. Many cultivators resisted the collectivization drive or only half-heartedly cooperated. As a consequence, with floods and famine ravaging the country, the distribution system falling into chaos and supply bottlenecks developing, more than 20 million died between 1959 and 1962. Output, both in the agricultural and industrial sectors, following an initial surge, dipped sharply during these years.

The 'Great Leap' departure also had serious repercussions for China's external relations, serving as the last straw which prompted the Soviet Union's increasingly estranged new Khrushchev leadership to formally break off relations. The Soviet Union had been subject to mounting criticisms from Mao for its 'hegemonistic' and 'revisionist' policy approach and the severing of diplomatic ties was accompanied by the withdrawal of technical advisers in August 1960.

The failure of the 'Great Leap' experiment served to reduce the influence of Mao between 1962 and 1965. Instead, a successful 'recovery programme' was instituted, under the leadership of the CCP first vice chairman, and new state president, the Moscow-trained Liu Shaoqi (1900–1970). This involved the reintroduction of private farming plots and markets, a reduction in the size of communes, and a restoration of income differentials and material incentives. Mao soon struck back, however, against what he termed a return to the 'capitalist road', and against the recrudescence of a new, bureaucratic governing elite, by launching the 'Great Proletarian Cultural Revolution' (GPCR) between 1966 and 1969.

The GPCR was a broad-front 'rectification campaign' directed against 'rightist' elements in the CCP, with the aim of re-establishing the supremacy of ideology (Maoism) over economics, or 'putting politics in command', of re-emphasizing egalitarian communist virtues and of bringing to the fore a new, and more radical, leadership generation. During the campaign, Mao, supported by the PLA chief, Lin Biao (1908–71), and the Shanghai-based 'Gang of Four', encouraged student (Red Guard) demonstrations against incumbent party and government leaders. The 'Gang of Four' was a grouping comprising Mao's wife, Jiang Qing (1914–91), the radical intellectuals, Zhang Chunqiao and Yao Wenyuan, and the former millworker, Wang Hongwen. The chief targets were Liu Shaoqi, who was dismissed in October 1968 and died in prison in 1969, Deng Xiaoping (b. 1904), head of the CCP Secretariat, and Peng Zhen, mayor of Beijing. Each of them was forced out of office and publicly disgraced. The campaign grew anarchic, however, during 1967, necessitating direct intervention by the PLA and the dispersal of the Red Guards into the countryside to 'learn from the peasants'.

Traditional government institutions fell into abeyance during the Cultural Revolution and new 'Three-Part Revolutionary Committees', comprising Maoist party officials, trade unionists, and PLA commanders, took over the administration. By 1970, however, Mao, concerned with the mounting public disorder, sided with the long-serving and pragmatic prime minister, Zhou Enlai (Chou En-lai; 1898–1976), leader of the centrist faction within the CPC, and gradually set about restoring order and reconstructing a balanced party-state system. A number of 'ultra-leftists' were ousted during August 1970 and in September 1971 the PLA commander and defence minister, Lin Biao, died en route to Outer Mongolia, after a failed coup attempt.

During 1972–73 a rehabilitation of purged cadres, including Deng Xiaoping and finance minister, Li Xiannian, commenced, while, overseas, a new policy of détente towards the United States was launched. This reconstruction movement was climaxed by the summoning of the National People's Congress (NPC) for the first time in 11 years, in January 1975, to ratify a new state constitution and approve a new, long-term economic strategy, termed the 'Four Modernizations'. This strategy, involving agriculture, industry, defence, and science and technology, aimed at bringing China on a par with the West by the year 2000.

The reconstruction process was temporarily halted in 1976 when, following the deaths of Zhou Enlai and Mao Zedong, in January and September respectively, a violent succession struggle between the leftist 'Gang of Four', led by Jiang Qing, and moderate 'rightists', grouped around Vice Premier Deng Xiaoping, was unleashed. Deng was forced into hiding by the 'Gang'. However, it was Mao's 'centre-left' protégé, Hua Guofeng (b. 1920), who was appointed CCP Chairman in September 1976, having already been selected as prime minister in January 1976.

Hua, in a pre-emptive move, proceeded to arrest the 'Gang', in October 1976, on charges of treason, and held power as a stop-gap leader between 1976 and 1978, implementing Zhou Enlai's 'Four Modernizations' programme. His authority was progressively challenged, however, by Deng Xiaoping, who was restored to office in March 1977, following wall-poster campaigns in Beijing. By December 1978, after further popular campaigns, Deng, who enjoyed substantial support among the state bureaucracy and military hierarchy, had gained effective control of the government, establishing a majority in the Politburo.

State and judicial bodies began to meet regularly again, the late Liu Shaoqi was rehabilitated as a party hero and major economic reforms were introduced. These involved the dismantling of the commune system and the introduction of direct farm incentives under a new 'responsibility system', as well as the encouragement of foreign investment in coastal enclave 'Special Economic Zones'.

By June 1981, Deng's paramountcy was assured by the installation of his protégés Hu Yaobang, as CCP chairman, later general secretary, and Zhao Ziyang (b. 1918) as prime minister, in June 1981 and September 1980 respectively. The 'Gang of Four' were sentenced to life imprisonment, Yao Wenyuan receiving 20 years, in January 1981, following a dramatic 'show trial'. A year later, in September 1982, Hua Guofeng was ousted from the Politburo, together with a number of senior colleagues, and in December 1982 a definitive new state constitution was adopted by the NPC. This restored the post of state president, which had been abolished in January 1975, to which office Li Xiannian was elected. The military was placed under firmer party control and a new code of civil rights was introduced.

The new 'Deng administration' took the form of a collective leadership, with Hu Yaobang (1915–89) assuming control of party affairs, Zhao Ziyang overseeing state administration, and Deng Xiaoping, a CCP vice chairman and chairman of the State Central Military Committee (SCMC) and the CCP's Central Military Commission (CMC), the 'power behind the throne', concentrating on the formulation of the longer-term strategy, and maintaining a close eye on the PLA.

The triumvirate proceeded to pursue a three-pronged policy programme. The first aim was to streamline the party and state bureaucracies and promote to power new, younger, and better educated technocrats. Second, they sought to curb the influence of the PLA through the retirement of senior commanders and a reduction in manpower numbers from 4.2 million to 3 million. The triumvirate's third priority was for economic modernization, based on the extension of market incentives, 'market socialism', and local autonomy, through the introduction of a new 'open-door' policy to encourage foreign trade and investment.

By 1986 the policies had succeeded in effecting the replacement of half the CCP's provincial-level officers. The new economic reforms met with immediate success in the rural sector, agricultural output more than doubling between 1978–85. They had adverse side effects, however, widening regional and social income differentials and fuelling a wave of 'mass consumerism', thus creating serious balance of payments and inflationary problems. These problems were exacerbated in 1984 when price reform in the urban industrial sector began to be implemented. In the political sphere, the new, pro-Western 'open-door' strategy and liberalization programme served to generate, predominantly intelligentsia, demands for fuller internal democratization. These calls culminated in a wave of major student demonstrations which swept across the country in December 1986. As a consequence of his failure to act promptly to check the disturbances, party chief Hu Yaobang was forced to resign in January 1987.

The departure of Hu, Deng Xiaoping's closest associate, appeared to imperil the future of the post-1978 Dengist reform (gai-ge) programme, as more conservative forces, grouped around the senior figures of the Shanghai-born Politburo member Chen Yun (1905–95) and NPC Standing Committee chairman, Peng Zhen, sought to halt the pace of change and re-establish firm central party control. As part of this strategy, a campaign against what was termed 'bourgeois liberalization', or Western ideas, was launched by the CCP's conservative wing, during the spring of 1987. The more traditional Maoist virtues of frugality and self-reliance were stressed. However, the Dengist 'reform wing' of the CCP held its corner, Zhao Ziyang being temporarily elevated to the positions of both party general secretary and prime minister.

At the CCP's 13th National Congress, held in October 1987, a 'work report' presented by Zhao that described the PRC as still in the 'initial stages of socialism', and thus requiring pragmatic resort to capitalist methods, was accepted. This document stressed the need for continuing reform, including price reform, though at a somewhat more cautious pace; an extension of the 'open-door' strategy; and an enhanced separation between the party and state machines. At the Congress, and during its immediate aftermath, personnel changes were also effected which served to shift the balance on the CCP's Central Committee (CC) and Politburo significantly towards the 'reform faction'. A clutch of young new technocrats and successful mayors were inducted into the Politburo, replacing 'old guard' oppositionist figures, including Chen Yun and Peng Zhen. Deng Xiaoping also retired from both the Politburo and CC, but retained his position as head of the CMC.

However, in November 1987, shortly after the Congress, Li Peng (b. 1928), the Moscow-trained adopted son of Zhou Enlai, replaced Zhao Ziyang as acting prime minister and was formally confirmed in the position when the 7th NPC met for its inaugural session in March 1988. Viewed as a conservative, centralist, reformer, this move suggested that the Dengist reform wing had not triumphed completely and that factional and strategy differences still remained at senior party levels. As 1988 progressed economic problems, emanating from the price deregulation strategy, mounted, with supply bottlenecks developing, as a consumer buying spree gained pace, particularly in the booming coastal provinces. The inflation rate rocketed to between 20–30%. This forced a sharp application of the brakes on economic reform, following an emergency CC session held in September, and the introduction of an austerity budget by Li Peng in March 1989.

A month later, following the death of the revered Hu Yaobang, students in Beijing took to the streets in prodemocracy demonstrations. These disturbances spread to provincial cities and gained in strength during May 1989, at the time of the visit to Beijing of the reformist Russian Soviet leader, Mikhail Gorbachev. The government effectively ceded control of the capital for a week to the students, buttressed by workers, as an intense CCP power struggle developed between conservatives, led by the unpopular Li Peng, and 'liberals', aligned to Zhao Ziyang. Li Peng, supported by Deng Xiaoping, gained the immediate upper hand and martial law was proclaimed and troops despatched to subdue the students. The PLA's officers refused, however, to use force against the demonstrators, creating a stalemate situation. However, at the beginning of June 1989, with the protest movement beginning to lose momentum, 27th Army troops, loyal to President Yang Shangkun (b. 1907), were sent into Tiananmen Square, in the centre of Beijing, to reclaim the capital, brutally shooting dead more than 1,300 unarmed protesters. This action put the hardline Li–Deng–Yang triumvirate in immediate control of the Chinese polity. A month later, Zhao Ziyang was ousted as CCP leader and replaced by the Shanghai party chief, Jiang Zemin (b. 1926). A crackdown against dissidents was launched, thousands being arrested. Martial law continued to be imposed in Beijing until January 1990 and throughout 1990–92 prodemocracy activists were brought to trial and given severe prison sentences.

Deng Xiaoping retired from his last official post in 1990. However, he continued to remain the nation's paramount leader, controlling the direction of change. From 1992, Deng sought again to promote a new phase of economic reform and improved relations with the West. This formed part of an Indonesian-influenced strategy of combining 'market socialism' with political authoritarianism. This Deng sought to underpin through personnel changes at the CCP's 14th Congress, held in October 1992. Elderly 'old guard' conservatives,

including President Yang Shangkun, Defence Minister Qin Jiwei, and the economics and organization specialists Yao Yilin (1917–94) and Song Ping, were persuaded to retire from the Politburo. They were supplanted by a clutch of younger, provincial leaders and economic reformers, in their 50s and 60s, notably Zhu Rongji, the former mayor of Shanghai, and Hu Jintao, former party chief in Guizhou province and Tibet. In addition, nearly half the members of the CCP's Central Committee were replaced.

The Chinese economy, after stalling during 1989–90, picked up strongly again from 1991 in response to the continuing, liberalizing reforms. Annual growth averaged, to 1995, officially 12%, although Western specialists have suggested the rate was closer to 8%. However, there were adverse concomitant developments, notably double-digit inflation, a sharp widening in social and regional inequalities in wealth, and the increasing level of urban crime and CCP corruption. In December 1994 and April 1995, Yao Yilin and Chen Yun, two important 'old guard' leaders died and by the summer of 1995 there was increasing concern over the health of Deng Xiaoping. Now in his 90s, and virtually blind and deaf and unable to stand or walk unaided, Deng's influence as 'paramount leader' appeared to be nearing an end. This was suggested by the arrest, on corruption charges, of a number of Deng associates in 1995. Deng's protégé, the CCP leader Jiang Zemin, who also became state president in March 1993, has begun to build up a power-base within the PLA and has brought into the CCP Politburo a 'Shanghai clique' of firm supporters. As a result, the chances of a relatively stable succession on the death of Deng have improved. Qiao Shi (b. 1924), the current chairman of the Chinese parliament and the former head of the security services and the CCP's personnel department, is viewed as an alternative, and more reform-minded, successor.

In foreign affairs, China's 1960 rift with Khrushchev's Soviet Union over policy differences became irrevocable in 1962 when Russia sided with India during a brief Sino-Indian border war. Relations with the Soviet Union deteriorated further in 1969 after border clashes in the disputed Ussuri river region. China pursued instead a nonaligned, 'Three Worlds', strategy, projecting itself as the spokesperson for Third World nations, although it achieved a nuclear capability by 1964.

During the early 1970s, concerned with Soviet expansionism, a rapprochement with the United States was effected, bringing China's entry into the United Nations, at Taiwan's expense, in 1971 and culminating in the establishment of full Sino-American diplomatic relations in January 1979. Relations with the West remained warm during the 1980s, under the Deng administration, with economic contacts broadening and solutions to the Hong Kong and Macao sovereignty questions being agreed with Britain and Portugal, on the basis of a pragmatic, 'one nation, two systems' formula.

From the mid-1980s, with the coming to power of the reformist leadership of Mikhail Gorbachev in the Soviet Union, Sino-Soviet relations thawed. Helped by progress over the divisive regional problems of Afghanistan and Cambodia and by border demarcation agreements, a heads-of-government–party summit between the two countries eventually took place in May 1989 and in May 1991 Jiang

Zemin made the first visit by a CCP leader to Moscow since 1957. An agreement demarcating the eastern section of the Sino-Soviet border was signed. After the collapse of communism in the Soviet Union in the autumn of 1991, China maintained amicable relations with the new Russian republic and, after a peace agreement for Cambodia was signed in Paris in October 1991, its relations with Vietnam were fully normalized in November 1991.

China's relations with the West received a sharp setback as a result of the government's barbaric actions in June 1989. The United States imposed an embargo on sales of military equipment and scaled back its government contacts. The European Union and Japan also imposed sanctions during 1989–91. With the Chinese vote on the UN Security Council being courted during the 1990–91 'Gulf crisis', relations with the 'developed nations' gradually improved, with visits being paid to China during late 1991 by senior leaders from the United States, United Kingdom, and Japan. However Sino-US relations cooled again from 1993, with the accession to power in the United States of the Clinton administration.

INDIA

Republic of India
Bharat Janarajya

Capital: Delhi

Social and economic data
Area: 3,287,263 km^2
Population: 896,600,000*
Pop. density per km^2: 273*
Urban population: 26%**
Literacy rate: 50%**
GDP: $255,000 million**; per-capita GDP: $290**
Government defence spending (% of GDP): 2.4%**
Currency: Indian rupee

Economy type: low income
Labour force in agriculture: 63%**
*1994
**1992

Ethnic composition
Seventy-two per cent of the population is of Indo-Aryan ethnic stock, 25%, predominantly in the south, Dravidian, and 3% Mongoloid. The official language is Hindi, spoken by 30% of the population, concentrated in northern and central India, with English used as an associate official language. There are also 17 recognized regional languages and more than 1,500 local dialects. Eight per cent of the population speak Bengali, 8% Telugu, 8% Marathi, 7% Tamil, 5% Urdu, and 5% Gujarati.

Religions
Eighty-three per cent of the population is Hindu, 11% Muslim, predominantly of the Sunni sect, 2% Christian, chiefly Roman Catholic, and 2% Sikh.

Political features
State type: liberal democratic
Date of state formation: 1947
Political structure: federal
Executive: parliamentary
Assembly: two-chamber
Party structure: multiparty
Human rights rating: 54%
International affiliations: AfDB, AG (observer), AsDB, CP, CW, ESCAP, G-15, G-24, G-77, IAEA, IBRD, ICC, ICFTU, IMF, IWC, LORCS, NAM, OAS (observer), SAARC, UN, WTO

Local and regional government
The country is divided into 25 substantially self-governing states and seven Union Territories, governed by administrators or lieutenant governors appointed by the president. Below them are divisions, districts, municipalities, development blocks, and villages. Districts are administered by appointed 'district collectors', while corporations and councils (*panchayats*) operate at the urban and subdistrict rural level, although elections have been infrequent. Jharkhand, a traditional tribal hill region in southern Bihar, was granted autonomy in October 1994 after a long campaign for self-determination which was led by the Jharkhand Mukti Morcha (Jharkhand People's Party).

Head of state
President Shankar Dayal Sharma, since 1992

Head of government
Prime Minister P V Narasimha Rao, since 1991

Political leaders since 1970*
1966–77 Indira Gandhi (Congress), 1977–79 Morarji Desai (Janata), 1979–80 Chaudhury Charan Singh (Lok Dal), 1980–84 Indira Gandhi (Congress: I), 1984–89 Rajiv Gandhi (Congress: I), 1989–90 V P Singh (Janata Dal), 1990–91 Chandra Shekhar (Janata Dal: S), 1991– P V Narasimha Rao (Congress: I/Congress)

*Prime ministers

Political system

India is a federal republic whose January 1950 constitution, with 397 articles and nine schedules, making it one of the longest in the world, contains elements from both the American and British systems of government. It comprises 25 self-governing states, as shown in Table 51, each of which is administered by a figurehead governor appointed by the federal president, for a five-year term, on the advice of the prime minister.

Each state has a Legislative Assembly, or Vidhan Sabha, of between 30 and 425 members, popularly elected for a five-year term. Five of the larger states, Bihar, Jammu and Kashmir, Karnataka, Maharashtra, and Uttar Pradesh (UP), have a second, smaller, legislative chamber called a Legislative Council or Vidhan Parishad. An executive Council of Ministers, headed by a chief minister, drawn from the Legislative Assembly, and responsible to it, is appointed on the basis of Assembly support.

The states have primary control over education, health, police, and local government, and work in consultation with the centre in the economic sphere. In times of crisis, central rule, or 'President's rule', can be temporarily imposed.

There are, in addition, seven Union Territories: the Andaman and Nicobar Islands; Chandigarh; Dadra and Nagar Haveli; Daman and Diu; Delhi; Lakshadweep, and Pondicherry. Each is governed by a lieutenant governor or administrator appointed by the federal president. Delhi and Pondicherry also have elected assemblies, or councils.

The federal government has sole responsibility in the fields of citizenship, defence, external trade, and foreign affairs, grouped under 97 headings in the constitution, and plays a key role in economic affairs. This, combined with its monopoly control over such 'growth taxes' as income tax, corporation tax, and customs and excise, the states relying on land and sales taxes and federal grants for their revenue, has served to weight the Indian federal system in the centre's favour compared, for example, with the US federal model.

The titular, executive head of the federal or 'Union' government is the president, who is elected for a five-year term by a large electoral college composed of members from both the federal and the state assemblies and, since 1992, the Delhi and Pondicherry Union Territories. Real, *de facto* executive power is, however, wielded by a prime minister and a 20–25-member Cabinet, termed the Council of Ministers, drawn from the majority party or coalition within the federal parliament.

The prime minister is served by his or her own influential advisors and often reserves for himself, or herself, a number of important ministerial portfolios. For example, Prime Minister Narasimha Rao is also minister of defence, electronics, industry, ocean development, science and technology, Jammu and Kashmir affairs, atomic energy, and space research.

The federal assembly is a two-chamber body, comprising a dominant, 545-member, lower house, the House of the People (Lok Sabha), which has final authority over financial matters and 543 of whose members are directly elected for a five-year term from single-member constituencies, by universal adult suffrage. Since 1989 the minimum voting age has been 18.

There is also a 245-member upper house, the Council of States (Rajya Sabha), 237 of whose members are indirectly elected, a third at a time for six-year terms, by state assemblies, on a regional quota basis. The remaining two seats in the Lok Sabha are reserved for Anglo-Indians, nominated by the president, while eight representatives of the Rajya Sabha are also reserved for presidential nominees.

To become law, bills require the approval of both chambers of the assembly, before formally receiving presidential assent. Ordinary amendments to the constitution require the approval of a two-thirds majority of the members of each house present and voting, and a simple majority of the total membership, to be followed by the president's assent. However, amendments which affect the distribution of powers between the centre and states, the representation of states in parliament, and the workings of the adjudicatory Supreme Court and High Courts require ratification by at least half the state legislatures as well, to become law. Since 1950, more than 70 amendments have been adopted.

Political parties

The dominant national political party, which has held power for all but six years, from 1977 to 1979 and 1989 to 1991, since independence, has been the Congress Party. Under British rule it functioned as a 'catch-all' umbrella organization for the nationalist movement, being originally formed by A O Hume (1829–1912) in 1885, under the designation Indian National Congress, as a moderate, port-city-based, intelligentsia pressure group. The movement's support base broadened and its policy outlook grew more radical during the interwar years, under the charismatic leadership of Mahatma Gandhi and the Western-educated Kashmiri Brahmin socialist, Jawaharlal Nehru. After splits, in 1969, 1978, 1981, 1987, and 1995, the main body of the party is today termed the All India Congress Committee and is led by P V Narasimha Rao.

The contemporary Congress remains a broad, secular-based, cross-caste and cross-religion coalition, which advocates a moderate socialist policy approach and nonalignment in foreign affairs. It is liberally financed by the major Indian industrial conglomerates.

Its support base has been strongest traditionally in the 'Hindi belt' of northern and central India and in adjoining western India, from which regions it has drawn most of its leaders, and weakest in the Dravidian south. However, recently its support in the Hindi north has waned. The party is a mass organization, claiming a membership of over 10 million, but is controlled from above by a small 20-member 'High Command', the Congress Working Committee.

In 1978 the main body of the party, led by Indira Gandhi, who was later assassinated in 1984, adopted the designation Congress (I), the 'I' standing for Indira. Being viewed as redundant, the attachment 'I' was dropped in 1993. In May 1995 the party split once again, this time at its grassroots. A breakaway Congress (Tiwari) party, seeking a return to the party's 'traditional' emphasis on minorities, the poor, and lower castes, was formed by Narain Dutt Tiwari, a veteran politician from the important northern state of Uttar Pradesh, Arjun Singh, a former cabinet minister and 16 Congress parliamentary deputies. However, the great bulk of the parliamentary party and party apparatus remained firmly behind Prime Minister Narasimha Rao, who headed what became termed the dominant Congress (Rao) wing. Congress (Tiwari) claimed the right to use on ballot papers Congress's famous symbol, the open hand, an important identifier in a nation where illiteracy remained widespread. However, in June 1995 the Indian Election Commission rejected this claim.

The principal national-level opposition parties are the Bharatiya Janata Party (BJP: Indian People's Party), the Janata Dal, the Samajwadi Janata Party, the Communist Party of India (CPI), and the Communist Party of India-Marxist (CPI-M).

The BJP was founded in 1980 and is an urban, middle-class and Hindu higher-caste orientated, radical right-wing Hindu grouping led by L K Advani and claiming 7.5 million members. Its roots go further back to the Jana Sangh, founded in 1951 but which later merged with the Janata Party. Initially, the BJP was a relatively moderate force, but since polling poorly in the 1984 general election it has become a staunchly Hindu-chauvinist force. It has used the Babri Masjid Ramjanmabhumi issue at Ayodhya to mobilize the Hindu community across northern India. Three even more radical forces on the militant Hindu right are Shiv Sena, led by Balram Thackeray and rooted in western India; the Rashtriya Swayamsevak Sangh (RSS), founded as a paramilitary organization in 1925 by Dr Keshav Hedgewar, and banned in 1948, 1976, and between 1992–93; and the Vishwa Hindu Parishad (VHP), banned between 1992–95, whose purpose is to disseminate the doctrine of Hindu nationalism.

The Janata Dal (People's Party) was formed in October 1988 through the merger of four important centrist and centre-left parties: the Janata (estd. 1977), the Lok Dal-B (estd. 1984), the Congress (Socialist; estd. 1984), and the Jan Morcha (People's Front; estd. 1987). It originated as an anti-Congress (I) body, led by the Jan Morcha's founder and leader, V P Singh, but split during 1990, after securing power. In 1992 three breakaway factions were formed, the most important two being Janata Dal (A), led by Ajit Singh, son of the late Jat 'prosperous peasant' leader, Charan Singh, and Janata Dal (B), led by S R Bommai. Another breakaway from the Janata Dal is the Samajwadi Janata Party (SJP; Socialist People's Party), formed in 1991 and led initially by Chandra Shekhar, but now by the 'middle peasant' leader Devi Lal. The Janata Dal party, and its offspring, have drawn particularly strong support from Hindu lower castes and, being secular in outlook, have recently drawn away from Congress Muslim support.

The states of India				Table 51
State	Area (sq km)	Population (m) 1991	Capital	Ruling party * (June 1995)
Andhra Pradesh	275,068	66.508	Hyderabad	Telugu Desam
Arunachal Pradesh	83,743	0.865	Itanagar	Congress
Assam	78,438	22.414	Dispur	Congress
Bihar	173,877	86.374	Patna	Janata Dal
Goa	3,702	1.170	Panaji/Panjim	Congress–Maharashtrawadi Gomantak Party (MGP)
Gujarat	196,024	41.310	Gandhinagar	Bharatiya Janata Party (BJP)
Haryana	44,212	16.464	Chandigarh	Congress
Himachal Pradesh	55,673	5.171	Simla	Congress
Jammu & Kashmir	222,236	7.719	Srinagar	President's rule
Karnataka	191,791	44.977	Bangalore	Janata Dal
Kerala	38,863	29.099	Trivandrum	Congress
Madhya Pradesh	443,446	66.181	Bhopal	Congress
Maharashtra	307,690	78.937	Bombay/Mumbai	Shiv Sena–BJP
Manipur	22,327	1.837	Imphal	Congress (in coalition)
Meghalaya	22,429	1.775	Shillong	Congress (in coalition)
Mizoram	21,081	0.690	Aizawl	Congress (in coalition)
Nagaland	16,579	1.210	Kohima	Congress
Orissa	155,707	31.660	Bhubaneswar	Congress
Punjab	50,362	20.281	Chandigarh	Congress
Rajasthan	342,239	44.006	Jaipur	Bharatiya Janata Party (BJP)
Sikkim	7,096	0.406	Gangtok	Sikkim Democratic Front (SDF)
Tamil Nadu	130,058	55.859	Madras	All-India Anna Dravida Munnetra Kazhagam (AIADMK)
Tripura	10,486	2.757	Agartala	President's rule
Uttar Pradesh	294,411	139.112	Lucknow	President's rule
West Bengal	88,752	68.078	Calcutta	Communist Party of India (Marxist)

* The party which provided the chief minister in November 1995

The CPI is a 460,000-member pro-Moscow party, which was formed in 1925, and is led by Indrajit Gupta.

The CPI-M dates from 1964. It has 600,000 members, was formerly pro-Beijing and is orientated towards the landless rural labourer. Its leading member is the reformist West Bengal chief minister, Jyoti Basu, and its general secretary is Harkishan Singh Surjeet.

In addition to these national organizations, there are numerous profederalist regional-level parties, the most important of which are the All-India Anna Dravida Munnetra Kazhagam (AIADMK), the Dravida Munnetra Kazagham (DMK), the Telugu Desam (Telugu Nation), the Jammu and Kashmir National Conference Party (JKNCP), the Shiromani Akali Dal (Akali Religious Party), the Asom Gana Parishad (AGP: Assam People's Council) and the Bahujan Samaj Party (BSP).

The AIADMK was established in 1972, in Tamil Nadu, and is led by Jayalalitha Jayaram, chief minister of Tamil Nadu and the former mistress of the film star, Marudud Gopalan Ramachandran, who died in January 1988. The DMK (estd. 1949) also operates in Tamil Nadu and, led by Muthuvel Karunanidhi, claims 1.6 million members.

The Telugu Desam was established in 1982, in Andhra Pradesh, and now has 2.6 million members. It is led by another former film star, N T Rama Rao.

The JKNCP dates from 1931 and, led by Dr Farook Abdullah, has 1 million members.

The Akali Religious Party was formed in 1920, in Punjab. It has 1 million members, but is currently split.

The AGP was formed in 1985 and is led by Prafulla Kumar Mahanta.

The BSP, based in the large north Indian state of Uttar Pradesh (UP), is a populist party orientated towards low-caste and Harijan ('untouchable') voters. Led by Kanshi Ram and in alliance with the Samajwadi Party, it secured control of the UP state assembly in the elections of November 1993. In June 1995, the BSP's Mayawati became chief minister of UP. She was the first Dalit ('untouchable') to head a state government, but was forced from office in October 1995.

India's opposition parties have been notoriously fractious, faction-ridden bodies, subject to frequent splits and subsequent reformations in new guises. Personality and policy differences have tended to frustrate the formation of a united opposition to the Congress party, with the notable exception of the successes of 1977 and 1989.

Latest elections

In the most recent Lok Sabha elections, held in May–June 1991, Congress (I) captured 227 seats and its ally, the AIADMK, 11. The BJP, which had been performing particularly strongly before the assassination of Rajiv Gandhi in May 1991, won 119 seats and 25% of the national vote. The electoral coalition of V P Singh's National Front, which included the Janata Dal (JD) and Telugu Desam (TD), and its Left Front (communist) allies won 126 seats: JD, 55; TD, 13; CPI, 13; and CPI-M, 35. The SJP, led by the outgoing premier, Chandra Shekhar, held on to just five seats, while Shiv Sena won four seats, and the Jharkhand Mukti Morcha, six. Only 511 Lok Sabha seats were contested initially.

The latest biennial elections to the Rajya Sabha were held in February–March 1994. They left Congress as the largest single party, with more than 100 of the 245 seats.

Political history

The Indian subcontinent, with the exception of the Dravidian south, was first unified by the Mauryan regime, 321–184 BC, whose emperor, Asoka (c. 273–232 BC), was converted to Buddhism. Later, north central India was reunited by the Gupta dynasty, c. 300–500 AD, during which period Brahmanical Hinduism re-established its dominance. Arab traders and invaders began to spread the Islamic faith in western and northwestern regions from the 7th century, the process deepening with the establishment, over much of northern, central, and western India, of the Delhi Sultanate, 1206–1525, and Mughal Empire, 1525–1780s, by Muslim conquerors from Central Asia. The south, however, which was the site of the Hindu Vijayanagar kingdom during the 14th and 15th centuries and was, later, only partially conquered by the Mughals, remained only tangentially exposed to Muslim influences.

Under British rule, which was established in stages between 1757 and 1856 and was to last until 1947, the subcontinent began, helped by the spread of railways and the creation of an extensive English-speaking bureaucracy, to be effectively unified for the first time. Nevertheless, during this period of the Raj, or British rule, almost half the land area, mainly the interior, remained free from direct British government. Instead, it was left to the control of 562 semi-independent, though loyal, 'princely states'.

During the later 19th century, Indian national consciousness began to emerge among the intelligentsia community, and was reflected in the creation, in 1885, of the Indian National Congress (INC), which campaigned for greater autonomy and eventual independence. The new nationalist movement grew more extensive and radical during the interwar years, as economic pressures mounted. The progressive self-government concessions made by the Government of India, including the 'dyarchy reforms' of 1919–21, which handed over much of provincial administrative responsibilities to elected assemblies, helping to inculcate a generalized respect for regular electoral processes, failed to satisfy the 'freedom fighters', Mahatma Gandhi (1869–1948) and Jawaharlal Nehru (1889–1964). They led a series of civil disobedience campaigns for which activity they were repeatedly imprisoned.

The Indian subcontinent was eventually granted independence in August 1947 and, as a result of a split in the nationalist movement between the secular INC and the communalist Muslim League, led by Muhammad Ali Jinnah (1876–1948), the country was partitioned along religious lines, with initial bloody consequences. The result was a predominantly Hindu India and a Muslim-dominated Pakistan. Pakistan was, itself, divided into two, widely separated, western (Sind–Punjab–NW Frontier) and eastern (East Bengal) sectors, with the Indian land mass in between.

For more than two years after August 1947, India temporarily remained under the supervision of a governor general appointed by the British monarch, while a new constitution was framed and approved. This was achieved by

January 1950, involving, in the process, the integration of former princely states and the restructuring of the old British provinces into new states, with boundaries based on linguistic lines. When the process was completed a fully independent, federal republic was proclaimed.

During its early years, the new republic faced problems in the resettlement of millions of Hindu refugees who had fled from Pakistan at the time of partition, losing, in the process, a similar number of Muslims who had moved out in the opposite direction. This resulted in a number of border skirmishes with its new neighbour over Kashmir.

Domestically, under the leadership of Prime Minister Nehru, limited land reforms and a new socialist economic programme were introduced. The programme, which involved protectionism, an emphasis on heavy industries and state planning, was initially successful. Meanwhile, the sovereignty of French- and Portuguese-held territories within India, including Chandernagore, Pondicherry, and Goa, was recovered between 1950 and 1961. Resort to force was necessary in the case of Goa.

In its external relations, India remained within the Commonwealth and played a leading role in the formation of the Non-Aligned Movement in 1961. It also, however, became involved in border clashes with communist China, in October 1962.

In May 1964, Prime Minister Nehru died and was briefly succeeded as national leader by his close associate, the Benares-born 'minister without portfolio', Lal Bahadur Shastri (1904–66). The country became entangled in a second border conflict with Pakistan over Kashmir between August and September 1965 before Shastri died, in January 1966.

His successor as INC leader and prime minister was Indira Gandhi (1917–84), the daughter of Jawaharlal Nehru. She adhered to the broad outlines of her father's policy programme, but also developed closer links with the Soviet Union, with whom India signed a 15-year economic and military assistance agreement in 1973.

In December 1971, Indian troops invaded East Pakistan in support of the local separatist government. After a 12-day war, they succeeded in defeating Pakistan's forces and oversaw the creation of the new independent, and pro-Indian, state of Bangladesh. This military success, despite contemporary economic difficulties, boosted the national standing of Prime Minister Gandhi. However, her personalized style of control had begun to foment divisions within the ruling INC, precipitating an initial split, in November 1969, in which the Gujarat-born Morarji Desai (1896–1995), a former deputy prime minister and 1966 party leadership challenger, together with a number of fellow senior colleagues, left to form a new Congress (O, or Organization).

Criticism of the prime minister's autocratic methods mounted in June 1975 when, having been found guilty of electoral malpractice during the March 1971 general election by the High Court, in her Allahabad constituency, and having been banned from holding elective office for six years, she imposed a draconian 'State of Emergency', involving the temporary outlawing of opposition parties and the imposition of tight censorship controls. Almost 1,000 of Mrs Gandhi's political opponents were imprisoned, under the provisions of the Maintenance of Internal Security Act. Despite her later being cleared of malpractice by the Supreme Court, in November 1975, the 'Emergency' continued for two years, during which time a harsh and unpopular, compulsory birth-control programme, by sterilization, was introduced under the supervision of Sanjay Gandhi (1946–80), Indira's youngest son.

The 'State of Emergency' was eventually lifted in March 1977 to allow parliamentary elections to take place. In this contest, the opposition parties, who had united under the umbrella of the newly formed Janata Party, were swept to power with a landslide victory. The new party's leader, Morarji Desai, defeated Indira Gandhi in her home constituency.

The new Janata government, the first non-INC administration since independence, headed by Prime Minister Desai, swiftly introduced constitutional amendments to reverse those pushed through by Indira Gandhi in 1975–76, thus restoring the 'democratic balance'. The Desai coalition was gradually undermined, however, by mounting economic difficulties and internal factional strife. This culminated, in July 1979, in the defection of many Janata members to a new secular party, the Lok Dal, under the leadership of the former health minister, Raj Narain, and home minister, Charan Singh. Desai was eventually toppled as prime minister in July 1979 and a coalition, under the leadership of Charan Singh, assumed power. A month later, however, after only 24 days in office, the Charan Singh government was overthrown.

In the Lok Sabha elections, which followed in January 1980, Indira Gandhi's renamed and revamped Congress (I), promising a firmer and more decisive approach to government after the drift of the Janata years and faced with opposition disarray, was returned to power, gaining a landslide majority.

The new administration proceeded to record success in the economic sphere, helped by the spread of the 'Green Revolution' in the agricultural sector, which resulted in high yields of wheat and rice. It was beset, however, by mounting problems of intercaste violence and regionalist unrest, centred in Gujarat, where there was caste strife, Muslim-dominated Kashmir, southern India and Assam, where violence was aimed at Bangladeshi immigrants. This resulted in Congress (I)'s loss of control of a string of state assemblies.

The most serious unrest occurred in the prosperous Punjab. Here initial moderate Sikh demands for greater religious recognition and a resolution of water and land disputes with neighbouring states, escalated into more extreme calls for the creation of a separate state of 'Khalistan'. In June 1984, Indira Gandhi, concerned with the mounting level of disorder in the province, sent Indian troops into the Golden Temple at Amritsar to dislodge the young Sikh extremist leader, Sant Jarnail Singh Bhindranwale (1947–84), and his armed followers. This 'storming' operation, which caused widespread damage to a revered holy shrine, as well as resulting in the death of Bhindranwale and hundreds of his 'disciples', provoked a Sikh backlash which served to radicalize and spread militancy through the community. Across India, Sikh troop regiments immediately mutinied and, four months later, in October 1984, the prime minister was assassinated by her Sikh bodyguards in the garden of her residence in Delhi. This, in turn, provoked savage Hindu retaliation in Delhi, in November 1984, involving the massacre of 2,000 Sikhs by vigilantes, before the new prime minister, Rajiv Gandhi (1944–91), Indira's eldest son, was able to restore order.

In the new general election which followed, in December 1984, Congress (I), benefiting from a wave of public sympathy, succeeded in securing a record victory, with its highest share, 49%, of the national vote since independence. The new prime minister, Rajiv Gandhi, a former airline pilot who had only reluctantly been persuaded into politics in 1980, following the death of his younger brother, was a popular leader. He was viewed as an upright, managerial 'non-politician', unsullied by the corruptions of the political game. He proceeded to project himself as a forward-looking and healing leader, pledging, under the slogan 'bringing India into the 21st century', to modernize and inject greater market efficiency into the Indian economy and to resolve the Punjab, Assam, Kashmir, and northeastern hill states' regional disputes.

Early deregulationary economic reforms, assaults on bureaucratic 'red tape', support for the launching of Indian space satellites, and the spread of computer technology promised to give substance to these visions, while an early move was made to resolve the Punjab dispute and even greater progress made in Assam, Kashmir, and the hill areas, including Mizoram. Here 25 years of rebellion were ended and it became a new state of the Indian Union.

By 1987, however, Rajiv Gandhi's national standing had been seriously diminished. In the economic sphere, the reformist zeal of 1985–86 had lost its impetus and prospects seemed poor, with the country in the grip of its worst drought of the century. In the external sphere, the Indian army, which had been sent to northern Sri Lanka to 'police' the July 1987 Jayawardene Peace Accord, had become bogged down in a war against its fellow community. Internally, Sikh–Hindu ethnic violence remained a serious problem in Punjab, with communalist Hindu chauvinism gaining in strength in adjoining regions. Politically, Congress (I) support had slumped, the party enduring reverses in state polls, as well as the defection of a number of elder party members who were opposed to the centralization of power within the hands of a tight-knit 'Doon clique' of young Gandhi associates. There were also public disputes between President Giani Zail Singh and the prime minister.

Most serious of all, however, the reputation that had initially been assigned to Rajiv Gandhi as the 'Mr Clean' of Indian politics had been seriously sullied by the uncovering by finance minister V P Singh (b. 1931) of the 'Bofors scandal', involving financial 'kick-backs' received by, it was alleged, government-connected Indian 'front organizations', for facilitating a major arms contract with the Swedish munitions firm.

Although cleared of any personal impropriety in this affair, the 'Bofors scandal' served to undermine popular confidence in the Gandhi administration, while at the same time vaulting on to the national stage V P Singh as a zealous crusader against corruption. Singh, along with other prominent 'dissident' members, was dismissed from Congress (I) in

July 1987 and proceeded to form a new 'political forum', the Jan Morcha, in October. Following his election to the Lok Sabha, in a by-election held in his native Allahabad in June 1988, Singh became the focus for an opposition unity drive, culminating in the formation of the new National Front and Janata Dal, in October 1988.

To contest the general election of November 1989, a broad anti-Congress (I) electoral pact was forged, comprising the Janata Dal and the regionally based DMK and Telugu Desam. This ensured that the number of seats captured by Congress (I) fell dramatically from 400 in December 1984 to just 192 and a minority National Front coalition government, headed by V P Singh, was formed after the election. A major objective of this new Singh administration was the lowering of racial tensions. However, as early as January 1990 Muslim separatist violence erupted in Kashmir. This forced the imposition of direct rule and resulted in a deterioration in relations with Pakistan. Interethnic violence similarly reached new heights in Punjab and became so serious in Assam that President's rule had to be imposed in November 1990. However, relations were improved with neighbouring Bhutan, Nepal (which had been subjected to a partial border blockade during 1989), and Sri Lanka, where the Indian Peacekeeping Force, sent by Rajiv Gandhi in July 1987, was withdrawn in March 1990.

From the summer of 1990 V P Singh's Janata Dal government was rocked by three developments. First, a decision by the prime minister to advocate implementation of the eight-year-old recommendations of the Mandal Commission on job reservations for disadvantaged castes provoked a bloody caste war in the cities of northern India. Second, from September 1990 there was serious Hindu–Muslim communal conflict, as Hindu militants of the Vishwa Hindu Parishad (VHP: World Hindu Council) pressed for the construction of a temple venerating the warrior-god Rama on the site of a 16th-century Muslim mosque in the north Indian holy city of Ayodhya. Third, Chandra Shekhar, a leading figure within the former Janata Party and a long-standing Singh opponent, established himself as the leader of a rebel faction within the National Front administration.

On 7 November 1990, shortly after troops had fired on Hindu fanatics in Ayodhya, the Singh government was voted from office and Chandra Shekhar, supported by the Haryana-based 'middle peasant' leader Devi Lal, took over as prime minister. Shekhar's minority administration, which was kept in power by the puppet-master support of Rajiv Gandhi's Congress (I), lasted only 115 days. By shelving the proposals of the Mandal Commission, it lessened intercaste tensions. However, regional and communal strife continued, claiming more than 5,000 lives during 1990, the great majority in Punjab. Meanwhile, the Indian economy, after bumper harvests during 1989–90, suffered from the higher oil prices which resulted from the 1990–91 Gulf conflict.

Shekhar, after falling out with his Congress (I) backers, resigned as premier in March 1991. His small, breakaway SJP party was trounced in the ensuing May–June 1991 general election. This election campaign was the most violent in the history of the Indian Republic, claiming several hundred lives, and was marked by the assassination of Rajiv Gandhi by a bomb strapped to a kamikaze Tamil Tiger female terrorist. Gandhi's Italian-born widow, Sonia, declined entreaties to take over as Congress (I) leader. Instead, the experienced southerner, P V Narasimha Rao (b. 1921), assumed the helm of Congress (I).

The most notable feature of the May–June 1991 election was the high level of support, a quarter of the national vote, received by the Hindu-chauvinist BJP, which polled particularly strongly in the northern 'Hindi belt'. However, a late, sympathy vote surge of support for Congress (I) was sufficient to enable Narasimha Rao to form a minority administration. After delayed elections were held in Punjab in February 1992, a Congress (I) majority was achieved. The new Rao government embarked on an ambitious freer market economic programme, slashing subsidies, allowing the rupee to float, encouraging foreign investment, and scrapping industrial licensing. It also announced in September 1991 that it would adopt the recommendations of the Mandal Commission. However, in December 1992 the country was rocked by a fresh outbreak of Hindu–Muslim violence, claiming 1,200 lives, after Hindu militants stormed and tore down the Ayodhya mosque. The government reacted by ordering the arrest of the leaders of the BJP and VHP, banning the VHP, and, with the Supreme Court's approval, dismissing the BJP administrations in Uttar Pradesh, Himachal Pradesh, Madhya Pradesh, and Rajasthan, where President's rule was declared.

From 1993, communal violence subsided somewhat. However, bloody insurgencies continued in Kashmir, where 150,000 Indian troops were stationed, and the weekly death toll exceeded 50 people, and in the northeastern hill states of Assam, Nagaland, and Manipur. With the administration of Narasimha Rao facing criticism for favouring the rich rather than the poor with its new economic programme, for perceived corruption, and for alienating Muslims over the Ayodhya issue, Congress, as it was now designated, became increasingly divided and endured crushing defeats in state elections in Karnataka and Andhra Pradesh, the latter being Narasimha Rao's home state, in December 1994. The human resources minister, Arjun Singh, immediately resigned from the government. This established him as a potential challenger to Rao, but the prime minister reacted swiftly by securing Singh's expulsion from Congress in February 1995.

By the spring of 1995, following humiliating defeats in the western Indian states of Maharashtra and Gujarat, where the Hindu-chauvinist Shiv Sena and BJP triumphed, and Bihar, won by a Janata Dal party orientated towards lower-caste voters, the states ruled by Congress accounted for barely a quarter of India's population. Despite strong growth in the economy, Congress seemed unlikely to secure a majority of seats in the 1996 federal election. This became even less likely in May 1995, when a new rift occurred within its ranks after the ousted Arjun Singh and the veteran north Indian politician, N D Tiwari, formed the new breakaway Congress (Tiwari). This claimed the support of 16 Congress members of parliament. In July 1995 a report by the independent Vohra Commission, set up in 1993, disclosed that large areas of northern India were controlled by mafia gangs which enjoyed the patronage of local politicians. In Uttar Pradesh, 180 of the 425 legislators had criminal records and here, and in adjoining Bihar, thugs were routinely engaged to capture polling booths and stuff ballot boxes.

INDONESIA

Republic of Indonesia (ROI)
Republik Indonesia

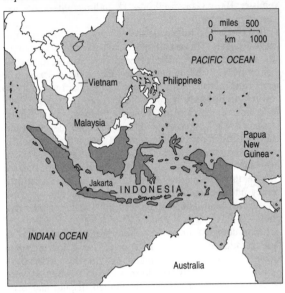

Capital: Jakarta

Social and economic data
Area: 1,904,569 km^2
Population: 194,600,000*
Pop. density per km^2: 102*
Urban population: 30%**
Literacy rate: 82%**
GDP: $138,000 million**; per-capita GDP: $730**
Government defence spending (% of GDP): 1.4%**
Currency: rupiah
Economy type: low income
Labour force in agriculture: 47%**

*1994
**1992

Ethnic composition
The country is heterogenous in social composition, comprising more than 300 ethnic groups, the majority of which are of Malay stock. The most important Malay communities are the Javanese, who comprise a third of the population, followed by the Sundanese, 7%, and Madurese, 3%. The Chinese, 2%, constitute the largest non-Malay community, with substantial numbers of Indians, Melanesians, Micronesians and Arabs, invariably regionally based, also to be found. The official national language is Bahasa Indonesia, a form of Trade Malay, but 25 local languages, predominantly Javanese, Madurese and Sundanese, and 250 local dialects, are also spoken.

Religions
Eighty-two per cent of the population is Sunni Muslim and 10% Christian. A third of Christians are Roman Catholics and two-thirds Protestants and other denominations. The

Protestant Batak of Sumatra, the Christian Evangelical Minahasan of Sulawesi, the Protestant Moluccans, and the Ibans of Kalimantan constitute the most important Christian communities. Two per cent of the population is Hindu, residing mainly in Bali, and 5% adheres to tribal religions. The country has the largest Muslim community, some 160 million, in the world. The majority of Muslims are, however, nominal, following an amalgam of animistic, Muslim, and Hindu beliefs and rituals. Aceh province in west Sumatra, where Islamic Sharia law is acknowledged, is an exception. The official state 'religion' is the secular ideology of Pancasila, based on five general principles: a belief in one supreme God; a just and civilized humanity; the unity of Indonesia; democracy, led by the wisdom of deliberations (*musyawarah*) among representatives; and social justice for the whole of the people of Indonesia.

Political features

State type: authoritarian nationalist
Date of state formation: 1949
Political structure: unitary
Executive: unlimited presidential
Assembly: one-chamber
Party structure: multiparty*
Human rights rating: 34%
International affiliations: APEC, AsDB, ASEAN, CP, ESCAP, G-15, G-77, IAEA, IBRD, ICC, ICFTU, IMF, IsDB, LORCS, NAM, OIC, OPEC, UN, WTO

*With one party predominating

Local and regional government

The country is divided into 24 provinces (*propinsi*), including East Timor, a metropolitan district (Jakarta) and two special autonomous districts (Aceh and Yogyakarta). Each is headed by a centrally appointed governor, two-thirds of whom are drawn from the military. Within the provinces are 246 districts or regencies (*kabupaten*), administered by regents (*bupats*); 54 municipalities (*kota madya*), under the charge of mayors (*walis*); and 3,349 subdistricts (*kecamatan*), headed by a *tjamat*. There is a three-tier system of elected provincial, regency, and village assemblies at local and regional levels.

Head of state and of government

President T N J Suharto, since 1967

Political leaders since 1970

1966–   T N J Suharto (Golkar)

Political system

Under the constitution of August 1945, which was amended in 1950 and 1969, the supreme political body in Indonesia is, in theory, the 1,000-member People's Consultative Assembly (Majelis Permusyawaratan Rakyat: MPR). This consists of 500 members of the House of Representatives and 500 selected representatives from 147 regional assemblies and 353 functional and political groups, including about 200 from the armed forces. It meets at least once every five years to elect an executive president and vice president and to determine the constitution and the 'broad lines of the policy of the State and Government'. All decisions, in accordance with the tradition of *musyawarah*, are taken unanimously.

The House of Representatives (Dewan Perwakilan Rakyat: DPR) functions as a single-chamber legislature and comprises 400 directly elected members and 100 presidential appointees, three-quarters of whom represent the armed forces. It meets at least once a year and elections are held every five years.

All statutes require the House's approval. Individual DPR members may submit draft bills. To become law, however, they need to be ratified by the president, who enjoys veto rights. As in the MPR, legislation is adopted by consensus, rather than voting, the chamber acting as a legitimator of presidential initiatives.

At the head of the executive, and the most powerful political figure in the country, is the president. Presidents are elected by the MPR for a renewable five-year term. They work with an appointed cabinet, exercise, as has already been noted, the right of veto over House of Representatives' bills and appoint governors for each of Indonesia's 27 provinces and special autonomous districts. In March 1995 the president's cabinet had 40 members, the majority of whom were specialist technocrats, and a quarter were serving or retired military commanders. Each of these cabinet ministers is responsible only to the president.

The president is assisted by several advisory agencies, including the Supreme Advisory Council (DPA: Dewan Pertimbangan Agung), National Development Council, and the National Security and Political Stabilization Board. During periods of emergency, the president has additional authority to enact ordinances which have the force of law, for up to a year, without parliamentary ratification.

Political parties

The dominant and governing political party in Indonesia is Golkar (Joint Secretariat of Functional Groups: Sekretariat Bersama Golongan Karya), led by President Suharto. The party was formed in 1964 by a group of senior army officers as a means of establishing a loose alliance of sectional interests, farmers, the fishing community, professionals, factory workers, young people, the older generation and women, so as to counter the growing influence of the Indonesian Communist Party (PKI). This enjoyed national support of around 15% during the 1950s, before being banned in 1966.

Golkar was brought under government control in 1968 and was transformed into the civilian arm of President Suharto's military regime. The party has an extensive national organization, but is tightly controlled from above by an elite, 45-member Central Committee, comprising senior state officials and army officers, all close to the president. It has been described as 'not so much a political party as ... the political arm of the bureaucracy', and is designed to restrict to a minimum the number of assembly seats obtained by other, genuine, political parties. Golkar currently claims a membership of 25 million and its first civilian, Harmoko, was elected its chairperson in October 1993.

There are two permitted 'opposition parties': the Indonesian Democratic Party (PDI: Partai Demokrasi Indonesia), and the United Development Party (PPP: Partai Persatuan Pembangunan).

The PDI was formed in 1973 through the enforced merger of five non-Islamic nationalist and Christian parties. It is heir

to the radical and once influential, Sukarno-linked, Indonesian Nationalist Party (PNI). However, today it is viewed as
being deeply penetrated by state intelligence officers. Its
leader has, traditionally, been effectively appointed by the
government. However, the current leader, the popular
Megawati Sukarnoputri, daughter of former President
Sukarno, who was elected the PDI's chair in December 1993,
is more independent and nationalistic in outlook, attracting
support from moderate Muslims and some members of the
military.

The PPP was also formed in 1973, by the merger of four
Islamic Parties, including the Nahdlatul Ulama and Indonesian Muslims' Party. It is led by Ismael Hassan Metareum, is
Islamic in outlook, and enjoys strong support in Aceh
province and in east and central Java. However, its four constituent elements remain poorly fused. On non-Muslim
issues, the PPP's members generally support government
initiatives.

To be officially registered, political parties must subscribe
to the state philosophy of Pancasila and have a membership
which covers more than a quarter of Indonesia. This has prevented the formation of narrowly regionalist-based groupings. Since 1975, only Golkar, the PDI and the PPP have
been permitted to function. Also, the two non-Golkar parties
are debarred from organizing below the district level. To
compensate for these restrictions, the state provides parties
with funds to cover administrative, campaign, and leadership
expenses.

The following regionally based separatist groups are in
conflict with the government: Front for an Independent
East Timor (Frente Revolucionario de Este Timor Indepen-
dente: Fretilin, estd. 1974), which seeks independence
for East Timor; the Free Papua Movement (Organizasi
Papua Merdeka: OPM: estd. 1963), which seeks unification
of Irian Jaya with Papua New Guinea; and the Free Aceh
Movement (estd. 1990), which campaigns for Aceh's
independence.

Latest elections

In the most recent DPR elections, which were held on 9 June
1992, Golkar, with 68% of the national vote, down 5% on its
1987 share, captured 282 of the 400 available seats. The
Muslim-backed PPP won 62 seats and 17% of the vote, while
the PDI garnered 56 seats on a 15% vote share. Turnout was
90.4%, with voting, as usual, taking place in multimember
provincial constituencies, based on a simple party list proportional representation system.

The election was viewed as relatively fair and the most
open and peaceful of the 'New Order' era. However, the
campaign speeches of the two 'opposition parties' were subjected to prior government vetting and it was apparent that
many votes were cast on a 'patronage basis'. The PDI
attacked the close relationship between the Suharto government and big business, hinting at nepotism and corruption.

In the concurrent regional assembly elections, Golkar
gained control of all the country's 27 provinces and
autonomous districts for the second time.

General Suharto (retired) was unanimously re-elected
president, as sole candidate, for a sixth consecutive five-year
term by the MPR on 10 March 1993.

Political history

Indonesia constitutes the largest archipelago nation in the
world, comprising 13,667 mountainous and volcanic islands,
6,000 of which are inhabited. They are separated east–west
by 5,271 kilometres and north–south by 2,210 kilometres.
The islands were settled by immigrants from South China
between 3000–500 BC, displacing the original Melanesian
population. During the early centuries of the Christian era,
they came under the influence of Hindu and Buddhist priests
and traders, who spread their culture and religion and later,
from 700 AD onwards, established substantial Hindu
empires. Islam was introduced during the 13th century by
Gujarati and Persian traders and had become the chief archipelago religion by the 15th century. Portuguese traders followed, in the early 16th century, and established lucrative
spice-trading posts.

The Portuguese commercial monopoly over the 'spice
islands' was successfully challenged by the Dutch, in 1595,
and the archipelago, now designated the Netherlands Indies,
was placed, between 1602 and 1798, under the supreme control of the Dutch East India Company. Initially, during the
17th century, the Dutch had concentrated purely on trade,
establishing new trading centres, while leaving internal
administration to indigenous Indonesian kingdoms. During
the 19th century, however, direct Dutch rule was imposed.
The islands were proclaimed a Dutch colony in 1816 and a
sugar-based plantation economy was established on Java. In
1922, the Netherlands Indies were designated an integral part
of the Netherlands kingdom.

During the 1920s and 1930s the rural economy faced
mounting difficulties including, in 1926, a communist-
inspired revolt. A nationalist movement developed, under the
leadership of the pro-Communist Indonesian Nationalist
Party (PNI), which was established in 1926, and headed by
the charismatic Achmed Sukarno (1902–70). This was suppressed by the Dutch administration, the PNI's leaders being
imprisoned and exiled between 1929 and 1932, but, in March
1942, following the occupation of the islands by Japanese
forces, the party was installed in power as an anti-Western
puppet government.

When Japan surrendered to the Allies, in August 1945,
President Sukarno proclaimed Indonesia's independence
from the Netherlands. The Dutch challenged this by launching military expeditions, between 1946 and 1949, before
eventually agreeing to transfer sovereignty in December
1949. At the same time, a 'special union' was established
between the two countries. This union was abrogated by
Indonesia in February 1956.

The new republic was planned as a federation of 16 constituent regions, but was made unitary in August 1950. This
naturally resulted in the dominance of Java, provoking
revolts in Sumatra and the predominantly Christian South
Moluccas. The paramount political figure in the new republic was President Sukarno, who, believing in the concept of
'guided democracy', ruled in an authoritarian manner and
pursued an ambitious, expansionist, and nationalist foreign
policy. He succeeded in effecting the transfer of Netherlands
New Guinea (Irian Jaya) to Indonesia, in May 1963, but
failed, after a confrontation with Malaysia, in the cases of
Sabah and Sarawak in North Borneo.

In September 1965, amid deteriorating economic conditions, caused by extravagant government overspending and corruption, a coup was attempted against Sukarno by groups connected with the 2.5-million-strong Indonesian Communist Party (PKI). This was firmly put down, with tens of thousands of PKI supporters losing their lives, by army chief of staff, General T N J Suharto (b. 1921). He then proceeded to assume power as emergency ruler in March 1966.

General Suharto ended Indonesia's hostility towards Malaysia over Sabah and Sarawak in August 1966, and formally replaced Sukarno as president in February 1967. He then proceeded to institute what was termed a 'New Order'. This involved the concentration of political power in the hands of a coterie of army and security force (*Kopkamtib*) officers and, mainly American-educated, technocrat planners; the propagation of a new secular state philosophy of Pancasila, stressing unity and social justice; the pursuit of a liberal, free-enterprise and 'open-door' economic policy; the fierce suppression of communist political activity; and the tight control of ordinary party political activity. All opposition groups were fused, by diktat, into two, 'neutered' units in 1973.

Aided by income from rising oil exports, significant industrial and agricultural growth was achieved during the 1970s, self-sufficiency in rice production being attained, for example, by the early 1980s. Per-capita GDP rose by 4.8% per annum in real terms between 1965 and 1985. In addition, Indonesia's territorial borders were extended by the forcible annexation of the predominantly Catholic former Portuguese colony of East Timor, in 1975–76.

Suharto's authoritarian methods, however, promoted opposition from many quarters. The opposition came from left-wing organizations, radical Muslims, and tribal separatist groups in the outlying islands of Irian Jaya and East Timor. In Irian Jaya there was the Free Papua Movement (OPM) and in East Timor, the Fretilin (Front for an Independent East Timor) and UDI independence fronts.

Following the suppression of an OPM-organized rebellion in Irian Jaya, the Suharto government instituted, in 1986, a 'transmigration programme', based on the resettlement there, and on other sparsely peopled 'outer islands', of a projected 65 million Javanese, by the year 2006. This scheme, which began in 1987, encountered strong opposition from indigenous Melanesians, prompting more than 10,000 refugees to emigrate to adjoining Papua New Guinea. In East Timor, meanwhile, it was reported that between 100,000 and 200,000 Timorese, a third to a sixth of the population, died from famine, disease, and continuing internal warfare during the decade immediately following the province's annexation. The United Nations refused to recognize Indonesian sovereignty over East Timor, which continued to be imposed through military force, although travel restrictions were partially eased from 1988.

During the early 1980s economic problems developed as world oil prices fell, oil providing 70% of Indonesia's foreign exchange earnings. The annual GDP growth rate dropped to 3.5% between 1980 and 1985, while the country's population continued to expand at a compound rate of 3.3%. Despite these difficulties, national support for Golkar rose nine points over its 1982 level to 73% in the general

election of April 1987. A year later, in March 1988, Suharto was unanimously re-elected, as the sole candidate, for a fifth five-year presidential term.

In April 1991 a 45-member Democracy Forum was launched by leading members of the religious and cultural intelligentsia, including Abdurrchman Wahid, leader of the Nahdlatul Ulama, the country's largest Muslim association, and in August 1991 a Forum for the Purification of People's Sovereignty was set up by General Hartono Resko Dharsono, the country's most prominent dissident, who had been released from prison in September 1990. They aimed to promote more democratic values in a state that remained authoritarian – the latter was shown most clearly in the army's massacre on 12 November 1991 of between 50 and 180 demonstrators during a funeral ceremony in Dili, East Timor, and the subsequent execution of a further 60–80 'subversives'.

Despite a pick-up in the rate of economic growth, averaging 7% per annum from 1989, support for Golkar fell to 68% of the national vote in the June 1992 general election. Reacting to this result, the party has sought to somewhat reduce its links with the military and tolerate a somewhat greater degree of political openness (*keperbukaan*) and decentralization. Suharto was re-elected for a sixth consecutive term as state president in March 1993, but intimated in March 1994 that he did not intend to seek a further, seventh term.

In its external relations, Indonesia has for a long time pursued a nonaligned foreign policy, hosting the Bandung Conference of Third World nations in 1955 and the tenth summit of the Non-Aligned Movement in August 1992. It has also been a prominent member of ASEAN since its inception in 1967. Under General Suharto, however, the country's relations, political and economic, with the West have notably improved, although the Netherlands did suspend its foreign aid after the November 1991 Dili massacre.

JAPAN

Nippon/Nihon ('The Land of the Rising Sun')

Capital: Tokyo

Social and economic data
Area: 371,815 km^2
Population: 125,000,000*
Pop. density per km^2: 336*
Urban population: 77%**
Literacy rate: 100%**
GDP: $3,730,000 million**; per-capita GDP: $30,000**
Government defence spending (% of GDP): 1.6%**
Currency: yen
Economy type: high income
Labour force in agriculture: 6%**

*1994
**1992

Ethnic composition
More than 99% of the population is of Japanese ethnic stock, with Japanese the official language.

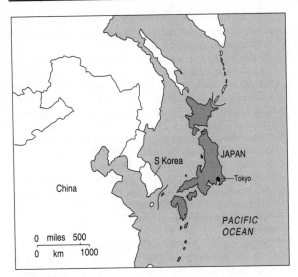

China

S Korea

JAPAN

Tokyo

PACIFIC
OCEAN

0   miles 500

0   km   1000

Religions
Around 40% of the population adheres to Shintoism, an indigenous religion embracing the worship of ancestors and nature, 38% adheres to the Buddhist faith, and 4% to a range of Christian denominations. Shintoism and Buddhism are non-exclusive and overlap. Since the World War II many new cults have emerged. They are known collectively as the New Religions (Shinko Shukyo), many being Buddhist offshoots.

Political features
State type: liberal democratic
Date of state formation: 5th century
Political structure: unitary
Executive: parliamentary
Assembly: two-chamber
Party structure: multiparty
Human rights rating: 82%
International affiliations: AfDB, AG (observer), APEC, AsDFB, BIS, CP, EBRD, ESCAP, G-5, G-7, G-10, IAEA, IBRD, ICC, ICFTU, IDB, IEA, IMF, IWC, LORCS, NEA, OAS (observer), OECD, UN, WTO

Local and regional government
The country is divided into nine regions, which are further subdivided into 47 prefectures, each of which is administered by an elected governor and has an elected assembly. Below, there are elected city, town, and village chief executives and assemblies. Local bodies are substantially dependent, however, on the central government for funding and policy direction.

Head of state
Emperor Akihito, since 1989

Head of government
Prime Minister Ryutaro Hashimoto, since 1996

Political leaders since 1970*
1964–72 Eisaku Sato (LDP), 1972–74 Kakuei Tanaka (LDP), 1974–76 Takeo Miki (LDP), 1976–78 Takeo Fukuda (LDP), 1978–80 Masayoshi Ohira (LDP), 1980–82 Zenko

Suzuki (LDP), 1982–87 Yasuhiro Nakasone (LDP), 1987–89 Noboru Takeshita (LDP), 1989 Sosuke Uno (LDP), 1989–91 Toshiki Kaifu (LDP), 1991–93 Kiichi Miyazawa (LDP), 1993–94 Morihiro Hosokawa (JNP), 1994 Tsutomu Hata (Shinseito), 1994–96 Tomiichi Murayama (SDPJ) 1996– Ryutaro Hashimoto (LDP)

*Prime ministers

Political system
Japan's 99-article, November 1946, constitution was framed by the occupying allied forces, with the intention of creating a consensual, parliamentary form of government and avoiding an overconcentration of executive authority. The head of the state is the emperor, whose functions are purely ceremonial, being described as 'the symbol of the State and of the unity of the people'. Real power is concentrated in the elected assembly and is exercised by a prime minister and cabinet.

The Japanese assembly, the Diet (Kokkai), is a two-chamber body composed of a 252-member upper house, the House of Councillors (Sangiin), and a 511-member lower house, the House of Representatives (Shugiin). The former has 152 representatives, elected from 47 prefectural constituencies on the basis of the 'limited vote' system, and 100 elected nationally by proportional representation. Under the 'limited vote' system electors cast a single vote, the candidates with the highest number of votes in each single-, or multi-member, constituency being returned in rank order. Electors are given an additional, separate, vote for the extra 100 members. To be included in this national ballot, parties must submit a list of at least ten candidates, at least five of whom are existing Diet members, or they must have won at least 4% of the vote at the previous election. Each councillor serves a six-year term, half the chamber being elected every three years.

Members of the House of Representatives are elected for a four-year term, subject to dissolution, in large, 3–5 member constituencies, again on the basis of the 'limited vote'. The ballot is restricted to those of 20 years and over.

Under the terms of an electoral reform act, which was approved by the Diet in January 1994, the House of Representatives' multimember constituencies, which have been blamed for encouraging 'money politics', are to be replaced at the next election by 300 single-member constituencies. A further 200 deputies in the new 500-member House will be returned by proportional representation on the basis of regional contests. Electors will thus, as in Germany, have two votes: one for a single-member candidate and the other for a proportional representation candidate. In an effort to reduce parties' reliance on business donations, the state financing of political parties is also to be introduced.

The House of Representatives is the dominant, and more important, of the two chambers of parliament. It is able to override vetoes on bills imposed by the House of Councillors if a two-thirds majority of those present is obtained. It also has paramountcy on financial questions. In practice, interhouse disputes, when they arise, are resolved by the convening of a special Joint Conference Committee. In both chambers, legislative business is effected through a system of Standing and Special Committees, with stress placed on achieving a consensus. Also, the opposition is allowed to chair a number of important committees. The legislature convenes at least once a year for a session which must last at least 150 days, but is usually far longer.

To amend the constitution, a two-thirds majority vote of all members of each chamber of the Diet is required, followed by a majority affirmation by the electors in a special referendum. Despite support for changes among elements within the ruling Liberal Democratic Party (LDP), the 'blocking' strength of the opposition parties has meant that no fundamental amendments to the 1946 'American constitution' have so far been made.

Executive administration is entrusted to a prime minister, chosen by the majority grouping within the Diet, who selects a cabinet of about 20 to 25 members. All are collectively responsible to the assembly, which can unseat the government by a successful 'no-confidence' motion. Cabinet members oversee the work of both government ministries and agencies and must, according to the rules of the constitution, be civilians. The majority, including the prime minister, must also be members of the Diet. The cabinet functions in a consensual, collective manner, with individual ministers working closely with their respective departmental senior bureaucrats, who, in reality, are the crucial policy-framing figures.

The post of prime minister, with its important patronage powers, was, between 1955 and 1993, assigned to the president of the LDP. The frequent changes in personnel occupying the post thus resulted from the desire of party faction leaders to rotate occupancy of this 'plum' position, rather than from substantive 'political' factors. In addition, cabinet posts were also liberally distributed between senior faction members, ministers rarely serving more than two years in a post.

Japan possesses a 15-justice Supreme Court, whose members are appointed by the cabinet, with the exception of the high judge, who is appointed by the Emperor, on the nomination of the cabinet. Once appointed, judges serve until the legal retirement age, but are subject to approval in decennial popular referenda. The Supreme Court enjoys administrative control over lower courts and the power of judicial review. It is able to determine the constitutionality of any law. In practice, however, as a result of the Japanese preference for settling disputes by negotiation and mediation, its use of these powers has been unusually limited.

Political parties

The dominant political party in Japan is the Liberal Democratic Party (LDP: Jiyu-Minshuto), led by Ryutaro Hashimoto. It monopolized power for nearly four decades after its formation, but failed to win House of Representatives' majorities in 1976, 1979, and 1983. In 1993 it was finally ousted from office, but it gained a share of power in 1994 at the heart of an improbable 'grand coalition' which included its traditional opponent, the Social Democratic Party of Japan (SDPJ).

Although tracing its origins back to the first parties established in the 1870s, the LDP was constituted in its present form in November 1955, when two conservative parties, the Liberals, led by Taketora Ogata, and the Japan Democratic Party, led by Prime Minister Ichiro Hatoyama, united.

Traditionally, the party has enjoyed strong support in rural areas, these constituencies being currently substantially over-represented in the Diet, in voter–deputy terms, vis-à-vis the growing urban districts. It also enjoys liberal funding from the business community, both small and large, and has developed, during its years in government, close links with the bureaucracy. About a quarter of LDP Diet members are former civil servants, often of senior rank.

Although viewed as 'conservative' in its ideological outlook, the LDP is, in reality, more of a 'catch-all' organization, embracing a broad and shifting variety of domestic and foreign affairs policy ideas which are applied in a pragmatic and corporatist manner. Its uniting principles, however, are a belief in the efficacy of private enterprise, support for the development of a welfare state, and a continuation of Japan's alliance with the United States.

Membership of the LDP was put at 3 million in 1990, corresponding to 2.4% of the total population. However, the party lacks an effective constituency, grass-roots, organization in the West European sense and is notably divided into factions based on personalities, rather than ideology.

In the early 1990s, there were half a dozen important factions, the leading one being the Takeshita faction, which contained more than 100 Diet members. These groupings, which involve the development of personalized patron–client ties between senior leaders and younger aspirants, have operated as a means of promoting the ministerial interests of the former, while advancing the careers of the latter, by step-by-step progression up the political ladder. Based on the Japanese emphasis on the neo-Confucianist principles of duty and obligation and traditional respect for family and personal ties, currently a third of the LDP's Diet members are related to another member by blood or marriage. The existence of factions has served to institutionalize competition within the party. At the local level, factional groupings bargain for acceptance of their members as party candidates in multimember constituencies. However, the ultimate goal of a faction is to secure for its leader the coveted post of LDP president. This is assigned biennially by a majority vote of the party's Diet members. Between 1955 and 1993 this post went with that of prime minister.

Undermined by financial scandals involving faction leaders, notably Takeshita, Kiichi Miyazawa, and Shin Kanemaru, the LDP's hegemony crumbled during the early 1990s and the party splintered in 1993, with the formation of two new parties, Shinseito (Japan Renewal Party) and Shinto Sakigake (New Party Harbinger), by ex-members of the LDP who were committed to reform of Japan's political system. Shinseito included many former members of the LDP faction led by Tsutomu Hata and the ambitious LDP secretary-general, Ichiro Ozawa. Sakigake was led by Masayoshi Takemura. A year earlier, in 1992, another centre-right reform party, the Japan New Party (JNP), was set up by Morihiro Hosokawa, a former LDP governor.

More than 10,000 political parties are registered as functioning in Japan. Only five parties other than the LDP and its recent offshoots are, however, significant forces. The second ranking party in the country and leading opposition body is the 127,000-member Social Democratic Party of Japan (SDPJ: Nippon Shakaito), formerly known as the Japan

Socialist Party (JSP). The SDPJ traces its roots back to the Socialist Party, which was established in 1925, but was allowed to play only a tangential role in interwar politics. The JSP, itself, was set up in November 1946 and temporarily held power between May 1947 and March 1948. The party subsequently split, in 1951–52, over its response to the US-Japanese Peace Treaty, but reunited in 1955. Formerly, it favoured a democratic socialist economic strategy and the establishment of a nonaggressive mutual security system, embracing Japan, China, the United States, and the USSR. However, since April 1990 it has adopted a social democratic policy programme and in September 1994 abandoned its traditional pacifist stance. Strongest in urban areas and among unionized workers, it is closely linked to the General Council of Trade Unions of Japan (Sohyo), with a membership of over 4 million. Support for the party has, however, fallen somewhat since the 1960s, when its share of the national vote stood at 27–29%. The party's formation, in 1994, of a 'grand coalition' with its traditional enemy, the LDP, and Sakigake, has created unease and divisions within the SDPJ and in January 1995 deputies from the right wing of the party, led by former chairperson Sadao Yamahana, formed a new parliamentary bloc, the Minshu Rengo–Minshu Shinto Club (Democratic League–Democratic New Club). In May 1995, at an extraordinary national convention, the SDPJ voted in favour of a leadership plan to dissolve the party and form a new one.

Further to the left stands the Japanese Communist Party (JCP: Nippon Kyosanto), which was founded in 1922, though subsequently banned until 1945, its leaders being imprisoned or exiled. Support for the JCP has increased since the early 1970s, following its assertion of independence from both the Sino and Soviet communist ideological camps, its renouncing of a call for violent revolution, and its focusing on economic and social improvement. The JCP is a mass party, with around 460,000 members. It is organized on hierarchical, 'democratic centralist' lines and controlled by a Presidium (Politburo) chaired by Kenji Miyamoto.

Occupying centre-left ground is the 'humanitarian socialist' Komeito (Clean Government Party), which was formed in November 1964 as the political wing of the 8-million-member Soka Gakkai Buddhist sect, Value Creation Society, which was itself established in 1930. It has a membership of 210,000. The party has campaigned for greater honesty in politics and improving the lot of the poor. It draws much of its support from workers, especially female, in small and medium-sized urban industries. The party's religious affiliation has, however, tended to hamper its development.

Also on the centre left is the Democratic Socialist Party (DSP: Minshato), formed in January 1960 by a right-wing faction which broke away from the JSP, in opposition to its alleged Marxist tendencies. The DSP favours the operation of a mixed economy, with greater welfare provision and selective nationalization. It currently has a membership of 72,000.

The United Social Democratic Party (USDP: Shaminren), formed in 1977 as a minor breakaway from the JSP, is also a minor political force of some note.

In December 1994, in an important political development, a new opposition coalition party was formed, Shinshinto (New Frontier Party). This combined the JNP, Shinseito, the DSP, and Komeito, which would be disbanded. Ichiro Ozawa was elected leader of the party in December 1995. The DSP and Komeito leaders, Takashi Yonezawa and Koshiro Ishida, are its vice presidents. It served to reverse the recent trend towards the fragmentation of Japanese party politics and to establish an effective two-party system, pitting the New Frontier Party against the incumbent LDP, SDPJ, and Sakigake coalition.

Latest elections

The most recent House of Representatives elections were held on 18 July 1993 and resulted in the first national defeat for the LDP since the party's formation in 1955. The LDP, with a 37% share of the national vote compared to 46% in 1990, won 223 of the 511 contested seats, 52 fewer than in 1990. The Shinseito and Shinto Sakigake parties, formed just before the election as breakaways from the LDP, captured 55 and 13 seats, and 10% and 3% of the popular vote respectively, while the one-year-old JNP secured 35 seats and an 8% share of the vote. The main opposition force, the SDPJ, polled less strongly than in 1990, winning just 70 seats and 15% of the vote, while Komeito captured 51 seats and 8% of the vote, the JCP and DSP 15 seats each, based on 8% and 4% respective vote shares, and Shaminren, four seats. Nine hundred and fifty-five candidates, including just 70 females, contested the elections, held in 129 multimember constituencies, but turnout, at 67%, was low by Japanese standards. Twelve female deputies secured election.

The latest elections for half the seats of the 252-member House of Councillors were held on 23 July 1995 and saw a sharp fall in support for the SDPJ, which retained only 16 of its 41 contested seats, and voter apathy, with turnout, at 44.5%, a record low. The new opposition Shinshinto party won 40 seats, the LDP 49, the JCP 8, and Sakigake 3. After this election, the ruling LDP–SDPJ–Sakigake coalition held 151 of the 252 upper house seats, with the LDP's share standing at 110.

Political history

Originally inhabited by Ainu people, Japan was invaded and settled from an early date by Manchu-Koreans and Malayans. In the 5th century AD the country was unified by the Yamato state, and, in the 6th century, Buddhism was introduced from Korea and Confucianist culture from China. During the 7th century a centralized monarchy on Chinese lines was established, but by the 12th century power had devolved to regional potentates, subservient to a paramount generalissimo, termed shogun. After a period of decentralization, the Tokugawa family, initially under the leadership of Iyeyasu (1542–1616), reunified the country during the later 16th century, establishing a new capital at Edo, now Tokyo, in central Honshu and creating a bureaucratized and demilitarized quasi-feudal system. From this date, despite self-imposed isolation from the outside world, considerable economic progress was made.

Military pressure from the Western powers, particularly the United States, forced an end to this isolation in the mid-19th century and, fearing colonial invasion, reformist elements within the *samurai* or military caste bureaucracy united with southwestern regional lords (*daimyo*) to overthrow the Tokugawa Shogunate, 1603–1867, and restore executive power to the young emperor Meiji Tenno in 1867. His family, based at Kyoto, had previously been Tokugawa puppets. To buttress imperial authority, Shintoism was established as the state religion, and the emperor was defined as the 'Divine Ruler'. During the next two decades after this 'Meiji Restoration', the feudal system was abolished, *samurai* and *daimyo* lords were pensioned off, the land system was reformed, and a new constitutional system, with an elected assembly and Westernized legal code, was established.

The radical reforms of the early Meiji era constituted a 'revolution from above', carried out by a small clique of nationalistic members of the former Tokugawa bureaucracy, termed the 'Genro', who were to remain the real power wielders, rather than the emperor, until the strengthening of party government during the interwar years. Impelled by a concern to 'catch up' with the West, they oversaw the rapid development of new industries and the build-up of a modern new army and navy. In conflicts in 1894–5 and 1904–5 respectively, China and Russia were defeated, and new colonies were secured, in the form of Formosa, now Taiwan, South Manchuria, Korea, and south Sakhalin. Rapid economic advance was achieved during the World War I and during the 1920s, the 'Taisho era', and there was movement towards democracy and party government, after the electorate had been substantially enlarged by the Reform Acts of 1919 and 1925. The 1925 Act established universal male suffrage for those of 25 years and over.

During the later 1920s, however, with economic conditions deteriorating, army leaders and ultra-nationalists gained the upper hand, launching the nation on an ultimately destructive phase of imperialist expansion. This began with the occupation of Manchuria in 1931, was followed by the invasion of China in 1937, and then war with the United States and Britain, after Japan's pre-emptive attack on the US Pearl Harbor naval base in Hawaii, in December 1941. Initially, during the early stages of the war, Japan successfully took control of much of the Asia–Oceania region, between Burma and the Philippines. By 1944, however, it was in retreat and, on 15 August 1945, following the United States' dropping of atomic bombs on Hiroshima and Nagasaki, Emperor Hirohito (1901–89) was compelled to tender the nation's unconditional surrender. An Allied control commission assumed charge and Japan was placed under military occupation by Allied, chiefly United States, troops, commanded by General Douglas MacArthur (1880–1964). In April 1952 the US-Japanese Peace Treaty came into force and full sovereignty was regained.

As a consequence of Japan's military defeat, Korea was made independent, Manchuria and Formosa were returned to China, and the small, former German, Pacific islands, that had been mandated to Japan after World War I, were now placed by the United Nations under American trusteeship. Japan was subsequently to regain the islands of Ryukyu, in 1972, and Bonin and Volcano, in 1968, from the United States. However, despite frequent appeals, the Northern Territories, which include the islands of the Shikotan and Habomai group, and the southernmost Kurils, which include Kunashiri and Etorofu, are still controlled by the Russian Federation and have not been returned.

During the immediate postwar phase of Allied rule, between August 1945 and April 1952, a sweeping 'democratization campaign' was launched, involving radical land, social, and educational reform and the framing of a new 'Peace constitution', in 1946. Under it, Emperor Hirohito was persuaded to renounce his claims to divinity and become a figurehead constitutional monarch, while the nation, through Article 9, committed itself to a pacific foreign policy. During the 1950s Japan concentrated on economic reconstruction, retreating towards neutralism in foreign affairs, under the protection of the American umbrella provided by the September 1951 Security Pact.

Postwar Japanese politics were dominated by the new Liberal Democratic Party (LDP), which was formed in 1955 by the merger of existing conservative parties. It was to provide the country with a regular succession of prime ministers. Real decision-making authority, however, became focused on a broader, consensual, corporatist grouping of politicians, senior civil servants, and directors of the major *zaibatsu* finance and industrial houses. Through a paternalist, guided approach to economic development, which was epitomized by the operations of the influential Ministry for International Trade and Industry (MITI), and by the inspired targeting of, and investment in, promising new transport, consumerdurable, and electronics growth industries, the Japanese economy expanded dramatically during the 1950s and 1960s, with GDP regularly advancing at an annual rate of 10%. During these years, Japan was also rehabilitated within the international community, entering the United Nations in 1958, re-establishing diplomatic relations with Western nations, and, following the lead taken by America's Nixon presidency, with communist China, in 1972.

In 1960 and 1968–9 Japan's hitherto tranquil internal politics were rocked by violent demonstrations against alleged American domination, involving the anarchic 'Red Army' terrorist organization. These were followed, in December 1974, by the resignation of Prime Minister Kakuei Tanaka (1918–93), in the wake of a bribery scandal, involving the American Lockheed Corporation. This culminated in Tanaka's arrest and resignation from the LDP, in July 1976, and his later conviction and sentence to four years' imprisonment, in October 1983. This scandal seriously tarnished the image of the LDP and led to the loss of its majority in the House of Representatives in the general election of December 1976. It also resulted in the formation of the New Liberal Club, as a breakaway grouping. The LDP remained in power, however, as the largest single party within the Diet.

During the 1970s and early 1980s, Japanese economic growth continued, though at a reduced annual rate of 4.5%, the country making a major impact on the markets of the United States and Europe, as an exporter of electrical goods, machinery, motor vehicles, and new high-technology items. By 1985 Japan had become the world's largest exporter of manufactured goods, surpassing the United States and (West) Germany. The growth in Japan's trade surplus and, in particular, the concentration of the country's export activity in a few sensitive sectors, served to create resentment overseas, however, as economic recession began to grip Europe and the United States between 1979 and 1982. This led to calls for Japan to open up its internal market to foreign exporters and to assume a greater share of the defence burden for the Asia–Pacific region. Prime ministers Takeo Miki (1974–76), Takeo Fukuda (1976–78), Masayoshi Ohira (1978–80), and Zenko Suzuki (1980–82) firmly resisted these pressures, and the Japanese government, in 1976, imposed a rigid 1% of GNP limit on the level of defence spending permissible.

However, under Prime Minister Yasuhiro Nakasone (b. 1917), who assumed power in November 1982, a review of policy was instituted. Nakasone favoured a strengthening of Japan's defence capability, a re-evaluation of attitudes towards the country's past, and the introduction of a more liberal, open-market economic strategy at home. These proposed policy departures proved controversial and could only partially be implemented. However, the forthright Nakasone emerged as a popular national figure and, after becoming, in November 1984, the first prime minister since Eisaku Sato, who had governed between 1964 and 1972, to be re-elected as LDP leader for more than one term, succeeded in securing a landslide victory in the July 1986 general election. In this contest, the LDP, after having experienced its worst ever reverse in the previous national poll of December 1983, achieved its highest level of popular support since 1963 and a record number of seats in the House of Councillors.

Soon after the July 1986 election the by-laws of the LDP were altered so as to allow party presidents a one-year extension beyond the normal limit of two two-year terms each, thus effectively extending Nakasone's tenure as prime minister until November 1987. During his final year in office, Nakasone introduced a sweeping tax reform bill, aimed at restoring 'justice and flexibility' to an archaic system, but was forced, because of Diet opposition, to make major compromises, including the withdrawal of plans to introduce a 5% value-added tax (VAT). Despite this political 'defeat', Nakasone remained sufficiently influential within the LDP, and popular outside, to effectively hand pick his successor as party and national leader. He nominated LDP secretary general, Noboru Takeshita (b. 1924), after a factional deadlock within the party.

The new prime minister pledged a continuation of his predecessor's domestic and foreign policies, including improving and extending the country's diplomatic relations, reintroducing a tax reform bill, and making a determined effort to reduce its record $86,690-million balance-of-payments surplus. Takeshita had notable personal success in the area of tax reform, a bill being passed by the House of Representatives in 1988 which lowered income tax and introduced a national sales tax at 3%. This measure proved, however, to be electorally unpopular. More seriously, the new government's popular standing was undermined by the eruption, in July 1988, of the 'Recruit Cosmos scandal'. This involved 'insider' share dealing, indirectly and directly, by senior party figures including Takeshita, Nakasone, and Finance Minister Kiichi Miyazawa (b. 1919). The latter resigned in December 1988, to be followed by Justice Minister Takashi Hasegawa and Deputy Prime Minister Ken

Harada in January 1989. Finally, in April 1989, with the government's and the LDP's popularity ratings standing at the unprecedentedly low levels of 4% and 25% respectively, Takeshita announced that he would resign as soon as the annual budget was passed and a successor found. His replacement, in June 1989, was the former foreign minister, Sosuke Uno (b. 1922).

After barely 53 days in office, Uno, who was dogged by a geisha sex scandal and whose party endured loss of control of the upper house in the elections of July 1989, announced his intention to step down, in turn, as soon as a successor could be found. This marked an inauspicious start to the new Heisei ('achievement of universal peace') era, which had been proclaimed following the death, in January 1989, of Hirohito (*Showa*) and the accession to the imperial throne of his son, Akihito (b. 1933). In August 1989, Uno's eventual successor as premier was Toshiki Kaifu (b. 1932), a former education minister and a member of the LDP's small, scandal-free Komoto faction. He formed a new cabinet whose members were comparatively young and which, in an attempt to counter the growing appeal to women of the JSP, led by Ms Takako Doi (b. 1929), included two women. The JSP gained 50 seats in the February 1990 Diet election, but the LDP held on to power, capturing 46% of the national vote, down 3% on 1986.

During the Gulf conflict of 1990–91, Japan pledged $13 billion to support the US-led anti-Iraq coalition. Prime Minister Kaifu failed in his attempt to persuade the Diet to approve a bill authorizing the sending there of unarmed, noncombatant military personnel. However, in 1992 a modified Peacekeeping Cooperation Act was passed. Kaifu also failed to secure passage of an electoral reform bill. Though embarrassed from the autumn of 1991 by new securities and crime syndicate (*yakuza*) scandals, the LDP, led by the popular Kaifu, polled strongly in the local elections of April 1991. Nevertheless, Kaifu was replaced in October 1991 as LDP leader and prime minister by the Recruit-implicated ex-finance minister, Kiichi Miyazawa.

The new administration was faced by economic slowdown. Its standing was further damaged by the Sagawa Kyubin financial scandal in which many leading figures within the LDP, including the Takeshita faction to 'kingmaker', Shin Kanemaru, who was arrested and sent for trial, were implicated. Kanemaru's removal led the powerful Takeshita faction split into two groups, led by Keizo Obuchi, who had the support of Noboru Takeshita, and by Tsutomu Hata (b. 1936), who was backed by the LDP's secretary general, Ichiro Ozawa (b. 1942). The Hata faction, which was committed to reform of the Japanese political system in an effort to end the scourge of 'money politics', eventually broke with the LDP in June 1993. By voting with the opposition on a no-confidence motion, it brought down the Miyazawa administration and when a general election was called, Hata and Ozawa formed the new Shinseito (Japan Renewal Party) party. Along with Shinto Sakigake (New Party Harbinger), which had been concurrently formed by LDP rebels, and the Japan New Party, set up in 1992 by Morihiro Hosokawa (b. 1938) with the intention of cleansing the political system, and the older centrist and left-of-centre Komeito, DSP, and SDPJ, Shinseito succeeded in ousting the LDP from power in the general election of July 1993, as LDP support slumped to just 37% of the national vote.

The new party coalition government was headed by the popular Morihiro Hosokawa, who was drawn from a distinguished *samurai* (military caste) and was a member of the LDP until 1990, with Tsutomu Hata, serving as foreign minister and deputy prime minister. Its top priorities were to reform the system for electing Diet members and funding political parties and to reflate the economy. A watered-down constitutional reform bill was accepted by both chambers of the Diet in January 1994, providing for replacement of the House of Representative's multimember constituencies by 300 single-member constituencies, with a further 200 deputies to be returned by proportional representation. However, financial scandals, albeit relatively minor, involving Ozawa and Hosokawa, surfaced during 1993–94 and persuaded Hosokawa to resign in April 1994. He was replaced as prime minister by Tsutomu Hata, on 25 April 1994, but immediately the SDPJ left the ruling coalition. This was ascribed to the party's concern that they had been excluded from a new parliamentary group, Kaishin (Innovation), which had been formed by Ozawa and comprised the JNP, Shinseito, the DSP, and recent new defectors from the LDP. Hata thus headed a minority administration and, facing the prospect of defeat on a no-confidence motion, resigned as prime minister on 25 June 1994.

An improbable 'grand coalition' government was formed on 29 June 1994 by the SDPJ, LDP, and Sakigake, with the SDPJ's chairperson, Tomiichi Murayama (b. 1924), serving as prime minister and the LDP's president until September 1995, Yohei Kono (b. 1937), as foreign minister and deputy prime minister. The SDPJ and LDP, erstwhile enemies, were united by a shared opposition to the political aspirations of Ichiro Ozawa and concern at what they viewed as the overly rapid pace of recent economic deregulation and political reform. The coalition created divisions within both the SDPJ and LDP, but also encouraged the opposition to unite in a new coalition party, Shinshinto (New Frontier Party: NFP) in December 1994, one month before a serious earthquake struck the city of Kobe, claiming 6,000 lives and damage estimated at $40 billion. Shinshinto brought together and superseded the JNP, DSP, Komeito, and Shinseito. Led by the popular, former LDP premier, Toshiki Kaifu, and assisted by Ichiro Ozawa, it comprised 214 Diet members and represented a serious future electoral threat to the LDP. The political mood remained uncertain through 1995 as the economy was afflicted by recession, rising levels of unemployment, a falling stockmarket, and decreasing bank reserves, while the public was concerned by the activities of the Aum Shinrikyo religious cult, which was implicated in a terrifying and fatal poison-gas attack in March 1995 on the Tokyo subway. In July 1995, the SDPJ polled poorly in elections to the House of Councillors. Murayama remained as prime minister and in August 1995 made a formal apology for Japanese atrocities during World War II. However, Yohei Kono stood down as the LDP's leader in September 1995 in the face of a challenge from Ryutaro Hashimoto, the populist-conservative international trade and industry minister who became prime minister in 1996.

KAZAKHSTAN

Republic of Kazakhstan
Kazak Respublikasy

Capital: Almaty (Alma-Ata)*
*To be replaced as capital in 2000 by the northern city of Akmola

Social and economic data
Area: 2,717,300 km^2
Population: 17,200,000*
Pop. density per capita: 6*
Urban population: 58%**
Literacy rate: 97%**
GDP: $30,700 million**; per-capita GDP: $1,800**
Government defence spending (% of GDP): 3.9%**
Currency: tenge
Economy type: middle income
Labour force in agriculture: 22%**

*1994
**1992

Ethnic composition
Forty per cent of the population is of Kazakh ethnic stock, 38% ethnic Russians, 6% German, 5% Ukrainian, 2% Uzbek, and 2% Tatar. All nationalities are guaranteed equal status by the constitution, but there have been increasing tensions in eastern Kazakhstan between the Russian-speaking Cossack community and ethnic Kazakhs. In northern Kazakhstan ethnic Russians form a majority of the population and separatist sentiments are growing. The official language, since 1989, has been Kazakh, a member of the Central Turkic language group, but Russian is also used as a language of interethnic communication.

Religions

The Kazakhs, who were converted to Islam in the 19th century, are predominantly Sunni Muslims of the Hanafi school. Since 1985, many new mosques have been opened. The ethnic Russians adhere to the Russian Orthodox Church and there are also significant Protestant, chiefly Baptist, and Roman Catholic communities. The republic is a secular state.

Political features

State type: authoritarian nationalist
Date of state formation: 1991
Political structure: unitary
Executive: unlimited presidential
Assembly: two-chamber
Party structure: multiparty
Human rights rating: N/A
International affiliations: CIS, EBRD, ECO, IAEA, IBRD, IMF, NACC, OIC (observer), OSCE, PFP, UN

Local and regional government

There are 19 regions and two cities, each with elected local governments, and below there are city and rural districts, towns, and villages with local councils.

Head of state (executive)

President Nursultan Nazarbayev, since 1990

Head of government

Prime Minister Akezhan Kazhageldin, since 1994

Political leaders since 1970

1989– Nursultan Nazarbayev (ex-communist independent)*

*Leader of the Communist Party from 1989 and president from 1990

Political system

Under the terms of the constitution of January 1993, Kazakhstan has a limited presidential executive system. Supreme executive power is held by a president popularly elected for a five-year term and who must have a fluent knowledge of Kazakh. The president works with a prime minister and a Council of Ministers of some 30 members. Legislative authority is held by the 177-member Supreme Kenges. One hundred and thirty-five of its members are elected for four-year terms in single-member constituencies, the other 42 are drawn from a 'state list' selected by national and regional government officials. However, President Nazarbayev dismissed the Supreme Kenges in March 1995 and governed by decree, pending the election of a new parliament. It is expected that the latter will be a smaller two-chamber body if proposed constitutional changes, set to be put before the public in a referendum later in 1995, are approved.

Political parties

The main political parties are the Socialist Party of Kazakhstan, known until September 1991 as the Kazakh Communist Party (KCP); the pro-Nazarbayev Congress of People's Unity of Kazakhstan (SNEK), which opposes radical nationalism and promotes social and ethnic harmony and is led by Kuanysh Sultanov; and the centrist People's Congress of Kazakhstan (NKK; estd. 1991), led by Olzhas Sulimeinov, a former environmental campaigner. An important nationalist opposition party is the Republican Party (Azat), led by Kamal Ormantayev. It forms part of a 32-member 'constructive opposition bloc' in the Supreme Kenges, formed in May 1994, which is concerned at preventing the growth of 'political dictatorship' and includes the NKK, the Socialist Party, the nationalist Jeltoqsan National Democratic Party, the Workers' Movement of Kazakhstan, and the ethnic Slav Lad ('harmony') movement, led by Aleksandra Dokuchayeva.

Latest elections

The most recent Supreme Kenges elections were held on 7 March 1994 and resulted in victory for supporters of President Nazarbayev. The pro-Nazarbayev SNEK won 30 seats, the Trades Union Federation, 11, the NKK, 9, the Socialist Party, 8, Lad ('harmony') Movement of ethnic Slavs, 4, and 59 nominal independents were elected. Turnout was officially put at 73.5%. Sixty per cent of the seats were won by ethnic Kazakhs. Opposition candidates had difficulty in gaining publicity during the campaign and faced harassment by the authorities, with 220 candidates being disqualified by appointed local election committees. However, in March 1995 the Constitutional Court voided the results of the general election on the grounds that the principle of 'one man, one vote' had been offended and constituency boundaries had been tampered with.

The last direct presidential election was held on 1 December 1991 and the unopposed victor was the incumbent Nursultan Nazarbayev, who secured 98.8% of the vote. On 29 April 1995 Nazarbayev's tenure was extended by a plebiscite to December 2000, thus postponing an election due in 1996. It was claimed officially that Nazarbayev received a 95.4% vote in this referendum, with turnout at 90%.

Political history

The Kazakhs are descendants of Mongol and Turkic tribes who settled in the region early in the Christian era. They established their own distinctive tribal confederation, the Kazakh Orda, between the late 15th and early 17th centuries, but then split into large nomadic federations, known as the Large, Middle, and Lesser Hordes led by Khans (chiefs). The Hordes, militarily threatened by Oirot Mongols from the east, turned to the Russian tsar for protection during the 18th century. Russian control became gradually tighter between 1822 and 1848, with the Khans being deposed, and in the later 19th century many Russian and Ukrainian peasants were resettled in the region. This caused resentment, leading to a fierce rebellion against Russian rule in 1916 in which 150,000 were killed. The Russian Revolution of 1917 led to civil war in Kazakhstan, but in 1920 it joined the USSR as an autonomous republic and became a full union republic in 1936. During the early 1930s more than a million people died in Kazakhstan as a result of starvation and repression associated with the Soviet agricultural collectivization programme. During the early 1940s, under the orders of the Soviet dictator Josef Stalin, large numbers of Germans were deported from the Volga region to the republic. Northern Kazakhstan was the site of the Soviet leader Nikita Khrushchev's ambitious 'virgin lands' agricultural extension programme during the 1950s, which not only led to overcropping and harvest failures during the early 1960s and desiccation of the Aral Sea, but also to a large influx of Russian settlers, who had numbered just 20% of the population in 1926, turning the Kazakhs into a minority in their own republic. Nuclear testing sites established in eastern Kazakhstan, new industries, and the Baikonur space centre at Leninsk also drew in Slav settlers.

There were violent nationalist riots in the capital, Almaty, in December 1986 when the long-serving and corrupt Brezhnevite Kazakh Communist Party (KCP) leader, Dinmukahmed Kunayev, was effectively sacked by the reformist Soviet leader Mikhail Gorbachev and replaced by an ethnic Russian, Gennadi Kolbin. Four people died. In June 1989 Nursultan Nazarbayev (b. 1940), an astute, nationalist-minded, 'reform-communist' who had been the republic's prime minister since 1984, assumed leadership of the KCP and in February 1990 became the republic's President. Nazarbayev embarked on a pragmatic programme of cultural and market-centred economic reform, involving the privatization of the service and housing sectors, and drawing on the advice of outside South Korean and Singaporean economists, and also pressed for greater economic autonomy for the republic, which declared its sovereignty in October 1990.

During the spring of 1991 President Nazarbayev, a member of the Politburo of the Communist Party of the Soviet Union, pressed for the signing of a new USSR Union Treaty 'of sovereign states with equal rights', and 94% of the electorate supported continuation of the Union in the all-USSR referendum of March 1991. Nazarbayev also stood out against the August 1991 anti-Gorbachev attempted coup in Moscow, describing it as 'illegal and unconstitutional' and tendering his resignation from the Communist Party of the Soviet Union and its Politburo. Soon after the coup was thwarted, the KCP was abolished. However, Nazarbayev played a key role in ensuring that the 'uncontrolled disintegration' of the USSR was averted and that non-Slav republics joined the new Commonwealth of Independent States (CIS), which was formed on 21 December 1991 at Almaty.

The independence of Kazakhstan, which was the last of the republics of the USSR to leave the Union, was formally recognized by the United States and other Western nations in January 1992 and it was admitted into the Conference on Security and Cooperation in Europe (CSCE, later the OSCE) in the same month. It became a member of the United Nations in March 1992. Kazakhstan inherited substantial nuclear forces from the USSR, including 1,410 warheads of SS-18 strategic missiles. However, the Nazarbayev administration pledged to gradually remove these, commencing in 1992 with tactical weapons, and to become nuclear-free. The latter pledge was achieved in 1995. In December 1993 the state ratified the START-1 disarmament treaty and Nuclear Non-Proliferation Treaty. Kazakhstan was also at the forefront of the formation, in 1994, of a structured economic, social and military union with neighbouring Kyrgyzstan and Uzbekistan, entailing coordination of economic, monetary, and labour policies and the free movement of goods, services, capital, and labour among the states.

President Nazarbayev, who secured a popular mandate in December 1991, which was reratified by a referendum held in April 1995, sought to rule in a non-party and non-sectarian consensual manner and to press on with market-centred and outward-looking economic reforms, while limiting the pace of political change. However, there were indications of creeping authoritarianism by the mid-1990s, with the president ruling by decree and avoiding a direct election in 1996. Mass privatizations commenced in November 1993, with the aim of privatizing a third of the economy by mid-1995, and joint-venture agreements were signed with foreign companies to develop the nation's immense gas, oil, and uranium reserves. However, during the early 1990s the restructuring programme led to annual declines in GDP exceeding 10% and a spiralling rate of inflation, causing popular unrest, while the emigration of hundreds of thousands of ethnic Russians and Germans also damaged the economy. The government of Prime Minister Sergei Tereshchenko, after being criticized by President Nazarbayev and by parliamentary deputies for its handling of the economy, resigned in October 1994 and Akezhan Kazhageldin became prime minister. The new administration sought to improve relations with Russia, which still controlled nearly all of the oil pipelines out of Central Asia, by signing an agreement in Moscow in January 1995 which provided for the establishment of joint armed forces by the end of 1995 and closer economic ties. However, bills to give the Russian language equal status to Kazakh, in an effort to assuage the country's large and important ethnic Russian minority, and to allow the privatization of land, were rejected by parliament. This prompted President Nazarbayev, taking advantage of a Constitutional Court ruling that the recent March 1994 general elections had been technically illegal as a result of a tampering with constituency boundaries, to dissolve parliament in March 1995 and rule by decree until fresh elections were held. A new constitution, approved in a referendum in August 1995 was criticized as reducing democratic freedoms by banning the formation of trade unions in state institutions, preventing dual citizenship, and replacing the Constitutional Court with a Constitutional Council, whose decisions would be subject to presidential veto.

NORTH KOREA

Democratic People's Republic of North Korea (DPRK)
Chosun Minchu-chui Inmin Konghwa-guk

Capital: Pyongyang

Social and economic data
Area: 120,538 km^2
Population: 23,100,000*
Pop. density per km^2: 192*
Urban population: 59%**
Literacy rate: 90%**
GDP: $29,000 million**; per-capita GDP: $1,285**
Government defence spending (% of GDP): 25.2%**
Currency: North Korean won
Economy type: middle income
Labour force in agriculture: 32%**

*1994
**1992

Ethnic composition
With the exception of a Chinese minority of 50,000, the population is fully Korean. The official language is Korean.

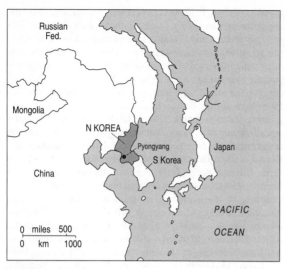

Russian Fed.

Mongolia

N KOREA

Pyongyang

S Korea

Japan

China

PACIFIC

OCEAN

0 miles 500
0 km 1000

Religions
Buddhism, Confucianism, Chondism, and Daoism are the traditional religions. Today, however, they enjoy apparently little support, their practice having been actively discouraged by a communist regime which sponsors atheism.

Political features
State type: communist
Date of state formation: 1948
Political structure: unitary
Executive: communist
Assembly: one-chamber
Party structure: one-party (E)
Human rights rating: 20%
International affiliations: ESCAP, G-77, IAEA, LORCS, NAM, UN

(E) – Effective

Local and regional government
The country is divided into nine provinces and two cities, below which there are urban districts, regular cities, and more than 150 counties. Each political unit has a Local People's Assembly, elected every four years at the provincial level and every two years below, which convenes once a year and 'elects' a Local People's Committee as its permanent executive organ.

Head of state
President Kim Jong Il, since 1994

Head of government
Prime Minister Kang Song San, since 1992

Political leaders since 1970*
1948–94 Kim Il Sung (KWP), 1994–   Kim Jong Il (KWP)

*Communist Party leader

Political system
North Korea's original socialist constitution was adopted in September 1948, being based closely on the 1936 USSR's 'Stalin constitution' model. It was superseded in December 1972 by the current 149-article version, which describes the People's Republic as a 'socialist state' in the stage of the 'dictatorship of the proletariat'. Significant, specifically Korean, departures from the earlier Soviet model are included in the document, most notably the stress that is placed on national self-reliance, called *chuche sasang*, or *juche*, the use of mass mobilization tactics (*chongsalli*), and all-pervasive party control (*te an*). In addition, the document also specifically embraces, in Article 5, the goal of national reunification, by 'peaceful means'.

Under the 1972 constitution, the sole and supreme organ of state power is the Supreme People's Assembly (SPA), or Choe Ko In Min Hoe Ui, a one-chamber body which comprises 687 members elected for four-year terms in single-member constituencies from a list of candidates put forward by the Democratic Front for the Reunification of the Fatherland (DFRF), which dates from 1946. The SPA convenes twice a year for short sessions, lasting several days, in the spring and autumn and 'elects' a 15-member Standing Committee to act for it when it is not sitting. It also elects a 15-member Central People's Committee (CPC), which the constitution describes as the 'supreme leadership organ of state power'. This is headed by the president of the republic.

The CPC determines domestic and foreign policy, can issue decrees and oversees the work of People's Committees below. It also supervises the day-to-day central executive, in the shape of the State Administrative Council (SAC), a 46-member body comprising 17 departmental ministers, 14 state commission chairpersons and nine vice premiers. The SAC is headed by the prime minister, who is elected by the SPA. Members of the SAC are appointed and dismissed by the CPC.

It is, however, the president of the republic who is the leading figure in the DPRK's presidentialist political system. Elected for renewable four-year terms by the SPA, the president is commander in chief of the armed forces and chairperson of the National Defence Commission. In addition, the president is empowered to issue edicts, preside over SAC meetings and 'guide' the work of the CPC.

The controlling force, and sole permitted political party, in the DPRK is the Communist Party (Korean Workers' Party: KWP). The party leads the broader DFRF mass organization, which includes the minor Korean Social Democratic Party and the Chondoist Chongu Party, and puts forward a single slate of candidates in elections. Its leading members also hold senior state posts.

The overriding and distinctive feature of the DPRK political system has been the extent to which it was dominated between 1948 and 1994 by a charismatic leader, Kim Il Sung (1912–94), who served as both KWP general secretary and state president. Depicted, in a Confucianist manner, as the nation's 'fatherly leader' and 'Sun of Mankind', Kim Il Sung established an extraordinarily pervasive personality cult. A unique 'socialist dynasty' was constructed, with his son, Kim Jong Il, the 'designated heir', taking over as the new 'Great Leader' and effective state leader on his father's death in July 1994. In addition, Kim Il Sung's younger brother, Kim Yong-Ju, re-emerged in December 1993, after 18 years in the political wilderness, to become a member of the KWP's Politburo and a state vice president.

Political parties

The ruling Korean Workers' Party (KWP: Chosun No-Dong Dang) was established in October 1945, with the title Korean Communist Party (KCP), in the North Korean zone occupied by Soviet forces. It was a coalition of communist-leaning groups who had variously been based in the USSR, China, the 'Yanan faction', and Manchuria and Korea, where they operated underground as anti-Japanese resistance fighters, prior to World War II. In August 1946 the party adopted the designation North Korean Workers' Party (NKWP), when its Chinese-trained wing, termed the New People's Party, merged with the KCP. In June 1949 it assumed its present name when the NKWP merged with the banned South Korean Workers' Party, led by Pak Hon-Yong.

The party was led, until his death in 1994, by the peasant-born Kim Il Sung, who had originally founded the Manchuria-based Korean People's Revolutionary Army in 1932. It enjoyed strong initial Soviet support. By the mid-1950s, following a series of purges of opposing factions, Kim established an unchallenged control over the party machine and, thereafter, proceeded to develop a unique, personalized, and Maoist- and Korean-nationalist influenced policy approach, officially termed 'Kim Il Sungism', which diverged significantly from post-Stalin Soviet communism. Founded on 'mass-line' mobilization methods and based on constant propagandizing, tight secret police control, and blanket censorship, it has moulded the most highly regimented and controlled society in the contemporary world.

The KWP is organized hierarchically on 'democratic centralist' lines, with small, 3–100-member, workplace 'cells' established at its base, district, and county committees higher up, all leading to a supra 2,000-member national Party Congress. The Party Congress, which is formally the supreme party organ, convenes, in theory, quinquennially, although only three Congresses were, in fact, called between 1961 and 1980. It 'elects' a Central Committee (CC) of about 250 members to assume authority when it is not in session. The CC meets several times a year in full session and, in turn, 'elects' a Politburo, with around 16 full and 18 non-voting 'alternate members', and a Secretariat, headed by the general secretary, to control party, and state, affairs. The Politburo has been dominated traditionally by an 'inner cabinet', or Presidium, but by the spring of 1995, following the deaths of Kim Il Sung and Oh Jin Woo, Kim Jong Il was left as the sole surviving Presidium member.

Membership of the KWP in 1987 totalled 3 million, which constituted 14.6% of the total population: one of the highest ratios in the communist world. This represented a 50% advance on the 1976 total.

Two loyal and subservient noncommunist parties are permitted to function under the umbrella of the DFRF and enjoy SPA representation: the Korean Social Democratic Party (KSDP) and the Chondoist Chongu Party (CCP: Ch'ondogyo Yong Friends' Party). The KSDP was established in 1945 and was known, until 1981, as the Korean Democratic Party. The CCP was formed in 1946 and its members adhere to the syncretic, Taoist–Buddhist–Confucian, religious faith.

Latest elections

The most recent SPA 'elections' were held on 22 April 1990, with all 687 DFRF candidates being returned unopposed. Turnout was put at more than 99%.

Political history

Korea was, according to legend, founded as a state in 2333 BC by the Tangun dynasty. More recent archaeological evidence suggests that the country was invaded and colonized by nomadic tribes from Manchuria and Siberia during the 3rd millennium BC. The descendants of these conquerors established three regional kingdoms, the Koguryo, Shilla, and Paekche at around the time of Christ. Of these, the economically and culturally advanced Buddhist Shilla kingdom, with its capital at Kyongju, was subsequently to emerge as the dominant one, absorbing the others and unifying the peninsula, between 668 and 1000 AD. This Shilla dynasty was succeeded by, first, the Koryu and, then, the Chosun, or Yi, dynasty, 1392–1910. During the Yi period, Korea lost its full autonomy, becoming a vassal of China and being subjected to periodic invasions by Mongol and Japanese forces. The country was now also exposed to Confucianism, this philosophy displacing Buddhism as the dominant intellectual force. During the later 19th century, expansionary Japan began to challenge China as the paramount power in the Korean region, before formally annexing the peninsula in 1910, turning it into a colony, administered by a governor general, based at Seoul, now in South Korea.

Under the Japanese, Korea rapidly developed, new heavy industries being established in the coal-rich north and commercialized agriculture being promoted in the south. Japanese rule was, however, bitterly opposed, since the gains from economic growth were largely monopolized by immigrant Japanese nationals, and Korean workers were forcibly conscripted as low paid factory and mine labour. In addition, the new rulers' determined attempt to eradicate Korean culture and enforce the adoption of the Japanese language and customs was deeply resented. Both communist and right-wing nationalist, exiled, resistance movements thus began to emerge during the interwar period.

Following Japan's surrender in August 1945, at the close of World War II, Korea was divided, at the 38th parallel, into two military occupation zones, with Soviet forces in the North and American in the South. In the northern zone the Soviets installed, in February 1946, a 'North Korean Provisional People's Committee', manned predominantly by Moscow-trained Korean communists, including Kim Il Sung. This held power, introducing a radical programme of land reform and nationalization, until the election of a Supreme People's Assembly in 1947. This was based on a 'unity list' of communist-approved candidates. A year later, following the founding of the pro-American 'Republic of Korea', south of the 38th parallel, by the conservative nationalist leader Dr Syngman Rhee (1875–1965), North Korea was formally declared a 'Democratic People's Republic', in September 1948, under the leadership of the Korean Workers' Party (KWP). Soviet Red Army troops initially remained in the country, but finally withdrew, in December 1948.

The two new Korean republics each claimed full jurisdiction over the entire peninsula and, on 25 June 1950, North

Korea, seeking immediate unification by force, launched a large-scale invasion of the South, rapidly reaching Seoul. Thus began the three-year-long Korean War, which, following the intervention of the United States, on the side of the South, and China, on the side of the North, ended in stalemate, but claimed the lives of 2 million people.

The 38th parallel border line between North and South was re-established by the armistice agreement of July 1953 and a UN force patrolled a 4,000-metre-wide demilitarized buffer zone (DMZ) which had been created. North Korea, however, never fully accepted this agreement and remained committed to reunification during the succeeding decades. As a result, despite the establishment in 1972 of a North–South coordinating committee to promote peaceful unification, relations with the South have remained tense and hostile. Border incidents have been frequent and in October 1983 four South Korean cabinet ministers were assassinated in Rangoon (Yangon), in Burma (Myanmar), following a bombing incident organized by two North Korean army officers. In addition, a maze of North Korean-dug, secret, tank-sized tunnels under the DMZ were uncovered by the UN border command in October 1978.

Domestically, the post-1948 period has seen economic development in a planned socialist manner in the DPRK. During the 1950s, factories and financial institutions were nationalized and agriculture collectivized, with overall priority being given to heavy industries and rural mechanization in investment programmes. The growth rate of the North Korean economy has, however, lagged considerably behind that of its more populous southern neighbour, which began to move ahead of the traditionally richer North, in terms of per-capita GDP, during the 1960s. Today, South Koreans are more than five times as affluent as 'Northerners'. The maintenance of substantial armed forces, exceeding 800,000 and consuming a quarter of GDP, has been a factor in checking North Korea's growth. So has the autarchic, self-reliant policy stance of the KWP leadership, although there has been some relaxation, in a more market-orientated and 'open-door' direction, since the late 1980s.

Politics in North Korea became dominated from the later 1980s by the 'succession question' as Kim Il Sung approached his 80s. After falling out with his brother, Kim Yong-Ju, ten years his junior, in 1975, Kim Il Sung sought to establish his son, Kim Jong Il (b. 1942), as sole heir designate. Kim Jong Il accompanied Kim Il Sung on diplomatic and factory tours, became 'Armed Forces Supreme Commander', presided over key party and state government meetings, and his portrait was placed on public display across the country. However, elements within the Workers' Party and armed forces, concerned at his lack of military experience and rumours of his lavish personal lifestyle, appeared to oppose Kim's succession aims. On the eventual death of Kim Il Sung, in July 1994, Kim Jong Il, known formerly as the 'Dear Leader' was reported by the state media to have been placed 'at the head of the party, administration, and people's armed forces'. He assumed his father's title of 'Great Leader' and the Pyongyang media sought to present a transmigration of political personality from father to son. In February 1995 Oh Jin Woo (1916–95), the defence minister and de facto number two in North Korea for more than 20

years, also died. It remained surprising, however, to Western observers that still, by the summer of 1995, Kim Jong Il had not formally been invested as state president and general secretary of the KWP or seen often in public since his father's death. This fed rumours that Kim Jong Il was himself seriously ill. A possible rival existed in his uncle, Kim Yong-Ju, who returned to the KWP Politburo in December 1993.

In its external relations, North Korea adopted a determinedly neutral stance in the Sino-Soviet dispute, signing a friendship and mutual assistance treaty with China in July 1961, while at the same time continuing to draw substantial economic and military aid from the Soviet Union, with whom links became closer from the 1970s. Overall stress, however, was placed on nationalistic self-reliance (juche), the country remaining largely isolated from external contacts.

From the start of the 1990s, as a result of mounting domestic economic shortages and the collapse of communism in Eastern Europe, depriving it of Russian economic aid, North Korea sought to bring to an end its economic isolation. In November 1990, anxious to attract inward investment in Chinese-style 'special economic zones', the first formal contacts were made with Japan, ending four decades of bitter hostility. In September 1990 Prime Minister Yon Hyong Muk made an unprecedented three-day visit to South Korea. This paved the way for North Korea's admission, simultaneously with South Korea's, into the UN in September 1991 and on 13 December 1991 a nonaggression pact was signed by the two states. This provided for the establishment of a military hotline to prevent accidental conflict, the restoration of cross-border communication links, the reunion of divided families, and the liberalization of commerce. In June 1995 North Korea, with its economy in turmoil, agreed to accept 150,000 tonnes of emergency rice supplies from South Korea.

During recent years there has been great Western concern that North Korea has been embarking on a nuclear weapons development programme. In January 1992 North Korea signed a Nuclear Safeguards Agreement, providing for international inspection of its nuclear facilities. In October 1994 the United States and North Korea signed an accord which provided for US diplomatic recognition and economic assistance if North Korea replaced its existing nuclear technology, abandoned its alleged nuclear weapons programme, and submitted itself to international nuclear inspection.

SOUTH KOREA

Republic of Korea (ROK)
Daehan-Minkuk

Capital: Seoul

Social and economic data
Area: 98,222 km^2
Population: 44,500,000
Pop. density per km^2: 453*
Urban population: 74%**
Literacy rate: 96%**
GDP: $330,000 million**; per-capita GDP: $7,500**
Government defence spending (% of GDP): 4.2%**
Currency: South Korean won

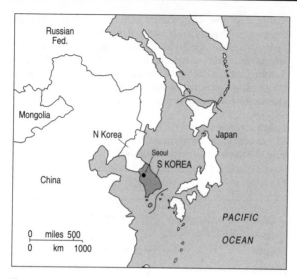

Economy type: high income
Labour force in agriculture: 16%**

*1994
**1992

Ethnic composition
With the exception of a small Nationalist Chinese minority, the population is almost entirely of Korean ethnic stock. The official language is Korean.

Religions
Mahayana Buddhism, which claims more than 8 million adherents, or 20% of the total population, is the principal religion, along with Christianity, with 8.5 million believers, three-quarters of whom are Protestants, belonging to the Presbyterian Church of Korea, the Korean Methodist Church, and smaller denominations, and a quarter of whom are Roman Catholics. Other important smaller religions are Confucianism, Won Buddhism, and Chundo Kyo, a syncretic religion, combining Shaman, Buddhist, and Christian doctrines, which was developed by nationalists during the later 19th century. Christianity was first introduced during the later 16th century and has been at the forefront of the human rights struggle. Freedom of worship and conscience is guaranteed under the constitution.

Political features
State type: emergent democratic
Date of state formation: 1948
Political structure: unitary
Executive: limited presidential
Assembly: one-chamber
Party structure: multiparty
Human rights rating: 59%
International affiliations: AfDB, APEC, AsDB, CP, EBRD, ESCAP, G-77, IAEA, IBRD, ICC, ICFTU, IMF, IWC, LORCS, OAS (observer), UN, WTO

Local and regional government
The country comprises nine provinces and six special cities of provincial status: Seoul, Pusan, Taegu, Inchon, Kwangju,

and Taejon. Below them, counties, towns and villages are the administrative units. Under reforms introduced by President Kim Young-Sam, provincial governors, city mayors and more than 4,650 provincial assembly and local council deputies were elected for the first time from June 1995.

Head of state (executive)
President Kim Young-Sam, since 1993

Head of government
Prime Minister Lee Soo Sung, since 1995

Political leaders since 1970
1962–79 Major General Park Chung-Hee (DRP), 1979–80 Choi Kyu-Hah (DRP), 1980–88 General Chun Doo-Hwan (DJP), 1988–93 Roh Tae-Woo (DJP/DLP), 1993– Kim Young-Sam (DLP)

Political system
The current, Sixth Republic, constitution, adopted in February 1988, supersedes the earlier constitutions of 1980 (Fifth Republic), 1972 (Fourth Republic), and 1948 (First–Third Republics). By previous standards, it is a liberal document, guaranteeing the preservation of a 'plural party system'; the fair management of election contests, by a nine-member Central Election Management Committee (CEMC); the citizen's right of *habeas corpus* and freedom of speech, press, assembly, and association; and establishing a nine-member Constitutional Court (CC) to police its maintenance. Included within the constitution is the aspiration of the 'peaceful unification of the Korean peninsula ... based on the principles of freedom and democracy'.

Legislative power rests with the 299-member single-chamber National Assembly (*Kuk Hoe*), 237 of whose members are elected for fixed four-year terms, on a first-past-the-post basis, in single-member constituencies. The remaining 62 seats are filled on the basis of proportional representation. Parties require a minimum of 20 seats within the Assembly to be recognized as an official negotiating faction.

The National Assembly convenes annually for a regular session of up to 100 days and also meets in 'extraordinary sessions', at the request of the president or three-quarters of its members. It has the authority to impeach the president and recommend the removal of the prime minister or any other minister; propose changes to the constitution, a two-thirds majority being required, followed by public approval in a referendum; and appoint a third of the members of the CEMC and CC. Approval from the National Assembly is also required for the president's appointment of holders of senior   judicial office.

Executive authority lies with the president, who is directly elected for a single, nonrenewable five-year term. Presidents govern with the assistance of an appointed cabinet, called the State Council, of between 15 and 30 members and headed by a prime minister. Serving members of the armed forces are debarred from cabinet office. The president is also empowered to appoint a third of the members of the CEMC and CC, as well as the chief justice and justices of the Supreme Court, subject to the National Assembly's assent.

Additionally, presidents may take issues directly to the public through the use of referenda. They may issue vetoes, which can be overridden by the National Assembly, and assume broad emergency powers, during times of emergency, subject to Assembly agreement. They cannot, however, dissolve the National Assembly.

The political structure established by the 1987 Constitution is a mixture of the American and French presidential models, with significant checks built in so as to strengthen the National Assembly vis-à-vis the president. In this respect it differs from the preceding 1972 and 1980 constitutions, and may engender instability during periods when party control over the executive and Assembly is split.

Political parties

The Democratic Liberal Party (DLP), led by Kim Young-Sam, is the dominant political force in the Republic of Korea today. It was formed in February 1990 when the ruling Democratic Justice Party (DJP) merged with the opposition parties, the Reunification Democratic Party (estd. 1987), led by the Presbyterian, Kim Young-Sam, and the New Democratic Republican Party (estd. 1987), led by former premier and former intelligence agency head Kim Jong-Pil. The DJP was formed in January 1981, as a 'government party', by the country's newly installed leader, General Chun Doo-Hwan. The party was strongly supported and generously financed by the business community, whose interests it promoted in a corporatist manner. It was also backed by the armed forces. In addition to these important bases, it developed a mass membership of more than 1 million, mainly in the north and east-centre of the country, and particularly in rural areas. The DJP's political forerunner was the Democratic Republican Party (DRP), which was established in February 1963 as a governing party to lend civilian legitimacy to the military regime of Major General Park Chung-Hee. In March 1995 a split in the DLP occurred, when Kim Jong-Pil, a former secret police chief, who accused the DLP government of being 'too soft' in its relations with North Korea and internal dissidents, set up a new, business-orientated ultra-conservative party, the United Liberal Democratic party (ULD), which subsumed the New People's Party in May 1995. He was replaced as DLP chairperson by Lee Coon Koo.

The main opposition party is the Democratic Party (DP). It was formed in September 1991 through the merger of the Roman Catholic, Kim Dae-Jung's New Democratic Party, itself the heir to the Party for Peace and Democracy (PPD; estd. 1987), with Lee Ki-Taek's smaller Democratic Party. It is a more left-of-centre force than the DLP, drawing its support from lower social strata, and has been led since March 1993 by Lee Ki-Taek. The party's chief support base is the southwestern Cholla region, but it is also strong in Seoul as a result of the in-migration of many people from Cholla.

In September 1995 a new rival centre-left party to the DP, the National Congress for New Politics (NCNP), was formed by Kim Dae-Jung, who had ended his two years' 'retirement' from politics. It immediately attracted 54 legislator defectors from the DP, making it the largest opposition group in the National Assembly.

Also significant is the centrist, pro-business New Democratic Party (NDP), led by Kim Dong-Kil. It was formed in 1994 through the merger of the United People's Party

(UPP), which was established in January 1992, under the designation Unification National Party (UNP), by Chung Ju Yung, founder of the Hyundai group, the country's second-largest industrial conglomerate, and the New Political Reform Party (NPRP; estd. 1992). The UNP/UPP's founder, Chung, was convicted in November 1993 for violations of the electoral law and given a suspended jail sentence.

Latest elections

The results of the most recent National Assembly elections, held in March 1992, were as follows:

	% Votes	Seats
DLP	39	149
DP	29	97
UNP	17	31
Others	15	22
Total	100	299

Turnout was 71.9% and party support was highly regionalized. The DP polled strongest in the underdeveloped southwestern region of Cholla, in the environs of Kwangju, while the DLP did best in North Kyongsang, Roh Tae-Woo's home area, and in the southeastern port of Pusan, Kim Young-Sam's home city.

In the presidential election of 18 December 1992, the DLP's candidate, Kim Young-Sam, was elected with 41% of the vote, defeating Kim Dae-Jung (DP), with 33%, Chung Ju-Yung (UPP), with 16%, and minor candidates, with 9%.

In inaugural local elections, held in June 1995, the ruling DLP polled poorly, winning only five of the 15 most important mayoral and gubernatorial contests. The newly formed ULD took three governorships in the provinces of North and South Chungchong and Kangwon and the mayorship of Taejon, and the DP four key posts, including the mayorships of Seoul and Kwangju and governorships of South and North Cholla provinces.

Political history

The Republic of Korea was formed from the zone south of the 38th parallel of latitude, which had been occupied by American troops after the Japanese surrender in August 1945. The American military government remained in charge of the country until, following national elections, in May 1948, an independent republic was declared three months later. Dr Syngman Rhee (1875–1965), the royal-born and American-educated leader of the rightist Liberal Party, who had been previously exiled, became the nation's first president, under a constitution which was based partially on the United States model.

During its first two years the republic had to deal with a series of problems. They included a massive influx of more than 2 million refugees who had fled from the communist regime in the North and the return of people from forced labour in Japan and Manchuria. It then experienced invasion and bitter warfare during the 1950–53 Korean War.

President Syngman Rhee, whose autocratic and nationalistic regime, known as the 'First Republic', had been accused of corruption and nepotism, resigned in April 1960, following student-led disorder. A new, parliamentary style, constitution, giving greater powers to the Assembly, was adopted and the opposition Democratic Party (DP) leader, Chang Myon, was appointed prime minister. This parliamentary regime (Second Republic) was characterized, however, by chronic political instability, precipitating a military coup, led by Major General Park Chung-Hee (1917–79), in May 1961. The National Assembly was dissolved, martial law imposed, and a military junta, the 'Supreme Council for National Reconstruction', was initially put into office. During this period, the Korean Central Intelligence Agency (KCIA) was also established, under the direction of Colonel Kim Jong-Pil, a relative of Park, and a government-sponsored party, the Democratic Republican Party (DRP), was created.

This paved the way for a return to 'civilian' rule, under a restored presidential system, with Park Chung-Hee, the DRP's nominee, elected president in December 1963. He had narrowly defeated the opposition New Democratic Party (NDP) candidate, Yun Po-Sun.

President Park proceeded to embark on a major programme of export-led industrial development, through a series of five-year plans, and the extension of 'soft loan' financial support to integrated conglomerates (*chaebol*), in a determinedly corporatist manner. Benefiting from the nation's plentiful supply of well educated, industrious and low paid workers, the programme proved to be a remarkable success, with more than 9% and 20% per annum rates of GDP and industrial growth being, respectively, attained during the 1960s and 1970s. As a result, South Korea emerged as a major exporter of consumer goods, including textiles, footwear, and electronics, and industrial products, such as steel, ships, and petrochemicals. This 'economic miracle' fundamentally transformed the socio-economic base of what had been a predominantly agrarian economy. A huge urban-industrial sector was now developing through a process of in-migration.

This buoyant economy, with incomes rising for middle- and upper-middle urban groups, provided a material basis for the Third Republic regime, enabling Park, aided, the opposition claimed, by ballot-rigging and vote-buying, to narrowly defeat the NDP nominees, Yun Po-Sun and Kim Dae-Jung (b. 1924), in the presidential contests of 1967 and 1971.

Despite the economic growth achieved, opposition to the authoritarian and repressive character of the Park regime, and to the country's growing links with despised Japan, began to mount during the 1970s. In response, martial law was imposed in October 1972 and a new '*yushin*' ('revitalizing') constitution, strengthening the president's powers, was adopted. This was done by a national referendum, in November 1972, which established a Fourth Republic.

Elections to the newly created presidential electoral college, the National Conference for Unification (NCU), and the now 'neutered' National Assembly, then followed, in December 1972. With more bribery and rigging, the DRP won a sweeping majority. The 2,359-member NCU duly ratified Park as president for a new six-year term.

Two years later, in May 1975, a severe clamp-down on political dissent was launched, with the enactment of 'Emergency Measure Number Nine' (EMNN), making it a crime to criticize the yushin system and thus, in practice, the incumbent regime. Thousands of political opponents were jailed or placed under house arrest, including Second Republic president, Yun Po-Sun, and NDP leader, Kim Dae-Jung. The latter was kidnapped by KCIA forces while in a Tokyo hotel.

For the NCU elections of May 1978, which were followed by Park's re-election as president in July, there was a brief political 'thaw'. However, with economic conditions briefly deteriorating, as the republic experienced its first year of negative growth since the war, and with the inflation rate surpassing 30%, worker and student protests erupted during 1979. These disturbances escalated, following the expulsion of NDP leader Kim Young-Sam (b. 1927) from the National Assembly for alleged 'subversive activities'. Then, in October 1979, President Park was assassinated by Kim Jae Gyu, the head of the KCIA, in a coup attempt.

Martial law was briefly imposed before an interim government was set up, under the leadership of the former prime minister, Choi Kyu-Hah. This introduced a number of liberalizing reforms, including the release of opposition leader Kim Dae-Jung, in February 1980, and the rescindment of EMNN. However, with antigovernment demonstrations gaining strength, a new clamp-down on dissidents was launched in May 1980, involving the arrest of 30 political leaders, including Kim Dae-Jung, the reimposition of martial law, and the closure of the National Assembly. Riots immediately erupted in Kim's home city of Kwangju. They were forcibly suppressed by paratroopers with, according to official sources, the loss of 189 lives. Outside observers put the true figure at more than 2,000.

In August 1980, Choi Kyu-Hah resigned as president, to be replaced by the leader of the army and former military intelligence chief, the American-trained Major General Chun Doo-Hwan (b. 1931). After a referendum, a new constitution was adopted in October 1980. It abolished the NCU and restricted the presidency to a single, nonrenewable, seven-year term. Martial law was lifted in January 1981 and, after Chun Doo-Hwan was elected president by a new 5,278-member electoral college, in February 1981, a new Fifth Republic was proclaimed. National Assembly elections followed, in which Chun's newly formed Democratic Justice Party (DJP), secured a substantial majority.

Under President Chun, the pace of economic growth accelerated once more. However, internal and external criticism of the suppression of civil liberties continued. A measure of cautious liberalization was to be seen prior to the February 1985 National Assembly elections, involving the release of many political prisoners and the return from exile in the United States, where he had been since 1982, of Kim Dae-Jung. In these elections the New Korea Democratic Party (NKDP), which had recently been formed as a vehicle for the opposition leaders, Kim Young-Sam and Kim Dae-Jung, secured 30% of the direct votes so that, when the new Assembly convened, 102 of its 276 members adopted the party's whip. The DJP held 148 seats, too few to force through fundamental constitutional changes.

Buoyed by their strengthened parliamentary position, the opposition forces launched, outside the Assembly, during 1986 and 1987, a major new campaign for democratic constitutional reform, as the February 1988 date for President Chun's step-down from power approached. The NKDP campaigned for a new system of government, based on direct presidential elections. The DJP countered with a proposal for a new prime ministerial system.

The scale of student unrest escalated in April and June 1987, now drawing support from ordinary workers and the middle classes. Two events triggered off this new spate of dissidence. The first was President Chun's announcement that the reform process would be suspended until after the Olympic Games had been held in Seoul, in September 1988. The second was the nomination of Roh Tae-Woo (b. 1932), a former Korean Military Academy colleague of Chun's, as its presidential candidate for forthcoming indirect elections.

Roh Tae-Woo unexpectedly responded to the growing popular movement against him by submitting a pragmatic, and relatively liberal, eight-point plan of political, constitutional and electoral reform to President Chun. Its key elements included the formation of a new consensual, nonparty, interim cabinet; the establishment of a bipartisan committee to draft a new constitution; the liberalization of labour and censorship laws; and the release from detention, and the restoration of the full political rights, of prominent opposition figures. The 'Roh plan' was accepted and in October 1987 a new constitution was approved in a national referendum. Adopted in February 1988, it provided for a directly elected presidency, serving a nonrenewable five-year term.

In the presidential contest, which was held in December 1987, Roh Tae-Woo, the DJP's nominee, although securing only 36% of the popular vote, emerged victorious, as a result of the candidacy of both Kim Young-Sam and Kim Dae-Jung, respective leaders of the recently formed Reunification Democratic Party (RDP) and Party for Peace and Democracy (PPD), which served to split the opposition's vote. Electoral fraud on the part of the governing party was alleged, but was substantially unproved.

Roh Tae-Woo formally replaced Chun Doo-Hwan as president of the new Sixth Republic in February 1988. However, in the National Assembly elections of April 1988 the opposition regrouped and succeeded in preventing the DJP from securing a majority in the new legislature for the first time since the party's creation. Political conflict calmed during the summer of 1988, as the nation hosted the Olympic Games. However, after the Olympic Games student unrest erupted periodically and calls for reunification of the peninsula grew in strength. After televised investigative work of National Assembly committees uncovered corruption among his close friends and relatives, former President Chun was forced to publicly apologize, in November 1988, on national television for his administration's misdeeds.

In February 1990, when the DJP merged with two opposition parties to form the Democratic Liberal Party (DLP), a stable governing majority was secured. However, in May 1991 more than 250,000 people, mainly students, demonstrated against the government and six attempted suicide after the police had beaten to death a young protester. In the general election of March 1992 the DLP lost its National Assembly majority unexpectedly, but was able, with the support of independent deputies, to hold on to power. The DLP's candidate, the former dissident, Kim Young-Sam, comfortably won the presidential election of December 1992 and succeeded Roh as president in February 1993. The defeated veteran opposition leader, Kim Dae-Jung retired from active politics until August 1995, when he founded a new political party as a vehicle for a further presidential bid in 1997.

Kim Young-Sam, the first South Korean president since 1960 not to have military connections, immediately launched a vigorous anticorruption drive. This claimed many victims in the military and business community and the assets of senior civil servants and politicians were controversially made public. An unpopular decision to open the previously protected rice market to imports, under the terms of a GATT (later WTO) agreement, persuaded Kim to replace his prime minister in December 1993. However, despite a temporary slowdown in GDP growth during 1992–93 from its customary annual rate of 9%, President Kim, with his relatively open governing style, retained a high public approval rating and the level of student protests diminished significantly. From 1994 the Kim administration encouraged greater competition, privatization, and deregulation within the still booming South Korean economy, as part of a 'globalization' (*segyehwa*) initiative. However, in June 1995 the ruling DLP, which had been weakened by a split in its ranks in March 1995, when Kim Jong-Pil left to form the ultra-conservative United Liberal Democratic (ULD) party, polled poorly in the country's first ever local elections. It won only a third of the provincial governorships and city mayorships, with the opposition centre-left Democratic Party (DP) and new ULD performing strongly. In October 1995 former president Roh Tae Woo admitted publicly that during his five-year rule he had secretly amassed 500 billion won (£400 million) in a party slush fund, retaining 170 billion won for personal use after he left office in 1993.

Externally, the constant threat of invasion from the North has been a key factor in South Korean politics since 1953, helping to justify stern rule. The country has been forced to devote significant resources to modernizing its armed forces, which number 630,000 and annually consume around 5% of GDP, even though they have been supported by more than 35,000 American troops. Both political and economic relations with the United States have remained close since 'liberation' and the United States currently provides a market for 40% of the republic's exports. Anti-American sentiment is, however, strong among opposition groups.

Close political economic links have also been developed with Japan. In recent years, however, as part of what has been termed a reunification directed 'Northern policy', there has been a normalization of diplomatic relations with communist China, in August 1992, and since 1990 relations with North Korea have improved dramatically. Both Koreas were admitted into the United Nations in September 1991 and on 13 December 1991 a nonaggression and confidence-building pact was signed in Seoul. This provided for the restoration of cross-border communications, the reunion of divided families, and the freer movement of people and ideas. On 31 December 1991 both states agreed at Panmujon to ban the testing, deployment, or possession of nuclear weapons. In response, the United States has agreed to withdraw its nuclear weapons from South Korea and reduce its troop strength in the republic. In 1995, South Korea was persuaded by the United States to give North Korea two 'safe' nuclear reactors, to persuade it to abandon its suspected atomic-weapons programme, and also supplied the North, whose economy was fast deteriorating, with emergency shipments of rice.

KYRGYZSTAN (KYRGYZIA)

Republic of Kyrgyzstan
Kyrgyzstan Respublikasy

Capital: Bishkek (formerly Frunze)

Social and economic data
Area: 198,500 km^2
Population: 4,600,000*
Pop. density per km^2: 23*
Urban population: 38%**
Literacy rate: 97%**
GDP: $3,800 million**; per-capita GDP: $840*
Government defence spending (% of GDP): 1.7%**
Currency: som
Economy type: low income
Labour force in agriculture: 32%**

*1994
**1992

Ethnic composition
Fifty-three per cent of the population are of Kyrgyz ethnic stock, 22% Russian, 13% Uzbek, 3% Ukrainian, and 2%

German. The official language is Kyrgyz, a Turkic language written in the Cyrillic script.

Religions
The principal religion is Islam, with the majority of ethnic Kyrgyz, Uzbeks, and Tajiks being Sunni Muslims of the Hanafi school. Many new mosques have opened since 1991. There is a Russian Orthodox Christian minority.

Political features
State type: emergent democratic
Date of state formation: 1991
Political structure: unitary
Executive: limited presidential
Assembly: two-chamber
Party structure: multiparty
Human rights rating: N/A
International affiliations: CIS, EBRD, ECO, ESCAP, IBRD, IMF, NACC, OIC, OSCE, PFP, UN

Local and regional government
The country is divided into six administrative regions (*oblasts* or *dubans*) and the municipality of Bishkek. There are also elected councils at city and rural district level.

Head of state (executive)
President Askar Akaev, since 1990

Head of government
Prime Minister Apas Jumagulov, since 1993

Political leaders since 1970
1990– Askar Akaev (ex-communist independent)

Political system
Since February 1995 the Republic of Kyrgyzstan has had a two-chamber legislature, the Zhogorku Kenesh, comprising a 70-member People's Assembly and a 35-member Legislative Assembly. Deputies are elected for five-year terms by the majoritarian system, which provides for a second, and exceptionally a third, ballot 'run-off' race in contests in which there is no clear first round majority. The state president, who has supreme executive power, has, since 1991, been popularly elected for a five-year term. There is a limit of two consecutive terms and the constitution stipulates that the president must have a fluent command of Kyrgyz. The president, who has decree powers, works with a cabinet of some 25 members. This is headed by a prime minister, who acts as the parliamentary manager for the president. The current constitution was approved in May 1993, but was amended substantially in October 1994. Future changes to the constitution require approval in a national referendum.

Political parties
There were 12 registered political parties in 1995. The majority of parties are weak and ill-organized and most parliamentary deputies are independents. The best organized party is the 10,000-member Party of Communists of Kyrgyzstan, which was banned in August 1991, but revived in June 1992. It is led by Sheraly Sadykov. Other significant parties are the Kyrgyz nationalist Ata Meken and Erkin Kyrgyzstan, the pro-Akaev Social Democratic Party (estd.

1993), the multiethnic Party of Kyrgyzstan Unity, the Democratic Movement of Kyrgyzstan, and the Agrarian Labour Party (estd. 1995).

Latest elections

The most recent legislature elections, the first since independence, were held on 5 and 19 February 1995 for the 35-member Legislative Assembly and the 70-member People's Assembly. Turnout was registered at 61% and 1,000 candidates contested the elections, which were largely free of poll violence. Thirteen candidates secured the required 50% of the vote majority on the first ballot. More than four-fifths of the candidates and roughly two-thirds of those elected were unaffiliated independents.

In the country's first popular presidential election, held on 12 October 1991, the incumbent Askar Akaev was elected unopposed, with 95.3% of the vote. Turnout was put at more than 90%.

Political history

Peopled mainly by horse-breeding, mountain-dwelling nomads, the Turkic-speaking descendants of the Mongol invaders who swept across Asia from the 13th century, Kyrgyzstan was annexed by Russia in 1864. It formed part of an independent Turkestan republic between 1917 and 1924, was then an autonomous republic within the USSR and, from 1936, became a full republic within the Soviet Union. Land reforms and agricultural collectivization during the 1920s and 1930s resulted in the settlement of many nomadic Kyrgyz, but also met with strong opposition from local armed groups (*basmachi*).

Long viewed as a bastion of conservatism, in the March 1991 USSR constitutional referendum the republic's voters overwhelmingly endorsed, with 88% in favour, the maintenance of the Union, while its Communist Party (CP) supported the August 1991 anti-Gorbachev attempted coup in Moscow. However, Askar Akaev (b. 1944), a 'reform communist' who had assumed the republic's presidency in November 1990, in the aftermath of Kyrgyz–Uzbek border riots that claimed between 300 and 1,000 lives in the densely settled Fergana Valley, condemned the coup as 'anti-constitutional' and overturned an attempt by local KGB and army chiefs to overthrow his government. On 28 August 1991, he resigned from the Soviet Communist Party and ordered the suspension of the republic's CP and the nationalization of its property. On 31 August 1991 the republic's parliament (Supreme Soviet) voted to declare independence from the USSR. After the Moscow coup was thwarted, Akaev was offered, but declined to accept, the position of USSR vice president by the Soviet leader Mikhail Gorbachev. He was returned, unchallenged, as Kyrgyzstan's president on 12 October 1991 in what was the republic's first ever popular contest.

Kyrgyzstan joined the Commonwealth of Independent States (CIS), which was formed in December 1991, but has also sought to develop close relations with Turkey, with whom it shares linguistic traditions. Its independence was recognized by the United States and other Western states in January 1992. It was admitted into the Conference on Security and Cooperation in Europe (CSCE, later the OSCE) in the same month and into the United Nations in March 1992. Kyrgyzstan soon became described as the 'real centre of democracy' within former Soviet Central Asia since its former Communist Party, though revived in June 1992, was substantially destroyed and greatly discredited. During 1991, with nationalism increasing in the new state, more than 100,000 ethnic Russians left the country. This led to fears of a 'brain drain'. The economy, previously heavily reliant on Moscow subsidies, underwent substantial restructuring and price liberalization from 1991. Commercial ties began to be developed with Western capitalist states, but in the short term a decline in GDP was registered, until 1995, and a sharp rise in inflation and levels of crime, these effects being exacerbated by departure from the rouble zone in May 1993 and adoption of its own currency, the som.

During 1993 the Akaev administration became destabilized by allegations of corruption made by conservative communists and nationalists who dominated the 350-member legislature, the Uluk Kenesh, which had been elected during the Soviet era. In December 1993 the prime minister, Tursenbek Chyngyshev, and vice president, Feliks Akulov, were forced to resign, with Apas Jumagulov, a former Communist premier, returning to replace Chyngyshev. However, Akaev, supported by pro-reform deputies, hit back in January and October 1994 by placing before the voters, in two national referenda, a confidence motion and a constitutional reform package, which entailed the replacement of the Uluk Kenesh by a smaller, elected bicameral body. The first plebiscite, on Akaev's reform programme, secured a 96% approval rating and in February 1995 a new, pro-Akaev parliament was elected.

Priorities of the president have been the privatization of land, restoration of Russian as a national language, alongside Kyrgyz, as a means of stemming the continuing exodus of skilled Russians, and preservation of the CIS, which is of great economic value to Kyrgyzstan. Akaev is also keen to ensure that Kyrgyzstan remains a secular state and to prevent the spread of Islamic fundamentalism from such neighbouring states as Tajikistan. Meanwhile, close ties have been established with the neighbouring states of Kazakhstan and Uzbekistan, with whom Kyrgyzstan forged an economic union in May 1994. This deepened into a social and military union in July 1994. In addition, in February 1995 an Interstate Council, with a rotating annual chair, was formed to devise common policy and to govern the trilateral union.

LAOS

The Lao People's Democratic Republic (LPDR)
Saathiaranagroat Prachhathippatay Prachhachhon Lao

Capital: Vientiane (Viengchane)

Social and economic data

Area: 236,800 km^2
Population: 4,600,000*
Pop. density per km^2: 19*
Urban population: 20%**
Literacy rate: 84%**
GDP: $1,200 million**; per-capita GDP: $270**

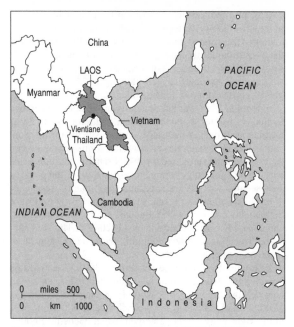

China

LAOS

PACIFIC
OCEAN

Myanmar

Vietnam

Vientiane
Thailand

INDIAN OCEAN

Cambodia

Indonesia

0 miles 500
0 km 1000

Government defence spending (% of GDP): 8.3%**
Currency: new kip
Economy type: low income
Labour force in agriculture: 70%**

*1994
**1992

Ethnic composition
Sixty per cent of the population is Laotian, predominantly Lao Lum, 35% hill tribes, and 5% Vietnamese and Chinese. Lao is the principal, and official, language, spoken by two-thirds of the population, with French also widely used. The non-Lao tribal ethnic groups, particularly the Meo, have forcibly opposed the new regime's challenges to their traditional way of life.

Religions
An estimated 58% of the population adheres to traditional Theravada Buddhism. A secular state was officially established in 1975, but the 1991 constitution respects all lawful activities of followers of Buddhism and other religious faiths. Thirty-five per cent of the people follow tribal, predominantly animist, religions; while, prior to the communist takeover, Roman Catholicism claimed 35,000 adherents.

Political features
State type: communist
Date of state formation: 1954
Political structure: unitary
Executive: communist
Assembly: one-chamber
Party structure: one-party
Human rights rating: N/A
International affiliations: AsDB, ASEAN (observer), CP, ESCAP, G-77, IBRD, IMF, LORCS, NAM, UN, WFTU

Local and regional government
The country is divided into 17 provinces (*khoueng*), administered by People's Revolutionary Committees, which are headed by a governor, appointed by the state president, and controlled by the ruling Lao People's Revolutionary Party (LPRP). In the northern highlands, where non-Lao ethnic groups predominate, a greater measure of self-government is enjoyed. Below the provinces, the units of administration are districts (*muong*), cantons (*tasseng*), and villages (*ban*). At the subprovincial level there are People's Councils and Committees which, in theory, are subject to triennial election.

Head of state
President Nouhak Phoumsavan, since 1992

Head of government
Prime Minister General Khamtay Siphandon, since 1991

Political leaders since 1970
1962–75 Prince Souvanna Phouma, 1975–92 Kaysone Phomvihane (LPRP), 1992– General Khamtay Siphandon (LPRP)*

*Communist Party leader

Political system
The LPDR's first constitution was endorsed in August 1991 by the then existing legislature, the Supreme People's Assembly. This describes the LPDR as a 'people's democratic state' in which the communist party, the Lao People's Revolutionary Party (LPRP), dominates as the leading organ and sole permitted political party. Elected bodies function according to the top-down principle of democratic centralism, but in the economic sphere private enterprise is accepted as part of a market-orientated economy subject to state intervention.

The legislature, the National Assembly, comprises 85 members popularly elected every five years. It meets in ordinary session twice a year and elects as executive head of state a president, who also serves a five-year term, subject to possible removal by the National Assembly. The president promulgates laws adopted by the National Assembly and, with the Assembly's approval, appoints or dismisses the prime minister and members of the Council of Ministers (COM), or cabinet. The COM comprises an 'inner cabinet' of around 20 ministers or chairpersons of committees and 60 deputy ministers and vice chairpersons. It has the task of framing the economic plan and budget and overseeing the day-to-day work of state ministries, committees, and local bodies. Senior members of the controlling LPRP monopolize key state positions.

Political parties
The ruling Lao People's Revolutionary Party (LPRP: Phak Pasason Pativat Lao) originated as the Lao Independence Front, which was founded in 1951 by Prince Souphanouvong, a member of the royal family, as a breakaway wing from the Communist Party of Indo-China, which was founded in 1930 by the Vietnamese communist, Ho Chi Minh. The movement became known as the Pathet Lao (Lao People's Front) in 1954 and was taken over by the North Vietnamese-backed Kaysone Phomvihane in 1955, although

Prince Souphanouvong remained its figurehead leader in negotiations with the incumbent government. Under the designation People's Party of Laos, it played a leading role in the Laotian Patriotic Front during the 1960s, functioning as a guerrilla wing, before adopting its present name in 1972.

The LPRP is organized hierarchically, with a stepped series of local, or branch, district and provincial committees, leading up to an 'elected' national Congress. In the past, the Congress has met irregularly, only two being called between 1955 and 1972. Since 1982, it has been convened at regular five-yearly intervals. The most recent session, the fifth, was in March 1991. The Congress ratifies the party programme and 'elects' a Central Committee (CC) to act when it is not sitting. The CC is presently composed of 55 full members.

The CC, in turn, 'elects' a smaller ten-member Politburo and Secretariat, headed by General Khamtay Siphandon. The Politburo, in accordance with the precepts of 'democratic centralism', dominates both party and state machines. Four of its current members are military figures.

In 1986, membership of the LPRP stood at 44,000, a figure which constituted barely 1% of the total population. This was one of the lowest party:citizen ratios in the communist world, although membership had more than doubled since the late 1970s. Rigorous entry rules are imposed, with the aim of maintaining the LPRP as a disciplined and committed 'vanguard' force. The party dominates the broader Lao Front for National Reconstruction (LFNR), which was established in 1979 as the successor to the Laotian Patriotic Front mass organization. The LFNR includes within its ranks representatives of economic and social 'interest groups' and is designed to mobilize nonparty support for government policy.

A number of illegal political groupings operate from external bases, particularly in hill tribe regions, as armed opposition to the communist regime. These include the Royalist, United Lao Liberation Front, led by General Vang Pao, which draws support from among the Hmong (Meo) tribes, and the United Front for the National Liberation of the Lao People.

Latest elections

The most recent elections to the National Assembly were held on 20 December 1992. The 85 seats were contested by 154 candidates approved by the Lao Front for National Reconstruction. Turnout was recorded at 99.3% of eligible voters.

Political history

Laos was first occupied by Chinese immigrants during the 4th and 5th centuries AD and adopted Buddhism during the 7th century. Between the 11th–13th centuries it constituted part of the culturally advanced Khmer Empire and became subject to immigration by Lao from Thailand. Not until the 14th century, when the region was united by the legendary King Fa Ngum, was an independent Laos kingdom established.

Initially visited by Europeans in the 17th century, Laos became a French protectorate between 1893 and 1945, and consisted of the three principalities of Luang Prabang, Vientiane, and Champassac. After a brief occupation by the Japanese during World War II, the French re-established

control in 1946, despite opposition from the Chinese-supported Lao Issara (Free Laos) nationalist movement. The country was granted semi-autonomy in 1949, when, under the constitutional monarchy of the king of Luang Prabang, Sisavang Vong, it became an Associated State of the French Union. In December 1954, following the Geneva Agreements, Laos secured full independence.

A sporadic civil war subsequently broke out between two factions of former supporters of the Lao Issara. The first was a moderate, royalist-neutralist, group, led by Prince Souvanna Phouma, who served as prime minister on several occasions. It had supported the 1949 French compromise and was the recognized government for the bulk of the country. The second was a more extreme, communist resistance group, the Pathet Lao (Land of the Lao), led by ex-Prince Souphanouvong (1909–95), the half-brother of Prince Souvanna, and Kaysone Phomvihane (1920–92). This was supported by China and the Vietminh, who were in control of much of northeastern Laos.

Following the Vientiane Agreement of 1957, a coalition government was temporarily established. This soon collapsed, however, after the May 1958 National Assembly elections had produced an inconclusive result. In 1960 a third, right-wing, force emerged when General Phoumi Nosavan, backed by the royal army, overthrew Prime Minister Souvanna Phouma and set up a pro-Western government, headed by Prince Boun Gum. A new Geneva Agreement was signed in 1962, establishing a tripartite broad-spectrum government, under the leadership of Prince Souvanna Phouma.

Fighting continued, however, between the Pathet Lao, assisted by North Vietnam, and the neutralists and the right-wing, assisted by the United States. The fighting was exacerbated by the neighbouring Vietnam War, until the Vientiane Agreement of 1973 established a cease-fire line, dividing the country northwest to southeast. The communists were given two-thirds of the country, including the Plain of Jars and the Bolovens Plateau, but the Souvanna Phouma government was made responsible for two-thirds of the population.

All foreign forces, North Vietnamese, Thai, and American, were to be withdrawn, and both sides received equal representation in Souvanna Phouma's provisional government of 1974. In 1975, however, the communist Pathet Lao, now renamed the Lao People's Front, following success in Assembly elections, seized full power. King Savang Vatthan, who had succeeded his father in October 1959, abdicated in November and Laos became a 'People's Democratic Republic' under the presidency of Prince Souphanouvong. Prince Souvanna Phouma remained as an 'adviser' to the government, but the real controlling force was now the LPRP leader and prime minister, Kaysone Phomvihane.

The new administration, which inherited a poor, war-ravaged economy, initially attempted to rapidly reorganize the country along socialist lines, nationalizing businesses and industries and collectivizing agriculture. However, faced with mounting food shortages and the flight of more than 250,000 refugees to Thailand, it began to modify this approach in 1979. The private sector was now allowed to continue to operate in a number of spheres and production incentives were introduced, with the stress now being placed on a gradual, step-by-step 'transition to socialism'.

In 1981, the country's first five-year plan came into force. However, in 1985–86, under pressure from the new reformist leadership of Mikhail Gorbachev in the Soviet Union, which supplied the country with considerable economic aid, further 'liberalization' reforms were introduced in the economic sphere, including the adoption of a new 'socialist business accounting system', which freed managers to set prices and wages and required enterprises to make a profit. In the rural sector, more than half the cropped area was privately farmed.

Politically, the country has remained subject to firm LPRP control since 1975. However, since the late 1980s, threatened by the collapse of communism elsewhere in the world, there have been moves, under the new national slogan of 'democracy and prosperity', towards a 'normalization' and liberalization of the political process. Local elections were held in 1988, and national elections followed in March 1989. In August 1991 the communist republic's first constitution was adopted. While confirming the LPRP's 'leading role', it contained no explicit references to socialism and provided for an executive presidency: this position being filled by Kaysone Phomvihane, who replaced Phoumi Vongvichit (1908–94), the acting head of state since 1986. The former vice premier, defence minister and supreme commander of the Lao People's Army, General Khamtay Siphandon (b. 1923) replaced Phomvihane as prime minister. Five months earlier, in March 1991, at the LPRP's fifth congress, a number of leading 'old guard' revolutionaries, including Souphanouvong and Vongvichit, left the Politburo. In his keynote address, the party's president, Kaysone Phomvihane, called for an acceleration of the pace of restructuring ('New Economic Mechanism'), including the dismantling of collective farms and a full return to private farming, and in April 1991 and June 1993 the IMF, encouraged by the country's market-based reforms, approved major loans.

Following Kaysone Phomvihane's death in November 1992, Nouhak Phoumsavan was elected state president by a special session of the legislature. Strong economic growth, averaging more than 6% per annum, was registered during the early 1990s, and helped to improve living standards, with foreign investment, principally from Thailand, beginning to increase.

Diplomatically, after 1975 Laos remained closely tied to the Soviet Union, until its demise in 1991, and neighbouring communist Vietnam. Initially Vietnam stationed 50,000 troops in the country, as many as the whole Laotian army. However, by 1989 Vietnam's troops had been withdrawn. Relations with neighbouring Thailand, which Laos accuses of having 'expansionist' designs, were strained during the 1970s and 1980s, border disputes intermittently breaking out in disputed regions. In addition, Laos accused both Thailand and China of providing assistance to rebel groups which operate in border tracts in the south and north. However, from the early 1980s, for economic reasons, there has been a significant improvement in relations with both countries and with Western states. A security and cooperation agreement was signed with Thailand in July 1991 and an agreement was entered into to provide for the phased repatriation of more than 60,000 Lao refugees who had fled to Thailand during the 1970s and 1980s. In April 1994 an Australian-financed 'Friendship Bridge' was opened, connecting Vientiane to the

northern Thai town of Nong Khai, and in November 1994 a draft agreement was signed with Thailand, Cambodia, and Vietnam on developing the Mekong River basin. Diplomatic relations with the United States were upgraded to full ambassadorial level in November 1991 and in May 1995 the United States lifted its 20-year-old aid embargo.

MALAYSIA

The Federation of Malaysia (FOM)
Persekutuan Tanah Melaysiu

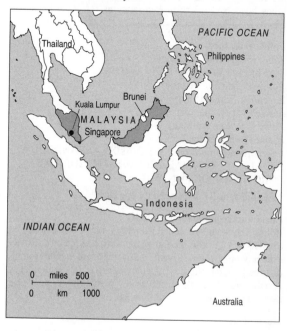

Capital: Kuala Lumpur

Social and economic data
Area: 329,758 km²
Population: 19,200,000*
Pop. density per km²: 58*
Urban population: 45%**
Literacy rate: 78%**
GDP: $57,600 million**; per-capita GDP $3,050**
Government defence spending (% of GDP): 4.4%**
Currency: ringgit or Malaysian dollar
Economy type: middle income
Labour force in agriculture: 26%**

*1994
**1992

Ethnic composition
Fifty-eight per cent of the population is Malay, four-fifths of whom live in rural areas, 32% is ethnic Chinese, four-fifths of whom are in towns, and 9% is Indian, chiefly Tamil. The official language is Bahasa Malaysia (Malay), but Chinese, Tamil, and English are also spoken. The primacy of ethnic Malays has been built into the constitution, with the offices of head of state and prime minister being open only to this

community. The distribution of Malays across the country is, however, uneven. In East Malaysia, ethnic Malays comprise less than a third of the population, Ibans and Kadazans predominating in Sarawak and Sabah, respectively.

Religions

Fifty-four per cent of the population is Sunni Muslim, 19% Buddhist, 7% Christian, nearly a third of whom live in East Malaysia, 12% follow the Chinese Confucianist and Daoist faiths, while many of the indigenous tribes of Sabah and Sarawak are animist. Islam is the official state religion, with the Yang Di-Pertuan Agong serving as the Federation's religious head, and rulers in each state as the local heads of Islam.

Political features

State type: liberal democratic
Date of state formation: 1957
Political structure: federal
Executive: parliamentary
Assembly: two-chamber
Party structure: multiparty*
Human rights rating: 61%
International affiliations: APEC, AsDB, ASEAN, CP, CW, ESCAP, G-15, G-77, IAEA, IBRD, ICFTU, IDB, IMF, LORCS, NAM, OIC, UN, WTO

*Though actually dominated by one party

Local and regional government

Below the state and federal territory level, the country is divided into 130 administrative districts, headed by a district officer, who is a civil servant. Below these are *mukims* (small districts), administered by *penghulus* (religious leaders). Sabah and Sarawak differ from West Malaysia, being divided into residencies and divisions.

Head of state

Paramount Ruler Ja'afar ibni Abdul Rahman (ruler of Negri Sembilan), since 1994

Head of government

Prime Minister Datuk Seri Dr Mahathir bin Mohamad, since 1981

Political leaders since 1970*

1970–76 Tun Abdul Razak (UMNO), 1976–81 Datuk Hussein bin Onn (UMNO), 1981–   Datuk Seri Dr Mahathir bin Mohamad (UMNO)

*Prime ministers

Political system

Malaysia is a federation of 13 states: Johore, Kedah, Kelantan, Malacca, Negri Sembilan, Pahang, Penang, Perak, Perlis, Sabah, Sarawak, Selangor, and Trengganu, plus the capital city, Kuala Lumpur, and the island of Labuan, which are separate Federal Territories. Each state has its own written constitution, head of state (sultan or Yang di-Pertuan Negeri) and elected 14–56-seat Legislative Assembly, led by a chief minister (Menteri Besar) and cabinet, and with powers to legislate on matters outside the federal parliament's sphere.

The federation is headed, under the constitution of 1957, by a constitutional monarch, the Paramount Ruler, Yang di-Pertuan Agong. The monarch is elected, by secret ballot, for five-year terms by and from among the hereditary rulers of nine of the states: Malacca, Penang, Sabah, and Sarawak being the exceptions. For this purpose, a special Conference of Rulers (Majlis Raja) is convened. The Paramount Ruler's powers are similar to those of the British monarch, including discretion in the appointment of the prime minister (Perdana Mentri) and in granting a dissolution of parliament. In normal circumstances, however, the monarch acts on the advice of the elected prime minister and cabinet, who wield effective executive power. The monarch has no powers of veto, but until a constitutional amendment was passed in May 1994, could delay legislation by returning it to parliament for reconsideration.

The federal legislature, or parliament (Parlimen), is a two-chamber body composed of a 70-member upper house, called the Senate (Dewan Negara) and a 192-member House of Representatives (Dewan Rakyat). The Senate comprises 40 members nominated by the monarch, four from the two Federal Territories, and two elected by each of the 13 state Legislative Assemblies. All serve a six-year term. The members of the House of Representatives are elected for five-year terms from single-member constituencies by universal adult suffrage. The constituency system is weighted in favour of Malays in the countryside and against the Chinese in the towns. The House of Representatives is the dominant chamber, the Senate having only delaying powers over bills originating in, and approved by, the lower chamber: one month over money bills and one year over other bills.

The majority party or coalition in the House of Representatives provides the prime minister, who selects an executive council of ministers (Juma'ah Mentri), or cabinet, from within parliament, as the government of the day. The prime minister also holds additional portfolios, such as home affairs and national and rural development. The cabinet is collectively responsible to parliament.

To amend the constitution, a two-thirds vote in the federal parliament is required.

Malaysia's federal system is substantially weighted towards the centre, the federal parliament enjoying sole authority to legislate in the fields of external affairs, defence and internal security, justice, except for Islamic law, industry, commerce, finance, education, transportation, and communication. In all other cases, federal legislation takes precedence over state law whenever a conflict arises. In addition, the states enjoy few significant sources of revenue.

It is in the spheres of land and natural resource management and local administration that state authority is greatest. Exceptions are the two East Malaysia (Borneo) states of Sabah and Sarawak. They enjoy a greater measure of autonomy, having been granted special safeguards in matters of land law, local government, finance, official religion, and official language.

Political parties

The principal political party in the Federation of Malaysia is the United Malays National Organization (UMNO), which, headed by Prime Minister Dr Mahathir bin Mohamad, is orientated towards native Malays and dominates a multiparty National Front (NF: Barisan Nasional) coalition, which contests national and state elections. The UMNO was originally formed in May 1946 to 'fight for independence and safeguard the interests of the indigenous people'. Since independence, the party has set as its aim the 'safeguarding of Malay interests', the promotion of national unity, and the pursuit of a 'neutral foreign policy'.

Dissension grew within UMNO during 1987–88, culminating in a High Court ruling in February 1988, which, as a result of irregularities in the party's internal elections of April 1987, declared the UMNO to be an 'unlawful' body. It therefore had to be disbanded, and a New UMNO (UMNO Baru) was immediately founded by Dr Mahathir. By June 1988 this grouping had a membership of 200,000, compared with the old UNMO's 1.4 million. Dissident UMNO members, led by former prime minister, Tunku Abdul Rahman, and former trade and industry minister, Tunku Tan Sri Razaleigh Hamzah, were forced outside and in May 1989 formed an alternative party, Semangat '46 (Spirit of 1946).

Thirteen other parties are currently also members of the ruling National Front coalition, the majority being communally or regionally based. The most important is the Chinese-orientated Malaysian Chinese Association (MCA), a conservative grouping, formed in 1949, which currently claims a membership of 500,000 and is led by Dr Ling Liong Sik. Another Chinese-orientated party within the NF is the 140,000-strong Gerakan Party (PGRM: Malaysian People's Movement Party), a socialist grouping, formed in 1968, and currently led by Dr Lim Keng Yaik. Orientated towards the Indian community is the 400,000-member Malaysian Indian Congress (MIC), which was established in 1946, and is led by Datuk S Samy Vellu.

Also within the ruling coalition are the People's Progressive Party (PPP); the Sarawak National Action Party (SNAP; estd. 1961); the Sarawak United People's Party (SUPP; estd. 1959); the United Sabah National Organization (USNO); the Parti Bansa Dayak Sarawak (PBDS; estd. 1983); the Parti Pesaka Bumiputra Bersatu (PPBB); and the Sabah-based People's Justice Movement (AKAR) and Liberal Democratic Party (LDP), both of which were admitted into the NF in July 1991.

The principal opposition party in the Federation is the predominantly Chinese, 12,000-member Democratic Action Party (DAP), led by Lim Kit Siang. Formed in 1966, the DAP advocates the establishment of a multiracial society based on the principles of democratic socialism. Also important is the Islamic-radical, 300,000- member Pan-Malayan Islamic Party (PAS: Parti Islam Se Malaysia), which was formed in 1951 and advocates the establishment of a fully Islamic society.

The Parti Bersatu Sabah (PBS), set up in 1985 by the Roman Catholic ex-chief minister of Sabah state, Datuk Joseph Pairin Kitangan, and a member of the NF until October 1990, is also a member of the opposition, drawing its support from the Christian Kadazan-Dusin people. Smaller, regional parties operate at the state level.

Latest elections
In the most recent House of Representatives elections, which were held on 24–25 April 1995, in tandem with elections to the 13 state legislative assemblies, the ruling National Front coalition captured 162 of the 192 House of Representatives seats and 64% of the vote, a 10% advance on its performance in 1990. The Chinese DAP, the largest opposition party in the new parliament, retained just 9 of the 20 seats it had held before the election and the opposition won no parliamentary seats in seven of the country's 13 states. The fundamentalist PAS held on to control of Kelantan state. However, the other states were won by the National Front, which won 339 of the 394 available state assembly seats. The election campaign was characterized by the state-controlled media adopting a slavishly pro-government line and the opposition being hampered by the banning of public rallies.

Political history
The history of the country is better understood on the basis of a knowledge of its geographical location. The Federation of Malaysia is divided into two broad regions: in the west, Peninsular Malaysia, comprising 11 states and 83% of the total population, and Eastern Malaysia, which includes the states of Sabah and Sarawak, in the north and east of the island of Borneo. The southern and central portion of the island forms part of Indonesia. The small, independent coastal Sultanate of Brunei is encircled by Eastern Malaysia and the two broad regions of Malaysia are separated by 640 kilometres of the South China Sea.

The regions of present-day Malaysia formed part of the Buddhist Sri Vijaya empire between the 9th and 14th centuries, an empire which was eventually overthrown by a Javanese Hindu kingdom. Islam was subsequently introduced and a substantial empire was built up, prior to the Portuguese conquest of Malacca in 1511. Thereafter the area came, successively, under Dutch, 1641–1795, British 1795–1817, and, again, Dutch, 1818–24, control.

From the mid-1820s, British sovereignty was progressively established over the Malaysia region, and a tin and rubber export-based economy was developed, particularly in the west. Chinese and Indian Tamil labourers were imported to work in the mines and on the plantations. Despite British presence, local state chiefs were allowed to retain considerable political autonomy. Initially, in 1826, only the states of Singapore, Penang, and Malacca were formally incorporated into the British Colony of the Straits Settlement. But in 1874 British protection was extended to Perak, Selangor, Pahang, and Negri Sembilan. In 1895 they collectively formed the Federated Malay States. Johore came under British protection in 1885. Then, between 1910 and 1930, protection treaties were entered into with Kedah, Perlis, Kelantan, and Trengganu, which, together with Johore, were known as the Unfederated Malay States. Finally, after World War II, and following the extension of British control over Sarawak, in 1948, the protectorates in Borneo and the Malay Peninsula were unified to form, in February 1948, the Federation of Malaysia (FOM) Crown Colony.

Following several years of communist insurrection, the FOM was granted independence, within the Commmonwealth, in August 1957. Six years later, in September 1963, Britain relinquished sovereignty over its crown colonies of Sabah and Sarawak, and a new 14-state FOM was formed. North Borneo had been a British territory since 1881 and administered by the North Borneo Company until 1946. Sarawak was a British territory which had been ruled by the Brooke family since 1841. This new Federation initially included the internally self-governing state of Singapore. However, in August 1965, Singapore, alleging discrimination against its Chinese community, seceded from the FOM.

During its early years, between 1963 and 1966, the existence of the FOM was contested by guerrillas supported by the Sukarno government of Indonesia, while, in 1968, the Philippines disputed the sovereignty of East Malaysia. Tunku (Prince) Abdul Rahman (1903–90) was the country's first prime minister, between 1963 and 1969, governing in a successful, consensual, and multiracial manner at the head of the Alliance Party, which had been established in 1952. Then, in August 1969, serious anti-Chinese race riots erupted in Kuala Lumpur, forcing the formation of an emergency administration. These riots followed a fall in support for the ruling United Malays National Organization (UMNO) in the federal elections and were indicative of a deeper Malay resentment of the economic success and wealth of the Chinese business community.

The disturbances prompted the resignation of Tunku Abdul Rahman in September 1970 and the creation, by his successor as prime minister, Tun Abdul Razak, of a broader ten-party, later 13, National Front governing coalition, to succeed the Alliance Party. The coalition included in its ranks previous opposition parties. In addition, a major 'New Economic Policy' was launched in 1971, with the aim of raising the share of businesses owned by ethnic Malays (Bumiputras) from a level of 4% to 30% by 1990. It was also planned to extend the use of pro-Malay 'affirmative action' quota systems for university entrance and company employment. At the same time, greater stress was placed on rural development, in an effort to achieve a better 'economic balance'.

During the 1970s, Malaysia enjoyed healthy rates of economic growth, of more than 7%, but the problem of communist guerrilla actions near the Thailand border re-emerged after 1975. Relations with the Chinese community also deteriorated in the later 1970s as a result of the federal government's initial refusal to accept 'boat people' refugees, fleeing from Vietnam. Even more serious was the revival of a fundamentalist Islamic movement in the western and northern provinces.

Dr Mahathir bin Mohamad (b. 1925), formerly the deputy prime minister and trade and industry minister, became the new leader of the UMNO and prime minister in July 1981 and proceeded to pursue a more narrowly Islamic and pro-Malay strategy than his predecessors. In addition, he embarked on an ambitious new industrialization programme, seeking to 'look east' and emulate Japan. He secured re-election in April 1982 and August 1986, but, between these dates, began to encounter growing opposition from his Malaysian Chinese Association (MCA) coalition partners. He was also faced with Christian–Moslem ethnic conflict in Sabah and a sudden slowdown in economic growth in 1985, as a result of the fall in world tin, rubber, and palm oil commodity prices. Internal UMNO opposition to Dr Mahathir also began to surface in 1987, when, in April, trade and industry minister, Tunku Razaleigh Hamzah, unsuccessfully, but only by a

small margin, challenged for the party's presidency. Two months later, Razaleigh and his closest supporters were dismissed from their cabinet posts.

During the autumn of 1987 racial tensions worsened, Chinese language education and religion emerging as divisive issues. Fearing a renewed outbreak of riots, Prime Minister Mahathir, in October–November, ordered the arrest and detention without trial of 106 politicians, including the DAP leader and deputy leader Lim Kit Siang and Karpal Singh. Among the people arrested were journalists, lawyers, and pressure group leaders. The action was taken under the provisions of the Internal Security Act (ISA). Press censorship regulations were also tightened, and several journals were forced to cease publication. These moves served to heighten intraparty opposition to Mahathir, to the extent that the party's moderate wing, led by Razaleigh and supported by former prime minister, Tunku Abdul Rahman, charged the prime minister with increasing authoritarianism. Eleven dissident members from this wing filed a legal suit, claiming that the party's leadership election of the previous year had been improperly conducted. Their claims were upheld by the High Court, in February 1988, which ruled that delegations taking part in the elections had not been legally registered and that, as a result, the UMNO was 'an unlawful society', and the 1987 elections were null and void.

This created a serious constitutional crisis, putting in doubt the legal status of the incumbent government. However, with the support of the head of state, Tunku Mahmood Iskandar, and with subsequent favourable judicial rulings, Prime Minister Mahathir weathered the storm. Initially, the Razaleigh–Rahman wing of the UMNO attempted to register a new successor party, 'UMNO Malaysia', but the application was rejected by the Registrar of Societies. Dr Mahathir responded by applying to form a 'New UMNO' (UMNO Baru), which excluded dissident members of the old UMNO. This application was accepted by the registrar.

Despite surviving the immediate political crisis of February 1988, Dr Mahathir's public standing was seriously weakened in the short term. The new UMNO Baru was defeated heavily in an opposition-engineered by-election in August 1988. Additional controversy was aroused by the passage of a constitutional amendment, in March 1988, which limited the power of the judiciary to interpret laws and the dismissal, in July 1988, of the lord president of the Supreme Court for alleged 'anti-government bias'. The National Front recovered sufficiently to secure a further clear victory in the October 1990 general election, although its share of parliamentary seats fell from the 84% achieved in August 1986 to just 71%.

In November 1993 finance minister Anwar Ibrahim was elected deputy president of UMNO, thus becoming the obvious heir-apparent to Dr Mahathir. In March 1994 Joseph Pairin Kitangan, chief minister of Sabah since 1985, was forced to resign after being undermined by a conviction for corruption which he had denied. A new UMNO government was formed in the state. This left only one state in the federation, Kelantan, with an opposition administration.

In foreign affairs, Malaysia joined ASEAN in 1967 and originally, during the Tunku Abdul Rahman era, adopted a pro-Western, anticommunist posture. From the 1970s, however, its relations with the communist powers improved, while closer links were also developed with Islamic nations. The country has advocated the creation of a zone of 'peace, freedom and neutrality' in Southeast Asia. In November 1993, concerned at the possibility of United States domination of the region, Malaysia boycotted the inaugural summit of the Asia Pacific Economic Cooperation (APEC) forum.

In the economic sphere, the government has, since the mid-1960s, pursued a system of indicative economic planning, based on the framing of five-year plans. In addition, in 1985, a ten-year Industrial Master Plan (IMP) was introduced, with the aim of fostering long-term development of the manufacturing sector. Joint venture projects have also been entered into with Japanese car manufacturing companies, while special tax and export incentives have been offered by the state's Malaysian Industrial Development Authority, in an effort to attract greater inward investment. These moves, involving a slackening of restrictions on foreign ownership, meant that the 1971 goal of achieving 30% ethnic Malay equity ownership by 1989 had, of necessity, to be revised. In 1986 the Malay share stood at 18%. The 'New Development Policy' (NDP), which was launched in June 1991 to replace the expiring 'New Economic Policy', was consequently less discriminatory against non-Malays. It aimed to achieve an eightfold increase, 7% per annum, in national income by the year 2020, by which date Malaysia, it envisaged, will have become a 'fully developed state'. Between 1986 and 1995 the annual rate of GDP growth averaged 8% and the UMNO increased its parliamentary majority in the general election held in April 1995, securing its biggest victory since independence in 1957.

MALDIVES

The Republic of the Maldives
Dhivehi Raajjeyge Jumhooriyyaa

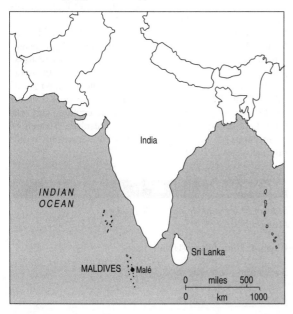

Capital: Malé

Social and economic data
Area: 298 km²
Population: 223,000*
Pop. density per km²: 748*
Urban population: 31%**
Literacy rate: 98%**
GDP: $135 million**; per-capita GDP: $650**
Government defence spending (% of GDP): 0%***
Currency: rufiyaa
Economy type: low income
Labour force in agriculture: 6%**

*1994
**1992
***There are no armed forces

Ethnic composition
The indigenous population comprises four 'ethnic strains': Dravidian, in the northern islands; Arab, in the middle islands; Sinhalese, in the southern islands; and Negro, or Ravare. Dhivehi, or Maldivian, is the syncretic official national language. There is also an Indian linguistic and religious immigrant minority.

Religions
The majority of the population, more than 90%, are Sunni Muslims. Islam is the state religion and Sharia law is enforced.

Political features
State type: authoritarian nationalist
Date of state formation: 1965
Political structure: unitary
Executive: unlimited presidential
Assembly: one-chamber
Party structure: no parties
Human rights rating: N/A
International affiliations: AsDB, CP, CW, CP, ESCAP, G-77, IBRD, IDB, IMF, NAM, OIC, SAARC, UN, WTO

Local and regional government
The country is divided into 20 administrative districts, comprising the capital, which is subject to direct central administration, and the 19 atolls, each of which is governed by an atoll chief (*verin*), appointed by the president. The chief is assisted by an elected committee. Each island is subject to the jurisdiction of a headman (*kateeb*), also appointed by the president.

Head of state and head of government
President Maumoon Abdul Gayoom, since 1978

Political leaders since 1970
1968–78 Ibrahim Nasir (independent), 1978– Maumoon Abdul Gayoom (independent)

Political system
The current constitution was adopted in November 1968 and is an amended version of an earlier 1964 document which was drawn up by the celebrated British constitutional lawyer, Sir Ivor Jennings. It provides for a single-chamber Citizens' Council (Majlis) of 48 members, and an executive president,

nominated by the Majlis and then elected by referendum. They all serve a five-year term. Forty of the Majlis' members are elected by universal adult suffrage, two each being returned by the National Capital Island and the 19 constituent atolls, and eight are appointed by the president. The Majlis meets three times a year, acting principally as a debating forum. The president appoints and leads a cabinet, whose members are individually responsible to the Majlis. In March 1995 the cabinet had 23 members and President Gayoom held the key portfolios of defence, national security, and finance and treasury. There has also been, since July 1985, a 15-member, president-appointed, Special Consultative Council, which advises on economic matters and held discussions, in 1990, on the advantages of promoting greater freedom of speech. Women are precluded from holding political office.

Political parties
There are no political parties in the Maldives, candidates standing for election on the basis of their 'personal influence' and clan loyalties.

Latest elections
In the most recent presidential election, or, rather, referendum, held on 1 October 1993, Maumoon Abdul Gayoom was re-elected unopposed for a fourth consecutive term, securing more than 92% of the popular vote. Non-party elections to the Majlis were last held in December 1994.

Political history
The Maldives comprise 1,196 small coral islands, 203 of which are inhabited, grouped in 19 atolls, situated in the North Indian Ocean, 650 kilometres southwest of Sri Lanka. The islands lie barely a metre above a rising sea level and the country faces the risk of disappearing beneath the waves if sea levels rise as a consequence of global warming. The original population, which was Dravidian, was displaced during the 9th century by seafaring Arabs, who introduced Islamic practices. During the 16th century, the islands came under Portuguese rule, before becoming a dependency of Ceylon, now Sri Lanka, from the mid-17th century, when Sinhalese and Indian colonies were established. Under the designation 'Maldive Islands', though still remaining a dependency of Ceylon, they were placed under British protection in 1887 and enjoyed a measure of internal self-government under a hereditary sultan.

Between January 1953 and February 1954 a republic was briefly established, before the sultanate, now subject to election, was restored, with Ibrahim Nasir serving as prime minister. In July 1965, with anti-British sentiment rising and reflected in a secessionist rebellion in Suvadivan in 1959–60, the islands were granted full independence outside the Commonwealth, under the new designation 'Maldives'. Three years later, after a referendum, the sultan was deposed and a republic was again established, with the then prime minister, Ibrahim Nasir, elected president. He governed with the aid of a prime minister, Ahmed Zaki, until March 1975, when this post was abolished, after an attempt by Zaki to secure a Majlis no-confidence vote against the president. A fully presidential system was then adopted.

Between 1956 and 1975 Britain had a Royal Air Force staging post on the southern island of Gan and its closure meant a substantial loss of income. The president, nevertheless, refused an offer from the USSR, in October 1977, to lease the former base, saying that he did not want it used for military purposes again, nor leased to a superpower.

In 1978 President Nasir announced that he would not stand for re-election for a third term and the Majlis nominated Maumoon Abdul Gayoom (b. 1937), a former university lecturer in Islamic studies and later a member of Nasir's cabinet, as his successor. He was then elected unopposed in a popular presidential 'referendum', in July 1978, winning 90% of the votes cast. Nasir, meanwhile, left the country for Singapore but was called back to answer charges of embezzling government funds. He denied the charges and attempts to extradite him were unsuccessful. Despite rumours of a plot by groups connected with Nasir to overthrow him, Gayoom was re-elected for a further five years in September 1983, securing 95.6% of the popular vote.

During his period in charge, the country, despite a rapid population growth of over 3% per annum, has enjoyed substantial economic progress, with annual GDP growth averaging nearly 10%. This has primarily been the result of the promotion of the tourist industry, which generates 20% of current GDP. A further 15% is generated by the fishing industry, in which 20% of the labour force is engaged. The president has also concentrated on the development of poor rural regions and social provision, such as education and health services.

In foreign affairs, while adhering to his predecessor's general policy of nonalignment and close links with the Arab nations of the Middle East, Gayoom brought the Maldives back into the Commonwealth as a full member in June 1985. The country is also a founder member of the South Asian Association for Regional Cooperation (SAARC).

President Gayoom was re-elected in September 1988, but was challenged in November 1988 by an abortive coup led by Abdullah Luthufi, an exiled businessman from the southern atoll of Adu, which had demanded secession during the 1970s. He had recruited a force of around 200 Tamil mercenaries in Sri Lanka. After fierce fighting, which claimed 20 lives, the rebels, who appeared to enjoy the backing of former President Nasir, captured the presidential palace and forced Gayoom into hiding. However, order was restored after the intervention, at Gayoom's request, of 300 paratroops sent by India, in fulfilment of its role as a member of SAARC: the Maldives lacked an army of its own. Luthufi and his co-conspirator, Sagar Nasir, were captured and sent for trial and Gayoom re-installed as President. Sixteen of those captured, including Luthufi, were sentenced to life imprisonment in 1989.

MONGOLIA

State of Mongolia/Mongolian Republic
Mongol Uls

Capital: Ulaanbaatar (Ulan Bator)

Social and economic data
Area: 1,565,000 km^2
Population: 2,400,000*

Pop. density per km²: 1.5*
Urban population: 49%**
Literacy rate: 93%**
GDP: $860 million**; per-capita GDP $400**
Government defence spending (% of GDP): 6.9**
Currency: tugrik
Economy type: low income
Labour force in agriculture: 30%**

*1994
**1992

Ethnic composition
Ninety per cent of the population is Mongol, 4% Kazakh, 2% Chinese, and 2% Russian. Khalkha Mongolian is the official language.

Religions
Tibetan Buddhism (Lamaism) has been the traditional religion for the Mongol community. It was suppressed during the communist era, but there has been a revival during recent years. The Kazakhs of western Mongolia are Sunni Muslims by descent.

Political features
State type: emergent democratic
Date of state formation: 1921
Political structure: unitary
Executive: limited presidential
Assembly: one-chamber
Party structure: multiparty
Human rights rating: N/A
International affiliations: AsDB, ESCAP, IAEA, IBRD, IMF, G-77, LORCS, NAM, UN, WFTU

Local and regional government
The country is divided into 18 provinces (*aymags*) and one municipality (Ulaanbaatar), with appointed governors (*dzasag darga*) and elected local assemblies.

Head of state (executive)
President Punsalmaagiyn Ochirbat, since 1990

Head of government
Prime Minister Puntsagiyn Jasray, since 1992

Political leaders since 1970* 1958–84 Yumjaagiyn Tsedenbal (MPRP), 1984–90 Jambyn Batmunkh (MPRP), 1990– Punsalmaagiyn Ochirbat (MPRP/independent)

*Communist Party leaders

Political system
Under the new, noncommunist, constitution of February 1992, Mongolia has a 76-member parliament, the People's Great Hural (Assembly). Deputies are elected for four-year terms and parliamentary sessions must be held at least every six months for not less than 75 working days. The voting age is set at 25 years and there are 26 constituencies. Election is by simple majority, provided candidates secure the support of at least 50% of the electorate of their constituency. The executive president is elected directly for a four-year term. Candidates must be at least 45 years old and be resident (for at least five years) ethnic Mongolians. The president works with a prime minister and a cabinet of some 20 members elected by the parliament and may veto legislation. These vetoes can be overturned by a two-thirds majority vote in the Great Hural. This new democratic constitution permits both private ownership and the imposition of forced labour.

Political parties
The dominant party is the Mongolian People's Revolutionary Party (MPRP) which originated as a broad front of radical nationalist forces, inspired by the 1917 Russian Bolshevik revolution, who were opposed to China's attempts to restore its sovereignty over Mongolia in 1919. In 1921 those with communist leanings met in the USSR to form the Mongolian People's Party, which was renamed the MPRP in 1924, constituting the nucleus of the country's new 'Provisional People's Government'. The MPRP was divided between a radical left wing and a conservative, moderate right wing during the 1920s and 1930s and subject to repeated factional conflicts, until party strongman, Marshal Horloogiyn Choybalsan, established his dominance between 1939–52. Under Choybalsan, the regular party machinery fell into disuse, only two congresses meeting, as power became personalized. Under his successors, however, a regularized structure was re-established. It is now a reform-socialist body, led by Budgragchaagyn Dash-Yondon. The party is organized hierarchically on 'democratic centralist' lines, with a nine-member Party Leadership Council at its apex.

The principal opposition party is the Mongolian National Democratic Party (MNDP), which was formed in October 1992 through the merger of the Mongolian Democratic Union (MDU; estd. 1989), the Mongolian Party of National Progress (MPNP), the Mongolian United Party (MUP), and the Party for Mongolian Renaissance. Led by Davaadorjyn Ganbold, it advocates market economics, a revival of traditional Mongolian culture, and a neutral foreign policy.

Latest elections

The most recent People's Great Hural elections were held in June 1992. The MPRP captured 70 of the 76 seats, based on a 57% share of the national vote. The three-party opposition coalition, comprising the MDP, the MPNP, and the MUP, and termed the Democratic Coalition, won 17% of the vote but only four seats. The Mongolian Social Democratic Party (MSDP; estd. 1990), captured 10% of the vote and one seat. The election was contested by 293 candidates and turnout was recorded at 95.6%.

The country's first ever direct presidential election was won by the incumbent Punsalmaagiyn Ochirbat on 6 June 1993. Ochirbat, a former member of the MPRP, but who stood in this election as the nominee of a coalition of the MNDP and MSDP, comfortably defeated the MPRP's official candidate, Lodongiyn Tudev, who was less committed to political and economic reform.

Political history

The area, dominated by nomadic tribes, was united by Genghis Khan (c. 1162–1227) during the early 13th century, and formed the nucleus of a vast Mongol empire which stretched across Asia, reaching its zenith under Genghis' grandson, Kublai Khan (1214–94). It was then conquered by China during the 17th century, being known as the Chinese province of 'Outer Mongolia' between 1689 and 1911. Following the Chinese 'republican revolution' of 1911, Mongolian nationalists proclaimed the country's independence and, receiving the support of Tsarist Russia, succeeded in gaining semi-autonomy, under the leadership of a traditionalist Buddhist monarchy, in the shape of a 'reincarnated' lama. Chinese sovereignty was asserted again in 1915 and, taking advantage of the turmoil in Russia, formal control was reintroduced in 1919. The new Soviet government came, however, to the support of Mongolian nationalists, helping them to overthrow Chinese rule for the last time in July 1921. Constitutionally, Mongolia continued to remain subject to China's formal sovereignty until January 1946, an October 1945 plebiscite having unanimously favoured full independence, but a November 1921 treaty with the Russian Soviet Federal Socialist Republic guaranteed its autonomy.

Initially, the newly independent state was subject to joint control by the monarchy and an MPRP-dominated 'People's Government'. However, on the death of King Javdzandamba Hutagt VIII in June 1924, the monarchy was abolished and a 'People's Republic' proclaimed. In November 1924 a Soviet-style constitution was adopted and a programme of 'defeudalization' launched. This involved the expropriation of the previously dominant nobility, the collectivization of agriculture, predominantly herding, and the destruction of Lama Buddhism. An armed uprising by anti-government forces, in 1932, was forcibly suppressed, with Soviet assistance. At least 100,000 people were killed in the purges of this period.

The dominant figure in the new state, following purges between 1936–39, became the former independence fighter, Marshal Horloogiyn Choybalsan, who combined the offices of MPRP leader and prime minister and ruled in a strict Stalinist manner, with minimal consultation. On his death, in January 1952, the two posts were respectively divided between Dashiyn Damba and Yumjaagiyn Tsedenbal, a Soviet-educated economist, until, in November 1958, Tsedenbal once again combined the positions and emerged as the dominant figure, but governing in a more cautious and consensual manner than his predecessor. A new constitution was adopted in July 1960, in recognition of the 'higher stage' of socialist development which had been attained.

Throughout the interwar period Mongolia remained closely dependent on the Soviet Union militarily, economically, and politically. Its MPRP leaders were all trained in Moscow and by the 1980s 95% of its foreign trade was with the USSR and Eastern Europe. This close interdependence received formal recognition in 1962, when Mongolia joined Comecon, and in January 1966, when a 20-year friendship, cooperation, and mutual assistance pact with the USSR was signed. This served to further sour relations with neighbouring communist China which, at this time, was in ideological dispute with the Soviet Union. As a consequence, border incidents between the two countries became frequent during the early 1970s.

Internally, Mongolia remained substantially isolated from the outside world during the 1970s, but experienced considerable economic change as new urban industries developed and settled agriculture spread. Politically, MPRP leader Yumjaagiyn Tsedenbal remained the dominant figure, assuming the post of head of state in May 1972, on the death of the long-serving Jamsrangiyn Sambuu, who had been head of state since 1954. Jambyn Batmunkh took over Tsendbal's post of prime minister. Tsedenbal finally retired, on the grounds of ill-health, in August 1984, and was replaced as party leader and head of state by Jambyn Batmunkh. Dumaagiyn Sodnom, Batmunkh's deputy, became the new prime minister.

Mongolia's political leadership had traditionally been notoriously conservative and loyal to the 'Moscow line'. However, following the accession to power in the Soviet Union of Mikhail Gorbachev in 1985, the country was encouraged to be more innovative and to broaden its outside contacts. A large-scale reorganization of government ministries was launched between 1986 and 1988, as a means of streamlining decision-taking and enhancing efficiency. In the diplomatic sphere, the level of cultural exchanges with China significantly increased and ambassadorial relations with the United States were established in January 1987. Also, between 1987 and 1990, the number of Soviet troops stationed within the country was reduced. Finally, a more tolerant attitude was adopted towards traditional social customs and religion. This encouraged a revival in Mongolian nationalism.

Influenced by events in Eastern Europe, an opposition grouping, the Mongolian Democratic Union (MDU), was formed illegally in December 1989 and during 1990 it spearheaded a campaign demanding greater democratization. As a result of this pressure, senior figures within the MPRP, including Batmunkh and Sodnom, were forced to resign in March 1990 and were later charged with corruption. Punsalmaagiyn Ochirbat (b. 1942), formerly the minister of external economic relations, became head of state and the People's Great Hural amended the constitution so as to end the communists' monopoly of power.

In the multiparty elections of July 1990 the remodelled MPRP captured 83% of parliament's seats and Ochirbat was subsequently elected indirectly state president. Members of the opposition Mongolian Democratic Party, successor to the MDU, were brought into a new administration which embarked on an ambitious programme of economic transformation, moving from central planning to a market economy by 1994. Prices were freed, the currency was devalued massively, a new banking system and stock exchange were established, industries and agriculture were privatized, via a voucher-conversion scheme, and the country joined the IMF and Asian Development Bank (AsDB). In the short term, the process of transition was painful. GDP fell by 10% during 1991 and by 9% during 1992, as the collapse of the Soviet Union led to the ending of its economic aid and supplies of energy, as well as the full withdrawal of Red Army troops. A seventh of the labour force was idle as the country found it difficult to find new markets for its products.

In the wake of the anticommunist repercussions of the failed August 1991 anti-Gorbachev coup in the USSR, President Ochirbat and other senior state officials resigned formally as members of the MPRP. A new constitution was adopted in February 1992 and in a general election held in June 1992 the MPRP held on to power. Puntsagiyn Jasray, an economist, became prime minister in July 1992 and President Ochirbat, now an independent supported by the MNDP and MSDP, was directly elected state president in June 1993. During 1993 the economy contracted by a further 8%, despite pledges of economic aid from Japan, loans from the IMF, and the signing of a Friendship and Cooperation Treaty with Russia. This provoked popular opposition to the government and in April 1994 there was a brief hunger strike by leading figures in the MDU and MSDP who accused the administration of corruption and ineffective economic reforms.

MYANMAR (BURMA)

Union of Myanmar/Burma* (UOM)
Myanmar Naingngandaw

*The designation Burma was officially dropped in May 1989, but is still used by the opposition and by the Western media

Capital: Yangon (Rangoon)

Social and economic data
Area: 676,552 km^2
Population: 44,600,000*
Pop. density per km^2: 66*
Urban population: 25%**
Literacy rate: 81%**
GDP: $17,000 million**; per-capita GDP: $385**
Government defence spending (% of GDP): 10.5%**
Currency: kyat
Economy type: low income
Labour force in agriculture: 64%**

*1994
**1992

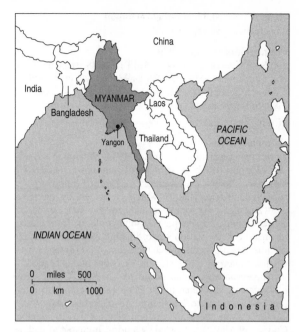

Ethnic composition
Burmans, who predominate in the fertile central river valley and southern coastal and delta regions, constitute the ethnic majority, comprising 72% of the total population. Out of more than a hundred minority communities, the most important are the Karen, 7% of the population, the Shan, 6%, Indians, 6%, Chinese, 3%, Kachin, 2%, and Chin, 2%. The indigenous minority communities, who predominate in mountainous border regions, show considerable hostility towards the culturally and politically dominant Burmans, undermining national unity. The official language is Burmese, spoken by 80% of the population.

Religions
Eighty-seven per cent of the population is Theravada Buddhist, 5% Christian, 4% Sunni Muslim, 3% animist, and 1% Hindu. Animism and Christianity are concentrated among the ethnic minority communities.

Political features
State type: military
Date of state formation: 1948
Political structure: unitary
Executive: military
Assembly: one-chamber
Party structure: multiparty
Human rights rating: 17%
International affiliations: AsDB, CP, ESCAP, G-77, IAEA, IBRD, IMF, LORCS, NAM, UN, WTO

Local and regional government
The country is divided into 14 administrative divisions, including seven states and seven provinces. Below them there are townships, wards, and village-tracts, each with an elected People's Council controlled by an inner Executive Committee.

Head of state and head of government

General Than Shwe, since 1992

Political leaders since 1970

1962–88 General U Ne Win (BSPP)*, 1988 Brigadier General Sein Lwin (BSPP)*, 1988 Dr Maung Maung (BSPP)*, 1988–92 General Saw Maung (military), 1992– General Than Shwe (military)

*Ruling party leaders

Political system

Under the constitution of January 1974, Myanmar is a unitary republic. The highest organ of state power is the 485-member People's Assembly (Pyithu Hluttaw), a single-chamber legislature which is elected by universal adult suffrage every four years and convenes twice a year for short sessions. The People's Assembly elects, from among its members, the nation's coordinating executive, the 29-member State Council, which includes a representative from each of Myanmar's 14 states and divisions and is headed by a chairperson who acts as president. The State Council also has authority, delegated by the People's Assembly, to interpret and promulgate legislation. To undertake day-to-day administration, the State Council elects a 16–20 member Council of Ministers, headed by a prime minister, as well as three judicial bodies: the Council of People's Justices, the Council of People's Attorneys, and the Council of People's Inspectors.

The constitution was suspended in September 1988 and all state organs and institutions were abolished and superseded by an army-run 19-member State Law and Order Restoration Council (SLORC) and martial law was proclaimed. The SLORC's chairperson, Than Shwe, serves as head of state and as prime minister and defence minister. He shares ultimate power with Lieutenant General Khin Nyunt, first secretary of the SLORC and head of the Directorate of Defence Services Intelligence, who is a protégé of Myanmar's former strongman, U Ne Win. From 1993 a 699-member National Convention, comprising representatives of the SLORC and ten opposition parties, including the National League for Democracy, began to meet periodically to discuss the framing of a new constitution. The junta is anxious that any new constitution will guarantee the military a continuing, significant political role, on the model of Indonesia.

Political parties

Since 1962 the controlling force in the UOM has been the National Unity Party (NUP), known until September 1988 as the Burma Socialist Programme Party (BSPP or Lanzin Party). It is closely intertwined with the military. With the passage of the Law to Protect National Solidarity, in March 1964, Myanmar legally became a one-party state. However, following the popular unrest of 1988, opposition parties began to reform.

The BSPP was established in July 1962 as a 'political arm' by the new military regime of General U Ne Win which had recently seized power. The party organized itself on quasi-communist lines, with a hierarchy of ward, village and district branches at its lower levels and a controlling 280-member Central Committee and 17-member Central Executive Committee (CEC), 'elected' by a supra 1,000-member quadrennial Congress, at its apex. It was assigned a 'leading role' in state affairs, with members of its CEC monopolizing senior executive posts. In 1985 membership of the BSPP was put at 2.3 million, a figure which constituted 6.1% of the total population.

From September 1988, when the multiparty system was relegalized, opposition parties rapidly re-emerged. The most important new party to be formed was the National League for Democracy (NLD), a broad grouping which was the successor to the Democracy and Peace (Interim) League (DPIL). The DPIL had been illegally established in August 1988 by the former prime minister U Nu, former president, U Mahn Win Maung, the influential former chief of staff and defence minister, General Thura Tin U, and Aung San Suu Kyi, the United Kingdom-based daughter of the assassinated national hero, Aung San.

Party formation accelerated from October 1988, so that by March 1989 it was reported that 22 registered political groupings had been recognized by the ruling military government. However, with the coming to power of the SLORC severe restrictions were placed on effective opposition party activity and by April 1992 only ten legal political parties remained.

Outside the formal party system, armed ethnic minority insurgent groups have been engaged in guerrilla warfare in border regions against the incumbent BSPP and preceding regimes since independence. The outlawed, 10,000 member, Burmese Communist Party (BCP: White Flag Party) is the most serious insurgent force. Formed in 1946, when the Communist Party, which was established in 1939, split into White and Red Flag factions, it remains an unreconstructed Stalinist body, which enjoyed military backing from China until recent years. It established *de facto* control of parts of northern Myanmar during the 1980s through establishing an alliance with Wa tribespeople. However, the Wa mutinied in 1989 and signed a peace treaty with Myanmar's ruling military junta. This forced the BCP's leaders to flee into exile in China.

Anti-communist groups have operated during recent decades in Karen, in the southeast, Kachin, in the northeast, Shan, in the east, Arakan, in the southwest, Chin, in the west, and Palaung, Mon, Lahu, and Pa-O. They have been organized since 1975 within the 35,000-guerrilla-strong National Democratic Front (NDF). The NDF's goal is to re-establish a federal state based on national self-determination. In 1988 the NDF created the Democratic Alliance of Burma (DAB) to incorporate a further 11 dissident groups, including monks, students, and expatriates. However, since 1991 an increasing number of rebel groups have entered into cease-fire agreements with the ruling SLORC, including the Shan, Palaung, and Pa-O, in 1991, the Kachin, in 1993, and the Mon, in 1995. This has left the Karen isolated as the chief remaining rebel force.

Latest elections

The most recent elections to the People's Assembly were held on 27 May 1990, when the opposition National League for Democracy, despite state intimidation, won, surprisingly, 392 of the 485 contested seats. It attracted 60% of the national vote, compared to the NUP's 21%. The NUP won just 10 seats, while the Shan Nationalities League for Democracy captured 23, and the Arakan League for Democracy, 11. The military junta subsequently prevented the Assembly from convening.

Political history

As early as 850 AD, a Burmese state was established, with its capital inland at Pagan. The country was overrun by the Mongols during the later 13th century, but a new Toungoo dynasty was uneasily established in 1486. The nation was reunited by Alaungpaya in 1752, and the port of Rangoon (Yangon) selected as the new capital. Later, however, during the 19th century, with the imperialist intrusion of Britain, this state was gradually dismembered. Following the Anglo-Burmese War of 1824–26, the Arakan coastal strip between Chittagong and Cape Negrais was ceded to British India. Then, in 1852, after defeat in the second Burmese War, Lower Burma, including Rangoon, was annexed by the British. Finally, in 1886, after Thibaw, the last Burmese king, had precipitated a third Burmese War, Upper Burma was conceded.

Britain immediately reunited these annexed portions to form the 'province of Burma', which was governed as part of British India, until constituted as a Crown Colony, with a degree of internal self-government, in 1937. It developed into a major rice, teak, and later oil, exporter, drawing into its coastal urban-commercial centres thousands of immigrant workers from India and China.

During World War II, Myanmar was invaded and occupied by Japan between 1942 and 1945, encouraging the flight of many of the more recent Indian émigrés. The Japanese proceeded to install a government of anti-British nationalists, headed by Ba Maw, and granted the country nominal independence. However, the nationalists, led by Aung San (1914–47) and U Nu (1907–95), both of whom had earlier been imprisoned by the British for their pro-independence activities, later turned against their 'patrons', founding the Anti-Fascist People's Freedom League (AFPFL), which collaborated with the British in their drive against the Japanese occupiers.

The country was liberated by Allied forces, in 1945, and achieved full independence outside the British Commonwealth, under the designation of 'Union of Burma', on 4 January 1948. A parliamentary democracy was established in which the socialist AFPFL, led by Prime Minister U Nu, held power and states were specially created for the Shan, Karen, Kachin, Chin, and Kayah minority peoples, who enjoyed a substantial measure of autonomy as part of a 'limited federal' system. The new republic was weakened, however, by a mounting internal insurgency movement, involving communist guerrillas, Karen tribespeople and other dissatisfied ethnic group separatists.

In 1958 a split within the AFPFL precipitated a political crisis which persuaded U Nu to 'invite' General U Ne Win (b. 1911), the army Chief of Staff, to form an emergency caretaker government. This administration, which lasted for two years, was the prelude to a full-scale military coup in March 1962 and the abolition of the parliamentary system. General U Ne Win, claimed that parliamentary government had proved unworkable in Myanmar and assumed power as head of a Revolutionary Council composed of fellow military officers. He abrogated the 1948 constitution and established a strong, centralized one-party state.

Following a referendum in December 1973, a new presidential-style unitary constitution was adopted in 1974, and the Revolutionary Council was dissolved. The existing military leaders resigned their titles to become civilian rulers, through the vehicle of a specially constituted Burma Socialist Programme Party (BSPP).

Ne Win was elected president and re-elected again in 1978, before stepping down to be replaced by another former army chief of staff, General U San Yu (b. 1919), in November 1981. The new post-1962 military-BSPP government adopted an external policy of neutralist isolationism. Domestically, it pursued an unique, self-reliant, Buddhist-influenced and state-dominated socio-economic strategy, termed the 'Burmese Way towards Socialism'. It was founded on strict price control in the agricultural sector, where farming was allowed to remain in private hands, and state enterprises in the commercial–industrial sector. This programme, coupled with the continuing internal insurgency, had a debilitating effect on the country's economy, turning Myanmar into one of the poorest, in terms of per-capita GDP, countries in the Asia–Pacific region. This fact was recognized in December 1987 by the UN's grant of 'least developed country' (LDC) status.

Public dissatisfaction with the deteriorating economic situation first became evident in 1974 and 1976 and assumed the form of food shortage riots and student demonstrations. A decade later, in September 1987, new student demonstrations erupted in Yangon after the introduction of precautionary demonetization measures, soon after the domestic trading of rice, which was now in short supply, had been freed from existing restraints. Further, more widespread and better organized, anti-government student and workers' riots followed, in March and June 1988. These were sternly repressed by the armed forces and riot police, at the cost of several hundred lives.

Concerned about the mounting political and economic chaos, an extraordinary BSPP Congress was convened in July 1988 to review the situation. At this meeting, Ne Win, San Yu, and Maung Maung Kha resigned from their respective positions as party leader, state president, and prime minister respectively, and were replaced by Brigadier-General Sein Lwin, who became both president and BSPP chairperson, and Thura U Tun Tin, who assumed the position of prime minister. A series of liberalizing economic reforms was also ratified.

This failed, however, to calm the situation. Instead, in late July and early August 1988, unrest escalated, with more than 100,000 people taking part in demonstrations demanding the removal as president of the reviled Sein Lwin, a 'hardliner' with a long history of dissident repression, and the installation of a new, democratically elected government. Strikes and demonstrations spread to northern urban centres and attracted the support of Buddhist monks and mutinous navy and air force personnel.

With government control of the country rapidly disintegrating, monks and demonstrators began to take charge of several city administrations. Following the killing of 3,000 unarmed demonstrators by riot police on 12 August 1988, and after only 17 days in office, Sein Lwin resigned as BSPP leader and president. A week later he was replaced in both posts by a civilian, the Western-educated former attorney-general, Dr Maung Maung. Despite the apparent 'reformist' credentials of the new national leader, strikes and demonstrations continued, mainly because of the new president's close links with Ne Win, who continued to remain a decisive 'behind-the-scenes' figure.

Caving in to popular pressure, at a new, hastily convened, emergency BSPP Congress on 10 September 1988, the leadership finally approved the holding of a free multiparty general election 'within three months'. A week later, however, with internal disorder continuing, the armed forces, led by former defence minister General Saw Maung, assumed power, in an effort to stabilize the situation. All state institutions were declared abolished and power was transferred to a 19-member military State Law and Order Restoration Council (SLORC), headed by Saw Maung. A night curfew was imposed and all gatherings of more than four people outlawed.

The new military regime, after initially killing hundreds of demonstrators in Yangon, legalized the formation of political parties. However, opposition leaders, notably Aung San Suu Kyi (b. 1945; the daughter of the late Aung San), U Nu, and Tin U, were debarred from standing in the People's Assembly elections which were held in May 1990. To the SLORC's surprise, this general election resulted in a landslide victory for the opposition National League for Democracy (NLD), which won 60% of the popular vote compared to the humiliating 21% secured by the pro-military BSPP, which had been renamed the National Unity Party (NUP). However, the ruling junta refused to accept the people's verdict and did not permit the new People's Assembly to convene. In December 1990 a 'parallel government', headed by Dr Sein Win (a cousin of Suu Kyi), was formed in the eastern city of Manerplaw, in territory controlled by the insurgent Democratic Alliance of Burma (DAB), on the border of Thailand. It was supported by Karen ethnic rebel forces, but was denounced by the bulk of the main opposition force, whose leader, Suu Kyi, held under house arrest from July 1989, was, in October 1991, awarded the Nobel Peace Prize for her 'non-violent struggle for democracy and human rights'. The former prime minister, U Nu, who later died in February 1995, was also kept under house arrest until April 1992, and in 1991 his Socialist Party was outlawed.

Throughout the period from 1989 there were reports of serious human rights abuses, including abduction, torture, and murder, by the security forces and the universities remained closed until August 1992. In addition, the ruling junta continued to wage dry season offensives against Karen ethnic insurgents in the east and moved 75,000 troops into the southwestern Arakan state in an attempt to stamp out a Muslim-led pro-independence movement. This prompted the flight of 200,000 Rohingya Muslims to Bangladesh during 1991–92, many of whom were repatriated from 1993. In response, the West imposed sanctions against Myanmar, which, through opium shipments from the northern Shan and Wa state regions, part of the so-called 'Golden Triangle', had become the source for 60% of the world's heroin. However, the states of ASEAN continued to pursue a policy of 'constructive engagement'.

In April 1993 General Saw Maung stepped down as junta leader on the grounds of deteriorating mental health, believing himself to be the reincarnation of a Burmese king. He was succeeded at the head of the SLORC and as prime minister by General Than Shwe, the former defence minister and deputy commander in chief. However, real power in the junta was believed to rest with the younger Lieutenant General Khin Nyunt, head of military intelligence, who was the protégé of the still influential, though ailing, Ne Win and had close links with China. In September 1992 martial law was officially lifted, but human rights abuses continued, with an estimated 2,000 political prisoners languishing in jail. The junta, which had earlier signed a peace agreement in 1989 with the powerful Wa tribe, situated in the far northeast, reached a cease-fire agreement with the Kachin Independence Army (KIA) in October 1993, ending 30 years of hostility between the Kachins and the Yangon regime. This formed part of a new conciliatory approach to the nation's pro-autonomy ethnic minorities. Cease-fire agreements were signed with a further 12 minorities between 1993–95. However, the most important rebel group, the Karens, were subjected to a major military drive which succeeded in toppling the DAB regime based at Manerplaw in January 1995, forcing the Karens to flee south and into Thailand. In the economic sphere, the junta has, since 1989, pursued a more liberal economic course than the preceding Ne Win regime. Foreign inward investment and tourism, in particular, have been encouraged, as well as the gas, oil and logging industries, and economic growth of 6% was registered during 1994. In July 1995, the prodemocracy leader Suu Kyi was released unconditionally from house arrest by the SLORC.

NEPAL

Kingdom of Nepal
Nepal Adhirajya

Capital: Katmandu

Social and economic data
Area: 141,181 km^2
Population: 21,100,000*
Pop. density per km^2: 149*
Urban population: 12%**
Literacy rate: 26%**
GDP: $3,500m**; per-capita GDP: $170**
Government defence spending (% of GDP): 1.3%**
Currency: Nepalese rupee
Economy type: low income
Labour force in agriculture: 91%**

*1994
**1992

Ethnic composition
Eighty per cent of the population is of Indo-Nepalese ethnic stock, which includes the Gurkhas, the Paharis, the Newars

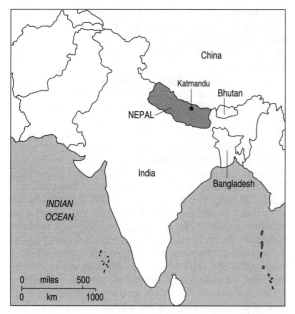

China

Katmandu

Bhutan

NEPAL

India

Bangladesh

INDIAN
OCEAN

0   miles   500

0   km   1000

and the Tharus. The remaining 20% is of Tibeto-Nepalese descent, concentrated in the north and east and surviving mainly as subsistence farmers. There is a caste system on the Indian model. Nepali is the official language and is spoken by 58% of the population. Bihari, spoken by 19% of the population, Maithir, by 12%, and Bhojpuri are also important, with English used as the main second language. Since July 1991 nearly 100,000 refugees from Bhutan have arrived in eastern Nepal.

Religions
Ninety per cent of the population are Hindus, 5% Buddhists and 3% Sunni Muslims. Hinduism is the official state religion and the king is regarded as the incarnation of the Hindu god Vishnu.

Political features
State type: emergent democratic
Date of state formation: 1768
Political structure: unitary
Executive: parliamentary
Assembly: two-chamber
Party structure: multiparty
Human rights rating: 69%
International affiliations: AsDB, CP, ESCAP, G-77, IBRD, IMF, LORCS, NAM, SAARC, UN

Local and regional government
The country is divided into 14 zones for local administration, each of which is headed by an appointed commissioner. Below, there are 75 districts, administered by a district officer. There are 3,524 villages (*gaon*) and 14 towns (*nagar*).

Head of state
King Birendra Bir Bikram Shah Dev, since 1972

Head of government
Prime Minister Sher Bahadur Deuba, since 1995

Political leaders since 1970
1955–72 King Mahendra Bir Bikram Shah, 1972- King Birendra Bir Bikram Shah Dev*, 1991–94 Girija Prasad Koirala (NCP), 1994–95 Man Mohan Adhikari (UNCP), 1995–   Sher Bahadur Deuba (NCP)

*From 1991 power was shared between the king and the prime minister.

Political system
Under the constitution of November 1990, Nepal is a pluralist, parliamentary democracy headed by a constitutional monarch. It has a two-chamber legislature, comprising a 205-member, directly elected House of Representatives (Pratinidhi Sabha) and a 60-member National Council (Rashtriya Sabha), which consists of ten appointees of the king, 35 members (including three women) elected by the lower house and 15 elected from the country's five development zones by an electoral college. The term for the House is five years and for the National Council, six years. Executive power is vested in the Council of Ministers, which is headed by a prime minister drawn from the House of Representatives' majority party grouping. The prime minister is appointed by the king, but their power, in accordance with the 'Westminster model', derives from their party's support. The constitution explicitly guarantees freedom of expression, press, peaceful assembly, association, and movement.

Political parties
Political parties were banned between January 1961 and April 1990, but did function unofficially. There are now two main political parties: the left-of-centre Nepali Congress Party (NCP), which dates from 1947 and was led between 1972 and 1994 by Ganesh Man Singh; and the United Nepal Communist Party (UNCP). The latter was formed in January 1991 by the merger of the Marxist-Leninist and Maoist factions of the Communist Party of Nepal (CPN; estd. 1949) and is led by the Maoist, Man Mohan Adhikari. It is also known as the Unified Marxist-Leninist Party (UML).

There are three other political parties of significance: the monarchist Rashtriya Prajatantra Party (RPP); the Nepal Mazdoor Kisan Party (NMKP); and the Sadhbhavan Party (SP). Political parties must register with the Election Commission to be officially recognized, with at least 5% of candidates presented at elections being female.

Latest elections
In the most recent House of Representatives elections, held on 15 November 1994, the UNCP, with strong support in Katmandu, won 88 of the 205 contested seats, the NCP, 83, the monarchist RPP, 20, the NMKP, 4, the SP, 3, and independent candidates, 7. Voter turnout, at 58%, was 7% below the level registered in the 1991 general election and five people were killed in election clashes.

Elections to the National Council were held in June 1991 and the NCP won 31 seats.

Political history
Nepal is a mountainous independent kingdom lying between India and China. Only 14% of the land is cultivated, the remainder being under forest, river bed, or snow. A third of the population live in the southern lowland 'terai' and

two-thirds in the central hilly region, predominantly in the Vale of Katmandu. It was formerly an assortment of small principalities, and was unified by the Gurkha King, Prithwi Narayan Shah, in 1768. In 1792 a commercial treaty was signed with Britain and in 1816, after the year-long Anglo-Nepali 'Gurkha War', a British Resident was allowed to reside at Katmandu and the kingdom became a British dependent 'buffer-state'.

During the remainder of the 19th century, Nepal remained an isolated, traditionalist outpost on the border of British India, its main value being the supply of Gurkha troops to the British Indian army. This created a 'remittance economy'. From 1846, effective executive power was wielded by the Rana family, who controlled the office of prime minister, making the monarch a titular figurehead.

In 1923 Britain formally recognized Nepal as a fully independent state. The country was, however, still bound by treaty obligations to the United Kingdom until 1947, the year of India's independence. In 1951, the controlling Rana oligarchy was overthrown in a 'palace revolution', supported by the Nepali Congress Party (NCP), and the monarchy, in the person of King Tribhuvan Bir Bikram Shah, was restored to power. In 1959, King Mahendra Bir Bikram Shah, who had succeeded him in 1955, promulgated the nation's first constitution, creating a two-chamber assembly, with a popularly elected lower House. Following elections, the NCP's pro-Indian socialist leader, Bisweswor Prasad Koirala, became prime minister but soon clashed with the king over policies. King Mahendra dissolved the assembly in December 1960 and put a ban on political parties the following month. In December 1962 he introduced a new constitution providing for a tiered, nonparty system of village councils (*panchayats*), an indirectly elected National Assembly and a prime minister appointed by the monarch.

King Mahendra died in January 1972 and was succeeded by his son Birendra Bir Bikram Shah Dev (b. 1945), who, faced with mounting agitation for political reform led by B P Koirala, held a referendum on the constitution in May 1980. A majority of 54.8% voted for a royal-backed, 'suitably reformed', *panchayat* system, in preference to a multiparty alternative. As a result, the constitution was amended, in December 1980, to provide for direct, though still nonparty, elections to the National Assembly. The first elections, which were held in May 1981, led to the defeat of a third of the progovernment candidates and returned a more independent-minded National Assembly. In July 1983 the new body proceeded to unseat Prime Minister Surya Bahadur Thapa, through a 'no-confidence' motion, despite his enjoyment of royal support, and put into office Lokendra Bahadur Chand.

Opposition to the banning of political parties increased in 1985, resulting in terrorist bombings in June. As a consequence, a stringent antiterrorist law was approved by the National Assembly, in August 1985, and more than 1,000 dissidents were arrested. In May 1986, new elections to the National Assembly returned an increased number of members opposed to the nonparty *panchayat* system, and led to the replacement of Prime Minister Chand by Marich Man Singh Shrestha, who had previously been chairman of the Assembly. In an effort to improve the image of the *panchayat* system, the government instituted a stringent anticorruption

drive during 1987. At the same time, however, strict curbs were placed on opposition activity, more than 100 supporters of the banned NCP, including its president, being arrested in the early months of 1988. Tight censorship controls were also imposed.

In the spring of 1990, inspired by events in Eastern Europe, there were mass prodemocracy demonstrations and strikes, coordinated by the NCP-led Movement for the Restoration of Democracy. These were met initially by a strong state response: 150 protesters were shot dead by the police and the NCP's leaders were placed under house arrest. However, after three months, in April 1990, King Birendra bowed to the mounting pressure. He replaced the hardline Shrestha as premier with Lokendra Bahadur Chand and, after talks with opposition leaders, agreed to lift the ban on political parties, abolish the *panchayat* system and renounce his absolute authority. An interim government was installed, headed by the NCP's K P Bhattarai, who had spent 14 years as a political prisoner, and in September 1990 the king approved a new draft constitution. Promulgated in November 1990, it transferred political power from the monarchy to an elected government. Marking the culmination of a 15-month democratization process, a general election was held on 12 May 1991. The NCP secured a narrow majority of seats in the new House of Representatives and its general secretary, G P Koirala, was appointed prime minister on 26 May 1991.

Within a year, the new government was confronted with large, Communist Party (UNCP)-led, demonstrations in Katmandu and Patan, protesting against the prevailing economic austerity. These escalated into a general strike on 6 April 1992 during which 12 demonstrators were killed when police fired into the crowd. A further 30 people were killed during violent UNCP-organized, anti-government protests which had erupted in June–July 1993 after the death of two communist leaders in a suspicious road accident. Crippled by a power struggle within the NCP, between Koirala, party leader Ganesh Man Singh, and party president Krishna Prasad Bhattarai, the government was faced with a series of parliamentary 'no-confidence' motions during 1994. These culminated, on 10 July 1994, in the government's defeat when 36 dissident NCP deputies united with the left-wing opposition. King Birendra dissolved parliament and called fresh elections for November 1994, with Koirala staying on as caretaker prime minister despite UNCP entreaties that a coalition government be formed instead.

The 15 November 1994 general election produced a 'hung parliament', in which the UNCP was the largest single party but was 15 seats short of a overall majority. A minority administration was thus formed by the communists, headed as prime minister by Man Mohan Adhikari (b. 1920), who had spent 17 years in prison for anti-monarchy activities. Adhikari, now a 'reform-communist', pledged that the new administration would encourage the private sector but also seek to help the landless through land reform. However, the new government, after the withdrawal of backing by the NCP in December 1994, found itself with insufficient support to rule effectively and in June 1995, at the request of Prime Minister Adhikari, King Birendra dissolved parliament. New elections were called for November 1995, with

Adhikari remaining premier in an interim capacity. The opposition NCP, RPP, and SP, which together held a small potential one-seat majority in the House of Representatives, filed petitions to the Supreme Court, claiming that the king's actions had been unconstitutional. The Supreme Court ruled in the opposition's favour in August 1995 and in September 1995 Adhikari resigned, after defeat on a no-confidence vote. He was replaced as prime minister by Sher Bahadur Deuba, leader of the NCP, who headed a centrist coalition which included the royalist Rashtriya Prajatantra Party (RPP).

In its external relations since the war, Nepal has traditionally been closely tied to India, entering into a mutual assistance pact soon after the latter's independence. In recent years, however, Nepal has pursued a more neutral, non-aligned course, seeking to create a 'zone of peace' in southern Asia and to maintain cordial relations with both its neighbours, India and China. In particular, commercial links with China have increased recently. This has been resented by India, who imposed a partial blockade of the country between 1989 and 1990 as a result of a dispute over the renegotiation of expired transit and trade treaties.

Economically and socially, Nepal remains a backward country, rates of literacy continuing to be low, and per-capita living standards depressed by over-rapid population expansion, currently 2.6% per annum, and adverse agricultural conditions. Almost a sixth of current GDP is derived from overseas development aid.

PAKISTAN

Islamic Republic of Pakistan Islami Jamhuria-e-Pakistan

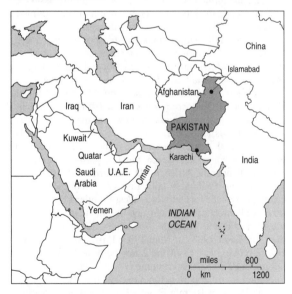

Capital: Islamabad

Social and economic data
Area: 803,943 km²
Population: 128,100,000*

Pop. density per km²: 159*
Urban population: 33%**
Literacy rate: 35%**
GDP: $53,300 million**; per-capita GDP: $420**
Government defence spending (% of GDP): 6.6%**
Currency: Pakistan rupee
Economy type: low income
Labour force in agriculture: 44%**

*1994
**1992

Ethnic composition
Pakistan possesses four principal, regionally based, and antagonistic ethnic communities: Punjabis in the Punjab; Sindhis in Sind; Baluchis in Baluchistan; and, fiercely independent, Pathans (Pushtans) in the North-West Frontier Province. Urdu and English are the official languages. However, 64% of the population speaks Punjabi, 12% Sindhi, 9% Baluchi, 8% Pushtu, and only 20% speaks Urdu, and 2% English.

Religions
Almost 91% of the population is Sunni Muslim and 5% Shia Muslim. Some 1.7% is Hindu and 1.3% is Christian, including 950,000 Roman Catholics, 400,000 adherents to the Protestant Church of Pakistan, and 340,000 to the United Presbyterian Church of Pakistan. Islam is the state religion.

Political features
State type: emergent democratic
Date of state formation: 1947
Political structure: federal
Executive: parliamentary
Assembly: two-chamber
Party structure: multiparty
Human rights rating: 42%
International affiliations: AsDB, CP, CW, ECO, G-24, G-77, ESCAP, IAEA, IBRD, ICC, ICFTU, IMF, IsDB, LORCS, NAM, OAS (observer), OIC, SAARC, UN, WTO

Local and regional government
Below the provinces, the highest level of local administration is the division, followed by the district and then the *tashil* and *taluka*. Commissioners and deputy commissioners operate at the divisional and district levels, alongside elected councils. Since October 1994, the Northern Areas (that part of Kashmir which is controlled by Pakistan, and is known as Azad Kashmir) has had an elected, 24-member council, with legislative, financial and executive powers.

Head of state
President Sardar Farooq Ahmad Khan Leghari, since 1993

Head of government
Prime Minister Benazir Bhutto, since 1993

Political leaders since 1970*
1969–71 General Agha Muhammad Yahya Khan (military), 1971–78 Zulfiqar Ali Bhutto (PPP), 1978–88 General Mohammad Zia ul-Haq (military), 1988 Ghulam Ishaq Khan (independent), 1988–90 Benazir Bhutto (PPP), 1990 Ghulam Mustafa Jatoi (NPP), 1990–93 Nawaz Sharif (IDA),

1993 Mir Balakh Sher Mazari (independent), 1993 Nawaz Sharif (IDA/PML), 1993 Moeenuddin Ahmad Qureshi (independent), 1993– Benazir Bhutto (PPP)

*A mixture of military leaders, presidents, and prime ministers, reflecting the shifts that have taken place in Pakistan's turbulent political system

Political system

Under the restored constitution of April 1973, Pakistan is a federal republic, comprising four provinces: Sind, with a population of 28 million; Punjab, 69 million; North-West Frontier Province, 16 million; and Baluchistan, 6 million. The provinces are administered by centrally appointed governors and local governments drawn from elected Provincial Assemblies and headed by chief ministers. There are also tribal areas, with a total population of 3 million, which are administered directly by the federal government. Responsibility for education, labour, health, industry, social welfare, agriculture, and roads legislation is entrusted to the provinces.

Primary power resides, however, with the central government, which is headed by a president, who is elected for a renewable, five-year term at a sitting of the members of the federal assembly and representatives from the four provincial assemblies. The president must be a Muslim. The presidency was originally a titular post, but following the constitutional amendments of March 1985, the office holder was given powers to dissolve the National Assembly, and appoint and dismiss the prime minister, the cabinet, and provincial governors. The president, therefore, emerged as the dominant political figure. However, following the death, in August 1988, of General Zia, the primacy of this office has diminished and the president is now expected to act on the advice of the prime minister.

The federal legislature consists of two chambers: a lower house, called the National Assembly, and an upper chamber, the Senate. The National Assembly has 217 members, comprising 207 directly elected for five-year terms by universal adult suffrage (minimum age 21 years) with ten further seats being reserved for Christians, Hindus, Parsis, and other minorities. The Senate has 87 members, elected, a third at a time, for six-year terms by Provincial Assemblies and tribal areas, in accordance with a quota system. The country's four provincial assemblies each elect 19 senators, the tribal areas, eight, and the Federal Capital Territory of Islamabad has three representatives who are elected by members of the Provincial Assemblies. The federal legislature convenes twice a year, for not less than 130 working days, in sessions which are not more than 120 days apart.

The National Assembly is the more powerful of the two chambers, having sole jurisdiction over financial affairs. The Senate has mainly an advisory role, with the right to send back to the National Assembly, only once, bills of which it disapproves. Joint National Assembly and Senate sittings are convened to iron out differences, by majority vote, on a small number of bills. To become law, bills must be passed by both chambers and must also be approved by the president, who has the power of veto. The presidential veto may, however, be overridden by a simple majority of both chambers.

Day-to-day government is in the hands of a prime minister, drawn from and responsible to the National Assembly, and a cabinet of some 20 members. A prime minister and government can be removed by a no-confidence motion which is supported by two-thirds of the members of the National Assembly and which specifically names a successor. If this is defeated, a further motion cannot be tabled until at least six months later.

Political parties

Political parties have been permitted to operate since December 1985, but under tight registration restrictions, which were not eased until 1988.

The currently dominant party is the Pakistan People's Party (PPP), led by Benazir Bhutto. The PPP was formed in 1967, by Zulfiqar Ali Bhutto, a member of a wealthy Sind land owning family, to campaign for democracy, moderate Islamic socialism, a nonaligned foreign policy, and the creation of a federal state. It drew the bulk of its support from student, industrial worker, and peasant ranks and from the provinces of Sind, especially its rural areas, and Punjab. In December 1993 a rift developed within the PPP, when, Nusrat Bhutto (b.1934), the mother of Benazir, who had been the party's co-chair since 1986, was ousted after she became estranged from her daughter as a result of declaring political support for her son, Murtaza Bhutto, head of the banned al Zulfiqar organization, who had been arrested on terrorist charges when he returned to Pakistan from abroad in November 1993. In March 1995 Murtaza Bhutto formed a breakaway faction of the PPP.

The chief opposition party is the Pakistan Muslim League (PML-Nawaz). The PML traces its roots back to the All-India Muslim League, which was originally founded in 1906, with particularly strong roots in the North Indian province of Uttar Pradesh. Following the death of the PML's leader, Muhammad Ali Jinnah, in 1948, and the assassination, three years later, of its influential prime minister, Liaquat Ali Khan, the party suffered a relative decline. In 1979 it split into two factions, the pro-government Pagara Group, named after the Sind-based religious leader, the Pir of Pagara, and which came to support General Zia ul-Haq, and the anti-Zia Chattha (later renamed the Qasim) Group. This second faction joined the opposition Movement for the Restoration of Democracy (MRD), in 1981. The PML is a conservative party, traditionally viewed as the mouthpiece of large landlords and local 'clan chiefs'. For the November 1988 National Assembly elections, the PML joined with eight other conservative and Muslim parties to form the Islamic Democratic Alliance (IDA). During 1988 the Pagara group of the PML also split into two factions: the Fida Group, led by the former North-West Frontier Province governor, Fida Mohammed Khan; and the Junejo group, allied to the former Prime Minister Mohammad Khan Junejo, who died in March 1993. In May 1993, Prime Minister Nawaz Sharif broke away from the latter body to form his own, dominant PML-Nawaz grouping.

Numerous other parties function. The four most important are the Pakistan Islamic Front (PIF); the Awami National Party (ANP); the National Democratic Alliance (NDA); and the Mohajir Qaumi Mahaz (MQM: Mohajir National Movement).

The PIF is an alliance of Islamic groups formed in 1993. Its key constituent element is the fundamentalist, right-wing,

Jamaat-e-Islami Pakistan (JIP: Islamic Assembly), which was established in 1941 and seeks the establishment of a Sunni Islamic state.

The ANP (People's National Party), founded in 1986 by an amalgamation of socialist groups, is a notable left-wing force, with a strong local base in the North-West Frontier Province.

The NDA was formed in 1992 by six parties and two independent groups, including the Jamhuri Watan Party and the National People's Party (NPP), which was formed in 1986 by the former Chief Minister of Sind, Ghulam Mustafa Jatoi, by breakaway members of the PPP who were critical of Benazir Bhutto's allegedly autocratic leadership style and overly moderate, middle-class orientated, polices, embracing, for example, the 'privatization' of selected state industries and the abandonment of the call for land reform.

The MQM, formed in 1986, is a Sind-based party, led by Altaf Hussain and orientated towards the middle class, Urdu-speaking Mohajir community, who migrated to the province from India at the time of Partition. Since then they have opposed recent ethnic-quota employment restrictions and campaign for recognition of Mohajirs as the country's fifth nationality. Though narrowly based, the MQM has been a rising political force during recent years, scoring heavily in Karachi and Hyderabad in the local and National Assembly elections since 1987 as ethnic tensions and violence have increased. Its leader, Altaf Husain, has been in self-imposed exile in London since mid-1992 and in June 1994 was sentenced in absentia by a Karachi court to 27 years imprisonment for alleged involvement in the maltreatment of soldiers in Sind in 1991. The dominant Altaf faction of the MQM is opposed by a breakaway Haqiqi faction.

Party loyalties are weak and fickle in Pakistan and are based predominantly on patronage and regional ties. The major parties are themselves internally divided between provincial and personality-based factions.

Latest elections
In the most recent National Assembly elections, which were held on 6 October 1993, the Pakistan People's Party (PPP) won 86 of the 202 contested seats, with a 38% share of the national vote, whereas the PML-Nawaz, with a 41% share of the vote, captured just 73 seats. PML-Junejo won 6 seats, the PIF, 3, the ANP, 3, and parties within the NDA, 4. Turnout was just 41%, falling to 10% in Karachi, where the MQM advocated a poll boycott in protest against alleged army discrimination against MQM candidates. Polling had to be suspended in five constituencies for reasons which included the deaths of candidates.

In the provincial elections, which were held three days after the National Assembly contests, the PPP and its allies won control of the two key provinces of Sind and Punjab. The PML-Nawaz and its allies secured power in the North-West Frontier Province, but no single group emerged dominant in Baluchistan.

After the last Senate elections, held in March 1994 for a third of the chamber, the PPP, with 23 out of 87 seats, was the largest single party grouping.

In the last, indirect election of the state president, on 13 November 1993, the Baluchi former foreign minister Farooq Ahmad Khan Leghari, the PPP's candidate, defeated the incumbent and PML-Nawaz-backed Wasim Sajjad Jan by 274 votes to 168.

Political history
The Indus Valley region of contemporary Pakistan supported an advanced, city-based ancient civilization, the Harappan, between 2500 and 1600 BC. The north of the region was later invaded by Aryans from the west, about 2000–1500 BC, and thereafter by successive waves of conquering peoples from Central Asia and beyond, including Muslims from the 10th century AD. These invaders continued on into the North Indian plains, establishing a series of empires with regional capitals in both India and Pakistan. The Mughals, from 1526, constituted the last of these 'conquest empires', prior to the establishment of British sovereignty over the Indian subcontinent. Formal British control was extended over the Punjab and Sind, following wars against local regimes, notably the Sikh 'successor state' in the Punjab, during the 1840s, and over Baluchistan and the North-West Frontier Province in 1896. Subsequent British rule in Pakistan was notable for its substantial investment in major canal irrigation projects in the West Punjab and northern Indus Valley, establishing this tract as a major wheat and cotton exporting area and drawing in settlers from the east. Because of a perceived threat from Russia to the North-West Frontier there was a concentration there of military installations and personnel.

Following the development of a cross-community nationalist movement in the Indian subcontinent, from the mid-1880s, a separate All-India Muslim League was established in 1906 to campaign specifically for Muslim interests. This body was initially dominated by Muslims from north India, before, in 1916, Muhammad Ali Jinnah (1876–1948), a Muslim lawyer educated in Karachi and England, became the League's president. During the interwar period the League veered between campaigning for independence from British rule within a national federation and seeking to establish a separate Muslim state.

In 1933, Choudhary Rahmat Ali invented the name 'Pakistan', or, in Urdu, 'Pure Nation', for a fully independent Muslim territory which would embrace the four provinces of Sind, Baluchistan, Punjab, and the North-West Frontier. Four years later, he called for the inclusion of the Muslim majority areas of Bengal within such a state. Fearing domination by the Hindu majority within India, these ideas were finally adopted by Jinnah in 1940, resulting, in August 1947, in the partitioning of the Indian subcontinent into Hindu and Muslim majority spheres, in accordance with boundaries hastily established by the Radcliffe Commission. More than 7 million Muslims moved into Pakistan from India, while a similar number of Hindus and Sikhs moved in the opposite direction in the days and months preceding and following the Partition. Terrible violence resulted wherever the two refugee courses passed each other.

Independent Pakistan was formally constituted as a Dominion within the British Commonwealth, with the British monarch as head of state. It comprised the five former, and frequently antagonistic, British Indian states of Baluchistan, East Bengal, the North-West Frontier Province, Sind, and West Punjab. It was more broadly divided between an eastern and western section, separated by 1,610 kilometres of Indian territory, and differing substantially in culture, language, and geography. The only thing that united the two sections was religion. The charismatic and respected Jinnah became the country's first governor general (GG) and president of the new Constituent Assembly, but, already gravely ill at the time of independence, he died in September 1948. Khwajah Nazimuddin, Ghulam Mohammad, and Iskander Mirza followed in the post of GG, before a republic was declared, in March 1956, and an 'Islamic' constitution was adopted. This constitution was abrogated in October 1958 and military rule imposed, following a coup by General Mohammad Ayub Khan (1907–74).

The country enjoyed rapid economic growth during the 1960s but mounting regional tension between demographically dominant East Pakistan and West Pakistan, where political and military power was concentrated. Following serious strikes and riots in March 1969, General Ayub Khan stepped down to be replaced by commander in chief, General Agha Muhammad Yahya Khan (1917–80). Pakistan's first elections with universal adult suffrage were subsequently held, in December 1970, the intention being to elect an assembly which would then frame a new constitution. They resulted in the Awami League of Sheikh Mujibur Rahman, which proposed autonomy, gaining a majority of seats in East Pakistan and the Pakistan People's Party (PPP) gaining a majority in the West. East Pakistan declared its independence from the West in March 1971, precipitating a civil war which resulted, following Indian troop intervention on East Pakistan's side in December 1971, in the emergence of the independent republic of Bangladesh.

As a consequence of this defeat, General Yahya Khan resigned and passed power in West Pakistan to the PPP's populist leader, Zulfiqar Ali Bhutto (1928–79). He proceeded to introduce a new federal parliamentary constitution, in April 1973, and a socialist economic programme of land reform and nationalization. From the mid-1970s, however, the Sind-based Bhutto faced growing regional opposition, particularly from Baluchistan and from Pathans campaigning for an independent Pakhtoonistan. He was also confronted with deteriorating economic conditions.

Bhutto won a majority in the March 1977 Assembly elections, but was accused of ballot-rigging by the Pakistan National Alliance (PNA) opposition. Riots ensued and, following four months of unrest, the Punjabi Muslim army chief of staff, General Mohammad Zia ul-Haq (1924–88), seized power in a bloodless coup in July 1977. Martial law was imposed and Bhutto was imprisoned for alleged murder. He was hanged in April 1979.

Between 1979 and 1981 Zia imposed severe restrictions on political activity. Economic growth revived, however, helped by a new pro-business strategy, by remittance inflows from workers in the Middle East and by American aid, following the December 1979 Soviet invasion of Afghanistan. This led, additionally, to the influx of more than 3 million refugees, three-quarters of them being housed in the North-West Frontier Province and 20% in Baluchistan.

At home, the general introduced a broad Islamization programme, aimed at deepening his support base and appeasing Islamic fundamentalists. This was opposed, however, by middle-class professionals and by the country's Shia minority. In March 1981, nine banned opposition parties, including the PPP, formed the Movement for the Restoration of Democracy (MRD) alliance, campaigning for a return to parliamentary government. The military government responded by arresting several hundred opposition politicians. A renewed democracy campaign was launched in the autumn of 1983, resulting in considerable anti-government violence in Sind province.

From 1982, however, General Zia slowly began enlarging the civilian element in his government and, in December 1984, held a referendum on the Islamization process. He obtained a majority for his proposals but the participation level was low. Nevertheless, the result was taken as legitimizing his continuance as president for a further five-year term.

In February 1985 direct elections were held to the National and Provincial Assemblies, but on a nonparty basis. The opposition, as in December 1984, boycotted the poll, and the resultant turnout was only 53%. A new civilian cabinet was, nevertheless, formed and an amended constitution was adopted. In December 1985, martial law and the ban on political parties were lifted, military courts were abolished and military administrators stepped down in favour of civilians. Opposition campaigns for democratization continued, however, with Benazir Bhutto (b. 1953), the Oxford- and Harvard-educated daughter of Zulfiqar Ali Bhutto, returning from self-exile in London, in April 1986, to launch a major autumn campaign for immediate 'open elections'. Riots erupted in Lahore, Karachi, and rural Sind, the tensions being exacerbated by clashes between rival local and immigrant communities. These led to the temporary arrest of the PPP's leaders and the despatch of troops to Sind.

In May 1987, concerned with a downturn in the economy, the slow pace of implementation of the Islamization programme, continuing law and order problems and with the growing independence of Prime Minister Mohammad Khan Junejo, President Zia summarily dismissed the Junejo government, dissolved the National Assembly and provincial legislatures and promised fresh elections within 90 days, as required by the constitution. Zia proceeded, in June–July 1988, to put together a new 18-member interim government, but without a prime minister. He also issued a presidential ordinance which decreed that the Sharia, the Islamic legal code, would immediately become the country's supreme law. He then outlined plans for the introduction of a formal presidential system and set 16 November 1988 as the date for new National Assembly elections.

Barely a month later, however, on 17 August 1988, the president was killed in a mysterious military air crash near Bahawalpur, 160 kilometres west of the Indian border, in east-central Pakistan. The crash was viewed by many as sabotage, with dissident elements within the Pakistan armed forces, or underground Afghan secret service agents, being variously blamed.

General Zia's death placed the country's political system in confusion, with no obvious successor apparent, within the government or the military forces. Pakistan's senior army commanders had been killed with Zia in the air crash. The elderly senate chairperson, Ghulam Ishaq Khan, took over as interim president, pledging to oversee the holding of the forthcoming national elections.

These were held, as scheduled, in November, and were preceded by intense party jockeying, involving the break-up of the MRD and the formation of a new nine-party conservative Muslim, anti-Bhutto, and anti-PPP, Islamic Democratic Alliance (IDA), by elements from the Muslim League and incumbent Zia loyalists. The PPP, advocating a moderate, centrist policy programme and declaring its intention to seek a 'fresh start' and avoid retribution for past actions against its members, succeeded in emerging as the dominant force in the contest. Benazir Bhutto was duly sworn in as prime minister in December 1988.

The new government faced many problems, including a deteriorating economy, exacerbated by a population growth of more than 3% per annum, and the difficulties of adjusting to changing circumstances in bordering Afghanistan. More specifically, its majority, which was based partially on a coalition with the Karachi-based Mohajir Qaumi Movement (MQM), remained fragile, while opposition remained strong in the IDA-controlled Punjab, among conservative Muslim religious leaders (mullahs), and among the military. These circumstances constrained the policy choices of the new administration, which pledged itself to continue to follow a free-market economic programme, maintain support for the Afghan mujaheddin, and leave untouched the country's substantial military budget.

In November 1989 Bhutto narrowly survived a confidence vote, held a month after the MQM had withdrawn its support. Nine months later, in August 1990, President Ghulam Ishaq Khan controversially dismissed the Bhutto government on accusations of incompetence, and, though subsequently untried, charges of corruption and abuse of power. The National Assembly was also dissolved, with Ghulam Mustafa Jatoi serving as a caretaker prime minister. Bhutto's husband, Asif Ali Zardari, also faced corruption charges, which were to be later dropped during 1993–94. In the ensuing general election, held in October 1990, the IDA, supported by the military, state bureaucracy, and mullahs, swept to victory, winning 105 of the 207 elective seats to the PPP's 45. Mian Mohammad Nawaz Sharif (b. 1949), formerly chief minister of Punjab, became prime minister. The first premier not to be drawn from the country's social elite, he embarked on a free-market economic programme, which included privatization and deregulation. Additionally, in May 1991, a Sharia bill, incorporating Islamic laws and designed to create an Islamic welfare state, was enacted and Sharif advocated a reduction in the executive powers of the state president as set out in the Eighth Amendment of 1985. During the summer of 1991 Sharif's reform programme became disrupted by labour unrest and terrorist incidents and the prime minister's own position became weakened by the uncovering of a financial corruption scandal which, it was alleged, involved members of his family.

During 1992 an 'Operation Clean-up' anti-crime and terrorism crackdown was launched in Sind, drawing criticism from the MQM for its heavy-handedness. However, with the IDA and PML beginning to fissure and large-scale anti-government demonstrations and marches being organized by Benazir Bhutto and the newly formed opposition National Democratic Alliance (NDA), Sharif's position became untenable by the spring of 1993. On 18 April 1993, accusing the prime minister of 'maladministration, nepotism, and corruption', President Ghulam Ishaq Khan dismissed Sharif, appointed Mir Balakh Sher Mazari as interim prime minister, dissolved the National Assembly, and called fresh elections. Unexpectedly, the Supreme Court ruled, on 26 May 1993, that President Khan's action was unconstitutional and ordered Sharif to be returned to power. However, within two months, on 18 July 1993, after Sharif had created a crisis in Punjab through imposing federal government rule over the province, both Prime Minister Sharif and President Khan were persuaded to resign from their posts after pressure was exerted by the military.

The former chairperson of the Senate, Wasim Sajjad Jan, and an apolitical former vice president of the World Bank, Moeenuddin Ahmad Qureshi, took over as popular caretaker president and prime minister respectively until the general election of October 1993. This poll returned to power Benazir Bhutto, heading a PPP-led coalition administration which was supported by the Awami National Party and the PML-Junejo. A month later, the PPP's candidate, Sardar Farooq Ahmad Khan Leghari (b. 1940), formerly the foreign minister, was elected state president, defeating the incumbent Sajjad Jan. During 1994–95 there was escalating ethnic and Shia versus Sunni Muslim sectarian violence in Sind, particularly Karachi, claiming more than 1,500 lives. The turmoil was blamed by the government on MQM extremists who had become urban guerrillas. There was also turmoil in the North-West Frontier Province, where Islamic fundamentalism was growing in strength, and where, in April 1994, a PPP-led administration was controversially installed after a PML-Nawaz-led coalition had been ousted in February 1994.

In foreign affairs, Pakistan has experienced strained relations with India throughout the post-independence period, being involved in border wars over Kashmir in 1965 and East Pakistan in 1971. The country left the Commonwealth in 1972, following the acceptance of the new state of Bangladesh, and has been allied with China since the 1950s, mainly because of their shared hostility to India. During the 1980s, with the Soviet Union occupying neighbouring Afghanistan, it developed close relations with the United States. It also joined the Non-Aligned Movement in 1979 and improved its ties with the Islamic states of the Middle East and Africa, sending 11,000 troops to Saudi Arabia to guard Islamic shrines during the 1990–91 Gulf conflict. Following the Soviet pull-out from Afghanistan in 1989 and the establishment of a mujaheddin government in Kabul in 1992, the United States' relationship with Pakistan has cooled, and in October 1990, under the terms of the Pressler Amendment, US economic and military aid was suspended after the United States learned that Pakistan was seeking to develop nuclear weapons. This action has fuelled anti-Americanism, which has been drawn upon by Islamic fundamentalist extremist forces. Tensions with India have also increased since 1989 as a result of the outbreak of a civil and religious war in Kashmir. Pakistan rejoined the Commonwealth in October 1989.

SINGAPORE

Republic of Singapore
Republik Singapura

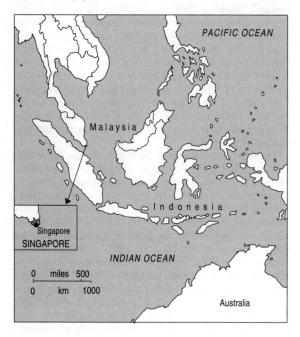

Capital: Singapore City

Social and economic data
Area: 623 km²
Population: 2,900,000*
Pop. density per km²: 4,654*
Urban population: 100%*
Literacy rate: 91%**
GDP: $39,500m**; per-capita GDP: $13,800**
Government defence spending (% of GDP): 5.2%**
Currency: Singapore dollar
Economy type: high income
Labour force in agriculture: 0.3%**

*1994
**1992

Ethnic composition
Seventy-seven per cent of the population is of Chinese ethnic stock, predominantly Hokkien, Teochew, and Cantonese, 15% Malay, and 7% Indian, chiefly Tamil. The national language is Malay, but Chinese (Mandarin), Tamil and English, the language of administration, are also official languages.

Religions
The majority, 54%, of Chinese are Buddhists or Daoists; Malays and Pakistanis are Sunni Muslims, 15% of the population; Indians are Hindus 4%; and Europeans, Eurasians, and other communities are Christians, 13%. The country is, however, a secular state, with religion, unlike neighbouring Malaysia and Indonesia, not a significant aspect of national life.

Political features
State type: liberal democratic*
Date of state formation: 1965**
Political structure: unitary
Executive: parliamentary
Assembly: one-chamber
Party structure: multiparty*
Human rights rating: 60%
International affiliations: AsDB, APEC, ASEAN, CP, CW, ESCAP, IAEA, IBRD, IMF, NAM, UN, WTO

*Though dominated, in practice, by one party
**As a fully independent state

Local and regional government
For administrative purposes, Singapore Island is divided into five districts: Singapore City, Katong, Serangoon, Bukit Panjang, and Jurong. There is no elected tier of local government, but 20–50-member Citizens' Consultative Committees have been established in each electoral district, staffed by nominees of the local member of parliament and subject to the approval of the Prime Minister's Office. The task of these Committees is both to serve as a medium through which the government can 'educate' the local people on government policies and to act as a feedback channel, through which popular needs and grievances are made known. They are also employed for the administration of a number of public works programmes and to mediate in local ethnic disputes.

Head of state
President Ong Teng Cheong, since 1993

Head of government
Prime Minister Goh Chok Tong, since 1990

Political leaders since 1970
1959–90 Lee Kuan Yew (PAP), 1990–   Goh Chok Tong (PAP)

Political system
Because of its small size, Singapore has a single-tier system of government. The constitution of December 1965, an amended version of an earlier, June 1959, constitution, has provided for a single-chamber Parliament, whose 81 members are elected for five-year terms by universal adult suffrage from 40 single-member wards, two 'non-constituency' seats (with restricted voting rights), intended for opposition candidates, and, since 1988, 13 three-member Group Representation Constituencies (GRC) through a simple plurality voting system. At least one member of the 'team' contesting the multimember GRCs must be of non-Chinese racial origin. In addition, since 1990 the government has been able to nominate up to six politically neutral MPs. These unelected MPs may serve for up to two years and can vote on all legislation except that concerning financial and constitutional matters. All parliamentary bills, with the exception of defence, public security, and the budget, are subject to the prior scrutiny of a 21-member Presidential Council, which was established in 1967, and is chaired by a chief justice. Its task is to ensure that proposed legislation does not discriminate against any ethnic or religious community.

Executive power is held by a prime minister and 15-member cabinet drawn from the majority party within Parliament. The prime minister is served by an influential Prime Minister's Office, which contains an anti-pollution unit, a corrupt practices investigation bureau, an election department, and a city district secretariat, which liaises with local citizens' consultative committees. First and second deputy prime ministers assist the prime minister in their responsibilities.

The state president was formerly elected indirectly by Parliament and occupied a ceremonial position. However, the constitutional amendment of January 1991 enhanced the authority of the president, conferring the power of veto of the budget and key cabinet decisions, control over spending of the country's financial reserves, and the right to appoint senior officials. The president is now directly elected for a six-year term, but stringent eligibility rules – restricting candidates to former cabinet members, senior civil servants, or managers of major companies – ensure that the president is drawn from the country's political-economic establishment.

The bulk of decisions in Singapore are taken behind the scenes through consultation between the Prime Minister's Office and an elite of around 300 well educated and loyal technocrats who staff senior posts in the state bureaucracy and in statutory boards and public corporations. They are renowned for their honesty and efficiency. For this reason, the country has been termed an 'administrative state', power being exercised in a paternalistic, though authoritarian, manner.

Although nominally a pluralist 'liberal democracy', the ruling Political Action Party (PAP), led since December 1992 by Prime Minister Goh Chok Tong, tends to dominate the political scene. Since independence, it has tightly controlled all aspects of public and political life, including the mass media, labour unions, defence and police establishments, and educational and social welfare systems.

Political parties

The People's Action Party (PAP) was originally formed in November 1954 by a small group of lawyers, trade unionists, journalists, and intellectuals, under the direction of Lee Kuan Yew, a Cambridge-educated barrister, in response to a mounting, Chinese-supported, communist nonviolent campaign for 'immediate independence for a free and noncommunist Malaya'. The PAP initially won only three seats from the 30 available in the Legislative Assembly elections of 1955. In the following election, in 1959, however, it established itself as the majority party, a position which it has held ever since. In its policy stance, the PAP has veered rightwards since its inception, originally describing itself as a 'democratic socialist' body. Today it adheres to a conservative, free-market economic programme and is strongly anti-communist in outlook. Efficiency, uninterrupted economic growth, and the creation of a 'multi-ethnic, multilingual, secular society', imbued with the national values of austerity, discipline, and unity, are the party's, and hence the country's, guiding goals. The PAP has also, however, placed strong emphasis on social welfare, having invested generously in education, public housing, and health and social provision. It has branches in each of the country's electoral constituencies and a membership of around 30,000. It is, however, tightly controlled from above by a 20-member Central Executive Committee, headed by Secretary-General Goh Chok Tong.

There are currently 20 registered opposition parties, the majority, however, are 'paper entities', having no real organizational base. The two most important parties are the Workers' Party (WP) and the Singapore Democratic Party (SDP).

The WP was originally established in 1957 as a socialist grouping which favoured greater labour union and civil freedom. It fell into abeyance during the later 1960s before being revived in 1971 by the Sri Lankan-born lawyer, Joshua Benjamin Jeyaretnam, who assumed its leadership and later won a parliamentary by-election in the low-income district of Ansom, in October 1981. He retained this seat at the general election of December 1984. Jeyaretnam was, however, subsequently harassed by the government and forced out of Parliament, in November 1986. In 1988 the WP merged with the Socialist Front (Barisan Socialis). In 1993 Jeyaretnam endeavoured to contest the direct presidential election, but was refused a certificate of eligibility by the official Presidential Election Commission on the grounds that he lacked the requisite 'integrity, good character and reputation'.

The SDP was formed in 1980 and was led until 1993 by the London-trained barrister, Chiam See Tong.

All opposition parties operate in difficult circumstances, their leading members having been subjected to a mixture of crude and subtle harassment by state institutions since the early 1970s. Several have been bankrupted in libel, defamation, and tax fraud suits, bankrupts being debarred from political activities by law.

Latest elections

In the most recent parliamentary elections, which were held on 31 August 1991, the PAP won 61% of the national vote and 77 of the 81 available seats. The opposition SDP, with 12% of the vote, won three seats, and the Workers' Party, with a 14% vote share, one seat. The PAP was unopposed in 41 constituencies.

In the country's first direct presidential election, held on 28 August 1993, Ong Teng Cheong, secretary-general of the National Trades Union Congress and the former deputy prime minister and chairperson of the PAP, secured 59% of the vote, defeating Chua Kim Yeow, president of the Development Bank of Singapore.

Political history

Singapore Island was leased as a trading post in 1819 from the Sultan of Johore by the British East India Company (EIC), on the advice of Sir Stamford Raffles (1781–1826), at a time when it was a swampy jungle. Seven years later, in 1826, Singapore, Malacca, and Penang were incorporated as the Straits Settlements, remaining under the charge of the EIC. The territory, retaining the designation Straits Settlements, passed to the British Crown in 1858 and formed a Crown Colony between 1867 and 1942. It had a burgeoning deep-water port complex to which Chinese coolies and Indian clerks were drawn. During World War II, the island was a vital British military base. It had been designed to be invulnerable to naval attack, but was invaded by land and occupied by the Japanese between February 1942 and September 1945. Singapore returned to British administration after Japan's surrender, becoming a separate Crown Colony in 1946 and fully self-governing, with Lee Kuan Yew (b. 1923) as prime minister, between 1959 and 1963. It joined the Federation of Malaysia in September 1963, but, following Malay-Chinese race riots in 1964, seceded in August 1965, claiming discrimination against its Chinese citizens. A new independent republic of Singapore was thus formed in September 1965, remaining in the Commonwealth and maintaining close commercial and defence ties with neighbouring Malaysia.

The new republic's internal political affairs were dominated by Prime Minister Lee Kuan Yew's People's Action Party (PAP), which gained a monopoly of all parliamentary seats in the elections between 1968 and 1980. Under Lee's stewardship, Singapore developed rapidly as a commercial and financial entrepôt and as a centre for new export industries, GDP growing at an average annual per-capita rate of more than 8% during the 1960s and 1970s. As a consequence, by the early 1980s it enjoyed the highest per-capita standard of living in Asia outside Japan and the Sultanate of Brunei and had developed an extensive social welfare system. These advances were achieved by a combination of private enterprise, in the trading and financial spheres, and careful state planning and infrastructural support, in the industrial. It was also the result of a willingness on the part of the country's population to accept authoritarian state direction, including the effective control of trade unions, in a benevolent, Confucianist manner.

During the early 1980s, however, as the country endured a brief halt in its growth course, opposition to the Lee regime began to surface, and then grow. In the December 1984 parliamentary elections, the PAP's share of the popular vote fell from 76% to 63% and two opposition parties, the Workers' Party (WP) and Singapore Democratic Party, won national-level seats for the first time.

This partial reverse encouraged Prime Minister Lee to take a progressively firmer line against the expression of dissent by both the media and political activists. As part of this process, in November 1986, J B Jeyaretnam, leader of the WP and a member of Parliament, was sentenced to one months' imprisonment and fined S$5,000 for perjury in connection with bankruptcy proceedings. This fine was a sufficient sum, under the terms of the constitution, to deprive him of his parliamentary seat and debar him from standing for election for five years.

Despite these actions, and helped by a once again booming economy, the PAP held its vote share steady at 62% in the September 1988 general election, capturing all but one of the available parliamentary seats. In November 1990 Lee stepped down as prime minister, handing over power to his deputy, Goh Chok Tong (b. 1941). However, he remained as a senior minister within the cabinet, while his Cambridge-educated son, Brigadier-General Lee Hsien Loong (b. 1952), served as deputy prime minister and trade and industry and defence minister. Despite suffering from cancer, Lee Jr was clearly being groomed to later succeed Goh Chok Tong as premier.

Buoyed by a level of economic growth which had averaged 8% per annum since 1989, support for the PAP

remained stable at 61% in the general election of August 1991. Since the late 1980s a privatization programme has been followed, reducing the number of state-owned corporations, and there has been some transfer of labour-intensive operations to neighbouring Malaysia and Indonesia, where labour costs are lower.

In its external relations, Singapore closely allied itself with the United States between 1965 and 1974. Since the mid-1970s, however, it has pursued a neutralist foreign policy, improving its contacts with communist China and playing an active role as a member of ASEAN. In general, however, diplomatic relations in Singapore are viewed as an extension of trade relations, the overriding goal being to promote exports and attract inward investment and technology flows.

SRI LANKA

Democratic Socialist Republic of Sri Lanka
Prajathanthrika Samajawadi Janarajaya Sri Lanka

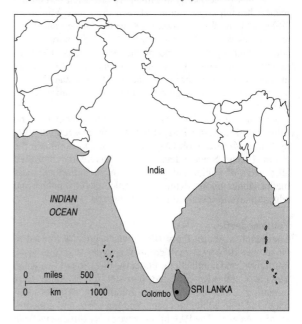

Capital: Colombo

Social and economic data
Area: 64,453 km^2
Population: 17,900,000*
Pop. density per km^2: 278*
Urban population: 22%**
Literacy rate: 88%**
GDP: $9,500 million**; per-capita GDP: $550*
Government defence spending (% of GDP): 4.7%**
Currency: Sri Lankan rupee
Economy type: low income
Labour force in agriculture: 43%**

*1994
**1992

Ethnic composition

Seventy-three per cent of the population is Sinhalese, 19% Tamil, and 7% Moors or Muslims, who are concentrated especially in the east. The Tamil community, which remains poorly integrated, is divided between the long-settled 'Sri Lankan Tamils', 11% of the population, who reside in northern and eastern coastal areas, and the more recent immigrant 'Indian Tamils', 8%, who settled in the Kandyan highlands as tea plantation workers during the 19th and 20th centuries. The latter's descendants were disenfranchised from 1948, but in 1989 voting rights were granted to 320,000 'Indian Tamils'. Sinhala, and, since 1988, Tamil are the official languages.

Religions

Seventy per cent of the population, predominantly Sinhalese, is Buddhist, of the Theravada sect, 15%, mainly Tamil, is Hindu, 8% is Christian, chiefly Roman Catholic, and 7% adheres to Sunni Islam. The 1978 constitution accords Buddhism the foremost place among religions and makes it the state's duty to protect and foster Buddhism. However, freedom of religious choice is also constitutionally guaranteed.

Political features

State type: liberal democratic
Date of state formation: 1948
Political structure: unitary
Executive: dual
Assembly: one-chamber
Party structure: two-party
Human rights rating: 47%
International affiliations: AsDB, CP, CW, ESCAP, G-24, G-77, IAEA, IBRD, ICC, ICFTU, IMF, LORCS, NAM, SAARC, UN, WFTU, WTO

Local and regional government

Following constitutional amendments adopted in 1987–88, a network of eight upper-tier provincial councils, with the northern and eastern provinces merged into one unit, and 68 lower-tier district councils (*pradeshiya sabhas*) has been established.

Head of state (executive)

President Chandrika Bandaranaike Kumaratunga, since 1994

Head of government

Prime Minister Sirimavo R D Bandaranaike, since 1994

Political leaders since 1970

1970–77 Sirimavo Bandaranaike* (SLFP), 1977–88 Junius Richard Jayawardene*/** (UNP), 1989–93 Ranasinghe Premadasa** (UNP), 1993–94 Dingiri Banda Wijetunga** (UNP), 1994– Chandrika Kumaratunga** (SLFP/People's Alliance)

*Prime minister, in parliamentary system
**Executive president

Political system

Under the constitution of September 1978, Sri Lanka has a presidential form of government based loosely on the French 'dual-executive' model. The head of state and chief executive is the president who is directly elected by universal adult suffrage for a six-year term. A two-term limit applies and voting is by the single transferable vote system. The victor is required to secure at least 50% of the national poll and electors are asked to list both first and, transferable, second preferences. The president appoints and dismisses cabinet ministers, including the prime minister, who functions as the president's 'parliamentary manager'. The president is also commander in chief of the armed forces, can hold selected ministerial portfolios, can dissolve parliament 'at will', and may submit to national referendum matters of national importance. Junius Richard Jayawardene, who was president between 1978 and 1988, was particularly influential and, during his last years of office, held six departmental portfolios, including defence, civil security, plan implementation and higher education. His successor, Ranasinghe Premadasa, combined the posts of president and prime minister. The current incumbent, Chandrika Kumaratunga, although she has pledged to abolish what she views as a 'gravely harmful' executive presidency, holds the finance, defence, policy planning and implementation, and Buddhist affairs portfolios.

Parliament, known as the National State Assembly, is a single-chamber body, which has supreme legislative authority and meets once a year for a session of up to four months. Currently it comprises 225 members who are directly elected by a 'modified' system of proportional representation, involving preferential voting, for six-year terms. The country is divided into 22 multimember constituencies, from which 196 deputies are returned, with the remaining 29 being elected from party lists on the basis of the total national vote of each party. A 12.5% of the vote cut-off level applies for representation. There are no by-elections, with parties being able to appoint successors to deputies who retire or die. A two-thirds parliamentary majority, followed by approval in a national referendum, is required to alter the constitution.

Political parties

Sri Lanka has traditionally been a classic two-party state, power alternating between the centre-right United National Party (UNP: Eksath Jathika Pakshaya) and the left-of-centre Sri Lanka Freedom Party (SLFP: Sri Lanka Nidahas Pakshaya).

The UNP, whose political roots go back to the interwar Ceylon National Congress (CNP), was founded in 1946 by the pro-Western liberal-conservative, Don Stephen Senanayake, and, after independence, was the country's first governing party, between 1948 and 1956. Its neglect of the poor, and of Sinhala-Buddhist sensitivities, led to electoral defeat in 1956, persuading the party to adopt a new, democratic-socialist, policy programme in 1958. Following an even heavier reversal in 1970, the UNP was remodelled as a mass party by Junius Richard Jayawardene, who was related by marriage to both of the wealthy and influential, upper-caste, Senanayake and Bandaranaike families. The goal of *dharmishta*, or a just and righteous society, was espoused and greater stress placed on rural development, although private enterprise and foreign investment were also encouraged. This strategy enabled the UNP to broaden its support base from its original dependence on the urban and privileged to a much wider electorate. Jayawardene's successor as state president and UNP leader, the lowly born Ranasinghe Premadasa, continued this populist approach. The Democratic United National Front (DUNF), led by Gamini Dissanayake, was formed in 1991 as a breakaway from the UNP by anti-Premadasa deputies. In 1994 Dissanayake returned to the UNP fold, becoming its presidential candidate, before being assassinated in October 1994.

The SLFP was founded in 1951 by the Oxford-educated barrister, Solomon W R Bandaranaike, previously a prominent member of both the CNP and the UNP government. He sought to construct a non-Marxist left-of-centre alternative to the ruling party. In 1956 Bandaranaike and the SLFP secured power, after heading a Sinhala–Buddhist-orientated united front, directed against the UNP. However, conservative elements defected from the party in 1959, leading to a swing to the left in the policies which were adopted when it was in power, between 1960 and 1964 and, under the leadership of Solomon Bandaranaike's widow, Sirimavo, between 1970 and 1977. During its long period in opposition after 1977, the SLFP machine atrophied and power became centralized within the ranks of the influential Bandaranaike family. The party's policy stance also shifted towards the centre. To contest the parliamentary and presidential elections of 1994, a centre-left People's Alliance coalition was formed under the SLFP's leadership.

More than a dozen other minor political parties currently operate in Sri Lanka. The most important, which was officially banned in August 1983 as a result of its separatist stance, is the Tamil United Liberation Front (Tamil Vimukthi Peramuna: TULF, estd. 1949), which, with its headquarters in Jaffna, is orientated towards the Tamil community and seeks to establish a separate autonomous Tamil region in the north and east to be known as Eelam. Also banned from 1971–77, after it had staged its first insurrection, and from 1983–88, was the Marxist- and Sinhalese-extremist People's Liberation Front (Janatha Vimukti Peramuna: JVP, estd. 1964), which was greatly weakened by military action against it in 1989–90.

Other significant parties are the Eeelavar Democratic Front (EDF), a Tamil-separatist group; the People's United Front (Mahajana Eksath Peramuna: MEP), a left-wing Sinhalese Buddhist body; the Trotskyist Lanka Equal Society Party (Lanka Sama Saamaja Party: LSSP), formed in 1937; the Communist Party of Sri Lanka (CPSL; estd. 1943); the Ceylon Workers' Congress (CWC; estd. 1939), which represents the interests of Indian Tamil tea plantation workers; and the Sri Lanka Muslim Congress (SLMC), led by Mohammed Ashraff, which was founded as an eastern regional grouping in 1980, before becoming a national party in 1986. In May 1995 the LSSP, CPSL, CWC, SLMC, and the DUNF each held a seat in the 22-member SLFP-dominated cabinet of Prime Minister Sirimavo Bandaranaike.

Latest elections

The most recent parliamentary election, held on 16 August 1994, resulted in victory for the People's Alliance, a left-wing coalition led by the SLFP's Chandrika Bandaranaike Kumaratunga. The Alliance won 105 of the contested seats, the ruling UNP 94 seats, the SLMC, 7, the TULF, 5, the Independent Group (Jaffna) (Eelam People's Democratic Party),

9, and the Democratic People's Liberation Front (estd. 1988), 3. Turnout was high, except in the Jaffna region where the Liberation Tigers of Tamil Eelam (LTTE) successfully organized a boycott. During the month-long campaign, 19 people were killed.

In the presidential election, which was held on 9 November 1994, Prime Minister Kumaratunga, representing the SLFP-dominated People's Alliance, secured an overwhelming victory. She captured a record 62% of the national vote, defeating the little known Srima Dissanayake of the UNP, who won 35% of the vote, and four other candidates. Turnout exceeded 60%.

Political history

The island of Sri Lanka which was known as Ceylon until 1972, was conquered by Sinhalese invaders from India about 550 BC and became a centre for Buddhism from the 3rd century BC. Arab and Portuguese spice traders later introduced Islam and Christianity respectively. Coastal areas, but not the central kingdom of Kandy, became subject to foreign control from 1505 onwards, including Portugal (1505–1658), Holland (1658–1796), and Britain (1796–1802). Finally, in 1802, Ceylon became a British Crown Colony.

Under British rule, 'Sri Lankan Tamils', who had been settled in the northern and eastern regions for centuries, took up English education and progressed rapidly in administrative careers. In addition, new 'Indian Tamils' immigrated to work on the tea and rubber plantations which had been developed in the central highlands region around Kandy. Conflicts between the Sinhalese majority and Tamil minority began to surface during the 1920s, as nationalist politics developed. In 1931, universal adult suffrage was introduced for an elected assembly and executive council, in which power was shared with the British, before, in February 1948, independence was achieved.

Between 1948 and 1972, Sri Lanka remained within the British Commonwealth as a Dominion, with a two-chamber parliamentary system on the 'Westminster model'. This comprised a directly elected House of Representatives, an indirectly elected Senate, and a titular governor general, who was the representative of the Commonwealth monarch. The liberal-conservative United National Party (UNP), led consecutively by Don Stephen Senanayake (1884–1952) and Dudley Senanayake (1911–73), initially held power. In 1956, however, the radical socialist, and more narrowly Sinhalese-nationalist, Sri Lanka Freedom Party (SLFP), led by Solomon Bandaranaike (1899–1959), gained an electoral victory, at the head of the People's United Front (Mahajana Eksath Peramuna: MEP) coalition.

Once in power, it established Sinhalese, rather than English, as the official language to be used for entrance to universities and the civil service. This precipitated Tamil riots in 1958, while the dissatisfaction of the more extremist Sinhalese culminated in the prime minister's assassination, by a Buddhist monk, in September 1959. Solomon Bandaranaike's widow, Sirimavo Bandaranaike (b. 1916), took over as prime minister and proceeded to hold office until 1977, except for UNP interruptions, under Dudley Senanayake, between March and June, 1960, and between 1965 and 1970. She was the world's first female prime minister and implemented a radical economic programme of nationalization and land reform; a pro-Sinhalese educational and employment policy; and an independent nonaligned defence policy. In 1972, a new republican constitution was adopted in which the Senate upper chamber was abolished and the new national name Sri Lanka, which is Sinhalese for 'Resplendent Island', was assumed.

During the 1970s economic conditions deteriorated, spawning a serious wave of strikes in 1976, while Tamils complained bitterly of discrimination. For example, from 1956 onwards the Tamils' share of government posts fell dramatically. All this bred a separatist movement which demanded the creation of an independent Tamil state (Eelam) in the north and east. The Tamil United Liberation Front (TULF) coalition was formed in 1976 to campaign for this goal and emerged as the second largest party in parliament in the elections of July 1977. These were fought under the old simple plurality voting system and brought a landslide victory for the UNP, led by Junius Richard Jayawardene (b. 1906).

The new Jayawardene government proceeded to remodel the constitution on French presidential lines in 1978. It discarded simple plurality voting and introduced a new free-enterprise economic programme, which, initially, proved to be successful. The government's position was strengthened by the decision of a presidential commission in October 1980 to deprive Sirimavo Bandaranaike of her civil rights for six years, as a result of alleged abuses of power during her period in office. The administration faced mounting unrest, however, in the north and east among Tamil separatist guerrillas, the Liberation Tigers of Tamil Eelam (LTTE), forcing the frequent imposition of a state of emergency.

Initially the UNP profited from a polarization of Sinhalese and Tamil opinion, and Jayawardene was re-elected president in October 1982. Two months later a popular referendum showed 55% in favour of prolonging the life of the UNP-dominated National State Assembly by six years. The referendum turnout was 77%. However, in 1983, the level of terrorist-organized violence escalated, with more than 900 people, mainly Tamils in the Jaffna area, being killed. This adversely affected foreign exchange earnings from the tourist industry and discouraged inward investment. Legislation was introduced to outlaw separatist organizations, including the TULF, in August 1982. All-party talks aimed at solving the Tamil dispute took place, under Indian mediation, in 1984, 1985, and 1986, but broke down as a result of differences over the degrees of autonomy to be conceded. Meanwhile, by 1987 more than 300,000 Tamils, faced with a Sinhalese backlash, had fled from Sri Lanka to India and elsewhere.

By 1987 the LTTE had established almost *de facto* control of the northern Jaffna region, and the economy was in a debilitated condition. Unemployment stood at 27%, inflation at 15%, and the annual GDP growth rate at 1.5%, compared with 6% between 1977 and 1983. In July of that year a Peace Accord, aimed at solving the 'Tamil issue', was signed by President Jayawardene and the Indian prime minister, Rajiv Gandhi. The plan's provisions included elevating Tamil and English to the status, alongside Sinhala, of official languages; the creation of eight, new, elected provincial coun-

cils, with the Tamil-dominated northern and eastern provinces being merged, subject to a referendum in the area; the repatriation of 130,000 Tamil refugees from South India; the disarming of Tamil militants, in return for a general amnesty; and the outlawing of LTTE training on, and supply from, the Indian mainland. Implementation of the Peace Accord in the Jaffna area was to be overseen by a 7,000 strong Indian Peace Keeping Force (IPKF).

This caused a storm of opposition from Sinhalese extremists, viewing the entry of Indian troops as an 'imperialist' invasion. More moderate Sinhalese elements, including the SLFP and several senior UNP government ministers, including Prime Minister Ranasinghe Premadasa (1924–93), strongly criticized the Accord as a 'sell-out' to Tamil interests and protest riots erupted in the Colombo region. An assassination attempt was made on the life of President Jayawardene by the resurfaced Sinhala-chauvinist People's Liberation Front (JVP) in August 1987.

Implementation of the Peace Accord in the Jaffna area by the IPKF met with initial success, but in October 1987 the surrender of arms by the LTTE ceased. The IPKF, which brought in more than 50,000 reinforcements, succeeded in gaining control of Jaffna city, but the LTTE militants, led by the elusive Velupillai Prabhakaran, escaped and established new guerrilla bases in rural areas to the east, inflicting casualty losses of between 600 and 700 on the IPKF. Meanwhile, in the south of the country, JVP terrorist attacks on UNP officials continued, claiming more than 500 lives.

Nevertheless, in April 1988, despite continuing interethnic violence, elections were held for four of the newly created provincial councils, the UNP capturing 57% of the elective seats and control of all the councils. The United Socialist Alliance (USA), a loose grouping of small opposition parties who supported the July 1987 Peace Accord, secured 41% of the seats. The SLFP boycotted the polls. These were followed, in November 1988, by provincial elections in the northern and eastern provinces. The LTTE were unsuccessful in their attempts to force a boycott of an election in which the Tamil, radical, Eeelam People's Revolutionary Front (EPRLF) and Eelam National Democratic Liberation Front (ENDLF) successfully participated, voter attendance being remarkably high.

A month later the presidential election followed. With President Jayawardene unable, under the provisions of the constitution, to seek a further term, Prime Minister Premadasa stood as the UNP candidate and was opposed by Sirimavo Bandaranaike heading a seven-party alliance, which included the Sri Lanka Muslim Congress (SLMC). Opposition to the July 1987 Peace Accord was her principal rallying call. Initially she publicly pledged to abrogate the agreement and demand the withdrawal of the IPKF 'within 24 hours of being elected', but later moderated her stance. Prime Minister Premadasa, in contrast, called only for a 'renegotiation' of the Accord and a phased withdrawal of Indian troops, something that was already underway.

The election campaign was marred by disruptive JVP-induced violence and intimidation, which claimed between 10–20 lives a day and prevented polling in a number of areas. Despite opposition claims of voting 'distortion', Premadasa emerged the victor. A member of the lowly Dhobi, laundrymen's, caste, he became Sri Lanka's first national leader since independence not to be drawn from the influential Goyigama elite. A crucial factor behind Premadasa's electoral victory had been the popular support generated by the programme of poverty alleviation and housing improvement that he had implemented during his ten years as prime minister. This programme he pledged to continue as president.

The 'state of emergency' imposed in May 1983 was briefly lifted in January 1989 as campaigning moved underway for National State Assembly elections. Despite the continuation of terrorist disruptive tactics, these elections were successfully held on schedule in February 1989, with the UNP securing a narrow parliamentary majority. The finance minister, Dingiri Banda Wijetunga (b. 1922), was appointed prime minister a month later, retaining his departmental portfolio. Round-table negotiations were held with Tamil Tiger leaders during May-June and October 1989 and the IPKF was withdrawn in March 1990. However, despite these reconciliatory moves, the 13-month-long Tiger cease-fire broke down in June 1990 and the civil war, with its two fronts in the north and south, resumed. The death toll exceeded 1,000 a month, with around 100 people a week being detained under the emergency laws. The government reacted by renewing its military offensive against the Tigers and the JVP, whose leader, Rohana Wijeweera, died in November 1989 while in army hands.

At the end of August 1991 President Premadasa suspended parliament for a month after an impeachment motion, supported by UNP dissidents led by Lalith Athulathmudali and Gamini Dissanayake, was tabled. It alleged 24 cases of abuse of power, corruption, and illegal family deals, and was prompted by concern that the executive presidential system had resulted in an autocratic over-concentration of power. In December 1991, eight erstwhile UNP deputies, who were expelled from the party and thus parliament, formed the anti-Premadasa Democratic National United Front (DUNF).

Athulathmudali was assassinated in April 1993, apparently by Tamil Tiger terrorists, and a week later, on 1 May 1993, President Premadasa was killed in a bomb explosion in Colombo, with the LTTE again officially blamed. Parliament voted for Prime Minister Wijetunga to take over as president, with Industry Minister Ranil Wickremasinghe being appointed the new premier. Under President Wijetunga the military offensive against the LTTE continued, with some success, but lacking the populist touch of his predecessor, support for the UNP waned in local elections held during 1993–94. Against a backcloth of annual GDP growth of more than 4% since 1991 and of 7% during 1993, President Wijetunga gambled in June 1994 by dissolving parliament and calling early legislative elections to be held in August 1994. These elections were won narrowly by the SLFP-dominated People's Alliance, led by Chandrika Bandaranaike Kumaratunga, the daughter of the SLFP's president, Sirimavo Bandaranaike, and the widow of a popular film actor who had been assassinated in 1988. Kumaratunga became prime minister on 19 August 1994 and formed a coalition government, with a cabinet comprising ministers from the SLFP, DUNF, SLMC, the Lanka Equal Society Party, and two small leftwing parties. She pledged to press for an amendment of the constitution to abolish the executive presidency and return to a parliamentary system of government, create 300,000 new jobs within a year, and start peace talks with the LTTE in an effort to end the ongoing civil war which had claimed more than 50,000 lives. Three months later, on 9 November 1994, Kumaratunga was herself popularly elected state president, defeating by a landslide margin the UNP's little-known candidate, Srima Dissanayake, who stood in place of her murdered husband, Gamini Dissanayake. She appointed her mother, Sirimavo Bandaranaike, prime minister on 14 November 1994, with the intention that they would later exchange roles once the presidency had been made a purely ceremonial position.

Peace talks were held with the LTTE from October 1994. These resulted in a temporary cease-fire coming into effect in January 1995, which broke down in April 1995. Major differences still existed between the positions of the two sides, so that the negotiation of a permanent political settlement and peace appeared to be still a significant way off. However, in July 1995 the government floated the idea of the creation of a new federal republic, comprising eight substantially autonomous regions, as a possible solution to the impasse. Concurrently, it launched a major military offensive, 'Operation Leap Forward', to drive the Tamil Tigers from the Jaffna peninsula. This led to 400,000 Tamils being made refugees.

Sri Lanka remains a member of the Commonwealth and Non-Aligned Movement and joined the South Asian Association for Regional Cooperation (SAARC) in 1985. Its relations with India, which deteriorated during the early 1980s, as a result of the latter's alleged support for Tamil guerrillas, improved after the accession of Rajiv Gandhi as Indian prime minister in 1984.

TAIWAN

The Republic of China (ROC)
Chung Hua Min Kuo

Capital: Taipei

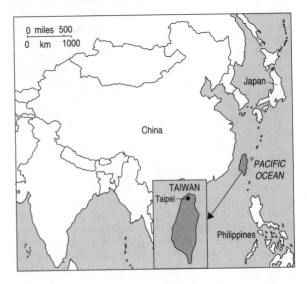

Social and economic data

Area: 36,000 km^2
Population: 21,000,000*
Pop. density per km^2: 583*
Urban population: N/A
Literacy rate: 93%**
GDP: $184,500m**; per-capita GDP: $9,000**
Government defence spending (% of GDP): 5.5%**
Currency: new Taiwan dollar
Economy type: high income
Labour force in agriculture: 12%**

*1994
**1992

Ethnic composition

Ninety-eight per cent of the population is Han Chinese and 2% aboriginal by descent. Some 87% are Taiwan-born and 13% 'mainlanders'. The official language is Northern Chinese, Mandarin.

Religions

The predominant religion, with more than 5 million adherents, or a quarter of the total population, is Buddhism of the Mahayana and Theravada schools. There are also 3.3 million, or 16%, adherents to Taoism, 300,000, or 2%, Roman Catholics, 200,000, or 1%, members of the Presbyterian Church in Taiwan which was established in 1865, and 60,000 followers of Islam. The philosophy of Confucianism also has a wide following.

Political features

State type: emergent democratic
Date of state formation: 1949
Political structure: unitary
Executive: limited presidential
Assembly: one-chamber
Party structure: multiparty
Human rights rating: 50%
International affiliations: APEC, AsDB, BCIE, ICC, ICFTU

Local and regional government

The country has two special municipalities, Taipei and Kaohsiung, which are governed by directly elected mayors. In addition, there are five municipalities, Taichung, Keelung, Tainan, Chiai, and Hsinchu, and 16 counties (*hsien*), each of which has its own elected local governing body. The task of deciding on the provincial budget and administrative policies and of overseeing the work of appointed provincial governors has been delegated to a Provincial Assembly, which works in conjunction with the central government.

Head of state

President Lee Teng-hui, since 1988

Head of government

Prime Minister Lien Chan, since 1993

Political leaders since 1970

1949–75 Chiang Kai-shek (KMT), 1975–88 Chiang Ching-kuo (KMT), 1988–   Lee Teng-hui (KMT)

Political system

Taiwan operates under a constitution adopted in January 1947 by the Republic of China (ROC), but which was substantially amended during 1991–92. It provides for a multi-layered, five-power system of government, combining both presidential and parliamentary executive features.

At the apex of the political system is a powerful executive president, who has traditionally been elected indirectly for a six-year term by the National Assembly (Kuo-Min Ta-Hui), a 'super-parliament' which has no legislative functions, but which has the authority to amend the constitution. However, from 1996 the president will be directly elected by the public for a four-year term. The president serves as head of state, commander in chief of the armed forces and has the authority to promulgate laws and appoint members of the Control Yuan. As chief executive, the president works with an appointed, 20–25-member, cabinet, termed the Executive Yuan, which is headed by a prime minister. It is responsible for policy formulation and executive administration.

The government is responsible to a single-chamber working assembly, or parliament, the Legislative Yuan (Li-Fa Yuan). The Legislative Yuan currently comprises 164 members, directly elected for a three-year term on the basis of proportional representation, from lists of candidates. In 1947 the assembly comprised 933 members, of whom 525 fled from the mainland. The Legislative Yuan holds two sessions a year, of around eight months in duration, and is empowered to hear administrative reports presented by the Executive Yuan and amend government policy. Party blocs with as few as 10% of the seats may introduce legislation.

The overarching National Assembly, which meets infrequently to elect the president and vice president, currently comprises 405 members, 325 of whom had been elected in December 1991 and 80 in December 1986. The 1991 intake comprised 225 who had been directly elected for a four-year term and 100 who had been appointed on a proportional basis from political parties winning at least 5% of the vote, including 20 presidential appointees from among overseas Chinese. Formerly, the National Assembly was a much larger, supra 1,000-member, body, having comprised deputies who had been originally elected, in 1947, from constituencies in mainland China. These fell under communist Chinese control in 1949, making new elections impossible. The original elected members were thus allowed to retain their seats during the ensuing decades, being termed 'life members', while fresh elections were held only for seats vacated by deceased members. The newcomers, termed 'supplementary members', represented Taiwan-based, 'limited-term' seats and were subject to re-election every six years. In 1947 the National Assembly had 3,330 members and roughly half of these later moved, in 1949, from the mainland to Taiwan. By 1988 natural attrition had reduced the number to around 920, of whom 106 comprised 'supplementary members', representing 'government-controlled, Taiwan-situated, constituencies'.

Three other governmental bodies exist: the 29-member Control Yuan; the Judicial Yuan; and the Examination Yuan. They have, respectively, the tasks of investigating the work of the executive, interpreting the constitution, and overseeing entrance examinations to public offices.

Political parties

The ruling Nationalist Party of China (Chung-kuo Kuo-min-tang or Kuomintang: KMT) was founded in November 1894 as the 'Hsing Chung Hui' by Dr Sun Yat-sen, who played a prominent role in the overthrow of China's Manchu regime in the 'Republican Revolution' of 1911. The party assumed the name Kuomintang (Guomindang) in October 1919 and was led by the Japanese-trained military general Chiang Kai-shek from 1925. Under Chiang's leadership the party, which had been moderately socialist in stance under Dr Sun, veered to the right and established close links with business-men, gentry landlords, and industrialists. It terminated the tactical anti-warlord alliance which it had maintained with the Chinese Communist Party (CPC) since the early 1920s, in a violent putsch in Shanghai in April 1927, and Chiang proceeded to establish control over much of China. In October 1928 he set up a new National Government. This Nationalist regime evolved in an authoritarian, quasi-fascist manner, acquiring a large German-trained army, in an effort to expunge Mao Zedong's CPC guerrilla threat. In 1937, however, when the Japanese invaded China, the Nationalists were forced into hiding in the western province of Sichuan. Weakened by this enforced retreat, they proved ill-equipped to take on the strengthened CPC when a civil war for control of China began in 1946, after Japan's departure from the country.

The contemporary Taiwan-based KMT declares as its aim the implementation of the 'three principles of the people'. The first is the liberation of the Chinese mainland from com-munist control and the establishment of a 'democratic, pros-perous and peaceful China', founded on a free-market economy, but with an equitable distribution of wealth. The second is the rejuvenation of the national culture. The third is to 'remain in the camp of democracy'.

Since 1924, the party has been organized on 'democratic centralist' lines similar to those of the Soviet Union's Com-munist Party. The KMT's supreme organ is the 2,100-dele-gate National Congress which meets for a week every five years, the most recent meeting being the 14th in August 1992, to ratify leadership decisions and 'elect' a Central Committee to undertake its work when it is not sitting. This Central Committee has 210 full members and 100 alternate, non-voting, members. The party is dominated by a 31-member Central Standing Committee (CSC), headed by a chairperson, assisted by a General Secretary, which controls appointments. Membership of the KMT was estimated at 2.4 million in 1990, constituting 12% of the total population. Substantial numbers are native Taiwanese, securing political and professional advancement from party membership.

The KMT has become increasingly factionalized during recent years. A liberal faction, dominated by native Tai-wanese, has coalesced around the figure of State President and Party Chairman Lee Teng-hui. It has been opposed by a conservative 'one China' faction grouped around the former Prime Minister Hau Pei-tsun and comprising predominantly second-generation mainlanders, i.e. those born in Taiwan but of mainlander parents, who emphasized the need for the regime to maintain its claim to be the legitimate government of all China. This rift became formalized in 1993 when 30 conservative legislators resigned from the KMT in May and

formed a New Alliance Nationalist Party. Later, in August 1993, six conservative dissidents, led by Jaw Shau-kung, and critical of the pace of recent reform and the leadership style of Lee Teng-hui, also left the KMT to found the Chinese New Party (CNP). This merged with the Chinese Social Democra-tic Party (CSDP; estd. 1991) in November 1993, retaining the designation CNP. Reflecting the divisions within the KMT, four vice chairperson posts were created at the August 1993 Congress to be filled by faction leaders.

The principal opposition party in Taiwan is the Democra-tic Progressive Party (DPP), which was formed, illegally, in September 1986, to campaign for the lifting of martial law and to contest the December 1986 assembly elections. The DPP is the heir to an earlier, informal, nonparty 'Tangwai' opposition grouping which had operated since the 1970s. Its leader, the veteran dissident Shih Ming-Teh, had spent 25 years in prison on sedition charges. The party advocates the establishment of direct trade, tourist, and postal links with the Chinese mainland and 'self-determination' for Taiwan. In 1993 it had a membership of around 20,000. In the December 1986 Legislative Yuan elections, the DPP won more than 20% of the national vote. It then became weakened by inter-nal, moderate-versus-radical, factional rivalries and by the formation of breakaway groups. The most notable of these is the Kungtang, or Workers of Labour Party, which adheres to a potentially popular, moderate, nonviolent programme of social improvement. The DPP adopted an aggressive pro-independence stance at the time of the December 1991 National Assembly elections and polled disappointingly, capturing less than a quarter of the national vote. Subse-quently, the party shifted emphasis to issues of social welfare and government corruption, and secured more than 40% of the national vote in the local elections of November 1993 and captured the mayorship of Taipei in December 1994.

Other recently formed opposition parties include the Democratic Liberal Party (DLP) and the China Freedom Party (CFP). The DLP was established in September 1987 and seeks to 'promote political democracy and economic lib-erty for the people of Taiwan'. The CFP was formed in 1987 and campaigns for the holding of free elections and the liber-alization of relations with the mainland. Two other parties date back to the pre-1949 period and still hold a number of seats in the National Assembly and Legislative Yuan, which they secured in the 1947 elections, and so are effectively tied to the KMT in a 'common front'. They are the Young China Party (YCP), which was formed in 1923, and is a small pro-KMT and pro-unification, anticommunist grouping, and the China Democratic Socialist Party (CDSP) which dates from 1932.

Latest elections

The most recent National Assembly elections were held in December 1991. The KMT, based on a 71% vote share, cap-tured 180 of the 225 directly elected seats and the DPP, with a 24% vote share, 41 seats. The KMT won 75 of the propor-tional seats and the DPP, 25. The elections were contested by 667 candidates from 17 parties.

The last Legislative Yuan elections were held on 19 December 1992 when the Kuomintang won 102 seats, the DPP, 50, and others, nine.

The most recent indirect presidential contests, held in March 1990, resulted in the incumbent Lee Teng-hui being re-elected unopposed.

Political history

Taiwan, which lies 145 kilometres off the Chinese mainland, was originally peopled by aborigines of Malayan descent. It was later settled by Chinese from the 6th century AD onwards, first slowly and then, from the 14th century, at a rapid pace. The bulk of these immigrants were drawn from the adjacent mainland provinces of Guangdong and Fujian. Known as Formosa, or 'The Beautiful', the island was briefly occupied, and controlled by, first, the Spanish and Dutch (1624–61) and, then, a Chinese Ming general, Cheng Ch'engkung, during the mid- and later 17th century, before being annexed by China's Imperial rulers, the Manchu Qing, in 1683. This encouraged further in-migration from the mainland, so that by 1800 a permanent Chinese ethnic majority had been established. Taiwan was subsequently ceded to Japan in 1895, under the terms of the Treaty of Shimonoseki, which concluded the 1895 Sino-Japanese war, and was only regained, by the Nationalist (Kuomintang) regime, after Japan's surrender to the Allies in August 1945.

In December 1949, Taiwan became the refuge for the right-wing Nationalist forces of Generalissimo Chiang Kaishek (1887–1975), President of the Chinese Republic since 1928, which had been compelled to evacuate the mainland after their defeat at the hands of the Communist troops of Mao Zedong. Chiang and his million or so Nationalist followers, although constituting a minority of only 15%, proceeded, violently, to put down a Taiwanese rebellion in February 1947, and then dominated the island, maintaining an army of 600,000, in the hope of reconquering the mainland over which they still claimed sovereignty. They continued to be recognized as the legitimate government of China, under the designation 'Republic of China' (ROC) by the United States. The ROC leaders themselves viewed Taiwan as just one of their country's constituent 35 provinces. They also occupied China's United Nations General Assembly and Security Council seats until October 1971. Then, following a rapprochement between communist China and the United States, they were finally expelled and their seats taken over by the People's Republic (PRC).

During the Korean War (1950–53), Taiwan was protected by US naval forces, the country signing a mutual defence treaty with the United States in December 1954. Benefiting from this security, Taiwan enjoyed a period of rapid economic growth during the 1950s and 1960s, and emerged as an export-orientated consumer goods producer, acquiring the description of a newly industrializing country (NIC). In the process, Taiwan's socio-economic base was fundamentally moved away from its former dependence on agriculture towards the industrial and service sectors. Thus, while, in 1950, 60% of the island's population had been engaged in agricultural activities and only 18% in industrial, by 1986 the relative shares were 28% and 42%. This transformation was wrought, first, during the 1950s, by the institution of a radical, anti-gentry, 'land-to-the-tiller', land reform programme, which dramatically boosted agricultural output. Second, the change in the rural sector was accompanied by the launching

of a determined state-guided programme of import substitution and export-led industrialization. This was based on a succession of four-year economic plans, beginning in 1953, and substantial infrastructure and human resources investment. Low wages, a disciplined workforce, and an expanding American market for the country's wares provided the means and stimulus for this transformation and, in response, the economy proceeded to expand at a 'miracle' rate of more than 8% per annum throughout the 1950s, 1960s, and 1970s. First producing textile goods, then electrical 'consumer durables' and then heavy machinery and petrochemicals, Taiwan is now very much involved in high technology computer production. The country's per-capita income, which had been below that of 'low-income' mainland China in 1949, spectacularly leapfrogged into the higher ranges of the world's middle-income countries. Today, with GDP growth still averaging 7% per annum, it is the second wealthiest nation, of substantial size, after Japan, in Asia.

During these 'miracle' years, political change failed to match economic change. Political power was monopolized by the Kuomintang (KMT) and armed forces, led by President Chiang Kai-shek, martial law being imposed and opposition activity outlawed. Constrained by its unification goals, an ossified political system was set up, no elections being held for assembly seats which had originally been secured in mainland constituency elections in 1947. During the 1970s, however, the Taiwanese government was forced to adjust to rapid external changes as the United States' administrations, under Richard Nixon (1969–74), Gerald Ford (1974–77), and Jimmy Carter (1977–81), adopted a new policy of détente towards communist China. This process gathered momentum after the death of Mao Zedong, in September 1976. It culminated in January 1979 in the full normalization of Sino-American relations, the severing of American-Taiwanese diplomatic contacts, and the annulment of America's 1954 Mutual Security Pact. Other Western nations followed suit during the 1970s and early 1980s, leaving, by 1988, only 22 countries with formal diplomatic links.

These far-reaching developments in the diplomatic sphere, coupled with changes within the ageing KMT, and the death of Chiang Kai-shek in April 1975, prompted a gradual review of Taiwanese policies, domestic and external. This reappraisal was set in train by the KMT's pragmatic, new leader, Chiang Ching-kuo (1910–88). He was the son of Chiang Kai-shek and had been prime minister from 1972 to 1978, KMT chairperson from 1975 to 1988, and State President from 1978 to 1988.

The outcome of the review was the adoption of a new programme of halting democratization and 'Taiwanization'. Thus, in December 1972, elections were held for 53 'vacated seats' within the National Assembly and 52 in the Legislative Yuan. There was also an increasingly rapid induction of native Taiwanese into the ruling KMT. Elections for further National Assembly and Legislative Yuan 'supplementary' seats were held in 1975, 1980, and 1983. In these 'contests' the KMT won overwhelming victories over the independent 'Tangwai', 'outside-the-party', candidates. Then, in the December 1986 elections for 80 National Assembly and 73 Legislative Yuan seats, the participation of an opposition party was tolerated. This was the Democratic Progressive

Party (DPP), which had recently been illegally established by 135 dissident politicians, led by Chiang Peng-chien. The DPP captured 22% of the popular vote and the KMT 69%. Finally, in July 1987, martial law was lifted and replaced by a new national security law. Under the terms of this, and related laws, the operation of political parties other than the KMT was at last permitted, but subject to regulation and in conformity with constitutional precepts, most notably the forswearing of support for communism and Taiwanese independence. Civilians were freed from the jurisdiction of military courts, press restrictions were lifted, and demonstrations legalized. There was a resultant wave of protest marches by farmers, environmentalists, and regime opponents in 1988.

The process of political liberalization accelerated markedly during 1986 and 1987 as President Chiang Ching-kuo, afflicted by ailing health, sought to both pave the way for a stable succession and secure himself a favourable place in history. Chiang eventually died, in January 1988, and was succeeded, as both state president and KMT chairperson, by Lee Teng-hui (b. 1923), the former mayor of Taipei and the country's vice president since March 1984. Unusually, he was both Taiwanese-born and a devout Christian. The new president was one of a number of 'modernizers' who had been promoted by Chiang Ching-kuo, and formed a 'technocrat' faction within the KMT. Included in this group were KMT General Secretary Lee Huan, and, initially, head of the joint chiefs of staff, the mainland-born Hau Pei-tsun.

President Lee immediately set about accelerating the pace of political reform, as well as instituting a programme of economic liberalization, entailing deregulation, privatization and a greater opening to international economic forces. In February 1988, the KMT's governing CSC approved a plan for drastically restructuring the country's legislature. Its key points were the phasing out, by 1992, through 'voluntary retirement' on substantial pensions, of between 150-200 'life-term' mainland constituency members and the replacing of them with new members representing Taiwanese constituencies. Five months later, at the KMT's 13th National Congress, held between 7 and 13 July, President Lee succeeded in packing the party's new Central Committee with 80% of his own candidates and in removing ten old guard conservative members from the CSC. Several days later, a major cabinet reshuffle in the Executive Yuan was effected, five ministers being replaced, including those in charge of finance and economic affairs. A new clutch of Western-educated, Taiwan-born technocrats was moved in. These changes strengthened significantly the reformist wing within both the party and state machines.

In the December 1989 Legislative Yuan elections the Kuomintang's vote share rose to 59% and the DPP increased its number of seats from 12 to 24. Controversially, however, in October 1991, the DPP, led by Hsu Hsin-liang, introduced a new clause into its charter which advocated Taiwanese independence and called for a plebiscite on the issue, despite the fact that calling for independence remained (until a change in the law in May 1992) a seditious offence. In the subsequent December 1991 National Assembly elections, which were held after the 566 last remaining 'life members' had resigned formally from their legislative posts, the DPP was clearly damaged by this stance. The KMT secured a landslide victory, winning 78% of the 325 seats at stake. This left it in a secure position to push through further liberalizing reform of the constitution.

In 1992 the Sedition and National Security laws were revised so that advocacy of independence and communism were no longer a criminal offence and a number of political prisoners were released. In February 1993 Lien Chan, a committed reformer, replaced the more conservative General Hau Pei-tsun as prime minister. This increased tensions within the KMT between its liberal, predominantly native Taiwanese, and conservative, predominantly second-generation mainlander wings. A formal split occurred in August 1993, at the time of the party's 14th Congress, when the Chinese New Party (CNP) was set up by conservative defectors led by Jaw Shau-kang. Support for the KMT fell below 50%, to 47.5%, for the first time ever in the local elections of November 1993 and in December 1994 the DPP secured a striking victory in the Taipei mayoral contest. In the latter election, the KMT's candidate finished third, behind both the DPP's Chen Shui-bian and the CNP's leader.

In its external relations, the KMT government, despite decreasing international support for its cause since the early 1970s, has continued to claim legitimate sovereignty in mainland China. The United States, under the terms of the March 1979 Taiwan Relations Act, has continued to supply the country with military weapons, for 'defensive purposes', but in steadily diminishing quantities. Meanwhile, since the early 1980s, the new post-Mao leadership in mainland China has launched a succession of initiatives geared towards achieving reunification in a federalist manner. Under these proposals Taiwan would officially become part of China, while retaining considerable autonomy as a 'special administrative region'. As such, it would maintain its own armed forces as well as a capitalist economic system. The model for this scheme, termed 'one country, two systems', has been the formula which has been accepted by Britain and Portugal for the transfer of sovereignty in their dependencies of Hong Kong and Macao during the late 1990s.

Between 1981 and 1987, the Taipei government met these PRC initiatives with its traditional response, the 'three nos': no contact, no negotiation, and no compromise with the mainland regime. During the closing months of the Chiang Ching-kuo administration, however, a significant relaxation of this stance became apparent and human contacts between the two states were allowed to increase. This approach has been continued by President Lee.

On 1 May 1991 the president declared an official end to the 42 years of 'civil war' ('Period of Communist Rebellion') between the two Chinas and revoked the 'Temporary Provisions', adopted in 1948, which had blocked major political reform. For the first time, the existence of a Communist Party-led government in Beijing was recognized officially and on 28 April 1991 the first Taiwanese delegation visited Beijing. Nevertheless, in 1994 Taiwan, still fearful of invasion from the mainland, devoted 27% of total budgetary expenditure and 5% of GDP to defence spending and, with armed forces of 485,000, had the twelfth largest army in the world. In June 1995 Taiwan offered the United Nations $1 billion if it would agree to restore the membership it lost in 1971.

TAJIKISTAN

Republic of Tajikistan
Respubliki Tojikiston/Jumhurii Tojikiston

Capital: Dushanbe

Social and economic data
Area: 143,100 km^2
Population: 5,700,000*
Pop. density per km^2: 40*
Urban population: 31%**
Literacy rate: 97%**
GDP: $2,700 million**; per-capita GDP: $480**
Government defence spending (% of GDP): 4.4%**
Currency: Tajik rouble
Economy type: low income
Labour force in agriculture: 43%**

*1994
**1992

Ethnic composition
Sixty-two per cent of the population is of Tajik ethnic stock, 24% Uzbek, 8% ethnic Russian, 1% Tatar, 1% Kyrgyz, and 1% Ukrainian. The official language, since 1989, has been Tajik, which belongs to the southwest Iranian language group and is similar to Farsi (Persian).

Religions
Most Tajiks are Sunni Muslims (Hanafi school), as are ethnic Uzbeks. However, Pamirs, concentrated in the province of Gorny-Badakhshan, adhere to the Shia Isma'ili sect. The fabulously wealthy Western-based Prince Karim Aga Khan is their 49th Imam, acting as their spiritual leader and benefactor. There are also Russian Orthodox Church and Jewish minority communities.

Political features
State type: authoritarian nationalist
Date of state formation: 1991
Political structure: unitary
Executive: unlimited presidential
Assembly: one-chamber
Party structure: multiparty*
Human rights rating: N/A
International affiliations: CIS, EBRD, ECO, EOC, ESCAP, IBRD, IMF, NACC, OIC, OSCE, UN

*Though effectively dominated by one party

Local and regional government
There are 19 administrative regions and the municipality of Dushanbe, and below, with elected local councils, city and rural districts, towns, and villages.

Head of state (executive)
President Imamoli Rakhmanov, since 1992

Head of government
Prime Minister Jamshed Karimov, since 1994

Political leaders since 1970
1982–85 Rakhmon Nabiyev (CPT)*, 1985–91 Kakhar Makhkamov (CPT)*, 1991 Kadriddin Aslonov (CPT), 1991–92 Rakhmon Nabiyev (CPT), 1992 Akbarsho Iskandrov (independent), 1992– Imamoli Rakhmanov (CPT)

*Communist Party leader

Political system
Under the terms of the November 1994 constitution, Tajikistan has a presidentialist political system. Executive authority is vested in a popularly elected president, who works with a cabinet headed by a prime minister. The legislature, the Supreme Assembly, comprises 181 members directly elected in accordance with the two-ballot majoritarian system, a second ballot 'run-off' race being held in contests in which there is no clear first-round majority. Exceptionally, third-round repeat elections are required if seats remain unfilled after the second ballot. Presidential and legislature terms are four years.

Political parties
The strongest and best organized political party in the republic is the Communist Party of Tajikistan (CPT), which supports President Rakhmanov. Between 1990 and 1992 three significant anticommunist opposition parties developed: the 15,000-member secular Democratic Party of Tajikistan (DP; estd. 1990); the Islamic Renaissance Party (IRP), led by Said Abdullah Nuri and Haji Akbar Turandjonzonda; and Rastokhez (Rebirth). They secured power briefly in 1992, but were banned by the Supreme Court in June 1993 since they continued to engage in guerrilla war against the CPT-led government. The DP split in June 1995 when Shodmon Yusuf was dismissed and replaced as party leader by Jumaboy Niyazov, a former political prisoner. In November 1994 a new opposition force, the Party of Popular Unity and Justice, was founded by the former Prime Minister Abdumalik Abdullojanov.

Latest elections

The most recent legislature elections were held on 26 February and 12 March 1995. Turnout during the first ballot ranged from 60% in the capital Dushanbe to an official 100% in one constituency in the eastern region of Gorny-Badakhshan, and averaged 84%. One hundred and sixty-two seats were filled on the first ballot, with 40% of seats being uncontested, while 19 required a second-ballot run-off contest in March 1995. Two seats remained unfilled after the second round. Opposition parties, complaining of intimidation of their candidates and of widespread violation of the election law, widely boycotted the polls, which resulted in overwhelming victory for candidates from or sympathetic to the CPT and People's Party of Tajikistan (estd. 1994), which supported President Rakhmanov.

The latest presidential election was held on 6 November 1994 and resulted in victory for the incumbent Imamoli Rakhmanov, who secured 58% of the popular vote, compared with 35% for his opponent, the ex-prime minister, Abdumalik Abdullojanov. Rakhmanov received particularly strong support from his native region of Khatlon in the south and from the capital, Dushanbe, while his rival polled strongest in his home town of Khodzhent (Leninabad) and the eastern region of Gorny-Badakhshan, which is peopled by ethnic Pamirs who seek independence and support the Lali Badakhshan political movement. Abdullojanov claimed that the contest had been tarnished by vote-rigging.

Political history

The Tajiks are distinguished from their Turkic neighbours by their Iranian language and traditionally sedentary lifestyle. By the 8th century AD they had emerged as a distinct ethnic group and established semi-independent territories under Uzbek tutelage during the medieval period. Northern Tajikistan came under Tsarist Russia rule between 1860 and 1900, while the south was annexed by the Emirate of Bukhara. There was initial resistance, by *basmachi* guerrillas, to the imposition of Soviet control after the 1917 Russian Revolution, but in 1924 the Tajik Autonomous Soviet Socialist Republic was formed and in 1929 it became a full constituent republic of the Soviet Union.

There were repressions of Tajiks during the 1930s Stalinist era of collectivization and in 1978 there was a large anti-Russian riot in which 13,000 participated. With the coming to power in Moscow of the reformist Mikhail Gorbachev in 1985 an anticorruption drive was launched in the Central Asian republics and there was some relaxation of censorship. Accused of tolerating nepotism and corruption, the leader of the Communist Party of Tajikistan (CPT) since 1982, Rakhmon Nabiyev, was replaced in late 1985 by Kakhar Makhkamov. With greater freedom of expression being now tolerated in this glasnost ('openness') era, there was a resurgence in Tajik consciousness during the late 1980s. In 1989 a Rastokhez ('Revival') Popular Front was established and Tajik was declared the state language, with teaching of its traditional Arabic script recommencing in state schools.

However, the outbreak of violent interethnic clashes in Dushanbe in February 1990, after it was rumoured that Armenian refugees were to be settled there, resulted in the CPT regime pursuing a more hardline stance. A state of emergency was maintained throughout 1990 and the nascent opposition parties, Rastokhez, the Democratic Party, and the Islamic Renaissance Party (IRP), were refused official registration.

Makhkamov was indirectly elected, by the parliament (Supreme Soviet), executive president of the republic in November 1990 and the population voted 90% in favour of preserving the USSR in the all-Union constitutional referendum held in March 1991. However, the CPT and Makhkamov supported initially the attempted anti-Gorbachev coup staged by conservative communists in Moscow in August 1991. However, there were prodemocracy demonstrations in Dushanbe, led by the three opposition parties, and, after a vote of no confidence, Makhkamov was forced to resign as president on 31 August 1991. Under acting president Kadriddin Aslonov, a declaration of independence was made on 9 September 1991, and the activities of the CPT, temporarily renamed the Socialist Party of Tajikistan (SPT), were banned on 22 September 1991. However, a day later, at a special session of the CPT-dominated Supreme Soviet, this ban was overturned. Aslonov was replaced as president by Rakhmon Nabiyev, the former Brezhnev-appointed CPT leader, and a three-month state of emergency was imposed.

Following more than a week of popular protest, hunger strikes, and civil disobedience, orchestrated by the opposition Union of Democratic Forces, Nabiyev agreed to resuspend the SPT, lift the state of emergency, legalize the opposition parties, step down as president, and hold direct elections on 24 November 1991. Opposed by six other candidates, including the liberal-minded film producer Davlat Khudonazarov, who was backed by Rastokhez and the IRP, Nabiyev comfortably won the election, capturing 57% of the vote to Khudonazarov's 30%. Nabiyev drew strongest support from the industrialized northern region of Khojand and from the rural Kulyab region in the south. However, the opposition, and outside observers, claimed that the balloting had been rigged. The SPT reverted to its former designation, the CPT, in January 1992.

Tajikistan joined the Commonwealth of Independent States (CIS) on its inception in December 1991 and the Conference on Security and Cooperation in Europe (CSCE) in January 1992, but immediate recognition by the United States was denied. This was because there were fears that Nabiyev, a hardline conservative ruling a uranium-rich but cash-poor republic, might be tempted to help such pariahs of the Islamic world as Libya fulfil their nuclear ambitions. US recognition was eventually forthcoming and in March 1992 Tajikistan became a member of the United Nations.

The government pledged to replace the Cyrillic alphabet imposed by Russia in the 1930s with an Arabic alphabet and, as part of the revival of Islamic tradition, new mosques began to be constructed with Iranian and Saudi Arabian finance, raising the total number from 18 in 1989 to more than 2,500 in 1992.

From the spring of 1992 the Nabiyev regime faced increasing opposition from Islamic and democratic groups, based especially in the Kurgan-Tyube region of the far south and the Garm valley, east of Dushanbe. There were also violent anti-Nabiyev demonstrations in the capital, led initially by Pamiris. These grew fiercer from August 1992, eventually forcing Nabiyev to resign on 7 September 1992. With the support of Islamic and democratic groups, the chairman of the Supreme Soviet, Akbarsho Iskandarov, took over as interim head of state with the task of ending the civil war. However, fighting intensified, with Islamic and democratic groups forming a Popular Democratic Army (PDA) coalition to fight Nabiyev and his allied Tajik People's Front (TPF) Kulyabi militia, which was led by Sangak Safarov. Iskandarov, who controlled effectively only the Dushanbe area, thus resigned as head of state on 10 November 1992 and the office of president was abolished. Power was assumed by the new chairman of the Supreme Soviet, Imamoli Rakhmanov, a communist collective farm chairman from the Kulyab region. The new government was sympathetic to Nabiyev and its forces allied with the TPF to restore control over Dushanbe and much of the country, with the exception of the Garm Valley and Gorny-Badakhshan in the east. The six-month-long civil war had claimed more than 20,000 lives and led to 600,000 becoming refugees, with 70,000 fleeing to neighbouring Afghanistan. Safarov was killed in March 1993 and Nabiyev died of a heart attack a month later. From March 1993 peacekeeping forces from the CIS were sent to the republic to help ensure that order was maintained and to patrol the border with Afghanistan, where rebel guerrilla groups were now based.

The economy of Tajikistan, already the poorest of the ex-republics of the USSR on independence in 1991, was affected adversely by the break-up of the union and was damaged further by the 1992–93 civil war, which caused economic losses estimated at 300,000 million roubles. The pace of market-centred economic reform was also particularly slow and GDP declined by 25% in both 1993 and 1994. Blamed for the poor state of the economy, Abdumalik Abdullojanov was dismissed as prime minister in December 1993 and replaced by Abduljalil Samadov. He, in turn, was replaced by Jamshed Karimov in December 1994. The post of President, which had been abolished in 1993, was re-established following a constitutional referendum held in November 1994, and Rakhmanov was popularly elected to the post in the same month, defeating his challenger, Abdullojanov.

However, the new president ruled in an increasingly authoritarian manner, with tight curbs being maintained on opposition activities in an effort to curb the spread of Islamic fundamentalism. The republic also remained closely allied to Russia, which provided more than half of the state's budget and had 25,000 troops stationed there, with opposition to the regime remaining strong in Gorny-Badakhshan and little progress being achieved in peace talks with the opposition Islamic rebels.

THAILAND

Kingdom of Thailand
Prathet Thai or Muang Thai

Capital: Bangkok

Social and economic data
Area: 513,115 km^2
Population: 56,900,000*

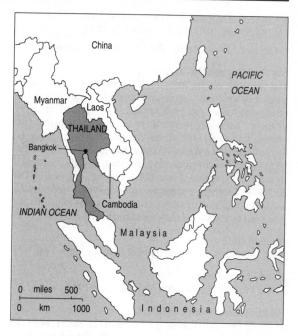

Pop. density per km^2: 111*
Urban population: 23%**
Literacy rate: 93%**
GDP: $115,000 million**; per-capita GDP: $2,040**
Government defence spending (% of GDP): 2.7%**
Currency: baht
Economy type: middle income
Labour force in agriculture: 63%**

*1994
**1992

Ethnic composition
Seventy-five per cent of the population is of Thai ethnic stock and 14% is ethnic Chinese, one-third of whom reside in Bangkok. Thai Malays constitute the next largest minority, followed by hill tribes. A substantial Kampuchean (Khmer) refugee community also resides in the country in border camps. The official language is Thai, or Siamese, with English being used as a universal second language.

Religions
Ninety-five per cent of the population is Buddhist, 4% is Sunni Muslim, predominantly ethnic Malays based in the south, while 0.5%, or 305,000, are Christians, three-quarters of whom are Catholics. Theravada Buddhism is the state religion.

Political features
State type: emergent democratic
Date of state formation: 1350
Political structure: unitary
Executive: parliamentary*
Assembly: two-chamber
Party structure: multiparty
Human rights rating: 62%

International affiliations: APEC, AsDB, ASEAN, CP, ESCAP, IAEA, IBRD, IMF, NAM, UN, WTO

*With special features: see **Political system**, below

Local and regional government

The country is divided into 73 provinces (*changwats*), headed by centrally appointed governors (*phuwaratchakan changwats*). Each province, in turn, is subdivided into 5–10 districts, each administered by a district officer (*nai amphoe*). Some 44,000 villages (*muban*) below are governed by elected chiefs (*phuyaiban*) who are removable by the district officer. The governor and provincial officials are advised by appointed provincial assemblies (*sapha changwats*). The Bangkok-Thonburi connurbation, in which 10% of the nation's population lives, constitutes a separate municipality, governed by an elected mayor and municipal council.

Head of state

King Bhumibol Adulyadej (King Rama IX), since 1946

Head of government

Prime Minister Banharn Silpa-archa, since 1995

Political leaders since 1970*

1963–73 General Thanom Kittikachorn (military), 1973–75 Dr Sanya Dharmasakti Thammasak (independent), 1975 Seni Pramoj (DP), 1975–76 Kukrit Pramoj (SAP), 1976 Seni Pramroj (DP), 1976–77 Thanin Kraivichien (independent), 1977–80 General Kriangsak Chomanan (military), 1980–88 General Prem Tinsulanonda (independent), 1988–91 Major General Chatichai Choonhavan (Thai Nation), 1991–92 Anand Panyarachun (independent), 1992 Narong Wongwan (Samakkhi Tham), 1992 General Suchinda Kraprayoon (military), 1992 Meechai Ruchuphan (independent), 1992 Anand Panyarachun (independent), 1992–95 Chuan Leekpai (DP), 1995– Banharn Silpa-archa (Thai Nation)

*Prime minister or military leader

Political system

Under the constitution of December 1991, as amended in May–June 1992 and January 1995, which superseded earlier documents of 1932, 1946, 1947, 1949, 1952, 1959, 1968, 1971, 1974, 1976, 1977, and 1978, Thailand is ruled by a hereditary constitutional monarch, working with an appointed and elected two-chamber National Assembly. The monarch, who remains a respected and revered figure and retains significant political power, acts as both head of state and head of the armed forces. He appoints a prime minister, on the advice of the National Assembly, selecting the person best able to secure majority support. The monarch is advised by an appointed 12-member Privy Council and has the authority to dissolve the National Assembly and call new elections. In addition, the monarch, acting on the advice of the prime minister, may veto bills, with a two-thirds National Assembly majority being required for this act to be overturned.

The upper house of the National Assembly, the Senate (Wuthisapha), comprises at present 270 members who are appointed for a six-year term by the monarch on the recommendation of the prime minister. Senators must not be members of any political party and must be at least 35 years of age. In practice, traditionally the vast majority have been drawn from the armed forces and the police, giving these institutions an effective 'blocking position' in the Thai political system. Under the terms of a constitutional amendment passed in January 1995, the Senate is to be reduced to two-thirds the size of the lower house, i.e. to 240 members, and Senators may not hold direct or indirect interests in government business concessions.

The lower house, the House of Representatives (Saphaphutan), comprises 391 members who are elected from single-member constituencies by universal adult suffrage for four-year terms. The chamber is subject to dissolution within this period. Representatives must be members of a political party and at least 25 years old. The voting age was reduced from 20 to 18 years in the January 1995 constitutional amendment.

The National Assembly debates and approves bills, while the Senate scrutinizes and may veto draft legislation. Joint meetings of the Senate and the House, chaired by the house speaker, are required for the passage of money bills, important legislation, but not, since May 1992, no-confidence motions.

The prime minister (Kayoke Rathamontri) is appointed by the monarch, and a selected 25–30 member cabinet, called the Council of Ministers, constitutes the country's political executive. It is responsible for both policy formulation and day-to-day administration. The prime minister and cabinet ministers may not be serving military officers, government employees, or have an interest in government business concessions. Additionally, since May 1992, there has been a requirement that the prime minister must be drawn from the ranks of elected deputies. The prime minister also heads the National Economic Development Board, the National Security Council, and the National Research Council and is served by a special policy-formulating advisory board, comprising academics and specialists. He enjoys extensive emergency powers, making him the most influential figure in the Thai political system. The strength of his influence is closely followed, however, by that of the army leadership.

Political parties

More than 20 political parties currently function. The most important seven are: the Democrat Party (DP: Prachatipat); the New Aspiration Party (NAP); the Palang Dharma Party (PDP); the Thai Nation (Chart Thai) party; Chart Pattana; the Social Action Party (SAP: Kij Sangkhom); and Nam Thai. The two most popular, and best organized, parties are the DP and Thai Nation.

The DP was established in 1946 and is a moderate, liberal grouping. It is the country's oldest legal political party and enjoys strong support in southern provinces. Led by Chuan Leekpai, it spearheaded the 1992 prodemocracy movement. The New Aspiration Party was formed in 1990 and is led by the former supreme military commander and deputy prime minister during 1990, General Chaovalit Yongchaiyut. The Righteous Force PDP (Palang Dharma), an austere anticorruption Buddhist party, was formed in 1988 by the charismatic Governor of Bangkok, Major General Chamlong Srimuang. The latter resigned as party leader in May 1995 and the PDP was taken over by the billionaire media tycoon Thaksin Shinawatra. Along with Ekkaparb (Solidarity), formed in 1989 through the merger of the Community Action Party, the Prachachon Party, Ruam Thai, and the Progressive Party, these four parties successfully contested the September 1992 general election together as the National Democratic Front and subsequently formed a coalition government which lasted until May 1995.

Thai Nation was formed in 1974. It is a right-wing, cash-rich pro-business party, dominated traditionally by the military. It has a firm popular base in the central and northeastern provinces. Its former leader, ex-premier Chatichai Choonhavan, formed the breakaway Chart Pattana (National Development) in 1992 and joined the government coalition in December 1994. Led by Banharn Silapa-archa, Thai Nation emerged as the largest party in parliament after the July 1995 general election.

The SAP, which also dates from 1974, is a moderate conservative grouping founded by Kukrit Pramoj (1911–1995), who was prime minister during 1975–76. It was a member of the Democrat-led coalition during 1992–93.

The Nam Thai was formed in 1994 by Amnuay Viravan, a former banker and deputy prime minister.

Other parties with recent parliamentary representation are Seritham (Justice Freedom; estd. 1992); Muan Chon (Mass) Party (estd. 1985), led by Police Captain Chalerm Yubamrung; the Thai Citizens' Party (Prachakorn Thai), a far-right, Bangkok-based monarchist body led by Samak Sundaravej, and dating from 1981; and Rassadorn (Citizens' Party; estd. 1981). The country's oldest political party, the Communist Party of Thailand (CPT), which dates from 1925, is currently illegal.

Thailand's political parties are loosely constructed, patronage-linked coalitions. Once elected, party members are substantially independent, each enjoying his own firm local base. Changes of party affiliation, in response to inducements, are frequent. In 1995 the going rate for buying an MP, whose loyalty was up for sale and who was willing to switch parties, was said to be 10 million baht ($400,000). Only the Democrat Party, which has more than 80 branches, Thai Nation, and the Social Action Party have extended local party organizations.

Latest elections

In the most recent House of Representatives elections, which were held on 2 July 1995, the most successful party was the Thai Nation. It won 92 of the 391 seats, with the Democrat Party finishing in second place, with 86 seats. Third and fourth positions were occupied by the New Aspiration and Chart Pattana (National Development) parties, winning 57 and 53 seats respectively, while the Palang Dharma (Moral Force) Party, with 23 seats, and Prachakorn Thai Party, 18 seats, together won most seats in the capital, Bangkok. As always in Thailand, the election was marked by violence and, especially, vote-buying, with an estimated 17 billion baht ($680 million) being disbursed during the 45-day campaign. Thai Nation was particularly active in vote-buying in rural areas in the north, but failed to win any seats in Bangkok, where voters are better educated. Overall turnout was 62 %.

Political history

Thailand supported a Bronze Age civilization as early as 4000 BC. Control over the country was later contested territorially by Malay, Khmer, Thai, and Mon tribes, before a unified Thai nation, termed Siam, was eventually founded in 1350. In 1826 and 1855 treaties of friendship and trade established Britain as the paramount power in the region and opened Siam to foreign commerce. The country was never formally colonized, however, being established, instead, as a neutral and independent buffer kingdom between British Burma and French Indochina, by the Anglo-French diplomatic agreements of 1896 and 1904.

After World War I, a movement for national renaissance developed, which culminated, in 1932, in a coup against the absolute ruler, King Prajadhipok, and the establishment of a constitutional monarchy and an elected, representative system of government. Political parties developed in the new parliament and the name of Muang Thai, 'Land of the Free', was adopted in 1939. During World War II Thailand was occupied by the Japanese between 1941 and 1945. The Thai government collaborated, although a guerrilla resistance movement also operated. A period of instability followed the Japanese withdrawal and King Ananda Mahidol was assassinated in 1946, before the army seized power in a coup in 1947, led by Field Marshal Pibul Songgram.

The army retained control during the next two decades, ruling through a military junta whose leadership was periodically changed by a series of bloodless coups. Field Marshal Pibul Songgram dominated between 1947 and 1957, Field Marshal Sarit Thanarat between 1957 and 1963, and General Thanom Kittikachorn between 1963 and 1973. The monarch, in the person of King Bhumibol Adulyadej (b. 1927), operated as a figurehead ruler and experiments with elected assemblies were undertaken between 1957 and 1958 and 1968 and 1971. During this era of junta rule, Thailand allied itself with the United States and encountered serious communist guerrilla insurgency along its borders with Laos, Kampuchea, and Malaysia.

Despite achievements in the economic sphere, the junta was overthrown, after violent student riots in October 1973. A democratic constitution was adopted in October 1974, establishing a constitutional monarchy and a National Assembly, to which free elections were held in 1975 and 1976. A series of coalition governments followed, but they lacked stability and, following further student demonstrations, the military assumed power again in 1976–77, annulling the 1974 constitution. Initially, the Army Supreme Commander, General Kriangsak Chomanan, held power between 1977 and 1980 and promulgated a new constitution in December 1978. This strengthened the position of the military and established a mixed civilian-military form of government, under the monarch's direction. However, General Kriangsak was forced to give way to General Prem Tinsulanonda in October 1980. He formally relinquished his army office and headed a series of civilian coalition governments which were formed after the parliamentary elections of April 1983 and July 1986.

Coups, led by junior military officers, were attempted in April 1981 and September 1985, the latter involving General Kriangsak. They were easily crushed, however, by Prime

Minister Prem, who governed in a cautious apolitical manner, retaining the confidence of the army leadership, state bureaucracy, business community and monarchy. Under Prem's stewardship, the country achieved a rapid rate of economic growth, of more than 9% per annum, and began the process of establishing Thailand as an export-orientated newly industrializing country (NIC). During the spring of 1988, following the introduction of legislation, allegedly at the United States government's behest, to tighten up copyright regulations, divisions began to widen within the ruling four-party coalition. This prompted Prem, who was also concerned that a personal impropriety might be publicized in a forthcoming 'no-confidence' motion, to call, in April, for a dissolution of parliament. This request was acceded to by King Adulyadej.

Following the subsequent general election, in July 1988, a new five-party ruling coalition, consisting of the Thai Nation, Democrat (DP), Social Action (SAP), Rassadorn, and United Democratic parties, was constructed, which, once again, asked Prem to come into parliament and assume its leadership. Prem, however, surprisingly declined this offer on 'personal grounds'. Instead, power passed to the former Deputy Prime Minister, Chatichai Choonhavan, leader of the Thai Nation party.

Chatichai pursued a similar pro-business policy course to his predecessor, but, after criticism of government corruption, was overthrown in February 1991 in a bloodless military coup – the nation's 17th since the abolition of the absolute monarchy in 1932. This coup was led by General Sunthorn Kongsompong, the supreme military commander, and by General Suchinda Kraprayoon, the army chief. Anand Panyarachun (b. 1932) took over as civilian interim prime minister, but his government was subject to the ultimate control of the military junta, which held direct charge of the defence and interior ministry portfolios. The framing of a new constitution, which enshrined the military's *de facto* authority by enabling it to appoint 270 senators, provoked large-scale demonstrations in Bangkok in November 1991. Nevertheless, the constitution was endorsed in December 1991.

In the general election of March 1992 the three leading pro-military parties, the airforce-linked Samakkhi Tham, Thai Nation, and the New Aspiration Party (NAP), secured more than half of the 360 contested seats. Narong Wongwan, leader of Samakkhi Tham, became prime minister, heading a five-party coalition. However, within a month, after the United States had denied him a visa as a result of alleged drug offences, he was replaced by the non-elected General Suchinda. This appointment provoked the largest street protests witnessed in Bangkok for two decades and Major General Chamlong Srimuang, leader of the opposition Palang Dharma (PDP), an austere Buddhist 'moral force' party, commenced a hunger strike. The army response was firm. But, after between 50 and 100 protesters were killed during riots on 17–19 May 1992, King Bhumibol Adulyadej intervened and called for harmony. On 24 May 1992 General Suchinda resigned and fled the country. Two days later, the recently imposed state of emergency was lifted and a package of constitutional reforms was agreed. These included a reduction in the power of the military-appointed Senate and

a requirement that, in future, the prime minister should be an elected member of parliament.

The respected Anand Panyarachun returned as interim prime minister, until elections held in September 1992 brought to power a four-party civilian coalition government of so-called 'prodemocracy angels'. The coalition was dominated by the DP, whose leader Chuan Leekpai (b. 1938) became prime minister, and the PDP. The DP had captured 79 seats in the 360-member House of Representatives and the PDP 47 seats, while the main opposition party, Thai Nation, had won just 77 seats. The SAP, with 22 seats, also joined the coalition and General Chaovalit Yongchaiyut, leader of the NAP, which had 51 seats, and a former supreme military commander, became interior minister. The government pledged to eradicate corruption, decentralize administration, liberalize the financial system, reform education, and promote rural development, via redistributing state land to the rural poor.

The governing coalition was weakened in September 1993 when the SAP left. However, the small Seritham (Justice Freedom) party, with eight deputies, joined in the same month and Chart Pattana (National Development), led by Chatichai Choonhavan and which had 60 deputies, in December 1994. The Leekpai government was relatively successful in its policy goals and achieved annual GDP growth of around 8%. However, in May 1995 the coalition was fractured by a withdrawal of support by the PDP, on the grounds of 'political righteousness', after it was revealed that its land reform programme, which had resulted in 600,000 poor rural families receiving 4.4 million acres of land, had, in a few cases, benefited wealthy families with connections to the DP. Faced with certain defeat in an impending 'no-confidence' motion, Prime Minister Leekpai dissolved parliament and called a snap general election for 2 July 1995. This was narrowly won by Thai Nation, led by Banharn Silpa-archa, who subsequently put together a seven-party coalition government. It included support from the PDP, SAP, NAP, Nam Thai, and Prachakorn Thai Party and had as its defence minister Chaovalit Yongchaiyudh and, as deputy prime minister, the media tycoon Thaksin Shinawatra, but excluded the DP.

Thailand's external relations during the past two decades have been dominated by the civil war in neighbouring Cambodia and Laos, which resulted in the flight of more than 500,000 refugees to Thailand after 1975 and provided justification for continued quasi-military rule and the maintenance of martial law. In addition, border concerns encouraged a tightening of Thailand's relations with its ASEAN allies, who became sponsors of the Cambodian Royalist movement, and led to a thawing in relations with communist China.

TURKMENISTAN

Republic of Turkmenistan
Turkmenostan

Capital: Ashkhabad (Ashgabat)

Social and economic data
Area: 488,100 km^2
Population: 4,000,000*

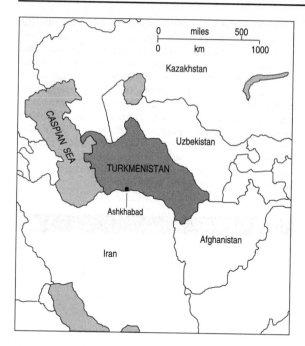

Pop. density per km²: 8*
Urban population: 45%**
Literacy rate: 98%**
GDP: $4,900 million**; *per-capita GDP*: $1,270**
Government defence spending (% of GDP): 3.8%**
Currency: manat
Economy type: middle income
Labour force in agriculture: 43%**

*1994
**1992

Ethnic composition

Seventy-two per cent of the population is of Turkmen ethnic stock, 10% ethnic Russian, 9% Uzbek, 3% Kazakh, and 1% Ukrainian. The official language is Turkmen, a member of the Southern Turkic language group. Under the terms of a December 1993 accord signed with Russia, Turkmenistan's 400,000 ethnic Russians have been permitted to hold joint Turkmen and Russian nationality.

Religions

The population is predominantly Sunni Muslim, but the state is secular.

Political features

State type: authoritarian nationalist
Date of state formation: 1991
Political structure: unitary
Executive: unlimited presidential
Assembly: one-chamber
Party structure: one-party*
Human rights rating: N/A
International affiliations: CIS, EBRD, ECO, EOC, ESCAP, IBRD, IMF, NACC, OIC, OSCE, PFP, UN

*Effective

Local and regional government

There are five regions, with elected councils operating at the district, town, and village level below.

Head of state and of government

President Saparmurad Niyazov, since 1990

Political leaders since 1970

1985–   Saparmurad Niyazov (CPT/DPT)*
*Niyazov was leader of the republic's Communist Party and prime minister from 1985 and head of state from 1990

Political system

Under the constitution of May 1992, Turkmenistan has a strong presidentialist form of government. The president serves as both head of state and head of government (prime minister), with decree powers, and as supreme commander of the armed forces. A personality cult has been developed. Public buildings have been renamed after Niyazov, a public holiday has been established to celebrate his birthday, and large portraits have been erected on major roads to a president who has been officially styled Turkmenbashi, 'leader of the Turkmen'. The president is directly elected for a five-year term, but in January 1994 President Niyazov's current term was extended, by plebiscite, until 2002. Legislative authority is held by the 50-member Majlis (parliament), popularly elected for a five-year term, and the president works with a Council of Ministers of some 35 members. Parliamentary candidates need to secure more than 50% of the vote, with there being a provision for a second 'run-off' ballot. There is also a People's Council (Khalk Maslakhaty), which comprises the members of the Majlis plus 50 representatives elected from the regions of Turkmenistan and acts as a supervisory organ and to debate important political and economic issues.

Political parties

The dominant political party is the 116,000-member Democratic Party of Turkmenistan (DPT), led by President Niyazov. Before 1991 it was known as the Communist Party of Turkmenistan (CPT). It is the only party which is allowed to effectively operate, with opposition figures facing repression. Agzybirlik (Unity) was formed in 1989 as a Turkmen 'popular front' nationalist force.

Latest elections

The most recent Majlis elections were held on 11 December 1994. All candidates were drawn from the ruling DPT or were 'independents' and were elected unopposed. Turnout was officially recorded at 99.8%.

The last presidential election was on 21 June 1992 when the incumbent Saparmurad Niyazov was returned to power, unopposed, with 99.5% of the vote. Niyazov's term in office was extended until 2002 by a national referendum held on 15 January 1994 and carried with the support of 99.9% of voters; only 212 Turkmen voted 'no', officially.

Political history

The principal Turkmen tribes are the Tekkes of Merv and Attok, the Ersaris, the Yomuds, and the Gokluns, all speaking varieties of a Turkic language and descended from the nomadic Oghuz and Mongol tribes who swept across Asia between the 10th and 13th centuries. This isolated region was conquered by Tsarist Russia between 1869 and 1900, with an estimated 150,000 Turkmen being killed in the 1881 battle of Gok Tepe. In 1916 the Turkmens rose up in revolt against Russian rule and an autonomous Transcaspian government was formed after the Russian Revolution of 1917. The Soviet Red Army re-established Russian control in 1919 and it became part of the Turkestan Soviet Socialist Autonomous Republic in 1921, before becoming a constituent republic of the USSR in 1925. Sporadic guerrilla resistance against the Soviet overlords, and their programme of agricultural collectivization and secularization, nearly 500 mosques being closed, continued into the 1930s. However, the Russians brought improvements in social, health, and educational facilities, and some economic progress. Much of the republic's land was barren until the Soviet-built Kara Kum Canal brought millions of acres of desert to life, stimulating cotton production, although living standards remained very low.

The nationalist movement was more muted in Turmenistan than in other former Soviet Central Asian republics. In September 1989 a 'popular front' organization, Agzybirlik, concerned with cultural and environmental issues, was formed illegally by Turkmen intellectuals. In May 1990 Turkmen replaced Russian as the official state language and in August 1990 Turkmenistan's legislature, the Supreme Soviet, declared the republic's 'sovereignty'. However, in the March 1991 USSR constitutional referendum the population voted to maintain the Union, and the attempted anti-Gorbachev coup in Moscow in August 1991 was initially supported by President Niyazov (b. 1940), an old Soviet hand, who had led the republic's Communist Party since 1985. However, in an October 1991 referendum there was an overwhelming 94% vote in favour of independence. It was duly declared.

Turkmenistan joined the Commonwealth of Independent States (CIS) on its inception in December 1991 and was admitted into the Conference on Security and Cooperation in Europe (CSCE, later the OSCE) in January 1992. It became a member of the United Nations in March 1992. Since independence, economic and diplomatic links with neighbouring Iran have improved and the new state joined the Economic Cooperation Organization (ECO), founded by Iran, Pakistan, and Turkey in 1975, which aimed to reduce customs tariffs and eventually form a customs union. In October 1994, along with Turkey, Azerbaijan, Kazakhstan, Kyrgyzstan, and Uzbekistan, it signed the 'Istanbul declaration' pledging to seek deepened economic and cultural cooperation with its 'Turkic brothers'.

The Niyazov regime has remained communist-dominated, intolerant of opposition, and increasingly personalized. Indeed, the growing personality cult surrounding the president and the decision to cancelled scheduled presidential elections due in 1997 and extend Niyazov's term in office by a plebiscite, duly held in Janury 1994, prompted the foreign minister, Khalyberdy Atayev, to resign in December 1993. Disruptions in inter-republican trade brought about by the dissolution of the USSR in December 1991 affected Turkmenistan less severely than many other republics because of its abundant natural energy resources. These have been

sufficient to enable the state to provide free electricity and gas to its citizens during 1993. A programme of cautious economic reform has been pursued, entailing the successful introduction of a new currency, the manat, in November 1993, gradual price deregulation for nonessential items, and the encouragement of foreign investment in developing the country's huge natural gas and oil reserves. Seven free economic zones, with exemptions from land tax, have been established for the latter purpose. However, GDP declined in each of the years between 1993–95 and there has been no real privatization. The new state, with its strict, secular leadership, has avoided the religious conflict and interethnic violence experienced in nearby Tajikistan.

UZBEKISTAN

Republic of Uzbekistan
Ozbekiston Republikasy/Ozbekistan Jumhuriyati

Capital: Tashkent

Social and economic data
Area: 447,400 km^2
Population: 21,900,000*
Pop. density per km^2: 49*
Urban population: 40%**
Literacy rate: 85%**
GDP: $19,900 million**; per-capita GDP: $950**
Government defence spending (% of GDP): 2.8**
Currency: som
Economy type: low income
Labour force in agriculture: 40%**

*1994
**1992

Ethnic composition

Seventy-one per cent of the population is of Uzbek ethnic stock, 8% is ethnic Russian, concentrated in the urban centres, 4% Tajik, 3% Kazakh, and 2% Tatar. Uzbek, from the Eastern Turkic language group, is the official language.

Religions

The predominant religion is Islam, mainly from the Sunni sect (Hanafi school). The influence of the Wahhabis and Sufism is well established in the country's south. The ethnic Slav communities are predominantly Orthodox Christians, and there are also 65,000 European Jews and 28,000 Central Asian Jews.

Political features

State type: authoritarian nationalist
Date of state formation: 1991
Political structure: unitary
Executive: unlimited presidential
Assembly: one-chamber
Party structure: one-party (effective)*
Human rights rating: N/A
International affiliations: CIS, EBRD, ECO, IAEA, IBRD, IMF, NACC, NAM, OSCE, PFP, UN

*Opposition activities are restricted

Local and regional government

There are 12 administrative regions and, below, there are city and rural districts and towns and villages with elected councils.

Head of state (executive)

President Islam Karimov, since 1990

Head of government

Prime Minister Abdulhashim Mulatov, since 1991

Political leaders since 1970

1990– Islam Karimov (UCP/PDP)

Political system

Under the terms of the December 1992 constitution, Uzbekistan is a secular state with a limited presidential political system. Supreme executive authority is held by a state president, who is directly elected for up to two consecutive five-year terms. The current incumbent, Islam Karimov, had his second term approved in March 1995 by a plebiscite.

There is a 250-member legislature, the Oli Majlis (Supreme Assembly), to which deputies are elected for five-year terms by a two-ballot majoritarian system, a second ballot 'run-off' race being held in contests in which there is no clear first-round majority winner. A prime minister and cabinet of some 25 members is drawn from the legislature, but they are subordinate to the President, who, with the approval of the Constitutional Court, may also dissolve the Oli Majlis.

Political parties

The principal political party is the People's Democratic Party of Uzbekistan (PDP), which is the reform-socialist successor to the formerly dominant Uzbekistan Communist Party (UCP). Set up in 1991 and led by President Karimov, it claims

a membership of 340,000. Its ally is the Fatherland Progress Party (FP: Vatan Taraqioti), which was created by the government as a party of business. It is supported by Khalq Birligi (People's Unity), formed in May 1995. The main opposition parties are Birlik (Unity Popular Front; estd. 1989), led by Adbdurakhim Pulatov and which claims a membership of 54,000; Erk (Freedom Democratic Party; estd. 1990), led by Mohammed Salikh and which favours a mixed economy; and the Islamic Renaissance Party, which advocates the establishment of an Islamic-based political system. In 1991 all religious political parties were banned and in 1992 Birlik was also outlawed. In February 1995, a new opposition party, the pro-Islamic Adolat ('Justice') Social Democratic Party of Uzbekistan was formed by Anwar Jurabayev. It claimed to have 6,000 members and the support of 47 recently elected parliamentary deputies and applied for official recognition. A centrist, intelligentsia-led party, the National Revival Democratic Party, was formed in June 1995.

Latest elections

The most recent parliamentary elections were held on 25 December 1994 and 22 January 1995. Only two parties, the PDP and the allied FP, were allowed to participate, with the PDP winning 69 of the 250 Oli Majlis seats, the FP, 14, and nominees of local authorities, 167. It was estimated that 120 of the latter were also PDP members. Turnout was reported at 93.6% and 643 candidates participated, with 205 of the majoritarian races being settled in the first round.

The last presidential election was held on 29 December 1991, when Islam Karimov, then chairperson of the Supreme Soviet (parliament), faced with one opponent, secured 85.9% of the vote. Karimov's tenure as president was extended a further five years, until 2000, in a plebiscite held on 26 March 1995, which secured 99.6% support, with turnout officially recorded at 99.3%.

Political history

The Uzbeks are Turkic-speaking descendants of the Mongol invaders who swept across Asia from the 13th century and mixed with more sedentary Central Asians. During the 18th and 19th centuries the region was politically dominated by the khanates of Samarkhand, Kokand, and Bukhara. From 1865 Turkestan was conquered gradually by Tsarist Russia, with the emir of Bukhara becoming a vassal, and in 1876 Kokand was subjugated. The Tashkent soviet (people's council) gradually extended its authority between 1917 and 1924, with the emir of Bukhara being deposed in 1920. Uzbekistan became a constituent republic of the USSR in 1925, although nationalist guerrilla (*basmachi*) resistance continued for a number of years.

Russia's communist rulers sought to secularize the republic during the 1920s and 1930s. Muslim schools, courts, and mosques were closed and clergy persecuted, while new national symbols and a new literary language were promoted through investment in state education. Skilled ethnic Russian workers also immigrated into urban centres as industries began to be developed. During World War II, in 1944, some 160,000 Meskhetian Turks were forcibly transported to Uzbekistan from their native Georgia under orders from the Soviet dictator, Joseph Stalin.

After the war, Uzbekistan became a major cotton-growing region, producing two-thirds of Soviet output. However, the associated irrigation projects contributed to the desiccation of the adjoining Aral Sea, with grave environmental and health consequences. The Uzbek Communist Party (UCP) leadership, who controlled the republic like a feudal fief, was notorious for the extent of its corruption and for its obedience to Moscow. In return, Uzbekistan received large financial subsidies.

From the late 1980s, as Moscow, under the direction of Mikhail Gorbachev, began to tolerate greater political openness (glasnost), there was an upsurge in Islamic consciousness. This provoked violent clashes with Meskhetian, Armenian, and Kyrgyz minority communities, particularly in the Ferghana Valley, which had become a hotbed for Wahabi Islamic militancy. In September 1989 an Uzbek nationalist organization, the Birlik ('Unity') People's Movement, was formed. The UCP, under the leadership of an old Soviet hand Islam Karimov (b. 1938), responded, in an outflanking nationalist move, by declaring the republic's 'sovereignty' in June 1990 and replacing Russian administrators with Uzbeks. However, the republic's population voted, in the March 1991 all-Union referendum, in favour of preserving the USSR as a 'renewed federation of equal sovereign republics'.

President Karimov did not immediately condemn the August 1991 attempted anti-Gorbachev coup in Moscow. However, once the coup was defeated, the UCP broke its links with the Communist Party of the Soviet Union (CPSU) and on 31 August 1991 the republic declared its independence. Uzbekistan joined the post-Soviet Commonwealth of Independent States (CIS) on its inception in December 1991 and was admitted into the Conference on Security and Cooperation in Europe (CSCE) in January 1992. It became a member of the United Nations in March 1992.

Karimov was directly elected president on 29 December 1991, receiving 86% of the popular vote. At home, he has embarked on a strategy of gradualist, market-centred economic reform. However, political authoritarianism has been maintained. Communist Party cells have been banned from the armed forces, the police, and civil service and the UCP changed its designation in 1991 to the People's Democratic Party (PDP). Nevertheless, the former UCP apparatus and personnel remained very much in control, with opposition groups harassed and banned, and the media is under state control. In December 1994–January 1995 elections, from which the opposition was banned from participating, a compliant, pro-Karimov legislature was returned and Karimov's tenure as President was extended in March 1995 for a further five years in a Soviet-style rubber-stamp plebiscite.

In February 1992 Uzbekistan joined the Economic Cooperation Organization (ECO), founded by Iran, Pakistan, and Turkey in 1975, which aimed to reduce customs tariffs and eventually form a customs union. In particular, links with Turkey have been strengthened, with Turkish taught in schools, alongside the Uzbek and English languages and in place of Russian. It also established an economic, military, and social union with neighbouring Kazakhstan and Kyrgyzstan in January and July 1994, negotiated a treaty on economic integration and policy coordination with Russia in March 1994, and has encouraged foreign investment in its energy resources and industrial joint ventures. Being largely self-sufficient in energy and foodstuffs, and with large gold resources, Uzbekistan was not so badly affected by the collapse of the USSR as many other Central Asian states. Nevertheless, the pace of economic reform has been slow for reasons of internal stability, after violent student-led food riots erupted in Tashkent in January 1992 following initial price liberalization. The emigration, since independence, of skilled ethnic Russian industrial workers and bureaucrats has also had adverse economic consequences, the inflation rate, at 270% in 1994, is dangerously high, food rationing has been in force since 1991, and GDP declined continuously between 1993–95.

Aided by an inflow of funds from Saudi Arabia, a revival of Islamic teaching and studies has been witnessed since independence. However, President Karimov, anxious to avoid the political turmoil caused by ethnic unrest and Islamic fundamentalism in neighbouring Tajikistan, has pursued a determinedly secularist stance. In May 1995 he advocated publicly that the five former Soviet Central Asian republics of Kazakhstan, Kyrgyzstan, Tajikistan, Turkmenistan, and Uzbekistan should create a common, unified Turkic republic of 'Turkestan'.

VIETNAM

The Socialist Republic of Vietnam (SRV)
Cong Hoa Xa Hoi Chu Nghia Viet Nam

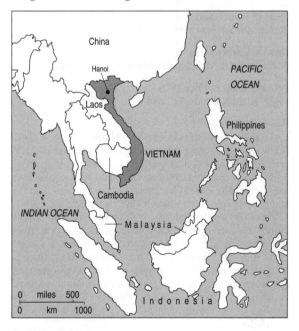

Capital: Hanoi

Social and economic data
Area: 329,566 km^2
Population: 70,900,000*
Pop. density per km^2: 215*

Urban population: 20%*
Literacy rate: 88%**
*GDP**: $12,200m**; per-capita GDP: $180**
Government defence spending (% of GDP): 4.3%**
Currency: dong
Economy type: low income
Labour force in agriculture: 62%**

*1994
**1992

Ethnic composition
Eighty-eight per cent of the population is Viet, also known as Kinh, and imbued with a strong sense of national identity; 2% is Chinese, or Hoa, being predominantly based in South Vietnam and engaged in commercial activities; 2% is Khmer; and the remaining 8% belongs to more than 50 minority nationalities, the most important of which are the Hmong, Meo, Muong, Nung, Tay, Thai, and Tho, who live mainly along the border with China, in the North, and are tribal groups. Vietnamese (Quoc-Ngu) is the main and official language.

Religions
The principal religion, followed by 55% of the population, is Buddhism, of the Mahayana, 'Greater Wheel', variety, in the North and the Theravada, 'Lesser Wheel', sect in the South, with the cult of ancestor worship in clan temples being a conspicuous element in it. Confucianism and Daoism are also important related religions. Caodaism, a syncretic, ethical religion, which was developed in the 1920s, claims 5 million adherents, predominantly in the Mekong delta, while Hoa Hoa, a Buddhist-orientated anti-communist sect, founded in 1939, used to have 1.5 million members, chiefly in the western Mekong delta, in South Vietnam. Roman Catholicism claims 6 million followers and Protestant denominations 180,000. Under the constitution complete freedom of worship has been guaranteed. In practice, however, restrictions have been periodically enforced, involving the 're-education' of anti-regime Buddhist and Christian groups.

Political features
State type: communist
Date of state formation: 1954
Political structure: unitary
Executive: communist
Assembly: one-chamber
Party structure: one-party*
Human rights rating: 27%
International affiliations: AsDB, ASEAN, ESCAP, IAEA, IBRD, IMF, NAM, UN

*Effectively

Local and regional government
The country is divided into 36 provinces, 3 municipalities, Hanoi, Haiphong and Ho Chi Minh City, and one special zone, Vung Tau-Con Dao, all directly under the control of the central authority. There are also 443 districts and town wards and 9,504 rural communes and street blocks. People's Councils operate and are elected at four-yearly intervals, in multi-candidate contests, in the case of the provinces, and every two years at other levels. The People's Councils elect

People's Committees as their executive organs, each unit being responsible and accountable to the body immediately above, in accordance with the precept of 'democratic centralism'. Their work is supervised by the Communist Party committee at the same level.

Head of state
President General Le Duc Anh, since 1992

Head of government
Prime Minister General Vo Van Kiet, since 1991

Political leaders since 1970
1965–75 Lieutenant General Nguyen Van Thieu*, 1969–75 Le Duan (Lao Dong)**, 1975–86 Le Duan (CPV)***, 1986 Truong Chinh (CPV)***, 1986–91 Nguyen Van Linh (CPV), 1991–   Do Muoi (CPV)***

*South Vietnam leader
**North Vietnam (DRV) leader
***Communist Party leaders

Political system
Vietnam, excluding the American client regime in the South, has had four constitutions since World War II. The first, which was adopted in November 1946, was a moderate, nonsocialist 'united front' document, drawing significantly from both the United States and French systems, and providing for 'the transformation of the country on a democratic basis'. Its replacement, which was adopted in December 1959, was unashamedly socialist, giving pride of place to central planning and collectivization and describing the state as 'a people's democracy, advancing step by step to socialism'. The third constitution, adopted in December 1980, described the country as in a 'period of transition to socialism on the national scale', with the 'socialization of production' yet to fully be attained in the South. It borrowed much from the Soviet Union's 1977 'Brezhnev constitution', explicitly prescribing a 'leading' and 'vanguard' role to the ruling Communist Party of Vietnam (CPV). It was replaced in April 1992 by a new 148-article constitution which, while re-emphasizing the CPV's leading role, also explicitly recognized the rights of citizens to engage in private enterprise, enshrining recent market-centred economic reforms.

Under the current constitution of 1992, the highest state authority and sole legislative chamber is the National Assembly (Quoc Hoi), a body which is composed of 395 members directly elected every five years by universal adult suffrage in multimember constituencies. Electors choose from a list of candidates selected by the Fatherland Front and its affiliated organization, with an element of choice being theoretically available, there being more candidates than seats. In addition, under the new 1992 election law, independent candidates are permitted. To be elected a candidate must secure 50% of the vote, a second contest being held if this is not achieved.

The National Assembly formally has the authority to decide on 'fundamental questions' of domestic and foreign policy and has the task of adopting the economic plan and state budget. To amend the constitution a two-thirds majority is required. The Assembly also elects from within it a president to serve as the formal head of state, as chairperson of the

Council on National Defence and Security, and as commander in chief of the armed forces.

Day-to-day government is carried out by a cabinet, headed by a chairperson, or prime minister. It is 'elected' by and responsible to the National Assembly and, in its absence, the president. It has overall jurisdiction over the management of the Socialist Republic of Vietnam's domestic and external affairs; frames the budget, economic plan, and state laws and decrees; and supervises the work of both the central bureaucracy and local government bodies.

The dominating and leading force in the Socialist Republic is the CPV, which has been headed since 1991 by General Secretary Do Muoi. The party controls the Vietnam Fatherland Front mass organization, which puts up candidates in state election contests. Leading members of the CPV also occupy key positions in the state hierarchy although, under the terms of the 1992 constitution, the CPV is supposed to be prohibited from involvement in the day-to-day running of the government.

Political parties

The ruling Communist Party of Vietnam (CPV: Dang Cong san Viet-Nam) was founded in February 1930 through the union, under Comintern instructions, of three small existing communist groups, the most important of which was the Vietnamese Revolutionary Youth League, which was established in 1925. Initally designated the Indochinese Communist Party (ICP), it was led by the Paris- and Moscow-trained Ho Chi Minh and had an initial membership of 211, backed by 2,000 active collaborators, predominantly drawn from the ranks of the intelligentsia. In June 1941 the party, which now had a formal membership of 2,000 and was supported by 40,000 followers, adopted a new strategy of guerrilla resistance, against Japanese occupation, following the example set by Mao Zedong in China. A 'united front' organization, the Viet Minh, was established for this purpose. By such means the party was swept to power in September 1945, although a further nine years of warfare ensued until its control, in the north, was recognized. In the meantime, following the separation of the Laotian and Cambodian sections, the party adopted a new name, the Lao Dong (Workers') Party, in February 1951, and became purely Vietnam-based. In December 1976, following the successful unification of North and South, the present designation of CPV was adopted.

The CPV is organized hierarchically on 'democratic centralist' lines. At the base there are local party cells (*chi bo*), which are established in factories, cooperatives, villages, wards, and army units, and which have 3–10 members each. Above, there are party organizations, committees 'elected' by congresses, at the district, provincial and municipal levels, with, at the apex, a national Party Congress, convened quinquennially. The Party Congress is, theoretically, the supreme authority within the CPV. It meets for a week and has the task of approving the party programme and 'electing' a Central Committee (CC) of some 160 members to assume its powers in its absence. The most recent, seventh, Party Congress, was held in June 1991, the previous Congresses having been in 1935, 1951, 1960, 1976, 1982, and 1986. A special mid-term National Conference was held in January 1995. The CC, which meets twice a year, in turn, 'elects' a Politburo of about 13 members, headed by a General Secretary, and a Secretariat of about nine members. These function as the real controlling bodies in the party and state structures, with a system of consensual, though factionalized, collective leadership operating. This leadership is of a gerontocratic nature, reflecting the continuing influence of Confucianist political notions.

Membership of the CPV currently stands at 1.8 million, or 2.6% of the total population, which is a low proportion by comparative communist state standards. Membership surged from a figure of barely 5,000 in 1945 to 760,000 in 1951, before falling during the 1950s, as stricter entry criteria were applied. Thereafter, the total climbed relatively slowly to 1.1 million in 1970 and 1.5 million in 1976. Reliable data on the party's social composition are lacking. However, in general, it appears that the bulk are drawn from peasant and white-collar backgrounds, the proportion who are described as 'blue-collar workers' constituting less than 10% of the total.

Two other parties, the trader-orientated Democratic Party (Dang Dan Chu), which was formed in 1944, and the intelligentsia-orientated Socialist Party (Dang Xa Hoi), which dates from 1946, are allowed to operate, but not to compete with the CPV. They participate in the Viet-Nam Fatherland Front, a CPV-dominated mass organization, which was established in North Vietnam in 1955 as a mobilizing body and successor to the League for National Union of Vietnam (Lien-Viet), which itself had, in 1946, grown out of the Viet Minh. In January 1977 the Fatherland Front absorbed the South Vietnam-based National Liberation Front and the Alliance of National Democratic and Peace Forces.

Latest elections

The most recent National Assembly elections were held on 19 July 1992. The 395 seats were contested by 601 candidates, including 63 non-Communists, seven members of the clergy, and more than 100 former Assembly members. Voters' concerns were ventilated in pre-election public meetings and by-elections held subsequently for three undecided seats. The military's share of representation in the new Assembly fell from 19% to 7%.

Political history

The Vietnamese are descended from Mongoloid nomads who settled in the Red River delta region in the north more than 2,000 years ago. The region came under Chinese control from the late 2nd century BC, directly between 111 BC and 938 AD, and indirectly thereafter. In southern Vietnam, the Mekong delta region, however, an independent Indianized kingdom (the Fu-nan), held sway between the 1st and 6th centuries AD. From the mid-10th century Vietnam enjoyed substantial independence, in the 15th century a united, north and south, kingdom being established. This disintegrated during the 17th and 18th centuries, and several small regionally based independent kingdoms took its place, but it was temporarily re-established in the early 19th century by Emperor Nguyen Anh.

The country, which had been exposed to European, initially Portuguese, commercial influence since the 16th century, was conquered by France between 1858 and 1884 and divided into the protectorates of Tonkin (North Vietnam) and Annam (South-central Vietnam) which, together with Laos and Cambodia, which embraced Cochin China, the southernmost tip of Vietnam, formed the French Indochinese Union. The Vietnamese protectorates were unified administratively in 1887, with a single governor generalship being created, thus improving physical north–south links.

During the colonial period, a French expatriate-run plantation economy, based mainly on rubber and rice, was established in southern Vietnam, drawing in press-ganged migrant labourers from the densely populated and heavily taxed north and centre. This dislocated existing social patterns and bred an impoverished and embittered peasantry. During World War II, the country was occupied by Japan between 1940 and 1945, although a pro-Vichy French administration remained in place until March 1945. Then the Emperor of Annam, Bao Dai, was appointed as a figurehead ruler. In opposition to this regime, the Viet Minh (Independence) League was formed by the Indochinese Communist Party (ICP) leader, Ho Chi Minh (1892–1969). It proceeded to wage a determined rural-based guerrilla war, which, during a period of severe economic difficulties, won considerable popular backing. The Viet Minh established a chain of rural enclaves, or 'base areas', within the Japanese occupied territory, steadily gaining in strength. Finally, in August–September 1945, with famine stalking the country and claiming the lives of 2 million people, and with the Japanese forces in disarray, it successfully mobilized the population in a revolutionary uprising which swept away the Bao Dai puppet regime and established a new Democratic Republic of Vietnam (DRV), with Ho Chi Minh as president, and a communist-dominated government in control.

France refused to recognize the new republic and, re-establishing control in the Saigon area, attempted to reconquer the country in the Indo-China War of 1946–54. The French set up a noncommunist state in the south in 1949, but, after their defeat at Dien Bien Phu, in May 1954, agreed, in the Geneva Accords of July 1954, to a cease-fire and the partitioning of the country along the 17th parallel of latitude. Ho Chi Minh was recognized as state president and Communist Party chairman in the communist-controlled DRV in the North, which had its capital at Hanoi, while Ngo Dinh Diem, the former premier to Bao Dai, headed the pro-Western and anticommunist regime in the South, which was termed the Republic of Vietnam (ROV), and had its capital at Saigon.

The Diem regime, and its repressive military successors, were opposed by former members of the Viet Minh, who became known as the Viet Cong, and then, from December 1960, the National Liberation Front. The two sides became engaged in guerrilla warfare, the National Liberation Front being supplied with military aid by North Vietnam and China, and the Diem regime by the United States. After the Tonkin Gulf incident, in August 1964, when North Vietnamese torpedo boats allegedly attacked two American destroyers, the United States became directly involved militarily in what was to be called the Vietnam War. Meanwhile, Diem had been overthrown, in November 1963, in a coup led by Lieutenant General Nguyen Van Thieu who, from June 1965, emerged as the nation's new 'strongman'.

Between 1964 and 1968 the scale of America's military involvement escalated. Major bombing campaigns were waged in the North and US troop strength was built up to a peak of 545,000. From 1969, however, as a result of mounting casualties and domestic opposition, including, most importantly, opposition from Congress, the United States began to withdraw its forces gradually and to sue for peace. A cease-fire agreement was signed in Paris in January 1973, but was breached by the North Vietnamese, who proceeded to move southwards, surrounding and capturing Saigon, which they renamed Ho Chi Minh City, in April 1975.

A new Socialist Republic of Vietnam was proclaimed in July 1976, and a programme to integrate the more affluent, capitalist South was launched. Land reform and collectivization had already been carried out in the North, as had the introduction of a central planning system and the launching of a heavy industrialization drive.

The new republic was to encounter considerable problems. The economy was in ruins, more than 3 million people, including a million guerrillas, having been killed and 4 million maimed during the struggles of the preceding two decades. Fifty-seven per cent of the population had been made homeless, and 70% of the country's industrial capacity had been destroyed by American bombing. Also, the new communist administration faced opposition from the intelligentsia, many of whom were now imprisoned, and from rural groups, who refused to cooperate in the drive to collectivize southern agriculture.

In December 1978 Vietnam was at war again, toppling the pro-Chinese Khmer Rouge government in Kampuchea (Cambodia) led by the brutal Pol Pot, which it alleged was showing expansionary ambitions, and installing a puppet administration led by Heng Samrin. A year later, following accusations of the maltreatment of ethnic Chinese living in Vietnam, China mounted a brief, but largely unsuccessful, punitive invasion of North Vietnam, between 17 February and 16 March 1979. These actions, coupled with the contemporary campaigns against private businesses in the South, induced the flight of an estimated 700,000 Chinese and middle-class Vietnamese from the country in 1978–79. Many of them left by sea and became known, internationally, as the 'boat people'.

In addition, economic and diplomatic relations were severed with China, its former close ally, and Vietnam moved more closely into the Soviet orbit. It was admitted into the Comecon in June 1978 and signed a Treaty of Friendship and Cooperation in November 1978.

Between 1976 and 1985, despite the receipt of substantial economic aid from the Eastern Bloc, planned growth targets were not attained. This forced policy adjustments, involving the extension of material incentives and the decentralization of decision-taking, in 1979 and 1985. In July 1986 the death was announced of Le Duan, the CPV's, and thus the country's, effective leader since September 1969, when Ho Chi Minh died. Then, at the December 1986, 6th CPV Congress, several of the prominent, septuagenarian and octogenarian, 'old guard' leaders retired. They included Prime Minister Pham Van Dong, President Truong Chinh, and senior Politburo member Le Duc Tho, who later died in October 1990.

These significant departures were followed by important policy changes under the direction of the party's pragmatic new leader, Nguyen Van Linh (b. 1914). They were termed 'renovation', or *doi moi* ('new road'), and included permitting the private marketing of agricultural produce and the establishment of private businesses; the scrapping of collective farms and freeing of food prices; and the encouragement of foreign 'inward investment' in joint ventures. The measures were to have most success in the more entrepreneurial and export-orientated South. In general, however, the country faced a severe economic crisis from 1988, with hyperinflation (exceeding 300% pa), rapid population growth (2.1% per annum), the loss of vital economic aid from the disintegrating Soviet Union, famine conditions in rural areas, and rising urban unemployment inducing a further flight of 'boat people' refugees during 1989–90, principally to Hong Kong.

Liberalization also extended to the political sphere during 1987–88, when more than 10,000 political prisoners, including former high-ranking members of the pre-1976 Republic of Vietnam government, were released from 're-education'. Do Muoi (b. 1917), a supporter of Nguyen Van Linh's policies, took over as CPV general secretary at the party's seventh Congress, held in June 1991. Two months later, Vo Van Kiet (b. 1922), a leading advocate of capitalist-style reform, replaced Do Muoi as prime minister. Le Duc Anh (b. 1920), a former defence minister and political conservative, was elected state president in September 1992. The new *doi moi* reforms, which aim to create a 'multisector economy under the capitalist option', began to have a beneficial impact from 1990, being buttressed, in May 1992, by a new constitution which explicitly guaranteed economic freedoms and, in Article 58, the right of citizens to own property. From 1993 annual GDP growth averaged around 8% and inflation 10–20%. In addition, a determined attempt was made to improve Vietnam's external relations, so as to secure economic aid and reduce the defence burden, which had consumed a crippling third of state expenditure.

In June 1988 the staged withdrawal of Vietnam's 140,000 troops stationed in Cambodia commenced. The process, which also included the removal of troops from Laos, was completed in October 1989 and in October 1991 a Cambodian peace agreement was signed. This enabled Vietnam's diplomatic relations with China to be normalized, after a 12-year breach. Commercial links also began to be established with ASEAN states, with plans being made for Vietnam to join this organization. The US embargo on trade and investment, imposed in 1975, was eased in April 1992 and finally lifted in February 1994. Rapprochement was furthered in January 1995 when the governments of Vietnam and the United States opened liaison offices in each other's capital cities and in July 1995 full diplomatic relations were re-established. Japan resumed its provision of development assistance in November 1992 after a 14-year freeze and IMF loans began to be granted to Vietnam from October 1993. It became a full member of ASEAN in July 1995.

Central America and the Caribbean

The region we have called Central America and the Caribbean contains 21 sovereign states. Eight are on the American mainland and 13 are islands, or island groups, within that part of the Atlantic Ocean usually referred to as the Caribbean Sea, or simply the Caribbean.

This is the smallest of the nine regions in areal size and the second smallest in population. It extends over 2.7 million square kilometres, or 2% of the world's land area, compared with figures of 15% for North America and 13% for South America. The total population is 152 million, or 2.7% of the world's total, compared with 5.1% in North America and 5.5% in South America. However, with three-quarters of the population contributed by just three states, Mexico, Cuba ,and Guatemala, the region includes a substantial number of small states. Indeed, nine have populations of less than half a million, and five have less than 150,000. All of these small countries, or 'micro-states', form part of island groupings in the Caribbean Sea.

In political terms Central America and the Caribbean is a strongly pluralistic region, 20 of the 21 states being liberal or emergent democracies. The one notable exception is Cuba, which has a defiantly communist regime. The historical backgrounds of all the countries have had a marked impact on their present political systems.

The 11 former British colonies, which are now independent members of the Commonwealth, all display the key characteristics of the 'Westminster model', including a two-party system, a parliamentary executive, a simple plurality voting system, and even an officially recognized opposition to the party in power. All, except Belize, are island states.

In contrast, most of the countries which were formerly under Spanish rule, and which are situated on the American mainland, have adopted political systems more in line with that of the United States, with executive presidents, whose powers are balanced and limited by elected assemblies.

Haiti and Panama have recently emerged from military-dominated rule and Panama has adopted the United States' style of limited presidency while Haiti has a dual executive, broadly on the French model. Cuba has a distinctive, populist, communist system, dominated by its charismatic leader, Fidel Castro.

Another interesting difference between the former British and former Spanish colonies is that the Commonwealth group are all post-1945 creations, six of them having been fully independent states only since 1975, whereas the 'Spanish empire' countries are mostly 19th-century creations, the youngest, Panama, having achieved full sovereignty as long ago as 1903.

In many ways the region is one of striking contrasts, with few signs of unity. For example, it is easier to fly from Jamaica to the Dominican Republic via Miami, in other words a round trip of some 1,600 kilometres, than to attempt to travel by the direct route of less than 800 kilometres. Frontier formalities also restrict international movement, with strict passport and customs controls operating even between Commonwealth countries.

The one feature all the Central American and Carribbean states have in common is the fact that they live in the shadow of the northern colossus, the United States. In other words, they are in America's 'back yard'. US interest in the region stems from the Monroe Doctrine of 1823, when the then secretary of state warned off European powers from interfering in what he saw as his country's domestic affairs.

The Spanish-American War of 1898, fought mainly over Cuba, reaffirmed the dominance of the United States and this strategic paternalism was rekindled as recently as 1983, when US forces, without consulting Britain, the British Crown, or the Commonwealth Secretariat, were given orders to invade Grenada. The United States was also instrumental, through its backing of the right-wing Contra army, in securing the removal of the left-wing Sandinista government, at the ballot box, in Nicaragua in 1990. A year earlier, it had intervened directly to depose Panama's military strongman General Manuel Noriega, who was involved in drug trafficking, and in 1994 sent troops to Haiti to help return to power the democratically elected exiled president, Jean-Bertrand Aristide.

In trade and culture, United States influence has grown dramatically in the post-World War II years. For example, 72% of the Dominican Republic's exports are to the United States, and 61% of those of Trinidad and Tobago. Exports from the United States to countries in the region are similarly high. Over 60% of tourists to Caribbean countries come from the United States, compared with less than 10% from Europe, or from Commonwealth countries, such as Canada.

Economically, it is not a rich region by European standards, but, on the other hand, only five of the 21 states, the Dominican Republic, Guatemala, Haiti, Honduras, and Nicaragua, fall into the 'low income' category, and some of them only marginally so, while the Bahamians enjoy a 'high income' status.

Despite the current evidence of disunity, there are encouraging signs that the countries of the Caribbean wish, and intend, to function in a more cohesive fashion. The Caribbean Community and Common Market (CARICOM) was founded in 1973, in Trinidad, as a successor to the Caribbean Free Trade Association. Its declared purpose is to further the integration process which the Association began and its members include Antigua and Barbuda, the Bahamas, Barbados, Belize, Dominica, Grenada, Guyana, Jamaica, St Christopher and Nevis, St Lucia, St Vincent and the Grenadines, and Trinidad and Tobago, as well as Montserrat, which is still a British possession. Recently, in 1994, CARICOM sponsored the formation of the Association of Caribbean States (ACS) trade grouping. On the mainland, some of the Central American states have developed closer ties with their Hispanic neighbours in the south.

It makes good sense for the Caribbean countries, with their small populations and vulnerable economies and frontiers, to work more closely together, but the proximity of the United States cannot be ignored. The Organization of American States (OAS), which includes 19 of the Central American and Caribbean countries, as well as 10 of the 11 South American states, has its headquarters in Washington DC and is very much an instrument of US' foreign policy. However, the North American Free Trade Agreement (NAFTA) between the United States, Canada, and Mexico is perhaps a sign of greater US willingness to be a partner, rather than a dominant neighbour.

Recommended reading

Booth, J and Seligson, M *Elections and Democracy in Central America*, University of North Carolina Press, 1989

Leiken, R (ed.) *Central America*, Pergamon, 1984

Central America and the Caribbean: social, economic, and political data

Country	Area (sq km)	c. 1992–94 Population (m)	c. 1992–94 Pop. density per sq km	c. 1992 Adult literacy rate (%)	World ranking	Income type	c. 1991 Human rights rating (%)
Antigua	440	0.079	180	88	84	middle	n/a
Bahamas	13,940	0.300	21	89	82	high	n/a
Barbados	430	0.260	605	99	8	middle	n/a
Belize	22,970	0.200	9	91	77	middle	n/a
Costa Rica	51,100	3.300	65	88	84	middle	90
Cuba	110,860	10.900	98	98	34	middle	30
Dominica	750	0.072	96	94	66	middle	n/a
Dominican Republic	48,072	7.600	156	69	119	low	78
El Salvador	21,390	5.500	257	67	121	middle	53
Grenada	345	0.091	264	98	34	middle	n/a
Guatemala	108,890	10.000	92	46	157	low	62
Haiti	27,750	6.900	249	35	169	low	n/a
Honduras	112,090	5.600	50	57	136	low	65
Jamaica	10,991	2.500	227	96	52	middle	72
Mexico	1,958,201	90.000	45	87	89	middle	64
Nicaragua	120,254	4.100	34	57	136	low	75
Panama	77,080	2.600	34	86	92	middle	81
St Kitts	261	0.044	168	98	34	middle	n/a
St Lucia	620	0.156	242	82	99	middle	n/a
St Vincent	390	0.117	300	96	52	middle	n/a
Trinidad	5,130	1.300	253	95	59	middle	84
Total/average/range	2,691,954	151.619	56	35–99			30–90

Key:
A	appointed	F	federal	SP	simple plurality
AMS	additional member system	PL	party list	U	unitary
E	elected	PR	proportional representation		

Table 52

World ranking	Date of state formation	State structure	State type	Executive type	Number of assembly chambers	Party structure	Lower house electoral system
	1981	U	Lib-dem	Parliamentary	2	two	SP
	1973	U	Lib-dem	Parliamentary	2	two	SP
	1966	U	Lib-dem	Parliamentary	2	two	SP
	1981	U	Lib-dem	Parliamentary	2	two	SP
21	1821	U	Lib-dem	Lim-pres	1	two	PR-PL
93	1899	U	Communist	Communist	1	one	SP
	1978	U	Lib-dem	Parliamentary	1	multi	mixed-E/A
38	1844	U	Lib-dem	Lim-pres	2	multi	PR-PL
72	1830	U	Lib-dem	Lim-pres	1	multi	SP
	1974	U	Lib-dem	Parliamentary	2	multi	SP
57	1839	U	Lib-dem	Lim-pres	1	multi	PR-AMS
	1804	U	Em-dem	Dual	2	multi	SB
53	1838	U	Lib-dem	Lim-pres	1	two	PR-PL
43	1962	U	Lib-dem	Parliamentary	2	two	SP
56	1821	F	Lib-dem	Lim-Pres	2	multi	PR-AMS
40	1838	U	Em-dem	Lim-pres	1	two	PR-PL
35	1903	U	Em-dem	Lim-pres	1	multi	SP
	1983	F	Lib-dem	Parliamentary	1	multi	SP
	1979	U	Lib-dem	Parliamentary	2	two	SP
	1979	U	Lib-dem	Parliamentary	1	two	SP
29	1962	U	Lib-dem	Parliamentary	2	multi	SP

Lib-dem	liberal democratic
Em-dem	emergent democratic
Lim-pres	limited presidential

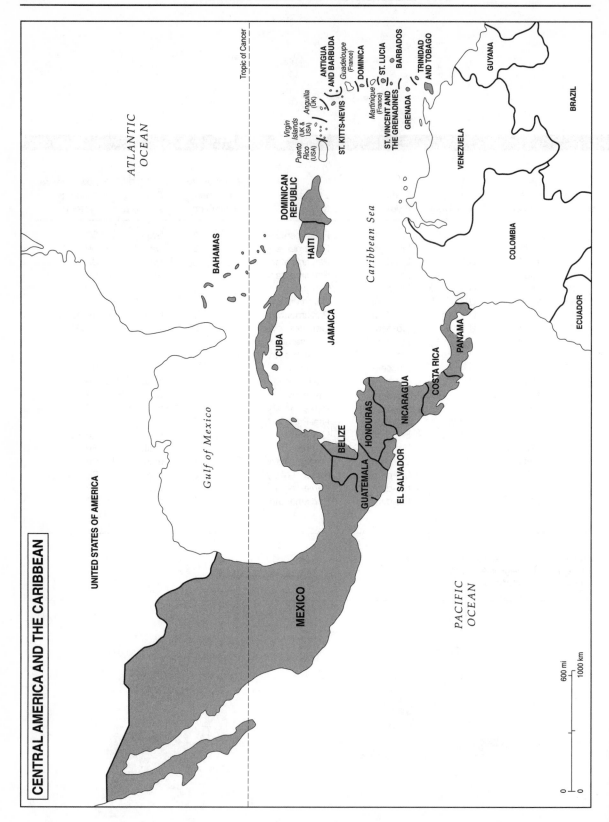

CENTRAL AMERICA AND THE CARIBBEAN

UNITED STATES OF AMERICA

ATLANTIC OCEAN

Gulf of Mexico

MEXICO

PACIFIC OCEAN

Tropic of Cancer

BAHAMAS

CUBA

JAMAICA

HAITI

DOMINICAN REPUBLIC

Caribbean Sea

BELIZE

GUATEMALA

HONDURAS

EL SALVADOR

NICARAGUA

COSTA RICA

PANAMA

Virgin Islands (UK & USA)

Puerto Rico (USA)

Anguilla (UK)

ST. KITTS-NEVIS

ANTIGUA AND BARBUDA

Guadeloupe (France)

DOMINICA

Martinique (France)

ST. LUCIA

BARBADOS

ST. VINCENT AND THE GRENADINES

GRENADA

TRINIDAD AND TOBAGO

VENEZUELA

COLOMBIA

GUYANA

BRAZIL

ECUADOR

600 mi

1000 km

ANTIGUA AND BARBUDA

State of Antigua and Barbuda

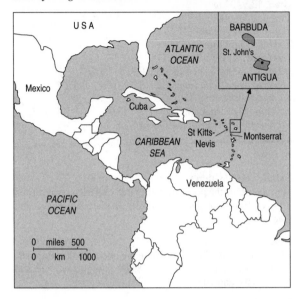

Capital: St John's

Social and economic data
Area: 440 km^2
Population: 79,000*
Pop. density per km^2: 180*
Urban population: 47%**
Literacy rate: 88%**
GDP: $185 million**; per-capita GDP: $2,340**
Government defence spending (% of GDP): 0.9%**
Currency: Eastern Caribbean dollar
Economy type: middle income
Labour force in agriculture: N/A

*1994
**1992

Ethnic composition
The population is almost entirely of African Negro descent.

Religions
Christianity is the dominant religion, the majority of the population, about 60,000, being Anglican.

Political features
State type: liberal democratic
Date of state formation: 1981
Political structure: unitary
Executive: parliamentary
Assembly: two-chamber
Party structure: two-party
Human rights rating: N/A
International affiliations: ACP, ACS, CARICOM, CW, IBRD, IMF, IWC, NAM (observer), OAS, OECS, UN, WTO

Local and regional government
The two islands of Antigua and Barbuda, which are about 50 kilometres apart, are divided into seven parishes for administrative purposes. Barbuda, the smaller of the two islands (161 km^2), has a considerable degree of internal autonomy.

Head of state
Queen Elizabeth II, represented by Governor General Sir James Carlisle since 1992

Head of government
Prime Minister Lester Bird, since 1994

Political leaders since 1970
1981–94 Vere C Bird (ALP), 1994– Lester Bird (ALP)

Political system
Antigua and Barbuda constitute an independent sovereign nation within the Commonwealth, retaining the British monarch as head of state. The constitution dates from independence, in 1981. The governor general represents Queen Elizabeth of the United Kingdom and is appointed on the advice of the Antiguan prime minister in office at the time of the appointment.

The executive is parliamentary and operates in a similar fashion to that in the United Kingdom, the prime minister being chosen, normally after a general election, by the governor general as the person most likely to have the support of the assembly. Once appointed, the prime minister chooses the cabinet and all are responsible to the assembly. The leader of the party with the second largest seat holding in the House of Representatives is automatically the official leader of the opposition.

The assembly, or parliament, consists of two chambers, the 17-member Senate and the 17-member House of Representatives. Senators are appointed for a five-year term by the governor general, 11 on the advice of the prime minister, four on the advice of the leader of the opposition, one at their own discretion and one on the advice of the Barbuda Council, representing the island of Barbuda. Members of the House of Representatives are elected by universal adult suffrage, through a simple plurality voting system, for a similar term.

Political parties
There are some four active political parties, the three most significant being the Antigua Labour Partry (ALP), the United Progressive Party (UPP), and the Barbuda People's Movement (BPM).

The ALP was formed in 1968 and has a moderate, centre-left orientation.

The UPP before 1992 was called the United National Democratic Party (UNDP), which was, itself, the result of a merger between two smaller parties, the United People's Movement (UPM), founded in 1982, and the National Democratic Party (NDP), which had been established only the year before. The UPP has a centrist orientation.

The BPM is a left-of-centre grouping based in Barbuda.

Latest elections
In the March 1994 general election Lester Bird and the ALP had another victory, winning 11 of the 17 seats in the House of Representatives. The UPP won five seats.

Political history

Antigua was visited by Christopher Columbus (1451–1506) in 1493 and colonized by the British in the 17th century. The neighbouring island of Barbuda was annexed in 1860. Between 1860 and 1959 it was administered by Britain within a federal system known as the Leeward Islands and in 1967 given the status of associated state and full internal independence, with Britain retaining responsibility for defence and foreign affairs. What had been the Legislative Council became the House of Representatives, the post of administrator was restyled governor and the chief minister became premier.

The ALP had held power since 1946 and in the first general election as an associated state, in 1971, its main opposition, the Progressive Labour Movement (PLM), won a decisive victory, its leader, George Walter replacing Vere Bird (b. 1910), leader of the ALP, as premier. The PLM fought the next election, in 1976, on a call for early independence whereas the ALP urged caution until a firm economic foundation had been laid. The electorate preferred the more gradualist approach and the ALP won.

Two years later, in 1978, the government declared itself satisfied that the country was now ready for full independence but opposition from the inhabitants of the island of Barbuda delayed the start of constitutional talks. The territory eventually became independent, as the State of Antigua and Barbuda, on 1 November 1981.

Since independence the ALP government has followed a foreign policy of nonalignment, but retaining close links with the United States, which it actively assisted in the invasion of Grenada in 1983.

In September 1993 Vere Bird retired from the ALP leadership and was succeeded by his son, Lester, who later led the party to another victory in the January 1994 general election.

THE BAHAMAS

The Commonwealth of the Bahamas

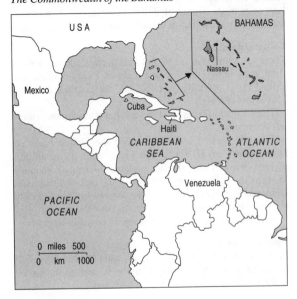

Capital: Nassau (on New Providence)

Social and economic data
Area: 13,940 km^2
Population: 300,000*
Pop. density per km^2: 21*
Urban population: 75%**
Literacy rate: 89%**
GDP: $2,800m**; per-capita GDP: $11,320**
Government defence spending (% of GDP): 0.5%**
Currency: Bahamian dollar
Economy type: high income
Labour force in agriculture: 5%**

*1994
**1992

Ethnic composition
About 85% of the population is black, of African origin, and 15% of European ancestry, mostly British, American, and Canadian.

Religions
Most people are Christian. There are about 50,000 Baptists, 40,000 Roman Catholics, 38,000 Anglicans, 12,000 Methodists, and 10,000 Seventh Day Adventists.

Political features
State type: liberal democratic
Date of state formation: 1973
Political structure: unitary
Executive: parliamentary
Assembly: two-chamber
Party structure: two-party
Human rights rating: N/A
International affiliations: ACP, ACS, CARICOM, CDB, CW, IBRD, IMF, NAM, OAS, UN

Local and regional government
Local administration is based on 18 natural island groupings. The islands of New Providence, where the national capital is located, and Grand Bahama have elected councils. The other 16 have district commissioners appointed by the central government.

Head of state
Queen Elizabeth II, represented by Governor General Orville Turnquest since 1995

Head of government
Prime Minister Herbert Ingraham, since 1992

Political leaders since 1970
1968–92 Sir Lynden Oscar Pindling (PLP), 1992–   Hubert Ingraham (FNM)

Political system
Bahamas is an independent sovereign nation within the Commonwealth, accepting the British monarch as head of state and an appointed, resident governor general as her representative. The constitution, which came into effect at independence in 1973, provides for a two-chamber assembly consisting of a Senate and House of Assembly. The governor

general appoints a prime minister and cabinet drawn from and responsible to the assembly. The leader of the second largest party in the House of Assembly is the official leader of the opposition.

The Senate has 16 members appointed by the governor general, nine on the advice of the prime minister, four on the advice of the leader of the opposition, and three after consultation with the prime minister. The House of Assembly has 49 members, elected by universal adult suffrage through a simple plurality voting system. The assembly has a maximum life of five years and is subject to dissolution within that period.

Political parties

There are four active political parties, but a two-party system operates through two major groupings: the Progressive Liberal Party (PLP); and the Free National Movement (FNM).

The PLP is a centrist party and was founded in 1953. It was in power from independence, in 1973 to 1992.

The FNM was formed in 1972 by a coming together of the United Bahamian Party (UBP) and PLP dissidents. Its orientation is centre-left.

Latest elections

In the August 1992 general election the FNM had a landslide victory, winning 33 of the House of Assembly seats. The PLP won the other 16 seats.

Political history

The islands were first visited in 1492 by Christopher Columbus (1451–1506), when inhabited by Arawak Indians. The Bahamas became a British colony in 1783 and were given internal self-government in 1964. The first elections for a National Assembly on a full adult voting register were held in 1967. The PLP, drawing its support mainly from voters of African origin, won the same number of seats as the European-dominated UBP and Sir Lynden Pindling (b. 1930), the PLP leader, by drawing support from outside his own party, became prime minister. In the 1968 elections the PLP scored a resounding victory and this success was repeated in 1972, enabling Pindling to lead his country into full independence, within the Commonwealth, in 1973. A tourist-based economy was subsequently developed, with, today, 70% of GDP contributed by this activity. Ninety per cent of the visitors are from the United States.

With the opposition parties in some disarray, Pindling increased his majority in 1977 but by 1982 the FNM had regrouped and were more convincing opponents. Despite this, and despite allegations of government complicity in drug trafficking, the PLP was again successful at the 1982 general election and Pindling's leadership was unanimously endorsed at a party convention in 1984. The 1987 general election, fought again against a background of alleged drug trafficking, was similarly won by the PLP, but with a reduced majority.

The August 1992 general election saw a massive swing towards the FNM and its leader, Hubert Ingraham, ended Pindling's 25 years of power.

BARBADOS

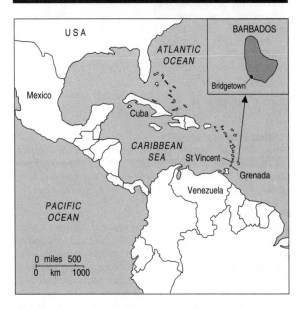

Capital: Bridgetown

Social and economic data

Area: 430 km^2
Population: 260,000 million*
Pop. density per km^2: 605*
Urban population: 46%**
Literacy rate: 99%**
GDP: 1,600 million**; per-capita GDP: $6,350**
Government defence spending (% of GDP): 0.7%**
Currency: Barbados dollar
Economy type: middle income
Labour force in agriculture: 8%**

*1994
**1992

Ethnic composition

About 80% of the population is of African descent, about 16% of mixed race, and about 4% of European origin, mostly British. English is the official language.

Religions

There are about 150,000 Anglicans, about 24,000 Roman Catholics, and significant numbers of other Christian faiths.

Political features

State type: liberal democratic
Date of state formation: 1966
Political structure: unitary
Executive: parliamentary
Assembly: two-chamber
Party structure: two-party
Human rights rating: N/A
International affiliations: ACP, ACS, CARICOM, CW, IBRD, IMF, NAM, OAS, SELA, UN, WTO

Local and regional government

Elected local government bodies were abolished in 1969 and replaced by 11 parishes, each administered by the central government.

Head of state

Queen Elizabeth II, represented by Governor General Dame Nita Barrow since 1990

Head of government

Prime Minister Owen Arthur, since 1994

Political leaders since 1970

1966–76 Errol Barrow (DLP), 1976–85 'Tom' Adams (BLP), 1985–86 Bernard St John (BLP), 1986–87 Errol Barrow (DLP), 1987–94 Erskine Lloyd Sandiford (DLP), 1994– Owen Arthur (BLP)

Political system

The country is a constitutional monarchy, with a resident governor general representing the United Kingdom monarch. The constitution dates from independence in 1966 and provides for a system of parliamentary government on the British model, with a prime minister and cabinet drawn from and responsible to the assembly.

This consists of two chambers, the Senate and the House of Assembly. The Senate has 21 members appointed by the governor general, 12 on the advice of the prime minister, two on the advice of the leader of the opposition and the rest on the basis of wider consultations. The House of Assembly has 28 members elected by universal adult suffrage, through a simple plurality voting system. The assembly has a maximum life of five years and is subject to dissolution within this period.

The governor general appoints the prime minister on the basis of likely support in the House of Assembly. He or she also appoints the leader of the party with the second largest number of seats in the House as the official leader of the opposition.

Political parties

There are three active political parties, the most significant being the Barbados Labour Party (BLP) and the Democratic Labour Party (DLP).

The BLP was founded in 1938 and has a moderate, left-of-centre, social-democratic orientation.

The DLP was formed in 1955, mainly from BLP dissidents, and has a roughly similar political stance.

Latest elections

In the September 1994 general election the BLP had a sweeping victory, winning 19 seats, to the DLP's eight.

Political history

Barbados became a British colony in 1627 and remained so, being famous for its sugar production, until it achieved full independence, within the Commonwealth, in November 1966. After riots in the country in 1937, moves towards a more independent political system began in the 1950s. Universal adult suffrage was introduced in 1951, with the BLP winning the first general election. Ministerial government was established in 1954 and the BLP leader, Sir Grantley Adams (1898–1971), became the first prime minister. In 1955 the DLP was formed by party activists disenchanted with the BLP. Six years later full internal self-government was achieved and in the general election in December 1961 the DLP was victorious under its leader, Errol Barrow (1920–87). When Barbados attained full independence in 1966 Barrow became the new nation's first prime minister.

The DLP was re-elected in 1971 but in the 1976 general election the BLP, led now by Sir Grantley Adams' son 'Tom', ended Barrow's 15 years of power. Both parties were committed to maintaining a free enterprise system, with tourism being encouraged, and alignment with the United States. However, the DLP government established diplomatic relations with Cuba in 1972 and the BLP administration supported the US invasion of Grenada in 1983. In 1981 the BLP was re-elected but Adams died suddenly in 1985 and was succeeded by his deputy, Bernard St John, a former BLP leader. In the 1986 general election the DLP, led by Barrow, was returned to power, winning 24 of the 27 seats in the House of Assembly. Errol Barrow died in 1987 and was succeeded by Erskine Lloyd Sandiford (b. 1937).

Dame Nita Barrow, sister of Errol Barrow, became governor general in 1990 and in the following year the DLP was re-elected, but with a reduced majority. In June 1994 Sandiford lost a confidence vote and sought a dissolution of the assembly. He was replaced as DLP leader by David Thompson. In the September 1994 elections the BLP, under Owen Arthur, had a resounding victory, winning 19 of the 28 seats.

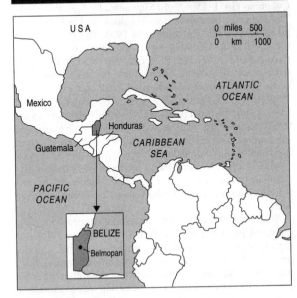

Capital: Belmopan

Social and economic data
Area: 22,970 km^2
Population: 200,000*
Pop. density per km^2: 9**
Urban population: 51%**

Literacy rate: 91%**
GDP: $300 million**; per-capita GDP: $1,720**
Government defence spending (% of GDP): 2%**
Currency: Belizean dollar
Economy type: middle income
Labour force in agriculture: N/A

*1994
**1992

Ethnic composition
There is a wide mix of races, comprising Creoles, mestizos, Caribs, East Indians, and Europeans, including Spanish, British, and Canadian Mennonites. The 1991 census showed that the Spanish-speaking population, boosted by economic immigrants, outnumbered the native black Creoles for the first time.

Religions
Christianity is the chief religion, about 64% of the population being Anglicans and Methodists. There are also about 100,000 Roman Catholics.

Political features
State type: liberal democratic
Date of state formation: 1981
Political structure: unitary
Executive: parliamentary
Assembly: two-chamber
Party structure: two-party
Human rights rating: N/A
International affiliations: ACP, ACS, CARICOM, CW, IBRD, IMF, NAM, OAS, SELA, UN, WTO

Local and regional government
For administrative purposes, the country is divided into six districts, ranging in population from under 12,000 to over 50,000. Local elections are usually contested as strongly as national elections.

Head of state
Queen Elizabeth II, represented by Governor General Dr Norbert Colville Young since 1993

Head of government
Prime Minister Manuel Esquivel, since 1993

Political leaders since 1970
1965–84 George Price (PUP), 1984–89 Manuel Esquivel (UDP), 1989–93 George Price (PUP), 1993– Manuel Esquivel (UDP)

Political system
Belize is a constitutional monarchy, with a resident governor general representing the United Kingdom monarch. The constitution dates from independence in September 1981 and provides for parliamentary government on the British model, with a prime minister and cabinet drawn from the assembly and responsible to it.

The two-chamber National Assembly consists of the Senate and the House of Representatives. The Senate has eight members appointed by the governor general for a five-year term, five on the advice of the prime minister, two on the advice of the leader of the opposition, and one after wider consultations. The House of Representatives has 29 members elected by universal adult suffrage, through a simple plurality voting system. The governor general appoints the prime minister on the basis of majority support in the House of Representatives and the leader of the party with the next largest number of seats as the official leader of the opposition.

Political parties
The two active political parties are the People's United Party (PUP) and the United Democratic Party (UDP).

The PUP was founded in 1950 by a small group, believing strongly in the need for national independence and social justice, who called themselves the People's Committee. The group soon split up but one of the founders, George Price, remained to create the PUP. Its orientation is left-of-centre.

The UDP was formed in 1974 by the merger of three groups, the People's Development Movement, the Liberal Party, and the National Independence Party. It is moderately conservative and is held together more by its opposition to the PUP than by a coherent ideology.

Latest elections
In the June 1993 general election the UDP scored an unexpected victory, winning 16 seats to the PUP's 13.

Political history
In ancient times Belize was one of the sites of the Mayan Indian civilization. Colonized as early as the 17th century, British Honduras, as it was then called, was not recognized as a British colony until 1862. A 1954 constitution provided for partial internal self-government, with Britain retaining responsibility for defence, external affairs, and internal security. The first general election under the new constitution was won by the PUP, led by George Price (b. 1919). PUP won all the subsequent elections until 1984. In 1964 full internal self-government was granted and Price became prime minister, working with a two-chamber assembly. In 1970 the nation's capital was moved from Belize City to the new town of Belmopan and in 1973 the whole country became known as Belize. Between the 1950s and 1980s the economy relied heavily on sugar exports, but has subsequently diversified into citrus exports and tourism.

The frontier with Guatemala had long been a source of dispute and in 1975 British troops were sent to defend it. Two years later negotiations with Guatemala began but no final conclusion was reached. In 1980 the United Nations called for full independence for Belize but a constitutional conference, which was called in 1981, broke up because of a dispute over Guatemala's demand for territory rather than just access to the Caribbean. Eventually, in September 1981, full independence was achieved and George Price became the first prime minister of the new nation. Britain agreed to leave troops to protect the frontier and to assist in the training of Belizean forces.

In 1984 PUP's 30 years of uninterrupted rule ended and the new prime minister was the UDP leader, Manuel Esquivel, but in 1989 PUP returned with a working majority. Four years later Esquivel unexpectedly returned to power, the UDP winning 16 of the House of Representatives' seats.

In 1984 Britain reaffirmed its undertaking to protect Belize's frontier and, despite renewed talks with Guatemala in 1985, no permanent solution to the dispute between the two countries was found until 1991, when diplomatic relations between the two countries were restored after Guatemala at last recognized Belize's sovereignty. By the end of 1993 Britain felt the situation sufficiently secure to announce that it would no longer have responsibility for the country's defence.

COSTA RICA

Republic of Costa Rica
República de Costa Rica

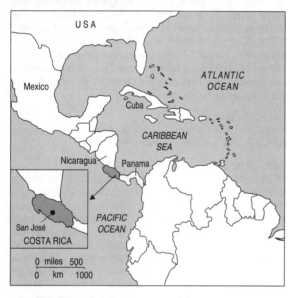

Capital: San José

Social and economic data
Area: 51,100 km^2
Population: 3,300,000*
Pop. density per km^2: 65*
Urban population: 48%**
Literacy rate: 88% **
GDP: $4,900 million**; per-capita GDP: $1,780**
Government defence spending (% of GDP): 1.3%**
Currency: colon
Economy type: middle income
Labour force in agriculture: 25%**

*1994
**1992

Ethnic composition
About 97% of the population is of European descent, mostly Spanish and about 2% is of African origin.

Religions
Roman Catholicism is the official religion and about 90% of the population practises that faith, although all beliefs are tolerated.

Political features
State type: liberal democratic
Date of state formation: 1821
Political structure: unitary
Executive: limited presidential
Assembly: one-chamber
Party structure: two-party
Human rights rating: 90%
International affiliations: ACS, AG (observer), ALADI (observer), BCIE, CACM, IAEA, IBRD, IMF, IWC, NAM (observer), OAS, SELA, UN, WTO

Local and regional government
The country is divided into seven provinces, ranging in population from about 150,000 to nearly 900,000. Each province is administered by a governor who is appointed by the president. The provinces are subdivided into cantons and the cantons into districts. There is an elected council for each major city in a canton.

Head of state and head of government
President José Maria Figueres, since 1994

Political leaders since 1970
1970–74 José Figueres Ferrer (PLN), 1974–78 Daniel Oduber Quiros (PLN), 1978–82 Rodrigo Carazo (CU), 1982–86 Luis Alberto Monge Alvárez (PLN), 1986–90 Oscar Arias Sánchez (PLN), 1990–94 Rafael Angel Calderon (PUSC) 1994–   José Maria Figueres (PLN)

Political system
The 1949 constitution provides for a president popularly elected for a four-year term, assisted by two vice presidents similarly elected. The president selects and appoints their own cabinet.

There is a single-chamber Assembly, consisting of 57 members, elected through a party list system of proportional representation, for a four-year term. Voting is compulsory.

Political parties
Out of more than 20 political parties, two have dominated the political scene for many years. They are the National Liberation Party (PLN) and what is now called the Christian Socialist Unity Party (PUSC).

The PLN began to form in 1948 and was officially founded in 1951. It is a left-of-centre, social democratic party and is affiliated to the Socialist International.

In its present form, the PUSC is a development from the Unity Party which was formed in 1978 as a coalition of four parties to oppose the PLN. It became the United Coalition (CU) and then, with other similarly orientated centrist groupings, the PUSC, in 1984.

Latest elections
In the February 1994 presidential elections José Maria Figueres (PLN), the son of the former president, won a narrow victory over his PUSC opponent, Miguel Angel Rodríguez.

In the simultaneous assembly elections the PLN won 28 seats, the PUSC 25, and independents 4.

Political history
Costa Rica, formerly inhabited by Guaymi Indians, was first colonized by Spain in the early 16th century and became an

independent nation, within the Central American Federation, in 1821. It seceded from the Federation in 1838. European immigrants were attracted to the country to run and work small farms. Apart from a period of military dictatorship between 1870 and 1882, and a brief civil war in 1948 because of a disputed presidential election, it has been one of the most democratically governed states in Latin America.

Present-day Costa Rica dates from the civil war of 1948 when the army, under José Figueres, restored order and adopted a new constitution. Figueres abolished the army, relying on the civil guard for the country's future defence, and then surrendered power to a civilian government. He soon returned, however, to become president the following year. He cofounded the PLN, nationalized the banks, and introduced a comprehensive social security system. He was re-elected in 1953.

There followed 16 years of mostly conservative rule, when some of the PLN policies were reversed. Then, in 1974, Daniel Oduber won the presidency for the PLN. He returned to socialist policies, extending the welfare state and establishing friendly relations with communist states. Communist and left-wing political parties were legalized.

In 1978 Rodrigo Carazo, leader of the conservative Unity Coalition (CU), became president. His presidency was marked by a disastrous collapse of the economy and allegations of involvement in illegal arms trafficking between Cuba and El Salvador.

The conservative administration was ended in 1982 when Luis Alberto Monge Alvárez, a former trade union official and cofounder, with Figueres, of the PLN, won a convincing victory in the presidential election. To reverse the damage done by the Carazo government, he introduced a 100-day emergency economic programme. He also maintained a policy of strict neutrality.

His government came under increasing pressure from the United States to abandon its neutral stance and condemn the left-wing Sandinista regime in Nicaragua. It was also urged to re-establish a national army. The pressures were resisted and in 1983 Monge reaffirmed his country's neutrality. However, relations with Nicaragua deteriorated after border clashes between Sandinista forces and the Costa Rica civil guard, so that, in 1985, Monge reluctantly agreed to create an antiguerrilla guard, trained by the United States.

This increased doubts about Costa Rica's declared policy of neutrality but in 1986 the United Kingdom university-educated Oscar Arias Sánchez (b. 1940), leader of the PLN, won the presidential election on a neutralist platform, defeating the pro-US candidate, Rafael Angel Calderón. Arias worked vigorously for peace in the area, in 1987 proposing a Central American Peace Agreement which was signed by the leaders of Nicaragua, El Salvador, Guatemala, and Honduras. It failed to halt the fighting in Nicaragua but contributed to the start of direct talks between the Nicaraguan government and the Contra rebels the following year.

A deteriorating economy produced public disenchantment and in 1990 the PLN lost both the presidential and assembly elections, but, with economic growth resuming, it returned in February 1994 and José Maria Figueres, the 39-year-old son of the former president, José Figueres Ferrer, assumed power.

CUBA

The Republic of Cuba
La República de Cuba

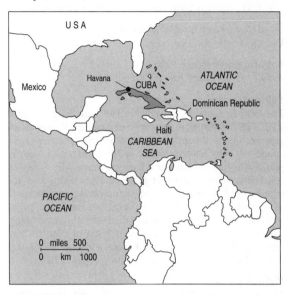

Capital: Havana

Social and economic data
Area: 110,860 km^2
Population: 10,900,000*
Pop. density per km^2: 98*
Urban population: 75%**
Literacy rate: 98%**
GDP: $20,000 million**; per-capita GDP: $1,886**
Government defence spending (% of GDP): 3.7%**
Currency: Cuban peso
Economy type: middle income
Labour force in agriculture: 25%**

*1994
**1992

Ethnic composition
The majority of the population is of mixed Spanish and African or Spanish and Indian origin. About a third are European and a tenth African.

Religions
All religions are permitted and there is no established church. Around 40% of the population is Roman Catholic.

Political features
State type: communist
Date of state formation: 1899
Political structure: unitary
Executive: communist
Assembly: one-chamber
Party structure: one-party
Human rights rating: 30%
International affiliations: ACS, ALADI (observer), IAEA, NAM, OAS (suspended 1962), SELA, UN, WTO

Local and regional government
The country is divided into 14 provinces varying in population from just under 60,000 to nearly 2 million. Within the provinces are 169 municipalities, each with an elected assembly, which, in turn, elects an executive committee.

Head of state and head of government
Dr Fidel Castro Ruz, since 1976

Political leaders since 1970
1959–   Fidel Castro Ruz (PCC)

Political system
The 1976 constitution, amended in 1992, created a socialist state with the National Assembly of People's Power as its supreme organ. It consists of 589 deputies directly elected (since 1993) by universal adult suffrage, through a simple plurality voting system, for a five-year term. The National Assembly, which holds twice-yearly sessions, elects 31 of its members to form the Council of State. It also elects the head of state who is president of the Council, head of government, and first secretary and chairman of the Political Bureau of the only authorized party, the Communist Party of Cuba (PCC). Fidel Castro thus occupies all the key positions within the state and the party, where ultimate political power lies.

Political parties
The origins of the PCC date back to 1925 when a socialist party was formed by a group of left-wing activists. In 1943 it became known as the People's Socialist Party (PSP). When Castro seized power in 1959 some of the old guard of the PSP found his methods and ideological leanings too anarchic for their comfort and were reluctant to give him their full support. Meanwhile Castro was leading his own movement and in 1961 the misgivings within the PSP were sufficiently allayed to allow it to merge, in 1961, with Castro's movement and other socialist groups, into the Integrated Revolutionary Organization (ORI). Two years later this became the United Party of the Socialist Revolution (PURS) and finally, in 1965, the Communist Party of Cuba (PCC).

It is a Marxist–Leninist party organized on top-down, Leninist 'democratic centralist' lines, with a 225-member Central Committee, a Political Bureau, Secretariat, and five Commissions.

Latest elections
The first direct elections to the National Assembly were held in February 1993. All the 589 deputies elected were PCC nominees.

Political history
After being under Spanish rule from the 16th century, Cuba was ceded to the United States in 1898, at the end of the Spanish–American War. This followed anticolonial uprisings between 1868–78 and 1895–98. It became independent in 1902 but the United States retained its naval bases and a right to intervene in internal affairs until 1934. In 1933 an army sergeant, Fulgencio Batista (1901–73) seized and held on to power until 1944, when he retired. In 1952, however, he seized power again in a bloodless coup and began another period of rule which many of his fellow countrypeople found oppressive.

In the following year a young lawyer and son of a sugar planter, Dr Fidel Castro Ruz (b. 1927), tried to overthrow him but was defeated. He went into exile to prepare for another coup, returning in 1956 but was again unsuccessful. He fled to the hills, with Argentine-born Dr Ernesto ('Che') Guevara (1928–67) and ten other fighters, to form a guerrilla force to fight the increasingly corrupt Batista regime.

In 1959 Castro's forces were finally successful and Batista was deposed, to great popular acclaim, and forced into exile in the Dominican Republic. The 1940 constitution was immediately suspended and replaced by a 'Fundamental Law', with all power vested in a Council of Ministers led by Castro as prime minister and his brother, Raúl, as his deputy. Che Guevara, who had assisted in the overthrow of Batista, was, reputedly, made Castro's 'number three'.

The following year all US businesses in Cuba were appropriated without compensation, provoking the United States into breaking off diplomatic relations. In 1961 it went further, sponsoring, in April, a full-scale but abortive invasion, the 'Bay of Pigs' episode. In December of the same year Castro announced that Cuba was now a communist state and would follow a Marxist–Leninist programme of economic development, entailing radical land reform, the nationalization of industries, and investment in education and healthcare.

In 1962 Cuba was expelled from the Organization of American States (OAS), which had originally been formed as a regional agency of the United Nations, but had become increasingly dominated by the United States. The 1961–63 administration of John F Kennedy (1917–63) in Washington then initiated a full political and economic blockade. Castro's response was to tighten his relations with the Soviet Union which, in the same year, supplied missiles, with atomic warheads, for installation on Cuban soil. A tense crisis was averted when, at the American president's insistence, they were dismantled. In 1965 Che Guevara left Cuba, ostensibly to fight causes in other parts of the world.

Between 1965 and 1972, with help from the Soviet Union, Cuba made substantial economic and social progress. However, many Cubans, concerned at the restrictions in their political rights, sought exile abroad, particularly in Florida. In 1972 Cuba became a full member of the Council for Mutual Economic Assistance (CMEA), a Moscow-based organization linking communist states. Cuba was to export sugar to the communist states and receive in return foodstuffs, machinery, and oil and by the 1980s 85% of its trade was with CMEA members. In 1976 a referendum approved a new socialist constitution and Fidel Castro and his brother were elected president and vice president. The following five years saw Cuba playing an increasingly assertive role in world affairs, particularly in Africa, usually to the disquiet of the United States.

In 1981, after being re-elected for another term, Castro offered to discuss foreign policy with the US administration but the offer was not accepted. Castro's support for Argentina, against Britain, during the 1982 Falklands conflict, cooled relations with the United States but improved them with other Latin American countries. The US invasion of Grenada in 1983 lowered the diplomatic temperature again. From the mid-1980s, as the Soviet Union, under the reformist leadership of Mikhail Gorbachev, abandoned the

'Brezhnev doctrine' of suppporting Third World revolutions, Cuba adopted a more conciliatory posture in its international relations, including those with the United States. In 1988 it signed a peace treaty with South Africa, providing for the withdrawal of Cuban forces from Angola. As a further indication of Cuba's return to the fold of international politics, in September 1988 it established formal relations with the European Community.

Despite the demise of the Soviet Union in 1991 and the almost universal abandonment of communism, Castro maintained his commitment to the ideology. However, by the early 1990s there were signs of some liberalizing of his regime, with the holding of direct municipal and national elections for the first time in 1992–93 and moves towards a more market-orientated economy. This was forced by a worsening economic crisis, as the country, faced with the collapse of the CMEA, tried to find new markets and sources of foreign exchange. There were serious fuel shortages and food rationing, encouraging the flight of thousands more Cubans to Florida. A US embargo on trade with Cuba remained in force, but the prospects of Cuba rejoining the OAS began to improve as a result of its political and economic reforms. In September 1995 Cuba's parliament passed a law permitting foreign ownership in nearly all parts of the economy.

DOMINICA

Commonwealth of Dominica

Capital: Roseau

Social and economic data
Area: 750 km^2
Population: 72,000 million*
Pop. density per km^2: 96*
Urban population: 57%**
Literacy rate: 94% **

GDP: $136 million*; per-capita GDP: $1,680**
Government defence spending (% of GDP): 0%***
Currency: East Caribbean dollar
Economy type: middle income
Labour force in agriculture: 31%**

*1994
**1992
***The Defence Force was disbanded in the 1980s after its involvement in attempted coups against the DFP administration

Ethnic composition
Most of the inhabitants are descended from African slaves who were brought to the island as plantation labourers in the 17th and 18th centuries. A small number of the original people of Dominica, the Arawaks, remain.

Religions
The vast majority of the population is Christian, about 80% Roman Catholic.

Political features
State type: liberal democratic
Date of state formation: 1978
Political structure: unitary
Executive: parliamentary
Assembly: one-chamber
Party structure: multiparty
Human rights rating: N/A
International affiliations: ACP, ACS, CARICOM, CW, IBRD, IMF, IWC, NAM (observer), OAS, OECS, UN, WTO

Local and regional government
For administrative purposes Dominica is divided into ten parishes.

Head of state
President Crispin Sorhaindo, since 1993

Head of government
Prime Minister Edison James, since 1995

Political leaders since 1970
1961–74 Edward Le Blanc (DLP), 1974–80 Patrick John (DLP), 1980–95 Dame Mary Eugenia Charles (DFP), 1995– Edison James (DUWP)

Political system
Dominica is an independent republic within the Commonwealth. The constitution dates from independence, in 1978, and is broadly modelled on the parliamentary system of the United Kingdom. It provides for a single-chamber, 30-member, House of Assembly. Twenty-one are representatives, elected by universal adult suffrage, through a simple plurality voting system, and nine are senators appointed by the president, who is head of state. Five of the senators are appointed on the advice of the prime minister, who is head of government, and four on the advice of the official leader of the opposition, who is the leader of the party with the second largest number of Assembly seats. The Assembly has a life of five years.

The president is elected by the Assembly for a five-year term, renewable once only, and appoints the prime minister on the basis of support in the Assembly. The prime minister chooses the cabinet and all are collectively responsible to the Assembly.

Political parties

There are three active political parties, the Dominica Freedom Party (DFP), the Labour Party of Dominica (LPD), and the Dominica United Workers' Party (DUWP).

The DFP was founded in 1970 as a centre-right party, drawing its leaders from the wealthier sections of the community but also receiving support from the poorer, rural sector.

The LPD was founded in 1985 as an alliance of three parties, the Dominica Labour Party (DLP), the Dominica Liberation Movement (DLM), and the United Dominica Labour Party (UDLP). The DLP dates from 1961, when it was formed to represent the labour movement. The alliance has a left-of-centre orientation.

The DUWP was formed in 1988 and has moved to replace the LPD as the main opposition party. It has a left-of-centre orientation.

Latest elections

In the 1995 general election the DUNP won 11 of the 21 elected Assembly seats and the DFP and LPD five each.

Political history

A British colonial possession since the 18th century, Dominica was part of the Leeward Islands federation until 1939. In 1940 it was transferred to the Windward Islands and remained attached to that group until 1960, when it was given a separate, semi-independent, status, with a chief minister and a Legislative Council. In 1961 the leader of the Dominica Labour Party (DLP), Edward LeBlanc, became chief minister and, after 13 years in office, retired, to be succeeded by Patrick John (b. 1937). The DLP held office until full independence was achieved in 1978 and its leader, John, became the first prime minister under a new constitution.

Opposition to John's increasingly authoritarian style of government soon developed and in the 1980 elections the DFP won a convincing victory on a free-enterprise policy programme. Its leader, Eugenia Charles (b. 1919), a London-trained barrister, became the Caribbean's first woman prime minister, John losing his seat in the Assembly. In 1981 John was thought to be implicated in a plot to overthrow Charles' government and a state of emergency was imposed. The following year he was tried and acquitted. He was retried in 1985, found guilty, and given a 12-year prison sentence.

A regrouping of left-of-centre parties resulted in the Labour Party of Dominica (LPD) becoming the main opposition to the DFP, but in the 1985 elections it was unable to prevent Eugenia Charles being re-elected. Under her leadership, Dominica developed strong links with France and the United States and in 1983 contributed a small contingent to the US-backed invasion of Grenada. In 1990 there were provisional moves to integrate with St Lucia, St Vincent, and Grenada into a Windward Islands federation.

In April 1994 the government declared a state of emergency, following industrial protests about its economic policies, but

eventually the storm was weathered. After losing the 1995 general election to the DUWP, led by Edison James, Dame Eugenia Charles announced her retirement from politics and she was replaced as DFP leader by Brian Alleyne.

DOMINICAN REPUBLIC

República Dominicana

Capital: Santo Domingo

Social and economic data

Area: 48,072 km^2
Population: 7,600,000*
Pop. density per km^2: 156*
Urban population: 62%**
GDP: $5,500 million**; per-capita GDP: $790**
Government defence spending (% of GDP): 1.3%**
Currency: Dominian Republic peso
Economy type: low income
Labour force in agriculture: 46%**

*1994
**1992

Ethnic composition

About 73% of the population are mulattoes, of mixed European and African parentage, about 16% European, and 11% African.

Religions

Roman Catholicism is the established religion and about 90% of the population adheres to it, although there is complete freedom for other beliefs.

Political features

State type: liberal democratic
Date of state formation: 1844
Political structure: unitary
Executive: limited presidential

Assembly: two-chamber
Party structure: multiparty
Human rights rating: 78%
International affiliations: ACP, ACS, ALADI (observer), CARICOM (observer), G-11, IAEA, IBRD, IMF, NAM (guest), OAS, SELA, UN, WTO

Local and regional government
The country is divided into 30 provinces and the National District. Each province has a governor, appointed by the president. The provinces are subdivided into municipalities, each with a mayor and an elected council.

Head of state and head of government
President Joaquín Balaguer Ricardo, since 1986

Political leaders since 1970
1966–78 Joaquín Balaguer Ricardo (PRSC), 1978–82 Silvestre Antonio Guzmán (PRD), 1982–86 Jorge Blanco (PRD), 1986– Joaquín Balaguer Ricardo (PRSC)

Political system
Although not a federal state, the Dominican Republic has a highly devolved system of regional and local government. The 1966 constitution provides for a president, popularly elected for a four-year term, and a two-chamber Congress, of Senate and Chamber of Deputies, elected for a similar term. Elections to the Senate are by a simple plurality voting system and to the Chamber by means of a party list system of proportional representation. The Senate has 30 members and the Chamber of Deputies 120. The president is head of government as well as head of state and chooses their own cabinet.

Political parties
There is a wide range of political parties, the three most significant being the Dominican Revolutionary Party (PRD), the Christian Social Reform Party (PRSC), and the Dominican Liberation Party (PLD).

The PRD was founded in Havana in 1939 by a group of antigovernment exiles. It became active in the Dominican Republic after the death of the dictator, Rafael Trujillo. It is a moderate left-of-centre party and now, led by José Francisco Peña Gómez, has about 400,000 members.

The PRSC was formed in 1961, after Trujillo's assassination, by the merger of several Christian, socialist, and other democratic groups. It has an independent, centre-right orientation.

The PLD was formed in 1973 by Juan Bosch, who had originally founded the PRD and then abandoned it. It has a strongly nationalist, left-wing orientation.

Latest elections
The results of the May 1994 presidential and assembly elections were strongly disputed, the PRSC claiming a narrow victory in the presidential contest and the PRD in both chambers of the Congress. In the face of this criticism, repeat elections were scheduled for November 1995.

Political history
Originally inhabited by Carib and Arawak Indians, the island, then known as Hispaniola (which included Haiti), was visited by Christopher Columbus (1451–1506) in 1492

and the Spanish established in 1496, at Santo Domingo, the first European settlement in the Western hemisphere. The western third of the island, comprising Haiti, was ceded by Spain to France in 1697 and from 1795 Santo Domingo also came briefly under French rule. Between 1803–21 several native republics held sway and then in 1844, after two decades of rule by Haiti, the Dominican Republic was formally established. The country was later temporarily occupied by US military forces, between 1916 and 1924. In 1930 the elected democratic government of Horacio Vázquez was overthrown in a military coup and General Rafael Trujillo Molina (1891–1961) began a long and ruthless personal dictatorship until he was assassinated in 1961.

In the following year the country's first free elections were won by Dr Juan Bosch (b. 1909), founder and leader of the left-wing party PRD. Bosch, himself, had been in exile for more than 30 years. He attempted to institute agrarian and labour reforms, but within a year he too was overthrown by the military who set up their own three-man ruling junta. An attempt to re-establish Bosch in 1965 was defeated, with the help of US troops, and in 1966 Joaquín Balaguer Ricardo (b. 1907), a protégé of Trujillo, and leader of the PRSC, won the presidency. A new, more democratically orientated, constitution was adopted and Balaguer, despite his links with Trujillo, proved to be a popular leader, being re-elected in 1970 and 1974.

The 1978 election was won by the PRD candidate, Silvestre Antonio Guzmán, and the PRD was again successful in the 1982 election when Jorge Blanco, the party's left-wing nominee, became president-designate. However the sitting president, Guzmán, committed suicide before he had finished his full term, after allegations of fraud by his family. An interim president was, therefore, chosen before the start of Blanco's term in August.

Despite his left-wing credentials, Blanco steered a restrained course in foreign policy, maintaining good relations with the United States and avoiding too close an association with Cuba. The state of the economy began to worsen, however, and in 1985 the Blanco administration was forced to adopt harsh austerity measures in return for IMF help. The PRD became increasingly unpopular and it was not suprising when the PRSC, under the veteran Joaquín Balaguer, returned to power in 1986. He retained the presidency, despite allegations of fraud by his opponents, in 1990 and 1994. By 1993 the rate of inflation, which had stood at over 100% in 1990, had been brought down to just 3%, but the unemployment level was nearly 30%. Complaints about malpractices in the May 1994 presidential and assembly elections resulted in an undertaking to rerun them in late 1995.

EL SALVADOR

The Republic of El Salvador
La República de El Salvador

Capital: San Salvador

Social and economic data
Area: 21,390 km^2
Population: 5,500,000*

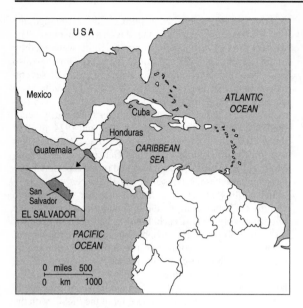

Pop. density per km²: 257*
Urban population: 45%**
Literacy rate: 67%**
GDP: $5,742 million**; per-capita GDP: $1,044**
Government defence spending (% of GDP): 2.7%**
Currency: Salvadorean colon
Economy type: middle income
Labour force in agriculture: 40%**

*1994
**1992

Ethnic composition
El Salvador has a largely homogeneous population. About 92% of the people are mestizos, 6% Indians, and 2% of European origin.

Religions
Roman Catholicism is the dominant religion, about 80% of the population following that faith. There are also about 200,000 Protestants.

Political features
State type: liberal democratic
Date of state formation: 1830
Political structure: unitary
Executive: limited presidential
Assembly: one-chamber
Party structure: multiparty
Human rights rating: 53%
International affiliations: ACS, ALADI (observer), BCIE, CACM, IAEA, IBRD, IMF, NAM (observer), OAS, SELA, UN, WTO

Local and regional government
The country is divided into 14 departments, ranging in population from about 140,000 to nearly 700,000. Each department is administered by a centrally appointed official. Within the departments there are municipalities, with elected mayors.

Head of state and head of government
President Armando Calderón Sol, since 1994

Political leaders since 1970
1967–72 Fidel Sánchez Hernández (PCN-military), 1972–77 Arturo Armando Molina (PCN-military), 1977–79 Carlos Humberto Romeros Mena (PCN-military), 1979–80 military junta, 1980–82 José Napoleón Duarte (PDC-military), 1982–84 Alvaro Magana Borja (independent-military), 1984–89 José Napoleón Duarte (PDC), 1989–94 Alfredo Cristiani Burkard (ARENA), 1994– Armando Calderón Sol (ARENA)

Political system
The 1983 constitution, amended in 1985, provides for a single-chamber Legislative, or National, Assembly of 84 members, elected by universal adult suffrage, through a simple plurality voting system, for a three-year term. The president is popularly elected for a five-year term. The president is assisted by a vice president and a Council of Ministers (cabinet), whom they appoint.

Political parties
Of the 11 officially recognized political parties, the most significant are the Christian Democrats (PDC), the National Republican Alliance (ARENA), the Farabundo Martí National Liberation Front (FMLN), and the National Conciliation Party (PCN).

The PDC was formed in 1960. It is strongly anti-imperialist and favours Latin American integration.

ARENA was founded in 1981. It has a strong right-wing orientation and is led by President Calderón Sol.

The FMLN was a guerrilla group. It translated itself into a political party in 1992. It has a left-wing orientation.

The PCN is another right-wing grouping which fought the 1985 elections on a joint platform with ARENA. It dates from 1961.

Latest elections
The ARENA candidate, Armando Calderón Sol, won the March–April 1994 presidential elections with 68.2% of the vote in the second round run-off.

In the March 1994 assembly elections the results were as follows:

	Seats
ARENA	39
FMLN	21
PDC	18
PCN	4
Others	2

Political history
El Salvador became a Spanish colony in 1523 and achieved independence, within the Federation of Central American States, in 1821. This federation dissolved in 1838 and it became a fully sovereign state. Since then there has been a history of frequent coups and political violence. In the 1930s a peasant uprising, led by Agustín Farabundo Martí, was put

down with, reputedly, some 30,000 lives lost and there were three more military takeovers in 1944, 1948, and 1960. Wide income differentials, with wealth and power concentrated in the hands of a relatively few families, has exacerbated social tensions.

Following another coup, in 1961, the conservative Party of National Conciliation (PCN) was established, winning all the seats in the National Assembly. The PCN stayed in power, with reports of widespread violations of human rights, until challenged, in 1979, by a socialist guerrilla movement, the Farabundo Martí National Liberation Front (FMLN). A civilian-military junta deposed the president and promised to introduce a democratic system of government with free elections. Elections were postponed, however, as the violence continued. In 1980 the Archbishop of San Salvador, Oscar Romero (1917–80), who was a well-known champion of human rights and had been nominated for the Nobel Peace Prize, was shot dead in his cathedral. The murder of three American nuns and a social worker prompted US President Jimmy Carter to suspend economic and military aid.

In December 1980 José Napoleón Duarte (1925–90), founder of the Christian Democratic Party (PDC) in 1960 and leader of a left-of-centre coalition, was sworn in as president. The US administration of Ronald Reagan gave him its backing, as an anticommunist, and encouraged him to call elections in 1982. The left-wing parties refused to enter the contest which was held amid great violence, at least 40 people being killed on election day. It was eventually won by the extreme right-wing National Republican Alliance (ARENA) party. As the FMLN continued its activities, some 1,600 Salvadorean troops, trained in the United States, and US military advisers were said to be actively involved in the conflict, along with extreme right-wing death squads. It was estimated that about 35,000 people were killed between 1979 and 1982.

A new constitution came into effect in 1983 but guerrilla activity continued. Duarte won the 1984 presidential election and in 1985 the PDC had a convincing victory in the Assembly. It was announced, in June 1988, that President Duarte had had tests in Washington which confirmed that he had terminal cancer. Despite this condition, and consequential absences for treatment, the president remained in office until June 1989, when he was succeeded by Dr Alfredo Cristiani, from ARENA.

Later that year the FMLN agreed to talk with the new president and a peace agreement was signed in December 1991, bringing to an end the 12-year-long civil war. Having transformed itself into a political party, it presented a strong challenge to ARENA in the 1994 presidential and assembly elections. However, the ruling party won most seats and retained the presidency in the person of Armando Calderón.

GRENADA

The State of Grenada

Capital: St George's

Social and economic data
Area: 34,500 km^2
Population: 91,000*

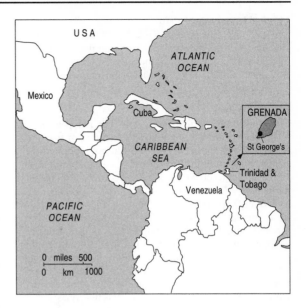

Pop. density per km^2: 264*
Urban population: 63%**
Literacy rate: 98% **
GDP: $200 million**; per-capita GDP: $1,900**
Government defence spending (% of GDP): N/A
Currency: East Caribbean dollar
Economy type: middle income
Labour force in agriculture: 25%**

*1994
**1992

Ethnic composition
The majority of the population is of black African descent.

Religions
The great majority of people, 82%, are Roman Catholics.

Political features
State type: liberal democracy
Date of state formation: 1974
Political structure: unitary
Executive: parliamentary
Assembly: two-chamber
Party structure: multiparty
Human rights rating: N/A
International affiliations: ACP, ACS, CARICOM, CW, IBRD, IMF, IWC, NAM, OAS, OECS, SELA, UN, WTO

Local and regional government
The country is divided into six parishes, each administered by an appointed district commissioner. The capital of St George's is administered by the central government.

Head of state
Queen Elizabeth II, represented by Governor General Sir Reginald O Palmer since 1992

Head of government
Prime Minister Keith Mitchell, since 1995

Political leaders since 1970

1967–79 Sir Eric Gairy (GULP), 1979–1983 Maurice Bishop (NJM), 1983 Hudson Austin (military), 1983–84 interim council 1984–89 Herbert Blaize (NNP), 1989–91 Ben Jones (TNP), 1991–95 Nicholas Braithwaite (NDC), 1995 George Brizan (NDC), 1995– Keith Mitchell (NNP)

Political system

The constitution, which dates from full independence in 1974, has created a system modelled on that of the United Kingdom, with a resident governor general, representing the British monarch, as the formal head of state and a prime minister and cabinet drawn from and collectively responsible to parliament.

Parliament consists of two chambers, a 15-member House of Representatives, elected by universal adult suffrage, through a simple plurality voting system, and a Senate of 13, appointed by the governor general, seven on the advice of the prime minister, three on the advice of the leader of the opposition and three after wider consultation. The official opposition is the party with the second largest number of seats in the House. The normal parliamentary term is five years.

Political parties

There are four political parties, the main ones being the National Democratic Congress (NDC), the Grenada United Labour Party (GULP), and the National Party (TNP).

The NDC was formed following the US invasion in 1989. It has a centrist orientation.

The TNP emerged from a coalition of centrist parties which came together as the New National Party (NNP) in 1984.

GULP dates from 1950 and is Grenada's oldest party. Its orientation is nationalist. Formerly left-of-centre, it has shifted increasingly rightwards.

Latest elections

In the June 1995 general election the NNP, led by Keith Mitchell, won 8 of the 15 House of Representatives' seats, the NDC, 5, and GULP, 2.

Political history

Grenada was visited by Christopher Columbus (1451–1506) in the 15th century but not colonized until about 200 years later. French settlers came from Martinique and ousted the local Caribs. Then, after being ceded to Britain in 1783, retaken by France and ceded to Britain again, it became a British colony in 1887. In 1958 it joined the Federation of the West Indies, until its dissolution in 1962, and then was granted internal self-government in 1967. It achieved full independence within the Commonwealth in 1974.

The early political life of the nation was dominated by two figures, Eric Gairy (b. 1922), a trade union leader who founded the Grenada United Labour Party (GULP) in 1950, and Herbert Blaize (1918–89), of the Grenada National Party (GNP). On independence, in 1974, Gairy was elected prime minister. He was knighted in 1977 but his rule was regarded as increasingly autocratic and corrupt and in 1979 he was replaced, in a bloodless coup, by the leader of the left-wing party, the New Jewel Movement (NJM), Maurice Bishop.

Bishop suspended the 1974 constitution, established a People's Revolutionary Government (PRG) and announced the formation of a People's Consultative Assembly to draft a new constitution. He promised a nonaligned foreign policy but became increasingly convinced that the United States was involved in a plot to destabilize his administration. This was strenuously denied. Relations with Britain and the United States deteriorated, while Grenada's links with Cuba and the Soviet Union grew stronger. In 1983 Bishop tried to improve relations with the United States and announced the appointment of a commission to draft a new constitution. This conciliatory attitude was opposed by the more left-wing members of his regime, resulting in a military coup, during which Bishop and three of his colleagues were executed.

A Revolutionary Military Council (RMC), led by General Hudson Austin, took control. In response to the outcry caused by the executions, Austin promised a return to civilian rule as soon as possible but on 25 October 1983 about 1,900 US troops, accompanied by 300 from Jamaica and Barbados, invaded the island. It was not clear whether the invasion was in response to a request from the governor general or on the initiative of the Organization of Eastern Caribbean States (OECS). In any event, concerned that Grenada might become a Cuban base, the United States readily agreed to take part. Neither Britain nor other members of the Commonwealth appeared to have been consulted. The RMC forces were defeated and Austin and his colleagues arrested.

In November 1983 the governor general appointed a non-political interim council and then the 1974 constitution was reinstated. Several political parties which had gone into hiding re-emerged. After considerable manoeuvring, an informal coalition of centre and left-of-centre parties resulted in the formation of the New National Party (NNP), led by Blaize. In the 1984 general election the NNP won 14 seats in the House of Representatives and Blaize became prime minister. The United States had withdrawn most of its forces by the end of 1983 and the remainder by July 1985.

Early in 1989 Blaize relinquished the NNP leadership and was succeeded by Keith Mitchell. He continued as prime minister, however, although suffering from terminal cancer. He died in December 1989 and was replaced by a close supporter, Ben Jones, pending a general election. The 1991 general election resulted in Nicholas Braithwaite, the NDC leader, becoming prime minister. In September 1994 Braithwaite resigned the NDC leadership but remained prime minister. He resigned that post in February 1995 and the new party leader, George Brizan, became head of government. His tenure was short-lived as the NNP, led by Keith Mitchell, won the June 1995 general election. He inherited an economy with a low inflation rate, of only 5%, but with an unemployment level of nearly 25%.

GUATEMALA

Republic of Guatemala
República de Guatemala

Capital: Guatemala City

Social and economic data
Area: 108,890 km²
Population: 10,000,000*
Pop. density per km²: 92*
Urban population: 40%**
Literacy rate: 46%**
GDP: $8,200 million**; per-capita GDP: $910**
Government defence spending (% of GDP): 1%**
Currency: quetzal
Economy type: low income
Labour force in agriculture: 54%**

*1994
**1992

Ethnic composition
The population consists mainly of two ethnic groups, Indians and ladinos. The word *ladino* is used to describe all non-Indians, including Europeans, black Africans, and mestizos. The Indians are descendants of the highland Mayas.

Religions
The great majority of the people are Christians, mostly Roman Catholics, 65%, with a largely Evangelical Protestant, 34%, minority.

Political features
State type: emergent democratic
Date of state formation: 1839
Political structure: unitary
Executive: limited presidential
Assembly: one-chamber
Party structure: multiparty
Human rights rating: 62%
International affiliations: ACS, ALADI (observer), BCIE, CACM, G-24, IAEA, IBRD, IMF, NAM, OAS, SELA, UN, WTO

Local and regional government
The country is divided into 22 departments, including Guatemala City, ranging in population from about 100,000 to 1.75 million, each administered by a governor appointed by the president.

Head of state and head of government
President Ramiro de León Carpio, since 1993

Political leaders since 1970
1970–74 Carlos Araña Osorio (MLN-military), 1974–78 Kjell Laugerud García (MLN-military), 1978–82 Fernando Romeo Lucas García (MLN-military), 1982–83 Efrain Ríos Montt (military), 1983–86 Oscar Humberto Mejía Victores (military), 1986–91 Mario Vinicio Cerezo Arevalo (PDCG), 1991–93 Jorge Serrano Elias (MAS), 1993– Ramiro de León Carpio (independent)

Political system
The 1986 constitution provides for a single-chamber National Congress of 80 members, 68 of whom are directly elected in departmental congressional districts and 12 on a national basis, by proportional representation. They serve a five-year term. The president is also directly elected for a similar term. He or she appoints a cabinet and is assisted by a vice president. Presidents are not eligible for re-election.

Political parties
There are some 11 political parties, the most significant being the Guatemalan Christian Democratic Party (PDCG), the Centre Party (UCN), the Revolutionary Party (PR), the Movement of National Liberation (MLN), the Democratic Institutional Party (PID), the Solidarity and Action Movement (MAS), the Guatemalan Republican Front (FRG), the National Advancement Party (PAN), and the Social Democratic Party (PSD).

The PDCG was founded in 1968. It is a Christian, centre-left party.

The UCN dates from 1984 and is a centre party.

The PR was originally founded in 1944 and reformed in 1957. It has a radical orientation.

The MLN is an extreme right-wing party which dates from 1960.

The PID is a moderate conservative party which was formed in 1965.

The MAS, FRG, PAN, and PSD in 1990 formed a right-of-centre coalition.

Latest elections
In the November 1990 presidential election the MAS candidate, Jorge Serrano Elias, won in a second round of voting, securing 68% of the votes cast, the UCN candidate, Jorge Carpio Nicolle, winning the remaining 32%. Serrano resigned in June 1993, with two-and-a-half years of his tenure of office remaining, and the Congress elected Ramiro de León Carpio, an independent member, as his successor, pending new elections in November 1995.

In the August 1994 National Congress elections right-wing parties, led by the FRG, with 32 seats, and the PAN, with 24 seats, achieved a clear majority. The PDCG captured 13 seats and the UCN, 8. Turnout was little more than 20%.

Political history
Guatemala was a site for the ancient Mayan Indian civilization. It later became a Spanish colony in 1524, but obtained

its independence successively from Spain in 1821, then Mexico and, in 1827, from the Federation of Central American States. A republic was finally established in 1839. It was then ruled by a succession of dictators until the presidency of Juan José Arevalo, in 1944, and his successor, Colonel Jacobo Arbenz Guzmán (1913–71). Their socialist administrations both followed programmes of reform, which included the expropriation of large estates and the redistribution of the land to landless peasants, but Arbenz's nationalization of the plantations of the United Fruit Company, in 1954, so alarmed the United States government that it sponsored a revolution, led by Colonel Carlos Castillo Armas, who then assumed the presidency.

He was assassinated in 1963 and the army continued to rule until 1966. There was a brief return to constitutional government until the military returned, in 1970. The next ten years saw a spate of political violence, in which it was estimated that more than 50,000 people died. In the 1982 presidential election the government candidate won but his opponents complained that the election had been rigged and, before he could take office, there was a coup by a group of young right-wing officers who installed General Ríos Montt (b.1926) as head of a three-man junta. He soon dissolved the junta, assumed the presidency, and embarked upon a policy of fighting corruption and ending violence. The antigovernment guerrilla movement was, however, growing, being fuelled by the suppression of the left. It was countered by repressive measures by Montt, so that by the beginning of 1983 opposition to him was widespread. After several unsuccessful attempts to remove him, a coup, led by General Mejía Victores, was successful.

Mejía Victores declared an amnesty for the guerrillas, the ending of press censorship, and the preparation of a new constitution. This was adopted in 1985 and in the elections which followed the Guatemalan Christian Democratic Party (PDCG) won a majority in the Congress as well as the presidency, Mario Vinicio Cerezo Arevalo (b. 1942) becoming its first civilian president for 20 years.

After the 1991 elections the new president, Jorge Serrano Elias, took a firm line against military dissidents. He also, surprisingly, restored diplomatic relations with Belize, whose territory had been claimed by Guatemala. In May 1993, citing student and industrial unrest as his reason, President Serrano, with some army support, attempted to impose an authoritarian regime on the country. In a rare display of unity, trade union, civic, and some army groups opposed the move, forcing Serrano to step down. The vice president, Gustavo Espina Salguero, then proclaimed himself president but this move was also blocked and in June 1993 the National Congress appointed a national unity government, headed by the human rights ombudsman, Ramiro de León Carpio (b. 1942).

Despite his seemingly impeccable credentials, President de León, faced with violent opposition and the continuation of guerrilla activity by the Guatemalan Revolutionary National Unity (URNG) movement, found his popularity falling and became increasingly dependent on army support. In January 1994 a referendum was held proposing to bring forward the congressional elections, so as to enable corrupt deputies to be ousted, and to decentralize government spending. Eighty per cent of voters supported this presidential initiative, although turnout was a paltry 16%. In the August 1994 congressional elections right-wing parties won a majority of seats and there were fears of a return to the autocratic governments the country had experienced in previous years. At the same time, the UN-sponsored peace talks with the URNG had made only slow and hesitant progress. New presidential elections were scheduled for late 1995.

HAITI

The Republic of Haiti
La République d'Haïti

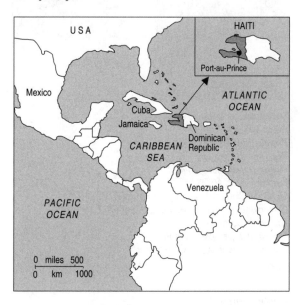

Capital: Port-au-Prince

Social and economic data
Area: 27,750 km^2
Population: 6,900,000*
Pop. density per km^2: 249*
Urban population: 30%**
Literacy rate: 35%**
GDP: $2,600 million**; per-capita GDP: $360**
Government defence spending (% of GDP): 2.3%**
Currency: gourde
Economy type: low income
Labour force in agriculture: 50%**

*1994
**1992

Ethnic composition
About 95% of the population is of black African descent, the remainder being mulattos or Europeans.

Religions
About 80% of the population follows Roman Catholicism, which is the official religion. Voodoo is also a folk religion.

Political features
State type: emergent democratic
Date of state formation: 1804
Political structure: unitary
Executive: dual
Assembly: two-chamber
Party structure: multiparty
Human rights rating: N/A
International affiliations: ACP, ACS, CARICOM (observer), IAEA, IBRD, IMF, OAS, SELA, UN, WTO

Local and regional government
The country is divided into nine departments, which are further subdivided into *arrondissements* and then communes. Departments are administered by appointed prefects and each commune has an elected mayor.

Head of state (executive)
President Jean-Bertrand Aristide, since 1994

Head of government
Prime Minister Smarck Michel, since 1994

Political leaders since 1970
1964–71 François Duvalier (National Unity Party), 1971–86 Jean-Claude Duvalier (PNP), 1986–88 Lieutenant General Henri Namphrey (military), 1988 Leslie Manigat (civilian), 1988–90 General Prosper Avril (military), 1990–91 Jean-Bertrand Aristide (FNCD), 1991–94 General Raoul Cedras (military), 1994– Jean-Bertrand Aristide (FNCD)

Political system
The constitution of 1950 was revised in 1957, 1964, 1971, 1983, and 1985 and then replaced with a new version in 1987. Between 1957 and 1986 the Duvalier family, father and then son, ruled Haiti with absolute power, maintaining their positions with the help of a private army. Although the constitution provided for an elected National Assembly, it had become a façade for the Duvaliers' own dictatorships.

In 1986 Henri Namphrey led a military coup and established a Governing Council, with himself as head and the future of democratic government in Haiti was again under test. Although a new constitution was introduced in 1987, providing for the sharing of executive power between a president, prime minister and two Houses of Congress, together with an independent judiciary, the congressional elections held in November 1987 and January 1988 were viewed by outside observers as largely fraudulent and the military was seen as retaining considerable power behind the façade of the civilian government.

The civilian government which was restored at the beginning of 1988 was overthrown later in the year by the military, again casting doubt over Haiti's democratic future, despite the new regime's promises to establish 'an irreversible democracy'. The 1990 election of a truly civilian government again raised hopes, but these were dashed a year later when military intervention was resumed.

The 1987 constitution provides for a two-chamber assembly consisting of a Senate of 27 members and a Chamber of Deputies, or National Assembly, of 83 members, elected by universal adult suffrage through a two-ballot majoritarian voting system, for a five-year term. There is also provision for a 'dual executive', with power being shared between a president, popularly elected for a five-year term, and a prime minister, appointed by the president on the basis of assembly support. The prime minister chooses a cabinet in consultation with the president.

Political parties
The two most significant parties are the National Front for Change and Democracy (FNCD) and the National Alliance for Democracy and Progress (ANDP).

The FNCD was formed to oppose the Duvalier regime. It is a loose coalition of peasants, trade unionists, and intellectuals, with a left-of-centre orientation and is headed by President Aristide.

The ANDP was formed to fight the 1990 election. Its orientation is also left-of-centre.

Latest elections
In the December 1990 presidential election Father Jean-Bertrand Aristide, the FNCD candidate, was elected with 67.5% of the popular vote, defeating ten other candidates. His nearest rival, Marc Bazin (ANDP) obtained 14.2% of the vote.

National Assembly and Senate elections were also held in 1990, but military intervention prevented the implementation of their results. New elections were planned for 1995.

Political history
First visited by Christopher Columbus (1451–1506) in 1492, Spain ceded Haiti, which comprised the western part of the island of Hispaniola, to France in 1697. Haiti became an independent state in 1804, after an uprising against French colonial rule, which had been led by the former slave, Toussaint l'Ouverture (1746–1803). Between 1822–44 Haiti also ruled the Dominican Republic, which comprised the eastern half of Hispaniola. Within Haiti there was constant friction between the African-descended Haitians and the mulattos and between 1915 and 1924 the country's political instability brought a period of United States intervention and rule. In the 1940s and 1950s there was a series of coups, the last being in 1956, which resulted in Dr François Duvalier (1907–71), a country physician who believed in voodoo, being elected president in 1957. After an encouraging start, the Duvalier administration degenerated into a personal dictatorship, ruthlessly maintained by a private militia, the Tonton Macoutes, and backed by the United States, which viewed him as a prop against communism. In 1964 Duvalier, 'Papa Doc', cemented his position by amending the constitution to make himself life president, with the power to nominate his son as his successor. On his death in 1971 Jean-Claude Duvalier (b. 1951) therefore came to the presidency at the age of 19 and soon acquired the name of 'Baby Doc'. Although the young Duvalier repeatedly promised a return to democratic politics, there was little real change and popular opposition to the regime mounted.

In 1985 Duvalier announced a further reform of the constitution, including the legalization of political parties, but this was not enough to prevent his overthrow in 1986. He went into exile in the south of France. The task of establishing democratic government fell to the new regime led by

Lieutenant General Henri Namphrey. In 1987 a new constitution was adopted, providing for democratic government and an independent judiciary, but congressional elections in 1987 and 1988 were deemed largely fraudulent by outside observers. Leslie Manigat was elected president but was ousted in a military coup, led by General Prosper Avril, eight months later. Avril installed a largely civilian government, but a few months later handed over power again to the military.

After a period of turbulence and uncertainty, presidential and congressional elections were held at the end of 1990, resulting in the election of a left-wing peasant Catholic priest, Jean-Bertrand Aristide (b. 1953), who immediately tried to end army corruption and return to genuine civilian rule. He was ousted by the army, led by General Raoul Cedras,and police chief Colonel Michel François in September 1991, and forced into exile. A provisional government, backed by the military, was installed, despite wide international criticism, and a reign of terror was instituted by the secret police.

While Aristide was exiled in the United States, three years of economic pressure, through United Nations-backed trade sanctions and eventually a naval blockade, and the illegal flight of thousands of Haitians to the United States so weakened the Haitian economy that in September 1994 the former US president, Jimmy Carter, was able to broker an agreement with the Cedras regime, allowing US troops to enter the country without opposition and restore President Aristide.

In October 1994 Cedras stood down, having been granted an amnesty, and Aristide returned as the legitimate president. He appointed a former businessman, Smarck Michel, as prime minister and said that he was renouncing the priesthood so that he could concentrate on his political duties.

HONDURAS

The Republic of Honduras
La República de Honduras

Capital: Tegucigalpa

Social and economic data
Area: 112,090 km^2
Population: 5,600,000*
Pop. density per km^2: 50*
Urban population: 45%**
Literacy rate: 57%**
GDP: $3,000 million**; per-capita GDP: $580**
Government defence spending (% of GDP): 1.3%**
Currency: lempira
Economy type: low income
Labour force in agriculture: 65%**

*1994
**1992

Ethnic composition
About 90% of the population is of mixed Indian and Spanish descent and known as ladinos, or mestizos. There are also Salvadorean, Guatemalan, American, and European minorities.

Religions
Almost 85% of the population is Roman Catholic and 15% belongs to Protestant Evangelical churches.

Political features
State type: liberal democratic
Date of state formation: 1838
Political structure: unitary
Executive: limited presidential
Assembly: one-chamber
Party structure: two-party
Human rights rating: 65%
International affiliations: ACS, ALADI (observer), BCIE, CACM, IBRD, ICFTU, IMF, LORCS, NAM, OAS, SELA, UN, WTO

Local and regional government
The country is divided into 18 departments which are further subdivided into municipalities. The municipalities have councils elected at the same time and in the same way as the National Assembly.

Head of state and head of government
President Carlos Roberto Reina Idiaquez, since 1993

Political leaders since 1970
1965–71 General Oswaldo López Arellano (PLH), 1971–72 Ramón Ernesto Cruz Ucles (PNH), 1972–74 General Oswaldo López Arellano (PLH), 1974–78 General Juan Melgar Castro (military), 1978–81 General Policarpo Paz García (military), 1981–84 Roberto Suazo Córdova (PLH), 1984–86 General Walter López Reyes (military), 1986–89 José Simeón Azeona del Hoyo (PLH), 1989–93 Rafael Leonardo Callejas (PNH), 1993– Carlos Roberto Reina Idiaquez (PLN)

Political system
The 1982 constitution, which underwent a major revision in 1985, provides for the election of a president, who is both head of state and head of government, by universal adult

suffrage for a four-year term. A single-chamber National Assembly is elected, through a party list system of proportional representation, for a similar term. The size of the Assembly may be amended in the light of population changes. It currently has 128 members. The president may not serve two terms in succession.

Political parties
There are some four political parties and a number of organized guerrilla groups. The two most significant parties are the Liberal Party of Honduras (PLH) and the National Party of Honduras (PNH).

The PLH appeared in its present form in 1980 but its origins go back to the 1890s. It has a number of internal factions which sometimes oppose the leadership. It has a centre-right orientation.

The PNH was formed in 1902, and underwent a major reorganization in 1916. It is a traditional right-wing party and, like the PLH, it too has its own internal factions.

Latest elections
In the November 1993 presidential election the PLH candidate, Carlos Roberto Reina, secured 52.4% of the vote and his PNH opponent, Osvaldo Ramos Soto, 40.7%.

The PLH also won a majority in the November 1993 National Assembly elections, capturing 71 seats to the PNH's 55.

Political history
Formerly a site of the ancient Mayan civilization, Honduras became a Spanish possession from the early 16th century. It broke away in 1821 to form a federation of Central American States with El Salvador, and achieved full independence in 1838 when this federation dissolved. There was political instability and wars with neighbouring states throughout much of the 19th and early 20th centuries and US involvement was significant, with the United Fruit Company controlling much of the country's crucial banana production. In 1925 there was a brief civil war and from 1939 to 1949 a dictatorship was established by the leader of the National Party (PNH). Then the government constantly changed hands in a series of military coups, with General Oswaldo López Arellano holding power for much of the period between 1963–74.

In 1980 civilian rule returned, but the army retained control of security and was able to veto cabinet appointments. Although the 1981 general election was won by the Liberal Party (PLH) and its leader, Dr Roberto Suazo, became president, real power was still in the hands of General Gustavo Alvárez, the commander in chief of the army, who, in 1982, managed to secure an amendment to the constitution which reduced government control over the armed forces. General Alvárez was virtually in charge of foreign policy, working closely with the United States and agreeing, in 1983, to the establishment of naval and air bases in Honduras. The American CIA was also active in providing assistance to Nicaraguan counter-revolutionaries based in Honduras.

In 1984 Alvárez was ousted by a group of junior officers and Honduras' close relationship with the United States came under review. In the same year divisions arose within the PLH over selection procedures for the party's presidential candidates and two years later the electoral law was changed. In the elections of 1986 Suazo was not eligible to stand for the presidency and the main PLH candidate was José Azeona. Although the PNH nominee won most votes, the revised constitution made Azeona the eventual winner.

In 1989 the PNH, led by Rafael Callejas, won both the presidential and assembly elections but in November 1993 the situation was reversed and the PLH returned to power, with Carlos Reina as president. Under Reina, the economy began to improve, with economic growth of 5% during 1993 and inflation in single figures. However, the unemployment rate exceeded 40%.

JAMAICA

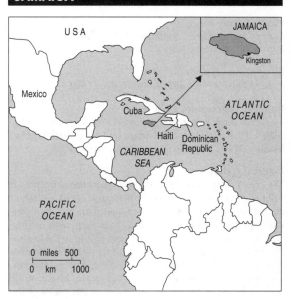

Capital: Kingston

Social and economic data
Area: 10,991 km^2
Population: 2,500,000*
Pop. density per km^2: 227*
Urban population: 54%**
Literacy rate: 96%**
GDP: $3,000 million**; per-capita GDP: $1,260**
Government defence spending (% of GDP): 0.9%**
Currency: Jamaican dollar
Economy type: middle income
Labour force in agriculture: 25%**

*1994
**1992

Ethnic composition
Nearly 80% of the population is of pure African descent and about 15% of mixed African-European origins. There are also Chinese, Indian, and European minorities.

Religions
The great majority of people are Christians, the largest number being Anglicans. There is also a large Rastafarian community.

Political features

State type: liberal democratic
Date of state formation: 1962
Political structure: unitary
Executive: parliamentary
Assembly: two-chamber
Party structure: two-party
Human rights rating: 72%
International affiliations: ACP, ACS, CARICOM, IAEA, IBRD, IMF, NAM, OAS, SELA, UN, WTO

Local and regional government

For administrative purposes, the country is divided into 14 parishes, each with an elected council.

Head of state

Queen Elizabeth II, represented by Governor General Howard Cooke since 1991

Head of government

Prime Minister Percival J Patterson, since 1992

Political leaders since 1970

1967–72 Hugh Shearer (JLP), 1972–80 Michael Manley (PNP), 1980–89 Edward P G Seaga (JLP), 1989–92 Michael Manley (PNP), 1992– Percival J Patterson (PNP)

Political system

The constitution came into force on independence in 1962. It follows closely the unwritten British model, with a resident constitutional head of state, in the shape of the governor general, representing the British monarch, who appoints a prime minister and cabinet, collectively responsible to the assembly. This consists of two chambers, an appointed 21-member Senate and a 60-member elected House of Representatives. Thirteen of the senators are appointed on the advice of the prime minister and eight on the advice of the leader of the opposition. Members of the House are elected by universal adult suffrage, through a simple plurality voting system, for a five-year term. It is subject to dissolution within that period.

Political parties

There are three active political parties, the two which have been the main adversaries in the political contest since independence being the Jamaica Labour Party (JLP) and the People's National Party (PNP).

The JLP was founded by Sir Alexander Bustamente in 1943 as the political wing of the Bustama Industrial Trade Union. It has a moderate, centrist orientation, and supports free enterprise in a mixed economy and cooperation with the United States.

The PNP was formed in 1938 by Norman Manley. It has a left-of-centre social-democratic orientation and believes in the pursuit of socialist principles within a self-sufficient, national framework, although this stance has been moderated in recent years. In October 1995 a new centrist party was formed by Bruce Golding, a former chairperson of the JLP.

Latest elections

In the March 1993 general election the PNP won a landslide victory, securing 52 of the House of Representatives' 60 seats, and Percival Patterson, who had succeeded Michael

Manley in 1992, continued as prime minister. The JLP won the other eight seats.

Political history

Visited by Christopher Columbus (1451–1506) in 1494, Jamaica was initially ruled by Spain from the early 16th century, with many of the indigenous Arawak Indians dying as a result of exposure to new diseases brought from the 'Old World'. Jamaica was a British colony from 1655. During the 1930s depression social and economic problems led to rioting and a developing political awareness. The country was granted internal self-government in 1959 and then full independence within the Commonwealth in 1962. The two leading political figures in the early days of independence were Sir Alexander Bustamente (1884–1977), the Spanish-raised adopted son of an Irish planter, and Norman Manley (1893–1969), a skilled barrister who became prime minister in 1955. Bustamente's Jamaica Labour Party (JLP) won the 1962 election and was again successful in 1967 under Bustamente's successor, Hugh Shearer. Then the PNP, under Norman Manley's son Michael (b. 1923), came into office in 1972.

Michael Manley was a strong advocate of social reform and economic independence from the developed world. Despite high unemployment, his party was returned to power in 1976 with an increased majority but by 1980 the economic position had worsened and, rejecting the conditions attached to an IMF loan, Manley sought support for his policies of economic self-reliance.

The 1980 general election campaign was extremely violent, despite calls by Manley and the leader of the JLP, Edward Seaga (b. 1930), for moderation. The outcome was a surprisingly decisive victory for the JLP. It won 51 of the 60 seats in the House of Representatives. Seaga thus received a mandate for a return to a renewal of links with the United States and an emphasis on free enterprise. He severed diplomatic links with Cuba in 1981.

In 1983 Seaga called an early snap election, with the opposition claiming they had been given insufficient time to nominate their candidates. On this occasion the JLP won all 60 seats. There were violent demonstrations when the new parliament was inaugurated and the PNP said it would continue its opposition outside the parliamentary arena.

In the February 1989 general election Michael Manley's PNP won a landslide victory, after which he hastened to assure the nation and the world that he intended to pursue moderate economic policies and establish good relations with the United States.

In March 1992 Manley resigned because of ill health and the PNP immediately elected Percival Patterson (b. 1935) as his successor. In the March 1993 snap general election Patterson had a personal success, increasing his party's House of Representatives seat holding by seven.

MEXICO

United States of Mexico
Estados Unidos Mexicanos

Capital: Mexico City

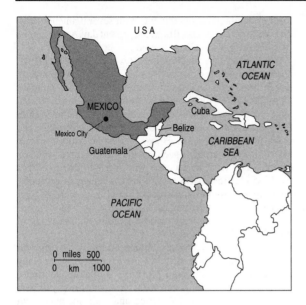

Social and economic data
Area: 1,958,201 km^2
Population: 90,000,000*
Pop. density per km^2: 45*
Urban population: 74%**
Literacy rate: 87%**
GDP: $330,000 million**; per-capita GDP: $3,750**
Governemt defence spending (% of GDP): 0.5%**
Currency: Mexican peso
Economy type: middle income
Labour force in agriculture: 23%**

*1994
**1992

Ethnic composition
About 60% of the population are mestizos, of Spanish-American and American-Indian parentage, about 30% are Indians, and the rest are mainly of European origin.

Religions
About 92% of the population is Roman Catholic. There is also a 5% Protestant Evangelical minority. Roman Catholicism was the established religion until 1857 and it is still under a measure of state control.

Political features
State type: liberal democratic
Date of state formation: 1821
Political structure: federal
Executive: limited presidential
Assembly: two-chamber
Party structure: multiparty*
Human rights rating: 64%
International affiliations: AVS, AG (observer), ALADI, APEC, BCIE, CARICOM (observer), G-3, G-15, G-24, IAEA, IBRD, IMF, IWC, NAFTA, NAM (observer), OECD, RG, SELA, UN, WTO

*Though dominated by one party

Local and regional government
Mexico is a federal republic of 31 states and a federal district, based on Mexico City. It displays several of the features of the United States federal system, with each state having its own constitution, governor, and single chamber assembly, termed the Chamber of Deputies, directly elected for six-year and three-year terms respectively. In broad terms, the powers of the federal government are set out in the federal constitution and the residue resides with the states. Within the states there are over 2,000 municipalities, each with an elected council.

Head of state and head of government
President Ernesto Zedillo Ponce de León, since 1994

Political leaders since 1970
1970–76 Luis Echeverria Alvárez (PRI), 1976–82 José Lopéz Portillo (PRI), 1982–88 Miguel de la Madrid Hurtado (PRI), 1988–94 Carlos Salinas de Gortari (PRI), 1994– Ernesto Zedillo Ponce de León (PRI)

Political system
The constitution dates from 1917, following the 1910 revolution which proclaimed a drastic change in land ownership, new labour legislation and a reduction in the powers of the Roman Catholic Church. Since then it has been amended several times, most recently in 1993, but its essential provisions remain. It provides for a president, who is both head of state and head of government, and a two-chamber National Congress of Senate and Chamber of Deputies, broadly based on the United States model. The Senate has a six-year term and the deputies serve for three years. The president is directly elected for a six-year term and chooses the cabinet.

The Senate has 128 members, each state and the Federal District being represented by four senators. Three of these are elected by majority election and the fourth by proportional representation.

The Chamber has 500 members, 300 representing single-member constituencies, being elected by a majority vote, and 200 elected by proportional representation, from party lists. The voting system is intended to give due weight to the minority parties, with the majority party in the Chamber being limited to no more than 315 seats.

Political parties
There are some six active parties, the most significant being the Institutional Revolutionary Party (PRI), the National Action Party (PAN), and the Party of the Democratic Revolution (PRD).

The PRI was formed in 1929 as the natural successor to the parties of the revolutionary period of Mexico's history and then called the National Revolutionary Party. It was redesignated as the Mexican Revolutionary Party in 1938. It is a broad-based party which has been a dominant force in Mexican politics for many years. It has a moderate, corporatist orientation.

The PAN was formed in 1939. Its orientation is moderate, Christian, centre-right reformist. Its leader is Carlos Castillo Peraza.

The PRD was formed in 1988 as an opposition force to the PRI. It has a left-of-centre reformist orientation.

Traditionally, the opposition PAN and PRD have been granted a number of congressional seats and the occasional state governorship by the dominant PRI in exchange for keeping their attacks on the regime within bounds. In this way, a unique multiparty dictatorship has survived for nearly 70 years. However, in recent years the increasingly confident PAN has begun to eschew such deals and now presses for outright power.

Latest elections

In the August 1994 presidential election the PRI candidate, Ernesto Zedillo, won with 48.8% of the vote, his nearest rival, the PAN candidate, Diego Fernández, securing 25.9%. This was the lowest ever victory margin for the PRI since its formation in 1929.

The results of the August 1994 congressional elections were as follows:

	Senate seats	Chamber of Deputies seats
PRI	64	300
PAN	24	119
PRD	8	71
Other parties	–*	10

*The fourth senator for each state was set to be elected in 1997

As in previous polls, the opposition charged the PRI with ballot-rigging and an independent monitoring group described the elections as 'definitely not clean'.

Political history

In early times Mexico was the site of a number of advanced Indian civilizations, notably the Mayas, based in the Yukatan peninsula, the Toltecs, and the Aztecs, who founded the city of Tenochtitlán in 1325 and under Montezuma II (1466–1520) established an extensive empire. This was overthrown by Spanish conquistador invaders, led by Hernando Cortés (1485–1547), between 1519–21. Centuries of economic exploitation and harsh repression by the Spanish colonial authorities created a vigorous movement for independence. This was eventually achieved in 1821, following a guerrilla war led by Vicente Guerrero. Mexico's early history as an independent nation was marked by civil and foreign wars, notably with the United States between 1846–48, which resulted in the loss of Mexican territories north of the Rio Grande, including Texas, New Mexico, and California. Under Porfirio Diaz (1830–1915), who was president between 1877–80 and 1884–1911, there was considerable economic modernization and growth, with railroads being developed with American finance, but there was political repression and a lack of social reform. This provoked his overthrow in 1911 by the reformist Francisco Madero (1873–1913) and the populist revolution of the same year, led by Emiliano Zapata (1879–1919). Zapata sought to reclaim land taken by the Spanish from indigenous Mexicans, but was driven into retreat in 1915 and assassinated in 1919. In 1917 Mexico adopted a new constitution, designed to establish a permanent form of democratic government. With several amendments, that constitution has lasted until the present day. A programme of social reform was also launched.

The broadly based Institutional Revolutionary Party (PRI) has dominated Mexican politics since the 1920s, pursuing largely moderate and, traditionally, left-of-centre policies. During the 1930s much of the economy was nationalized and large estates were divided. Its popularity was damaged from the 1970s by the country's poor economic performance and rising international debts. However, despite criticisms from vested interest groups, such as the trade unions and the Church, the PRI scored a clear win over all other parties in the 1985 elections, with no serious challenger in evidence. Soon afterwards the government's problems were exacerbated by a massive earthquake in Mexico City, which caused thousands of deaths and made hundreds of thousands of people homeless.

Mexico has been strongly influenced by its proximity to the United States. Its constitution, for example, reflects many aspects of that of its more powerful neighbour. At times, however, the Mexican government has been strongly critical of US policy in Central America and, as a member, with Colombia, Panama, and Venezuela, of the Contadora Group, has argued strongly for the withdrawal of all foreign advisers from the region.

With the price of oil, a vital export earner, falling sharply, the economic situation worsened so much in the 1980s that the Mexican government, after prolonged negotiations, felt obliged, in 1986, to sign an agreement with the IMF. This provided loans sufficient to keep the country solvent for several years. The agreement was extended in 1992. Two years later the Free Trade Agreement between the United States and Canada was expanded to include Mexico and retitled the North American Free Trade Agreement (NAFTA).

In the 1988 presidential election the PRI candidate, Carlos Salinas de Gortari (b. 1948), won by a small margin amid claims of election frauds. The PRI also increased its majority in the 1988 assembly elections. President Salinas then embarked on an ambitious programme of market-centred economic reform, encouraging inward investment with considerable success.

In 1989 the first non-PRI state governor was elected, when the National Action Party (PAN) won in Baja California state. In November 1993 the PRI chose Luis Donaldo Colosio as its candidate for the 1994 presidential elections. However, the country was thrown into turmoil when, in March 1994, Colosio was assassinated while attending a political rally in Baja California. Ernesto Zedillo (b.1952) was chosen as Colosio's replacement. Meanwhile, Indian groups, led by the mysterious figure of Commandante Marcos, had rebelled in January 1994 in the southern state of Chiapas, operating under the banner of the Zapatista National Liberation Army (EZLN), demanding political reform and land distribution. They took control of part of the territory, declaring it independent. A peace agreement was reached in December 1994 but the situation continued to be unsettled.

The PRI enjoyed successes in the August 1994 presidential and congressional elections, Zedillo taking the supreme office and the party securing a majority, though much reduced, in both chambers. However, the opposition claimed that there had been electoral fraud in a number of regions, notably Chiapas, where the PRI controversially secured the state governorship. Instability of the political system was again in focus when, in September 1994, the PRI secretary general, José Francisco Ruiz, was killed in Mexico City. In December 1994 Zedillo was sworn in as president, but within weeks he was faced by a grave currency crisis, with foreign investors, concerned at continuing political instability and Mexico's high level of indebtedness, seeking to sell their clearly overvalued peso holdings. Sharp devaluations in the peso became necessary and support was received from the new Clinton administration in the United States. This helped stabilize the situation, but inflation rose sharply during 1995 and there was a sudden contraction in GDP and deep spending cuts. New privatizations of the ports, railroads, and airways were also announced. In March 1995 it was revealed that former president, Carlos Salinas, had gone into exile, following the arrest of his brother, Raoul, on murder and corruption charges. In August 1995 the PRI's president, Maria de los Angeles Moreno, resigned after a string of bad election results, which saw the PRI lose the governorships of several more states to the opposition PAN.

NICARAGUA

Republic of Nicaragua
República de Nicaragua

Capital: Managua

Social and economic data
Area: 120,254 km^2
Population: 4,100,000*
Pop. density per km^2: 34*
Urban population: 61%**
Literacy rate: 57%**
GDP: $1,447 million**; per-capita GDP $360**
Government defence spending (% of GDP): 13.4%**

Currency: Gold cordoba
Economy type: low income
Labour force in agriculture: 46%**

*1994
**1992

Ethnic composition
Over 70% of the population is of mixed Indian, Spanish, and African blood. About 9% is of pure African descent and 5% pure Indian.

Religions
All religions are tolerated. About 90% of the population is Roman Catholic and there is a strong following of the Protestant Moravian Church, particularly along the Atlantic coast.

Political features
State type: emergent democratic
Date of state formation: 1838
Political structure: unitary
Executive: limited presidential
Assembly: one-chamber
Party structure: two-party
Human rights rating: 75%
International affiliations: ACS, ALADI (observer), BCIE, CACM, IAEA, IBRD, IMF, NAM, OAS, SELA, UN, WTO

Local and regional government
The country is divided into 16 departments, ranging in population from about 30,000 to over 800,000. Below the department level are municipalities, with elected councils, but limited powers.

Head of state and head of government
President Violeta Barrios de Chamorro, since 1990

Political leaders since 1970
1967–79 Anastasio Somoza Debayle (military), 1979–85 junta (FSLN), 1985–90 Daniel Ortega Saavedra (FSLN), 1990– Violeta Barrios de Chamorro (UNO)

Political system
The 1986 constitution, amended in November 1994, provides for a president, who is head of state and head of government, and a 90-member single-chamber National Assembly. The president is elected by universal suffrage for a five-year non-renewable term, and is assisted by a vice president, elected in the same way, and an appointed cabinet. The National Assembly is also elected by universal suffrage, through a party list system of proportional representation, for a six-year term.

Political parties
There are some 22 active political parties, 14 of them operating within the National Opposition Union (UNO), a diverse coalition, ranging from conservatives on the right to communists on the left. The other main political force is the Sandinista National Liberation Front (FSLN).

The UNO was constructed to fight the then ruling FSLN in the 1990 elections. It is led by President Barros and is right-of-centre.

The FSLN was founded in 1960 to pursue a guerrilla struggle against the ruling Somoza regime. Between 1979 and 1990 it was the principal government party. It is a Marxist–Leninist grouping, but is divided between moderate reformist and hardline wings. Its leader is the hardline Daniel Ortega.

Latest elections

In the February 1990 presidential election the FSLN candidate, Daniel Ortega, was defeated by the leader of the UNO coalition, Violeta Barrios de Chamorro, who obtained 54.7% of the vote.

In the simultaneous Assembly elections UNO won 51 seats to the FSLN's 39.

Political history

Nicaragua, formerly inhabited by Indian tribes, was conquered by Spain in 1552. It achieved independence from Spanish rule in 1821 and was briefly united with Mexico and then with the United Provinces of Central America, before becoming fully independent in 1838. In 1912, as the political situation deteriorated, at the Nicaraguan government's request, the United States established military bases in the country but their presence was opposed by a guerrilla group, led by Augusto César Sandino. The United States withdrew its forces in 1933 but not before it had established and trained a National Guard, commanded by a trusted nominee, General Anastasio Somoza Garcia (1896–1956).

Sandino was assassinated in 1934, reputedly on Somoza's orders, but some of his followers continued their guerrilla activity on a small scale. The Somoza family began a near-dictatorial rule which was to last for over 40 years. During this time they developed wide business interests and amassed a huge personal fortune, while political opponents were exiled. General Somoza was elected president in 1936 and stayed in office until his assassination in 1956 when he was succeeded by his son, Luis Somoza Debayle (1922–67). In 1960 the left-wing Sandinista National Liberation Front (FSLN), named after the former guerrilla leader, was formed with the object of overthrowing the Somozas by revolution. This was not to happen, however, for some 17 years. Luis Somoza was followed as president in 1967 by his brother, Anastasio Somoza Debayle (1925–80), who was to head an even more notorious and oppressive regime. In July 1979, after considerable violence and loss of life, Somoza was ousted and fled the country. He was later assassinated in Paraguay in 1980.

The FSLN established a provisional Junta of National Reconstruction led by Daniel Ortega Saavedra (b. 1945), who had earlier spent seven years in prison for his involvement in urban guerrilla activities; published a statute guaranteeing civil rights; and appointed a Council of State, prior to an elected National Assembly and, later, a new constitution.

Nicaragua's relations with the United States deteriorated rapidly with the election of the conservative Republican Ronald Reagan as US president in November 1980. He froze the package of economic assistance arranged by his Democrat predecessor, Jimmy Carter, alleging that the Sandinista government was supporting attempts to overthrow the administration in El Salvador. In March 1982 the Nicaraguan government declared a state of emergency in the wake of attacks on bridges and petroleum installations. The Reagan administration embarked on a policy of destabilizing the Sandinista government by actively supporting the counter-revolutionary forces (the 'Contras'), with bases in Honduras, and by covert CIA operations to undermine the economy. In February 1985 President Reagan denounced Ortega's regime, saying that his objective was to 'remove it in the sense of its present structure'.

A Central American Peace Agreement, instigated by President Oscar Arias Sánchez of Costa Rica, was signed in Guatemala by leaders of Nicaragua, El Salvador, Guatemala, Honduras, and Costa Rica in August 1987, but it failed to halt the fighting. In January 1988, however, President Ortega instituted direct talks with the rebels and the US Congress refused to vote additional military aid to them. In October 1988 President Reagan announced that he would be seeking no more aid for the Contras.

In February 1989 the presidents of Guatemala, El Salvador, Honduras, and Costa Rica agreed to disarm the Contra rebels and Ortega undertook to hold new elections in February 1990 and to restore civil rights to everyone. These elections resulted in wins for the broad-based right-of-centre National Opposition Union (UNO) coalition at both presidential and Assembly levels, Violeta Barrios de Chamorro becoming president. However, the defection to the FSLN of ten UNO deputies after the election left the president without a clear Assembly majority. In addition, President Chamorro inherited an economy which was in ruins after more than a decade of civil war, with an estimated 60% of the population unemployed.

In February 1994, after months of negotiations, a final peace accord was signed with the residue of the rebels, known as Recontras, who had hitherto stayed aloof from negotiations.

In November 1994 the constitution was amended, reducing the presidential term from six to five years, and barring consecutive terms of office. Also, in a bid to destroy nepotism, the constitution now barred relatives of serving presidents from standing for election.

PANAMA

The Republic of Panama
La República de Panamá

Capital: Panama City

Social and economic data
Area: 77,080 km^2
Population: 2,600,000*
Pop. density per km^2: 34*
Urban population: 54%**
Literacy rate: 86% **
GDP: $6,000 million**; per-capita GDP: $2,400**
Government defence spending (% of GDP): 1.2%**
Currency: balboa
Economy type: middle income
Labour force in agriculture: 25%**

*1994
**1992

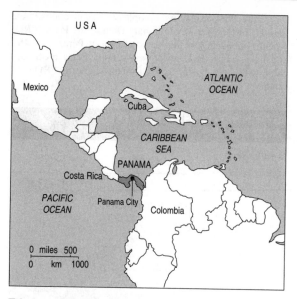

Ethnic composition

About 70% of the population are mestizos, of Spanish-American and American-Indian parentage, and are called Panamenos. About 14% are West Indian, 10% white American or European, and 6% Indian.

Religions

Eighty-five per cent of the population is Roman Catholic and Roman Catholicism is a quasi-state religion. There are also Evangelical Protestant and Jewish minorities.

Political features

State type: emergent democratic
Date of state formation: 1903
Political structure: unitary
Executive: limited presidential
Assembly: one-chamber
Party structure: multiparty
Human rights rating: 81%
International affiliations: AG (associate), ALADI (observer), IAEA, IBRD, IMF, IWC, NAM, OAS, SELA, UN

Local and regional government

The country is divided into nine provinces and three autonomous Indian reservations. Each province has a governor, appointed by the president. The provinces are further subdivided into districts, each with its own mayor.

Head of state and head of government

President Ernesto Pérez Balladares, since 1994

Political leaders since 1970

1968–78 General Omar Torrijos Herrera (military), 1978–82 Aristedes Royo Sánchez (effective military), 1982–84 Ricardo de la Espriella (effective military), 1984–85 Nicolás Ardito Barletta (effective military), 1985–88 Eric Arturo Delvalle (effective military), 1988–89 Manuel Solis Palma (effective military), 1989–94 Guillermo Endara Galimany (ADOC), 1994– Ernesto Pérez Balladares (PRD)

Political system

The constitution underwent a major revision in April 1983, following a referendum. This has resulted in a new, single-chamber Legislative Assembly of 72 members, elected by universal adult suffrage, through a simple plurality voting system, for a five-year term. The president is elected in the same way for a similar period of office. He or she is assisted by two elected vice presidents and an appointed cabinet.

Political parties

There are some 13 political parties, nine of them functioning in three main blocs. The most significant individual parties are the Democratic Revolutionary Party (PRD), the Arnulfista Party (PA), the Authentic Liberal Party (PLA), the National Liberal Republican Movement (MOLIRENA), and the Papa Egoro Movement (MPE).

The PRD was founded in 1979 by supporters of General Torrijos and the army, headed by General Antonio Noriega. It now has a centre-right orientation.

The PA was formed in 1990 and has a left-of-centre orientation.

The PLA was an ally of the PA in the 1994 elections and has a similar orientation.

MOLIRENA was formed in 1982. It has a right-of-centre orientation.

The MPE was founded in 1991 and has a moderate, centre-left orientation. It is led by Rubén Blades.

Latest elections

In the May 1994 elections there were three main electoral blocs: Pueblo Unido, led by the PRD; Alianza Democrática, led by the PA, and including the PLA; and Cambio 94, led by MOLIRENA. The MPE fought the elections independently.

The Pueblo Unido candidate, Ernesto Pérez, won the presidential election with 33.3% of the vote, and the bloc also won most seats, but not an overall majority, in the Legislative Assembly. In the latter, the PRD captured 21 seats, the PA, 12, the MPE, 6, MOLIRENA, 5 and other parties, 27 seats.

Political history

Established as a Spanish colony early in the 16th century, Panama became part of Spanish New Granada (Columbia) in 1821 and, with the help of the United States, achieved full independence in 1903. The US support was a form of enlightened self-interest because, at the same time, it bought the rights to build the Panama Canal, connecting the Atlantic and Pacific Oceans. This was eventually opened in 1914. Under the original 1903 treaty the United States was given control of a ten-mile wide strip of territory, known as the Canal Zone, in perpetuity. At the same time, Panama was guaranteed US protection and an annuity. In 1939 Panama's protectorate status was ended by mutual agreement, and in 1974 the two countries agreed to negotiate an eventual complete transfer of the canal to Panama, despite opposition from the US Congress.

In 1977 two treaties were signed by Panama's president, General Omar Torrijos Herrera, and the US president, Jimmy Carter. One transferred the canal and the other guaranteed its subsequent neutrality. A referendum in Panama approved the change but the US Senate demanded amendments to the effect that, after the complete transfer of all facilities in 1999 only Panamanian forces would be stationed in the zone, and that the United States would have the right to use force to keep the canal open if it became obstructed. On this revised basis, the two treaties were finally approved.

The 1980s saw a deterioration in the state of Panama's economy, with opposition to the austerity measures which the government introduced to try to halt the decline. In the 1984 elections, after a very close result, Dr Nicolás Ardito Barletta, the Democratic Revolutionary Party (PRD) candidate, was declared the winner, but in 1985 he resigned, amid speculation that he had been forced to by the commander of the National Guard, General Manuel Noriega (b. 1940). Relations between Panama and the United States deteriorated with the departure of President Barletta, the US administration of President Ronald Reagan announcing a cut in its financial aid. Barletta was succeeded by Eric Arturo Delvalle, who immediately set about seeking a national consensus on economic policy. US criticism continued, Noriega being accused of drug trafficking. In February 1988 President Delvalle attempted to dismiss Noriega as head of the armed forces and was immediately voted out of office by the National Assembly and replaced by the former education minister, Manuel Solis Palma. Delvalle's downfall was seen as further evidence of the power and influence of General Noriega, who had become the country's *de facto* ruler. US support for the former president was also seen as a reason for his demise. The US government's immediate reaction was to increase its forces in the Canal Zone, as a show of military strength, and to put economic pressure on Panama by freezing its assets in the United States.

With mounting unrest in the country, a group of Panamanian officers, led by Police Chief Leonidas Macias, attempted a coup but this was quickly foiled by troops loyal to Noriega. The US administration then attempted to negotiate the general's departure by offering to drop federal charges against him for drug trafficking but the attempted deal had the effect of discrediting the Reagan administration and strengthening support for Noriega.

In May 1989 the elections for the Legislative Assembly were clearly fraudulent and were eventually declared invalid. The United States put more pressure on Noriega to resign and strengthened its Canal Zone garrison. Then, in December 1989, US troops were ordered to enter the country by force to arrest him. The mission was code-named 'Operation Just Cause'. After seeking refuge in the Vatican embassy, Noriega eventually gave himself up and was taken to Florida for trial, and in 1992 was found guilty of drugs offences. He was given a 40-year prison sentence. In October 1993 he was also convicted of murder in Panamanian courts. The US authorities installed Guillermo Endara as president in December 1989. He was said to have won the earlier invalid election and now embarked on an economic reform programme, including privatization.

The influence of the military in Panama was progressively reduced and in December 1991 the Assembly formally dissolved the army. However, a referendum held in November 1992 rejected a reform package, which would have outlawed the creation of a standing army. The position was eventually clarified in August 1994, when the Legislative Assembly overwhelmingly approved a constitutional amendment abolishing the army 'in order to avoid a return to military rule'.

In May 1994, in the first completely free elections in the nation's history, the Revolutionary Democratic Party (PRD) won the presidency, in the person of Ernesto Pérez (b. 1946), and most seats in the Legislative Assembly. Pérez, a US-educated millionaire businessman, formed a minority PRD government.

ST CHRISTOPHER (ST KITTS) AND NEVIS

St Kitts-Nevis

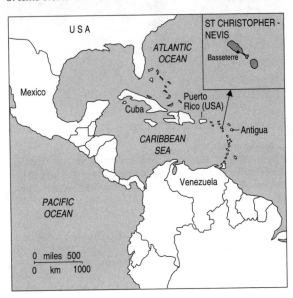

Capital: Basseterre

Social and economic data
Area: 261 km^2
Population: 44,000*
Pop. density per km^2: 168*
Urban population: 41%**
Literacy rate: 98%**
GDP: $165 million**; per-capita GDP: $4,100**
Government defence spending (% of GDP): N/A
Currency: Caribbean dollar
Economy type: middle income
Labour force in agriculture: N/A

*1994
**1992

Ethnic composition
The population is almost entirely of African descent.

Religions
The majority of the population belongs to the Anglican, 36%, and Methodist, 32%, Protestant churches, with a Roman Catholic, 11%, minority.

Political features
State type: liberal democratic
Date of state formation: 1983

Political structure: federal
Executive: parliamentary
Assembly: one-chamber
Party structure: multiparty
Human rights rating: N/A
International affiliations: ACP, ACS, CARICOM, CW, IBRD, IMF, IWC, OAS, OECS, UN, WTO

Local and regional government
Despite the smallness of the land area and population, a limited federal system operates. Nevis island has its own Assembly, of five elected and three nominated members, a prime minister and cabinet and a deputy governor general representing the British monarch. Nevis has the constitutional right to secede from the union with St Christopher, subject to approval in a referendum. The two islands are divided into parishes, for administrative purposes, St Kitts having nine and Nevis five parishes.

Head of state
Queen Elizabeth II, represented by Governor General Sir Clement Arrindell since 1983

Head of government
Prime Minister Denzil Douglas, since 1995

Political leaders since 1970
1967–78 Robert Bradshaw (SKLP), 1978–79 Paul Southwell (SKLP), 1979–80 Lee L Moore (SKLP), 1980–95 Kennedy Alphonse Simmonds (PAM-NRP coalition), 1995– Denzil Douglas (SKLP)

Political system
The islands of Saint Christopher, often called St Kitts, and Nevis are a federation constituting an independent state within the Commonwealth. Although the total population is only about 44,000 it has, in effect, a federal constitution which dates from independence in 1983 and provides for a parliamentary system for the two islands, on the lines of that of the United Kingdom. The governor general is the formal head of state, representing the British monarch.

There is a single-chamber National Assembly of 14 members. Eleven representatives are popularly elected for five years by universal adult suffrage, through a simple plurality voting system, and three senators are appointed by the governor general: two on the advice of the prime minister and one on the advice of the leader of the opposition. The governor general also appoints the prime minister and cabinet who are drawn from and responsible to the Assembly. As in the United Kingdom, the leader of the second largest party in the Assembly is the official leader of the opposition.

Political parties
There are currently five political parties, the four most significant being the People's Action Movement (PAM), the Nevis Reformation Party (NRP), the Saint Kitts-Nevis Labour Party (SKLP), and the Concerned Citizens' Movement (CCM).

The PAM was formed in 1965. It has a centre-right orientation.

The NRP was created in 1970 as the focus of a movement to secure the separation of Nevis from St Kitts. It has a centrist orientation.

The SKLP is the country's oldest political organization, dating back to the Workers' League of 1932. It is a moderate, left-of-centre party.

The CCM is a recently formed centrist party.

Latest elections
In the July 1995 general election the SKLP won 7 National Assembly seats, the CCM, 2, the PAM, 1, and the NRP, 1.

Political history
St Christopher (known locally as Liamuiga), visited by Christopher Columbus (1451–1506) in 1493, was the first British colony in the West Indies, dating back to 1623, and Nevis was settled very soon afterwards. Anguilla (see Chapter 8) was joined to the two islands in 1816 and between 1871 and 1956 they were administered as part of the Leeward Islands Federation. Sugar cane planting became the mainstay of the economy. After World War I a campaign began for the islands' independence. The Labour Party (SKLP) was formed in 1932 as the vanguard of the independence movement. Saint Christopher–Nevis–Anguilla joined the West Indies Federation in 1956 and remained in membership until its dissolution in 1962. There was an abortive attempt to form a smaller East Caribbean Federation and then the three islands became Associated States, with internal self-government, within the Commonwealth, in 1967.

Robert Bradshaw, leader of the SKLP, became the first prime minister and was re-elected in 1971 and 1975. In 1970 the Nevis Reformation Party (NRP) was formed, calling for separation for Nevis, and the following year Anguilla, disagreeing with the government in St Christopher, chose to return to being a British dependency. Bradshaw died in 1978 and was succeeded by his deputy, Paul Southwell, but he, too, died the following year to be replaced by Lee L Moore.

The 1980 general election produced a 'hung' Assembly and, although the SKLP won more than 50% of the popular vote, a PAM–NRP coalition government was formed, with the People's Action Movement (PAM) founder and leader, Dr Kennedy A Simmonds (b. 1936), as prime minister. Full independence was scheduled for 1983 and the SKLP argued there there should be a general election before then but this was rejected by the government, in the face of sometimes violent opposition.

On 1 September 1983 St Christopher and Nevis became a fully independent federal state, within the Commonwealth, with an opportunity for Nevis to secede, under certain conditions, being written into the constitution. In the 1984 general election the PAM–NRP coalition was decisively returned to office.

The 1993 general election produced an inconclusive result and a minor political crisis, as Simmonds tried to construct a new government. Because of demonstrations outside government offices, the governor general declared a one-day state of emergency but, eventually, a PAM–NRP administration was agreed, with Simmonds continuing as prime minister.

A snap election in July 1995 resulted in a win for the SKLP and its leader, Denzil Douglas, became prime minister. The islands' proximity to Colombia have placed them within direct line of the 'cocaine route' and in 1995 the growth of drug trafficking became apparent, with retaliations by drug dealers as the police tried to stamp out the menace.

ST LUCIA

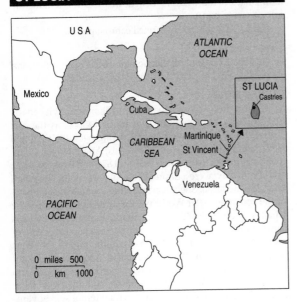

Capital: Castries

Social and economic data
Area: 620 km²
Population: 156,000*
Pop. density per km²: 242*
Urban population: 47%**
Literacy rate: 82%**
GDP: $450 million**; per-capita GDP $2,900**
Government defence spending (% of GDP): N/A**
Currency: East Caribbean dollar
Economy type: middle income
Labour force in agriculture: N/A

*1994
**1992

Ethnic composition
The great majority of the population is of African descent.

Religions
Eighty per cent of the population is Roman Catholic. The rest belongs mainly to the Anglican or other Protestant churches.

Political features
State type: liberal democratic
Date of state formation: 1979
Political structure: unitary
Executive: parliamentary
Assembly: two-chamber
Party structure: two-party
Human rights rating: N/A
International affiliations: ACP, ACS, CARICOM, CW, IBRD, IMF, IWC, NAM, OAS, OECS, UN, WTO

Local and regional government
The country is divided into 16 parishes, each representing a town or village. They have partly elected and partly appointed councils.

Head of state
Queen Elizabeth II, represented by Governor General Stanislaus A James since 1989

Head of government
Prime Minister John G M Compton, since 1982

Political leaders since 1970
1964–79 John Compton (UWP), 1979–81 Allan Louisy (SLP), 1981–82 Winston Cenac (SLP), 1982– John Compton (UWP)

Political system
The constitution dates from independence in 1979. It provides for a constitutional monarchy with a parliamentary system based broadly on that of the United Kingdom. There is a two-chamber Parliament, comprising a Senate, of 11 appointed members, and a House of Assembly, of 17 members, elected from single-member constituencies by universal adult suffrage, through a simple plurality system of voting. Members of the Senate are appointed by the governor general, six on the advice of the prime minister, three on the advice of the leader of the opposition and two after wider consultation. Parliament has a life of five years but is subject to dissolution within that period. The governor general appoints a prime minister and cabinet on the basis of House of Assembly support. They are all drawn from and responsible to it. The leader of the party with the second highest number of seats in the House is the official leader of the opposition.

Political parties
There are three active political parties, the United Workers' Party (UWP), the St Lucia Labour Party (SLP), and the Progressive Labour Party (PLP).
  The UWP was founded in 1961 by John Compton as a breakaway from the SLP, which itself developed from the Workers' Union in the late 1940s. The PLP was formed in 1981 by SLP dissidents. All three parties have moderate, left-of-centre orientations.

Latest elections
In the April 1992 general election the UWP won for a third, consecutive time, taking 11 of the Assembly seats and the SLP captured the other six.

Political history
Saint Lucia was ceded to Britain by France at the Treaty of Paris of 1814 and remained a British colony within the Windward Islands federal system until 1960. The federal system was ended and, in 1967, it acquired internal self-government as a West Indies Associated State. The founder and leader of the United Workers' Party (UWP), John Compton (b. 1926), a UK-trained barrister, became prime minister with the St Lucia Labour Party (SLP) forming the opposition. In 1975 the Associated States agreed to seek independence separately and, in February 1979, after prolonged negotiations, St Lucia achieved full independence within the Commonwealth, with Compton as prime minister.
  Later that year the SLP returned to power under its leader, Allan Louisy, but a split developed within the party and in 1981 Louisy was forced to resign, being replaced by the Attorney General Winston Cenac. Soon afterwards George

Odlum, who had been Louisy's deputy, left, with two other SLP members, to form a new party, the Progressive Labour Party (PLP). For the next year the Cenac government had to fight off calls for a change of government which culminated in a general strike. Cenac eventually resigned and in the general election held in May 1982 the UWP won a decisive victory enabling John Compton to return as prime minister. The UWP retained its control of the House of Assembly in the 1987 and 1992 elections.

Banana production remains crucial to the country's economy, providing 40% of export earnings, and a fall in prices in 1993 resulted in unrest and strikes by farmers and agricultural workers. Unemployment is high, but tourism is being developed. In 1991 exploratory moves were made towards a Windward Islands Federation, with Dominica, Grenada and St Vincent, but little progress was subsequently evident.

ST VINCENT AND THE GRENADINES

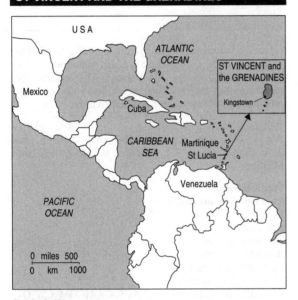

Capital: Kingstown

Social and economic data
Area: 390 km²
Population: 117,000*
Pop. density per km²: 300*
Urban population: 25%**
Literacy rate: 96%**
GDP: $187 million**; per-capita GDP: $1,750**
Government defence spending (% of GDP): N/A
Currency: Caribbean dollar
Economy type: middle income
Labour force in agriculture: 50%**

*1994
**1992

Ethnic composition
Most of the original, indigenous Caribs have disappeared and the population is now largely of African origin.

Religions
The great majority of people are Christian: Anglicans, 42%, Methodists, 21%, or Roman Catholics, 12%.

Political features
State type: liberal democratic
Date of state formation: 1979
Political structure: unitary
Executive: parliamentary
Assembly: one-chamber
Party structure: two-party
Human rights rating: N/A
International affiliations: ACP, ACS, CARICOM, CW, IBRD, IMF, IWC, OAS, OECS, UN, WTO

Local and regional government
For administrative purposes, the country is divided into five parishes with 13 divisions within them.

Head of state
Queen Elizabeth II, represented by Governor General David Jack since 1985

Head of government
Prime Minister James F Mitchell, since 1984

Political leaders since 1970
1967–72 Milton Cato (SVLP), 1972–74 James Mitchell (PPP), 1974–79 Milton Cato (SVLP–PPP coalition), 1979–84 Milton Cato (SVLP), 1984– James Mitchell (NDP)

Political system
The constitution dates from independence in 1979. It provides for a constitutional monarchy with a parliamentary system of government based in several respects on that of the United Kingdom, a resident governor general representing the British monarch. There is a single-chamber House of Assembly, with 21 members. Of these, 15 representatives are directly elected by universal adult suffrage, through a simple plurality voting system, four senators are appointed by the governor general on the advice of the prime minister and two senators are appointed on the advice of the leader of the opposition. The Assembly has a life of five years but is subject to dissolution within that time. The governor general appoints a prime minister and cabinet who are drawn from and responsible to the Assembly. The leader of the party with the second largest number of seats in the Assembly is the official leader of the opposition.

Political parties
There are some four active political parties, the two most significant being the New Democratic Party (NDP) and the Unity Labour Party (ULP).

The NDP was formed in 1975 by James Mitchell, a former member of the St Vincent Labour Party (SVLP) and prime minister. It has a right-of-centre orientation.

The ULP was formed in 1994 by a merger of the SVLP and the Movement for National Unity (MNU). It has a moderate centre-left orientation.

Latest elections
In the February 1994 general election the NDP won 12 Assembly seats and James Mitchell continued as prime

minister. The remaining three seats were won by a centre-left alliance, led by the ULP.

Political history

The island of St Vincent was visited by Christopher Columbus (1451–1506) in 1498 on St Vincent's day. Possession was disputed by France and Britain during the 17th and 18th centuries, but in 1783, under the terms of the Treaty of Versailles, the island, along with the Grenadines, a chain of 32 tiny islands and cays, was finally ceded to Britain. The colony was part of the West Indies Federation until it was dissolved in 1962. The islands then acquired internal self-government in 1969 as an Associated State, within the Commonwealth. They achieved full independence, still within the Commonwealth, as St Vincent and the Grenadines, in October 1979.

Until the 1980s two political parties dominated politics in the islands, the St Vincent Labour Party (SVLP) and the People's Political Party (PPP). Milton Cato, SVLP leader, was prime minister at independence but his leadership was challenged in 1981 when a decline in the economy and his attempts to introduce new industrial relations legislation resulted in a general strike. Cato survived mainly because of divisions in the opposition parties and in 1984, hoping to take advantage of these divisions, he called an early general election. The New Democratic Party (NDP), which had been formed by an SVLP defector and former prime minister, James Mitchell (b. 1931), won a surprising victory, which was confirmed in 1989, when the NDP won all 15 elective seats.

In September 1991 provisional moves were made to integrate with Dominica, Grenada and St Lucia into a Windward Islands Federation and, after being re-elected in February 1994, Prime Minister Mitchell said he would still pursue the proposal.

Banana production and tourism are the staples of the islands' economies.

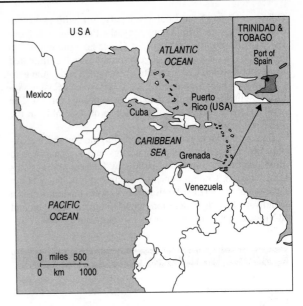

TRINIDAD AND TOBAGO

The Republic of Trinidad and Tobago

Capital: Port of Spain

Social and economic data
Area: 5,130 km^2
Population: 1,300,000*
Pop. density per km^2: 253*
Urban population: 66%**
Literacy rate: 95%**
GDP: $4,888 million**; per-capita GDP: $3,730**
Government defence spending (% of GDP): 1.4%**
Currency: Trinidad and Tobago dollar
Economy type: middle income
Labour force in agriculture: 12%**

*1994
**1992

Ethnic composition
There are two main ethnic groups, one comprising Africans, who were originally brought in as slaves to work on the sugar plantations, and the other East Indians, who came to the country as indentured labourers from India after the abolition of slavery in the 1830s. There are also minorities of Europeans, Afro-Europeans, and Chinese. The original Carib population has largely disappeared. Today the country is 40% Indian, 40% black, and 20% mixed race.

Religions
About 34% of the population is Roman Catholic, about 25% Hindu, about 15% Anglican and about 6% Sunni Muslim.

Political features
State type: liberal democratic
Date of state formation: 1962
Political structure: unitary
Executive: parliamentary
Assembly: two-chamber
Party structure: multiparty
Human rights rating: 84%
International affiliations: ACP, ACS, CARICOM, CW, G-24, IBRD, IMF, NAM, OAS, SELA, UN, WTO

Local and regional government
The country is divided into four self-governing cities, six counties, and the semi-autonomous island of Tobago. The local government system displays some of the features of the unreformed system of the United Kingdom, with elected councillors and aldermen being politically responsible for the provision of local services.

Head of state
President Noor Mohammed Hassanali, since 1987

Head of government
Prime Minister Patrick Manning, since 1991

Political leaders since 1970
1959–81 Eric Williams (PNM), 1981–86 George Chambers (PNM), 1986–91 Arthur Robinson (NAR), 1991– Patrick Manning (PNM)

Political system

Trinidad and Tobago is an independent republic within the Commonwealth. The 1976 constitution provides for a president, who is a constitutional head of state, and a two-chamber assembly, consisting of a Senate of 31 members and a House of Representatives of 36 members. The president appoints the prime minister and cabinet who are collectively responsible to the House of Representatives. The leader of the party with the second largest number of seats in the House is the official leader of the opposition. The president also appoints the 31 senators, 16 on the advice of the prime minister, six on the advice of the leader of the opposition, and nine after wider consultation. The 36 members of the House of Representatives are elected by universal adult suffrage, through a simple plurality voting system. The assembly has a life of five years.

Tobago island was given its own House of Assembly in 1980. It has 15 members, 12 popularly elected and three chosen by the majority party. It achieved full internal self-government in 1987.

Political parties

There are some four major political parties. They are the National Alliance for Reconstruction (NAR), the People's National Movement (PNM), the United National Congress (UNC), and the Movement for Social Transformation (Motion).

The NAR was formed in 1984 as a coalition of moderate, left-wing parties. It became a united, separate party in 1986. It has a nationalistic, left-of-centre orientation.

The PNM was founded in 1956 by Eric Williams, a well-known Caribbean historian. It had its origins in the Teachers' Economic and Cultural Association. The PNM has a nationalistic, moderate centrist stance. It seeks to appeal to all races, but its chief constituency is black.

Until the 1991 general election the NAR and the PNM had dominated the country's politics. This domination was challenged by the formation of the UNC, led by Basdeo Panday, and Motion.

The UNC was formed by NAR dissidents in 1989 and draws its support from the Indian community. Motion was formed in the same year. Both have left-of-centre orientations.

Latest elections

In the November 1995 general election the PNM won 17 seats, with 48% of the vote, and the UNC also 17, with a 45% vote share. The NAR won the remaining two seats in Tobago.

Political history

Trinidad was colonized by Spain in the 16th century and ceded to Britain, under the Treaty of Amiens, in 1802. Tobago had been colonized by Dutch, English, and French settlers and became a British colony, in the Windward Islands group, in 1814. The two islands became a joint British Crown Colony in 1899 and, after World War II, movement towards self-government, and eventual independence, began.

The country's first political party, the People's National Movement (PNM), was formed by Dr Eric Williams, a renowned historian, in 1956, and when the colony was granted internal self-government in 1959 he became the first chief minister. Between 1958 and 1961 it was a member of the Federation of the West Indies but withdrew and achieved full independence, within the Commonwealth, in 1967, Dr Williams becoming the first prime minister. His moderate policies provoked an army mutiny and Black Power revolt in 1970.

A new constitution was adopted in 1976 which made the country a republic. The former governor general, Ellis Clarke, became the first president and Dr Williams continued as prime minister. He died in March 1981 without having nominated a successor and the president appointed George Chambers for an interim period until the PNM formally adopted him as leader, in May 1981. In the general election of that year the PNM marginally increased its majority, while the leader of a moderate left-wing party grouping, the Trinidad and Tobago National Alliance, Arthur 'Ray' Robinson (b. 1926), a former deputy leader of the PNM, was leader of the opposition.

In the next few years the National Alliance was reorganized into a more credible party, as the National Alliance for Reconstruction (NAR), and in the 1986 general election it swept the PNM from power and Arthur Robinson, a UK-trained barrister, became prime minister. By 1988 the fall in world oil prices had had an adverse effect on the economy, resulting in strains within the NAR and the government. In July 1990 an attempted coup by 120 Islamic fundamentalists, who held parliamentarians and ministers hostage, shooting Prime Minister Robinson in the legs, was foiled after a six-day siege. Disenchantment with Robinson led to an astonishing defeat for his party in the December 1991 general election, its seat holding dropping from 33 to two. Patrick Manning, leader of the triumphant PNM, became the new prime minister.

In August 1995 the speaker of the House of Representatives, Occah Seapaul, was placed temporarily under house arrest for refusing to resign after allegedly bringing her position into disrepute after trying unsuccessfully to sue a former business partner for defrauding her. A state of emergency was briefly imposed. The opposition parties described the speaker's detention as madness.

A general election, held in November 1995, produced a dead heat between the PNM and the predominantly Indian UNC. A UNC-led government led by Basdeo Panday and supported by the Tobago-based NAR was expected to be formed.

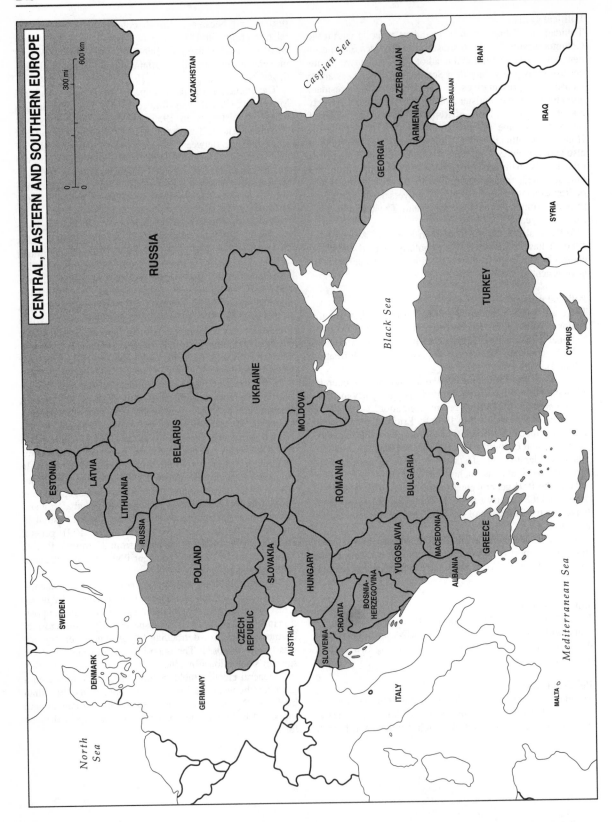

CENTRAL, EASTERN AND SOUTHERN EUROPE

300 mi
600 km

North Sea

Mediterranean Sea

Black Sea

Caspian Sea

RUSSIA

KAZAKHSTAN

AZERBAIJAN

AZERBAIJAN

ARMENIA

GEORGIA

IRAN

IRAQ

SYRIA

TURKEY

CYPRUS

UKRAINE

MOLDOVA

BELARUS

ESTONIA

LATVIA

LITHUANIA

RUSSIA

POLAND

CZECH REPUBLIC

SLOVAKIA

HUNGARY

AUSTRIA

SLOVENIA

CROATIA

BOSNIA-HERZEGOVINA

YUGOSLAVIA

ROMANIA

BULGARIA

MACEDONIA

ALBANIA

GREECE

SWEDEN

DENMARK

GERMANY

ITALY

MALTA

Central, Eastern, and Southern Europe

Before 1991 it was sensible to view Central and Eastern Europe as a politically homogenous block. There were nine states, Albania, Bulgaria, Czechoslovakia, East Germany, Hungary, Poland, Romania, the Soviet Union, and Yugoslavia, each having a communist political system. However, between 1989–91 communism collapsed; the federations of Czechoslovakia, Russia, and Yugoslavia splintered into 22 separate sovereign states; East Germany was reunited with the Federal Republic of Germany; and emergent democratic regimes were widely established across the region. Thus for this second edition, Eastern Europe, essentially a political construct, has been replaced by a more coherent geographical entity, Central, Eastern, and Southern Europe. This new region embraces the postcommunist successor states of Central and Eastern Europe as well as the three Southern European states, Cyprus, Greece, and Turkey, but excludes the five countries of 'Turkestan' (Kazakhstan, Kyrgyzstan, Tajikistan, Turkmenistan, and Uzbekistan), which were formerly part of the Soviet Union but are rightly part of Asia.

The 25 states of Central, Eastern, and Southern Europe, including Russia, the world's largest country, cover 20 million square kilometres. This is equivalent to almost a sixth of the world's land area. However, with a combined population of 435 million, the region accounts for only 8% of the global population, and its GDP of $976 billion is 4% of the world's total. Per-capita GDP in the region averaged $2,241 in c. 1992. Three-quarters of the states have middle incomes, five low incomes and only two, Cyprus and Greece, high incomes.

Politically, the region comprises 20 emergent democracies, two authoritarian nationalist regimes and three liberal democracies: Cyprus, Greece, which is a member of the European Union and NATO, and Turkey, which is also a member of NATO. However, as noted in Chapter 3, at least seven of the region's emergent democracies (Albania, Belarus, Georgia, Macedonia, Moldova, Romania, and Yugoslavia) are still very much in an embryonic state and possess a number of authoritarian nationalist features, while democracy in Bosnia-Herzegovina has been nonfunctioning as a result of the ongoing civil war. The republican form of government is uniform across the region and only three states have federal structures: Bosnia-Herzegovina, Russia, and Yugoslavia. In half the region's states the limited presidential executive type is found, with the parliamentary executive in a quarter, the dual executive in four, and the unlimited presidential in two. All of the countries have multiparty systems. However, in many of the states party structures are weakly developed and, consequently, government coalitions fragile and unstable. For example, 29 minor parties secured representation in Poland's parliament in October 1991 and in 1993 between 5–7 parties held seats in the parliaments of Bulgaria, the Czech and Slovak republics, Hungary, and Romania. This is because these states are currently situated in only the first or second phase, that of 'basic democracy' and constitution-building, of the three-phase transition from communist totalitarianism to a mixed

economy-based political pluralism that has been posited by Zbigniew Brzezinski. Entry into the crucial third phase, one characterized by a full legal and entrepreneurial culture and the existence of a stable party system, may take anything between 10–20 years. In three-quarters of the region, the electoral system is based on proportional representation. Elsewhere, the second ballot majoritarian system is employed in five states and the single plurality in one.

Socio-economically Central, Eastern, and Southern Europe is a middle income, or 'Second World', region. However, the pattern of income distribution and spending differs significantly from that found in a similar middle-income region, Latin America, with the state, as a result of the legacy of communism, playing a much greater role in economic and social life. For example, in 1992 social spending on welfare, education, and health accounted for 25% of GDP in Central and Eastern Europe compared to just 10% in Latin America. In addition, government defence spending exceeded 3% of GDP in 18 of the region's states, compared to just three states in South America, and was between 7–11% in Russia, Cyprus Ukraine, and Yugoslavia.

Since 1989 the nations of Central and Eastern Europe have abandoned central planning and embraced the market to differing degrees and with varying measures of success. One consequence of this 'transition to capitalism' was a severe contraction in regional and national GDPs, by at least 20%, between 1989–94. In addition, rates of inflation and unemployment increased sharply as uncompetitive, state-subsidized enterprises were left to compete in an 'open economy' and as prices were freed. In some states, notably Poland, Ukraine, Russia, Belarus, Georgia, and Yugoslavia, hyperinflation was experienced during the early 1990s, forcing the adoption of austere stabilization programmes. Only since 1995 has a broad-based growth in GDP been registered within the region.

The most successful and smoothest transition from a planned economy to the free market in Central and Eastern Europe occurred in the Czech Republic, which benefited from its inheritance of a skilled and well-educated workforce and a relatively advanced industrial economy, but also from political stability after 1989, substantial foreign inward investment and the adoption of sensible policies, including a successful mass privatization initiative. In the three Baltic republics of Estonia, Latvia, and Lithuania, and in Hungary, Slovenia, Bulgaria, Slovakia, and Poland, where a radical 'shock therapy' programme was pursued between 1990–93, the transition was also relatively successful. Elsewhere, a combination of political instability and ethnic disputes, which led to civil wars in Armenia, Azerbaijan, Croatia, Bosnia, Yugoslavia, and in parts of Moldova and southern Russia, stymied market-centred economic reform programmes.

The 'market transition' has been associated with considerable social suffering for those who have lacked the skills to adjust and prosper in the new competitive environment. This led to popular disillusionment with some of the more radical liberal-conservative parties, disciples of the Reaganite–Thatcherite 'new right' vision of the unbridled free market, which had initially come to power in Central Europe in 1989–90 after the collapse of communism. As a consequence, in the second wave of postcommunist elections held in Central and Eastern Europe between 1992–95, voters rejected 'new right' conservative parties such as Isamaa in Estonia and the internally divided and politically inexperienced, intelligentsia-led centre-right Popular Front and nationalist coalitions that had held power in Lithuania, Poland, Hungary, and Bulgaria. In their place, they returned to office either maverick populists, such as Vladimir Meciar in Slovakia and Alexander Lukashenko in Belarus, or experienced reformed communists, who pledged to maintain a strong 'social safety net' within the framework of a German-style 'social market economy'. Elsewhere in the region, in Azerbaijan, Georgia, Romania, Russia, Ukraine, and Yugoslavia, ex-communists had never really left power. Clearly then, outside Cyprus, Greece, and Turkey, the communist legacy remains strong, continuing to shape and influence political developments. To understand current political dynamics in Central and Eastern Europe, it is necessary to go beyond the present and examine the historical process by which communism became established and so entrenched in the region during the postwar era and also analyse the forces which led to its dramatic collapse between 1989–91.

The birth and death of communism in Central and Eastern Europe: 1917–91

The first communist regime was established in 1917 in the Soviet Union (USSR) when, following the March and October revolutions, the Tsarist autocracy was toppled and a new socialist republic, under the 'guiding hand' of the Communist Party of the Soviet Union (CPSU), was created. This embraced the current sovereign states of Armenia, Azerbaijan, Belarus, Estonia, Georgia, Latvia, Lithuania, Moldova, Russia, and Ukraine. The other communist political executives in Central and Eastern Europe dated from the end of World War II. In most cases, they were set up with Soviet support soon after their liberation from Nazi occupation, as the Red Army advanced westwards in 1944.

The actual method by which these communist systems were established and the degree of popular support which they initially enjoyed varied substantially from country to country.

In the cases of Poland, the newly created German Democratic Republic (GDR), and Romania, the new system was arbitrarily imposed by fiat.

In Bulgaria and Hungary, more subtle quasi-parliamentary means were pursued, with the Soviet-linked, indigenous communist parties (CPs) initially forming a 'Popular Front' coalition with moderate socialist and radical-centrist groupings. Then, between 1947 and 1949, by establishing control over the media, police, and state electoral commissions, the CPs, despite enjoying less than 15% of popular support, won majorities in the elected assemblies and proceeded to remodel the constitutions in a new one-party direction.

In Czechoslovakia the CP inherited a stronger prewar base and enjoyed broad popular support, so that it was able to secure the majority of the national vote in the free election of May 1946.

Finally, in Albania and Yugoslavia, the new communist regimes, which assumed control in 1944–45, differed significantly from those to the northwest, having been established, without direct Red Army aid, by local guerrilla resistance leaders, Enver Hoxha in Albania and Marshal Tito in Yugoslavia. Because of their 'Partisan' anti-Nazi activities, they initially enjoyed popular support.

By 1949, all the states of contemporary Central and Eastern Europe had communist systems firmly in place. They were initially structured, with the notable exception of Tito's Yugoslavia, in close conformity with the 'Stalinist model' then prevailing in the USSR. This involved tight, hierarchical party control over all aspects of political, social, and cultural life; the promotion of leadership 'personality cults'; the terroristic use of secret police to suppress internal political opposition and dissent; and, in the economic sphere, agrarian collectivization, bureaucratic central planning, and concentration on heavy industrialization.

However, with the maverick exception of Hoxha's Albania, which broke with the USSR in 1961 in opposition to Khrushchev's denunciation of the Stalin era, 'Stalinization' was never fully completed in the Central European satellites. Bulgaria came closest. Elsewhere, internal opposition, pressing for more liberal and inclusive political structures, periodically surfaced in the form of workers' revolts and intelligentsia campaigns, forcing prudent changes of course. In the cases of East Berlin in 1953, Hungary in 1956, and Prague in 1968, Soviet or Warsaw Pact troops had to be employed to restore CP control. In Poland, in December 1981, martial law was imposed by the country's own military forces as a means of suppressing a serious internal challenge to the incumbent Polish United Workers' Party regime.

In Central and Eastern Europe the postwar era was thus characterized, on the one hand, by broad stability and on the other by periodic challenges to the authority of the ruling CPs. The stability was achieved by tight links with their dominant eastern neighbour, the USSR, through the economic, military, and political structures of Comecon, the Warsaw Treaty Organization, and the Comintern. Only the Balkan states of Albania and Yugoslavia remained aloof from these. The recurrent periods of opposition forced policy adjustments and partial departures from the Soviet model in both the political and economic spheres. The sociocultural heterogeneity of this region, coupled with a history of subjection to autocratic, external rule, economic backwardness, and nascent democratization during the interwar decades, were crucial factors helping to explain these conflicting trends. They resulted in the creation of a unique 'political culture'.

With the exception of the Muscovy (RSFSR) heartland of what was the Soviet Union, which formed the core for the successive Kiev-based (10th–12th centuries), Moscow-based (1462–1709) and St Petersburg (Leningrad)-based (1709–1917) Russian empires, state creation came late to Central and Eastern Europe. Albania, Armenia, Bulgaria, Czechoslovakia, Georgia, Hungary, Lithuania, Macedonia, Poland, Romania, Ukraine, and Yugoslavia (Serbia) had formed the cores of ancient and medieval kingdoms, but none had emerged as a substantially coherent nation-state until the late 19th and early 20th centuries. The majority were formed only at the close of World War I.

Before this, and because of their strategically important position between Asia and Northwestern Europe, they found themselves at various times under the authority of either the Turkish, Austrian, German, or Russian empires. As a consequence, Central and Eastern Europe was exposed to a variety of influences, religious, legal, scriptural, and institutional.

Although differing in detail, all the empires had a common autocratic-bureaucratic character. This served to rule out autonomous political evolution in a liberal-democratic direction. Similarly, it checked the growth of national cultural traditions, fostering, instead, localized, subregional identities. These legacies are still apparent today. They generated, on the one hand, deferential and subservient attitudes to those in positions of authority and, on the other hand, regional divisions which have tended to undermine the cohesion of national movements, pro- or antigovernment.

In the economic sphere, the centuries of control by alien empires resulted in 'peripheral' Central and Eastern Europe's relative underdevelopment compared with that of adjoining Western Europe. This arose partly from resource deficiencies, but, more significantly, from the retention of outmoded socio-economic structures, most notably serfdom, more than a century after they had been discarded in the West. Industrial development was consequently retarded and began only fitfully at the close of the 19th century, with the state playing a directing role and large capital-intensive factories becoming the norm. This tended to restrict the growth of urban working-class communities and a virile middle class. Only in eastern Germany and in parts of Czechoslovakia, Slovenia, and West Poland did a more rounded development occur.

During the interwar years, there were significant changes in the East European political and socio-economic scene as new states came into existence and tentative experiments were made with new liberal-democratic constitutional forms. The exception, of course, was the USSR where, under Stalin's lead, attention was focused on establishing 'socialism in one country', by a radical restructuring of the nation's economic and political system.

Elsewhere, the 1919 Treaty of Versailles had established new parliamentary structures, supported by broad franchises and generous proportional representation electoral systems. Unfortunately, the new states were, in many respects, arbitrary territorial constructions, below the foundations of which lay the seeds of internal religious and ethnic conflicts. These differences worked themselves through into the political systems, resulting in a multiplicity of parties achieving assembly representation and creating chronic governmental instability.

Reacting against this, the conservative-nationalist parties who gained the upper hand over centrist-liberal groups during the mid- and later 1920s, proceeded, in all the Central and East European states, with the notable exception of Czechoslovakia, to abrogate parliamentary forms of government and establish new monarchic or presidential autocracies of a quasi-fascist kind.

The resulting regimes, such as those of King Boris in Bulgaria (1934–43), Admiral Horthy in Hungary (1920–44), King Karol in Romania (1930–40), King Zog in Albania (1928–39), Ullmanis in Latvia (1934–39), Voldemaras and Smetona in Lithuania (1926–29 and 1929–40), Marshals Pilsudski and Smigly-Rydz in Poland (1926–35 and 1935–39), and King Alexander and Regent Paul in Yugoslavia

(1929–34 and 1934–39) continued to hold power until the outbreak of World War II. During this period the socialist and communist parties, which had drawn between 10–20% of the national vote during the early 1920s, were proscribed and forced underground.

The interwar years were, therefore, with the notable exception of economically advanced and socially differentiated Czechoslovakia, a period of abortive democratization. Despite its initial failure, this democratic experiment was to have a long-term impact on the 'political culture' of the region, tending to undermine traditional attitudes of political subservience and shifting popular political expectations in a more pluralist direction than in what was the Soviet Union.

During the early postwar period the economic performance of Central and Eastern Europe was creditable, GDP advancing at an average annual rate of 4.5% between 1950 and 1979. As part of this growth process, there was fundamental structural transformation, with a major rural to urban-industrial shift occurring, and the proportion of the population engaged in agriculture fell from 45% in 1960 to 25% in 1985. However, from the later 1970s, as the economies of Central and Eastern Europe 'matured', growth rates slumped. Between 1980 and 1985 regional GDP advanced by only 2% per annum, while in strife-torn and debt-encumbered Poland and Yugoslavia negative growth was recorded.

During this same period, the nations of the Warsaw Pact were faced with an economically crippling 'Cold War' arms race with the West, driven both by innovative new technologies and by the anticommunist rhetoric of the American president, Ronald Reagan (1981–88). This concatenation of developments persuaded Mikhail Gorbachev, who became leader of the CPSU in March 1985, to sanction a radical three-pronged new course for communism in the Soviet Union and its 'satellites'. The centrepiece of the Gorbachev programme was encouragement of market-centred and decentralized economic reforms under the slogan 'perestroika' (economic restructuring) in an effort to inject new life into the region's stagnating economies. This was coupled, second, with détente and military retrenchment overseas, evidenced by the withdrawal of Soviet troops from Afghanistan in 1989, as the existing 'Brezhnev doctrine' of expansionist support for all left-leaning regimes was replaced with a new 'Sinatra doctrine' which accepted that the governments and peoples of USSR 'satellite states' should be allowed to develop in their 'own way'. Third, believing that, for the programme of economic reform to be successful, it needed to be accompanied by greater political freedoms, on a 'social democratic' model, Gorbachev encouraged political openness (glasnost), tolerance of the expression of religious and ethnic identities, and a measure of democratization and 'socialist pluralism' in the political process.

The 'Gorbachev experiment' was a bold and idealistic attempt to breathe new life into communist systems which had become increasingly sclerotic. However, ultimately it was to prove to be a failure since it failed to deliver the promised economic improvements, with living standards deteriorating across Central and Eastern Europe between 1985–89, and because it ignited dangerously divisive and destabilizing nationalist and ethno-religious separatist elements frozen for half a century by communist regimes that had propagated atheism and 'socialist patriotism'.

One basic indicator of the profound sociocultural heterogeneity of Central, Eastern, and Southern Europe is the religious affiliations of its peoples. Within the region, four principal faiths are to be found, with regional concentrations of support. Roman Catholicism predominates in the westerly states of Poland, Lithuania, the Czech and Slovak republics, Croatia, Slovenia, Hungary, and the western Ukraine, most of which were at one time under Austrian imperial control. Protestantism is found in the west-central states of eastern Germany, Estonia, Latvia, the Czech Republic, and Hungary. Eastern Orthodoxy, with its Armenian, Georgian, Greek, Macedonian, Serbian, Romanian, Russian, and Ukrainian branches, is practised in the eastern and southern Slav lands of Armenia, Belarus, Bulgaria, Cyprus, Georgia, Greece, Macedonia, Moldova, Romania, Russia, and Yugoslavia. Islam is the predominant religion in Albania, Azerbaijan, northern Cyprus and southern portions of Bulgaria, the USSR, and Yugoslavia.

The most spiritually homogenous states in Central, Eastern, and Southern Europe are Poland, where 95% of the population are baptized as Catholics, and Greece, where 98% are adherents to the Greek Orthodox faith. The most spiritually heterogenous states are Bosnia-Herzegovnia, with its contending Muslim, Serbian Orthodox, and Croatian Catholic communities and Cyprus, with its Greek Orthodox and Muslim divisions which have led to the partitioning of the island.

The distribution of ethnic and national groups closely follows that of religious communities, adding a further dimension to community rivalries. The most culturally diverse state within the region, not surprisingly when account is taken of its size, is Russia, which embraces more than 100 ethnic-language groups. There have also been intense intrastate ethnic rivalries in Czechoslovakia, between Czechs and Slovaks, leading to the country's division in 1993, and in the Transylvania region of Romania, between Magyar Hungarians and Romanians, precipitating an interstate political crisis in 1988. Even more serious have been the

Central, Eastern, and Southern Europe: social, economic, and political data

Country	c. 1992–94 Area (sq km)	c. 1992–94 Population (m)	c. 1992 Pop. density per sq km	Adult literacy rate (%)	World ranking	c. 1991 Income type	Human rights rating (%)
Albania	27,393	3.300	120	75	112	middle	n/a
Armenia	29,800	3.600	121	99	8	low	n/a
Azerbaijan	86,600	7.300	84	97	44	low	n/a
Belarus	207,600	10.300	50	98	34	middle	n/a
Bosnia-Herzegovina	51,129	4.500	88	93	70	low	n/a
Bulgaria	110,994	8.900	80	95	59	middle	83
Croatia	56,538	4.900	87	97	44	middle	n/a
Cyprus	9,250	0.725	75	91	77	high	n/a
Czech Republic	78,864	10.400	132	99	8	middle	97
Estonia	45,100	1.600	35	99	8	middle	n/a
Georgia	69,700	5.500	79	99	8	low	n/a
Greece	131,944	10.200	78	93	70	high	87
Hungary	93,033	10.500	113	97	44	middle	97
Latvia	64,589	2.700	42	99	8	middle	n/a
Lithuania	65,200	3.800	58	98	34	middle	n/a
Macedonia	25,713	2.000	78	89	82	low	n/a
Moldova	33,700	4.400	131	96	52	middle	n/a
Poland	304,463	38.500	126	99	8	middle	83
Romania	229,027	23.400	102	97	44	middle	82
Russia	17,075,400	149.200	9	99	8	middle	54
Slovakia	49,035	5.300	108	99	8	middle	n/a
Slovenia	20,251	2.000	99	99	8	middle	n/a
Turkey	779,450	59.600	76	81	102	middle	44
Ukraine	603,700	52.200	86	98	34	middle	n/a
Yugoslavia	102,173	10.600	104	93	70	middle	55
Total/average/range	20,350,646	435,425	21	75–99			44–97

Key:

AMS	additional member system	SB	second ballot	Em-dem	Emergent democratic
PL	party list	SP	simple plurality	Auth-nat	Authoritarian nationalist
PR	proportional representation	Lib-dem	Liberal democratic	Unlim-pres	Unlimited presidential

ethnic rivalries in Yugoslavia. These resulted in the ruling communist party becoming factionalized along ethnic-regional lines and ultimately, in 1991, to secession from the federation by Croatia and Slovenia.

In the Soviet Union, which had comprised 15 'sovereign republics', it was the release of long pent-up ethnic tensions and nationalist aspirations by Mikhail Gorbachev's glasnost policy which ultimately proved to be corrosive of the entire communist edifice. In the three Baltic republics and in Armenia, Georgia, and the western Ukraine nationalist sentiment was especially powerful and during 1990–91 'sovereignty' and independence declarations were issued by the parliaments of these states. In addition, revenues and resources were held back from the centre, crippling the USSR's tightly integrated planned economy, while the Red Army troops became embroiled in policing internal ethnic conflicts, notably in the Baltic, Caucasus, and Central Asian regions. In August 1991 a last-ditch effort was made by communist hardliners to recentralize political and economic authority within the Union, with Gorbachev being ousted. However,

this ill-organized putsch lasted just 61 hours and destroyed any lingering popular legitimacy that the CPSU may have held. Gorbachev subsequently returned to power, but his credibility was fatally diminished and within four months the Soviet Union had been dissolved and communism abandoned.

The collapse of communism occurred two years earlier in the 'satellite states' of Central Europe. There the pacesetters for reform were Hungary, where in February 1989 an internally reformed communist party abandoned its constitutionally guaranteed leading role and established a new pluralist political system, and Poland, where in April 1989 a historic accord was reached between the communist party and the Solidarity free trade union, in which the formation of opposition parties was sanctioned and the state's media monopoly lifted. In East Germany, Czechoslovakia, and Bulgaria, intelligentsia-led 'Popular Front' organizations, heirs to earlier human rights bodies such as Charter '77, sprang up between 1988–89 to press for democratization. Large-scale prodemocracy demonstrations were held during 1989–90,

Table 53

World ranking	Date of state formation	State structure	State type	Executive type	Number of assembly chambers	Party structure	Lower house electoral system
	1912	U	Em-dem	Lim-pres	1	multi	PR-AMS
	1991	U	Auth-nat	Unlim-pres	1	multi	PR-AMS
	1991	U	Auth-nat	Unlim-pres	1	multi	PR-AMS
	1991	U	Em-dem	Lim-pres	1	multi	SB
	1992	F	Em-dem/trans	Lim-pres	2	multi	SB
30	1908	U	Em-dem	Parliamentary	1	multi	PR-PL
	1991	U	Em-dem	Lim-pres	2	multi	PR-PL
	1960	U	Lib-dem	Lim-pres	1	multi	SP
9	1993	U	Em-dem	Dual	2	multi	PR-PL
	1918/1991	U	Em-dem	Dual	1	multi	PR-PL
	1991	U	Em-dem/trans	Lim-pres	1	multi	PR-AMS
26	1829	U	Lib-dem	Parliamentary	1	multi	PR-PL
9	1918	U	Em-dem	Parliamentary	1	multi	PR-AMS
	1920/1991	U	Em-dem	Parliamentary	1	multi	PR-PL
	1919/1991	U	Em-dem	Dual	1	multi	PR-AMS
	1992	U	Em-dem	Lim-pres	1	multi	SB
	1991	U	Em-dem	Lim-pres	1	multi	PR-PL
30	1918	U	Em-dem	Lim-pres	2	multi	PR-PL
33	1881	U	Em-dem	Lim-pres	2	multi	PR-PL
69	1547/1917/1991	F	Em-dem	Lim-pres	2	multi	PR-AMS
	1993	U	Em-dem	Parliamentary	1	multi	PR-PL
	1991	U	Em-dem	Dual	2	multi	PR-AMS
85	1923	U	Lib-dem	Parliamentary	1	multi	PR-PL
	1918/1991	U	Em-dem	Lim-pres	1	multi	SB
68	1918/1992	F	Em-dem	Lim-pres	2	multi	PR-AMS

Lim-pres	Limited presidential
Trans	Transitional

exerting sufficient popular pressure to persuade the ruling communist parties to step down from power peacefully and hold multiparty elections. Only in Albania and Romania, where the reviled dictator Nicolae Ceauşescu was forced from office and executed in December 1989, was the transition violent. Elsewhere, the collapse of communist regimes occurred with a whimper rather than a bang. The once dominant ruling parties were undermined by their lack of popular legitimacy, their out-of-touch and gerontocratic leadership, their inept economic management, and, perhaps most crucially, by the refusal of the Soviet Union to provide, or threaten to provide, external military support on the models of East Berlin in 1953, Budapest in 1956, and Prague in 1968.

Recommended reading

Ascherson, N '1989 in Eastern Europe: Constitutional Representative Democracy as a 'Return to Normality'?', Chap. 12 in J Dunn (ed.) *Democracy: The Unfinished Journey 508 BC to AD 1993*, Oxford University Press, 1992

Garton Ash, T *We the People: Revolution of '89 Witnessed in Warsaw, Budapest, Berlin and Prague*, Granta, 1990

Banac, I (ed.) *Eastern Europe in Revolution*, Cornell University Press, 1992

Berglund, S and Dellenbrant, J A (eds) *The New Democracies in Eastern Europe: Party Systems and Political Cleavages*, Edward Elgar, 1994

Brzezinski, Z *The Grand Failure: The Birth and Death of Communism in the Twentieth Century*, Macdonald, 1989

Glenny, M *The Rebirth of History: Eastern Europe in the Age of Democracy*, Penguin, 1990

Hawkes, N (ed.) *Tearing down the Curtain: The People's Revolution in Eastern Europe*, The Observer, 1990

Lewin, M *The Gorbachev Phenomenon: A Historical Introduction*, Hutchinson Radius, 1989

Roskin, M G *The Rebirth of East Europe*, Prentice-Hall, 1991

Sakwa, R *Russian Politics and Society*, Routledge, 1993

Shopflin, G *Politics in Eastern Europe 1945–1992*, Blackwell, 1993

Sword, K (ed.) *The Times Guide to Eastern Europe: The Changing Face of the Warsaw Pact*, Times Books, 1990

White, S, Batt, J and Lewis, P G (eds) *Developments in East European Politics*, Macmillan, 1993

ALBANIA

Republic of Albania
Republika e Shqipërisë

Capital: Tiranë

Social and economic data
Area: 27,393 km^2
Population: 3,300,000*
Pop. density per km^2: 120*
Urban population: 36%**
Literacy rate: 75%
GDP: $3,600 million**; per-capita GDP: $1,125**
Government defence spending (% of GDP): 3.5%**
Currency: lek
Economy type: middle income
Labour force in agriculture: 48%**

*1994
**1992

Ethnic composition
Ninety per cent of the population is of Albanian, non- Slavic, ethnic stock and 8% is ethnic Greek. In recent years relations with Greece have been strained by Greek allegations that the Greek community, concentrated in southern Albania, has been subjected to persecution. The official language is Albanian, with the Gheg dialect being spoken in the north and the Tosk in the south. Many Albanians work abroad, particularly in Greece, with drachma remittances contributing a quarter of GDP.

Religions
Historically, 70% of the population has adhered to Islam, Sunni and Bektashi; 20%, predominantly in the south, to the Eastern Orthodox Church; and between 5–10%, mainly in the north, to Roman Catholicism. Between 1967 and 1990 Albania officially declared itself an 'atheist state', outlawing all forms of religious worship and organization.

Political features
State type: emergent democratic
Date of state formation: 1912
Political structure: unitary
Executive: limited presidential
Assembly: one-chamber
Party structure: multiparty
Human rights rating: N/A
International affiliations: COE, EBRD, ECE, IAEA, IBRD, IMF, LORCS, OIC, OSCE, PFP, UN

Local and regional government
Albania is divided into 26 districts (*rreth*) for the purpose of local government.

Head of state (executive)
President Dr Sali Berisha, since 1992

Head of government
Prime Minister Aleksander Meksi, since 1992

Political leaders since 1970
1944–85 Enver Hoxha (PLA)*, 1985–92 Ramiz Alia (PLA)*, 1992–   Dr Sali Berisha (PDS)**

*Communist Party leaders
**President

Political system
The 1991–92 constitution provides for a single-chamber, 140-member People's Assembly (Kuvendi Popullor). One hundred of its members are directly elected in individual constituencies by a two-ballot, majority vote system for a four-year term. The remaining 40 seats are allocated on a proportional representation basis. An executive president, who is also commander in chief of the armed forces, is elected by the Assembly in a secret ballot for a maximum of two consecutive five-year terms. A successful candidate needs to secure a two-thirds majority of the votes cast. The president exercises the duties of the People's Assembly when it is not in session. A prime minister, appointed by the president, and Council of Ministers (COM), or cabinet, approved by the Assembly, has day-to-day charge of the government.

Political parties
There are two principal political parties: the Albanian Democratic Party (Partia Demokratike Shqipërisë: PDS) and the Socialist Party of Albania (Partia Socialiste Shqipërisë: PSS).

The PDS was formed in December 1990 by members of the Tiranë intelligentsia, including Dr Sali Berisha, in order to challenge the country's one-party communist regime. Led until March 1995 by Edouard Selami, it favours political pluralism and market-centred economic reform. Much of its support is drawn from the country's north.

The southern-based PSS, known until June 1991 as the Party of Labour of Albania (PLA), is the 'reform-socialist' successor to the former ruling communist party. The PLA was founded, with Yugoslav assistance, in November 1941 by a French-educated schoolteacher, Enver Hoxha, as a small 200-member underground body. It organized itself on Leninist 'democratic centralist' pyramidal lines and between the 1950s and 1980s adhered to the classic Marxist–Leninist–Stalinist doctrines which were being abandoned by those whom the PLA viewed as 'revisionists' elsewhere in the communist world. By 1986 full party membership stood at 128,000, corresponding to 4.2% of the total population. An 'Enverist' rump of the PLA, led by Hysni Milloshi, broke away from the remainder of the party when it was relaunched as the PSS in 1991, but it was outlawed subsequently by a June 1992 People's Assembly law on political organizations.

Other significant parties formed in recent years include the Social Democratic Party of Albania (PSDS) and the Albanian Republican Party (PRS), which have held ministerial posts in the PDS-led government of Sali Berisha; and the Human Rights Union (EAD), which is orientated towards the 400,000 Greek Albanians concentrated in the south of the country. The interests of Albania's ethnic Greek community are also promoted illegally by the banned OMONIA ('Concord') organization.

Latest elections

The most recent People's Assembly elections were held on 22 and 29 March 1992. The Democratic Party secured 92 of the 140 elective seats, including 90 of the 100 which were directly elected, attracting 62% of the national vote. The PSS, with 26% of the vote, won 38 seats, the PSDS, 7 seats, the EAD, 2 seats, both directly elected, and the PRS one seat. Voter turnout exceeded 90% of those registered.

Political history

Albania successively formed part of the Byzantine and Ottoman Empires between the 5th century and 1347 and between 1468 and 1912. It achieved independence in November 1912, but was then occupied by Italy between 1914 and 1920. In 1925 a republic was proclaimed, with Prime Minister Ahmed Bey Zogu (1895–1961), a conservative Muslim landlord, as president. Three years later, he was enthroned as King Zog I and was to reign continuously as an absolute monarch until Albania was occupied once again by Italian forces in April 1939. The country remained backward and rural-based, 80% of the population being dependent on agriculture in 1930, with a feudal Islamic landholding structure still surviving.

During World War II a communist-led National Liberation Front (NLF) was established, in 1941, with help from Yugoslav communists. Under the leadership of Enver Hoxha (1908–85), the NLF emerged as the most successful resistance group in the country and in 1944 forced the withdrawal of German forces, who had entered Albania in the previous year. Liberation was thus achieved without Soviet Red Army assistance.

In November 1944 the NLF, now known as the Democratic Front, following the purge of noncommunist elements, assumed power and called elections in December 1945, based on a single list of communist party-sponsored DFA candidates. The new Constituent Assembly proclaimed Albania a republic in January 1946, forcing the deposed King Zog to continue to live in exile. A Soviet-style communist constitution was adopted in March 1946, with the PLA now the sole legal political party.

At first, the new regime was closely allied to Yugoslavia, its armed forces being controlled by Yugoslav advisers and the economic plans of both Balkan states being coordinated. Yugoslavia's expulsion from the Cominform in 1948, following an ideological rift between Stalin and Tito, provided an opportunity for this state of dependency to be severed. Instead, Albania developed close economic links with the Soviet Union between 1949 and 1955, entering Comecon in 1949 and the Warsaw Pact in 1955.

During the late 1950s and early 1960s Soviet-Albanian relations progressively deteriorated as the country's leader, Enver Hoxha, a committed Stalinist, refused to accept Khrushchev's 'revisionist' denunciations of the Stalin era and his rapprochement overtures to Yugoslavia. Following attacks on the Soviet leadership by Hoxha, the USSR terminated its economic aid in June 1961 and broke off diplomatic relations in December 1961. Albania responded by ceasing cooperation within Comecon in 1962 and formally withdrawing in 1968 from the Warsaw Treaty Organization, after the Soviet invasion of Czechoslovakia. Close ties were now developed, instead, with Mao Zedong's communist China.

Inside the country, a strict Stalinist economic and political system was imposed by Hoxha, involving rural collectivization, industrial nationalization, central planning, totalitarian one-party control, the frequent purging of cadres to prevent the emergence of an elitist governing stratum, and the propagation of a 'cult of personality' centred upon Hoxha himself. A major drive against the Islamic and Christian religions was also launched, in 1967, involving the closure of more than 2,000 mosques and churches, in an effort to create the world's 'first atheist state' and expunge all remaining centrifugal tendencies.

Initially, between 1946 and 1954, Hoxha combined the key posts of PLA leader and state premier but in 1954 he was replaced in the second post by Mehmet Shehu, who remained as COM chairperson until his death in December 1981. Shehu was officially reported to have committed suicide but nonofficial sources suggest he was 'liquidated' after having been involved in a leadership struggle against Hoxha. His replacement was his deputy, Adil Carcani.

The 'Hoxha experiment', with its stress on national self-reliance, the 1976 constitution forbidding the acceptance of foreign credits, and on the minimization of urban–rural and blue- and white-collar income differentials, despite progress in the agricultural and energy spheres, left Albania with the lowest per-capita income in Europe by the time of the leader's death in 1985. Internationally, the country became one of the most isolated in the world, diplomatic relations with communist China having been severed in 1978, following the post-Mao leadership's accommodation with the United States.

Ramiz Alia (b. 1925), the Moscow-trained president of the presidium of the People's Assembly, was elected first secretary of the PLA on Hoxha's death in April 1985. The new regime, although pledging to uphold the independent policy line of its predecessor, began to make policy adjustments in both the foreign and domestic spheres. External contacts broadened and the number of countries with which Albania has diplomatic relations increased from 74 in 1978 to 111 in 1988. This diplomatic 'thaw' was accompanied by a growth in two-way external trade. Internally, political reforms remained limited, but in the economic sphere, new incentives, in the form of wage differentials for skilled tasks, were slowly introduced.

Opposition to the PLA regime began to mount during 1990 around the northwest border town of Shköder and, in early June 1990, unprecedented antigovernment street demonstrations erupted in Tiranë. Faced with a government crackdown, thousands of demonstrators sought refuge in foreign embassies and were later allowed to leave the country. In December 1990, amid continuing protests which were threatening an economic collapse, the PLA leadership announced that opposition parties would be allowed to operate and the ban on religious activity would be lifted. In response, the pluralist Democratic Party was formed, under the leadership of Dr Sali Berisha (b. 1945), a cardiologist from Tiranë. In February 1991 a huge bronze statue of Enver Hoxha was toppled in Tiranë by demonstrators and there were riots in several other towns. President Alia responded by replacing his unpopular prime minister, Adil Carcani, with the more reform-minded Fatos Nano and imposing presidential rule. Tanks were also moved into the streets of the capital and, fearing a hardline coup, thousands of Albanians fled by sea to Greece, Yugoslavia, and Italy.

In the spring of 1991 diplomatic relations with the United States and United Kingdom, suspended since 1946, were restored. In multiparty elections held in March–April 1991, the ruling PLA, polling strongly in rural areas, won 169 of the 250 seats in the new People's Assembly, a two-thirds majority sufficient to enable it to effect constitutional changes. The opposition's frustration was vented in anticommunist riots in Shköder, with four people being shot dead by the police, including the local PDS leader.

A new interim constitution was adopted in April 1991, the country being renamed the Republic of Albania and the PLA's leading role rescinded. The People's Assembly elected Ramiz Alia as executive president, replacing the former presidium, and commander in chief of the armed forces. In June 1991 an all-party 'government of national stability' was appointed, with Ylli Bufi, the former food minister, as prime minister and a PDS member as deputy premier. The PLA renamed itself the Socialist Party of Albania (PSS) on 13 June 1991, with Fatos Nano as its chairperson, and in July 1991 a land privatization act restored land to peasants dispossessed under the communist regime.

Unrest, food riots, and anticommunist demonstrations continued during 1991 and, complaining of manipulation, the PDS withdrew from the coalition, forcing Prime Minister Bufi's resignation on 6 December 1991. He was replaced on 18 December 1991 by the former nutrition minister, Vilson Ahmeti, who became Albania's first noncommunist premier, and in January 1992 a number of former communist officials, including Enver Hoxha's widow, Nexhmije Hoxha, were arrested on corruption charges. (Nexhmije Hoxha was subsequently sentenced to 11 years' imprisonment in May 1993 and her eldest son, Ilir Hoxha, to one year in jail in June 1995.) In the March 1992 general election, the PDS won a convincing

victory and the new Assembly elected Dr Sali Berisha as state president on 6 April 1992, voting him increased executive powers. On 13 April 1992 Aleksander Meksi, from the PDS, became prime minister, heading a PDS-dominated coalition administration. The former president, Ramiz Alia, was arrested in September 1992 and charged with the misuse of state funds and abuse of power and in July 1993, in what appeared to be a politically motivated move, Fatos Nano was also charged with corruption. (Alia was later convicted in September 1994, at what amounted to a political 'show trial', and was sentenced to eight years' imprisonment, while the former prime minister, Adil Carcani, received a five-year suspended prison term. However, in July 1995 Alia was released, following an appeal court ruling).

From 1993 the economy began to recover, with GDP growth of 8% being registered during that year and the monthly inflation rate falling to 1.5%. However, relations with neighbouring Greece were strained during 1994–95 by Greek claims that the ethnic Greek community residing in southern Albania were facing discrimination. Despite the economic improvement, popular support for the PDS waned during 1994. This was shown by the failure in November of a PDS-sponsored referendum on a new draft constitution. Despite a turnout of 84%, only 42% backed the proposed changes. President Berisha reacted by increasing the degree of state control over the media, with newspaper distribution in Tiranë being restricted to government-owned kiosks and state bookshops from June 1995.

In October 1995 a 'law against communist genocide' was passed, banning from running in national and local elections until 2002 any person who had been a member of parliament or the Central Commitee or Politburo of the Communist Party before May 1991. In July 1995 Albania acceded to the Council of Europe.

ARMENIA

Republic of Armenia
Hayastani Hanrapeut'yun

Capital: Yerevan

Social and economic data
Area: 29,800 km²
Population: 3,600,000*
Pop. density per km²: 121*
Urban population: 68%
Literacy rate: 99%**
GDP: $3,140 million**; per-capita GDP: $900**
Government defence spending (% of GDP): 3.6%**
Currency: dram
Economy type: low income
Labour force in agriculture: 10%**

*1994
**1992

Ethnic composition
Ninety-one per cent of the population is of Armenian ethnic stock, 5% Azeri, 2% Russian, and 2% Kurd. The official language is Armenian, a distinct Indo-European language.

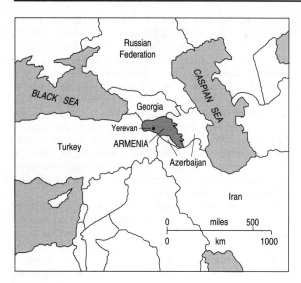

Religions

The population is predominantly Christian, with the leading denominations being the Armenian Apostolic Church, which has supported the nationalist movement, the Russian Orthodox Church, and Protestant churches. The number of Muslims has declined as a result of the exodus of many Azerbaijanis. Kurds are also adherents of Islam.

Political features

State type: authoritarian nationalist
Date of state formation: 1991
Political structure: unitary
Executive: unlimited presidential
Assembly: one-chamber
Party structure: multiparty*
Human rights rating: N/A
International affiliations: BSECZ, CIS, EBRD, IAEA, IBRD, IMF, NACC, NAM (observer), OSCE, UN

*Although opposition activity is restricted

Local and regional government

Armenia is divided into 67 districts (*rayons*) for local government, with an additional *rayon* to administer Yerevan.

Head of state (executive)

President Levon Ter-Petrossian, since 1990

Head of government

Prime Minister Hrand Bagratian, since 1993

Political leaders since 1970

1990–   Levon Ter-Petrossian (APM)

Political system

Armenia has an executive presidency, with the president being directly elected for a five-year term since 1991. Under the terms of the constitution adopted in 1995, there is a 190-member legislature, the National Assembly, to which deputies are elected for a five-year term. Election is by a German-style additional member system, with voters casting two ballots. One is to elect a deputy for one of the 150 single-

member constituencies, by the second ballot majoritarian system, and the other is for a party list, with 40 deputies being elected proportionately, allocated to parties winning more than 5% of the national vote. The president, whose powers are greatly strengthened under the 1995 constitution, works with a subordinate prime minister and council of ministers of some 30 members. There is also a vice president.

Political parties

The governing party is the Armenian Pan-National Movement (APM), formed in 1989 as an anticommunist nationalist party and led by Levon Ter-Petrossian. The Communist Party of Armenia (CPA), which formerly dominated the republic, was suspended in September 1991, but relegalized in 1992. Other political parties include the extreme-nationalist National Self-Determination Union (NSDU), which, led by Paruyr Ayrykian, seeks recovery of lands lost to Turkey after World War I; the 40,000-member Armenian Revolutionary Federation (ARF: Dashnaktsutyun), which was formed in 1890 and was the ruling party in independent Armenia between 1918–20, but was banned under Soviet rule; and the National Unity opposition coalition. The ARF, after being accused of involvement in terrorism, was suspended by presidential decree in December 1994. This ban was confirmed by the Supreme Court in January 1995.

Latest elections

The most recent presidential election was held on 16 October 1991 and was won by the APM's leader, Levon Ter-Petrossian, who won 83% of the national vote.

Legislative assembly elections were last held on 5 and 29 July 1995, with the ruling APM securing a clear victory, winning 119 seats, based on a 43% share of the vote. International observers from the OSCE described the contest as 'generally free but not fair', with the government of President Ter-Petrossian being accused of intimidating its opponents, and ten political parties being banned for improperly registered applications. The women's organization, Shamiram, with 17% of the vote, captured eight seats, the Communist Party 12% of the vote and seven seats, the NSDU 6% and three seats, and the ARF 2% and one seat. Forty-five independents were elected and 13 parties contested, with a turnout of 55%.

Political history

Formerly an ancient kingdom in an area extending into what is now the Van region of Turkey and part of northwestern Iran, Armenia reached the height of its power under King Tigranes I, 'the Great', between c. 95 and 55 BC, becoming the strongest state in the Roman east and controlling an empire that stretched from the Mediterranean to the Caucasus. Afterwards, it was dominated by foreign powers. This bred an intense, defensive national consciousness. Christianity became the official religion in 301 AD and the country fell under the sway of the Byzantine Empire, then the Muslim Turks, from the late 11th century, the Mongols in the 13th century, and the Ottomans from the 16th century.

With the advance of Russia into the Caucasus during the early 19th century, Russia taking east Armenia between 1813 and 1828, there was a revival in Armenian culture and, inspired by the successes of the Greek and Balkan peoples, a struggle for independence. This provoked an Ottoman back-lash in west Armenia and growing international concern at Armenian maltreatment: the 'Armenian question'. In 1915 an estimated 1,750,000 Armenians were massacred and deported by the Turks. The territory was conquered by Russia in 1916, but, after the Versailles settlement, briefly became an independent state in 1918. Two years later it was occupied by the Red Army. Along with Azerbaijan and Georgia, it formed part of the Transcaucasian Soviet Social-ist Republic, but became a constituent republic of the USSR in 1936 and a showpiece for Stalinist industrial develop-ment.

The glasnost (openness) initiative launched by Mikhail Gorbachev, who became Russia's communist leader in 1985, reawakened Armenian national identity. In 1988 demands for reunion with neighbouring Nagorno-Karabakh (Nagorny Karabakh), an Armenian Orthodox Christian-dominated enclave situated within the predominantly Muslim republic of Azerbaijan, led to riots, strikes, and, ulti-mately, during 1989–91, to a bloody civil war, necessitating the intervention of Soviet troops. The Armenian Pan-National Movement (APM), which was formed in Novem-ber 1989 by Levon Ter-Petrossian (b. 1945) and Vazguen Manukyan, and the militant Karabakh Committee were at the fore of this growing nationalist campaign. The campaign included attempts to secure full control over the Azerbaijani-peopled autonomous region of Nakhichevan, situated within Armenia, causing the flight of almost 200,000 Azeris from the republic. This fuelled anticommunist feeling and in the May 1990 elections to the republic's Supreme Soviet (par-liament) nationalists, particularly the APM, polled strongly and Ter-Petrossian and Manukyan were chosen as president and prime minister respectively, defeating communist chal-lengers.

On 23 August 1990 a declaration of independence was made, but it was ignored by Moscow and the international community. The republic boycotted the March 1991 USSR referendum on the preservation of the Soviet Union and in April 1991 the property belonging to the Communist Party of Armenia (CPA) was nationalized. Four months later, the CPA dissolved itself.

In a referendum held on 21 September 1991, shortly after the collapse of an attempted anti-Gorbachev coup by com-munist hardliners in Moscow, 99% of Armenians voted for secession from the USSR, with turnout reaching 94%. Two days later, independence was formally proclaimed by Presi-dent Ter-Petrossian, but this failed to secure Western recog-nition. A cease-fire agreement, brokered by the presidents of the Russian Federation and Kazakhstan, was signed by Armenia and Azerbaijan on 24 September 1991. It provided the basis for a negotiated settlement to the Nagorno-Karabakh dispute, including the disarming of local militias, the return of refugees, and the holding of free elections in the enclave. However, the agreement collapsed in November 1991 when the Azerbaijan parliament, dominated by com-munists-turned-nationalists, voted to annul Nagorno-Karabakh's autonomous status. Red Army troops were gradually withdrawn from the enclave, leaving it vulnerable to Azeri attacks. In response, after a referendum and elec-tions in December 1991, Nagorno-Karabakh's parliament

declared its 'independence', precipitating an intensification of the conflict.

On 16 October 1991, in the republic's first direct elections, Ter-Petrossian was overwhelmingly reconfirmed as presi-dent, capturing 83% of the national vote. On 21 December 1991 Armenia agreed to join the new confederal Common-wealth of Independent States (CIS), which was formed to supersede the Soviet Union, and in January 1992 was accorded diplomatic recognition by the United States and admitted into the Conference on Security and Cooperation in Europe (CSCE, later the OSCE). It also became a full and independent member of the United Nations.

Since independence most land has been returned to pri-vate ownership. However, Armenia's GDP has declined by nearly 10% per annum. The Nagorno-Karabakh dispute with Azerbaijan, which has claimed more than 18,000 Armenian and 5,000 Azerbaijani lives since 1988 and made over 1 mil-lion people refugees, and unrest in western Georgia during 1993 resulted in supply routes being blocked, leading to severe energy and food shortages. There has also been a huge influx of refugees to Yerevan, doubling the city's pop-ulation, and parts of the country have still not fully recov-ered from a devastating earthquake in 1988, which claimed 20,000 lives. Nevertheless, taking advantage of the weak-ness of the Azerbaijani regime, the ethnic Armenians of Nagorno-Karabakh extended the area under their territorial control during 1993–94, being allegedly aided by Armenia, before a cease-fire agreement was signed in May 1994.

In February 1993 Hrand Bagratian replaced Khosrov Haroutunian as prime minister. Subsequently, the pace of economic reform began to accelerate, with a new privatiz-ation and price liberalization programme being launched in March 1995. However, popular support for President Ter-Petrossian and the APM dipped to a low level during 1994–95 and there were demands for fresh elections and large antigovernment demonstrations in Yerevan in July and November 1994. The president's response, in December 1994, was to suspend by decree the chief opposition party, the ARF, and close down 11 antigovernment newspapers. Parliamentary elections, held in July 1995, resulted in vic-tory for the ruling APM and a constitution, strengthening presidential powers, was concurrently approved. How-ever, the election was tarnished by intimidation of the oppo-sition.

AZERBAIJAN

Republic of Azerbaijan
Azerbayjan Respublikasy

Capital: Baku

Social and economic data
Area: 86,600 km^2
Population: 7,300,000*
Pop. density per km^2: 84*
Urban population: 53%**
Literacy rate: 97%**
GDP: $5,800 million**; per-capita GDP: $800**
Government defence spending (% of GDP): 2.9%

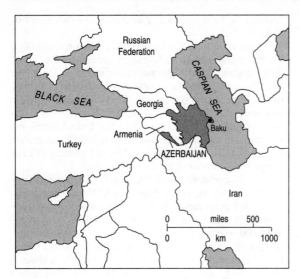

Currency: manat
Economy type: low income
Labour force in agriculture: 19%**

*1994
**1992

Ethnic composition
Eighty-three per cent of the population is of Azeri ethnic stock, 6% Russian, and 6% Armenian. The official language is Azerbaijani, a member of the South Turkic language group.

Religions
Ethnic Azeris are predominantly Muslim, 70% adhering to the Shi'ite Ithna sect and 30% the Sunni (Hanafi school). There are also sizeable Russian Orthodox and Armenian Apostolic Christian communities.

Political features
State type: authoritarian nationalist
Date of state formation: 1991
Political structure: unitary
Executive: unlimited presidential
Assembly: one-chamber
Party structure: multiparty*
Human rights rating: N/A
International affiliations: BSECZ, CIS, EBRD, ECO, ESCAP, IBRD, IMF, NACC, OIC, OSCE, PFP, UN

*Although opposition activity is restricted

Local and regional government
There are two autonomous regions within Azerbaijan, Nagorno-Karabakh and Nakhichevan (which is actually situated within Armenia), nine independent cities, and 54 districts, with elected local governments.

Head of state (executive)
President Geidar Aliyev, since 1993

Head of government
Prime Minister Fuad Kuliyev, since 1994

Political leaders since 1970
1990–92 Ayaz Mutalibov (CPA/Republican Democratic Party), 1992 Isa Gambarov (PFA/Musavat), 1992–93 Abulfez Elchibey (PFA), 1993–   Geidar Aliyev (New Azerbaijan)

Political system
Azerbaijan currently has a presidentialist political system, although the political system has remained in a state of flux since the overthrow of President Elchibey in June 1993. The executive president is directly elected for a four-year term and works with a prime minister and Council of Ministers of some 30 members. The current legislature is the 50-member Milli Majlis (National Assembly), an interim rump parliament which replaced the 350-seat Supreme Soviet in late 1991. Deputies are elected for four-year terms by a majority system, with a second ballot 'run-off' race being held in contests in which there is no clear first-round majority.

It was announced in August 1995 that there would be a new 125-member, single-chamber parliament, with 80% of the members elected in single seat constituencies and 20% by proportional representation.

Political parties
The principal political parties are the Popular Front of Azerbaijan (PFA: Khalqu Jibhasi), the New Azerbaijan (Yeni Azerbaijan), the Communist Party of Azerbaijan (CPA), the Muslim Democratic Party (Musavat), the Party for National Independence (Istikal; estd. 1992), led by Etibar Mamedov, and the Social Democratic Party (estd. 1990).

The PFA is a democratic nationalist body formed in 1989 and is led by former president, Albufaz Elchibey. Since the coming to power of President Aliyev, it has been subject to a crackdown by security forces who have accused it of seeking to destabilize the regime. In May 1995 the PFA's leader, Elchibey, advocated creation of a 'greater Azerbaijan', unifying Azerbaijan with northern Iran.

New Azerbaijan was set up in 1993 to support the presidency of Geidar Aliyev, a former communist.

The CPA, which is led by Sayad Sayadov, was suspended in 1991 and briefly renamed the Republican Democratic Party, but was reconstituted in November 1993. It was banned again in September 1995 by the Supreme Court after it was accused of intending to destroy the country's independence.

Musavat promotes Islamic values and the unity of Turkic peoples. It functioned between 1911–20 and was re-established in 1992 led by Isa Gambarov and became an ally of the PFA. Its general secretary is Niyazi Ibrahimov.

In March 1995 the Grey Wolves opposition party was banned by President Aliyev.

Latest elections
The most recent direct presidential election was held on 10 October 1993 and won by Geidar Aliyev, who secured 98.8% of the vote, with turnout recorded at 97%. None of the major opposition parties put forward candidates and the election was dominated, according to outside observers, by biased pro-Aliyev media propaganda.

Legislative elections to the Supreme Soviet were last held on 12 November 1995. Turnout was 86% and a pro-Aliyev majority was returned.

Political history

Azerbaijan shares a common language and culture with Turkey, but, prior to its conquest by Tsarist Russia in the early 19th century, it was a province of Persia. Today, 15 million Shi'ite Azeris live across the border in Iran. The name Azerbaijan is derived from the independent state first established in the region in the 4th century BC by Atrophates, a vassal of Alexander III (356–323 BC) of Macedon. During the mid-18th century there were independent khanates in the area, but these became Russian protectorates after 1805. During the late 19th century, Baku became the centre of an important oil industry.

A member of the Transcaucasian Federation in 1917, it became an independent republic in 1918, with Gyanja (Kirovabad) as the capital, but was occupied by the Red Army in 1920 and was subsequently forcibly secularized. During the 1930s there were peasant uprisings against the Stalinist collectivization of agriculture and a series of violent purges of the Azerbaijani Communist Party (CPA). Despite these purges, the CPA became notorious for the extent of its corruption, being described as a 'state-run mafia'. This persuaded the reformist Mikhail Gorbachev, who became leader of the Soviet Communist Party (CPSU) in 1985, to engineer the dismissal in October 1987 of Geidar Aliyev (b. 1923), who had been the CPA's leader since 1969 and a member of the CPSU's Politburo since 1982.

Taking advantage of the new openness (glasnost) encouraged by Gorbachev, there was a growth in Azerbaijani nationalism from the later 1980s. This was spearheaded by the Azerbaijani Popular Front (PFA), which was established in 1989, and was fanned by the dispute with Christian Armenia over Armenian-peopled Nagorno-Karabakh (Nagorny Karabakh) and Azerbaijani-peopled Nakhichevan, two neighbouring enclaves, with the status of Azerbaijani autonomous regions, in Azerbaijan and Armenia respectively.

This dispute over control, which reawakened centuries-old enmities, flared up into full-scale military and economic civil war from December 1989, prompting Azerbaijani calls for secession from the Soviet Union. It led, in January 1990 to the despatch of Soviet troops to Baku to restore order and communist authority, and the imposition of a state of emergency. Opportunistically, the CPA, under the leadership of Ayaz Mutalibov, allied itself with the nationalist cause. It rejected compromise in the Nagorno-Karabakh dispute and adopted a new state flag and designation in December 1990. In the September 1990 Supreme Soviet (legislature) elections, the Popular Front, having been on the verge of power before the January 1990 crackdown, was convincingly defeated by the CPA. Azerbaijanis voted overwhelmingly in favour of preserving the Union in the March 1991 USSR constitutional referendum – although the opposition claimed turnout was only 20%, rather than the officially claimed 75% – and the August 1991 anti-Gorbachev coup in Moscow was warmly welcomed by President Mutalibov, who ordered militia and tanks on to the streets of Baku to break up demonstrations. These had been organized by the Popular Front and had been supported by Geidar Aliyev, a former leader of the CPA who was now chairperson of the legislature of Nakhichevan, whose people had voted against the March 1991 USSR referendum proposal.

However, with the failure of the Moscow coup, Mutalibov resigned from the CPA, which was soon disbanded, and on 30 August 1991 independence was declared and the state of emergency, still in force in Baku, was lifted. On 8 September 1991, Mutalibov was directly elected state president as the sole candidate in a contest which was boycotted by the opposition National Democratic/ People's Front and was characterized by fraudulent practices. Mutalibov won 84% of the vote.

On 21 December 1991 Azerbaijan joined the new Commonwealth of Independent States (CIS), which superseded the Soviet Union. Turkey recognized its independence in November 1991, but the United States and other Western nations withheld recognition because of Azerbaijan's poor human rights record and its 'aggressive policy' towards Nagorno-Karabakh. However, in January 1992 it was admitted into the Conference on Security and Cooperation in Europe (CSCE, later the OSCE) and became a member of the United Nations in March 1992. As another measure of its independence, the new state began to form its own independent armed forces. Diplomatic and commercial links with Turkey were established and relations with Shi'ite Iran improved. In February 1992 the republic joined the Economic Cooperation Organization (ECO), founded by Iran, Pakistan, and Turkey in 1975, which aimed to reduce customs tariffs and eventually form a customs union. Also in February 1992 Azerbaijan reverted from the Cyrillic alphabet, imposed by Moscow in 1937, to the Latin alphabet.

In March 1992 President Mutalibov resigned, as a result of mounting nationalist opposition to Azeri deaths, which were approaching 5,000, and defeats in Nagorno-Karabakh, which he had placed under direct presidential rule in January 1992, and was replaced by Yakub Mamedov, the chairperson of the legislature, now known as the National Assembly. An internal power struggle developed and Mutalibov was briefly restored to power in May 1992 by the National Assembly and a state of emergency was declared, However, after the parliament building had been stormed by Popular Front supporters, Mutalibov was ousted again and replaced as interim president by Isa Gambarov, chairperson of the PFA. On 7 June, the Popular Front leader, Albufaz Elchibey (b. 1938), was directly elected state president, capturing 59% of the national vote and defeating four rival candidates.

Morale improved in the armed forces with the coming to power of the nationalist Elchibey and a number of military successes were initially recorded between June and October 1992 in the struggle with Armenia over Nagorno-Karabakh. Thereafter, however, Azeri troops suffered a succession of disastrous military defeats which destabilized the Elchibey regime and left Armenian forces in control of a tenth of Azerbaijan's territory. This culminated in the president's overthrow in June 1993 in a military coup led by Colonel Surat Guseinov, a wealthy wool merchant who had established his own private army in the Gandja area of western Azerbaijan to fight the Armenians in Nagorno-Karabakh. It was rumoured that he was in receipt of Russian military support. Geidar Aliyev, leader of the Nakhichevan autonomous region, became the new head of state, while Guseinov served as prime minister and 'supreme commander'. Elchibey fled to Nakhichevan and a referendum was held on 29 August 1993 in which it was officially claimed that only 2% of Azerbaijanis expressed 'trust' in the ousted president. The PFA, whose leadership and supporters became subjected to a security crackdown, including arrests, disputed the veracity of the poll's reported results. Aliyev was duly elected state president on 10 October 1993, in a contest boycotted by the opposition parties.

The new, and authoritarian, Aliyev regime developed closer ties with Russia, which replaced Turkey, courted by Elchibey, as Azerbaijan's main regional ally. However, militarily Azerbaijan continued to lose ground to Armenia in the dispute over Nagorno-Karabakh, with a fifth of Azerbaijani territory, including the Lachin corridor which links Armenia with the enclave, being controlled by Armenians by the spring of 1994. However, hopes of an end to the six-year-old conflict were raised in May 1994 when a cease-fire agreement was reached in Moscow in May 1994. In October 1994 President Aliyev was faced by a coup attempt led by Surat Guseinov, who, as a result, was replaced as prime minister by Fuad Kuliyev. A further attempted coup, led by the deputy interior minister, Ravshan Javadov, was foiled in March 1995 and the state of emergency imposed in October 1994 was extended. Another coup plot, hatched by supporters of former president, Mutalibov, was foiled in August 1995 and three months later parliamentary elections were held, from which 15 opposition parties, including the PFA, were banned from participating.

Since independence Azerbaijani GDP has declined at an average rate of more than 10% per annum and inflation has spiralled as a result of the disruption of former ties with the ex-Soviet Union and the conflict with Armenia over Nagorno-Karabakh and Nakhichevan, which has resulted in the influx of an estimated 900,000 refugees into the republic and a quarter of annual spending being consumed by the military. A market-centred economic reform programme involving price liberalization and privatization is being gradually implemented and joint ventures have been negotiated with Western companies to develop the oilfields of the Caspian Sea.

BELARUS (BYELORUSSIA)

Republic of Belarus*
Respublika Belarus

*Belarus is the UN's preferred English language transliteration of the republic's name, although Byelarus, Bielarus, and Byelorussia are also widely used

Capital: Minsk (Mensk)

Social and economic data
Area: 207,600 km^2
Population: 10,300,000*
Pop. density per km^2: 50*
Urban population: 67%**
Literacy rate: 98%**
GDP: $30,100 million**; per-capita GDP: $2,925**+
Government defence spending (% of GDP): 3.3%**
Currency: Belarussian rouble, or zaichik (to be replaced, it is planned, by the Russian rouble)

Economy type: middle income
Labour force in agriculture: 19%**

*1994
**1992
+Per-capita GDP has decreased significantly since 1992

Ethnic composition
Seventy-eight per cent of the population is of Belarussian ('eastern Slav') ethnic stock, 13% is ethnic Russian, 4% Polish, 3% Ukrainian, and 1% Jewish. The official language since 1990 has been Belarussian, an eastern Slavonic tongue written in the Cyrillic script, but which is only the main tongue for 4% of the population. Russian, the most widely spoken language in the republic, was made a co-equal 'state' language in 1995, after a referendum held on the issue.

Religions
The population is predominantly Christian, most ethnic Belarussians and Russians belonging to the Eastern Orthodox Church. There are also 2 million Roman Catholics, who include ethnic Poles and Uniates, or 'Greek Catholics', and more than 200 Baptist churches. The small ethnic Tatar community adheres to Islam.

Political features
State type: emergent democratic
Date of state formation: 1991
Political structure: unitary
Executive: limited presidential
Assembly: one-chamber
Party structure: multiparty
Human rights rating: N/A
International affiliations: CIS, EBRD, ECE, IBRD, IMF, NACC, OSCE, UN

Local and regional government
For the purposes of local government, Belarus is divided into six regions (*oblasts*) and the capital city of Minsk. Below these there are districts (*rayons*), cities, towns, and villages,

with local councils. In October 1994 'primary level' soviets, i.e. village and some town councils, were abolished.

Head of state (executive)
President Alexander Lukashenko*, since 1994

*Also transliterated as Lukashenka

Head of government
Prime Minister Mikhail Chigir, since 1994

Political leaders since 1970
1990–94 Vyacheslav Kebich (BCP)*, 1991–94 Stanislav Shushkevich (independent)**, 1994 Mechislav Grib (BCP)**, 1994– Alexander Lukashenko (independent)***

*Prime minister (in a dual executive to 1994)
**Head of state
***Executive president

Political system
Under the terms of the constitution of March 1994, Belarus has a democratic-pluralist, limited presidential political system. The executive president is directly elected for a maximum of two five-year terms. The president serves as head of state and commander of the armed forces, appoints the cabinet and prime minister and may declare a state of emergency, but cannot dissolve parliament. Candidates for the presidency may be nominated either by 100,000 citizens or 70 parliamentary deputies. The legislature, the Supreme Council, comprises 260 members, elected directly for four-year terms by a majority system, with a second ballot 'run-off' race being held in contests in which there is no clear first-round majority winner. Turnout must be at least 50% for an election result to be valid and sufficient deputies, 174 (or two-thirds of 260), must be returned to form a parliamentary quorum, so that further 'repeat elections' may be held. From the majority grouping within the Supreme Council, a prime minister (chairperson of the Council of Ministers) is drawn. There exists within the Council of Ministers an inner cabinet, or collegium, comprising the prime minister, the deputy prime minister, and the ministers of finance, interior, and foreign affairs.

Political parties
The principal political parties in Belarus are the Belarus Communist Party (BCP), the Belarus Patriotic Movement (BPM), the Belarussian Popular Front (BPF, or 'Adradzhenye'), the Peasants' Party (estd. 1990), the Christian Democratic Union of Belarus, and the Socialist Party of Belarus (estd. 1994).

The 15,000-member BCP was suspended in August 1991 after the anti-Gorbachev putsch in Moscow, but was relegalized in June 1992.

The BPF was formed in 1988 as a democratic nationalist umbrella force and in 1994, led by Zenon Poznyak, claimed a membership of 500,000. It promotes the concept of a 'Baltic–Black Sea community' embracing Belarus, Ukraine, and the Baltic States, advocates Czech-style market-centred economic reform, and seeks supremacy for the Belarussian language, although 96% of Belarussians speak Russian as their main tongue.

The BPM was formed in November 1994 as a populist force supporting President Lukashenko.

Latest elections
The most recent, and first direct, presidential elections were held on 23 June and 10 July 1994. Six candidates contested the first round, with Alexander Lukashenko, a young independent pro-Russian populist, dubbed the 'Belarussian Zhirinovsky', topping the poll with 45% of the national vote. He defeated the conservative communist prime minister, Vyacheslav Kebich, who captured 17% of the vote, the moderate nationalist former head of state Stanislav Shushkevich, 10%, Zenon Poznyak, a human-rights campaigner representing the Belarussian Popular Front, 14%, Alexander Dubko (Peasant's Party), 6%, and Vasil Novikau (Communist Party), 5%. Turnout reached 79%. In the second round 'run-off' with Kebich, Lukashenko won an 80% share of the vote. He attracted support from both the young and, by promising to reimpose tighter state controls over the economy, the elderly, offering 'simple solutions to complicated problems'. The election was viewed as free and fair, although the printing of the only independent newspaper, *Svabada* ('Freedom'), was mysteriously halted during the campaign and there were occasions when the electricity was turned off in halls where Lukashenko was speaking.

The first two rounds of the most recent legislature elections were held on 14 and 28 May 1995. Only 18 of the 260 seats were filled in the first round and a further 101 in the second, as a consequence both of voter apathy and limited media coverage, with turnout falling below the required level of 50% for a contest to be valid, and a multiplicity of candidates, which prevented a clear majority winner emerging. Of the 2,348 candidates contesting the first round, 43% were independents, and 432 candidates contested the second round. Twenty-four of the elected deputies were members of the Belarussian Communist Party and 26 from the Peasants' Party, with the remainder being chiefly independents and directors and chairs of state and collective farms. The Supreme Council was inquorate after the first two rounds, but further elections in December 1995 filled 79 more seats.

Political history
Having been subject to centuries of Lithuanian, Polish, Russian, and then Soviet rule, Belarus's claims to a separate national identity are somewhat tenuous. A medieval Belarussian state did develop around the city of Polotsk on the Dvina river, but from the 13th century it became incorporated within the Slavonic Grand Duchy of Lithuania and from 1569 there was union with Poland. Belarussia, or 'White Russia', was brought into the Russian Empire in the late 18th century by Catherine the Great (1729–96). It served as Russia's land bridge to the West and as an important agricultural region. From the later 19th century there was an upsurge in national consciousness and, amid the chaos of the Bolshevik Revolution in Russia, an independent Belarussian National Republic was proclaimed on 25 March 1918. However, it failed to receive international recognition. Instead, in January 1919, a Belarussian Soviet Republic was established, with some loss of territory to Poland. Initially, national culture and language were encouraged until the Soviet leader, Joseph Stalin, launched a 'Russification' drive from 1929, which resulted in more than 100,000 people, predominantly writers and intellectuals, being executed near Minsk between

1937 and 1941. Agriculture was also collectivized despite peasant resistance. Under the terms of the 1939 Nazi–Soviet pact, western and eastern Belarussia were reunified, regaining lands lost to Poland and Lithuania in 1921, but the country then suffered severely under German invasion and occupation between 1941 and 1944. An estimated 1.3 million died, including the bulk of its large Jewish population.

'Russification' continued between the 1960s and mid-1980s, with the teaching of the Belarussian language dwindling, strict state censorship being imposed, and large-scale immigration by ethnic Russians occurring. However, with the coming to power of the new Soviet leader, Mikhail Gorbachev, in 1985 and the launching of the glasnost (political openness) initiative, there was an urban-based and intelligentsia-led national cultural revival. Influenced by developments in the neighbouring Baltic Republics, a Belarussian Popular Front (BPF: Adradzhenye), demanding greater autonomy, was established in October 1988. In the wake of the April 1986 Chernobyl nuclear reactor disaster in Ukraine, which rendered one-fifth of the republic's agricultural land and one-sixth of its forests unusable and forced the resettlement of several hundred thousand people from southern Belarus, the Belarussian Ecological Union (BEU) was also formed. Despite official and media restrictions, both the Popular Front and the BEU contested the March–April 1990 Belarussian parliamentary (Supreme Soviet) elections under the Democratic Bloc banner and captured more than a quarter of the 310 elective seats, polling strongest in the larger cities of Mensk and Gomel. In response, a Declaration of State Sovereignty was issued in July 1990 and Belarussian was re-established as the republic's official state language from September 1990.

Having been an industrially advanced republic within the Soviet Union, specializing in the assembly of lorries, tractors, motorcycles, and televisions and the production of fertilizers and petrochemicals, a switch to self-management and self-financing of nonstrategic industries began in January 1990. Belarus had a reputation as a cautious and 'compliant' republic within the USSR. In the March 1991 all-Union referendum on the preservation of the USSR, 83% of those participating – turnout was also 83% – supported Gorbachev's proposal to form a 'renewed federation of equal sovereign republics'. However, in April 1991 the republic was rocked by a series of workers' strikes and demonstrations in Mensk and other cities demanding not just higher wages, to counteract recent price rises, but also the removal of the Belarus Communist Party (BCP) government. Four months later, in August 1991, Belarussia's communist head of state, Nikolai Dementei, expressed support for the anti-Gorbachev attempted coup launched in Moscow by communist hardliners. After the coup failed, Dementei resigned and the republic's Supreme Soviet declared Belarussia's independence on 25 August 1991. The BCP was also suspended. On 19 September 1991 the Supreme Soviet voted to adopt the name of Republic of Belarus and elected Stanislav Shushkevich (b. 1934), a university physicist who was the son of a famous Belarussian poet who was silenced in the 1930s and who was an advocate of democratic reform and the swift transition to a market economy, as its chairperson and thus *de facto* state president. Shushkevich played an important role

in the creation in December 1991 of a new Commonwealth of Independent States (CIS), the confederal successor to the USSR, with Mensk being chosen as the CIS's initial centre.

In January 1992 Belarus was formally recognized as an independent state by the United States and other Western countries and was admitted into the Conference on Security and Cooperation in Europe (CSCE, later the OSCE). It had been a member of the United Nations since its foundation in 1945.

After independence, Belarus's new administration, with Shushkevich sharing power with Vyacheslav Kebich, a pro-Russian BCP politician and former industrial manager who became prime minister in 1990, was cautious in its implementation of market-centred economic reform. Privatization and price liberalization was introduced very gradually, the machine-building and chemicals industries were slowly restructured, and the country remained heavily dependent upon Russia for its industrial raw materials. This was explained by the resistance of both Kebich and the Supreme Soviet, which was dominated by communists, to significant economic changes. Indeed, a 75% profits tax was imposed on those private firms which did exist. The new state inherited a substantial arsenal of nuclear weapons from the USSR. These the Shushkevich administration pledged to remove gradually, beginning, in 1992, with tactical nuclear weapons and in February 1993 ratifying the START-1 and Nuclear Non-Proliferation treaties. However, in December 1993 a collective security treaty was signed with the CIS, which substantially subordinated Belarus's military policy to Russia's.

The condition of the Belarus economy deteriorated rapidly between 1992 and 1994, with inflation reaching 40% a month and industrial production being nearly halved as it adjusted to the loss of key markets in Russia and elsewhere in the ex-Soviet Union. Living standards also fell sharply to near Albanian levels. In January 1991, in an effort to stabilize the economy, the Kebich government entered into negotiations with Russia for the proposed exchange of the republic's *zaichiki* ('little hare') coupons, which were introduced in 1992, for Russian roubles at a 1:1 rate. This promised to enable Belarus to secure access to Russian oil and raw materials at Russia's low domestic prices, but meant the surrender of monetary sovereignty to Moscow. However, the deal was criticized by nationalists and the independent trade unions and remained unratified.

Accused of unproven corruption by a communist-dominated parliamentary commission, the nationalist-minded Stanislav Shushkevich was ousted as head of state in January 1994, following a no-confidence vote, and was replaced by Mechislav Grib, a lawyer and former general of the Soviet Union's interior ministry. Both Shushkevich and, with the backing of the BCP, Prime Minister Kebich contested direct elections to a new position of executive president in June–July 1994, but the surprise winner, by a landslide margin, was Alexander Lukashenko (b. 1955). A 39-year-old former collective farm boss who had risen to become chairman of the Supreme Soviet's anticorruption commission, Lukashenko fought the election on an anticorruption and an earthy populist platform. He pledged a 'job and home for every Belarussian', spot checks on the income sources of the owners of villas in suburban Mensk, price freezes 'to end inflation', large credits to prop up agriculture and industry, and the establishment of a Slav union with Russia. Indeed, Lukashenko boasted that he had been the only Belarussian deputy to vote against the disintegration of the Soviet Union in December 1991.

However, apparently reneging on campaign pledges, in July 1994 President Lukashenko appointed a cabinet, headed by Prime Minister Mikhail Chigir, which was largely supportive of continued market-centred economic reforms. Milk and bread prices were liberalized in August 1994 and the idea of monetary union with Russia shelved. However, a friendship and cooperation treaty was signed with Russia in February 1995. With new parliamentary elections set for 14 May 1995, President Lukashenko sought to hold a concurrent referendum asking the people to give him more powers over the still deteriorating economy and in the battle against crime, and to amend the constitution so as to enable him to dissolve parliament at will. Nationalist-minded Popular Front deputies in parliament protested against this authoritarian move and the president's pro-Russian policies, and went on hunger strike. President Lukashenko responded by sending in troops to storm the parliament building in April 1995 and dissolve the legislature pending the new elections.

In the 14 May 1995 referendum, voters overwhelmingly approved, by a 4:1 margin, with turnout at 65%, reducing the country's independence vis-à-vis Russia and strengthening President Lukashenko's powers. They agreed to restore Russian as an equal official language with Belarussian, restore the Soviet flag and symbols of Belarus, supported plans for economic integration with Russia (a customs union being established in May 1995), and gave the president his requested dissolution powers. The simultaneous parliamentary elections were marked by voter apathy, with repeat elections being scheduled for the winter since less than half the electorate bothered to vote. Indeed, many electors followed the controversial lead of the president who crossed out all the names of candidates in his electoral district, stating that none was worth voting for. Those deputies which were returned were predominantly unreformed communists. The parliament remained inquorate and unable to sit after voter apathy, encouraged by the state media, worsened in the second round. The result of the May 1995 referendum brought closer the prospect of a Slavic reunion with Russia, the chief stumbling block being Russia's concern that the cost of union would be too cripplingly high for its currently weakened economy: the cost for Russia of monetary union alone was estimated at more than $2 billion.

BOSNIA-HERZEGOVINA

Republic of Bosnia-Herzegovina
Bosnia i Hercegovina

Capital: Sarajevo

Social and economic data
Area: 51,129 km²
Population: 4,500,000*
Pop. density per km²: 88*
Urban population: 36%**

Literacy rate: 93%**
GDP: N/A; per-capita GDP: N/A
Government defence spending (% of GDP): 48.7%**
Currency: Bosnia-Herzegovina dinar (the Croatian kuna is used in Bosnian Croat dominated areas and the Yugoslav dinar in Serb areas)
Economy type: low income
Labour force in agriculture: N/A

*1994
**1992

Ethnic composition
The republic contains a complex mosaic of ethnically mixed communities. According to the 1994 census, 44% of the population is ethnic Muslim, 31% Serb, 17% Croat, and 6% 'Yugoslav'. Croats are most thickly settled in southwestern Bosnia and western Herzegovina and Serbs in eastern and western Bosnia. However, the civil war since 1991 has led to large-scale population movements, with hundreds of thousands of, principally, Croats and Muslims fleeing as refugees to neighbouring states. The war has also claimed more than 200,000 lives, the greatest proportion being Muslims. The main language is Serbo-Croat, with Muslims and Croats using the Roman alphabet, while Serbs use the Cyrillic script.

Religions
Prewar figures state that forty-four per cent of the population adheres to Sunni Islam, 33% to the Serbian Eastern Orthodox Christian faith, and 17%, comprising ethnic Croats, is Roman Catholic. The Muslim community is composed of chiefly Bosnian Muslims, Slavs who converted to Islam during the Ottoman period, but also includes some Albanian and Turkish Muslims.

Political features
State type: emergent democratic/transitional
Date of state formation: 1992

Political structure: federal/transitional
Executive: limited presidential
Assembly: two-chamber
Party structure: multiparty
Human rights rating: N/A
International affiliations: COE, NAM (guest), OIC (observer), OSCE, UN

Head of state
President Dr Alija Izetbegović, since 1990

Head of government
Prime Minister Haris Silajdzic, since 1993

Political leaders since 1970
1990– Dr Alija Izetbegović (SDA)

Local and regional government
As a result of the continuing civil war, local government institutions have been superseded by effective military rule by locally dominant ethnic militias, although it is envisaged that the new Muslim-Croat Federation of central Bosnia will be divided into eight cantons with a significant degree of autonomy and that municipalities will have their own local administrations.

Political system
The political system of Bosnia-Herzegovina has been in an unsettled condition, as a result of the bitter civil war which has raged since 1991. In mid-1995 the country was effectively partitioned between two contending states, a Muslim-Croat federation, which controlled central parts of the country, as well as the enclave of Bihac, situated in north-western Bosnia, and a self-proclaimed Serb republic, Republika Srpska, based at Pale, near Sarajevo, which controlled eastern and much of western Bosnia-Herzegovina.

The internationally recognized government of the republic was headed by the Bosnian Muslim Dr Alija Izetbegović, who was president of the directly elected seven-member Collective State Presidency since November 1990. Izetbegović held power under the constitution of 1974, which had been extensively amended between 1989 and 1991. This had provided, in accordance with traditions inherited from the Yugoslav Republic, for rotating leaderships, balanced ethnic representation, and 'ethnic vetoes' on key issues. The president was elected by the other members of the Collective State Presidency. Under this constitution, the legislature, the Assembly, comprises two chambers, the 130-member Chamber of Citizens and the 110-member Chamber of Communes, with deputies directly elected by a majority system, there being a second-round 'run-off' race in contests where no candidate secures a majority of the vote in the first round. A prime minister and cabinet of ministers are drawn from the Assembly.

In May 1994, following an accord signed in March 1994 by the Croatian government and Bosnia's Muslim and ethnic Croat leaders, a new Muslim-Croat federation was formed, which would operate parallel to existing executive institutions of the Muslim-dominated Republic of Bosnia-Herzegovina and the self-styled 'Croatian Republic of Herceg-Bosna', which comprised territoried controlled by ethnic Croats. The federation was to be divided into eight

Swiss-style cantons, four of which were majority-Muslim, two were Croat, and two (Mostar and Travnik) were multi-ethnic. It was to be linked eventually to Croatia in a loose confederation with economic and monetary union and coord-inated defence policies. A constituent assembly was formed in May 1994, which elected Kresimir Zubak, who had replaced the separatist Mate Boban as leader of the Bosnian Coats in February 1994, as president of the Federation, a chiefly ceremonial position, with Ejup Ganic, from the Bosn-ian Collective State Presidency, as vice president. However, Izetbegović remained head of state, while Haris Silajdzic continued as prime minister of a joint cabinet of the Republic of Bosnia-Herzegovina and the Federation of Bosnia-Herze-govina. This cabinet contained 11 Muslims and 6 Croats. It was envisaged that, once political conditions had returned to normal, the new federation would have a weak presidency and the federal government, headed by the prime minister, would be responsible for defence, economic affairs, and for-eign policy. The offices of prime minister and president would be rotated annually or biannually between Muslim and Croat representatives, while a Confederative Council would later be established, with its chair rotating annually between representatives of Croatia and Bosnia-Herzegovina.

The Serb-controlled regions of Bosnia-Herzegovina refused to enter into such a federation and, instead, had their own elected assembly, as well as a president, Dr Radovan Karadžić, since December 1992, and a prime minister.

Under the terms of the November 1995 Dayton Accord, there was to be a new central government, with a rotating presidency, elected parliament and Constitutional Court for the new united state – Sarajevo was to be the united capital, but the Bosnian–Croat federation and Bosnian Serb republic would continue as subsidiary entities.

Political parties
The main political parties in Bosnia-Herzegovina are ethni-cally based. They comprise the Party of Democratic Action (SDA), the Serbian Renaissance Movement (SPO), the Croatian Christian Democratic Union of Bosnia-Herzegov-ina (HDZ), and the League of Communists (LC) and Social-ist Alliance (SA).

The SDA is the main Muslim nationalist organization in the republic and was founded in 1990 by President Izetbe-gović.

The SPO was formed in 1990 by Dr Radovan Karadžić as a Serbian-nationalist force under the designation Serbian Democratic Party (SDS).

The HDZ, which is affiliated to Franjo Tudjman's HDZ in Croatia, is a Croat nationalist party which was formed in 1990 by Mate Boban and has been led since July 1994 by Dario Kordic.

The LC, and its mass organization ally, the SA, was the former ruling party in the republic until 1990. It adopted the designation Socialist Democratic Party in 1990, becoming a reform-socialist party.

Latest elections
The last Assembly elections in the Republic of Bosnia-Herzegovina were held on 18 November and 2 and 9 Decem-ber 1990 and resulted in the SDA winning 86 of the 240

available seats in the two chambers of parliament. The SDS captured 82 seats, the HDZ, 44, the LC–SA, 20, and the Alliance of Reform Forces, 13.

The seven-member Collective State Presidency was also directly elected on 18 November 1990.

Political history

Once the Roman province of Illyria, the area of Bosnia and Herzegovina which forms the southwestern component of the contemporary state enjoyed brief periods of independence in medieval times, before being conquered by the Ottoman Turks in 1463. It remained part of the Ottoman Empire until the late 19th century and many of the Slav inhabitants were converted to Sunni Islam. Following a Bosnian revolt (1875– 76) against Turkish rule, it became an Austrian protectorate in 1878, eventually being annexed by the Austrian Habsburgs in 1908, following the Turkish Revolution of that year. It was the assassination in Sarajevo on 28 June 1914 of Archduke Franz Ferdinand (1863–1914), the heir to the Austro-Hungarian Empire, by a Bosnian Serb student, Gavrilo Princip (1895–1918), which precipitated World War I. In 1918, following the collapse of the Habsburg Empire, Bosnia and Herzegovina were incorporated in the new Kingdom of Serbs, Croats, and Slovenes, which became known as Yugo-slavia in 1929. After invasion by Nazi Germany in 1941, it was included in the Ustasa puppet state of 'Greater Croatia' until the communist Partisan resistance leader, Marshal Tito (1892–1980), established his provisional government at liberated Jajce in Bosnia in November 1943. Bosnia-Herzegovina was kept undivided because of its ethnic and religious mix of Orthodox Christian Serbs, Roman Catholic Croats, and Muslim Serbo-Croat-speaking Slavs and it became a republic within the Yugoslav Socialist Federal Republic in November 1945.

During the 1960s in an effort to create a counterpoint to the increasingly hostile Serb and Croat communities, Tito encouraged a strengthening of the position of the Slav Muslims, who were granted a distinct ethnic status in the 1971 census and were given a share in power through a rotating collective presidency, introduced in 1971. However, the republic's communist leadership became notorious for its corruption, racketeering, and authoritarianism and from 1980 there was an upsurge in Islamic nationalism and worsening Muslim-Serb ethnic tension from 1989. Multiparty republic assembly elections were held in November–December 1990 and resulted in the defeat of the ruling League of Communists (LC) and the formation of a coalition government by Muslim, Serb and Croat nationalist parties. This complicated the republic's dealings with Serbia. From the spring of 1991 the Serb-against-Croat civil war in neighbouring Croatia spread disorder into Bosnia-Herzegovina, with ethnic Croats establishing barricades to attempt to prevent the predominantly Serb Yugoslav National Army (JNA) from moving through into Croatia. In August 1991, the republic's president, Dr Alija Izetbegović (b. 1925), a devout Muslim lawyer and former anticommunist political prisoner, expressed concern that Serbia intended to divide up Bosnia-Herzegovina between Serbia and Croatia, with a reduced Muslim buffer state inbetween, and appealed for support from Turkey and the European Community (EC).

From September 1991 border areas began to fall into Serbian hands and Serbs began to form autonomous enclaves within the republic. In October 1991 the Bosnian parliament proclaimed the republic's 'sovereignty', but this was rejected by ethnic Serbs, who established an alternative assembly and held a referendum in November 1991 on remaining within the rump Yugoslav federation. In response, Muslims and Croats formed an alliance in the republic's parliament and voted, in January 1992, to seek recognition of independence by the EC. A subsequent referendum, held on 29 February–3 March 1992 at the EC's request, resulted in an overwhelming pro-independence vote. However, this referendum was boycotted by Bosnian Serbs, who were fierce opponents of independence. Independence from Yugoslavia was declared on 3 March 1992. Violent ethnic clashes ensued, with bombings in several Bosnian cities, and on 27 March 1992 Serb leaders proclaimed their own 'Serbian Republic of Bosnia and Herzegovina', stating their desire to remain in Yugoslavia. Despite the worsening situation, the EC and the United States officially recognized the country's independence on 7 April 1992 and in May 1992 Bosnia-Herzegovina was admitted into the United Nations (UN).

In the spring of 1992 Serb militia units, led by Dr Radovan Karadžić (b. 1945), an accomplished psychiatrist and poet, and effectively backed by Serbia, took control of border towns in eastern Bosnia. They also launched attacks on the capital, Sarajevo. As Croats, led by militia leader Mate Boban, who was designated president of the Croatian Community of Herceg-Bosna, and the ill-armed Muslims also struggled to gain disputed territory, a state of emergency was declared. A number of cease-fires were quickly broken. By the end of May 1992 hundreds had been killed and hundreds of thousands had been rendered homeless by the all-out civil war. Bosnian Serbs had established control over an area stretching from the northwest to the southeast, comprising seven-tenths of the country. They expelled or killed Muslims and Croats from these occupied zones as part of an 'ethnic cleansing' process, with the aim of establishing a more homogenous Serb population. They established a network of detention camps where atrocities, including torture, rape, and arbitrary executions, were reportedly perpetrated. Meanwhile, Croats dominated large portions of the western part of the country, comprising a fifth of Bosnia-Herzegovina, aiming to later unite these territories with their home republic so as to form a new 'Greater Croatia'.

The UN called for the withdrawal of the JNA by 19 May 1992 and imposed economic sanctions against Serbia. In June 1992 the UN Security Council voted to deploy UN forces in Bosnia so as to ensure the supply of humanitarian aid and to protect besieged Sarajevo airport. This mandate was extended in August 1992 to allow the UN's 'blue beret' troops, the UN Protection Force in the former Yugoslavia (UNPROFOR), to use force to protect relief supplies and the first UN troops arrived in Bosnia in November 1992. The UN and EC appointed Cyrus Vance, a former US State Department secretary, and Lord David Owen (b. 1938), a former British foreign minister, to act as mediators and reach a political settlement with the Bosnian Serbs, Bosnian Muslims, and Bosnian Croats. A Vance–Owen peace plan, providing for a federal, ethnic-based Bosnia, was accepted in principle in January 1993 by the Croats and Serbs, but Muslim politicians expressed initial reservations. The Muslims later agreed to the plan, but it was rejected by the self-styled Bosnian Serb Assembly in April 1993 and overwhelmingly in a referendum of Bosnian Serbs held on 15–16 May 1993, which involved the simultaneous endorsement of the establishment of a Bosnian Serb state.

By September 1993 it became accepted that the establishment of a federation of ten cantons, with three for each community and Sarajevo shared by all, was no longer feasible, and the UN and EC mediators, Thorvald Stoltenberg, a former foreign minister of Norway who replaced Vance as UN negotiator in April 1993, and Lord Owen entered into discussions in Geneva with the contending parties and drew up new plans to partition the country into three separate states organized on ethnic lines. This was criticized as rewarding ethnic cleansing and military aggression, but was viewed as the only practicable solution. However, the three communities, particularly the Serbs, disagreed on where boundaries should be drawn. As a result interethnic fighting continued, with Croats attacking the Muslim city of Mostar in February 1994 and Serbs bombarding Gorazde, a Muslim enclave in eastern Bosnia, in April–May 1994. By the latter date, the number of UN forces deployed in the country had reached 22,000. Their chief tasks were the 'containment' of fighting, the airlifting of relief food and medical aid into starving, isolated eastern Bosnia, the enforcement of a 'no-fly zone' over Bosnia, and the protection of militarily vulnerable 'UN safe areas', as designated by the UN in May 1993. These included Gorazde, which was defended by NATO air strikes against Serb forces in April 1994, yet, nevertheless, effectively fell to Bosnian Serb forces, Tuzla, Zepa, Bihac, and Srebrenica.

In March 1994 the Bosnian Croats and Muslims, formerly adversaries until a cease-fire was signed in February 1994, agreed, under United States prompting, to sign an accord providing for the establishment of a new Bosnian Muslim-Croat Federation of ethnically delineated cantons, with Sarajevo as its neutral capital (see *Political system* above) and the long-term goal of forming a confederation with Croatia. This new Muslim-Croat coalition began to change the military balance in the republic, although the Bosnian army, which included more than 200,000 troops, continued to be deprived of weapons with which to defend itself by an international arms embargo. On 9 June 1994 the UN Special Envoy, Yasushi Akashi, negotiated a temporary cease-fire in the civil war. This was flouted within days. However, in July 1994 the recently formed 'Contact Group', which comprised diplomats from the United States, Russia, Britain, France, and Germany, put together a peace plan. This provided for 51% of the country's territory being accorded to the Bosnian Muslim-Croat Federation, comprising much of central Bosnia and Herzegovina, as well as the eastern enclaves of Zepa, Gorazde, and Srebenica and the western outposts of Bihac and Orasje. The remaining 49% of the land area would be governed by the Bosnian Serbs, with Sarajevo placed under UN administration for several years, Mostar administered by the European Union (EU) and the UN also controlling thin strips of territory to link central Bosnia with its outlying enclaves. The UN and EU threatened to impose

strict sanctions if the plan was rejected. The Bosnian Muslim-Croat Federation accepted the proposal. However, the Bosnian Serbs, unwilling to give up 21% of the country, rejected the plan, following a referendum held on 27–28 August 1994. This was despite pressure to accept being imposed by Slobodan Milošević, the nationalist-minded president of Serbia, whose republic's economy had been damaged gravely by international sanctions which had been imposed in May 1992 as punishment for Serbian support of the Karadžić regime. Serbia responded by imposing an economic blockade on the Bosnian Serbs for all but humanitarian aid from August 1994, while the United States announced, in November 1994, that its forces in the Balkan region would no longer enforce the international arms embargo against Bosnia-Herzegovina, thus making it easier for the Bosnia-Croat Federation to build up its military strength.

In December 1994 the former US president, Jimmy Carter, negotiated a four-month cease-fire accord, which took effect from 1 January 1995. However, there were fears that a new wave of fighting would break out once the truce expired. The two contending parties, the Bosnian Muslim-Croat Federation and the Bosnian Serbs, had used the period of peace to regroup and rearm. The former, with 150,000 troops and 115 tanks, had agreed a military cooperation pact with Croatia and had become increasingly confident of its military strength and ability. The latter, with 75,000 troops and 400 tanks, while now denied assistance from Serbia, which appeared to be moving towards recognition of the borders of Bosnia-Herzegovina in exchange for a lifting of crippling UN sanctions, had closened their ties with the ethnic Serbs of the 'Republic of Krajina', in neighbouring eastern Croatia.

In May 1995 the Bosnian crisis intensified when Bosnian Serbs took 370 UN peacekeepers as hostages against further NATO air strikes and bombarded Muslim civilians in the 'safe area' of Tuzla. The West reacted by sending out a 12,500-troop Rapid Reaction Force to protect the 22,500-strong UNPROFOR. By 17 June 1995, following mediation by Serbia, the release of all the Bosnian Serb-held UN hostages had been secured. Ignoring belated UN air strikes, in July 1995 the Bosnian Serbs captured the UN 'safe areas' of Srebrenica and Zepa, situated in eastern Bosnia-Herzegovina, forcing more than 40,000 Muslim civilians to flee and allegedly murdering at least 4,000 Muslim troops. With the Bosnian Serbs' army chief, General Ratko Mladic, now apparently beyond the control of the civilian leader Dr Radovan Karadžić, they also attacked the Muslim enclave of Bihac in western Bosnia-Herzegovina and shelled Sarajevo. However, these actions provoked an effective riposte by the Croatian army, which overran the Serb-held 'Republic of Krajina' in August 1995 and launched assaults on Serb positions in western and southern Bosnia-Herzegovina.

The four-year-long conflict had wrecked the already poor economy of Bosnia-Herzegovina. It had claimed around 200,000 lives, injured many more, and rendered more than 1.5 million people homeless refugees. In July 1995 the US Senate voted to lift the arms embargo on Bosnia, although this was vetoed by President Clinton. Meanwhile, a number of Western countries, disillusioned by the failure of

UNPROFOR to prevent the fall of 'safe areas', now advocated the withdrawal of UNPROFOR. However, in September 1995 progress towards a peace deal was made when the Bosnian Serbs agreed 'in principle' to recognize the sovereignty of the Bosnian Muslim-Croat Federation on condition that the separate Bosnian Serb state, 'Respublika Srpska', comprising 49% of the territory, was also inter-nationally recognized.

Under US prompting, the foreign ministers of Bosnia, Croatia, and Serbia met in New York and agreed on the preliminary outlines of a new constitution for post-war Bosnia. This provided for a common parliament and elected presidency. From 12 October 1995 a 60-day cease-fire came into force and in November 1995 negotiations between leaders of Bosnia, Croatia, and Serbia began in Dayton, Ohio, USA. In the same month Bosnia and Serbia opened liaison offices in their respective capitals.

The Dayton talks produced an historic accord, on 21 November 1995, accept'd by the leaders of Bosnia, Croatia and Serbia. This provided for the country to remain a single state, with free, supervised elections, a rotating presidency, the return of refugees and the banning from public office of indicted war criminals. The peace plan was policed from January 1996 by a 60,000-strong NATO force, replacing the UN mission.

BULGARIA

Republic of Bulgaria
Republika Bulgariya

Capital: Sofia

Social and economic data
Area: 110,994 km²
Population: 8,900,000*

Pop. density per km²: 80*
Urban population: 69%**
Literacy rate: 95%**
GDP: $13,000 million**; per-capita GDP: $1,500**
Government defence spending (% of GDP): 2.9%**
Currency: lev
Economy type: middle income
Labour force in agriculture: 17%**

*1994
**1992

Ethnic composition
The Bulgarians, who constitute around 90% of the population, are a Southern Slavic race. Nine per cent of the population are ethnic Turks, who during the later 1980s were subjected to government pressure to adopt Slavic names and to resettle elsewhere. In 1989 an estimated 340,000 fled to Turkey, but 140,000 came back after the 'Bulgarization' programme and legal discrimination was abandoned in 1990. The official language is Bulgarian, a Slavonic tongue written in the Cyrillic alphabet.

Religions
Eighty-seven per cent of the religiously active population adheres to the Bulgarian Orthodox faith and 9%, predominantly ethnic Turks, to Islam. In addition, there are 65,000 adherents to the Latin branch of Roman Catholicism and 30,000 to its Bulgarian, Byzantine-Slavrite, branch, 60,000 Protestants, as well as 10,000 followers of the Armenian Orthodox Church. Religious freedom is guaranteed by the 1991 constitution.

Political features
State type: emergent democratic
Date of state formation: 1908
Political structure: unitary
Executive: parliamentary
Assembly: one-chamber
Party structure: multiparty
Human rights rating: 83%
International affiliations: BIS, BSECZ, COE, DC, EBRD, ECE, IAEA, IBRD, ICFTU, IMF, LORCS, NACC, NAM (guest), PFP, OSCE, UN, WEU (associate partner), WFTU

Local and regional government
There are nine regions (*oblasti*), including the capital, each administered by a governor appointed by the Council of Ministers. Municipalities have councils, elected every four years, and executive mayors.

Head of state
President Zhelyu Zhelev, since 1990

Head of government
Prime Minister Zhan Videnov, since 1995

Political leaders since 1970
1954–89 Todor Zhivkov (BKP)*, 1989–90 Petar Mladenov (BKP/BSP)*, 1990–91 Alexander Lilov (BKP/BSP)+, 1990– Zhelyu Zhelev (UDF)**, 1990 Andrei Lukanov (BKP/BSP)***, 1990–91 Dimitur Popov (independent)***,

1991–92 Filip Dimitrov (UDF)***, 1992–94 Lyuben Berov (MRF)***, 1994–95 Reneta Indzhova (UDF)***, 1995– Zhan Videnov (BSP)***

*Communist party leader and state president
**State president
***Prime minister
+Communist party leader

Political system

Under its July 1991 constitution, Bulgaria is a parliamentary republic. It has a single-chamber, 240-member parliament, the National Assembly or Duma, which is elected every five years by universal suffrage (for adults at least 21 years old), through a system of proportional representation, with a 4% threshold for party representation. The prime minister and cabinet, or Council of Ministers (COM), are drawn from the group able to command a majority in the Assembly. For the government to be overthrown in a no-confidence motion the opposition must secure an absolute majority of the votes, that is 121. A state president, who is also commander in chief of the armed forces, is popularly elected for a five-year term in a two-round majoritarian election. The president's powers are principally ceremonial, but the office holder has certain emergency powers and may return legislation to the National Assembly for further consideration, but can be overruled. Candidates for the presidency must be at least 40 years old and resident in Bulgaria for at least five years before the election. This residency qualification prevented Simeon II, the pretender to the Bulgarian throne, who had lived in exile since 1946, from contesting the 1992 presidential election. A turnout level of at least 50% is required for a presidential election result to be valid. The separation of powers between the legislature, executive, and judiciary is monitored by a 12-member Constitutional Court. Amendments to the constitution must be carried by a majority of three-quarters of the National Assembly's members in three ballots on three different days. A new constitution may only be adopted by an elected 400-member Grand National Assembly.

Political parties

There are three principal political parties in Bulgaria: the excommunist Bulgarian Socialist Party (BSP: Bulgarska Sotsialisticheska Partiya); the right-of-centre Union of Democratic Forces (UDF: Sayuz na Demokratichni Sili, SDS); and the Turkish community-orientated Movement for Rights and Freedoms (MRF: Dvizhenie za Prava i Svobodi, DPS).

The BSP is the successor to the formerly dominant Bulgarian Communist Party (BKP: Bulgarska Komunisticheska Partiya). It adopted its present name in April 1990 and is led by Zhan Videnov. Arguably the least 'reform-socialist' of the excommunist parties of Central Europe, it favours improved links with Russia and the construction of a social safety net to cushion the impact of the transition to a market economy. The BKP was formed in 1919 by a radical faction that split away from the Bulgarian Social Democratic (Workers') Party, which had been established in 1891. From its earliest days, it was closely tied to the Russian communist movement. Banned within Bulgaria in 1923, it was forced underground during much of the interwar period. The party has

been organized traditionally on pyramidal, Leninist 'democratic centralist lines', being controlled by a small Politburo. By 1986 the BKP's membership had risen to 932,000, representing 10.4% of the country's total population. Membership of the BSP was put, in 1992, at 475,000.

The UDF was formed in December 1989 as an umbrella alliance of anticommunist forces committed to political pluralism and market-centred reform. It is led by Filip Dimitrov and is an increasingly fractious coalition, embracing economic liberals, environmentalists, independent trade unions, intellectuals, and nationalists. Much of its support is drawn from the urban middle classes.

The 95,000-member MRF, founded in 1990, is orientated towards Bulgaria's rural-based Turkish minority community and is led by the former dissident philosopher, Ahmed Dogan.

More than 50 other political parties function, including the Bulgarian Agricultural People's Union-United (BAPU), a peasant organization, which was founded as the Agrarian Party in 1899, and was allowed to operate under communist rule as a force subservient to the BKP.

Latest elections

The most recent National Assembly elections were held on 18 December 1994 and resulted in victory for the excommunist BSP. In alliance with two minor parties, the Ecoglasnost Political Club and the Alexander Stamboliiski Agrarian Party, the BSP won 44% of the national vote and 125 of the Assembly's 240 seats. The incumbent UDF captured just 24% of the vote and 69 seats, the Bulgarian National Agrarian Union/People's Union/Democratic Party, 7% of the vote and 18 seats, while the MRF and Bulgarian Business Bloc (BBB) each secured 5% of the vote and 15 and 13 seats respectively. A further 50 parties contested the election but failed to surmount the 4% vote threshold for representation. Turnout was 75%.

A direct presidential election was held on 12 and 19 January 1992. It was won by Zhelyu Zhelev, a former dissident philosopher, representing the UDF, who captured 53% of the second ballot 'run-off' vote, defeating Velko Vulkanov, an independent supported by the BSP, who had campaigned on an anti-Turkish platform.

Political history

Settled by the Slavs in the late 6th century, the area covered by contemporary Bulgaria was conquered in the 7th century by Turkish Bulgars who merged with the local population. They adopted Eastern Orthodox Christianity in the later 8th century and established powerful empires in the 10th and 12th centuries. From 1396 Bulgaria formed part of the Ottoman Empire. National liberation revolts occurred during the later 19th century, being aided by the defeat of the Ottomans in 1878 by the Russian Tsar Alexander II, but full independence was not achieved until 1908.

During World War I, Bulgaria allied itself with Germany, and, after its early defeat, lost Aegean coastal lands which it controlled to the Allied forces. The retreating troops mutinied and proclaimed a republic. The uprising was, however, suppressed, with German military aid. After the war, support for the left-wing Social Democratic and Agrarian parties increased and in 1919 an independent Agrarian government was formed under the leadership of Alexander Stamboliiski. It introduced a series of radical measures, including land reform, before being overthrown in a fascist coup in June 1923, in which Stamboliiski was murdered. A further coup in 1934 established a monarchical-fascist dictatorship under the leadership of King Boris III. The country remained backward, with more than 70% of the labour force employed in agriculture.

In 1941 Bulgaria again allied itself with Germany, joining in the occupation of Yugoslavia and declaring war on Britain and the United States. King Boris mysteriously died in 1943, following a visit to Hitler, and was succeeded by his young son, Simeon II. The country was subjected to German occupation, and then invaded by the USSR in September 1944.

The Soviet Union put into power a communist-inclined anti-fascist alliance, the Fatherland Front, under the leadership of General Kimon Georgiyev. Within the Front, the Bulgarian Communist Party (BKP), led by Georgi Dimitrov (1882-1949), who had returned from exile, controlled the key interior and justice ministries and set about purging the bureaucracy and armed forces of opposition elements.

In September 1946, following a referendum, the monarchy was abolished and a new People's Republic proclaimed. In October 1946, elections were held to the Grand National Assembly (Sobranje) on a single Fatherland Front basis, with the Communists gaining 277 of the 465 seats. A new, Soviet-style constitution was then drafted and adopted in December 1947, establishing a single-party state.

The new regime, headed, respectively, by BKP first secretaries Georgi Dimitrov and Vulko Chervenkov, the brother-in-law of Dimitrov, between 1945 and 1949 and between 1950 and 1954, proceeded to nationalize industrial and financial institutions and introduce cooperative farming, central planning, and repressive police control in a Stalinist manner. Political opponents were summarily executed, including the Agrarian Party leader, Nikola Petkov.

The more moderate Todor Zhivkov (b. 1911) succeeded Chervenkov as BKP leader in 1954. He pursued a determined industrialization programme, creating significant growth in the engineering and electronics sectors during the 1960s. In May 1971 he introduced a new presidential constitution. This enabled him to relinquish the chair of the Council of Ministers (COM), a post he had held since 1962, and become president of the newly formed State Council. Stanko Todorov became chairman of the COM, holding the post continuously until 1981, when he was replaced by Grisha Filipov.

Under Zhivkov, who enjoyed particularly close relations with the Soviet leader, Leonid Brezhnev, Bulgaria emerged as one of the USSR's most loyal satellites. Only limited political and economic reforms were tolerated at home, industrial growth being based on the formation of large, integrated State Economic Organizations (SEOs). Externally, Bulgaria strictly adhered to Brezhnev's 'Moscow line' during international disputes and became a closely integrated member of Comecon and the Warsaw Treaty Organization. During the 1980s the country faced mounting economic problems and, prompted by Mikhail Gorbachev, who became the new reformist Soviet leader in 1985, a haphazard series of administrative and economic reforms, under

the slogan *preustroistvo* ('restructuring'), were introduced and a new generation of leaders promoted to power. The reforms involved greater decentralization in the planning process, based on factory 'management'; greater openness in party affairs; the introduction of market efficiency principles ('the new economic mechanism') to eliminate weak enterprises; the streamlining of the state bureaucracy; and the launching of a series of campaigns against corruption and inefficiency. However, these measures proved insufficient for reformers inside and outside the BKP and, influenced both by public demonstrations and the dramatic changes which were occurring in other Soviet satellites and backed by the army and Soviet leadership, Zhivkov was replaced as BKP leader and state president on 10 November 1989 by the foreign minister, Petar Mladenov (b. 1936). In January 1990 the BKP's 'leading role' in the political system was terminated, enabling opposition parties and independent trade unions to function. In addition, political prisoners were freed and the secret police wing responsible for the surveillance of dissidents was abolished.

In February 1990, as an estimated 200,000 UDF supporters gathered in Sofia to demand an end to BKP rule, Alexander Lilov, a reformer, became BKP leader and Andrei Lukanov was appointed prime minister, replacing Georgi Atanasov, who had been premier since 1986. A special commission was established to investigate allegations of nepotism and fraud by the administration of Todor Zhivkov, who was placed under house arrest. Zhivkov was subsequently tried in September 1992, found guilty and sentenced to seven years' imprisonment, while Atanasov was sentenced to ten years' imprisonment for embezzlement. As part of the new reform drive, private farming was made legal once again and price controls were eased, resulting in shortages of foodstuffs and spiralling inflation. The BKP renamed itself the Bulgarian Socialist Party (BSP) in April 1990 and in a multiparty general election held on 10 and 17 June 1990 captured 47% of the national vote and 211 of the 400 elective seats. The opposition liberal-conservative Union of Democratic Forces (UDF), formed in December 1989, won 36% of the vote and claimed that the contest had been marred by ballot-rigging.

Petar Mladenov resigned the presidency in July 1990 and was succeeded by the UDF's leader, Dr Zhelyu Zhelev (b. 1935), a former philosophy professor. Following mass demonstrations and a general strike, Andrei Lukanov was also replaced as prime minister in December 1990 by the independent Dimitur Popov, who headed a caretaker coalition government. A new constitution was adopted in July 1991, defining the country as a parliamentary republic with a 'democratic, constitutional and welfare state'. By October 1991 prices had increased tenfold and unemployment stood at 300,000. The October 1991 general election, held under the new constitution, resulted in a hung parliament, with the UDF edging out the BSP, capturing 34% of the national vote and 110 of the 240 elective seats, but not securing an overall majority. The BSP secured 33% of the vote and 106 seats. This left the ethnic Turkish community-orientated MRF holding the balance of power with 24 seats, based on an 8% vote share.

A minority UDF government was duly formed, the first noncommunist administration in Bulgaria for 46 years, with

Filip Dimitrov, an ex-Green Party lawyer, becoming prime minister. Western aid to the republic began to slowly increase and the United States reduced its import tariffs imposed on Bulgarian goods. Zhelyu Zhelev became Bulgaria's first directly elected president in January 1992, but the new UDF administration soon encountered mounting dissension as the economic situation deteriorated, after a GDP fall of 26% in 1991 led to severe food and fuel shortages and the rationing of basic commodities. There were strikes by miners, public transport workers, civil servants, and teachers in July and September 1992 and in October 1992 the MRF and BSP voted together to bring down the Dimitrov administration. Lyuben Berov (b. 1925), an academic economist and member of the MRF, became the new prime minister in December 1992, heading an MRF and BSP-backed 'government of experts'.

The new administration pressed ahead with gradualist economic reforms, with a programme to privatize 500 medium-to-large state enterprises, on the Czech 'mass privatization' voucher model, being approved in August 1993. It also signed a ten-year treaty of friendship and cooperation with Russia in April 1993. However, Berov secured little positive support in a series of seven no-confidence votes which were held during 1994 and in September 1994 the prime minister tendered his resignation. He was replaced in October 1994, in a caretaker capacity, by Reneta Indzhova from the UDF, who was the former head of the Privatization Agency and who became the country's first female prime minister.

The general election, held on 18 December 1994, resulted in a clear victory for the BSP, which captured 44% of the national vote to the divided UDF's 24%, and a parliamentary majority. The BSP profited from growing nostalgia for the communist era, especially among the old, living on fixed incomes, and rural communities who were concerned by the country's economic decline and high rates of inflation (120% during 1994), unemployment (20%), and crime. In addition, unlike other central European states, opposition parties were unable to benefit from a strong nationalist or anti-Russian sentiment. Indeed, Bulgarians shared a common Slavonic and Orthodox Christian heritage with the Russians and had never rebelled during the communist era or required the deployment of Red Army troops.

The Moscow-trained Zhan Videnov, leader of the BSP since December 1991, but still only 35 years old, became the new prime minister in January 1995. He put together a cabinet, which comprised a number of independent technocrats, and pledged to work towards closer relations with Russia and to reduce the pain of market reform through giving more attention to social and welfare issues, in a 'social-market' manner, while continuing with privatization.

CROATIA

Republic of Croatia Republika Hrvatska

Capital: Zagreb

Social and economic data
Area: 56,538 km²
Population: 4,900,000*

Pop. density per km²: 87*
Urban population: 51%**
Literacy rate: 97%**
GDP: $7,500 million**+; per-capita GDP: $1,530**+
Government defence spending (% of GDP): 5.9%**
Currency: kuna (formerly the Croatian dinar)
Economy type: middle income+
Labour force in agriculture: N/A

*1994
**1992
+Estimates for Croatia's GDP vary widely, ranging from $7,900 million to $20,900 million for 1990, before the civil war caused considerable damage

Ethnic composition
In 1991 77% of the republic's population were ethnic Croats, a south Slavic people, 12% ethnic Serbs, and 1% Slovenes. However, the civil war of 1991, subsequent 'ethnic cleansing' (involving the forcible expulsion by one ethnic group of another to create a more homogenous population) in Croat and Serb-dominated areas, and the protracted conflict in neighbouring Bosnia have been associated with large-scale population movements. More than 300,000 Croats have been displaced from Serbian enclaves within the republic and there are an estimated 500,000 refugees from Bosnia in the republic. Serbs are most thickly settled in areas bordering Bosnia-Herzegovina, particularly in the Krajina region, between Bosnia and the Adriatic coast, and in Slavonia, in eastern Croatia. However, more than 150,000 fled from Krajina to Bosnia-Herzegovina and Serbia, following the region's recapture by the Croatian army in August 1995. The official language, since 1991, has been Croatian, though Serbian is widely spoken. Both languages are versions of Serbo-Croat, but the Roman Catholic Croats use the Latin script, while the Eastern Orthodox Serbs use the Cyrillic script.

Religions

Most Croats adhere to the Roman Catholic faith, while Serbs are predominantly Serbian Eastern Orthodox Christians. There are small Muslim, Protestant, and Jewish minorities.

Political features

State type: emergent democratic
Date of state formation: 1991
Political structure: unitary
Executive: limited presidential
Assembly: two-chamber
Party structure: multiparty
Human rights rating: N/A
International affiliations: COE, IAEA, IBRD, IMF, NAM (observer), OSCE, UN

Local and regional government

For the purpose of local administration, the republic is divided into 21 counties, 420 municipalities, and 61 towns. Between 1991 and 1995, one-third of the country, divided into four zones adjoining Bosnia-Herzegovina, was ruled by technically illegal ethnic Serb regimes. The largest Serb-controlled enclave was the self-declared 'Republic of Serbian Krajina' (RSK) which had its own Serb-elected parliament, with a president, Milan Martic, and prime minister, Borislav Mikelic. It included smaller Serb enclaves in Slavonia. The UN Confidence Restoration Operation (UNCRO) supervised an uneasy truce in these zones. However, the Croat army retook Western Slavonia in May 1995 and Krajina in August 1995. This left only Eastern Slavonia, adjoining Serbia in the northeast, under the control of Croatian Serbs. In the formerly Italian-ruled peninsula of Istria, situated along the Adriatic coast in the far northwest of Croatia, there is a growing separatist movement, led by the Istrian Democratic Assembly (IDS).

Head of state (executive)

President Dr Franjo Tudjman, since 1990

Head of government

Prime Minister Zlatko Matesa, since 1995

Political leaders since 1970*

1990–   Dr Franjo Tudjman (HDZ)

*Executive president

Political system

Under the terms of the December 1990 constitution Croatia has a mixture of a presidential and parliamentary system. However, such is the charismatic authority of the current incumbent of the office of president, Franjo Tudjman, that at present the form of executive is best characterized as 'limited presidential' rather than 'dual'. The president is directly elected for a five-year term and serves as head of state, representing the country abroad, and supreme commander of the armed forces, appoints and dismisses the prime minister and members of the government, calls referenda, calls elections for parliament, and, at times of crisis or war, has decree powers. During the 1991–92 civil war, a war cabinet, the Special Council, was established, which was chaired by the State Council. The parliament, known as the Assembly (Sabor), is a two-chamber body, comprising an 80-member lower house, the Chamber of Deputies, or Representatives (Predstavnicki Dom), and a 63-seat upper house, the Chamber of Districts, or Municipalities (Zupanski Dom). Lower-house deputies are popularly elected for four-year terms, while three upper-chamber representatives are elected from each of the republic's 21 counties. The Chamber of Deputies is the most influential of the two houses, approving laws, adopting the state budget, and deciding on wars and peace. The upper house can, however, propose legislation and, after a bill is adopted by the lower chamber, return laws for reconsideration. The prime minister and cabinet, though appointed by the president, need to be able to command a majority within the Chamber of Deputies. From January 1993 proportional representation replaced first-past-the-post as the electoral system used in the republic. Three lower chamber seats are guaranteed to the country's Serbian minority.

Political parties

There are seven significant parties in Croatia: the Christian Democratic Union (HDZ), the Croatian Social Liberal Party (HSLS), the Social Democratic Party of Change (SDP), the Croatian Party of Rights (HSP), the Croatian Peasant Party (HSS), the Croatian National Party (HNS), and the Serbian National Party (SNS).

The HDZ is a right-of-centre Christian democratic nationalist force, led by President Franjo Tudjman, and is the dominant party in Croatia, controlling both houses of parliament. Formed in 1989, it has been subject during recent years to divisions between its right and liberal, or left, wings, particularly over the issue of whether or not to pursue an active military policy in Bosnia-Herzegovina. This culminated, in April 1994, in Stipe Mesic and Josip Manolic, respectively chairs of the lower and upper chambers of parliament and leaders of the liberal wing, leaving to form the breakaway Croatian Independent Democrats (HND), claiming the support of 16 deputies. The HND was critical of Tudjman's allegedly 'dictatorial' leadership style and the support given to the Bosnian Croat Army's campaign in southern Bosnia.

The HSLS, a centrist force led by Drazen Budisa, is the chief opposition party.

The SDP is the reform-socialist successor to the formerly dominant Croatian League of Socialists, or communist party, later known as the Party of Democratic Renewal (PDR). It adopted its current name in 1991.

The HSP is an ultranationalist Croat-orientated body. It has a paramilitary wing, the Croatian Defence Association (HOS), which has been involved in fighting in the Croatian civil war and has been linked with anti-Serb incidents. The activities of the HSP are kept under close surveillance and in November 1991, Dobroslav Paraga, the party's then leader, was arrested on charges of terrorism. He was subsequently acquitted in November 1993.

The HSS, led by Zlatko Tomcic, is orientated towards rural interests, notably peasants, and the SNS to the Serbian minority.

There are also three small parties which campaign for regional autonomy: the Istrian Democratic Assembly (IDS), the Dalmatian Action Party (DA), and the Rijeka Democratic Alliance (RDA).

Latest elections

The most recent elections to the Chamber of Deputies,held in October 1995, were won by the governing HDZ. With 45% of the votes, it won 42 of the seats, falling short of the two-thirds majority which would have enabled the constitution to be amended to increase the president's powers. The HSS–IDS–HNS alliance secured 18% of the vote, the HSLS 12%, the SDP 9% and the HSP 5%; 290,000 Bosnian Croats voted in the election.

The HDZ also secured a clear majority of seats, 37 out of 63, to the upper house, the Chamber of Districts, in the elections held on 7 February 1993.

The HDZ's leader, Dr Franjo Tudjman, won the direct presidential election held on 2 August 1992, attracting 57% of the vote. His nearest rival, Drazen Budisa of the HSLS, captured 22% of the vote and there were six other candidates. Voting rights in this, and the concurrent parliamentary election, were extended to Croats in Bosnia-Herzegovina and to anyone with a Croat parent or who intended to apply for Croat citizenship.

Political history

Part of Pannonia in Roman times, the region was settled by Carpathian Croats in the 7th century. Formed into a kingdom under Tomislav in 924, for eight centuries from 1102 it enjoyed autonomy under the Hungarian crown, except for Slavonia, in the east, which between 1526 and 1699 was held by the Ottoman Turks. In the 19th century, Croatia formed part of the Austro-Hungarian Habsburg Empire. After World War I and the dissolution of the Habsburg Empire in 1918, it became a constituent part of the new kingdom of the Serbs, Croats, and Slovenes, known from 1929 as Yugoslavia. The Roman Catholic Croats resented the domination of this kingdom by Serbs, who were Eastern Orthodox Christians, and a Croat terrorist organization, the Ustasa, became active during the 1930s. This body was responsible for the assassination, in 1934, of King Alexander I of Yugo-slavia, who was a Serb and had set up a royal dictatorship in 1929, during a state visit to France. During World War II, after the Germans occupied Yugoslavia, a Nazi puppet state, 'Greater Croatia', was established from April 1941 under the 'Poglavnik' (leader) Ante Pavelic (1889–1959), the Herzegovina-born Ustasa leader. This included most of Bosnia-Herzegovina and parts of Serbia, as well as the modern republic. As many as 500,000 Serbs, 55,000 Jews, and thousands of Romanies (gypsies) were brutally massacred in extermination camps by this Croatian fascist regime, which sought to establish a 'pure' Croat Catholic republic. The Ustasa state met with fierce resistance from the communist Partisans and, after a bitter civil war, was overthrown in 1944.

In November 1945, Croatia became a constituent republic within the communist-dominated Yugoslav Socialist Federal Republic, whose dominant figure, Marshal Tito, was a Croatian who had led the Partisan resistance to the Pavelic regime. Along with neighbouring Slovenia, Croatia became one of the richest republics in the federation, with a thriving agricultural sector, substantial manufacturing industries, and a burgeoning tourist industry along the Dalmatian, or Adriatic, coast. Haunted by memories of the Ustasa regime, the federal republic's communist leadership treated with hostil-

ity expressions of Croatian nationalism, which they equated with fascism. However, Croats grew increasingly to resent the economic subsidies that the republic paid to poorer members of the federation in the east and south and also the fact that the federation and even the League of Communists of Croatia (LCC), following a purge of its Croat leadership in 1972, were dominated by Serbs. Consequently, from the 1960s there was an upsurge in Croat nationalism. Initially it took the form, in the Maspok ('mass movement'), of a cultural revival, but, from the 1970s, a violent separatist movement began to gain ground, which was not appeased by Tito's construction of a looser federation in 1974.

Nationalist agitation continued through the 1980s and there was mounting industrial unrest from 1987 as spiralling inflation caused a sharp fall in living standards. In an effort to court popularity and concerned at the Serb chauvinism of Slobodan Milošević, Communist Party chief and president of Serbia from 1986, the LCC, later renamed the Party of Democratic Renewal (PDR), adopted an increasingly anti-Serb line from the mid-1980s. In addition, following Slovenia's lead, it allowed the formation of rival political parties from 1989.

However, in the first multiparty republic elections, which were held in April–May 1990, the PDR was comprehensively defeated by the right-wing nationalist Croatian Democratic Union (HDZ). Led by the former Tito Partisan and revisionist historian, the retired General Dr Franjo Tudjman (b. 1922), who had been imprisoned in 1972 and 1981 for his nationalist activities and who advocated the creation of a 'Greater Croatia', which would include Bosnia-Herzegovina, the HDZ won almost a two-thirds assembly majority. This was based on a 42% share of the republic's vote. Tudjman was duly elected state president by the Sabor (parliament) on 30 May 1990.

As president, Tudjman was initially conciliatory, declaring his government's aim to be simply a demand for greater autonomy. However, in February 1991 the Croatian Assembly, in conjunction with that of neighbouring Catholic Slovenia, issued a proclamation calling for secession from Yugoslavia and the establishment of a new confederation which would exclude Serbia and Montenegro. It also ordered the creation of an independent Croatian army.

Concerned at possible maltreatment in a future independent Croatia, in March 1991 Serb militants announced the secession from Croatia of the self-proclaimed 'Serbian Autonomous Region of Krajina', situated in western Croatia between the Adriatic coast and the border with Bosnia-Herzegovina. Centred on Knin and economically underdeveloped, Krajina contained 250,000 Serbs. The region's full traditional name, 'Vojna Krajina', meant 'military frontier'. In a referendum held on 12 May 1991 there was 90% support in Krajina for it remaining with Serbia and Montenegro, in a residual Yugoslavia. A week later, on 19 May 1991, Croatia's electors voted overwhelmingly, by a 94% margin, for independence within a loose confederation of Yugoslav sovereign states and on 25 June 1991 the Croatian government, in concert with the Slovenian government, issued a unilateral declaration of independence.

From July 1991, despite Croatia agreeing to suspend implementation of its independence declaration for three months, there was an escalating conflict between Croatian government forces and the Serb-dominated Yugoslav army (JNA) and civil war between Serbs and Croats within Croatia. Independent Serbian 'governments' were proclaimed in Krajina and also in Eastern and Western Slavonia. A succession of cease-fires ordered by the Yugoslav federal presidency and European Community (EC) observers passed unobserved and by September 1991 a third of Croatia had fallen under Serb control. The most intense fighting took place around the towns of Osijek and Vukovar in Slavonia, near Croatia's eastern border, as Serbs sought to link together Krajina and Serbia in a new 'Greater Serbia'. Three thousand people, mainly Croats, died in the attempted defence of Vukovar. Croatia's ports were besieged and at least 500,000 people had been made refugees. The fighting lasted longer than in Slovenia since the Serb-dominated Yugoslav federal authorities were unwilling to accept the loss of a republic which contained such a substantial Serb minority.

Rich in oil, Croatia retaliated with an oil-supply blockade on Serbia and announced, in October 1991, that it had formally severed all official relations with Yugoslavia. At the same time, attacks were launched on federal army barracks within the republic. By the end of 1991 the conflict had claimed as many as 10,000 lives. However, on 2 January 1992 a peace plan was successfully brokered in Sarajevo by the United Nations (UN) envoy, Cyrus Vance. This provided for an immediate cease-fire, the full withdrawal of the JNA from Croatia, and the deployment, from February 1992, of 14,000 UN 'blue beret' troops, the UN Protection Force in Yugoslavia (UNPROFOR), later known as the UN Confidence Restoration Operation (UNCRO), in contested Krajina and Eastern and Western Slavonia, while demilitarization was effected and a political settlement worked out. This accord was disregarded by the breakaway Serb leader in Krajina, Milan Babic, but was recognized by the main Croatian and Serbian forces. Under German pressure, the independence of Croatia and Slovenia was recognized by the EC and the United States on 15 January 1992 and in May 1992 Croatia was admitted to the UN.

During 1992 an uneasy truce lasted within Croatia and its four Serb-controlled enclaves. The JNA withdrew from the republic in mid-May 1992 and the Serbs ended their 238-day siege of the port and tourist resort of Dubrovnik on 28 May. However, UNCRO was unsuccessful in its efforts to enforce demilitarization in the Serb enclaves and there was sporadic Croat–Serb fighting in Krajina and Slavonia, as well as reports of forced expulsions of minority communities, part of an 'ethnic cleansing' process. Tensions were strained further by the outbreak of civil war in neighbouring Bosnia-Herzegovina, where Bosnian Serbs were the initial aggressors, but where Croats also sought, initially, to establish by force their own independent enclaves. The crisis in Bosnia led to an influx of hundreds of thousands of refugees into Croatia.

Presidential and parliamentary elections held in Croatia in August 1992 resulted in the re-election of President Tudjman and the governing HDZ, whose control over the media had been tightened during 1992. However, the ethnic disputes in Krajina, Slavonia, and Bosnia were fomenting widening divisions between the HDZ's extreme nationalist right wing, which advocated Croat military action in Bosnia to carve out

a new 'Greater Croatia', and its liberal left wing, which favoured establishing a defensive military alliance with the Bosnian Muslim government so as to pool resources against the common Serb threat. President Tudjman sided with the latter faction on 1 March 1994 when he signed the Washington agreement with the Bosnian Muslims and Bosnian Croats. This provided for a cease-fire in fighting between Muslims and Croats in Bosnia, the formation of a Muslim-Croat Federation in Bosnia-Herzegovina and included the long-term goal of confederation with Croatia.

The Croatian economy was devastated by the civil war of 1991–92 and the subsequent Croat–Serb tensions. GDP fell by 45% between 1990 and 1992, with the Dalmatian coast tourist industry and foreign investment collapsing; the annual inflation rate rose to more than 500%; wartime physical damage amounted to at least $15 billion; the maintenance of a refugee population of 500,000 was consuming a fifth of the annual budget; while the armed forces, which numbered more than 100,000, were an even greater resource drain. Despite these distractions, the HDZ administration continued to press on with market-centred economic reforms, including privatization, driven on by the eventual goal of seeking entry into the European Union.

In January 1993 Croat forces violated the 1992 UN peace agreement, launching a military offensive into Serb-held Krajina. This, and an 'Operation Blitz' offensive in May 1995, which resulted in the recapture of Western Slavonia, met with some success. However, still, by mid-1995, Serbs continued to control around 27% of Bosnia. Their position appeared to be effectively safeguarded by UNCRO. In the 'Republic of Serbian Krajina' (RSK), which included Serb-inhabited parts of Slavonia, the Serbs had their own parliament and, in January 1994, elected as president the moderate nationalist, Milan Martic, who replaced the more extreme Milan Babic. In March 1995 President Tudjman agreed reluctantly to sanction an extension of UNCRO's mandate in Croatia, but insisted that the force must be scaled down in size and should concentrate on policing the borders between Croatia and Bosnia and Serbia.

In August 1995, taking advantage of increasing international revulsion at the actions of the Bosnian Serbs, who had launched brutal offensives against Muslim UN 'safe area' enclaves within Bosnia-Herzegovina, including Bihac, adjoining Croatia, a lightning advance into Serbian Krajina was launched in August 1995 by more than 150,000 Croat army troops. Heavily overwhelmed, the 50,000 Serb irregulars defending the self-proclaimed republic were forced to withdraw into western Bosnia-Herzegovina and within 30 hours the Croats had recaptured Knin, capital of the Krajina region. Three UN peacekeepers were killed during the 'Operation Storm' blitzkrieg assault, which was followed by Croat raids into Serb-held areas of adjoining Bosnia-Herzegovina. At least three-quarters of the Serb inhabitants of Krajina, numbering 200,000, fearing reprisals by the Croats, fled east into Bosnia and Serbia, producing a self-imposed form of 'ethnic cleansing'. By September 1995 only the narrow belt of Eastern Slavonia, lying in northeast Croatia along the country's border with Serbia, remained in the hands of Croatian Serbs. There were 1,500 UN peacekeepers in Eastern Slavonia and plans were made to withdraw UN 7,500 troops stationed in Krajina and Western Slavonia. A snap general election, held in October 1995, resulted in a clear victory for Tudjman's HDZ. In November 1995 Serbia agreed to hand back control over Eastern Slavonia to Croatia over a two-year period, with international administration in the interval.

CYPRUS

Republic of Cyprus
Kipriakí Dimokratía
(and Turkish Republic of Northern Cyprus
Kibris Cumhuriyeti)

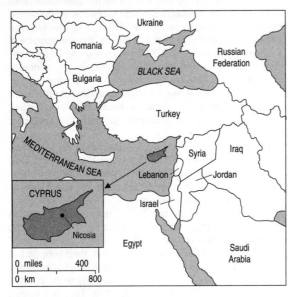

Capital: Nicosia

Social and economic data
Area: 9,250 km^2
Population: 725,000*
Pop. density per km^2: 75*
Urban population: 54%**
Literacy rate: 91%**
GDP: $5,800 million**; per-capita GDP: $8,000**
Government defence spending (% of GDP): 7.5%**
Currency: Cyprus pound
Economy type: high income
Labour force in agriculture: 17%**

*1994
**1992

Ethnic composition
About 80% of the population have Greek origins and are Greek-speaking, while about 18% have Turkish roots and speak Turkish, living in the northern part of the island, within the self-styled Turkish Republic of Northern Cyprus.

Religions
There are about 444,000 members of the Greek Orthodox Church, mainly in the south, and about 105,000 Muslims, mainly in the north.

Political features
State type: liberal democratic
Date of state formation: 1960
Political structure: unitary
Executive: limited presidential
Assembly: one-chamber
Party structure: multiparty
Human rights rating: N/A
International affiliations: ACP (associate), CE, CSCE, CW, IAEA, IBRD, ICC, ICFTU, IMF, NAM, OIC, UN, WTO

Local and regional government
For administrative purposes, the country is divided into six districts, ranging in population from just over 30,000 to over 230,000.

Head of state and head of government
Greek: President Glafkos Clerides, since 1993
(Turkish: Rauf Denktaş, since 1976)

Political leaders since 1970
1960–74 Archbishop Makarios III (EOKA), 1974 Nicos Sampson (military), 1974–77 Archbishop Makarios III (DEKO), 1977–88 Spyros Kyprianou (DEKO), 1988–1993 Georgios Vassilou (independent), 1993– Glafkos Clerides (DISY)

Political system
The 1960 constitution provided for power-sharing between Greek and Turkish Cypriots, on a basis of numerical parity, but in 1963 the Turks declined to participate and the following year set up a separate community in northern Cyprus, refusing to acknowledge the Greek government in the south. The Greek Cypriot government claims to be the government of all Cyprus and is generally accepted as such, except by the Turkish community. There are, therefore, two republics, each with its own president, council of ministers, assembly, and judicial system. The self-styled 'Turkish Republic of Northern Cyprus' even has its own representatives overseas. Greek Cyprus has a president, elected for five years by universal adult suffrage, through a second ballot voting system, and a single-chamber assembly, the House of Representatives, with 80 members, elected by simple plurality and also for five years. Twenty-four of the seats are reserved for Turkish members but, since they have never been taken up, all the current 56 members are Greek. The president appoints and heads a council of ministers.

Turkish Cyprus adopted a separate constitution, after a referendum in 1985, providing for a president, Council of Ministers, and assembly similar to that in the southern part of the island. This separate government has only received external recognition from Turkey. In 1988 the newly elected president, Georgios Vassilou, pledged himself to construct a national government and to work speedily towards an end to the division of the island. Later that year talks between him and the Turkish Cypriot leader began, under United Nations auspices, but did not come to a successful conclusion. His successor, Glafkos Clerides, continued the search for unity.

Political parties
Of seven political parties, the four most significant in the Greek sector are the Democratic Party (DEKO), the Progres-

sive Party of the Working People (AKEL), the Democratic Rally (DISY), and the Socialist Party–National Democratic Union of Cyprus (SK–EDEK).

DEKO was formed in 1976. It has a centre-left orientation and believes that the solution to Cyprus's problems lies in a federal strategy, achieved through the good offices of the United Nations.

AKEL was formed in 1941 as the successor to the Communist Party of Cyprus. Although its orientation is socialist, it was not formally aligned with the Soviet bloc. It supported the candidature of Georgios Vassilou for the presidency in 1988, even though he himself stood as an independent.

DISY was formed in 1976. In 1977 it absorbed the Democratic National Party (DEK) into its ranks. It has a centrist orientation and supports the idea of Western nations taking an active part in bringing Cyprus's racial and religious troubles to an end.

SK–EDEK was formed in 1969 as the Socialist Party of Cyprus. It supports the idea of a nonaligned, independent, unitary, and demilitarized Cyprus, with a socialist social and economic structure.

Latest elections

In the May 1991 House of Representatives elections the results were as follows:

	% votes	Seats
DISY	35.8	20
AKEL	30.6	18
DEKO	19.5	11
SK–EDEK	10.9	7

In the 1993 presidential election the results were as follows:

1st Ballot:	Glafkos Clerides (DISY)	36.7%
	Georgios Vassilou (independent)	44.2%
	Paschalis Paschalides (EDEK)	18.6%
2nd Ballot:	Glafkos Clerides	50.3%
	Georgios Vassilou	49.7%

Political history

Originally Greek, Cyprus was conquered by the Turks in 1571 and then by the British in 1878, and annexed in 1914. In 1955 a guerrilla war against British rule was started by Greek Cypriots seeking 'Enosis', or unification with Greece. The chief organization in this campaign was the National Organization of Cypriot Combatants (EOKA) and its political and military leaders were the Head of the Greek Orthodox Church in Cyprus, Archbishop Makarios III (1913–77), and General George Grivas (1898–1974). Because of their activities Makarios and other Enosis leaders were deported by the British government in 1956.

After three years of intensive negotiations, Makarios was allowed to return to Cyprus and, with the granting of full independence in 1960, was elected president of the new Greek–Turkish state. As part of the independence agreement, Britain was allowed to retain its military and naval bases on the island.

Relations between the Greek and Turkish political leaders deteriorated and in 1963 the Turks withdrew from power-sharing and fighting broke out between the two communities. The following year a United Nations (UN) peacekeeping force was established to keep the two sides apart. After a prolonged period of mutual hostility, relations improved to the extent that talks were resumed, with the Turks arguing for a federal state and the Greeks wanting a unitary one.

In 1971 General Grivas returned to the island and started a guerrilla campaign against the Makarios government, believing that it had failed the Greek community. Three years later Grivas died and Makarios carried out a purge of his supporters but in 1974 he himself was deposed by Greek officers of the National Guard and Nicos Sampson, who was a political extremist calling again for Enosis, was appointed president. Makarios fled to Britain.

At the request of the Turkish Cypriot leader, who feared the extremism of Sampson, Turkey sent troops to the island, taking control of the northern region and dividing Cyprus along what became known as the 'Attila Line', cutting off about a third of the total territory. Later in 1974 Sampson resigned, the military regime which had appointed him collapsed, and Makarios returned. The Turkish Cypriots had, however, by now established their own *de facto* independent government for what they called the 'Turkish Federated State of Cyprus' (TFSC), with Rauf Denktaş (b. 1924) as president.

In 1977 Makarios died and was succeeded by Spyros Kyprianou (b. 1932), who had been president of the House of Representatives. He saw the way forward through international mediation and in 1980 UN-sponsored peace talks between the Greek and Turkish communities were resumed. The Turkish Cypriots offered to hand back about 4% of the territory they controlled and to resettle 40,000 of the 200,000 refugees who had fled to the north, but this failed to satisfy the Greek Cypriots and stalemate was reached. The Turks wanted equal status for the two communities, equal representation in government and firm links with Turkey. The Greeks, on the other hand, favoured an alternating presidency, strong central government and representation in the assembly on a proportional basis. Between 1982 and 1985 several attempts by the Greek government, in Athens and the UN to find a compromise solution failed and the Turkish Republic of Northern Cyprus (TRNC), with Denktaş as president, was formally declared, but recognized only by Turkey.

In 1985 a summit meeting between Denktaş and Kyprianou failed to reach agreement and the UN secretary general drew up proposals for a bizonal federal Cyprus, with a Greek president and a Turkish vice president but this was not found acceptable. Meanwhile, both Kyprianou and Denktaş had been re-elected.

The dispute between the two communities seemed to be insoluble until the election of the independent candidate Georgios Vassilou (b. 1931) to the presidency in 1988. Vassilou seemed likely to be better placed to find a solution because of his lack of involvement in party politics. He immediately set about creating a government of national unity and taking steps to bridge the Greek–Turkish divide. However, despite a series of talks with the Turkish-Cypriot leader, under UN auspices, hopes of reunification remained unfulfilled.

In the 1993 presidential elections the leader of Democratic Rally (DISY), Glafkos Clerides (b. 1920), narrowly defeated Vassilou. Clerides continued to seek a solution to the island's divisions and in May 1995 talks between representatives of the two communities were resumed.

CZECH REPUBLIC

Česká Republika

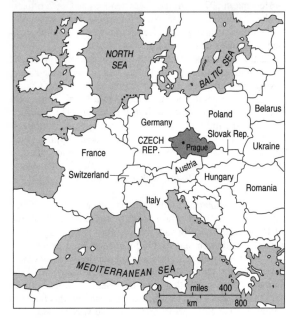

Capital: Prague (Praha)

Social and economic data
Area: 78,864 km^2
Population: 10,400,000*
Pop. density per km^2: 132*
Urban population: N/A+
Literacy rate: 99%**
GDP: $29,000**; per-capita GDP: $2,815**
Government defence spending (% of GDP): 3.1%**
Currency: koruna
Economy type: middle income
Labour force in agriculture: 9%**

*1994
**1992
+73% in Czechoslovakia in 1990

Ethnic composition
The bulk of the population is of Czech ethnic stock, a Western Slav race. There is also a sizeable Slovak minority and small Polish, German, and Hungarian minorities. The official language is Czech, but 4% of the population speaks Slovak.

Religions
Around 40% of the population is Roman Catholic. Significant minorities adhere to the Czech Hussite Church (172,000), the Presbyterian Evangelical Church of Czech Brethren (168,000), and the Eastern Orthodox Church.

Political features
State type: emergent democratic
Date of state formation: 1993*
Political structure: unitary
Executive: dual
Assembly: two-chamber
Party structure: multiparty
Human rights rating: 97%
International affiliations: BIS, CEI, CERN, COE, EBRD, ECE, IAEA, IBRD, ICFTU, IMF, LORCS, NACC, NAM (guest), OECD, OSCE, PFP, UN, VG, WEU (associate partner), WTO

*Czechoslovakia was formed in 1918

Local and regional government
The country is divided into eight regions (*kraje*), one of which is the city of Prague, which are subdivided into municipalities for the purposes of local administration.

Head of state
President Václav Havel, since 1993*

*President of Czechoslovakia from 1989

Head of government
Prime Minister Václav Klaus, since 1992

Political leaders since 1970+
1969–87 Gustáv Husák (CPCZ)*, 1987–89 Miloš Jakeš (CPCZ)*, 1989 Karl Urbanek (CPCZ)*, 1989– Václav Havel (Civic Forum/independent)**, 1992– Václav Klaus (CDP)***

+Leaders of Czechoslovakia to 1993
*Communist Party leaders
**State president
***Prime minister

Political system
Under the terms of the December 1992 constitution, which came into force on 1 January 1993 when the federal republic of Czechoslovakia split into two separate Czech and Slovak republics, the Czech Republic has a dual executive political system. Most executive authority is wielded by the prime minister on the parliamentary model. However, the state president, although largely a ceremonial figure, has the power to veto legislation and, in certain circumstances, may dissolve the lower house of parliament. The present incumbent, Václav Havel, wields considerable moral authority, having played a key role in the struggle against communist authoritarianism.

Legislative power resides with a two-chamber parliament, which comprises the 200-member Chamber of Deputies, the lower house, and the 81-member Senate. The Chamber of

Deputies is elected for four years under a system of proportional representation by universal suffrage, the minimum voting age being 18 years. Senators are directly elected for six-year terms in a staggered manner, with one-third being subject to election every two years. The Senate was initially expected to be elected in 1993, but delays have resulted in the postponement of its first elections until 1996. Both houses meet in a joint session to form an electoral college to elect the state president for a maximum of two consecutive five-year terms. The president appoints and dismisses the prime minister, is supreme commander of the armed forces, represents the state in external affairs, and appoints, with the Senate's consent, the judges of the 15-member Constitutional Court, who serve ten-year terms, and the chair and deputy chairs of the Supreme Court. The prime minister, appointed by the president, appoints a Council of Ministers (COM), or cabinet, of some 20 members that commands a majority in the Chamber of Deputies to assume charge of day-to-day executive government.

Previously, before the Czech Republic became a separate state in January 1993, each of the two national republics had its own constitution, assembly, and government, while the federal republic of Czechoslovakia also had its own two-chamber Federal Assembly. This comprised the directly elected 200-member Chamber of the People, which included 134 deputies from the Czech Republic, and the 150-member Chamber of Nations, with 75 Czech members. Both chambers elected a state president, who appointed a prime minister and government. There were special procedural safeguards to prevent domination by either nationality, for example separate voting by Czech and Slovak deputies when adopting the economic plan and budget, with majorities from both groups needed before they could be passed. The individual republics had special jurisdiction over such matters as culture, education, health, and justice, while the federal administration concentrated on economic, financial, and diplomatic issues.

Political parties

The main political parties in the Czech Republic are the right-of-centre Civic Democratic Party (CDP) and Civic Democratic Alliance (CDA); the left-of-centre Civic Movement (CM); the Communist Party of Bohemia and Moravia (KSCM); the centrist Agrarian Party, Liberal National Social Party (LNSP, formerly the Czech Socialist Party, or CSP) and Czech Social Democratic Party (CSDP); the Christian Democratic Union–Czech People's Party (CDU–CPP); the Moravian and Silesian nationalist Movement for Autonomous Democracy of Moravia and Silesia (MADMS); and the far-right Czech Republican Party.

The CDP, CDA, and CM were all formed in 1991 following a split in the Civic Forum (Obcanske forum), which was set up in 1989 as an intelligentsia-led umbrella body to spearhead the 'Velvet Revolution' prodemocracy movement. The 35,000-member CDP, led by Prime Minister Václav Klaus, is a right-of-centre anticommunist body, committed to the establishment of a Western-style free-market economy. The CDA, which has been a coalition partner of the CDP since 1992, is similar in outlook. The CM, set up by Jiri Dienstbier, is a more liberal left-of-centre force supportive of President Havel.

The 380,000-member KSCM, formed in 1991, is the reform-socialist successor to the formerly dominant Communist Party of Czechoslovakia (CPCZ: Komunista Strana Ceskoslovenska). The CPCZ originated in May 1921 as a left-wing breakaway faction from the Czechoslovak Social Democratic Party (estd. 1897). With an initial membership of 350,000, the party was multi-ethnic in character. It was allowed to operate legally throughout the interwar period, capturing more than 10% of the vote, but did not share power in any of the cabinets of that period. Membership declined to less than 100,000 and the party was forced underground when Hitler invaded the country. In 1945, however, the CPCZ received a massive influx of new members and captured 38% of the vote in the free elections of 1946. It later endured major purges during the early 1950s and immediately after the 'Prague Spring' of 1968. As a result, party membership contracted from 1.68 million in 1962 to 1.17 million in 1971. In 1986 it rose again to 1.68 million, representing 10.8% of the total population. Following a split in the KSCM in July 1993, after the traditionalist Miroslav Grebenicek was elected the party's new leader, the breakaway Party of the Democratic Left was formed by the reformist Jiri Svoboda.

The Agrarian Party, formed in 1990 to seek compensation for farmers whose property was confiscated during collectivization, and the CSP, an urban white-collar middle-class orientated party formed in 1948 by elements from the Czechoslovak National Socialist Party (estd. 1897), contested the 1992 Czech National Council elections, along with the Green Party (estd. 1989), under the banner of the 'Liberal Social Union (LSU)'. In June 1993 the CSP, which had been tolerated during the communist era, renamed itself the Liberal National Social Party (LNSP) and left the LSU and a month later the LSU's two remaining members joined with the CSDP, which was re-established in 1989 after being banned in 1948, and the Christian Social Union (CSU), to form the moderate-left 'Realism Bloc'.

The CDU–CPP, formed in 1992, is a centre-right body, incorporating the Czech People's Party, a Roman Catholic party founded in 1919 and permitted to function during the communist era.

The MADMS advocates the establishment of a self-administered Republic of Moravia and Silesia situated in the east of the Czech Republic.

Latest elections

The most recent Chamber of Deputies elections were held on 5–6 June 1992 when the Czech Republic was part of Czechoslovakia and the Chamber was known as the Czech National Council. The CDP emerged as the largest single party, capturing 76 of the 200 seats, based on a 30% share of the vote. The Left Bloc, dominated by the KSCM, won 35 seats, with 14% of the vote. Six other parties each captured between 5% and 7% of the vote and gained representation: the CSDP, 16 seats; the Liberal Social Union, 16; the CDU–CPP, 15; the Association for the Republic–Czech Republican Party, 14; the CDA, 14; and the MADMS, 14 seats. Nineteen per cent of the vote was captured by other smaller parties which failed to surmount the 5% threshold for representation.

Political history

An independent state of Czechoslovakia emerged in October 1918 following the dissolution of the Austro-Hungarian Habsburg Empire at the close of World War I. It incorporated the Czech lands of Bohemia and Moravia, which had been under Austrian rule since the 16th century, and Slovakia, which had been ruled by Hungary for nearly 1,000 years. Despite the problems posed in integrating the diverse ethnic groups within the new nation, Czechoslovakia was the only East European state to retain a parliamentary democracy throughout the interwar period. This took the form of a five-party coalition government, dominated by the Agrarian and National Socialist parties, under the leadership of the influential Slovak-born Tomáš Masaryk (1850–1937), who was president between 1918 and 1935. It was made possible by the relatively advanced state of the country's economic and social development. In 1930, for example, as few as a third of the population were involved in agricultural activities, while 40% of males were employed in the industrial sector.

During the later 1930s, with the rise to power of the Nazi leader Adolf Hitler in Germany, opposition to the government was fomented by German- and Magyar-speaking irredentists. This provided the pretext for the Munich Agreement of September 1938 between Britain, France, Germany, and Italy under which Czechoslovakia was forced to surrender its Sudeten German districts to Nazi Germany. Six months later, the German army invaded and annexed the remainder of the country. President Eduard Beneš (1884–1948) immediately resigned in opposition to these actions, setting up a government in exile in London.

During World War II, the Czech lands were subjected to direct German occupation, although Slovakia was granted 'independent' status in 1944 and Bohemia–Moravia was governed as a 'protectorate'. Liquidation campaigns were directed against the intelligentsia and in 1942 the inhabitants of Lidice were massacred. The country was liberated in 1945 by Soviet and American troops, including a Soviet-trained native contingent under the direction of General Ludvík Svoboda (1895–1975). A government of national unity was immediately formed, with Beneš as president, but with communists occupying prominent ministries, including the interior, which included the police, and information. Communists also dominated local administration. Two million Sudeten Germans were summarily expelled.

In elections to the 300-member Constituent National Assembly in May 1946, the left, which included communists and social democrats, achieved a narrow majority, enabling the CPCZ leader, Klement Gottwald (1896–1953), to become prime minister. By 1948 the CPCZ was in full control, seizing power in a coup in February 1948 and, under the National Front banner, winning a single-list ballot victory in May 1948, following the framing of a new, Soviet-style constitution. Beneš duly resigned as president in June 1948 and was succeeded by Gottwald.

Czechoslovakia's historic provinces were abolished in 1948, the country being divided, first, into 19 and then, under the new constitution of July 1960, 12 regions. Earlier, in 1945, the nation's leading industries and financial institutions had been taken into state ownership and a programme of agricultural collectivization launched.

During the 1950s, under Presidents Gottwald, Antonin Zapotocky, and Antonin Novotný (1904–75), a strict Stalinist regime was maintained, opposition members being purged. Policy adjustments began to be made, however, from the mid-1960s, as a result of mounting pressure from students and intellectuals, particularly among the Slovaks, and from deteriorating economic conditions.

In January 1968 the orthodox CPCZ leader Antonin Novotný was replaced by the reformist Slovak, Alexander Dubček (1921–92). In March 1968 the war hero, General Svoboda, became president and in April 1968 Oldřich Černik was appointed prime minister. The new regime embarked on a major liberalization programme (the 'Socialist Democratic Revolution'), promising the restoration of freedom of assembly, speech, and movement; the imposition of restrictions on the secret police; decentralized economic reform; and the introduction of elements of democratized political pluralism. These proposed changes, despite assurances that Czechoslovakia would remain within the Warsaw Pact and that the CPCZ would retain its leading political role, were viewed with suspicion by the Soviet Union and on 20–21 August 1968, 600,000 Soviet, Bulgarian, East German, Hungarian, and Polish troops invaded Czechoslovakia to restore the orthodox line and eradicate an experiment which had been termed 'socialism with a human face'.

Following the Soviet invasion, a major purge of liberals within the CPCZ was launched, party membership falling by a third, and Dr Gustáv Husák (b. 1913), a Slovak Brezhnevite, replaced Dubček as CPCZ leader in April 1969, and Lubomír Štrougal, a Czech, was appointed prime minister in January 1970. However, General Svoboda remained as president until May 1975, successfully negotiating the phased withdrawal of Soviet troops. A new federal constitution was adopted in October 1968, satisfying the nationalist aspirations of the country's Slovak minority.

In 1973 an amnesty was extended to some of the 40,000 who had fled Czechoslovakia after the 1968 invasion, signalling a slackening of repression. However, in 1977, following the signature of a human rights manifesto, 'Charter 77', by more than 700 intellectuals and former party officials, in response to the 1975 Helsinki Agreements, a new crackdown commenced. The arrest of dissidents continued in May 1981 during the Polish 'Solidarity' crisis.

Under the leadership of Gustáv Husák, Czechoslovakia emerged during the 1970s and early 1980s as a loyal ally of the Soviet Union. Minor economic reforms were introduced, but ideological orthodoxy and strict party control were maintained in the political sphere. However, after the accession of the reformist Mikhail Gorbachev to the Soviet leadership in 1985, pressure for economic and administrative reform mounted. In December 1987, while remaining president, Husák was replaced as CPCZ leader by Miloš Jakeš (b. 1922), a Czech-born economist. Working with the reformist technocrat Ladislav Adamec, prime minister since October 1988, he began to introduce a reform programme (*prestavba*, 'restructuring') on the USSR's perestroika model. His approach was cautious, and dissident activity, which became increasingly widespread during 1988–89, was suppressed.

Influenced by events elsewhere in Eastern Europe, a series of, initially student-led, prodemocracy rallies were held in

Prague's Wenceslas Square from 17 November 1989. Support for the protest movement rapidly increased after the security forces' brutal suppression of the early rallies, injuring more than 500 people, and by 20 November 1989 there were more than 400,000 demonstrators in Prague and a growing number in Bratislava. An umbrella opposition movement, Civic Forum, was swiftly formed under the leadership of the playwright and Charter 77 activist Václav Havel (b. 1935), which attracted the support of prominent members of the small political parties that were members of the ruling CPCZ-dominated National Front coalition.

With the protest movement continuing to grow, Jakeš resigned as CPCZ leader on 24 November 1989 and was replaced by Karel Urbanek, a South Moravian, and the party's ruling Politburo was purged. Less than a week later, following a brief general strike, the National Assembly voted to amend the constitution to strip the CPCZ of its 'leading role' in the government, and thus of its monopoly on power. Opposition parties, beginning with Civic Forum and its Slovak counterpart, Public Against Violence (PAV), were legalized. On 7 December 1989 Adamec resigned as prime minister and was replaced by Marián Čalfa, who formed a 'Grand Coalition' government in which key posts, including the foreign, financial, and labour ministries, were given to former dissidents. Čalfa resigned from the CPCZ in January 1990, but remained premier.

On 27 December 1989 the rehabilitated Alexander Dubček, who had addressed mass protest rallies in Prague and Bratislava, in November 1989, was sworn in as chair of the Federal Assembly, and on 29 December 1989 Václav Havel became president of Czechoslovakia. The new reform government immediately extended an amnesty to 22,000 prisoners, ended censorship, secured agreements from the CPCZ that it would voluntarily give up its existing majorities in the federal and republic assemblies and state agencies, and promised multiparty elections for June 1990. These were won by the Civic Forum and PAV, which captured 46% of the federal vote to the CPCZ's 14%, and Marián Čalfa continued at the head of a new Civic Forum–PAV dominated government. The Čalfa administration announced plans for reducing the size of the armed forces, called on the USSR to pull out its 75,000 troops stationed in the country, and applied for membership of the IMF and World Bank. Václav Havel was re-elected president, unopposed, for a further two years by the new Federal Assembly on 5 July 1990.

Some devolution of power was introduced in 1990 to ameliorate friction between the Czech and Slovak republics. A bill of rights was passed in January 1991, and moves were made towards price liberalization and privatization of small businesses. In May 1991 a bill was passed to return property nationalized after 25 February 1948 to its original owners, the first such restitution measure in Eastern Europe. The name 'Czech and Slovak Federative Republic' was adopted in April 1990 and in November 1990 the Slovak Republic declared Slovak the official language of the republic, a move promoted by the Slovak National Party, which had organized pro-autonomy rallies and demonstrations in the republic during the second half of 1990.

During the opening months of 1991, Civic Forum began to split into two distinct factions: a centre-right faction under the leadership of finance minister, Václav Klaus (b. 1941), designated the Civic Democratic Party (CDP) in April 1991; and a social-democratic group, the Civic Forum Liberal Club, renamed the Civic Movement in April 1991, led by foreign minister, Jiri Dienstbier and deputy prime minister, Pavel Rychetsky. In March 1991 PAV also split when Slovak premier Vladimir Meciar formed a splinter grouping, the Movement for a Democratic Slovakia (MDS), pledged to greater autonomy from Prague. In April 1991 he was dismissed as head of the Slovak government by the presidium of the Slovak National Council (parliament) because of policy differences. Protest rallies were held in the Slovak capital of Bratislava by Meciar supporters. Jan Carnogursky, leader of the Christian Democratic Movement, junior partner in the PAV-led ruling coalition, took over as Slovak premier.

In July 1991, a month after the final withdrawal of Soviet troops from the state, the USSR agreed to pay the equivalent of US $160 million to Czechoslovakia in compensation for damage done to the country since the 1968 USSR invasion. In August 1991, the phased privatization of Czech industry commenced, with 50 of its largest businesses put up for sale on international markets. Friendship treaties were signed with France, Germany, and the Soviet Union in October 1991. In the same month, PAV became a liberal-conservative political party, and was renamed the Civic Democratic Union–Public Action Against Violence, led by Martin Porubjak.

With the major political parties already divided into separate Czech and Slovak groups, it was anticipated that the outcome of the June 1992 general election would determine whether or not the country would break up into separate Czech and Slovak states. In the Czech republic, the right-of-centre CDP polled strongly and a CDP-dominated four-party coalition government, with the Civic Democratic Alliance, the CDU–CPP, and the Christian Democratic Party, was formed, with Václav Klaus becoming Czech prime minister. In the Slovak republic, the pro-independence MDS, led by Vladimir Meciar, triumphed. Its success was attributed, in part, to its campaign against the federal government's economic reforms, which had led to a rise in the unemployment level to 10% in the more backward Slovak republic, against just 2.5% in the more advanced Czech republic. The MDS also emerged, with 57 seats, as the second largest party group in Czechoslovakia's 300-member Federal Assembly, and used this position to block concurrence on a new federal agreement and further its separatist demands.

Because of its largely bloodless nature, the progressive democratization of Czechoslovakia from 1989 had been called the 'Velvet Revolution'. During 1992–93 the federal republic witnessed an ordered and peaceful 'velvet divorce'. On 17 July 1992 the Slovak National Council (parliament) issued a symbolic declaration of Slovak sovereignty. Also in July 1992, a transitional federal government was formed, being dominated by members of the CDP and MDS, with Jan Strasky (CDP) as prime minister. Negotiations on the division of federal assets and liabilities, applying a 2:1 ratio to reflect the relative size of the Czech and Slovak populations, and on the mechanics of the separation of the two republics progressed during the remainder of 1992. The 'divorce' proved amicable since Czech leaders saw the advantage of independence for a republic which was more economically developed than Slovakia. In addition, the dissolution occurred against a background of only muted public concern, with opinion polls suggesting that more than 60% of Czechs and Slovaks actually opposed the country's division. However, despite President Havel's repeated calls for a referendum to be held on the issue, the break-up was left to be decided by elected politicians. A new Czech Republic constitution was adopted in December 1992 and came into force on 1 December 1993, when Slovakia achieved independence and a separate Czech Republic was established. A customs union treaty was signed in October 1992 and a treaty of good neighbourliness on 17 December 1992 to consummate the 'divorce', and the former president of Czechoslovakia, Václav Havel, was elected president of the new state in January 1993. Václav Klaus remained prime minister and the Czech National Council, elected in June 1992, was redesignated the Chamber of Deputies, being due for re-election in 1996.

In June 1993 the Czech Republic became a member of the Council of Europe (COE) and, while indicating its longer-term goal of joining the European Union (EU), signed a friendship and cooperation treaty with Russia in August 1993.

The centre-right Klaus administration concentrated 1992–95 on implementing market-centred economic reforms so as to establish a Western-style capitalist economy. Although GDP declined significantly, by as much as a quarter, between 1991–93 and there were associated problems of rising crime and corruption, the Czech reform programme was one of the most successful in Central Europe. Service-sector led growth began to be registered from 1994 and inflation was kept down to around 10% per annum. In January 1993 VAT was introduced and the Prague stock exchange was reopened in April 1993 after more than 50 years' closure. By 1994 the private sector's share of GDP had surpassed 50% and more than 6 million Czechs had participated in the first wave of mass privatizations, carried out via an innovative voucher scheme. Encouraged by its political stability, significant Western, especially German, investment was attracted to the new state which entered the OECD in November 1995.

ESTONIA

Republic of Estonia
Eesti Vabariik

Capital: Tallinn

Social and economic data
Area: 45,100 km²
Population: 1,600,000*
Pop. density per km²: 35*
Urban population: 72%**
Literacy rate: 99%**
GDP: $4,600 million*; per-capita GDP: $3,000*
Government defence spending (% of GDP): 4.5%**
Currency: kroon
Economy type: middle income
Labour force in agriculture: 13%**

*1994
**1992

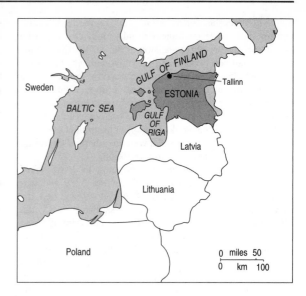

Ethnic composition
Sixty-two per cent of the population are ethnic Estonians, a Finno-Ugric people, 30% Russian, 3% Ukrainian, 2% Belarussian, and 1% Finnish. Estonian, a language closely related to Finnish, has been the republic's official language since 1989, although 85% of ethnic Russians are unable to speak Estonian.

Religions
The population is predominantly Christian, with most ethnic Estonians belonging to the Evangelical Lutheran Church and ethnic Russians to the Russian Orthodox Church.

Political features
State type: emergent democratic
Date of state formation: 1918/1991
Political structure: unitary
Executive: dual
Assembly: one-chamber
Party structure: multiparty
Human rights rating: N/A
International affiliations: BC, BIS, CBSS, COE, EBRD, ECE, IAEA, IBRD, ICFTU, IMF, NACC, OSCE, PFP, UN, WEU (associate partner)

Local and regional government
The republic contains 15 counties or districts (*maakond*), which are subdivided into communes (*vald*), and six towns.

Head of state (executive)
President Lennart Meri, since 1992

Head of government
Prime Minister Tiit Vahi, since 1995

Political leaders since 1970
Head of state: 1988–92 Arnold Rüütel (Kindel kogu), 1992– Lennart Meri (Isamaa); Prime minister: 1988–90 Indrek Toome (CPE), 1990–92 Edgar Savisaar (EPF), 1992– Tiit Vahi (independent excommunist), 1992–94

Mart Laar (Isamaa), 1994–95 Andres Tarand (independent/Greens), 1995– Tiit Vahi (Coalition Party)

Political system

Under the terms of the constitution of July 1992, Estonia has a democratic parliamentary political system, with a strong presidency. The current president, Lennart Meri, was directly elected. However, in future the president will be indirectly elected, for a maximum of two consecutive five-year terms, by the Parliament (Riigikogu). The president, who must be an Estonian citizen by birth and at least 40 years old, represents Estonia in diplomatic relations, is commander in chief of the armed forces, initiates amendments to the constitution, and nominates the prime minister. The legislature, Riigikogu, comprises 101 members popularly elected for four-year terms on the basis of proportional representation, with a 5% cut-off limit for representation. An executive prime minister, nominated by the president, is drawn from the legislature and works with a Council of Ministers, or cabinet, of some 15 members.

Political parties

The most important political parties in Estonia are: the Coalition Party (KMU); Isamaa (National Fatherland Party, or Pro Patria); the Estonian Reform Party (ERP); the Centre Party (CP); the Estonian National Independence Party (ENIP; estd. 1988); the Communist Party of Estonia (CPE); Our Home is Estonia; and the Estonian Social Democratic Party (ESDP).

The Coalition Party, led by Prime Minister Tiit Vahi, is a left-of-centre force which favours a German-style 'social market economy' and includes a number of former communists. It is allied to the Rural Union bloc, which includes the Estonian Rural People's Union (ERPU; estd. 1994), which is orientated towards agrarian interests. Led by the former state president, Arnold Rüütel, a Brezhnev-era politician who favours state subsidies for agriculture and preserving collective farms, it is a successor to the early nationalist body, Kindel kogu (Secure Home), which included a number of former communists.

Isamaa, or the Union of Fatherland, the ruling party between 1992–95, is a right-wing nationalist body founded in 1992 by Mart Laar, a strong advocate of a free-market economic strategy.

The ERP, formed in November 1994 by Siim Kallas, the former president of the Bank of Estonia, also favours a free-market economic policy, including the scrapping of income tax, but seeks improved relations with Russia and Estonia's ethnic Russian community.

The CP, led by Edgar Savisaar, is a successor to the Estonian Popular Front (EPF: Rahvarinne), a moderate nationalist umbrella organization formed in 1988.

The ENIP, a radical nationalist force, originated in 1987 as the Estonian Group for the Publication of the Molotov–Ribbentrop Pact (MRP–AEG).

The CPE was originally formed in 1920 and renamed itself the Estonian Democratic Labour Party in 1992. Along with the Our Home is Estonia and the ESDP, it draws much of its support from ethnic Russians.

Latest elections

The most recent, and second post-independence, legislature elections were held on 5 March 1995. The largest number of seats, 41 out of the 101 available, was won by the Coalition Party in alliance with the ERPU Rural Union, based on a 32% share of the vote. The ERP won 19 seats, with 16% of the vote; Edgar Savisaar's Centre Party, 16 seats, with 14% of the vote; Isamaa, 8 seats and just 8% of the vote; the Moderates Bloc, led by the former prime minister, Andres Tarand, and the ethnic Russian-orientated Estonia is our Home, each won 6 seats and 6% of the vote, while the far-right Republican Conservative People's Party won 5 seats, with 5% of the vote.

The last presidential election, held on 20 September 1992, produced no outright winner. The incumbent Arnold Rüütel (Kindel kogu) captured 42% of the national vote, Lennart Meri (Isamaa), 30%, Rein Taagepera (EPF), 24%, and Lagle Parek (ENIP), 4%. As no single candidate secured an absolute majority of votes, the task of electing the president was devolved to the Riigikogu, who chose Lennart Meri on 5 October 1992. Only those Estonians, or their descendants, who were citizens of the country in 1940 were allowed to vote in the 1992 elections. This effectively disenfranchised 38% of the republic's population.

Political history

Independent states were formed in the area now known as Estonia during the 1st century AD and the Vikings mounted an invasion in the 9th century AD. In the 13th century southern Estonia came under the control of the Teutonic Knights, German crusaders, who converted the inhabitants to Christianity, while Talinn joined the Hanseatic League, the union of European commercial towns that stretched from London to Novgorod. The Danes, who had taken control of northern Estonia, sold this area to the Teutonic Knights in 1324, but by the 16th century German nobles owned much of the land. In 1561 Sweden took control of the north and also wrested the south from Poland in 1625. The Swedes continued to rule the whole country until control was ceded to Tsarist Russia in 1721. Repressive Russian government and German economic control spurred an Estonian nationalist movement during the late 19th century. It focused initially on cultural themes, but after the turn of the century pro-independence political parties began to be formed.

Estonia was occupied by German troops during World War I. The Russian Red Army forces, who tried to regain power in 1917, after the Russian Revolution, were overthrown by Germany in March 1918, after Estonian nationalists, led by Konstantin Pats, had proclaimed independence on 24 February 1918. Soviet authority was restored in November 1918, but it was overthrown again, by German and British forces, in May 1919 and a democratic republic was established. In January 1921 the major Western powers recognized Estonia's independence. The 1920s saw cultural and economic advances and major land reforms. However, in March 1934, at a time of deep economic depression, the liberal-democratic parliamentary system was overthrown by Konstantin Pats in a quasi-fascist coup. Political parties were banned and an authoritarian presidentialist system was established.

In August 1939, as part of the supplementary protocol to the Molotov–Ribbentrop Pact, Germany and the USSR secretly agreed that Estonia should come under Russian influence and the country was incorporated into the USSR as the Estonian Soviet Socialist Republic in August 1940. Mass deportations of 60,000 Estonians to Siberia followed. In July 1941 Estonia was again occupied by Germany, prompting large-scale emigration to the West, but the USSR regained control in September 1944. The process of 'sovietization' was continued, involving agricultural collectivization, the development of heavy industries, deportations of Estonians, and the immigration of ethnic Russians. There was sporadic resistance from the 'forest brethren' (*metsavennad*) guerrillas until the mid-1950s and, thereafter, dissent focused on cultural issues. In particular, there was great antipathy towards the creeping 'Russification' of a republic which had been 92% ethnic Estonian in 1939.

From 1985, encouraged by the policies of glasnost (openness) and perestroika (economic restructuring) espoused by the Soviet Union's new leader, Mikhail Gorbachev, nationalist dissent became more vocal. In April 1988 an Estonian Popular Front (EPF) was unofficially formed, advocating the transformation of the USSR into a truly confederal body, and in August 1988 the more radical Estonian National Independence Party (ENIP) began to campaign, via mass rallies, for full independence. The EPF included a number of members of the Communist Party of Estonia (CPE), which began to respond to the changing public mood. On 16 November 1988 the CPE-dominated Supreme Soviet (parliament) adopted a declaration of sovereignty, which included a power of veto over Soviet legislation, and a new constitution which allowed private property and placed land and natural resources under Estonian control. However, the USSR's Supreme Soviet rejected this declaration as unconstitutional. In January 1989 Estonia's parliament also voted to replace Russian with Estonian as the republic's official language and, in November 1989, denounced the 1940 incorporation of the republic into the USSR as a 'forced annexation'.

In February 1990 the Communist Party's monopoly of power was abolished and a multiparty political system became established. In elections held in March 1990, pro-independence candidates won a majority of seats in the Supreme Soviet and a coalition government was formed, with the EPF's leader, Edgar Savisaar, becoming prime minister in April 1990. Arnold Rüütel, an adaptable communist-era politician who had previously been chairman of the presidium of the Supreme Soviet, and thus effective head of state, remained as head of state. Unofficial elections were also held concurrently, in March 1990, to a rival nationalist parliament, the Congress of Estonia, for which the franchise was limited to those who had been citizens of the pre-1940 Estonian Republic and their descendants.

On 8 May 1990 Estonia's Supreme Soviet issued an effective declaration of independence and the state emblems and name of the pre-1940 Republic of Estonia were restored. However, the Russian president, Mikhail Gorbachev, anulled the declaration as unconstitutional and there were protests and strikes by ethnic Russians in Tallinn. Estonians, concerned at the USSR's attempted military intervention in Latvia and Lithuania in January 1991, boycotted the March 1991 all-Union referendum on the future of the USSR and, instead, held a plebiscite on independence, which, with a turnout of 83%, resulted in 78% voting in favour of independence. By the summer of 1991 the republic had embarked on a programme of privatization and the prices of agricultural products had been freed. On 20 August 1991, in the midst of the attempted anti-Gorbachev coup in the USSR, which led to Red Army troops being moved into Tallinn to seize the television transmitter and the republic's main port being blocked by the Soviet navy, Estonia declared its full and immediate independence (it had been in a 'period of transition' since March 1990) and outlawed the Communist Party. On 6 September 1991 this declaration was recognized by Moscow and on 17 September, along with the other Baltic States, Estonia was admitted into the United Nations (UN) and the Conference on Security and Cooperation in Europe (CSCE, later the OSCE).

Prime Minister Edgar Savisaar and his cabinet resigned in January 1992 after failing to alleviate food and energy shortages. Tiit Vahi, the former transport minister, formed a new government which included seven key ministers unchanged from the previous cabinet. A new constitution, which had been framed by a Constitutional Assembly including equal numbers of delegates from the Supreme Soviet and the Congress of Estonia, was approved in a national referendum held in June 1992. Voting in the parliamentary and general elections which followed in September 1992 was restricted, by the new Citizenship Law, to persons who had been citizens of pre-1940 Estonia and their descendants. The elections resulted in victory for the Isamaa conservative-nationalist alliance, which won 29 of the 101 seats in the new Riigikogu. A coalition government was formed with the ENIP and Moderate Group, with Isamaa's Mart Laar (b. 1960), a 32-year-old historian and political disciple of Britain's conservative leader, Margaret Thatcher, becoming prime minister and Lennart Meri (b. 1929), a former foreign minister, president.

The new Laar administration, which included a 28-year-old foreign minister and 29-year-old interior minister, embarked on an ambitious programme of market-centred economic reform, involving large-scale privatization, with 80% of state-owned enterprises being sold by 1995. In the short term GDP declined during 1992–93, but from 1994 growth in the economy resumed, being aided by substantial foreign investment. The withdrawal of the remaining Soviet troops stationed in Estonia was also successfully negotiated, with the last troops leaving on 29 August 1994, and Estonia entered the Council of Europe in May 1993. Despite these successes, popular support for the abrasive Laar and the Isamaa party slumped to barely 5% by mid–1994. One factor was the controversial law on aliens, passed in July 1993, which defined the 500,000 former Soviet citizens in Estonia as 'foreigners' who would be required to apply for a residency permit or face expulsion. Another was the cutbacks that had been made in social spending. In September 1994 the prime minister was defeated in parliament on a no-confidence motion. This followed revelations that Laar had secretly ordered the sale in October 1992 of 2,000 million Russian roubles to the breakaway Russian republic of Chechnya.

Andres Tarand, the environmental minister who was a member of the Green movement, became caretaker prime minister in October 1994, holding power at the head of a broad-based coalition until elections were held in March 1995. These resulted in a crushing defeat for Isamaa, which attracted less than 8% of the national vote, and victory for the centre-left in the form of the Coalition Party and Rural People's Union, led respectively by Tiit Vahi and Arnold Rüütel. A new coalition government was formed in April 1995 by Vahi, a former communist-era factory manager, which included members of the Centre Party. It was expected to pursue a 'social market' economic programme, with a bias to the agricultural sector, and seek to improve relations with Russia and the state's own, and now discriminated against, ethnic Russian minority community. However, the new government remained committed to Estonia's integration into Western and European institutions, signing a trade and cooperation agreement with the European Union in June 1995. Following a scandal involving the interior minister, Edgar Savisaar, the government collapsed in October 1995, but a new Vahi-led coalition with the ERP was formed a month later.

GEORGIA

Republic of Georgia
Sakartvelos Respublica

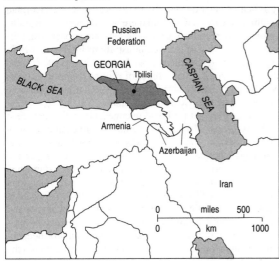

Capital: Tbilisi

Social and economic data
Area: 69.700 km^2
Population: 5,500,000*
Pop. density per km^2: 79*
Urban population: 56%**
Literacy rate: 99%**
GDP: $4,670 million**; per-capita GDP: $850**
Government defence spending (% of GDP): 3.8%**
Currency: Georgian coupon
Economy type: low income
Labour force in agriculture: 22%**

*1992
**1994

Ethnic composition
Seventy per cent of the population is of Georgian ethnic stock, 8% is Armenian, 7% ethnic Russian, 5% Azeri, 3% Ossetian, 2% Abkhazian, and 2% Greek. Georgian, a non-Indo-European language, is the official language.

Religions
Around 80% of the population belongs to the Christian Georgian Orthodox Church. Islam is professed by Azeris, Abkhazians, Adzharians, and Kurds.

Political features
State type: emergent democratic/transitional
Date of state formation: 1991
Political structure: unitary
Executive: limited presidential
Assembly: one-chamber
Party structure: multiparty
Human rights rating: N/A
International affiliations: BSECZ, CIS, IBRD, IMF, OSCE, PFP, UN

Local and regional government
There are two 'autonomous republics', Abkhazia and Adzharia. Abkhazia, situated in the far northwest of the republic, has an area of 8,600 square kilometres and a population of 538,000, with its capital at Sukhumi. It was a republic during the 1920s, but was incorporated into Christian Georgia in 1931 and Georgians were resettled there. By 1990 ethnic Georgians comprised 46% of its population and ethnic Abkhazians, a Turkic-speaking Muslim people who have sought secession, only 18%. Adzharia, situated in the southwest, has an area of 3,000 square kilometres and a population of 382,000, with its capital at Batumi. South Ossetia, situated in the north-centre of the republic, with its capital at Tskhinvali, is an 'autonomous region'. Its inhabitants, 66% Ossetian, an East Iranian people, have been traditionally pro-Russian, with North Ossetia forming part of the Russian Federation. The minorities in these territories seek autonomy and, in the case of the South Ossetians, reunion, within the Russian Federation, with North Ossetia. Below there is a hierarchy of provinces, or regions, rural territories, districts, municipalities, and villages.

Head of state (executive)
President Eduard Shevardnadze, since 1992

Head of government
Prime Minister Otar Patsatsia, since 1993

Political leaders since 1970
1990–92 Zviad Gamsakhurdia (Round Table), 1992 Military Council, 1992– Eduard Shevardnadze (independent/CUG)

Political system
Georgia's political system is in a transitional state as a result of the continuing internal unrest caused by the Abkhazia dispute. A decree on state power was passed on 6 November 1992 to act as the interim constitution. This provided for a 235-member legislature, the Supreme Soviet, to which 150 deputies are elected by proportional representation and 85 by the first-past-the-post system, for four-year terms. The

Supreme Soviet's chairperson served as executive head of state, or *de facto* president. Since November 1995 the president has been directly elected for a five-year term, renewable once only. The head of state, who is also commander in chief of the armed forces, governs with a cabinet of ministers, which includes a prime minister. In September 1993 the head of state, Eduard Shevardnadze, was conferred emergency powers to rule by decree and the Supreme Soviet dissolved itself temporarily. In August 1995, a new constitution came into force.

Political parties

Georgia has an exceptionally fragmented multiparty system, which is riven by clan and regional rivalries. Dozens of parties compete for power, but many have large military components and are based on kinship or loyalty to charismatic leaders.

The most significant of the myriad of parties which operate are; the Citizens' Union of Georgia (CUG); the National Democratic Party of Georgia (NDPG); the Round Table/Free Georgia Bloc; the Georgian Popular Front (GPF); the Georgian Communist Party (GCP); and the National Independence Party (NIP).

The CUG is a party formed by head of state Eduard Shevardnadze in September 1993.

The NDPG was founded in 1981 by Giorgi Chanturia to campaign for Georgian independence. The party has been supportive of the Shevardnadze regime. Chanturia was assassinated in December 1994.

The Round Table–Free Georgia group was founded by Zviad Gamsakhurdia, a longstanding nationalist dissident, to contest the 28 October and 11 November 1990 Supreme Soviet elections. Its leader died in December 1993.

The GPF was formed in July 1989 as a moderate nationalist, prodemocratization umbrella force.

The GCP was the ruling party in Georgia until 1990 and has been a pro-independence nationalist body since 1989. It was banned in August 1991, in the wake of the unsuccessful Soviet coup attempt, but was revived in June 1994 under the leadership of Major General Paneleimon Giorgadze.

The NIP is an extreme nationalist body.

Latest elections

The most recent legislative elections were held on 5 November 1995. No single party dominated the contest, but the largest number of seats was won by the pro-Shevardnadze CUG, with 24% of the vote. The centre-right opposition NDPG and All Georgian Union of Revival attracted 8% and 7% support. Eight other parties won seats.

Eduard Shevardnadze was directly elected president on 5 November 1995, with 75% of the vote, defeating Jumber Patiashivili, the former communist chief. Turnout was 64%.

Political history

Georgia was converted to Christianity in the 4th century AD, when the first Georgian state was established. From the 7th century, with the weakening of the Persian and Byzantium empires, an independent Georgian feudal kingdom was created by the Gagrationi house, tracing its ancestry to King David. The kingdom became especially powerful between the late 11th and early 13th centuries, under David II

(1089–1125) and Queen Tamara, who died in 1212, and the Georgian Church became an independent body. Thereafter the country fell under the sway of Persian, Mongol, and Turkish imperial powers, before being annexed by Tsarist Russia in 1801. Tbilisi (Tiflis) developed into an important commercial centre under the Tsars; however, the Georgian language and church were gradually suppressed.

On 26 May 1918, amid turmoil in the Russian Empire, Georgia reasserted its independence but, denied economic help from the West and with its ports subject to blockade, its rebellion was crushed by the Red Army in February 1921. Between 1922 and 1936 Georgia entered the USSR as part of the Transcaucasian Federation, along with Armenia and Azerbaijan, before becoming a full republic in 1936. There was rapid industrial development between the 1920s and 1950s, but considerable resistance to rural collectivization, and political purges were instituted during the 1930s by Lavrenti Beria (1899–1953), the Transcaucasia party leader, under the orders of the Soviet leader, Joseph Stalin, himself an ethnic Georgian. During World War II, Stalin ordered the deportation of 200,000 Meskhetians from southern Georgia to Central Asia.

During the 1950s and 1960s, Georgia's administration became notorious for its laxity and corruption. A drive against crime and corruption was launched between 1972 and 1985 by Eduard Shevardnadze (b. 1928), leader of the Georgian Communist Party (GCP), and there was accelerated 'Russification'. This provoked a growing nationalist backlash, witnessed in the form of mass demonstrations in Tbilisi in 1978 and 1981, terrorist incidents, and the founding, in 1977, of the Initiative Group for the Defence of Human Rights in Georgia by the university lecturer Zviad Gamsakhurdia (1939–93), the son of a famous Georgian novelist.

With the glasnost (political openness) initiative launched by the reformist Mikhail Gorbachev, who became the new Soviet leader in 1985, there was an intensification of the nationalist campaign in the later 1980s, with the separatist National Democratic Party of Georgia (NDPG), established in 1981, becoming increasingly assertive and a Georgian Popular Front (GPF) being formed in July 1989. This fuelled anti-Georgian feeling among the republic's Abkhazian and Ossetian minority communities. The Tiananmen-style massacre in Tbilisi of at least 20 peaceful Georgian pro-independence demonstrators by Soviet troops, firing toxic gas, on the night of 8–9 April 1989 added momentum to the nationalist movement and during 1989–90, with its old-guard leadership purged, the GCP joined the secessionist camp. In November 1989 the republic's Supreme Soviet declared the supremacy of Georgian laws over all-Union laws and in February 1990 the constitution was amended to abolish the GCP's guaranteed monopoly on power.

After the seven-party Round Table–Free Georgia nationalist coalition triumphed in Georgia's 28 October and 11 November 1990 free multiparty Supreme Soviet elections, capturing 64% of the vote and 155 of the 250 seats, Zviad Gamsakhurdia was chosen as state president on 14 November 1990, while Tengiz Sigua, also from the Round Table–Free Georgia group, became prime minister. The GCP, despite also adopting a nationalist stance, won only 64 seats. The new parliament voted, in January 1991, to establish a republican National Guard and end conscription to the Soviet Red Army.

In March 1991 all parts of Georgia, except the pro-Union autonomous territories of Abkhazia and South Ossetia, boycotted the all-Union USSR constitutional referendum. Instead, the republic held a plebiscite on independence on 31 March 1991, which secured 93% approval, with a turnout of 95%. Independence was declared on 9 April 1991 and a campaign of civil disobedience against Soviet interests was launched. On 26 May 1991 Gamsakhurdia became the first republic president in the USSR to be directly elected, winning 87% of the vote and defeating five other candidates. However, voting did not take place in Abkhazia or South Ossetia. President Gamsakhurdia failed to strongly denounce the anti-Gorbachev coup in Moscow in August 1991, prompting the resignation in protest of Prime Minister Tengiz Sigua. However, the GCP was banned in the wake of the failed Moscow coup.

From September 1991 Gamsakhurdia became an increasingly dictatorial president, banning opposition parties, arresting political opponents, and instituting tight press censorship. This led to a growing popular protest movement, fuelled further by government troops firing on the crowds. With disorder mounting, Gamsakhurdia declared a state of emergency on 24 September 1991. He ordered the arrest in October 1991 of most of the leadership of the nationalist NDPG, headed by Giorgi Chanturia. However, the power struggle intensified, as the president's opponents resorted to force to oust him, and from December 1991 Gamsakhurdia had to take refuge in a basement bunker in the shell-shattered Tbilisi parliament building. He fled to Armenia on 6 January 1992 and later to the Chechen republic in southern Russia. Distracted by these events, Georgia failed to join the new Commonwealth of Independent States (CIS), which was established in December 1991 after the USSR had been dissolved. Although the United States withheld diplomatic recognition of Georgia until conditions on human rights and democracy could be met, it officially acknowledged the republic's independent status. In January 1992 Georgia was admitted into the Conference on Security and Cooperation in Europe (CSCE, later the OSCE) and in July 1992 into the United Nations (UN).

The leaders of the anti-Gamsakhurdia rebel troops, Tengiz Kitovani, a former schoolmate of Gamsakhurdia's and a commander of a faction of the Georgian National Guard which broke away to oppose the Gamsakhurdia regime from August 1991, and Dzhaba Ioseliani, a former convict and playwright who was commander of the paramilitary Mkhedrioni ('the Horsemen'), established a Military Council. Tengiz Sigua returned as prime minister, but fresh elections were promised for April 1992. Subsequent rebellion by Gamsakhurdia supporters, 'Zviadists', between January and July 1992, which were especially strong in the fugitive president's home region of western Georgia, was crushed by the Military Council. In February 1992, Chanturia and Temur Zhorzholiani, leader of the Monarchist Party, travelled to Spain to meet the Bagrations, descendants of Georgia's royal family, with the aim of returning with the heir to Tbilisi in preparation for a coronation the following year. However, in March 1992, the republic's former communist leader and former Soviet foreign minister, Eduard Shevardnadze,

returned to Georgia and the ruling Military Council transferred its powers to a newly created 50-member, all-party State Council, chaired by Shevardnadze and including Sigua, Kitovani, and Ioseliani.

In July 1992 the autonomous republic of Abkhazia declared its independence, forcing Shevardnadze to deploy the Georgian National Guard as a bloody armed conflict erupted. The situation was calmer elsewhere, notably in the secessionist autonomous region of South Ossetia, where a cease-fire agreement was signed in July 1992, ending two years of fighting which had claimed the lives of more than 1,000 Ossetians and 400 Georgians and had led to thousands fleeing to North Ossetia, in the Russian Federation. This made it possible, in August 1992, for Shevardnadze to lift the state of emergency imposed by Gamsakhurdia. Elections to the Supreme Soviet, held in October 1992, were boycotted in South Ossetia and in parts of Abkhazia and western Georgia and produced an inconclusive outcome. However, Shevardnadze secured popular approval as head of state, winning 95% of the national vote in an uncontested election.

The major problem facing Shevardnadze was the continuing conflict in Abkhazia. In August 1990, following fighting with Georgian government troops which claimed more than 100 lives and led to 50,000 fleeing to southern Russia, Vladislav Ardzinba, leader of the independence campaign and chairperson of the Abkhazian parliament, fled north from the capital, Sukhumi. However, the Abkhazians, receiving support from Russian nationalist volunteer fighters, launched a counter-offensive from October 1992, shelling Georgian troops stationed in Sukhumi. In July 1993, under the terms of a peace deal mediated by the CSCE, some Georgian troops were withdrawn from the autonomous republic. This enabled Abkhazian forces to humiliatingly defeat the Georgian army and capture the Black Sea resort of Sukhumi on 16 September 1993, forcing Shevardnadze temporarily into hiding and 120,000 civilians to flee into western Georgia. In the wake of this debacle, supporters of ousted ex-president, Gamsakhurdia, launched a new rebellion. To save the situation, Shevardnadze was moved to turn, reluctantly, to Russia for military aid to crush the dual insurgencies. The price for this was an agreement, in October 1993, that Georgia would enter the CIS in December 1993, thus ceding significant political and economic sovereignty. In addition, it was agreed that 20,000 Russian troops could remain stationed in four bases in Georgia, including some strategic Black Sea ports, for at least 25 years.

With Russian aid the Gamsakhurdia rebellion was crushed in November 1993 and its leader died in December 1993, apparently committing suicide. In May 1994 a cease-fire agreement was reached with Abkhaz rebels, with considerable autonomy being ceded to the republic and 2,500 Russian peacekeeping troops being deployed in the autonomous republic. This promised to end four years of fighting which, by official estimates, had claimed 30,000 lives and led to the flight of 250,000 Georgian refugees. In November 1994 the Abkhazian parliament issued a sovereignty declaration, but in February 1995 the autonomous republic's nationalist leaders announced that they would shelve their demands for independence in the light of Russia's invasion of the Chechen republic.

The economic damage wrought by the internal conflicts in Abkhazia and South Ossetia and the civil war between pro- and anti-Gamsakhurdia supporters was enormous. During 1991–92 alone output fell by 60% and during 1993 and 1994 the annual fall in real GDP, averaged 35%. Inflation exceeded 5,000% per annum by 1994, the budget deficit was the equivalent of 60% of GDP and there were severe fuel and food shortages, with bread rationing being imposed as Abkhazia's productive agricultural land was placed temporarily out of use. There was also a surge in the level of crime and political terrorism, as mafia gangs and paramilitaries increased their influence. In February 1994 the powerful Mkhedrioni irregulars were disbanded and in January the unregistered paramilitary National Liberation Front maintained by former defence minister, Tengiz Kitovani, was disarmed. This formed part of a general demilitarization drive. The Mkhedrioni was later reconstituted as the Rescue Corps, which was itself substantially disarmed in May 1995. A friendship and cooperation treaty was signed with Russia in February 1994 and economic and commercial agreements seemed to pave the way for Georgia's re-entry into the rouble zone. With the granting of a large IMF loan to the republic in December 1994, the launching of a mass privatization campaign in April 1995, and a reduction in the monthly rate of inflation to below 3% during the first half of 1995, the economic outlook began to improve somewhat. In August 1995 Eduard Shevardnadze survived a car bomb assassination attempt, blamed variously on the paramilitary Mkhedrioni and mafia groups and a former interior minister. He convincingly won the November 1995 presidential election.

GREECE

Hellenic Republic
Elliniki Dimokratia

Capital: Athens

Social and economic data
Area: 131,944 km^2
Population: 10,200,000*
Pop. density per km^2: 78*
Urban population: 64%**
Literacy rate: 93%**
GDP: $75,000**; per-capita GDP: $7,184**
Government defence spending (% of GDP): 5.5%*
Currency: drachma
Economy type: high income
Labour force in agriculture: 25%**

*1992
**1994

Ethnic composition
Over 97% of the population is Greek. The main minorities are Turks, Slavs, and Albanians.

Religions
The Eastern Orthodox Church is the established religion and it has about 9 million adherents, or most of the population. There are also about 47,000 Roman Catholics, 5,000 Protestants, and 5,000 Jews.

Political features
State type: liberal democratic
Date of state formation: 1829
Political structure: unitary
Executive: parliamentary
Assembly: one-chamber
Party structure: multiparty
Human rights rating: 87%
International affiliations: CE, CERN, CSCE, EEA, EU, IAEA, IBRD, IMF, NACC, NAM (guest), NATO, OECD, UN, WEU, WTO

Local and regional government
Although the 1975 constitution prescribes that 'the administration of the States shall be organized on the basis of decentralization', Greece has tended to be a highly centralized state. In 1983 measures were introduced to devolve more power to the ten regions into which the country is divided and the departments into which they, in turn, are subdivided.

Head of state
President Costis Stephanopoulos, since 1995

Head of government
Prime Minister Andreas Papandreou, since 1993

Political leaders since 1970
1967–73 Colonel George Papadopoulos (military), 1973–74 Lt-Gen Phaidon Ghizikis (military), 1974–80 Constantine Karamanlis (ND), 1981–89 Andreas Papandreou (PASOK), 1989 Tzannis Tzannetakis (ND–Communist coalition), 1989 Yannis Grivas (caretaker administration), 1989–90 Xenophon Zolotas (caretaker administration), 1990 Yannis Grivas (caretaker administration), 1990–93 Constantine Mitsotakis (ND), 1993–   Andreas Papandreou (PASOK)

Political system
The 1975 constitution provides for a parliamentary system of government, with a president, who is head of state, a prime minister, who is head of government, and a single-chamber

Parliament. The president is elected by Parliament for a five-year term. They appoint the prime minister on the basis of parliamentary support. Amendments to the constitution in 1986 transferred virtually all executive powers from the president to the prime minister. The president and the cabinet are collectively responsible to Parliament. This has 300 members, all elected by universal adult suffrage, through a party list system of proportional representation, for a four-year term. Bills passed by Parliament must be ratified by the president, whose veto, however, can be overridden by absolute majority of the total number of members of Parliament.

Political parties

There are some 17 political parties, the two most significant being the Panhellenic Socialist Movement (PASOK) and the New Democracy Party (ND).

PASOK was formed in 1974 by the incorporation of the Democratic Defence and the Panhellenic Liberation Movement, two organizations committed to the removal of the military regime which had been dominating Greek politics. Although strongly nationalistic, it favours socialization through international cooperation.

The ND was also formed in 1974. It is a broad-based, centre-right party, favouring social reform through a free enterprise system. It is a strong supporter of EU and NATO membership.

Latest elections

The results of the October 1993 general election were as follows:

	% votes	seats
PASOK	46.9	170
ND	39.3	111
Other parties	13.8	19

Political history

Historically the birthplace of democracy, Greece became an independent modern nation-state in 1829 and a constitutional monarchy in 1843. Relations with neighbouring Turkey were strained for much of the 19th century, resulting in an unsuccessful war in 1897 and a more successful one in 1912–13. Politics were dominated between 1910 and 1935 by Eleutherios Venizelos (1864–1936), who was prime minister for nearly half the period. The monarchy was removed between 1923 and 1935, when King George II (1890–1947) was restored by the army, but was to remain dependent upon the military leader General Ioannis Metaxas (1871–1941). Soon after the outbreak of World War II an attempted invasion by Italy was successfully resisted but a determined onslaught by Germany proved too powerful and occupation followed.

During the German occupation, between 1941 and 1944, a communist-dominated resistance movement armed and trained a guerrilla army and after the war the National Liberation Front, as it was called, attempted to create a socialist state. If the Greek royalist army had not been massively assisted by the United States, this undoubtedly would have happened. As it was, the monarchy, in the shape of King Paul (1901–64), was re-established, and in 1964 he was succeeded by his son, Constantine II (b. 1940).

Dissatisfaction with the performance of the government and conflicts between the king and his ministers resulted in a coup, in 1967, led by Colonel George Papadopoulos (b. 1919). The monarchy was replaced by a new regime, which, despite its democratic pretensions, was little more than a military dictatorship. All political activity was banned and opponents of the government were forced out of public life. In 1973 Greece declared itself a republic and Papadopoulos became president.

A civilian cabinet was appointed but before the year was out another coup brought Lieutenant General Phaidon Ghizikis to the presidency, with Adamantios Androutsopoulus as prime minister. The failure of the government to prevent the Turkish invasion of Cyprus led to its downfall and a former prime minister, Constantine Karamanlis (b. 1907), was recalled from exile to form a new Government of National Salvation. Karamanlis immediately ended martial law, press censorship, and the ban on political parties and in the 1974 general election his New Democracy Party (ND) won a decisive majority in Parliament. A referendum held the same year emphatically rejected the idea of a return of the monarchy and in 1975 a new constitution for a democratic 'Hellenic Republic' was adopted, with Constantine Tsatsos as the new president.

The ND won the 1977 general election with a reduced majority and in 1980 Karamanlis resigned as prime minister and was elected president. The following year Greece became a full member of the European Community, having been an associate since 1962. Meanwhile, the ND found itself faced with a growing challenge from the Panhellenic Socialist Movement (PASOK) which won an absolute majority in Parliament in the 1981 general election. Its leader, Andreas Papandreou (b. 1919), the son of a prominent left-of-centre republican politician, became Greece's first socialist prime minister.

PASOK had been elected on a radical socialist platform, which included withdrawal from the European Community, the removal of US military bases, and a sweeping programme of domestic reform. Important social changes, such as lowering the voting age to 18, the legalization of civil marriage and divorce, and an overhaul of the universities and the army, were carried out, but, instead of withdrawing from Europe, Papandreou was content to obtain a modification of the terms of entry, and, rather than close US bases, he signed a five-year agreement on defence and economic cooperation. Despite introducing tight austerity measures to deal with growing inflation, PASOK won a comfortable majority in the 1985 elections, and in March 1986 the constitution was amended, limiting the powers of the president in relation to those of the prime minister.

In 1988 relations with Turkey showed a marked improvement. Papandreou met Prime Minister Turgut Özal of Turkey for talks in Switzerland and later Özal paid a visit to Athens, the first by a Turkish prime minister for over 35 years. Later in 1988 the personal life of Prime Minister Papandreou became difficult. It was announced that he and his wife were about to divorce and that he had a heart condition for which he underwent surgery.

In 1989 Papandreou sought a renewal of his mandate but the general election result was inconclusive, resulting in a short-lived coalition between the conservative ND and the Communists, led by Tzannis Tzannatakis. This collapsed and a caretaker government was formed prior to another general election in April 1990.

The ND won half the assembly seats and its leader, Constantine Mitsotakis, was able to form Greece's first single-party government for a decade. The main events during this administration were the election of the former ND leader, Constantine Karamanlis, as president, the signing of an agreement for siting US bases in Greece, the ratification of the Maastricht Treaty on European unity, and the clearing of Andreas Papandreou of corruption charges levelled against him.

In September 1993 Mitsotakis called a general election to renew his mandate but failed, PASOK winning a clear majority and the veteran politician Papandreou returning to office. In March 1995 Costis Stephanopoulos was elected president by Parliament.

HUNGARY

Republic of Hungary
Magyar Köztársaság

Capital: Budapest

Social and economic data
Area: 93,033 km²
Population: 10,500,000*
Pop. density per km²: 113*
Urban population: 66%**
Literacy rate: 97%**
GDP: $32,000 million**; per-capita GDP: $3,050**

Government defence spending (% of GDP): 2%**
Currency: forint
Economy type: middle income
Labour force in agriculture: 14%**

*1994
**1992

Ethnic composition
The majority, 93%, of the population is native Hungarian, or Magyar, of non-Slavic stock. There exist, in addition, minorities of about 170,000 Germans, 120,000 Slovaks, 50,000 Croats, and 20,000 Romanians. There is also a large Romany, gypsy, community of around 600,000, which has its own elected governing body. Hungarian (Magyar) is the main language.

Religions
About 60% of the population is Roman Catholic. Until the 1960s, this church was subject to state repression, the primate Cardinal József Mindszenty being imprisoned and given a life sentence. A quarter of the population is Protestant, the principal denominations being the Presbyterian Reformed Church of Hungary, with 2 million members, and the Lutheran Church of Hungary, with 430,000 adherents. The Jewish community numbers around 90,000 people.

Political features
State type: emergent democratic
Date of state formation: 1918
Political structure: unitary
Executive: parliamentary*
Assembly: one-chamber
Party structure: multiparty
Human rights rating: 97%
International affiliations: BIS, CEFTA, CEI, CERN, COE, DC, EBRD, ECE, HG, IBRD, IMF, LORCS, NACC, NAM (guest), OAS (observer), OSCE, UN, VG, WFTU, WTO

*Although the president has some executive powers

Local and regional government
For local administration, the country is divided into 19 counties (*megyed*) and the capital city, subdivided into 22 districts and local councils, elected every five years.

Head of state
President Arpád Göncz, since 1990

Head of government
Prime Minister Gyula Horn, since 1994

Political leaders since 1970
1956–88 János Kádár (HSWP)*, 1988–89 Károly Grósz (HSWP)*, 1989–90 Rezsö Nyers (HSP)*, 1990–93 József Antall (MDF)**, 1993–94 Peter Boross (MDF)**, 1994– Gyula Horn (HSP)**

*Communist Party leader
**Prime minister

Political system
Under the terms of the 'transitional constitution', adopted in October 1989, Hungary is a unitary state with a one-cham-

ber 386-member National Assembly (Orszaggyules). Its members are elected for four-year terms under a mixed system of direct and proportional representation. One hundred and seventy-six are directly elected, on a potential two-ballot majoritarian run-off basis, from single-member constituencies; a maximum of 152 are returned from 20 regional, county and metropolitan multi-member constituencies via lists on a proportional basis (with a 5% cut-off limit being applied to determine representation); and a minimum of 58 are elected indirectly from party-nominated national 'compensation' lists, designed to favour smaller parties able to muster at least 5% of the vote. The National Assembly, which meets at least twice a year, elects the state president, for a maximum of two five-year terms, and a Council of Ministers (COM), or cabinet, of some 15 members headed by a prime minister. The president, who must be at least 35 years old, has the authority to initiate legislation, hold plebiscites, and appoint higher civil servants. National Assembly decisions are only valid if carried by a majority when a quorum of at least half its members is present. Constitutional changes require a two-thirds majority. The 15-member Constitutional Court ensures compliance with the constitution.

Political parties

More than 50 political parties operate in Hungary today, supported by partial state funding. Six of these are significant organizations: the Hungarian Socialist Party (HSP: Magyar Szocialista Párt, or MSzP); the Hungarian Democratic Forum (Magyar Demokrata Fórum: MDF); the Christian Democratic People's Party (Kereszténydemokrata Néppárt: KDNP); the Independent Smallholders' Party (Fuggetlen Kizgazda es Pólgari Párt: FKgP); the Alliance of Free Democrats (Szabad Demokratak Szövetsége: SzDSz); and the Federation of Young Democrats–Hungarian Civic Party (Fiatal Demokraták Szövetsége-Magyar Pólgari Párt: FIDESz–MPP).

The HSP is the reform-socialist successor to the formerly ruling Hungarian Socialist Workers' Party (HSWP), adopting its current name and changed political stance in October 1989. The 67,000-member HSP is led by Gyula Horn. The former HSWP was itself an offspring of the Hungarian Communist Party (HCP), which was founded in November 1918 and which, in alliance with the Hungarian Social Democratic Party (HSDP), which dated from 1890, briefly established a 133-day 'Soviet Republic' under the leadership of Béla Kun, between March and August 1919. It was proscribed and forced underground by the succeeding Horthy dictatorship, many of its thousand or so members fleeing to Moscow. There, the party was purged and 'Stalinized'. With Soviet military support, it moved into a dominant position in the country from 1945, forcing the left wing of the HSDP to merge and form a new United Workers' Party, in 1948. It was renamed the Hungarian Workers' Party (HWP) in 1949 and the HSWP in 1956, being substantially reconstituted, following the 'national uprising' of that year. Party membership totalled 1.5 million in the immediate post-World War II period, but, after falling to 500,000 in 1962, grew to 880,000 in 1987, representing 8.3% of the total population. Many members left the party between 1987 and 1989. A rump HSWP, led by Gyula Thurmer, continued to function after

the party's reconstitution in September 1989, but secured only 4% of the first-round vote in the March 1990 general election and thus no parliamentary representation.

The MDF was founded in September 1988 by a group of Populist intellectuals as an umbrella body embracing reformist communists, Christian Socialists, and Christian Democrats. Under the leadership of József Antall, who died in December 1993, it developed into a centre-right nationalist force. The KDNP (estd. 1989) and FKgP (estd. 1988) are, similarly, right-of-centre bodies, but the FKgP split during 1992 into two rival factions. The FKgP has advocated the restoration to its original owners of land collectivized after 1947. In June 1993 an extreme nationalist and anti-Semitic faction of the MDF, led by Istvan Csurka, a prominent novelist, and Lajos Horvath, broke away to from the new Hungarian Justice and Life Party (MIEP).

The SzDSz, led now by Ivan Petö, was formed by dissident intellectuals in November 1988 as a radically pro-Western and pro-free-market party. Closely related is the FIDESz, which, formed in March 1988, gained a reputation as the most militant of the anticommunist pluralist forces. It originated as a liberal-minded youth party, but in April 1993 lifted its age limit of 35 for members and elected Viktor Orbán, aged 30, as its chairperson. During 1993 opinion polls suggested that the FIDESz was the country's most popular party. However, its performance in the May 1994 general election was disappointing and it adopted the new designation FIDESz–MPP in April 1995.

Latest elections

In the most recent National Assembly elections, held on 8 and 29 May 1994, the excommunist HSP secured a convincing victory, capturing 209 of the 386 available seats, based on a 33% share of the national vote. The incumbent MDF, despite using the state media to attack the HSP as an autocratic party, finished in a humiliating third position, winning just 12% of the popular vote and 37 seats. It finished behind the Alliance of Free Democrats, which captured 70 seats, based on a 20% poll share. The Independent Smallholders' Party, with 9% of the vote, won 26 seats; the Christian Democratic People's Party, 7% and 22 seats; and the Federation of Young Democrats, 7% and 20 seats. Two other parties, the Agrarian Association and the Liberal Civic Alliance (Entrepreneurs' Party), each won a single seat. The far-right anti-Semitic Hungarian Justice and Life Party (MIEP), led by the ex-MDF member Istvan Csurka, attracted just 1.6% of the national vote. Turnout was 69% in the first round and 55% in the second, when 174 seats were decided by a first-past-the-post run-off contest. In the event, only 125 seats, rather than the expected 152, were filled from regional party lists, leaving 85, rather than the anticipated 58, to be allocated to national lists for the six parties which succeeded in surmounting the 5% threshold required for representation.

Political history

Having previously been subjected to Roman and Germanic rule, a Magyar kingdom was first established in 1000 AD by St Stephen (c. 977–1035), who converted the country's inhabitants to Christianity. From the early 14th century the nation again came under foreign control, with the south and centre falling to the Turks from the 16th century. They were replaced in the later 17th century by the Austrian Habsburgs. Lajos Kossuth (1802–94) led a Hungarian renaissance during the mid-19th century, with an independent republic being proclaimed and serfdom abolished in 1848–49. This was quickly suppressed by joint Austrian and Russian forces and an Austro-Hungarian empire was re-established within which Hungary enjoyed substantial self-government.

Full independence was finally obtained in 1918, following the dismemberment of the Austro-Hungarian Empire at the close of World War I. A brief 'Soviet Republic' experiment during 1919 was suppressed by Romanian and Czechoslovak troops and a conservative dictatorship was then established, under the leadership of the regent, Admiral Nikolaus Horthy de Nagybánya (1868–1957).

The new regime restricted the franchise to only 27% of the population, paving the way for perpetual dominance by the right-wing Party of Unity, although during the later 1930s the fascist Arrow Cross party emerged as a serious challenger. Only limited advances were achieved in the economic sphere during these years, with still, in 1930, more than half the population remaining dependent upon agricultural activities. In these circumstances, the subsequent 1930s depression had a particularly adverse effect on the country.

On the outbreak of World War II, Admiral Horthy allied Hungary with Germany and the Axis powers, joining Adolf Hitler in the invasion of the Soviet Union in 1941. In March 1944, however, the country was overrun by Soviet forces and the Horthy regime toppled. A provisional five-party coalition government was formed in December 1944, headed by General Miklos. It included the communist agriculture minister, Imre Nagy (1895–1958), who set about distributing land to the peasants as a means of broadening the party's support base. In addition, the Communist Party (HCP) held a majority of seats in the temporary Assembly and was given control of the police forces.

In free elections held in November 1945, the HCP secured 17% of the total votes and 70 of the 409 seats. The Smallholders' Party emerged as the most popular force, capturing a majority of seats, but the HCP, with Soviet support, succeeded in forcing the formation of a coalition with other leftist parties. It then proceeded to introduce a programme of nationalization and central economic planning. In February 1946 a republic was inaugurated and from June 1948, when the HCP and HSDP merged to form the HWP, all other political parties were outlawed. This was followed, in August 1949, by the adoption of a new Soviet-style constitution.

Under HWP leader Mátyás Rákosi, a strict Stalinist regime was imposed between 1946 and 1953, involving forced collectivization and the launching of a wave of secret police terror. Liberalization in the economic sphere began tentatively between 1953 and 1955, when Imre Nagy, supported by the Soviet premier, Georgi Malenkov, replaced Rákosi as prime minister. However, Nagy, in turn, was removed in April 1955, after the fall of Malenkov.

In 1956, in the wake of the Soviet leader Nikita Khrushchev's denunciation of Stalin in his February 'secret speech', pressure for democratization mounted. Rákosi stepped down as HWP leader in July and, following student

and worker demonstrations in Budapest on 23 October, Nagy was recalled as prime minister and János Kádár (1912–89) was appointed general secretary of the HWP. Nagy proceeded to lift restrictions on the formation of political parties, released the anticommunist primate, Cardinal József Mindszenty (1892–1975), and announced plans for Hungary to withdraw from the Warsaw Pact and become a neutral power. These changes were, however, opposed by Kádár, who set up a rival government in East Hungary. He then returned to Budapest, with Soviet tanks, and overthrew the Nagy government on 4 November 1956. Two hundred thousand refugees fled to the West during the 1956 'Hungarian National Uprising' and 2,500 citizens were killed.

In the immediate wake of this 'rebellion', the HWP was purged and reconstituted as the HSWP. Several years of repression followed, with 2,000 participants in the uprising, including Nagy, being executed and many others deported to the USSR. During the 1960s, however, Kádár proceeded to introduce pragmatic, liberalizing reforms, including a decentralization of economic planning, styled, in 1968, the 'New Economic Mechanism'. This gave Hungary the reputation of being one of the freest and most market-orientated Eastern European states. It became a member of the IMF and the World Bank in 1982, and enjoyed a considerable improvement in living standards. Greater participation in local affairs was also encouraged as part of this 'self-governing' process. Externally, Hungary emerged as a loyal member of the Warsaw Pact and Comecon during the 1960s and 1970s.

Hungary's relations with Moscow improved significantly during the post-Brezhnev era, with the perestroika (economic restructuring) programme adopted by the reformist Mikhail Gorbachev, who became Soviet leader in 1985, being influenced by Hungary's 'market socialism' experiment. Between 1987 and 1988 there were further reforms, including more price deregulation, the creation of a stock market, the introduction of value-added tax (VAT), and the establishment of 'enterprise councils'.

As elsewhere in Eastern and Central Europe, change came quickly to Hungary from 1988. In May 1988, two months after a large prodemocracy march was held in Budapest, Kádár, who had become an obstacle to reform, was replaced as HSWP general secretary by Károly Grósz (1930–96), the prime minister since June 1987, and two reformers, the economist Rezsö Nyers and Imre Pózsgay, were brought into the Politburo. Kádár was moved upstairs to the new ceremonial post of party president. These changes were designed to usher in a new phase of political reform, with the stated aims of achieving a clearer separation between party and state and of introducing a new system of 'socialist pluralism' in which noncommunist parties would be admitted into a more influential, decision-taking parliament, censorship laws would be relaxed, the HSWP would no longer have a guaranteed leading role in society, and independent trade unions would be allowed to form. Outside momentum was added to this process by the formation of 'reform clubs' by intellectuals and dissidents, under the 'Network of Free Initiatives' umbrella organization. These were superseded, in September 1988, by the Hungarian Democratic Forum (MDF), an umbrella movement for opposition groups, and several dozen other political parties were formed during 1989 and 1990.

In February 1989 the official interpretation of the events of 1956 was also radically revised, it being now seen as a 'popular uprising' rather than a 'counter-revolution', and in June 1989 Imre Nagy was posthumously rehabilitated, cleared of alleged past crimes by the Supreme Court, and reburied in a state funeral attended by 300,000 people. The border with Austria was opened in May 1989, with adverse effects for East Germany's communist regime, as thousands of East Germans escaped to the West via Hungary. Two months later, as the reform momentum continued to build up, Grósz was forced to share power with the more radical trio of Nyers, Pózsgay, and Miklós Németh (prime minister since November 1988), as a four-person ruling praesidium was formed. The HSWP had earlier, in February 1989, agreed to abandon the clause in the constitution guaranteeing the party a leading political role.

In October 1989 a series of significant constitutional changes, the result of round-table talks held with opposition groups through the summer, were approved by the National Assembly. These included the adoption of a new set of electoral rules, the banning of workplace communist party cells, and the change of the country's name from the 'People's Republic' to simply 'Republic'. Also in October 1989 the HSWP changed its name to the Hungarian Socialist Party (HSP), and adopted Pózsgay as its presidential candidate. Grósz, and other conservatives, refused to play an active role in the renovated party, which had become a 'social-democratic' pluralist force. Despite these changes, the HSP's standing was damaged badly by the January 1990 'Danubegate scandal', when it was revealed that the secret police had bugged opposition parties and passed the information obtained to the HSP. The HSP polled disastrously in the March–April 1990 multiparty general election, attracting, in the first round, only 11% of the national vote to the MDF's 25%, the SzDSz's 21%, the Independent Smallholders' 12%, the FIDESz's 9%, and the KDNP's 7%. After the election, a MDF-dominated coalition government was formed in May 1990, embracing the KDNP and Independent Smallholders' Party and independents, and headed by the MDF leader, Dr József Antall (1932–93), a former museum director, who became prime minister. Arpád Göncz (b. 1922), a former dissident playwright, translator, and a member of the SzDSz, who was jailed between 1956 and 1963 for opposing the communist regime, was elected state president by the legislature in August 1990, replacing Mátyás Szuros, who had been acting president since October 1989. The new right-of-centre administration declared its aims as withdrawal from the Warsaw Pact, to seek membership of the European Union, and to effect a full transition to a Western-style market economy.

Externally, events moved swiftly during 1990. The Soviet Union was asked, in February 1990, to withdraw its troops and the government announced, in June 1990, that Hungary would no longer participate in Warsaw Pact military exercises. As the Warsaw Pact and Comecon had disbanded by July 1991, the country was able to move towards the West more directly. Hungary joined the Council of Europe (COE),

becoming its first Eastern European member, in November 1990 and, on schedule, in June 1991 the last Soviet troops withdrew from the country. In February 1991 Hungary signed the Visegrad declaration of economic, political, and security cooperation with Poland and Czechoslovakia (which became two separate states from 1 January 1993), while treaties of cooperation were signed with Russia and Ukraine in December 1991. In March 1994 it applied for full membership of the European Union.

Of all the former Soviet satellite states, Hungary experienced the smoothest transition towards a market economy during the early 1990s, although GDP did decline by more than 20% between 1990–93. This was probably because it was the first to adopt a policy of self-management and privatization, even before the downfall of the communist regime in 1989. Although economic problems persisted, including an increase in unemployment to 12% of the workforce, Hungary provided a gradualist model for other 'newly freed' East European states to be compared to the 'shock therapy' model of Poland. In January 1991 the forint was devalued by 15% in an effort to boost exports and in June 1991 a Compensation Bill for owners of land and property expropriated under the communist regime was approved by the National Assembly. It was hoped that, by clearing up the uncertainty over ownership, the bill would stimulate the privatization programme and inward investment. By the start of 1994, with the economy beginning to grow again, around 40% of the workforce were employed by the private sector and nearly half of the 2,000 state enterprises which existed in 1989 had been either sold or liquidated.

Politically, the period between 1982 and 1984 was one of relative stability, but there were growing strains within the MDF-led ruling party. In June 1992 the Independent Smallholders' Party split into two factions, one of which supported the Antall administration, while the other allied itself with the opposition. A year later, in June 1993, a split also occurred in the MDF, with its vice chairperson, Istvan Csurka, leaving to form the extreme nationalist and anti-Semitic Hungarian Justice and Life Party (MIEP). During 1993 the health of Prime Minister Antall, who was suffering from lymph gland cancer, deteriorated progressively and on his death, in December 1993, the interior minister, Peter Boross (b. 1928), took over as prime minister.

The MDF trailed throughout 1993–94 in the opinion polls behind the HSP and the FIDESz and in the general election of May 1994 was able to secure a mere 12% of the national vote, finishing behind the HSP, which attracted 33% of the vote, and the SzDSz, with 20% popular support. The HSP was in a position to form a majority administration on its own, but chose instead to form a powerful socialist-liberal coalition government with the SzDSz Alliance of Free Democrats and which controlled 72% of the legislature's seats. Gyula Horn (b. 1932), a trained economist who had been a member of the procommunist militia which had fought against democrats in 1956, but was later a reformist foreign minister during the final period of communist rule in 1989–90, became prime minister on 15 July 1994. A member of the left wing of the HSP, he constructed a 14-member technocratic cabinet, which included three representatives of the SzDSz, and pledged to adopt a less nationalist posture than the preceding MDF administration. In particular, efforts were made to improve relations with neighbouring Slovakia and Romania where large ethnic Hungarian communities resided. The Horn administration became beset by divisions over economic policy, leading to the resignation of its staunchly promarket finance minister, László Bekesi, in January 1995 and the dismissal, in the same month, of the privatization chief, Ferenc Bartha. However, in March 1995 a radical economic reform package was unveiled by the Horn administration which, in a dramatic policy U-turn, sought to institute major cuts in public spending, including social and welfare programmes, so as to reduce the level of indebtedness and to boost exports via devaluing the forint by more than a quarter and increase the pace of privatization. In June 1995 the popular Arpád Göncz was re-elected by Hungary's parliament for a second term as state president, being backed by the SzDSz and HSP.

LATVIA

Republic of Lavia
Latvijas Republika

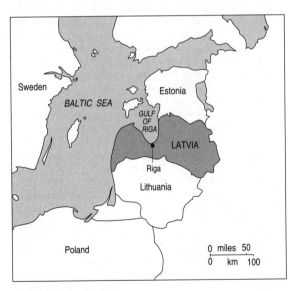

Capital: Riga

Social and economic data
Area: 64,589 km^2
Population: 2,700,000*
Pop. density per km^2: 42*
Urban population: 72%**
Literacy rate: 99%**
GDP: $5,300 million**; per-capita GDP: $2,050**
Government defence spending (% of GDP): 3%**
Currency: lat
Economy type: middle income
Labour force in agriculture: 17%**

*1994
**1992

Ethnic composition
Fifty-three per cent of the population is of Latvian ethnic stock, 34% is ethnic Russian, 4% Belarussian, 3% Ukrainian, 2% Polish, and 1% Lithuanian. The official language, since 1988, has been Latvian, or Lettish, a member of the Baltic group of Indo-European languages which is written in the Latin script. Only a quarter of ethnic Russians are fluent in Latvian.

Religions
The predominant religion is Christianity, with most ethnic Latvians belonging to the Lutheran or Roman Catholic churches, and most ethnic Russians are Russian Orthodox or Old Believers. During the period of Soviet rule, until the late 1980s, many churches were closed and the clergy imprisoned.

Political features
State type: emergent democratic
Date of state formation: 1920/1991
Political structure: unitary
Executive: parliamentary
Assembly: one-chamber
Party structure: multiparty
Human rights rating: N/A
International affiliations: BC, BIS, CBSS, COE, EBRD, ECE, IAEA, IBRD, IMF, NACC, OSCE, PFP, UN, WEU (associate partner)

Local and regional government
Latvia is divided into 26 districts, 56 towns, and 37 urban settlements for the purposes of local government.

Head of state
President Guntis Ulmanis, since 1993

Head of government
Prime Minister Andris Skele, since 1995

Political leaders since 1970
1990–93 Ivars Godmanis (LPF), 1993–94 Valdis Birkavs (Latvian Way), 1994–95 Maris Gailis (Latvian Way), 1995–   Andris Skele (independent)

Political system
Under the restored constitution of 1922, Latvia is a democratic parliamentary republic. Legislative authority is vested in the 100-seat Saeima, whose members are elected for three-year terms on the basis of proportional representation, with a 5% cut-off limit being applied to determine representation. Executive power is held by a prime minister, drawn from the majority party or grouping in the Saeima and Council of Ministers, comprising 12 ministries. The Saeima elects a president to serve as titular head of state, also for three years.

Political parties
Latvia, like many other central European postcommunist states, has a diffused multiparty system, comprising numerous recently formed and poorly organized bodies.

Currently, the most important parties are: the Latvian Way (Latvijas Cels); the Latvian National and Conservative Party

(LNNK); Harmony for Latvia and Rebirth for the National Economy (HLRNE); the centrist Ravnopravie (Equal Rights); For the Fatherland and Freedom (FFF); the Latvian Peasants' Union (LZS); the Union of Christian Democrats (CDU); the middle-of-the-road Democratic Centre Party; the populist extremist Movement for Latvia; and Master in Your Home (Saimnieks) party.

The Latvian Way was formed in February 1993 as a right-of-centre force which favours development of a market economy, private ownership of land, and Baltic cooperation. The then head of state, Anatolijs Gorbunovs, was a founder member and the party includes a number of excommunists.

The 12,000-member LNNK is a right-wing nationalist force founded in June 1988 by Eduards Berklavs under the designation National Independence Movement of Latvia. It adopted its present name in June 1994.

HLRNE and Ravnopravie are committed to the extension of Latvian citizenship to all ethnic Russians.

The FFF is an extreme nationalist body which advocates a 'Latvia for the Latvians' policy. The LZS was originally formed in 1917, as the Latvian Farmers' Union, and was re-established in 1990 to fight for the interests of the agrarian community. The 1,500-member CDU is a centre-right body established in 1991. In September 1994 the LNNK, FFF, LZS, and CDU formed an opposition coalition, termed the National Bloc, within Latvia's parliament.

The formerly dominant party before the elections of June 1993 was the 150,000-member Latvian Popular Front (LPF: Latvijas Tautas Fronte), which was set up in 1988 as a moderate umbrella nationalist organization.

The Latvian Communist Party (CPL), which split in 1990, a breakaway Democratic Labour Party of Latvia being formed, and was banned in August 1991, also failed to secure parliamentary representation in June 1993.

The Movement for Latvia, led by Joachim Siegerist, a German citizen and former LNNK deputy, advocates reduced taxes, greater foreign inward investment, closer ties with Russia, and a tough approach to fighting crime and corruption.

Saimnieks, which is led by Ziedonis Cevers, a former leader of the Young Communists, and is dominated by the former communist *nomenklatura*, seeks to protect agriculture, with tariffs and the stopping of land privatization.

Latest elections

The most recent parliamentary elections were held in October 1995. They produced a hung parliament in which two populist extremist parties attracted most support, with 15% of the vote each. These were the Movement for Latvia and the Master in Your Home party, winning 16 and 18 seats. Nine parties surmounted the 5% threshold for representation. The ruling Latvian Way, led by Maris Gailis, saw its vote share more than halved, to below 15%, but, with 17 seats, remained at the hub of a new multi-party coalition government. Almost a third of the population were unable to vote in the election. These were chiefly Russian speakers, many of whom failed to pass the Latvian language and history tests, and the five-year minimum residency requirement for citizenship.

Political history

The area now known as Latvia was invaded by the Vikings in the 9th century and the Russians in the 10th century. After lengthy resistance, it was taken over by German crusaders, the Teutonic Knights, in the 13th century and governed by them for more than 200 years, with the inhabitants being converted to Christianity. More changes of control followed, by Poland, Lithuania, and Sweden, during the 16th and 17th centuries, before Tsarist Russia took over in 1710. By 1800 all of Latvia had come under Russian control. The Latvian independence movement began to emerge in the early 1900s. During World War I, Latvia was partially occupied by the Germans and on 18 November 1918 proclaimed its independence. This was achieved after Soviet forces were expelled by German, Polish, and Latvian troops between May 1919 and January 1920.

A democratic parliamentary constitution, based on pure proportional representation, was adopted in 1922. The dominant party was the Latvian Farmers' Union, led by Karlis Ulmanis, which introduced successful land reforms. However, there were 18 changes of government from 1922 until May 1934, when, at a time of economic depression, Ulmanis assumed power in a bloodless coup. Ulmanis dissolved the legislature, the Saeima, banned all political parties, and became president in 1936. In August 1939 a secret German–Soviet agreement assigned Latvia to Russian rule and in July 1940 Latvia was incorporated as a constituent republic of the USSR. During World War II, Latvia was again occupied by German forces from July 1941, but the USSR regained control in 1944.

There were mass deportations of Latvians to Russia and Central Asia, the immigration of ethnic Russians (in 1935 three-quarters of the population had been ethnic Latvian), the development of heavy industries and collective farms, and the establishment of one-party communist rule. Repression of Latvian cultural and literary life was particularly extreme during the 1960s and 1970s as a result of a purge of the Communist Party of Latvia (CPL) instituted by the Soviet leader Nikita Khrushchev, which saw the replacement of Latvian-born members with those born in the USSR, termed *latovichi*.

As in the other Baltic republics, nationalist dissent grew from 1980, influenced by the Polish example and by the glasnost (political openness) and perestroika (economic restructuring) initiatives launched by Mikhail Gorbachev, who became the new Soviet leader in 1985. An Environmental Protection Club (EPC) was formed in 1986, the pro-independence National Independence Movement of Latvia (LNNK) in June 1988, and the intelligentsia-led Latvian Popular Front (LPF) in October 1988 as an umbrella force, which included many communists and claimed a membership of 250,000, to campaign for political pluralism and autonomy. In September 1988 Latvia's prewar flag was relegalized and official status accorded to the Latvian language. In July 1989, with many members of the CPL having been won over to the nationalist cause, Latvia's parliament, the Supreme Soviet, declared its sovereignty and economic independence from the USSR.

The CPL's constitutional guarantee of a monopoly of power was abolished in January 1990 and in elections held to the Supreme Soviet in March–April 1990 the LPF secured a clear victory, capturing 131 of the 201 contested seats. The LPF's deputy chairperson, Ivars Godmanis, became prime minister and Anatolijs Gorbunovs, from the CPL, became the new head of state. The Supreme Soviet was renamed the Supreme Council and a number of articles of the 1922 constitution were restored as the new parliament announced, in May 1990, that Latvia's incorporation into the USSR in 1940 was illegal and the republic was now commencing a transitional period that would lead to full political and economic independence. At the same time, the CPL split into two separate Moscow-linked and independent wings. An unofficial alternative parliament, the Congress of Latvia, was also established in May 1990 after voting by citizens of the pre-1940 republic and their descendants. This was dominated by the LNNK.

The Soviet leader, Mikhail Gorbachev, anulled Latvia's declaration of independence in May 1991 and during 1991 non-Latvians organized anti-independence strikes and demonstrations. In January 1991, fearing a complete break-up of the Union, Soviet interior ministry (OMON) paratroopers were sent to seize key installations in Riga, killing one civilian. This enabled Alfred Rubiks, leader of the pro-Moscow wing of the CPL to set up the 'Committee of Public Salvation' as a rival government to the legitimate one headed by Godmanis. However, following internal and international protests, the Soviet forces withdrew later in January 1991. Latvia boycotted the March 1991 all-Union referendum on the continuance of the USSR and held, instead, a plebiscite on independence, which received 73.7% support, based on a turnout of 87.6%. On 21 August 1991, in the midst of the failed anti-Gorbachev coup in the USSR, which led to Red Army troops seizing the radio and television station in Riga, the republic declared its full and immediate independence. The CPL was also outlawed and Rubiks imprisoned. This declaration was recognized by the Soviet government and Western nations on 6 September 1991 and the new state was admitted to the United Nations (UN) and Conference on Security and Cooperation in Europe (CSCE, later the OSCE).

The LPF administration headed by Godmanis instituted market-centred economic reforms, with a new national currency, the lat, being introduced to replace the rouble in March 1993 and the service sector, particularly banking, being encouraged. However, in the short term, the republic suffered from disruption of traditional trading relations with the USSR and shortages of fuel and raw materials. As a consequence, GDP declined by 8% in 1991 and by more than 25% in 1992, while inflation and crime increased sharply. In 1992 a controversial provisional new citizenship law was also introduced which required those who had not been, or were not the descendants of, citizens of the pre-1940 republic to apply for naturalization. The requirements for naturalization included knowledge of the Latvian language and residence of 16 years in Latvia.

The general election, held on 5–6 June 1993, resulted in a complete defeat for the unpopular LPF, which failed to win a seat in the new Saeima, and brought to power a more centrist government coalition, with Valdis Birkavs (b. 1942), from the recently formed Latvian Way, becoming prime minister and Guntis Ulmanis (b. 1939), from the Latvian Peasants' Union

(LZS), president. Ethnic Russians had been effectively excluded from voting in this election, with the franchise being restricted to citizens of the interwar Latvian Republic and their descendants. In July 1994 the withdrawal of LZS support led to the resignation of Prime Minister Birkavs and his replacement, in September 1994, by Maris Gailis, also from the Latvian Way. The new coalition government included Birkavs as foreign minister and deputy prime minister. The final withdrawal of Russian troops from Latvia was completed in August 1994 and during 1994–95 the economy began to grow. In June 1995 a trade and cooperation agreement was signed with the European Union (EU), offering the eventual prospect of joining the EU. In December 1995, after a general election producing a hung parliament, Andris Skele (b. 1958), an independent entrepreneur, became prime minister.

LITHUANIA

Republic of Lithuania
Lietuvos Respublika

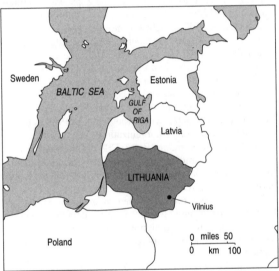

Capital: Vilnius

Social and economic data
Area: 65,200 km^2
Population: 3,800,000*
Pop. density per km^2: 58*
Urban population: 70%**
Literacy rate: 98%**
GDP: $7,000 million**; per-capita GDP: $1,850**
Government defence spending (% of GDP): 3%**
Currency: litai
Economy type: middle income
Labour force in agriculture: 17%**

*1994
**1992

Ethnic composition
Eighty per cent of the population is of Lithuanian ethnic stock, 9% is ethnic Russian, 7% Polish, 2% Belarussian, and

1% Ukrainian. Lithuanian, a Baltic tongue which used the Latin script, replaced Russian as the official language in 1988. Interethnic relations have deteriorated in recent years.

Religions
Ethnic Lithuanians are predominantly Roman Catholics and in 1992 three-quarters of the republic's population followed this faith. Ethnic Russians, Belarussians, and Ukrainians largely adhere to the Russian Orthodox Church or are Old Believers.

Political features
State type: emergent democratic
Date of state formation: 1919/1991
Political structure: unitary
Executive: dual
Assembly: one-chamber
Party structure: multiparty
Human rights rating: N/A
International affiliations: BC, BIS, CBSS, COE, EBRD, ECE, IAEA, IBRD, IMF, NACC, OSCE, PFP, UN, WEU (associate partner)

Local and regional government
The republic is divided into 44 districts, 92 towns, and 22 urban settlements for the purposes of local government.

Head of state
President Algirdas Brazauskas, since 1993

Head of government
Prime Minister Adolfas Slezevicius, since 1993

Political leaders since 1970
Head of state: 1988–90 Algirdas Brazauskas (CPL), 1990–93 Vytautas Landsbergis (Sajudis), 1993– Algirdas Brazauskas (LDLP); Prime minister: 1990–91 Kazimiera Prunskiene (CPL), 1991–92 Gediminas Vagnorius (independent), 1992 Aleksandras Abisala (Sajudis), 1992–93 Bronislovas Lubys (independent), 1993– Adolfas Slezevicius (LDLP)

Political system
Under the terms of the constitution of October 1992, which is modelled on that of 1938, Lithuania is a democratic-pluralist state, with a predominantly parliamentary form of executive, though the president retains considerable authority in the selection of the prime minister. A proposal to introduce an executive presidency was rejected in a referendum held in May 1992.

Legislative authority is vested in the 141-deputy Seimas, or parliament, which is directly elected, in accordance with a mixed system of majority voting and proportional representation, for a four-year term. Candidates must be aged 25 years or more and the Seimas meets for two regular four-month sessions each year. The state president is directly elected for a maximum of two consecutive five-year terms and must be at least 40 years old. With the approval of the Seimas, the president appoints a prime minister who shares executive power with a 15–20-member Council of Ministers. The president also has an active role in foreign affairs.

Political parties
Currently the dominant political party in Lithuania is the Lithuanian Democratic Labour Party (LDLP), which was formed in December 1990 as the reform-socialist successor to the Lithuanian Communist Party (LCP), which broke away from the Soviet Communist Party in December 1989 and was outlawed in August 1991. The LDLP is divided between a faction which supports accelerated market-centred economic reform and an agrarian lobby which opposes land reforms. The party favours improved relations with Russia and other ex-Soviet states.

The chief opposition party is the Homeland Union–Lithuanian Conservatives (Tevynes Santara), which was formed in May 1993 to succeed Sajudis (Lithuanian Restructuring Movement), set up in June 1988 to spearhead Lithuania's drive for independence. The Homeland Union is a right-of-centre nationalist force, modelled on the British Conservative Party, led by former president, Vytautas Landsbergis. Closely aligned is the centre-right Christian Democratic Party of Lithuania, which was first formed in 1905 and was re-established in February 1989. The left-of-centre Lithuanian Social Democratic Party originated in 1896 and was also re-established in 1989.

Latest elections
The most recent legislature elections were held on 25 October and 15 November 1992 and resulted in victory for the excommunist LDLP, which captured 73 of the 141 seats in the Seimas. The formerly dominant Sajudis won, in alliance with the Citizens' Charter of Lithuania, only 30 seats, the Christian Democratic Party, 16, the Social Democratic Party, 8, the Polish Union, 4, and other parties, 10.

The last presidential election was held on 14 February 1993 and was won by the LDLP's Algirdas Brazauskas, who secured 60% national support. His only opponent was Stasys Lozoraitis, Lithuania's ambasssador to the United States who had been an émigré for 50 years. Five other candidates, including the incumbent President Landsbergis, withdrew from the contest.

Political history
Lithuania became a separate nation at the end of the 12th century and the German crusaders, the Teutonic Knights, who tried to invade it in the 13th century were driven back, enabling the country to extend its territorial limits almost as far as Moscow to the east and the Black Sea to the south. In the 16th century Lithuania joined Poland in a single state, and in 1795 both came under the control of tsarist Russia. Revolts in 1831 and 1863 failed to win independence. A more organized nationalist movement emerged in the 1880s, but self-government was refused by the Russians in 1905.

During World War I, Lithuania was occupied by German troops. After the war, it declared independence on 16 February 1918 but the USSR claimed Lithuania as a Soviet republic. There was an uprising, supported by Germans and Poles, and in 1919 a democratic republic was established. A coup, in December 1926, led by Antanas Smetona, brought back authoritarian rule until, in 1939, it was invaded by Nazi Germany and later handed over, in the secret Molotov–Ribbentrop pact, to the Soviet Union. Following Germany's invasion of the USSR in 1941, Lithuania revolted against Soviet rule and established its own government. However, the Germans soon occupied the country until Soviet rule was restored in 1944. Some 210,000 people, including 165,000 Jews, were killed during the brutal Nazi occupation of 1941–44. As in Estonia and Latvia, there was fierce guerrilla resistance to the imposition of Soviet rule until the early 1950s and the 'sovietization' policies of forcible agricultural collectivization and persecution of the Roman Catholic Church. The Russian authorities reacted by deporting an estimated 570,000 Balts to Siberia during the late 1940s.

An intelligentsia- and Roman Catholic Church-led dissident movement was in place during the 1960s and 1970s, producing illegal *samizdat* publications. This grew in strength during the early and mid-1980s, influenced by the Polish example and encouraged by the policies of glasnost (political openness) and perestroika (economic restructuring) espoused by Mikhail Gorbachev, who became the new Soviet leader in 1985. In 1987 the Lithuanian Freedom League (LFL) was set up by dissidents recently released from prison and began to organize public demonstrations. In June 1988 a popular front, the Lithuanian Restructuring Movement (Sajudis), was formed to campaign for increased autonomy, and on 17 November 1988 Lithuania's parliament, the Supreme Soviet, recognized Lithuanian as the state language and readopted the flag and other state symbols of the independent interwar republic.

During 1989 the Lithuanian Communist Party (LCP) became increasingly nationalistic in an attempt to win public support and on 18 May 1989 the CPL-dominated Supreme Soviet passed a declaration of sovereignty which asserted the supremacy of Lithuanian legislation over all-Union laws. Later in the year, the LCP's monopoly of political power was abolished and a multiparty system was sanctioned, freedom of religious expression was re-established, and, in December 1989, the LCP split in two, with the majority faction formally breaking away from the Communist Party of the Soviet Union (CPSU) and establishing itself as a social-democratic Lithuanian-nationalist body. These moves took place against the background of an increasing level of popular participation in nationalist demonstrations, with more than 1 million people forming a 'human chain' extending from Tallinn in Estonia to Vilnius in Lithuania in August 1989 to protest against the 50th anniversary of the Nazi–Soviet Baltic Pact.

In the parliamentary elections of February–March 1990 Sajudis and its allies won a clear majority of seats, 88 out of 141, and the party's chairperson, Vytautas Landsbergis (b. 1932), a former music professor, was elected the country's new head of state, replacing Algirdas Brazauskas (b. 1932), leader of the LCP since 1988. On 11 March 1990 Landsbergis unilaterally proclaimed the restoration of Lithuania's independence and the Supreme Soviet was renamed the Supreme Council. The Soviet Union responded by imposing an economic blockade on 16 April 1990. By June 1990 Lithuania had exhausted its energy reserves and in July 1990 its Supreme Council was forced to suspend the independence declaration in order to have the blockade lifted. Criticized by militant nationalists as being too concil-

iatory towards Moscow, Kazimiera Prunskiene, a member of the LCP who had been prime minister since March 1990, resigned on 8 January 1991 and went into exile. She was replaced by Gediminas Vagnorius. This change of prime minister took place at a time of national crisis, with Soviet interior ministry (OMON) paratroops being sent to Vilnius to occupy Communist Party buildings which had been nationalized by the Lithuanian government after President Landsbergis had rescinded the suspension of the declaration of independence. On 13–14 January 1991, 13 civilians were killed when the OMON black beret troops seized the radio and television centre in Vilnius, but, faced with internal and international condemnation, the Soviet forces began to withdraw in late January 1991. The Soviet action increased support for independence among ethnic Lithuanians who, on 9 February 1991, gave 90% approval to the re-establishment of an independent Lithuania in a referendum in which turnout reached 84%.

In the wake of the failed anti-Gorbachev coup in the Soviet Union in August 1991, Lithuania's declaration of independence was formally recognized by the Soviet government and Western nations on 6 September 1991. The new state became a full member of the United Nations (UN) and was admitted into the Conference on Security and Cooperation in Europe (CSCE, later the OSCE). In July 1992, having been criticized by opposition deputies for his authoritarian governing style, Vagnorius resigned as prime minister and was replaced by Aleksandras Abisala, a close ally of President Landsbergis. However, Sajudis endured a crushing defeat in elections to the new legislature, the Seimas, which were held in October–November 1992. The party was accused of mismanaging economic reform, comprising price liberalization and privatization, which had resulted in GDP declining by 13% during 1991 and 76% of families being officially reported as living in poverty in 1992. The excommunist LDLP, now a social-democratic force supportive of a market economy, secured a parliamentary majority and its leader, Vytautas Brazauskas, became the new head of state and Bronislovas Lubys (b. 1938), prime minister. The new government was a coalition which included six members of the previous administration, but no members of Sajudis, which preferred to remain in opposition.

On 14 February 1993 Brazauskas was directly elected state president, convincingly defeating Stasys Lozoraitis, a Lithuanian émigré, and then announced his formal resignation from the LDLP. In March 1993 Adolfas Slezevicius became the new prime minister and on 31 August 1993 Russia removed the last of its remaining troops stationed in Lithuania. During 1993 the Lithuanian economy remained in severe recession and the governing party was itself divided over the optimal pace of economic reform. A free trade agreement was entered into in September 1993 with the other Baltic States, Estonia and Latvia, and relations were improved with neighbouring Poland, with whom a Friendship and Cooperation Treaty was signed in April 1994, despite the continuing campaign of Lithuania's Polish minority community for Polish to be recognized as one of the republic's official languages. In June 1995 a trade and cooperation agreement was signed with the European Union (EU).

MACEDONIA

Republic of Macedona (official internal name)
Republika Makedonija
The Former Yugoslav Republic of Macedonia (FYRM,
international name)

Capital: Skopje

Social and economic data
Area: 25,713 km²
Population: 2,000,000*
Pop. density per km²: 78*
Urban population: 54%*
Literacy rate: 89%*
GDP: $1,600 million*; per-capita GDP: $800*†
Government defence spending (% of GDP): N/A
Currency: Macedonian denar
Economy type: low income
Labour force in agriculture: N/A

*1992
†Alternative estimates place per-capita GDP as high as
$1,800

Ethnic composition
Sixty-six per cent of the population is, according to 1991 and
1994 official censuses, of Macedonian ethnic stock, 22% is
ethnic Albanian, 5% Turkish, 3% Romanian, 2% Serb, and
2% Muslim, comprising Macedonian Slavs who converted
to Islam during the Ottoman era and known as Pomaks. This
ethnic breakdown is disputed by Macedonia's ethnic Albanian population, who, concentrated in the west of the republic,
claim that they form 40% of the population and seek autonomy. It is also contested by ethnic Serbs, who claim that they
number 250,000, and neighbouring states. Macedonian, a
Slavic language closely related to Bulgarian, is the official

language, but minority languages, such as Albanian, are used
at the local level.

Religions
Macedonia is a predominantly Christian state. More than
60% of the population adheres to the autocephalous (independent) Macedonian Orthodox Church, but there is a large
Sunni Islam minority, comprising around 25% of the population and including mainly ethnic Albanians.

Political features
State type: emergent democratic
Date of state formation: 1992
Political structure: unitary
Executive: limited presidential
Assembly: one-chamber
Party structure: multiparty
Human rights rating: N/A
International affiliations: COE, IAEA, IBRD, IMF, OSCE
(observer), PFP, UN

Local and regional government
The basis unit of local government has, traditionally, been
the local commune or township.

Head of state (executive)
President Kiro Gligorov, since 1991

Head of government
Prime Minister Branko Crvenovski, since 1992

Political leaders since 1970*
1991–   Kiro Gligorov (SDSM)

*Executive president

Political system
The November 1991 democratic-pluralist constitution
describes the state as one based on citizenship rather than ethnicity. It provides for a 120-member single-chamber National
Assembly (Sobranje), elected by universal adult suffrage for a
four-year term, with provision for its size to be increased to
140 members. Elections are on a majority basis, with a second
round 'run-off' contest being held in constituencies where no
candidate wins at least 50% of the vote in the first round, and,
exceptionally, repeat elections being held subsequently. The
president, who is head of state and of the armed forces, is
directly elected for a similar term. He or she appoints the prime
minister as head of government. Other ministers are elected
by the National Assembly. The prime minister and other
ministers cannot concurrently be members of the Assembly.

Political parties
The main parties in Macedonia are the ruling Alliance of
Macedonia (SM) bloc; the Party of Democratic Prosperity of
Albanians in Macedonia (PDPSM); the Internal Macedonian
Revolutionary Organization–Democratic Party for Mace-
donian National Unity (VMRO–DPMNE); and the Democ-
ratic Party of Macedonia (DPM).

The SM is an alliance of three parties, the excommunist
Social Democratic Alliance of Macedonia (SDSM), which is
led by Prime Minister Branko Crvenovski and President
Kiro Gligorov, the Liberal Party (LP); and the left-wing

Socialist Party of Macedonia (SPM; estd. 1990). The reform-socialist SDSM was known until 1991 as the League of Communists of Macedonia–Party for Democratic Reform, which, formed in 1943, had been the ruling party in the republic during the communist era.

The PDPSM, formed in 1990, is a predominantly Albanian and Muslim party which, although splitting into two rival factions in February 1994, has participated in the SM-led governing coalition. It seeks to improve conditions for the Albanian minority in Macedonia.

The VMRO–DPMNE and DPM are the two main opposition parties. The VMRO–DPMNE is the most staunchly nationalist force in the country. It originated in 1893 as an opponent of the partition of Macedonia and a supporter of the idea of forming a Southern Slav federation of Macedonians, Bulgarians, and Serbs. Refounded in June 1990, it secured the largest number of parliamentary seats in the November–December 1990 general election. However, in the October–November 1992 Sobranje elections it failed to win any seats. It claimed that the results were rigged, but its pro-Bulgarian stance is believed to have lost its support. The DPM, formed in 1993 by Petar Goshev, is a free-market nationalist body.

Latest elections

The most recent parliamentary elections were held on 16 and 30 October and 13 November 1994. The third round was required to fill 11 seats which had been undecided after two rounds of voting. The ruling three-party Alliance of Macedonia (SM) won 95 of the 120 available seats, of which 58 were won by the SDSM, 29 by the Liberal Party, and 8 by the SPM. The ethnic Albanian-orientated PDPSM captured 10 seats and the National Democratic Party 4 seats. The nationalist VMRO–DPMNE, formerly the Sobranje's largest party, failed to win a seat, while the other opposition force, the DPM, won just 1 seat. Both these parties claimed that there had been ballot-rigging and boycotted the second and third rounds, demanding the elections to be annulled. Turnout ranged between 50% and 60% in the first two rounds, but reached 78% in the third-round contests.

The last presidential election was held on 14 October 1994 and was won by the incumbent Kiro Gligorov, an excommunist backed by the SM, who attracted 69% of the vote, defeating Ljubisha Georgievski, a theatre director representing the VMRO–DPMNE, with 19% of the vote. Turnout was 76%, but the election was tainted by allegations of ballot-rigging which led the State Electoral Commission to order a repeat poll in 11 constituencies.

Political history

Macedonia was an ancient country of southeast Europe between Illyria, Thrace, and the Aegean Sea, becoming a significant kingdom under Alexander the Great (356–323 BC), who conquered Greece, Egypt, and the Persian Empire. In 148 BC it became a province of the Roman Empire. Macedonia was settled by Slavs in the 6th century, but then suffered a series of conquests, by Bulgars in the 7th century, by Byzantium in 1014, by Serbia in the 14th century, and by the Islamic Ottoman Empire in 1371. Following the First Balkan War of 1912, Macedonia was partitioned, with its Greek-speaking areas being assigned to Greece and the remainder divided between Bulgaria and, the area that constitutes the present republic, Serbia. During World War I, Bulgaria temporarily occupied the region. After the war, Serbian Macedonia became part of the new federal kingdom of Yugoslavia, but, with Serbian being imposed as the official language, demands for greater autonomy continued to be made. During World War II, Macedonia was again occupied by Bulgaria between 1941 and 1944. A separate Macedonian republic was formed in 1945 when Yugoslavia, now under communist control, was reorganized on Soviet federal lines by Marshal Tito. During the postwar period, Macedonia, predominantly agricultural, remained the least developed part of Yugoslavia, but it received effective subsidies from the other richer republics. The Macedonian language and cultural identity was encouraged as a means of countering any lingering pro-Bulgarian sentiment. The republic's Albanian Muslim community also grew progressively, and tension resurfaced between ethnic Macedonians and the Serb-dominated federal government.

After the death of the Yugoslav president, Tito, in 1980, it became increasingly apparent that the federal structure would not hold. Internal pressures and the monumental changes that occurred in the Soviet bloc countries following the advent to the leadership of the USSR of the reformist Mikhail Gorbachev in 1985 stimulated nationalist fervour based on ethnic and religious differences and growing fears of Serb-nationalist expansionism. In 1988, influenced by developments in the neighbouring Albanian-dominated autonomous province of Kosovo, in Serbia, there were large nationalist demonstrations by ethnic Albanian students in western Macedonia. In mid-1989 the ruling League of Communists of Macedonia (LCM) agreed to relinquish its dominant role. This paved the way for multiparty elections to the republic's parliament in November–December 1990 in which nationalist parties, notably the Internal Macedonian Revolutionary Organization–Democratic Party for Macedonian National Unity (VMRO–DPMNE), polled strongly. However, the overall result of this contest was inconclusive and an all-party coalition 'Government of Experts', though dominated by the VMRO–DPMNE, was formed in March 1991, with the independent Nikola Kljusev as prime minister. Indirect presidential elections held on 27 January 1991 resulted in Kiro Gligorov (b. 1918), a pragmatic former communist, being chosen by the parliament as the new head of state. The secession of Croatia and Slovenia from the Yugoslav socialist federation in June 1991 gave impetus to Macedonia's drive for full autonomy, and the Macedonian government, formerly supportive of the continuance of the Yugoslav federation but now concerned that a reduced 'rump Yugoslavia' would be dominated by Serbia, held a referendum on independence on 8 September 1991. This poll was boycotted by the republic's substantial ethnic Albanian and Serb minorities, but received overwhelming support from the majority ethnic Macedonian community.

Sovereignty was declared by the Macedonian parliament in September 1991 and independence in January 1992. Swift recognition was accorded by neighbouring Bulgaria and also by Turkey, but not by Serbia or by Greece, the latter being concerned that it might imply a territorial claim on its own northern province of Macedonia. In an unofficial referendum, also held in January 1992, Macedonia's Albanian community voted by a 99.9% margin for autonomy, as the 'Republic of Ilirida', with many harbouring the desire to unite with neighbouring Albania and Kosovo province in Yugoslavia to form an enlarged 'greater Albania' ruled from Tiranë. Serbia effectively acceded to Macedonia's independence in March 1992 by sanctioning the full withdrawal of federal Yugoslav troops from the republic and in April 1992 the new Yugoslav constitution referred only to the republics of Serbia and Montenegro. Macedonia was eventually admitted into the United Nations (UN) on 8 April 1993 under the designation 'The Former Yugoslav Republic of Macedonia', and a 700-strong multinational UN force was stationed in the republic to help ensure its integrity. In December 1993 it was recognized by the states of the European Union and in February 1994 by Russia and the United States. However, Greece continued to campaign for the designation 'Skopje' to be used instead and remained concerned that Macedonia's November 1991 constitution contained a reference to speaking for 'all Macedonians' and that its flag carries the Vergina Star of the Macedonian dynasty of Alexander the Great. As a consequence, in February 1994, with a new Papandreou government in power, Greece suspended diplomatic ties and imposed a trade embargo on Macedonia, excepting only foodstuffs and medical supplies. This action caused severe damage to the Macedonian economy which was already crippled by the disruption of trade with Serbia, against whom international sanctions were in force, with GDP halving between 1989–94 and inflation exceeding 30% a month by 1994 and the unemployment level being estimated at more than 30% during 1993.

In October 1991 the VMRO–DPMNE withdrew from the coalition 'Government of Experts', complaining that it was being excluded from the decision-making process, and in July 1992 Branko Crvenovski became prime minister, heading a new administration dominated by the excommunist Social Democratic Alliance of Macedonia (SDSM), which he led. The administration sought to gradually introduce market-centred economic reforms and improve relations with neighbouring countries. The Crvenovski administration included ministers from the ethnic Albanian-orientated Party of Democratic Prosperity (PDPSM), although two of its senior figures, Husein Haskaj, the deputy defence minister, and Mithad Emini, were arrested in November 1993 and later convicted, in June 1994, for plotting to organize an Albanian-funded 'All-Albanian Army' in the Albanian peopled region of Testovo, situated in northwest Macedonia. Crvenovski continued as prime minister and Gligorov as president after parliamentary and presidential elections, held in October–November 1994, saw the SDSM and its allies gaining a clear victory over the nationalist VMRO–DPMNE, although there were allegations of poll irregularities. As energy shortages worsened, a state of emergency was declared in December 1994. In September 1995 Greece finally officially recognized Macedonia and restored diplomatic relations after Macedonia agreed to redesign its flag and change two articles of its constitution to remove any suggestion of possible claims on the Greek province of Macedonia. In October 1995 President Gligorov was seriously injured in a car-bomb assassination attempt in Skopje.

MOLDOVA

Republic of Moldova
Republica Moldoveneasca

Capital: Chişinău (formerly Kishinev)

Social and economic data
Area: 33,700 km²
Population: 4,400,000*
Pop. density per km²: 131*
Urban population: 48%**
Literacy rate: 96%**
GDP: $5,637 million**; per-capita GDP: $1,280**
Government defence spending (% of GDP): 1.2%**
Currency: leu
Economy type: middle income
Labour force in agriculture: 32%**

*1994
**1992

Ethnic composition
Sixty-five per cent of the population is of Moldovan (Romanian) ethnic stock, 14% Ukrainian, 13% ethnic Russian, 4% Gagauzi, 2% Bulgarian, and 2% Jewish. Romanian (Moldovan), a Romance language written in the Latin script, has been the official language since 1989. Russian and Turkish, spoken by the Gagauz, are minority languages.

Religions
The population is predominantly Christian, adhering principally to the Russian Eastern Orthodox Church. Despite their Turkish origins, the Gagauz also adhere to Orthodox Christianity. There is a small Jewish minority.

Political features
State type: emergent democratic
Date of state formation: 1991
Political structure: unitary
Executive: limited presidential

Assembly: one-chamber
Party structure: multiparty
Human rights rating: N/A
International affiliations: BSECZ, CIS, COE, IBRD, IMF, NACC, OSCE, PFP, UN

Local and regional government
The country comprises 38 districts and 10 cities for the purposes of local government. The Gagauz minority, concentrated around Komrat in southwestern Moldova, concerned at growing nationalism among the country's Romanian majority, have attempted to establish a separate 'Republic of Gagauzia' since 1990. Ethnic Russians, who dominate the region east of the Dnestr river in the far east of the country, have also sought to establish their own separate 'Dnestr Soviet Republic', with its capital at Tiraspol. Both the Gagauz and the Dnestr regions have been granted special autonomous status by the August 1994 constitution.

Head of state
President Mircea Snegur, since 1990

Head of government (executive)
Prime Minister Andrei Sangheli, since 1992

Political leaders since 1970*
1990–   Mircea Snegur (excommunist independent)

*President

Political system
Under the terms of the August 1994 constitution, Moldova is a 'presidential, parliamentary republic'. The constitution seeks to enshrine political pluralism and free ethnic and linguistic expression. It also bars the stationing of foreign troops on Moldovan soil, establishing 'permanent neutrality' for the state, and grants special autonomous status to the Gagauz and Dnestr regions. The country has had an executive presidency since 1991, with decree powers granted in 1993 and the authority to appoint and dismiss cabinet ministers. The state president is directly elected, for a five-year term, and appoints a prime minister and cabinet, or Council of Ministers. The legislature, the Moldovan Parliament (Parlamentul), has 104 members who are directly elected by proportional representation for four-year terms.

Political parties
Thirty parties contested the most recent, February 1994, parliamentary elections, but only four party blocs were sufficiently popular to gain representation. These were the Agrarian Democratic Party (ADP); the Socialist Party and Yedinstvo/Unity Movement bloc; the Peasants and Intellectuals bloc; and the Christian Democratic People's Front (CDPF).

The ADP is a nationalist-centrist force, which favours cooperation within the Commonwealth of Independent States (CIS). President Snegur was a member of the ADP until June 1995, but resigned since he believed that some ADP leaders opposed further economic reform and sought to reduce his presidential powers. In August 1995, he became leader of the new centrist Party of Revival and Conciliation (PRC).

The Socialist Party is the reform-socialist successor to the Communist Party of Moldova, which was banned in August 1991, but relegalized in September 1993. It favours closer ties with Russia.

The Peasants and Intellectuals bloc is a pro-Romanian body, as is the CDPF, formed in 1992 as successor to the nationalist Moldavian Popular Front (MPF; estd. 1989). Both advocate Moldova's reintegration into Romania.

In the breakaway Dnestr Republic the dominant party is the Patriotic Bloc.

Another party of some significance is the Gagauz Halky (Gagauz People's Movement), which represents the 150,000-strong Gagauz minority community and advocates Gagauz separatism.

Latest elections
The most recent parliamentary elections were on 27 February 1994. The ADP, which attracted 43% of the national vote, emerged as the largest single force and achieved a parliamentary majority, capturing 56 of the 104 available seats. The Socialist Party and Yedinstvo/Unity Movement bloc, representing the Slavic population, won 28 seats, based on a 22% vote share, the Peasants and Intellectuals bloc, 11 seats and 9% of the vote, and the CDPF, 9 seats, with 8% of the vote. Altogether, 30 parties contested the election, but most, including the Social Democratic Party (3.5%), the Democratic Labour Party (2.6%) and the Reform Party (2.5%), fell below the 4% of the national vote cut-off threshold for representation. The poll was boycotted in the separatist Dnestr region.

The last presidential election was held on 8 December 1991 and was won by Mircea Snegur, the existing head of state (chairman of the Supreme Soviet), who, with the backing of the Moldovan Popular Front, won 98% of the national vote. Snegur was unopposed, after two challengers withdrew.

Political history
Formerly a principality in Eastern Europe, occupying an area divided today between the republic of Moldova and modern Romania, the region was independent from the 14th to the 16th century, when it became part of the Ottoman Empire. Its eastern part, Bessarabia, was ruled by Russia between 1812 and 1917, when it declared its independence, but was transferred to Romania in 1918. After Nazi Germany recognized the USSR's interest, in the secret Molotov–Ribbentrop pact of August 1939, Romania was forced to cede Bessarabia in June 1940 and it was joined with part of the Soviet/Ukrainian-controlled Autonomous Moldavian Republic to form the Moldavian Socialist Republic in August 1940. Before and after World War II, the republic was brutally 'sovietized'. The intelligentsia and *kulak* (rich peasant farmer) communities were liquidated or deported to Central Asia, agriculture was collectivized, private enterprises were taken over by the state, and ethnic Russians and Ukrainians were settled in the republic. Previously predominantly agricultural, Moldova witnessed significant urban and industrial growth from the 1950s.

Encouraged by the glasnost (political openness) instituted by Mikhail Gorbachev, who became the Soviet Union's new leader in 1985, and the Baltics' independence movement, there was an upsurge in Moldovan nationalism during the late 1980s. This took the form, initially, of a campaign for language reform and for reversion from the Cyrillic to the Latin alphabet. In 1988 a Moldavian Movement in Support of Perestroika (economic restructuring) was formed and in May 1989, after large demonstrations in Chişinău, the Moldavian Popular Front (MPF) was established. In August 1989 the MPF persuaded the republic's parliament (Supreme Soviet) to make Romanian the state language and reinstate the Latin script. This provoked demonstrations and strikes by the republic's Russian speakers and led the 150,000-strong, Turkish-speaking but Orthodox Christian, Gagauz minority, concentrated in the southwest, to campaign for autonomy.

In November 1989, after MPF radicals had staged a petrol bomb assault on the interior ministry headquarters in Chişinău, the conservative leader of the Moldavian Communist Party (MCP), Semyon Grossu, was dismissed and replaced by the more conciliatory Pyotr Luchinsky. In the wake of the Chişinău riots, with interethnic strife worsening, a temporary state of emergency was imposed and a ban placed on public meetings. This restricted campaigning for the February 1990 Supreme Soviet elections. Nevertheless, the MPF polled strongly and, as a result, 40% of the deputies returned were aligned to the MPF and a further 30% were sympathetic to its aims. In April 1990 the new Supreme Soviet elected Mircea Snegur (b. 1940), a reform-nationalist MCP member who was supported by the MPF, as its chairperson and effective head of state, and in May 1990 Mircea Druc, an MPF reform-economist, became prime minister.

After this election and the leadership changes of April–May 1990, the movement towards independence gathered momentum. A 'sovereignty' declaration was made by the Supreme Soviet in June 1990 and a republican guard was established in November 1990. The republic decided to boycott the March 1991 USSR referendum on the preservation of the Union because of concern that it might worsen interethnic tensions. However, 650,000 people, predominantly ethnic Russians, defied the official boycott and voted overwhelmingly for the Union. During the August 1991 attempted anti-Gorbachev coup in Moscow by communist hardliners, which was denounced by President Snegur but supported by the Dnestr and Gagauz regions, there were large prodemocracy demonstrations in Chişinău. After the coup, MCP activity was banned in workplaces and on 27 August 1991 the republic formally declared its independence. Immediate recognition was accorded by Romania. However, the highly industrialized, predominantly ethnic Russian-peopled Dnestr region in the east, centred around Tiraspol and with a population of 700,000, which had been part of Ukraine until 1940, declared its own independence from Moldova on 2 September 1991 and adopted a separate constitution. The declaration and a subsequent plebiscite on independence, held in December 1991, were rejected by Moldova.

Moldova joined the Commonwealth of Independent States (CIS) on its inception on 21 December 1991 and was admitted into the Conference on Security and Cooperation in Europe (CSCE, later the OSCE) in January 1992. It became a member of the United Nations (UN) in March 1992. However, following pro-unification border rallies, the Moldovan and Romanian presidents met in January 1992 to discuss the possibility of union. Snegur, who was directly elected state president in December 1991 in an unopposed contest, favoured a gradual approach towards unification with Romania.

In January 1992, as armed conflict in the secessionist Trans-Dnestr escalated, having broken out in December 1991, a state of emergency was imposed by President Snegur. By June 1992 the fighting between the Dnestr region's Slav militia and the Moldovan army had claimed 700 lives and had led to 50,000 refugees fleeing to Ukraine. It was alleged that the Dnestr militia received Russian nationalist support. The conflict was ended in July 1992 by the signing of a Moldovan-Russian peace agreement. This provided for the continued stationing of Russian 14th Army troops in the region to help maintain the peace and the grant of 'special status' within Moldova to the area. In effect, the region had broken away from Moldova and, controversially, Lieutenant General Alexander Lebed, the Russian nationalist commander of the 14th Army, was later elected to the Dnestr Supreme Soviet in September 1993. Lebed was later dismissed from the Russian army, by President Yeltsin, in June 1995.

In July 1992 the MPF-dominated government fell as a result of lack of popular support for its policy of seeking reintegration into Romania and the rapidly deteriorating performance of the economy as a transition was sought from a command to a market economy. In 1991 real GDP fell by 12% and during the first half of 1992, as a result of the Trans-Dnestr conflict and a devastating drought, a further 28% decline was registered. Moldova was particularly dependent on Russia for fuel supplies and Ukraine for access to the Black Sea. Andrei Sangheli, the former agriculture minister, took over as prime minister, heading a 'government of national accord' formed in July 1992, whose principal support was drawn from the Agrarian Democratic Party (ADP) and the Conciliation group of ethnic Russian deputies.

The new administration concentrated on attempting to improve the economy, through beginning privatization, initially in the service sector, in October 1993, and introducing a new currency, the leu, in November 1993 to replace the Russian rouble. This programme began to have some effect by 1995, by which time the decline in GDP, which had exceeded 20% in 1994, was halted and inflation had been greatly reduced. In addition, from 1993, President Snegur, realizing that pro-Romanian parties were becoming increasingly unpopular, abandoned his earlier policy of seeking closer ties with Romania and concentrated, instead, on improving relations with Russia, seeking full membership of the CIS, which was achieved in April 1994, and strengthening Moldovan statehood. This policy proved electorally popular, with the pro-Russian ADP and Socialist Party polling strongly in the February 1994 parliamentary elections, attracting 65% of the national vote, while the pro-Romanian Peasants and Intellectuals bloc and Christian Democratic People's Front, the successor to the MPF, won less than 17% support. Underlining this public mood, a national referendum on continued independence from Romania and Russia, which was held on 6 March 1994, won 95% approval, based on a turnout of 75%. In August 1994 Russia agreed to fully withdraw its 14th Army troops, still stationed in the Dnestr region, by 1997. Moldova acceded to the Council of Europe in July 1995.

POLAND

Republic of Poland
Polska Rzeczpospolita

Capital: Warsaw (Warszawa)

Social and economic data

Area: 304,463 km^2
Population: 38,500,000*
Pop. density per km^2: 126*
Urban population: 63%**
Literacy rate: 99%**
GDP: $83,823 million**; per-capita GDP: $2,180**
Government defence spending (% of GDP): 2.5%**
Currency: zloty
Economy type: middle income
Labour force in agriculture: 25%**

*1994
**1992

Ethnic composition

Ninety-eight per cent of the population are ethnic Poles, a Western-Slav race. There are also small ethnic German, Ukrainian, and Belarussian minorities. The rights of the 500,000-strong German minority in Poland to their own culture, language, and religion have been recognized in a treaty of good neighbourliness and friendly cooperation with Germany, which also confirms the Oder–Neisse border. The official language is Polish.

Religions

Ninety-five per cent of the population adheres to the Roman Catholic faith; 2%, or 870,000, to the Polish Autocephalous Orthodox Church; and 100,000 to Protestant denominations, mainly the Evangelical Augsburg Church. The Roman Catholic Church is an influential institution with a buoyant membership. It is closely connected with the idea of Polish nationhood and played an important role, particularly during the primacy of Cardinal Stefan Wyszyński, in the campaign for human rights. The Catholic Church was granted full legal status in May 1989.

Political features

State type: emergent democratic
Date of state formation: 1918
Political structure: unitary
Executive: limited presidential
Assembly: one-chamber
Party structure: multiparty
Human rights rating: 83%
International affiliations: CEFTA, CERN, COBSS, COE, IAEA, IBRD, IMF, NACC, NAM (guest), OSCE, PFP, UN, VG, WEU (associate partner), WTO

Local and regional government

The country is divided into 49 provinces (*voivodships*) administered by appointed governors and 2,348 elected and autonomous local councils.

Head of state (executive)

President Alexander Kwasniewski, since 1990

Head of government

Prime Minister Jozef Oleksy, since 1995

Political leaders since 1970

1970–80 Edward Gierek (PZPR)*, 1980–81 Stanislaw Kania (PZPR)*, 1981–90 General Wojciech Jaruzelski (PZPR)*, 1990–95 Lech Wałesa (Solidarity/independent)** 1995–   Alexander Kwasniewski (SLD)**

*Communist Party leaders
**Democratic executive president

Political system

Under the revised constitution, adopted between 1989 and 1992, Poland has a limited presidential political system, although the interim constitution fails to define the president's powers clearly. The executive president is directly elected for a maximum of two consecutive five-year terms in a two-round majority contest. The president, who must be at least 35 years old, has responsibility for military, foreign, and police affairs and has the authority to appoint the prime minister, who commands a majority in the Sejm, dissolve parliament, call referenda, veto bills, and impose martial law. There is a two-chamber legislature, the National Assembly (Zgromadzenie Narodowe), comprising a 460-member lower assembly, the Sejm (parliament), and a 100-member upper chamber, the Senate (Senat). Deputies are elected to the Sejm for four-year terms by means of proportional representation in free multiparty contests. Three hundred and ninety-one Sejm deputies are elected from 37 multimember electoral districts and 69 through national party lists. Under the terms of electoral regulations adopted in May 1993, parties (except national minority groups) must gain 5% of the national vote to qualify for seats (with alliances needing at least 8%), and bonus seats, from the national list, are awarded to parties which attract more than 7% support. The Senate is elected on a provincial basis, each province returning two senators, except Warsaw and Katowice, which elect three. The Sejm passes bills, adopts the state budget and economic plan, and appoints a 24-member executive council of ministers, headed by a chairperson, or prime minister. The Senate has the power of veto in specified areas, which can be overridden by a two-thirds Sejm vote. The prime minister administers with a cabinet, or council of ministers. Ministers are appointed by the president, but it has been uncertain whether they can be dismissed by the president without restraint.

Political parties

Since the collapse of communism, numerous political parties have been formed, but most have been short-lived and able to attract only small shares of the national vote. In the October 1991 general election, for example, 29 parties secured representation in the Sejm, but no single party was able to win more than 12% of the vote. The September 1993 general election, encouraged by changes to the electoral law (see *Political system*) saw a reduction in the number of parties securing representation to seven, but again no party polled more than 20% of the vote.

Currently, there are seven significant parties in Poland: the Democratic Left Alliance (Sojusz Lewicy Demokratycznej: SLD); the Polish Peasant Party (PSL); the Freedom Union (UW); the Labour Union (UP); the Non-Party Bloc in Support of Reforms (BBWR); the Confederation for an Independent Poland (KPN); and the Conservative Liberal Movement (RKL).

The 60,000-member SLD was formed in 1990, as the Social Democracy Party, to be the reform-socialist successor to the Polish United Workers' Party (Polska Zjednoczona Partia Rabotnicza: PZPR), the dominant party in Poland until 1989. The SLD, led by the young and charismatic Alexander Kwasniewski, favours the building of a market economy, but seeks to ensure that its social costs to poorer sections of society are alleviated. It also proposes abolition of the Senate. The preceding PZPR was heir to the Communist Workers' Party of Poland (KPRP) which was founded in 1918 by Marxist wings of the nationalist Polish Socialist Party (PPS), which dated back to 1892 (and was later illegally revived in 1987), and the internationalist Social Democracy of the Kingdom of Lithuania and Poland Party (SDKPiL), which was established as long ago as 1895. The KPRP later changed its name to the Communist Party of Poland (KPP) in 1925, but was forced to operate underground when proscribed by the Piłsudski regime. Because of its close Soviet links, it enjoyed little domestic support, membership standing at barely 10,000, and it was dissolved by Stalin in 1938. Four years later the pro-Moscow Polish Workers' Party (PPR) was established as a successor body. It was divided into two wings, a Moscow-based Stalinist faction, led by Boleslaw Bierut, and a 'native' anti-German resistance wing led by party first secretary, Władysław Gomułka. Gomułka was ousted by Bierut as leader in 1948 and the party was soon afterwards merged with the PPS to form the PZPR. In 1987 membership of the PZPR stood at 2.13 million, or 5.7% of the total population.

The 200,000-member centre-left rural sector-orientated PSL was formed in 1990 to replace the United Peasants' Party (ZSL), which, along with the intelligentsia-orientated Democratic Party (SD; estd. 1939), had been permitted to operate during the communist period under the umbrella of the PZPR-led Patriotic Movement for National Rebirth (PRON) mass organization. The ZSL was established in 1948 as a successor to the earlier peasant nationalist movement, the Polish People's Party.

The UW, led since April 1995 by Leszek Balcerowicz, a former finance minister, was formed in April 1994 by Tadeusz Mazowiecki through the merger of Mazowiecki's Democratic Union (DU) and the Liberal Democratic Congress (KLD; estd. 1988). Both former parties had their roots in the Solidarity free-trade union movement, the DU being formed in 1991 as a centrist successor to the Citizens' Movement–Democratic Action (ROAD), formed in 1990. The left-wing Labour Union (UP), known formerly as Labour Solidarity, also had its roots in Solidarity, along with the BBWR, a Christian Democratic right-of-centre alliance formed in 1993 by Lech Wałesa and backed by the Catholic Church. Two other parties which had their roots in Solidarity are the centre-right Centre Alliance (estd. 1990) and the Peasant Alliance (PL), which united in May 1994 with three other right-wing bodies, including the Christian National Union (estd. 1989), to form the Covenant for Poland 'confederation'.

The KPN is a right-wing body formed in 1979.

The RKL is a right-wing party, formed in April 1995 by Czeslaw Bielecki, prime minister in 1991, and Andrzej Olechowski, foreign minister in 1993–95.

Latest elections

The most recent Sejm elections were held on 19 September 1993 and were characterized by a significant swing to the left and the eclipse of the by now fragmented Solidarity movement, resulting in a return to power of the SLD and PSL, successor parties to the communist era PZPR and ZSL. With the new electoral arrangements in force (see *Political system*) designed to favour larger parties, only seven parties and alliances secured representation, compared with 29 in 1991. The SLD attracted 20% of the vote and won 171 of the Sejm's 460 seats, while the PSL, with 15% of the vote, captured 132 seats. The centre-left DU secured 11% of the vote and 74 seats, the left-wing Labour Union, 7% of the vote and 41 seats, the right-wing KPN, 6% of the vote and 22 seats, and the pro-Wałesa BBWR, 5% of the vote and 16 seats. The only other parties to win seats were German minority organizations, which won 4 seats, being specifically exempted from the 5% cut-off rule. Thirty-five per cent of the vote was won by minor parties which failed to surmount the minimum vote share threshold for representation. These included Homeland (formerly Catholic Electoral Action), which won 6.4% of the vote, Solidarity, 4.9%, the Centre Alliance, 4.4%, the Liberal Democratic Congress (KLD), 4%, Stanislaw Tyminski's Party X, 2.7%, and the Peasant Alliance (PL), 2.3%. Turnout, at 52%, was 9% up on 1991. Concurrent elections, on a provincial basis, to the 100-seat Senate resulted in the SLD capturing 37 seats, the PSL, 36, Solidarity, 10, the DU, 4, and others, 13.

The last direct presidential elections were held on 5 and 19 November 1995. Lech Wałesa won 48% in the second round vote, Alexander Kwasniewski, the leader of the reformed communists, 52%, Jacek Kuron, a former dissident had attracted support in the first round. There were 10 other candidates

Political history

During the medieval period, particularly from the 14th century, Poland was an influential Central European power under its own Jagellion dynasty, which ruled between 1386 and 1572. When it was united with Lithuania in 1569, Poland became the largest country in Europe. Defeat in the mid-17th century in a war against Russia, Sweden, and Brandenburg brought about its decline and a century later the country was partitioned between Russia, ruling the east, Prussia, the west, and Austria, the south-centre, where a measure of autonomy was granted. There were uprisings in 1830 and 1863 against the repressive Russian regime, leaving behind a legacy of deep antipathy.

At the close of World War I, in November 1918, a fully independent Polish republic was established. Marshal Józef Piłsudski (1867–1935), the founder of the PPS, was elected the country's first president and, taking advantage of upheavals in the Soviet Union, he proceeded to launch an advance into Lithuania and the Ukraine which reached stalemate in 1921. Politically, the immediate postindependence years were characterized by instability, with 14 multiparty coalition governments holding power between 1918 and 1926. Marshal Piłsudski then seized complete power in a coup in May 1926 and proceeded to govern in an increasingly autocratic manner until his death in 1935. The country remained backward, only pockets of industrialism existing at Lodsz and in Upper Silesia, with, in 1930, 60% of the total population remaining dependent upon agricultural activities.

A military regime, under the leadership of Śmigly-Rydz, remained in power until the German invasion of September 1939. Western Poland was immediately incorporated into the Nazi Reich, while the remainder of the country, except for a brief Soviet occupation of East Poland between 1940 and 1941, was treated as a colony and endured tremendous suffering. A third of the educated elite were liquidated, while, in all, 6 million Poles lost their lives – half of them Jews, slaughtered in concentration camps. By the middle of 1944, parts of eastern Poland had been liberated by Soviet Red Army forces, allied with Polish troops commanded by General Rola-Zymierski, and a communist-dominated multiparty coalition government was set up at Lublin. In March 1945 the remaining German forces were driven out of the country.

The Soviet Union immediately recognized the 'Lublin coalition' as the Provisional Government of all Poland, but this was challenged by the Polish exile government, based in London and backed by the Western Allies. It was headed, as prime minister, by the peasant leader Stanislaw Mikolajcyk (1901–67). Following the Yalta Conference, in February 1945, it was agreed to set up a joint government, but this was dominated by the Lublin coalition and PPR, which secured effective control of the security police and armed forces. Their position was further strengthened when, at the manipulated Sejm elections of January 1947, the Lublin coalition's list of candidates, the 'Democratic Bloc', secured 80% of the votes and 88% of the 444 seats. A month later, a 'People's Republic' was proclaimed, with the PPR predominant, and in October 1947 Mikolajcyk fled to the West.

The new regime was faced with immediate resettlement problems as a result of the drastic 240-kilometre westward shift of the borders of the Polish state engineered at the Potsdam Conference in July 1945. Under the terms of this agreement, Poland's eastern frontier was set at the 1921 Curzon Line, with 180,000 square kilometres in the east, almost half of 'old Poland', being lost to the Soviet Union, while 100,000 square kilometres of former German territories along the line of the Oder and Neisse rivers were added from the west.

A Soviet-style one-party constitution was adopted in July 1952 and a harsh Stalinist form of rule instituted by Boleslaw Bierut, the PZPR leader between 1948 and 1956. This involved rural collectivization and the persecution of Catholic Church opponents, including the arrest, in 1953, of Cardinal Wyszyński (1901–81). During this period, Poland also joined Comecon, in 1949, and the Warsaw Pact, in 1955, and remained under close Soviet supervision, with the USSR's Marshal Konstantin Rokossovsky serving as minister for war between 1949 and 1956.

In June 1956 serious strikes and riots, resulting in 53 deaths, erupted in Poznań in opposition to Soviet exploitation and food shortages. This prompted the reinstatement of the more pragmatic, 'nativist', Władysław Gomułka (1905–82) as PZPR first secretary and the introduction of a series of moderate reforms, involving, most importantly, the reintroduction of private farming (by the mid-1980s 85% of Poland's cropped area was privately tilled), the release of Cardinal Stefan Wyszyński, and toleration of Catholicism.

Sudden food price rises, in December 1970, caused a further outbreak of strikes and rioting in Gdańsk, Gdynia, and Szczecin. These demonstrations had to be forcibly suppressed. This led to Gomułka's replacement as PZPR leader by the Silesia party boss and leader of the party's technocratic faction, Edward Gierek (b. 1913), who proceeded to institute a new economic reform programme directed towards achieving a rapid rise in living standards and production of consumer goods. The country became heavily indebted, however, to foreign creditors and further strikes and demonstrations took place at Radom and Ursus, in June 1976, on the announcement of a proposal to raise food prices.

Opposition to the Gierek regime, which was accused of gross corruption, mounted in 1979, following a visit paid to his homeland by the recently elected Pope John Paul II (b. 1920), the former Cardinal Wojtyla of Kraków. Strikes commenced in Warsaw in June 1980, following a poor harvest and meat price rises, and rapidly spread across the country. The government attempted initially to appease workers by entering into pay negotiations with unofficial strike committees, but, at the Gdańsk shipyards, demands emerged for permission to form free independent trade unions. The government conceded this request and recognized the right to strike, resulting in the formation, in August 1980, in Gdańsk, of the Solidarnosc (Solidarity) union, under the leadership of the electrician, Lech Wałesa (b. 1943).

In September 1980, the ailing Gierek was replaced as PZPR first secretary by Stanislaw Kania, but the unrest continued as the 10-million-member Solidarnosc campaigned for a five-day working week and a rural Solidarnosc was established. Meanwhile, inside the PZPR, rank and file pressure began to grow for greater democratization, and a quarter of the party's members actually joined Solidarnosc. With mounting food shortages and PZPR control slipping, Kania was replaced as PZPR leader by the joint prime minister and defence minister, General Wojciech Jaruzelski (b. 1927), in October 1981.

With Soviet military activities taking place on Poland's borders, martial law was imposed on 13 December 1981. Trade union activity was banned, the leaders of Solidarnosc arrested, a night curfew imposed, and a Military Council of National Salvation established, headed by Jaruzelski. Five months of severe repression ensued, resulting in 15 deaths and 10,000 arrests. The actions of the Polish government were condemned by the United States administration and economic sanctions were imposed.

In June 1982 curfew restrictions were eased, prompting further serious rioting in August. Three months later, Lech Wałesa was released and in December 1982 martial law was suspended, and then formally lifted in July 1983. Pope John Paul II visited Poland in June 1983 and called for conciliation. The authorities responded in July by dissolving the Military Council and granting an amnesty to political prisoners and activists. This amnesty was broadened in July 1984, with the release of 35,000 prisoners and detainees on the 40th anniversary of the People's Republic, prompting the American government to relax its economic sanctions. The residual sanctions were later fully removed, in February 1987.

The Jaruzelski administration pursued pragmatic reform, including liberalization of the electoral system. The political atmosphere remained tense, however, and was strained by the murder of Father Jerzy Popieluszko (1947–84), a pro-Solidarnosc priest, by members of the security forces in October 1984, by the continued ban on Solidarnosc and by a threat, which was eventually withdrawn in February 1986, to try Lech Wałesa for slandering state electoral officials when disputing the October 1985 Sejm turnout figures. Economic conditions and farm output slowly improved, but Poland's foreign debt remained huge. During 1988 the nation's shipyards, coalmines, ports, and steelworks were paralysed by a wave of Solidarity-led strikes for higher wages to offset the effect of recent price rises. With its economic strategy in tatters, the government of Prime Minister Zbigniew Messner resigned, being replaced in December 1988 by a new administration headed by the reformist communist Mieczyslaw Rakowski, and the PZPR's Politburo was infused with a new clutch of technocrats.

After six weeks of PZPR–Solidarity–church negotiations, an historic accord was reached in April 1989 under whose terms Solidarity was relegalized, the formation of opposition political associations was tolerated, legal rights were conferred on the Catholic Church, the state's media monopoly was lifted, and a new 'socialist pluralist' constitution was drafted. In the subsequent National Assembly elections, held in June 1989, Solidarity captured all but one of the Sejm and Senate seats for which they were entitled to contest: 55% of the Sejm's seats had been reserved for contests between candidates from the Patriotic Movement for National Rebirth (PRON), the PZPR broad front organization; 10% for nationalist dignitaries; and the remaining 161 (35%) for non-

PRON candidates. Jaruzelski was elected president by parliament in July 1989.

In September 1989 a 'grand coalition' was formed with Tadeusz Mazowiecki (b. 1927), editor of Solidarity's newspaper, as prime minister. Jaruzelski continued as president. The new government, which attracted generous financial aid from Western powers, proceeded to dismantle the command economy and encourage the private sector. A tough austerity programme approved by the IMF was also instituted to address the problem of hyperinflation, which ran at 550% in 1989.

In January 1990 the PZPR voted to disband itself and reform as the Social Democracy Party (SLD). In April 1990 the Sejm voted to restore 3 May (the anniversary of the creation of the 1791 constitution) as national day and to cancel the 22 July (anniversary of the 1944 Lublin Manifesto establishing communist rule) as a national holiday. Censorship was also abolished in April 1990. During 1990 real GDP in Poland fell by 12% and unemployment rose to over 1 million. In July 1990, 40 members of the 259-strong Solidarity caucus, under the leadership of Zbigniew Bujak and Wladyslaw Frasyniuk, established the Citizens' Movement–Democratic Action Party (ROAD) to provide a credible alternative to the Wałesa-orientated Solidarity Centre Alliance (SCA), which had been established in May 1990.

In the first round of direct presidential elections, held on 25 November 1990, the rupture within Solidarity was exposed as both Prime Minister Mazowiecki and Lech Wałesa contested for the position. Having run a populist campaign, Wałesa topped the poll with a 40% vote share and Mazowiecki, defending an unpopular government, finished in third position, with 18% of the vote, behind Stanislaw Tyminski, a previously obscure, right-wing, returned émigré Canadian entrepreneur, who captured 23% of the vote. In the second round, held on 9 December 1990, Wałesa defeated Tyminski by a large margin.

The defeated Mazowiecki resigned as prime minister in December 1990 and the newly elected Wałesa stood down from the Solidarity chair and was sworn in as president. He chose for prime minister an economist and former Solidarity activist, Jan Krzysztof Bielecki (b. 1951), and the new government included the IMF-backed finance minister, Leszek Balcerowicz, and other ministers from the outgoing administration. They pledged to consolidate the free market they had introduced, and the first privatization share sales were held in January 1991, with mixed success.

In the short term, the new 'shock therapy' programme of radical market-centred restructuring reform resulted in a continuing sharp decline in living standards – real GDP falling by around 10% in 1991 – and growing public discontent and industrial unrest as unemployment climbed to more than 2 million (11% of the workforce) by December 1991. Bielecki offered his resignation in late August 1991, complaining that he no longer enjoyed the support of a Sejm that still contained many communists. Parliament refused to either accept the resignation or approve the government's crucial proposed budget cuts. President Wałesa urged it to confer emergency powers to enable the government to rule by decree until the general election. However, this plea was rejected, creating an impasse, although Bielecki agreed to stay on as prime minister, pending elections.

The October 1991 general election was Poland's first post-communist, fully free, multiparty contest. With a generous system of pure proportional representation being operated and party roots being still weak, 29 parties were successful in winning Sejm seats. No dominant party emerged from the voting, with the best performances being recorded by Mazowiecki's Democratic Union (DU), which attracted 12% of the national vote, and the Wałesa-orientated Centre Alliance and Polish Peasant Party (PSL), which each won 9% of the vote. In the light of this unsettled outcome, President Wałesa proposed that he should combine the positions of president and prime minister for two years, heading a 'national unity' grand coalition government. However, this failed to gain broad support. An attempt was then made to construct a left-of-centre coalition led by Broneslaw Geremek. This foundered, and in December 1991 Wałesa reluctantly allowed Jan Olszewski, a former Solidarity defence lawyer and a representative of the Centre Alliance, to set about forming a five-party centre-right coalition government. This government pledged to pursue a more gradual approach to market-orientated reform and, in particular, to slow down the privatization programme by concentrating instead on helping ailing state industries.

In October 1991 a treaty was signed with the Soviet Union providing for the withdrawal of all Soviet combat troops by 15 November 1992 and the remainder by the end of 1993. This agreement was substantially upheld by the new Russian administration, with the last Russian troops actually leaving Polish soil in September 1994. During 1992 unemployment continued to rise, reaching 2.5 million (14% of the workforce) by the year's end, as the demise of the intensive, inefficient state-owned industry of the communist era progressed. However, the 'shock therapy' reform programme began to have an effect. The annual rate of inflation was brought down from 684% in early 1990 to 60% in early 1992 and during that year the Polish economy became the first in Eastern Europe to resume growth after the collapse of communism, with the private sector now accounting for more than 50% of economic activity.

Despite these achievements, the Olszewski government remained unpopular and in June 1992 fell after losing a no-confidence motion in the Sejm. In July 1992 Hanna Suchocka, from the DU, became the new, and Poland's first female, prime minister, leading a new seven-party coalition government. The Suchocka coalition was beset by constant internal wranglings and in May 1993, after refusing the strike demands of 600,000 teachers and health-care workers, was itself brought down in a no-confidence motion. However, Suchocka remained as prime minister in a caretaker capacity until new parliamentary elections were held in September 1993. These elections were held under new electoral rules, which, with a 5% threshold having been introduced for gaining seats, were designed to ensure that a smaller number of large parties achieved representation. To general surprise, the Democratic Left Alliance (SLD) and PSL, which were successors to the ruling parties of the communist era, the PZPR and ZSL, returned to power, attracting 36% of the vote between them and capturing 303 of the 460 available Sejm seats. These reform-socialist parties benefited from public dissatisfaction with the social costs of the transition to a market economy, from some concern about a strict abortion law approved in January 1993, and also from the failure of right-of-centre parties to construct a broad-based alliance to contest the poll. The centre-left DU attracted 11% of the vote, and won 74 seats, while the Non-Party Bloc in Support of Reforms (BBWR), a movement launched by President Wałesa in June 1993, secured barely 5% of the vote and just 16 seats.

Waldemar Pawlak (b. 1959), a former farm manager who was now leader of the PSL, was appointed prime minister in October 1993, forming a coalition government with the excommunist SLD which commanded sufficient seats, a two-thirds majority in both houses, to press through an amendment of the constitution. Although a number of the new government's ministers had held power during the communist period, the Pawlak administration pledged to continue to work towards the construction of a market-based economy, while seeking to ensure, through increased welfare spending, that costs were distributed more equitably and suffering was alleviated. In addition, with Andrzej Olechowski, a pro-Wałesa independent, being appointed foreign minister, the administration reaffirmed Poland's desire to join NATO and, at some future date, the European Union.

Between 1993–95 the economic upturn began to gather pace, with annual GDP growth averaging nearly 5%. However, Prime Minister Pawlak clashed increasingly with President Wałesa, who accused Pawlak of stalling the process of mass privatization, blocking measures which favoured the Catholic Church, and putting more emphasis on rebuilding ties with Russia than improving links with the West. In February 1995, after the pro-West Olechowski had resigned as foreign minister and the prime minister and president had been unable to agree on a suitable defence minister, President Wałesa presented Pawlak with the ultimatum that he must resign or otherwise face a dissolution of the legislature. Pawlak gave way and resigned, being replaced as premier in March 1995 by Jozef Oleksy, the former Sejm speaker and a former communist who had held a position in the communist cabinet of 1988. Oleksy agreed to appoint Wałesa nominees to the key cabinet portfolios of defence, foreign affairs and the interior ministry. The 1994–95 power struggle between the right-of-centre Wałesa, seeking to present himself as the defender of the postcommunist market and social reforms, and the left-of-centre SLD–PSL administration helped to boost the popularity rating of the president. Nevertheless, he was defeated in the November 1995 presidential election by Alexander Kwasniewski, leader of the SLD.

ROMANIA

Rômania

Capital: Bucharest

Social and economic data
Area: 229,027 km^2
Population: 23,400,000*
Pop. density per km^2: 102*
Urban population: 55%**
Literacy rate: 97%**

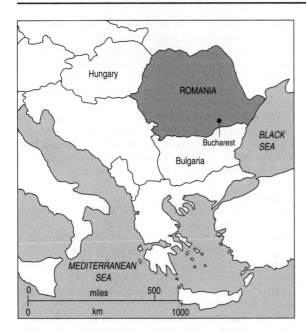

GDP: $24,438 million**; per-capita GDP: $1,045**
Government defence spending (% of GDP): 4.2%**
Currency: leu
Economy type: middle income
Labour force in agriculture: 29%**

*1994
**1992

Ethnic composition
Eighty-nine per cent of the population is ethnic Romanian, a non-Slavic race. There exist within the country substantial Hungarian, German, and Serbian minorities. The Hungarians number 1.6 million and are concentrated in Transylvania, in the northwest, a region which formed part of Hungary prior to 1918 and was traditionally more affluent than neighbouring parts of Romania. During the later 1980s, plans by Nicolae Ceauşescu to demolish 7,000 villages here and replace them with 500 new agro-industrial complexes, involving the dispersed resettlement of ethnic Hungarians, formed part of a controversial forced assimilation, or 'Romanization', policy, which precipitated a diplomatic crisis between Hungary and Romania in 1988. There was further unrest in Transylvania in March 1990 when violent clashes between ethnic Hungarian and Romanian nationalists led to the exodus of some Hungarians. The official language is Romanian, a Romance language.

Religions
Nearly 80% of the population adheres to the Romanian Orthodox Church, a body which is organized into patriarchates. There are also 1.5 million Roman Catholics, belonging chiefly to the Latin and Romanian, or Byzantine rite, sects. Among Protestant churches, which draw support from the German and Hungarian ethnic communities, the Reformed (Calvinist) Church currently has 700,000 members, while the Pentecostal Church has 250,000 adherents.

Islam has 55,000 followers, mostly among the Turkish-Tatar community.

Political features
State type: emergent democratic
Date of state formation: 1881
Political structure: unitary
Executive: limited presidential
Assembly: two-chamber
Party structure: multiparty
Human rights rating: 82%
International affiliations: BSECZ, COE, DC, IAEA, IBRD, IMF, NACC, NAM (guest), OSCE, PFP, UN, WEU (associate partner), WTO

Local and regional government
The country is divided into 40 counties (*judete*), excluding the municipality of Bucharest, for the purpose of local administration, with municipalities below.

Head of state
President Ion Iliescu, since 1989

Head of government
Prime Minister Nicolae Vacaroiu, since 1992

Political leaders since 1970
1965–89 Nicolae Ceauşescu (PCR)*, 1989– Ion Iliescu (NSF/independent)**

*Communist Party leader
**Democratic executive president

Political system
Under the December 1991 constitution, Romania has a limited presidential, pluralist political system. An executive president is directly elected for a maximum of two four-year terms in a two-round majority contest. The president appoints the prime minister, who in turn appoints the cabinet, or Council of Ministers. Candidates are eligible for election to the presidency if supported by at least 100,000 electors and, once elected, the president may not remain a member of a political party. The legislature comprises two chambers, a 341-member lower house, the Chamber of Deputies, in which 13 seats are set aside for representatives of the country's national minorities, and a 143-member upper chamber, the Senate. Both are elected for four-year terms by means of proportional representation in multiparty contests. Candidates for the Senate must be at least 30 years old and those for the Chamber, 21 years. Former members of the Securitate are ineligible for election. Romania's former King, Michael I, lives in exile in Switzerland and has been refused entry into the country since April 1992.

Political parties
In common with the other postcommunist states of Central Europe, Romania has a fluid party system. At the time of the September 1992 general election there were 91 registered political parties. Currently, the most important political parties are: the Social Democracy Party of Romania (PSDR); the Romanian National Unity Party (RNUP); the Greater Romania Party (Romania Mare); the Democratic Party–National Salvation Front (DP–NSF); the National Salvation

Front (NSF); the Hungarian Democratic Union of Romania (HDUR); the Christian Democratic–National Peasants' Party (CD–PNC); and the Socialist Labour Party (SLP).

The PSDR was established in July 1993 as a body supportive of President Iliescu through the merger of the Democratic National Salvation Front (DNSF), the Republican Party, and the Romanian Socialist Democratic Party. Its key constituent element, the social-democratic DNSF, was formed in April 1992 by supporters of President Iliescu after a split occurred in the NSF, the centre-left body which had been formed in December 1989 by Ion Iliescu and Petre Roman to fight for political democracy and the transition to a market economy. The PSDR, which contains many excommunists and favours only limited reforms, is supported in government by the RNUP (estd. 1990), a right-wing anti-Hungarian Romanian nationalist body led by Gheorghe Funar, mayor of the Transylvanian capital, Cluj, and the far-right ultranationalist and anti-Semitic Romania Mare, led by Corneliu Vadim Tudor.

The centre-left DP–NSF is the remnant of the NSF which is led by former prime minister, Petre Roman, and is now in opposition to the Iliescu–Vacaroiu government. It is more promarket in outlook than the PSDR.

The HDUR, formed in 1990 and led by Bela Marko, campaigns for the grant of 'special status' to ethnic Hungarians in Romania. The mainstream opposition parties have refused to cooperate with the HDUR, viewing it as an extreme nationalist force.

The CD–PNC is a tolerant centre-right promarket opposition body and the most important constituent element of the 18-party Democratic Convention of Romania (DCR), which contested the 1992 parliamentary and presidential elections. It was formed in 1990 through the merger of the CD and the traditional PNC, which had been first established in 1869, but banned by the communists in 1947.

Prior to the December 1989 revolution, the dominant and sole legal political party in Romania was the Romanian Communist Party (PCR). However, it was banned in December 1989, although the SLP was formed in 1990 by former members. The PCR was established in May 1921 by a left-wing section of the Social Democratic Workers' Party (SDWP), which was itself originally founded in 1893. The party was proscribed by the Romanian government in 1924 and forced underground, during which period it developed close links with Moscow. It merged with the SDWP in October 1947 to form the Romanian Workers' Party, changing its name to the PCR in July 1965. Membership of the PCR stood at 3.69 million in 1987, or 16.2% of the total population, the highest proportion for any East European communist state. In 1962 membership had been just 0.9 million.

Latest elections

The most recent, and first postcommunist, multiparty parliamentary elections were held on 27 September 1992 and resulted in seven parties, or party alliances, gaining representation in the Chamber of Deputies and eight in the Senate. The most successful party was the DNSF, which attracted 28% of the national vote and won 117 of the 328 contested Chamber of Deputies seats and 49 of the 143 Senate seats. The centre-right Democratic Convention of Romania (DCR), a coalition

of 18 parties, won 20% of the vote and 82 and 34 seats in the respective houses; the National Salvation Front won 10% of the vote and 43 and 18 seats; the Romanian National Unity Party, 8% of the vote and 30 and 14 seats; and the Hungarian Democratic Union of Romania, 7% and 27 and 12 seats. International monitors judged the election to be 'flawed, but not fraudulent'.

The last direct presidential election was held on 27 September and 11 October 1992 and was won on the second run-off ballot by Ion Iliescu of the DNSF, who defeated Emil Constantinescu of the DCR by a 61% to 39% margin. Four other candidates had contested the first round.

Political history

Romania was the site of the Dacian kingdom, which was occupied by the Romans between 106 and 271 AD, and Christianity was introduced. Later, under the influence of neighbouring Byzantium, the people became Orthodox Christians. From medieval times, Romanians lived in the three autonomous kingdoms of Wallachia, Moldavia, and Transylvania, which fiercely resisted the westward expansion of the Ottoman kingdom.

Part of the Ottoman Empire from the 15th century, and then subject to Russian suzerainty, between 1829 and 1856, a Romanian nation-state was initially formed by Prince Alexandru Ioan Curza, between 1859 and 1866, by the union of the principalities of Moldavia and Wallachia. The Great Powers recognized Romania's full independence in 1881, under King Carol I (1839–1914). The country, having fought on the Allied side during World War I, extended its boundaries in 1918, receiving Transylvania and Bukovina from the dismembered Austro-Hungarian Empire, as well as, until 1940, Bessarabia, from Russia. It thus emerged as the largest state in the Balkans.

During the interwar period Romania remained economically backward, with 72% of its population dependent upon agriculture. It enjoyed a brief experiment with representative institutions, until, in 1930, as a means of countering the growing popularity of the Fascist 'Iron Guard' mass movement, King Carol II (1893–1953) abolished the democratic constitution of 1923 and established his own dictatorship.

Early in World War II, the country was forced to surrender Bessarabia, North Transylvania, and South Dobruja to the Soviet Union, Hungary, and Bulgaria respectively, in accordance with the August–September 1940 Vienna Arbitration and Craiova Treaty. Additionally, as a result of German pressure, King Carol II abdicated, handing over power to General Ion Antonescu, who, ruling in the name of Carol's son King Michael (b. 1921), signed the Axis Pact, in November 1940, allying Romania with Nazi Germany. This was followed, in June 1941, by Romania's declaration of war on the Soviet Union. Between 1941–44 the Antonescu regime allowed thousands of Jews to be killed or deported to Nazi concentration camps in Poland.

In August 1944, with the Red Army on Romania's borders, King Michael supported a coalition of left and centre parties, including the Romanian Communist Party (PCR), to oust the Antonescu regime. Romania subsequently joined the war against Germany and in the Paris Peace Treaty, of February 1947, recovered Transylvania, but lost South Dobruja to Bulgaria and Bessarabia and North Bukovina to the Soviet Union.

The initial postliberation government was a broadly based coalition, termed the National Democratic Front (NDF), under the leadership of General Santescu. Then, in March 1945, under Soviet pressure, a communist-dominated administration was set up, nominally headed by the radical peasants' Ploughmans' Front leader, Petru Groza. Parliamentary elections were held in November 1946, in which the NDF stood as the Bloc of Democratic Parties, polling 80% of the votes. In the following year, all the noncommunist parties were dissolved and King Michael I was forced to abdicate. This paved the way for the adoption of a one-party Soviet-style republican constitution in April 1948.

A programme of industrial nationalization and agricultural collectivization was immediately launched by the new regime and there was a rapid purge of opposition leaders, so as to firmly establish the PCR in power. Soviet troops remained in the country, however, until 1958. The dominant political personality between 1945 and 1965 was PCR leader and head of state, Gheorghe Gheorghiu-Dej (1901–65). He took Romania into Comecon in 1949 and the Warsaw Treaty Organization in 1955.

On his death in March 1965, power passed to Nicolae Ceauşescu (1918–89), who immediately oversaw the framing of a new constitution, in June 1965, which placed greater emphasis on national autonomy. Under Ceauşescu, who was created state president in 1975, Romania adopted a foreign policy line independent of the Soviet Union, condemning the 1968 invasion of Czechoslovakia and refusing to participate directly in Warsaw Pact manoeuvres or to allow Soviet troops to cross its borders. Additionally, Ceauşescu called for multilateral nuclear disarmament and the creation of a Balkan nuclear-weapons-free zone. He also maintained warm relations with communist China.

At home, the secret police (Securitate) maintained a tight Stalinist rein on dissident activities, while a Ceauşescu personality cult was propagated, with almost 40 members of the president's extended family, including his wife Elena and his son Nicu, occupying senior state and party positions. Economic difficulties mounted as Ceauşescu, pledging himself to repay the country's accumulated foreign debt, embarked on an austerity programme. This led to food shortages and widespread power cuts in the winters from 1985 onwards. The army occupied power plants and in 1987 brutally crushed workers' strikes and demonstrations at Braşov.

After a referendum in 1986, military spending was cut by 5%. Ceauşescu was re-elected general secretary of the PCR in 1984 and 1989 and state president in 1985. He remained steadfast in his policies, ruling out any question of economic or political reform on the 'Gorbachev model' in the Soviet Union, even calling in the spring of 1989 for Warsaw Pact nations to intervene to prevent the opposition Solidarity movement from assuming power in Poland. The country's relations with neighbouring Hungary also reached crisis point during 1988–89 as a result of a Ceauşescu 'systemati-̦ zation plan' to demolish 7,000 villages and replace them with 500 agro-industrial complexes, in the process forcibly resettling and assimilating Transylvania-based ethnic Hungarians.

The unexpected overthrow of the Ceauşescu regime occurred dramatically in December 1989. It was sparked off by the government's plans to exile a dissident, ethnic Hungarian Protestant pastor, László Tökes (b. 1952), to a remote village. Ethnic Hungarians and Romanians joined forces in the city of Timişoara to form an anti-Ceauşescu protest movement. Hundreds of demonstrators were killed in the state's subsequent crackdown on 17 December 1989. Four days later, an officially sponsored mass rally in Bucharest for President Ceauşescu, who had returned from Iran, backfired when the crowd chanted anti-Ceauşescu slogans and civilians were shot dead in subsequent violent clashes with the security forces. Disturbances spread swiftly to other parts of the country, prompting Ceauşescu to declare a state of emergency. Divisions between the military, who were unwilling to open fire on demonstrators, and the Securitate rapidly emerged and on 22 December 1989 the army Chief of Staff, General Stefan Gusa, turned against the president and called on his soldiers to 'defend the uprising'. Ceauşescu attempted to flee by helicopter, but was caught near Tirgoviste and summarily tried by a military tribunal. He was found guilty of genocide, corruption, and destruction of the Romanian economy, and was executed, along with his wife, on Christmas Day.

Battles between Ceauşescu-loyal Securitate members and the army ensued in Bucharest, with several thousand being killed, but the army seized the upper hand. A National Salvation Front (NSF) was established in late December 1989, embracing former dissident intellectuals, reform communists and military leaders. At its head was Ion Iliescu (b. 1930), a Moscow-trained communist engineer, while Petre Roman (b. 1947), an academic without political experience, was appointed prime minister. The Front's council proceeded to relegalize the formation of alternative political parties and draft a new constitution. Faced with grave economic problems, it initiated a ban on the export of foodstuffs, the abandonment of Ceauşescu's 'systematization programme', the dissolution of the Securitate, the abolition of the PCR's leading role, and the relegalization of small-plot farming (with cooperative farmland being returned to its original owners) and abortion (all contraception had been banned by Ceauşescu).

In April 1990 a new Romanian Intelligence Service, accountable to parliament, was set up to replace the disbanded Securitate. The government legalized the Eastern Orthodox Church and the Vatican re-established diplomatic relations. In May 1990 Ion Iliescu won the country's first free presidential elections since World War II, capturing 85% of the vote, and the NSF secured an overwhelming victory in the concurrent parliamentary elections. However, these victories heightened tension between Romanians and the Hungarian ethnic minority in Transylvania. Moving towards a legal market economy, the government cut subsidies, the leu was devalued, and prices were allowed to float. Industrial exports slumped and strikes and protests increased until the government agreed to postpone its price liberalization programme. Refugees continued to leave the country and there were demonstrations against the government during December 1990 and January 1991, especially in Timişoara and Bucharest.

The second stage of price liberalization commenced in April 1991, despite trade-union protests against the sharply rising cost of living and level of unemployment (over 1 million). At the same time the leu was devalued by 72% to meet the loan conditions set by the IMF and as a step towards internal convertibility by 1992. In the same month a new treaty on cooperation and good neighbourliness was signed with the USSR, which obliged the two states 'not to take part in any type of alliance directed against either of them'.

In August 1991 President Iliescu signed a law to allow for the privatization of all state enterprises except utilities, with adult Romanians being given a 30% stake in state-owned ventures. In November 1991 the leu was made internally convertible. Prices rose 400% during 1991 and hundreds of thousands were on short-time work. GNP fell during 1991 by 12%.

In September 1991 Prime Minister Petre Roman resigned after three days of riots in Bucharest by thousands of striking miners, protesting against soaring prices and a fall in their living standards. Theodor Stolojan, the finance minister and a proponent of accelerated price liberalization, took over as premier, forming a new, cross-party, coalition government in October 1991. He promised to remain politically neutral and vowed not to stand in the 1992 elections.

A national referendum in December 1991 overwhelmingly endorsed a new constitution which guaranteed pluralism, human rights, and a free market. This cleared the path for a general election in 1992. Romania's 2 million-strong Hungarian minority opposed the new constitution on the grounds that it failed to grant special minority or language rights.

The September–October 1992 parliamentary and direct presidential elections resulted in the pro-Iliescu Democratic National Salvation Front (DNSF), which was an offshoot from the NSF, emerging as the largest single party, with 28% of the national vote, and Iliescu being re-elected state president by a convincing margin. After the elections, the DNSF formed a coalition government with the Agrarian Democratic Party of Romania (ADPR), with Nicolae Vacaroiu (b. 1943), an economist, as prime minister. The new administration pressed on with economic reform, including privatization, but the pace was slow compared to other Central European states and the economy continued to deteriorate, with the unemployment level exceeding 10%. This provoked student and labour unrest, notably by coalminers, but also including, on 28 January 1994, a general strike by more than a million workers. In March 1994, in an effort to strengthen the position of the minority Vacaroiu administration, which had only narrowly survived a series of no-confidence motions instigated during 1993–94 by the more reformist-minded opposition, two right-wing extreme nationalist parties, Romania Mare and the Romanian National Unity Party (RNUP), were brought into the coalition. However, this action persuaded the ADPR to withdraw and increased the sense of concern among ethnic Hungarians, who had been appeased during 1993 by such concessions as the granting of more Hungarian language teaching and Hungarian street signs, and further strained relations with Hungary. Two RNUP members were brought into the cabinet in August 1994 and in January 1995 a governing pact was signed with

the anti-Semitic Romania Mare and with the Socialist Labour Party (SLP), the successor to the PCR. These events led to increasing Western concern over the future development of democracy in Romania.

RUSSIA (ROSSIYA)

Republic of the Russian Federation*
Rossiyskaya Federativnaya Respublika

*Known until 1991 as the Russian Soviet Federal Socialist Republic (RSFSR)

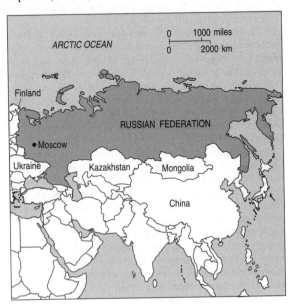

Capital: Moscow

Social and economic data
Area: 17,075,400 km^2
Population: 149,200,000*
Pop. density per km^2: 9*
Urban population: 74%**
Literacy rate: 99%**
GDP: $387,476 million**; per-capita GDP: $2,600**
Government defence spending (% of GDP): 7%**
Currency: rouble
Economy type: middle income
Labour force in agriculture: 13%**

*1994
**1992

Ethnic composition
The population is predominantly, 83%, of ethnic or 'Great Russian' stock, an eastern Slav race. There are also significant Tatar, 4%, Ukrainian, 3%, Chuvash, 1%, Belarussian, 1%, Bashkir, 1%, and Chechen, 1%, minorities. The official language is Russian, but more than 100 minor languages are also spoken within the federation. The Tatar, Bashkir, and Chechen peoples have campaigned for full autonomy during recent years.

Religions

The Russian Orthodox is the most important church, claiming 40 million adherents, constituting 27% of the total population, with many new churches having been built since the late 1980s. There are also small Roman Catholic, Protestant, Islamic, and Jewish communities. The principal adherents to Islam are Volga Tatars, Chuvash, Bashkirs, and the Chechens, and the Ingush and Ossetians of the northern Caucasus region. Despite large-scale emigration since the 1970s, the Jewish community in the Russian Federation numbers 2 million, being concentrated in the main urban centres.

Political features

State type: emergent democratic
Date of state formation: 1547*/1917**/1991***
Political structure: federal
Executive: limited presidential
Assembly: two-chamber
Party structure: multiparty
Human rights rating: N/A
International affiliations: BSECZ, CERN (observer), CIS, COBSS, COE, DC, IAEA, IBRD, IMF, IWC, NACC, OSCE, PFP, UN Security Council (permanent member)

*Ivan IV became the first Russian Tsar
**The communist Union of Soviet Socialist Republics (USSR)
***The contemporary Russian Federation

Local and regional government

The Russian Federation includes 21 republics, with a combined population of around 25 million. The populations of the republics range from nearly 4 million in the most populous, Bashkortostan (Bashkiria) and Tatarstan, to under 200,000 in the smallest. Sixteen of these republics were autonomous republics within the RSFSR during the communist period, namely, (capitals in brackets): Bashkortostan (Ufa); Buryatia* (Ulan-Ude); Chechnya (Grozny); Chuvashia (Cheboksary); Daghestan (Makhachkala); Kabardino-Balkaria (Nalchik); Kalmykia (Elista); Karelia* (Petrozavodsk); Komi* (Syktyvkar); Mari-El (Yoshkar-Ola); Mordovia* (Saransk); North Ossetia (Vladikavkaz, formerly Ordzhonikidze); Sakha, or Yakutia* (Yakutsk); Tatarstan (Kazan); Tuva (Kizyl); and Udmurtia* (Izhevsk). Four were formerly autonomous regions (*oblasts*), namely, Adygeya*, Gorno-Altai*, Karachevo-Cherkassia and Khakassia*, while the Ingushetia republic was newly created in June 1992. Ethnic Russians form a majority of the population in only nine of the republics, viz. those marked with an asterisk. The unit called Russia comprises the parts of the Russian Federation that are not included within any of the other 21 republics and, with five-sixths of the Federation's total population, is divided into 68 administrative regions (*oblasts* and *krais*) and autono-mous territories and districts, which have considerable devolved authority.

Head of state

President Boris Yeltsin, since 1990

Head of government

Prime Minister Viktor Chernomyrdin, since 1992

Political leaders since 1970

USSR*: 1964–82 Leonid Brezhnev (CPSU), 1982–84 Yuri Andropov (CPSU), 1984–85 Konstantin Chernenko (CPSU), 1985–91 Mikhail Gorbachev (CPSU); Russian Federation: 1990– Boris Yeltsin (ex-CPSU independent)

*Communist Party leaders

Political system

The Russian Federation's December 1993 constitution provides for a presidentialist executive system, checked by a two-chamber legislature, the Federal Assembly. The president, who is directly elected for a maximum of two five-year terms, serves as head of state and the armed forces and chooses and appoints the prime minister and Council of Ministers (cabinet). The president, who is advised by his own 'kitchen cabinet' of trusted friends and officials, may issue decrees, veto parliamentary legislation, and sets out the government's political and economic policy in an annual address to the Federal Assembly. The president also appoints and heads a Security Council, which is concerned with defence issues, and proposes the chair of the Central Bank, the prosecutor general, and key members of the judiciary. Furthermore, since January 1994 the security services and the interior, defence, and foreign affairs ministries have been directly subordinate to the presidency. Candidates for the presidency must be nominated by a minimum number of electors: 250,000 in 1991, though there are proposals to raise the figure to as many as 1.5 million for the 1996 contest.

The bicameral Federal Assembly consists of a 450-seat lower house, the State Duma, and a 178-seat upper chamber, the Federation Council. In December 1993, 225 members were directly elected to the State Duma for a two-year term in single-member constituencies on the basis of first-past-the-post, but with the proviso that turnout must be at least 25% for the result to be valid. The other 225 members were drawn from national party lists on the basis of proportional representation, with a 5% qualification threshold being imposed. Electors thus have two votes: one for a local constituency and one for the national list. President Yeltsin has sought to increase the proportion of Duma deputies who are directly from constituencies from a half to two-thirds, that is to 300 out of 450, since it is argued that constituencies are more accountable to the electorate and that the list system has tended to favour extremist, as opposed to centrist, parties. The Federation Council comprises two deputies elected, on a first-past-the-post basis, from each of Russia's 89 regions and republics. The Federal Assembly is relatively weak *vis-à-vis* the president. It may not consider presidential decrees and, while it may oust a government through a vote of no confidence, for which an absolute majority is required (i.e. 226 Duma votes), it must do so twice within three months before the president is forced to take action. The president can then either form a new government or dissolve the Assembly and call fresh elections. However, the Federal Assembly may impeach the president if both chambers pass a vote in favour and there is agreement from both the Supreme Court and the Constitutional Court, a body which was established in October 1991 to supervise Russian laws and treaties with foreign states, and to examine territorial disputes. In addition, the president may not dissolve the Duma during the first 12 months after its election.

Although the 1993 constitution has sought to claw back powers to the centre, the Russian Federation's 21 republics and 68 regions have equal rights and considerable authority, the republics having their own constitutions, elected governments, and budgets. They effectively determine the pace and direction of economic and social reforms, having the main control over land ownership and being responsible for 80% of state welfare spending.

Political parties

Formerly a one-party communist state, Russia has seen the formation of numerous political parties since political pluralism was tolerated from the start of the 1990s, but few have been substantial or lasting. Party ties and loyalties are weak and many politicians are elected as independents, drawing on local support bases, and form opportunistic alliances within parliament. Parties must collect at least 200,000 signatures to be able to contest the parliamentary elections.

In mid-1995 there were 250 registered parties, with around ten significant political parties, or blocs, which can be arranged ideologically into three broad, and well-balanced, groupings: conservative excommunist; radical right-wing nationalist and populist; and liberal-centrist or right-of-centre promarket and propluralism bodies.

The conservative excommunist bloc comprises the Communist Party of the Russian Federation (CPRF), which has been led since December 1992 by the Russian nationalist Gennady Zyuganov and was relegalized in October 1993; the allied centre-left Agrarian Party, led by Mikhail Lapshin, which favours the continuance of collective state farming and large state subsidies for the rural sector; and the Women of Russia Party. The CPRF, which favours firmer state control over the economy, is the only slightly reformed heir to the formerly dominant Communist Party of the Soviet Union (CPSU). It claims a membership of 550,000 and prints its own newspaper, *Pravda Rossii* ('Russia's Truth'). The CPSU was founded in 1903, following a split in the Russian Social Democratic Workers' Party (RSDWP), established in 1898 by Georgi Plekhanov (1857–1918), between a majority (Bolshevik) wing led by V I Lenin, which saw the need, in Russian conditions, to organize the party as a tightly disciplined vanguard of professional revolutionaries ready to lead a sudden worker–peasant revolution, and a minority (Menshevik) wing led by Martov, which favoured a traditional mass org-anization and viewed the attainment of socialism as still distant, and needing to be initially preceded by a bourgeois revolution. In 1912, Lenin's Bolsheviks formally set themselves up as a separate group and became the sole permitted party within the Soviet Union when they seized power from the Mensheviks in the revolution of October 1917. The party, which had a membership of 23,600 on the eve of the revolution, subsequently changed its name to the All-Russian Communist Party (Bolsheviks) in 1918, to the All-Union Communist Party (Bolsheviks) in 1925, and to the CPSU in 1952. By 1987 the party had a membership of 19 million and more than 440,000 'workplace cells'. Organized on top-down 'democratic-centralist' principles, the CPSU was controlled by a small, circa 12-member Politburo and Secretariat, which were 'appointed' by a circa 300-member Central Committee which, in turn,

was 'appointed' by a quinquennial, circa 5,000-member Party Congress.

The most important extreme-nationalist and right-wing populist party in the Russian Federation is the misleadingly titled Liberal Democratic Party of Russia (LDPR). Led by the xenophobic Vladimir Zhirinovsky and formed in 1990, the LDPR advocates tough measures to crack down on crime and a fancifully expansionist foreign policy with the aim of establishing a 'Greater Russia', incorporating former Soviet states and also parts of Central Europe, the Middle East, and Asia. The LDPR is dominated by Zhirinovsky who was re-elected as leader for a ten-year term in April 1994 and has absolute power to appoint and dismiss party officials. Another extreme-nationalist party is the Congress of Russian Communities, formed in 1995 by Alexander Lebed, a popular ex-general. Somewhat more moderate is Power to the People, led by Sergei Baburin and the former communist prime minister, Nikolai Ryzhkov, which seeks to recreate the former Soviet Union, and the communist-nationalist Great Power (Derzhava) party, led by Aleksandr Rutskoi, a former vice president who has declared his candidacy for the presidency in 1996. The latter is described as a 'social patriotic movement' and claims a membership of 1 million people.

A large number of liberal-centrist and pro-market-reform parties operate in the Federation, but they currently remain small and quarrelsome. The most significant centre-right party is Russia's (Democratic) Choice (estd. 1993), which is a bloc of radical reformers led by Yegor Gaidar, the architect of Russia's market-centred reform programme up to 1994, and which includes Gennady Burbulis, a former close aide to President Yeltsin. It incorporates Democratic Russia, which was formed in 1990, believes in 'freedom, property, legality' and draws most support from Moscow and St Petersburg. Until December 1994, and the invasion of Chechnya, Russia's Choice supported President Yeltsin.

Another significant centrist grouping, also formed in 1993, is the Yabloko bloc, which is led by the popular prorform economist, Grigori Yavlinsky, and the Russian ambassador to the United States, Vladimir Lukin. It favours gradualist, as opposed to radical 'shock therapy', market-centred reforms.

Four other, more conservative, notable centrist parties are the Party of Russian Unity and Accord (PRUA; estd. 1993), the Civic Union for Stabilization, Justice and Progress (CUSJP; estd. 1993), the Movement for Democratic Reforms (MDR); and the Democratic Party of Russia (DPR; estd. 1990). The PRUA, led by two deputy prime ministers, Sergei Shakhrai and Aleksandr Shokhin, appeals to the regional and industrial lobbies and the poor. The CUSJP, led by Arkadi Volsky, is the successor to the Civic Union, formed in 1992. The MDR is led by the mayor of St Petersburg, Anatoly Sobchak. The DPR, led until October 1994 by Nikolai Travkin, originated as the radical wing of the Democratic Platform in the CPSU.

During 1994–95 a number of splits occurred in these core party blocs, with small new offshoot parties being formed. In January 1994 more than 60 independent parliamentary deputies formed a new bloc, termed the New Regional Policy, while in May 1995, in a particularly significant development, the prime minister, Viktor Chernomyrdin, became leader of the new Russia is Our Home party. The latter, a centre-right pro-Yeltsin centrist force, sought to appeal to those who sought 'progress without shocks or revolutions, who are tired of disorder and lies, (and) who are proud of Russian statehood', and claimed the support of almost all government ministers and many regional leaders. Also in May 1995, the leftist Accord (Soglasiye) bloc was formed, embracing elements from the Agrarian Party and Agrarian Union and with Ivan Rybkin, chairperson of the State Duma, as its leader. The other significant new party is Forward Russia, led by the nationalist-populist reformer Boris Fedorov.

Latest elections

The most recent State Duma elections were held on 17 December 1995. The Communist Party (CPRF) polled most strongly, attracting 22% of the federal vote and winning more than 150 seats. The allied Agrarians and Power to the People parties won more than 30 further seats. Communist support was greatest in the central and southern regions, beyond the Urals. The ultra right-wing LDPR, drawing in high levels of support in military districts, the far east and 'frontier' districts, secured 11% of the vote (half its 1993 result) and 51 seats. The centrist Our Home is Russia party and Yabloko bloc, with 10% and 7% of the vote, won 54 and 46 seats respectively and polled strongest in the cities of Moscow and St Petersburg. The nationalist Congress of Russian Communities and liberal Russia's Democratic Choice each secured only 4% national support, winning 5 and 10 seats respectively. 37 other parties attracted less than 5% support, thus failing to secure a share of the 225 seats filled proportionately. There were 2,687 candidates for the single-seat constituencies and more than 80 independents were elected. The latter included Andrei Kozyrev, the foreign minister, who was forced to resign since under the constitution a deputy may not be a minister. Turnout was reported up on the December 1993 level of 55%.

The most recent, and first direct, presidential election was held on 12 June 1991. Six candidates contested, with the incumbent Boris Yeltsin attracting 57% support, the former Soviet prime minister, Nikolai Ryzhkov, 17%, and the right-wing demagogue, Vladimir Zhirinovsky, 8%.

Political history

The Russian Federation, as it is now called, was the 'Muscovy' heartland of the Soviet Union. It was originally settled by nomadic Slavs, Turks, and Bulgars between the 3rd and 7th centuries before, in the 9th and 10th centuries, Viking chieftains established a Russian dynasty based around the town of Novgorod in the northwest. The centre of control moved to Kiev between the 10th and 12th centuries, and this formed the capital of the first Russian Empire. Its peoples were converted to Eastern Orthodox Christianity, which had been introduced by Greek missionaries from Byzantium, or Constantinople.

Mongol-Tatar rule was subsequently imposed over the east and centre of the country, during the 13th and 14th centuries, with Belarussia and the Ukraine ruled by Poland. It was not until the late 15th century that a new Russian Empire was established by Ivan III, 'the Great' (1440–1505), and the

capital became located in what is now Moscow. The empire was considerably extended in scope by Ivan IV, 'the Terrible' (1530–84), who assumed the title tsar in 1547 and resumed control of the northwest, annexed Kazan and Astrakhan and began the colonization of Siberia. Under the subsequent tsars and tsarinas, Peter I, 'the Great' (1672–1725) and Catherine II, 'the Great' (1729–96), the Baltic lands, the Crimea, West Ukraine, and eastern Poland were added, and the capital was moved to St Petersburg in the northwest. Under Tsar Alexander II (1818–81; ruled 1855–81), the borders of the Russian Empire were further extended, being pushed east to the Pacific and south into Central Asia.

Although militarily a 'great power' by the later 19th century, the country remained economically and politically backward compared with its neighbours in Western Europe, from which it remained culturally isolated. Serfdom persisted until 1861 and it was not until 1906, following the abortive revolution of 1905, that the country's first constitution and national representative assembly, the Duma, were established. The Duma was elected on a narrow franchise, with, in 1910, barely 2.4% of the population enjoying the right to vote. It thus did little to temper the despotic character of the tsarist regime.

At the start of the 20th century a state-led crash industrialization programme was belatedly launched, but towards the close of World War I, when its armed forces were in retreat and the economy was in ruins, the tsarist autocracy was finally overthrown in the revolution of March 1917 by a combination of disaffected soldiers, workers, peasants, and Russian Social Democratic Workers' Party (RSDWP) activists. Tsar Nicholas II (1868–1918) abdicated and a republic was declared, headed first by Prince Georgi Lvov (1861–1925) and then by the agrarian-populist Socialist Revolutionary Party leader, Aleksandr Kerensky (1881–1970).

This provisional government was soon itself overthrown, in the 'October Revolution' of 1917, by the Bolsheviks, led by the charismatic, white-collar intellectual, Vladimir Ilyich Lenin (1870–1924), who had recently returned from exile in Zurich, and the Ukrainian Jew who had played a directing role in the 1905 revolution, Leon Trotsky (1879–1940). This second 'revolution' was, in fact, a coup, rather than a popular uprising. This is demonstrated by the fact that the Bolsheviks polled only 25% of the votes in the free elections held to the Constituent Assembly in November 1917, compared with the 63% secured by other socialist parties. Lenin, however, ignored the result of this election, swiftly dissolved the Constituent Assembly in January 1918, and established, instead, one-party control through an extensive system of Bolshevik-dominated soviets ('peoples' councils').

The initial four years of the new Bolshevik regime were consumed with repelling external attacks by the allied powers and Poland and fighting an internal civil war against a combination of pro-tsarist, 'bourgeois democrat', socialist revolutionary and Menshevik 'White' forces. These problems were eventually overcome and, in December 1922, the Soviet Union (USSR) was formally established as a federation and a new constitution was adopted in 1923.

The problems of reconstruction meant that, in the economic sphere, a pragmatic mixed-enterprise approach was initially pursued, between 1921 and 1927, under the title of the 'New Economic Policy' (NEP). Peasants were allowed to till their own land and small- and medium-sized private industries operated, while the 'commanding heights' of the economy were brought under state control. This social democratic strategy was gradually abandoned, however, by Lenin's successor as party leader, Joseph Stalin (1879–1953), the son of a poor Georgian cobbler-serf.

Seeking to rapidly transform the nation from an agrarian to a top-ranking industrial power and, in the process, fundamentally rearrange its socio-economic base in a socialist direction, he embarked, from 1927, on a radical programme of forced collectivization and heavy industrialization, founded on a system of firm, party-controlled, central planning. The first Five-Year Plan was introduced in 1928.

Stalin's programme of 'socialism in one country' was opposed by some of his leading party colleagues, including Trotsky, who favoured an internationalist policy of fomenting supportive revolutions abroad. Other opponents were Trotsky's 'leftist' supporter, Lev Kamenev (1883–1936), the moderate pro-NEP 'rightist', Nikolai Bukharin (1888–1938), the 'Old Bolshevik', Grigori Zinoviev (1883–1936), and the Leningrad (St Petersburg) Party leader, Sergei Kirov (1888–1934). Stalin's response was a series of ruthless party purges and 'liquidations' which were launched during the 1920s and 1930s. As a result, party membership fell from 3.5 million in 1933 to 1.9 million in 1938.

In the economic sphere, Stalin's ambitious transformatory programme had significant results, Soviet industry recording a growth rate of 16% per annum between 1929 and 1940, its blue-collar workforce quadrupling in size and the country's urban population doubling. However, the social and political costs were enormous. Millions of 'rich peasants' (*kulaks*) were executed or sent to labour camps in Siberia, agricultural produce was forcibly marketed, depressing rural per-capita living standards, and the countryside was squeezed to provide investment income for industry. Both the party and state political structures were disfigured, democratic consultation giving way to personalized control, supported by the intrusive and terroristic use of the NKVD secret police, under the direction of Stalin's Georgian crony, Lavrenti Beria (1899–1953).

The Stalin regime, although unpopular with rural groups and with the intelligentsia, did, however, receive support from a number of sections of Soviet society. These included the new postrevolution generation of socialist educated 'worker-bureaucrats' who had benefited from the new opportunities for rapid advancement. Support also came from urban workers and the military, the groups which had been the prime beneficiaries of the 'forced industrialization' strategy. In addition, during World War II, Stalin's role as a determined leader (*Vozhd*), successfully standing up to German Nazi aggression in a bitter struggle, termed the 'Great Patriotic War', in which 25 million Russians perished, brought him broad popular nationalist support.

The Red Army's success in repelling Germany's forces in 1943 re-established the country as a 'great power' and at the close of World War II it was able to gain effective dominance over Eastern Europe, setting up a series of satellite socialist governments, as well as securing the direct annexation of Baltic and Polish territories in the northwest and a substantial area in Moldova and West Ukraine in the southwest, which

had formerly been controlled by Romania. During the immediate postwar period these gains were consolidated, and indirect support was provided to anticolonial movements in the Far East. The USSR therefore became established as a globally active 'Superpower' and this approach inaugurated a new East–West 'Cold War' era.

On Stalin's death in March 1953 a collective leadership, which included the Communist Party's (CPSU) first (general) secretary, Nikita Khrushchev (1894–1971), the prime minister, Georgi Malenkov (1901–88), the foreign minister, Vyacheslav Molotov (1890–1986), as well as the first deputy prime ministers, Nikolai Bulganin (1895–1975) and Lazar Kaganovich (1893–1991), assumed power. They swiftly combined to remove NKVD chief Beria, in December 1953, and proceeded to introduce a new legal code which regularized the political system. However, although agreed on the need to reform and 'humanize' the 'Stalin system', strong intraleadership differences soon emerged over the exact emphasis and direction of new policy approaches. As a consequence, a fierce succession contest developed between 1953 and 1958.

Khrushchev emerged as the victor, succeeding in first ousting the 'antiparty' triumvirate of Malenkov, Molotov and Kaganovich in June 1957, and then Bulganin, who had succeeded Malenkov as prime minister in 1955, in June 1958. Khrushchev was now able to combine the key posts of prime minister and CPSU first secretary. Once installed in power, Khrushchev introduced a radical new party programme, at the 22nd CPSU Congress of October 1961, which envisaged rapid agricultural, industrial and technological development, to enable the Soviet Union to move ahead of the United States in economic terms by 1980, and for the nation to attain full communism.

To achieve these goals, an ambitious 'virgin lands' cultivation campaign was launched in underdeveloped Kazakhstan, with the aim of swiftly boosting agricultural output. In addition, a programme of decentralized industrial management was unveiled, based on the formation of new regional economic councils (*sovnarkhozy*). Material incentives were also introduced in the rural sector.

In the political, social, and diplomatic spheres, Khrushchev introduced radical new party rule changes, directed towards curbing the authority of entrenched officials (*apparatchiki*); sanctioned a cultural 'thaw'; and enunciated the new principle of 'peaceful co-existence' with the West, as a means of diverting resources away from the defence sector.

These reforms enjoyed initial success and following the explosion of its first hydrogen bomb in 1953 and the launching of a space satellite, the *Sputnik I*, in 1957, the Soviet Union appeared to be emerging for the first time as a serious technological rival to the United States. However, Khrushchev's liberalization policy and his denunciation of the errors and crimes of the 'cult of personality' Stalin era, at the 20th Party Congress in February 1956, had serious repercussions among the Soviet Union's East European satellites, encouraging a nationalist revolt in Hungary. A breach in relations with China also resulted and his administrative reforms were fiercely opposed by senior party and state bureaucrats.

After a series of poor harvests in overcropped Kazakhstan, workers' riots in Soviet cities, and the Cuban missile crisis climbdown of 1962, opposition to Khrushchev began to coalesce, and at the Central Committee meeting of October 1964 the party leader was dismissed and forced into retirement.

A new and conservative collective leadership assumed power, centred around the figures of the former head of state Leonid Brezhnev (1906–82), First Deputy Prime Minister Alexei Kosygin (1904–80), Party Organization Secretary Nikolai Podgorny, and Party Ideology Secretary Mikhail Suslov (1902–82). They immediately abandoned Khrushchev's *sovnarkhozy* and party reforms and reimposed strict censorship in the cultural sphere. Priority was now given to the expansion and modernization of the Soviet armed forces, including the creation of a naval force with a global capability. This, coupled with the Soviet invasion of Czechoslovakia in 1968 to suppress a gathering reform movement, resulted in a renewal of the East–West 'Cold War' between 1964 and 1970.

During the later 1960s and early 1970s, Leonid Brezhnev, by inducting his supporters into the CPSU Politburo and Secretariat, established himself as the dominant figure within the Soviet polity. He continued to govern, however, in a cautious and consensual manner, bringing into the Politburo, in April 1973, leaders from all the significant centres of power, including the KGB, in the person of Yuri Andropov (1914–84), the army, Marshal Andrei Grechko, and the diplomatic service, Andrei Gromyko (1909–89).

Working with Prime Minister Kosygin, Brezhnev introduced a series of minor economic reforms and gave new priority to agricultural and consumer goods production. In 1977 he oversaw the framing of a new constitution which established a settled new political system in which the limits for dissent were clearly set out and which described the state as in a stage of 'developed socialism' whose future development would rely increasingly on the technocratic use of scientific innovation.

Brezhnev, who became the new state 'president' in May 1977, emerged as an international statesperson during the 1970s, frequently meeting Western leaders during what was a new era of détente. The landmarks of this period were the SALT-1 and SALT-2 Soviet-American arms limitation agreements of 1972 and 1979 and the Helsinki Accord of 1975, which brought Western recognition of the postwar division of Eastern Europe.

During this détente era there was a new cultural 'thaw' which resulted in the emergence of a vocal dissident movement, led by the nuclear physicist Dr Andrei Sakharov (1921–89). The political and military influence of the Soviet Union was also extended into Africa and the 'Horn' with the establishment of new communist-leaning governments in Angola in 1975, Mozambique in 1974, Ethiopia in 1975, and South Yemen in 1978.

The détente era was eventually ended, however, by the Soviet invasion of Afghanistan in December 1979 and the Polish crisis of 1980–81, ushering in a further 'Cold War' era and a period of domestic repression. Sakharov, for example, was arrested and sent into internal exile in 1980.

During its final years the Brezhnev administration, with its leader physically incapacitated by a series of strokes, and his rivals jockeying for position to succeed him, was characterized by policy sclerosis, mounting corruption, and economic stagnation.

On Brezhnev's death in November 1982, Yuri Andropov, a former KGB chief, was elected CPSU chairperson by his Politburo colleagues. He proceeded, energetically, to introduce a series of substantive economic reforms, styled the 'enterprise management' initiative, which were aimed at streamlining and decentralizing the planning system and inculcating greater labour discipline. Andropov also launched a major campaign against corrupt and complacent party and state bureaucrats. These measures had a perceptible impact on the Soviet economy during 1983.

The reform impetus waned, however, when Andropov died in February 1984 and was succeeded by the cautious and elderly Konstantin Chernenko (1911–85), a man who had previously served as Brezhnev's political secretary and closest aide. Chernenko held power as a stopgap leader for 13 months, his sole initiative being a renewed search for détente with the United States which was rejected by the hardline Reagan administration.

On Chernenko's death in March 1985, power was transferred to a new generation led by Mikhail Gorbachev (b. 1931), the protégé of Yuri Andropov and a former agriculture secretary, who, at the age of 54, was the CPSU's youngest leader since Stalin. Although elected on a divided Politburo vote, Gorbachev vigorously took up the reins of reform, sharply criticizing the preceding Brezhnev era. His reform prescription was three-pronged.

First, in the economic sphere, under the slogan of *perestroika*, or 'restructuring', he pressed for greater decentralization in decision-taking. Farmers and factory managers were to be freed from pettifogging bureaucratic interference and there was to be increased emphasis on material incentives, cost accounting, and factory self-financing, as part of a new *khozrachiot* or 'market socialist' system. Second, working with the new prime minister, Nikolai Ryzhkov (b. 1929), a former industrial manager, he set about radically overhauling the party and state bureaucracies, replacing cautious Brezhnevite placemen with ambitious technocrats. To support these political changes, Gorbachev, under the slogan *glasnost*, or 'openness', encouraged criticism of bureaucratic inefficiencies and opened up a free discussion in the media of existing problems, reform options, and previous party history. Third, he embarked on a détente initiative abroad in the hope of achieving an arms reduction agreement with the United States, which would allow resources to be diverted to the civilian sector. Working with his emollient foreign minister, the Georgian Eduard Shevardnadze (b. 1928), he made skilful use of the international television media to put the US Reagan administration on the defensive over the issues of space weapons and nuclear testing.

Following summit meetings held in Geneva in November 1985, Reykjavik in October 1986, and Washington in December 1987, Gorbachev signed an Intermediate-Range Nuclear Forces (INF) Treaty with the United States, designed to eliminate medium- and shorter-range nuclear missiles stationed in Europe. As part of this détente process, the USSR also agreed on a phased withdrawal, by February 1989, of all of its 100,000 troops from Afghanistan, ending a ten-year entanglement which had cost the lives of 13,000 Soviet soldiers, and a unilateral 500,000 reduction in the size of its armed forces within two years, including the withdrawal of 50,000 troops and 5,000 tanks from Europe. In effect, Gorbachev had signalled his intention of abandoning the 'Brezhnev doctrine' of ratchetlike Soviet military expansion overseas.

The new Soviet leader consolidated his position at the CPSU's 27th Congress, held in March 1986, by ousting a number of ailing senior Brezhnevites from the controlling Politburo and Secretariat and replacing 40% of the party's Central Committee. However, during 1987–88, as Gorbachev pressed for an acceleration (*uskoreniye*) in the reform process, including adoption of a comprehensive economic revitalization plan, the 'New Economic Mechanism', he began to encounter increasing domestic opposition. This came from both conservatives within the CPSU, grouped around ideology chief Yegor Ligachev (b. 1920), and a smaller group of party radicals, led by Boris Yeltsin (b. 1931), the Moscow party chief until his dismissal in November 1987. Gorbachev faced additional problems, with the eruption of serious nationalist challenges to his administrations in a number of the USSR's 15 Union Republics, notably the three Baltic republics, Kazakhstan and Armenia, Azerbaijan, and Georgia in the region of Transcaucasia, and the continued sluggish performance of the economy. A new opposition group, the Democratic Union, was formed in Moscow in 1988 and there were Russian language demonstrations in Leningrad (St Petersburg), where the tsarist flag was raised.

In an effort to add momentum to the reform process, in June 1988 Gorbachev convened a special 4,991-member All-Union Party Conference, the first since 1941. At this meeting a radical constitutional overhaul was approved. A new 'superlegislature', the 2,250-deputy Congress of the USSR People's Deputies (CUPD), was created, from which a full-time bicameral working parliament, the 542-member Supreme Soviet, was subsequently to be elected, headed by a state president with increased powers. The members of this CUPD were to be chosen in competition with one another and inner-party democracy was to be introduced to the CPSU, replacing top-down 'democratic centralism'. The authority of the local soviets ('people's councils') was enhanced and their structures made more democratic, while, in the economic sphere, it was agreed to reintroduce private leasehold farming, reform the price system, and allow part-time private enterprise in the service and small-scale industry sectors.

The June 1988 reforms constituted the most fundamental reordering of the Soviet policy since the 'Stalinist departure' of 1928, entailing the creation of a new type of 'socialist democracy' (*demokratizatsiya*) and accountability, as well as a new mixed economic system. The CUPD elections of March–April 1989 showed clear opposition to conservative apparatchiks and in May 1989 the new CUPD elected Gorbachev as its chair, and thus as state president. Gorbachev continued to strike against conservative and 'old guard' opponents during 1988–89, demoting Ligachev to the lowly agriculture portfolio. In addition, in 1989, as further evidence of his abandonment of the 'Brezhnev doctrine', the Soviet president sanctioned the establishment of noncommunist and 'reform-communist' governments elsewhere in Eastern Europe. As a consequence, the ruling communist regimes in Poland, Czechoslovakia, East Germany, Bulgaria, Hungary, and Romania were overthrown in a wave of 'people's power' during 1989–90. Responding to these developments, in February 1990, the CPSU Central Committee decided to create a new directly elected state executive presidency on US and French models. In March 1990, the Soviet parliament authorized private ownership of the means of production, which had been forbidden since the 1920s. Further constitutional amendments passed during 1990 supported the right of self-determination, including the secession of republics, and terminated the CPSU's monopoly of power.

The Gorbachev reform programme showed signs of running out of control during 1989–90 as a result both of growing nationalist tensions – which in April 1989 and January 1990 had prompted the despatch of troops to the Caucasus region, first to break up demonstrations in Tbilisi, Georgia, and then to attempt to quell a civil war between Armenia and Azerbaijan over the disputed enclave of Nagorno-Karabakh – and mounting popular discontent over the failure of perestroika to improve living standards.

In their December 1989 summit meeting in Malta, Gorbachev and the new US president, George Bush, declared an official end to the Cold War. This opened up the prospect of the USSR securing 'most-favoured nation' trading status with the United States, membership of GATT, and an influx of Western investment. However, throughout 1990 the political and economic situation deteriorated. In pluralist elections held at local and republic levels, anticommunist nationalist and radical deputies polled strongly, particularly in the Baltic republics and in major cities. The new republican governments, including the RSFSR in June 1990, issued declarations of state economic and political sovereignty and, in the case of the Baltics, independence in March–May 1990. These were ignored by Moscow, which, instead, imposed a temporary economic blockade on Lithuania. As the year progressed, a 'war of laws' developed between the centre and the republics, who kept back funds, which contributed to a worsening of the federal budget deficit, and the system of central economic planning and resource distribution began to break down. As a consequence, with crime and labour unrest also increasing, the USSR's national income fell by at least 4% during 1990 and was to decline by a further 15% during 1991. Indeed, mounting food shortages led to rationing and an emergency international airlift of food aid during the winter of 1990–91.

The CPSU also began to fracture during 1990 as a result of nationalist challenges within the republics and divisions over the direction and pace of economic and political reform between conservatives, who had grouped themselves in the 'Soyuz' and 'Communists for Russia' factions, liberals, in the 'Communists for Democracy' faction, and radicals, aligned to the 'Democratic Platform'. A split was formalized at the 28th CPSU Congress, held in July 1990, when Boris Yeltsin, who was indirectly elected president of the Russian Republic (RSFSR) in May 1990, and Gavriil Popov and Anatoly Sobchak, respectively the radical mayors of Moscow and St Petersburg, resigned their party membership. Earlier, in the RSFSR, a new Russian Communist Party had also been formed and in September 1990 the Russian Federation's parliament adopted the 'Shatalin Programme' of rapid market-centred economic reforms, although this was soon shelved in the face of public opposition.

In December 1990, concerned at the gathering pace of economic and political disintegration and ethnic strife, President Gorbachev, now immensely unpopular, with his public approval rating in single figures, persuaded the Soviet parliament to vote him increased emergency powers and approve a new federalized political structure. Subsequently, under pressure from the 'Soyuz' group, the military, and the KGB secret service, a clear rightward shift in policy became apparent. This was manifested by the appointment of the conservative Valentin Pavlov as prime minister, Gennady Yanayev as vice president, and the hardline Boris Pugo (1937–91) as interior minister; by the resignation of Foreign Minister Eduard Shevardnadze, who warned that a new dictatorship was impending; by the dispatch in January 1991 of black beret paratroopers to Vilnius and Riga in Lithuania and Latvia to seize political and communications buildings; and by a retightening of press and television censorship. In protest, striking Kuzbas coalminers called, between March and May 1991, for Gorbachev's resignation.

From the spring of 1991, after his March 1991 proposal to preserve the USSR as a 'renewed federation of equal sovereign republics' secured public approval by 76% of participating voters in a Unionwide referendum, which was boycotted by six republics, Gorbachev again attempted to reconstruct a centre-left reform alliance with liberals and radicals. In April 1991, a pact aimed at achieving stable relations between the federal and republican governments and with promoting economic reform was signed by the presidents of nine republics: the three Baltic states, Armenia, Georgia, and Moldova were the republics which refused to sign. Two months later, the draft of a new Union Treaty, entailing a much greater devolution of authority and the establishment of a new two-chamber federal legislature and a directly elected executive president, was also approved by nine republics. In July 1991 Gorbachev's standing was further enhanced by the signing, in Moscow, of a Strategic Arms Reduction Treaty (START), to reduce the number of US and Soviet long-range nuclear missiles. At home, however, Boris Yeltsin, who in June 1991 was directly elected president of the giant Russian Federation, pressed for even greater reform and in July 1991 Communist Party cells were banned from operating in factories, farms, and government offices within the Russian Republic. In the same month a Democratic Reform Movement was formed by Shevardnadze, Sobchak, and Popov.

These liberal-radical initiatives raised disquiet among CPSU conservatives and in June 1991 Prime Minister Pavlov unsuccessfully attempted to persuade the Soviet parliament to vote him extra powers. Two months later, on Monday 19 August 1991, a day before the new Union Treaty was to be signed, an attempted anti-Gorbachev coup was launched by a reactionary alliance of leaders of the CPSU apparatchiki, the military-industrial complex, the KGB, and the armed forces. It was declared in the early hours of the morning that President Gorbachev, who was on holiday in the Crimea, was ill and that Vice President Gennady Yanayev would take over as president, as part of an eight-person emergency committee, which also included Prime Minister Pavlov, Defence Minister Dmitri Yazov, KGB Chief Vladimir Kryuchkov, and Interior Minister Boris Pugo. This committee assumed control over radio and television, banned demonstrations and all but eight newspapers, imposed a curfew, and sent tanks into Moscow. They failed, however, to arrest the Russian president, Boris Yeltsin, who defiantly stood out against the plotters as the head of a democratic 'opposition state' barricaded in the Russian parliament building, the so-called 'White House', where external telephone links remained in operation. Yeltsin called for a general strike and the reinstatement of President Gorbachev. On Wednesday morning, having failed to wrest control of the 'White House' and win either international or Unionwide acknowledgement of the change of regime, and having endured large demonstrations in Moscow, St Petersburg, Kishinev (in Moldova), and Lviv (in Ukraine), the coup disintegrated. The junta's inept leaders were arrested, with the exception of Pugo, who committed suicide, and in the early hours of Thursday 22 August 1991 President Gorbachev, fully reinstated, arrived back in Moscow. There were 15 fatalities during the crisis.

In the wake of this failed attempted coup established CPSU structures, as well as the Union itself, rapidly disintegrated in the face of a popular backlash which saw such icons of communism as the Felix Dzerzhinsky statue outside the KGB headquarters in Moscow being toppled and the Red Flag being burned and replaced by traditional tsarist symbols. President Gorbachev initially misjudged the changed mood, intimating his continued faith in the popularly discredited CPSU and seeking to keep to a minimum the necessary changes in personnel and institutions. However, forced by pressure exerted by the public and by Boris Yeltsin, whose stature both at home and abroad had been hugely enhanced, a succession of far-reaching reforms were instituted which effectively sounded the death knell of Soviet communism and resulted in the fracturing of the Union.

The new federal cabinet was selected effectively by Yeltsin and was staffed largely with radical democrats from the Russian Republic, with Ivan Silaev, prime minister in the RSFSR since June 1990, becoming federal prime minister. Yeltsin also declared himself to have assumed charge of the armed forces within the Russian Republic and, at a heated session of the Russian parliament, pressurized President Gorbachev into signing a decree suspending the activities of the Russian Communist Party. In addition, a new Russian national guard was established and control assumed over all economic assets in the republic. Recognizing the changed realities, President Gorbachev announced on 24 August 1991 that he was immediately resigning as general secretary of the CPSU and ordered the party's discredited Central Committee to dissolve itself.

The attempted coup of August 1991 speeded up the movement towards dissolution of the Soviet Union. During the coup, when Red Army tanks were sent into their capitals with orders to seize radio and television stations, the Estonian and Latvian parliaments followed the earlier example of Lithuania and declared independence. After the coup the largely conservative-communist controlled republics of Azerbaijan, Belarus, and Uzbekistan, as well as the key republic of Ukraine, also joined the Baltics, Georgia, Moldova, and Armenia in declaring their independence. Their governments acted partly in the hope of shoring up their authority and privileges and partly because they feared Russian domination of the existing USSR and possible future territorial disputes.

At an emergency session of the Congress of People's Deputies held in September 1991, the Union was partially salvaged through the negotiation of a new Union Treaty in which each republic was to be allowed to decide its own terms of association, with much greater power being devolved from the centre in what represented a new loose confederation, or 'Union of Sovereign States', though with the armed forces retained under a single military command. Ten republics – the three Baltic states, Georgia, and Moldova being the exceptions – declared a willingness to sign this agreement. The Congress also voted on 5 September 1991 to establish a new system of government in which the CUPD would be abolished and its powers would be assumed by a revamped two-chamber Supreme Soviet, with its upper chamber being chosen by the republics and its decisions ratified by the latter, a State Council (government), comprising President Gorbachev and the heads of the ten republics, and an Inter-Republican Economic Committee, with equal representation from all 15 republics and chaired by Ivan Silaev. It also acknowledged the rights of republics to secede, opening the way on 6 September 1991 for President Gorbachev to formally recognize, by decree, the independence of the Baltic states.

The possibility of forging a new decentralized union receded as 1991 progressed. Concerned at the accumulation of political and economic authority by Russia, other republics began to seek full independence so as to escape Russian domination, including Armenia, Azerbaijan, Georgia, Moldova, and, crucially, Ukraine, and refused to sign new economic and political agreements. Participation in the new Supreme Soviet and State Council was patchy, their gatherings attracting members from, at most, ten republics. Although a declaration of intent to maintain a 'common economic zone' of inter-republican free trade and to uphold existing factory ties was initialled in October 1991, along with a civic and interethnic accord, the republics proved unable to agree on specific details of a proposed new economic and political union. As a consequence, President Gorbachev occupied the position of a figurehead leader, possessing little real authority, although his position was slightly strengthened by the return of Shevardnadze to head the foreign ministry in November 1991. Instead, the pre-eminent leader in the new USSR, governing significantly from the former office of the CPSU Politburo, was Russia's president, Boris Yeltsin, who now also combined the position of Russian prime minister. In November 1991 the Russian Republic took over control of the Soviet money supply and exchange rate, and began implementing a market-centred economic reform programme. On 14 November 1991 preliminary agreement was reached on the formation of a new 'Union of Sovereign States', but at a subsequent meeting,

held on 25 November 1991, the republican delegations which attended refused to initial the treaty.

On 8 December 1991, a week after a referendum on independence was held in Ukraine, the three most powerful republics, Russia, Belarus, and Ukraine, agreed to form a new Commonwealth of Independent States (CIS), a military and economic grouping of sovereign states. This development was denounced by President Gorbachev, but by mid-December the five Central Asian republics of Kazakhstan, Kyrgyzstan, Tajikistan, Turkmenistan, and Uzbekistan had announced that they would also join the CIS. Accepting the inevitable, President Gorbachev agreed on a transfer of power from the centralized USSR government to the CIS. The remaining republics, Armenia, Azerbaijan, and Moldova, with the exception of Georgia, which was distracted by civil war, joined the others in signing agreements on 21 December 1991 to establish the new Commonwealth, or alliance, of Independent States. The formal dissolution of the USSR came on 25 December 1991, when Gorbachev resigned as president, and in the same month the United States and European Community accorded the Russian Federation diplomatic recognition as an independent state.

The new Russian Federation, despite the weakness of its economy, remained a 'great power' and the most significant of the post-Soviet successor states. It inherited much of the former USSR's strategic and diplomatic assets, including a permanent seat on the United Nations Security Council, embassies overseas, and a considerable conventional and nuclear military arsenal. It was admitted into the Helsinki Conference on Security in Europe (CSCE, later the OSCE) in January 1992 and sought to use its membership of the new CIS as a means of maintaining its economic and strategic hegemony in Eastern Europe and Central Asia. Containing almost half the population of the former USSR and around 70% of its agricultural and industrial output, the republic was a vast federation, spanning 11 time zones, stretching 2,000 miles from the Arctic Ocean to China, comprising numerous autonomous republics, regions, and districts and catering for distinct non-Russian ethnic groups, including Tatars, Chechens, Chuvash, Dagestanis, Buryats, Yakuts, Kalmyks, and Chuchi, each with its own parliament and laws. After 1990 many of these autonomous areas made sovereignty or independence declarations, most conspicuously oil-rich and predominantly Muslim Tatarstan, where Russia's largest ethnic minority resided, gas-rich Bashkiria, Siberian Yakutia, and Chechnya–Ingushetia, situated in the southwest. In March 1992, 18 of Russia's 20 republics signed a treaty agreeing to remain within a loose federation: Tatarstan and Chechnya–Ingushetia, which later became two separate republics, dissented. The Russian Federation also faced the threat of territorial claims and border conflicts with neighbouring republics, since 25 million ethnic Russians lived outside the federation. Of particular concern was the Russian-dominated Crimea, which formed part of Ukraine.

Russia's immediate concern from 1992, however, was the rapid deterioration in living standards and shortages of food and consumer goods as a result of price liberalization and the restructuring of commerce, the defence sector, and industry as the republic sought to effect the transition from a planned to a market economy. The government conceded that output would drop by 20% during the first quarter of 1992 and inflation during the year was to exceed 2,000%. This prompted mounting criticism from within parliament, from its speaker, or chairperson, the Russian nationalist Ruslan Khasbulatov (b. 1943), who in January 1992 called for the government's resignation, and from Russia's vice president, Aleksandr Rutskoi, an Afghan war veteran who believed that privatization should have preceded price liberalization. Fears began to mount that Yeltsin might be challenged by a military-backed nationalist coup.

In December 1992 Yegor Gaidar, a committed promarket economic reformer who was blamed for the dismal state of the economy, was ousted as Russian prime minister by the 1,033-member Congress of Russian People's Deputies, the federation's conservative excommunist dominated parliament, although Gaidar was to return as an economics minister in September 1993. Viktor Chernomyrdin (b. 1938), a more cautious former communist apparatchik whose former career had been as head of the huge state gas concern Gazprom, became the new premier and in March 1993 the Congress sought to limit President Yeltsin's powers to rule by decree and cancelled a planned constitutional referendum. Yeltsin struck back by temporarily imposing 'special rule', pending the holding of this referendum. Held on 25 April 1993, the plebiscite gave a clear, 53–59%, vote of confidence to the Yeltsin presidency and its reform programme, but apathy was such, turnout being 64%, that the approval level failed to reach the supra 50% absolute majority of the electorate which was required for a constitutional reform to be carried.

President Yeltsin's battle with the obstructive, conservative Russian parliament continued throughout 1993 and on 21 September 1993, faced with its unveiling of proposals to reduce the presidency's powers and derail proposed economic reforms, notably the mass privatization programme, Yeltsin summarily dissolved the Congress and the subordinate Supreme Soviet, a bicameral standing body elected from the Congress, and, anxious to bring a rapid end to the political stalemate, called fresh parliamentary elections for 11–12 December 1993. The Congress responded by voting to impeach Yeltsin, arguing that his dissolution of parliament had been unconstitutional, and designated the vice president, Aleksandr Rutskoi, as the new 'acting president'. Supported by speaker Khasbulatov, 'president' Rutskoi took refuge in the parliament building. A two-week siege of parliament ensued, which, claiming at least 145 lives, was broken on 4 October after troops, following the orders of Defence Minister General Pavel Grachev, were sent on 4 October 1993 to arrest the putschists, resulting in the surrender of Rutskoi and Khasbulatov. Later, in February 1994, Rutskoi, Khasbulatov, and others involved in the 'October rebellion' were granted an amnesty and released from detention.

A new Russian parliament was elected on 12 December 1993 and a constitution, based on the French model, which increased the powers of the presidency, was approved narrowly in a concurrent plebiscite. However, the parliament elections failed to resolve the political uncertainty in the country since the outcome was inconclusive. The extreme right-wing nationalist-populist Liberal Democratic Party,

led by the xenophobic Vladimir Zhirinovsky (b. 1947), captured 23% of the national vote and emerged as the largest single party in the new State Duma, while the Communist Party of Russia and its Agrarian Party and Women of Russia allies attracted a further 28% of the vote. A new coalition cabinet was formed in January 1994, which was headed by the centrist Prime Minister Viktor Chernomyrdin and retained the reformist Anatoly Chubais as minister for privatization and Andrei Kozyrev (b. 1951) as foreign minister, but the two leading radical reformers, the economy and finance ministers, Yegor Gaidar and Boris Fedorov, resigned, being replaced by more centralist 'Soviet-style economists' and members of the Communist-aligned Agrarian Party, as Prime Minister Chernomyrdin declared that the 'period of market romanticism had ended'. The economy had contracted by a further 8% during 1993, the inflation rate remained high, and there was a new scourge of organized crime. However, by 1994, 30% of state-owned enterprises had been privatized and the private sector produced 62% of officially recorded GDP. In 1995 positive growth in GDP was at last registered.

During 1994 Russia was hit by a major currency crisis in October, which led to the dismissal of the finance minister and central bank chief. However, overseas, in its 'near abroad', the country's influence increased significantly, as its forces were called upon to help restore order after civil wars erupted in Armenia, Georgia, and Tajikistan in former-Soviet Transcaucasia and Central Asia and the CIS became a more effective body. In June 1994 Russia joined NATO's Partnership for Peace (PFP). Internally, an autonomy agreement was reached with Tatarstan in February 1994. However, relations with the mountainous republic of Chechnya, situated in the Caucasus region, which had proclaimed its independence from Russia as early as November 1991, deteriorated greatly. This autonomous republic was the home base of Ruslan Khasbulatov and a centre of organized crime. Civil war broke out in the region in September 1994 as opposition forces, supported by Khasbulatov, attempted to overthrow Chechnya's president, General Dzhokar Dudayev, and the Russian army invaded the republic in December 1994 in an effort to reimpose central control, thus setting an example to other secessionist-minded republics. The army met with fierce guerrilla resistance and the fighting, which lasted several months and claimed the lives of 1,800 Russian soldiers and an even greater number of Chechen guerrillas and civilians, led to a third of the Chechen population being made refugees, consumed resources equivalent to more than 1% of Russian GDP, and gravely tarnished the reputation of President Yeltsin. On 30 July 1995 a peace deal, brokered by Prime Minister Chernomyrdin, was signed by the contending parties. It provided for an immediate cease-fire, demilitarization of the republic, enhanced autonomy and the holding of elections in December 1995.

By the spring of 1995 Yeltsin's public approval rating had fallen to single figures and centrist democratic parties, notably Russia's Choice, led by Yegor Gaidar, withdrew their backing from the Yeltsin regime. This resulted, in June 1995, after 140 people had been killed in the southern Russian town of Budyonnovsk following the mishandling of a Chechen hostage siege, in the Duma passing a motion of no confidence in the government. To prevent defeat in a second no-confidence motion, which would have precipitated the holding of early parliamentary elections, President Yeltsin sacked the interior minister, head of the security service and the deputy prime minister in late June 1995. The president, whose public appearances had become infrequent and erratic, with his health deteriorating, was seen increasingly as having become, like Gorbachev in 1990–91, a prisoner of a conservative military-nationalist grouping. His prospects of re-election in 1996 appeared increasingly remote, leading to mounting fears that, in a swing back to authoritarianism, the presidential elections might be cancelled. In the meantime, Prime Minister Chernomyrdin, who formed his own political party in May 1995, was establishing himself as the most serious establishment challenger for the presidency. In November, the prime minister was given temporary control over security and foreign policy after President Yeltsin was hospitalized following his second serious heart attack in 1995.

SLOVAKIA

Slovak Republic
Republika Slovenska

Capital: Bratislava

Social and economic data
Area: 49,035 km²
Population: 5,300,000*
Pop. density per km²: 108*
Urban population: N/A+
Literacy rate: 99%**
GDP: $11,000 million**; per-capita GDP: $2,080**
Government defence spending (% of GDP): 2.3%**
Currency: Slovak koruna

Economy type: middle income
Labour force in agriculture: 12%**

*1994
**1992
+73% in Czechoslovakia in 1990

Ethnic composition
Eighty-seven per cent of the population is of Slovak ethnic stock and 11% is ethnic Hungarian (Magyar). There are also small Czech (1%), Moravian, Silesian, and gypsy communities. Slovak, a member of the western Slavonic group, has been the sole official language since 1996. The large ethnic Hungarian minority, who live in the south of the state, have been demanding greater cultural and educational autonomy and new laws guaranteeing minority rights.

Religions
Sixty per cent of the population is Roman Catholic. The Protestant Slovak Lutheran (Evangelical) Church has 330,000 members, the Reformed Christian Church of Slovakia, 89,000 adherents, and the Orthodox Church, 55,000 members.

Political features
State type: emergent democratic
Date of state formation: 1993*
Political structure: unitary
Executive: parliamentary
Assembly: one-chamber
Party structure: multiparty
Human rights rating: N/A
International affiliations: BIS, CE, CEI, CEFTA, CERN, DC, EBRD, ECE, IAEA, IBRD, ICFTU, IMF, LORCS, NACC, OSCE, PFP, UN, VG, WEU (associate partner), WFTU, WTO

*Czechoslovakia was formed in 1918

Local and regional government
The republic is divided into four regions, one of which is the city of Bratislava, which are subdivided into 38 municipalities for the purpose of local government.

Head of state (ceremonial)
President Michal Kovac, since 1993

Head of government
Prime Minister Vladimir Meciar, since 1994

Political leaders since 1970*
1990–91 Vladimir Meciar (PAV), 1991–92 Jan Carnogursky (CDM), 1992–94 Vladimir Meciar (MDS), 1994 Jozef Moravcik (DUS), 1994– Vladimir Meciar (MDS)

*Prime minister

Political system
Under the terms of the September 1992 constitution, which came into force on 1 January 1993, Slovakia has a parliamentary political system. There is a single-chamber legislature, the National Council of the Slovak Republic, whose 150 members are elected by universal adult suffrage for a four-year term through a system of proportional represent-

ation. The state president, who is elected by the National Council for a maximum of two consecutive five-year terms, served, until June 1995, as commander in chief of the armed forces, appoints the prime minister, represents the republic internationally, and may declare a referendum and state of emergency. Successful candidates for the presidency need to receive three-fifths majority support from the legislature. A president can be removed from office if the National Council passes a no-confidence resolution with a 60% majority. The prime minister, drawn from the grouping holding at least 60% support from the National Council, is executive head of government and nominates a cabinet of about 15 members. There is provision for a national referendum to be held if a petition is signed by at least 350,000 citizens. For a referendum to be valid, turnout must exceed 50%.

Political parties

The seven main political parties in Slovakia are the Movement for a Democratic Slovakia (MDS), the Democratic Union of Slovakia (DUS), the Party of the Democratic Left (PDL), the Association of Workers of Slovakia (ZRS), the Christian Democratic Movement (CDM), the Slovak National Party (SNP), and the Hungarian Coalition.

The centre-left nationalist-populist MDS was formed in March 1991 by Vladimir Meciar as a breakaway from the moderate Public Against Violence (PAV), which was set up in 1989 as an intelligentsia-led umbrella body to spearhead the prodemocracy movement in Slovakia. The MDS pressed for full autonomy for the Slovak Republic and was instrumental in securing the dissolution of Czechoslovakia and the formation of independent Slovakia in January 1993.

The centrist DUS was formed in February 1994 as a breakaway from the MDS by Jozef Moravcik and merged in April 1994 with the Alliance of Democrats, which had been formed in June 1993 by Milan Knazko, after his dismissal from the Meciar government and the MDS.

The PDL is the reform-socialist successor to the formerly dominant Communist Party of Slovakia. It was formed in 1991 and is led by Peter Weiss. The left-wing Association of Workers of Slovakia (ZRS) was formed in April 1994 as a breakaway from the PDL and is led by Jan Luptak, a former bricklayer.

The CDM, led by Jan Carnogursky, is a right-of-centre force, in favour of rapid transition to a Western-style full market economy, which was formed in 1990. The SNP is a strongly nationalist party set up in 1990 and led now by Jan Slota. It was weakened in February 1994 when its leader, Ludovit Cernak, left to form a new centre-right party, the National Democratic Party.

The Hungarian Coalition is an electoral alliance of parties orientated towards Slovakia's large ethnic Hungarian minority community. It comprises the Hungarian Civic Party, the Hungarian Christian Democratic Movement, and Egyutteles (Coexistence).

Latest elections

The most recent elections to the National Council were held on 30 September–1 October 1994. The largest number of seats, 61 out of the 150 available, was won by the MDS, which attracted 35% of the vote and ran in coalition with the

small Farmers' Party of Slovakia (RSS). The excommunist PDL dominated the Common Choice bloc, which also comprised the Social Democratic Party, the Green Party, and the Farmers' Movement, and won 18 seats, based on a 10% vote share. The Hungarian Coalition and CDM, each with 10% of the vote, won 17 seats apiece; the DUS, with a 9% vote share, 15 seats; the ZRS, with 7% of the vote, 13 seats; and the SNP, with 5% of the vote, 9 seats. Twelve other party groupings contested the election and attracted 13% of the national vote, but fell individually below the 5% cut-off threshold for individual party representation and 10% threshold applied to coalitions of four or more groups. Turnout was 76%.

Political history

In the 9th century AD Slovaks and Czechs, both western Slavic peoples, were united under the Great Moravian Empire. But from the 10th century, following the empire's dissolution, Czechs formed an independent kingdom which lasted until the Habsburgs assumed control in the 16th century, while Slovaks came under Hungarian rule and remained under the latter's tutelage until the 20th century. Slovak national revival movements were mounted during the 19th century and in October 1918, following the dismemberment of the Austro-Hungarian Habsburg Empire at the end of World War I, the independent state of Czechoslovakia was formed, reuniting the Slovak and Czech peoples.

Slovaks resented the fact that economic development in interwar Czechoslovakia was concentrated in the Czech lands and that, while Roman Catholics predominated in Slovakia, the central government in Prague was anti-clerical. However, Slovak demands for the establishment of a federal system, in which the Slovak lands would be granted autonomy, were rejected. In October 1938, following the September 1938 Munich Agreement which ceded to Nazi Germany predominantly German-peopled areas of Czechoslovakia, Slovak autonomy was declared by Slovak nationalists. The German dictator, Adolf Hitler, responded by agreeing to the establishment of a separate, pro-Nazi Slovak state in March 1939 under the fascist leadership of Jozef Tiso. Jews, in particular, were persecuted by the Tiso regime, which lasted until April 1945, despite an armed rebellion, the 'Slovak National Uprising', being mounted in August 1944.

During the early 1950s, with a communist state being established in Czechoslovakia (see *Czech Republic, Political history*), Slovak nationalism was forcibly suppressed, with even the Slovak-born Gustáv Husák (b. 1913), who was later to become communist party leader in Czechoslovakia between 1969 and 1987, being imprisoned. However, there was economic development, with heavy industry being introduced into Slovakia. In January 1968, another Slovak-born politician, Alexander Dubček (1921–92), rose to become leader of the ruling Communist Party of Czechoslovakia (CPCZ) and instituted the 'Prague Spring' political reforms. These met with Soviet disapproval and an invasion by Czechoslovakia's Warsaw Pact allies in August 1968 and Dubček's dismissal. Husák, who replaced Dubček as CPCZ leader, introduced a new federal constitution in 1969, which granted Slovakia its own government and legislature, the

Slovak National Council, and greater autonomy in the cultural, educational, and judicial spheres.

Continued repression of the Roman Catholic Church and Slovak nationalists during the 1970s and early 1980s meant that when, in the later 1980s, political openness began to be encouraged by the new Soviet leader, Mikhail Gorbachev, the anticommunist prodemocracy movement was especially strong in Slovakia. In 1989 the Public Against Violence (PAV) umbrella grouping was formed in the republic to spearhead this protest campaign and in November 1989 large mass rallies were held in Bratislava and were addressed by the formerly disgraced Alexander Dubček.

In the June 1990 Federal Assembly and National Council multiparty elections, which were held after the CPCZ had renounced its monopoly of power and a new postcommunist reformist administration, headed by Prime Minister Marian Calfa and President Václav Havel (b. 1935), had assumed power in Prague, the PAV polled particularly strongly in Slovakia. So did the Slovak National Party (SNP), an extreme nationalist party which, critical of Czech predominance in the political and economic affairs of Czechoslovakia, campaigned for the republic's full independence. Vladimir Meciar (b. 1931), a founding member of the PAV, became Slovak prime minister after the election, heading a PAV-dominated coalition administration. Throughout 1990 the SNP organized pro-autonomy rallies and demonstrations in Slovakia as the political temperature rose. The moderate-nationalist PAV administration attempted to appease this nationalist sentiment by declaring Slovak the official language of the republic in November 1990. Then, in March 1991, Prime Minister Meciar formed a breakaway faction from the PAV, termed the Movement for a Democratic Slovakia (MDS), whose platform was greatly increased autonomy for Slovakia within a much looser federation. In response, the Slovak National Council replaced Meciar as prime minister with Jan Carnogursky, leader of the centre-right Christian Democratic Movement (CDM).

The federation's fate was decided by the outcome of the 5–6 June 1992 federal and republic elections, which resulted in Meciar's MDS becoming the second largest party group in the Federal Assembly and the dominant group in the Slovak National Assembly. Meciar became Slovak prime minister again, heading an MDS-dominated, but SNP-supported, administration, and on 17 July 1992 the Slovak National Council voted overwhelmingly to declare Slovak sovereignty. Agreement was reached in the summer of 1992 with the Czech Republic prime minister, Václav Havel, on the arrangements for separation and in September 1992 a new Slovak constitution was adopted by the Slovak National Council.

It was agreed that federal assets and liabilities should, in accordance with relative population strengths, be apportioned 2:1 between the Czech and Slovak republics and property on a territorial basis. In October 1992 a customs union treaty was signed by the two republics, providing for the abolition of trade restrictions between the two states on independence, and in December 1992 a cooperation agreement was signed. On 1 January 1993 all remaining federal structures were dissolved and the new separate Czech and Slovak republics were created. Slovakia was automatically admitted into the UN, CSCE (later the OSCE), IMF, and World Bank, while the Slovak National Council, elected in 1992, remained as the legislature, with Meciar as prime minister. After two rounds of voting by the legislature had not produced a winner with the requisite three-fifths majority support, Michal Kovac (b. 1930), the deputy leader of the MDS and a former banker who had been chair of Czechoslovakia's Federal Assembly from 1992, was elected state president on a third vote on 15 February 1993. On assuming the presidency, in March 1993, he dropped his membership of the MDS and was to emerge as a political rival to Meciar.

The new state was faced with grave economic problems. The attempt to move from a planned economy to a market economy and to find new markets for its increasingly obsolete steel, chemicals, and arms heavy industries had led to a sharp fall in GDP between 1991–93 and an increase in the unemployment level to more than 15% and, with a new national currency being introduced, inflation to 30%. There were also accusations of corruption in the privatization process. Not until 1994 did GDP begin to grow again. Relations with Hungary, a member with Slovakia of the Visegrad Group (VG), which promotes economic integration in Central Europe, were also strained by the issue of the large Hungarian minority resident in Slovakia, who were campaigning for cultural and educational autonomy. However, a Treaty of Friendship and Cooperation was later signed by the two states in March 1995. In addition, the country was less politically stable than the neighbouring Czech Republic. The MDS's coalition with the SNP was an uneasy one and between March and November 1993 there were, temporarily, no SNP ministers within the cabinet. There were also splits within the MDS after the foreign minister, Milan Knazko, was dismissed in March 1993 and went on to form the Alliance of Democrats as a liberal, right-of-centre party.

Slovakia entered the Council of Europe in June 1993, reflecting the country's increasingly pro-Western orientation. In February 1994 the MDS split again when Deputy Prime Minister Roman Kovac and Foreign Minister Jozef Moravcik (b. 1945) joined a new anti-Meciar party faction, the Alternative of Political Realism (APR), later termed the Democratic Union for Slovakia (DUS), which called for the establishment of 'a government of politically nonaligned experts'. Within days they were dismissed from the MDS and resigned from the cabinet, creating a government crisis. In February 1994 the SNP was also weakened by the defection of its former leader, Ludovit Cernak. Following defeat in a no-confidence vote in the National Council and deteriorating relations with President Kovac, who expressed 'serious reservations about the style and ethics of Meciar's politics', Vladimir Meciar resigned as prime minister on 14 March 1994. Jozef Moravcik, now leader of the DUS, was appointed interim prime minister, pending new elections. He headed a broad-based five-party coalition government including members from the excommunist Party of the Democratic Left (PDL), the Christian Democratic Movement (CDM), the Alliance of Democrats, which had been formed by Milan Knazko, the DUS, and the conservative National Democratic Party, formed by Cernak. The new government succeeded in halting the rise in unemployment and inflation, as the economy began to grow once more, cut back the budget deficit, and introduced a voucher privatization programme on the Czech model. Despite these achievements, the governing coalition was defeated in the general election of September–October 1994, capturing just 29% of the national vote to the populist MDS's 35%, which won 61 of the 150 National Council seats.

On 13 December 1994 Meciar was sworn in again as prime minister, heading an MDS-dominated 'red-brown' coalition government with the ultranationalist SNP, the left-wing Association of Slovak Workers (ZRS), and the Farmers' Party of Slovakia (RSS), which had been the MDS's electoral partner. The new populist-nationalist government immediately postponed the planned second wave of mass privatization, based on coupon sales, and pledged to revitalize the arms industry and boost pensions and teachers' salaries.

In May 1995 the National Council passed, with a 53% majority, a vote of no confidence in President Kovac over his alleged failure to control the domestic intelligence service, and Prime Minister Meciar, who resented the independent stance adopted by the president, called for Kovac's resignation. Kovac, enjoying strong popular support, refused to step down, although in June 1995 the National Council stripped the president of his role as head of the armed forces. In September 1995, as part of an alleged campaign of intimidation orchestrated by supporters of Prime Minister Meciar, the son of President Kovac was mysteriously kidnapped and beaten up.

SLOVENIA

Republic of Slovenia
Republika Slovenija

Capital: Ljubljana

Social and economic data
Area: 20,251 km^2
Population: 2,000,000*
Population density per km^2: 99*
Urban population: 49%**
Literacy rate: 99%**
GDP: $10,655 million**; per-capita GDP: $5,330**
Government defence spending (% of GDP): 3.3%**
Currency: tolar
Economy type: middle income
Labour force in agriculture: 13%**

*1994
**1992

Ethnic composition
Ninety per cent of the population is of Slovene ethnic stock, 3% is ethnic Croat, and 2% Serb. Slovene, which resembles Serbo-Croat and is written in Roman characters, is the official language, but Hungarian and Italian are also widely used in ethnically mixed areas and 5% of the population speak Serbo-Croat.

Religions
The population is predominantly, more than 90%, Roman Catholic, with minority Serbs adhering to the Serbian Orthodox faith.

Political features
State type: emergent democratic
Date of state formation: 1991
Political structure: unitary
Executive: dual
Assembly: two-chamber
Party structure: multiparty
Human rights rating: N/A
International affiliations: COE, IAEA, IBRD, IMF, NAM (guest), OSCE, PFP, UN, WTO

Local and regional government
There are 62 local government districts.

Head of state
President Milan Kucan, since 1990

Head of government
Prime Minister Dr Janez Drnovsek, since 1992

Political leaders since 1970
1990– Milan Kucan (PDR/excommunist independent)*, 1990–92 Lojze Peterle (SKD)**, 1992–   Dr Janez Drnovsek (LDS)**

*President
**Prime minister

Political system
Under the December 1991 constitution Slovenia has predominantly a parliamentary pluralist political system, but the president retains a degree of moral authority which enables the system to be currently characterized as 'dual executive'. The president is directly elected for a maximum of two five-year terms. Their power is chiefly ceremonial. The legislature comprises two chambers, the 90-member National

Assembly (Drzavni Zbor) and the 40-member National Council (Drzavni Svet). The National Assembly is elected for four years and comprises 38 directly elected deputies, 50 members selected on a proportional basis by an electoral commission from among parties that have secured at least 3% of the national vote and two nonelected representatives of the Hungarian and Italian minorities. The National Council serves a five-year term and comprises 22 directly elected members and 18 chosen indirectly by an electoral college to 'represent various social, economic, trading, political and local interest groups'. The National Assembly is the most significant chamber and the prime minister, who is formally appointed by the president, must be able to command a majority within it. The National Council performs principally an advisory function, but a new government needs to be approved by the Council and it may propose laws to the Assembly and demand that the latter review its decision on a law before promulgating it.

Political parties

The principal political parties in Slovenia are the Liberal Democracy of Slovenia (LDS), the Slovenian Christian Democrats (SKD), the Slovenian Nationalist Party (SNS), the Slovenian People's Party (SLS), and the Associated List of Social Democrats (ZLSD).

The LDS and SKD currently form the governing coalition. The LDS is a centrist force which was formed in 1990 out of the Union of Socialist Youth, a communist youth organization. Led by Prime Minister Dr Janez Drnovsek, it has abandoned its former socialist orientation and in March 1994 merged with the Democratic Party (DS), the Green Alliance (ZS) and the excommunist Socialist Party to increase its strength in the National Assembly to 30 seats out of 90. The DS originated in 1990 after a split in the Slovenian Democratic Union (estd. 1989), the first party to be formed in opposition to the communists.

The SKD is a right-of-centre conservative party, formed in 1989 and led by former premier, Lojze Peterle.

The SNS is a right-wing nationalist body and the SLS is also a conservative force which originated, in 1989, as the Slovenian Farmers' Association.

The excommunist ZLSD is an alliance of four left-of-centre parties formed to contest the 1992 parliamentary elections: the Social Democratic Union (estd. 1990), the Workers' Party of Slovenia (estd. 1990), the Democratic Party of Pensioners, and the Social Democratic Reform of Slovenia.

Latest elections

The most recent parliamentary and presidential elections, the first since independence, were held on 6 December 1992.

In the presidential contest, the incumbent excommunist, but now standing as an independent, Milan Kucan was re-elected, securing 64% of the popular vote. He defeated seven challengers, with Ivan Bizjak of the SKD finishing second with 21% of the poll. Turnout was 76%.

Eight parties secured representation in the National Assembly. The five most successful were the centre-left LDS, which attracted 24% of the national vote and won 22 of the 90 seats; the right-of-centre SKD, with 15% of the vote

and 15 seats; the four-party left-of-centre Associated List of Social Democrats, with 14% of the vote and 14 seats; the right-wing nationalist SNS, with 10% of the vote and 12 seats; and the agrarian-conservative SLS, with 9% of the vote and 10 seats. Turnout was 85% and 25 parties and coalitions contested this poll.

Political history

The area corresponding to contemporary Slovenia was settled by the Slovenes in the 6th century and later by the Slavs and Franks, from 788, before coming under Hungarian domination between 907–55. It was absorbed in the Austro-Hungarian Habsburg Empire from 1335, forming part of the Austrian crownlands of Carniola, Styria, and Carinthia. From 1848 the Slovenes began their struggle for national unification and this was largely achieved in December 1918 following the collapse of the Habsburg Empire. The territory was incorporated, along with the Serbs, Croats, and Montenegrins, into the Kingdom of the Serbs, Croats, and Slovenes, which became known as Yugoslavia in 1929. However, a sizeable Slovene community lived under Italian rule in Istria, until borders were rearranged after World War II.

Unlike in neighbouring Croatia, there were few Slovenian demands for autonomy during the 1930s. During World War II the region was occupied by Germany and Italy and in 1941 an anti-Nazi Slovene Liberation Front was formed. This became allied with Marshal Tito's communist-led all-Yugoslav Partisan army and with British and American forces. After the war, in November 1945, Slovenia became a constituent republic of the communist Yugoslav Socialist Federal Republic. Benefiting from its Habsburg legacy, it was the most economically advanced and politically liberal republic within the federation, helping to subsidize the poorer southeastern republics.

From the 1980s, however, there was economic decline and, particularly after the death of the federation's leader, Marshal Tito, increasing nationalist unrest. The leadership of the ruling Slovene League of Communists (LCS) responded by pressing for greater autonomy within the federation to enable the republic to pursue a strategy of economic liberalization and political pluralism. In 1989 opposition parties were legalized and a free, multiparty election was held in April 1990. Despite renaming themselves the Party of Democratic Reform (PDR) and adopting a social democratic programme, the now reformed communists were convincingly defeated by the six-party Democratic Opposition of Slovenia (DEMOS), a nationalist, centre-right coalition, which campaigned for independence within a year and attracted a 55% share of the national vote. However, the PDR's reformist leader, Milan Kucan (b. 1941), who was an outspoken opponent of the nationalist-populist president and communist party leader of Serbia, Slobodan Milošević, was popularly elected state president, renouncing his party membership once installed in office.

After the parliamentary elections, a new DEMOS-dominated government was formed with Lojze Peterle, leader of the right-of-centre Slovenian Christian Democrats (SKD), as prime minister. It sought to promote the formation of a new loose Yugoslav confederation. However, this was resisted by an increasingly assertive Serbia. On 2 July 1990 the Slovenian National Assembly declared the sovereignty of the republic, with its laws now taking precedence over federal legislation. Following a referendum on independence, which was held on 23 December 1990 and received 89% support, plans began to be made for secession. An independent army, the Slovenian Territorial Defence Force, was established in the spring of 1991 and on 8 May 1991 it was announced that the secession of both Slovenia and Croatia from the federation would take place on 25 June 1991.

Around 3,000 soldiers from the federal Yugoslav National Army (JNA), which was dominated by Serbians, moved to the Slovenian border on 27 June 1991 and around 70 died during a week of sporadic clashes with the new Slovenian army. The European Community (EC) sought to broker a cease-fire, but could not prevent an aerial bombardment of Ljubljana on 2 July 1991, the first bombardment of a European city since World War II. However, during its short campaign against the new Slovenian forces, the JNA endured a number of reverses, and the federal government agreed later on 2 July 1991 to accept the EC cease-fire terms of a three-month suspension of Slovenia's declaration of independence and the withdrawal of the JNA from the republic. This was successfully implemented as the focus of the Serb-dominated JNA's activity switched to Croatia, with its much larger Serb minority.

On 8 October 1991, after the three-month moratorium on disassociation had expired, Slovenia proclaimed its full independence and introduced its own currency, the tolar. Slovenia's independence was formally recognized by the EC in January 1992 and by the United States in April 1992, and in May 1992 it became a member of both the United Nations (UN) and Conference on Security and Cooperation in Europe (CSCE, later the OSCE). On 23 December 1991 Slovenia adopted a new constitution and on 30 December the ruling DEMOS coalition, which had become undermined by increasing factionalism, dissolved itself. Peterle continued as prime minister until April 1992, when his government was defeated in a no-confidence motion and Dr Janez Drnovsek, leader of the Liberal Democratic Party (LDS), took over as premier.

The parliamentary and presidential elections of December 1992 resulted in little change, with Kucan being re-elected state president, although this position had been made largely ceremonial by the new constitution, and Drnovsek continuing as prime minister, heading a LDS, SKD, and, until its withdrawal in March 1994, Social Democratic Party of Slovenia (SDSS) centrist coalition government. Benefiting from its greater ethnic homogeneity and its location adjoining Italy and Austria, Slovenia managed to successfully divorce itself from the tragic events elsewhere in the former Yugoslavia between 1992–95 and, although relations with Croatia and Serbia remained strained, it was able to concentrate on building a competitive market economy and its drive for associate membership of the European Union. Between 1989–93 GDP fell by 20% in the republic and unemployment climbed to 14% of the workforce. However, from 1994 the economy began to grow again, the pace of privatization had accelerated, the inflation rate had been brought down to a manageable 1% a month, and the exchange rate was stable.

TURKEY

Republic of Turkey
Türkiye Cumhuriyeti

Capital: Ankara

Social and economic data
Area: 779,450 km^2
Population: 59,600,000*
Pop. density per km^2: 76*
Urban population: 64%**
Literacy rate: 81%**
GDP: $114,000 million**; per-capita GDP: $1,954**
Government defence spending (% of GDP): 4.1%**
Currency: Turkish lira
Economy type: middle income
Labour force in agriculture: 50%**

*1992
**1994

Ethnic composition
Over 90% of the population can be said to be Turks but only about 5% can claim Turki or Western Mongoloid ancestry. Most people are descended from earlier conquerors of their country, such as the Greeks.

Religions
About 99% of the people are Muslims, mainly of the Sunni sect. Islam was the state religion for a brief period, between 1924 and 1928.

Political features
State type: liberal democratic
Date of state formation: 1923
Political structure: unitary
Executive: parliamentary
Assembly: one-chamber

Party structure: multiparty
Human rights rating: 44%
International affiliations: ACP (associate), CE, CERN, CSCE, ECO, IAEA, IBRD, IMF, NACC, NATO, OECD, OIC, UN, WEU (associate), WTO

Local and regional government
The country is divided into 74 provinces and 2,074 municipalities. The provinces have appointed governors and there are elected assemblies at all levels.

Head of state (executive)
President Suleiman Demirel, since 1993

Head of government
Prime Minister Tansu Ciller, since 1993

Political leaders since 1970
1965–71 Süleiman Demirel (JP), 1971–73 'nonparty' leaders (military), 1973–74 Bülent Eçevit (RPP–NSP coalition), 1974–75 transitional coalition, 1975–78 Süleiman Demirel (JP coalition), 1978–79 Bulent Ecevit (RPP coalition), 1979–80 Süleiman Demirel (JP), 1980–83 General Kenan Evren (military), 1983–89 Turgut Özal (ANAP), 1989–91 Yildirim Akbulut (ANAP), 1991 Mesut Yilmaz (ANAP), 1991–93 Süleiman Demirel (DYP), 1993– Tansu Ciller (DYP)

Political system
After a military coup in 1980, a National Security Council (NSC) was installed with its president as head of state. In 1982, a new constitution was adopted, and later amended in 1987. It provides for a single-chamber National Assembly of 550 members, elected through a weighted party list system of proportional representation, for a five-year term. Parties must obtain at least 10% of the popular vote before they can win representation in the National Assembly. The executive president is elected by the Assembly for a seven-year term. They then appoint a prime minister to lead the government. The relationship between the president and prime minister is not entirely clear particularly in matters of constitutional authority.

Political parties
Political activities were banned between 1980 and 1983 when new parties were allowed to form. There are now some 15 active groups, the five main ones being the Motherland Party (ANAP), the Republican People's Party (CHP) the True Path Party (DYP, formerly TPP), the Welfare party (REFAH), and Bülent Eçevit's Democratic Left party (DSP).

The centre-left CHP was formed in 1931 by Demal Atatürk and in 1995 merged with the Social Democratic Populist party.

ANAP was founded in 1983 by Turgut Özal. It has a nationalist-Islamic right-of-centre orientation.

The SHP was originally formed in 1985 by a merger of the Populist and Social Democratic parties.

The DYP originates from 1983 when it replaced the old Justice Party. It merged with the Citizen Party in 1986. It has a centre-right pro-Western stance.

Refah, led by Necmettin Erbakan (b. 1926), is an Islamic fundamentalist body, opposed to membership of NATO and the EU.

Latest elections
The results of the 24 December 1995 general election were as follows:

	% votes	National Assembly seats
Refah	21.3	158
ANAP	19.7	132
DYP	19.2	135
DSP	14.7	75
CHP	10.8	50

Political history
During the Middle Ages Turkey's power and influence were legendary and the Ottoman Empire spread into southern Russia, Hungary, Syria, Arabia, Egypt, and Cyprus. Its power began to decline in the 17th century, as the armies of Russia and Austria pushed the Turks back towards the Bosporus. Britain and France, however, saw Turkey's value as a bulwark against Russia's imperialist ambitions and fought the Crimean War (1853–56) to defend its frontiers.

Towards the end of the 19th century the Ottoman Empire began to disintegrate and Turkey was spoken of as 'the sick man of Europe'. The European powers were quick to take advantage of this weakness, France seizing Tunis in 1881, and Britain, Egypt in 1882. The final humiliation came after World War I when Turkey had allied itself with Germany and shared in its defeat. The Treaty of Sèvres finished the Ottoman Empire and the army, led by Kemal Atatürk (1881–1938), removed the sultan in 1922 and proclaimed a republic in 1923.

Atatürk (CHP) ruled with a firm hand until his death in 1938. During this time he secularized and Westernized his nation, emancipated women and turned Turkey into a modern industrial state, substituting national pride for the old Islamic loyalties.

Atatürk was succeeded by Ismet Inonu (1884–1973), who continued his predecessor's work, but in a more pluralist fashion. During World War II Inonu allied himself with Britain and the United States, although he delayed entering the war until near its end, in 1945. He liberalized the political system and was then defeated in Turkey's first free elections, held in 1950, which were won by the Democratic Party (DP), led by Celal Bayar and Adnan Menderes (1899–1961). Bayar became president and Menderes prime minister.

In the post-1945 period Turkey felt itself threatened by the USSR and joined a number of collective defence organizations, including NATO in 1952 and the Baghdad Pact in 1955. This became the Central Treaty Organization (CENTO) in 1959 and was eventually dissolved in 1979. Turkey strengthened Western links and by 1987 was making overtures about possible membership or association with the European Community.

In 1960 the government was overthrown in a military coup and President Bayar was later imprisoned and Menderes executed. A new constitution was adopted in 1961 and civilian rule restored even though the leader of the coup, General Cemal Gürsel became president. There followed a series of civilian governments, led mainly by Ismet Inonu, now very much an elder statesman, until 1965, when the Justice Party (JP), led by Süleiman Demirel (b. 1924), came to power.

Following strikes and student unrest, the army forced Demirel to resign in 1971 and for the next two years the country came under military rule again. A civilian government was restored in 1973 in the shape of a CHP coalition led by Bulent Eçevit (b. 1925). The following year Turkey sent troops to Cyprus to protect the Turkish-Cypriot community, resulting in the effective partition of the island. Ecevit's government fell when he refused to annex north Cyprus and in 1975 Suleiman Demirel returned at the head of a right-wing coalition.

Elections held in 1977 were inconclusive and Demirel precariously held on to power until 1978 when Ecevit returned, leading another coalition. He was faced with a deteriorating economy and outbreaks of sectional violence and by 1979 had lost his working majority and resigned. Demirel returned in November but the violence continued and in September 1980 the army stepped in and set up a National Security Council (NSC), with Bülent Ulusu as prime minister. Martial law was imposed, political activity suspended, and a harsh regime established.

Law and order were eventually restored but at a high cost in the loss of civil liberties, and, in the face of strong international pressure, work was begun on the draft of a new constitution. In May 1983 political parties were allowed to operate again. The old parties reformed under new names and in November three of them fought the Assembly elections, the conservative Motherland Party (ANAP), the Nationalist Democracy Party (MDP), and the Populist Party (SDHP). ANAP won a narrow, but clear, majority and its leader, Turgut Özal (1927–93), became prime minister.

Following a referendum in September 1987, the political ban on the opposition leaders, Süleiman Demirel and Bülent Eçevit, was removed and in a relatively free and open general election two months later Prime Minister Turgut Özal and ANAP retained their National Assembly majority. Immediately after the election Bulent Ecevit announced his retirement from active politics and in November 1989 Turgut Özal was elected as Turkey's first civilian president for more than 60 years. In November 1989 Yildirim Akbulut, speaker of the National Assembly and ANAP leader, was appointed prime minister. Two years later he lost the party leadership and President Özal appointed his successor, Mesut Yilmaz, as head of government.

Dissatisfaction with the state of the economy reduced ANAP's popular support and the inconclusive 1991 general election resulted in a coalition government of the DYP and the SHP, with Süleiman Demirel as prime minister.

Internationally, Turkey had supported the US-led coalition in the Gulf War and awaited a reply to its 1989 application for EC membership. Its human rights record and unresolved dispute with Cyprus were obstacles to full international recognition.

The death of Turgut Özal in April 1993 brought Süleiman Demirel to the presidency and appointed Tansu Ciller (b. 1946), as the country's first female prime minister. In 1995 military actions against Kurds in northen Iraq put a strain on the relationship with Turkey's NATO allies. In December 1995 a customs union deal was agreed with the EU, but the concurrent general election produced a 'hung parliament'.

UKRAINE

The Ukraine
Ukraina

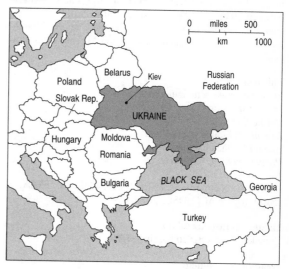

Capital: Kiev (Kiyev)

Social and economic data
Area: 603,700 km²
Population: 52,200,000*
Pop. density per km²: 86*
Urban population: 68%**
Literacy rate: 98%**
GDP: $94,831 million**; per-capita GDP: $1,820**
Government defence spending (% of GDP): 7.2%**
Currency: karbovanets (coupon)***
Economy type: middle income
Labour force in agriculture: 24%**

*1994
**1992
***To be replaced by the grivna

Ethnic composition
Seventy-three per cent of the population is of Ukrainian ethnic stock, 22% is ethnic Russian, 1% is Jewish, and 1% Belarussian. Some 1.5 million émigrés live in the United States and 750,000 in Canada. Ethnic Russians are most densely settled in industrialized eastern Ukraine and in Crimea. The official state language is Ukrainian, an Eastern Slavonic language written in the Cyrillic script.

Religions

The population is predominantly Christian, adhering chiefly to the Ukrainian Eastern Orthodox Church. This Church originated as the Ukrainian Autocephalous Orthodox Church (UAOC), but split in 1930 when the communist regime incorporated it into the Russian Orthodox Church, as the Ukrainian Orthodox Church (UOC). A UAOC continued to operate underground and was revived in 1990. Today it is known as the Ukrainian Orthodox Church (Kievan Patriarchy), while the UOC operates as the Moscow Patriarchy. The Catholic Church is strong in Western Ukraine and Transcarpathia. Known as the Uniate Church, it was established in 1596 by Orthodox clergy who retained Eastern rites and liturgies while acknowledging the primacy of the Pope. The Uniate Church operated underground in Ukraine between 1946 and 1990 and today claims 5 million adherents. Ethnic Poles adhere to the Latin-rite Catholic Church. There are small Protestant, Jewish, and Muslim communities.

Political features

State type: emergent democratic
Date of state formation: 1918/1991
Political structure: unitary
Executive: limited presidential
Assembly: one-chamber
Party structure: multiparty
Human rights rating: N/A
International affiliations: BSECZ, CIS, COE, DC, IAEA, IBRD, IMF, NACC, OSCE, PFP, UN

Head of state (executive)

President Leonid Kuchma, since 1994

Head of government

Prime Minister Evhen Marchuk, since 1995

Political leaders since 1970

1973–89 Vladimir Shcherbitsky (UCP)*, 1989–90 Volodymyr Ivashko (UCP)*, 1990–94 Leonid Kravchuk (excommunist independent)**, 1994– Leonid Kuchma (excommunist independent)**

*Communist Party leader
**Executive president

Local and regional government

Ukraine comprises 24 provinces or regions (*oblasts*) and one metropolitan area, Kiev. Below there are city and rural districts, towns, and villages, with elected councils. Crimea, situated in the far south of Ukraine, adjoining the Black Sea, is an autonomous republic with special status. It has an area of 25,881 square kilometres and a population of 2.55 million, with its capital at Sevastopol. Part of the Russian Federation until 1954, it contains a large ethnic Russian majority, as well as Crimean Tatars who were forcibly deported from their homeland in 1944, but have begun to return since 1989. The autonomous republic has been opposed to Ukraine's independence and, despite Ukraine granting it greater autonomy in April 1992, its parliament declared its sovereignty in May 1994.

Political system

Ukraine's constitution dates back to 1978, during the communist era, but was substantially modified during the early 1990s to provide for political pluralism and to create a presidency with significant executive authority. The state president is directly elected for a five-year term, has decree powers, and appoints a prime minister and cabinet, able to command support within parliament. The legislature, the Supreme Council (Supreme Soviet), or Verkhovna Rada, comprises 450 deputies who are popularly elected for four-year terms by the majoritarian system. Under the terms of the election law adopted in November 1993, there is provision for the polling to take place over several rounds, if necessary. A candidate can be elected in the first round if able to secure more than 50% of the vote, with turnout also exceeding 50%. Run-off elections are then held between the two leading candidates in constituencies where voting failed to produce a clear majority. However, further rounds of voting may be required if turnout falls below 50% in the run-off contests. Indeed, despite repeat elections being held in July, August, and November 1994, after the first two rounds in March and April 1994, 45 Supreme Council seats remained to be filled at the close of 1994. The division of executive authority in Ukraine between the president and prime minister is confused in the current constitution and, in practice, has varied between 1991 and 1995. However, in June 1995 parliament voted the president full control over ministerial appointments and enhanced decree powers.

Political parties

There is no clear governing party in Ukraine and currently the parliament is dominated by independents, comprising managers of state-owned factories and collective farms, academics, and private *biznesmeni*, with no firm party links. A large number of parties do, however, function. The most important are the Ukrainian Communist Party (UCP) and its allies, the Peasant's Party of Ukraine (PPU) and the Ukrainian Socialist Party (USP); four moderate-nationalist parties, Rukh, the Ukrainian Republican Party (URP), the Congress of Ukrainian Nationalists (CUN), and the Democratic Party of Ukraine (DPU); two extreme-nationalist bodies, the Ukrainian National Assembly (UNA) and the Ukrainian Conservative Republican Party (UCRP); and six small centrist parties, the Inter-Regional Reform Block (IRRB), led by President Kuchma, the Ukrainian Democratic Renaissance Party (UDRP), the Civil Congress of Ukraine (CCU), the Social Democratic Party of Ukraine (SDPU), the Labour Party, and the Christian Democratic Party of Ukraine (CDPU).

The UCP was the dominant and only permitted political party in Ukraine until 1990. It was banned in October 1991, but was relegalized in October 1993 and emerged as the largest single party in parliament after elections held between March and November 1994. The UCP, led by Petro Simonenko, stands for closer political and economic ties with Russia and a partial return to central planning. Ideologically, it is supported by the 1.6 million-member PPU (estd. 1992), which seeks to retain the collective farm system and opposes privatization, and the 10,000-member USP, formed in 1991 as a breakaway from the UCP and led by Oleksandr

Moroz, who became speaker of the Supreme Council in May 1994.

The moderate-nationalist Rukh emerged in 1988 as the Ukrainian People's Movement for Restructuring, an umbrella 'popular front' body which pressed for political pluralism and independence from the Soviet Union. It became a formal political party in 1993 and claims 60,000 full members and 500,000 associate members. Its leader is Vyacheslav Chornovil.

The 12,000-member URP was formed in 1990 as a successor to the Ukrainian Helsinki Union (estd. 1988) and the 4,000-member DPU was established in 1990. Both advocate withdrawal from the Commonwealth of Independent States (CIS).

The SDPU, formed in 1990, advocates the creation of a federal Ukraine.

Latest elections

The most recent elections to Ukraine's Supreme Council were held in two rounds on 27 March and 10 April 1994. Only 49 of the 450 contested seats were filled in the first round and a further 289 in the second round. Further repeat elections had to be held in July, August, and November 1994 for seats where turnout fell below the level of 50% required, by Ukrainian electoral law, to validate contests. However, the overall turnout was 75% in the first round and 66% in the run-off second round. Of the 338 seats filled by the end of the second round, nearly half the deputies, 163, were unaffiliated, but many were members of the old provincial *nomenklatura* (communist ruling class). The largest single-party grouping was the UCP, with 86 deputies, to whom were closely allied the Peasant Party and Ukrainian Socialist Party, with 18 and 14 seats respectively. The second largest party was Rukh, with 20 seats. The moderate nationalist URP won 8 seats and the Congress of Ukrainian Nationalists, 5 seats; the extreme-nationalist UNA and UCRP won 3 and 2 seats respectively; and the six centrist parties noted in the *Political parties* section won 17 seats between them. The first round was contested by 5,833 candidates, three-quarters of whom were independents. This was encouraged by the electoral law which does not permit party affiliations to be printed on ballot papers.

The latest presidential election was held, in two rounds, on 26 June and 19 July 1994. Seven candidates contested the first round in which the incumbent president, Leonid Kravchuk, attracted 37.7% of the vote, while the former prime minister, Leonid Kuchma, captured 31.3%, and the Supreme Council chair, Oleksandr Moroz, 13%. In the run-off race, Kuchma, securing 52% of the vote, unexpectedly defeated Kravchuk, who polled only 45%. Kuchma, backed by the UCP, swept Russified eastern Ukraine and Crimea, while Kravchuk, supported by Ukrainian nationalists, won 90% of the vote in large tracts of western Ukraine. Turnout was 71%.

Political history

'Ukraine' means 'borderland' and Ukrainians belong to the southern branch of Eastern Slavs. Their country formed the heartland of the medieval state of Kievan Rus which emerged in the 9th century. Uniting Ukrainians, Russians

(Muscovites), and Belarussians, it became the leading power in eastern Europe, before being destroyed by Mongol invasion in the 13th century. Christianity was adopted from Byzantium in 988 AD and the region came under Catholic Polish rule from the 14th century, with the peasantry being reduced to serfdom. In 1648 there was a revolt against Polish oppression led by Cossacks, composed originally of runaway serfs, and a militarist state was established by *hetman* (elected leader) Bohdan Khmelnytsky (d. 1657). In 1667 East and West Ukraine were partitioned between Muscovy and Poland.

Under the Russian tsar, Peter I, the publication of Ukrainian books was banned in 1720. Later, in 1783, serfdom was introduced into Eastern Ukraine, or 'Little Russia', as it was known. In the late 18th century, Russia also secured control over all of Western Ukraine, except for Galicia in the far west, which was annexed by Austria in 1772. The 19th century witnessed a Ukrainian cultural revival and the establishment of secret nationalist political organizations, especially in Galicia, where Austrian rule was relatively liberal. During the late 19th and early 20th centuries there was rapid economic development and urbanization in the fertile and mineral-rich Russian Ukraine, but under the later tsars suppression of Ukrainian culture and 'Russification' intensified.

In January 1918, after the overthrow of the tsar, an independent Ukrainian People's Republic was proclaimed, allying itself with the Central Powers (Germany and Austria–Hungary), although a Soviet government was established in Kharkov in the east. The Germans installed a conservative *hetman* regime, which was popularly overthrown at the close of World War I. After two years of civil war, Western Ukraine (Galicia–Volhymia) was transferred to Polish rule, while the rest of the country came under Soviet control, becoming a constituent republic of the USSR in December 1922. In the mid-1920s a conciliatory policy of 'Ukrainization' was pursued. However, during the 1930s, under the Soviet leadership of Joseph Stalin, there was a mass purge of intellectuals, *kulaks* (rich farmers), and the destruction of the Ukrainian Autocephalous (Independent) Orthodox Church. During the manmade 'collectivization famine' of 1932–33 at least 7 million peasants died.

Polish-controlled Western Ukraine was occupied by the Red Army from September 1939 until the Nazi German invasion of the USSR in June 1941. This led to mass deportations and exterminations of more than 5 million Ukrainians and Ukrainian Jews. In 1944 Moscow ordered the deportation en masse to Central Asia of Crimean Tatars, who were accused of collaboration. After World War II, Soviet-ruled Ukraine was enlarged to include territories formerly under Polish (Western Ukraine), Czechoslovak (Transcarpathian Ukraine), and Romanian (North Bukovina and part of Bessarabia) control and became a founding member of the United Nations (UN) in 1945.

Western Ukraine remained the site of partisan resistance by the Ukrainian Insurgent Army (UPA) until the early 1950s and, as part of a 'sovietization' campaign, there were mass arrests and deportations to Siberia of 500,000 people and inward migration of ethnic Russians. The Uniate Church was proscribed in 1946 and forcibly merged with the Russian

Orthodox Church. After the death of Stalin in 1953, Ukraine was treated in a more conciliatory fashion by Nikita Khrushchev, Soviet leader until 1964, who had been the Ukrainian Communist Party (UCP) leader between 1938 and 1947. In February 1954, to 'celebrate' the 300th anniversary of Slavic 'fraternal union', Crimea was transferred back to Ukraine's jurisdiction and in the 1960s there was a Ukrainian literary revival and growth of the dissident movement.

In 1972–73 a crackdown on dissent was launched and Vladimir Shcherbitsky, a close ally of the Soviet leader Leonid Brezhnev, replaced the more liberal Petro Shelest as UCP leader. However, from the mid-1970s Helsinki Monitoring Groups became active and the Uniate Church continued to operate underground in Western Ukraine. In the wake of the Chernobyl nuclear power plant disaster in April 1986, which may, indirectly, have claimed thousands of lives from radiation sickness and contaminated much surrounding agricultural land, a popular environmentalist movement, Green World (estd. 1987), emerged in Ukraine.

Emboldened by the glasnost (political openness) and perestroika (economic restructuring) initiatives launched by Mikhail Gorbachev, who became the Soviet Union's new leader in 1985, nationalist and proreform demonstrations increased. At the forefront of this popular movement was the People's Movement of Ukraine for Restructuring (Rukh), which was established in November 1988. In September 1989, following a strike by Donbass coalminers, Shcherbitsky was ousted as UCP leader; in December 1989 the Uniate Church was allowed to reregister; and in the March 1990 republic Supreme Soviet elections, 'reform communist' and Rukh candidates in the Democratic Bloc polled strongly in urban areas and western Ukraine. In all, the Democratic Bloc won 170 of the 450 Supreme Soviet seats and in July 1990 the new parliament declared the republic's economic and political sovereignty.

Ukrainian nationalist sentiment developed a head of steam from the autumn of 1990. In October 1990 protest marches by 100,000 students in Kiev forced the resignation of Prime Minister Vitaly Masol and in the spring of 1991 striking Donbass coalminers called for the resignation of the Soviet president, Mikhail Gorbachev. The republic participated in the March 1991 all-Union referendum on the future of the USSR, with 70% approving Gorbachev's proposals for a 'renewed federation'. However, in Western Ukraine an additional question on independence received 90% support. In May 1991, the republic's Supreme Soviet agreed to hold a referendum on independence later in the year. Ukraine's president, Leonid Kravchuk (b. 1934), formerly the UCP's pragmatic ideology chief, was slow to condemn the August 1991 attempted anti-Gorbachev coup launched in Moscow by communist hardliners, which had provoked a series of Rukh-led prodemocracy rallies in Lviv (Lvov). However, after the coup's failure, Kravchuk swiftly donned nationalist colours, banning the UCP and declaring the republic's provisional independence on 24 August 1991, pending the referendum. There was a resounding 90% vote in favour of independence in the 1 December 1991 plebiscite and, simultaneously, Kravchuk was popularly elected president. He captured 62% of the vote, defeating the ex-dissident Vyacheslav Chornovil who, as leader of Rukh and leader of the

radical Lviv regional council, attracted a 23% share of the vote, and five other challengers.

Ukraine joined the Commonwealth of Independent States (CIS) on its inception on 21 December 1991, and its independence was swiftly recognized by Canada, home to around 1,000,000 Ukrainians, as well as by Ukraine's central European neighbours, the United States, and the European Union. In January 1992, Ukraine was admitted into the Helsinki Conference on Security and Cooperation in Europe (CSCE, later the OSCE).

Ukraine inherited a substantial nuclear arsenal. It was pledged by President Kravchuk that the country would ratify fully the START-1 treaty and become a nuclear-free state by 1994, while establishing an independent 200,000–400,000-strong army. However, Ukrainian nationalists were in favour of retaining some nuclear weapons. A programme of market-centred economic reform and privatization was launched, with some prices being freed in January 1992. Coupons were introduced as a secondary currency to the rouble, pending the creation of an independent currency, the grivna. However, the continued strength of excommunist apparatchiks in the bureaucracy and parliament served to frustrate successful implementation of the economic programme between 1991 and 1994, with prices being reregulated from February 1992. There were also postindependence quarrels with Russia over the division of the Red Army and the Black Sea fleet, over which Russia and Ukraine held joint sovereignty, and unsatisfactory relations with the Crimean autonomous republic, which, with its 70% ethnic Russian community, issued an independence declaration of its own in September 1991.

In October 1992 Leonid Kuchma (b. 1938), a former manager of the world's largest missile factory at Dnepropetrovsk, became prime minister and attempted to steer through parliament a programme of gradual market reform and closer economic relations with Russia. He assumed power at a time when the Ukrainian economy was rapidly collapsing. GDP declined by 10% in 1991, 15% in 1992, and 20% in 1993, the annual inflation rate shot up to more than 3,000% during 1993 and there was periodic labour unrest. Unable to gain parliamentary support for more radical reforms, Kuchma resigned as premier in September 1993 and President Kravchuk began to take firmer control over government policy, with a more cautious, centrally controlled economic strategy being adopted.

Elections to the Ukrainian parliament in March–April 1994, the first to be held since independence, resulted in the UCP and allied parties continuing as the largest force and in June 1994 the excommunist Vitaly Masol, who had been premier between 1987–90, became prime minister. In the presidential elections of June–July 1994 the country's division between a nationalist west and a pro-Russian eastern majority was clearly demonstrated. The incumbent president, Kravchuk, backed effectively by the nationalist Rukh, polled strongly in Western Ukraine, winning as much as 94% of the vote in the regions of Lviv, Ternopil, and Ivano-Frankivsk. However, his challenger, the former prime minister, Leonid Kuchma, backed by the UCP and advocating closer ties with Russia, swept Eastern and Central Ukraine, capturing as much as 90% of the vote in Crimea. As a consequence, Kuchma, somewhat surprisingly, was elected the new state president, defeating Kravchuk on the second run-off ballot by a margin of 52% to 45%.

The new Kuchma administration and Supreme Council ratified the Nuclear Non-Proliferation Treaty in November 1994, giving up its inherited nuclear arsenal and receiving, in return, pledges of substantial American economic aid. This brought about a significant, and unexpected, improvement in Ukraine's relations with the West. A large $2.5 billion loan was provided to Ukraine by the IMF on the condition that a tough monetary stabilization plan, entailing tight public spending restrictions, price liberalization, and privatization, was adhered to. This brought the monthly inflation rate down to 5% by the spring of 1995. In March 1995, in an effort to speed up the pace of market-centred economic change, President Kuchma replaced Vitaly Masol, an anti-reformer, as prime minister with Evhen Marchuk, a former head of the Ukrainian Secret Service, who was nevertheless viewed as a pragmatist. However, the communist-dominated Supreme Council continued to block radical reforms, with the consequence that by 1995 barely 2% of state enterprises had been privatized. In April 1995 parliament sought to oust the proreform Marchuk government. However, in June 1995, faced by the threat that Kuchma would hold a national referendum asking Ukrainians whether they 'trust President or parliament', it relented and approved a 'constitutional accord' which gave the president full control over ministerial appointments, without needing to refer to parliament for approval, and enhanced the president's decree powers.

During 1994 the autonomous republic of Crimea became increasingly assertive in its drive for greater autonomy. In January 1994 the pro-Russian Yuri Meshkov was elected the republic's president and, following a March 1994 referendum on autonomy, in May 1994 the Crimean Assembly approved an effective sovereignty declaration. Enjoying a personal mandate in Crimea, President Kuchma and Ukraine's parliament reacted in March 1995 by annulling Crimea's constitution and sacking Meshkov. In April 1995 Kuchma assumed direct control over the Crimean Republic for four months. The Russian government of President Yeltsin acquiesced, insisting that Crimea remained an internal affair for Ukraine. However, a friendship and cooperation treaty between Ukraine and Russia remained to be signed and Ukraine was still only an 'associate member' of the CIS's economic union and an 'observer' at its Inter-Governmental Assembly.

YUGOSLAVIA

The Federal Republic of Yugoslavia (FRY),
including the republics of Serbia and Montenegro
Federativna Republika Jugoslavija

Capital: Belgrade

Social and economic data
Area: 102,173 km^2
Population: 10,600,000*
Pop. density per km^2: 104*
Urban population: 50%**

Literacy rate: 93%**
GDP: $15,900 million**; per-capita GDP $1,500**
Government defence spending (% of GDP): 10.6%**
Currency: New Yugoslav dinar
Economy type: middle income
Labour force in agriculture: 26%**

*1994
**1992

Ethnic composition
According to the 1991 census, 62% of the population of the rump federal republic is ethnic Serb, 17% Albanian, 5% Montenegrin, 3% 'Yugoslav', and 3% Muslim. Serbs predominate in the republic of Serbia, where they form, excluding the autonomous areas of Kosovo and Vojvodina, 85% of the population and in Vojvodina they comprise 55% of the population. Albanians constitute 77% of the population of Kosovo; Montenegrins comprise 69% of the population of the republic of Montenegro; and Muslims predominate in the Sandzak region which straddles the Serbian and Montenegrin borders. Since 1992 an influx of Serb refugees from Bosnia and Kosovo has increased the proportion of Serbs in Serbia, while many ethnic Hungarians have left Vojvodina, and, faced by harassment by Serb militias, an estimated 500,000 Albanians have left Kosovo. Serbo-Croat in its Serbian form, written in Cyrillic script, is the main language, but Albanian is widely spoken in Kosovo.

Religions
Nearly 75% of the population adheres to the Eastern Orthodox faith, belonging to the Serbian Orthodox Church and the Montenegrin Orthodox Church, which was re-established in November 1993, while 19%, chiefly in Kosovo and Montenegro, follows Sunni Islamic beliefs. There is also a small Roman Catholic minority in Vojvodina.

Political features

State type: emergent democratic
Date of state formation: 1918/1992*
Political structure: federal
Executive: limited presidential
Assembly: two-chamber
Party structure: multiparty
Human rights rating: N/A
International affiliations: AG (observer), CERN (observer), G-24, IAEA, NAM, OSCE (suspended), UN (suspended), WTO

*The present 'rump federation' was formed in 1992

Local and regional government

As the rump of a larger state, the present federal republic consists of the two republics of Montenegro (area: 13,812 km²; population: 0.65 million) and Serbia (area: 88,361 km; population: 9.95 million) and, within Serbia, the autonomous provinces of Vojvodina (area: 21,508 km²; population: 2.4 million) and Kosovo–Metohija (area: 10,817 km²; population: 2 million). Each republic and autonomous province has its own elected assembly, although the Kosovo assembly was dissolved in 1990 by the government of the republic of Serbia. Within each republic and province there are locally elected councils.

Head of state

President Zoran Lilic, since 1993

Head of government

Prime Minister Radoje Kontic, since 1993

Political leaders since 1970*

1944–80 Marshal Tito (SKJ)**, 1992–93 Dobrica Cosic (SPS)***, 1993– Zoran Lilic (SPS)***, 1989– Slobodan Milošević (SPS)****, 1990– Momir Bulatovic (SDPCG)*****

*There was an annually rotating, republic-based leadership from 1980–92
**Communist Party leader
***Federal president
****President of the Serbian republic
*****President of Montenegro

Political system

Formerly a socialist federation of six republics, following the breakaway of Slovenia, Croatia, Bosnia-Herzegovina, and Macedonia in 1991–92, a new constitution was adopted in April 1992 for the 'rump federation' of the republics of Serbia and Montenegro. This has provided for a two-chamber Federal Assembly (Savezna Skupstina), consisting of a 138-member Chamber of Citizens and a 40-member Chamber of the Republics. In the Chamber of Citizens 108 seats are directly elected from the republic of Serbia and 30 from Montenegro. Half of the Serbian seats are elected by single-member constituencies through a majoritarian system of voting and half by a party list system. Six of the Montenegro seats are elected from single-member constituencies and the rest by the party list system. The Chamber of Republics has 20 members selected by each of the two republican parlia-

ments so as to reflect party strengths. The combined assemblies elect an executive federal president who chooses a prime minister to chair a cabinet of some 15 members. The constitution provides that the president and prime minister must be drawn from different republics. There is also a Supreme Defence Council, which comprises the federal president and prime minister, the presidents of Serbia and Montenegro, and the chief of general staff of the Yugoslav army.

In practice, although the Federal Assembly is empowered to declare a state of emergency in a constituent republic without reference to its assembly and the federation is supreme in defence matters, the authority of the federal government is, in general, much less than that of the individual republics of Serbia and Montenegro. Each functions as a virtually independent state, with its own legislature and political executive. Serbia has a 250-member National Assembly and a directly elected executive president, while in Montenegro the Assembly comprises 125 members and the president is also directly elected. Under the Serbian constitution of September 1992 the formerly autonomous regions of Vojvodina and Kosovo–Metohija within Serbia no longer have autonomy.

Political parties

The dominant parties in the two constituent republics of Yugoslavia are the Socialist Party of Serbia (SPS) and the Montenegrin Social Democratic Party (SDPCG), which are reform-socialist heirs to the League of Communists of Yugoslavia (SKJ), formerly the ruling party in a wider federation. Radical nationalist, centre-right, leftist and ethnic-orientated parties also operate in each republic, the most important being the Serbian Radical Party (SRS); the People's Assembly Party (NSS), formerly known as the Serbian Democratic Movement (DEPOS); the Democratic Party (DS); the Democratic Party of Serbia (DSS); the Democratic Community of Vojvodina Hungarians (DZVM); the Democratic Party of Albanians/Party of Democratic Action (DPA/PDA); and the New Socialist Party of Montenegro (NSPM).

The SKJ was founded in April 1919 under the title of the Socialist Workers' Party of Yugoslavia (Communist) (SWPY) by a union of socialist organizations based in Serbia, Croatia, Slovenia, and Bosnia. With a membership of 60,000, it changed its name to the Communist Party of Yugoslavia (CPY) in June 1920 and in the Yugoslav Constituent Assembly elections of that year emerged as the third largest grouping, capturing 0.2 million votes and 59 seats. A year later it was banned and forced underground, its membership dwindling to several hundred during the early 1930s. The Croatian-born Josip Broz (Tito) assumed the party's leadership in 1937, and began building up membership. He later developed it into a popular 'Partisan', anti-Nazi, liberation force during World War II, so that it was eventually able to assume power in November 1943. The designation SKJ was adopted in 1952 to symbolize its alignment on a new, non-Soviet-linked, socialist course. Membership of the SKJ in 1987 stood at 2.10 million, corresponding to 9.1% of the total population and in December 1994 Branko Loza became the party's new president.

The SPS was formed in 1990 through a merger of the SKJ's Serbian branch, the League of Communists of Serbia, and the Socialist Alliance of the Working People of Serbia. Under the leadership since 1986 of Slobodan Milošević, a populist demagogue, it has become increasingly identified with Serb nationalism.

The SDPCG was known until 1991 as the League of Communists of Montenegro. It supports the continuation of a Yugoslav federation, but is less nationalist than the SPS.

The SRS is an extreme right-wing Serbian nationalist body, whose paramilitary wing, the Chetnik movement, was implicated in fighting in Croatia and Bosnia during 1991–93. In November 1993 the party's leadership, including Dr Vojislav Seselj, commander of the Chetniks, was arrested on charges of the commission of war crimes in Croatia and Bosnia and in September 1994 Seselj was jailed for four months after being involved in a scuffle in parliament. The SRS abolished its Chetnik paramilitary wing in April 1994, but in January 1995 half of its members left to join a new ultra-right-wing party, the Nikola Pasic Serbian Radical Party (SRS–NP), formed by Jovan Glamocanin.

The NSS is a centrist Christian-democratic opposition force, led by Slobodan Rakitic, which was known until January 1995 as the DEPOS bloc. DEPOS was an umbrella opposition grouping which was dominated by the right-wing nationalist Serbian Renewal Movement (SPO), led by Vuk Draskovic. The SPO's advocacy from 1992 of the forcible creation of a 'Greater Serbia' encompassing the Serb-occupied Krajina region of Croatia and most of Bosnia-Herzegovina led to more moderate elements within DEPOS seeking to sever the SPO's links with the broader movement.

The DS and DSS are moderate nationalist forces which are allied with the SPS and SDPCG in the federal coalition government.

The DZVM, formed in 1990, supports the interests of the ethnic Hungarian minority in Vojvodina, and the DPA/PDA, the ethnic Albanian community, along with the pro-independence Democratic Alliance of Kosovo, which is led by Dr Ibrahim Rugova.

The NSPM was formed in 1992 through the merger of the Socialist Party of Montenegro and the People's Party.

Latest elections

The most recent federal elections were held on 20 December 1992 and resulted in the SPS winning 47 of the 138 seats in the Chamber of Citizens; the SDPCG, 17; the SRS, 34; DEPOS, 20; the NSPM, 9; the DS, 5; and the DZVM, 3 seats.

The last elections in Serbia were held on 20 December 1993 and resulted in the SPS, with 37% of the vote, capturing 123 of the available 250 National Assembly seats, an advance of 22 seats on its performance in December 1992. DEPOS won 45 seats (down 4); the SRS, damaged by the arrest of its leaders in November 1993 on charges of the commission of war crimes during fighting in Croatia and Bosnia, 39 seats (down 34); the DS, 29 (up 22); the DSS, 7; the DZVM, 5; and the DPA, 2. Turnout was 62%, but the poll was largely boycotted by ethnic Albanians in Kosovo and Muslims in the Sandzak region. The most recent Serbian presidential election was held on 20 December 1992 and was won by the incumbent Slobodan Milošević, who, polling strongly in small towns and rural areas, captured 56% of the vote, defeating Milan Panić, the federal prime minister, who

attracted 34% of the vote but claimed that there had been wide-scale electoral malpractice.

Assembly elections were last held in Montenegro on 20 December 1992 and were won by the SDPCG, which attracted 43% of the vote.

Political history

Formerly under Roman rule, during the early medieval period the republics of what became Yugoslavia in 1918 existed as substantially independent entities. The kingdom of Serbia was the most important, being the nucleus of an extensive Balkan empire during the 14th century. From the late 14th to the mid-15th centuries much of eastern, southern, and central Yugoslavia, Bosnia-Herzegovina, Macedonia, and Serbia, was conquered by Turks and incorporated into the Ottoman Empire. Mountainous Montenegro was an exception and survived as a sovereign principality. During this period northwestern Yugoslavia, consisting of the republics of Croatia and Slovenia, became part of the Austro-Hungarian Habsburg Empire. They were to enjoy, however, a greater measure of political autonomy than the Turk lands.

Uprisings against Turkish rule in the early 19th century won Serbia a similar degreee of autonomy, before full independence was achieved in 1878. The new kingdom of Serbia proceeded to enlarge its territory, at the expense of Turkey and Bulgaria, during the Balkan Wars of 1912–13. However, it was not until December 1918, following the collapse of the Austro-Hungarian Empire, that Croatia and Slovenia were 'liberated' from foreign control. A new 'Kingdom of the Serbs, Croats and Slovenes' now came into existence, with the Serbian Peter Karageorgevich (1844–1921), Peter I, assuming its leadership, as a constitutional monarch, and working with an elected legislative assembly. Montenegro joined the union after its citizens had voted for the deposition of their own ruler, King Nicholas.

Peter I died in August 1921 and was succeeded by his son and regent, Alexander I (1888–1934), who renamed the country Yugoslavia, or 'Nation of the Southern ('Yugo') Slavs'. Faced with opposition from Croatian federalists at home and from the Italians abroad, in January 1929 he established a Serbian-dominated military dictatorship. The country remained backward during this period, with more than three-quarters of the population dependent on agricultural activities.

Alexander I was assassinated in October 1934 in Marseilles by a Macedonian with Croatian dissident links. His young son, Peter II, succeeded him and a regency under the boy's uncle, Paul, was set up and came under increasing influence from Nazi Germany and Italy. The regency was briefly overthrown in a coup by pro-Allied airforce officers in March 1941, precipitating a successful invasion by German troops. Peter II (1923–70; reigned 1934–45) fled to safety in England, while two guerrilla groups began resistance activities. One was the pro-royalist Serbian-based Chetniks, or 'Army of the Fatherland', led by General Draza Mihailović (1893–1946), and the other the communist Partisans, or 'National Liberation Army', led by Josip Broz, to be later known as Marshal Tito (1892–1980).

The communist Partisans, comprising, towards the end of the war, 800,000 men, gained the upper hand in their struggle with the Axis forces and at liberated Jajce, in Bosnia, Tito established a provisional government, called the 'Executive Committee of National Liberation', in November 1943. Two years later, in November 1945, following the expulsion, with only limited Soviet assistance, of the remaining German forces, a new Yugoslav Federal People's Republic was proclaimed.

Following Constituent Assembly elections, based on a single list of candidates for the communist-dominated People's Front, a new Soviet-style federal constitution was adopted in January 1946 which established the dominance of the Communist Party of Yugoslavia (CPY, known from 1952 as the League of Communists, or SKJ) and during the succeeding years remaining royalist opposition was expunged. Although at first closely linked with the USSR, Tito objected to Soviet 'hegemonism', broke with Stalin in 1948, and proceeded to introduce his own independent brand of communism. This was given shape in the Constitutional Law of January 1953, which established the framework of a more liberal and decentralized system, based on the concept of workers' self-management and supporting the notion of private farming. As a result, by the 1980s 85% of Yugoslavia's cropped area was privately tilled. Having established himself as the clearly dominant force in the Yugoslav polity, Tito also assumed the newly created post of president of the Republic in 1953. This was a position which he was to hold until his death in May 1980.

In foreign affairs, the country, which had been expelled from Cominform in June 1948 and which remained outside the Warsaw Treaty Organization and Comecon, sought to establish for itself an intermediate position between East and West, playing a leading role in the creation of the nonaligned movement in 1961.

Domestically, the nation endured continuing regional discontent, particularly in Croatia, where a violent separatist movement gained ground in the 1960s and early 1970s. To deal with these problems, Tito initially encouraged further decentralization and devolution of power to the constituent republics in amendments to the constitution which were introduced between 1966 and 1968. In addition, a system of collective leadership and a regular rotation of office posts was introduced in July 1971, in an effort to prevent the emergence of regional cliques. Partial corrective recentralization was, however, a feature of the February 1974 constitution.

On Tito's death in May 1980 the position of executive president, which he had been accorded for life under the terms of the 1974 constitution, was effectively abolished and a collective and rotating (between republics) presidential leadership assumed power instead. However, this new collective leadership, lacking a dominant, 'guiding hand' personality at its head, became subject to internal cleavages, resulting in fudged policy paralysis, and confused demarcation lines emerging between differing federal and republican executive bodies.

In these circumstances, there was a recrudescence of regionalist conflict, with a serious popular movement emerging in 1981–82 among the Albanians of Kosovo autonomous province who campaigned for full republican status. These demonstrations had to be suppressed by the armed forces. In Bosnia-Herzegovina and Croatia, unrest emerged among the

Muslim and Catholic communities respectively during the mid–1980s. This regionalist discontent was aggravated by a general decline in living standards after 1980, caused by a mounting level of foreign debt, whose servicing absorbed 10% of GDP, and a spiralling inflation rate, which reached 200% in 1988 and 700% in 1989.

In 1987–88, the federal government, under the leadership of Prime Minister Branko Mikulic (b. 1928), a Bosnian, introduced a radical 'market socialist' package, in an effort to restructure the economy. This involved the freeing of prices and wages from residual controls, the introduction of a federal value-added tax (VAT), and a new bankruptcy law. The private sector was extended further and foreign inward investment, in special free-trade zones, was encouraged. There was also a general switch towards an 'indicative', rather than central, planning system. The short-term consequence of this programme was, however, an austerity wage freeze, sparking off a wave of industrial strikes, and a rise in the unemployment level to above 1 million, or 15% of the workforce. Following a wave of strikes and mounting internal disorder, Mikulić was replaced as prime minister in January 1989 by Ante Marković, a reformist Croatian.

In the political sphere, constitutional amendment proposals were put forward by the federal presidency in 1988, aimed at enhancing the federal government's authority and abolishing the right of veto enjoyed by republican and provincial assemblies. In addition, an emergency 'Extraordinary Party Conference' was convened in May 1988, in an effort to formulate fresh solutions to the economic and political crisis. At this meeting, the system of regional rotation employed for filling the top party post was temporarily abandoned, and the new SKJ leader, Stipe Suvar, was elected in a competitive ballot. The party remained acutely divided, however, between regionally based liberal Slovenian and conservative Serbian wings on the questions of decentralization and democratization.

However, the most significant development from the late 1980s was the emergence of a new prospective national 'strongman' (*vozd*) in the form of the SKJ's Serbian party leader since 1986, Slobodan Milošević (b. 1941). A populist hardliner, Milošević lent his support to grassroots campaigns to terminate Kosovo and Vojvodina's autonomous province status and fully integrate the regions within Serbia. These aims were substantially secured in March 1989 when the Vojvodina and Kosovo assemblies, following Serbian pressure, endorsed earlier changes to the Serbian constitution which served to return control over their defence, state security, foreign relations, justice, and planning to Serbia. These actions immediately triggered a wave of violent ethnic riots in Kosovo which claimed at least 29 lives. In addition, Milošević was seen to have been behind street protests in Titograd in October 1988 which forced the resignation of the entire state and party leadership of the Montenegro republic and its replacement with pro-Serbian cadres. His 'Serbian nationalist' stance and conservative policy prescriptions were firmly opposed, however, by the rich northwestern republics of Croatia and Slovenia. The growing schism within the ruling SKJ was confirmed in January 1990 when the party's congress had to be abandoned after a walkout by the Slovene delegation.

In late July 1990 the Serbian assembly voted to dissolve the Kosovo assembly and in September 1990 a new multiparty constitution came into force in the Serbian republic, which effectively stripped Kosovo and Vojvodina of their autonomy. Kosovo's ethnic Albanian community reacted by calling a general strike on 3 September 1991 and by convening an underground parliament that proclaimed a new, unrecognized constitution for the province. In multiparty elections held in Serbia in December 1990 Milošević was re-elected president of the republic by a landslide margin and the communists, renamed the Socialist Party of Serbia (SPS), also retained a convincing assembly majority. The communists were also re-elected in Montenegro. However, in Croatia, Slovenia, Bosnia-Herzegovina, and Macedonia, following multiparty elections held between April and November 1990, new noncommunist government coalitions came to power. These called for the establishment of a looser confederation. Prime Minister Marković was sympathetic to these wishes and formed the Alliance of Reform Forces in July 1990 which advocated the preservation of Yugoslav unity within a pluralist federation. However, Milošević refused to compromise. Instead, as Croatia and Slovenia pressed for secession from the federation, the Serb minority community in Croatia, activated by memories of wartime persecution by Croatia's Ustasa regime, was encouraged to demand the creation of autonomous regions to be allied within a new 'Greater Serbia'. In March 1991 there were large anti-Milošević and anticommunist demonstrations in Belgrade by a crowd of 30,000. These spread to Novi Sad in Vojvodina, but were crushed violently by riot police and tanks.

By the spring of 1991, following Croatia and Slovenia's issuing in February 1991 of a joint notice of secession, to become effective in June, Yugoslavia's collective presidency had broken down and federal institutions had become progressively Serbianized. On 15 March 1991 the state president, Borisav Jovic, a Serbian, dramatically resigned, after other members of the collective state presidency refused to support his plan to introduce martial law across the country. There were fears that his departure might presage a military takeover in Yugoslavia.

On 25 June 1991 both Slovenia and Croatia issued unilateral declarations of independence, or 'dissociation', from the Yugoslav federation, though declaring their continued willingness to discuss the formation of a new, much looser Yugoslav confederation. This precipitated, from 27 June 1991, military confrontations between the federal army and republican forces, with more than 100 people being killed in four days of fighting. A European Community (EC) delegation of foreign ministers brokered a cease-fire at the end of June, including a three-month suspension in implementation of Slovenia's declaration of independence and withdrawal of the Yugoslav National Army (JNA) from Slovenia. However, between July and Sept 1991 civil war intensified in ethnically mixed Croatia, between Serbian Chetnik guerrillas and Croats, particularly near its eastern border (especially the towns of Osijek and Vukovar) and in the Krajina region, where 250,000 Serbs lived. Several hundred died in fighting during July 1991 and a similar number in August. It became uncertain who (politicians or the military) now controlled the country at the federal level. Furthermore, the JNA had

become factionalized, with many units refusing to heed the call by President Stipe Mesic, a noncommunist Croatian, for a return to barracks.

A new cease-fire was ordered by the federal presidency on 7 August 1991, after the EC – which viewed Serbia as the real aggressor, seeking, via the JNA and rebel Serb militias within Croatia, to carve out a new 'Greater Serbia' – threatened to apply economic sanctions against the republic. However, again it failed to hold and by September 1991 around a third of Croatia was under Serb control and at least 120,000 people had become refugees. Oil-rich Croatia responded by imposing an oil supply blockade on Serbia and attacking federal army barracks within the republic. Later in September 1991, Serbian forces attacked the Croatian port of Dubrovnik, laying siege to the city. This persuaded the EC to impose an economic embargo on the republic in November 1991.

Concerned at Serb expansionist ambitions, the republic of Bosnia-Herzegovina proclaimed its sovereignty in October 1991 and a referendum on independence was held in Macedonia in September 1991. The latter received overwhelming support, although it was boycotted by the Albanian and Serbian minorities. In Kosovo, an unofficial referendum on sovereignty was also held in September 1991 and similarly received overwhelming support. A provisional unofficial government was elected, being accorded immediate recognition by Albania. The Yugoslav federal government effectively collapsed between September and October 1991 as Croat, Slovene, Bosnian, and Macedonian representatives resigned from federal bodies, including the federal presidency. On 3 October 1991 four of the eight members of the collective state presidency, drawn from Serbia, Montenegro, Kosovo, and Vojvodina, voted to take on the powers of the Yugoslav assembly, despite the meeting falling short of the five members required for a quorum. In effect, Serbia was left dominating a 'rump Yugoslavia', comprising two ethnically close republics and two autonomous regions, one of which, Kosovo, was secessionist minded. On 5 December 1991 Stipe Mesic resigned from the federal presidency, declaring that 'Yugoslavia no longer exists'. On 20 December 1991 the federal prime minister, Ante Marković, also resigned.

In early January 1992 a peace plan was successfully brokered in Sarajevo by UN envoy Cyrus Vance which provided for an immediate cease-fire in Croatia, withdrawal of the Yugoslav army, and the deployment of 10,000 UN troops in contested Krajina and eastern and western Slavonia until a political settlement was worked out. This accord was disregarded by the breakaway Serb leader in Krajina, Milan Babic, but was recognized by the main Croatian and Serbian forces. The independence of Slovenia and Croatia was recognized by the EC and the United States on 15 January 1992 and that of Bosnia-Herzegovina in April 1992. Macedonia also declared its independence in January 1992.

In April 1992 a new federal constitution was adopted for the 'rump Yugoslavia' and in the May–June 1992 federal elections Dobrica Cosic, a Serb writer, was elected federal president and Milan Panic became prime minister in July 1992. In concurrent elections held illegally in Kosovo, the ethnic Albanian-dominated Democratic Alliance of Kosovo secured a clear victory and proclaimed the foundation of a new 'Republic of Kosovo', with Ibrahim Rugova as president. Meanwhile fighting continued in Bosnia-Herzegovina, where Serb irregulars, driven by the vision of a 'Greater Serbia', seized 70% of the republic's land area, with thousands of non-Serbs being killed or evicted from their homes as part of an abhorrent policy of 'ethnic cleansing'. Concern for ethnic minorities in Serbia, notably in Kosovo where ethnic Albanians were being subjected to harassment by Serb militias led by Zeljko Raznjatovic (known as 'Arkan'), and Serbia's attempted 'carve-up' of the newly independent Bosnian republic prompted the United States to deny recognition of the 'new Yugoslavia' and to call for the country's expulsion from the Conference on Security and Cooperation in Europe (CSCE, later the OSCE) and its removal from its UN seat.

Fresh elections to the republican and federal parliaments, held on 20 December 1992, resulted in the former communist SPS and Montenegrin Social Democratic Party (SDPCG) emerging as the largest single party in each republic, with a plurality of the vote, and Slobodan Milošević being re-elected as Serbia's president. However, the neofascist Serbian Radical Party (SRS) and the nationalist Democratic Movement of Serbia (DEPOS) also polled strongly, forcing the SPS to share power in a socialist-nationalist coalition government in Serbia. Milošević's opponent in the Serbian presidential election was the federal prime minister, Milan Panic, who was swiftly ousted on 29 December 1992, following defeat in a no-confidence motion and was replaced, in February 1993, by a Milošević ally, Radoje Kontic, who headed a SPS and SDPCG federal coalition government. In June 1993 the federal president, Dobrica Cosic, was also removed, at Milošević's instigation, and replaced by the pro-Milošević Zoran Lilic (b. 1953) and in new Assembly elections in Serbia in December 1993 the SPS achieved a near majority, winning 123 of the 250 available seats.

Throughout 1992–94 the economies of Serbia and Montenegro were devastated by the impact of international economic sanctions imposed, by the EC from November 1991 and by the UN in May 1992 and April 1993, as a result of the federal republic's continuing indirect support of ethnic Serbs fighting in Bosnia-Herzegovina and the Republic of Krajina, within Croatia, and its refusal to recognize Croatia and Bosnia. Output slumped to barely 30% of the prewar level,

nearly half the population were unemployed, hyperinflation, with prices rising in Serbia at the rate of 5% an hour in December 1993, exceeded the levels seen in Germany in the 1920s, and there were severe shortages of fuel, food, and medicine, precipitating a wave of strikes by industrial and transport workers. This economic hardship intensified nationalist feeling in Serbia, but was resented by Montenegrins, whose president, Momir Bulatovic, pursued an increasingly independent line.

During 1994 the Serbian leadership began to give increased emphasis to economic reconstruction. A new currency, known popularly as the 'super dinar', was introduced in January 1994. This, and the formation in February 1994 of a new national unity coalition government in Serbia, headed by a new prime minister, Mirko Marjanovic, a former company manager, and supported by the New Democracy party, formerly a member of the opposition DEPOS bloc, resulted in a sharp reduction in the inflation level. More importantly, President Milošević came to accept the need for the Serbians of Bosnia to agree to a peace plan devised by the five-nation Contact Group, comprising diplomats from Russia, the United States, France, Germany, and Britain, which would give them control over 49% of Bosnia-Herzegovina. When the Bosnian Serbs' leader, Dr Radovan Karadžić (b. 1945), rejected this proposal, the Yugoslav Federation imposed an economic blockade on the Bosnian Serbs and the Milošević-controlled Serbian media began to charge the Bosnian Serb leadership with wartime racketeering and corruption. The blockade held during 1994–95 and was rewarded by the UN suspending a number of international sanctions, including the reopening of international flights to Belgrade and the Montenegrin port of Bar. A full suspension of sanctions was promised if Yugoslavia would recognize the existence of Bosnia-Herzegovina and Croatia. In August 1995 President Milošević rejected appeals by Radovan Karadžić and Milan Martic, the respective leaders of the Bosnian and Krajina Serbs, to provide military aid as the Croatian army launched offensives against the self-proclaimed 'Republic of Serbian Krajina' and the Bosnian Serbs.

In November 1995 Serbia played a key role in the US-brokered Dayton peace accord for Bosnia-Herzegovina and finally accepted the separate existence of Croatia and Bosnia. As a consequence, in December 1995 the United States lifted its economic sanctions against Yugoslavia.

Central and Southern Africa

The region we have defined as Central and Southern Africa covers, as Table 54 shows, an area of more than 24 million square kilometres, nearly seven times larger than Northern and Western Europe, and comparable in size to Asia. It has a comparatively low population density, however: less than a quarter of that of Northern and Western Europe and less than a fifth of that of Asia. Lying mostly between the Tropic of Cancer and the Tropic of Capricorn it enjoys a mainly tropical or subtropical climate, although marked variations can be found between the Atlantic and Indian Ocean coasts and between the mountainous and low-lying areas. The great majority of the inhabitants of the region are indigenous black Africans. Even in South Africa only about 27% of the population is not of black ethnic stock.

As Table 1 in Part I reveals, 45 of the 48 states in Central and Southern Africa, or over 93%, are of post-1945 origin. Before that time virtually the entire region was controlled by one or other of the major European powers, yet the 'scramble for Africa', as it has been described, began comparatively late in the 19th century, the big 'share out' taking place between 1870 and 1914. Table 55, below, gives the distribution of 46 of the current 48 states between the European colonial powers during this period. This distribution does not necessarily indicate the European power which was the first to exploit a particular country, but the settlement finally agreed after much bargaining by the major powers during the late 19th and early 20th centuries.

Ethiopia and Eritrea, which were then one state, and Liberia were the exceptions to the rule. Ethiopia managed to retain its independence from the 11th century, and Eritrea was only briefly occupied by Italy between 1882 and 1923. Liberia was created by the American Colonization Society, as a home for liberated American slaves, and formally recognized as the Free and Independent Republic of Liberia by Britain and France in 1847.

Historically and culturally the most arresting aspect of Central and Southern Africa is its tribal nature. This has resulted in a great variety in its political systems and considerable social and political disunity. Although most of the European powers, initially at any rate, attempted to export their own tried and tested systems of democratic government, as civilizing and unifying devices, after independence most were significantly changed and adapted to suit local conditions, or were replaced with something much more authoritarian.

For example, of the 17 countries which were under British control during the first half of this century, only four, Botswana, Gambia, Mauritius, and, tentatively, Uganda, had pluralistic, democratic systems before the 1990s. The rest were either one-party states or under military rule. None of the 16 states which were part of the French colonial empire had, before the 1990s, suceeded, or even attempted, to fashion a pluralist democracy.

There are some good and valid reasons for this pattern of political systems and it would be unwise to compare them with contemporaneous states in other parts of the world in any censorious fashion. The need to cohere tribal loyalties into a sense of national identity and pride was clearly a major

imperative. Examples of what can happen if tribal feelings are allowed to run completely free are to be found in the civil wars in Nigeria and the Congo (Zaire), in the early 1960s, and the more recent civil wars in Ethiopia and Sudan and killings by Hutus and Tutsis in Burundi and Rwanda.

It should also be remembered that the cultural histories of the people of Central and Southern Africa are much different from those of many of their counterparts in other parts of the world. Tribal decision-making was conducted on the basis of discussion, leading to a consensus enunciated by the chief, and the proliferation of one-party systems is, to a great extent, a modern manifestation of this approach.

Furthermore, the comparative sophistication of Western-style political systems was not necessarily appropriate for communities where levels of literacy were still comparatively low. For example, Table 47 shows adult literacy levels of less than 40% for 47% of the states in Central and Southern Africa, compared with under 5% of the states in Central America and the Caribbean, under 11% of those in the Middle East and North Africa, and under 18% of Asian countries. Within this overall picture there are, however, considerable variations, with literacy rates ranging from under 20% in Burkina Faso, Congo, Djibouti, and Gabon to over 60% in Botswana, Ethiopia, Kenya, Mauritius, South Africa, Zaire, Zambia, and Zimbabwe. The high literacy level of 83% in Mauritius has contributed to the establishment, and maintenance, of a sophisticated, multiparty political system.

The 'scramble for Africa' in the 19th century has been matched by the 'scramble for democracy' in that continent during the last decade of the 20th century. The break-up of the Soviet Union in 1991, and the demise of communism as a 'model ideology' for postcolonial states, has dramatically changed the political map of Central and Southern Africa. Using the criterion of the establishment of a liberal democratic system in the past decade, the region now has among its political types the largest proportion of emergent democracies, nearly 63%, of any in the world. Indeed, 42% of the world's 72 emergent democracies are situated within this region. If the two well-established liberal democracies, in Botswana and Mauritius, are added, then Central and Southern Africa has been transformed from a continent dominated by one-party, authoritarian or militarist political systems to one which can begin to be compared with other regions with much stronger democratic heritages. However, as emphasized in Chapters 3 and 6, a strong caveat exists. The competitive element remains weak in many of Africa's fledgling democracies and the military remains an influential background force. However, it is hoped that, over time, stable multiparty systems will develop across the region.

The distribution of religions throughout Central and Southern Africa tends to reflect patterns of colonization based sometimes on trade and sometimes on missionary fervour. For example, the countries where Islam is the main, or a major, religion, which include Burkina Faso, Chad, Comoros, Djibouti,.Eritrea, Gambia, Guinea, Mali, Mauritania, Niger, Nigeria, Senegal, Sierra Leone, Somalia, Sudan, and Tanzania, are found near the early Arab coastal or northern trading routes, which predate European exploitation. On the other hand, the countries where Christians are in the majority, such as Angola, Burundi, Cape Verde, the Central

Central and Southern Africa: social, economic, and political data

Country	Area (sq km)	c. 1992–94 Population (m)	c. 1992–94 Pop. density per sq km	c. 1992 Adult literacy rate (%)	World ranking	Income type	c. 1991 Human rights rating (%)
Angola	1,246,700	10.300	8	42	160	low	27
Benin	112,622	5.100	45	23	184	low	90
Botswana	582,000	1.400	2	74	114	middle	79
Burkina Faso	274,200	9.800	34	18	186	low	n/a
Burundi	27,830	6.000	215	34	171	low	n/a
Cameroon	475,442	12.500	26	54	141	low	56
Cape Verde	4,033	0.400	99	37	166	low	n/a
Central African Republic	622,984	3.300	5	27	177	low	n/a
Chad	1,284,000	6.000	5	30	174	low	n/a
Comoros	1,860	0.600	323	48	153	low	n/a
Congo	342,000	2.400	7	16	188	low	n/a
Côte d'Ivoire	322,460	13.400	42	54	141	low	75
Djibouti	23,200	0.500	22	12	189	low	n/a
Equatorial Guinea	28,100	0.400	14	50	149	low	n/a
Eritrea	93,679	3.500	37	n/a		low	n/a
Ethiopia	1,106,200	51.300	46	62	129	low	13
Gabon	267,667	1.300	5	12	189	middle	n/a
Gambia	11,300	0.900	80	27	177	low	n/a
Ghana	238,540	16.400	69	60	131	low	53
Guinea	245,860	6.300	26	24	182	low	n/a
Guinea-Bissau	36,130	1.000	28	37	166	low	n/a
Kenya	580,646	26.100	45	69	119	low	46
Lesotho	30,350	1.900	63	59	134	low	n/a
Liberia	97,754	2.800	287	40	161	low	n/a
Madagascar	587,041	13.300	23	53	145	low	n/a
Malawi	118,480	10.700	90	48	153	low	33
Mali	1,240,000	10.100	8	32	173	low	n/a
Mauritania	1,030,700	2.200	2	34	171	low	n/a
Mauritius	2,040	1.100	539	83	98	middle	n/a
Mozambique	799,380	15.300	19	27	177	low	53
Namibia	824,292	1.600	2	38	163	middle	n/a
Niger	1,267,000	8.500	7	28	176	low	n/a
Nigeria	923,768	119.300	129	51	147	low	49
Rwanda	26,340	7.800	296	50	149	low	48
São Tomé	964	0.121	128	57	136	low	n/a
Senegal	197,000	7.900	40	38	163	low	71
Seychelles	450	0.069	153	58	135	middle	n/a
Sierra Leone	71,740	4.500	63	21	185	low	67
Somalia	637,660	9.500	15	24	182	low	n/a
South Africa	1,222,037	40.800	33	80	105	middle	50
Sudan	2,505,800	27.400	11	27	177	low	18
Swaziland	17,400	0.800	46	55	140	low	n/a
Tanzania	945,090	28.800	29	46	157	low	41
Togo	56,790	3.900	69	43	159	low	48
Uganda	241,139	19.200	80	48	153	low	46
Zaire	2,345,000	41.200	18	72	117	low	40
Zambia	752,620	8.900	12	73	115	low	57
Zimbabwe	390,759	10.900	28	67	121	low	65
Total/average/range	24,259,047	577.490	24	12–83			13–90

Key:

A	appointed	PR	proportional representation	Em-dem	Emergent democratic
AMS	additional member system	SB	second ballot	Nat-soc	Nationalistic socialist
E	elected	SP	simple plurality	Auth-nat	Authoritarian nationalist
F	Federal	U	unitary	Unlim-pres	Unlimited presidential
PL	party list	Lib-dem	Liberal democratic	Lim-pres	Limited presidential

Table 54

World ranking	Date of state formation	State structure	State type	Executive type	Number of assembly chambers	Party structure	Lower house electoral system
97	1975	U	Em-dem	Lim-pres	1	two	PR-PL
21	1960	U	Em-dem	Lim-pres	1	multi	SP
37	1966	U	Lib-dem	Lim-pres	1	two	SP
	1960	U	Em-dem	Lim-pres	1	multi	SP
	1962	U	Auth-nat	Unlim-pres	1	two	SP
66	1960	U	Em-dem	Lim-pres	1	multi	SP
	1975	U	Em-dem	Lim-pres	1	two	SP
	1960	U	Em-dem	Lim-pres	2	multi	SB
	1960	U	Em-dem	Lim-pres	1	multi	SP
	1975	F	Em-dem	Lim-pres	2	two	SB
	1960	U	Em-dem	Lim-pres	2	multi	SB
40	1960	U	Em-dem	Lim-pres	1	multi	SB
	1977	U	Em-dem	Lim-pres	1	multi	SP
	1968	U	Em-dem	Lim-pres	1	multi	SP
	1993	U	Nat-Soc	Unlim-pres	1	multi	mixed-E/A
106	11th C	F	Em-dem	Lim-pres	1	multi	mixed-E/A
	1960	U	Em-dem	Lim-pres	1	multi	SB
	1965	U	Military	Military	1	two	SP
72	1957	U	Em-dem	Lim-pres	1	multi	SP
	1958	U	Em-dem	Lim-pres	1	multi	SP
	1974	U	Em-dem	Lim-pres	1	multi	SP
83	1963	U	Auth-nat	Unlim-pres	1	multi	SP
	1966	U	Em-dem	Parliamentary	2	multi	SP
	1847	U	Military	Military/trans	2	trans	SP
	1960	U	Em-dem	Lim-pres	2	multi	SP
90	1964	U	Em-dem	Lim-pres	1	multi	mixed-E/A
	1960	U	Em-dem	Lim-pres	1	multi	SB
	1960	U	Em-dem	Lim-pres	2	multi	SB
	1968	U	Lib-dem	Parliamentary	1	multi	SP
72	1975	U	Em-dem	Lim-pres	1	two	SP
	1990	U	Em-dem	Lim-pres	1	two	SP
	1960	U	Em-dem	Lim-pres	1	multi	SP
77	1960	F	Military	Military	2	multi	SP
80	1962	U	Auth-nat	Unlim-pres	1	multi	SP
	1975	U	Em-dem	Lim-pres	1	multi	SP
45	1960	U	Nat-soc	Unlim-pres	1	multi	PR-AMS
	1976	U	Em-dem	Lim-pres	1	multi	PR-AMS
51	1961	U	Military	Military	1	multi	SP
	1960	F*	Military	Military	1	one	mixed-E/A
75	1910	U	Em-dem	Lim-pres	2	multi	PR-PL
103	1956	F	Military	Military	1	trans	A
	1968	U	Absolutist	Absolutist	2	one	mixed-E/A
87	1961	U	Nat-soc	Unlim-pres	1	multi	mixed-E/A
80	1960	U	Em-dem	Lim-pres	1	multi	SB
83	1962	U	Auth-nat	Unlim-pres	1	multi	mixed-E/A
88	1960	U	Auth-nat	Unlim-pres	1	one	trans
65	1964	U	Em-dem	Lim-pres	1	two	SP
53	1980	U	Nat-soc	Unlim-pres	1	one	mixed-E/A

Trans	Transitional
*	Federal system is inoperative as a consequence of civil war.

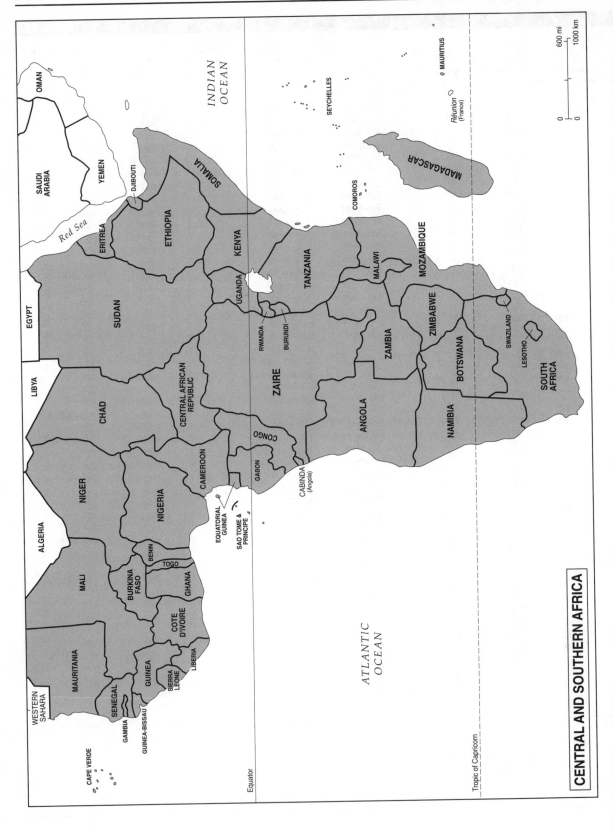

CENTRAL AND SOUTHERN AFRICA

European control of central and southern Africa 1870–1914				Table 55
Great Britain	Botswana			Côte d'Ivoire
	Gambia			Djibouti
	Ghana			Gabon
	Kenya			Guinea
	Lesotho			Madagascar
	Malawi			Mali
	Mauritius			Mauritania
	Namibia (then part of South Africa)			Niger
	Nigeria			Senegal
	Seychelles			Somalia (part)
	Sierra Leone		Portugal	Angola
	Somalia (part)			Cape Verde
	South Africa			Guinea-Bissau
	Sudan			Mozambique
	Swaziland			São Tomé e Príncipe
	Uganda		Germany	Burundi
	Zambia			Cameroon
	Zimbabwe			Rwanda
France	Benin			Tanzania
	Burkina Faso			Togo
	Central African Republic		Spain	Equatorial Guinea
	Chad		Belgium	Zaire
	Comoros		Italy	Eritrea
	Congo			Somalia (part)

African Republic, Congo, Equatorial Guinea, Gabon, Ghana, Guinea-Bissau, Kenya, Lesotho, Madagascar, Malawi, Namibia, Rwanda, São Tomé e Príncipe, the Seychelles, South Africa, Swaziland, Uganda, Zaire, Zambia, and Zimbabwe, came under the influence of European missionaries.

Although comparably rich in natural resources in many areas, Central and Southern Africa is still economically poor in relation to most other regions, 88% of the states having low incomes, only six in the middle-income category and none, including potentially wealthy countries such as Nigeria and South Africa, falling into the high-income group. The bulk of international aid, and particularly assistance in food supplies, is still directed to this region, which has 10% of the world's population but produces barely 1% of global GDP. During the 1980s the region found itself caught in the vice of a rapidly growing population, notwithstanding serious famines in the precarious Sahel belt running between Senegal and Somalia, notably in Ethiopia, and an escalating AIDS epidemic in parts of Eastern and Central Africa, and a sluggish economy. The latter was not improved by the paucity of intraregional cooperation. The dramatic political changes of recent years may, it is hoped, stimulate corresponding economic improvements, as skills are improved and resources directed away from the defence sector into more productive channels. It is possible also that, with the ending of apartheid

in South Africa and the collapse of the Soviet Union removing two key sources of discord, intraregional cooperation will improve. A hopeful sign was the decision in August 1995 of the leaders of the 12-nation Southern African Development Community (SADC) to work towards establishing a free-trading southern African economic community by the year 2000.

Recommended reading

Arnold, G (ed.) *Political and Economic Encyclopaedia of Africa*, Longman, 1993

Bayatt, J-F *The State in Africa: The Politics of the Belly*, Longman, 1993

Chazan, N, Mortimer, R, Ravenhill, J and Rothchild, D *Politics and Society in Contemporary Africa*, Lynne Rienner, 1992

Diamond, L, Linz, J and Lipset, S M (eds) *Democracy in Developing Countries*, Vol. 2, *Africa*, Lynne Rienner, 1988

Hyden, G and Bratton, M (eds) *Governance and Politics in Africa*, Lynne Rienner, 1992

Maguire, K *Politics in South Africa: From Vorster to de Klerk*, W & R Chambers, 1991

ANGOLA

The Republic of Angola
A República de Angola

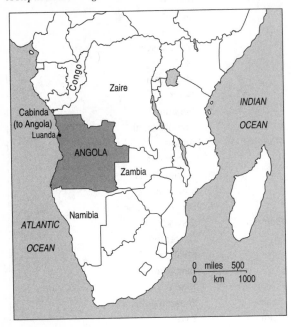

Capital: Luanda

Social and economic data
Area: 1,246,700 km²
Population: 10,300,000*
Pop. density per km²: 8*
Urban population: 27%**
Literacy rate: 42%**
GDP: $6,100 million**; per-capita GDP: $610**
Government defence spending (% of GDP): 32.4**
Currency: new kwanza
Economy type: low income
Labour force in agriculture: 69%**

*1994
**1992

Ethnic composition
There are eight main tribal groups, the Bakonga, the Mbunda, the Ovimbundu, the Lunda-Tchokwe, the Nganguela, the Nyaneka-Humbe, the Hiriro, and the Ambo, and about 100 subgroups. There was a major exodus of Europeans in the early 1970s and there are now about 30,000 left, mainly Portuguese. The official language is still Portuguese.

Religions
Most of the population adheres to traditional animist beliefs, but Roman Catholicism also attracts a following from around 60% of the people.

Political features
State type: emergent democratic
Date of state formation: 1975

Political structure: unitary
Executive: limited presidential
Assembly: one-chamber
Party structure: two-party
Human rights rating: 27%
International affiliations: ACP, CEEAC (observer), IBRD, IMF, Lusophone, NAM, OAU, SADC, UN, WTO

Local and regional government
The country is divided into 18 provinces, each governed by a Provincial Commissioner who is an *ex officio* member of the central government.

Head of state (executive)
President José Eduardo dos Santos, since 1979

Head of government
Prime Minister Marcelino José Carlos Moco, since 1992

Political leaders since 1970
1975–79 Agostinho Neto (MPLA), 1979–   José Eduardo dos Santos (MPLA–PT)

Political system
Formerly a one-party state, in 1991 a new constitution was adopted, providing for an executive president, popularly elected for five years, renewable only twice, and a 223-member National Assembly, elected for four years by a system of proportional representation. The Assembly includes three seats reserved for Angolans abroad. These are currently unfilled. The president appoints a prime minister and Council of Ministers (cabinet). In 1995 two vice-presidential posts were created.

Political parties
There are over 30 political parties, the three most significant being the People's Movement for the Liberation of Angola (MPLA), the National Union for the Total Independence of Angola (UNITA), and the National Front for the Liberation of Angola (FNLA).

The MPLA was formed in 1956 as a 'liberation movement' with the specific aim of securing the country's independence from Portugal. When independence was obtained in 1975 it became the party of government and in 1977 it was reconstructed to become a Marxist–Leninist 'vanguard' party, adopting the title the People's Movement for the Liberation of Angola–Workers' Party (MPLA–PT). It was the only legally permitted party until 1991. In December 1990 it abandoned Marxism–Leninism for 'democratic socialism'.

UNITA, formed in 1966, was a rebel group, backed by South Africa, and is now the main opposition to the MPLA.

The FNLA originated in 1962 as a rebel group which was to receive US backing. It is led today by Holden Roberto and is part of a 14-party Democratic Civilian Alliance, which was established in 1994.

Latest elections
Multiparty elections held in September 1992 resulted in a clear victory for the MPLA, which, with 53.7% of the national vote, won 129 National Assembly seats. UNITA, with 34.1% of the vote, captured 70 seats, and the FNLA, with 2.4% of the vote, 5 seats. Although the poll was viewed

as generally fair by United Nations observers, the result was disputed by the UNITA leader, Jonas Savimbi, and the civil war resumed. In the concurrent presidential election, the incumbent president, dos Santos, won the first round, with 49.6% of the vote to the 40% cast for Savimbi, but narrowly fell short of the required first-round absolute majority. No date for the second round of the elections was announced. However, in November 1994 dos Santos and Savimbi signed a peace accord, providing for the completion of the 1992 elections and interim power sharing.

Political history

Angola had been colonized by Portugal as early as the 17th century and became an overseas province in 1951. A strong independence movement began in the 1950s, with guerrilla warfare organized by the People's Movement for the Liberation of Angola (MPLA), which was based in the Congo. Two other nationalist movements were formed, the National Front for the Liberation of Angola (FNLA) and the National Union for the Total Independence of Angola (UNITA) and the struggle for independence developed, in 1961, into a civil war. The MPLA attracted support from socialist and communist states, UNITA was helped by the Western powers, including the United States, and the FNLA was backed by the 'non-left' power groups of southern Africa, chiefly South Africa.

After the granting of full independence in 1975 there was a return to a confused state of civil war, with the MPLA and UNITA the main contestants and foreign mercenaries helping the FNLA. By 1975 the MPLA, led by Dr Agostinho Neto and with the help of mainly Cuban forces, was in control of most of the country and the People's Republic of Angola was established, with Luanda as its capital and Neto as its first president. It soon won international recognition. In the meantime, the FNLA and UNITA had proclaimed their own People's Democratic Republic of Angola, based in Nova Lisboa, renamed Huambo, in the west-central area of the country.

President Neto died in 1979 and was succeeded by José Eduardo dos Santos (b. 1942), who maintained the policy of retaining strong links with the Soviet bloc. UNITA guerrillas, supported by South Africa, continued their guerrilla operations and in 1980 and 1981 South African forces made direct raids into Angola to attack bases of the South West Africa People's Organization (SWAPO), who were fighting for the independence of Namibia, whose claims Angola supported.

By 1982 there were international diplomatic moves to end the hostilities. In 1984 the FNLA surrendered to the MPLA and in 1983 South Africa proposed a complete withdrawal of its forces if it could be assured that the areas it vacated would not be filled by Cuban or SWAPO units. The Angolan government accepted the South African proposals and a settlement was concluded, known as the Lusaka Agreement, whereby a Joint Monitoring Commission (JMC) was set up to oversee the South African withdrawal. In 1985 South Africa announced that its withdrawal had been completed and the JMC was wound up. Relations between the two countries deteriorated however when, in 1986, new South African raids into Angola occurred. UNITA also continued to receive South African and American support.

By 1988 there was clear evidence that South Africa would welcome an opportunity of withdrawing from the conflict and secret talks between its country's representatives and those of Angola and Cuba were held in London under US auspices. The continued South African occupation of Namibia remained the main stumbling block to a lasting settlement. At the end of 1988, however, an agreement was eventually signed. This provided for the full withdrawal of South African and Cuban forces.

In May 1991 a US, Russian, and Portuguese-brokered peace accord between the Angolan government and UNITA was signed at Estoril, Portugal, and the rebel leader in exile, Jonas Savimbi (b. 1934), returned. Multiparty elections held in September 1992 were disputed by Savimbi and, to avoid a renewal of the civil war, President dos Santos agreed to annul the result and hold fresh elections. At first this seemed to appease Savimbi but later fighting broke out again. During 1993 the actions of UNITA forfeited of it any remaining international support and, from September, a UN oil and arms embargo was imposed against the alternative UNITA regime, which controlled 70% of the country. International pressure forced Savimbi to agree to a provisional cease-fire in December 1993. This did not hold. However, in November 1994, after government forces captured the UNITA stronghold of Huambo, a definitive cease-fire accord was signed, with agreement at last reached on how the second round of the presidential elections would be conducted. In the interim, it was agreed to share power, with UNITA being given four full ministerial positions and Savimbi being offered the post of vice president in 1995. The economic situation facing the government was appalling, with inflation at more than 2,000% and much infrastructure having been destroyed.

BENIN

The Republic of Benin
La République du Bénin

Capital: Porto Novo

Social and economic data

Area: 112,622 km²
Population: 5,100,000*
Pop. density per km²: 45*
Urban population: 40%**
Literacy rate: 23%**
GDP: $2,050 million**; per-capita GDP: $410**
Government defence spending (% of GDP): 1.5%**
Currency: franc CFA
Economy type: low income
Labour force in agriculture: 60%**

*1994
**1992

Ethnic composition

Ninety-nine per cent of the population is indigenous African, distributed among 42 tribes, the largest being the Fon, the Adja, the Yoruba, and the Bariba. There is a small European, mainly French, community. The official language is French.

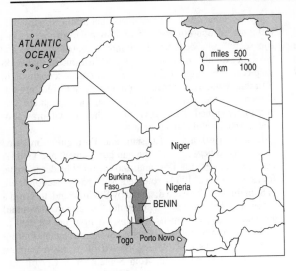

ATLANTIC OCEAN

0 miles 500
0 km 1000

Niger

Burkina Faso

Nigeria

BENIN

Togo Porto Novo

Religions
Sixty-five per cent of the population follows traditional animist beliefs, about 13% is Muslim, 12% Roman Catholic, and 3% Protestant.

Political features
State type: emergent democratic
Date of state formation: 1960
Political structure: unitary
Executive: limited presidential
Assembly: one-chamber
Party structure: multiparty
Human rights rating: 90%
International affiliations: ACP, BOAD, CEAO, ECOWAS, Francophone, FZ, IBRD, IMF, NAM, OAU, OIC, UEMOA, UN, WTO

Local and regional government
The country is divided into six provinces, which are further subdivided into 78 districts. A significant amount of general and financial policy-making has been devolved.

Head of state and head of government
President Nicéphore Soglo, since 1991

Political leaders since 1970
1970–72 Hubert Maga (civilian–military triumvirate), 1972 Justin Ahomadegbe (civilian–military triumvirate), 1972–91 Colonel Mathieu Kerekou (military/PRPB), 1991– Nicéphore Soglo (PRB–UTDR Coalition)

Political system
The former constitution was based on a Fundamental Law (Loi Fondamentale) of 1977 which made it a one-party state, dominated by the Benin People's Revolutionary Party (PRPB), committed to the path of 'scientific socialism'. In 1990 a new pluralist constitution was approved by referendum. It provides for an executive president, elected by universal suffrage for a five-year term, renewable once only. There is a single-chamber 64-member National Assembly, similarly elected for a five-year term. The president appoints a Council of Ministers (cabinet), which he or she heads, and has decree powers. There is a Constitutional Court.

Political parties
There are over 20 parties, several of them contesting elections in small blocks, and varying from time to time in their alignments. The most significant are the governing group, the Union for the Triumph of Democratic Renewal (UTDR), which shares power with the National Democratic Rally (RND) and President Soglo's Benin Renaissance Party (PRB), which was formed in 1992. Other parties include the National Party for Democracy and Development (PNDD), the Party for Democratic Renewal (PRD), the Social Democratic Party (PSD), and the National Union for Solidarity and Progress (UNSP).

The general orientation of most parties is left-of-centre.

Latest elections
In the March 1991 multiparty presidential elections Nicéphore Soglo defeated the incumbent president, Mathieu Kerekou, in the second round, winning 67.6% of the vote.

In the 1991 assembly elections no party or block won an overall majority. The results were as follows:

	Seats
UTDR	12
PNDD/PRD	9
PSD/UNSP	8
RND	7
Others	28

Political history
Benin used to consist of a number of small, generally warring, principalities, the most powerful being the Kingdom of Dahomey, which was established in the 17th century. The area was conquered by the French in 1892 and became the French Protectorate of Dahomey. It was made part of French West Africa in 1904, and in 1958 became a self-governing dominion within the French Community. In 1960 it became a fully independent state.

For the next 12 years it went through a period of acute political instability, with swings from civilian to military rule, including five army coups, and with disputes between the inhabitants of the northern, central, and southern regions. In 1972 the Deputy Chief of the army, Colonel Mathieu Kerekou (b. 1933), established a military regime pledged to give fair representation to each region, governing through an appointed National Council of the Revolution (CNR). In 1974 he announced that the country would follow a path of 'scientific socialism', based on Marxist–Leninist principles, and the following year the nation's name was changed from Dahomey to Benin.

In 1977 the CNR was dissolved and a civilian government formed, with Kerekou elected as president and head of state. He was re-elected in 1984 and 1989. After some initial economic and social difficulties, the Kerekou government showed signs of growing stability and in 1987 the president resigned from the army to demonstrate his commitment to genuine democracy. In 1989 he disavowed Marxism–Leninism and embarked on a new course towards a market economy.

In March 1990, following a constitutional conference, it became obvious that a transition to full democratic government would proceed at a faster pace than Kerekou had anticipated. He appointed as prime minister Nicéphore Soglo (b. 1933), a former World Bank administrator, and in the March 1991 free presidential elections was defeated by his protégé. Soglo subsequently ruled with a ten-party coalition, known as Le Renouveau, and attracted Western economic assistance.

BOTSWANA

The Republic of Botswana

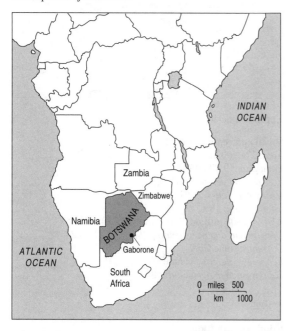

Capital: Gaborone

Social and economic data
Area: 582,000 km^2
Population: 1,400,000*
Pop. density per km^2: 2*
Urban population: 27%**
Literacy rate: 74%**
GDP: $3,797 million**; per-capita GDP: $2,790**
Government defence spending (% of GDP): 3.8%**
Currency: franc CFA
Economy type: middle income
Labour force in agriculture: 26%**

*1994
**1992

Ethnic composition
About 94% of the population is Tswana, 5% Bushman, and the rest is European. The official language is English.

Religions
The majority of the population follows traditional animist beliefs and about 30% is Christian.

Political features
State type: liberal democratic
Date of state formation: 1966
Political structure: unitary
Executive: limited presidential
Assembly: one-chamber
Party structure: two-party
Human rights rating: 79%
International affiliations: ACP, CW, IBRD, IMF, NAM, OAU, SADC, UN, WTO

Local and regional government
The country is divided into nine districts, ranging in population from under 20,000 to over 300,000 and six independent townships. Each has an elected council and is mainly responsible for primary education, licensing, and collecting taxes in its own locality.

Head of state and head of government
President Sir Ketumile Masire, since 1980

Political leaders since 1970
1966–80 Sir Seretse Khama (BDP), 1980– Sir Ketumile Masire (BDP)

Political system
The 1966 constitution contains features which blend the British system of parliamentary accountability with the distinctive tribal nature of the country. It provides for a National Assembly of 46 members, 40 elected by universal adult suffrage, four elected by the Assembly itself, all through a simple plurality voting procedure, plus the speaker and the attorney general. It has a life of five years. The president is elected by the Assembly for its duration and is an *ex officio* member of it. There is also a House of Chiefs of 15, consisting of the chiefs of the country's eight principal tribes, plus four members elected by the chiefs themselves and three elected by the House in general. The president is answerable to the Assembly. He or she may delay a bill for up to six months and then either sign it or dissolve the Assembly, putting both it and him or herself up for election. The House of Chiefs is consulted by the president and the Assembly in matters affecting them. The president chooses and appoints a cabinet which is answerable to the Assembly.

Political parties
The main political parties are the Botswana Democratic Party (BDP) and the Botswana National Front (BNF). There are four other smaller parties or political groupings. The BDP was formed in 1962 and has a moderate centrist orientation. The BNF was formed in 1967 and its support comes mainly from the urban working class. Its stance is moderate left-of-centre.

Latest elections

In the October 1994 National Assembly elections the BDP won 26 of the 40 seats with a 53.1% share of the vote, the BNF winning 13 seats with a 37.7% vote.

In October 1994 Masire was re-elected by the National Assembly for a fourth presidency.

Political history

With South Africa to the south and east, Zimbabwe to the northeast, and Namibia to the west and north, Botswana occupies a delicate position geographically and politically. It was originally Bechuanaland and, at the request of local rulers who feared an invasion by Boer farmers, became a British protectorate in 1885. When the British Parliament passed the Union of South Africa Act in 1910, making South Africa independent, it made provision for the possibility of Bechuanaland eventually becoming part of South Africa, but stipulated that this would not happen without the consent of the local inhabitants. Successive South African governments requested the transfer but the chiefs always resisted it, preferring full independence to a South African takeover.

In 1960 a new constitution was agreed, providing for a Legislative Council but still under the control of a British high commissioner. In 1963 high commission rule was ended and in the Legislative Council elections the newly formed Bechuanaland Democratic Party (BDP) won a majority of seats. Its leader, the Oxford University-educated Seretse Khama (1921–80), had been deposed as chief of the Bangangwato tribe in 1950, following his marriage to an Englishwoman two years before. He was in exile in England and returned to lead his party as president. In 1966 the country, renamed Botswana, became an independent state within the Commonwealth and Sir Seretse Khama, as he had now become, was the new nation's first president.

He continued to be re-elected until his death in 1980 when he was succeeded by the vice president, Dr Quett Masire (b. 1925). Dr Masire was re-elected in 1984. Since independence Botswana has earned a reputation for political and economic stability and has successfully followed a path of nonalignment. From time to time it was provoked by South Africa, which accused it of providing bases for the African National Congress (ANC). This was always denied by both Botswana and the ANC itself. South Africa had also persistently pressed Botswana to sign a nonaggression pact, similar to the Nkomati Accord, agreed with Mozambique, but it always refused to do so. In 1985 South African forces raided the capital, Gaborone, allegedly in search of ANC guerrillas, killing 12 people, for which Botswana demanded compensation. The ending of apartheid in South Africa and the establishment of a multiracial government from 1993 did much to normalize relations between the two countries.

Dr Masire was knighted and adopted the first name of Ketumile, in preference to Quett. In the 1994 elections the BDP retained power with a reduced majority, its share of the national vote falling by 12% compared to 1989, and he was re-elected for the third time. Since independence, the formerly impoverished economy of Botswana has been transformed by diamond mining, which first began in 1967. Annual GDP growth rates have averaged nearly 10% and diamonds currently account for 50% of GDP. However, the unemployment rate is 30% in Gaborone, prompting many to migrate to work in South Africa.

BURKINA FASO

Republic of Burkina ('Land of Upright Men')
République de Burkina

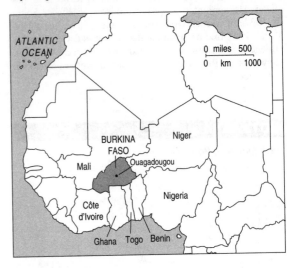

Capital: Ouagadougou

Social and economic data

Area: 274,200 km²
Population: 9,800,000*
Pop. density per km²: 34*
Urban population: 17%**
Literacy rate: 18%**
GDP: $2,908 million**; per-capita GDP: $290**
Government defence spending (% of GDP): 3.2%**
Currency: franc CFA
Economy type: low income
Labour force in agriculture: 84%**

*1994
**1992

Ethnic composition

There are over 50 tribes in the country. They include the nomadic Mossi, 48% of the population, the Fulani, 10%, and the Gourma, 5%. The settled tribes include: in the north, the Lobi-Dagari, 7%, and the Mande, 7%; in the southeast, the Bobo, 7%; and in the southwest the Senoufo, 6%, and the Gourounsi, 5%. The official language is French.

Religions

Fifty-seven per cent of the population follows traditional, animist religions, about 40% is Sunni Muslim, and there are about 1 million Christians, the vast majority being Roman Catholics.

Political features

State type: emergent democratic
Date of state formation: 1960

Political structure: unitary
Executive: limited presidential
Assembly: one-chamber
Party structure: multiparty
Human rights rating: N/A
International affiliations: ACP, BOAD, CEAO, CILISS, ECOWAS, Francophone, FZ, IBRD, IMF, NAM, OAU, OIC, UEMOA, UN, WTO

Local and regional government
For administrative purposes, the country is divided into 30 provinces, administered by governors, and subdivided into 300 departments.

Head of state (executive)
President Blaise Compaoré, since 1987

Head of government
Prime Minister Roch Christian Kabore, since 1994

Political leaders since 1970
1966–80 Colonel Sangoulé Lamizana (military), 1980–82 Colonel Zerbo (military), 1982–83 Major Jean-Baptiste Ouédraogo (military), 1983–87 Captain Thomas Sankara (military), 1987–92 Captain Blaise Compaoré (military), 1992–   Captain Blaise Compaoré (ODP–MT-led coalition)

Political system
The June 1991 constitution provides for an executive president, directly elected by universal suffrage for a seven-year term, renewable once only. There is a single chamber, 107-member assembly, the Assembly of People's Deputies (ADP), which is elected for a five-year term. The president appoints a prime minister, subject to the ADP's veto, and a Council of Ministers (cabinet). There is provision in the constitution for the formation of a second, nominated consultative chamber, the Chamber of Representatives, comprising 120 members serving three-year terms.

Political parties
Of the many registered political parties the most significant is the Popular Front (FP), a multi-party grouping formed to support President Compaoré. It includes the Organization for Popular Democracy (ODP–MT), the Movement for Democratic Progress (MDP), the Union of Burkina Democrats and Patriots (UDPB), the centre-left Union of Social Democrats (USD), and the left-of-centre National Convention of Progressive Patriots Socialist Party (CNPP–PSD).

Other political parties include the radical-nationalist pro-Sankara United Social Democracy Party (PDSU).

Latest elections
In the May 1992 assembly elections the ODP–MT won 78 of the 107 seats, amid claims of fraud by its opponents, who boycotted the poll. The CNPP–PSD captured six seats.

In December 1991 President Compaoré was re-elected when opposition candidates withdrew. There were widespread voting abstentions.

Political history
Formerly known as Upper Volta, Burkina Faso was a province of French West Africa. In 1958 it became a self-governing republic and two years later achieved full independence, with Maurice Yaméogo as its first president. A military coup in 1966 removed Yaméogo and installed Colonel Sangoulé Lamizana as president and prime minister. He suspended the constitution, dissolved the National Assembly, put a ban on political activities, and set up a Supreme Council of the Armed Forces as the instrument of government. In 1969 the ban on political activities was lifted and in the following year a referendum approved a new constitution, based on civilian rule, which was to come into effect after a four-year transitional period.

However, General Lamizana announced, in 1974, a return to rule by the army and the dissolution of the National Assembly. Three years later political activities were again permitted and in the 1978 elections the Volta Democratic Union (UDV) won a majority in the National Assembly and Lamizana was elected president, but a deteriorating economy led to a wave of strikes and he was overthrown in a bloodless coup in 1980.

Colonel Zerbo, who had led the coup, formed a Government of National Recovery, suspended the constitution again and dissolved the National Assembly. In 1982 Zerbo was, in turn, ousted by junior officers and Major Jean-Baptiste Ouédraogo emerged as leader of a new military regime, with Captain Thomas Sankara as prime minister. In 1983 Sankara led another coup and seized supreme power, and a National Revolutionary Council (CNR) was set up.

In 1984 Sankara announced that the country would be known as Burkina Faso ('Land of Upright Men'), symbolizing a break with its colonial past, and launched literacy and afforestation programmes in what was an immensely poor country. The government strengthened ties with neighbouring Ghana and established links with Benin and Libya. In October 1987 President Sankara was killed, allegedly accidentally, in a coup led by a close colleague, Captain Blaise Compaoré, who then succeeded him.

An attempt to overthrow him in 1989 was foiled but public pressure grew for a more democratic form of government. Eventually a new multiparty constitution was approved, in a June 1991 national referendum, and provision was made for free elections. Compaoré was elected president in December 1991 and his ruling party group won the assembly elections in May 1992, amid claims of widespread fraud and an opposition boycott.

BURUNDI

The Republic of Burundi
La République du Burundi

Capital: Bujumbura

Social and economic data
Area: 27,830 km^2
Population: 6,000,000*
Pop. density per km^2: 215*
Urban population: 6%**
Literacy rate: 34%**
GDP: $1,193 million**; per-capita GDP: $210**
Government defence spending (% of GDP): 2.6**

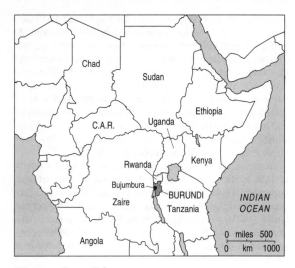

Currency: Burundi franc
Economy type: low income
Labour force in agriculture: 91%**

*1994
**1992

Ethnic composition

There are two main tribes in the country: the agriculturalist Hutu, comprising about 85% of the population, and the predominantly pastoralist Tutsi, about 14%. A virtual tribal apartheid has been operated for many years by the traditionally Tutsi-controlled government and massive killings of Hutus were reported in 1988. Violence on an even greater scale occurred in 1993 and again in 1995. There is a small Pygmy minority, comprising about 1% of the population, and a few Europeans and Asians. The official languages are Kirundi and French.

Religions

About 60% of the population, mostly Hutus, are Roman Catholic, most of the other inhabitants following traditional beliefs, mainly in a God 'Imana'. There are also about 160,000 Pentacostalists and 60,000 Anglicans.

Political features

State type: authoritarian nationalist
Date of state formation: 1962
Political structure: unitary
Executive: unlimited presidential
Assembly: one-chamber
Party structure: two-party
Human rights rating: N/A
International affiliations: ACB, CEEAC, CEPGL, Francophone, IBRD, IMF, KBO, NAM, OAU, UN, WTO

Local and regional government

For administrative purposes, the country is divided into 15 provinces, administered by governors. The provinces are further subdivided into districts and communes.

Head of state (executive)

President Sylvestre Ntibantunganya, since 1994

Head of government

Prime Minister Antoine Nduwayo, since 1995

Political leaders since 1970

1966–76 Captain Michel Micombero (UPRONA), 1976–87 Colonel Jean-Baptiste Bagaza (military), 1987–93 Major Pierre Buyoya (military), 1993 Melchior Ndadye (Frodebu), 1993–94 Cyprien Ntaryamira (Frodebu), 1994– Sylvestre Ntibantunganya (Frodebu)

Political system

The March 1992 constitution provides for an executive president, directly elected by universal suffrage for a five-year term, renewable once only, and a single-chamber 81-member National Assembly, similarly elected and serving a similar term. The National Assembly chooses a prime minister who, in turn, appoints a Council of Ministers, which he or she heads. The constitution specifically bans ethnically and regionally based parties, and requires party leaderships to be equally representative of the Hutu and Tutsi communities.

Political parties

The two most significant parties are the Front for Burundian Democracy (Frodebu) and the Union for National Progress (UPRONA).

Frodebu was founded in 1992 and has a left-of-centre orientation and receives strong Hutu support.

UPRONA was the only legally permitted party until 1992. It was founded in 1958, while the country was a monarchy, and given its monopoly position by royal decree in 1966. It is a socialist party with a strong nationalist orientation, and receives significant Tutsi support.

In 1994 a new left-of-centre party was formed, the Front for Allies of Change (FAC).

Operating in exile in Zaire, the National Council for the Defence of Democracy (CNDD) represents Hutu extremists and has a 30,000-strong armed wing, the Force for the Defence of Democracy.

Latest elections

The June 1993 presidential election was won by Melchior Ndadye (Frodebu), a Hutu, defeating the incumbent president, Buyoya (UPRONA).

In the June 1993 National Assembly elections Frodebu won 65 seats, with a 71% vote share, and UPRONA the other 16 seats, with a 21% vote share.

Political history

The country now called Burundi was a semifeudal Tutsi kingdom known as Urundi which became part of the empire of German East Africa in 1899. During World War I it was occupied by Belgian forces and later, as part of Ruanda–Urundi, was administered by Belgium as a League of Nations, and later United Nations, trust territory.

As a prelude to full independence, elections in 1961 were supervised by the United Nations (UN), and won by the Union for National Progress (UPRONA), which had been formed by Louis, one of the sons of the reigning king, Mwambutsa IV. Louis became prime minister but was assassinated after only two weeks in office and succeeded by his brother-in-law, André Muhirwa.

In 1962 Urundi separated from Ruanda, and, as Burundi, was given internal self-government and then full independence. The minority Tutsi community were to dominate the government during the next 30 years. In 1966 King Mwambutsa IV, after a 50-year reign, was deposed by another son, Charles, with the assistance of the army, and the constitution was suspended. Later in the year Charles, now Ntare V, was himself deposed by his prime minister, Captain Michel Micombero, who declared Burundi a republic. Micombero was a member of the Tutsi tribe whose main rivals were the numerically superior Hutus. In 1972 the deposed Ntare V was killed, allegedly by Hutus, and this provided an excuse for the Tutsis to carry out a series of large-scale massacres of Hutus. An estimated 100,000 were killed and many also fled the country. In 1973 amendments to the constitution made Micombero president and prime minister and in the following year UPRONA was declared the only legal political party, with the president as its secretary general.

In 1976 Micombero was himself deposed in an army coup led by Colonel Jean-Baptiste Bagaza (b. 1946), who was appointed president by a Supreme Revolutionary Council. He was assisted by a prime minister. The following year the prime minister announced a return to civilian rule and a five-year plan to eliminate corruption and secure social justice. In 1978 the post of prime minister was abolished and in 1981 a new constitution, providing for a National Assembly, was adopted after a referendum. In the 1984 election Bagaza, as the only presidential candidate, secured over 99% of the votes cast.

In September 1987 another coup, led by Major Pierre Buyoya, ousted Bagaza and a Military Council for National Redemption was established. Despite Buyoya's promises to improve the human rights situation in Burundi, discrimination against the Hutus continued to be practised by the Tutsi minority and widespread killings were reported in 1988, many of them allegedly by Tutsi soldiers, and there was a large exodus of Hutu refugees to Rwanda. In October 1988 the appointment of the first Hutu prime minister provided a hint of rapprochement between the two tribes.

In March 1992 a new constitution was adopted and in the first ever multiparty presidential elections in June 1993 Buyoya, a Tutsi, was defeated by the Frodebu candidate, Melchior Ndadye, a Hutu. In the same month Frodebu won a majority in the National Assembly. Ndadye's new government included a mixture of Hutus and Tutsis.

In October 1993 President Ndadye was killed in a coup by the Tutsi-controlled army and was succeeded in January 1994 by a fellow Hutu, Cyprien Ntaryamira. Three months later, in April 1994, Ntaryamira was killed when an aircraft in which he was returning with the president of neighbouring Rwanda was shot down, allegedly by dissident Tutsis. Their deaths unleashed ethnic killings on a scale never before experienced, with three-quarters of a million fleeing to Rwanda, leading to a refugee crisis. The carnage escalated in Rwanda.

The speaker of the National Assembly, Sylvestre Ntibantunganya, another Hutu, became acting president and was confirmed in that post in September 1994. Meanwhile, in an effort to avoid the tribal violence in Rwanda, the leaders of all the main political parties signed a four-year power-sharing agreement and in February 1994 Anatole Kanyenkiko, a Tutsi with a Hutu mother and Hutu wife, was appointed prime minister. Twelve months later he was replaced by Antoine Nduwayo, another Tutsi.

In March 1995 there was another major outbreak of ethnic violence in the region, apparently initiated by dissident Tutsis. This time it was Burundi, and particularly the capital, Bujumbura, and not Rwanda, where most of the killings occurred. It was evident that, despite genuine attempts at democratic government and efforts to avoid ethnic clashes, the underlying tribal antipathies remained.

CAMEROON

The United Republic of Cameroon
La République unie du Cameroun

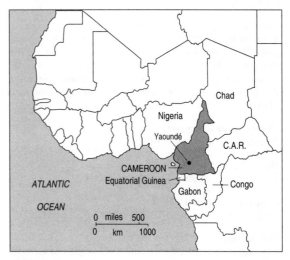

Capital: Yaoundé

Social and economic data
Area: 475,442 km^2
Population: 12,500,000*
Pop. density per km^2: 26*
Urban population: 42%**
Literacy rate: 54%**
GDP: $10,003 million**; per-capita GDP: $820**
Government defence spending (% of GDP): 1.1%**
Currency: franc CFA
Economy type: low income
Labour force in agriculture: 60%**

*1994
**1992

Ethnic composition
The main ethnic groups include the Cameroon Highlanders, 31%, the Equatorial Bantu, 19%, the Kirdi, 11%, the Fulani, 10%, the Northwestern Bantu, 8%, and the Eastern Nigritic, 7%. A majority of the population are French speakers, but a fifth are English speakers who, claiming that they are discriminated against in public employment, seek autonomy.

Both French and English have been designated as official languages.

Religions
About 40% of the population is Christian, mostly Roman Catholic, about 39% has traditional, animist beliefs, and about 21% is Muslim.

Political features
State type: emergent democratic
Date of state formation: 1960
Political structure: unitary
Executive: limited presidential
Assembly: one-chamber
Party structure: multiparty
Human rights rating: 56%
International affiliations: ACP, BDEAC, CEEAC, CEMAC, CW, Francophone, FZ, IAEA, IBRD, IMF, LCBC, NAM, OAU, OIC, UN, WTO

Local and regional government
The country is divided into ten provinces, ranging in population from under 400,000 to over 1.5 million. These are further subdivided into departments. A hierarchy of officials, responsible for regional and local administration, report to the president's representatives. Municipal elections took place in 1995.

Head of state (executive)
President Paul Biya, from 1982

Head of government
Prime Minister Simon Achidi Achu, since 1992

Political leaders since 1970
1960–82 Ahmadou Ahidjo (UNC), 1982– Paul Biya (RPDC)

Political system
Cameroon was a federal state until 1972 when a new constitution, revised in 1975, made it unitary. The constitution was further revised in 1991 and now provides for a president, who is head of state (and appoints a prime minister as head of government), directly elected by universal suffrage for a five-year term, and a single-chamber 180-member National Assembly similarly elected for the same term. All elections are conducted through the simple plurality system.

Political parties
More than 40 parties officially registered in preparation for the first multiparty elections in 1992. Since then there has been considerable fluidity in party compositions and several have been constituted into allied groups or changed their names. The most significant groups now are the Cameroon People's Democratic Movement (RDPC) and the Front of Allies for Change (FAC).

The RDPC was formed in 1966, under the name of the Cameroon National Union (UNC), by a merger of the governing party of each state of the original federation and the four opposition parties. The name was changed to RDPC in 1985. Its orientation is nationalist left-of-centre.

The FAC was formed in 1994 by 16 parties in opposition to the RDPC. At its core is the Social Democratic Front

(SDF). Its predecessor was the Union for Change. It has a centre-left orientation.

Other parties include the National Union for Democracy and Progress (UNDP; estd. 1991), which refused to join the FAC, and the Union of the Cameroon People (UPC).

Latest elections
In the October 1992 presidential elections Paul Biya (RDPC) was narrowly elected with 39.9% of the popular vote, his nearest rival, John Fru Ndi (SDF), securing 35.9%, while Bello Bouba Maigari (UNDP) attracted 19.2% of the vote.

The results of the March 1992 National Assembly elections were as follows:

	Seats
RDPC	88
UNDP	68
UPC	18
Others	6

Political history
Although subject to slave trading by the Belgians, Cameroon avoided colonial rule until 1884 when it became the German protectorate of Kamerun. After World War I the League of Nations gave France a mandate to govern about 80% of the area, mainly in the east and south, with Britain administering the remaining 20%. In 1946 both became United Nations trust territories.

In 1957 French Cameroon became a state within the French Community and three years later fully independent as the Republic of Cameroon. A 1961 plebiscite resulted in the northern part of British Cameroon deciding to merge with neighbouring Nigeria, which had recently obtained its independence, and the southern part joining the Republic of Cameroon. Together they became the Federal Republic of Cameroon, with French and English as the official languages. The former French zone was called East Cameroon and the former British part West Cameroon.

Ahmadou Ahidjo (1924–89), who had been elected the first president of the original republic in 1960, became president of the new federal republic and was re-elected in 1965. In 1966 it became a one-party state, when the two government parties and most of the opposition parties merged into the Cameroon National Union (UNC). Extreme left-wing opposition to the single party was finally crushed in 1971. In 1972 a new constitution abolished the federal system and in 1973 a new National Assembly was elected. In 1982 Ahidjo resigned, nominating Paul Biya (b. 1933), the prime minister since 1975, as his successor. Soon after taking office in 1983 Biya began to remove supporters of his predecessor and Ahidjo accused him of trying to create a police state, resigning from the presidency of the UNC. Biya was, nevertheless, re-elected in 1984 while Ahidjo went into exile in France. Biya strengthened his personal control by abolishing the post of prime minister and reshuffling his cabinet. He also announced that the nation's name would be changed from the United Republic of Cameroon to the

Republic of Cameroon. In 1985 the UNC changed its name to RPDC and Biya tightened his control still further by more cabinet changes. In 1988 he was re-elected for the second time.

Opposition to his autocratic regime grew, fuelled by a sharp decline in living standards, and at the end of 1991 he was forced to concede constitutional changes which would allow multiparty politics to operate.

He and a new National Assembly were elected under the revised constitution in 1992. However, the opposition claimed that there had been ballot-rigging. Pressure mounted during 1993 for further amendments to the constitution, including calls, from the English-speaking minority, for a return to the federal system. In November 1995 Cameroon was admitted to the Commonwealth.

CAPE VERDE

The Republic of Cape Verde
A República de Cabo Verde

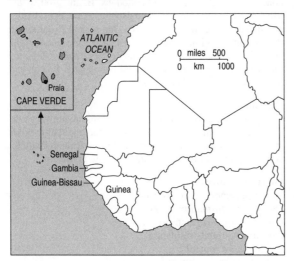

Capital: Praia

Social and economic data
Area: 4,033 km^2
Population: 400,000*
Pop. density per km^2: 99*
Urban population: 30%**
Literacy rate: 37%**
GDP: $312 million**; per-capita GDP: $780**
Government defence spending (% of GDP): 0.8%**
Currency: escudo
Economy type: low income
Labour force in agriculture: 54%**

*1994
**1992

Ethnic composition
About 60% of the population are mixed descendants of Portuguese settlers and African slaves and are called *mestiços* or

creoles. The rest are mainly African. The European population is very small. The official language is Portuguese.

Religions
About 98% of the total population is Roman Catholic.

Political features
State type: emergent democratic
Date of state formation: 1975
Political structure: unitary
Executive: limited presidential
Assembly: one-chamber
Party structure: two-party
Human rights rating: N/A
International affiliations: ACP, CILSS, ECOWAS, IBRD, IMF, Lusophone, NAM, OAU, UN

Local and regional government
Cape Verde is divided into two districts (*distritos*), each of which is subdivided into seven councils (*concelhos*). The island of Santo Antão comprises three councils and the island of São Tiago four councils.

Head of state (executive)
President Antonio Mascarenhas Monteiro, since 1991

Head of government
Prime Minister Carlos Alberto Wahnon de Carvalho Veiga, since 1991

Political leaders since 1970
1975–91 Aristedes Pereira (PAICV), 1991– Antonio Mascarenhas Monteiro (MPD)

Political system
The 1990 multiparty constitution provides for an executive president, elected by universal suffrage, through an absolute majority system of voting, and a 79-member National Assembly (AN), elected by universal suffrage by simple plurality voting. Both serve five-year terms. The prime minister is nominated by the AN and appointed by the president. The formation of parties on a religious or geographical basis is prohibited.

Political parties
The two most significant parties are the Movement for Democracy (MPD) and the African Party for the Independence of Cape Verde (PAICV).

The MPD, which was formed in 1990, has a moderate centrist orientation and advocates administrative decentralization.

The PAICV was, until 1990, the only legal party and was originally formed in 1956, before independence from Portugal in 1975, as the African Party for the Independence of Portuguese Guinea and Cape Verde (PAIGC), in anticipation of the eventual union of the two countries, but when this was abandoned it adopted its present name. Its orientation is African-Nationalist.

Latest elections
The country's first multiparty elections were held in January 1991. In the assembly elections the newly formed MPD defeated the ruling PAICV, winning 56 seats to the latter's 23.

In the February 1991 presidential elections President Pereira (PAICV) was defeated by a former Supreme Court judge, Antonio Mascarenhas Monteiro (MPD), by 73.5% to 26.5% of the votes cast.

Political history

The Cape Verde islands were colonized by the Portuguese in the 15th century and from the 1950s onwards a liberation movement developed. The mainland territory to which the Cape Verde archipelago is linked, Guinea, now Guinea-Bissau, was granted independence in 1974, and a process began for the eventual union of Cape Verde and Guinea-Bissau.

In 1975 Cape Verde secured its own independence from Portugal and a provisional government was set up, composed of Portuguese settlers and locally born members of the PAIGC. In the same year the first National People's Assembly was elected and Aristides Pereira (b. 1923), the founder and secretary general of the PAIGC, became president of the new state.

A constitution was adopted in 1980 making provision for the coming together of Cape Verde and Guinea-Bissau but by 1981 it had become clear that there was not enough support for the union so the idea was dropped and the PAIGC became the PAICV. Relations with Guinea-Bissau, which had cooled, gradually improved and under the guidance of Pereira, who was re-elected in 1981 and 1986, Cape Verde followed a careful policy of nonalignment and achieved considerable respect within the region. However, the decision in 1987 to decriminalize abortion offended many Catholics and unrest, from 1988, forced pluralist political reforms in 1990.

In the multiparty elections of 1991 the PAICV was heavily defeated by the recently formed Movement for Democracy (MPD) and the MPD's candidate, Antonio Mascarenhas Monteiro, won the presidency, on a low poll. Carlos Veiga was appointed prime minister and free market-orientated economic reforms were introduced.

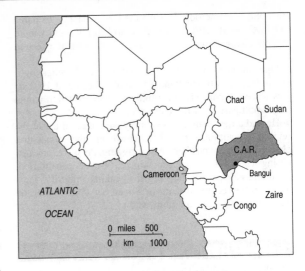

CENTRAL AFRICAN REPUBLIC

La République Centrafricaine

Capital: Bangui

Social and economic data

Area: 622,984 km^2
Population: 3,300,000*
Pop. density per km^2: 5*
Urban population: 48%**
Literacy rate: 27%**
GDP: $1,170 million**; per-capita GDP: $390**
Government defence spending (% of GDP): 2.4%**
Currency: franc CFA
Economy type: low income
Labour force in agriculture: 84%**

*1994
**1992

Ethnic composition

There are over 80 ethnic groups but 66% of the population falls into one of three: the Banda, 30%, the Baya-Mandjia,

29%, and the Mbaka, 7%. There are clearly defined ethnic zones: the forest region, inhabited by Bantu groups, the Mbaka, Lissongo, Mbimu, and Babinga; the river banks, populated by the Sango, Yakoma, Baniri, and Buraka; and the savannah region, where the Banda, Zande, Sara, Ndle, and Bizao live. Europeans number less than 7,000, the majority being French. The official language is French and Sangho is the national language.

Religions

Figures for adherents to particular religions are not very reliable but it is estimated that a quarter of the population holds traditional, animist beliefs, about a third is Roman Catholic and another third Protestant, and about 5% is Muslim.

Political features

State type: emergent democratic
Date of state formation: 1960
Political structure: unitary
Executive: limited presidential
Assembly: two-chamber
Party structure: multiparty
Human rights rating: N/A
International affiliations: ACP, BDEAC, CEEAC, CEMAC, Francophone, FZ, G-77, IBRD, IMF, NAM, OAU, UN, WTO

Local and regional government

On the basis of French experience, the country is divided into 16 prefectures, further subdivided into 52 subprefectures, below which there are communes.

Head of state (executive)

President Ange-Felix Patasse, since 1993

Head of government

Prime Minister Gabriel Koyambounou, since 1995

Political leaders since 1970

1965–79 Colonel Jean-Bédel Bokassa (military), 1979–81 David Dacko (MESAN), 1981–93 General André Kolingba (military), 1993– Ange-Felix Patasse (MLPC)

Political system

The original constitution, adopted following independence in 1960, was annulled in 1972 and then a new version, which came into force in 1981, was suspended in a military coup within months of its adoption and legislative powers, which were to be held by an elected National Assembly, were placed in the hands of a Military Committee for National Recovery (CMRN). Four years later the CMRN was dissolved and a new 22-member Council of Ministers, containing both military and civilian members, was established. A new constitution was approved by referendum in 1986. In August 1992 a 'Grand National Debate' was held to discuss the country's political future and agreement was reached to hold future multiparty elections.

The new constitution, adopted in January 1995, provides for an executive president, who is head of state, directly elected by universal suffrage for a six-year term, renewable once only. There is an 85-member National Assembly similarly elected for a five-year term, and an advisory Economic and Regional Council, half elected by the Assembly and half appointed by the president, who also appoints a prime minister to lead a Council of Ministers. All elections are by the two-ballot majoritarian system.

Political parties

Of more than ten active parties, the two most significant are the Central African People's Labour Party (MLPC) and the Central African Democratic Rally (RDC).

The MLPC was founded in 1979. It has a left-of-centre orientation.

The RDC was founded in 1987 and until 1993 was the only legal party. It was the organ of the former militarily controlled governing regime and has a right-of-centre orientation.

Latest elections

In the August–September 1993 presidential elections the president of the MLPC, Ange-Felix Patasse, with 52.5% of the vote, defeated Abel Goumba, the candidate of the Group of Democratic Forces (CFD), representing 14 opposition groups, in the second ballot. The incumbent president, Kolingba, finished in fourth place in the first ballot.

In the August–September 1993 Assembly elections the MLPC won 34 of the 85 seats, the RDC, 13, and smaller parties and independents, 38.

Political history

The territory of Oubangi-Chari came under French influence in 1889 and was given self-government within what was then French Equatorial Africa in 1958. Two years later it achieved full independence. The leading political figure was Barthélémy Boganda who had founded the Movement for the Social Evolution of Black Africa (MESAN) and had been a leading figure in the campaign for independence. He became the country's first prime minister. A year before full independence he was killed in an air crash and succeeded by his nephew, David Dacko (b. 1930), who became president in the independent nation in 1960. In 1962 he established a one-party state, with MESAN as the only legal political organization. Dacko was overthrown in a military coup in

December 1965 and the commander in chief of the army, Colonel Jean-Bédel Bokassa (b. 1921), assumed power.

Bokassa progressively increased his personal control of the political system and, in 1972, annulled the constitution and made himself life president. Two years later he awarded himself the title of Marshal of the Republic. In 1976 ex-president Dacko was persuaded to return as Bokassa's personal adviser and later that year the republic was restyled the Central African Empire (CAE). In 1977 Bokassa was crowned emperor at a lavish ceremony his country could ill afford. His rule became increasingly dictatorial and idiosyncratic, leading to revolts by students and, in April 1979, by school children, who objected to the compulsory wearing of school uniforms, manufactured by a company owned by the Bokassa family. Many of the children were imprisoned and it is estimated that at least 100 were killed, with the emperor, allegedly, being personally involved.

In September 1979, while Bokassa was in Libya, Dacko ousted him in a bloodless coup, backed by France. The country became a republic again, with Dacko as president. He initially retained a number of Bokassa's former ministers but, following student unrest, they were dropped and in February 1981 a new constitution was adopted, with an elected National Assembly. Dacko was elected president for a six-year term in March but opposition to him grew and in September 1981 he was deposed in another bloodless coup, led by the armed forces chief of staff, General André Kolingba. The constitution was suspended, as well as all political activity, and a military government installed. Undercover opposition to the Kolingba regime continued, with some French support, but relations with France improved following an unofficial visit by President François Mitterrand in October 1982.

By 1984 there was some evidence of an eventual return to constitutional government. The leaders of the banned political parties were granted an amnesty and at the end of the year the French president paid a state visit. In January 1985 proposals for a new constitution were announced and in September civilians were introduced for the first time into Kolingba's administration.

In 1986 former president and emperor, Bokassa, returned from exile and was tried for murder, illegal detentions and embezzlement of state funds. Although he was found guilty and sentenced to death, President Kolingba announced in March 1988 that, on the recommendation of the country's senior judges, he had decided to commute the death sentence.

Demands for a more democratic political system grew, with pressure also being applied by France, an important donor of economic aid. In August 1992 there was a 'Grand National Debate' where it was agreed that a new multiparty constitution should be introduced. In its final form, it was adopted in January 1995.

Multiparty presidential elections, originally scheduled for 1992, were cancelled with Kolingba in last place. They were eventually held in August–September 1993 and resulted in Kolingba's defeat by Ange-Felix Patasse, leader of the Central African People's Labour Party (MLPC), who was a former prime minister. In the following month the MLPC secured the largest seat holding in the National Assembly and Patasse appointed Jean-Luc Mandaba, the MLPC vice president, prime minister, heading a coalition government. In April 1995, anticipating a defeat in the National Assembly on a confidence motion, Mandaba resigned and was succeeded by Gabriel Koyambounou.

CHAD

The Republic of Chad
La République du Tchad

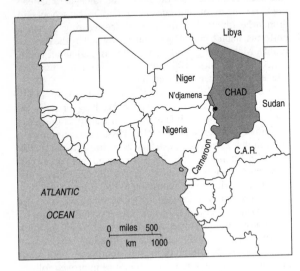

Capital: N'djamena

Social and economic data
Area: 1,284,000 km^2
Population: 6,000,000*
Pop. density per km^2: 5*
Urban population: 34%**
Literacy rate: 30%**
GDP: $1,083 million**; per-capita GDP: $190**
Government defence spending (% of GDP): 5.2%**
Currency: franc CFA
Economy type: low income
Labour force in agriculture: 83%**

*1994
**1992

Ethnic composition
Northern Chad is populated mainly by Arabs and the south by Pagan, or Kirdi, groups. There is no single dominant group in any region, the largest being the Sara, who comprise about a quarter of the total population. Europeans, mainly French, constitute a very small minority. The official languages are French and Arabic.

Religions
About 52% of the population is Sunni Muslim, living predominantly in the north, about 35%, predominantly in the south, follows traditional African animist religions, and about 5%, mainly the Sara, is Christian.

Political features
State type: emergent democratic*
Date of state formation: 1960
Political structure: unitary
Executive: limited presidential*
Assembly: one-chamber*
Party structure: multiparty
Human rights rating: N/A
International affiliations: ACP, BDEAC, CEEAC, CEMAC, CILSS, Francophone, FZ, IBRD, IMF, LCBC, NAM, OAU, OIC, UN, WTO

*In a state of transition

Local and regional government
Following French experience, the country is divided into 14 prefectures within which are 54 subprefectures, 27 administrative posts, and nine municipalities.

Head of state and head of government
President Idriss Déby, since 1990

Political leaders since 1970
1960–75 François Tombalbaye (PPT), 1975–79, General Félix Malloum (military), 1979–82 General Goukouni Oueddi (military), 1982–90 Hissène Habré (UNIR), 1990– Idriss Déby (MPS)

Political system
A provisional constitution of 1982, following a civil war, provided for a president and Council of Ministers (cabinet), appointed and led by the president. In October 1991 political parties other than the ruling MPS were permitted, provided they shunned 'intolerance, tribalism, regionalism, religious intolerance and ... recourse to violence'. A national conference was held early in 1993 which adopted a transitional charter, as a prelude to full democracy. An interim assembly, the 57-member Higher Transitional Council (CST), was established to function for 12 months, after which elections would be held. The transition period was later extended into 1996.

Political parties
Since 1991 some 30 parties have been authorized, the most significant being the Patriotic Salvation Movement (MPS), a coalition of a number of groups which were instrumental in overthrowing Hissène Habré in 1990.

Latest elections
There was a general election in July 1990 but five months later the government of President Habré was overthown. Multiparty elections were scheduled for 1996.

Political history
Chad, then called Kanem, was settled by Arabs from the 7th century onwards. From 1913 it was a province of French Equatorial Africa and then became an autonomous state within the French Community, in 1958, with François Tombalbaye as its prime minister. Full independence was achieved in 1960 and Tombalbaye was elected president. His party, the Sara-dominated Chadian Progressive Party (PPT), held 57 of the 85 National Assembly seats. He was soon faced with unrest, mainly because of disagreements between

the nomadic Arabs of the north, who saw Libya as a natural ally, and the Sara Christians of the south, who felt more in sympathy with neighbouring Nigeria.

A conflict began less on the basis of party divisions and more on the basis of loosely organized private armies, each loyal to a particular leader. By 1975 at least three groups claimed to be the true revolutionaries. In the north the Chadian National Liberation Front (Frolinat) led a revolt, the two leading figures in it being Goukouni Oueddi and the northerner, Hissène Habré.

Meanwhile Tombalbaye's attempts at 'Chadization' aroused opposition and in 1975 he was killed in a coup led by the former army Chief of Staff, Félix Malloum. Malloum made himself president of a Supreme Military Council but despite his appeals for national unity, Frolinat continued to oppose him, with support from Libya.

By 1978 Frolinat, now led by General Goukouni, had expanded its territorial control but was halted with the aid of French troops. Malloum tried to reach a political settlement by making the other former Frolinat leader, Hissène Habré, prime minister but in 1979 fighting broke out again and Malloum was forced to flee the country.

Conferences of rival groups in Nigeria eventually resulted in the formation of a provisional government (GUNT), with Goukouni as president. The Organization for African Unity (OAU) set up a peacekeeping force, composed of Nigerian, Senegalese, and Zairean troops, but this failed to prevent civil war breaking out between the armies of Goukouni and Habré.

By April 1981 Habré's Armed Forces of the North (FAN) were in control of half the country, forcing Goukouni to flee, eventually setting up a 'government in exile'. In 1983 a majority of OAU members agreed to recognize Habré's regime as the legitimate government but Goukouni, with Libyan support, fought on. After bombing raids by Libya, Habré appealed to France for help and 3,000 troops were sent as military instructors. Following a Franco-African summit, in August 1983, a cease-fire was agreed in December, the latitude line 16 degrees north eventually becoming the dividing line between the opposing forces. The Libyan president, Colonel Muammar Kadhafi, proposed a simultaneous withdrawal of French and Libyan troops and this was eventually accepted. Meanwhile Habré had dissolved the military arm of Frolinat and formed a new political party, the National Union for Independence (UNIR) but opposition to his regime grew.

In 1987 the Libyans intensified their military operations in northern Chad, producing an equal response from the Habré government, and renewed, if reluctant, support from France. It was announced in September 1987 that France, Chad, and Libya had agreed to observe a cease-fire proposed by the Organization of African Unity and in the same year Goukouni publicly backed Habré as the legitimate head of state. In May 1988 Colonel Kadhafi made a surprisingly generous offer to meet President Habré and resolve outstanding differences and in October 1988, with the civil war halted, full diplomatic relations between the two countries were restored.

A new constitution was approved in July 1990 but five months later the Patriotic Salvation Movement (MPS) rebel forces based in Sudan, led by Idriss Déby, the former Chadian army chief, and supported by Libya, defeated Habré's army and Deby was installed as president. The United States declined to recognize the new regime, because of its Libyan connections, but France agreed to send financial aid.

Despite attempted coups against it and the continuing activity of rebels, in 1991 and 1992 the Deby government retained control, promising the establishment of a democratic, multiparty political system in the near future. Following a National Conference in 1993, a transitional charter was adopted, prior to elections planned for 1994. The transition period was later extended to 1996.

COMOROS

The Federal Islamic Republic of Comoros
La République fédérale islamique des Comores

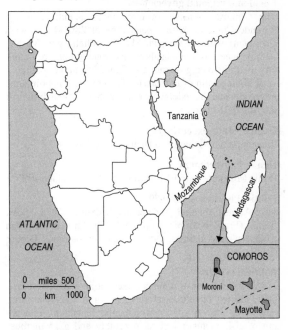

Capital: Moroni (on Njazidja)

Social and economic data
Area: 1,860 km²
Population: 600,000*
Pop. density per km²: 323*
Urban population: 29%**
Literacy rate: 48%**
GDP: $276 million**; per-capita GDP: $460**
Government defence spending (% of GDP): N/A
Currency: franc CFA
Economy type: low income
Labour force in agriculture: 83%**

*1994
**1992

Ethnic composition
The population is of mixed origin, Africans, Arabs, and Malaysians predominating. The principal ethnic group is the Antalaotra. The languages are French and Arabic.

Religions

The majority of the population (98%) is Sunni Muslim and Islam is the state religion. There are about 2,000 Roman Catholics.

Political features

State type: emergent democratic
Date of state formation: 1975
Political structure: federal
Executive: limited presidential
Assembly: two-chamber
Party structure: two-party
Human rights rating: N/A
International affiliations: ACP, AL, Francophone, FZ, IBRD, IMF, IOC, NAM, OAU, OIC, UN

Local and regional government

The Comoros consists of three main islands, Njazidja (Grande Comore), with a population of 280,000, Nzwani (Anjouan), with 210,000, and Mwali (Moheli), with 35,000. Although each of the islands has a certain amount of autonomy, with its own governor and Council, it all constitutes a very limited form of federalism. The president appoints the governors and the federal government has responsibility for the islands' resources.

Head of state (executive)

President Said Mohammed Djohar, since 1990

Head of government

Prime Minister Caabi El Yachroutu Mohamed, since 1995

Political leaders since 1970

1975 Admed Abdallah Abderemane (Udzima), 1975–78 Ali Soilih (Front National Uni), 1978–90 Ahmed Abdallah Abderemane (Udzima), 1990– Said Mohammed Djohar (RDR)

Political system

The June 1992 constitution provides for an executive president, elected by universal suffrage for a five-year term, renewable once only, and a two-chamber legislature, consisting of a 42-member Federal Assembly and a 15-member Senate. Members of the Assembly are elected by universal suffrage for a four-year term and the Senate consists of five members from each of the main islands, elected by an electoral college. They serve for six years. The president appoints a prime minister, as head of government, from the majority party in the Assembly.

Political parties

From 1979 Comoros was a one-party state, based on the Comoron Union for Progress (Udzima). Some 20 parties eventually emerged under the 1992 constitution, the most significant being the National Union for Democracy in the Comoros (UNDC) and the Rally for Democracy and Renewal (RDR).

The UNDC is an Islamic-nationalist grouping. It is part of a 12-party alliance, the Forum for National Recovery (FRN), formed in 1994, which also includes Udzima, which withdrew its support from President Djohar in November 1991.

The RDR was formed in 1993 and has a left-of-centre orientation.

Latest elections

In the 1990 presidential elections Said Mohammed Djohar defeated his UNDC opponent, Mohammed Taki, in the second round, with 55% of the vote to Taki's 45%.

In the December 1993 Assembly elections the RDR won 24 seats, the UNDC and its allies taking 18.

Political history

The Comoros islands of Grande Comore, Anjouan, Moheli, and Mayotte became a French colony in 1912 and were attached to Madagascar in 1914. They separated from Madagascar and their status changed to that of a separate French Overseas Territory in 1947. Internal self-government was obtained in 1961 and in 1974 referenda on independence were held on the four islands. The first three islands voted in favour of independence. They ceded unilaterally from France in July 1975, but maintained ties via a defence pact and aid donations. As 'The Comoros', they were admitted into United Nations membership in 1975, with Ahmed Abdallah Abderemane as the first president. However, the island of Mayotte, whose citizens had voted against independence, remained as a French dependency (see *Chapter 8*). In August 1975 a coup, led by Ali Soilih, deposed Abdallah and abolished the Assembly, resulting in a deterioration in relations with France. Ali Soilih was elected president and took on increased powers under a new constitution.

In 1978 Soilih was killed by French mercenaries, supposedly working for Abdallah. A federal Islamic republic was proclaimed, a new constitution adopted, establishing a single-party state, and Abdallah was elected president. With these changes, diplomatic relations with France were restored. In 1979 the Comoros became a one-party state and the powers of the federal government were increased. In the same year a plot by British mercenaries to overthrow Abdallah was foiled. In 1984 he was re-elected president and in the following year the constitution was amended, abolishing the post of prime minister and making Abdallah head of government as well as head of state, but in 1989 he was killed by rebel soldiers.

After months of uncertainty, with European mercenaries briefly ruling, in 1990 multiparty democracy was restored and Said Mohammed Djohar, a former president of the Supreme Court, was elected head of state. He sought to create a government of national unity, but was faced during 1991 and 1992 by several coup attempts. His administration was unstable, with the country's third transitional government being appointed in July 1992.

Multiparty assembly elections held in November 1992 resulted in no party winning a working majority but in December 1993 the Rally for Democracy and Renewal (RDR) won control and its leader, Mohamed Abdou Madi, was appointed prime minister. In October 1994 he was replaced by Halifa Houmadi. Following criticisms of his administration, in April 1995 Houmadi resigned and was succeeded by Caabi El Yachroutu Mohamed. In September 1995 the increasingly unpopular president, Djohar, was briefly overthrown in a coup by mercenaries, led by Colonel Bob Denard, a former French marine who was married to a Comoran and had been active in French Africa for more than three decades. Denard had been behind the coups of 1975 and 1978 and the assassination of President Abdallah in

1989. After six days 80-year-old President Djohar was restored to power by 600 French troops. A 'government of unity' was formed in November 1995, which included four ministers from parties which had backed the coup.

CONGO

The Republic of the Congo
La République du Congo

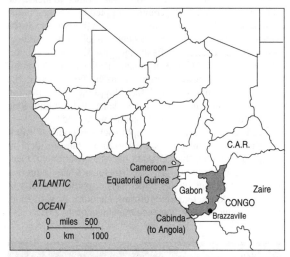

Capital: Brazzaville

Social and economic data
Area: 342,000 km²
Population: 2,400,000*
Pop. density per km²: 7*
Urban population: 42%**
Literacy rate: 16%**
GDP: $2,200 million**; per-capita GDP: $940**
Government defence spending (% of GDP): 3.8%**
Currency: franc CFA
Economy type: low income
Labour force in agriculture: 62%**

*1994
**1992

Ethnic composition
The vast majority of Congolese are Bantus and comprise 15 main ethnic groups and 75 tribes. The Kongo, or Bakongo as they are sometimes called, account for about 45% of the population, then come the Bateke, or Teke, about 20%, and then the Mboshi, or Boubangui, about 16%. The official language is French.

Religions
More than a quarter of the population follows traditional, animist beliefs, nearly half is Roman Catholic, and a fifth is Protestant. There are also about 40,000 Muslims.

Political features
State type: emergent democratic
Date of state formation: 1960

Political structure: unitary
Executive: limited presidential
Assembly: two-chamber
Party structure: multiparty
Human rights rating: N/A
International affiliations: ACP, BDEAC, CEEAC, CEMAC, Francophone, FZ, IBRD, IMF, NAM,OAU, UN, WTO

Local and regional government
The country is divided into nine provinces, each with its popularly elected regional council and executive committee. They act under the direction of commissars appointed by the central committee of the governing party.

Head of state (executive)
President Pascal Lissouba, since 1992

Head of government
Prime Minister General Jacques-Joachim Yhombi-Opango, since 1995

Political leaders since 1970
1968–77 Marien Ngouabi (PCT), 1977–79 Colonel Jacques-Joachim Yhombi-Opango (military), 1979–92 Denis Sassou-Nguesso (PCT), 1992– Pascal Lissouba (UPADS)

Political system
The Congo was a one-party state based on the Congolese Labour Party (PCT), until a new multiparty constitution was adopted in March 1992, following a referendum. This provides for an executive president and a two-chamber assembly, comprising a 125-member National Assembly and a 60-member Senate. The president is directly elected by universal suffrage for a five-year term and the National Assembly is similarly elected for the same length of term. Members of the Senate serve a six-year term. The second ballot voting system is used. The President appoints a prime minister and cabinet.

Political parties
Until the adoption of the new multiparty constitution in 1992 the only legal party was the Congolese Labour Party (PCT). There are now more than 60 active parties. The four most significant are the Pan-African Union for Social Democracy (UPADS); the Union for Democratic Renewal (URD), a seven-party alliance which includes the Congolese Movement for Democracy and Integral Development (MCDDI), led by Bernard Kolelas; the Rally for Democracy and Development (RDD), led by the prime minister, General Yhombi-Opango; and the PCT.

UPADS, led by President Lissouba, its coalition partner, the RDD, and the opposition MCDDI have moderate, left-of-centre orientations.

The PCT, now led by Denis Sassou-Nguesso, was formed in 1969 to replace the National Revolutionary Movement (MNR). It is a Marxist–Leninist party, committed to the path of what it calls 'scientific socialism', and is a member of the six-party United Democratic Forces (UDF) opposition coalition formed in 1994.

Latest elections
In the August 1992 multiparty presidential elections there were 17 candidates, the front runners being Pascal Lissouba

(UPADS), Bernard Kolelas (MCDDI), and Denis Sassou-Nguesso (PCT). The second ballot produced a straight fight between Lissouba and Kolelas, which Lissouba won.

The results of the 1992 Senate elections were as follows:

	Seats
UPADS	23
MCDDI	13
PCT	3
Other parties	21

In the May–June 1993 National Assembly elections UPADS won 69 of the 125 seats but the opposition parties contested the results and demanded fresh elections. Eventually, it was agreed to rerun elections in 11 disputed constituencies in October 1993. The final result still left UPADS with 47 seats. The URD won 28 seats, the PCT, 15, the Rally for Democracy and Social Progress (RDPS), 10, and other parties, 25 seats.

Political history

After years of exploitation by Portuguese slave traders, the Congo became a colony within French Equatorial Africa in 1910. It was declared an autonomous republic within the French Community in 1958 and Abbé Youlou, a Roman Catholic priest who involved himself in politics and was suspended by the church, was elected prime minister and then president when full independence was achieved in 1960. Two years later plans were announced for the creation of a one-party state but in 1963, following industrial unrest, Youlou was forced to resign.

A new constitution was approved and Alphonse Mossamba-Débat, a former finance minister, became president, adopting a policy of what he described as 'scientific socialism'. He declared the National Revolutionary Movement (MNR) to be the only permitted political party. In 1968 a military coup, led by Captain Marien Ngouabi, overthrew Mossamba-Débat and the National Assembly was replaced by a National Council of the Revolution. Ngouabi proclaimed a Marxist state but kept close economic links with France.

In 1970 the PCT, as the MNR had become known, became the sole legal party and three years later a new constitution provided for an Assembly chosen from a single party list. In 1977 Ngouabi was assassinated in a coup and eventually replaced by Colonel Joachim Yhombi-Opango. Two years later Yhombi-Opango, having discovered a plot to overthrow him, handed over the government to the Central Committee of the PCT and eventually Denis Sassou-Nguessou (b. 1943) became president.

Sassou-Nguessou steadily moved his country out of the Soviet sphere of influence and in 1982 the new regime received formal recognition by France In 1984 and 1989 Sassou-Nguessou was re-elected for further five-year terms but dissatisfaction with his administration grew and in a national conference on the country's political future, in February–June 1991, the president was severely criticized, his executive powers reduced, and an interim government, under

a prime minister, appointed until a new constitution was in place and multiparty elections were held.

The constitution was overwhelmingly approved, by referendum, and in March 1992 Pascal Lissouba became the country's first democratically elected president and his party, the Pan-African Union for Social Democracy (UPADS), the largest party in both the National Assembly and the Senate. Sassou-Nguessou took his defeat gracefully.

President Lissouba appointed Stéphane Bongho-Nouarra prime minister to lead a minority 'war cabinet' to tackle the economic problems of a country crippled by a huge burden of external debt. In November 1992 Bongho-Nouarra lost a vote of confidence and the president dissolved the National Assembly and called for fresh elections. They were eventually won by UPADS and in January 1993 General Yhombi-Opango was appointed prime minister. Followers of the opposition parties disputed the May–June 1993 election results, resulting in strikes and violence and a month-long curfew, during which some 40 people were killed.

In January 1995, in an attempt to achieve political stability, the prime minister resigned to allow the president to bring parties other than UPADS into the government. General Yhombi-Opango was asked to form a new administration, which now included members of parties formerly in opposition. Market-centred reforms, including privatization, were introduced under the encouragement of the IMF.

COTE D'IVOIRE

The Republic of the Ivory Coast
La République de la Côte d'Ivoire

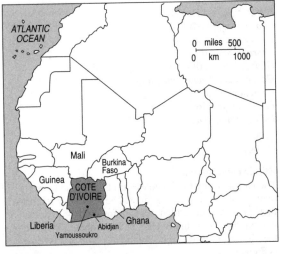

Capital: Abidjan (*de facto* and legislative); Yamoussoukro *de jure* and administrative)

Social and economic data
Area: 322,460 km²
Population: 13,400,000*
Pop. density per km²: 42*
Urban population: 42%**
Literacy rate: 54%**

GDP: $7,000 million**; per-capita GDP: $674**
Government defence spending (% of GDP): 1.4%**
Currency: franc CFA
Economy type: low income
Labour force in agriculture: 65%**

*1994
**1992

Ethnic composition
There is no single dominant ethnic group and the main tribes include the Agni, Baoule, Krou, Senoufou, and Mandingo. There are also about 2 million Africans who have settled from neighbouring countries, particularly Burkina Faso. Europeans number about 70,000. The official language is French.

Religions
About 60% of the population follows traditional, animist beliefs, about 20% is Sunni Muslim, and 15% Roman Catholic.

Political features
State type: emergent democratic
Date of state formation: 1960
Political structure: unitary executive/limited presidential
Assembly: one-chamber
Party structure: multiparty*
Human rights rating: 75%
International affiliations: ACP, BOAD, ECOWAS, FZ, G-24, IAEA, IBRD, IMF, NAM, OAU, UEMOA, UN, WTO

*Though dominated by one party

Local and regional government
The country is divided into 49 departments, each with its own elected council.

Head of state (executive)
President Henri Konan Bédié, since 1993

Head of government
Prime Minister Daniel Kablan Duncan, since 1993

Political leaders since 1970
1960–93 Félix Houphouët-Boigny (PDCI), 1993– Henri Konan Bédié (PDCI)

Political system
The constitution dates from independence in 1960 and was amended in 1971, 1975, 1980, 1985, 1986, 1990, and 1994. It provides for an executive president, who is head of state, elected by universal adult suffrage, through a majoritarian voting system of the second ballot, for a five-year term, and a single-chamber 175-member National Assembly, elected in the same way and also serving a five-year term. The president, who since 1994 must be Ivoirian by birth or have Ivoirian parents, appoints a prime minister, as head of government.

Political parties
A multiparty system has been operating since 1990 and there are now some 40 legal parties.

The ruling party is the Democratic Party of the Ivory Coast (PDCI), founded in the 1940s by Félix Houphouët-Boigny,

as a branch of the African Democratic Rally (RDA). It has a nationalistic free-enterprise orientation.

In October 1994 a split appeared in the PDCI and a breakaway party, the centrist Rally of Republicans (RDR), was formed. This is led by Djeny Kobina and supported by the former prime minister, Alassane Ouattara.

Among the opposition groups, the most significant are the Ivorian People's (or Popular) Front (FPI) and the Ivorian Labour (or Workers') Party (PIT). Both have left-of-centre orientations.

Latest elections
In November 1990, in the first multiparty Assembly elections since independence, none of the opposition parties had sufficient organization or finance to offer a real threat to the PDCI, which won 163 of the 175 seats. The opposition FPI won nine seats and the PIT one, but claimed electoral fraud. In 1994, 31 PDCI deputies broke away to form the RDR.

In October 1995 multiparty presidential and assembly elections, the incumbent president, Henri Konan Bédié, secured an overwhelming victory. Turnout was 45%, but the chief opposition parties boycotted the poll. There were several deaths during a violent campaign. The PDCI also secured a clear victory in the November 1995 assembly elections. It won 148 seats to the RDR's 13 and FPI's 11.

Political history
Formerly a province of French West Africa, which had been colonized in the 19th century, the Côte d'Ivoire was given self-government within the French Community in 1958 and then full independence in 1960, when a new constitution was adopted. Félix Houphouët-Boigny (1905–93), leader of the Democratic Party of the Ivory Coast (PDCI), was the country's first president. He maintained close links with France after independence and this support, combined with a good economic growth rate, gave his country a high degree of political stability. He was very much a pragmatist in politics and was criticized by some other African leaders for maintaining links with South Africa. He countered the criticism by arguing that a dialogue between blacks and whites was essential. As a strong believer in independence for black African states, he denounced Soviet and other forms of intervention in African affairs and travelled extensively to improve relations with the Western powers.

In the president's advancing years opposition to him grew, particularly as the economy deteriorated, with per-capita incomes falling by 25% between 1987 and 1993 as an IMF-promoted austerity programme was implemented. However, despite the appearance of rival parties, Houphouët-Boigny and the PDCI retained their control in multiparty elections in 1990. In December 1993 the veteran president died, at the age of 88, and, in accordance with the terms of the constitution, the president of the National Assembly, Henri Konan Bédié (b. 1934), became head of state for the remainder of the presidential term. This prompted the resignation of the disenchanted prime minister, Alassane Ouattara, who was replaced by Daniel Kablan Duncan. It was believed that new birth and residency restrictions for prospective presidential candidates, which were introduced in 1994, were designed to prevent the ambitious Ouattara from becoming a candidate.

In October 1995 President Konan Bédié and the PDCI won clear victories in multiparty elections that were boycotted by many opposition parties.

DJIBOUTI

The Republic of Djibouti
Jumhuriya Djibouti

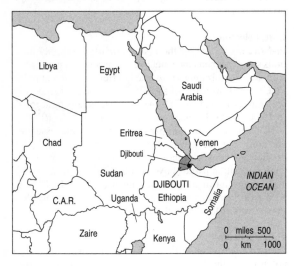

Capital: Djibouti

Social and economic data
Area: 23,200 km²
Population: 500,000*
Pop. density per km²: 22*
Urban population: 86%**
Literacy rate: 12%**
GDP: $340 million**; per-capita GDP: $730**
Government defence spending (% of GDP): 5.3%**
Currency: Djibouti franc
Economy type: low income
Labour force in agriculture: N/A

*1994
**1992

Ethnic composition
The population is divided chiefly into two Hamitic groups, the Issas (Somalis) in the south and the minority Afars (or Danakil) in the north and west. Ethnic rivalry between the two is intense. There are also minorities of Europeans, mostly French, as well as Arabs, Sudanese and Indians. The official language is French.

Religions
Virtually the whole population (95%) is Sunni Muslim.

Political features
State type: emergent democratic
Date of state formation: 1977
Political structure: unitary
Executive: limited presidential

Assembly: one-chamber
Party structure: multiparty*
Human rights rating: N/A
International affiliations: ACP, AL, IBRD, IGADD, IMF, NAM, OAU, OIC, UN

*Though dominated by one party

Local and regional government
For administrative purposes, the country is divided into five districts.

Head of state (executive)
President Hassan Gouled Aptidon, since 1977

Head of government
Prime Minister Barkat Gourad Hamadou, since 1981

Political leaders since 1970
1977–   Hassan Gouled Aptidon (RPP)

Political system
The September 1992 multiparty constitution, which was approved by a referendum, provides for an executive president, elected by universal suffrage, and serving a six-year term. There is a single-chamber assembly, the 65-member Chamber of Deputies, elected for a five-year term. The President, who is also commander in chief of the armed forces, appoints a prime minister and Council of Ministers (cabinet).

Political parties
Between 1981 and 1992 the only permitted party was the People's Progress (or Popular Rally for Progress) Party (RPP). Although other parties can now operate, the only one that has made any impact is the Democratic Renewal Party (PRD).

The RPP was formed in 1979 to replace the African People's League for Independence (LPAI), the dominant party before and after independence. Its orientation is basically nationalist.

The PRD was formed in 1992. It has a left-of-centre orientation.

The United Opposition Front (UOF) was formed in 1992 and includes the Front for the Restoration of Unity and Democracy (FRUD), an Afars' guerrilla movement formed in 1991.

Latest elections
In the December 1992 assembly elections all seats were won by the RPP.

In the May 1993 presidential contest President Gouled was re-elected with 60% of the vote, his nearest rival, the PRD candidate, obtaining 20%. Turnout was below 50%.

Political history
Djibouti, with its excellent deep port, became a French colony in 1862, being part of French Somaliland, and in 1945 was declared an overseas territory. In 1967 it was renamed the French Territory of the Afars and the Issas. There were frequent calls for independence, particularly from the Issas community, sometimes resulting in violence, and this goal was eventually achieved in 1977. Hassan Gouled Aptidon

(b. 1916), who had been active in the independence movement, was elected the first president.

In 1979 all existing political parties were combined to form the People's Progress Party (RPP) and the government embarked on the task of bringing together the two main tribes, the Issas, who traditionally had strong links with Somalia, and the Afars, who had been linked with Ethiopia, through a policy of 'rapid detribalization'.

In 1981 a new constitution was adopted, making the RPP the only legal party and providing for the election of a president after nomination by the RPP. President Gouled was subsequently elected. The following year a Chamber of Deputies was elected from a list of RPP nominees. Under Gouled, Djibouti pursued a largely successful policy of amicable neutralism with its neighbours, concluding treaties of friendship with Ethiopia, Somalia, Kenya, and the Sudan, and tried to assist the peace process in East Africa. Although affected by the 1984–85 droughts, it managed to maintain stability with the help of famine relief aid from the European Community.

The septuagenarian Gouled was re-elected in 1987 and again in 1993, after constitutional changes which allowed opposition parties to operate. Despite these changes, no party other than the RPP has made a significant impact on the political scene, so that Djibouti has remained a *de facto* one-party state. In 1991 an Afars-dominated movement, the Front for the Restoration of Unity and Democracy (FRUD), commenced guerrilla activities against the regime, in the northeast. However, in June 1994 FRUD signed a peace accord with the government.

EQUATORIAL GUINEA

The Republic of Equatorial Guinea
La República de Guinea Ecuatorial

Capital: Malabo

Social and economic data
Area: 28,100 km^2
Population: 400,000*
Pop. density per km^2: 14*
Urban population: 29%**
Literacy rate: 50%**
GDP: $132 million**; per-capita GDP: $330**
Government defence spending (% of GDP): 1.5%**
Currency: franc CFA
Economy type: low income
Labour force in agriculture: 66%**

*1994
**1992

Ethnic composition
Between 80% and 90% of the population is of the Fang ethnic group, of Bantu origin. Most of the other groups have been pushed to the coast by the Fang expansion. The official language is Spanish.

Religions
About 96% of the population is Roman Catholic. The rest follow traditional beliefs.

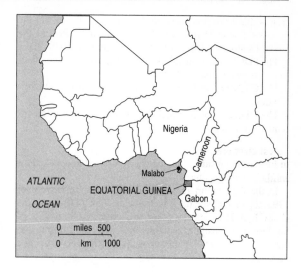

Political features
State type: emergent democratic
Date of state formation: 1968
Political structure: unitary
Executive: limited presidential
Assembly: one-chamber
Party structure: multiparty*
Human rights rating: N/A
International affiliations: ACP, BDEAC, CEEAC, CEMAC, FZ, IBRD, IMF, NAM, OAU, UN

*Though dominated by one party

Local and regional government
For administrative purposes, the country is divided into seven provinces.

Head of state (executive)
President Brigadier General (retired) Teodoro Obiang Nguema Mbasogo, since 1979

Head of government
Prime Minister Silvestre Siale Bileka, since 1993

Political leaders since 1970
1968–79 Francisco Macias Nguema (military), 1979–91 Teodoro Obiang Nguema Mbasogo (military), 1991– Brigadier General (retired) Teodoro Obiang Nguema Mbasogo (PDGE)

Political system
The November 1991 constitution, which was approved by referendum, provides for multiparty politics, with an executive president, who is head of state, elected by universal suffrage for a seven-year term. There is a single-chamber assembly, the 80-member House of Representatives, also popularly elected for a five-year term. The president appoints a prime minister and Council of Ministers.

Political parties
Until 1992 only one party was allowed to operate, the Democratic Party of Equatorial Guinea (PDGE). Of the other

groups that have since formed, the most significant are the People's Social Democratic Convention (CSDP) and the Social Democratic Union of Equatorial Guinea (UDSGE).

The PDGE was formed in 1987 as the government party. It has a strong nationalist orientation.

The CSDP was formed in 1992 and has a left-of-centre orientation.

The UDSGE was founded in 1990 and also has a left-of-centre orientation.

Latest elections
In June 1989 President Obiang was re-elected unopposed for another seven-year term.

In the first multiparty assembly elections, in November 1993, the PDGE won 68 of the 80 seats, the CSDP, 6, and the UDSGE, 5. The contest was strongly criticized for its lack of fairness by opposition and foreign observers. Turnout was barely 30%, with the main opposition parties encouraging a boycott.

Political history
After 190 years of Spanish rule, during which period a harsh plantation system was established, Equatorial Guinea became fully independent in 1968 with Francisco Macias Nguema as the nation's first president, heading a coalition government. He soon assumed dictatorial powers, however, and in 1970 outlawed all existing political parties, replacing them with one, the United National Party (PUN). Two years later he declared himself president for life and established a tight control of the press and radio. Between 1976 and 1977 there were many arrests and executions. He also established close relations with the Soviet bloc.

In 1979 he was overthrown in a coup led by his nephew, Colonel Teodoro Obiang Nguema Mbasogo, with at least the tacit approval of Spain. Macias was later tried and executed. Obiang expelled the many Soviet technicians and advisers and renewed economic and political ties with Spain. He banned political parties and ruled through a Supreme Military Council and withstood four coup attempts between 1981 and 1988. In 1982, after pressure was exerted by the United Nations, a new constitution was adopted, promising an eventual return to civilian rule, but nothing resulted. In 1991, responding to public pressure, President Obiang allowed a referendum which gave overwhelming support for a change to multiparty politics.

In the first multiparty assembly elections, in November 1993, the PDGE won a clear majority, amid allegations of vote-rigging by opposition politicians and foreign observers.

ERITREA

Capital: Asmara (Asmera)

Social and economic data
Area: 93,679 km^2
Population: 3,500,000*
Pop. density per km^2: 37*
Urban population: N/A
Literacy rate: N/A
GDP: $ 402 million**; per-capita GDP: $115**

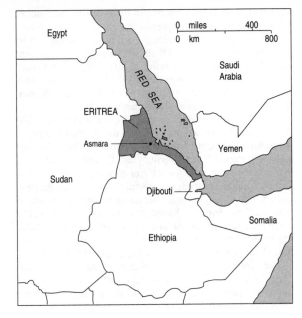

Government defence spending (% of GDP): N/A
Currency: Ethiopian birr
Economy type: low income
Labour force in agriculture: N/A

*1994
**1992

Ethnic composition
There are several ethnic groups, including the Amhara and the Tigrais. The main language is Tigrinya.

Religions
About 50% of the population follows Sunni Islam and the remainder adheres to Coptic Christianity.

Political features
State type: nationalistic socialist*
Date of state formation: 1993
Political structure: unitary
Executive: unlimited presidential*
Assembly: one-chamber
Party structure: multiparty
Human rights rating: N/A
International affiliations: ACP, COMESA, IBRD, IGADD, IMF, OAU, UN

*In a state of transition

Local and regional government
A regional system was inherited from Ethiopia but in May 1995 a new structure was approved, based on six administrative regions, further divided into subregions and villages.

Head of state and of government
President Issaias Afewerki, since 1993

Political leaders since 1970
1993–   Issaias Afewerki (EPLF/PFDJ)

Political system

The 1993 provisional constitution, amended in 1994, provides for a transitional government, functioning for not more than four years, after which a permanent constitution will be adopted. There is a single-chamber 150-member National Assembly, half nominated by the Central Committee of the People's Front for Democracy and Justice (PFDJ) and the rest popularly elected. Eleven seats are reserved for women. The Assembly elects the president, as head of state and government. The president, who is also commander in chief of the armed forces, appoints and chairs a cabinet (State Council).

Political parties

Although several parties function, the dominant one is the People's Front for Democracy and Justice (PFDJ). It changed its name in 1994 from the Eritrean People's Liberation Front (EPLF), in which guise it had been in the vanguard of the movement to secure independence from Ethiopia. It has a left-of-centre orientation.

Since independence the PFDJ's dominance has been challenged by breakaway factions, some of which have combined to form the opposition Eritrean National Pact Alliance.

Latest elections

Provision has been made for multiparty elections to take place within four years of independence.

Political history

Eritrea was occupied by Italy in 1882 and declared a colony in 1890. In 1935 it was used as a base for Italy's invasion of Ethiopia and designated part of Italian East Africa in 1936. In 1941, during World War II, Italian forces in Eritrea were defeated by the British and after the war the country was federated with Ethiopia in 1952 by the United Nations, and then made an Ethiopian province in 1962. This sparked a strong secessionist movement, which was to continue for 30 years as the Ethiopian military government fought hard to hold on to the province. In addition to the problems caused by the fighting between Ethiopian and Eritrean forces, there were severe famines caused by successive droughts.

The most durable secessionist force was the Eritrean People's Liberation Front (EPLF), founded in 1958. By 1977 it controlled much of the region, but then the new Ethiopian regime of Colonel Mengistu Haile Mariam, receiving military aid from the Soviet Union, turned back the tide until the late 1980s. In 1990 the EPLF's armed wing captured the strategic port of Massawa. This made the deployment of Ethiopian troops in the region untenable and in 1991 the Mengistu military regime was toppled in Ethiopia. After a referendum held in April 1993 showed overwhelming, 99.8%, support for independence, the EPLF declared the secession of Eritrea and in May 1993 this separate state was recognized by the new Ethiopian government. International recognition soon followed.

A transitional government was established by the EPLF, now renamed the People's Front for Democracy and Justice (PFDJ), with multiparty elections planned within the four-year period of transition, while a constitution was drafted. Issaias Afewerki was elected head of state and head of government by the PFDJ.

ETHIOPIA

The Federal Democratic Republic of Ethiopia

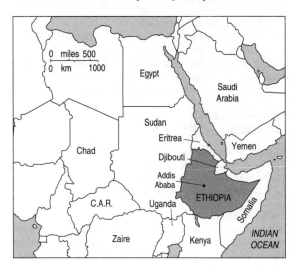

Capital: Addis Ababa

Social and economic data

Area: 1,106,200 km^2
Population: 51,300,000*
Pop. density per km^2: 46*
Urban population: 13%**
Literacy rate: 62%**
GDP: $5,904 million**; per-capita GDP: $120**
Government defence spending (% of GDP): 4.1%**
Currency: Ethiopian birr
Economy type: low income
Labour force in agriculture: 80%**

*1994
**1992

Ethnic composition

The country contains over 70 different ethnic groups, the two main ones being the Galla, mainly in the east and south of the central plateau, who comprise about 40% of the population, and the Amhara and Tigrais, largely in the central plateau itself, who constitute about 35% of the population. The official language is Amharic.

Religions

About 35% of the population is Sunni Muslim and 45% belongs to the Ethiopian Orthodox Church (Tewahida). There are also significant numbers of animists and Christians.

Political features

State type: emergent democratic*
Date of state formation: 11th century
Political structure: federal
Executive: limited presidential*
Assembly: one-chamber*
Party structure: multiparty
Human rights rating: 13%

International affiliations: ACP, COMESA, G-24, IAEA, IBRD, IGADD, IMF, NAM, OAU, UN

*In a state of transition

Local and regional government
Between 1952 and 1962 Ethiopia was a federation and then became a unitary state. In 1994 it returned to its federal status on the basis of nine states: Tigré, Afar, Amara, Oramia, Somali, Benshangui, Gambela, Harer, and Peoples of the South. Unusually, each state enjoys the right to secede.

Head of state and head of government
President Meles Zenawi, since 1991

Political leaders since 1970
1916–74 Haile Selassie (Emperor), 1974–77 General Tefere Bante (military), 1977–91 Colonel Mengistu Haile Mariam (WPE), 1991– Meles Zenawi (EPRDF)

Political system
A new constitution was ratified in December 1994. Under its terms, Ethiopia returned to federal status, based on nine states. Controversially, the constitution includes provision for any one of the nine states to secede from the federation. It also provides for a multiparty system, with a president, as head of state and government, and a 548-member federal assembly, all directly elected by universal suffrage.

Political parties
Until 1991 the only legal political party was the Marxist–Leninist Workers' Party of Ethiopia (WPE), which was established in 1984. Since then a number of parties in opposition to the WPE have been established, the most significant being the Ethiopian People's Revolutionary Democratic Front (EPRDF), which now dominates the political scene. Many of the other parties are regionally based.

The EPRDF was formed in 1989 through an amalgamation of smaller groupings, including the Tigré People's Liberation Front, the Ethiopian People's Democratic Movement, the Oromo People's Democratic Union, and the Afar Democratic Movement. The Tigréan people are the dominant force in the EPRDF, which has a left-of-centre orientation.

Latest elections
In July 1991 Meles Zenawi, the leader of the EPRDF, was elected president by the National Assembly.

In the country's first multiparty elections, in May 1995, the EPRDF secured a landslide victory in the federal assembly.

Political history
After a long period of subordination to Egypt, Ethiopia became independent in the 11th century as the Kingdom of Abyssinia. It survived the European scramble for Africa, defeating an attempted Italian invasion in 1896. In the 20th century, one man, Haile Selassie (1891–1975), came to dominate the country for more than 50 years. He became regent in 1916, king in 1928, and emperor in 1930, Westernizing the country. During the Italian occupation of Abyssinia between 1935–36 he lived in exile in England, but was retored to power in 1941 after the country was liberated by British

forces. In 1963 Emperor Haile Selassie promoted the foundation of the Organization of African Unity (OAU), which held its first conference in Addis Ababa. He was deposed by the armed forces in 1974, following a disastrous famine in 1973, high inflation, growing unemployment and demands for a more democratic form of government. His palace and estates were nationalized, the parliament was dissolved and the constitution suspended. He died in 1975 at the age of 83 in a small apartment in his former palace in Addis Ababa.

General Teferi Bante, who had led the uprising and had been made head of state, was killed in 1977 by fellow officers and Colonel Mengistu Haile Mariam (b. 1937) replaced him. A one-party Marxist–Leninist influenced regime was established, with collective farming promoted, with adverse consequences. Throughout the period of Haile Selassie's reign, and that of his predecessor, Emperor Menelik II, there had always been attempts by various regions which had been annexed to secede, particularly from Tigré and from Eritrea, which was ceded to Ethiopia in 1952. The 1975 revolution encouraged these secessionist movements to increase their efforts and the military government had to fight to hold on to Eritrea and the southeast region of Ogaden, where Somalian troops were assisting local guerrillas. The communist Soviet Union, which had adopted Ethiopia as a new ally, threatened to cut off aid to Somalia and Cuban troops assisted Mengistu in ending the fighting there. The struggle for independence by Eritrea and the adjoining province of Tigré continued. In the midst of this confusion there was acute famine in the northern provinces, including Eritrea, after the failure of the rains for three successive seasons. In addition to a massive emergency food aid programme from many Western nations, the Ethiopian government tried to alleviate the problem by resettling people from the northern area to the more fertile south. By 1986 more than half a million had been resettled.

In September 1987 civilian rule was formally reintroduced under a new constitution, with Mengistu elected as the country's first president. He was the only candidate and retained his emergency powers. The civil war continued until the leading opposition alliance, the Ethiopian People's Revolutionary Democratic Front (EPRDF), offered a cease-fire in July 1990, leading to the ousting of Mengistu in May 1991. He fled the country and the EPRDF established an interim government prior to elections. In July 1991 the EPRDF leader, Meles Zenawi, was elected president by the National Assembly. Meanwhile, drought conditions exacerbated Ethiopia's problems and led to many deaths, despite massive food aid from Western nations. With the end of hostilities, the EPRDF showed itself to be remarkably calm and disciplined. This augured well for future democratic development and the economic situation also began to improve, with private farming and the market sector being encouraged. However, unrest continued in the Oromo region, where some groups were pressing for the creation of an independent state of Oromia.

As part of the peace process, it was agreed that a referendum on Eritrean independence should be held. This was held in April 1993 and there was an overwhelming vote in favour. In May 1993 Eritrea was formally recognized by Ethiopia as a fully independent state.

A constituent assembly was elected in Ethiopia by multiparty elections held in June 1994, with the EPRDF winning the vast majority of the seats, and in December a new constitution was adopted, making Ethiopia a federal state. In the elections for a permanent assembly in May 1995 the EPRDF won a decisive majority.

GABON

The Gabonese Republic
La République gabonaise

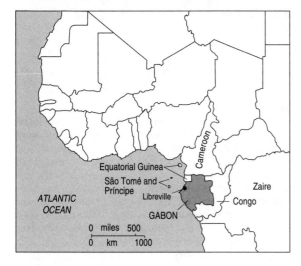

Capital: Libreville

Social and economic data
Area: 267,667 km²
Population: 1,300,000*
Pop. density per km²: 5*
Urban population: 47%**
Literacy rate: 12%**
GDP: $3,600 million**; per-capita GDP: $3,000**
Government defence spending (% of GDP): 2.5%**
Currency: franc CFA
Economy type: middle income
Labour force in agriculture: 76%**

*1994
**1992

Ethnic composition
There are 40 Bantu tribes in four main groupings: the Fang, the Eshira, the Mbede, and the Okande. There are also Pygmies and about 10% of the population is European, mostly French. The official language is French.

Religions
About 70% of the population is Christian, mainly Roman Catholic, and the rest mostly follows traditional animist beliefs.

Political features
State type: emergent democratic
Date of state formation: 1960

Political structure: unitary
Executive: limited presidential
Assembly: one-chamber
Party structure: multiparty
Human rights rating: N/A
International affiliations: ACP, BDEAC, CEEAC, CEMAC, FZ, G-24, IAEA, IBRD, IMF, NAM, OAU, OIC, OPEC, UN, WTO

Local and regional government
For administrative purposes, the country is divided into nine provinces, ranging in population from about 50,000 to nearly 200,000. These are, in turn, subdivided into 37 departments. The provinces are administered by governors and the departments by prefects, all appointed by the president.

Head of state (executive)
President Omar Bongo, since 1967

Head of government
Prime Minister Paulin Obame-Nguema, since 1994

Political leaders since 1970
1967–   Omar Bongo (PDG)

Political system
The 1991 constitution provides for an executive president, directly elected by universal suffrage for a five-year term, renewable once only, and a single-chamber 120-member National Assembly, elected for a five-year term. The president appoints a prime minister who, in turn, appoints a Council of Ministers (cabinet), in consultation with the president.

Political parties
Until 1990 the only legally permitted party was the Gabonese Democratic Party (PDG). There are now eight parties represented in the National Assembly, the two most significant, other than the PDG, being the Gabonese Progress Party (PGP) and the National Rally of Woodcutters (RNB).

The PDG was formed in 1968 by Omar Bongo, who dissolved the former ruling party, the Gabonese Democratic Bloc (BDG), and created a one-party state. The party has a strongly nationalist orientation and is a political vehicle for the president, who is its secretary general.

The PGP is a left-centre grouping formed in 1990.

The RNB was also formed in 1990 and incorporates the Movement for National Regeneration (MORENA). It too has a left-of-centre orientation.

Latest elections
Omar Bongo was re-elected president in December 1993 with a 51% vote share.

In the September 1990 multiparty assembly elections the PDG won 66 seats, the PGP, 19, and MORENA/RNB, 17. There were allegations of widespread fraud.

Political history
Gabon was a province of French Equatorial Africa from 1889 until it achieved full independence in 1960. There were then two main political parties, the Gabonese Democratic Bloc (BDG), led by the pro-French Léon M'ba (1902–67), and the Gabonese Democratic and Social Union (UDSG),

led by Jean-Hilaire Aubame. Although the two parties were evenly matched in popular support, M'ba became president on independence and Aubame foreign minister. In 1964 the BDG wanted the two parties to merge but this was resisted by the UDSG, whereupon M'ba called a general election. Before the elections took place M'ba was deposed in a military coup led by supporters of Aubame but, with the help of France, M'ba was restored to office. Aubame was later found guilty of treason and imprisoned. The UDSG was outlawed and most of its members joined the BDG.

In 1967 M'ba, although in failing health, was re-elected. He died later the same year and was succeeded by Albert-Bernard Bongo (b. 1935). In the following year he dissolved the BDG and established the Gabonese Democratic Party (PDG) as the only legal political party. Bongo was re-elected in 1973 and, announcing his conversion to Islam, changed his first name to Omar. He was re-elected in 1979, 1986, and 1993, pursuing a pro-Western policy course.

Gabon, with its great reserves of uranium, manganese, and iron, is the richest per-capita country in mainland Black Africa, and Bongo and his predecessors have successfully exploited these resources. Although operating an authoritarian regime, he managed to dilute any serious opposition to him. However, he was eventually forced to concede to mounting popular demands, including strikes and antigovernment riots, for a more democratic form of government and in 1990 a multiparty system was introduced. The PDG achieved narrow victories in the 1990 and 1993 multiparty assembly and presidential elections, although the opposition alleged fraud. A government of national unity, including opposition representatives, was formed by Prime Minister Casimir Oye M'ba. He was replaced as prime minister by Paulin Obame-Nguema (PDG) in October 1994 and national elections promised for 1996.

GAMBIA

The Republic of the Gambia

Capital: Banjul

Social and economic data
Area: 11,300 km²
Population: 900,000 million*
Pop. density per km²: 80*
Urban population: 24%**
Literacy rate: 27%**
GDP: $316 million**; per-capita GDP: $350**
Government defence spending (% of GDP): 3.7%**
Currency: dalasi
Economy type: low income
Labour force in agriculture: 84%**

*1994
**1992

Ethnic composition
There is a wide mix of ethnic groups, the largest being the Mandingo, comprising about 40% of the population. The other main groups are the Fula, the Wolof, the Jola, and the Serahuli. The official language is English.

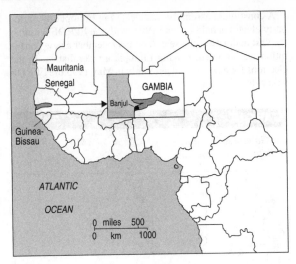

Religions
Eighty-eight per cent of the population is Sunni Muslim. The rest is mainly Anglican Protestant (9%) or animist, following the beliefs of the Jola tribe.

Political features
State type: military authoritarian
Date of state formation: 1965
Political structure: unitary
Executive: military
Assembly: one-chamber
Party structure: two-party
Human rights rating: N/A
International affiliations: ACP, CILSS, CW, ECOWAS, IBRD, IMF, NAM, OAU, OIC, OMVG, UN, WTO

Local and regional government
There is considerable variety in the forms of local government in Gambia. In the capital city there is an elected council and some areas have part-elected and part-appointed councils. In others authority rests with the tribal chiefs.

Head of state and head of government
Lieutenant Yahya Jameh, since 1994

Political leaders since 1970
1970–94 Sir Dawda Karaba Jawara (PPP), 1994– Lieutenant Yahya Jameh (military)

Political system
Gambia is an independent republic within the Commonwealth. The constitution dates from independence in 1970 and provides for a single-chamber assembly, the House of Representatives, consisting of 50 members, 36 directly elected by universal adult suffrage, through a simple plurality voting system, five elected by the chiefs, eight nonvoting nominated members and the attorney general, *ex officio*. It serves a five-year term. The president is elected by direct universal suffrage, again for a five-year term. He or she appoints a vice president, who is also leader of the House of Representatives, and a cabinet. In July 1994, following an army

coup, a military-controlled government was installed. This comprised a five-member Provisional Ruling Council of Patriotic Forces (PRCPF), headed by Lieutenant Yahya Jameh.

Political parties

There are four political parties, the two most significant being the People's Progressive Party (PPP) and the National Convention Party (NCP).

The PPP was formed in 1959 and in 1965 merged with the Democratic Congress Alliance and then, in 1968, with the Gambia Congress Party. In its various forms, it has been the dominant party since the granting of independence. There were calls at one time to make Gambia a one-party state but these were resisted by the president until 1994, Sir Dawda Jawara, who is also the party's secretary general. The PPP has a moderate centrist orientation and is a strong supporter of the Commonwealth.

The NCP dates from 1975. It is a left-of-centre party, advocating fairer sharing of the nation's wealth.

Following the military coup in July 1994, all political parties were banned.

Latest elections

In the April 1992 presidential election Sir Dawda Jawara (PPP) was re-elected with 58.4% of the popular vote. The NCP candidate, Sherif Mustapha Dibba, won 22%.

In the April 1992 elections for the House of Representatives the PPP won 25 seats, and the NCP, 6.

Political history

Originally united with Sierra Leone, Gambia became a British Crown Colony in 1843 and an independent colony within the British Empire in 1888. Political parties were formed in the 1950s, internal self-government was granted in 1963 and full independence within the Commonwealth was achieved in 1965, with Dawda K Jawara (b. 1924), a British university-educated veterinary surgeon, as prime minister.

Gambia declared itself a republic in 1970, Jawara becoming president, thus replacing the British monarch as head of state. He was re-elected in 1972, 1977, 1982, and 1987, with Gambia standing out as one of Africa's few stable and functioning multiparty democracies during these decades. In 1981 an attempted coup against him was thwarted with the help of Senegalese troops and this strengthened the ties between the two countries to such an extent that plans were announced for their merger into a confederation of Senegambia. This was, however, abandoned in 1989.

In the April 1992 presidential and assembly elections Jawara won a fifth term and the People's Progressive Party (PPP) held its majority, but in July 1994, following a coup led by junior army officers, President Jawara fled the country and was given asylum in Senegal. Lieutenant Yahya Jameh named himself president and established a Provisional Ruling Council of the Patriotic Armed Forces (PRCPF), promising to fight corruption and a return to real democracy. The international community condemned the coup and donor countries stopped their aid programmes. The lucrative tourist industry was also badly damaged. Two attempted countercoups, in November 1994 and January 1995, failed.

GHANA

The Republic of Ghana

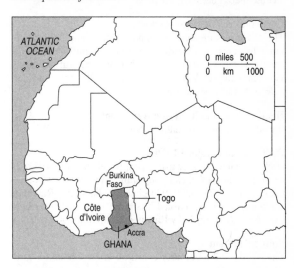

Capital: Accra

Social and economic data

Area: 238,540 km²
Population: 16,400,000*
Pop. density per km²: 69*
Urban population: 35%**
Literacy rate: 60%**
GDP: $5,850 million**; per-capita GDP: $356**
Government defence spending (% of GDP): 1.4%**
Currency: cedi
Economy type: low income
Labour force in agriculture: 59%**

*1994
**1992

Ethnic composition

There are over 75 ethnic groups in the country. The most significant are the Akan, in the south and west, comprising about 44% of the population. Then come the Mole-Dagbani, in the north, the Ewe, in the south, the Ga, in the region of the capital city, and the Fanti, in the coastal area. The official language is English.

Religions

About 30% of the population is Protestant, 25% Roman Catholic, 20% Sunni Muslim, and about 20% follow traditional animist beliefs.

Political features

State type: emergent democratic
Date of state formation: 1957
Political structure: unitary
Executive: limited presidential
Assembly: one-chamber
Party structure: multiparty*
Human rights rating: 53%

International affiliations: ACP, CW, ECOWAS, G-24, IAEA, IBRD, IMF, NAM, OAU, UN, WTO

*Though dominated by one party

Local and regional government

The country is divided into nine regions, ranging in population from just over 1 million to just over 2 million. They are subdivided into 58 districts, which, in turn, are further subdivided into 267 subdistricts. Tribal chiefs still wield considerable authority in some areas, however.

Head of state and head of government

President Flight Lieutenant Jerry Rawlings, since 1981

Political leaders since 1970

1969–72 General Akwasi Afrifa (military–PP), 1972–78 Colonel Ignatius Acheampong (military), 1978–79 Frederick Akuffo (military), 1979 Flight Lieutenant Jerry Rawlings (military), 1979–81 Hilla Limann (PNP), 1981– Flight Lieutenant (retired) Jerry Rawlings (military/NDC)

Political system

The April 1992 multiparty constitution for Ghana's Fourth Republic, which was approved in a referendum, provides for a president who is both head of state and head of government, elected by universal suffrage for a four-year term. There is a single-chamber 200-member House of Parliament, also elected by universal suffrage for a four-year term. The president appoints a vice president and Council of Ministers (cabinet), with the approval of Parliament.

There is also a 25-member Council of State, consisting of presidential nominees and representatives of the regions, to advise the president.

Political parties

The 1979 constitution was suspended in 1981 and all political parties were banned. When the ban was lifted in 1992 the National Democratic Congress (NDC) was formed by a coalition of pro-Rawlings groups. It has a centrist orientation.

Its main rivals are the left-of-centre New Patriotic Party (NPP) and the National Convention Party (NCP), both founded in 1992.

Latest elections

Rawlings was a clear winner in the November 1992 presidential elections, securing 58% of the popular vote.

In the December 1992 parliamentary elections the NDC won 189 of the 200 seats, following a boycott of the polls by the main opposition groups. The NCP won eight seats.

Political history

Ghana was formed by a merger of a British colony, the Gold Coast, which was established in 1874 after the Dutch were ousted, with a British administered United Nations Trust Territory which was part of Togoland. The great interior kingdom of Ashanti was conquered in 1898 and a successful cocoa-based economy was established. The country achieved full independence in 1957, with Dr Kwame Nkrumah (1909–72), who had been prime minister of the Gold Coast since 1952, as president. Nkrumah embarked on a policy of what he called 'African socialism' and established an author-

itarian regime. In 1964 he declared Ghana a one-party state, with the Convention People's Party (CPP), which he led, as the only legal political organization. He then dropped his original stance of international nonalignment and forged links with the Soviet Union and other communist countries.

His autocratic methods created many enemies and in 1966 he was deposed, while on a visit to China, and the leader of the coup, General Joseph Ankrah, established a National Liberation Council. It released many political prisoners and carried out a purge of CPP supporters. In 1969 Ankrah was replaced by General Akwasi Afrifa, who announced plans for a return to civilian government. A new constitution established an elected National Assembly and a nonexecutive presidency. A new grouping, the Progress Party (PP) won a big majority in the Assembly and its leader, Kofi Busia, was appointed prime minister. The following year Edward Akuffo-Addo became the civilian president.

However, the state of the economy worsened and, disenchanted with the civilian administration, the army seized power again in 1972. The constitution was suspended and all political institutions replaced by a National Redemption Council (NRC), under Colonel Ignatius Acheampong. In 1976 he, too, promised a return to civilian rule but critics doubted his sincerity and in 1978 he was replaced by his deputy, Frederick Akuffo, in a bloodless coup. Like his predecessors, Akuffo also announced a speedy return to civilian government but before elections could be held he, in turn, was deposed by junior officers led by Flight Lieutenant Jerry Rawlings (b. 1947). Rawlings, a populist, stated his intentions to be to root out widespread corruption and promote 'moral reform'.

In 1979 civilian rule was restored again, but two years later Rawlings seized power again, complaining about the incompetence of the government. He established a Provisional National Defence Council (PNDC), with himself as chair, again suspending the constitution, dissolving Parliament, and banning political parties. Although the policies of the charismatic Rawlings were initially supported, his failure to revive the economy caused discontent and resulted in a number of popular demonstrations and attempted coups.

Calls for a return to multiparty politics grew and in April 1992 a constitution for a new Fourth Republic was approved by referendum. In September 1992 Rawlings resigned his airforce commission to contest the presidential elections as a civilian and in November he was re-elected, amid claims of fraud by his opponents. During 1994 more than 6,000 people were killed in ethnic clashes in the country's Northern Region, forcing the imposition, for six months, of a state of emergency.

GUINEA

The Republic of Guinea
La République de Guinée

Capital: Conakry

Social and economic data
Area: 245,860 km^2
Population: 6,300,000*

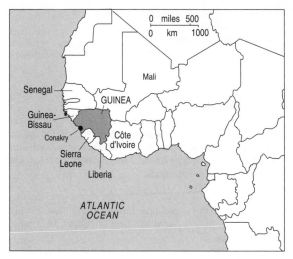

Pop. density per km²: 26*
Urban population: 27%**
Literacy rate: 24%**
GDP: $2,494 million**; per-capita GDP: $430**
Government defence spending (% of GDP): 1.3%**
Currency: Guinea franc
Economy type: low income
Labour force in agriculture: 78%**

*1994
**1992

Ethnic composition
There are some 24 tribal ethnic groups, the main ones being the Malinke, the Peul, and the Soussou. Since independence the government has tried to unify the country by breaking down traditional ethnic barriers. The official language is French.

Religions
About 90% of the population is Sunni Muslim and there are animist and Roman Catholic minorities.

Political features
State type: emergent democratic*
Date of state formation: 1958
Political structure: unitary
Executive: limited presidential
Assembly: one-chamber
Party structure: multiparty
Human rights rating: N/A
International affiliations: ACP, CEAO (observer), ECOWAS, IBRD, IMF, MRU, NAM, OAU, OIC, OMVG, UN

*In a state of transition

Local and regional government
The country is divided into eight provinces, each administered by an appointed governor. There are also elected provincial councils.

Head of state and head of government
President Lansana Conté, since 1984

Political leaders since 1970
1958–1984 Ahmed Sékou Touré (PDG), 1984– Major General Lansana Conté (military/PUP)

Political system
The 1991 constitution, amended in 1992, provides for a multiparty political system with a president who is head of state and head of government, elected by universal suffrage for a five-year term. It also provides for a 114-member single-chamber National Assembly elected in the same way for a similar term.

Political parties
Before April 1992 Guinea was a one-party state. Since then more than 40 parties have been officially recognized. The most significant are the Party of Unity and Progress (PUP), the Rally of the Guinean People (RPG), the Union of the New Republic (UNR), and the Party for Renewal and Progress (PRP).

The PUP is a centrist grouping supporting President Conté. The opposition RPG, led by Alpha Condé, UNR and PRP have left-of-centre orientations.

Latest elections
Lansana Conté won the December 1993 presidential elections with 51.7% of the popular vote.

In the 1995 National Assembly elections the results were as follows:

	Seats
PUP	71
RPG	19
UNR	9
PRP	9
Other parties	6

Political history
Guinea was formerly the colony of French Guinea from 1890, and part of French West Africa. It became fully independent in 1958, after a referendum had rejected, unlike other parts of French West Africa, a proposal to remain a self-governing colony within the French Community. The first president was Ahmed Sékou Touré (1922–84), who made the Democratic Party of Guinea (PDG) the only legal political organization and embarked upon a policy of socialist revolution. There were unsuccessful attempts to overthrow him in 1961, 1965, 1967, and 1970 and, suspicious of conspiracies by foreign powers, he put his country for a time into virtual diplomatic isolation. By 1975, however, relations with most of his neighbours had returned to normal and in 1978 there was reconciliation with France.

Touré initially trod a path of rigid Marxism, ruthlessly crushing opposition to his policies, but gradually moved towards a mixed economy, private enterprise becoming legal in 1979. His domestic regime was, nevertheless, authoritarian and harsh. Externally, he positively sought closer relations with the Western powers, particularly France and the United States. He was re-elected unopposed in 1980 but in

March 1984 died while undergoing heart surgery in the United States.

Before the normal machinery for electing his successor could be put into operation, the army staged a bloodless coup, suspending the constitution, outlawing the PDG, and setting up a Military Committee for National Recovery, with Major General Lansana Conté (b. 1945) at its head. He pledged to restore democracy and respect human rights, releasing hundreds of political prisoners and lifting restrictions on the press. Conté then implemented an IMF-approved economic reform programme and made strenuous efforts to restore his country's international standing through a series of overseas visits. He was successful enough to persuade some 200,000 Guineans who had fled the country during the Touré regime to return. Nevertheless, he continued to head an unelected military regime.

Antigovernment strikes and mass protests in 1991 persuaded the government to promise to allow at least one opposition party to function at some time in the future and in December 1991 a new constitution was announced. In April 1992 provision was made for multiparty politics, with a mixed military-civilian Transitional Committee for National Recovery being set up. A year later Conté won the open presidential election. The president's party, the Party of Unity and Progress (PUP), also won a convincing victory in the 1995 National Assembly elections.

GUINEA-BISSAU

Republic of Guinea-Bissau
República da Guiné-Bissau

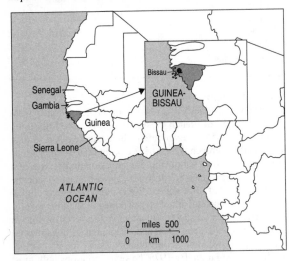

Capital: Bissau

Social and economic data
Area: 36,130 km²
Population: 1,000,000*
Pop. density per km²: 28*
Urban population: 20%**
Literacy rate: 37%**
GDP: $180 million**; per-capita GDP: $180**

Government defence spending (% of GDP): 3.7%**
Currency: Guinea peso
Economy type: low income
Labour force in agriculture: 82%**

*1994
**1992

Ethnic composition
The majority of the population originate from Africa and comprise five main ethnic groups, the Balante, in the central region, the Fulani, in the north, the Malinke, in the north-central area, and the Mandyako and the Pepel near the coast. The official language is Portuguese.

Religions
About 60% of the population follows traditional, animist beliefs, about 35% is Sunni Muslim, and about 5% Roman Catholic.

Political features
State type: emergent democratic
Date of state formation: 1974
Political structure: unitary
Executive: limited presidential
Assembly: one-chamber
Party structure: multiparty*
Human rights rating: N/A
International affiliations: ACP, CILSS, ECOWAS, IBRD, IMF, NAM, OAU, OIC, OMVG, UN, WTO

*Though dominated by one party

Local and regional government
The country is divided into eight regions and one autonomous section, based on the capital, Bissau. All have elected councils.

Head of state (executive)
President João Bernardo 'Niño' Vieira, since 1980

Head of government
Prime Minister Manuel Saturnino da Costa, since 1994

Political leaders since 1970
1973–80 Luiz Cabral (PAIGC), 1980–   Brigadier General João Bernardo 'Niño' Vieira (PAIGC)

Political system
Until 1992 Guinea-Bissau was a one-party state, the 1984 constitution describing the African Party for the Independence of Portuguese Guinea and Cape Verde (PAIGC) as 'the leading force in society and in the nation' and the state as an 'anti-colonialist and anti-imperialist republic'. Although Cape Verde chose not to be united with Guinea-Bissau, preferring independence, the title of the original party which served the two countries has been retained. The revised constitution provides for a directly elected 100-member National Assembly and a president, who is an executive head of state, similarly elected. The Assembly is elected for four years and the president for five years. The president, who is also commander in chief of the armed forces, appoints a prime minister and other ministers.

Political parties

The PAIGC was the only legally permitted party until 1991, when the Supreme Court ended 17 years of one-party rule by legalizing other groups. Now other parties operate, the most significant being the Guinea-Bissau Resistance Party–Bafata Movement (PRGB–MB), the Party for Social Renovation (PRS), and the Party of Renovation and Development (PRD).

The PAIGC was formed in 1956 and was originally the ruling party for both Guinea-Bissau and Cape Verde. It has a nationalistic, socialist orientation and has been organized on top-down Leninist lines.

The PRGB–MB was founded in 1986 in Lisbon. It has a centrist orientation.

The PRS was formed in 1992. It has a left-of-centre orientation.

The PRD is led by João da Costa, who was arrested in connection with a July 1993 attempted coup, but was later released.

Latest elections

João Vieira narrowly won the July 1994 presidential election, in the second round, with 52% of the vote.

In the July 1994 assembly elections the PAIGC won a clear majority, with 62 of the 100 seats.

Political history

Guinea-Bissau, as part of the Portuguese empire, was governed jointly with Cape Verde until 1879, when it became a separate colony, with the name Portuguese Guinea. Agitation for independence intensified after World War II and this resulted in the formation, in 1956, of the African Party for the Independence of Portuguese Guinea and Cape Verde (PAIGC). In the face of Portugal's refusal to grant independence, fighting broke out in 1961 and by 1972 the PAIGC claimed to be in control of two-thirds of the country. The following year the 'liberated areas' were declared independent and in 1973 a National People's Assembly was set up and Luiz Cabral appointed president of a State Council. Some 40,000 Portuguese troops were used to try to put down the uprising, suffering heavy losses. However, before a clear outcome was reached, a sudden coup in mainland Portugal proved a sufficient distraction to bring the fighting to an end and the PAIGC negotiated independence with the new government in Lisbon. In 1974 Portugal formally acknowledged Guinea-Bissau as a sovereign nation.

The PAIGC set about laying the foundations for a socialist state which was intended to include Cape Verde, but in November 1980, four days before approval of the constitution, the inhabitants of Cape Verde, feeling that Guinea-Bissau was being given preferential treatment in the constitutional arrangements, decided to withdraw. Cabral was deposed in a coup and Colonel João Vieira (b. 1939) became chair of a Council of Revolution. At its 1981 Congress, the PAIGC decided to retain its name, despite Cape Verde's withdrawal, and its position was confirmed as the only legal party, with Vieira, a party member since 1960, as its secretary general. Normal relations between Guinea-Bissau and Cape Verde were restored in 1982. Constitutional changes in 1984 created an executive presidency.

In January 1991, in response to public pressure, the PAIGC formally approved the introduction of 'integral multipartyism' and later that year a number of opposition parties were legalized. In July 1994 the PAIGC obtained a clear majority in the Assembly elections and in the following month Brigadier General Vieira had a narrow victory in the first multiparty presidential election, attracting 52% of the vote. In October 1994 Manuel Saturnino da Costa, the hardline secretary general of the PAIGC, was appointed prime minister. He inherited an economy which, crippled by high levels of external indebtedness and with inflation at 100%, was heavily reliant on foreign economic aid.

KENYA

Republic of Kenya
Jamhuri ya Kenya

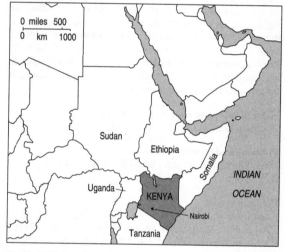

Capital: Nairobi

Social and economic data
Area: 580,646 km^2
Population: 26,100,000*
Pop. density per km^2: 45*
Urban population: 25%**
Literacy rate: 69%**
GDP: $8,500 million**; per-capita GDP: $325**
Government defence spending (% of GDP): 2.2%**
Currency: Kenya shilling
Economy type: low income
Labour force in agriculture: 81%**

*1994
**1992

Ethnic composition
The main ethnic groups are the Kikuyu, about 21%, the Luhya, 14%, the Luo, 13%, the Kalenjin, 11%, the Kamba, 11%, the Kisii, 6%, and the Meru, 5%. The official language is Swahili.

Religions
The adherence to religions varies from tribe to tribe and area to area. About 25% of the population is Roman Catholic, 24%

belong to Independent African Churches, 18% Protestant, 6% Sunni Muslim, chiefly near the coast and around Nairobi, and a fifth of the populace follows traditional animist beliefs.

Political features

State type: authoritarian nationalist
Date of state formation: 1963
Political structure: unitary
Executive: unlimited presidential
Assembly: one-chamber
Party structure: multiparty*
Human rights rating: 46%
International affiliations: ACP, COMESA, CW, IAEA, IBRD, IGADD, IMF, IWC, NAM, OAU, UN, WTO

*Though dominated by one party

Local and regional government

Regional and local governments display features from the days of British colonial rule. The country is divided into eight provinces, including the city of Nairobi, which are further subdivided into 40 districts. The provinces are administered by provincial commissioners and the districts by district commissioners. Below the commissioner level there are municipal councils, town councils, county councils, urban councils, and area councils.

Head of state and head of government

President Daniel arap Moi, since 1978

Political leaders since 1970

1964–78 Jomo Kenyatta (KANU), 1978– Daniel arap Moi (KANU)

Political system

Kenya became a republic, within the Commonwealth, in 1964 and the constitution dates from independence in 1963. It was amended in 1964, 1969, 1982, 1988, 1991, and 1992. It provides for a president, elected by universal adult suffrage for a five-year term, and a single-chamber National Assembly, serving a similar term.

A 1992 amendment requires a presidential candidate to win not only a majority of the national votes but to be endorsed by at least 25% of voters in at least five of the country's eight provinces. Critics of the amendment alleged that it was introduced to assist President Moi in the 1992 elections.

The Assembly has 202 members, 188 elected by universal adult suffrage, through a simple plurality voting system, 12 nominated by the president and the attorney general and speaker as *ex officio* members. From 1969 to 1982 Kenya was a one-party state in fact and then became one in law. In December 1991 a constitutional amendment, allowing multiparty politics, became effective. The vice president and Cabinet of Ministers are appointed by the president.

Political parties

Until 1991 the only legitimate party was the Kenya African National Union (KANU). Since 1992 opposition parties have been formed, the most significant being the Forum for the Restoration of Democracy–Asili (FORD–Asili), the Forum for the Restoration of Democracy–Kenya (FORD–Kenya), and the Democratic Party (DP).

The predecessor to KANU was the Kenya African Union (KAU), formed in 1944, mainly by members of the Kikuyu tribe. Jomo Kenyatta became its leader in 1947 and then KAU was proscribed in 1952, following the Mau Mau violence and Kenyatta's imprisonment. On his release, in 1961, he set about merging KAU with its rival, the Kenya African Democratic Union (KADU). KANU was subsequently formed, with Kenyatta as its leader. Its orientation is now nationalistic and centrist, and very much a political vehicle for the president.

FORD–Asili and FORD–Kenya were both formed in 1992 and have left-of-centre Luo and Luhya orientations.

The DP was founded a year earlier in anticipation of the restoration of multiparty politics. It, too, has a left-of-centre orientation and is kikuyu dominated.

In May 1995 a new centre-left party, Safina, was formed by Richard Leakey (b. 1944), renowned palaeoanthropologist. From November 1995 it formed the hub of an anti-KANU alliance, incorporating the DP, FORD-Asili, and FORD-Kenya.

Latest elections

In the first multiparty presidential elections, in December 1992, President Moi was re-elected for his fourth successive term. Although only securing 36% of the votes, those of his opponents were split, allowing him to win.

In the December 1992 Assembly elections KANU won 95 of the elected seats, FORD–Asili and FORD–Kenya won 31 each, and the DP, 23. There were accusations of progovernment intimidation during the poll.

Political history

An East African Protectorate was forcibly formed in 1895 by the British, which became the colony of Kenya in 1920. A white planting community settled in highland areas, displacing many Kikuyu, and during the 1920s a black protest movement developed. The country came close to civil war, as pronationalist groups carried out a campaign of violence. The Kenya African Union (KAU) was founded in 1944 and in 1947 Jomo Kenyatta (1894–1978), a member of Kenya's largest tribe, the Kikuyu, became its president. Three years later a secret society of young Kikuyu militants was formed, called Mau Mau, which had the same aims as KAU but sought to achieve them by violent means. Although Kenyatta disassociated himself from the Mau Mau risings of 1952–56, he was not trusted by the British authorities and was imprisoned in 1953.

The terrorist campaign had largely finished by 1956 and the state of emergency which had been imposed was lifted and Kenyatta released in 1961. The country was granted internal self-government in 1963 and Kenyatta, who had become leader of the Kenya African National Union (KANU), became prime minister and then president after full independence, within the Commonwealth, was obtained in 1964. He continued as president until his death in 1978, during which time his country achieved considerable stability and he became a widely respected world leader.

He was succeeded by the vice president, Daniel arap Moi (b. 1924), who built on the achievements of his predecessor, launching an impressive four-year procapitalist development plan. An attempted coup by junior airforce officers in 1982 was foiled and resulted, for a while, in political detentions and press censorship. The airforce and Nairobi University were also temporarily dissolved. In the same year the National Assembly declared Kenya a one-party state. President Moi was re-elected in 1983 and 1988 and his position seemed secure, but as his rule became increasingly autocratic, demands for multiparty politics grew. Moi resisted these calls until 1991, when, influenced by pressure exerted by foreign aid donors, a constitutional amendment allowed for this.

Nevertheless, his critics have also argued that he was not fully committed to pluralist politics. A constitutional amendment in 1992, which would seem to assist him in presidential elections, tended to support this view and there have been regular complaints about the fairness of the conduct of elections. President Moi and KANU were successful in the 1992 multiparty elections, soon after which FORD–Asili and FORD–Kenya agreed to form a united front to fight future elections. In 1993 a temporary suspension of parliament by the president provoked unrest in Nairobi and there were tribal clashes in the Rift Valley region. In 1994 the country was afflicted by a terrible drought, during which almost a fifth of the population was threatened by famine. In July 1995 it was claimed by the US-based Human Rights Watch Africa that more than 1,500 Kenyans had died as a result of political violence since 1991.

LESOTHO

The Kingdom of Lesotho

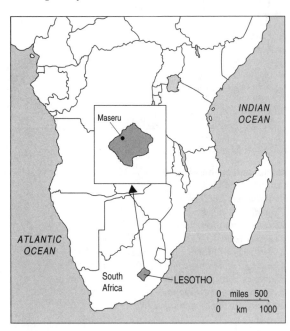

Capital: Maseru

Social and economic data
Area: 30,350 km²
Population: 1,900,000*

Pop. density per km²: 63*
Urban population: 21%**
Literacy rate: 59%**
GDP: $846 million**; per-capita GDP: $547**
Government defence spending (% of GDP): 5%**
Currency: loti
Economy type: low income
Labour force in agriculture: 23%**

*1994
**1992

Ethnic composition
Almost the entire population are Bantus, of Southern Sotho, or Basotho, stock. The official language is English.

Religions
About 45% of the population is Roman Catholic and 48% Protestant (Anglican and Lesotho Evangelical).

Political features
State type: emergent democratic
Date of state formation: 1966
Political structure: unitary
Executive: parliamentary
Assembly: two-chamber
Party structure: multiparty*
Human rights rating: N/A
International affiliations: ACP, COMESA, CW, IBRD, IMF, NAM, OAU, SADC, UN, WTO

*Though dominated by one party

Local and regional government
For administrative purposes, the country is divided into ten districts. Each district has an appointed coordinator and an elected council.

Head of state
King Moshoeshoe II, since 1995

Head of government
Prime Minister Ntsu Mokhehle, since 1993

Political leaders since 1970
1970–86 Chief Leabua Jonathan (BNP), 1986–90 General Justin Lekhanya (military), 1990–93 Colonel Elias Ramaema (military), 1993–   Dr Ntsu Mokhehle (BCP)

Political system
Lesotho is an independent hereditary monarchy within the Commonwealth. The original constitution, which dates from independence in 1966, was replaced in 1993 and provides for a king who is head of state but has no executive or legislative powers. A parliamentary system operates with a two-chamber legislature, the 65-member National Assembly and the Senate. Members of the National Assembly are elected by universal suffrage for a five-year term. The Senate consists of traditional chiefs and eight nominated members. There is a College of Chiefs with the traditional power of electing or removing the king by majority vote.

Political parties

There are five active parties, the two most significant being the Basotho Congress Party (BCP) and the Basotho National Party (BNP).

The BCP was the main opposition party but had been banned when Lesotho became virtually a one-party state. With the return of multiparty politics in 1993 it became overtly active again. It has a left-of-centre orientation.

The BNP was formed in 1958 by Chief Leabua Jonathan and soon became his personal political machine. It has a right-of-centre orientation.

Latest elections

In the March 1993 general election the BCP secured a landslide victory, winning all the 65 National Assembly seats.

Political history

Lesotho, founded as a state entity in the 1820s by the Sotho leader, Moshoeshoe I (c. 1790–1870), was formerly called Basutoland. As such, it became a British dependency in 1868 and then a colony. It was given internal self-government in 1965, with the paramount chief of the Basotho people since 1960, the Oxford-educated Moshoeshoe II (b. 1938) as king. It achieved full independence, as Lesotho, in 1966. The Basotho National Party (BNP), a conservative group favouring limited cooperation with South Africa, remained in power from independence until 1986. Its leader, Chief Leabua Jonathan, became prime minister in 1966 and after 1970, when the powers of the king were severely curtailed and he was forced into an eight-month exile in the Netherlands, the country was effectively under the prime minister's control.

From 1975 an organization called the Lesotho Liberation Army (LLA) carried out a number of attacks on BNP members, with the support, it was alleged, of the South African government. The South Africans denied complicity but, at the same time, pointed out that Lesotho allowed the then banned South African nationalist movement, the African National Congess (ANC), to use it as a base. Economically, Lesotho was dependent on South Africa but openly rejected the policy of apartheid. It came under pressure from Pretoria to sign a nonaggression pact, similar to the Nkomati Accord between South Africa and Mozambique, but Jonathan's government consistently refused to do so.

In January 1986 South Africa imposed a border blockade, cutting off food and fuel supplies to Lesotho, and a few weeks later the government of Chief Jonathan was ousted and replaced in a coup led by General Justin Lekhanya. He announced that all executive and legislative powers would be placed in the hands of the king, ruling through a Military Council, chaired by General Lekhanya, and a Council of Ministers. A week after the coup about 60 ANC members were deported to Zambia and on the same day the South African blockade was lifted.

In February 1990 General Lekhanya was removed from office and replaced by Colonel Elias Ramaema. At the same time King Moshoeshoe II was deposed and replaced by his son Letsie III (b. 1963). King Moshoeshoe went into exile. Soon after taking over the reins of government Ramaema announced that political parties would be allowed to operate again and King Moshoeshoe was allowed to return in July 1992, in the role of a tribal chief rather than monarch.

In early 1993 Colonel Ramaema kept his promise, relinquishing military control, and multiparty elections were held. The Basotho Congress Party (BCP) won all the assembly seats and its leader, Dr Ntsu Mokhehle, became prime minister. In January 1994 fighting broke out between rival army factions, a potential civil war being averted by prompt action by the Organization of African Unity (OAU).

In August 1994 King Letsie III dissolved the Assembly, dismissed the prime minister and said he would return the throne to his father, Moshoeshoe II. The leaders of South Africa, Zimbabwe, and Botswana intervened, giving King Letsie a deadline of 1 September for reinstating the elected government of Dr Ntsu Mokhehle and on 14 September 1994 this was done. In January 1995 King Letsie abdicated and King Moshoeshoe returned to the throne as a nonexecutive monarch.

LIBERIA

The Republic of Liberia

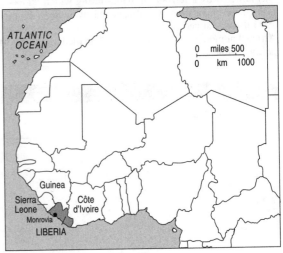

Capital: Monrovia

Social and economic data

Area: 97,754 km²
Population: 2,800,000*
Pop. density per km²: 287*
Urban population: 47%**
Literacy rate: 40%**
GDP: $811 million**; per-capita GDP: $353**
Government defence spending (% of GDP): 1.2%**
Currency: Liberian dollar
Economy type: low income
Labour force in agriculture: 74%**

*1994
**1992

Ethnic composition

Ninety-five per cent of the population are members of indigenous tribes, which include the Kpelle, the Bassa, the Gio, the Kru, the Grebo, the Mano, the Krahn, the Gola, the

Gbandi, the Loma, the Kissi, the Vai, and the Bella. The other 5% are descended from slaves repatriated from the United States. The official language is English.

Religions
Liberia is officially a Christian state but all religions are tolerated and traditional animist practices widely followed. The main Christian churches are Lutheran, Anglican, Roman Catholic, Baptist, and United Methodist, to which a quarter of the population belongs. A similar proportion, 24%, follows Sunni Islam.

Political features
State type: military authoritarian*
Date of state formation: 1847
Political structure: unitary
Executive: military collective presidential*
Assembly: two-chamber
Party structure: in transition
Human rights rating: N/A
International affiliations: ACP, ECOWAS, IAEA, IBRD, IMF, MRU, NAM, OAU, UN

*In a state of transition to emergent democracy

Local and regional government
The country is divided into nine counties, each administered by an appointed superintendent. In addition, there are six territories and the capital district of Monrovia.

Head of state and head of government
Chair of collective executive council: Wilton Sankawulo, since 1995

Political leaders since 1970
1944–71 William Tubman (TWP), 1971–80 William Tolbert (TWP), 1980–90 Samuel Kenyon Doe (NDPL), 1990–94 Amos Sawyer (NPFL), 1994–95 David Kpormakor (IGNU), 1995– Wilton Sankawulo (transitional collective government)

Political system
From 1980 to 1984 Liberia was under the military rule of a People's Redemption Council (PRC). In 1984 the PRC was dissolved and its functions taken over by an Interim National Assembly appointed by the president, pending a new constitution which came into effect in 1986. This provided for a two-chamber National Assembly, consisting of a Senate with 26 members and a House of Representatives of 64, elected by universal adult suffrage, through a simple plurality voting system, for a six-year term. The president was to be elected in the same way for a similar term. A civil war began in 1990 which threw the country into chaos before an interim government was established in 1991. This was replaced in 1993 by a collective presidency and then in March 1994 a transitional Interim Government of National Unity (IGNU) was appointed with United Nations backing, with a five-member Council of State and 35-member Transitional Legislative Assembly. However, this collapsed because of disagreements between the various warlords. They eventually signed a peace agreement, but the government remained in a transitional state.

Political parties
Until the Doe government collapsed in 1990 Liberia was virtually a one-party state, dominated by the Democratic Party of Liberia (NDPL).

The NDPL was formed in 1984 by Samuel Doe, as a modern equivalent of the True Whig Party (TWP), which had been the leading force in Liberia's politics since the early years of the state's creation.

The main groups involved in the 1994–95 coalition government were the National Patriotic Front of Liberia (NPFL), led by Charles Taylor, and the United Liberation Movement for Democracy in Liberia (Ulimo), led by Raleigh Seekie.

All parties have left-of-centre orientations.

In opposition are the Armed Forces of Liberia (AFL), led by General Hezekiah Bowen.

Latest elections
In the 1985 presidential election Samuel Doe won with 50.9% of the vote.

In the 1985 assembly elections the NDPL won 22 of the 26 Senate seats and 51 of the 64 House seats, in the face of allegations of electoral fraud.

In 1991 Amos Sawyer was re-elected interim president by rebel groups.

Political history
Liberia was founded in 1821 by the American Colonization Society as a settlement for black slaves from the southern United States. It became an independent republic in 1847 and between 1878 and 1980 politics were dominated by the True Whig Party, which provided all the country's presidents. William Tubman (1895–1971), a descendant of US slaves, was president from 1944 until his death in 1971 and was succeeded by the vice president, William R Tolbert, who was re-elected in 1975.

In 1980 Tolbert was assassinated in a military coup led by Master Sergeant Samuel Doe (b. 1950), who suspended the constitution, banned all political parties, and ruled through an appointed People's Redemption Council (PRC). The first Liberian of local ancestry to rule the nation, he proceeded to stamp out corruption in the public service, encountering considerable opposition and making enemies who were later to threaten his position.

A new draft constitution, providing for an elected two-chamber National Assembly and an elected president, was approved by the PRC in 1983 and by national referendum the following year. Political parties were allowed to function again, provided they registered with a new body, the Special Electoral Commission (SECOM). In August 1984 Doe founded the National Democratic Party of Liberia (NDPL) and announced that he proposed to stand for the presidency.

By early 1985, 11 political parties had been formed but only five eventually registered in time for the elections. Doe's party won clear majorities in both chambers of the Assembly, although there were complaints of election fraud, and Doe himself was elected president.

By 1990 there was considerable opposition to Doe which developed into a civil war, the government being challenged by Charles Taylor, a former state employee who had been charged with theft, and Prince Yormie Johnson, a friend of

Taylor who had broken away to form a splinter group. In the face of international efforts to find a solution, the war continued and in September 1990 Doe was captured and killed. Taylor's political wing, the National Patriotic Front of Liberia (NPFL), set up an interim government, headed by Amos Sawyer, an academic lawyer. Despite the installation of this government, and the signing of a peace agreement, in October 1991, rebel forces outside the mainstream groups continued to fight. A predominantly Nigerian West African military force, known as Ecomog, was sent in to the country to attempt to impose some order in a war that had claimed 150,000 lives and rendered 2 million homeless.

In August 1993 a collective presidency was agreed but this soon collapsed and was replaced by a transitional government, which was later disputed by the military leaders. Another peace agreement, between the NPFL, Ulimo, and the Armed Forces of Liberia, led by Hezekiah Bowen, was signed in September 1994 but fighting continued. In January and February 1995 Ghanaian-backed peace moves also foundered but in August 1995 an agreement, brokered by the Ghanaian president, Flight Lieutenant Jerry Rawlings, was accepted by Charles Taylor and the leaders of the other main military factions, George Boli and Alhaji Kromah. In September 1995 a collective executive, consisting of the three warlords and chaired by the academic, Wilton Sankawulo, was established as an interim administration until elections in 1996.

MADAGASCAR

The Democratic Republic of Madagascar
Repoblika Demokratika n'i Madagaskar

Capital: Antananarivo (Tananarive)

Social and economic data
Area: 587,041 km^2
Population: 13,300,000*
Pop. density per km^2: 23*
Urban population: 25%**
Literacy rate: 53%**
GDP: $2,760 million**; per-capita GDP: $230**
Government defence spending (% of GDP): 1.2%**
Currency: Malgasy franc
Economy type: low income
Labour force in agriculture: 81%**

*1994
**1992

Ethnic composition
There are 18 main Malagasy tribes of Malaysian-Polynesian origin. There are also minorities of French, Chinese, Indians, Pakistanis, and Comorans. Despite a common ethnic heritage, the inhabitants of the highlands, mainly the Merinas, have frequently found themselves in conflict with the coastal tribes, known as the *côtiers*. The official languages are Malagasy and French.

Religions
About 47% of the population follows traditional, animist beliefs and about 50% is Christian, of which about half is

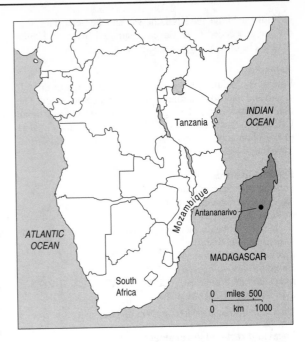

Roman Catholic and half Protestant. There is also a Muslim minority.

Political features
State type: emergent democratic
Date of state formation: 1960
Political structure: unitary
Executive: limited presidential
Assembly: two-chamber
Party structure: multiparty
Human rights rating: N/A
International affiliations: ACP, COMESA, Francophone, IAEA, IBRD, ICC, ICFTU, IMF, IOC, NAM, OAU, UN, WTO

Local and regional government
The country is divided into six provinces, with a three-tiered substructure, based on traditional village assemblies, or *fokonolona*.

Head of state (executive)
President Albert Zafy, since 1993

Head of government
Prime Minister Emmanuel Rakotovahiny, since 1995

Political leaders since 1970
1960–72 Philibert Tsiranana (PSD), 1972–75 General Gabriel Ramanantsoa (military), 1975–93 Lieutenant Commander Didier Ratsiraka (FNDR), 1993– Albert Zafy (Comité des Forces Vives)

Political system
The 1992 constitution provides for an executive president, who is head of state, and a two-chamber assembly, a 138-member National Assembly and a Senate. The president and

National Assembly are elected by universal suffrage for seven- and five-year terms respectively.

The Senate, comprising appointed and nominated members, should have been formed during 1995.

Political parties

Until 1990 the only permitted political movement was the National Front for the Defence of the Malagasy Socialist Revolution (FNDR). Its main opposition now is the Comité des Forces Vives.

The FNDR was formed in 1976 around the Advance Guard of the Malagasy Revolution (AREMA) which Didier Ratsiraka established as the nucleus of a single national party. Within the FNDR are six other groups, three of them left-wing and three left-of-centre.

The Comité des Forces Vives is also a coalition of left-of-centre groups, including the National Union for Democracy and Development (UNDD) and the Rasalama Active Forces Cartel (FVCR). It was formed in 1991.

Latest elections

The February 1993 presidential election was won convincingly by the leader of the Comité des Forces Vives, Albert Zafy, who secured 66% of the vote in the second round, defeating the incumbent president, Didier Ratsiraka.

In the June 1993 General Assembly elections the Comité des Forces Vives won 75 of the 138 seats.

Political history

Formerly a French colony, forcibly annexed in 1896, Madagascar became an autonomous state within the French community in 1958. This followed a nationalist uprising in 1947–48 that was suppressed with heavy loss of life. It achieved full independence, as a republic, in 1960. The country's history since independence has been greatly influenced by the competing interests of Madagascar's two main ethnic groups, the coastal tribes, known as the *côtiers*, and the highland people, represented by the Merina.

The first president of the republic was Philibert Tsiranana, leader of the Social Democratic Party (PSD), which identified itself with the coastal-based *côtiers*. In 1972 the army, representing the Merina, took control of the government and pursued a more nationalistic line than Tsiranana. This caused resentment among the *côtiers* and, with rising unemployment, led to a government crisis in 1975 which resulted in the imposition of martial law under a National Military Directorate and the banning of all political parties.

Later that year a new, socialist constitution was approved and Lieutenant Commander Didier Ratsiraka (b. 1936), a *côtier*, was elected president of the Democratic Republic of Madagascar. Political parties were allowed to operate again and in 1976 the Front-Line Revolutionary Organization (AREMA) was formed by Ratsiraka, as the nucleus of a single party for the state. By 1977 all political activity was concentrated in the left-wing National Front for the Defence of the Malagasy Socialist Revolution (FNDR) and all the candidates for the National People's Assembly were FNDR nominees. In 1977 the National Movement for the Independence of Madagascar (MONIMA), a radical socialist party, withdrew from the FNDR and was declared illegal. MONIMA's

leader, Monja Jaona, unsuccessfully challenged Ratsiraka for the presidency.

Despite social and political discontent, particularly among the Merinas, Ratsiraka was re-elected and AREMA marginally increased its Assembly seat total in the 1989 elections.

There were coup attempts against the government in 1990 and then in October 1991, after widespread civil unrest following the army's firing into a crowd during an August 1991 general strike, Ratsiraka was forced to surrender some of his powers and create a new unity government, which included opposition members. A referendum, in August 1992, gave clear support for a return to multiparty politics and a revised constitution was introduced, transferring some of the president's powers to a prime minister, as head of government. The coalition opposed to Ratsiraka, the Comité des Forces Vives, won both the February 1993 presidential and June 1993 Assembly elections, its leader Albert Zafy, becoming president. He appointed Francisque Ravony prime minister and this was confirmed by the National Assembly. In 1995 Zafy and Ravony disagreed over the issue of who had the authority to appoint the prime minister, the president or the Assembly. In a referendum held in September 1995 voters decided in favour of the president and a month later Ravony was replaced by Emmanuel Rakotovahiny (UNOD), who was an ally of Rafy.

MALAWI

The Republic of Malawi

Capital: Lilongwe

Social and economic data
Area: 118,480 km^2
Population: 10,700,000*
Pop. density per km^2: 90*

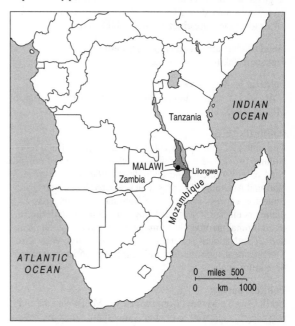

Urban population: 42%**
Literacy rate: 48%**
GDP: $1,904 million**; per-capita GDP: $180**
Government defence spending (% of GDP): 1%**
Currency: Malawi kwacha
Economy type: low income
Labour force in agriculture: 82%**

*1994
**1992

Ethnic composition
Almost all the people are indigenous Africans but divided ethnically into numerous tribes, the main ones being the Chewa, the Nyanja, the Tumbuka, the Yao, the Lomwe, the Sena, the Tonga, and the Ngoni. There are also Asian and European minorities. The official languages are English and Chichewa.

Religions
About 30% of the population is Protestant and 25% Roman Catholic. The remainder is mostly Sunni Muslim (16%) or follows traditional animist beliefs (20%).

Political features
State type: emergent democratic
Date of state formation: 1964
Political structure: unitary
Executive: limited presidential
Assembly: one-chamber
Party structure: multiparty
Human rights rating: 33%
International affiliations: ACP, COMESA, CW, IBRD, IMF, NAM, OAU, SADC, UN, WTO

Local and regional government
For administrative purposes, the country is divided into three regions, which are further subdivided into 24 districts. Regions are the responsibility of cabinet ministers and districts are administered by appointed commissioners. At a lower level there are chiefs' and subchiefs' areas.

Head of state and head of government
President Bakili Muluzi, since 1994

Political leaders since 1970
1966–94 Hastings Kamuzu Banda (MCP), 1994– Bakili Muluzi (UDF)

Political system
The June 1993 multiparty constitution, adopted after a referendum, provides for a president, who is head of state and head of government, and a single-chamber legislature, the National Assembly. The president is elected by universal suffrage for a five-year term. The National Assembly has 177 members elected in a similar way plus an unlimited number of additional members who may be nominated by the president. The National Assembly also serves a five-year term. The president appoints and leads ministers who are responsible to him or her.

Political parties
Until 1993 the Malawi Congress Party (MCP) was the only party legally allowed to operate. Now there are some seven other authorized parties, the most significant being the United Democratic Front (UDF) and the Alliance for Democracy (AFORD).

The MCP was founded in 1959 by Hastings Banda to lead the fight for independence. It became very much his personal political machine. Its orientation can best be described as right-wing multiracial.

The UDF was founded in 1992 and has a left-of-centre orientation.

AFORD was also formed in 1992 and in 1993 absorbed the Malawi Freedom Movement. It, too, has a left-of-centre orientation.

Latest elections
The leader of the UDF, Bakili Muluzi, was elected president in May 1994 with 47% of the vote, his nearest rival, Hastings Banda, obtaining 33.6%.

In the May 1994 National Assembly elections the UDF won 85 seats, the MCP, 55, and AFORD, 36.

Political history
Malawi, which came under British rule in 1891, was formerly the protectorate of Nyasaland. White settlers moved into its fertile south, taking African land. This led to a violent uprising in 1915, led by the Reverend John Chilembwe. Between 1953 and 1964, the country formed part of the white-dominated Central Africa Federation of Rhodesia and Nyasaland, which comprised what are now Zimbabwe, Zambia and Malawi. Dr Hastings Kamuzu Banda (b. c. 1903), through the Malawi Congress Party (MCP), led a campaign for independence, being imprisoned briefly in 1959, and in 1963 the Federation was dissolved. Nyasaland became independent, as Malawi, in 1964 and two years later a republic and a one-party state, with Dr Banda, who had been prime minister since 1963, as its first president.

Banda governed his country in a very personal way, brooking no opposition, and his foreign policies were, at times, rather idiosyncratic. He astonished his Black African colleagues in 1967 by officially recognizing the white-only republic of South Africa and, in 1971, became the first African head of state to visit that country. In 1976, however, he also recognized the socialist government in Angola.

In 1977 he embarked upon a policy of what can best be described as cautious liberalism, releasing some political detainees and allowing greater press freedom, but these moves proved insufficient to satisfy his critics, including important foreign aid donors, and in 1992, in the wake of industrial riots, he promised a referendum on constitutional change.

The referendum, held in June 1993, showed a clear, 63%, majority in favour of a multiparty system and a new constitution was drafted and approved. This included, in November 1993, the repeal of the institution of life presidency that had been conferred on Banda in 1971. In the May 1994 presidential and assembly elections the newly formed United Democratic Front (UDF) was victorious. Its leader, Bakili Muluzi (b. 1943), became president and a coalition government was formed, comprising the UDF and the Alliance for Democracy (AFORD). Early in 1995 the veteran Dr Hastings Banda, who had undergone brain surgery in 1993, and his former aide, John Tembo, who had headed the police and the MCP's armed youth wing, the Malawi Young Pioneers, were formally charged with the murder of political opponents in 1983. Banda was acquitted in December 1995.

MALI

The Republic of Mali
La République du Mali

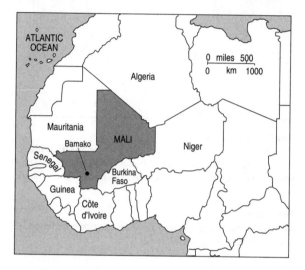

Capital: Bamako

Social and economic data
Area: 1,240,000 km^2
Population: 10,100,000*
Pop. density per km^2: 8*
Urban population: 25%**
Literacy rate: 32%**
GDP: $2,484 million**; per-capita GDP: $270**
Government defence spending (% of GDP): 1.9%**
Currency: franc CFA
Economy type: low income
Labour force in agriculture: 86%**

*1994
**1992

Ethnic composition
About half the population belongs to the Mande group of tribes, which include the Bambara, the Malinke, and the Sarakole. Other significant tribes are the Fulani, the Minianka, the Senutu, the Songhai, and the nomadic Tuareg in the north. The official language is French.

Religions
About 80% of the population is Sunni Muslim, about 2% is Christian, and the rest mostly follows traditional, animist beliefs.

Political features
State type: emergent democratic
Date of state formation: 1960

Political structure: unitary
Executive: limited presidential
Assembly: one-chamber
Party structure: multiparty
Human rights rating: N/A
International affiliations: ACP, BOAD, CEAO, CILSS, ECOWAS, Francophone, FZ, IAEA, IBRD, IMF, NAM, OAU, OIC, OMVS, UEMOA, UN, WTO

Local and regional government
The country is divided into six regions and 42 counties, or *cercles*, which are further subdivided into 279 *arrondissements*. All are administered by officials of the national government.

Head of state (executive)
President Alpha Oumar Konare, since 1992

Head of government
Prime Minister Ibrahim Boubacar Keita, since 1994

Political leaders since 1970
1968–91 Lieutenant Moussa Traoré (military/UDPM), 1991–92, Lieutenant Colonel Amadou Toumani Toure (military), 1992– Alpha Oumar Konare (ADEMA)

Political system
The January 1992 multiparty constitution, approved by referendum, provides for an executive president, who is head of state, and a single-chamber legislature, the National Assembly. The president and the Assembly are elected by universal suffrage for five-year terms. Of the 129 members of the National Assembly, 13 represent the interests of Malians abroad. The president appoints the prime minister, as head of government, and he or she in turn appoints other ministers.

Political parties
Until 1991 the only legally permitted party was the Malian People's Democratic Union (UDPM). Now more than 40 parties have been officially recognized, the most significant being the Alliance for Democracy in Mali (ADEMA), the National Committee for Democratic Initiative (CNID), the Assembly for Democracy and Progress (RDP), the Civic Society, and the Democracy and Progress Party (PDP).

The UDPM has a women's wing (UNFM) and a youth wing (UNJM). It was founded in 1976, in accordance with the 1974 constitution, as the government party. Although it is a socialist party and organized on Marxist–Leninist lines, its predominant orientation is nationalistic.

ADEMA is the main partner in the coalition government formed in 1992. The PDP and the Civic Society are the others. They all have left-of-centre orientations. The CNID and RDP left the coalition in 1994.

The chief Tuareg rebel group is the Unified Movement and Fronts of Azawad (MFUA).

Latest elections
In the March 1992 National Assembly elections ADEMA won 76 of the 116 seats but the turnout was very low.

In the second round of the April 1992 presidential elections the ADEMA leader, Alpha Oumar Konare, was elected with 69% of the votes cast.

Political history
Because of its comparatively isolated position, Mali escaped European contact until France conquered the region between 1880 and 1895 and established a colony. It then was called French Sudan and formed part of French West Africa. In 1959, with Senegal, it formed the Federation of Mali. Senegal soon left and Mali became a fully independent republic in 1960, with Modibo Keita as its first president.

Keita imposed an authoritarian socialist regime but the failure of his economic policies led to his removal in an army coup in 1968. The constitution was suspended and all political activity banned, the government being placed in the hands of a Military Committee for National Liberation (CMLN) with Lieutenant Moussa Traoré as its president and head of state. The following year he became prime minister as well.

Traoré promised a return to civilian rule and in 1974 a new constitution was adopted, formally making Mali a one-party state. A new national party, the Malian People's Democratic Union (UDPM), was announced in 1976. Despite opposition from students to a one-party state and objections by the army to civilian rule, Traoré successfully made the transition so that by 1979 Mali had a constitutional form of government, but with ultimate power lying in the party and the military establishment.

In March 1991, following violent demonstrations against one-party rule, Traoré was ousted by troops led by Lieutenant Colonel Amadou Toumani Toure, who set up an interim government, pending a new multiparty constitution. This was adopted in January 1992 and in April 1992 the main opposition party, the Alliance for Democracy in Mali (ADEMA) won both the assembly and presidential elections. Alpha Oumar Konare (b. 1946) became president and Younoussi Toure, prime minister. However, following student unrest the latter resigned and was succeeded, in April 1993, by a national unity government, headed by Abdoulaye Sekou Sow. Further student riots, in February 1994, led to the appointment of Ibrahim Boubacar Keita as prime minister. A peace pact was signed at Bamako in 1992 with Tuareg rebels, who had been fighting in northern Mali.

MAURITANIA

Islamic Republic of Mauritania
Jumhuriyat Mauritaniya al-Islamiya

Capital: Nouakchott

Social and economic data
Area: 1,030,700 km^2
Population: 2,200,000*
Pop. density per km^2: 2*
Urban population: 50%**
Literacy rate: 34%**
GDP: $1,000 million**; per-capita GDP: $500**
Government defence spending (% of GDP): 2.9%**
Currency: ouguiya
Economy type: low income
Labour force in agriculture: 69%**

*1994
**1992

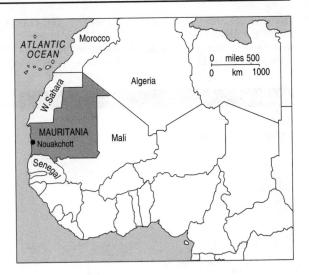

Ethnic composition
Over 80% of the population is of Moorish, or Moorish-black origin. About 18% is black African, concentrated in the south, and there is a small European minority. The official language is Arabic.

Religions
Islam is the state religion and almost the entire population is Sunni Muslim of the Malekite rite.

Political features
State type: emergent democratic
Date of state formation: 1960
Political structure: unitary
Executive: limited presidential
Assembly: two-chamber
Party structure: multiparty*
Human rights rating: N/A
International affiliations: ACP, AL, AMF, AMU, CEAO, CILSS, ECOWAS, IBRD, IMF, NAM, OAU, OIC, OMVS, UN, WTO

*Though dominated by one party

Local and regional government
The country is divided into 12 regions plus the capital district of Nouakchott. Each region has its own governor and within it are departments, administered by prefects, and within the departments, *arrondissements*. There are appointed regional assemblies.

Head of state (executive)
President Maawiya Ould Sid'Ahmed Taya, since 1984

Head of government
Prime Minister Sidi Mohamed Ould Boubacar, since 1992

Political leaders since 1970
1960–78 Mokhtar Ould Daddah (PPM), 1978–79 General Moustapha Ould Mohamed Salek (military), 1979 Colonel Ahmed Ould Bouceif (military), 1979–84 Colonel Mohamed Khouni Ould Haidalla (military), 1984–   Colonel Maawiya Ould Sid'Ahmed Taya (military/PRDS)

Political system

The July 1991 multiparty constitution provides for an executive president, who is head of state, and a two-chamber assembly, consisting of the Senate and the National Assembly. The president is elected by universal suffrage for a six-year term. The 56-member Senate is indirectly elected for a six-year term and the 79-member National Assembly is directly elected by universal suffrage for a five-year term. There are three advisory bodies, the Constitutional Council, the Supreme Islamic Council, and the Economic and Social Council. The president appoints the prime minister, as head of government.

Political parties

Since the legalization of parties in 1991 some 18 have been recognized, the four most significant being the Social Democratic Republican Party (PRDS), the Mauritanian Party for Renewal (MPR), the Rally for Democracy and National Unity (RDNU), and the Union of Democratic Forces.

The PRDS was founded in 1991 as the political vehicle of President Taya. It has a left-of-centre orientation.

The MPR and RDNU were also founded in 1991, with similar orientations.

Latest elections

In the January 1992 presidential elections Ould Taya won an outright victory in the first round, with 62.7% of the votes. Opposition parties disputed the result.

Complaining of ballot-rigging, the opposition boycotted the March 1992 National Assembly elections, allowing the PRDS to win 67 of the 79 elective seats. The MPR and RDNU each won one seat.

Political history

French influence was first apparent in Mauritania in the 17th century and, after a period of partial colonization in 1903, it became a full colony, and part of French West Africa, in 1920. It was given internal self-government, within the French Community, in 1958 and full independence in 1960. Moktar Ould Daddah, leader of the Mauritanian People's Party (PPM), was elected president in 1961.

In 1975 Spain ceded the western part of the Sahara to Mauritania and Morocco, leaving it to them to decide how to share it. Without consulting the Saharan people, Mauritania occupied the southern area, leaving the rest to Morocco. A resistance movement developed against this occupation, called the Popular Front for Liberation, or the Polisario Front, with the support of Algeria, and both Mauritania and Morocco found themselves engaged in a guerrilla war, forcing the two countries, who had formerly been rivals, into a mutual defence pact. Mauritania's economy was gravely weakened by the conflict and in 1978 President Daddah was deposed in a bloodless coup led by Colonel Mohamed Khouni Ould Haidalla. Single-party rule was imposed under the Military Committee for National Salvation.

Peace with the Polisario was eventually achieved in August 1978, when Mauritania renounced its claim to Western Sahara, allowing diplomatic relations with Algeria to be restored. Diplomatic relations with Morocco were broken in 1981 when Mauritania formally recognized the Polisario

regime in Western Sahara (see **Chapter 8**). Normal relations were restored in 1985.

Meanwhile, in December 1984, while Colonel Haidalla was attending a Franco-African summit meeting in Burundi, Colonel Maawwiya Ould Sid'Ahmed Taya (b. 1943), the prime minister since 1981, led a bloodless coup to overthrow him. During 1991 calls for a more democratic political system grew and a referendum produced a massive vote in favour of multiparty elections. President Ould Taya acceded to this popular demand. The constitution was changed and a number of opposition parties formed, but the president was not universally trusted. He won the presidential election in January 1992, amid claims of poll-rigging, and the opposition boycotted the March 1992 assembly elections, allowing the president's party, the PRDS, a clear win.

MAURITIUS

The Republic of Mauritius

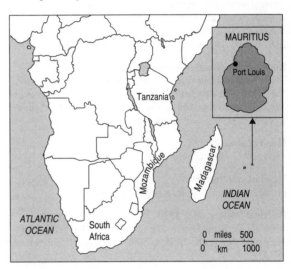

Capital: Port Louis

Social and economic data

Area: 2,040 km^2
Population: 1,100,000*
Pop. density per km^2: 539*
Urban population: 37%**
Literacy rate: 83%**
GDP: $2,889 million**; per-capita GDP: $2,700**
Government defence spending (% of GDP): 0.3%**
Currency: Mauritian rupee
Economy type: middle income
Labour force in agriculture: 19%**

*1994
**1992

Ethnic composition

There are five principal ethnic groups within the islands: French, black Africans, Indians, Chinese, and Mulattos, or Creoles. Indo-Mauritians predominate, constituting 67% of the population, followed by Creoles, 29%, Sino-Mauritians, 3.5%, and Europeans, 0.5%. The communities have sharply differing values and occupations so that interethnic rivalries are intense. English is the official language but Creole is spoken by more than 50% of the population, Hindi by 22%, and Bhojpuri by 19%.

Religions
Fifty-one per cent of the population is Hindu, 17% Sunni Muslim, 30% Christian, mostly Roman Catholic, and less than 1% is Buddhist. Roman Catholicism is the oldest religion and on Rodrigues island, where 90% of the population is European or Creole, almost all are adherents to it.

Political features
State type: liberal democratic
Date of state formation: 1968
Political structure: unitary
Executive: parliamentary
Assembly: one-chamber
Party structure: multiparty
Human rights rating: N/A
International affiliations: ACP, COMESA, CW, IAEA, IBRD, IMF, IOC, NAM, OAU, SADC, UN, WTO

Local and regional government
The island of Mauritius is divided into nine districts, while the island of Rodrigues has one of its two representatives on the Legislative Assembly acting as 'Minister for Rodrigues'. Locally, there are elected urban and village councils.

Head of state
President Cassam Uteem, since 1992

Head of government
Prime Minister Dr Navin Ramgoolam, since 1995

Political leaders since 1970
1968–82 Sir Seewoosagur Ramgoolam (MLP), 1982–95 Sir Aneerood Jugnauth (MSM), 1995 Dr Navin Ramgoolam (MLP)

Political system
Mauritius is an independent republic within the Commonwealth. The constitution dates from independence in 1968 and was amended in 1969 and 1991. It provides for a president, who is formal head of state, and a single-chamber National Assembly. There is a parliamentary-type executive, with a prime minister appointed by the president from the National Assembly on the basis of Assembly support. The president also appoints a Council of Ministers, on the advice of the prime minister, and all are collectively responsible to the Assembly. The president is elected by the Assembly for a five-year term. The Assembly has either 70 or 71 members: 62 elected by universal adult suffrage, through a simple plurality voting system, in multimember constituencies, with eight 'additional members' selected by the president, in consultation with the judiciary, from among the 'runners up' at the general election. This is done in an effort to ensure a balance in representation between the islands' different ethnic groups. The attorney general, if not an elected member, is the other Assembly member. The Assembly serves a five-year term. The island of Mauritius has 20 three-member constituencies and Rodrigues island has one two-member constituency. One of the elected members is designated Minister for Rodrigues.

Political parties
There are some 14 active political parties, the five most significant being the Mauritius Socialist Movement (MSM), the Mauritius Labour Party (MLP), the Mauritius Social Democratic Party (PMSD), the Mauritian Militant Movement (MMM), and the Organization of Rodriguan People (OPR).

The MSM was formed in 1983 as a successor to the Mauritius Socialist Party, which itself was an outgrowth from the Mauritian Militant Movement. It has a moderate socialist orientation, and campaigned to make Mauritius a republic within the Commonwealth.

The MLP describes itself as 'democratic socialist', but is really a centrist body, orientated towards Hindu Indians. It was originally formed in 1936 to campaign for the rights of cane-field workers and proceeded to dominate Mauritian politics up to 1982. It is led by Navin Ramgoolam.

The PMSD is also an old-established party, but of a more conservative hue. Drawing its support from Franco-Mauritian landowners and the Creole middle classes, it is pro-Western, anticommunist, and determinedly Francophile in its policy outlook. It joined the MSM-led coalition government in February 1995.

The MMM was formed in 1970 as a workers' party, enjoying strong backing from the trade union movement and boasting broad cross-community membership. It has a left-wing orientation and is led by Paul Bérenger. The party split in 1993 and the faction which remained within the government coalition adopted the designation Renouveau Militant Mauricien (RMM), under the leadership of Prem Nababsing.

The OPR is a small party representing the inhabitants of Rodrigues island.

Latest elections
In the December 1995 general election the MSM was defeated by the opposition MLP–MMM coalition, which won all the 62 elected assembly seats.

Political history
The Republic of Mauritius is in the Indian Ocean east of Madagascar and consists of the island of Mauritius and the dependencies of Rodrigues island, Agalega island, and the Cargados Carajos, or St Brandon islands.

Mauritius island, then uninhabited, was discovered by the Dutch in 1598 and named after Prince Maurice of Nassau. It was colonized during the 17th century, but abandoned in 1710. The French reoccupied it, with Rodrigues, in 1715 and established sugar cane plantations to be worked by imported African slaves. During the Napoleonic War of 1803–15 the island group was captured by Britain and then formally ceded to it by France in 1814. From then until 1903 it was administered with the Seychelles as a single colony. As a separate colony, Mauritius developed rapidly to become a major sugar cane producer. With the abolition of slavery in 1834, a switch from imported African workers to indentured labour from India took place. Although originally brought in on short-term contracts, many Indian immigrants chose to stay, establishing the ethnic pattern which exists today.

Following several decades of campaigning for self rule, spearheaded by the Mauritius Labour Party (MLP), the islands were granted internal self-government in July 1957 and full independence, within the Commonwealth, in March 1968. The MLP's leader, Dr Seewoosagur Ramgoolam, who had been chief minister since September 1961, became the country's first prime minister.

During the 1960s Mauritius enjoyed rapid economic growth on the basis of a strong market for sugar. This made possible a substantial rise in social spending and the successful implementation of an urgently needed population control programme. However, in the early 1970s, as export markets declined and economic conditions generally deteriorated, opposition to the Ramgoolam government grew, led by the newly formed left-wing Mauritius Militant Movement (MMM), headed by Paul Bérenger. It played a leading role in organizing a wave of strikes in 1971, the government responding by imposing a state of emergency and postponing the Legislative Assembly elections which were due in August 1972.

The governing MLP and Mauritius Social Democratic Party (PMSD) coalition eventually broke up in December 1973, but Ramgoolam stayed in power by establishing a new alliance with the Muslim Committee of Action (CAM). In the December 1976 general election the MMM emerged as the largest single party, but Ramgoolam succeeded in forming a new governing coalition of the MLP, CAM, and PMSD. Against a background of rising unemployment and industrial unrest, the ruling coalition was eventually defeated in the election of June 1982, the MMM, in alliance with the Mauritius Socialist Party (PSM), winning all 60 seats on Mauritius island. The PSM's leader, Aneerood Jugnauth (b. 1930), became the new prime minister, promising to pursue radical policies, based on nonalignment in foreign affairs, the extension of state control of the economy, and a proposal to make Mauritius a republic within the Commonwealth. Within a year, however, sharp differences emerged within the coalition, including Jugnauth's objection to a MMM campaign to make Creole the national language. He dissolved the coalition in March 1983 and formed a new MSM minority administration.

Lacking a working majority, Jugnauth had to call for fresh elections in August 1983. These resulted in the MSM forming an electoral alliance with the MLP and PMSD and Jugnauth becoming prime minister again, on the understanding that the MLP's leader, Sir Seewoosagur Ramgoolam, as he now was, would be made president if Mauritius became a republic. When the government failed to secure legislative approval for this constitutional change, Ramgoolam was appointed governor general on the retirement of the existing holder of the post, in December 1983. He died two years later and was replaced as governor general by Sir Veerasamy Ringadoo, a former finance minister.

The new MSM, MLP, and PMSD coalition was weakened in February 1984, when the MLP withdrew, but it remained in office with the support of 11 dissident MLP members. Then, in December 1985, its reputation was tarnished when an attempt was made to 'cover up' a Mauritius–Netherlands

drugs smuggling scandal involving MSM and PMSD members. Despite these difficulties, improvements in the economy enabled a new alliance of the three parties to secure another majority in the 1987 general election.

A coalition of the MSM, MMM, and OPR won the 1991 general election and in the following year republican status was achieved. In 1993 the MMM split. Those deputies remaining within the government coalition formed the Renouveau Militant Mauricien (RMM), while the remaining deputies, under the leadership of Paul Bérenger, formed an opposition pact with the MLP. In 1995 Mauritius joined the Southern African Development Community (SADC).

In December the MLP–MMM secured a landslide general election victory and Navin Ramgoolam became prime minister.

MOZAMBIQUE

The Republic of Mozambique
A República de Moçambique

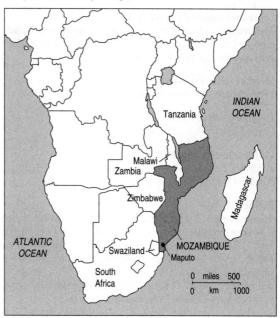

Capital: Maputo

Social and economic data
Area: 799,380 km^2
Population: 15,300,000*
Pop. density per km^2: 19*
Urban population: 30%**
Literacy rate: 27%**
GDP: $1,256 million**; per-capita GDP: $80**
Government defence spending (% of GDP): 9.8%**
Currency: metical
Economy type: low income
Labour force in agriculture: 85%**

*1994
**1992

Ethnic composition

The majority of people belong to local tribal groups, the largest being the Makua-Lomue, comprising about 38% of the population. The other significantly large group, of about 24%, is the Tsonga. The official language is Portuguese.

Religions

Most people, 60%, follow traditional animist beliefs, while 15%, or 2 million people, are Sunni Muslims, and 14% Roman Catholics.

Political features

State type: emergent democratic
Date of state formation: 1975
Political structure: unitary
Executive: limited presidential
Assembly: one-chamber
Party structure: two-party
Human rights rating: 53%
International affiliations: ACP, COMESA, CW, IBRD, IMF, Lusophone, NAM, OAU, SADC, UN, WTO

Local and regional government

The country is divided into 11 provinces, including Maputo city, within which are districts, cities, and localities. Each province has a governor and elected assembly.

Head of state (executive)

President Joaquim Alberto Chissano, since 1986

Head of government

Prime Minister Pascoal Mocumbi, since 1994

Political leaders since 1970

1975–86 Samora Machel (Frelimo), 1986– Joaquim Alberto Chissano (Frelimo)

Political system

The November 1990 multiparty constitution provides for an executive president, directly elected for a five-year term, renewable twice only, and a single-chamber Assembly of the Republic with 250 members also directly elected by universal suffrage for a five-year term. The president, who is also commander in chief of the armed forces, appoints the prime minister and a Council of Ministers (cabinet).

Political parties

Until 1990 the National Front for the Liberation of Mozambique (Frelimo) was the only legally permitted party. It was formed in 1962 and reconstituted in 1977 as a 'Marxist–Leninist vanguard party'. From 1990 it became a 'free-market' party.

There are now more than 20 other parties, the most significant being the civilian arm of the Mozambique National Resistance (MNR or Renamo), which, with South African support, fought a civil war with Frelimo between 1980 and 1992. It has a right-of-centre orientation.

Latest elections

In the October 1994 presidential elections Chissano won 53% of the vote, defeating the Renamo leader, Afonso Dhlakama, who obtained 33%.

The results of the October 1994 Assembly elections were as follows:

	% votes	Seats
Frelimo	44.3	129
Renamo	37.9	112
Others	17.8	9

Political history

Mozambique became a Portuguese colony in 1505 and was subsequently exploited, with forced labour, for its gold and ivory, as well as being a source of slaves for export. Guerrilla groups had actively opposed Portuguese rule from the early 1960s, the various left-wing factions combining to form Frelimo. As the government in Lisbon came under increasing strain, Frelimo's leader, Samora Machel (1933–86), demanded nothing short of complete independence and, in 1974, internal self-government was granted, with Joaquim Chissano (b. 1939), a member of Frelimo's Central Committee, as prime minister. A year later full independence was achieved and Machel became the country's first president.

He was immediately faced with the problem of hundreds of thousands of Portuguese settlers departing, leaving no trained replacements in key economic positions. Two activities had been the mainstay of the Mozambique economy, transit traffic from South Africa and Rhodesia and the export of labour to South African mines. Although Machel declared his support for the African National Congress (ANC) in South Africa, and the Patriotic Front in Rhodesia, he knew that he still had to coexist and trade with his two white-governed neighbours. He put heavy pressure on the Patriotic Front for a settlement of the guerrilla war and this eventually bore fruit in the Lancaster House Agreement of 1979 and the eventual electoral victory of Robert Mugabe, a reliable friend of Mozambique.

From 1980 onwards the country was confronted with the twin problems of widespread drought, which affected most of southern Africa, and attacks by dissidents, under the banner of the Mozambique National Resistance (Renamo), also known as the MNR, who were covertly, but strongly, backed by South Africa. These attacks were concentrated on Mozambique's vital and vulnerable transport system. Machel, showing considerable diplomatic skill, had, by 1983, repaired relations with the United States, undertaken a successful European tour and established himself as a respected African leader. His sense of realism was shown in his relations with South Africa. In March 1984 he signed the Nkomati Accord, under which South Africa agreed to deny facilities to the MNR and Mozambique, in return, agreed not to provide bases for the banned ANC. Machel took steps to honour his side of the bargain but was doubtful about South Africa's good faith. On 19 October 1986 he died in an air crash near the South African border on a return flight from Zambia. Despite the suspicious circumstances of his death, a subsequent inquiry pronounced it as an accident.

The following month Frelimo's Central Committee elected the foreign minister, and former prime minister,

Joaquim Chissano, as his successor. In his acceptance speech, Chissano pledged himself to carry on with the policies of his predecessor. Chissano strengthened the ties Machel had already forged with Zimbabwe and Britain and in February 1987 took the unprecedented step of informally requesting permission to attend the Commonwealth Heads of Government summit in Vancouver in October. This was seen by some observers as a prelude to a request for Commonwealth membership, but the Commonwealth secretary general, Sir 'Sonny' Ramphal, described such speculation as misleading. Mozambique's economic problems were aggravated in the early months of 1987 by food shortages, following another year of drought.

Despite the Nkomati Accord, South Africa continued to train and arm the MNR. Mozambique's reply was to mount a Front Line States regional army with a combination of Zimbabwean, Tanzanian, and Mozambique troops. In May 1988 it was announced that Mozambique and South Africa had agreed to revive a joint security commission which had originally been set up under the Nkomati Accord and in September 1988 President P W Botha of South Africa paid a visit to Mozambique. In December 1988 the Tanzanian government announced the withdrawal of its troops, initiating a relaxation of tension and guerrilla activity, and in 1990 a partial cease-fire was agreed.

Meanwhile, Chissano abandoned one-party rule, to make his regime more acceptable, and peace talks with the MNR opened in 1991. In August 1992 a peace accord was agreed and a treaty signed by Chissano and the MNR leader, Afonso Dhlakama, in October. This provided for a permanent cease-fire, to be monitored by 6,000 United Nations troops, and the disarmament of Renamo.

After Frelimo's victories in the multiparty presidential and assembly elections, in November 1994, the MNR leadership said it would cooperate with the government in the post-election era. IMF-promoted economic reforms, aimed at reconstructing the devastated economy, provoked fuel price riots in Maputo in November 1993. In 1995 Mozambique, which is surrounded by six Commonwealth countries, was accepted into Commonwealth membership. The use of English had been increased and the country's laws and institutions adapted to fit Commonwealth practice.

NAMIBIA

The Republic of Namibia
Republiek van Namibie

Capital: Windhoek

Social and economic data
Area: 824,292 km^2
Population: 1,600,000*
Pop. density per km^2: 2*
Urban population: 29%**
Literacy rate: 38%**
GDP: $1,854 million**; per-capita GDP: $1,030**
Government defence spending (% of GDP): 2.2%*
Currency: Namibian dollar

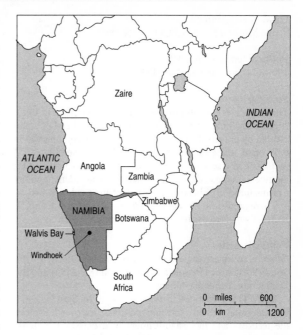

Economy type: middle income
Labour force in agriculture: 44%**

*1994
**1992

Ethnic composition
Eighty-five per cent of the population is black African, 51% of whom belong to the Ovambo tribe. The rest includes the pastoral Nama and Bushmen. There is a 6% white minority. The official languages are Afrikaans and English.

Religions
Christianity is the main religion, practised by 85% of the population. Among the Christians, 50% are Lutherans, 20% Roman Catholics, 6% members of the Dutch Reformed Church, and 6% Anglicans.

Political features
State type: emergent democratic
Date of state formation: 1990
Political structure: unitary
Executive: limited presidential
Assembly: one-chamber*
Party structure: two-party
Human rights rating: N/A
International affiliations: ACP, COMESA, CW, IAEA, IBRD, IMF, NAM, OAU, SADC, UN, WTO

*But with a second advisory chamber

Local and regional government
The country is divided into 13 regions, each with an elected council, and administrative districts.

Head of state (executive)
President Sam Nujoma, since 1990

Head of government
Prime Minister Hage Geingob, since 1990

Political leaders since 1970
1990–　Sam Nujoma (SWAPO)

Political system
The multiparty constitution dates from independence in 1990. It provides for an executive president, who is head of state, elected by universal suffrage for a five-year term, renewable only once, and a directly elected National Assembly of 72 members, also serving for five years, plus up to six nonvoting members nominated by the president. The president appoints a prime minister as head of government and a cabinet.

There is also a 26-member advisory National Council, indirectly elected by the regions, serving a six-year term.

Political parties
Of some seven active parties the two most significant are the South-West Africa People's Organization (SWAPO) and the Democratic Turnhalle Alliance (DTA).

SWAPO was founded in 1958 and is led by Sam Nujoma. Campaigning for full and unconditional independence for the territory and the establishment of a classless socialist society, it was banned in 1960 and forced to operate from bases in neighbouring Angola and Zambia. It has a left-of-centre orientation.

The DTA was formed in 1977 and is a coalition of moderate centrist African, coloured, and white parties.

Latest elections
Sam Nujoma won the December 1994 presidential election, obtaining 76.34% of the vote.

The results of the concurrent National Assembly elections were as follows:

	% votes	Seats
SWAPO	73.9	53
DTA	20.8	15
Other parties	5.3	4

Political history
Deterred by the coastal Namib Desert, European penetration of Namibia was delayed until the 18th century. British and Dutch missionaries first moved into the area, before, in 1884, Britain incorporated a small enclave around Walvis Bay in Cape Colony, while the Germans forcibly annexed the remainder of the territory in the same year. In 1903–4 there were massacres of the Herero people and, in 1915, during World War I, South African forces seized control of the German colony.

Administration of the area, now designated South West Africa (SWA), was entrusted to the Union of South Africa under the terms of a League of Nations mandate in 1920 and, in 1925, a limited measure of self-government was granted to the territory's European inhabitants. After World War II, South Africa applied, in 1946, to the newly established United Nations (UN) for the full incorporation of the man-dated lands, rich in diamonds and uranium, within its Union. This demand was rejected and, instead, South Africa was called upon to prepare a trusteeship agreement for the area.

The South Africans, however, rejected this request and instead proceeded to integrate South West Africa more closely with Pretoria, granting the territory's white voters representation in the Union's parliament in 1949 and extending to it its own apartheid laws in October 1966. In response to these measures, the South West African People's Organization (SWAPO) was established in 1958 by an Ovambo, Sam Nujoma (b. 1929), to lead a campaign for an end to racial discrimination and for the granting of full independence from South Africa. The organization was harassed by the South African authorities and its more radical wing, led by Nujoma, was forced into exile in 1960. Later, from the mid-1960s, Nujoma's exiled party established a military wing, the People's Liberation Army of Namibia (PLAN), and, utilizing bases in Angola and Zambia, proceeded to wage a guerrilla war of attrition against the South African occupying army.

South Africa's continued occupation of Namibia, as South West Africa was redesignated by the UN in 1968, met with an increasing challenge by international bodies from the late 1960s and was declared illegal by the International Court of Justice in 1971. Three years later the UN Security Council passed a resolution requiring South Africa to begin a transfer of power to Namibians by the end of May 1975 or face UN action. South Africa's prime minister, B J Vorster, responded by expressing willingness to enter into negotiations on Namibian independence, but not with SWAPO, an organization which the UN had, in 1973, formally recognized as the 'authentic representative of the Namibian people'.

During the mid-1970s the military conflict in Namibia and the bordering region escalated as Pretoria attempted, unsuccessfully, to topple the new Marxist government which had come to power in neighbouring Angola in 1975. Tentative moves towards a settlement were made in 1978, with the holding of tripartite talks between SWAPO, South Africa, and the five Western members of the UN Security Council, the 'Contact Group'. At the conclusion of these discussions, SWAPO and the Pretoria regime conditionally accepted proposals involving a reduction in the level of South African troops and the release of political prisoners as the prelude to the holding of UN-supervised elections. These proposals were incorporated in UN Security Council Resolution 435 of September 1978. However, South Africa subsequently retracted, holding instead in December 1978, under its own terms, elections which were boycotted by SWAPO and not recognized by the West. A long period of political and military stalemate followed during which South Africa continued its armed offensive against Angola and the PLAN, and, at the same time, attempted to establish in Namibia a stable pro-Pretoria regime, based on a conservative coalition termed the Democratic Turnhalle Alliance (DTA). This experiment came to an end, however, in January 1983 when the DTA's leader, Dirk Mudge, resigned following disagreements with Pretoria and direct rule was reimposed.

Negotiations between Pretoria, the Western powers, neighbouring African states, and Namibian political forces continued during the succeeding years, but repeatedly foundered on South Africa's insistence that any withdrawal of its military forces from both Angola and Namibia should be linked to the departure of the 50,000 Cuban troops stationed in Angola. In June 1985 South Africa established a new 'puppet regime' in Namibia, termed the 'Transitional Government of National Unity' (TGNU). It was dominated by political representatives drawn from the white and black ethnic minority communities, and contained only one minister from the dominant Ovambo tribe. The TGNU, which failed to gain recognition from the UN or Western powers, attempted to reform the apartheid system in Namibia and adopt a new draft constitution, but was seriously divided between its conservative and moderate wings. In particular, more reformist, nonwhite elements within the TGNU sought to move away from a political structuring based on ethnic, rather than national or geographical, lines. This was firmly opposed, however, by the South African administrator general, Louis Pienaar, since it would destroy the safeguards, called 'minority rights', which had been established to protect white interests.

During 1987–88 major strides towards resolving the Namibian–Angolan issues began finally to be made. A pathfinding agreement was signed by the South African and Angolan governments in August 1988, providing for an immediate cessation of military activities, followed by a rapid withdrawal of South African and Cuban forces from Angola and South Africa's troops from Namibia.

In April 1989 a strong UN peacekeeping force was stationed in Namibia, as a prelude to freely open internationally supervised elections later in the year. The elected assembly would then adopt and approve a new independence constitution. Sam Nujoma, the SWAPO president, returned in September and elections for a Constituent Assembly in November were won decisively by his party. The new constitution was adopted in February 1990 and Nujoma was sworn in as president of the independent mineral-rich republic of Namibia in March 1990. Namibia immediately entered the Commonwealth.

The Walvis Bay enclave, the only deep-water port on Namibia's coast, became a matter of dispute between the Namibian and South African governments but eventually, in August 1993, the government in Pretoria surrendered its sovereignty over it. The dramatic political changes in South Africa during 1993–94 were warmly welcomed in Namibia and close relations between the two countries were cemented. SWAPO won the December 1994 National Assembly elections and Nujoma was re-elected for another term. The parliamentary majority SWAPO secured was sufficiently large, at greater than two-thirds, to enable it to amend the constitution if it wished.

NIGER

The Republic of Niger
La République du Niger

Capital: Niamey

Social and economic data
Area: 1,267,000 km^2
Population: 8,500,000*

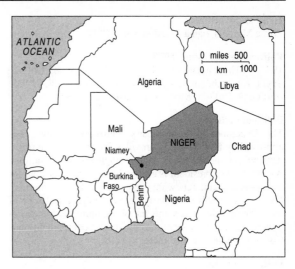

Pop. density per km^2: 7*
Urban population: 19%**
Literacy rate: 28%**
GDP: $2,233 million**; per-capita GDP: $290**
Government defence spending (% of GDP): 1.3%**
Currency: franc CFA
Economy type: low income
Labour force in agriculture: 85%**

*1994
**1992

Ethnic composition
Three tribes make up over 75% of the population. They are the Hausa, mainly in the central and southern areas, the Djerma-Songhai, in the southwest, and the Beriberi-Manga, in the east. There is also a significant number of the Fulani tribe, mainly nomadic, and, in the north, the Tuareg. The official language is French.

Religions
About 85% of the population is Sunni Muslim. Most of the rest follow traditional animist beliefs.

Political features
State type: emergent democratic
Date of state formation: 1960
Political structure: unitary
Executive: limited presidential
Assembly: one-chamber
Party structure: multiparty
Human rights rating: N/A
International affiliations: ACP, BOAD, CEAO, CILSS, ECOWAS, Francophone, FZ, IAEA, IBRD, IMF, IsDB, LCBC, NAM, OAU, OIC, UEMOA, UN, WTO

Local and regional government
The country is divided into seven departments, each headed by a prefect, assisted by a regional advisory council. Within the departments are 32 *arrondissements* and 150 communes.

Head of state (executive)
President Mahamane Ousmane, since 1993

Head of government
Prime Minister Hama Amadou, since 1995

Political leaders since 1970
1958–74 Hamani Diori (NPP), 1974–87 Lieutenant Colonel Seyni Kountché (military), 1987–93 Colonel Ali Seybou (military), 1993– Mahamane Ousmane (CDS)

Political system
The December 1992 multiparty constitution, which was approved by a referendum, provides for an executive president, who is head of state, and a single-chamber National Assembly. The president is elected by universal suffrage for a five-year term, renewable once only. The 83-member National Assembly is similarly elected for the same length of term. The president appoints the prime minister, as head of government, and, on the prime minister's recommendation, a Council of Ministers (cabinet).

Political parties
Of some 18 registered parties, the four most significant are the National Movement for a Development Society–Nassara (MNSD–Nassara), the Social Democratic Convention–Rahama (CDS–Rahama), the Niger Party for Democracy and Socialism–Tarayya (PNDS–Tarayya), and the Niger Alliance for Democracy and Progress–Zaman Lahiya (ANDP–Zaman Lahiya).

The MNSD–Nassara was formed in 1988 as the MNSD and was the only permitted party until 1991, when it changed its name. It has a left-of-centre orientation.

The CDS–Rahama, the PNDS–Tarayya, and the ANDP–Zaman Lahiya are all left-of-centre parties formed in 1991.

The CDS–Rahama and ANDP–Zaman Lahiya are part of the coalition, the Alliance of the Forces for Change (AFC). PNDS–Tarayya was also part of the AFC until 1994.

Latest elections
Mahamane Ousmane (CDS–Rahama) won the February–March 1993 presidential elections in the second ballot run-off, with 55.42% of the vote, Tandja Mamadou (MNSD–Nassara) obtaining 44.58%.

The results of the January 1995 National Assembly elections were as follows:

	Seats
MNSD–Nassara	29
CDS–Rahama*	24
PNDS–Tarayya	12
ANDP–Zaman Lahiya*	9
Other AFC parties*	7
Other non-AFC parties	2

* Contesting as Alliance of the Forces for Change

Political history
Formerly part of French West Africa from 1901, Niger achieved full independence in 1960. Hamani Diori (1916–89), the prime minister since 1958, was elected president and re-elected in 1965 and 1970. Maintaining very close and cordial relations with France, Diori seemed to have established one of the most stable regimes in Africa, and the discovery of uranium deposits promised a sound economic future. However, his practice of suppressing opposition to his party, the Niger Progressive Party (NPP), coupled with a severe drought between 1968 and 1974, resulted in widespread civil disorder and, in April 1974, he was ousted in a coup led, reluctantly, by the French-trained army Chief of Staff, Lieutenant Colonel Seyni Kountché (1931–87).

Kountché suspended the constitution and established a military government with himself as president. He immediately set about trying to restore the economy and negotiating a more equal relationship with France, through a cooperation agreement signed in 1977. Threatened by possible droughts and consequential unrest, Kountché tried to widen his popular support by liberalizing his regime but died in November 1987, while undergoing surgery in a Paris hospital, and was succeeded by the army Chief of Staff, Colonel Ali Seybou.

Seybou was confirmed as president in December 1989 but calls for a multiparty political system developed and in August 1991 he was divested of most of his executive powers, which were transferred to a transitional 15-member High Council of the Republic (HCR).

In March 1992 the transitional government collapsed, amid economic problems and tribal unrest, spearheaded by the secessionist-minded nomadic Tuaregs in the north, and calls for multiparty politics were renewed. Following a referendum in December 1992, a new constitution was approved and two months later Mahamane Ousmane was elected president. In the concurrent assembly elections an alliance of left-of-centre parties, the Alliance of the Forces for Change (AFC), won an absolute majority. In September 1994 the PNDS–Tarayya withdrew its support from the governing coalition, forcing a general election. In the subsequent January 1995 elections the AFC was returned but with a reduced majority.

NIGERIA

The Federal Republic of Nigeria

Capital: Abuja

Social and economic data
Area: 923,800 km^2
Population: 119,300,000*
Pop. density per km^2: 129*
Urban population: 37%**
Literacy rate: 51%**
GDP: $33,000 million**; per-capita GDP: $323**
Government defence spending (% of GDP): 0.6%**
Currency: naira
Economy type: low income
Labour force in agriculture: 45%**

*1994
**1992

Ethnic composition
There are more than 250 tribal groups in the country, the main ones being the Hausa and Fulani in the north, the

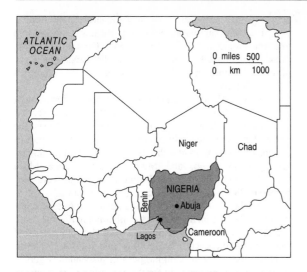

Yoruba in the south, and the Ibos in the east. The non-African population is relatively small and numbers no more than about 30,000. The official language is English.

Religions
About half the population is Sunni Muslim, settled predominantly in the north, about 35% is Christian, divided between Roman Catholics and Protestants, found chiefly in the south, and the remainder mostly follow traditional animist beliefs.

Political features
State type: military authoritarian
Date of state formation: 1960
Political structure: federal
Executive: military
Assembly: two-chamber
Party structure: multiparty
Human rights rating: 49%
International affiliations: ACP, CW,* ECOWAS, G-15, G-24, IAEA, IBRD, IMF, LCBC, NAM, OAU, OPEC, UN, WTO

*Membership suspended 1995

Local and regional government
The country is divided into 30 states plus a federal capital. There are also some 500 local government councils.

Head of state and head of government
Chair of PRC, General Sanni Abacha, since 1993

Political leaders since 1970
1966–1975 Colonel Yakubu Gowon (military), 1975–79 General Olusegun Obasanjo (military), 1979–83 Shehu Shagari (NPN–NPP coalition), 1983–85 Major General Muhammed Buhari (military), 1985–93 Major General Ibrahim Babangida (military), 1993 Ernest Shonekan (interim), 1993– General Sanni Abacha (military)

Political system
Nigeria is a federal republic of 30 states. The constitution is based on one of 1979 which was amended following a military coup in December 1983. Another coup in 1985 made

further changes. The president was made head of state, commander in chief of the armed forces, and chair of the Armed Forces Ruling Council (AFRC).

The draft of a new constitution was published in 1988 and implemented in stages. It provides for an executive president and a two-chamber assembly, consisting of a 91-member Senate and a 593-member House of Representatives, all elected by universal suffrage. The constitution contains strong elements of the United States model, the president being given power to veto legislation and the assembly power to override that veto by a two-thirds majority vote.

Currently, the president, who assumed power in a bloodless coup in November 1993, suspending the parliament, is head of state and head of government, presiding over a miliary-dominated Provisional Ruling Council (PRC) and a Federal Executive Council. There is no legislative assembly.

Political parties
The ban on political parties imposed in 1979 was lifted in 1989 and then gradually parties were approved under conditions stipulated by the Provisional Ruling Council. In November 1993 parties were banned again and the new ban was lifted in 1995.

The two most significant parties are the Social Democratic Party (SDP) and the National Republican Convention (NRC).

The SDP, led by Moshood Kashimawo Olawale Abiola, was formed in 1989. It has a left-of-centre orientation.

The NRC was also formed in 1989. It has a right-of-centre orientation.

Latest elections
The results of the July 1992 assembly elections were as indicated in the table below.

Success in the June 1993 presidential elections was claimed by M K O Abiola, the SDP candidate, who declared himself president, but the elections were annulled by the ruling Council.

	Senate seats	House of Representatives seats
SDP	52	314
NRC	37	275
	(2 seats decided in by-elections)	(4 seats decided in by-elections)

Political history
The British founded a colony at Lagos in 1861 and gradually extended it by absorbing surrounding areas until by 1914 it had become Britain's largest African colony. It achieved full independence, as a constitutional monarchy within the Commonwealth, in 1960 and became a republic in 1963. The republic was based on a federal structure, introduced in 1954, so as to accommodate the regional differences and the many tribes.

The ethnic differences, including the fact that groups of tribes were in different parts of the vast country, always contained the ingredients for a potential conflict. The discovery of oil in the southeast in 1958 made it very much richer than the north and this exaggerated the differences.

Nigeria's first president, in 1963, was Dr Nnamdi Azikiwe (b. 1904), who had been a banker, then established an influential newspaper group and played a leading part in the nationalist movement, pressing for independence. He came from the eastern Ibo tribe. His chief rival was Sir Abubakar Tafawa Balewa (1912–66), who was prime minister from 1957 until he was assassinated in a military coup in 1966. The coup had been led by mainly Ibo junior officers, from the eastern region. The offices of president and prime minister were suspended and it was announced that the state's federal structure would be abandoned.

Before this took place, the new military government was overturned in a countercoup by a mostly Christian faction from the north, led by Colonel Yakubu Gowon (b. 1934). He re-established the federal system and appointed a military governor for each region. Soon afterwards thousands of Ibos in the north were slaughtered. In 1967 a conflict developed between Gowon and the military governor of the eastern region, Colonel Chukwuemeka Odumegwu-Ojukwu, about the distribution of oil revenues, which resulted in Ojukwu's declaration of an independent Ibo state of Biafra. Gowon, after failing to pacify the Ibos, ordered federal troops into the eastern region and a civil war began. It lasted until January 1970, when Biafra surrendered to the federal forces.

In 1975 Gowon was replaced in a bloodless coup led by Brigadier Murtala Mohammad, but he was killed within a month, in a coup led by General Olusegun Obasanjo, who announced a gradual return to civilian rule and in 1979 the leader of the National Party of Nigeria (NPN), Shehu Shagari, became president.

In December 1983, following a deterioration in the economy caused by falling oil prices, Shagari's government was deposed in another bloodless coup, led by Major General Muhammed Buhari, who established a military adminis-tration. In 1985 there was another peaceful coup which replaced Buhari with a new military government, led by Major General Ibrahim Babangida (b. 1941), the army Chief of Staff. He promised a return to a democratic civilian government in 1989, but in 1987 announced that the transition would not now take place until 1992. A draft constitution was debated in the assembly throughout 1988 but agreement on its final form was not reached. In 1989 the ban on political activity was lifted and parties were approved within strict criteria. Assembly elections were held in July 1992, the Social Democratic Party (SDP) winning a majority of seats, but it was announced that the National Assembly would not be opened until after presidential elections had taken place. These were held in June 1993 and the SDP candidate, Chief Moshood Abiola, claimed victory. President Babangida refused to accept the result and declared the elections void.

After much manoeuvring, the two main parties, the SDP and the NRC, agreed to form an interim government which excluded Abiola, who left the country. In August 1993 Babangida stepped down and handed over power to an interim, nonelected government, led by Chief Ernest Adegunle Shonekan. Meanwhile, Abiola had returned and in November 1993 the Nigerian High Court ruled that the military government was illegal. A week later Shonekan was

removed in a bloodless coup and General Sanni Abacha seized power, banning all political parties, arresting Abiola and reinstating the 1979 constitution. On taking power, Abacha announced that he would establish a National Constitutional Conference (NCC) to determine the country's political future.

In October 1994 the High Court ruled that the detention of Abiola was illegal and in December 1994 the NCC recommended that military rule should continue until at least the end of 1995, despite the lifting of the ban on political parties in June of that year. In March 1995, the former ruler, General Olusegun Obasanjo, and Major General Shehu Musa Yar'Adua were accused of plotting a coup and were sentenced to 25 years' imprisonment, after a secret trial.

In October 1995 General Abacha attempted to ease international pressure on his regime by announcing that the death sentences on 14 other coup plotters would be commuted and that there would be a return to civilian rule in 1998. However, in November 1995 the Commonwealth suspended Nigeria's membership as punishment for the execution of nine human rights activists, including Ken Saro-Wiwa (1941–1995), who had led a campaign for self-determination for the minority Ogoni tribe and for environmental protection.

RWANDA

The Republic of Rwanda
Republika y'u Rwanda
La République rwandaise

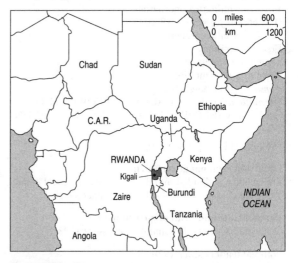

Capital: Kigali

Social and economic data
Area: 26,340 km²
Population: 7,800,000*
Pop. density per km²: 296*
Urban population: 6%**
Literacy rate: 50%**
GDP: $2,304 million**; per-capita GDP: $320**
Government defence spending (% of GDP): 7.3%**
Currency: Rwanda franc

Economy type: low income
Labour force in agriculture: 93%**

*1994
**1992

Ethnic composition
About 84% of the population belongs to the Hutu tribe, most of the others being Tutsis. There are also Twa and Pygmy minorities. The official languages are Kinyarwanda and French.

Religions
About a quarter of the population follows traditional animist beliefs, nearly half is Roman Catholic, 8% is Protestant, and 8% Sunni Muslim.

Political features
State type: authoritarian nationalist*
Date of state formation: 1962
Political structure: unitary
Executive: unlimited presidential*
Assembly: one-chamber
Party structure: multiparty*
Human rights rating: 48%
International affiliations: ACP, CEEAC, CEPGL, COMESA, IBRD, IMF, KBO, NAM, OAU, UN, WTO

*In a state of transition

Local and regional government
The country is divided into 11 prefectures which are further subdivided into 145 communes, or municipalities. The communes are administered by appointed governors and have elected councils.

Head of state (executive)
President Pasteur Bizimungu, since 1994

Head of government
Prime minister Pierre-Celestin Rwigyema, since 1995

Political leaders since 1970
1962–73 Grégoire Kayibanda (Democratic Republican Movement–Parmehutu), 1973–94 Major General Juvénal Habyarimana (military/MRND), 1994 Theodore Sindikubgabo (interim), 1994– Pasteur Bizimungu (FPR interim)

Political system
The 1978 constitution, amended in 1991, provides for an executive president and a single-chamber 70-member assembly, the National Development Council (CND). The president and the CND are elected by universal adult suffrage, through a simple plurality voting system, for a five-year term. The president, who may be re-elected up to the age of 60, appoints a prime minister and a Council of Ministers (cabinet). Since July 1994 a Transitional National Assembly has been formed and multiparty elections are scheduled for 1999.

Political parties
Until 1991 Rwanda was a one-party state, the sole legal party being the National Revolutionary Development Movement (MRND). When the constitution was amended other parties were accepted, among them the Rwanda Patriotic Front

(FPR), the Republican Democratic Party (MDR), the Liberal Party (PL), the Social Democratic Party (PSD), and the Christian Democratic Party (PDC).

The MRND was formed in 1975. It has a nationalist socialist orientation and is Hutu dominated. It was implicated in the April–July 1994 genocide of thousands of Tutsis.

The FPR represents the Tutsi minority community who were ousted from government in the 1960s. It is led by President Bizimungu, a Hutu.

The MDR evolved from groups formed in the 1960s and in the early 1990s it split into two factions, a mainly Hutu, progovernment group, and a multi-ethnic, antigovernment group. Both have left-of-centre orientations.

The PL was formed in 1991 and it, too, split into pro- and antigovernment factions in the early 1990s. It has a moderate, centrist orientation.

The PSD was formed in 1991 as a breakaway from the MRND.

The PDC was formed in 1990. It has a Christian centrist orientation.

Latest elections
In the December 1988 one-party National Development Council (CND) elections, 70 deputies were elected from a list of 140 MRND nominees.

In the December 1988 presidential election General Habyarimana was the sole candidate.

Political history
In the 16th century the Tutsi tribe moved into the country and took over from the indigenous majority Hutus, establishing a feudalistic kingdom. Then, at the end of the 19th century German colonizers arrived and forced the Tutsi king to allow the country to become a German protectorate. It was linked to the neighbouring state of Burundi within the empire of German East Africa until after World War I, when it came under Belgian administration as a League of Nations, later United Nations, trust territory.

In 1961 the monarchy was abolished and Ruanda, as it was then called, became a republic. It achieved full independence in 1962 as Rwanda, with Grégoire Kayibanda as its first president. Fighting broke out in 1963 between the two main tribes, the Hutu and the Tutsi, resulting in the loss of, it is estimated, some 20,000 lives, before an uneasy peace was agreed in 1965. Kayibanda was re-elected President in 1969 but by the end of 1972 the tribal warfare had restarted and in July 1973 the head of the National Guard, Major General Juvénal Habyarimana (1937–94), led a bloodless coup, ousting Kayibanda and establishing a military government.

Meetings of the assembly were suspended and all political activity banned until a new ruling party was formed. It was the National Revolutionary Development Movement (MRND) and was the only legally permitted political organization. A referendum held at the end of 1978 approved a new constitution designed to fulfil Habyarimana's promise, in 1973, to return to normal constitutional government within five years, and cautious moves in this direction were started in 1990.

In the same year the Rwanda Patriotic Front (FPR), an army consisting mainly of Tutsi refugees, invaded the country from neighbouring Uganda, with the object of overthrowing the Hutu-dominated Habyarimana government. Much of the north was occupied and guerrilla fighting continued until, in October 1992, a power-sharing agreement between the government and the FPR was concluded, resulting in the signing of an agreement in Arusha, Tanzania, in August 1993.

In April 1994 President Habyarimana was killed when the aircraft in which he was returning with the Burundi president, Cyprien Ntaryamira, was shot down on its approach to Kigali airport. His death unleashed violence on an unprecedented scale and destroyed the peace accord which had been signed the previous year. The speaker of the assembly, Theodore Sindikubgabo, became president with a transitional, Hutu-dominated government headed by Prime Minister Jean Kambanda. The new government was rejected by the FPR, who resumed fighting, forcing the government to flee from Kigali. It was estimated that more than 500,000 people, mainly Tutsis, had been killed and 2 million displaced as refugees, many fleeing to Zaire, Burundi, and Tanzania as a result of the frenzied clashes between Hutu militias and the Tutsi-dominated FPR. A French humanitarian mission, Opération Turquoise, attempted to protect refugees and stem the spread of cholera and dysentry in the overcrowded refugee camps.

In July 1994 the FPR declared victory and established a coalition government led by Faustin Twagiramungu, a Hutu member of the Republican Democratic Party (MDR), as prime minister and Pasteur Bizimungu, of the FPR, as president, but excluding the MRND. Major General Paul Kagame, the FPR's military leader, became vice president and defence minister. Despite this seeming rapprochement, there were still reports of Hutus being killed by Tutsi soldiers.

As more evidence of rapes and genocide was revealed, steps were started to investigate allegations, the United Nations Security Council adopting a Resolution to establish an International Criminal Tribunal in Arusha, Tanzania, instead of in Kigali, as the Rwandan government had planned.

In March 1995 there was another major outbreak of ethnic violence in neighbouring Burundi and it was feared that it might spread to Rwanda. It failed to do so but presented the government in Kigali with another refugee problem, as thousands of Hutus fled from Burundi to avoid Tutsi attacks. It was reported that many Hutu refugees had died in the ensuing confusion, either by being trampled to death, or at the hands of Rwandan, mainly Tutsi, soldiers. In August 1995 President Bizimungu dismissed Prime Minister Twagiramungu following his open criticism of the domination of his government by the FPR. The new prime minister, Pierre-Celestin Rwigyema (MDR), was another Hutu.

SAO TOME E PRINCIPE

The Democratic Republic of São Tomé e Príncipe
A República Democrática de São Tomé e Príncipe

Capital: São Tomé

Social and economic data
Area: 964 km^2
Population: 121,000*
Pop. density per km^2: 128*
Urban population: 26%**

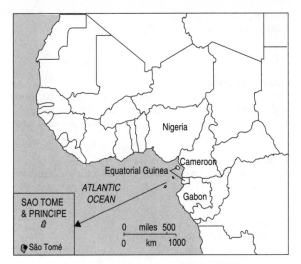

Literacy rate: 57%**
GDP: $42 million**; per-capita GDP: $340**
Government defence spending (% of GDP): N/A
Currency: dobra
Economy type: low income
Labour force in agriculture: 54%**

*1994
**1992

Ethnic composition
The population is predominantly African. The official language is Portuguese.

Religions
About 70% of the population is Christian, mostly Roman Catholic.

Political features
State type: emergent democratic
Date of state formation: 1975
Political structure: unitary
Executive: limited presidential
Assembly: one-chamber
Party structure: multiparty
Human rights rating: N/A
International affiliations: ACP, CEEAC, IBRD, IMF, NAM, OAU, UN

Local and regional government
For administrative purposes, the country is divided into seven counties. Six of them are on São Tomé. The smaller island of Príncipe forms one county in itself, with internal autonomy.

Head of state (executive)
President Miguel Trovoada, since 1991

Head of government
Prime Minister Carlos da Graça, since 1994

Political leaders since 1970
1975–91 Manuel Pinto da Costa (MLSTP), 1991–   Miguel Trovoada (independent)

Political system

The August 1990 multiparty constitution, approved by a referendum, provides for an executive president, who is head of state, and a single-chamber 55-member National Assembly. The president is elected by universal suffrage for a five-year term, limited to two successive terms. The National Assembly is elected in the same way for a four-year term. The president appoints the prime minister and ministers on the latter's advice.

Political parties

Until 1990 the only legal party was the Movement for the Liberation of São Tomé e Príncipe–Social Democratic Party (MLSTP–PSD). There are now some five other parties, the most significant being the Democratic Convergence Party–Reflection Group (PCD–GR) and the Independent Democratic Action (ADI).

The MLSTP–PSD was founded in 1972 by Manuel Pinto da Costa from an earlier nationalistic group. It has a nationalist and socialist orientation and is led by Carlos da Graça.

The PCD–GR was formed in 1987 by a breakaway faction of the MLSTP. It has a moderate left-of-centre orientation and is led by Norberto José d'Alva Costa Alegre.

The ADI was founded in 1992. It has a centrist orientation.

Latest elections

The March 1991 presidential election was won by the independent, Miguel Trovoada.

The results of the October 1994 National Assembly elections were as follows:

	Seats
MLSTP–PSD	27
PCD–GR	14
ADI	14

Political history

The two islands of São Tomé e Príncipe were first colonized by the Portuguese in the late 15th century. They became important trading posts for ships on their way to the East Indies, supplying sugar and later cocoa and coffee, which was produced using forced labour. They were declared an overseas province of Portugal in 1951 and were given internal self-government in 1973. An independence movement, the Movement for the Liberation of São Tomé e Príncipe (MLSTP), led by Dr Manuel Pinto da Costa (b. 1937) and formed in Gabon in 1972, took advantage of a military coup in Portugal, in 1974, and persuaded the new government in Lisbon to formally recognize it as the sole representative of the people of the islands. Full independence followed, in July 1975, with a one-party socialist regime being established.

Dr Pinto da Costa became the first president and in December a National People's Assembly was elected. During the first few years of his presidency there were several unsuccessful attempts to depose him and, with a worsening economy, Pinto da Costa began to reassess his country's international links which had made it overdependent on the Eastern bloc and, in consequence, isolated from the West.

In 1984 he formally proclaimed that in future São Tomé e Príncipe would be a nonaligned state and gradually the country turned more towards nearby African states, as well as maintaining its links with Lisbon. However, an invasion and coup attempt in 1988 was only foiled with the help of Angolan and East European troops. In 1990, influenced by the collapse of communism in Eastern Europe, the MLSTP abandoned Marxism and, following a referendum in August 1990, a new, multiparty constitution was approved. Pinto da Costa retired in advance of assembly and presidential elections and in January 1991 his party, the MLSTP–PSD, was defeated by the Democratic Convergence Party (PCD–GR) in the National Assembly elections. With a parliamentary majority, the PCD's leader, Norberto José d'Alva Costa Alegre, became prime minister. The March 1991 presidential election was won by an independent candidate, Miguel Trovoada. In July 1994 the prime minister, in dispute with President Trovoada over control of the budget, was dismissed and replaced by Evaristo do Espirito Santo Carvalho, leader of the small People's Alliance (AP). In October 1994 the MLSTP–PSD, in early legislative elections, returned to power, although one seat short of an overall assembly majority. Its chairperson, Carlos da Graça, was appointed prime minister. With unemployment standing at 38% and the level of foreign indebtedness at $165 million, an attempted coup 'to recover the dignity of the country', was launched in August 1995 by junior army officers, led by Lieutenant Manual Quintas de Almeida. However, within days, power was handed back to the civilian government.

SENEGAL

The Republic of Senegal
La République du Sénégal

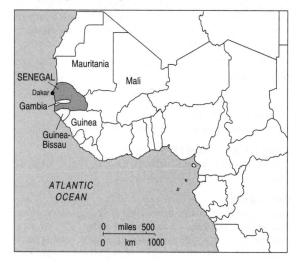

Capital: Dakar

Social and economic data
Area: 197,000 km^2
Population: 7,900,000*
Pop. density per km^2: 40*
Urban population: 41%**

Literacy rate: 38%**
GDP: $5,745 million**; per-capita GDP: $710**
Currency: franc CFA
Economy type: low income
Labour force in agriculture: 81%**

*1994
**1992

Ethnic composition

Senegal has a great ethnic diversity. The Wolof group are the most numerous tribes, comprising about 36% of the population. The Fulani comprise about 21%, the Serer 19%, the Diola 7%, and the Mandingo 6%. Within each main group are many individual tribes. The official language is French.

Religions

More than 90% of the population is Sunni Muslim, 5% Christian, chiefly Roman Catholic, and 5% follow animist traditional beliefs.

Political features

State type: nationalistic socialist
Date of state formation: 1960
Political structure: unitary
Executive: unlimited presidential
Assembly: one-chamber
Party structure: multiparty*
Human rights rating: 71%
International affiliations: ACP, BOAD, CEAO, CILSS, ECOWAS, FZ, G-15, IAEA, IBRD, IMF, IWC, NAM, OAU, OIC, OMVG, OMVS, UEMOA, UN, WTO

*Though dominated by one party

Local and regional government

The country is divided into ten regions, each with an appointed governor and elected assembly. There is a further subdivision into departments, *arrondissements* and villages. Departments are administered by prefects, *arrondissements*, by subprefects, and villages by chiefs.

Head of state

President Abdou Diouf, since 1981

Head of government

Prime Minister Habib Thiam, since 1993

Political leaders since 1970

1960–80 Léopold Sédar Senghor (UPS–PS), 1981– Abdou Diouf (PS)

Political system

The constitution dates from 1963 and has since been amended. It provides for a single-chamber 120-member National Assembly and an executive president, who is head of state and commander in chief of the armed forces. The president is directly elected by universal adult suffrage for a five-year term, limited to two terms. The Assembly is elected for a three-year term through the additional member majoritarian system of voting, with 70 deputies elected nationally by proportional representation and 50 representing single-member constituencies. The president appoints a prime minister as head of government.

Political parties

Between 1966 and 1974 Senegal was a one-party state, but now, although there are some 16 registered parties, two dominate the political scene. They are the Senegalese Socialist Party (PS), led by President Abdou Diouf, and the Senegalese Democratic Party (PDS).

The PS began in 1949 as the Senegalese Progressive Union (UPS). In 1976 it was reconstituted in its present form. It is a democratic socialist party.

The PDS was formed in 1976. It has a liberal centrist orientation.

Latest elections

In the February 1993 presidential election Abdou Diouf was re-elected with 58.4% of the vote, while his PDS rival won 32%.

In the May 1993 National Assembly elections, which were contested by six parties, the results were as follows:

	% votes	Seats
PS	56.6	84
PDS	30.2	27
Other parties	13.2	9

Political history

After 300 years as a French colony, Senegal became an independent republic in September 1960, with the poet–politician Léopold Sédar Senghor (b. 1906), leader of the Senegalese Progressive Union (UPS), which had spearheaded the independence movement after World War II, as its first president. An attempted federation with Mali in 1959–60 proved to be unsuccessful. In 1962 Senghor took over the post of prime minister and four years later, in 1966, made the UPS the only legal party. In 1970 he relinquished the office of prime minister to a young protégé, Abdou Diouf (b. 1935), who, in 1976, was to be named his successor. In 1973 Senghor was re-elected and began to honour his promise to allow the return to multiparty politics. In December 1976 the UPS was reconstituted to become the Senegalese Socialist Party (PS) and two opposition parties were legally registered. In the 1978 elections the PS won over 80% of the Assembly seats and Senghor was decisively re-elected. He retired at the end of 1980 and was succeeded by Diouf who immediately sought national unity by declaring an amnesty for political offenders and permitting more parties to register.

In 1980 Senegal sent troops to Gambia to protect it against a suspected Libyan invasion, and it intervened again in 1981 to thwart an attempted coup. As the two countries came closer together, agreement was reached on an eventual merger and the confederation of Senegambia came into being in February 1982, but this was abandoned in 1989. Senegal maintained close links with France, allowing it to retain military bases.

In the 1983 elections Diouf and his party were again clear winners and later that year he further tightened his control of his party and the government, abolishing the post of prime minister, but this was subsequently reinstated.

Despite open opposition, Diouf and the PS remained firmly in power and were decisively re-elected in 1988. The opening up of the party system, ironically, strengthened, rather than weakened, the one-party state. In April 1989 violent clashes over border grazing rights, in both Senegal and Mauritania, threatened to create a rift between the two countries but full diplomatic relations were restored in 1992.

In February 1993 Diouf was re-elected president and in the subsequent assembly elections, in May 1993, the PS was returned with a clear, though slightly reduced, majority. There were clashes between government forces and separatist rebels in the southern Casamance province during 1993. A cease-fire agreement was signed in July 1993 but it broke down in 1995.

SEYCHELLES

The Republic of the Seychelles

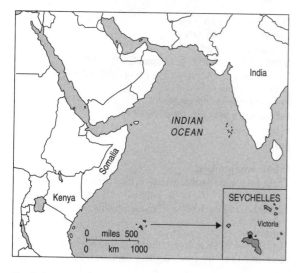

Capital: Victoria

Social and economic data
Area: 450 km^2
Population: 69,000*
Pop. density per km^2: 153*
Urban population: 50%**
Literacy rate: 58%**
GDP: $378 million**; per-capita GDP $5,500**
Government defence spending (% of GDP): 3.5%**
Currency: Seychelles rupee
Economy type: middle income
Labour force in agriculture: 10%**

*1994
**1992

Ethnic composition
The majority of the population is Creole, of mixed African–European parentage. There is a small European minority, mostly French and British. The official languages are English, French, and Creole.

Religions
About 90% of the population is Roman Catholic and Roman Catholicism is a quasi-state religion. About 7% is Anglican.

Political features
State type: emergent democratic
Date of state formation: 1976
Political structure: unitary
Executive: limited presidential
Assembly: one-chamber
Party structure: multiparty
Human rights rating: N/A
International affiliations: ACP, CW, IBRD, IMF, IOC, IWC, NAM, OAU, UN

Local and regional government
There is no local government as such, administration coming almost entirely from the centre.

Head of state and head of government
President France-Albert René, since 1977

Political leaders since 1970
1970–77 James Mancham (SDP), 1977–   France-Albert René (SPUP/SPFP)

Political system
Seychelles is a republic within the Commonwealth. The June 1993 multiparty constitution, which was approved in a referendum, provides for a president, who is head of state and head of government, and a single-chamber 33-member National Assembly. The president, who is also commander in chief of the armed forces, is elected by universal suffrage for a five-year term, and is limited to a maximum of three successive terms. Twenty-two members of the National Assembly are directly elected from single-member constituencies by universal suffrage and the remaining 11 are elected from a national list on a proportional basis.

Political parties
Until 1991 the only legally permitted party was the Seychelles People's Progresssive Front (SPPF). Now several other parties operate, the most significant being the Democratic Party (DP).

The SPPF was founded in 1964 as the Seychelles People's United Party (SPUP) and in 1978 adopted its present name. It has a nationalistic socialist stance and is led by President René.

The DP was formed in 1992 as the successor to the Seychelles Democratic Party (SDP), which, under James Mancham, was the governing party between 1970 and 1977. It has a left-of-centre orientation.

Latest elections
The incumbent president, France-Albert René (SPPF), won the July 1993 presidential elections, with a 59.5% vote share, defeating the DP candidate, Sir James Mancham, who obtained 36.7%.

The results of the July 1993 National Assembly elections were as follows:

	% votes	Seats
SPPF	57.5	27
DP	32.8	5
Others	9.7	1

Political history

Seychelles is a group of 115 islands, scattered over an area of more than a million square kilometres. They were colonized by the French in 1768, captured by the British in 1794, and formally ceded by France in 1814 to became a British Crown Colony in 1903.

In the 1960s several political parties were formed, campaigning for independence, the most significant being the Seychelles Democratic Party (SDP), led by James Mancham, and the Seychelles People's United Party (SPUP), led by France-Albert René (b. 1935). At a constitutional conference in London in 1970 René demanded complete independence while Mancham favoured integration with the United Kingdom. Agreement was not reached and so a further conference was held in 1975 when internal self-government was agreed.

The two parties then formed a coalition government, with Mancham as prime minister. Eventually full independence was achieved in June 1976. Seychelles became a republic within the Commonwealth, with Mancham as president and René as prime minister. The following year René staged an armed coup, while Mancham was attending a Commonwealth conference in London, and declared himself president. Mancham went into exile.

After a brief suspension of the constitution, a new one was adopted, creating a one-party state, with the SPUP being renamed the Seychelles People's Progressive Front (SPPF). René, as the only candidate, was formally elected president in 1979 and then re-elected for another five-year term in 1984. There were several unsuccessful attempts to overthrow him, including one staged by South African mercenaries in 1981. René followed a policy of nonalignment but maintained close links with Tanzania, which provided defence support.

A successful tourism-based economy was developed, providing the highest per-capita living standards in Africa.

In 1991 René promised to return to pluralist politics. In July 1992 a 20-member commission was popularly elected to draft a new constitution. Its first draft was rejected in a referendum held in November 1992, but in June 1993 a multi-party constitution was approved and adopted. Sir James Mancham, the former deposed president, returned and in the July 1993 presidential elections was defeated by René. The ruling SPPF also won a majority in the National Assembly.

SIERRA LEONE

The Republic of Sierra Leone

Capital: Freetown

Social and economic data
Area: 71,740 km²
Population: 4,500,000*

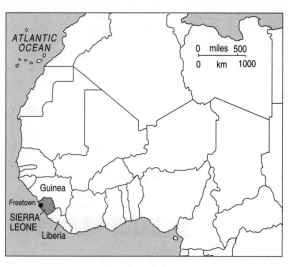

Pop. density per km²: 63*
Urban population: 31%**
Literacy rate: 21%**
GDP: $670 million**; per-capita GDP: $150**
Government defence spending (% of GDP): 2.5%**
Currency: leone
Economy type: low income
Labour force in agriculture: 70%**

*1994
**1992

Ethnic composition

There are some 18 tribal groups in the country, three of which comprise nearly 70% of the population. They are the Mende, the Tenne, and the Limbe. The official language is English.

Religions

Most people, 52%, follow traditional animist beliefs. There are Sunni Muslim (38%) and Anglican Christian (6%) minorities.

Political features

State type: military authoritarian*
Date of state formation: 1961
Political structure: unitary
Executive: military*
Assembly: one-chamber*
Party structure: multiparty*
Human rights rating: 67%
International affiliations: ACP, CW, ECOWAS, IAEA, IBRD, IMF, MRU, NAM, OAU, OIC, UN, WTO

*In a state of transition

Local and regional government

The country is divided into three provinces, Northern, Southern, and Eastern, plus the Western area, which includes Freetown. Each province has a cabinet minister responsible for it. The provinces are divided into districts, within which are 148 chiefdoms, each controlled by a tribal chief.

Head of state and head of government

Chair of NPRC, Captain Valentine E M Strasser, since 1992

Political leaders since 1970

1968–85 Siaka Stevens (APC), 1985–92 Major General Joseph Saidu Momoh (APC), 1992– Captain Valentine Strasser (military)

Political system

The 1991 constitution provided for a multiparty political system after 13 years of one-party rule but in April 1992 President Momoh was ousted in a coup led by Captain Valentine Strasser, who set up a 25-member military National Provisional Ruling Council (NPRC), later known as the Supreme State Council. He said he would re-establish civilian rule when order had been restored.

The former constitution provided for an executive president, directly elected for a seven-year term, and a 124-member House of Representatives, elected for five years.

Political parties

Between 1978 and 1991 the only permitted party was the All People's Congress (APC). Since then a number of parties have been formed, six of them combining into a coalition, the United Front of Political Movement (UNIFORM).

The APC was founded by Sierra Leone's first president, Siaka Stevens, in 1960. It has a moderate socialist orientation.

UNIFORM is a coalition of six parties formed in 1991, in opposition to the APC. They have a general left-of-centre orientation.

The Revolutionary United Front (RUF), led by Corporal Foday Sankoh, has been conducting a guerrilla war against the regime since May 1991.

Latest elections

The incumbent, Joseph Momoh, was elected president, as the sole candidate, in October 1985.

In the May 1986 general election there were 335 candidates for the 105 elected seats in the House of Representatives. All were APC nominees.

Multiparty elections were promised for 1996.

Political history

In 1787 the area which is now Sierra Leone was bought by English philanthropists to provide a settlement, called Freetown, for freed slaves and in 1808 it became a British colony. The interior was conquered in 1896. It achieved full independence, as a constitutional monarchy within the Commonwealth, in 1961, with Sir Milton Margai, leader of the Sierra Leone People's Party (SLPP), as prime minister.

Margai died in 1964 and was succeeded by his half-brother, Dr Albert Margai. The 1967 general election was won by the All People's Congress (APC), led Dr Siaka Stevens (1905–88), but the result was disputed by the army which assumed control and set up a National Reformation Council, forcing the governor general to temporarily leave the country. In the following year another army revolt brought back Stevens as prime minister and in 1971, after the 1961 constitution had been changed to make Sierra Leone a republic, he became president. He was re-elected in 1976 and the APC, having won the 1977 general election by a big margin, began to demand the creation of a one-party state. A new constitution, making the APC the sole legal

party, was approved by referendum in 1978 and Stevens was sworn in as president for another seven-year term.

As the date for the next presidential election drew near, Stevens, who was now 80, announced that he would not stand for re-election and an APC conference in August 1985 endorsed the commander of the army, Major General Joseph Saidu Momoh (b. 1937), as the sole candidate for party leader and president. He was formally elected in October 1985. Momoh appointed a civilian cabinet and immediately disassociated himself from the policies of his predecessor, who had been criticized for failing to prevent corruption within his administration.

In March 1991 President Momoh said he welcomed a return to multiparty politics and this was endorsed with 60% support in a referendum. However, Momoh was deposed in April 1992 and the army, led by the young officer, Captain Valentine Strasser (b. 1965), resumed control. Strasser said he was still committed to pluralist politics at some future date. Meanwhile, the government found itself involved in a continuing struggle with rebel forces operating from neighbouring Liberia, where a civil war was raging. The struggle had begun in 1991 when the rebels, fighting under the banner of the Revolutionary United Front (RUF), made several territorial gains in the southeast. They received support from the Liberian rebel group, the National Patriotic Front of Liberia (NPFL). The government responded by recruiting South African mercenaries and new conscripts to train and improve its small, ill-equipped army. An attempt, in November 1994, to negotiate a cease-fire failed and the guerrilla war continued, with foreign nationals being taken hostage by the RUF. The death toll exceeded 20,000 and there were 500,000 refugees in Sierra Leone and 250,000 in neighbouring Guinea and Liberia.

SOMALIA

Somali Democratic Republic
Jamhuuriyadda Dimuqraadiga Soomaaliya

Social and economic data

Area: 637,660 km^2
Population: 9,500,000*
Pop. density per km^2: 15*
Urban population: 35%**
Literacy rate: 24%**
GDP: $1,125 million**; per-capita GDP: $150**
Government defence spending (% of GDP): 6.2%**
Currency: Somali shilling
Economy type: low income
Labour force in agriculture: 76%**

*1994
**1992

Ethnic composition

Somalia is one of the most ethnically homogeneous countries in Africa. Ninety-eight per cent of the population is indigenous Somali, about 84% of Hamitic stock and 14% Bantu. However, the people are divided into some 100 clans, based on patrilineal ties that go back many generations, with

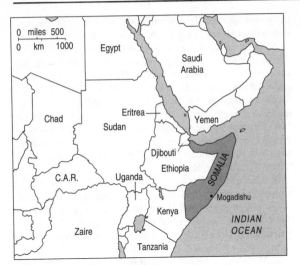

intense clan rivalries. The official language is Arabic and the national language Somali.

Religions
Islam is the state religion, most people being Sunni Muslims. There is also a Roman Catholic minority.

Political features
State type: military authoritarian*
Date of state formation: 1960
Political structure: federal*
Executive: military*
Assembly: one-chamber*
Party structure: one-party*
Human rights rating: N/A
International affiliations: ACP, AL, AMF (suspended), IBRD, IGADD, IMF, NAM, OAU, OIC, UN

*In a state of transition

Local and regional government
In March 1993 proposals were agreed for a federal system of government based on 18 regions, further subdivided into districts.

Head of state and head of government
President (interim) Ali Mahdi Mohammed, since 1991

Political leaders since 1970
1969–91 Major General Muhammad Siad Barre (SRSP),
1991–   Ali Mahdi Mohammed (USC)

Political system
At a conference in March 1993, 15 representatives of the main political factions agreed to set up a 74-member Transitional National Council (TNC), with three representatives from the 18 administrative regions, five from the capital, Mogadishu, and one from each of the factions who had signed the agreement. It was also agreed that a federal system would be established, but in May 1994 the leaders of the self-proclaimed Republic of Somaliland, covering the territory of the former British Somaliland, said they would never form a federal state with Somalia.

Political parties
Political parties in Somalia are based more on clans than ideology and so tend to function in different areas of the country. This clan division contributed to the civil war and the near anarchy after 1989.

The most dominant current grouping is the United Somali Congress (USC–Hawiye clan), based in Mogadishu and central Somalia. Other groups include the Somali Patriotic Movement (SPM–Darod clan), the Somali Salvation Democratic Front (SSDF–Majertein clan), the Somali Democratic Alliance (SDA–Gadabursi clan), the United Somali Front (USF–Issa clan), and the Somali National Movement (SNM).

The SPM was formed in 1989 in southern Somalia.

The SSDF was formed in 1981, also in the south.

The SDA is an alliance of various, mainly southern, groups and was formed in 1992.

The USF was formed in 1989 in the northwest.

The SNM is the ruling party in the self-declared independent 'Republic of Somaliland', situated in the northwest. It is led by Abdel-Rahman Ahmed Ali, who was the state's president between 1991–93.

Latest elections
Elections were promised in 1995 but could not be held due to the civil war.

In the 1984 Assembly elections members were chosen from a single list of 171 Somali Revolutionary Socialist Party (SRSP) candidates.

Political history
European interest in this part of Africa was stimulated by the opening of the Suez Canal in 1869. Britain, in the north in 1886, and Italy, in the south, established colonies and Somalia became a fully independent republic in 1960 through the merger of British and Italian Somaliland.

After achieving independence Somalia was involved in disputes with its neighbours because of its insistence on the right of all Somalis to self-determination, wherever they had settled. This applied particularly to those living in the Ogaden region of Ethiopia and in northeast Kenya. A dispute over the border with Kenya resulted in a break in diplomatic relations with the United Kingdom for five years, between 1963 and 1968. A dispute with Ethiopia led to an eight-month war, in 1978, in which Somalia was defeated by Ethiopian troops assisted by Soviet and Cuban weapons and advisers. There was a rapprochement with Kenya in 1984 and, in 1986, the first meeting for ten years between the Somalian and Ethiopian leaders.

The first president of independent Somalia was Aden Abdullah Osman and he was succeeded, in 1967, by Dr Abdirashid Ali Shermarke, of the Somali Youth League (SYL), which had become the dominant political party. In October 1969 President Shermarke was assassinated, providing an opportunity for the army to seize power, under the leadership of the commander in chief, Major General Muhammad Siad Barre (1910–95). He suspended the 1960 constitution, dissolved the National Assembly, and banned all political parties. He then formed a military government, the Supreme Revolutionary Council (SRC), to rule by decree, and the following year declared Somalia a socialist state.

In 1976 the SRC transferred power to a newly created Somali Revolutionary Socialist Party (SRSP) and in 1979 a new constitution for a socialist one-party state was adopted. In 1977 Somali guerrillas drove the Ethiopians out of the predominantly Somali-inhabited Ogaden, but, with support from the Soviet Union, the Ethiopians later regained the territory. Barre was re-elected in January 1987 but opposition to his regime grew in the north, led by the Ethiopian-backed Somali National Movement (SNM), operating across the Ethiopian border.

In August 1989 the SRSP announced a proposal to introduce a multiparty political system, an announcement viewed cynically by opposition groups, who began to resort to violence in different parts of the country. In January 1991 rebel forces took control of the national capital, Mogadishu, and Barre was forced to flee. Ali Mahdi Mohammed was made interim president by the United Somali Congress (USC).

Drought and the political confusion, as rival groups seized districts in the north and south, resulted in widespread famine. An international aid programme was mounted, but its work was constantly interrupted by the warring factions, who looted food convoys. In December 1992, following an initiative by outgoing US president, George Bush, 28,000 US troops entered the country, under United Nations (UN) auspices, as the United Task Force (UNITAF), ostensibly to protect aid supplies. Then, in an attempt to establish some sort of social and political order, they became involved in clan conflicts. Joined by other international forces, they became, in May 1993, the UN Operation in Somalia (UNOSOM-II). However, by the end of 1994 US, Canadian, French, South Korean, and Belgium contingents withdrew, reducing the strength of UNOSOM-II to 15,000 troops.

Fighting continued, particularly, from November 1991, between the forces of the Hawiye clan USC, led by Ali Mahdi Mohammed, and the Abgal subclan, which had broken with the USC, the Somali National Alliance (SNA), led by General Muhammad Farah Aidid. The situation became more confused until, in March 1994, a peace agreement between the two main rival warlords was concluded. The remit of UNOSOM-II was modified to give it a more peacekeeping and less interventionist role and plans were made for its progressive withdrawal. Even though there was still considerable instability, by March 1995 the last troops had, rather ignominiously, left the country, with the warlords General Aidid and Ali Mahdi Muhammed continuing to contest for power. It was revealed that the former president, Barre, had died in January 1995, in exile in Nigeria, at the age of 84.

In northwest Somalia an independent 'Republic of Somaliland', comprising much of the territory of former British Somaliland, was declared in 1991, with Abdel-Rahman Ahmed Ali, leader of the Somali National Movement (SNM), as its president. However, this failed to secure international recognition and by 1994 Ahmed Ali, who had been replaced as the republic's president by Muhammad Ibrahim Egal in May 1993, was advocating negotiations between north and south to sort out the country's problems. This proposal was rejected by President Ibrahim Egal.

SOUTH AFRICA

Republic of South Africa
Republiek van Suid-Afrika

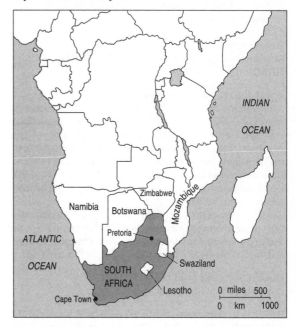

Capital: Pretoria (administrative), Bloemfontein (judicial), Cape Town (legislative)

Social and economic data
Area: 1,222,037 km²
Population: 40,800,000*
Pop. density per km²: 33*
Urban population: 50%**
Literacy rate: 80%**
GDP: $106,000 million**; per-capita GDP: $2,666**
Government defence spending (% of GDP): 3.3%**
Currency: rand
Economy type: middle income
Labour force in agriculture: 14%**

*1994
**1992

Ethnic composition
Seventy-three per cent of the population is black African, 15% white, of European stock, 9% previously known as coloured, of mixed African–European parentage, and 3% Asian. There are 11 official languages, including Afrikaans, English, Xhosa (21%), Zulu (16%), Sesotho, Swazi, Ndebele, Venda, and Tsonga.

Religions
Most whites and African–Europeans and about 60% of the Africans are Christians. There are over 2 million Roman Catholics, about 2 million Anglicans, and about 1.5 million members of the Dutch Reformed Church. About 60% of the Asians are Hindus and 20% Muslims. There are also about 120,000 Jews.

Political features

State type: emergent democratic
Date of state formation: 1910
Political structure: unitary
Executive: limited presidential
Assembly: two-chamber
Party structure: multiparty
Human rights rating: 50%
International affiliations: CW, IAEA, IBRD, IMF, IWC, NAM, OAU, SADC, UN, WTO

Local and regional government

Although it is not a federal state, South Africa has a strongly devolved system of government based on nine regions: Eastern Cape, Eastern Transvaal, Kwazulu/Natal, Northern Cape, Northern Transvaal, North West, Orange Free State, Pretoria/Witwatersrand/Vereeniging (PWV), and Western Cape. Each region has its own legislature of between 30 to 100 members, based on population size, elected by a proportional representation voting system.

The organs of the central government are regionally dispersed, the administrative capital being at Pretoria, in PWV, the seat of the judiciary in Bloemfontein, in the Orange Free State, and the National Assembly at Cape Town, in Western Cape.

Head of state and head of government

President Nelson Rolihlahla Mandela, since 1994

Political leaders since 1970*

1966–78 B J Vorster (NP), 1978–89 P W Botha (NP), 1989–94 F W de Klerk (NP), 1994– Nelson Mandela (ANC)

*Prime minister to 1984, president thereafter

Political system

The November 1993 multiparty Interim Constitution provides for a president, who is head of state and head of government, supported by at least two deputy presidents, and a two-chamber parliament, comprising a 400-member National Assembly and a 90-member Senate.

Members of the National Assembly are elected by a system of proportional representation, 200 being taken from national party lists and 200 from regional party lists. Members of the Senate are indirectly elected on the basis of ten from each of the nine regional legislatures.

The president is elected by the National Assembly. Any party with at least 20% of the national vote is entitled to nominate a deputy president, to be appointed by the president. The first deputy president, who acts as prime minister, is nominated by the majority party and the second deputy president by the second largest party in the National Assembly. Any party with at least 5% of the national vote is entitled to a number of cabinet portfolios, proportionate to the number of seats it has in the National Assembly. The president allocates the portfolios.

The present government is a transitional Government of National Unity and will function, along with the Interim Constitution, until 1999.

Political parties

Of over 30 political parties, the most significant are the African National Congress of South Africa (ANC), the National Party (NP), the Inkatha Freedom Party (IFP), the Freedom Front (FF), the Democratic Party (DP), the Pan-Africanist Congress (PAC), and the African Christian Democratic Party (ACDP).

The ANC was formed in 1912 and was banned from 1960 to 1990. In 1985 it opened its membership to all races. It has a moderate left-of-centre orientation and is led by president Nelson Mandela.

The NP was founded in 1912 and was the all-white ruling party until 1994. It now has a moderate right-of-centre orientation and is led by the former president, F W de Klerk.

The IFP was originally founded as an African Liberation Movement, with mostly Zulu support. It was reconstructed in 1990 as a multiracial party. It has a centrist orientation and is led by Chief Mangosuthu Buthelezi.

The FF was formed in 1994. It has a white, right-wing orientation and is led by General (retired) Constand Viljoen.

The DP was formed in 1989 by a merger of the Independent Party, the National Democratic Movement, and the Progressive Federal Party. It has a multiracial, moderate, centrist orientation.

The PAC was formed in 1959 by ANC dissidents. It has a black, left-of-centre, nationalist orientation.

The ACDP was formed in 1993. It has a Christian right-of-centre orientation.

Latest elections

The results of the April 1994 first nonracial multiparty National Assembly elections were as shown in the table below.

	% votes	Seats
ANC	62.6	252
NP	20.4	82
IFP	10.5	43
FF	2.2	9
DP	1.7	7
PAC	1.2	5
ACDP	0.5	2
Other parties	0.9	–

Political history

South Africa, where black African states had been long established, was first settled by Europeans in the 17th century. The Dutch were the first, establishing the colony of Cape Town in 1652, followed by the French and then the British. The descendants of the Dutch and French Huguenots were the farmers, or Boers, who established their first republic in Natal in 1839. The British, meanwhile, had annexed the Cape in 1814 and were moving in the same direction as the Boers (or Afrikaners). By the middle of the 19th century the British controlled the Cape and had acquired Natal in 1843 through helping the Boers defend themselves against the Zulus. The Boers then trekked northwards and westwards, in the Great Trek of 1835–37, and created republics in the

Transvaal and Orange Free State, which were later recognized by the British. The discovery of diamonds in 1867 and gold in the Witwatersrand in south Transvaal in 1886 led to rivalry between the British and the Boers, and this, together with Boer resentment of the British policy of imperialism and the fear of their culture being destroyed, resulted in a series of wars in 1880–81 and 1899–1902. The Boer resistance to British attempts to annex their republics was led by Paul Kruger (1825–1904). After fortunes had wildly fluctuated, the Boers were eventually defeated and peace was agreed with the signing of the Treaty of Vereeniging in 1902.

The eventual outcome was the passing by the British Parliament, in 1909, of the South Africa Act, which established a new British dominion called the Union of South Africa, consisting of the former colonies of the Orange River, Transvaal, the Cape, and Natal. The Act guaranteed equal status for people of British or Boer descent. The Union came into being in 1910, with Louis Botha (1862–1919), the Boer leader and soldier, as the first prime minister of the new state. An Afrikaner insurrection, led by Christian de Wet (1854–1922), was suppressed and German Southwest Africa, now Namibia, was conquered during 1914–15. In 1919 Botha was succeeded by his protégé, General Jan Christian Smuts (1870–1950).

Smuts, who was prime minister between 1919–24 and 1939–48, headed the South Africa Party, preaching toleration and conciliation, but the National Party (NP), which had been established in 1912 as an opposition movement, was much less liberal, particularly under its post-World War II leader, Daniel Malan (1874–1959). In 1912 the African National Congress (ANC) was also formed to campaign against white supremacy. It drew its support predominantly from the black and immigrant Asian communities and during the 1920s there was black industrial protest. During World War II, South Africa joined the Allied cause.

The NP came to power in 1948, under Malan, who introduced the policy of apartheid, or race segregation, attempting to justify it on the grounds of separate, but equal, development. Its effects, however, were to deny all but the white minority a voice in the nation's affairs and facilities and areas of residence were segregated into white, black, and coloured zones (the Group Areas Act). In the 1950s the ANC led a campaign of civil disobedience until it, and other similar movements, were, in 1960, declared illegal. In 1964 its leader, Nelson Mandela (b. 1918), was given life imprisonment for alleged sabotage. He was to become a central symbol of black opposition to the white regime.

Malan was succeeded in 1958 by Hendrik Verwoerd (1901–66), who refused to change his policies, despite criticisms from within the Commonwealth. Following a decision to assume republican status, in 1961, South Africa withdrew from the Commonwealth. Verwoerd remained in office until his assassination in 1966 and his successor, B(althazar) J(ohannes) Vorster (1915–83), continued to follow the same line. 'Pass laws', restricting the movement of blacks within the country, were introduced, causing international outrage, and ten 'homelands' (Bantustans) were established to contain particular ethnic groups. By the 1980s many of the white regime's opponents had been imprisoned without trial and it was estimated that more than 3 million people had been forcibly resettled in black townships between 1960 and 1980. This provoked responses from the black community in the form of strikes and an uprising in Soweto in 1976. Complaints of police brutality brought international condemnation, particularly when news was given of the death in police detention of the black community leader, Steve Biko (1946–77), in September 1977.

Despite this, the NP continued to increase its majority at each election, with the white opposition parties failing to make any significant impact. In 1978 Vorster resigned and was succeeded by P(ieter) W(illem) Botha (b. 1916), who seemed determined to resist the pressures from his party's extreme right-wing hardliners and give more scope to its liberal members. He embarked upon a policy of constitutional reform which would involve coloureds and Indians, but not blacks, in the governmental process. The inevitable clash occurred and in March 1982 Dr Andries Treurnicht (1921–93), leader of the hardline (verkrampte) wing, and 15 other extremists, were expelled from the NP. They later formed a new party, the Conservative Party of South Africa (CPSA), which advocated a new partitioning of the country, along racial lines.

Although there were considerable doubts about P W Botha's proposals within the coloured and Indian communities, as well as among the whites, he went ahead and, in November 1983, they were approved by 66% of the voters in an all-white referendum. The new constitution came into effect in September 1984. In 1985 a number of apartheid laws were amended or repealed, including the ban on sexual relations or marriage between people of different races and the ban on mixed racial membership of political parties, but the underlying inequalities in the system remained and the dissatisfaction of the black community grew. Serious rioting broke out in the black townships, with Soweto, near Johannesburg, becoming a focal point, and, despite the efforts of black moderates such as the Anglican Bishop of Johannesburg Desmond Tutu (b. 1931) to encourage peaceful resistance, violence grew.

Calls for economic sanctions against South Africa grew during 1985 and 1986 and at the Heads of Commonwealth conference in Nassau in October 1985, it was decided to investigate the likelihood of the South African government dismantling apartheid and thus avoiding the need to impose full sanctions. It was eventually concluded that there were no signs of genuine liberalization. Reluctantly, the British prime minister, Margaret Thatcher, agreed to limited measures, while some leading Commonwealth countries, notably Australia and Canada, took additional independent action. The US Congress eventually forced President Ronald Reagan to move in the same direction.

In the face of this international criticism, State President Botha announced that he would call elections in 1987 to seek a renewal of his mandate. The results were gains for the National and Conservative parties. Growing support for the Conservative Party was evidenced by wins in Assembly by-elections in March 1988. State President Botha's reaction, in April 1988, was to propose more 'constitutional reform', which would give blacks more control over their own affairs. The proposals were criticized by both whites and blacks. By South African standards Botha's plans were revolutionary but, nevertheless, the whites would retain the main levers of power. Despite this, there were signs of clandestine movements. It was announced in May 1988 that a group of white South African politicians opposed to apartheid, including two members of the House of Assembly, had had secret discussions in Germany with representatives of the ANC, which was being led in exile by Nelson Mandela's colleague, Oliver Tambo (1917–93).

In January 1989 State President Botha suffered a stroke and early in February announced that he was giving up the NP leadership but would remain president until the end of his current term and would not seek re-election. In an unusually speedy election the party leadership passed to F(rederik) W(illem) de Klerk (b. 1936) by a very narrow majority in a third ballot.

In June 1989 F W de Klerk announced a five-year plan for 'constitutional reform'. It was widely criticized by his opponents as a continuation of apartheid in a disguised form. However, after a tentative start, the new state president moved quickly and further than his critics had expected. In 1989 he ordered the release from prison of Walter Sisulu and other leading ANC members and, in February 1990, in a dramatic speech at the opening of the House of Assembly, he announced sweeping reforms, including the unbanning of the ANC, the lifting of the state of emergency, a moratorium on capital punishment, and the repeal of the Separate Amenities Act, which had segregated blacks from whites. A week later Nelson Mandela was released. All restrictions on the movement of Mandela and his ANC colleagues were lifted and during the following months he travelled widely, attracting considerable international support. In December 1990 Oliver Tambo returned to South Africa. Namibia also achieved independence from South Africa in 1990.

In June 1991 the remaining laws which had enshrined the apartheid system were repealed and in September 1991 President de Klerk announced that his proposals for constitutional change would be put to the white minority in a referendum. In March 1992 the referendum resulted in a 68.6% 'Yes' and a 31.4% 'No' vote for change.

The negotiations between the government and black representatives were impeded by friction between the ANC, whose supporters are chiefly Xhosas, and the Zulu Inkatha movement, led by Chief Mangosuthu Gatsha Buthelezi (b. 1928), the prime minister of the Zulu homeland of KwaZulu since 1972, who was accused of instigating violence against ANC members. The national security forces were also suspected of clandestinely encouraging Inkatha and other ANC opponents. In June 1992, 42 ANC supporters were killed at a political rally in the black township of Boipatong, near Johannesburg, allegedly by Inkatha supporters. Mandela immediately called off the constitutional talks, but they were later resumed.

In February 1993 Mandela and President de Klerk agreed to the formation of a government of national unity, after free elections. This was initially opposed by Chief Buthelezi, because he had not been consulted, and by white right-wing extremists who, in April, shot and killed a prominent ANC member, Chris Hani. In the same month Oliver Tambo suffered a stroke and died. In September 1993 a multiracial Transitional Executive Council (TEC) was established while

a new constitution was being agreed. The constitution was ratified in November and free nonracial elections were scheduled for April 1994. Meanwhile, in October 1993, in recognition of their efforts, Mandela and de Klerk were jointly awarded the Nobel Peace Prize.

The April 1994 elections resulted in a clear victory for the ANC and Nelson Mandela was elected president by the new National Assembly, with Thabo Mbeki being nominated first deputy president by the ANC and F W de Klerk nominated second deputy president by the NP.

In President Mandela's first administration the majority of portfolios went to the ANC but NP members were given, among others, the key posts of Provincial Affairs and Constitutional Development and Finance, while Chief Buthelezi was awarded Home Affairs.

The restoration of South Africa within the international community was confirmed in July 1994, when it returned to Commonwealth membership. It also joined the Organization of African Unity (OAU) in June 1994 and the Southern African Development Community (SADC). In November 1994 the Restitution of Lands Bill was passed, restoring land to dispossessed black people.

The dramatic changes in the country's political and social systems have aroused expectations among the black majority which the Mandela government will have difficulty in fulfilling in the time scale that some of its supporters expect. Nevertheless, it is certain that there will be no going back and that South Africa's future as Africa's leading state is assured. During 1995 levels of crime and violence rose to alarmingly new levels and in local elections, in November 1995, although the ANC achieved a clear victory, voter apathy was such that turnout slumped to barely 30% in some areas.

SUDAN

The Republic of Sudan
Al Jamhuryat al-Sudan

Capital: Khartoum

Social and economic data
Area: 2,505,800 km^2
Population: 27,400,000*
Pop. density per km^2: 11*
Urban population: 23%**
Literacy rate: 27%**
GDP: $8,316 million**; per-capita GDP: $330**
Government defence spending (% of GDP): 11.6%**
Currency: Sudanese pound
Economy type: low income
Labour force in agriculture: 64%**

*1994
**1992

Ethnic composition
There are over 50 ethnic groups and nearly 600 subgroups in the country, but the population is broadly distributed between Arabs, in the north, and black Africans, in the south. The Arabs are numerically greater and dominate national affairs, and the official language is Arabic.

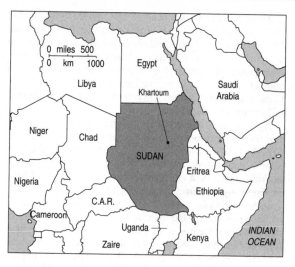

Religions

People of the north are mostly Sunni Muslims (70%) and Islam is the state religion. In the south they are mostly Christians (8%) or followers of traditional animist beliefs (20%).

Political features

State type: military authoritarian*
Date of state formation: 1956
Political structure: federal
Executive: military*
Assembly: one-chamber
Party structure: multiparty (in suspension)*
Human rights rating: 18%
International affiliations: ACP, AL, AMF (suspended), COMESA, IAEA, IBRD, IGADD, IMF, NAM, OAU, OIC, UN

*In a state of transition

Local and regional government

In February 1994 the country was divided into 26 states with governors, assisted by state ministers, appointed by the president. The states are (with the capitals in brackets): Bahr-al-Jabal (Juba), Upper Nile (Malakal), Red Sea (Port Sudan), Lakes (Rumbek), Gezira (Madani), Southern Darfur (Nyala), Jonglei (Bor), Southern Kordofan (Kaduqli), Khartoum (Khartoum), Sinnar (Sinjah), Eastern Equatoria (Kapoeta), Northern Bahr-al-Ghazal (Aweil), Northern Darfur (Fashir), Northern Kordofan (Ubayyid), Northern (Dunqulah), Gadaref (Gadaref), Western Kordofan (Fulah), Western Equatoria (Yambio), Western Bahr al-Ghazal (Wau), Western Darfur (Junaynah), Kassala (Kassala), Nahr-al-Nil (Damir), Warab (Warab), Unity (Bantu), White Nile (Radah), and Blue Nile (Damazin).

Head of state and government

President Lieutenant General Omar Hasan Ahmad al-Bashir, since 1989

Political leaders since 1970

1969–85 Colonel Gaafar Muhammad al-Nimeri (military/ SSU), 1985–86 General Swar al-Dahab (military), 1986–89 Sadiq al-Mahdi (NNUP–DUP coalition), 1989– Lieutenant General Omar Hasan Ahmad al-Bashir (military-influenced)

Political system

The 1973 constitution was suspended following a military coup in April 1985 and the country was placed under a 15-member Transitional Military Council (TMC). Another military coup in 1989 installed a Revolutionary Command Council (RCC) and an appointed 300-member Transitional National Assembly, prior to the reinstatement of democratic government. In October 1993 political reforms were announced, with democratic presidential and legislative elections promised for 1996.

Political parties

Political parties were officially banned in 1989, but the fundamentalist National Islamic Front (NIF) has influence over the RCC.

The Sudan People's Liberation Army (SPLA) is a militarily controlled political group, which has conducted a secessionist war, mainly in the Christian south, against the government since 1984. Since then it has split into two competing factions, led by Torit leader John Garang and the other by Riek Machar.

There are also parties which existed before 1989 and then went into exile.

Latest elections

Multiparty legislative elections were last held in April 1986.

Political history

In the early 19th century Egypt tried to gain control of the Sudan but was thwarted by the resistance of the many, fragmented tribes. In the 1880s, however, a fanatical religious leader, Abdullah al-Taashi, succeeded where Egypt could not. He launched a rebellion against Egypt, and its protector, Britain, leading to the fall of Khartoum. It was eventually recovered by a combined British-Egyptian force, led by Lord Kitchener (1850–1916), and an Anglo-Egyptian condominion was established in 1899. This lasted until Sudan achieved independence, as a republic, in 1956.

Two years later a coup ousted the civil administration and a military government was set up under a Supreme Council of the Armed Forces. In 1964 it, too, was overthrown and civilian rule reinstated, but, five years later, the army returned in a coup led by Colonel Gaafar Muhammad al-Nimeri (b. 1930). All political bodies were abolished, a Revolutionary Command Council (RCC) was set up, and the country's name was changed to the Democratic Republic of the Sudan. Close links were soon established with Egypt and in 1970 an agreement in principle was reached for eventual union. In 1972 this should have become, with the addition of Syria, the Federation of Arab Republics, but internal opposition blocked both developments.

In 1971 a new constitution was adopted, Nimeri confirmed as president, and the Sudanese Socialist Union (SSU) declared to be the only legally permitted party. Nimeri came to power in a left-wing revolution but soon turned to the West, and particularly the United States, for support. The most serious problem initially confronting him was the near civil war between the Muslim north and the non-Muslim south, which had started as long ago as 1955. He tackled it by agreeing, at a conference in Addis Ababa in 1972, to the three southern provinces being given a considerable degree of autonomy, including the establishment of a High Executive Council (HEC) to cater specifically for their distinctive needs. Towards the end of 1973 elections took place for a Regional People's Assembly for southern Sudan and some months later a National People's Assembly, for the whole country, was established.

By 1974 Nimeri had broadened his political base but his position still relied on army support. Three years later, as he felt his position to be more secure, he embarked on a policy of reconciliation, bringing some of his former opponents into his administration and then, in 1980, creating a high degree of devolution by reorganizing the country into six regions, each with its own assembly and a degree of executive autonomy. The National People's Assembly was dissolved, as powers had been devolved to the regional assemblies, and the southern HEC was also disbanded. There was still dissatisfaction, however, about a proposed redivision of the southern region.

In 1983 Nimeri was re-elected for a third term but his regional problems persisted and he was forced to send more troops from the north to the south. In trying to pacify the south he alienated the north and then caused considerable resentment among the non-Muslim southerners by announcing the imposition of strict Islamic laws to replace the existing penal code. By 1984 he was faced with widespread unrest, demonstrated by strikes in the north in protest against his economic policies and disillusionment in the south. The situation there had deteriorated so much that a separatist movement had emerged, the Sudan People's Liberation Movement (SPLM), whose troops, the Sudan People's Liberation Army (SPLA) had taken control of large areas in the region of the Upper Nile.

In March 1985 a general strike was provoked by a sharp devaluation of the Sudanese pound and an increase in bread prices but the underlying discontent was more deep-seated. While he was on a visit to the United States, Nimeri was deposed in a bloodless coup led by General Swar al-Dahab, a supporter of Nimeri who had been forced to take over because of the threat of an army mutiny. Swar al-Dahab set up a Transitional Military Council (TMC) and announced that he would hand over power to a civilian administration within a year. At the end of the year the country's name was changed to 'The Republic of Sudan'.

The SPLA's initial response to the 1985 coup was encouraging. It declared a cease-fire and then presented Swar al-Dahab with a series of demands. He tried to conciliate by suggesting the cancellation of the redivision of the southern region and the reinstatement of the HEC there but these concessions were not enough and fighting broke out again. This continued throughout 1985 but, although the SPLA refused officially to recognize the TMC, secret informal discussions were taking place between representatives of both sides.

A provisional constitution was adopted in October 1985 and an election held for a Legislative Assembly in April 1986. The election was fought by more than 40 parties but no one emerged with a clear majority. A coalition government was formed, with Ahmed Ali El-Mirghani of the Democratic Unionist Party (DUP) as head of state and Oxford-educated Sadiq al-Mahdi, of the Islamic-nationalist New National Umma (People's) Party (NNUP), as prime minister, heading a coalition Council of Ministers. The Assembly was charged with producing the draft of a permanent constitution. In another move towards reconciliation with the south, John Garang, the SPLA leader, was offered a seat on the Council of Ministers but declined it.

By 1987 the south had become even more unstable and was now in the throes of a civil war between the army and the SPLM. The situation there was aggravated by drought, famine, and an unprecedented influx of refugees from neighbouring states, such as Ethiopia and Chad, which had been experiencing their own internal conflicts.

In April 1988 Dr al-Mahdi announced the second break-up of his coalition and the formation of a new government of national unity. He was re-elected prime minister for another term and in May 1988 a new coalition was formed, which included members of the NNUP, DUP, and the fundamentalist National Islamic Front (NIF). In December 1988 a peace accord with the SPLA was signed, but fighting continued.

In July 1989 Dr al-Mahdi was removed in a coup led by Brigadier General Omar Hasan Ahmad al-Bashir, who suspended all political activity and established a Revolutionary Command Council (RCC). Bashir made peace overtures to the SPLA leader, Colonel John Garang, but rumours of agreements between the government and the rebels were subsequently discounted. Throughout 1990 and 1991 the situation continued to be unpredictable, with reports of many lives lost, particularly in the southeast, where the Islamic fundamentalist military government waged a ruthless campaign against the largely Christian and animist population.

In 1991 there was a reported split within the SPLA and, although this was denied, when the Sudanese government reconvened peace talks in May 1992, under the auspices of the Nigerian government, two SPLA delegations attended, the Torit faction, led by John Garang, and SPLA–United, led by Riek Machar. Although the negotiations ended in June 1992 with a communiqué committing all parties to 'peaceful negotiations' at a future date, fighting continued and the death toll continued to mount.

In September 1993 the regional Inter-Governmental Authority on Drought and Development (IGADD), whose members include Djibouti, Ethiopia, Kenya, Somalia, and Uganda, as well as Sudan, launched another peace initiative and agreement was reached between the Sudanese government and the two SPLA factions for talks later in the year.

In October 1993 President Bashir revealed a constitutional reform package, dissolved the RCC, and appointed a civilian government and in January 1995 the rival SPLA leaders, Garang and Machar, were reported to have agreed a cease-fire to a war that had cost thousands of lives and left nearly 2 million as refugees. Fresh IGADD-sponsored talks between the government and the rebels began in May 1994 but ended in deadlock in September 1994. With the fundamentalist NIF strongly influencing government policy, Sudan has emerged as a sponsor of Islamic extremism, including terrorism, across the region and has backed Libya and Iraq. In September 1995 two days of student-led rioting in Khartoum claimed several lives.

SWAZILAND

The Kingdom of Swaziland
Umbuso Weswatini

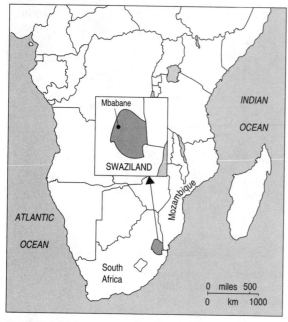

Capital: Mbabane (administrative), Lobamba (legislative and royal)

Social and economic data
Area: 17,400 km^2
Population: 800,000*
Pop. density per km^2: 46*
Urban population: 28%**
Literacy rate: 55%**
GDP: $720 million**; per-capita GDP: $900**
Government defence spending (% of GDP): N/A
Currency: lilangeni
Economy type: low income
Labour force in agriculture: 74%**

*1994
**1992

Ethnic composition
About 90% of the population is indigenous African, distributed among the Swazi, Zulu, Tonga, and Shangaan tribes. There are European and Afro-European, called Eurafrican, minorities numbering about 22,000. The official languages are English and siSwati.

Religions
About three-quarters of the people are Christians, chiefly Protestants (36%), Roman Catholics (11%), and members of Independent African Churches (28%), and about 20% follow traditional animist beliefs.

Political features
State type: absolutist

Date of state formation: 1968
Political structure: unitary
Executive: absolute
Assembly: two-chamber
Party structure: one-party
Human rights rating: N/A
International affiliations: ACP, COMESA, CW, IBRD, IMF, NAM, OAU, SADC, UN, WTO

Local and regional government
The country is divided into four regions, with regional councils consisting of representatives of the 40 chieftancies into which the nation is further subdivided.

Head of state (absolute)
King Mswati III, since 1986

Head of government
Prime Minister Prince Jameson Mbilini Dlamini, since 1993

Political leaders since 1970
1968–82 King Sobhuza II, 1982–83 Queen Dzeliwe, 1983–86 Queen Ntombi, 1986– King Mswati III

Political system
Swaziland is a monarchy within the Commonwealth. The 1978 constitution represents an attempt to combine a traditional pattern of government with the need for a more modern system of consultation and administration. It makes the monarch the head of state and the effective head of government, with a prime minister and Council of Ministers chosen by the monarch. There is a two-chamber assembly, the Libandla, consisting of a 30-member Senate and a 65-member National Assembly. Twenty senators are appointed by the monarch and ten are elected by the National Assembly from among its own members. Since 1993, 55 members of the National Assembly have been directly elected from candidates nominated by traditional local councils (*Tinkhundlas*), and ten are appointed by the monarch.

It was announced in 1994 that the king was to appoint a 15-member commission to draft a new constitution.

Political parties
Political activity by groups other than the Imbokodvo National Movement (INM) was banned in 1973 and this ban was formalized in the 1978 constitution. The INM was formed in 1964 and has a traditional nationalist orientation. It serves as a political instrument for the monarchy.

Since the announcement of constitutional reforms in 1993 a number of political groupings have re-emerged, but are as yet in an embryonic state.

Latest elections
Elections to the National Assembly were held, on a nonparty basis, in September and October 1993. Only three members of the Council of Ministers were re-elected, the prime minister being one who did not retain his seat.

Political history
Swaziland, which had formed a traditional kingdom for the Swazi peoples, was jointly ruled by the United Kingdom and the Transvaal republic, established by the Boers, from 1890

until the end of the South African war of 1899–1902. It then forcibly became a British protectorate in 1904 and, in 1907, a High Commision Territory. The United Kingdom Act of Parliament which established the Union of South Africa, in 1910, made provision for the possible inclusion of Swaziland, with other High Commission Territories, within the Union, but the British government said that this would never be done without the agreement of the people of the Territories. In the knowledge of this constitutional provision, the South African government repeatedly asked for Swaziland to be placed under its jurisdiction but this was resisted by the British government and by the people of Swaziland themselves. The requests ended when, in 1967, Swaziland was granted internal self-government and then achieved full independence, within the Commonwealth, in 1968.

The 1963 constitution, which the British government introduced before full independence, provided for a parliamentary system of government with King Sobhuza II as head of state. In 1973, with the agreement of the assembly, the king suspended the constitution and assumed absolute powers. Then in 1978 a new constitution was announced, providing for a two-chamber assembly, whose members would be partly appointed by the king and partly elected by an electoral college representing the 40 chieftancies.

King Sobhuza died in 1982 and, in accordance with Swazi tradition, the role of head of state passed to the queen mother, Dzeliwe, until the king's heir, Prince Makhosetive, reached the age of 21, in 1989. In August 1983, however, Queen Dzeliwe was ousted by another of King Sobhuza's wives, Ntombi, who was formally invested as queen regent in October. A power struggle developed within the royal family and in November 1984 it was announced that the crown prince would succeed to the throne in April 1986, three years before he would attain his majority. In April 1986 he was formally invested as King Mswati III (b. 1968).

During 1991 a royal commission toured the country, listening to peoples' views on constitutional change. Direct assembly elections were introduced in 1993 and in 1994 the king announced that he was to set up a commission, representative of the government and outside interests, to recommend a new constitution. A member of the South African Customs Union, Swaziland has close economic ties with South Africa and uses the South African rand alongside its own currency.

TANZANIA

The United Republic of Tanzania
Jamhuri ya Muungano wa Tanzania

Capital: Dodoma (legislative and official), Dar es Salaam (joint administrative)

Social and economic data
Area: 945,090 km²
Population: 28,800,000*
Pop. density per km²: 29*
Urban population: 22%**
Literacy rate: 46%**
GDP: $3,549 million**; per-capita GDP $130**

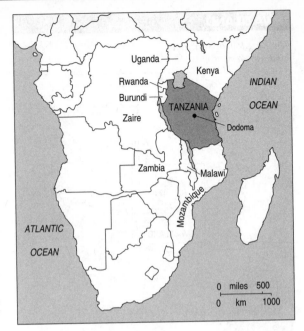

Government defence spending (% of GDP): 3.2%**
Currency: Tanzanian shilling
Economy type: low income
Labour force in agriculture: 79%**

*1994
**1992

Ethnic composition
Ninety-nine per cent of the population are Africans, and are ethnically classified as Bantus, but they are distributed among over 130 tribes. The main tribes are the Bantu, the Vilotic, the Nilo-Hamitic, the Khoisan and the Iraqwi. English and Swahili are the official languages.

Religions
About a third of the people are Sunni Muslims and about 97% of these live on the island of Zanzibar. The rest of the population are mainly Christians, in the Anglican, Greek Orthodox, Lutheran, or Roman Catholic (12%) churches, or follow traditional animist beliefs (35%).

Political features
State type: nationalistic socialist
Date of state formation: 1961
Political structure: unitary
Executive: unlimited presidential
Assembly: one-chamber
Party structure: multiparty*
Human rights rating: 41%
International affiliations: ACP, COMESA, CW, G-15, IAEA, IBRD, IMF, KBO, NAM, OAU, SADC, UN, WTO

*Though dominated by one party

Local and regional government
Zanzibar has its own constitution, providing for a president, elected by universal adult suffrage, through a simple plural-

ity voting system, for a five-year term, and a 45–55-member House of Representatives, similarly elected.

The country is divided into 20 mainland regions and two island divisions, of Zanzibar and Pemba, administered by appointed regional or divisional commissioners. On the mainland the regions are further subdivided into districts, and on Zanzibar the divisions are subdivided into areas. There are part elected and part appointed representative councils.

Head of state (executive)
President Benjamin Mkapa, since 1995

Head of government
First Vice President and Prime Minister Cleopa Msuya, since 1994

Political leaders since 1970
1964–85 Julius Nyerere (CCM), 1985–95 Ali Hassan Mwinyi (CCM), 1995– Benjamin Mkapa (CCM)

Political system
The 1977 constitution made Tanzania a one-party state, the party being the Revolutionary Party of Tanzania (CCM), but in 1992 legislation was passed allowing opposition parties to operate.

The constitution, as amended, provides for an executive president elected by universal suffrage for a five-year term, renewable once only. There is a single-chamber National Assembly of up to 291 members, 232 directly elected by universal suffrage through a simple plurality voting system, five elected by the Zanzibar House of Representatives, five allocated specifically for women, 15 representing party organizations, 12 nominated by the president, and 22 ex officio regional commissioners. The National Assembly also serves a five-year term. An Electoral Commission may review and, if necessary, increase the number of constituencies before each general election.

The president appoints two vice presidents from members of the National Assembly, one of whom is termed prime minister. The president also appoints and presides over a cabinet.

Political parties
Until 1992 the only legal party was the Revolutionary Party of Tanzania (CCM). It was founded in 1977 by an amalgamation of the Tanganyika African National Union (TANU), covering the mainland, and the Afro-Shirazi Party, covering the islands of Zanzibar, and its constitution pledged it 'to establish a socialist democratic state by self-help'. The party has a left-of-centre orientation.

After 1992 a number of other parties were formed to contest the 1995 multiparty elections. These included the Civic Party (Chama Cha Wananchi: CCW), the Tanzania People's Party (TPP), the Democratic Party (DP), the Zanzibar United Front (Kama-huru), the Liberal Democratic Party, the National Party for Construction and Reform– Mageuzi (NCCR–Mageuzi), the National League of Democrats (NLD), and the Movement for Multiparty Democracy (MMD). All date from 1992 or 1993.

The CCW, TPP, DP, Liberal Democrats, NCCR, NLD, and MMD have left-of-centre orientations. Kamahuru is a centrist, Zanzibar-based grouping.

Latest elections
In October 1995 the first multiparty elections to the National Assembly and the presidency were held. The ruling CCM claimed victory but the organiz-ation was so chaotic that the poll had to be rerun in many areas, including the commercial capital, Dar es Salaam. In November 1995 Benjamin Mkapa (CCM) was declared president, winning 62% of the vote, and the CCM captured 186 assembly seats to the opposition's 46

Political history
What is now Tanzania had strong links with Arab, Indian, and Persian traders long before Europeans arrived and there is still evidence of those links in the country's religions and customs. The Germans were the first Europeans to establish themselves on the mainland, and Tanganyika, as it was called, became part of German East Africa. Meanwhile, the British had declared Zanzibar a protectorate. Tanganyika was taken away from Germany after World War I and Britain was given a mandate to govern it. After World War II a movement for independence developed and in 1961 Tanganyika was given internal self-government and later the same year full independence, within the Commonwealth. Tanzania was founded by the merger of Tanganyika and Zanzibar in 1964.

Julius Nyerere (b. 1922) became the country's first prime minister in 1961, but gave up the post some six weeks after independence to devote himself to the development of the Tanganyika African National Union (TANU), which he had formed in 1954. However, in December 1962, when Tanganyika became a republic, he returned to become the nation's first president. Zanzibar became an independent sultanate in 1963 and, following an uprising, a republic within weeks. The Act of Union with the mainland was signed in April 1964 and Nyerere became president of the new United Republic of Tanzania. Despite the union, the island of Zanzibar has retained its own constitution.

Nyerere dominated the nation's politics for the next 20 years, being re-elected in 1965, 1970, 1975, and 1980, and became one of Africa's most respected politicians. Known throughout Tanzania as 'Mwalimu' ('teacher'), he established himself as a genuine Christian-socialist who attempted to put into practice a philosophy which he fervently believed would secure his country's future. He committed himself in the Arusha Declaration of 1967, the name coming from the northern Tanzanian town where he made his historic statement, to building a socialist state for the millions of poor peasants, through a series of village cooperatives (ujamas). In the final years of his presidency economic pressures forced him to compromise his ideals and accept a more capitalistic society than he would have wished, but his achievements have been many, including the best public health service on the African continent, according to United Nations officials, and a universal primary school system.

Relations between Tanzania and its neighbours have been variable. The East African Community (EAC) of Tanzania, Kenya, and Uganda, which was formed in 1967, broke up in 1977 and links with Kenya became uneasy, particularly as Kenya had embarked on a more capitalistic economic policy than Tanzania. In 1979 Nyerere sent troops into Uganda to support the Uganda National Liberation Front in its bid to overthrow President Idi Amin. This enhanced Nyerere's reputation but damaged his country's economy.

In March 1984 Nyerere announced his impending retirement and it was widely expected that he would be succeeded by the prime minister, Edward Sokoine, but he was killed in a road accident in the same year. The president of Zanzibar, Ali Hassan Mwinyi (b. 1925), was adopted as the sole presidential candidate by the CCM Congress in December 1985. In 1990 Nyerere retired as CCM chairman and was succeeded by Mwinyi. President Mwinyi, encouraged by the IMF, instituted a programme of economic liberalization.

In May 1992 legislation was passed permitting multiparty politics and soon afterwards a number of groups formed in anticipation of free elections in 1995. Ethnic unrest and violence in neighbouring Burundi created the influx into northern Tanzania of huge numbers of refugees during 1994 and 1995. Benjamin Mkapa was elected president in November 1995.

TOGO

The Togolese Republic
La République togolaise

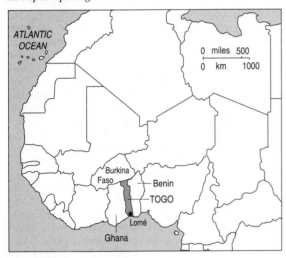

Capital: Lomé

Social and economic data
Area: 56,790 km^2
Population: 3,900,000*
Pop. density per km^2: 69*
Urban population: 29%**
Literacy rate: 43%**
GDP: $1,365 million*; per-capita GDP: $390**
Government defence spending (% of GDP): 2.8%**
Currency: franc CFA
Economy type: low income
Labour force in agriculture: 64%**

*1994
**1992

Ethnic composition
Most of the people in the north are of Sudanese Hamitic origin while those in the south are mostly black African.

They are distributed among some 37 different tribes. There are also European, Syrian, and Lebanese minorities. The official languages are French, Ewe, and Kabre.

Religions
About 50% of the population follows traditional animist beliefs, about 35% is Christian, chiefly Roman Catholic, and about 15% is Sunni Muslim.

Political features
State type: emergent democratic
Date of state formation: 1960
Political structure: unitary
Executive: limited presidential
Assembly: one-chamber
Party structure: multiparty
Human rights rating: 48%
International affiliations: ACP, BOAD, CEAO (observer), ECOWAS, Francophone, FZ, IBRD, IFM, NAM, OAU, UEMOA, UN, WTO

Local and regional government
The country is divided into four regions, administered by appointed inspectors, who are advised by elected councils.

Head of state (executive)
President General Etienne Gnassingbé Eyadéma, since 1967

Head of government
Prime Minister Edem Kodjo, since 1994

Political leaders since 1970
1967–91 General Etienne Gnassingbé Eyadéma (RPT), 1991–93 Joseph Kokou Koffigoh (transitional), 1993– General Etienne Gnassingbé Eyadéma (RPT)

Political system
The September 1992 multiparty constitution, which was approved in a referendum, provides for an executive president, who is head of state, and a single-chamber National Assembly. The president is elected by universal suffrage for a five-year term. The 81-member National Assembly is similarly elected for the same length of term. The president appoints the prime minister on the basis of assembly support.

Political parties
Until 1991 the only legal party was the Assembly of the Togolese People (RPT). Since then more than 60 parties have officially registered, the most significant, in addition to the RPT, being the Action Committee for Renewal (CAR) and the Togolese Union for Democracy (UTD).

The RPT was founded in 1969. It has a nationalist socialist orientation and is led by President Eyadéma.

The CAR and the UTD were formed in 1991. They have left-of-centre orientations.

For electoral purposes, the parties tend to form broad coalitions.

Latest elections
Etienne Gnassingbé Eyadéma won the August 1993 multiparty presidential election with 96.5% of the votes.

In the February 1994 National Assembly elections the CAR won 34 seats, the RPT, 35, and the UTD, 6.

Political history

Originally part of the Kingdom of Togoland, Togo was a German protectorate from 1884 to 1914, when the country was invaded by French and British forces. In 1922 it became a League of Nations mandated territory and responsibility for it was split between France and Britain. The French eastern part was administered separately, as French Togo, while the British part, called British Togoland, was included within the British Gold Coast. In 1957 the inhabitants of British Togoland chose to remain part of the Gold Coast, which was later to become Ghana, while French Togoland voted to become an autonomous republic within the French Union.

The new French Togolese republic was given internal self-government in 1956 and full independence in April 1960, and Sylvanus Olympio, leader of the United Togolese (UT) party, became the first president in an unopposed election in April 1961. In 1963 Olympio was overthrown and killed in a military coup and his brother-in-law, Nicolas Grunitzky, who had gone into exile, was recalled to become provisional president. A referendum approved a new constitution and Grunitzky's presidency was confirmed. In January 1967 he, in turn, was deposed in a bloodless military coup, led by Lieutenant General Etienne Gnassingbé Eyadéma (b. 1937). The constitution was suspended and Eyadéma assumed the presidency and banned all political activity. Six years later he founded a new party, the Assembly of the Togolese People (RPT), and declared it the only legal political organization.

There were several unsuccessful attempts to overthrow him and Eyadéma responded by promising a new constitution and multiparty elections. However, in August 1991, under pressure from foreign creditors and internal strikes, he was stripped of his powers by a national conference held to determine the country's political future. In addition, the RPT was dissolved and an appointed High Council of the Republic (HCR) replaced the National Assembly, with Joseph Kokou Koffigoh appointed as head of a transitional government. After some abortive attempts by loyal troops to restore Eyadéma's powers, there was some rapprochement between him and the HCR and it was agreed that a referendum on constitutional change would be held. This took place in September 1992 and showed an overwhelming desire for a return to full democracy. While the RPT in theory no longer existed, it was, in reality, still an active force. The other parties had coalesced into broad groupings, the main one being the Collective of Democratic Opposition-2 (COD-2), some 26 political organizations and trade unions, which included the Action Committee for Renewal (CAR) and the Togolese Union for Democracy (UTD). Early in 1993 unsuccessful talks were held in France between representatives of the main political groupings in an attempt to resolve the constitutional crisis and the situation became more complicated when Eyadéma and Koffigoh, having partly restored their relationship, in February 1993, agreed to form a new 'crisis government', headed by Koffigoh. This move was strongly opposed by COD-2 and the HCR.

In April 1993 Eyadéma and Koffigoh agreed a timetable for multiparty elections and as the situation improved in the following month, after direct talks between the president and representatives of COD-2, it was announced in June 1993 that Koffigoh had formed a new grouping of six parties, the Coordination of New Forces (CFN), in anticipation of the elections.

The presidential contest took place in August 1993 and Eyadéma was elected with more than 90% of the vote, amid allegations of ballot-rigging by his opponents. Assembly elections were eventually held in February 1994, in a tense atmosphere, after attempts had been made to assassinate Eyadéma. The CAR won 36 seats and its coalition partner, the UTD, 7, while Eyadéma's party, the RPT, obtained 35. Koffigoh's party, the Coordination of New Forces (CFN), secured only one seat. The result was later changed, after claims of irregularities, leaving the CAR with 34 seats, the UTD, 6, and the RPT, 35.

Koffigoh resigned and, after discussions, in April 1994 President Eyadéma appointed Edem Kodjo, the UTD leader, as prime minister. This was rejected by the CAR which withdrew from its partnership with the UTD. Eventually Kodjo formed a government consisting of UTD and RPT members with others from minor parties. The CAR, still dissatisfied with the election results and Kodjo's appointment, boycotted the National Assembly until August 1995.

UGANDA

The Republic of Uganda

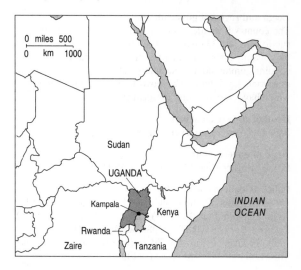

Capital: Kampala

Social and economic data
Area: 241,139 km²
Population: 19,200,000*
Pop. density per km²: 80*
Urban population: 12%**
Literacy rate: 48%**
GDP: $3,598 million**; per-capita GDP $190**

Government defence spending (% of GDP): 2.8%**
Currency: new Uganda shilling
Economy type: low income
Labour force in agriculture: 86%**

*1994
**1992

Ethnic composition
There are about 40 different tribes concentrated into four main groups: the Bantu, who are the most numerous, the Eastern Nilotic, the Western Nilotic, and the Central Sudanic. There are also Rwandan, Sudanese, Zairean, and Kenyan minorities. The official languages are English and Swahili.

Religions
Approximately 60% of the population is Christian, three-quarters Roman Catholic and the rest Protestant, about 6% is Sunni Muslim, and the remainder mostly follow traditional animist beliefs.

Political features
State type: authoritarian nationalist
Date of state formation: 1962
Political structure: unitary
Executive: unlimited presidential
Assembly: one-chamber
Party structure: multiparty*
Human rights rating: 46%
International affiliations: ACP, COMESA, CW, IAEA, IBRD, IGADD, IMF, KBO, NAM, OAU, OIC, UN, WTO

*Though dominated by one party

Local and regional government
The country is divided into ten provinces which are further subdivided into 38 districts. The provinces are administered by governors, appointed by the president, and they, in turn, appoint commissioners to administer the districts. At the grassroots level, there is a network of 'resistance councils', which have responsibility for local administration.

Head of state (executive)
President Yoweri Museveni, since 1986

Head of government
Prime Minister Kinti Musoke, since 1994

Political leaders since 1970
1966–71 Milton Obote (UPC), 1971–79 Major General Idi Amin Dada (military), 1979 Yusuf Lule (UNLF), 1979–80 Godfrey Binaisa (UNLF), 1980–85 Milton Obote (UPC), 1985–86 General Tito Okello (military), 1986– Yoweri Museveni (NRA–NRM broad coalition)

Political system
The 1969 constitution was revived in 1981. It provides for a single-chamber National Assembly of 126 members and an executive president who is head of state. He or she appoints a prime minister as head of government. The president and the Assembly are elected by universal adult suffrage, through a simple plurality voting system, for a five-year term.

In 1985 a military coup suspended the constitution and dissolved the National Assembly. A power-sharing agree-ment between the head of a Military Council, General Tito Okello, and Yoweri Museveni, leader of the National Resis-tance Army (NRA), which had been formed to overthrow the regime of Milton Obote, was concluded in December 1985 and this led to the dissolution of the Military Council and the establishment of a National Resistance Council (NRC), con-sisting of 210 elected and 68 presidentially appointed mem-bers, to act as a legislative body prior to the adoption of a new constitution. Its chairperson, President Museveni, acted as chief executive, appointing a prime minister. In March 1994 a Constituent Assembly, comprising 214 elected and 74 nominated members, was established to debate and agree a draft constitution.

Political parties
The activities of political parties were suspended in 1986, but they were not banned, and this suspension was extended for a further five years in 1990. Of the 'dormant' parties, the most significant are the National Resistance Movement (NRM), the Democratic Party (DP), the Conservative Party (CP), the Uganda People's Congress (UPC), and the Uganda Freedom Movement (UFM).

The NRM is the political wing of Yoweri Museveni's National Resistance Army (NRA). It was originally estab-lished in 1980 to oppose the regime of Milton Obote.

The DP was founded in 1953 and banned in 1969 when a one-party state was established. It has a centre-left orien-tation.

The CP dates from 1979. It has a centre-right orientation.

The UPC was formed in 1960 and was made the only legal party, by Milton Obote, between 1969 and 1971. It has a left-of-centre orientation.

The UFM was formed in 1987. It has a left-of-centre stance.

Latest elections
Nonparty elections to the Constituent Assembly in March 1994 resulted in President Museveni's supporters capturing 114 of the elective seats, the rest being distributed between UPC and DP supporters.

Political history
The British East Africa Company concluded treaties with local rulers to develop Uganda in the 1890s. In 1894 the ter-ritory was made a British protectorate and was divided into five regions, four of them governed directly by Britain, with the assistance of native chiefs, and one, Buganda, ruled by its traditional prince, the Kabaka, under the British Crown. In the 1950s internal self-government was given, with four provinces controlled by local ministers and Buganda by the Kabaka.

Uganda achieved full independence, within the Common-wealth, in 1962 with Dr Milton Obote (b. 1924), leader of the Uganda People's Congress (UPC) which he had founded in 1960, as prime minister. Buganda and the other four regions continued to enjoy a fair degree of self-government so that in 1963, when republican status was assumed, it was on a fed-eral basis and King Mutesa II (1924–69), the former Kabaka of Buganda, became president of the whole country, with Obote as his prime minister.

Obote wanted to establish a one-party state, to which the king objected. Having failed to win the argument by persuasion, Obote mounted a coup in 1966 and deposed King Mutesa. Obote took over as head of state as well as head of government, making himself executive president. One of his first acts was to end the federal status. After an attempt to assassinate him in 1969, Obote banned all opposition and established what was effectively a one-party state. In 1971 he was overthrown in an army coup led by Major General Idi Amin Dada (b. 1926), who suspended the constitution and all political activity and took legislative and executive powers into his own hands. Obote fled the country and took refuge in neighbouring Tanzania.

Amin proceeded to wage what he called an 'economic war' against foreign domination, resulting in mass expulsions of the economically successful Asian community, many of whom settled in Britain. Then in 1976 he claimed that large tracts of Kenya historically belonged to Uganda and also accused Kenya of cooperating with the Israeli government in a raid on Entebbe airport to free Jewish hostages held in a hijacked aircraft. Relations with Kenya became strained and diplomatic links with Britain were severed. During the next two years the Amin regime carried out a widespread campaign against any likely opposition, resulting in thousands of deaths and imprisonments.

In 1978, when he annexed the Kagera area of Tanzania, near the Uganda border, the Tanzanian president, Julius Nyerere sent troops to support the Uganda National Liberation Army (UNLA), which had been formed to fight Amin. Within five months Tanzanian troops had entered the Uganda capital, Kampala, forcing Amin to flee, at first to Libya and then to Saudi Arabia.

A provisional government, comprising a cross-section of exiled groups, the United Liberation Front (UNLF), was set up, with Dr Yusuf Lule as president. Two months later Lule was replaced by Godfrey Binaisa who, in turn, was overthrown by the army. A Military Commission made arrangements for national elections which were won by the UPC and Milton Obote came back to power. Obote's government was soon under pressure from a range of exiled groups operating outside the country and guerrilla forces inside and he was only kept in office because of the presence of Tanzanian troops. When they were withdrawn in June 1982 a major offensive was launched against the Obote government by the National Resistance Movement (NRM), led by Dr Lule and Yoweri Museveni (b. 1944), and its military wing, the National Resistance Army (NRA). By 1985 Obote was unable to control the army, which had been involved in indiscriminate killings, and was ousted in July 1985 in a coup led by General Tito Okello. Obote fled to Kenya and then Zambia, where he was given political asylum.

Okello had little more success in controlling the army and, after a short-lived agreement of power-sharing with the NRA, in January 1986 he left the country and fled to Sudan. Yoweri Museveni was sworn in as president in the same month and immediately announced a policy of national reconciliation, promising a return to normal parliamentary government within three to five years. He formed a cabinet in which most of Uganda's political parties were represented. The political stability provided by the new regime enabled the economy to improve, with Ugandan Asians being encouraged to return and reclaim their businesses.

In 1989 the National Resistance Council (NRC), which had replaced the National Assembly as an interim legislative body, extended its term of office to allow time for a new constitution to be drafted. In March 1993 a draft constitution was published by the government and 12 months later a Constituent Assembly was elected to debate it. The new constitution of September 1995 extended the rule of the NRC for a further five years. In July 1993, in an effort to increase his popularity, President Museveni reinstated the country's four tribal monarchies, with Ronald Metebi being crowned as a ceremonial king of the Buganda people, 26 years after the monarchy was abolished.

ZAIRE

The Republic of Zaire
La République du Zaïre

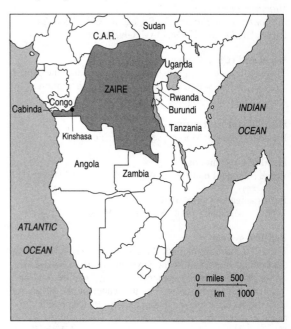

Capital: Kinshasa

Social and economic data
Area: 2,345,000 km²
Population: 41,200,000*
Pop. density per km²: 18*
Urban population: 29%**
Literacy rate: 72%**
GDP: $8,500 million**; per-capita GDP: $214**
Government defence spending (% of GDP): 3%**
Currency: new zaïre
Economy type: low income
Labour force in agriculture: 72%**

*1994
**1992

Ethnic composition

Almost the whole population is of African descent, distributed among over 200 tribes, the most numerous being the Kongo, the Luba, the Lunda, the Mongo, and the Zande. The official language is French and there are four national languages: Kiswahili, Tshiluba, Kikongo, and Lingala.

Religions

About half the population are Roman Catholics, 26% belong to Protestant churches and 17% to the Kimbanguist Protestant-African Church, while the remainder follow traditional animist beliefs.

Political features

State type: authoritarian nationalist
Date of state formation: 1960
Political structure: unitary
Executive: unlimited presidential
Assembly: one-chamber
Party structure: one-party
Human rights rating: 40%
International affiliations: ACP, CEEAC, CEPGL, G-24, IAEA, IBRD, IMF, NAM, OAU, UN, WTO

Local and regional government

The country is divided into ten regions, including the capital territory, below which are subregions. Administration is by appointed commissioners.

Head of state (executive)

President Marshal Mobuto Sese Seko, since 1965

Head of government

Prime Minister Léon Kengo Wa Dondo, since 1994

Political leaders since 1970

1965– Marshal Mobuto Sese Seko (MPR)

Political system

The 1978 constitution made Zaire a one-party state, based on the Popular Movement of the Revolution (MPR). The constitution provided for a president who was head of state and head of government as well as the leader of the MPR. As party leader he or she was automatically elected president for a seven-year term, renewable once only. There was provision for a single-chamber assembly, the National Legislative Council, with 210 members elected by universal adult suffrage, through a simple plurality voting system, for a five-year term. The president had power to appoint and preside over a National Executive Council, but ultimate power rested with the MPR.

In August 1991 a National Conference was convened to deliberate the country's political future. In April 1992 the Conference gave itself sovereign status and in August installed a new government. Four months later it established a 435-member High Council of the Republic (HCR) as the supreme interim legislative and executive authority, with powers to adopt the new constitution, which the Conference was drafting. Although the HCR was recognized by a number of foreign states, President Mobutu refused to accept it and said he would abide by the 1978 constitution.

This resulted in the creation of two rival governments, one appointed by the president and one by the HCR, which claimed the right to appoint the prime minister. The deadlock was finally ended in January 1994 when a transitional 730-member legislature, combining the HCR with the National Legislative Council, was agreed. It was given the title of the High Council of the Republic–Parliament of Transition (HCR–PT).

The powers of the prime minister were strengthened, at the expense of the president, and a time limit of 15 months (later extended to 39 months) was set before a referendum on the new constitution was held.

Political parties

The Popular Movement of the Revolution (MPR) was formed in 1967 as Zaire's only political party and was immediately fused into the state machinery, party officials being, at the same time, government officials. The party, led by President Mobuto, has an African socialist orientation.

After 1991 a number of opposition groups formed, the three most significant being the Sacred Union of Radical Opposition and Allies (Usoral), the Union for Democracy and Social Progress (UPDS), the Republican and Democratic Union (URD), and the Congolese National Movement–Lumumba (MNC).

The Usoral is an alliance of a number of small parties. Its overall orientation is left-of-centre.

The UPDS was formed in 1982 and also has a left-of-centre orientation.

The URD was a group that was expelled from Usoral in May 1994.

The MNC is a coalition of seven left-of-centre parties formed in 1994 to support the former prime minister, Patrice Lumumba.

Latest elections

In June 1994 President Mobutu appointed Leon Kengo as prime minister after he had obtained 72% of the vote in a ballot conducted by the HCR–PT.

Political history

Formerly ravaged by the slave trade, the region of what is now Zaire was, in the 1870s, claimed by King Leopold II (1835–1909) of Belgium as a personal colony, termed the Belgian Free State. This claim received international recognition in 1885. It ceased to be a personal possession and was renamed the Belgian Congo in 1907, emerging as an important exporter of minerals. In the post-World War II period an independence movement, spearheaded by the Congolese National Movement (MNC), gathered momentum and the Belgian government quickly acceded to the movement's demands, granting the country full independence in June 1960, as the Republic of the Congo. Many thought the Belgian government's decision too precipitate in that it produced a number of immediate problems which could have been anticipated and perhaps avoided.

The new state was intended to have a unitary structure and be governed centrally from Léopoldville (Kinshasa) by President Joseph Kasavubu and Prime Minister Patrice Lumumba (1925–61), the leader of the MNC, but Moise

Tshombe, a wealthy businessexecutive, argued for a federal solution and, becoming dissatisfied with the government's response to his requests, established his own political party and declared the rich mining province of Katanga, where he was based, an independent state, under his leadership.

Fighting broke out, which was not properly quelled by Belgian troops, and the United Nations Security Council agreed to send a force to restore order and protect lives. Meanwhile, there were disagreements between President Kasavubu and Prime Minister Lumumba on how the crisis should be tackled and this division between them prompted the Congolese army commander, Colonel Sese Seko Mobutu (b. 1930), who was then known as Joseph-Désiré Mobutu and was a member of the MNC, to step in and temporarily take over the reins of government. Lumumba was imprisoned and later released and five months later power was handed back to Kasavubu.

Soon afterwards it was announced that Lumumba had been murdered and the white mercenaries employed by Tshombe were thought to be responsible. The outcry which followed this announcement resulted in a new government being formed, with Cyrille Adoula as prime minister. During the fighting between Tshombe's mercenaries and United Nations forces the UN secretary general, Dag Hammarskjöld (1905–61), flew to Katanga province to mediate and was killed in an air crash on the Congolese–Northern Rhodesian border. The attempted secession of Katanga was finally stopped in 1963 when Tshombe went into exile, taking many of his followers with him to form the Congolese National Liberation Front (FNLC). In July 1964 Tshombe returned from exile and President Kasavubu appointed him interim prime minister until elections for a new government could be held.

In August 1964 the country embarked upon what was hoped to be a new era of stability, as the Democratic Republic of the Congo, but a power struggle between Kasavubu and Tshombe soon developed and again the army, led by Mobutu, intervened. He established what he called a 'second republic', in November 1965. Two years later a new constitution was adopted and in 1970 Mobutu was elected president.

The following year the country changed its name from Congo (Kinshasa) to the Republic of Zaire and in 1972 the Popular Movement of the Revolution (MPR) was declared the only legal political party. In the same year the president adopted the name of Mobutu Sese Seko. Mobutu carried out a large number of political and constitutional reforms which brought stability to what had once seemed an ungovernable country but the harshness of some of his policies brought international criticism as well as domestic opposition to his regime.

In 1990 he made some concessions to that opposition by agreeing moves towards multiparty politics and in 1991 new political parties were allowed to register. However, a promised constitutional conference was postponed and Mobutu tried to maintain his control by juggling with the post of prime minister among politicians likely to win popular support.

In August 1991 a national conference on the political future of Zaire began its deliberations and soon came into conflict with Mobutu. In its closing session, in December 1992, it dissolved the National Legislative Council and elected a 435-member transitional legislature, the High Council of the Republic (HCR). The HCR was dominated by opponents of Mobutu who, when it claimed the right to appoint a prime minister, retaliated by appointing a rival administration.

This confrontational situation persisted until June 1994 when it was agreed to merge the HCR with the National Legislative Council into a new transitional assembly, the High Council of the Republic–Parliament of Transition (HCR–PT). Léon Kengo Wa Dondo (URD) was elected prime minister by the HCR–PT and subsequently appointed by President Mobutu. Kengo immediately set about the task of ensuring domestic stability and restoring international confidence in the country, but he was soon faced with a currency crisis and was forced to close half of Zaire's foreign embassies because their upkeep could not be afforded. The country's problems were exacerbated when, in May 1995, news of an outbreak of the Ebola virus, for which there is no known vaccine or cure, was given. There was also a continuing secessionist movement in mineral-rich Shaba province (formerly Katanga) and tribal clashes in Kivu province and in August 1995 thousands of refugees were forcibly repatriated to Burundi and Rwanda. Such was the breakdown in law and order that Zaire's continuation as a nation-state was precarious.

ZAMBIA

The Republic of Zambia

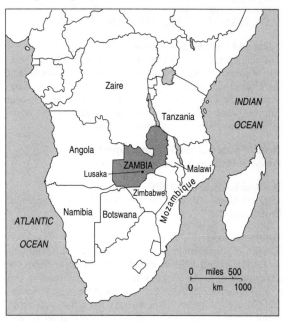

Capital: Lusaka

Social and economic data
Area: 752,620 km^2
Population: 8,900,000*
Pop. density per km^2: 12*
Urban population: 42%*

Literacy rate: 73%**
GDP: $2,931 million**; per-capita GDP: $330**
Government defence spending (% of GDP): 1.5%**
Currency: Zambian kwacha
Economy type: low income
Labour force in agriculture: 38%**

*1994
**1992

Ethnic composition

Over 95% of the population are indigenous Africans, belonging to more than 70 different tribes, the most numerous being the Bantu-Botatwe and the Bemba. The official languages are English, Tonga (16%), Bemba, Lozi, Nyanja, Kaonda, Lunda, and Luvale.

Religions

About 70% of people are Christians, about a third of them Roman Catholics and the rest Protestants. There are also substantial Muslim, animist, and Hindu minorities.

Political features

State type: emergent democratic
Date of state formation: 1964
Political structure: unitary
Executive: limited presidential
Assembly: one-chamber
Party structure: two-party
Human rights rating: 57%
International affiliations: ACP, COMESA, CW, G-15, IAEA, IBRD, IMF, NAM, OAU, SADC, UN, WTO

Local and regional government

The country is divided into eight provinces: Northern, Western, Southern, Eastern, Northwestern, Central, Luapula, and the Copperbelt, each with a responsible minister of state, working through civil servants. Below this level, local administration reflects some of the features of the unreformed English local government system.

Head of state and head of government

President Frederick Chiluba, since 1991

Political leaders since 1970

1964–91 Kenneth David Kaunda (UNIP), 1991–   Frederick Chiluba (MMD)

Political system

Zambia is an independent republic within the Commonwealth. Its August 1991 multiparty constitution provides for a president, who is head of state and head of government, and a single-chamber 150-member National Assembly. The president is elected by universal suffrage for a five-year term, renewable once only. The National Assembly is similarly and concurrently elected. There is an advisory body, the 27-member House of Chiefs, consisting of four chiefs from each of the Northern, Western, Southern and Eastern Provinces, three each from the Northwestern, Luapula, and Central Provinces, and two from the Copperbelt Province. The House of Chiefs may submit resolutions to the National Assembly and advises the president on matters referred to it.

Political parties

From 1972 to 1990 the United National Independence Party (UNIP) was the only legal political party. Now there are more than ten active parties, the most significant, in addition to the UNIP, being the Movement for Multiparty Democracy (MMD), the Multiracial Party (MRP), the National Democratic Alliance (NADA), and the Democratic Party (DP).

The UNIP was formed in 1959 as a breakaway group from the African National Congress (ANC), which called itself the Zambian African National Congress (ZANC). It changed to its present name in 1964. It has an African socialist orientation and is led by Kebby Musokotwane.

The MMD was formed in 1990 by a combination of trade unionists and some former members and opponents of the UNIP. It has a left-of-centre orientation and is led by President Chiluba. Subsequent splits in the MMD have resulted in the formation of two splinter parties: the National Party (NP) and the Caucus for National Unity (CNU).

The MRP is a moderate left-of-centre and, as its name indicates, multiracial party.

The NADA and DP were formed in 1991 and also have left-of-centre orientations.

Latest elections

In the October 1991 general election the MMD candidate, Frederick Chiluba, won the presidency, with 75.8% of the vote compared with Kenneth Kaunda's 24.21%.

The MMD also secured an overwhelming victory in the National Assembly, winning 125 seats to the UNIP's 25.

Political history

As Northern Rhodesia, Zambia was administered by the British South Africa Company of Cecil Rhodes (1853–1902) between 1889 and 1924, when it became a British protectorate. In 1953 it became part of a federation which included Southern Rhodesia, now Zimbabwe, and Nyasaland, now Malawi, but the mainly black Northern Rhodesians objected to the white dominance of Southern Rhodesia and, despite opposition from white settlers, started an independence movement. The Federation of Rhodesia and Nyasaland was dissolved in 1963 and Northern Rhodesia was granted internal self-government. Within months it became the independent republic of Zambia, within the Commonwealth, with Dr Kenneth Kaunda (b. 1924), leader of the United National Independence Party (UNIP), as its first president. In 1972 it was declared a one-party state and this brought a period of greater internal stability.

Externally, Zambia was economically dependent on neighbouring white-ruled Rhodesia and relations between the two countries deteriorated because of its support for the Patriotic Front, led by Robert Mugabe (b. 1924) and Joshua Nkomo (b. 1917). When Zimbabwe, as Rhodesia became, achieved independence in 1980 good relations were restored.

Despite his imposition of strict economic policies, Kaunda was convincingly re-elected in 1983 and 1988, but popular opposition to him grew. After a referendum held in 1990 on a return to multiparty democracy received strong support, President Kaunda agreed to end one-party rule. In October 1991, in the first multiparty elections for more than 20 years, Kaunda lost the presidency to the leader of the newly formed Movement for Multiparty Democracy (MMD), Frederick Chiluba (b. 1943), and his ruling party, the UNIP, was soundly defeated in the assembly elections. This was the first democratic change of government in English-speaking Black Africa. President Chiluba immediately removed the six-year-old state of emergency, but reimposed it in March 1993, claiming the threat of a coup. This led to a split in the MMD, with the National Party (NP) being formed by disillusioned MMD members, led by Arthur Wina (d. 1995), and attracting the allegiance of 17 deputies. In 1992 Kaunda gave up the UNIP leadership. A privatization drive was launched by President Chiluba, reversing the statist policies of his predecessor, but the economy was faced with the problem of high inflation (200% in 1993) and rapidly diminishing reserves of its staple export, copper.

ZIMBABWE

The Republic of Zimbabwe

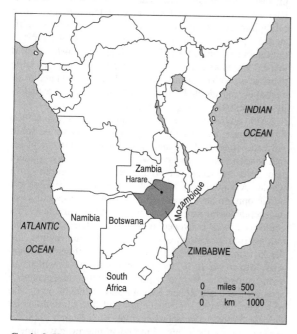

Capital: Harare (formerly Salisbury)

Social and economic data
Area: 390,759 km²
Population: 10,900,000*
Pop. density per km²: 28*
Urban population: 30%**
Literacy rate: 67%**
GDP: $5,900 million**; per-capita GDP: $570**
Government defence spending (% of GDP): 3.9%**
Currency: Zimbabwe dollar
Economy type: low income
Labour force in agriculture: 65%**

*1994
**1992

Ethnic composition
There are four distinct ethnic groups in the country: indigenous Africans, who account for about 95% of the population, Europeans, mainly British, who account for about 3.5%, and Afro-Europeans and Asians, who each comprise about 0.5%. The official language is English.

Religions
About 40% of the population follows traditional animist beliefs and about 30% is Anglican (Protestant) Christian, and 15% Roman Catholic.

Political features
State type: nationalistic socialist
Date of state formation: 1980
Political structure: unitary
Executive: unlimited presidential
Assembly: one-chamber
Party structure: one-party*
Human rights rating: 65%
International affiliations: ACP, CW, G-15, IAEA, IBRD, IMF, NAM, OAU, SADC, UN, WTO

*effectively

Local and regional government
The country is divided into eight provinces, administered by the central government. There are local authorities in cities and towns, with elected mayors and councils.

Head of state and head of government
Executive President Robert Gabriel Mugabe, since 1980

Political leaders since 1970
1964–79 Ian Smith (RF), 1979–80 Bishop Abel Muzorewa (ANC), 1980– Robert Gabriel Mugabe (ZANU–PF)

Political system
Zimbabwe is an independent republic within the Commonwealth. Its constitution dates from independence in 1980 and originally contained many features of the British parliamentary system. However seven amendments have made significant changes so that what originally approximated to a parliamentary executive is now a presidential one, and what was formerly a multiparty system has become, in effect, a one-party system.

In its amended form, the constitution provides for a president who is both head of state and head of government, with the title executive president. The current president was elected by a simple plurality of members of the assembly but future elections will be by universal adult suffrage, and the holder of the office will serve a six-year term. The president chooses and appoints a vice president and cabinet. He or she has power to veto a bill passed by the assembly but this veto can be overruled by a two-thirds assembly vote. In several respects the Zimbabwean presidency contains features of the limited executive of the United States.

The assembly consists of a single-chamber 150-member House of Assembly, with 120 members elected by universal adult suffrage, through a party list system of proportional representation, 12 nominated by the president, ten traditional chiefs, and eight provincial governors. Members serve a six-year term.

Political parties

The two main political parties, the Zimbabwe African National Union–Patriotic Front (ZANU–PF) and the Zimbabwe African People's Union (ZAPU), merged in 1987 to become ZANU–PF. Although ZANU–PF is not officially declared as the only legal party and other groups continue to function, they have little electoral impact so that Zimbabwe is, effectively, a one-party state.

ZANU–PF began in 1963 as the Zimbabwe African Union (ZANU), led by Robert Mugabe, breaking away from ZAPU, founded by Joshua Nkomo two years earlier. During the years of opposition to the white-dominated regime the two groups operated together as the Patriotic Front (PF) and between 1974 and 1979 both were banned. The two leaders returned to take a leading part in the independence negotiations in 1979–80 and the parties merged in 1987. The new combined party has an African socialist orientation.

A number of other parties exist but none has yet attracted sufficient support to present a serious challenge to the dominance of ZANU–PF.

Latest elections

In the April 1995 general election ZANU–PF won 118 of the 120 elective seats, being unopposed in 55 contests. The Reverend Ndabaningi Sithole was one of the two opposition deputies elected. Five leading opposition parties, led by Bishop Abel Muzorewa, head of the United Party (UP), boycotted what they termed 'fraudulent elections', with the state media vigorously promoting ZANU–PF and more than 100,000 being unable to vote as a result of chaotic registration.

Political history

Cecil Rhodes (1853–1902), through the British South Africa Company, began the exploitation of the rich mineral resources of the region north of South Africa in the 1880s, the area north and south of the Zambezi River becoming known as Rhodesia. When the British South Africa Company's charter expired in 1923 the southern section, or Southern Rhodesia, became a self-governing British colony and 30 years later, in 1953, it joined Northern Rhodesia (Zambia) and Nyasaland (Malawi) to form a multiracial Central African Federation. The federation's economy was to be built on labour from Nyasaland, mineral resources from Northern Rhodesia and expertise from Southern Rhodesia. Within ten years, however, the federation was dissolved and Northern Rhodesia, and Nyasaland went their separate and independent ways as the new states of Zambia and Malawi.

The degree of self-government to be enjoyed by Southern Rhodesia after disengagement from the federation was limited by the British government's insistence on retaining the power to veto any legislation which discriminated against black Africans. This was accepted by some, but not all, white Rhodesians. Among those who objected to it were the members of the Rhodesian Front Party (RF), a grouping of white politicians committed to maintaining racial segregation. Their leader, Winston Field, became the country's first prime minister.

Meanwhile, African nationalists were campaigning for full racial democracy and the African National Congress (ANC), which had been formed in 1934, was, in 1957, reconvened under the leadership of Joshua Nkomo (b. 1917). It was banned in 1959 and Nkomo went into exile to become leader of the National Democratic Party (NDP), which had been formed by some Congress members. When the NDP was also banned in 1961, Nkomo created the Zimbabwe African People's Union (ZAPU) and this, too, was declared unlawful in 1962. In 1963 a split developed within ZAPU, one group, led by the Reverend Ndabaningi Sithole (b. 1920), forming the Zimbabwe African National Union (ZANU), with Robert Mugabe (b. 1924) as its secretary general.

In April 1964 Field resigned and was replaced by Ian Smith (b. 1919), who rejected terms for independence proposed by Britain which would require clear progress towards majority rule. Four months later ZAPU and ZANU were banned and Nkomo and Mugabe imprisoned. In November 1965, after further British attempts to negotiate a formula for independence, Smith annulled the 1961 constitution and unilaterally announced Rhodesia's independence. Britain broke off diplomatic and trading links and the United Nations initiated economic sanctions, which were bypassed by many multinational companies. The British prime minister, Harold Wilson, had talks with Smith in 1966 and 1968 but they were abortive on both occasions. In 1969 Rhodesia declared itself a republic and adopted a new constitution, with white majority representation in a two-chamber assembly.

ZAPU and ZANU had begun a guerrilla war against the Smith regime, which at times was supported by armed South African police. In 1971 the draft of another agreement for independence was produced which the British government said must be acceptable to the Rhodesian people 'as a whole'. A commission was sent from Britain in 1972 to test public opinion and it reported back that the proposals were unacceptable. Informal discussions continued and in 1975 a conference was convened in Geneva, attended by deputations from the British government, the Smith regime, and the African nationalists, represented by the moderate Bishop Abel Muzorewa (b. 1925), president of the ANC, which had been formed in 1971 to oppose the earlier independence arrangements, and Robert Mugabe and Joshua Nkomo, who had been released from detention and had formed a joint Patriotic Front. An independence date of 31 March 1978 was agreed, but not the composition of an interim government. Smith prevaricated and at the beginning of 1979 produced a new 'majority rule' constitution, which contained an inbuilt protection for the white minority, but which he had managed to get Muzorewa to accept. In June 1979 Bishop Muzorewa was pronounced prime minister of what was to be called Zimbabwe Rhodesia.

The new constitution was denounced by Mugabe and Nkomo as another attempt by Smith to perpetuate the white domination, and they continued to lead the Zimbabwe African National Liberation Army from bases in neighbouring Mozambique. In August of that year the new British prime minister, Margaret Thatcher, attended her first Commonwealth Heads of Government conference in Lusaka. She was not expected to be sympathetic to the exiled black nationalists but, under the influence of the foreign secretary,

Lord Carrington, and the conference host, President Kenneth Kaunda of Zambia, she agreed to a constitutional conference in London at which all shades of political opinion in Rhodesia would be represented. The conference, in September 1979, at Lancaster House, resulted in what became known as the Lancaster House Agreement and paved the way for full independence. A member of the British Cabinet, Lord Soames (1920–87), was sent to Rhodesia as governor general, with full powers to arrange a timetable for independence.

Economic and trade sanctions were immediately lifted and a small Commonwealth Monitoring Force supervised the disarming of thousands of guerrilla fighters who brought their weapons and ammunition from all parts of the country. A new constitution was adopted and elections were held, under independent supervision, in February 1980. They resulted in a decisive win for Robert Mugabe's ZANU–PF party. The new state of Zimbabwe became fully independent in April 1980, with the Reverend Canaan Banana as president and Robert Mugabe as prime minister.

During the next few years a rift developed between Mugabe and Nkomo and between ZANU–PF and ZAPU supporters. Nkomo was accused of trying to undermine Mugabe's administration and was demoted and then dismissed from the cabinet. Fearing for his safety, he left the country, spending some months in Britain. ZAPU was also opposed to the proposal by ZANU–PF, in 1984, for the eventual creation of a one-party state.

Mugabe's party increased its majority in the 1985 and 1990 elections and, relations between the two leaders having improved, a complete merger took place in 1987. In the same year, as President Banana retired, Mugabe combined the roles of head of state and head of government and assumed the title of executive president, with Nkomo becoming vice president. In 1990 he proposed that the *de facto* one-party state should become one in law but this did not attract wide support.

Freak drought conditions in 1991 and 1992 placed great strains on the nation's economy and Mugabe's popularity, but no substantial rival had yet emerged to challenge his position. In the April 1995 general election ZANU–PF, winning votes in rural areas as a result of its land distribution scheme, secured another crushing victory. In October 1995 Ndabaningi Sithole, leader of the opposition ZANU-Ndonga, was arrested and charged with plotting a coup against Mugabe.

The Middle East and North Africa

This region extends from the Mediterranean Sea in the north to the Arabian Sea and the Tropic of Cancer in the south, and from the Atlantic Ocean in the west to the borders of Afghanistan and Pakistan in the east. It is mostly desert country, with the climatic conditions associated with this kind of terrain, and is traditionally the home of the nomad, forced into a life of wandering in search for vegetation. It is also, of course, with the notable exception of Israel, the land of the Arab. Indeed, the whole region is often referred to as the Arab world. The total population of the region is in excess of 269 million and is thinly dispersed over an area of more than 11 million square kilometres.

Islam is the dominant religion and is officially decreed as such in 14 of the 18 states. The kingdom of Saudi Arabia lies at the heart of this Islamic domain, housing the two cities most revered by Muslims, Mecca and Medina. In contrast, Israel is the home of Judaism, despite the presence of more than half a million Muslims. The other state in the region where a substantial number of its citizens do not follow Islamic codes is Lebanon, which has a Maronite Christian minority of nearly a million.

The Jewish question, of whether Israel can coexist with its Arab neighbours, has been at the heart of politics in this part of the world for more than 70 years, and for much of that time it was associated with the British and French presence in the Middle East.

After World War I, Britain, as one of the victors, was given control by the League of Nations of Iraq, Palestine, and Transjordan while France, as the other major European victor, acquired responsibility for Lebanon and Syria. The two European powers colluded in extending their control of the region, Britain taking Egypt under its protection and then, by a series of treaties with the ruling monarchs, most of the states in the Persian Gulf. Only Saudi Arabia retained its independence, under the skilful guidance of King Ibn Saud. France, in turn, took control of Morocco, Algeria, and Tunisia.

Meanwhile, Britain, while fulfilling its pledge to free the Arabs from Turkish rule, also promised, through the declaration by Foreign Secretary Arthur Balfour (1848–1930) in 1917, to establish in Palestine a 'National Home for the Jewish people'. This resulted in an increase in Jewish immigration during the 1920s and 1930s, in the face of growing Arab opposition. Even though the Balfour Declaration had been made, Britain, largely out of self-interest, tended to side with the Arab states, but the holocaust in Nazi Germany

Middle East and North Africa: social, economic, and political data

Country	Area (sq km)	c. 1992–94 Population (m)	c. 1992–94 Pop. density per sq km	c. 1992 Adult literacy rate (%)	World ranking	Income type	c. 1991 Human rights rating (%)
Algeria	2,381,750	27.100	11	57	136	middle	66
Bahrain	691	0.516	747	70	118	high	n/a
Egypt	997,738	56.100	56	48	153	low	50
Iran	1,648,000	63.200	38	54	141	middle	22
Iraq	438,317	19.900	45	60	131	middle	17
Israel	20,700	5.400	261	96	52	high	76
Jordan	98,000	4.400	45	80	105	middle	65
Kuwait	17,818	1.800	101	73	115	high	33
Lebanon	10,452	2.900	277	80	105	middle	n/a
Libya	1,775,500	5.500	3	64	127	middle	24
Morocco	458,730	27.000	59	50	149	middle	56
Oman	300,000	1.700	5	38	163	middle	49
Qatar	11,440	0.500	44	51	147	high	n/a
Saudi Arabia	2,150,000	16.500	8	62	129	high	29
Syria	184,050	13.800	75	65	124	middle	30
Tunisia	164,150	8.600	52	65	124	middle	60
United Arab Emirates	77,700	1.700	22	54	141	high	n/a
Yemen	540,000	13.000	26	39	162	low	49
Total/average/range	11,275,036	269.616	24	38–96			17–76

Key:

A	appointed	PR	proportional representation	Lib-dem	Liberal democratic
E	elected	SB	second ballot	Em-dem	Emergent democratic
F	federal	SP	simple plurality	Nat-soc	Nationalistic socialist
PL	party list	U	unitary	Islam-nat	Islamic nationalist

created such worldwide sympathy for the Jewish cause that it became impossible for anyone to resist the demands for an independent state of Israel. The rest of the account of the relations between Jews and Arabs is given in the political histories of the countries involved. It has been partly recounted at this stage because the current political situation in the region cannot be properly understood if this aspect of its history is overlooked.

In economic terms the Middle East and North Africa constitutes a relatively wealthy region, but that wealth is unevenly distributed. Bahrain, Israel, Kuwait, Qatar, Saudi Arabia, and the United Arab Emirates all enjoy high per-capita incomes, some comparable to, or better than, those of Northern and Western European states. The average citizen of Kuwait and the United Arab Emirates, for example, enjoys a higher living standard than his or her opposite number in the United Kingdom. At the other extreme, Egypt and Yemen have low-income economies, with Algeria, Iran, Iraq, Jordan, Lebanon, Libya, Morocco, Oman, Syria, and Tunisia all falling into the middle-income bracket. The wealth of most of the wealthiest countries has been derived from oil, while Israel has maintained its living standards through industry and enterprise, plus substantial subsidies from its friends in the Western world.

The comparatively high literacy rates in some of the richest states are a reflection of the generous, if paternalistic, way in which their rulers have invested their wealth in education and social services. On the other hand, there are other countries in the region, such as Egypt, Yemen, and Oman, where half or more of the population is illiterate. It is difficult to obtain an accurate picture of the degree of civil liberties enjoyed in some countries, particularly the absolutist states, but, with some few exceptions, human rights ratings over the region are not good.

The political systems of the 18 states, as shown in Table 56, fairly accurately reflect their respective cultures and histories. Seven have absolutist regimes and these can be mostly traced back to Islamic traditions and a long acceptance of monarchical rule. Four have been classified as nationalistic socialist systems, most of which were created as a reaction to domination by a European power and the need to establish a national, independent identity. One, Iran, with an Islamic nationalist regime, has not only embraced Islam as a faith but has incorporated it into its political system.

Six states can be said to have democratic systems, that of Israel being now well established but the other five of more recent origin. Egypt has had a pluralist political system, though dominated by one party, since 1971, Tunisia since

Table 56

World ranking	Date of state formation	State structure	State type	Executive type	Number of assembly chambers	Party structure	Lower house electoral system
52	1962	U	Nat-soc	Unlim-pres	1	one	SB
	1971	U	Absolutist	Absolutist	none	none	n/a
75	1922	U	Lib-dem	Lim-pres	1	multi	mixed-E/A
100	1499	U	Islam-nat	Unlim-pres	1	none	SB
104	1932	U	Nat-soc	Unlim-pres	1	one	PR–PL
39	1958	U	Lib-dem	Parliamentary	1	multi	PR-PL
53	1946	U	Absolutist	Absolutist	2	multi	SP
90	1961	U	Absolutist	Absolutist	1	none	SP
	1944	U	Em-dem	Dual	1	multi	PR-PL
99	1951	U	Nat-soc	Unlim-pres	1	one	SP
66	1956	U	Em-dem	Dual	1	multi	SP
77	1951	U	Absolutist	Absolutist	none	none	n/a
	1971	U	Absolutist	Absolutist	none	none	n/a
95	1932	U	Absolutist	Absolutist	none	none	n/a
93	1946	U	Nat-soc	Unlim-pres	1	one	SP
60	1956	U	Em-dem	Lim-pres	1	one	PR–AMS
	1971	F	Absolutist	Absolutist	none	none	n/a
77	1990	U	Em-dem	Lim-pres	1	multi	SP

Unlim-pres	Unlimited presidential
Lim-pres	Limited presidential

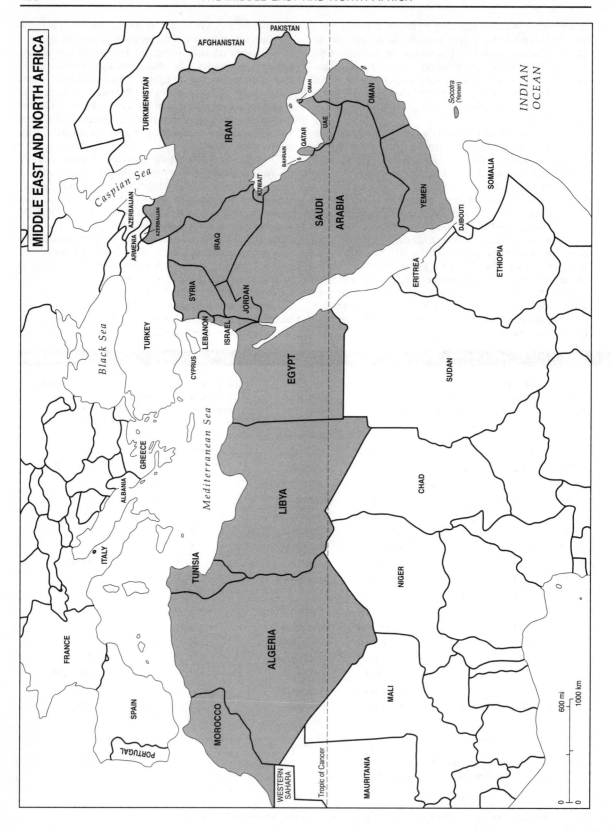

MIDDLE EAST AND NORTH AFRICA

1994, and Morocco since 1992, while Lebanon has struggled to maintain some semblance of democratic government since 1990, with internecine struggles always threatening to destroy it. The now united Yemen democracy is still in its infancy and its future remains precarious.

The continuing sense of insecurity in the region is evidenced by the high levels of government spending on defence in several countries. Defence expenditure in recent years has reached nearly 10% of the gross domestic product in Israel and Jordan and has well exceeded that figure in Iraq, Kuwait, Oman, and Saudi Arabia. These are considerably higher than the global average, with seven of the countries appearing in the world 'top 15' in terms of proportionate defence spending.

After the 1988 cease-fire in the Iran–Iraq war, there seemed a chance of peace returning to this troubled region but Iraq's invasion of Kuwait in 1990 again threw the Middle East into turmoil. Despite the prompt response by the Western powers, and the subsequent punitive measures taken, Iraq remains a threat to the region's stability as long as its leader, Saddam Hussein, controls its destiny.

Israel, and its relations with the Arab world, is the other key to long-lasting stability. The positive moves from the Arab side, mainly at the instigation of the United States, have changed the political climate and it is not inconceivable that during the next decade Israel's isolation may be finally ended and an independent Palestine state established.

Recommended reading

Ayubi, N *Political Islam: Religion and Politics in the Arab World*, Routledge, 1991

Cobban, H *The PLO*, Cambridge University Press, 1984

Luciani, G (ed.) *The Arab State*, Routledge, 1990

Ovendale, R *The Origins of the Arab–Israeli Wars*, 2nd edn., Longman, 1992

Ovendale, R *The Longman Companion to the Middle East since 1914*, Longman, 1992

Zubaida, S *Islam, the People and the State*, Tauris, 1993

ALGERIA

Democratic and Popular Republic of Algeria
El Djemhouria El Djazairia Demokratia Echaabia

Capital: Algiers (al-Jazair)

Social and economic data
Area: 2,381,750 km²
Population: 27,100,000*
Pop. density per km²: 11*
Urban population: 53%**
Literacy rate: 57%**
GDP: $48,000 million**; per-capita GDP: $1,832**
Goverment defence spending (% of GDP): 2.5%*
Currency: Algerian dinar
Economy type: middle income
Labour force in agriculture: 26%**

*1994
**1992

Ethnic composition
Ninety-nine per cent of the population is of Arab Berber origin, the rest being of European extraction, mainly French. Arabic is the official language but French is widely used.

Religions
Islam is the state religion and 99% of the population is Sunni Muslim.

Political features
State type: nationalistic socialist*
Date of state formation: 1962
Political structure: unitary
Executive: unlimited presidential
Assembly: one-chamber
Party structure: effectively one-party
Human rights rating: 66%

International affiliations: AL, AMF, AMU, G-24, IAEA, IBRD, IMF, NAM, OAPEC, OAU, OIC, OPEC, UN

*In a transitional state

Local and regional government
Revealing a combination of French and Arab influence, the country is divided into 48 departments or districts (*wilayat*), ranging in population from 2 million to less than 65,000, which are further subdivided into communes (*daira*). Each department and commune has an elected assembly. These assemblies are under the direct supervision of the minister of the interior, who appoints administrative governors (*wali*).

Head of state (executive)
President Liamine Zeroual, since 1994

Head of government
Mokdad Sifi, since 1994

Political leaders since 1970
1965–79 Houari Boumédienne (military), 1979–92 Benjedid Chadli (FLN), 1992 Mohammed Boudiaf (emergency government), 1992–94 Ali Kafi (emergency government), 1994– Lamine Zeroual (transitional government)

Political system
The current constitution was adopted in 1976 and amended substantially in 1989 and 1991. It created a socialist Islamic republic with originally the National Liberation Front (FLN) as the only legally permitted political party. The FLN nominated the president, who was then elected by popular vote for a five-year term. There is a single-chamber National People's Assembly of 430 deputies, elected for a five-year term by a majoritarian two-ballot voting system.

In 1989 a new constitution allowed parties other than the FLN to operate and multiparty elections to take place. However, in 1992 the constitution was suspended and elections cancelled when it appeared likely that Islamic fundamentalists would be voted into office. A five-member High State Council, with strong military representation, was appointed and its chair became state president. In 1995 efforts were made to persuade nonfundamentalist opposition parties to participate in a multiparty direct presidential election to be held under the majoritarian two-ballot system.

Political parties
From a number of radical Muslim organizations which were started from the 1920s onwards, calling for the expulsion of the French from Algeria, there developed a young socialist group who in 1954 formed the National Liberation Front (FLN), with a military wing, the National Army of Liberation (ALN). When full independence from France was obtained in 1962 the FLN became the only legal party. Some of the more radical figures in the independence movement had been imprisoned in France and one of them, Ahmed Ben Bella, returned to Algeria to take over the leadership of the party and become the country's first president. The FLN has a mass membership and its orientation is socialist, nationalist and Islamic.

The main Islamic opposition force is the Islamic Salvation Front (FIS), a fundamentalist organization, as its name implies. It was banned in 1992.

The other significant group is the National Socialist Forces Front (FFS), a left-of-centre, largely Berber, party formed illegally in 1963.

Latest elections
The first round of multiparty elections in December 1991 produced a decisive victory for the FIS. The ruling FLN Council cancelled the January 1992 second-round vote and President Chadli resigned. The explanation given was that the constitution was not functioning as had been intended.

Political history
Algeria was conquered by the French in the 1830s and soon became one of France's major colonies. French nationals were encouraged to settle in Algeria and become permanent residents, enjoying greater economic and political power than the local Muslim inhabitants. Unlike most of France's other overseas possessions, however, Algeria was regarded as an extension and part of mainland France. The disparity between the rights of the European minority and the Arab majority led to a bitter war for independence, led by the FLN, in 1954. Under considerable international pressure, the French president, Charles de Gaulle, in 1959 accepted the principle of national self-determination for Algeria and full independence was eventually achieved in 1962. The following year a one-party republic was created with Ahmed Ben Bella (b. 1916) as its first president.

In 1965 a military group, led by Colonel Houari Boumédienne (1925–78), deposed Ben Bella, suspended the constitution and ruled through a Revolutionary Council. In 1976 a new constitution, confirming Algeria as an Islamic socialist one-party state, was approved. Boumédienne died in 1978 after a long illness and there was a smooth transfer of power to Benjedid Chadli (b. 1929), secretary general of the FLN, who, in 1979, felt sufficiently confident of his position to release Ben Bella from the house arrest which had been imposed following the 1965 coup. In the same year the FLN adopted a new structure, with a Central Committee nominating the Party Leader who would automatically become president. Under this revised system, Chadli was re-elected in 1983.

During Chadli's terms as president significant steps were made in improving relations with France and the United States and in 1981 Algeria enhanced its international reputation by acting as an intermediary in securing the release of the American hostages in Iran. In 1988 diplomatic relations with Morocco were restored after a 12-year break and a similar restoration with Egypt was sought.

Despite Algeria's considerable wealth of natural resources, President Chadli was forced to introduce austerity measures which proved highly unpopular with consumers. This unpopularity was heightened by the feeling that he was moving away from the socialist principles of his predecessor, Boumédienne, and favouring an elite few at the expense of the majority. Acts of violence erupted in 1988, to which the army reacted promptly and harshly, but Chadli managed to moderate the uprisings by promising constitutional changes

which would make the government more responsive to popular opinion.

In 1989 the constitution was amended, allowing political parties other than the FLN to function, and in December 1991 the first multiparty assembly elections were held. A decisive win in the first round for the Islamic fundamentalist FIS resulted in the cancellation of the second round and Chadli's resignation.

He was replaced by a five-member High State Council (HSC), chaired by Mohammed Boudiaf. Five months later, in June 1992, President Boudiaf was assassinated, probably by fundamentalists, and Ali Kafi (b. 1928) became the new head of the HSC. Algeria's future as a democratic state seemed to be hanging in the balance.

The emergency government continued in the face of increased violence by Islamic extremists, spearheaded by the Armed Islamic Group (GIA), whose stronghold was Boufarik. In June 1993 proposals for a return to democratic government were unveiled and in August 1993 Redha Malik was appointed prime minister. However, the violence continued, claiming the death, among others, of a former prime minister, Kasdi Merbah. By October 1994 Islamic extremists were targeting foreigners, causing many of them to leave the country. The government's reaction became more determined and the army's dominant position was increased in January 1994 when General Liamine Zeroual was appointed president by the HSC.

In March 1994 a dialogue with the banned FIS was opened and in April 1994 a new government, under Prime Minister Mokdad Sifi, was formed. However, the violence continued and by mid-1995 the three-year war between the security forces and Islamic militants had claimed more than 40,000 lives. The economy was consequently damaged, with the level of unemployment exceeding 20%. In a further effort to secure peace, President Zeroual initiated a national dialogue with representatives of all of the main political groups.

The leaders of the FIS, who had been denied power and imprisoned, were released in July 1994 but, as the violence escalated, were reimprisoned in November 1994. The extremists continued their campaign of terror, hijacking a French airliner in December 1994. A multiparty presidential election was planned for November 1995. However, the FIS remained banned and the main left-wing opposition parties, the FLN and FSS, refused to participate, arguing that there needed to be national reconciliation before any election was held. Only the minor Algerian Movement for Justice and Development (MAJD) and National Party for Solidarity and Development appeared likely to put forward candidates.

BAHRAIN

State of Bahrain
Daulat al-Bahrain

Capital: Manama (Al Manamah)

Social and economic data
Area: 691,200 km^2
Population: 516,000*
Pop. density per km^2: 747*

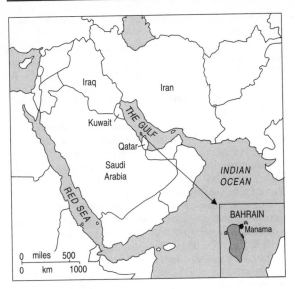

Urban population: 83%**
Literacy rate: 70%**
GDP: $3,985 million**; per-capita GDP: $7,870**
Government defence spending (% of GDP): 5.5%**
Currency: Bahrain dinar
Economy type: high income
Labour force in agriculture: 3%**

*1994
**1992

Ethnic composition
About 73% of the population is Arabic and about 9% Iranian. There are Pakistani and Indian minorities. Arabic is the official language but English is widely spoken.

Religions
Islam is the state religion and of the 475,000 Muslims, about 60% are Shi'ite and 40% Sunni. There are about 25,000 Christians.

Political features
State type: absolutist
Date of state formation: 1971
Political structure: unitary
Executive: absolute
Assembly: there has been no elected assembly since 1975
Party structure: none
Human rights rating: N/A
International affiliations: AL, AMF, DDS, GCC, IBRD, IMF, NAM, OAPEC, OIC, UN, WTO

Local and regional government
There is no recognizable local government system.

Head of state (executive)
Emir Sheikh Isa bin-Sulman al-Khalifa, since 1961

Head of government
Prime Minister Sheikh Khalifa bin-Sulman al-Khalifa, since 1970

Political leaders since 1970
1961–   Sheik Isa bin-Sulman al-Khalifa (Emir)

Political system
The 1973 constitution provided for an elected National Assembly of 30 members but it was dissolved in 1975 after the prime minister said he could not work with it. Bahrain is now governed by the emir, by decree, through a cabinet chosen by him and consisting mainly of his close relatives. Those who are not related are drawn from the wealthiest merchant families in the state. In 1992 the emir appointed a 30-member Consultative Council.

Political parties
There are no recognizable political parties.

Latest elections
There have been no elections since the dissolution of the assembly in 1975.

Political history
Bahrain is a traditional Arab monarchy and became a British Protected State in the 19th century, with government shared between the ruling sheikh and a British adviser. In 1928 Iran, then called Persia, claimed sovereignty but in 1970 accepted a United Nations' report showing that the inhabitants of Bahrain preferred independence.

In 1968 Britain, as part of a policy of reducing its overseas commitments, announced its intention to withdraw its forces and Bahrain joined two other territories which were also under British protection, Qatar and the Trucial States, now called the United Arab Emirates, to form a Federation of Arab Emirates. In 1971 both Qatar and the Trucial States left the Federation and Bahrain became an independent nation, signing a new treaty of friendship with Britain.

In 1973 a constitution was introduced providing for an elected National Assembly but two years later the prime minister, Sheikh Khalifa, complained of obstruction by the Assembly which was then dissolved. Since then the emir and his family have ruled with virtually absolute powers. Following the Iranian revolution of 1979, relations between the two countries became uncertain, with fears of Iranian attempts to disturb Bahrain's stability. Bahrain became a focal point in the Gulf region, its international airport the centre of Gulf aviation and the new Gulf University sited in the country. A causeway linking it to Saudi Arabia has also been constructed. Oil was discovered in Bahrain in the 1930s, providing the backbone for the country's wealth. Oil reserves are likely to be depleted early in the 21st century, but gas reserves will last a further 50 years and the economy has diversified to include a significant financial services sector.

In the 1990–91 Gulf War Bahrain supported the UN-sponsored action against Iraq and in October 1991 signed a defence cooperation agreement with the United States. In recent years Bahrain has been in dispute with Qatar over the sovereignty of the oil-rich Hawar islands, with respective claims being submitted to the International Court of Justice in The Hague.

EGYPT

Arab Republic of Egypt
Jumhuriyat Misr al-Arabiya

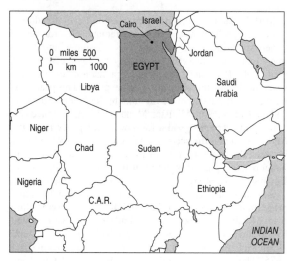

Capital: Cairo

Social and economic data
Area: 997,738 km^2
Population: 56,100,000*
Pop. density per km^2: 56*
Urban population: 44%**
Literacy rate: 48%**
GDP: $35,632 million**; per-capita GDP: $630**
Government defence spending (% of GDP): 4.8%**
Currency: Egyptian pound
Economy type: low income
Labour force in agriculture: 34%**

*1994
**1992

Ethnic composition
Native Egyptians comprise over 93% of the population, mainly of Hamitic stock. Arabic is the official language but English and French are also used.

Religions
Islam is the state religion and 90% of the population is Muslim, nearly all Sunni.

Political features
State type: liberal democratic*
Date of state formation: 1922
Political structure: unitary
Executive: limited presidential
Assembly: one-chamber
Party structure: multiparty*
Human rights rating: 50%
International affiliations: AG (observer), AL, AMF, DDS, G-15, G-24, IAEA, IBRD, IMF, NAM, OAPEC, OAU, OIC, UN, WTO

*Though dominated by one party

Local and regional government
For administrative purposes, the country is divided into 25 governorates, ranging in population from about 10,000 to over 5 million. Each has an appointed governor and elected council.

Head of state and head of government
President Hosni Mubarak, since 1981

Political leaders since 1970
1970–81 Anwar Sadat (ASU), 1981– Hosni Mubarak (NDP)

Political system
The 1971 constitution provides for a single-chamber People's Assembly (Majlis ash-Shaab) of 454 members, 10 nominated by the president and 444 elected from 222 constituencies. Four hundred of the candidates for election are chosen from lists prepared by the parties and the remaining 44 are independents. The second-ballot majoritarian system of voting is used. The Assembly serves a five-year term. The President is nominated by the Assembly and then elected by popular referendum for a six-year term. The president appoints one or more vice presidents and a Council of Ministers, and is eligible for re-election.

There is also a 210-member Advisory Council (Majlis ash-Shoura), partly elected and partly appointed.

Political parties
There are some 11 political parties, the four most significant being the National Democratic Party (NDP), the Socialist Labour Party (SLP), the Liberal Socialist Party, and the New Wafd Party.

The NDP was formed in 1978 as the official government party, absorbing the older Arab Socialist Party. It has a moderate centre-left orientation.

The SLP was also founded in 1978 and is the official opposition party. It has its origins in the Egyptian Youth party and has a centrist orientation.

The Liberal Socialist Party dates from 1978. It has a strong free-enterprise outlook, favouring an 'open-door' economic policy.

The New Wafd Party is Egypt's oldest political grouping, dating back to 1919. After being banned, it was reconstituted in 1978 under its current name, then disbanded and reformed in 1983. It is a strongly nationalist right-of-centre body.

Latest elections
The 1990 elections were boycotted by the three main opposition parties and the NDP won 348 of the 444 elected seats.

Political history
Egypt has existed as a unified state for more than 50 centuries, during which time it has come under Persian, Roman, and Byzantine rule. From the 16th century until 1882, when it was occupied by Britain, Egypt was part of the Turkish Ottoman Empire. In 1914 it was made a British protectorate and given nominal independence in 1922, under King Fuad I (1868–1936). He was succeeded in 1936 by King Farouk I (1920–65) and Britain agreed to recognize Egypt's full independence, announcing a phased withdrawal of its forces, except from the Suez Canal, Alexandria, and Port Said,

where there were important naval bases. The departure of the British was delayed by the start of World War II and the consequent campaign in Libya, which ended in the defeat of the German and Italian forces which had threatened the security of the Canal Zone. British troops were eventually withdrawn in 1946, except for the Suez Canal garrison.

In the immediate postwar years a radical movement developed, calling for an end to the British presence and opposition to Farouk for his extravagant lifestyle and his failure to prevent the growth of the new state of Israel. This led, in 1952, to a bloodless coup by a group of young army officers, led by General Mohammed Neguib (b. 1901) and Colonel Gamal Abdel Nasser (1918–70), who overthrew Farouk and replaced him with a military junta. The 1923 constitution was suspended and all political parties were banned. The following year Egypt declared itself a republic, with General Neguib as president and prime minister. In 1954 Nasser assumed the post of prime minister and an agreement was signed for the withdrawal of British troops from the Canal Zone by 1956. Then, following a dispute with Neguib, Nasser took over as head of state.

At home he embarked on a large-scale programme of social reform and abroad became a major force for the creation of Arab unity. In 1956 a new constitution was adopted, strengthening the presidency, to which Nasser was elected unopposed. Later that year British forces were withdrawn in accordance with the 1954 agreement. When the United States and Britain cancelled their offers of financial help to build the ambitious Aswan High Dam, Nasser responded by announcing the nationalization of the Suez Canal. In a contrived operation, Britain, France, and Israel invaded the Sinai Peninsula and two days later Egypt was attacked. Strong pressure from the United States brought a cease-fire and an Anglo-French withdrawal. The effect of the abortive Anglo-French operation was to push Egypt towards the USSR and enhance Nasser's reputation in the Arab world.

In 1958 Egypt and Syria merged to become the United Arab Republic (UAR), with Nasser as president, but three years later Syria withdrew, although Egypt retained the title of UAR until 1971. The 1960s saw several short-lived attempts to federate Egypt, Syria, and Iraq. Despite these failures Nasser enjoyed increasing prestige among his neighbours while at home, in 1962, he founded the Arab Socialist Union (ASU) as Egypt's only recognized political organization.

In 1967 Egypt, as the acknowledged champion of the Arab world, led an attack on Israel which developed into the Six-Day War. It ended ignominiously, with Israel defeating all its opponents, including Egypt. One result of the conflict was the blocking of the Suez Canal which was not opened again to traffic until 1975. Following Egypt's defeat, Nasser offered his resignation but was persuaded to stay on. In 1969, at the age of 52, he suffered a fatal heart attack and was succeeded by the vice president, Colonel Anwar Sadat (1918–81).

In 1971 a new constitution was approved and the title 'Arab Republic of Egypt' was adopted. Sadat continued Nasser's policy of promoting Arab unity but proposals to create a federation of Egypt, Libya, and Syria again failed. In 1973 an attempt was made to regain territory lost to Israel. After 18 days' fighting US Secretary of State Henry Kissinger (b. 1923) arranged a cease-fire, resulting in Israel's evacuation of parts of Sinai, with a UN buffer zone separating the rival armies. This US intervention strengthened the ties between the two countries while relations with the USSR cooled.

In 1977 Sadat, surprisingly, travelled to Israel, to address the Israeli parliament and make a dramatic plea for peace. Other Arab states were dismayed by this move and diplomatic relations with Syria, Libya, Algeria, and the Yemen, as well as the Palestine Liberation Organization (PLO), were severed. Despite this opposition, Sadat pursued his peace initiative and at the Camp David talks in the United States he and the Israeli Prime Minister, Menachem Begin, signed two agreements. The first laid a framework for peace in the Middle East and the second a framework for a peace treaty between the two countries. In 1979 a treaty was signed and Israel began a phased withdrawal from the Sinai Peninsula. Egypt was, in consequence, expelled from the Arab League.

Soon after his accession to the presidency, Sadat began a programme of liberalizing his regime, but met opposition from Muslim fundamentalists and in 1981 was assassinated by a group of them. He was succeeded by Lieutenant General Hosni Mubarak (b. 1928), who had been vice president since 1975. The line of succession from Nasser had thus been maintained, and, just as Sadat had continued the policies of his predecessor, so did Mubarak. In the 1984 elections the National Democratic Party (NDP), which Sadat had formed in 1978, won an overwhelming victory in the Assembly, strengthening Mubarak's position.

Egypt's relations with other Arab nations improved and in 1987 it was readmitted into membership of the Arab League. Domestically, Mubarak had increasing problems with Muslim fundamentalists, making him increasingly dependent on the support of the army.

In 1988 full diplomatic relations with Morocco were restored and full relations with Libya and Syria followed.

Egypt played a full part as one of the allies in the 1990–91 Gulf War against Iraq and has done much to reinstate itself as leader of the Arab world. The arrival of a more flexible Labour administration in Israel, in 1992, allowed Mubarak to play a pivotal role in Middle East peace negotiations, bridging the gap between the Arab and Western worlds. In October 1993, despite a deteriorating economy, with the rate of unemployment exceeding 20%, Mubarak was re-elected, unopposed, for a third term as president. In June 1995 he survived an assassination attempt, allegedly by fundamentalist militants, while attending an OAU meeting in Ethiopia.

IRAN

Islamic Republic of Iran
Jomhori-e-Islami-e-Irân

Capital: Tehran

Social and economic data
Area: 1,648,000 km^2
Population: 63,200,000*
Pop. density per km^2: 38*
Urban population: 58%**

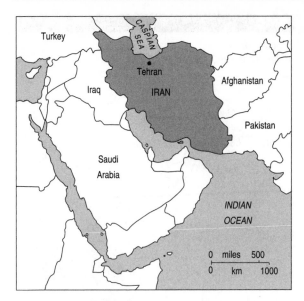

Literacy rate: 54%**
GDP: $131,000 million**; per-capita GDP: $2,189**
Government defence spending (% of GDP): 4.3%**
Economy type: middle income
Labour force in agriculture: 37%**

*1994
**1992

Ethnic composition
About 63% of the population is of Persian origin, 18% Turkic, 13% other Iranian, 3% Kurdish, and 3% Arabic. Farsi (Persian) is spoken by about half the population.

Religions
Islam is the state religion and most (97%) of the population are Shia Muslims. There is a minority of Sunni Muslims, and about 300,000 Christians and 80,000 Jews.

Religious leader
Ayatollah Sayed Ali Khamenei, since 1989

Political features
State type: Islamic authoritarian nationalist
Date of state formation: 1499
Political structure: unitary
Executive: unlimited presidential
Assembly: one-chamber
Party structure: no official parties
Human rights rating: 22%
International affiliations: CP, ECO, G-24, IAEA, IBRD, IMF, NAM, OIC, OPEC, UN

Local and regional government
Iran has a long tradition of strong local government and the country is divided into 24 provinces, 472 counties, and 499 municipalities. The provinces are administered by governor generals, the counties by governors, and the municipalities by lieutenant governors or *sherifs*.

Head of state and head of government
President Ali Akbar Hashemi Rafsanjani, since 1989

Political leaders since 1970
1953–79 Shah Mohammad Reza Pahlavi, 1979–80 Mehdi Bazargan (IRP), 1980–81 Abolhasan Bani-Sadr (IRP), 1981–89 Sayed Ali Khomeini (IRP), 1989– Ali Akbar Hashemi Rafsanjani (independent)

Political system
The constitution, which came into effect on the overthrow of the shah in 1979, provides for a president elected by universal adult suffrage and a single-chamber legislature, called the Islamic Consultative Assembly (Majlis ash-Shoura), of 270 members, elected by the majoritarian voting system of the second ballot. The president and the Assembly serve a term of four years. The president is the executive head of government. There is also a popularly elected 83-member Council of Experts, composed entirely of clerics, which appoints a religious leader (Wali Faqih) who exercises supreme authority as a quasi-head of state and ensures that decisions taken by the government comply with Islamic precepts.

Political parties
Although a number of political parties exist they are not officially recognized.

Latest elections
Elections to the Majlis ash-Shoura were held in April and May 1992. They resulted in an overwhelming number of successful candidates supporting President Rafsanjani.

In June 1993 Rafsanjani was re-elected for a second four-year term.

Political history
Persia, as Iran was known before 1935, has been a sovereign state since the end of the 15th century. It adopted its first democratic constitution in 1906 after revolutionaries had rebelled against the despotism of the shahs of the Qajar dynasty, who had ruled Persia since the 18th century. In the early part of the 20th century the country became the subject of British, Russian, and Turkish exploitation until a coup, in 1925, by Colonel Reza Khan, a Cossack officer, deposed the existing Shah and resulted in his election as shah, with the title Reza Shah Pahlavi. In 1941 he abdicated in favour of his son, Mohammad Reza Pahlavi (1919–80), who embarked on a massive programme of modernization to bring the country into the 20th century.

During World War II, Iran, as it had become, was occupied by British, American, and Russian troops until the spring of 1946. Anti-British and anti-American feeling grew and in 1951 the newly elected prime minister, Dr Mohammed Mussadeq, obtained legislative approval for the nationalization of Iran's largely foreign-owned petroleum industry. With American connivance, Mussadeq was deposed in a 1953 coup and the dispute over nationalization was settled the following year when oil drilling concessions were granted to a consortium of eight companies. The shah assumed complete control of the government and between 1965 and 1977 Iran enjoyed a period of political stability and economic growth, based on oil revenue.

In 1975 the shah had introduced a one-party political system, based on the Iran National Resurgence Party (Rastakhis), but opposition to his regime was becoming increasingly evident. The most effective challenge came from the exiled religious leader, Ayatollah Ruhollah Khomeini (1900–89), who carried on his campaign from France. He demanded a return to the principles of Islam and pressure on the shah became so great that in 1979 he left the country, leaving the way open for Khomeini's return.

Khomeini proceeded to appoint a provisional government but power was placed essentially in the hands of the 15-member Islamic Revolutionary Council, controlled by himself. Iran was declared an Islamic Republic and a new constitution, based on Islamic principles, was adopted. Relations with the United States were badly affected when a group of Iranian students seized 66 American hostages at the US embassy in Tehran, to give support to a demand for the return of the shah to face trial. Even the death of the shah, in Egypt in 1980, did little to resolve the crisis which was not ended until all the hostages were released in January 1981. The hostage crisis not only damaged US–Iranian relations but dealt a mortal blow to President Jimmy Carter's hopes of winning the US presidency for a second term.

In its early years several rifts developed within the new Islamic government and although by 1982 some stability had been attained, disputes between different factions developed again in the years that followed. Externally, the war with Iraq which broke out in 1980, following a border dispute, continued with considerable loss of life on both sides. By 1987 both sides in the war had increased the scale of their operations, each apparently believing that outright victory was possible. Then, in 1988, the leaders of the two countries, somewhat surprisingly, agreed to a cease-fire and the start of talks about a permanent solution to the dispute.

Not only was the end of the war seen in 1988 but also the beginnings of a rapprochement between Iran and the Western powers. The burden of the fighting, and the enormous loss of life, had obviously affected the attitude of the ruling regime, allowing more moderate elements, such as the speaker of the Assembly, to exercise greater influence. The restoration of diplomatic relations with Britain at the end of 1988 was reversed, however, because of Islamic opposition to the publication of *The Satanic Verses* by the British-based author, Salman Rushdie. Ayatollah Khomeini issued a fatwa, or public order, for his assassination and Iran seemed to have reverted to its extremist, unpredictable character. Then, in July 1989, Ayatollah Khomeini died. He was succeeded as religious leader by Ayatollah Ali Khamenei (b. 1940), while the pragmatic speaker of the Assembly, Hashemi Rafsanjani (b. 1934), became executive president. Apart from occasional setbacks and expressed suspicions about Iran's military intentions and its maltreatment of the Kurdish people of northern Iran, relations with the Western powers progressively improved. In June 1993 Rafsanjani was re-elected, but his efforts to promote free-market reforms to stimulate an ailing economy, with unemployment at 25%, have been repeatedly thwarted by the opposition of clerics.

IRAQ

Republic of Iraq
al-Jumhuriya al-'Iraqiya

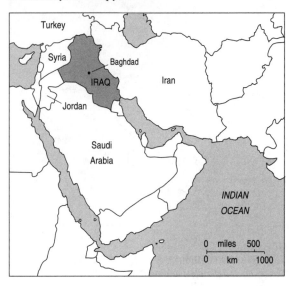

Capital: Baghdad

Social and economic data
Area: 438,317 km^2
Population: 19,900,000*
Pop. density per km^2: 45*
Urban population: 73%**
Literacy rate: 60%**
GDP: $41,000 million**; per-capita GDP: $2,104**
Government defence spending (% of GDP): 15.3%**
Currency: Iraqi dinar
Economy type: middle income
Labour force in agriculture: 13%**

*1994
**1992

Ethnic composition
About 79% of the population is Arab, 16% Kurdish, mainly in the northeast, 3% Persian, and 2% Turkish. The Kurds have, for a long time, pressed for greater autonomy which has been promised and then often replaced by harsh repressive measures. The official language is Arabic spoken by about 80% of the population.

Religions
Islam is the state religion and about 51% of the population is Shia Muslim and 43% Sunni Muslim. The Sunni are mainly in the north of the country and the Shia in the south.

Political features
State type: nationalistic socialist
Date of state formation: 1932
Political structure: unitary
Executive: unlimited presidential
Assembly: one-chamber

Party structure: one-party
Human rights rating: 17%
International affiliations: AL, AMF (suspended), IAEA, IBRD, IMF, NAM, OAPEC, OIC, OPEC, UN

Local and regional government

The country is divided into 15 provinces, administered by appointed governors, and three governorates, which together comprise a partially autonomous Kurdish region. Within the latter region, two rival Kurdish leaders, Massoud Barzani, head of the Kurdistan Democratic Party, and Jalal Talabani, leader of the Patriotic Union of Kurdistan, claim authority.

Head of state and head of government

President Saddam Hussein, since 1979

Political leaders since 1970

1968–79 Ahmed Hassan al-Bakr (Arab Socialist Ba'ath Party), 1979– Saddam Hussein (Arab Socialist Ba'ath Party)

Political system

The 1970 constitution, amended in 1973, 1974, 1980, and 1988, provides for a president who is head of state, head of government, and chair of a Revolutionary Command Council (RCC). Day-to-day administration is under the control of a Council of Ministers over which the president also presides. They are also regional secretary of the Arab Ba'ath Socialist Party which, although not the only political party in Iraq, so dominates the country's institutions as to make it virtually a one-party state. In effect, therefore, Iraq is ruled by the Arab Ba'ath Socialist Party through its regional secretary and other leading members. There is a 250-member National Assembly, elected for a four-year term by universal suffrage through a proportional representation voting system, but it has little real power.

Political parties

Although there are, in theory, a number of parties, in reality there is only one which has real political power, the Arab Ba'ath Socialist Party. It was originally founded in Damascus in 1947 and came to prominence in Iraq in 1968 and since then has dominated the country's politics. Its orientation is socialist and strongly nationalistic.

The chief opposition to the regime is the Iraqi National Congress, which operates in exile in London.

Latest elections

In the 1989 elections for the National Assembly the Arab Ba'ath Socialist Party, as part of the National Progressive Front coalition, won a majority of the 250 seats.

In September 1995 the National Assembly unanimously approved Saddam Hussein as the sole candidate, for a further seven-year term, in a national presidential plebiscite. This was held in October and there was officially a 99.96% vote in favour of Saddam Hussein, with turnout put at 99.47%.

Political history

Formerly part of the Turkish Ottoman Empire, Iraq was placed under British administration by the League of Nations in 1920. This was the start of a long, and generally amicable, relationship. In 1932 Iraq became a fully independent kingdom and the following year the reigning king, Faisal I (1885–1933), who had ruled since 1921, died, to be succeeded by his son, Ghazi. The leading figure behind the throne was the strongly pro-Western General Nuri el-Said (1888–1958), who held the post of prime minister from 1930 until 1958. In 1939 King Ghazi was killed in a motor accident and Faisal II (1935–58) became king at the age of three, his uncle Prince Abdul Ilah acting as regent until 1953 when the king assumed full powers.

In 1955 Iraq signed the Baghdad Pact, a regional collective security agreement, with the USSR seen as the main potential threat, and in 1958 joined with Jordan to form an Arab Federation, with King Faisal II as head of state. In July of that year, however, a revolution overthrew the monarchy and King Faisal, Prince Abdul Ilah, and General Nuri were all assassinated. The constitution was suspended and Iraq was declared a republic, with Brigadier Abdul Karim Kassem (1914–63) as head of a left-wing military regime. He withdrew from the Baghdad Pact in 1959 and, after tenuously holding on to power for five years, was killed in another coup in 1963.

The leader of this coup was Colonel Salem Aref. He established a new constitutional government, ended martial law and within two years had introduced a civilian administration. He died, however, in an air crash in 1966. His brother, who succeeded him, was, in turn, ousted in a revolution led by the Arab Ba'ath Socialist Party in 1968 and replaced by Major General Ahmed al-Bakr who concentrated power in the hands of a Revolutionary Command Council (RCC), taking for himself the posts of head of state, head of government, and chair of the RCC.

In 1979, Saddam Hussein (b. 1937), who for several years had been the real power behind the scenes, replaced al-Bakr as chair of the RCC and state president. Saddam Hussein, who had joined the Arab Ba'ath Socialist Party in 1957, had been forced to flee Iraq in 1959 after attempting to assassinate General Kassem, was imprisoned in 1964 for plotting to overthrow the succeeding regime, and had played a leading role in the 1968 revolution. In 1980 he introduced a 'National Charter', reaffirming a policy of nonalignment and a constitution which provided for an elected National Assembly. The first elections took place that year.

Externally, Iraq had, since 1970, enjoyed a fluctuating relationship with Syria, sometimes distant and sometimes close enough to contemplate a complete political and economic union. By 1980, however, the atmosphere was cool. Relations between Iraq and Iran had been tense for some years, with disagreement about the border between them, which runs down the Shatt-al-Arab waterway. The 1979 Iranian revolution made Iraq more suspicious of Iran's future intentions and in 1980 a full-scale war broke out.

Despite Iraq's potentially weaker military strength, Iran made little territorial progress and by 1986 it seemed as if a stalemate might have been reached. The fighting intensified however in late 1986 and early 1987, with heavy human and material losses on both sides. By 1988 Iraq was enjoying greater military success, then, somewhat unexpectedly, the Iranian government responded to an initiative by the United Nations secretary general and agreed to a cease-fire.

The end of hostilities freed Iraq's well disciplined army to deal with the Kurdish rebels who, in their quest for greater autonomy, had taken advantage of the government's preoccupation with the Iran–Iraq War. Many Kurds were reported to have fled the country into neighbouring Turkey or Iran.

In the early months of 1990 Iraq initiated a 'war of words' against neighbouring Kuwait, claiming that it held territory and oil reserves belonging to Iraq. In August 1990 the words turned into deeds and Kuwait was invaded and speedily occupied. Following initiatives by the United States, Britain, and France, the UN Security Council agreed to impose sanctions on Iraq and then, in February 1991, military attacks.

The ground war, following a massive use of air power, was short and effective, lasting just 100 hours, and Kuwait was freed. The UN cease-fire resolution imposed on Iraq, and enforced by economic sanctions and a special commission, required that it destroyed its chemical and biological weapons and ceased attempts to develop nuclear weapons. However, Saddam Hussein remained in power and, although much of his offensive capability was reduced, he was still able to persecute the Kurdish and Shia minorities in northern Iraq and the southern marshlands. This persuaded the West to declare 'safe haven' no-fly zones to protect these minority communities. Hopes in the West that internal opposition would weaken his position and eventually displace him were not fulfilled and in late 1994 there were even signs of military activity near the border with Kuwait. A show of strength by the United States dissipated that threat. In August 1995 Saddam Hussein's position seemed less secure as, with the economy in a state of collapse, a number of his key associates defected. These included two of Saddam Hussein's sons-in-law and their wives who fled to Jordan, whose ruler, King Hussein, was the cousin of Iraq's former king, Faisal II. Saddam Hussein fell back increasingly on the support of his sons, Udai and Qusai, heads of the intelligence services, both of whom were given vice presidential authority in May 1995.

ISRAEL

State of Israel
Medinat Israel

Capital: Jerusalem (not recognized by the United Nations)

Social and economic data
Area: 20,700 km²
Population: 5,400,000*
Pop. density per km²: 261*
Urban population: 92%**
Literacy rate: 96%**
GDP: $68,000 million**; per-capita GDP: $13,233**
Government defence spending (% of GDP): 9.8%**
Currency: new shekel
Economy type: high income
Labour force in agriculture: 2%**

*1994
**1992

Ethnic composition
About 85% of the population is Jewish. Most of the rest of the population is Arab. The official language is Hebrew,

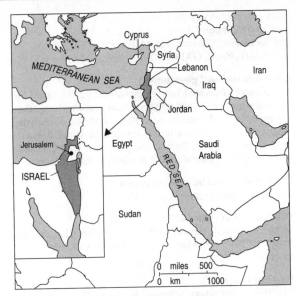

spoken by the majority of the population; Arabic is the second language and English is also used.

Religions
Judaism is the state religion and about 85% of the population professes to adhere to it. There are also about 527,000 Muslims and about 94,000 Christians.

Political features
State type: liberal democratic
Date of state formation: 1948
Political structure: unitary
Executive: parliamentary
Assembly: one-chamber
Party structure: multiparty
Human rights rating: 76%
International affiliations: AG (observer), CERN (observer), IAEA, IBRD, IMF, UN, WTO

Local and regional government
The country is divided into six administrative districts, each controlled by a district commissioner. Within the districts there are 31 municipalities and 115 local councils. There are also 48 regional councils, containing representatives from 700 villages. Elections for regional and local councils coincide with those for the Knesset (assembly) and also operate through a proportional representation voting system. Since 1994 Palestinians in the occupied territories of Gaza and the West Bank of the Jordan have enjoyed a measure of autonomy.

Head of state
President Ezer Weizmann, since 1993

Head of government
Prime Minister Shimon Peres, since 1995

Political leaders since 1970
1969–74 Golda Meir (Labour Party), 1974–77 Yitzhak Rabin (Labour Alignment coalition), 1977–83 Menachem Begin

(Likud coalition), 1983–84 Yitzhak Shamir (Likud coalition), 1984–86 Shimon Peres (Labour–Likud National Unity coalition), 1986–88 Yitzhak Shamir (Likud–Labour National Unity coalition), 1988–90 Yitzhak Shamir (Likud–Labour Party coalition), 1990–92 Yitzhak Shamir (Likud), 1992–95 Yitzhak Rabin (Labour-led coalition), 1995– Shimon Peres (Labour-led coalition)

Political system

Israel does not have a written constitution. In 1950 the single-chamber assembly, the Knesset, voted to adopt a state constitution by evolution over an unspecifed period of time. As in the other few states without written constitutions, such as the United Kingdom and New Zealand, a number of laws have been passed which are considered to have particular constitutional significance and they could, at some time, be codified into a single written document.

Supreme authority rests with the Knesset, whose 120 members are elected by universal adult suffrage, through a party list system of proportional representation, for a four-year term. It is, however, subject to dissolution within that period. The president is a constitutional head of state and is elected by the Knesset for a five-year term. The prime minister and cabinet are mostly drawn from, and collectively responsible to, the Knesset, but occasionally a cabinet member may be chosen from outside.

Political parties

There are currently some 28 political parties, several of the small ones being rather like religious pressure groups. The two most significant of the main parties are the Israel Labour Party and the Consolidation Party (Likud). The proportional representation voting system not only encourages the growth of small, specifically orientated, parties but also frequently results in broad-based coalition governments.

The Israel Labour Party was formed in 1968 by a merger of three existing Labour groups, Mapai, Rafi, and Achdut Ha'avoda. Mapai was the Israel Workers' Party and started life in 1930 but its origins go back to the turn of the century in Europe, and particularly in Russia. In its present form, the Labour Party has a generally moderate left-of-centre orientation.

Likud was founded in 1973 as an alliance of several right-of-centre groupings. Under its present leadership by Binyamin Netanyahu (b. 1949) it has adopted a much harder line than the Labour Party towards its Arab neighbours and Israeli–Palestinian relations generally.

Latest elections

The results of the June 1992 general election were as follows:

	Seats
Left bloc	61
Labour	44
Others	17
Right bloc	43
Likud	32
Others	11
Religious parties	16

Apart from Labour and Likud, the other parties securing representation included: the Meretz Party, 12 seats; the right-wing Tzomet Party, 6; the ultra-orthodox Shas Party, 6; the National Religious Party, 6; the United Tora Judaism Party, 4; the right-wing nationalist Moledet, 3; the Arab Democratic Party, 3; and the left-wing Palestinian Hadash Party, 3.

Political history

The Zionist movement, calling for an independent community for Jews in their historic homeland of Palestine, started in the 19th century, and in 1917 Britain declared its support for the idea. In 1920 Palestine was placed under British administration by the League of Nations and the British government was immediately faced with the rival claims of Jews who wished to settle there and the indigenous Arabs who were opposed to them. In 1937 Britain proposed two separate communities, Arab and Jewish, an idea which was accepted by the Jews but not by the Arabs, and fighting broke out between the two races. In 1947, after the murder of 6 million Jews in European concentration camps by Germany's Nazi regime, this plan for a partition was supported by the United Nations (UN). In 1948, when Britain ended its Palestinian mandate, Jewish leaders immediately proclaimed a new, independent State of Israel, with David Ben-Gurion (1886–1973) as prime minister.

Although it had no specific frontiers, the new state won wide recognition in the non-Arab world. Neighbouring Arab states reacted by sending forces into Palestine to crush the new nation but with no success. Indeed, when a cease-fire agreement had been reached, in 1949, Israel was left in control of more land than had originally been allocated under the UN partition plan. The non-Jewish occupied remainder of Palestine, known as the West Bank, was incorporated into Jordan. The creation of this *de facto* state encouraged Jewish immigration on a large scale, about 2 million having arrived from all over the world by 1962. Meanwhile, hundreds of thousands of Arab and indigenous Palestinian residents had fled from Israel to neighbouring countries, such as Jordan and Lebanon. In 1964 a number of exiled Palestinian Arabs founded the Palestine Liberation Organization (PLO), with the declared ultimate aim of overthrowing the State of Israel.

Throughout the 1960s there was considerable tension between Israel and Egypt, which, under President Gamal Abdel Nasser, had become an important leader in the Arab world. His nationalization of the Suez Canal in 1956 provided an opportunity for Israel, in collusion with Britain and France, to attack Egypt and occupy a part of Palestine which Egypt had controlled since 1949, the Gaza Strip. The British–French–Israeli attack on Egypt was soon called off under US and UN pressure and Israel was forced to withdraw from the Strip in 1957. Ten years later, the Six-Day War, as it was called, between Egypt and Israel, eventually left the Israelis with large territorial gains, including the whole of Jerusalem, the West Bank area of Jordan, the Sinai Peninsula in Egypt, and the Golan Heights in Syria. These were all immediately incorporated into the State of Israel.

Ben-Gurion resigned in 1963 and was succeeded by Levi Eshkol, leading a coalition government, and then in 1968 three of the coalition parties combined to form the Israel Labour Party. In 1969 Golda Meir (1898–1978), the Labour

Party leader, became prime minister, continuing in office until 1974. In 1973, during the final months of her last administration, another Arab–Israeli war broke out, coinciding with Yom Kippur, the holiest day of the Jewish year. Israel was attacked simultaneously by Egypt and Syria and after nearly three weeks of bitter fighting, resulting in heavy losses, cease-fire agreements were reached.

Golda Meir resigned in June 1974 and was succeeded by General Yitzhak Rabin (1922–95), heading a Labour-led coalition. In the 1977 elections the Consolidation (Likud) bloc, led by Menachem Begin (1913–92), won an unexpected victory and Begin became prime minister. Within five months relations between Egypt and Israel underwent a dramatic change, mainly because of initiatives by President Anwar Sadat of Egypt, encouraged by the US administration of President Jimmy Carter. Sadat made an unprecedented visit to Israel to address the Knesset and the following year the Egyptian and Israeli leaders met at Camp David, in the United States, to sign agreements for peace in the Middle East. A peace treaty was signed in Washington in March 1979 and the following year Egypt and Israel exchanged ambassadors, to the dismay of most of the Arab world. Israel withdrew completely from Sinai by 1982 but continued to occupy the Golan Heights. In the same year a major crisis was created when Israel, without consulting Egypt, advanced through Lebanon and surrounded West Beirut, in pursuit of 6,000 PLO fighters who were trapped there. A complete split between Egypt and Israel was narrowly avoided by the efforts of the US special negotiator, Philip Habib, who secured the evacuation from Beirut to various Arab countries of about 15,000 PLO and Syrian fighters in August 1982. Israel's alleged complicity in the massacre of hundreds of people in two Palestinian refugee camps increased Arab hostility.

Prolonged talks between Israel and Lebanon, between December 1982 and May 1983, resulted in an agreement, drawn up by US secretary of state, George Shultz (b. 1920), calling for the withdrawal of all foreign forces from Lebanon within three months. Syria refused to acknowledge the agreement and left some 40,000 troops, with about 7,000 PLO members, in the northeast, and Israel retaliated by refusing to withdraw its forces from the south. During this time Begin was faced with increasingly difficult domestic problems, including rapidly rising inflation. There was also growing opposition to his foreign policies and, in his private life, he had become depressed by the death of his wife. In September 1983 he resigned and Yitzhak Shamir (b. 1915) formed a shaky coalition. Elections in July 1984 failed to produce a conclusive result, with the Labour Alignment, led by Shimon Peres (b. 1923), winning 44 Knesset seats and Likud, led by Shamir, 41. Neither leader was able to form a viable coalition so eventually, after weeks of negotiation, it was agreed that a Government of National Unity would be formed, with Peres as prime minister for the first 25 months and Shamir as his deputy, and then a reversal of the positions. Peres was, therefore, in charge of the government until October 1986, when Shamir took over.

Meanwhile, the problems in Lebanon continued. In March 1984, under pressure from Syria, President Amin Gemayel of Lebanon rejected the 1983 treaty with Israel, but the Government of National Unity in Tel Aviv continued with its plans for the withdrawal of its forces, even though it might lead to outright civil war in southern Lebanon. Guerrilla groups of the Shia community of southern Lebanon took advantage of the situation by attacking and inflicting losses on the departing Israeli troops. Israel replied with ruthless attacks on Shia villages. Most of the withdrawal was completed by June 1985.

Several peace initiatives by King Hussein of Jordan failed, largely because of Israeli and US suspicions about the role and motives of the PLO, some of whose supporters were alleged to have been involved in hijacking and other terrorist incidents in and around the Mediterranean area. There were, however, signs of improvements in 1985. Prime Minister Peres met King Hussein secretly in the south of France and later, in a speech to the United Nations, Peres said he would not rule out the possibility of an international conference on the Middle East, with wide representation. PLO leader Yasser Arafat (b. 1929) also had talks with King Hussein and later, in Cairo, publicly denounced the use of terrorism by the PLO outside territories occupied by Israel.

Domestically, the Government of National Unity was having some success with its economic policies, inflation falling in 1986 to manageable levels, but differences developed between Peres and Shamir over the concept of an international peace conference. Towards the end of 1987 international criticism of Prime Minister Shamir's handling of an intifada (Palestinian uprising) in the occupied territories grew and this widened the gulf between him and Peres. Despite Foreign Minister Peres' support for a conference proposed by US secretary of state, George Shultz, Prime Minister Shamir resolutely opposed the idea.

Meanwhile, the deaths of Palestinians continued. In April 1988 the military commander of the PLO, and Yasser Arafat's closest colleague, Abu Jihad, was assassinated at his home in Tunis, allegedly by the Israeli secret service. His death triggered off an increase in violence in the occupied territories.

King Hussein's unexpected announcement in July 1988 that Jordan was shedding its responsibility for the West Bank and transferring it to the PLO seemed likely to have an impact on Israel's general election in November of that year. Prime Minister Shamir said he would abide by the Camp David Agreement and not try to annex the West Bank after Jordan's withdrawal, but would resist any attempt by the PLO to set up a Palestinian government there. Shimon Peres' reaction was more conciliatory.

The 1988 general election failed to produce a clear victory for either of the two main parties and, after months of discussion, Labour agreed to join another coalition with Likud, but this collapsed in 1990 and Shamir continued in power, with the help of religious groups.

In 1990 US secretary of state, James Baker (b. 1930), proposed a Middle East peace conference which Shamir at first opposed. Later he agreed to participate, providing the PLO was not directly represented. The conference began in 1991 but progress was slow because of Shamir's intransigence and the continuing policy of establishing Jewish settlements in the Palestine occupied territories. The success of Labour in the June 1992 general election brought a new sense of immediacy to the negotiations.

At the beginning of 1993 the ban on contacts with the PLO was lifted and later in the year Prime Minister Rabin and PLO leader, Yasser Arafat, signed an agreement which led to the withdrawal of Israeli forces from Jericho and the Gaza Strip in March 1994. Despite attempts by extremists on both sides to wreck it, the peace process continued with strong US encouragement. An agreement with Jordan was signed in October 1994 and in the same month, in recognition of their efforts, Rabin and Arafat were jointly awarded the Nobel Peace Prize. In September 1995, further Israeli–PLO talks produced an accord, signed in Washington, on the extension of Palestinian self-rule from Gaza and Jericho to most of the rest of the West Bank. Israeli troops were to be withdrawn over a six-month period, an elected 82-member Palestinian Council set up, to hold power for three years, many Palestinian prisoners to be released, and the PLO to revoke certain clauses in its 'covenant' calling for the destruction of Israel. However, there remained the threat that the deal might be wrecked by militants on either side, notably the extremist Palestinian Hamas group and 140,000 armed Jewish settlers living in the West Bank among 1.2 million Palestinians. These fears deepened in November 1995 when Prime Minister Rabin was assassinated by a Jewish right-wing extremist, when leaving a peace rally in Tel Aviv. The foreign minister, Shimon Peres, took over as prime minister but lacking Rabin's military background seemed less likely to ensure that the peace process would continue to attract support from a wide range of Israeli opinion.

JORDAN

Hashemite Kingdom of Jordan
al-Mamlaka al-Urduniya al-Hashemiyah

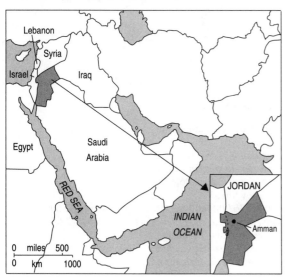

Capital: Amman

Social and economic data
Area: 98,000 km²
Population: 4,400,000*

Pop. density per km²: 45*
Urban population: 69%**
Literacy rate: 6%**
GDP: $6,560 million**; per-capita GDP: $1,640**
Government defence spending (% of GDP): 9.4%**
Currency: Jordanian dinar
Economy type: middle income
Labour force in agriculture: 10%**

*1994
**1992

Ethnic composition
The majority of the people are of Arab descent and there are minorities of Circassians, Armenians, and Kurds. The official and most widely used language is Arabic.

Religions
Eighty per cent of the population is Sunni Muslim. The king can trace his unbroken ancestry back to the prophet Muhammad. There is also a Christian minority.

Political features
State type: absolutist
Date of state formation: 1946
Political structure: unitary
Executive: semi-absolute
Assembly: two-chamber
Party structure: multiparty
Human rights rating: 65%
International affiliations: AL, AMF, IAEA, IBRD, IMF, NAM, OIC, UN

Local and regional government
The country is divided into eight governorates. Three of them are known collectively as the West Bank and responsibility for them was relinquished by Jordan in 1988.

Head of state and head of government
King Hussein ibn Talal, since 1952

Political leaders since 1970
1952– King Hussein ibn Talal

Political system
Jordan is not a typical constitutional monarchy on the Western model, since the king is effectively both head of state and head of government. The current constitution dates from 1952 but has been amended in 1974, 1976, and 1984. It provides for a two-chamber National Assembly of a Senate of 40, appointed by the king for an eight-year term, with half retiring every four years, and a House of Representatives of 80, elected by universal adult suffrage, through a simple plurality voting system, for a four-year term. The House is subject to dissolution within that period. The king governs with the help of a Council of Ministers (cabinet), whom he appoints and who are responsible to the Assembly. The cabinet is headed by a prime minister. Despite the existence of an elected assembly, Jordan has more absolutist than democratic characteristics, but there is evidence of gradual change.

Political parties

Political parties were banned in 1963, partially restored in 1971, banned again in 1976, and then allowed to operate in 1992.

By 1993, 21 parties had registered but independent groups, loyal to the king, still predominate. The most significant party is the Islamic Action Front (IAF), a fundamentalist party backed by the Muslim Brotherhood.

Latest elections

In the November 1993 House of Representatives elections the IAF emerged as the largest single party, with 16 seats, but conservative and centrist independents still dominated the House.

Political history

Palestine, which included the West Bank of present-day Jordan and Transjordan, which is the present-day East Bank, were part of the Turkish Ottoman Empire until it was dissolved after World War I. They were then both placed under British administration by the League of Nations. Transjordan acquired increasing control over its own affairs, separating from Palestine in 1923 and achieving complete independence when the British mandate expired in 1946. The mandate for Palestine ran out two years later, in 1948, whereupon Jewish leaders claimed it for a new state of Israel. Fighting broke out between Jews and Arabs until a cease-fire was agreed in 1949. By then Transjordan forces had occupied part of Palestine to add to what they called the new state of Jordan. The following year they annexed the West Bank.

In 1953 Hussein ibn Talal (b. 1935) came to the Jordanian throne at the age of 17, because of his father's mental illness, and has ruled the country since then. In February 1958 Jordan and Iraq formed an Arab Federation which came to an end five months later when the Iraqi monarchy was overthrown. During his reign, King Hussein I has survived many upheavals in his own country and neighbouring states, including attacks on his life, and has maintained his personal control of Jordan's affairs as well as playing an important role in Middle East affairs. His relations with his neighbours have fluctuated but on the whole his has been a moderating influence. The loss of the West Bank territories to Israel during the Six-Day War of 1967 severely damaged the Jordanian economy.

After the Israeli invasion of Lebanon in 1982, King Hussein found himself playing a key role in attempts to bring peace to that part of the world, establishing an acceptable working relationship with the Palestine Liberation Organization (PLO) leader, Yasser Arafat. By 1984 the Arab world was clearly split into two camps, with the moderates represented by Jordan, Egypt, and Arafat's PLO, and the militant radicals by Syria, Libya, and the rebel wing of the PLO. In 1985 King Hussein and Arafat put together a framework for a Middle East peace settlement. It would involve bringing together all the interested parties, including the PLO, but Israel objected to the PLO representation. Futher progress was hampered by the alleged complicity of the PLO in a number of terrorist operations in that year and King Hussein's attempts to revive the search for peace were unsuc-

cessful. In July 1988 King Hussein dramatically announced that he would cease to regard the West Bank as part of Jordan and would no longer have responsibility for its administration. His main motive seemed to be to provoke the PLO into taking over Jordan's previous role and accelerating the movement towards the creation of a Palestinian state.

The king's image as a peace broker was severely damaged by his support for Saddam Hussein during the 1991 Gulf War but success in the US-inspired Middle East peace talks helped his rehabilitation, and in 1994 a peace treaty with Israel was signed, under United States auspices. Since 1992, with the re-establishment of a multiparty system, a greater measure of political pluralism has been tolerated by King Hussein.

KUWAIT

State of Kuwait
Dowlat al-Kuwait

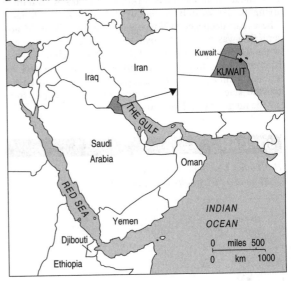

Capital: Kuwait

Social and economic data

Area: 17,818 km^2
Population: 1,800,000*
Pop. density per km^2: 101*
Urban population: 96%**
Literacy rate: 73%**
GDP: $36,000 million**; per-capita GDP: $20,000**
Government defence spending (% of GDP): 12.6%**
Currency: Kuwaiti dinar
Economy type: high income
Labour force in agriculture: 2%**

*1994
**1992

Ethnic composition

About 42% of the population is Kuwaiti, 40% non-Kuwaiti Arab, 5% Indian and Pakistani, and 4% Iranian. The official language is Arabic but English is also used in commercial transactions.

Religions
Islam is the state religion and most of the population is Muslim, about 70% Sunni and 30% Shi'ite.

Political features
State type: absolutist
Date of state formation: 1961
Political structure: unitary
Executive: absolute
Assembly: one-chamber
Party structure: none
Human rights rating: 33%
International affiliations: AL, AMF, BDEAC, DDS, GCC, IAEA, IBRD, IMF, NAM, OAPEC, OIC, OPEC, UN, WTO

Local and regional government
The country is divided, for administrative purposes, into four districts, each with an appointed governor.

Head of state (executive)
Emir Sheikh Jabir al-Ahmad al-Jabir as-Sabah, since 1977

Head of government
Crown Prince Sheikh Saad al-Abdullah as-Salim as-Sabah, since 1994

Political leaders since 1970
1965–77 Sheikh Sabah al-Salim as-Sabah, 1977– Sheikh Jabir al-Ahmad al-Jabir as-Sabah

Political system
The 1962 constitution was partly suspended by the emir in 1976 and reinstated in 1980. It vests executive power in the hands of the emir, who governs through an appointed prime Minister and Council of Ministers. The current prime minister is the emir's eldest son, the crown prince. There is a single-chamber National Assembly of 50 members, elected on a restricted suffrage, by adult Kuwaitis fulfilling strict residence requirements, for a four-year term, but in July 1986 it was dissolved, Sheikh Jabir III preferring to govern with an unelected consultative council. It was reconstituted and elections were held in 1992. Despite some semblance of constitutional government, Kuwait is, in effect, a personal monarchy and an absolutist state.

Political parties
No parties are allowed, but there are unofficial groups within the Assembly.

Latest elections
Elections were held in October 1992. There were 278 candidates, mostly independent, for the 50 National Assembly seats. Nineteen government supporters were elected, 12 liberals, and 19 Islamic fundamentalists.

Political history
Part of the Turkish Ottoman Empire from the 16th century, Kuwait made a treaty with Britain in 1899 enabling it to become a self-governing protectorate until it achieved full independence in 1961. Oil was first discovered in 1938 and

its large-scale exploitation began after 1945, transforming Kuwait City from a small fishing port into a thriving commercial centre. The oil revenues have enabled ambitious public works and education programmes to be undertaken.

Sheikh Abdullah al-Salim as-Sabah took the title of emir in 1961 when he assumed full executive powers. He died in 1965 and was succeeded by his brother, Sheikh Sabah al-Salim al-Sabah. He, in turn, died in 1977 and was succeeded by Crown Prince Jabir (b. 1928), who appointed Sheikh Saad al-Abdullah as-Salim as-Sabah as his heir apparent.

Kuwait has used its considerable wealth not only to improve its infrastructure and social services but also to enable it to serve as a strong supporter of the Arab cause generally.

Its association with Iraq has for long been precarious and in August 1990, after making territorial demands, Saddam Hussein invaded the country and occupied it. The emir fled to Saudi Arabia, while an American-led United Nations military coalition successfully defeated Iraq in the 'Operation Desert Storm' Gulf War of February 1991. Considerable material damage was sustained but it was hoped that, with the Sabah dynasty restored, Kuwait would live up to the democratic hopes of its liberators. However, although there have been some cautious moves towards more democratic institutions, it remains basically an absolutist state. With Saddam Hussein still in power, normal stable relations with Iraq have yet to be restored.

LEBANON

Republic of Lebanon/The Lebanon
al-Jumhouria al-Lubnaniya/al-Lubnan

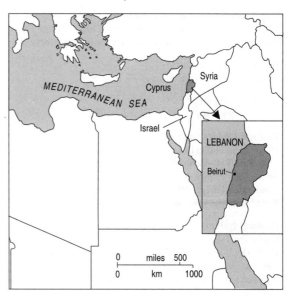

Capital: Beirut (Bayrouth)

Social and economic data
Area: 10,452 km^2
Population: 2,900,000*
Pop. density per km^2: 277*

Urban population: 85%**
Literacy rate: 80%**
GDP: $3,700 million**; per-capita GDP: $1,370**
Government defence spending (% of GDP): 4.4%**
Currency: Lebanese pound
Economy type: middle income
Labour force in agriculture: 14%**

*1994
**1992

Ethnic composition
About 90% of the population is Arab. There are Armenian, Assyrian, Jewish, Turkish, and Greek minorities. The official language is Arabic but French is also used.

Religions
There are about 1 million Shia Muslims, 900,000 Maronite Christians, associated with the Roman Catholic Church, 500,000 Sunni Muslims, 150,000 members of the Greek Orthodox Church, 200,000 Druzes, and 100,000 members of the Armenian Church.

Political features
State type: emergent democratic
Date of state formation: 1944
Political structure: unitary
Executive: dual
Assembly: one-chamber
Party structure: multiparty
Human rights rating: N/A
International affiliations: AL, AMF, G-24, IAEA, IBRD, IMF, NAM, OIC, UN

Local and regional government
The country is divided into five regional units, called *maofazats*, each administered by an appointed prefect.

Head of state (executive)
President Elias Hrawi, since 1989

Head of government
Prime Minister Rafik al-Hariri, since 1992

Political leaders since 1970
1970–76 Sulaiman Franjiya (military-led coalition), 1976–82 Elias Sarkis (Lebanese Front), 1982 Bachir Gemayel (assassinated before he assumed office), 1982–88 Amin Gemayel (Phalangist Party), 1988–89 Michel Aoun (military), 1989 René Mouawad (Maronite), 1989– Elias Hrawi (Maronite)

Political system
Under the 1926 constitution, which was amended in 1927, 1929, 1943, 1947, and 1990, legislative power is held by the National Assembly, whose 128 members, divided equally between Christians and Muslims, are elected by universal adult suffrage, through a party list system of proportional representation. The Assembly serves a four-year term. The president is elected by the Assembly for a six-year term. Presidents appoint a prime minister and cabinet who are collectively responsible to the Assembly. The 1990 amendment to the constitution reduced the powers of the president and increased those of the prime minister so as to achieve a better balance between them. The sharing of power between the two executives has some similarity with that provided for in the French constitution. In an attempt to preserve religious harmony, the constitution ensures that the president is always a Maronite Christian, while the prime minister is a Sunni Muslim and the speaker of the National Assembly is a Shia Muslim. The cabinet includes six Christians and five Muslims.

Political parties
There are currently some 19 political parties but membership of the National Assembly is more easily recognized in terms of religious groupings. The seven most significant parties are the Phalangist Party, the Progressive Socialist Party (PSP), the National Liberal Party (NLP), the National Bloc, the Lebanese Communist Party (PCL), the Amal group, and Hizbollah.

The Phalangist Party was established in 1936 by a group of young right-wing nationalists who were impressed by the growth of fascism in Nazi Germany. Their main aim was to secure independence from France. In its present form the party has moved nearer to the centre and can best be described as having a nationalistic Maronite Christian and radical orientation.

The PSP was founded in 1949 by Kamal Jumblat, the Druze leader. It is now led by his son, Walid. It has a moderate socialist orientation.

The NLP dates from 1958 and was formed by Camille Chamoun at the end of his presidential term. It has a centre-left orientation.

The National Bloc is a moderate, recently formed, Maronite grouping in the centre of the political spectrum.

The PCL was originally established in 1924 but did not become politically active unbtil 1936. It is a nationalist communist party and was once closely allied with its Syrian counterpart, but this link seems now to have been broken.

Amal is a Shia Islamic party led by Nabi Berri, while Hizbollah (Party of God) is an Islamic fundamentalist body.

Latest elections
Presidential elections were held in November 1989, after the assassination of René Mouawad, and Elias Hrawi was elected by 47 assembly members, five abstaining. A new election was due in November 1995 but President Hrawi's term was, with Syria's backing, extended a further three years by parliament.

The general election, held in three stages in August–September 1992, was boycotted by the Christian parties and resulted in a largely pro-Syrian National Assembly dominated by Amal and Hizbollah.

Political history
Originally part of the Turkish Ottoman Empire, Lebanon was administered by France, under a League of Nations mandate, from 1920 to 1941. Independence was declared in 1941, it became a republic in 1943, with a constitution that provided for power-sharing between the main religious groups, and achieved full autonomy in 1944. Historically, it has had strong links with Syria, but Lebanon has had a much richer mix of religions and cultures, including a large Christian community and Arabs of many sects. Christians and Muslims

lived peacefully together for many years and this social stability enabled Lebanon, until the mid-1970s, to become a major commercial and financial centre.

The thriving business district of Beirut was largely destroyed in 1975–76 and Lebanon's role as an international trader has been greatly reduced. After the establishment of the state of Israel in 1948, Lebanon was a natural haven for thousands of Palestinian refugees. The Palestine Liberation Organization (PLO) was founded in Beirut in 1964, with a large and destabilizing influx of Palestinians to Lebanon occurring after the 1967 Arab–Israeli war. It moved its headquarters to Tunis in 1982. The presence of PLO forces in Lebanon was the main reason for Israel's invasion and much of the subsequent civil strife. This internal fighting has been largely between left-wing Muslims and conservative Christian groups, mainly members of the Phalangist Party. There have also been differences between traditional Muslims, with pro-Iranian attitudes, such as the Shia, and the deviationist Muslims, such as the Druze, backed by Syria. In 1975 the fighting developed into a full-scale civil war.

A cease-fire was agreed in 1976 but fighting broke out again in 1978 when Israeli forces invaded south Lebanon in search of PLO guerrillas. The United Nations secured Israel's agreement to a withdrawal and set up an international peacekeeping force but to little avail. In 1979 Major Saad Haddad, a right-wing Lebanese army officer, with Israeli encouragement, declared an area of about 2,000 square kilometres in southern Lebanon an 'independent free Lebanon' and the following year Christian Phalangist soldiers took over an area north of Beirut. Throughout this turmoil the Lebanese government found itself virtually impotent. In 1982 the presidency was won by Bachir Gemayel (1947–82), the youngest son of the founder of the Phalangist Party, but, before he could assume office, he was assassinated and his brother, Amin (b. 1942), took his place.

Following exhaustive talks between Lebanon and Israel, under United States auspices, an agreement was signed in May 1983, declaring an end to hostilities and calling for the withdrawal of all foreign forces from the country within three months. Syria refused to recognize the agreement and left about 40,000 troops, with about 7,000 PLO fighters, in northern Lebanon. Israel responded by refusing to take its forces from the south. Meanwhile, a full-scale war blew up between the Christian Phalangists and the Muslim Druze soldiers in the Chouf Mountains, resulting in the defeat of the Christians and the creation of another mini-state, controlled by the Druze. The multinational force was drawn gradually, but unwillingly, into the conflict until it was eventually withdrawn in the spring of 1984.

Unsuccessful attempts were made in 1985 and 1986 to bring the civil war to an end as Lebanon, and particularly Beirut, saw its infrastructure and earlier commercial prosperity virtually destroyed in a battlefield for the Iranian-backed Shia Hizbollah ('Children of God') and the Syrian-backed Shia Amal. In May 1988 President Hafez al-Assad of Syria, after several previous abortive attempts, sent his troops into southern Beirut, with the agreement of Lebanon and Iran, to attempt to restore order and secure the release of the hostages still believed to be held there.

The end of Amin Gemayel's presidency in 1988 threatened to add a fresh dimension to Lebanon's troubles. Attempts to agree a suitable Maronite Christian successor in August of that year initially failed and the presidential election was postponed. When his term came to an end, in September 1988, Gemayel felt it necessary to establish at least a caretaker administration and appointed General Michel Aoun to head a military government. This decision was opposed by Prime Minister Selim El-Hoss, who set up his own rival administration.

In May 1989 the Arab League succeeded in arranging a truce and, despite Aoun's opposition, in November René Mouawad, a Maronite Christian, was made president. Within 17 days he was assassinated. Another Maronite, Elias Hrawi (b. 1930), was elected as his successor. Aoun continued to defy the elected president for another year but eventually surrendered. Gradually, a sense of normality returned to the country, and particularly Beirut, with the continuing presence of Syrian troops helping to preserve order. Progressively, Western hostages held there were released and the appointment as prime minister in October 1992 of the moderate businessexecutive, Rafik al-Hariri, offered promise of a lasting peace. However, Hizbollah guerrillas continued to control the Beka'a Valley and were active in the south of the country, provoking intermittent raids by Israeli forces which continued to occupy a buffer security zone.

LIBYA

The Great Socialist People's Libyan Arab State of the Masses
Daulat Libiya al-'Arabiya al-Elshtrakiya al-Jumhuriya

Capital: Tripoli (Tarabulus)

Social and economic data
Area: 1,775,500 km^2
Population: 5,500,000*
Pop. density per km^2: 3*

Urban population: 84%**
Literacy rate: 64%**
GDP: $27,320 million**; per-capita GDP: $5,551**
Government defence spending (% of GDP): 6.3%**
Currency: Libyan dinar
Economy type: middle income
Labour force in agriculture: 18%**

*1994
**1992

Ethnic composition

The great majority of people are of Berber and Arab origin, with a small number of Tebou and Touareg nomads and semi-nomads, mainly in the south. The official language is Arabic but English and Italian are used, particularly in commercial transactions.

Religions

Most of the population, over 96%, are Sunni Muslims but Islam is not the state religion. There are also about 38,000 Roman Catholics.

Political features

State type: nationalistic socialist
Date of state formation: 1951
Political structure: unitary
Executive: unlimited presidential
Assembly: one-chamber
Party structure: one-party
Human rights rating: 24%
International affiliations: AL, AMF, AMU, IAEA, IBRD, IMF, NAM, OAPEC, OAU, OIC, OPEC, UN

Local and regional government

For administrative purposes, the country is divided into 13 provinces (*baladiyat*). Below this level are municipalities. A feature of Libya's approach to government is the spread of people's committees, to encourage popular involvement, at all levels.

Head of state and head of government

Revolutionary Leader Colonel Muammar al-Kadhafi, since 1969

Political leaders since 1970

1969–   Muammar al-Kadhafi (ASU)

Political system

The 1977 constitution created an Islamic socialist state and the machinery of government is designed to allow the greatest possible popular involvement, through a large Congress and smaller secretariats and committees. There is a General People's Congress (GPC) of 1,112 members, which elects a secretary general who was intended to be the head of state. In 1979, however, Colonel Kadhafi, although still head of state, gave up the post of secretary general. The GPC meets at infrequent intervals, the most recent in January–February 1994, and is serviced by a General Secretariat, which is the nearest equivalent to an assembly in the Libyan system. The executive organ of the state is the 22-member General People's Committee, which is the equivalent of a Council of

Ministers or cabinet and replaces the structure of ministries which operated before the 1969 revolution.

Political parties

The Arab Socialist Union (ASU) is the only political party, although it has no official existence. Despite the elaborately democratic structure that has been created, ultimate political power rests with the party and the revolutionary leader, Colonel Kadhafi.

The ASU was formed by Colonel Kadhafi in 1971 as a mass party equivalent of the Arab Socialist Union of Egypt. Since its establishment he has tried to increase popular involvement almost to the extent of making its active membership too diffused. It has a radical left-wing orientation, accurately reflecting the predisposition of its leader.

Latest elections

It is difficult to identify elections in the conventional sense. GPC delegates are drawn from directly elected Basic People's Congresses, trade unions, 'popular committees', and professional organizations, with voting often being by a show of hands or a division into 'Yes' and 'No' camps.

Political history

Formerly an Italian colony, Libya was occupied and then governed by Britain from 1942 until it achieved independence, as the United Kingdom of Libya, in 1951, Muhammad Idris-as-Sanusi becoming King Idris. Formerly a poor country, the development of oil reserves since the 1960s has transformed the Libyan economy. The country enjoyed internal and external stability until a bloodless revolution in 1969, led by young nationalist officers, deposed the king and proclaimed a Libyan Arab Republic. Power was placed in the hands of a Revolution Command Council (RCC), with Colonel Muammar al-Kadhafi (b. 1942) as chairman and the Arab Socialist Union (ASU) as the only legally permitted political party.

The charismatic but unpredictable Kadhafi, who had been born into a nomadic family, was soon active in the Arab world, proposing a number of schemes for unity, none of which was permanently adopted. In 1972 it was for a federation of Libya, Syria, and Egypt and then, later in the same year, a merger between Libya and Egypt. In 1980 the proposal was for a union with just Syria and in 1981 with Chad. Domestically, Kadhafi tried to run the country on a socialist-Islamic basis, with people's committees pledged to socialism and the teachings of the Holy Koran. A constitution adopted in 1977 made him secretary general of the General Secretariat of a large General People's Congress (GPC), with over 1,000 members, but in 1979 he resigned the post so that he could devote more time to 'preserving the revolution'.

Kadhafi's attempts to establish himself as a leader of the Arab world have brought him into conflict with the Western powers, and particularly the United States. He became, in the eyes of US president Ronald Reagan, a threat to world peace similar to Fidel Castro, the communist leader of Cuba. In particular, the US administration objected to Libya's presence in Chad and its attempts to unseat the French–US-sponsored government of President Habré. The United States has linked Kadhafi to terrorist activities throughout the world, despite his denials of complicity, and the killing of a member of the US military in a bomb attack in Berlin in April 1986 prompted a raid by US aircraft, some of them based in Britain, on Tripoli and Benghazi, including Kadhafi's personal headquarters.

Within the Arab world, Kadhafi is seen as something of a maverick. In the spring of 1988, encouraged by a marked improvement in the state of the Libyan economy, he embarked on a dramatic programme of liberalization, freeing political prisoners and encouraging private businesses to operate.

He also made a surprisingly conciliatory offer to recognize the independence of Chad and give material help for the reconstruction of the country. In September 1988 Kadhafi, again surprisingly, won praise from Amnesty International by his announcement of the ending of a formal army and its replacement by a 'people's army', the Jamahariya Guard.

Early in 1989 the United States government accused Libya of building a chemical weapons factory. Soon afterwards, but in a supposedly unrelated incident, two Libyan fighter planes were shot down by aircraft operating with the US navy off the North African coast. Libyan extremists were allegedly involved in the destruction of a Pan-Am airliner over Lockerbie in Scotland in 1988 and, when Kadhafi refused to release two suspects for trial, the UN imposed trade sanctions in 1992.

His country's association with terrorist activities, always denied, have tended to make Kadhafi an international outcast, but there is increasing evidence of his desire to be rehabilitated. Against the background of a fast deteriorating economy, it was announced in October 1995 that up to 1 million foreign workers, chiefly from Chad, Mali, and Sudan would be expelled.

MOROCCO

The Kingdom of Morocco
al-Mamlaka al-Maghribiya

Capital: Rabat

Social and economic data
Area: 458,730 km^2
Population: 27,000,000*
Pop. density per km^2: 59*
Urban population: 47%**
Literacy rate: 50%**
GDP: $27,000 million**; per-capita GDP: $1,036**
Government defence spending (% of GDP): 3.8%**
Currency: dirham
Economy type: middle income
Labour force in agriculture: 46%**

*1994
**1992

Ethnic composition
Most of the population are indigenous Berbers. Pure Berbers are, however, gradually becoming less numerous than Arab-Berbers, although the distinction now has little social or political significance. There is a sizeable Jewish minority. The official language is Berber; French and Spanish are also spoken in certain regions.

Religions
Islam is the state religion and about 98% of the population is Muslim. There are also about 60,000 Christians, mostly Roman Catholics, and about 30,000 Jews.

Political features
State type: emergent democratic
Date of state formation: 1956
Political structure: unitary
Executive: dual
Assembly: one-chamber
Party structure: multiparty
Human rights rating: 56%
International affiliations: AL, AMF, AMU, IAEA, IBRD, IMF, NAM, OIC, UN, WTO

Local and regional government
The country is divided into 7 provinces and 41 prefectures. The four provinces of Spanish Sahara are also administered by Morocco; see ***Chapter 8***. The provinces and prefectures have appointed governors and prefects and there are indirectly elected councils.

Head of state (executive)
King Hassan II, since 1961

Head of government
Prime Minister Abdellatif Filali, since 1994

Political leaders since 1970
1961–   King Hassan II

Political system
Morocco is not a normal constitutional monarchy in that the king, in addition to being the formal head of state, also presides over his appointed cabinet and has powers, under the 1972 constitution, to dismiss the prime minister and other

cabinet ministers, as well as to dissolve the assembly. The executive thus displays aspects of the French model, particularly since a 1992 constitutional amendment, passed after a national referendum, gave greater powers to the assembly and prime minister.

The assembly consists of a Chamber of Representatives of 333 members, serving a six-year term. Two hundred and twenty-two are directly elected by universal adult suffrage, through a simple plurality voting system, and the remainder are chosen by an electoral college of local councillors and employers' and employees' representatives.

Political parties

There are currently 11 political parties, the seven most significant being the Constitutional Union (UC), the National Rally of Independents (RNI), the Popular Movement (MP), the National Democratic Party (PND), the National Popular Movement (MNP), Istiqlal, and the Socialist Union of Popular Forces (USFP).

The UC was formed in 1982 and has a right-wing orientation.

The RNI was founded in 1978 by an independent group of progovernment politicians. It has an essentially royalist orientation.

The MP was created in 1957 and legalized in 1959. It draws much of its support from the rural communities and has a moderate centrist orientation.

The PND was founded in 1981 as a result of a split within the RNI. It has a moderate nationalistic stance.

The MNP is a centre-right grouping.

Istiqlal was formed in 1943 as the independence party. It has a nationalistic centrist orientation.

The USFP started in 1959 as part of the National Union of Popular Forces (UNFP). Dissidents broke away in 1974 to found the USFP. It has a progressive socialist orientation.

No Islamic parties are permitted.

Latest elections

The centre-right parties fought the 1993 general election as the Entente Nationale (*wifaq*) bloc, comprising the UC, MP, PND, RNI, and MNP. The centre-left group was the Bloc Démocratique (*kutlah*) and included the USFP, Istiqlal, and smaller similarly minded parties.

The results were as follows:

	Seats by direct election	Seats by indirect election	Total
UC	27	27	54
USFP	48	4	52
MP	33	18	51
Istiqlal	43	7	50
RNI	28	13	41
MNP	14	11	25
PND	14	10	24
Other parties	15	21	36

Political history

After hundreds of years of being part of a series of vast Muslim empires, European influence came to Morocco in the 16th century, in the shape of the Portuguese. It was then the turn of the Spanish and French in the 19th century. In 1912 Morocco was split into Spanish and French protectorates and in 1925 the Rif rebellion stirred nationalist sentiment. The country became fully independent as the Sultanate of Morocco in 1956, with Mohammed V, who had been reigning since 1927, as head of state. The two former protectorates were soon joined by Tangier, which until then had been designated an international zone. The Sultan was restyled King Mohammed of Morocco in 1957 and died three years later, in 1960.

He was succeeded by the crown prince, who became King Hassan II (b. 1929). During his reign King Hassan has appointed numerous prime ministers and, despite several attempts to depose or kill him, has retained his personal position. Between 1960 and 1972 a number of constitutions were formulated in an attempt to find a successful marriage between personal royal rule and demands for a more democratic form of government. The most recent is the 1972 constitution, which was amended in 1992.

Most of King Hassan's reign has been dominated by Morocco's claims to what was Spanish Sahara, an area to the southwest of Morocco, considered to be historically Moroccan. Under pressure from King Hassan, who encouraged a 'Green March' of unarmed peasants into the territory, Spain agreed, in 1975, to cede the region to Morocco and Mauritania, leaving the eventual division to them. The local inhabitants, who had not been consulted, reacted violently through an independence movement, the Polisario Front, which won the support of Algeria. Within a year of Spain's departure, Morocco and Mauritania found themselves involved in a guerrilla war. Algeria's support for Polisario, which included permitting the establishment of a government in exile in Algiers, the Sahrawi Arab Democratic Republic (SADR), prompted King Hassan in 1976 to sever diplomatic relations. In 1979 Mauritania agreed a peace treaty with the Polisario forces, whereupon King Hassan immediately annexed that part of Western Sahara which Mauritania had vacated. Polisario reacted by raising the scale of its operations. In 1983 a summit meeting of the Organization of African Unity (OAU) proposed an immediate cease-fire, direct negotiations between Morocco and Polisario, and the holding of a referendum in Western Sahara on the issue of self-determination.

Morocco agreed in principle to the proposals but refused to deal directly with Polisario. Although the war was costly, it allowed King Hassan to capitalize on the patriotic fervour it generated among Moroccans. Then, in 1984, he surprised the world by signing an agreement with Colonel Kadhafi of Libya, who, until then, had been helping Polisario. At the same time, Morocco was becoming increasingly isolated, with more countries recognizing the SADR, which had embarked upon a new military and diplomatic offensive. The isolation showed signs of ending with the announcement in May 1987 that better relations with Algeria had been achieved. In November 1987 Polisario guerrillas agreed to a cease-fire in Western Sahara and South Morocco and in May 1988 Morocco and Algeria announced that they were resuming full diplomatic relations. Although a peace plan with the Polisario Front had been agreed, fighting continued until a cease-fire in 1991. Early in 1989 it was announced that diplomatic relations with Syria had been restored. Morocco was the only Maghreb state to send troops as part of the US-led coalition in the 1991 Gulf War.

In the 1993 general election, the first held since 1984, the centre-left parties improved their position in the direct elections, but the centre-right won more seats overall. After the results had been finally digested, the King appointed a new nonparty government, led by one of his most trusted ministers, Karim Lamrani, who continued in office. The king said the centre-left, the *kutlah*, had refused to form a government with his allies and the centre-right, the *wifaq*, said they needed a spell out of office to allow them to reconstruct. In May 1994 Lamrani was dismissed and replaced by another royal ally, Abdellatif Filali.

OMAN

Sultanate of Oman
Sultanat 'Uman

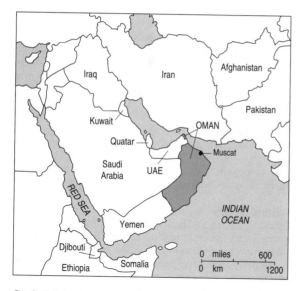

Capital: Muscat

Social and economic data
Area: 300,000 km²
Population: 1,700,000*
Pop. density per km²: 5*
Urban population: 11%**
Literacy rate: 38%**
GDP: $8,960 million**; per-capita GDP: $5,600**
Government defence spending (% of GDP): 15.3%**
Currency: Omani rial
Economy type: middle income
Labour force in agriculture: 50%**

*1994
**1992

Ethnic composition
The great majority of the population is Arab but there are also substantial Iranian, Baluchi, Indo-Pakistan, and East African minorities. The official language is Arabic but English is generally used in commercial transactions.

Religions
Islam is the state religion and about 75% of the population is Ibadi Muslim and the rest Sunni Muslim.

Political features
State type: absolutist
Date of state formation: 1951
Political structure: unitary
Executive: absolute
Assembly: there is no elected assembly
Party structure: none
Human rights rating: 49%
International affiliations: AL, AMF, DDS, GCC, IBRD, IMF, IWC, NAM, OIC, UN

Local and regional government
The country is divided into 41 provinces, or *wilayats*, each under the control of a provincial governor, or *wali*, appointed by the sultan.

Head of state and head of government
Sultan Qaboos bin Said, since 1970

Political leaders since 1970
1970– Sultan Qaboos bin Said

Political system
Oman has no written constitution and the sultan has absolute power, ruling by decree, but assisted by an appointed cabinet. There is no democratic assembly as such but he takes advice from an appointed cabinet. There is an advisory Consultative Council (Majlis) of 59 appointed members, taken from a list of candidates chosen by notables, provincial governors, and sheikhs.

Political parties
There are no political parties.

Latest elections
No free elections are held.

Political history
As Muscat and Oman, the country had a very close relationship with Britain, being under its protection from the 19th century. When its complete independence was recognized in 1951, as the Sultanate of Oman, the two countries signed a Treaty of Friendship. Said bin Taimur, who had been sultan since 1932 and whose dynasty went back to the 18th century, was overthrown by his son, Qaboos bin Said (b. 1940), in a bloodless coup in 1970. With the economy boosted by exploitation of vast oil reserves from the late 1960s, Qaboos bin Said embarked on a much more liberal and expansionist policy than that of his conservative father. Oman benefits from its natural wealth but conflicts in

neighbouring countries, such as Yemen, Iran, Iraq, and Afghanistan, have not only emphasized the country's strategic importance but put its own security at risk. The sultan has tried to follow a path of nonalignment, maintaining close ties with the United States and other NATO countries. Like most Middle East states in recent years, Oman has had to deal with militant Islamic extremists, seeking to destabilize the regime.

QATAR

State of Qatar
Dawlat Qatar

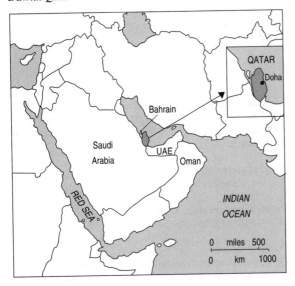

Capital: Doha

Social and economic data
Area: 11,440 km²
Population: 500,000*
Pop. density per km²: 44*
Urban population: 79%**
Literacy rate: 51%**
GDP: $6,673 million**; per-capita GDP: $15,140**
Government defence spending (% of GDP): 4.4%**
Currency: Qatar riyal
Economy type: high income
Labour force in agriculture: 3%**

*1994
**1992

Ethnic composition
Only about 25% of the population are indigenous Qataris, 40% being Arabs, and the others Pakistanis, Indians, and Iranians. The official language is Arabic but English is generally used in commercial transactions.

Religions
Islam is the state religion. Most people (98%) are Sunni Muslims of the strict Wahhabi persuasion.

Political features
State type: absolutist
Date of state formation: 1971
Political structure: unitary
Executive: absolute
Assembly: there is no assembly
Party structure: none
Human rights rating: N/A
International affiliations: AL, AMF, DDS, GCC, IAEA, IBRD, IMF, NAM, OAPEC, OIC, OPEC, UN

Local and regional government
Local government is the overall responsibility of the Minister of Municipal Affairs. Each of the largest towns has a partly elected and partly appointed municipal council.

Head of state and head of government
Emir Sheikh Hamad bin Khalifa al-Thani, since 1995

Political leaders since 1970
1949–72 Sheikh Ahmad al-Thani, 1972–95 Sheikh Khalifa bin Hamad al-Thani, 1995– Sheikh Hamad bin Khalifa al-Thani

Political system
A provisional constitution adopted in 1970 confirmed Qatar as an absolute monarchy, with the emir holding all executive and legislative powers. The emir appoints a Council of Ministers and lead them in the role of prime minister. There is a 30-member Advisory Council, with limited powers to question ministers.

Political parties
There are no political parties in the state.

Latest elections
There is no constitutional machinery for elections.

Political history
Formerly part of the Turkish Ottoman Empire, Qatar was evacuated by the Turks in 1914 and the British government gave formal recognition in 1916 to Sheikh Abdullah al-Thani as its ruler, guaranteeing protection in return for an influence over the country's external affairs.

In 1968 Britain announced its intention of withdrawing its forces from the Persian Gulf area by 1981 and Qatar decided to try to form an association with other Gulf states. Terms could not be agreed, however, and on 1 September 1971 the country became fully independent. A new Treaty of Friendship with Britain was signed to replace the former arrangements.

In the meantime the ruler, Sheikh Ahmad, had announced a provisional constitution which would provide for a partially elected consultative assembly, while retaining ultimate power in the emir's hands. However, in 1972, while Sheikh Ahmad was out of the country, his cousin the crown prince Sheikh Khalifa, who held the post of prime minister, led a bloodless coup and declared himself emir. He embarked upon an ambitious programme of social and economic reform, curbing the extravagances of the royal family. An

Advisory Council was appointed, in accordance with the 1970 constitution, and its membership was expanded in 1975.

Mineral-rich Qatar has had good relations with most of its neighbours and is regarded as one of the more stable and moderate Arab states, although there have been recent territorial disputes with Bahrain and Saudi Arabia. In 1990–91 it joined the United Nations' coalition forces against Iraq in the Gulf War.

In June 1995, in another bloodless coup, Sheikh Khalifa bin Hamad al-Thani was ousted by his son, the Crown prince and defence minister Sheikh Hamad bin Khalifa al-Thani.

SAUDI ARABIA

The Kingdom of Saudi Arabia
al-Mamlaka al-'Arabiya as-Sa'udiya

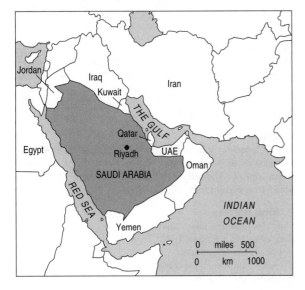

Capital: Riyadh

Social and economic data
Area: 2,150,000 km^2
Population: 16,500,000*
Pop. density per km^2: 8*
Urban population: 74%**
Literacy rate: 62%**
GDP: $126,000 million**; per-capita GDP: $7,942**
Government defence spending (% of GDP): 13.1%**
Currency: riyal
Economy type: high income
Labour force in agriculture: 48%**

*1994
**1992

Ethnic composition
About 90% of the population is Arab and 10% Afro-Asian. Arabic is the official language and widely spoken.

Religions
Islam is the state religion. The great majority of the population, 92%, is Sunni Muslim, chiefly of the Wahhabi sect, and the rest is Shia Muslim. Saudi Arabia is the centre of Islam, containing the two holiest places, Mecca and Medina.

Political features
State type: absolutist
Date of state formation: 1932
Political structure: unitary
Executive: absolute
Assembly: there is no elected assembly
Party structure: none
Human rights rating: 29%
International affiliations: AL, AMF, DDS, GCC, IAEA, IBRD, IMF, NAM, OAPEC, OIC, OPEC, UN

Local and regional government
The country is divided into 14 provinces which are subdivided into districts and subdistricts. Each province is administered by a governor general, each district by a governor, and each subdistrict by a headman. There are provincial councils whose members are elected by tribal chiefs.

Head of state and head of government
King Fahd Ibn Abdul Aziz al-Saud, since 1982

Political leaders since 1970
1964–75 King Faisal, 1975–82 King Khalid, 1982– King Fahd

Political system
Saudi Arabia is an absolute monarchy with no written constitution, no assembly, and no political parties. The king rules, in accordance with the ancient law of Islam, by decree. He appoints and heads a Council of Ministers (cabinet) whose decisions are the result of a majority vote, but always subject to the ultimate sanction of the king. The formation of a 60-member Consultative Council (Majlis al-Shura) in 1992, to be appointed every four years in accordance with the Islamic principle of 'consultation', suggested that tentative steps were being taken towards a more democratic form of government. In addition, in 1992 a law was passed limiting ministers to four years in office.

Political parties
There are no political parties.

Latest elections
There is no provision for free elections.

Political history
Originally part of the Turkish Ottoman Empire, modern Saudi Arabia is almost entirely the creation of King Ibn Saud (1880–1953), a Wahhabi who, after the dissolution of the Ottoman Empire in 1918, fought rival Arab rulers until in 1926 he had established himself as the undisputed King of the Hejaz and Sultan of Nejd (central Arabia). Six years later this area became the United Kingdom of Saudi Arabia. Oil was discovered in the late 1930s and commercially exploited from the 1940s, providing the basis of the country's great prosperity.

King Ibn Saud died in 1953 and was succeeded by his eldest son, Saud Ibn Abdul Aziz (1902–69). During King Saud's reign relations between Saudi Arabia and Egypt became strained and criticisms of the king within the royal family grew to such an extent that in November 1964 he was forced to abdicate in favour of his brother, Crown Prince Faisal Ibn Abdul Aziz (1904–75). Under King Faisal, Saudi Arabia became an influential leader among Arab oil producers.

In 1975 King Faisal was assassinated by one of his nephews and his half-brother, Khalid Ibn Abdul Aziz (1913–82), who had been made crown prince, succeeded him. Khalid was in failing health and found it increasingly necessary to rely on his other brother, Crown Prince Fahd (b. 1923), to perform the duties of government, so that he became the country's effective ruler. Saudi Arabia had by now become the most influential country in the Arab world, giving financial support to Iraq in its war with Iran and drawing up proposals for a permanent settlement of the Arab–Israeli dispute.

King Khalid died suddenly of a heart attack in 1982 and was succeeded by Fahd, his half-brother Abdullah becoming crown prince and his full brother, Prince Sultan, defence minister.

Saudi Arabia made an enormous financial contribution to the 1991 Gulf War against Iraq, as well as providing a base for allied operations.

In October 1994 the king announced the appointment of a Higher Council for Islamic Affairs, as an 'ombudsman of Islamic activity in educational, economic and foreign policy', and in August 1995 a major cabinet reshuffle was effected, bringing in 15 new faces. The latter were chiefly technocrats and included six members of the consultative Majlis al-Shura. However, the key defence, foreign affairs, and interior ministries remained firmly in the hands of royal princes. King Fahd has also instituted a gradually evolving policy of privatization.

SYRIA

Syrian Arab Republic
al-Jumhuriya al-'Arabiya as-Suriya

Capital: Damascus (Dimashq)

Social and economic data
Area: 184,050 km^2
Population: 13,800,000*
Pop. density per km^2: 75*
Urban population: 51%**
Literacy rate: 65%**
GDP: $14,234 million**; per-capita GDP: $1,070**
Government defence spending (% of GDP): 8.6%**
Currency: Syrian pound
Economy type: middle income
Labour force in agriculture: 30%**

*1994
**1992

Ethnic composition
More than 90% of the population are Arabs but there are enormous differences between them in language and regional affiliations and, to a lesser extent, religion. There are also differences between the settled and nomadic people. The official language is Arabic, with Kurdish as a minority tongue.

Religions
The great majority of people (90%) are Sunni Muslims, but Islam is not the state religion. The constitution merely says 'Islam shall be the religion of the head of state'. There are Shia Muslim and Druze minorities.

Political features
State type: nationalistic socialist
Date of state formation: 1946
Political structure: unitary
Executive: unlimited presidential
Assembly: one-chamber
Party structure: one-party
Human rights rating: 30%
International affiliations: AL, AMF, BADEA, DDS, G-24, IAEA, IBRD, IMF, NAM, OAPEC, OIC, UN

Local and regional government
The country is divided into 13 provinces which are further subdivided into administrative districts, localities, and villages. There are elected provincial assemblies and district and village councils.

Head of state and head of government
President Hafez al-Assad, since 1971

Political leaders since 1970
1970–   Hafez al-Assad (Ba'ath Arab Socialist Party)

Political system
The 1973 constitution provides for a president elected by universal adult suffrage, through a simple plurality voting system, for a seven-year term. The president is head of state,

head of government, secretary general of the Ba'ath Arab Socialist Party, and president of the National Progressive Front, the umbrella organization for five socialist parties which dominate the country's politics. Syria is therefore, in reality, if not in a strictly legal sense, a one-party state. There is a single-chamber 250-member assembly, the National People's Assembly (Majlis al-Sha'ab), also elected by universal adult suffrage, by simple plurality voting, for a four-year term. The president appoints vice presidents and governs with a prime minister and Council of Ministers whom he or she also appoints.

Political parties

Since 1972 political groups have operated as a single party under the name of the National Progressive Front.

Syria has a long history of left-wing politics and the National Progressive Front includes the Communist Party of Syria, a pro-Soviet party established in 1924, the Arab Socialist Party, the Arab Socialist Unionist Party, the Syrian Arab Socialist Union Party, and the Ba'ath Arab Socialist Party, which is the hub of the organization. It dates from 1947 and is the result of a merger of the Arab Revival Movement and the Arab Ba'ath Party, both of which were founded in 1940. The National Progressive Front has a pro-Arab socialist orientation.

Latest elections

The results of the August 1994 elections for the Majlis al-Sha'ab were as follows:

	Seats
National Progressive Front	167
Independents	83

Political history

Syria was part of the Turkish Ottoman Empire until 1918 and came under French control in 1920 as a result of a secret treaty, the Sykes–Picot Agreement, concluded by two British and French diplomats, Sir Mark Sykes and Georges Picot. They agreed the partitioning of the Turkish Empire, identifying the respective spheres of influence of Britain and France in the Middle East and North Africa. As part of the deal, France was given a free hand in Syria.

The Syrians resented the French occupation and there were several revolts in the 1920s and 1930s. As the Second World War II loomed, the government in Paris changed its policy, against the wishes of the French army in Syria, and promised independence. This was proclaimed in 1944 but, because of the reluctance of French officers to relinquish power, full independence did not come until 1946. There followed a period of military dictatorship and a series of coups. In 1958 Syria merged with Egypt, to become the United Arab Republic (UAR), but in 1961, following another army coup, it seceded and an independent Syrian Arab Republic was established.

In 1963 a government was formed mainly from members of the Arab Socialist Renaissance (Ba'ath) Party but three years later it was removed in another coup by the army. In 1970 the moderate wing of the Ba'ath Party, led by Lieutenant General Hafez al-Assad (b. 1928), seized power in yet another bloodless coup and in the following year Assad was elected president. Soon afterwards he formed the five main political parties into one broad group, under his leadership, as the National Progressive Front.

Since then President Assad has remained in office without any serious challenges to his leadership. In 1983 he was reported to have suffered a heart attack but recovered in an apparently weakened condition. This event aroused speculation about his possible successor but no specific name emerged.

Externally Syria has, under President Assad, played a leading role in Middle East affairs. In the Arab–Israeli Six-Day War of 1967 it lost territory to Israel and after the Yom Kippur War of 1973 Israel formally annexed the Golan Heights, which had previously been part of Syria. During 1976 Assad progressively intervened in the civil war in Lebanon, eventually committing some 50,000 troops to the operations. Relations between Syria and Egypt cooled after President Sadat's Israel peace initiative in 1977 and the subsequent Camp David agreement, but were restored in 1989.

Assad's authority was made evident in 1985 when he secured the release of 39 US hostages from an aircraft hijacked by the extremist Shia group Hizbollah ('Party of God') and he played a significant part in securing the release of Western hostages in Lebanon. The return of Lebanon to a degree of normality was very much the product of the actions of Assad, who sent in Syrian forces in 1990 to defeat the Lebanese Christian militia of Michel Aoun. His contribution to the defeat of his old rival, Saddam Hussein, when Syria supported the American-led United Nations military coalition against Iraq in the 1991 Gulf War, was also significant.

Formerly an international pariah as a result of its alleged sponsorship of terrorism, Syria's relations with the Western world, and particularly the United States, progressed positively during 1993 and 1994, into 1995. Prospects for an Israeli withdrawal from the Golan Heights were also improved after US-sponsored talks and a summit meeting in Alexandria between the presidents of Egypt and Syria and King Fahd of Saudi Arabia. Assad was re-elected for a fourth term as president in 1991 and, since the collapse of the Soviet Union, which used to be Syria's most important trading partner, has introduced a number of economic reforms to encourage investment and stimulate growth.

TUNISIA

Republic of Tunisia
al-Jumhuriya at-Tunisiya

Capital: Tunis

Social and economic data
Area: 164,150 km^2
Population: 8,600,000*
Pop. density per km^2: 52*
Urban population: 57%**
Literacy rate: 65%**

GDP: $12,417 million**; per-capita GDP: $1,444**
Government defence spending (% of GDP): 3.5%**
Currency: Tunisian dinar
Economy type: middle income
Labour force in agriculture: 22%**

*1994
**1992

Ethnic composition
About 10% of the population is pure Arab, the remainder being of Berber–Arab stock. There are small Jewish and French communities. The official language is Arabic but French is also widely spoken.

Religions
Islam is the state religion and about 99% of the population is Sunni Muslim. There are also Jewish and Christian (Roman Catholic) minorities.

Political features
State type: emergent democratic
Date of state formation: 1956
Political structure: unitary
Executive: limited presidential
Assembly: one-chamber
Party structure: effectively one-party
Human rights rating: 60%
International affiliations: AL, AMF, AMU, IAEA, IBRD, IMF, NAM, OAU, OIC, UN, WTO

Local and regional government
The country is divided into 23 governorates which are further subdivided into delegations and sectors, all administered by appointed officials. Municipalities are more democratically governed by elected councils.

Head of state and head of government
President Zine el-Abidine Ben Ali, since 1987

Political leaders since 1970
1956–87 Habib Bourguiba (PSD), 1987– Zine el-Abidine Ben Ali (PSD)

Political system
A new constitution was adopted in 1959, providing for a president who is both head of state and head of government, elected by universal adult suffrage through a simple plurality voting system for a five-year term and eligible for re-election. In 1985 Habib Bourguiba was made President for Life by the National Assembly, but in 1988 his successor announced a number of important constitutional changes. They included the abolition of the post of President for Life; a limitation on the presidency to a maximum of three five-year terms; the maximum age for presidential candidates to be set at 70; and the minimum age for assembly candidates to be reduced from 28 to 25. There is a single-chamber National Assembly of 163 members, serving a five-year term. One hundred and forty-four are elected by simple plurality voting and 19 seats are reserved for parties which did not win a majority in each of the country's 25 constituencies. This procedure was introduced in 1993 so as to ensure that there is always an opposition in the National Assembly. The president governs through an appointed Council of Minister, led by a prime minister.

Political parties
In 1963 Tunisia became a one-party state, the party being the Destourien Socialist Party (PSD), led by President Habib Bourguiba. Since 1981, however, additional parties have been officially recognized.

The PSD was formed in 1934 as a splinter group from the old Destour (Constitution) Party. It was renamed the Constitutional Democratic Rally (RDC) in 1988 and has a moderate, nationalistic socialist orientation. It continues to dominate the political scene but President Ben Ali has warned his followers to prepare themselves to operate in a more pluralistic system.

There are now some seven active political parties. The Movement of Democratic Socialists (MDS), the excommunist Renovation Movement (MR) and the banned radical Islamic Renaissance Party (al-Nahda) are the chief opposition parties.

Latest elections
In the March 1994 presidential election, Zine el-Abidine Ben Ali was re-elected as the only candidate, with more than 99% of the votes cast.

In the March 1994 National Assembly elections, the RCD won all 144 of the seats contested on the usual simple-majority list basis. The other 19 seats were distributed between six smaller parties and independents who came second in the national poll.

Political history
After being subjected to rule by Phoenicians, Carthaginians, Romans, Byzantines, Arabs, Spaniards, and Turks, Tunisia came under French control in 1883. After World War I an independence movement began to grow and in 1934 the Destourien Socialist Party (PSD) was founded by Habib

Bourguiba (b. 1903) to lead the campaign. Tunisia was granted internal self-government in 1955 and full independence in 1956, with Bourguiba as prime minister. A year later the monarchy was abolished and Tunisia became a republic, with Bourguiba as president.

A new constitution was adopted in 1959 and the first National Assembly was elected. Between 1963 and 1981 the Destourien Socialist Party (PSD) was the only legally recognized party but since that date others have been allowed to operate. President Bourguiba followed a distinctive line in foreign policy, establishing close links with the Western powers, including the United States, but joining other Arab states in condemning the US-inspired Egypt–Israeli treaty. He also allowed the Palestine Liberation Organization (PLO) to use Tunis for its headquarters from 1982. This led to an Israeli attack in 1985 which strained relations with the United States. Relations with Libya also deteriorated to such an extent that diplomatic links were severed in 1985.

Bourguiba ruled his country firmly and paternalistically and his long period in Tunisian politics made him a national legend, evidenced by the elaborate mausoleum which has been built in anticipation of his eventual departure. In November 1987, however, his younger colleagues became impatient and staged an internal coup, declaring him 'mentally and physically unfit for office' and forcing him to retire at the age of 84. The former prime minister, Zine el-Abidine Ben Ali (b. 1936), replaced him as president and chair of the ruling PSD and Hedi Baccouche was appointed prime minister. After taking up supreme office Ben Ali moved quickly to establish his own distinctive policy line and style. His new government showed itself to be more tolerant of opposition than Bourguiba's and in December 1987 over 2,000 political prisoners were granted an amnesty. They included 608 members of the fundamentalist Islamic Tendency Movement (MTI). As a further indication of greater liberalization, the unpopular State Security Court, established during Bourguiba's regime, was disbanded and there have been some moves towards privatization in the economy. In 1988 Ben Ali changed the PSD's name to the Constitutional Democratic Rally (RDC) and tightened his personal control of it by appointing two-thirds of the membership of its Central Committee. Despite competition from opposition parties, the RDC won virtually all the National Assembly seats in the 1994 elections.

The greater liberality in Tunisia in recent years has given encouragement to fundamentalists to flex their muscles, although their political vehicle, the Renaissance Party, is banned. Like other Middle East states, Tunisia has had to deal with the sometimes violent activities of Islamic militants.

UNITED ARAB EMIRATES

al-Imarat al-'Arabiya al-Muttahida

Capital: Abu Dhabi

Social and economic data
Area: 77,700 km^2
Population: 1,700,000*

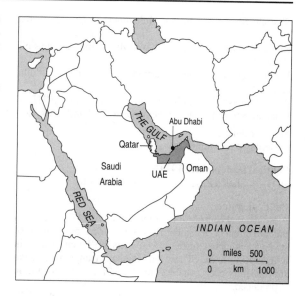

Pop. density per km^2: 22*
Urban population: 82%**
Literacy rate: 54%**
GDP: $32,813 million**; per-capita GDP: $19,300**
Currency: UAE dirham
Economy type: high income
Labour force in agriculture: 5%**

*1994
**1992

Ethnic composition
The Emirates have a very mixed population, including many immigrants. About 75% are Iranians, Indians, or Pakistanis and only about 25% Arabs. Arabic is the main language.

Religions
Sunni Islam is the state religion and it is almost universally followed.

Political features
State type: absolutist
Date of state formation: 1971
Political structure: federal
Executive: absolute
Assembly: there is no elected assembly
Party structure: none
Human rights rating: N/A
International affiliations: AL, AMF, DDS, GCC, IAEA, IBRD, IMF, NAM, OAPEC, OIC, OPEC, UN, WTO

Local and regional government
The country is a federation of seven self-governing emirates, each with its own absolute ruler.

Head of state and head of government
President Sheikh Zayed Bin Sultan al-Nahayan, since 1971

Supreme council of rulers
Abu Dhabi: **Sheikh Zayed Bin Sultan al-Nahayan, since 1966
Dubai: *Sheikh Maktoum Bin Rashid al-Maktoum, since 1990

Sharjah: Sheikh Sultan Bin Muhammad al-Quasimi, since 1972
Ras al-Khaimah: Sheikh Saqr Bin Muhammad al-Quasimi, since 1948
Umm al-Qaiwain: Sheikh Rashid Bin Ahmad al-Mu'alla, since 1981
Ajman: Sheikh Humaid Bin Rashid al-Nuami, since 1981
Fujairah: Sheikh Hamad Bin Muhammad al-Sharqi, since 1974

*Prime minister
**Deputy prime minister

Political leaders since 1970
1971–   Sheikh Zayed Bin Sultan al-Nahayan

Political system
A provisional constitution for the United Arab Emirates was put into effect in December 1971. It provided for the union of seven sheikhdoms, formerly known as the Trucial States, in a federal structure. These provisional arrangements have subsequently been extended, until a permanent constitution is produced.

In accordance with the provisional constitution, the highest authority is the Supreme Council of Rulers which includes the sheikhs of all the emirates. The Council elects two of its members to be president and vice president of the federal state. The president then appoints a prime minister and Council of Ministers. There is a federal National Council of 40 members appointed by the emirates for a two-year term and this operates as a consultative assembly. Each of the rulers is a hereditary emir and an absolute monarch in their own country.

Political parties
There are no political parties.

Latest elections
There are no popularly elected bodies.

Political history
The British government signed treaties with the sultans and sheikhs of seven emirates on the southern shores of the Persian Gulf and the Gulf of Oman during the 19th century and, from 1892, became responsible for their defence. Collectively, they were called the Trucial States. In 1952, on British advice, they set up a Trucial Council, consisting of all seven rulers, with a view to eventually establishing a federation.

In the 1960s they became very wealthy through the exploitation of oil deposits and, believing that they were now strong enough to stand alone, and as part of a policy of disengagement from overseas commitments, in 1968 the British government announced that it was withdrawing its forces within three years.

The seven Trucial States, with Bahrain and Qatar, formed a Federation of Arab Emirates, which was intended to become a federal state, but in 1971 Bahrain and Qatar decided to secede and become independent nations. Six of the Trucial States then agreed to combine to form the United Arab Emirates which came into being in December 1971. The remaining sheikhdom, Ras al-Khaimah, joined in February 1972. Sheikh Zayed, the ruler of Abu Dhabi, became the first president.

In 1976 Sheikh Zayed, disappointed with the slow progress towards centralization, announced that he would not accept another five-year term as president. He was persuaded to continue, however, with assurances that the federal government would be given more control over such activities as defence and internal security. In recent years the United Arab Emirates have played an increasingly important role in Middle East affairs and during the liberation of Kuwait in the 1991 Gulf War, losing 17 UAE nationals in the process. In 1987 diplomatic relations with Egypt were resumed and Sheikh Zayed paid an official visit to Cairo during which he signed a trade treaty between the two countries.

The collapse of the Bank of Credit and Commerce International (BCCI) in 1991 was estimated to have cost the UAE $10 billion. The government was highly critical of the Bank of England's role in the affair.

YEMEN

Republic of Yemen
al-Jamhuriya al-Yamaniya

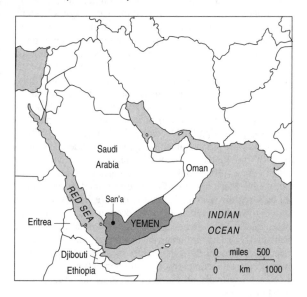

Capital: San'a (political), Aden (economic and commercial)

Social and economic data
Area: 540,000 km²
Population: 13,000,000*
Pop. density per km²: 26*
Urban population: 31%**
Literacy rate: 39%**
GDP: $6,746 million**; per-capita GDP: $540**
Government defence spending (% of GDP): 2.5%**
Currency: rial (north), dinar (south); both are legal currency throughout the country
Economy type: low income
Labour force in agriculture: 63%**

*1994
**1992

Ethnic composition

Until the departure of Yemenite Jews for Israel in 1948, they were the predominant ethnic group in the country. Now most of the population are Arabs. Arabic is the main language.

Religions

Most of the population are Muslims, divided roughly equally between the Sunni (54%) and Zaidist Shia (46%) orders. Islam is the state religion.

Political features

State type: emergent democratic
Date of state formation: 1990
Political structure: unitary
Executive: limited presidential
Assembly: one-chamber
Party structure: multiparty
Human rights rating: 49%
International affiliations: AL, AMF, IAEA, IBRD, IMF, NAM, OIC, UN

Local and regional government

The country is divided into 38 provinces and then further subdivided into districts and villages. There are appointed governors at the higher levels and traditional village headmen.

Head of state and head of government

President Ali Abdullah Saleh, since 1990

Political leaders since 1970

North Yemen: 1967–74 Abdur Rahman al-Iriani (Republican), 1974–77 Ibrahim al-Hamadi (military), 1977–78 Ahmed ibn Hussein al-Ghashmi (military), 1978–90 Ali Abdullah Saleh (GPC)

South Yemen: 1969–78 Salim Rubayi Ali (NF), 1978–80 Abdul Fattah Ismail (YSP), 1980–86 Ali Nasser Muhammad (YSP), 1986–90 Haider Abu Bakr al-Attas (YSP)

United Yemen: 1990–   Ali Abdullah Saleh (GPC)

Political system

The Republic of Yemen was founded on 22 May 1990, when North and South Yemen were united. A constitution was approved in May 1991, providing for a 301-member assembly, the House of Representatives, and a five-member Presidential Council. The constitution underwent major revision in September 1994, when the Presidential Council was abolished and a president, directly elected by universal suffrage, was instituted. The amended constitution defines the state as a multiparty democracy, with a market-based economy and Islamic sharia law as the source of all legislation. The assembly is also elected by universal suffrage and it and the president serve five-year terms, the president's term being renewable once only. The president appoints a Council of Ministers.

Political parties

Over 30 political parties were legalized after the publication of the draft constitution in December 1989, and out of these there emerged three main regionally based groupings: the General People's Congress (GPC), the Yemen Socialist Party (YSP), and the Yemen Reform Group (al-Islah).

The GPC is the power base of President Saleh and, with its main following in the north of the country, it has a left-of-centre orientation.

The southern-based YSP is the power base of Ali Salim al-Bid, who was the president of South Yemen before unification. It has a left-wing traditionally Marxist orientation.

Al-Islah was formed in 1990 as a coalition of the Muslim Brotherhood and the pro-Saudi tribal confederation of the north. It has a right-of-centre orientation.

Latest elections

The results of the April 1993 general election were as follows:

	Seats
GPC	121
al-Islah	62
YSP	56
Other parties	62

Political history

The Yemen Arab Republic, or North Yemen, was under Turkish rule from 1517 to 1918, when it secured its independence. The Imam Yahya became king and remained monarch until he was assassinated in 1948. His son, Imam Ahmad, succeeded him and ruled in what can best be described as a sadistic fashion, keeping the country isolated and backward, until he was deposed in a military coup in 1962.

The kingdom of Yemen was then renamed the Yemen Arab Republic (YAR), provoking a civil war between royalist forces, assisted by Saudi Arabia, and republicans, supported by Egypt. By 1967 the republicans, under Marshal Abdullah al-Sallal, had won. Later that year Sallal was deposed while on a foreign visit and a Republican Council took over.

Meanwhile, Britain had withdrawn from South Yemen and, with the installation of a repressive regime there, hundreds of thousands of South Yemenis fled to the YAR, many of them forming guerrilla groups with the aim of overthrowing the communist regime in South Yemen. This resulted in a war between the two Yemens from 1971 until 1972, when, under the auspices of the Arab League, a cease-fire was arranged. Both sides agreed to a union of the two countries but the agreement was not implemented.

In 1974 the pro-Saudi Colonel Ibrahim al-Hamadi seized power in North Yemen and by 1975 there were rumours of a possible attempt to restore the monarchy. In 1977 al-Hamadi was assassinated and another member of the Military Command Council, which al-Hamadi had set up in 1974, Colonel Ahmed ibn Hussein al-Ghashmi, took over. In 1978 a gradual move towards a more constitutional form of government was started, with the creation of an appointed Constituent People's Assembly, the dissolution of the Military Command Council and the installation of al-Ghashmi as president. In 1978, however, he was killed when a bomb exploded in a suitcase carried by an envoy from South Yemen.

This incident worsened relations between the two Yemens and war broke out once more. The Arab League again intervened to arrange a cease-fire and for the second time the two countries agreed to unite. This time, however, definite progress was made so that by 1983 a joint Yemen Council was meeting at six-monthly intervals.

In 1983 President Ali Abdullah Saleh (b. 1942) of North Yemen submitted his resignation to the Assembly, as his term of office neared its end. His resignation was refused and he was re-elected for a further five years. In 1988 his presidency was extended to a third term.

In the aftermath of the 1978 killing of al-Ghashmi, the president of South Yemen, Rubayi Ali, was deposed and executed. Two days later the three political parties in South Yemen agreed to merge to form a 'Marxist–Leninist vanguard party', the Yemen Socialist Party (YSP), and Abdul Fattah Ismail became its secretary general. In December Ismail was appointed head of state but four months later resigned, on the grounds of ill health. He subsequently went into exile and was succeeded by Ali Nasser Muhammad.

Meanwhile, in 1985 Ali Nasser Muhammad was re-elected secretary general of the YSP and its Political Bureau for another five years. He soon began taking steps to remove his opponents, his personal guard shooting and killing three Bureau members. This act of violence led to a short civil war and the eventual dismissal of Ali Nasser from all of his posts in the party and the government. A new administration was formed, with Haidar Abu Bakr al-Attas as president, chair of the Presidium of the Supreme People's Council, and secretary general of the YSP Political Bureau.

A more conciliatory climate had been created in the South and the new government, influenced by the loss of economic aid from the fast disintegrating Soviet Union, immediately committed itself to continuing the process of eventual union with the economically more prosperous YAR. In November 1987 the presidents of the two Yemens met for talks and in March 1988 a joint committee on foreign policy sat for the first time in Aden. A draft constitution for the two Yemens was published in December 1989, providing for a multiparty system of government, and in January 1990 the border between the two states was opened to allow free movement from both sides.

In May 1990 the new Republic of Yemen was established and the General People's Congress (GPC), of the north, led by Ali Abdullah Saleh, and the Yemen Socialist Party (YSP), of the south, led by Ali Salim al-Bid, formed an alliance. In the light of the history of disputes between the two formerly separate states, the unification process had been remarkably smooth, but Yemen's economy was fragile, particularly the south which had suffered from central planning, and its stability was severely threatened during the 1991 Gulf War, when its leaders opposed the US-led operations against Iraq. The first free elections in April 1993 resulted in the GPC winning most assembly seats, but not an overall majority. As a result, a three-party coalition government was established, with Saleh as president, al-Bid, vice president, and the former president of South Yemen, Haider Abu Bakr al-Attas, prime minister.

The general election was soon overshadowed by differences between the former north and south leaders, neither apparently willing to make concessions to the other. Soon after the elections al-Bid visited the United States, to consult with his opposite number, Al Gore, without discussing the matter with President Saleh. On his return al-Bid retired to his southern stronghold, refusing even to attend elections for the Presidential Council.

These incidents were symptomatic of a deeper-seated distrust which became so acute that by April 1994 civil war had broken out, with a new southern state, the Democratic Republic of Yemen (DRY), being proclaimed in May 1994. However, within two months the northern forces of President Saleh had inflicted a crushing defeat on those of the south. Saleh was magnanimous in victory and al-Bid fled into exile, where he headed a National Opposition Front.

In September 1994 Saleh introduced major constitutional changes, consolidating his own party's position, and in October formed a new two-party coalition with al-Islah. The cabinet was chaired by Prime Minister Abdel Aziz Abdel Ghani (GPC), with three other GPC members and one al-Islah member as his deputies. Having firmly secured his place, Saleh himself was re-elected president in October 1994.

North America

The northern half of the continent of America encompasses a vast region of over 19 million square kilometres, more than five times the size of Northern and Western Europe, or almost 15% of the world's surface. Despite this areal size, its inhabitants constitute only about 5% of the world population and it contains only two nation-states, Canada and the United States of America.

Geographically and climatically, it is a region of great contrasts and extremes. Parts of northern Canada and Alaska are well within the Arctic Circle while southern Florida is only a few degrees north of the Tropic of Cancer. The two countries share an enormous coastline, which includes the Arctic, Atlantic, and Pacific oceans, within which are the Bering Sea, the Beaufort Sea, Hudson Bay, and the Gulf of Mexico.

Although the overall population density of the region is low, there are areas of considerable concentration, for example, 25 United States cities have populations of 0.5 million or more, seven have in excess of 1 million, and New York contains more than 7 million people. Canada, with a much smaller population than its neighbour, does not display equivalent concentrations, but its two largest cities, Toronto and Vancouver, have populations of nearly 3 million and more than 1 million respectively.

North America is a markedly 'high-income' region, in fact the two countries which occupy it enjoy, between them, 29% of the world's annually created wealth. It follows naturally from this that Canadian and United States citizens experience very high living standards compared with most other people in the world.

Although the region was originally peopled by Native Americans and Inuit, the majority of today's inhabitants trace their histories back to European beginnings. Both Canada and the United States were once British colonies, Canada remaining a dependency, in one form or another, for over 280 years, while some of the states on the US eastern seaboard experienced colonial rule for about 200 years before violently winning their independence. Britain, however, was not the only European power to place its imprint on the region. France and Spain also vied for control, usually to secure a commercial advantage. Reminders of this early European exploit-ation are found in the French-speaking parts of Canada, in the southern states of the United States, particularly Louisiana, and in the Spanish-speaking communities of states such as California and New Mexico.

This colonial experience has affected the political cultures and structures of the two countries, but in different ways. Canada has retained its allegiance to the British Crown and has adhered to parliamentary institutions, even to the extent of calling one chamber of its assembly the House of Commons. The United States, on the other hand, has less kind memories of the past and has resolutely sought to ensure that individual political and social liberties can never be usurped by an autocratic executive again. Both countries rank high in human rights ratings but these have been achieved through different political routes.

Both, however, have federal structures of government, a fact that reflects the size of each country and its ethnic and cultural diversity. Within these federal systems can be seen the strong sense of independence still felt by individual provinces and states, each jealous of its right to retain a unique identity within the overall national picture. Both countries can be proud of a long history of political stability. For example, neither has been troubled by a serious threat to its established democratic system for more than 100 years.

Relations between the two states sharing this half continent have generally been civilized and correct, rather than warm. Canada has always been conscious of being close to 'big brother' and has been suspicious of moves to 'Americanize' the Canadian way of life, culturally as well as economically. Realistically, however, Canadian political leaders have recognized the existence of common needs and goals and have been happy to join the United States in mutually beneficial endeavours, such as the North Atlantic Treaty Organization (NATO). At the same time, they have recognized that, as a 'superpower', indeed, with the demise of the Soviet Union, the world's sole remaining superpower, the United States' interests are far wider than Canada's could ever be, or they would want them to be. In recent years this recognition of the need to share the region in a constructive way has resurfaced in the shape of the 1989 free trade agreement between Canada and the United States. In 1992 it was expanded to include Mexico, and given the title the North American Free Trade Agreement (NAFTA). Its aim is to progressively create, over a 10–15 year period, a common market of some 375 million people and give the two northern states opportunities to invest in Mexico's low-wage economy.

Recommended reading

Bowles, N *The Government and Politics of the United States*, Macmillan, 1993

Derbyshire, I *Politics in the United States: From Carter to Bush*, W & R Chambers, 1990

Jackson, R J, Jackson, D and Baxter-Moore, N *Politics in Canada: Institutions, Behaviour and Public Policy*, Prentice-Hall, 1986

CANADA

Dominion of Canada

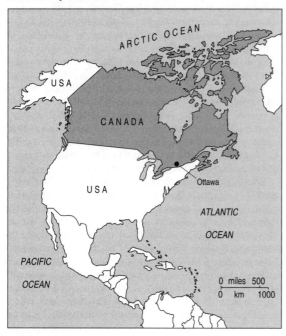

Capital: Ottawa

Social and economic data

Area: 9,970,610 km²
Population: 27,800,000*
Pop. density per km²: 3*
Urban population: 78%**
Literacy rate: 96%**
GDP: $566,000 million**; per-capita GDP: $20,320**
Government defence spending (% of GDP): 1.9%*
Currency: Canadian dollar
Economy type: high income
Labour force in agriculture: 5%*

*1994
**1992

Ethnic composition

About 45% of the population is of British origin, 29% French, 23% of other European stock, and about 3% indigenous Indians or Eskimos/Inuits, who, known now as the 'first nations', have pressed recently for a measure of self-government. The official languages are English and French.

Religions

There are about 11.2 million Roman Catholics, 900,000 Anglicans, 316,000 members of the Greek Orthodox Church, and 150,000 members of the Ukrainian Greek Orthodox Church.

Political features

State type: liberal democratic
Date of state formation: 1867
Political structure: federal
Executive: parliamentary
Assembly: two-chamber
Party structure: multiparty
Human rights rating: 94%
International affiliations: AG (observer), APEC, CSCE, CW, ESA (cooperating), G-7, G-10, IAEA, IBRD, IMF, NACC, NAFTA, NAM (guest), NATO, OAS, OECD, UN, WTO

Local and regional government

Canada is a federation of ten provinces: Alberta, British Columbia, Manitoba, New Brunswick, Newfoundland, Nova Scotia, Ontario, Prince Edward Island, Québec, and Saskatchewan, and two territories: Northwest Territories and Yukon. The provinces range in territorial size from Prince Edward Island, with 5,660 square kilometres, to Québec, with 3,246,389 square kilometres. Their populations vary from 122,506 for Prince Edward Island to 8,625,107 for Ontario. The size and populations of the territories are equally diverse. Yukon is the smaller, with 22,135 people within 531,844 square kilometres, compared with Northwest Territories, with 45,471 people spread over an area of 3,246,389 square kilometres.

Each province has a single-chamber assembly, popularly elected for a five-year term, and a premier who is appointed by the lieutenant-governor on the basis of support in the provincial assembly. Each premier heads an executive council.

North America: social, economic, and political data

Country	Area (sq km)	c. 1992–94 Population (m)	c. 1992–94 Pop. density per sq km	c. 1992 Adult literacy rate (%)	World ranking	Income type	c. 1991 Human rights rating (%)
Canada	9,970,610	27.800	3	96	52	high	94
United States	9,372,614	257.800	28	98	34	high	90
Total/average/range	19,343,224	285.600	15	96–98			90–94

Key:
SP	simple plurality	F	federal	Lib-dem	Liberal democratic	Lim-pres	Limited presidential

There is considerable decentralization from the federal government to the provincial governments, the respective powers being set out in the constitution, the former being essentially concerned with matters affecting the whole nation, and the latter purely provincial affairs.

Head of state
Queen Elizabeth II, represented by Governor General Ramon John Hnatyshyn since 1990

Head of government
Prime Minister Jean Chrétien, since 1993

Political leaders since 1970
1968–79 Pierre Trudeau (Liberal), 1979–80 Joe Clark (Progressive Conservative), 1980–84 Pierre Trudeau (Liberal), 1984 John Turner (Liberal), 1984–93 Brian Mulroney (Progressive Conservative), 1993– Jean Chrétien (Liberal), 1993 Kim Campbell (Progressive Conservative)

Political system
The constitution is based on five Acts of the British Parliament, the Quebec Act, 1774, the Constitutional Act, 1791, the Act of Union, 1840, the British North America Act, 1867, and the Canada Act, 1982. The British North America Act stated that the constitution should be similar in principle to that in Britain and the Canada Act gave Canada power to amend its constitution and added a Charter of Rights and Freedoms, to recognize the nation's multicultural background. Paradoxically, although Britain had always avoided adopting a written constitution for itself, it gave itself powers to prescribe for another sovereign state. The Canada Act therefore represented the formal ending of these powers and the guarantee of Canada's complete independence. Canada has, nevertheless, voluntarily retained the British monarch as a symbolic head of state and maintained its membership of the Commonwealth.

The federal parliament consists of two chambers, the Senate and the House of Commons. The 104 members of the Senate are appointed for life, or until the age of 75, by the governor general. They must be resident in the provinces they represent and, as persons of standing, are the equivalent of life peers in the British House of Lords. The House of Commons has 295 members elected by universal suffrage, through a simple plurality voting system. The federal prime minister is chosen by the governor general from the party which can command support in the House of Commons and, as in the British system, is accountable, with the cabinet, to the House of Commons. Parliament has a maximum life of five years but may be dissolved within that period. Again as in Britain, legislation must be passed by both chambers and then signed by the governor general.

Political parties
Of some 17 political parties, the most significant are the Progressive Conservative Party (PCP), the Liberal Party, the New Democratic Party (NDP), the Bloc Québécois, and the Reform Party.

The PCP was founded in 1854. In its earliest days it was staunchly pro-British, pro-Empire, and anti-American. It is now more internationalist and in closer harmony with its United States neighbour. It advocates individualism and free enterprise.

The Liberal Party of Canada developed in the late 19th century as the Canadian counterpart of the Liberal Party in Britain. It strongly supports the autonomy of Canada, the maintenance of universal welfare policies and freedom of trade, particularly within the continent of North America.

The NDP dates from 1961. Before then it was known as the Cooperative Commonwealth Federation, which had itself grown out of the United Farmers' Party and the Socialist Party of Canada. It has a moderate left-of-centre orientation and is a social democratic member of the Socialist International.

The Bloc Québécois was formed in 1990 as a Francophone separatist party, committed to independence for the French-speaking province of Québec. It is led in the federal parliament by Lucien Bouchard.

The Reform Party is a populist right-wing grouping, based largely in the western provinces.

Latest elections
In the 1993 House of Commons general election the results were as shown in the table on page 455.

Political history
Canada was discovered in 1497 by John Cabot (1425–1500), who thought he had found the route to China. In 1534

								Table 57
World ranking	Date of state formation	State structure	State type	Executive type	Number of assembly chambers	Party structure	Lower house electoral system	
15	1867	F	Lib-dem	Parliamentary	2	multi	SP	
21	1776	F	Lib-dem	Lim-pres	2	two	SP	

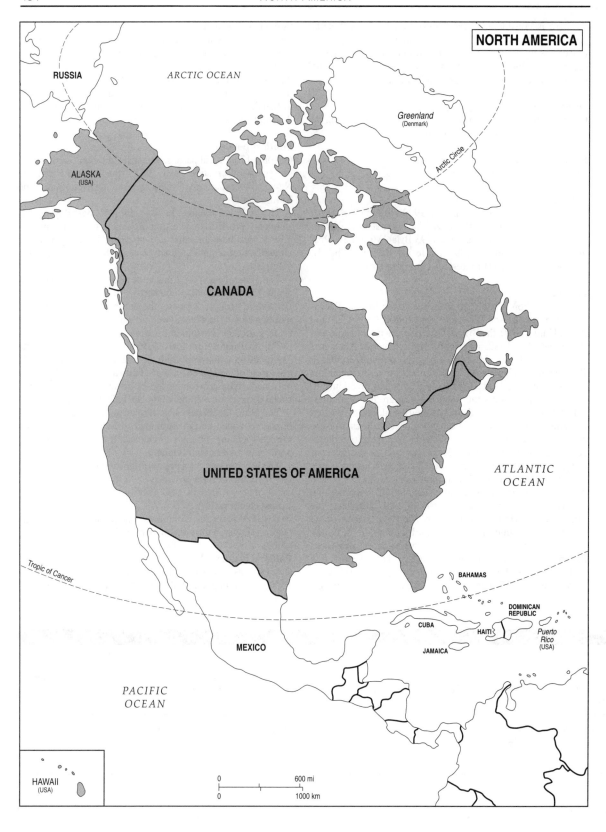

NORTH AMERICA

RUSSIA

ARCTIC OCEAN

Greenland
(Denmark)

Arctic Circle

ALASKA
(USA)

CANADA

ATLANTIC
OCEAN

UNITED STATES OF AMERICA

Tropic of Cancer

BAHAMAS

DOMINICAN
REPUBLIC

CUBA

HAITI

Puerto
Rico
(USA)

JAMAICA

MEXICO

PACIFIC
OCEAN

HAWAII
(USA)

0   600 mi
0   1000 km

	% votes	Seats
Liberals	41.6	177
Bloc Québécons	13.9	54
Reform Party	18.1	52
PCP	16.1	2
NDP	6.6	9

Jacques Cartier (1491–1557) landed and claimed the country for France and in 1583 Sir Humphrey Gilbert (1537–83) visited Newfoundland and claimed it for England. During the next two centuries both countries expanded their trading activities and colonization schemes, the rivalry inevitably leading to war. The former French colonists resented the British victory over France in 1759 and, in an effort to pacify them, in 1791 the country was divided into English-speaking Upper and French-speaking Lower Canada. The two parts were united in 1841 and in 1867 the self-governing dominion of Canada, within the British Empire, was founded.

From 1896 to 1911 the Liberal Party was in power under a French Canadian, Wilfred Laurier (1841–1919). His government fell because of dissatisfaction with his attempts to strengthen trade links with the United States and he was succeeded by Robert Borden (1854–1937), heading a Conservative administration. He successfully organized Canada for war in 1914 and was the first Dominion prime minister to attend an Imperial War Cabinet meeting. In 1921 the Liberals returned to office, under W L Mackenzie King (1874–1950), and they were to dominate Canadian politics for the next three decades, with Mackenzie King until 1948 and then with Louis St Laurent (1882–1973) until 1957.

The Progressive Conservatives returned to power in 1957, after 36 years in the wilderness. The Liberals, under Lester Pearson (1897–1972), returned to office in 1963 and Pearson remained prime minister until he was succeeded by former law professor Pierre Trudeau (b. 1919) in 1968. Trudeau maintained Canada's defensive alliance with the United States but sought to widen its influence on the world stage. At home he was faced with the problem of dealing with the separatist movement in Québec and set about creating what he called the 'just society'. Although a French Canadian himself, Trudeau was totally opposed to the idea of separatism for any part of the country. His success in achieving his objectives may be judged by his ability to win two elections in a row, in 1972 and 1974.

Then, in 1979, with no party having an overall majority in the Commons, the Progressive Conservatives, led by Joe Clark (b. 1939), formed a government. Later that year Trudeau announced his retirement from politics but when, in 1980, Clark was defeated on his government's budget proposals, Trudeau reconsidered his decision and, with the dissolution of parliament, won the general election with a large majority. Trudeau's third administration was concerned with the question of 'patriation', or the extent to which the Parliament in Westminster had power to determine the constitution of Canada. Eventually the position was resolved with the passing of the Canada Act of 1982, which was the last piece of legislation of the United Kingdom Parliament to have force in Canada.

In 1983 Clark was replaced as leader of the Progressive Conservatives by Brian Mulroney (b. 1939), a businessexecutive with no previous political experience, and in 1984 Trudeau retired to be replaced as Liberal leader and prime minister by John Turner (b. 1929), a former minister of finance. Within nine days of taking office, Turner called a general election and the Progressive Conservatives, under Mulroney, won the largest majority in Canadian history. Soon after forming his administration, Mulroney began an international realignment, placing less emphasis on links Trudeau had established with Asia, Africa, and Latin America, and more on cooperation with Europe and a closer 'special relationship' with the United States. One aspect of this closer cooperation was discussion about the possibility of greater freedom of trade between the two countries, culminating in a free-trade agreement which was signed in 1988.

The relationship between the federal government and the provinces was still a live political issue. In April 1987 Prime Minister Mulroney reached agreement with the ten provincial premiers in the Meech Lake Accord. This was intended to give all the provinces considerable powers in appointments to the Senate and Supreme Court, a veto over many possible constitutional amendments and financial compensation to any province which opted out of any new national shared-cost programme in favour of its own programme. The Accord was strongly criticized by former prime minister Trudeau as likely to destroy the equilibrium between Ottawa and the provinces which he had created and which Mulroney had inherited. The 1988 general election was fought mainly on the issue of the free-trade agreement negotiated with the United States, the Conservatives winning with a clear, but reduced, majority.

In August 1992 a constitutional reform package, replacing the Meech Lake Accord, and called the Pearson Agreement, was put together. This gave greater autonomy to the provinces, and a particular recognition to Québec, but, when put before the electorate in a referendum in October 1992, it was rejected. By this time Prime Minister Mulroney's popular standing had sunk to an unprecedented low and in February 1993 he resigned. In June he was succeeded by Canada's first woman prime minister, Kim Campbell (b. 1947).

In the general election, four months later, the PCP suffered a resounding defeat, its seat-holding in the House of Commons falling from 157 to two, and the separatist Bloc Québécois became the official opposition party. The Liberals increased their seat tally by nearly 100 and their leader, Jean Chrétien (b. 1934), became prime minister. Within two months Kim Campbell had resigned the PCP leadership and four months later another leading female politician, Audrey McLaughlin (b. 1936), gave up the NDP leadership. In Québec, where the Parti Québécois was in power under the leadership of Jacques Parizeau, a referendum on separation was held in October 1995. The separatists, drawing strong support from the province's French speaking majority, attracted 49.4% of the vote, with a 94% turnout.

UNITED STATES OF AMERICA (USA)

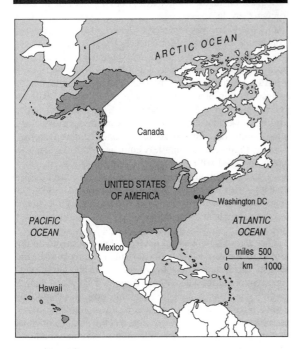

Capital: Washington DC

Social and economic data
Area: 9,372,614 km²
Population: 257,800,000*
Pop. density per km²: 28*
Urban population: 76%**
Literacy rate: 98%**
GDP: $5,920,199 million**; per-capita GDP: $23,500**
Government defence spending (% of GDP): 4.7%**
Currency: US dollar
Economy type: high income
Labour force in agriculture: 3%**

*1994
**1992

Ethnic composition
Approximately three-quarters of the population are of European origin, including 29% who trace their descent from British and Irish stock, 8% from German, 5% from Italian, and 3% each from Scandinavian and Polish. Twelve per cent are black, or African-Americans, 8% Hispanic, and 3% Asian and Pacific Islander. Blacks form 30% of the population of the states of the 'Deep South', namely Alabama, Georgia, Louisiana, Mississippi, and South Carolina. Asians are most thickly concentrated in California. Although the main language is English, there are significant Spanish-speaking minorities, especially in southern California, Texas, Arizona, and New Mexico, where Hispanics form 37% of the population.

Religions
More than 30% of the population, or 79 million, are Protestants, chiefly belonging to the Baptist (31 million), Methodist (12 million), Lutheran (8 million), Presbyterian (4.2 million), Anglican (2.4 million), Assemblies of God (2.2 million), United Church of Christ (1.7 million), Disciples of Christ (1.0 million), and Seventh Day Adventist (0.8 million) churches. Twenty-two per cent, or 59 million, are Roman Catholics, 2% (5.9 million) Jewish, 2% (4.2 million) Eastern, including Greek, Orthodox, 2% (4.3 million) Mormons, and 2% (4 million) Muslims, of whom 1.3 million are African-American 'Black Muslims'. The rest of the population professes no religion or belongs to small, distinctive sects or creeds. Church and state are strictly separated.

Political features
State type: liberal democracy
Date of state formation: 1776
Political structure: federal
Executive: limited presidential
Assembly: two-chamber
Party structure: two-party
Human rights rating: 90%
International affiliations: AfDB, AG (observer), ANZUS, APEC, AsDB, BIS, CP, EBRD, ECE, ECLAC, ESCAP, G-5, G-7, G-10, IAEA, IBRD, ICC, ICFTU, IDB, IEA, IMF, IWC, LORCS, NACC, NAFTA, NATO, NEA, OAS, OECD, OSCE, SPC, UN Security Council (permanent member), WTO

Local and regional government
Below the state level there are 3,100 counties, over 18,000 municipalities, and almost 17,000 townships, with wards and precincts below them. Office holders are elected to fill political and administrative and judicial posts at all these levels.

Head of state and of government
President William (Bill) J Clinton, since 1993

Political leaders since 1970*
1969–74 Richard M Nixon (R), 1974–77 Gerald R Ford (R), 1977–81 Jimmy E Carter (D), 1981–89 Ronald W Reagan (R), 1989–93 George H W Bush (R), 1993–   Bill Clinton (D)

*Executive president

Political system
The United States is a federal republic comprising 50 states and the District of Columbia. Under its 1787 constitution, which became effective in March 1789 and has since been subject to 27 amendments, the constituent states are reserved considerable powers of self-government. The federal, or central, government concentrated originally on defence, foreign affairs, and the coordination of 'interstate' concerns, leaving legislation in other spheres to the states, each with its own constitution, elected assembly (bicameral in all states except Nebraska), governor, Supreme Court, and local taxation powers. Since Roosevelt's 1930s 'New Deal', however, the federal government has increasingly impinged upon state affairs and become the principal revenue raising and spending agency.

The US federal government is characterized by a deliberate separation of the executive from the legislative and judicial functions. At the head of the executive branch of government is a president, elected every four years on a fixed date in November in a national contest by universal adult suffrage. Votes are counted at the state level on a first-past-the-post, winner-takes-all basis, with each state being assigned a slate of seats, equivalent to the sum of its congressional representatives, in a national 538-member Electoral College. This College later, in mid-December, formally elects the president. The victor is thus the candidate who secures the highest number of Electoral College votes, not necessarily the highest number of popular votes across the country. Once elected, the president, who must be at least 35 years of age, serves as head of state, commander in chief of the armed forces and head of the civil service. He or she is restricted, under the provisions of Amendment 22, which was adopted in 1951, to a maximum of two terms and, once elected, cannot be removed except through impeachment by Congress.

The president works with a personally selected cabinet team, subject to the Senate's approval, whose members are debarred from serving in the legislature. For this reason, the cabinet is composed of specialists who concentrate on the work of their own departments and who are frequently drawn from business or academic, rather than party political, backgrounds. To coordinate policy-making and draw up strategic plans, the president is served by an ever-growing White House Office of personal political aides and trouble-shooting assistants. This team is headed by a chief of staff, and includes the National Security Council (NSC), the Domestic Council, the Office of Management and Budget (OMB), and the Council of Economic Advisers (CEA) as functionalist support units.

The second branch of government, Congress, the federal legislature, consists of two equally powerful chambers, the 100-member Senate and the 435-member House of Representatives. Senators, who must be at least 30 years of age, serve fixed six-year terms, two being elected from each state in a state-wide race, regardless of size or population. A third are elected at a time, biennially, with no restrictions being placed on re-election.

Representatives, who must be at least 25 years of age, are elected from single-member constituencies of roughly equal demographic size, of 450,000 to 700,000, to serve for fixed two-year terms, again with no restrictions on re-election.

Congress has sole powers of legislation and operates through a system of specialized standing, select and investigative committees, which are composed of members drawn from parties in accordance with their relative strength in each chamber. They have the authority to call forth an array of witnesses from the executive branch and outside. These powerful committees, whose work is televised, are chaired by senior members of the party controlling the chamber and are liberally staffed by advisory assistants.

The Senate is the more powerful chamber of Congress, its approval being required for key federal appointments and for the ratification of foreign treaties. In addition, it is the Senate which hears cases of impeachment brought against federal officials.

The House of Representatives is of greatest importance in the fiscal sphere, all spending bills being required, under the terms of Section 7 of Article 1 of the constitution, to originate in this chamber. This makes the House's budget and finance committees particularly important.

The president needs to work with Congress to persuade it to adopt his or her policy programme, addressing it in January for an annual 'State of the Union' speech and sending periodic 'messages' and 'recommendations'. The president's success depends on the office holder's level of party support in Congress, bargaining skills, and current public standing. To become law, legislation, which is initially proposed by individual senators and representatives and worked upon in committee, requires the approval of both chambers of Congress. If differences arise, a special 'Joint Congressional Committee', composed of senior members drawn from both chambers, is convened to produce a compromise agreement. The president retains, however, the option of imposing vetoes which can only be overridden by two-thirds majorities in both Congressional houses.

Constitutional amendments require two-thirds majorities from both chambers of Congress and subsequent ratification by at least three-quarters, or 38, of the nation's 50 state legislatures, within a seven-year time span. Alternatively, it is possible for a constitutional amendment to be initiated by two-thirds of state legislatures, calling for the convening of a special National Constitutional Convention. Measures adopted at this convocation then require the subsequent approval by constitutional conventions in 38 states to become law.

The third branch of government, the judiciary, headed by the Supreme Court, interprets the written US constitution to ensure that a correct balance is maintained between federal and state institutions, and the executive and legislature, and that the civil rights enshrined in Amendments 1–10, 'The Bill of Rights', adopted in 1791, are upheld.

The Supreme Court consists of nine judges appointed by the president, subject to the Senate's approval, who serve life terms and are removable only through impeachment. Headed since 1986 by Chief Justice William H Rehnquist (b. 1924) and with a conservative majority, it is an unusually influential and potentially 'activist' body, enjoying the power to effectively veto legislation and overturn executive actions which it rules to be unconstitutional.

The United States is, in addition, responsible for the administration of a number of Pacific Island territories, including American Samoa and the US Virgin Islands, which are governed by local legislatures and a governor. They are described more fully in *Chapter 8*. Each of these territories, as well as the 'self-governing territories' of Puerto Rico and Guam, sends a nonvoting delegate to the US House of Representatives.

Political parties

Two broad 'catch-all' party coalitions, divided regionally and ideologically, dominate American politics: the Democrats and the Republicans. The first-past-the-post electoral system, the presidentialist nature of American politics, and the ability of the existing parties to embrace broad ranges of opinion have been key factors in fostering this party polarization and working against the emergence of additional third or fourth parties.

The Democratic Party (D) was originally founded in 1792 by Thomas Jefferson, one of the drafters of the Declaration of Independence of 1776, to defend the rights of individual states against the centralizing moves of the Federalists. First, under the designation Democratic Republicans and then, from 1828, Democratic Party, it held power almost continuously between 1800 and 1860. During the American Civil War, 1861–65, it became identified with the defeated rural Confederacy States of the South, a region which became a stronghold for the party, electing senators and representatives of a conservative and illiberal hue.

In the northeastern seaboard states, a substantially different, in terms of ideological outlook, Democratic Party emerged during the years between 1865 and 1920. It sought out and won over the majority of the new immigrant minority communities, the Irish, Poles, Italians, Catholics, and Jews, who flooded into the industrializing coastal cities during this period.

During the 1930s Great Depression, this new urban power base was strengthened when, under the leadership of Franklin D Roosevelt, the party pressed ahead with a 'New Deal' programme of social reform and state interventionism. This attracted to the Democrats a broad coalition of support, establishing the party, which had been overshadowed by the Republicans between 1861 and 1932, as the new majority party at both the local and congressional level. This is shown in Table 58 below.

Between 1933–68 the Democratic Party secured the presidency for its candidate during 28 of the 36 years and control of both chambers of Congress during all but four of these years. The party's northeastern wing, founded on a network of strong, worker-orientated, urban organizational 'machines', was dominant during these years, espousing a philosophy of liberalism which favoured an extended role for the federal government. During the 1960s, however, as this northeastern wing pressed for civil rights reform, desegregation, equal opportunity, and voting rights for the black community, the party's southern conservative 'Dixiecrat', or 'Boll Weevil', wing became increasingly alienated.

In presidential elections, southern electors began to vote regularly for Republican nominees, and, within Congress, 'historical', or 'yellow-dog', Democrat Dixiecrats voted against the Democrat presidents Kennedy and Johnson on social issues. Intraparty divisions widened during the later 1960s, as northern liberal opposition to the Vietnam War mounted, setting in train a drive to democratize the party's organizational structure and selection procedures, with the use of primary, or delegate election, contests open to all voters identifying themselves as party supporters. Election procedures replaced the caucus, or closed-door party meeting, and state convention, or open-door party meeting, systems.

The Democratic Party today is composed of at least five significant wings or tendencies. The first is a still sizeable, though now reduced, southern conservative, or neo-liberal, faction, sometimes referred to as the party's 'congressional wing'. The second is a larger, traditionally dominant grouping of northern 'New Deal' liberals, known as the 'presidential wing'. The third group consists of the radical prairie-populist liberals of the midwestern agricultural–industrial states, most notably Minnesota. The fourth, smaller, faction consists of the Trumanite 'Defense Democrats'. The fifth party faction, which is strongest outside Congress at the city government level, is the ultra-liberal 'Rainbow Coalition' movement.

The southern 'congressional wing', comprising around a dozen senators and 40 representatives, is organized in the Conservative Democratic Forum (CDF). This forms a 'swing' grouping within Congress, sometimes aligning with Republican congressmen in votes on economic, social, and defence issues. Southern conservatives and moderate liberals also work together in the influential Democratic Leadership Council (DLC). Founded in 1985, and incorporating state governors, the fiscally conservative but socially liberal DLC is the section of the party most closely associated with President Bill Clinton.

The northern 'presidential wing' is interventionist in both the economic and social spheres, and moderate on defence. It

Party control of the presidency and congress since 1859					Table 58
The presidency		Senate		House of Representatives	
Republican	1861–1865	Democrats	1859–1860	Republicans	1859–1874
Democrat	1865–1868	Republicans	1861–1878	Democrats	1875–1880
Republican	1869–1884	Democrats	1879–1880	Republicans	1881–1882
Democrat	1885–1888	Republicans	1881–1892	Democrats	1883–1888
Republican	1889–1892	Democrats	1893–1894	Republicans	1889–1890
Democrat	1893–1896	Republicans	1895–1912	Democrats	1891–1894
Republican	1897–1912	Democrats	1913–1918	Republicans	1895–1910
Democrat	1913–1920	Republicans	1919–1932	Democrats	1911–1916
Republican	1921–1932	Democrats	1933–1946	Republicans	1917–1932
Democrat	1933–1952	Republicans	1947–1948	Democrats	1933–1946
Republican	1953–1960	Democrats	1949–1952	Republicans	1947–1948
Democrat	1961–1968	Republicans	1953–1954	Democrats	1949–1952
Republican	1969–1976	Democrats	1955–1980	Republicans	1953–1954
Democrat	1977–1980	Republicans	1981–1986	Democrats	1955–1994
Republican	1981–1992	Democrats	1986–1994	Republicans	1995–
Democrat	1993–	Republicans	1995–		

adheres to many of the tenets of the Americans for Democratic Action (ADA) organization, which was established in 1947. Its leading representatives include Massachusetts Senator, Edward Kennedy (b. 1932), and New York State's former governor, Mario Cuomo.

The roots of the midwestern populists can be traced back to the People's Party, founded during the 1890s, and the Progressive Party, which operated during the interwar years to represent the interests of small farmers against those of big business.

The Trumanite 'Defense Democrats' were represented during the 1970s and 1980s by New York senator, Daniel Patrick Moynihan. While liberal in the economic and social sphere, they have favoured a firm, traditionally anticommunist, foreign policy.

The 'Rainbow Coalition' is a movement embracing black, Hispanic, feminist, student, homosexual, and antinuclear minority groupings, and has been led by the charismatic African-American civil rights leader, the Reverend Jesse Jackson (b. 1941).

All of these minority communities support the Democratic Party by overwhelming margins in elections. Catholics, Jews, unionized workers, and families on lower incomes constitute other important and, more general, Democrat support blocks.

The Republican Party (R), also popularly known as the Grand Old Party (GOP), was formed in Michigan in 1854 by a coalition opposed to slavery. It secured the election of its candidate, Abraham Lincoln, to the presidency in 1860, and became identified with the wealthy and industrializing victorious North during the Civil War. The party also won the support of people in the rural and small-town areas of the midwest. These included the long-settled Protestant majority community and the new frontier states of the Pacific coast. All this support was put together in an electoral coalition which dominated at the federal level until the early 1930s.

The Republicans were outflanked by Roosevelt during the 1930s and 1940s, then, under the leadership of Dwight D Eisenhower during the 1950s, came to accept the popular social and economic reforms of the 'New Deal' era and its aftermath, and, in the process, extended their support base. In ideological outlook, however, the Republicans continued to be positioned to the right of the Democrats in both the economic and social spheres. In terms of voter identification they also lagged behind their centre-left rivals, registering a national identification level of 35% compared to 45% by the Democrats.

During recent decades, the Republicans have dominated at the presidential level, having won five of the seven electoral contests held since November 1964. They enjoy a firm regional support base in the centre and west of the country and poll strongly amongst the white Protestant community and those on higher incomes. The party has made significant inroads into the traditionally Democrat-dominated South. It has attracted many elected Democrat defectors since the start of the Clinton presidency, including five representatives and senators and 100 state and local-level politicians since the November 1992 presidential election. After the November 1994 midterm congressional elections, the GOP held a majority of the South's House and Senate seats for the first time since the Civil War.

Ideologically, until the election of Richard Nixon as president in 1968, the GOP was dominated by a big business-orientated, and relatively liberal, northeastern 'Wall Street' wing, one of whose most prominent members was the influential former New York state governor, and vice president, Nelson A Rockefeller (1908–79). This northern liberal grouping has, however, contracted significantly since the 1970s, and is now reduced to a minority rump.

Instead, the Republicans have become dominated by a western and midwestern small-town majority grouping, described as the 'Main Street' wing, and epitomized by the figures of Barry Goldwater, Ronald Reagan, Kansas senator Bob Dole (b. 1923), Texas senator, Phil Gramm, both of whom are contesting the party's presidential nomination in 1996, and Newt Gingrich, house speaker from 1995. This wing adheres to a conservative and individualist 'small government' philosophy of reduced taxation, a balanced budget, and a Christian moral code. The Conservative Caucus, which is an organization established in 1974 by Howard Phillips, and the Heritage Foundation, established by Paul Weyrich, have served as lobbyists and think-tanks for this faction, which includes Empower America, a ginger organization formed by Jack Kemp (b. 1935), a representative from New Jersey, and Malcolm Forbes Jr, a billionaire publisher.

To the right of the new party mainstream stands an increasingly vocal Christian fundamentalist activist grouping, led by the Reverend Pat Robertson (b. 1930), who had established the Christian Broadcasting Network in 1960 and later formed the Freedom Council as a political pressure group, before challenging George Bush for the party's presidential nomination in 1988. By 1995 the Christian Coalition, directed by Ralph Reed (b. 1961), claimed 1.6 million members and dominated 18 state Republican parties and partly controlled 13 more.

Also standing on the far right of the GOP is Patrick Buchanan, a conservative columnist who served in the Reagan administration and contested for the party's presidential nomination in 1996, advocating extreme social conservatism and populist economic nationalism.

Each of the major parties has only a rudimentary national organization, with no official membership, and, although party politicians in Congress group together for committee assignment purposes, they seldom vote en bloc.

A four-day National Convention is convened every four years, during the summer immediately preceding a presidential contest, to elect a presidential candidate and adopt a party 'platform', which is a nonbinding manifesto. Delegates to these large, 2,200–4,200-member, bodies are elected through state-level primaries, caucuses, or conventions, and are pledged to vote for particular candidates.

Between Conventions, party business is carried on by a National Committee, elected by state parties. The Committee's primary functions are to set the rules for the presidential primaries and National Conventions and coordinate fund-raising activities. The Republican National Committee is the better organized, having made considerable progress in the use of modern direct-mail fund-raising and leafleting services since the early 1970s and thus established itself as an important source of finance for Senate, as well as presidential, campaigns.

Despite this progress, party organization remains concentrated at the state level. Here the true, localized 'party systems' of American politics are to be found. In comparison with West European political parties, however, state parties are informally organized, the choice of party candidates being unusually open because of the primary system of selection and because aspirants for office are heavily reliant on generating their own funding resources. They do this by drawing on donations from interest groups via Political Action Committees (PACs), to contest expensive, media-dominated elections. This pattern has fed through to Congress, where the legislative process is unusually atomized and individualistic.

Numerous minor parties also operate in the United States. None has, however, made any impact at either the state or federal level. For example, the most notable of the minor parties, the ultra-individualist and free-market Citizens' Party, which was established in 1971, has secured less than 1% of the vote in presidential contests. It did, however, win a seat in the Alaska state legislature in 1978. Of greater importance has been the independent presidential challenges by breakaway members from the major parties. For example, George Wallace, a renegade southern Democrat, secured 13% of the national vote and 46 Electoral College seats in November 1968 and John Anderson, a liberal-Republican, 7% of the popular vote, though no Electoral College seats, in November 1984. In November 1992, the maverick populist billionaire businessman, H Ross Perot, captured 19% of the national vote. This was the best third-candidate performance since 1912.

Latest elections

In the most recent presidential election, held on 3 November 1992, the Democrat challenger, Bill Clinton, secured a convincing victory over the incumbent Republican president, George Bush. Clinton captured 43% of the popular vote and 370 Electoral College seats to Bush's 37% and 168 seats. Bush won just 18 states, concentrated in the South and interior of the country, as well as the solidly conservative Alaska. Clinton dominated in the west and industrialized northeast, but was also able to win four states in the South, going some way towards reconstructing the Roosevelt–Johnson 'Democrat coalition' which had been destroyed by Richard Nixon and Ronald Reagan. The election was complicated by the candidacy of the Texan billionaire, H Ross Perot, who, running as a conservative–populist independent, actually outspent his two major party rivals in terms of television advertising. The contemporary recession and Perot's quixotic candidacy helped raise turnout to more than 54% of the voting-age population, an advance of 4% on the 1988 turnout level.

As usual, the November 1992 presidential election contest was preceded by a prolonged 'primary campaign' among an assortment of candidates seeking main party nomination by securing a majority of delegate votes at the July–August 1992 National Conventions. Officially, the nomination race commenced in February 1992, with caucuses at Iowa, followed by the New Hampshire primary, with a large 'Super Tuesday' of coordinated, mainly southern, caucuses and

primaries being held on 10 March 1992. In reality, unofficial campaigning for the Democrats' presidential nomination began as early as the spring of 1991, with the former Massachusetts senator, Paul Tsongas, declaring his candidacy on 30 April 1991.

In the end, six figures contested the Democrat nomination, but after 'Super Tuesday' the contest had been reduced to a battle between three candidates, Paul Tsongas, Jerry Brown, the former governor of California, and Bill Clinton, the governor of Arkansas. Despite reservations about possible flaws in his character, Clinton, well financed and with extensive ties throughout the Democratic Party, secured a clear and early victory.

President Bush was challenged for the Republican nomination by the controversial David Duke, a former member of the racist Ku Klux Klan, and the right-wing 'America First' economic nationalist, Pat Buchanan, but achieved the necessary National Convention delegates at an even earlier date than Clinton.

The most recent congressional and state elections were held on 8 November 1994 and resulted in a catastrophic defeat for the Democrats, who suffered from the unpopularity of President Clinton and recent congressional scandals involving leading Democrats. In the Senate contests, the Republicans gained 9 seats from the Democrats and a further seat via the defection to the party of a conservative southern Democrat. As a consequence, they regained control of the upper chamber for the first time since 1986, finishing with 53 seats to the Democrats' 47. Even more dramatic were the results in the House of Representatives elections. The Republicans gained 55 seats from the Democrats and wrested control of the chamber for the first time since 1954. The Democrats were left with just 204 House seats to the Republicans' 230, with the Socialist Bernie Sanders holding on to one seat in Vermont. The Republican landslide was completed by the gain of 11 state governorships from the Democrats, leaving the GOP with 30 out of 50 governorships, including control in seven of the eight largest states. One of the most prominent Democrats, Mario Cuomo, was defeated in his bid for re-election for a fourth term as New York State governor, while in Washington State, Tom Foley, a congressman for 30 years, became the first incumbent house speaker to be defeated since 1860. In the southern states the Republicans polled particularly strongly. State elections were also accompanied by the approval of a number of propositions (referenda) relating chiefly to taxation or to term limits for elected officials.

Political history

The land area covered by the contemporary United States of America (USA) was first settled by 'Indian' groups who migrated from Asia across the Bering land bridge over 25,000 years ago. Today, a million of their descendants survive, more than half living on reservations. European exploration of the continent commenced with the Norse in the 9th century. Later, during the 16th century, Florida and Mexico were colonized by the Spanish, and, during the 17th century, portions of the east coast, in New England and Pennsylvania, were occupied by the British, the Great Lakes and Louisiana by the French, New Jersey by the Dutch, and Delaware by the

Swedes. The Swedish and Dutch settlements were subsequently acquired by the British, who controlled the territory between New England and the Carolinas. Following the Anglo-French Seven Years' War, between 1756 and 1763, Canada, Florida, and East Louisiana were also brought under British sovereignty by the terms of the Treaty of Paris of 1763.

In 1775 the 13 English-speaking colonies of Connecticut, Delaware, Georgia, Maryland, Massachusetts, New Hampshire, New Jersey, New York, North Carolina, Pennsylvania, Rhode Island, South Carolina, and Virginia revolted against British colonial tax impositions, proclaiming their independence in July 1776. A provisional constitution, the Articles of Confederation, was adopted in 1777. Led by George Washington (1732–99) and with French aid, the confederated states succeeded in defeating the armies of George III in the War of American Independence, 1775–83.

A new constitution was drawn up for the independent federal republic in 1787, at the Philadelphia Convention, and came into force in 1789. A 'Bill of Rights' was added in 1791. This constitution provided for a directly elected House of Representatives, but, until the ratification of the 17th Amendment in 1913, only an indirectly elected Senate, whose members were chosen by state legislators. The president was selected by an Electoral College, with Washington, of the Federalist Party, being the first to occupy the position.

Initially, the United States extended west only to the Mississippi River and north to the Great Lakes. Louisiana, which was purchased from France, was added in 1803 and Florida, which was acquired from Spain, in 1819. Further former Spanish states, including California and Texas, joined the Union between 1821 and 1853, following a war with Mexico between 1846 and 1848.

In 1861 the American Civil War broke out between the cotton-growing southern Confederate states of Alabama, Arkansas, Florida, Georgia, Louisiana, Mississippi, North Carolina, South Carolina, Tennessee, Texas, and Virginia and the more industrialized and urbanized northeastern Federal states, over the issue of 'states' rights' and the maintenance of slavery in the South. More than 600,000 died in the conflict, the North triumphing after the surrender of General Robert E Lee (1807–70) to General Ulysses S Grant (1822–85) at Appomattox on 9 April 1865.

Northern troops subsequently occupied the South, between 1865 and 1877, during a 'Reconstruction Period', and constitutional Amendments 13–15, which abolished slavery and guaranteed blacks civil rights, were adopted. Five days after the South's surrender, however, the North's Republican president, Abraham Lincoln (1809–65), who had been re-elected for a second term in November 1864, was assassinated by John Wilkes Booth (1838–65).

During the half century following the Civil War, the northeastern seaboard states underwent rapid industrialization, more than 30 million overseas, predominantly European, immigrants being attracted to their cities. With the spread of railways, the agricultural frontier extended westwards towards the Rockies and Pacific, while the new territories of Alaska, which was purchased from Russia in 1867, and Hawaii, which was acquired in 1898, were added. Externally, the United States adhered to an isolationist policy, not entering World War I until 1917.

After the war, the franchise was extended to women in 1920 by Amendment 19, and economic growth continued until the Wall Street stock market crash of October 1929. Thereafter, the country was plunged into a severe industrial and agricultural depression, bringing mass unemployment. Franklin D Roosevelt (1882–1945), the Democrat former governor of New York, who was elected president in November 1932, responded to this crisis by abandoning the *laissez-faire* policies of his Republican predecessor, Herbert C Hoover (1874–1964), and launching, under the slogan 'New Deal', a radical programme of state intervention. 'Soft loans' were provided to agriculturists and local authorities, employment-generating public works projects were launched, farm prices raised, and old-age and unemployment insurance schemes introduced. These measures helped to alleviate the depression, although it was not until World War II that full employment was re-established.

Politically, this 'New Deal' programme drew to the Democratic Party new blocks of support, establishing it as the new, dominant, national party. Because of this, Roosevelt was re-elected president in 1936, 1940, and 1944, thus becoming the country's longest-serving leader.

The United States, after initially adhering to its isolationist stance, entered the World War II in December 1941, following Japan's attack on Pearl Harbor in Hawaii. Its navy subsequently defeated the Japanese fleet at the Battle of Midway in June 1942, and its army divisions helped turn the tide against Germany in Europe between 1943 and 1945. However, it was not until August 1945 and the dropping of atom bombs on Hiroshima and Nagasaki that Japan formally ceased hostilities and surrendered.

Having established itself as a global 'superpower', through its decisive actions between 1941 and 1945, the United States remained internationalist during the postwar era. Under the presidency of the Democrat, Harry S Truman (1884–1972), who served between 1945 and 1952, a 'doctrine' of intervention in support of endangered 'free peoples', and of containing the spread of communism, was devised by State Department Secretary (foreign minister) Dean Acheson (1893–1971). This led to America's safeguarding of Nationalist Taiwan in 1949 and its participation, under United Nations auspices, in the Korean War of 1950–53.

The United States, in addition, took the lead in creating new global and regional organizations designed to maintain the peace: the United Nations (UN) in 1945, the Organization of American States (OAS) in 1948, the North Atlantic Treaty Organization (NATO) in 1949, and the South East Asia Treaty Organization (SEATO) in 1954. It also launched the Marshall Plan, between 1947 and 1952, to strengthen the economies of its European allies.

Domestically, President Truman sought to introduce liberal reforms, with the aim of extending civil and welfare rights, under the slogan a 'Fair Deal'. These measures were blocked, however, by a combination of southern Democrats and Republicans, in Congress.

Truman's foreign policy was criticized as being 'soft on communism' between 1950 and 1952, as a wave of anti-Soviet hysteria, spearheaded by the work of Senator Joseph McCarthy (1908–57), swept the nation. This rightward shift in the public mood provided the basis for Republican victories in the congressional and presidential elections of November 1952. The popular military commander, General Dwight ('Ike') Eisenhower (1890–1969), became president and was re-elected by an increased margin in November 1956.

Working with Secretary of State John Foster Dulles (1888–1959), Eisenhower adhered to the Truman–Acheson doctrine of 'containment', while at home he pursued a policy of 'progressive conservatism', designed to encourage business enterprise.

The Eisenhower era was one of growth, prosperity, and social change, involving the migration of southern blacks to the northern industrial cities and a rapid expansion in the educational sector. In the southern states racial tensions emerged, as a new black rights movement developed under the leadership of Dr Martin Luther King (1929–68). Responding to these new demands and developments, the youthful Massachusetts Democrat, John F Kennedy (1917–63), on the promise of a 'New Frontier' programme of social reform, gained victory in the presidential election of November 1960. However, the new president, having emerged as a firm opponent of communism abroad, as evidenced by the Bay of Pigs Affair of 1961 and the Cuban Missile Crisis of 1962, and having proposed a sweeping domestic Civil Rights Bill, was assassinated in November 1963. It was left to his deputy and successor, the Texan Lyndon B Johnson (1908–73), to oversee the passage of Kennedy's 'Great Society' reforms.

These measures, which included the Equal Opportunities, Voting Rights, Housing, and Medicare Acts, guaranteed blacks new civil rights, including the effective right to vote in southern states, and significantly extended the reach of the federal government. They were buttressed by the judicial rulings of the Supreme Court chaired by Chief Justice Earl Warren (1891–1974), who occupied the post between 1953 and 1969.

Abroad, however, President Johnson became embroiled in the Vietnam War, 1964–75, which, with casualty numbers mounting, polarized American public opinion and created deep divisions within the Democratic Party.

Johnson decided not to run for re-election in November 1968 and the Democrat candidate, former vice president, Hubert H Humphrey (1911–78), was defeated by the experienced Republican, Richard M Nixon (1913–94). Nixon, a staunch conservative, encountered worsening student and racial conflicts at home but enjoyed greater success abroad. Working with National Security Advisor Henry Kissinger (b. 1923), he began a gradual disengagement from Vietnam and launched an imaginative new policy of *détente* which brought about improvements in relations with the Soviet Union, a Strategic Arms Limitation Treaty (SALT 1) being signed in 1972, and with communist China.

Faced by a divided opposition, led by the radical George McGovern (b. 1922), Nixon gained re-election by an overwhelming margin in November 1972. During the campaign, however, Nixon's staff illegally broke into the Democratic Party's headquarters, in the Watergate building, in Washington DC. The resulting 'cover-up' created a damaging scandal which, with a congressional impeachment impending, forced the resignation of the president in August 1974.

Watergate shocked the American public, eroding confidence in the presidency, Republicans, and the Washington establishment. The upright liberal Republican, Gerald R Ford (b. 1913), who had only been vice president since December 1973, succeeded Nixon as president. Maintaining the services of Kissinger, Ford adhered to his predecessor's policy of *détente*. He faced, however, a resurgent and hostile Democrat-dominated Congress which introduced legislation curbing the powers of the presidency, by means of the War Powers Resolution of 1973 which prohibits the president from keeping US forces in hostile situations for more than 90 days without congressional authorization, and forcing isolationism abroad. The new president also had to deal with an economic recession and fuel shortages. These had resulted from the 1973 Arab–Israeli War and the emergence of the Organization of Petroleum Exporting Countries (OPEC) who proceeded to force up world oil prices.

Ford contested the presidential election of November 1976, but was defeated by the 'born again' southern Christian and anti-Washington outsider, James ('Jimmy') E Carter (b. 1924), who promised a new era of open and honest government.

Carter, the former governor of Georgia, was a fiscal conservative, but social liberal, who sought to extend welfare provision through greater administrative efficiency. In addition, he pledged to end the fuel crisis by enforced conservation. This he substantially achieved through the Energy Acts of 1978 and 1980.

Overseas, President Carter pursued a 'new foreign policy' which emphasized human rights in America's foreign relations. In the Middle East, Carter came close to a peace settlement in 1978–79, effecting the Camp David Agreements of September 1978 between Egypt and Israel, followed by a peace treaty in March 1979. Also, in January 1979 America's diplomatic relations with communist China were fully normalized.

The Carter presidency was brought down, however, by a twin set of foreign policy crises in 1979–80: the fall of the Shah of Iran in January 1979 and the consequent Iranian Islamic Revolution, and the Soviet invasion of Afghanistan in December 1979. The president's vacillating leadership style, defence economies, and moralistic foreign policy were blamed for weakening America's influence abroad. As a consequence, there was a resurgence in anticommunist feeling and mounting support for a new policy of rearmament and selective interventionism.

Carter responded to this new mood by enunciating the hawkish Carter Doctrine of 1980. This asserted that the United States had a vital interest in the Gulf region, which it would defend by force. It also supported a major new arms development programme. The president's popularity plunged, however, during 1980 as, mainly because of a new round of OPEC-induced oil price rises, economic recession gripped the country. During the same period American embassy staff were held hostage by Shi'ite fundamentalists in Tehran.

The radical Republican Ronald W Reagan (b. 1911) benefited from Carter's difficulties and was swept to victory in the November 1984 presidential election, the Democrats also losing control of the Senate for the first time in 26 years.

The new president, like his predecessor, was an 'outsider politician' who, from being a former screen actor and governor of California, had risen to prominence as an effective television-skilled campaigner. Reagan, drawing support from the 'Moral Majority' movement and 'New Right', believed in a return to traditional Christian religious and family values and propounded a supply-side economic strategy, founded on reduced taxation, deregulation, and political decentralization, to get 'government off people's backs'.

In his approach to foreign affairs, Reagan rejected *détente* and spoke of the communist-controlled Soviet Union as an 'evil empire' which needed to be checked by a military build-up. He launched the space-based Strategic Defense Initiative (SDI) in 1983, and spoke of a readiness to employ force when necessary.

The early years of the Reagan presidency witnessed substantial reductions in taxation and sweeping cutbacks in federal welfare programmes. This created serious hardship, as economic recession gripped the nation between 1981 and 1983. The official unemployment rate rose from a level of 7.8% in May 1980 to a postwar high of 10.8% in November 1982. Abroad, the president's new foreign policy led to a sharp deterioration in Soviet–American relations, ushering in a new 'cold war' era during the Polish 'Solidarity' crisis of 1981.

By the autumn of 1983, however, the US economy began a strong neo-Keynesian recovery, the unemployment level falling to 7% in June 1984, and, helped by the successful invasion of Grenada by US marines in October 1983 to foil an alleged Marxist coup, President Reagan recovered his popularity and was swept to a landslide victory on a wave of optimistic patriotism in the presidential election of November 1984. He defeated the Democrat ticket of Walter Mondale (b. 1928) and Geraldine Ferraro (b. 1935) by a record margin.

During 1985 and 1986 public support for President Reagan was maintained, as a radical tax-cutting bill was successfully pushed through Congress. In 1986, however, clouds began to gather on the economic horizon as a huge budget and trade deficit developed, while overseas the president faced mounting public opposition to his policies in Central America. He also encountered a formidable new superpower adversary in the form of the new reformist Soviet leader, Mikhail Gorbachev. Gorbachev pressed for arms reductions during superpower summits held in Geneva in November 1985 and Reykjavik in October 1986.

The Reagan presidency was rocked in November 1986 by the Republican Party's loss of control of the Senate, following midterm elections, and the disclosure of a damaging 'Iran–Contragate' scandal, concerning American arms sales to Iran in return for the release of hostages, and the 'laundering' of profits to help the Nicaraguan Contra anticommunist guerrillas. This scandal dented public confidence in the administration and forced the resignation and dismissal of key cabinet members, including National Security Adviser Rear Admiral John Poindexter (b. 1936) in November 1986 and Chief of Staff Donald Regan (b. 1918) in February 1987.

Having reasserted presidential authority between 1981 and 1986, the ailing President Reagan began to forfeit power to a resurgent Congress during 1987. However, under the skilled leadership of his new chief of staff, Howard Baker (b. 1925), the president began to recover his standing in the national polls through emerging as a 'born again' convert to

détente. This was evidenced by his signing in Washington in December 1987 a historic agreement with the Soviet Union to scrap intermediate-range nuclear forces (INF).

Reagan's popularity transferred itself to Vice President George Bush (b. 1924) who, despite selecting the inexperienced Dan Quayle (b. 1947), a two-term senator from Indiana, as his running mate and despite opposition charges that he had been indirectly involved in the Irangate proceedings, defeated the Democrats' candidate Michael S Dukakis (b. 1933), the governor of Massachusetts, in the presidential election of November 1988. Bush captured 53% of the national vote to Dukakis's 46%, finishing ahead in 40 states. He thus became the first sitting vice president since the Democrat Martin Van Buren (1782–1862) in 1836 to secure the presidency through the ballot box.

Bush came to power, after six years of economic growth, at a time of uncertainty. Reagan's tax-cutting policy, while stimulating the economy and reducing the level of unemployment to just 5%, had led to mounting federal trade and budget deficits, which had served to turn the United States into a debtor nation for the first time in its history and had helped trigger a Wall Street share crash in October 1987.

Bush promised, on his inauguration, to 'make kinder the face of the nation and gentler the face of the world' and, despite his campaign rhetoric, sought to steer a more moderate and consensual course, both domestically and overseas, than his predecessor. There were minor domestic initiatives in the areas of education, drug control, and the environment, where problems had surfaced during the Reagan years. However, in general the first three years of the Bush presidency were dominated by events overseas, in particular the collapse of communism which occurred across Central and Eastern Europe from 1989. This made possible substantial defence economies and left America as the one remaining global superpower, with a long-awaited START (Strategic Arms Reduction Talks) treaty being signed with the Soviet Union in July 1991. Responding to the changed circumstances, President Bush spoke of building a 'new world order' in which the UN would play a more positive and interventionist role in supporting the spread and defence of liberal democracy. The Bush presidency was also characterized by greater US military assertiveness overseas, starting in December 1989 when 23,000 troops were sent to Panama to overthrow the corrupt Panamanian dictator, General Manuel Noriega. A year later, following Iraq's invasion and annexation of neighbouring Kuwait on 2 August 1990, President Bush played the leading role in constructing and dominating a UN coalition with the purpose of forcing Iraq's withdrawal. After economic sanctions and diplomatic negotiations had failed, this multinational coalition, which included 430,000 US ground troops, 1,300 fighter and support aircraft, 2,000 tanks, and 55 warships and was led by the American general, H Norman Schwarzkopf, embarked, from 17 January 1991, on 'Operation Desert Storm'. This involved massive air attacks on Iraqi positions and, from 23 February 1991, a ground offensive. It succeeded in its objectives, with Iraq accepting ceasefire and withdrawal terms on 3 March 1991.

As US commander in chief during 'Operation Desert Storm', President Bush's public approval rating climbed to 90% in the spring of 1991 and his re-election in 1992 appeared inevitable. However, the president had much less success on the domestic front. The economy was marred both by recession and a crippling budget deficit, which forced Bush during 1990 to recant on his 1988 campaign promise not to raise taxes. There were also mounting social tensions, linked to unemployment and growing drug abuse, as witnessed most dramatically by violent riots on 29 April 1992 among the 'underclass' of Los Angeles.

As 1992 progressed and the economy entered a 'second-dip' phase of the recession, the president's popularity slumped dramatically, with his position being worsened by new revelations suggesting his possible involvement in the 'Irangate' affair. Bush was criticized for his 'do-nothing' approach towards the domestic scene both by his Democrat challenger for the presidency, the neo-liberal Arkansas governor, Bill Clinton (b. 1946), and by the Texan billionaire, H Ross Perot (b. 1930), who entered the race as a well-funded conservative–populist independent, preaching the need for tough economic reform. The Bush campaign team attempted to attack perceived flaws in Clinton's character and to depict him as a 'tax and spend liberal'. However, these were resisted resolutely by a candidate who was drawn from the Democrat's more conservative southern wing. Running a skilful campaign, concentrating on a message of generational change and greater domestic intervention, Clinton secured a clear victory over the incumbent Bush in the November 1992 presidential election. Perot also polled surprisingly strongly, attracting 19% of the national vote, the highest share achieved by a third candidate since the 'Bull Moose' challenge of Theodore Roosevelt (1858–1919) in 1912. Drawing support from a wide range of social groups and geographical areas, Clinton had before him the prospect of consolidating this support so as to establish a new 'neo-liberal Democrat' electoral coalition which would replace the 'new Republican' coalition which had been constructed by Ronald Reagan.

During 1993 President Clinton faced repeated criticisms of his uncertain leadership and apparent lack of clear principles and strategy, especially overseas, where US intervention in Somalia in October 1993 resulted in the deaths of 18 members of the US military. His personal standing was also undermined by a series of allegations concerning sexual and financial misconduct, the latter, the 'Whitewater scandal', concerning the Clintons' financial dealings, while he was governor of Arkansas, with the Whitewater Development Corporation. Nevertheless, President Clinton's record of success in Congress, in terms of votes won, was the best of any president since 1953. The two most important measures passed were the deficit reduction budget package, approved in August 1993, and the North Atlantic Free Trade Agreement (NAFTA), ratified in November 1993. The former provided for a reduction in the federal deficit, which stood in 1993 at $255 billion, or 4% of GDP, by $496 billion over five years through a combination of spending cuts and tax increases, targeted at high earners and gasoline. The latter, a measure first proposed by President Bush, provided for the formation of a North American free trade zone, embracing Canada, Mexico, and the United States, with trade barriers being phased out over a 15-year period.

During 1994, with a special counsel being appointed to investigate the 'Whitewater affair' in January and congres-

sional hearings commencing in July, and with a former Arkansas state clerical worker, Paula Jones, filing sexual harassment charges against Clinton in May, President Clinton continued to be dogged by scandals. These were eagerly seized upon by the president's Republican opponents, whose congressional leadership was now directed by Newt Gingrich (b. 1943), an aggressive radical-right Reaganite whose vigorous campaigns against alleged 'Democrat sleaze' had already resulted in the toppling of key Democrat congressmen. President Clinton's key domestic reform measure, the overhaul of the country's health care system so as to provide, via a combination of market forces and federal regulations, health insurance for every US citizen, was entrusted to a task force overseen by Hillary Rodham Clinton, the president's formidable wife, who was an accomplished lawyer. The proposed package was unveiled in September 1992 and gained broad public support. However, the measure was effectively killed by the powerful private health care lobby and was rejected by Congress in September 1994.

This came as a crushing blow to the Clinton presidency and, despite a background of buoyant economic growth, the Democrats were heavily defeated in the congressional and state elections of November 1994. The midterm reverse was so great that the Republicans secured control of both chambers of Congress for the first time since 1954 and held 60% of state governorships. Newt Gingrich, orchestrator of the Republican campaign, became the new house speaker and effective leader of the opposition. During 1995 he sought to secure implementation of a radical ten-point conservative-populist manifesto, 'Contract with America'. This included pledges to secure a balanced budget, tackle rising crime levels, limit congressional terms, reform welfare, and drastically reduce the powers of the federal administration. With President Clinton being forced to share authority during 1995, Gingrich became a quasi prime minister in an uneasy 'dual administration'.

By mid-April 1995, the lower chamber had approved all but one of the elements of 'Contract with America', the congressional term limits bill being rejected. However, the Senate, led by majority leader, Bob Dole, a candidate for the Republican Party's presidential nomination in 1996, had passed only two measures. In June 1995 President Clinton issued the first veto of his administration, rejecting a package of cuts in education and training. However, he also indicated a determination to shift rightwards, responding to the changed public mood. He unveiled his own proposals for the achievement of a balanced budget by 2005, through major reductions in Medicare and other welfare costs, and seized the centre ground on such issues as school prayers, affirmative action, and family values, while portraying the Republicans as reckless extremists. This strategy enabled Clinton's public approval rating to climb to a respectable 47% in August 1995, with polls suggesting that he would defeat the frontrunner of the divided Republicans, Bob Dole, in a presidential election by a clear margin. The other leading candidates for the Republican Party's presidential nomination in 1996 were Phil Gramm, a conservative Texas senator who was backed by the Christian Coalition, and Patrick Buchanan, an ultra-conservative columnist.

Northern and Western Europe

The region Northern and Western Europe, as we have defined it, stretches from the Arctic Ocean in the north to the Mediterranean Sea in the south, and from the Atlantic Ocean in the west to the Adriatic in the east. It includes 23 nation-states, whose total populations amount to over 370 million, or over 85 million more than the total number of people inhabiting the whole of the North American continent. However, the land area occupied by these 23 countries is less than a fifth of that within the boundaries of the United States and Canada and accounts for only 2.7% of the world's total land area. We are, therefore, looking at a comparatively large region, fairly densely populated, but with this density greatest near the geographical centre and discernibly thinning out at the peripheries.

Climatically there are substantial variations, ranging from the tundra of northern Scandinavia to the warm temperate conditions enjoyed by those countries bordering the Mediterranean. Ethnically the differences are not as great and, with a few exceptions, most of the countries in this region have a common cultural heritage, a common Christian foundation, with a north–south Protestant–Catholic denominational division, and a shared history. There are distinct language differences, however, from country to country, the dominant tongues being English, French, German, and the Latin languages of Italy, Spain, and Portugal.

Paradoxically, although 15 of these 23 states are now members of the European Union, the history of the region has been one of division and war rather than cooperation and unity. Most of the major states have been rivals at one time or another and most have clashed militarily. England has been at war with Spain and France. France has clashed with most of Europe and, more recently, Germany has attempted to subjugate the entire continent. A desire to prevent a recurrence of war in Europe was the genesis of the European Community and that wish has been largely fulfilled, since the region has enjoyed peace and stability since World War II even though countries on its periphery have fared less well. Today, 15 of the states within the region are members of the European Union, with open frontiers for the movement of goods, capital, and people.

Despite containing less than 7% of the global population, Northern and Western Europe is a key region, containing most of the major political and economic powers. It was in this region where, during the post-Renaissance era, the world's first modern nation-states were formed and from this base the colonization of Africa, the Americas, and Asia was conducted. Indeed, as *Chapter 8* shows, the United Kingdom, France, and the Netherlands remain significant colonial powers.

Economically, the 23 states of Northern and Western Europe now have much in common. All operate some form of mixed economy, based partly on market forces and state intervention, although within this mixture sharp policy differences are evident. Whereas there has been a tendency in recent years for a majority of governing regimes to have a centrist orientation, a minority, the most notable among them being the United Kingdom, have shifted to the right. All 23 countries in the region have high-income economies. Indeed, 15 of the world's 20 wealthiest states are situated within Northern and Western Europe, with Liechtenstein, Switzerland, Luxembourg, and Denmark occupying positions in the world 'top five'. In 1992 average per-capita GDP in Northern and Western Europe exceeded $20,000 and the region generated almost a third of global GDP.

All the 23 states within Northern and Western Europe have comparatively high literacy rates, most being, in fact, in the 90%+ category. Urbanization levels are also high and human rights ratings, ranging from 87% in Spain to 99% in Finland, are the best in the world outside North America.

Some of the 23 states have significant regional problems within their national boundaries, based on linguistic, religious, or cultural differences. The most notable examples are to be found in Belgium, Spain, Italy, and the United Kingdom.

In Belgium differences between the Flemish-speaking north and the French-speaking south have resulted in a multiplicity of political parties, based on language distinctions as well as economic and social priorities. In reality, disagreements between the north and the south, and dissatisfaction with the peculiar position of Brussels, which is linguistically out of step with the rest of the country, owe as much to economic as to cultural disparities. However, in the 1991 general election more than a million Belgians voted for extremist and antipolitical parties and in 1993 it was decided to establish a federation of three states: Flanders, Wallonia, and Brussels.

In Finland demands for greater recognition of the Swedish-speaking minority are growing progressively weaker. In Norway language differences are based more on dialects and these are being gradually assimilated into a common rural–urban approach. The passion generated by linguistic minorities on the Danish–German and Austrian–Italian borders has diminished markedly in recent years.

Switzerland provides a good example of how language and cultural variations can be successfully accommodated without disrupting social and political harmony. The fact that a federal approach was taken is less important than the willingness, over a long period of time, to show a tolerant respect for cultural and social differences. The strength of the Swiss economy, and the high living standards enjoyed by its citizens, have also helped to create these harmonious relationships.

While Spain was under a virtual military dictatorship until the death of General Franco in 1975 the demands of Basque separatists could be kept in check by force. However, since the return to pluralist politics a different approach has been necessary. A substantial devolution of powers, short of full federalism, seems to have gone a long way towards meeting regional aspirations.

In Italy strong regional divisions have also promoted political decentralization. The chief divide exists between the economically backward south, the 'Mezzogiorno', and the industrially highly developed north. The federalist Northern League has established itself as the dominant force in the northern region of Lombardy.

What to do about Northern Ireland has been on the agenda of United Kingdom governments for more than half a century and a permanent answer has not yet been found. For the past two decades the approach has been to match violence with violence and an attempt to find a political solution, which would involve all sides in the argument, has so far been avoided. However, the agreement in September 1994 by the nationalist Irish Republican Army (IRA) to a cease-fire was a welcome development. The nationalist movement in Wales has now lost much of its momentum but calls for Scottish devolution, or even separation, have been revived and are likely to become stronger in the ensuing years. This is because, unlike Wales, the sense of nationalism in Scotland is based more on economic and social factors than on cultural differences.

Putting aside regional disputes, politically the 23 nations now show great similarities. Twenty-one have been classified as liberal democracies and one, Andorra, is an emergent democracy. The Vatican City State, as the centre of the Roman Catholic faith, is an absolutist theocratic regime.

A close examination of Table 59 below reveals the extent of the political similarities. Four, Austria, Belgium, Germany, and Switzerland, are federal states and the remaining 19 are unitary. Twelve have two-chamber assemblies and 10

are content with one. Eighteen have parliamentary executives; one, Switzerland, has a limited presidential executive; one, the Vatican City State, has an absolute executive; and in three, France, Finland, and Portugal, the executive is 'dual', with responsibility shared between a president and a prime minister. Finally, the voting systems in 19 states are based on proportional representation, while a majoritarian system is used in three countries: France, Monaco, and the United Kingdom.

It is in the areas of party politics and electoral systems that a clear majority–minority situation arises. Eighteen of the 23 states have multiparty politics operating whereas three, France, Malta, and the United Kingdom, have more polarized two-party systems.

It would be dangerous to draw too firm conclusions about the effects of voting systems on party structures from this small sample, but it can be said that multiparty politics and some form of proportional representation seem to go hand in hand in most countries in Northern and Western Europe. It can also be said that the fact that many have had coalition governments for most of the postwar period does not seem to have, in any way, diminished the degree of democracy they

Northern and Western Europe: social, economic, and political data

Country	Area (sq km)	c. 1992–94 Population (m)	c. 1992–94 Pop. density per sq km	c. 1992 Adult literacy rate (%)	World ranking	Income type	c. 1991 Human rights ranking (%)
Andorra	468	0.058	124	100	1	high	99
Austria	83,850	7.800	93	100	1	high	95
Belgium	30,528	10.068	329	100	1	high	96
Denmark	43,080	5.200	121	99	8	high	98
Finland	338,139	5.060	15	99	8	high	99
France	543,965	57.400	106	99	8	high	94
Germany	357,000	80.600	226	99	8	high	98
Iceland	102,850	0.300	3	99	8	high	n/a
Ireland	70,283	3.500	50	99	8	high	94
Italy	301,225	57.800	192	97	44	high	90
Liechtenstein	160	0.029	181	99	8	high	n/a
Luxembourg	2,590	0.400	154	100	1	high	n/a
Malta	316	0.400	1,266	81	102	high	n/a
Monaco	2	0.014	14,000	100	1	high	99
Netherlands	37,938	15.300	403	99	8	high	98
Norway	324,219	4.300	13	99	8	high	97
Portugal	92,080	9.900	107	85	94	high	92
San Marino	61	0.023	377	96	52	high	n/a
Spain	504,880	39.200	78	95	59	high	87
Sweden	449,700	8.700	19	99	8	high	98
Switzerland	41,290	6.900	168	99	8	high	96
United Kingdom	244,100	57.800	238	99	8	high	93
Vatican City State	0.3	0.001	2,250	100	1	high	n/a
Total/average/range	3,568,724.3	370.753	104	81–100			87–99

Key:

AMS	additional member system	I	indirect	PR	proportional representation
E	elected	LV	limited vote	SB	second ballot
F	federal	PL	party list	SP	simple plurality

have enjoyed, or their economic performances. Indeed, it can be cogently argued that the reverse is true.

In summary, although there are clear differences in approach to the political, economic, and social challenges facing them, the 23 states of Northern and Western Europe have more shared values than disagreements. Above all else, most have mature political systems which have survived many changes in the environments in which they function and this maturity has created a keen sense of reality and tolerance in their dealings with the rest of the world. Probably the most encouraging sign is that the nations of Northern and Western Europe, whether or not they are European Union members, are increasingly coming together, rather than drifting apart.

Recommended reading

Derbyshire, I *Politics in France: From Giscard to Mitterrand*, W & R Chambers, 1990

Derbyshire, I *Politics in Germany: From Division to Unification*, W & R Chambers, 1991

Derbyshire, I and Derbyshire, J D *Politics in Britain: From Callaghan to Thatcher*, W & R Chambers, 1990

Jacobs, F (ed.) *Western European Political Parties: A Comprehensive Guide*, Longman, 1989

Lane, J E and Ersson, S O *Politics and Society in Western Europe*, Sage, 1991

Mey, Y and Knapp, A *Government and Politics in Western Europe: Britain, France, Italy and Germany*, 2nd edn., Oxford University Press, 1993

Nicholson, F (ed.) *Political and Economic Encyclopaedia of Western Europe*, Longman, 1990

Roberts, G K and Lovecy, J *West European Politics Today*, Manchester University Press, 1988

Smith, G *Politics in Western Europe*, Gower, 1989

Table 59

World ranking	Date of state formation	State structure	State type	Executive type	Number of assembly chambers	Party structure	Lower house electoral system
1	1278	U	Em-dem	Parliamentary	1	multi	PR-AMS
14	1918	F	Lib-dem	Parliamentary	2	multi	PR-PL
12	1830	F	Lib-dem	Parliamentary	2	multi	PR-PL
4	940/1849	U	Lib-dem	Parliamentary	1	multi	PR-PL
1	1917	U	Lib-dem	Dual	1	multi	PR-PL
15	741	U	Lib-dem	Dual	2	multi	SB
4	1871/1949/1990	F	Lib-dem	Parliamentary	2	multi	PR-AMS
	1944	U	Lib-dem	Parliamentary	1	multi	PR-PL
15	1937	U	Lib-dem	Parliamentary	2	multi	PR-STV
21	1861	U	Lib-dem	Parliamentary	2	multi	PR-AMS
	1342	U	Lib-dem	Parliamentary	1	multi	PR-LV
	1848	U	Lib-dem	Parliamentary	1	multi	PR-PL
	1964	U	Lib-dem	Parliamentary	1	two	PR-STV
1	1297	U	Lib-dem	Parliamentary	1	none	SB
4	1648	U	Lib-dem	Parliamentary	2	multi	PR-PL
9	1905	U	Lib-dem	Parliamentary	2	multi	PR-PL
19	1128	U	Lib-dem	Dual	1	multi	PR-PL
	301	U	Lib-dem	Parliamentary	1	multi	PR-LV
26	1492	U	Lib-dem	Parliamentary	2	multi	PR-PL
4	1523	U	Lib-dem	Parliamentary	1	multi	PR-PL
12	1648	F	Lib-dem	Lim-pres	2	multi	PR-PL
18	1707	U	Lib-dem	Parliamentary	2	multi	SP
	1377/1929	U	Abs/Theo	Abs	n/a	none	n/a

STV	single transferable vote	Lib-dem	Liberal democratic	Theo	Theocratic
U	unitary	Em-dem	Emergent democratic		
Abs	Absolutist	Lim-pres	Limited presidential		

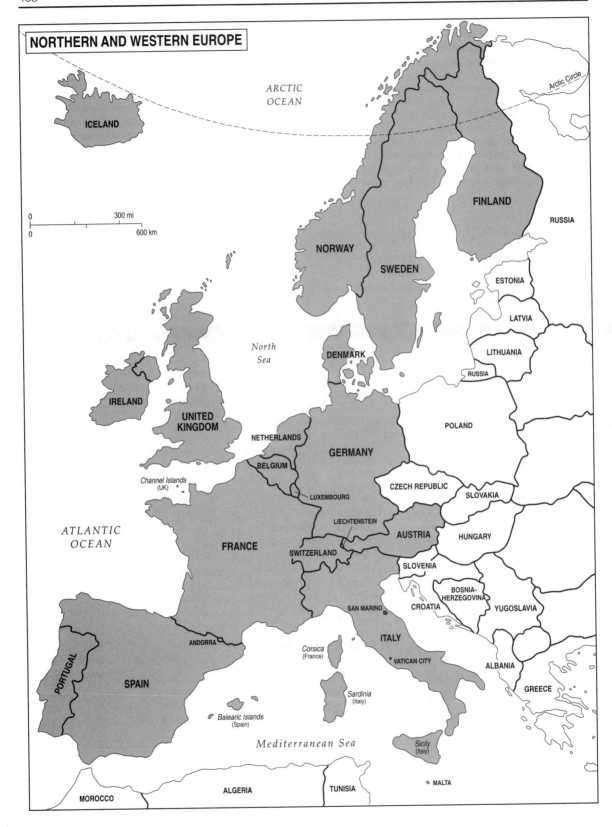

NORTHERN AND WESTERN EUROPE

ARCTIC OCEAN

ICELAND

Arctic Circle

0   300 mi
0   600 km

FINLAND

NORWAY

RUSSIA

SWEDEN

ESTONIA

LATVIA

North
Sea

DENMARK

LITHUANIA

RUSSIA

IRELAND

UNITED
KINGDOM

NETHERLANDS

BELGIUM

GERMANY

POLAND

Channel Islands
(UK)

LUXEMBOURG

CZECH REPUBLIC

SLOVAKIA

ATLANTIC
OCEAN

LIECHTENSTEIN

AUSTRIA

HUNGARY

FRANCE

SWITZERLAND

SLOVENIA

SAN MARINO

CROATIA

BOSNIA-
HERZEGOVINA

YUGOSLAVIA

PORTUGAL

ANDORRA

Corsica
(France)

ITALY

VATICAN CITY

ALBANIA

SPAIN

Sardinia
(Italy)

GREECE

Balearic Islands
(Spain)

Mediterranean Sea

Sicily
(Italy)

MOROCCO

ALGERIA

TUNISIA

MALTA

ANDORRA

Co-Principality of Andorra
Principat d'Andorra

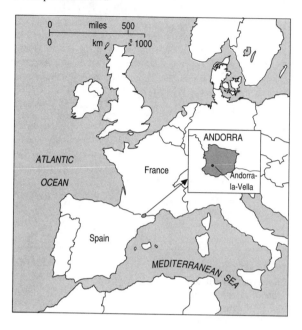

Capital: Andorra-la-Vella

Social and economic data
Area: 468 km²
Population: 58,000*
Pop. density per km²: 124*
Urban population: 94%**
Literacy rate: 100%**
GDP: $1,200 million**; per-capita GDP: $21,150**
Government defence spending (% of GDP): 0%
Currency: French franc and Spanish peseta
Economy type: high income
Labour force in agriculture: N/A

*1994
**1992

Ethnic composition
Twenty-five per cent of the population are Andorrans and 75% immigrant Spanish workers. Catalan is the local language.

Religions
Roman Catholicism is the chief religion.

Political features
State type: emergent democratic
Date of state formation: 1278
Political structure: unitary
Executive: parliamentary
Assembly: one-chamber
Party structure: multiparty
Human rights rating: 99%
International affiliations: CE, UN

Local and regional government
Andorra is divided into seven parishes, each administered by a communal council. Councillors are elected by universal suffrage for four-year terms.

Co-heads of state
Episcopal Co-Prince: Monsignor Dr Joan Marti Alanis, bishop of Seo de Urgel, Spain
French Co-Prince: Jacques Chirac, president of France, since 1995

Head of government
President of the Executive Council: Marc Forne, since 1994

Political leaders since 1982
1982–84 Oscar Ribas Reig, 1984–90 Josep Pintat Solens, 1990–94 Oscar Ribas Reig (AND), 1994–   Marc Forne (UL)

Political system
Andorra had no formal constitution and was governed on semifeudal lines until 1993 when a constitution was approved by referendum. It describes the country as an independent, democratic co-principality and places sovereignty in the hands of the people, yet retains elements of its feudal origins through joint heads of state, the bishop of Urgel, in Spain, and the president of the French Republic. They are represented by permanent delegates, the vicar general of the Urgel diocese and the prefect of the French *département* of Pyrénées-Orientales. Although administratively independent, it had no individual international status until 1993, when it became a full member of the United Nations and in the following year was admitted into the Council of Europe. The 1993 constitution provides for a 28-member assembly, the General Council of the Valleys, serving a four-year term. Fourteen are elected on a national basis and 14 in dual constituencies in each of the seven valleys. The Council submits motions and proposals to the permanent delegates for approval but the 1993 constitution has reduced the powers of the co-princes and their permanent delegates and increased those of the Andorran government, the Executive Council, which, for the first time, has power to raise revenue by income taxes and other fiscal means. The seven-member Executive Council is headed by a prime minister, who is called President of Government.

Political parties
Technically illegal until 1993, several groupings have emerged. They include the centrist National Democratic Grouping (AND), New Democracy (ND) and the National Andorran Coalition (CNA); the centre-right Liberal Union (UL); and the left-of-centre National Democratic Initiative (IDN).

Latest elections
In the December 1993 elections under the new constitution the AND won eight General Council seats, the UL five and the ND five. Other parties and independents obtained ten seats.

Political history
Andorra's independence is viewed as dating from 1278, when an agreement (*pareage*) was entered into between France and the bishop of Seo de Urgel in Spain for the state's co-rule. Since then, possessing only an unpaid ceremonial

militia, it remained dependent upon its larger neighbours for its security and continued existence.

Until 1970 only third-generation Andorran males had the vote. Now the franchise extends to all first-generation Andorrans of foreign parentage aged 28 or over. The electorate is still small, however, in relation to the total population, up to 75% of whom are foreign residents, who are constantly demanding political and nationality rights. Immigration, controlled by a quota system, is restricted to French and Spanish nationals intending to work in Andorra. Since the 1980s democracy, at first fragile, has gradually grown and in 1993 a national referendum overwhelmingly supported proposals for a democratic constitution. In the country's first elections under the new constitution, Oscar Ribas Reig, who had been head of government under the pre-constitution system, was elected president of the Executive Council, heading a broad coalition. Within less than a year he resigned the presidency, after losing the support of ND members of his coalition, and was succeeded by the UL leader, Marc Forne.

While maintaining its political and economic links with France and Spain, in 1993 Andorra became a full member of the United Nations and in the following year joined the Council of Europe.

Economically, the Co-Principality has progressed significantly during recent decades, utilizing its exemption, under the terms of an 1867 Franco–Spanish agreement, from the payment of import duties, to develop a growing tourist industry. About 10 million visitors currently pass through the state annually, purchasing low-priced consumer goods, while several thousand North Europeans use Andorra as a tax haven. This prosperity has been somewhat threatened, however, by the creation of a single European market.

AUSTRIA

Republic of Austria
Republik Österreich

Capital: Vienna

Social and economic data
Area: 83,850 km^2
Population: 7,800,000*
Pop. density per km^2: 93*
Urban population: 59%**
Literacy rate: 100%**
GDP: $171,000 million**; per-capita GDP: $22,000**
Government defence spending (% of GDP): 0.9%**
Currency: schilling
Economy type: high income
Labour force in agriculture: 8%**

*1994
**1992

Ethnic composition
Ninety-eight per cent of the population is German, 0.7% Croatian and 0.3% Slovene. German is the national language.

Religions
About 89% of the population is Roman Catholic, about 6% belongs to other Christian religions, and there are some 7,000 Jews.

Political features
State type: liberal democratic
Date of state formation: 1918
Political structure: federal
Executive: parliamentary
Assembly: two-chamber
Party structure: multiparty
Human rights rating: 95%
International affiliations: AG (observer), CE, CERN, EEA, ESA, EU, IAEA, IBRD, IMF, NAM (guest), OECD, OSCE, UN, WTO

Local and regional government
Austria is a federal republic divided into nine provinces or states (*Länder*), each with its own assembly and government. The states, with their populations, are: Wien (1.5 million), Niederösterreich (1.4 million), Oberösterreich (1.3 million), Steirmark (1.2 million), Tirol (0.6 million), Karnten (0.5 million), Salzburg (0.4 million), Vorarberg (0.3 million), and Burgenland (0.27 million). The assemblies (*Landtag*) are very similar to the lower house of the federal assembly. Executive power is exercized by governors elected by the provincial assemblies.

Although, constitutionally, Austria is a federal state, there is a high degree of centralization, the federal government being responsible for education, the police, the postal service, the railways, social policies, and taxation.

Head of state
President Thomas Klestil, since 1992

Head of government
Federal Chancellor Franz Vranitzky, since 1986

Political leaders since 1970
1970–83 Bruno Kreiksky (SPÖ), 1983–86 Fred Sinowatz (SPÖ–FPÖ coalition), 1986– Franz Vranitzky (SPÖ–ÖVP coalition)

Political system

The 1920 constitution was amended in 1929, suspended during the Hitler years, and reinstated in 1945. It provides for a two-chamber federal assembly, consisting of a National Council (Nationalrat) and a Federal Council (Bundesrat). The National Council has 183 members elected by universal adult suffrage, through a party list system of proportional representation, for a four-year term. It is subject to dissolution during this period. The Federal Council has 64 members elected by the provincial assemblies for varying terms, depending upon the life of each individual assembly. Each province provides a chair for the Federal Council for a six-month term of office. The federal president is the formal head of state and is elected by popular vote for a six-year term. The federal chancellor is head of government and chosen by the president on the basis of support in the National Council. He or she governs with a cabinet of their own choosing.

Political parties

There are currently 13 active political parties, the most significant being the Social Democratic Party of Austria (SPÖ), the Austrian People's Party (ÖVP), Freedom (FPÖ), the United Green Party of Austria (VGÖ), and the Green Alternative Party (ALV).

The SPÖ was founded in 1889 as the Social-Democratic Party. It advocates democratic socialism and the maintenance of Austria's neutrality.

The ÖVP was founded in 1945 as the Christian-Democratic Party. It describes itself as a 'progressive centre party'.

The FPÖ dates from 1955, and afterwards took over from the League of Independents, which was wound up in 1956. It has a right-wing but populist orientation and advocates social reform, immigration control and withdrawal from the EU. It changed its name from the Freedom Party of Austria to Freedom in 1995.

The VGÖ and ALV are ecological parties which have recently arrived on the political scene, both originating in 1982. The VGÖ is the more conservative of the two, the ALV being the result of a union, in 1987, between the Austrian Alternative List (ALO) and another Green party, the BIP. The VGÖ declined to take part in the merger.

Latest elections

In the 1992 presidential election Thomas Klestil (ÖVP) defeated his SPÖ rival, Rudolf Streicher, in the second ballot run-off, by 56.85% of the popular vote to 43.15%.

The results of the October 1994 Nationalrat elections (turnout 78.1%) were:

	% votes	Seats
SPO	35.2	65
OVP	27.7	52
FPO	22.6	42
Greens	7.0	13
Liberal Forum	5.7	11

The results of the 1993 Bundesrat elections were: ÖVP, 33 seats, SPÖ, 27 seats, and FPÖ, 9 seats.

Political history

The first Austrian Republic was proclaimed in November 1918 after the break-up of the Dual Monarchy of Austria–Hungary. A constituent assembly, which had been formed, voted to make Austria an integral part of Germany but the peace treaties ruled out any Austria–Germany union. With the rise of Nazism in Germany in the 1930s there was considerable pressure on Austria, culminating, in 1938, in the Anschluss, or union, making Austria a province of Greater Germany until the end of the war in 1945.

Austria returned to its 1920 constitution in 1945, with a provisional government led by Dr Karl Renner (1870–1950). The Allies had divided the country into four zones, occupied by the USSR, the United States, Britain, and France. The first postwar elections were held while the country was still occupied and resulted in an SPÖ–ÖVP coalition government. Austria's full independence was formally recognized in October 1955.

The first postwar noncoalition government was formed in 1966 when the ÖVP came to power with Josef Klaus as chancellor. In 1970 the SPÖ formed a minority government under Dr Bruno Kreisky (b. 1911) and increased its majority in the 1971 and 1975 general elections. In 1978 opposition to the government's proposals to install the first nuclear power plant nearly resulted in its defeat but it survived and, although the idea of a nuclear plant was abandoned, nuclear energy continued to be a controversial issue. In 1983 the SPÖ regime came to an end when it lost its overall majority and Kreisky resigned, refusing to join a coalition. The SPÖ decline was partly attributed to the emergence of new environmentalist groups, the VGÖ and the ALO. Dr Fred Sinowatz, the new Chair of the SPÖ, formed an SPÖ–FPÖ coalition government.

In April 1985 international controversy was aroused with the announcement that Dr Kurt Waldheim (b. 1918), former United Nations secretary general, was to be a presidential candidate. Despite allegations of his complicity in the Nazi regime, as a wartime officer in Yugoslavia, Waldheim was eventually elected president in January 1986. In June of that year Sinowatz resigned the chancellorship, for what he described as personal reasons, and was succeeded by Franz Vranitzky (b. 1937) but the SPÖ–FPÖ coalition broke up when an extreme right-winger, Jorg Haider (b. 1950), became FPÖ leader.

In the November 1986 elections the SPÖ tally of National Council seats fell from 90 to 80 and the ÖVP's from 81 to 77 while the FPÖ increased its seats from 12 to 18. For the first time the Green lobby was represented, the VGÖ won eight seats. Vranitzky offered his resignation but was persuaded by the president to try to form a 'grand coalition', between the SPÖ and the ÖVP, on the lines of Austria's first postwar government. Agreement was eventually reached and Vranitzky remained as chancellor with the ÖVP leader, Dr Alois Mock, as vice chancellor. Sinowatz denounced the coalition as a betrayal of socialist principles and resigned as chair of the SPÖ.

In the October 1990 Nationalrat elections the SPÖ held its position as the largest single party but its ÖVP partner lost a quarter of its votes and seats, the FPÖ taking up most of the ÖVP's losses. Vranitsky continued as chancellor with the ÖVP president as his deputy.

In July 1991, in a speech to the Nationalrat, Chancellor Vranitsky acknowledged that many Austrians, including some in prominent positions, had collaborated with the repressive measures and persecutions of Hitler's Third Reich. In August of the same year the European Community formally endorsed Austria's 1989 application for entry and full membership was achieved in January 1995.

In the October 1994 general election right-wing parties made significant gains, the FPÖ increasing its Nationalrat seat tally from 33 to 42, while the SPÖ registered a net loss of 15 seats. The SVÖ–ÖVP, socialist–conservative 'grand coalition', collapsed in October 1995, following budget disagreements and disillusionment with the reality of European Union membership, and its strict convergence criteria for monetary union. A general election was held in December 1995.

BELGIUM

Kingdom of Belgium
Royaume de Belgique
Koninkrijk België

Capital: Brussels

Social and economic data
Area: 30,528 km^2
Population: 10,068,000*
Pop. density per km^2: 329*
Urban population: 97%**
Literacy rate: 100%**

GDP: $200,000 million**; per-capita GDP: $20,000**
Government defence spending (% of GDP): 1.8%**
Currency: Belgian franc
Economy type: high income
Labour force in agriculture: 3%**

*1994
**1992

Ethnic composition
The northern part of the country consists mainly of Flemings, of Teutonic stock, who speak Flemish, while in the south the majority of people are Walloons, of Latin stock, who speak French.

Religions
About 88% of the population is Roman Catholic. There are also about 35,000 Jews and substantial minorities of a number of Protestant denominations, including the Lutheran Church, the Church of England, the United Belgian Protestant Church, the Belgian Evangelical Mission, and the Union of Evangelical Baptist Churches.

Political features
State type: liberal democratic
Date of state formation: 1830
Political structure: federal
Executive: parliamentary
Assembly: two-chamber
Party structure: multiparty
Human rights rating: 96%
International affiliations: AG (observer), BENELUX, BLEU, BOAD, CE, CERN, CSCE, EEA, ESA, EU, G-10, IAEA, IBRD, IMF, NACC, NATO, OECD, UN, WEU, WTO

Local and regional government
Since 1980 Flanders and Wallonia had regional 'subgovernments', each with an elected regional assembly, with certain cultural and economic powers. There was also a separate Walloon Cultural Council. In 1993 the constitution was amended to provide for a federation of three mainly autonomous regions, Brussels, Flanders, and Wallonia, so as to reflect the country's linguistic and cultural diversity. The new constitution moved powers from the Senate to the elected regional assemblies, each of which has a life of five years.

For administrative purposes, the nation is divided into provinces which are further subdivided into communes. Local government is conducted by a partnership of officials, appointed by the central government, and elected councillors, representing the views of the localities.

Head of state
King Albert, since 1993

Head of government
Prime Minister Jean-Luc Dehaene, since 1992

Political leaders since 1970
1968–72 Gaston Eyskens (CVP coalitions), 1972–74 Edmond Leburton (PSC coalition), 1974–78 Leo Tindemans

(CVP coalitions), 1978–79 Paul Vanden Boeynants (PSC coalitions), 1979–81 Wilfried Martens (CVP coalitions), 1981 Mark Eyskens (CVP coalition), 1981–92 Wilfried Martens (CVP coalitions), 1992– Jean-Luc Dehaene (CVP coalition)

Political system

The constitution dates from 1831 and was subsequently amended a number of times, rewritten in 1971 and further revised in 1993 to create a federation. The parliamentary system contains features found in both Britain and the United States. For example, the prime minister and cabinet are drawn from and responsible to the assembly, which, in turn, through a powerful committee system, exercises considerable control over the executive.

The assembly consists of two chambers, the Senate, with 71 members, and the Chamber of Representatives, with 150. Forty members of the Senate, whose powers were greatly reduced by the 1993 constitution, are nationally elected, through a party list system of proportional representation and 31 are coopted. The Senate has a life of four years. The Chamber of Representatives members are elected by universal adult suffrage, through a party list system of proportional representation, also for a four-year term.

The prime minister is appointed by the king on the basis of assembly support. The king then appoints a cabinet on the advice of the prime minister.

Political parties

There are currently 20 active political parties, most of them reflecting the linguistic and social divisions within the country. The most significant parties are the Dutch-speaking Social Christian Party (CVP), the French-speaking Social Christian Party (PSC), the Dutch-speaking Socialist Party (SP), the French-speaking Socialist Party (PS), the Flemish Liberals and Democrats (VLD), the French-speaking Liberal Reform Party (PRL), the People's Union (Volksunie), the French-speaking Democratic Front (FDF), and the Flemish Vlaams Blok.

The CVP was founded in 1945. It has a centre-left orientation. The PSC was formed at the same time and is the CVP's French-speaking equivalent. Collectively, the two parties now have over 180,000 members.

The SP is the Flemish wing of the Socialist Party and was founded in 1885. The PS is the French-speaking wing, which broke away in 1979. Both wings have left-of-centre orientations.

The VLD is the successor to the PVV which was the Flemish wing of the Liberal Party and was formed in 1961, to replace the former Liberal Party. The PRL is the French-speaking wing and dates from 1979. Before that it was known as the Walloon Freedom and Reform Party. Both wings have a moderate centrist orientation.

The Volksunie was founded in 1954 and argues for allowing full scope for the promotion of a Flemish identity.

The Vlaams Blok is a right-wing Flemish nationalist grouping, more extreme than the other Flemish parties.

Latest elections

The results of the 1995 general election were as follows:

	% votes	Chamber seats	Senate seats
CVP	17.2	29	7
VLD	13.1	21	3
PS	11.9	21	6
SP	12.6	20	5
PRL–FDF	10.3	18	6
PSC	7.7	12	5
Vlaams Blok	7.8	11	3
Volksunie	4.7	5	2
Other parties	14.7	13	3

Political history

What is now the modern Kingdom of Belgium has experienced many changes of rule under many different political regimes, from the Romans of pre-Christian times, to the French, then the Spanish, then the Austrians, and then the French again. It formed part of the French Empire between 1794 and 1815, after which it was united with the Netherlands. Linguistic, religious, and historical differences made the marriage an unhappy one and in 1830 the Belgians rebelled. The great powers intervened and Belgium was given international recognition as an independent kingdom, under Leopold I of Saxe-Coburg (1790–1865). From that date the country developed rapidly to become a significant industrial and commercial force.

The experience of two world wars fought on its territory has made Belgium acutely aware of the dangers of the pursuit of purely national ends and since 1945 it has played a major part in international cooperation in Europe, being a founder member of the Benelux Economic Union, the Council of Europe, and the European Community.

Its main internal political problems have stemmed from the division between French- and Dutch-speaking members of the population, aggravated by the polarization between Flanders in the north, which is predominantly Conservative, and French-speaking Wallonia in the south, which tends to be mainly Socialist. About 55% of the population is Dutch-speaking, 44% French-speaking, and the remainder speaks German. It has been a hereditary monarchy since 1830 and King Leopold III (1901–83), who had reigned since 1934, abdicated in 1951 in favour of his son, Baudouin I (1930–93).

Between 1971 and 1973, in an attempt to close the language and social divisions, amendments to the constitution were made. These involved the transfer of greater power to the regions, the inclusion of German-speaking members in the cabinet and linguistic parity in the government overall. Then, in 1974, separate Regional Councils and Ministerial Committees were established. In 1977 a coalition government, headed by Leo Tindemans (CVP), proposed the creation of of a federal Belgium, based on Flanders, Wallonia, and Brussels, but the proposals were not adopted and in 1978 Tindemans resigned. He was followed by another coalition government headed by Wilfried Martens (b. 1936). In 1980 the language conflict developed into open violence and it was eventually agreed that Flanders and Wallonia should have separate regional assemblies with powers to spend up to 10% of the national budget on cultural facilities, public health, roads, and urban projects. Brussels was to be governed by a three-member executive. In 1993 the constitution was amended to provide for this threefold federation, with a reduction in the legislative powers of the Senate and an increase in those of the elected regional assemblies.

Such was the political instability that by 1980 Martens had formed no fewer than four coalition governments. In 1981 a new coalition, led by Mark Eyskens (CVP), lasted less than a year and Martens again returned to power. Between 1981 and 1982 economic difficulties resulted in a series of damaging public sector strikes and in 1983 linguistic divisions again threatened the government.

Martens formed yet another coalition government after the 1985 general election but this broke up in 1987 and the prime minister was asked by the king to continue until after further elections. These were held in December 1987 but failed to produce a conclusive result and, after a series of exploratory talks between political leaders, Martens formed a CVP–PS–SP–PSC–Volksunie coalition in May 1988. After the November 1991 general election, in which 1 million people voted for extremist and antipolitical parties, he found it increasingly difficult to hold his coalition together and resigned. He was persuaded to carry on as a caretaker prime minister until, in March 1992, his CVP colleague, Jean-Luc Dehaene (b. 1940), was able to form a viable government.

In 1993 Dehaene, faced with deadlock in the coalition over a decision to reduce the budget deficit, offered his resignation but the king refused to accept it and eventually the dispute was resolved. King Baudouin, who had been a calming figure in the political process, died in July 1993 and was succeeded by his brother, Prince Albert (b. 1934).

DENMARK

Kingdom of Denmark
Kongeriget Danmark

Capital: Copenhagen

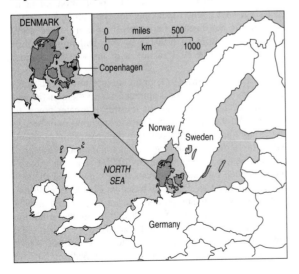

Social and economic data
Area: 43,080 km^2
Population: 5,200,000*
Pop. density per km^2: 121*
Urban population: 85%**
Literacy rate: 99%**
GDP: $134,000 million**; per-capita GDP: $25,927**
Government defence spending (% of GDP): 2%**
Currency: Danish krone
Economy type: high income
Labour force in agriculture: 6%**

*1994
**1992

Ethnic composition
The Danes are a branch of the Scandinavian race which embraces the whole peninsula, including Sweden, Norway, and Finland as well as Denmark. Danish is the national language.

Religions
The Danish Lutheran Church is the established church and about 91% of the population belongs to it.

Political features
State type: liberal democratic
Date of state formation: c. 940/1849
Political structure: unitary
Executive: parliamentary
Assembly: one-chamber
Party structure: multiparty
Human rights rating: 98%
International affiliations: AG (observer), CBSS, CE, CERN, EEA, ESA, EU, IAEA, IBRD, IMF, IWC, NACC, NATO, NC, OECD, OSCE, UN, WEU (observer), WTO

Local and regional government
Denmark is divided into 14 counties (*amstkommuner*), varying in population from about 47,000 to nearly 620,000, plus one city and one borough. All have elected councils. At a lower level there are 277 districts, each with an elected council and mayor.

The two autonomous dependencies, the Faroe Islands and Greenland, enjoy home rule, with elected assemblies and executives, as described in ***Chapter 8***. They also elect representatives to the national assembly, the Folketing.

Head of state
Queen Margarethe II, since 1972

Head of government
Prime Minister Poul Nyrup Rasmussen, since 1993

Political leaders since 1970
1973–75 Poul Hartling (Liberal), 1975–82 Anker Jörgensen (Social Democrat and coalition), 1982–1993 Poul Schlüter (Conservative coalition), 1993–   Poul Nyrup Rasmussen (Social Democrat-led coalition)

Political system
The 1849 constitution has been revised on several occasions, the last being in 1953. It provides for a hereditary monarch,

with no personal political power, and a single-chamber assembly, the Folketing. The prime minister and cabinet are drawn from and collectively responsible to the Folketing, which has 179 members, elected by adult franchise, 175 of the members representing metropolitan Denmark; two, the Faroe Islands and two, Greenland. Voting is by a party list system of proportional representation and the Folketing has a life of four years, but may be dissolved within this period if the government is defeated on a vote of confidence. The government, however, need only resign on what it itself defines as a 'vital element' of policy.

Political parties

The proportional representation voting system favours the growth of political parties with distinctively different attitudes and policies. There are currently some 15, the eight most significant being the Social Democrats (SD), the Conservative People's Party (KF), the Liberal Party (V), the Socialist People's Party (SF), the Radical Liberals (RV), the Centre Democrats (CD), the Progress Party (FP), and the Christian People's Party (KrF).

The SD was founded in 1871 on Marxist principles but now has a moderate left-of-centre orientation. Its members are drawn mainly from blue-collar workers and public service employees.

The KF was formed in 1916 by a mixture of landowners, intellectuals, and academics. It is a moderate, free enterprise party which accepts the need for state intervention to preserve the nation's social and economic balance.

The Venstre or V party is the Liberal Party of Denmark and was established in 1870. It is a centre-left grouping which supports free trade, a well-funded welfare system, but a minimum of state interference in other respects.

The SF was formed in 1959 by Aksel Larsen who had been the leader of the Danish Communist Party but was expelled because he refused to toe the Soviet line. As now constituted, it is a moderate, left-wing party which seeks to apply socialism in a distinctively Danish way.

The RV split from the Liberals in 1905 to pursue more radical policies. It is a strongly internationalist party which favours domestic policies of social reform, worker participation in industrial management, the control of monopolies, and the strengthening of private enterprise.

The CD is a moderate centrist party which was formed in 1973. It opposes extremes in politics and is a strong supporter of EU and NATO membership.

The FP began in 1972 as a strongly anti-bureaucratic movement, promoting such radical ideas as the abolition of income tax, the disbanding of the civil service, and a drastic reduction in legislation.

The KrF was founded in 1970 as an inter-denominational grouping which places emphasis on family values. It is a strong opponent of abortion and pornography.

The EU is a far-right party strongly opposed to European Union membership.

Latest elections

The results of the 1994 Folketing elections were as illustrated in the following table:

	% votes	Seats
SD	34.6	62
V	23.3	42
KF	15.0	27
SF	7.3	13
FP	6.4	11
RV	4.6	8
EU	3.1	6
CD	2.8	5
KrF	1.8	0
Independents	1	1

Political history

Part of a United Scandinavian Kingdom until the 15th century and then remaining linked with Norway until 1815, Denmark became an independent state in 1849. The constitution which was then adopted reaffirmed its status as a constitutional monarchy. Neutral in World War I, Denmark tried to preserve its neutrality in 1939 by signing a pact with Adolf Hitler, but was invaded by the Germans in 1940 and occupied until liberated by British forces in 1945.

Although traditionally a neutralist country, Denmark joined NATO in 1949 and the European Free Trade Association (EFTA) in 1960, resigning to join the European Community in 1973. Iceland was part of the Danish kingdom until 1945 and the other parts of non-metropolitan Denmark, the Faroe Islands and Greenland, were given special recognition by a constitution which has been successfully adapted to meet changing circumstances. The last rewriting occurred in 1953 when, among other things, provision was made for a daughter to succeed to the throne in the absence of a male heir, and a system of voting by proportional representation was introduced.

Moderate left-wing policies have tended to dominate Danish politics, and the voting system, often resulting in minority or coalition governments, has, on the whole, encouraged this moderate approach. In 1985 Denmark's tradition of neutrality was exemplified by evidence of a growing non-nuclear movement.

In the 1987 general election the centre-right coalition, led by Poul Schlüter (b. 1929), lost seven seats but Schlüter decided to continue with a minority government, holding 70 of the 179 Folketing seats. A government defeat over Denmark's non-nuclear defence policy prompted him to call a snap general election in May 1988. This resulted in slight gains for his centre-right coalition but overall an inconclusive result. The queen asked Schlüter to form a new government which he did in June 1988, on the basis of Conservative, Liberal, and Radical Liberal support, and the term of his coalition was renewed in the 1990 general election.

In June 1992 the Danish electorate sent shock waves through the European Community when, in a referendum, they declined to ratify the Maastricht Treaty on closer economic and political union by a narrow 49%:51% margin. Following a new referendum in May 1993, when 56.8% voted 'Yes', it was ratified.

In 1993 Prime Minister Schlüter resigned after a judicial inquiry had accused him of faling to reveal the truth about the prevention of Tamil refugees from Sri Lanka entering Denmark and he was replaced by Poul Nyrup Rasmussen (b. 1944), heading an SD-led coalition. Despite losses in the general election in the following year he narrowly retained his position by forming a minority SD–CD–RV coalition government, dependent on the support of left-wing parties.

FINLAND

Republic of Finland
Suomen Tasavalta

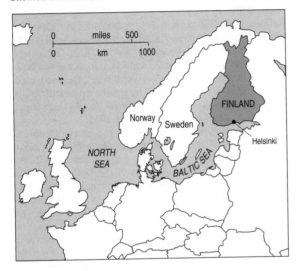

Capital: Helsinki

Social and economic data
Area: 338,139 km^2
Population: 5,060,000*
Pop. density per km^2: 15*
Urban population: 60%**
Literacy rate: 99%**
GDP: $90,000 million**; per-capita GDP: $18,000**
Government defence spending (% of GDP): 2%**
Currency: markka
Economy type: high income
Labour force in agriculture: 9%**

*1994
**1992

Ethnic composition
The great majority of Finns are descended from the inhabitants of Russia who were pushed northwards by Slav migrations. The majority speak Finnish, with a 6% minority speaking Swedish.

Religions
Ninety per cent of the population belongs to the Evangelical Lutheran Church.

Political features
State type: liberal democratic
Date of state formation: 1917
Political structure: unitary
Executive: dual
Assembly: one-chamber
Party structure: multiparty
Human rights rating: 99%
International affiliations: AG (observer), CBSS, CE, CERN, EEA, ESA (associate), EU, IAEA, IBRD, IMF, IWC, NAM (guest), NC, OECD, OSCE, PFP, UN, WTO

Local and regional government
The country is divided into 12 provinces (*laani*), each administered by an appointed governor. One of the provinces, Ahvenanmaa, which comprises the self-governing Åland Islands (pop. 0.024 million), also has an elected assembly (*landsting*) and local powers of legislation.

Head of state (formal and executive)
President Martti Ahtisaari, since 1994

Head of government
Prime Minister Paavo Lipponen, since 1995

Political leaders since 1970
1970 Teuve Aura (cabinet of experts), 1970–71 Ahti Karjalainen (KP-led coalition), 1971–72 Teuve Aura (caretaker cabinet), 1972 Rafael Paasio (SSDP), 1972–75 Kalevi Sorsa (SSDP-led coalition), 1975 Keijo Liinamaa (caretaker cabinet), 1975–77 Martti Miettunen (KP-led coalitions), 1977–79 Kalevi Sorsa (SSDP-led coalition), 1979–82 Mauno Koivisto (SSDP-led coalition), 1982–87 Kalevi Sorsa (SSDP-led coalitions), 1987–91 Harri Holkeri (KOK-led coalition), 1991–95 Esko Aho (KESK-led coalition), 1995– Paavo Lipponen (SSDP-led coalition)

Political system
Finland is a republic which combines a parliamentary system with a strong presidency. The single-chamber assembly, the Eduskunta, has 200 members, elected by universal adult suffrage, through a party list system of proportional representation, for a four-year term. The president is elected for six years by popular vote, or, if there is not a clear majority, by a 301-member electoral college, chosen by popular vote in the same way as the assembly. The president appoints a prime minister and a cabinet, called a Council of State, all members of which are collectively responsible to the Eduskunta.

The relationship between the president and the prime minister and the Council of State is unusual, the nearest equivalent being in France. The president is entrusted with supreme executive power, and can ignore even a unanimous decision reached in the Council of State, but the prime minister is concerned with the day-to-day operation of the government so that to some extent they can, at times, both act as heads of government. Both the president and the Eduskunta can initiate legislation and the president has a right of veto, but that veto can be overruled by a newly appointed assembly. Because of the system of proportional representation, there is a multiplicity of parties, and the prime minister invariably heads a coalition Council of State.

Political parties

There are some nine political parties, the most significant being the Finnish Social Democratic Party (SSDP), the National Coalition Party (KOK), The Finnish Centre Party (KESK), the Finnish Christian Union (SKL), the Swedish People's Party (SFP), the Finnish Rural Party (SMP), and the Left-Wing Alliance (VL).

The SSDP was founded in 1899 as a product of the growing working class movement. It has a moderate left-of-centre orientation. The KOK was formed in 1918. It has a moderate right-of-centre stance. The KESK dates from 1906 and is a radical centre party, promoting the interests of rural areas and favouring decentralized government. The SFP was founded in 1906 to represent the numerous Swedes who had become resident in Finland and established themselves as something of an elite group. The SMP dates from 1956 and seeks to defend the interests of small farmers, industrial workers, and those with small businesses. The Left-Wing Alliance was formed in 1980 by a merger of a number of left-wing parties, including the communists.

Latest elections

In the 1995 Eduskunta elections the results were as follows:

	% vote	Seats
SSDP	28.3	63
KESK	19.9	44
KOK	17.9	29
Others	33.9	54

In the 1994 presidential elections Martti Ahtisaari (SSDP) won 53.9% of the votes, his rival, Elisabeth Rehn (SFP), obtaining 46.1%.

Political history

Finland was formerly an autonomous part of the Russian Empire and during the 1917 Russian revolution it proclaimed its independence. The new Soviet regime initially tried to regain control but acknowledged its independence in 1920. In 1939 the Soviet Union's request for military bases in Finland was rejected and the two countries were involved in the 'Winter War', which lasted for 15 weeks. Finland was defeated and forced to cede territory. In the hope of getting it back, it joined Nazi Germany in attacking the Soviet Union in 1941 but agreed a separate armistice in 1944. It was again forced to cede territory and in 1948 signed the Finno–Soviet Pact of Friendship, Cooperation and Mutual Assistance (the YYA Treaty). This was extended in 1955, 1970, and 1983.

Although the Treaty requires it to repel any attack on the USSR through Finnish territory by Germany or its allies, Finland has adopted and maintained a policy of strict neutrality. It signed a trade treaty with the EEC in 1973 and a 15-year trade agreement with the USSR in 1977.

Finnish politics have been characterized by instability in governments, more than 60 having been formed since independence, including many minority coalitions. The presidency, on the other hand, has been very stable, with only two presidents in over 30 years. The unusual device of a dual executive has, therefore, countered the instability and provided a consistency which might otherwise have been lacking. The Social Democratic and Centre parties have dominated Finland's coalition politics for many years but the 1987 general election resulted in the Social Democrats entering government with their arch enemies, the Conservatives, and the Centre Party being forced into opposition. The Centre Party returned to power, however, in 1991 at the head of the country's first wholly nonsocialist coalition. In 1994 the political balance was restored when the SSDP won the presidency through their candidate, Martti Ahtisaari (b. 1937) and in the following year the party returned to power under its leader, Paavo Lipponen.

In recent years Finland has gradually relaxed its policy of strict neutrality, being admitted to the Council of Europe in 1989 and entering EU membership in 1995.

FRANCE

The French Republic
La République Française

Capital: Paris

Social and economic data
Area: 543,965 km²
Population: 57,400,000*
Pop. density per km²: 106*
Urban population: 74%**
Literacy rate: 99%**
GDP: $1,290,000 million**; per-capita GDP: $22,700**
Government defence spending (% of GDP): 3.4%**
Currency: French franc
Economy type: high income
Labour force in agriculture: 6%**

*1994
**1992

Ethnic composition

The population is overwhelmingly drawn from French ethnic stock, of Celtic and Latin origins, with a Basque minority residing in the southwest. There are, in addition, more than 4 million immigrants, constituting 7% of the population. A third of these are drawn from Algeria and Morocco in Muslim North Africa and reside mainly in the Marseilles Midi region and in northern cities. A further fifth originate from Portugal and a tenth each from Italy and Spain. French is the principal langauge, although small minorities speak Breton, Basque, and Occitan (the ancient language of Languedoc, in the south).

Religions

More than 80% of the population describe themselves as Roman Catholics, although barely 15% are regular church attenders. There are substantial Muslims (2.5 million; 30% residing in Marseilles), Protestant (850,000), and Jewish minorities.

Political features

State type: liberal democratic
Date of state formation: AD 741
Political structure: unitary
Executive: dual
Assembly: two-chamber
Party structure: multiparty
Human rights rating: 94%
International affiliations: AG (observer), BDEAC, BOAD, CERN, CE, EEA, ESA, EU, Francophone, FZ, G-5, G-7, G-10, IAEA, IBRD, IMF, IOC, IWC, NACC, NATO, OECD, OSCE, SPC, UN Security Council (permanent member), WEU, WTO

Local and regional government

There are 22 regional councils (*conseils régionaux*), concerned primarily with economic planning, which were originally set up in 1973 as indirectly elected advisory bodies and have since 1986 been directly elected. Below these are 96 metropolitan department (large county) councils (*conseils généraux*) and 36,673 village and town councils, or communes, to which two ballot council and mayoral elections are held every six years. Benefiting from recent decentralization initiatives, local mayors now control housing, transport, sport, schools, culture, welfare, and some aspects of law enforcement, and have some tax-raising powers. Many national-level French politicians are members of regional councils or mayors in their home areas, for example Prime Minister Alain Juppé is mayor of Bordeaux and former prime minister, Raymond Barre, is mayor of Lyon. However, since 1985, parliamentarians have been restricted to holding a maximum of two elected offices. Corsica, which was designated a *collectivité territoriale* in 1982, has its own directly elected legislative assembly, which has the authority to scrutinize National Assembly bills and to propose amendments applicable to the island. This is described in more detail in *Chapter 8*.

Head of state

President Jacques Chirac, since 1995

Head of government

Prime Minister Alain Juppé, since 1995

Political leaders since 1970

Presidents: 1969–74 Georges Pompidou (UDR), 1974–81 Valéry Giscard d'Estaing (RP/UDF), 1981–95 François Mitterrand (PS), 1995–   Jacques Chirac (RPR)

Prime ministers: 1969–72 Jacques Chaban-Delmas (UDR), 1972–74 Pierre Messmer (UDR), 1974–76 Jacques Chirac (UDR), 1976–1981 Raymond Barre (UDF), 1981–84 Pierre Mauroy (PS), 1984–86 Laurent Fabius (PS), 1986–88 Jacques Chirac (RPR)*, 1988–91 Michel Rocard (PS), 1991–92 Edith Cresson (PS), 1992–93 Pierre Bérégovoy (PS), 1993–95 Edouard Balladur (RPR)*, 1995–   Alain Juppé (RPR)

*Shared power with the socialist President Mitterrand in a 'cohabitation' dual-executive administration

Political system

Under the October 1958 Fifth Republic constitution, the nation's 17th since 1789, France has a two-chamber parliament (*parlement*) and a 'dual' or shared executive. The parliament comprises the National Assembly (Assemblée Nationale) and the Senate (Sénat). The 577 members of the National Assembly are elected for a five-year term, subject to dissolution during this period, from single-member constituencies on the basis of a two-ballot 'run-off' absolute majority voting system. The 321 members of the Senate are indirectly elected, a third at a time, triennially, for nine-year terms by an electoral college composed of local National Assembly members, mayors, department council members, and delegates from municipal councils. Twenty-two National Assembly and 13 Senate seats are elected by overseas departments and territories, and 12 Senate seats by French nationals abroad.

For the March 1986 National Assembly elections a party list system of proportional representation was employed, based on department level multimember constituencies. Within months of this contest, however, the new Chirac administration restored the traditional two-ballot 'run-off' system employed since 1958. Under this system, it is possible for candidates to be elected on the first ballot if they secure an absolute majority of the votes cast and at least one-quarter of the registered votes. Otherwise, a second poll is held a week later in which all the candidates who secured at least 12.5% of the total first ballot 'primary' vote are entitled to participate and which is decided on a relative majority or simple plurality basis. In practice, left- and right-coalition party pacts are invariably entered into locally for this second ballot, with low polling first-ballot candidates agreeing to stand down, turning the follow-up ballot into a head-to-head duel between two contestants. Three-quarters of National Assembly seats are, in general, decided on the second ballot.

The National Assembly, whose work is conducted through six large, 61- and 121-member, functional standing committees, is the more dominant of the two chambers. It examines the annual budget first; the prime minister is drawn from its ranks; while, most importantly, its members are in a position to overthrow the government on a censure or confidence motion.

The Senate, whose membership, as a consequence of its electoral base, is skewed towards centrist- and independent-minded rural and small town representatives, acts as a partial, and sometimes salutary, check. It has the authority to temporarily veto legislation passed by the National Assembly and force amendments in specially convened 'joint conciliation conferences'. Senate vetoes can, however, be overridden by a 'definitive vote' in the National Assembly.

In comparative terms, the most striking feature of the French parliament is its restricted powers vis-à-vis the political executive. Under the terms of Article 34 of the 1958 constitution, it may only pass laws in a 'restricted domain', incorporating areas such as taxation, civic rights, electoral laws, nationalization, and penal matters, and may only lay down general guidelines or 'principles' in the areas of education, labour law, national defence organization, local government and social security. In other policy spheres, the government, is empowered to legislate by executive decree. Even within areas inside its own domain, parliament may occasionally, for a specified period, delegate authority to the executive branch to rule by ordinances, countersigned by the president.

In addition, the French parliament is given, by Article 47, only 70 days to debate and vote on the annual budget. Once this period has elapsed, the government is permitted to impose the measure by ordinance. For other bills, the executive can employ 'guillotine' procedures, pledging its 'responsibility'. The bill then automatically proceeds if no opposition vote of censure is called and successfully passed within 24 hours. The executive can also insist on a single vote on the full text (*vote bloqué*) without accepting any floor amendments.

Finally, the parliamentary year was traditionally restricted, under the terms of Article 28, to a maximum length of only 170 days, distributed in two sessions between October–December and April–June. Outside this period the government was empowered to rule by decree. However, in August 1995 the constitution was amended to provide for an unbroken nine-month parliamentary session between October and June, with ministers being required to answer parliamentary questions once a week.

These restrictions on parliamentary authority were deliberately imposed by the framers of the 1958 constitution in an effort to strengthen the executive branch which had been notoriously weak during the Assembly-dominated Third (1870–1940) and Fourth (1946–58) Republics. In this purpose they have succeeded, though, in the process, the balance has, arguably, been shifted too greatly in the executive's favour. The newly elected President Chirac has redressed the balance somewhat, by extending the parliamentary session.

The authority of France's powerful executive is shared between the two figures of president and prime minister. The president is directly elected for a seven-year term by universal adult suffrage, candidates being required to gain an absolute poll majority either in a first ballot, open to a range of challengers, or in a second 'run-off' contest held a fortnight later between the two top-placed candidates who wish to participate again.

Once elected, the president combines the formal posts of head of state and commander in chief of the armed forces and assumes, by virtue of Article 5, the role of umpire, or 'guardian', of the constitution. The formal powers of the president are extensive, embracing the right to select the prime minister; preside over meetings of the Council of Ministers, or cabinet; countersign government bills; negotiate foreign treaties; initiate referenda; and dissolve the National Assembly and call fresh elections, subject to the qualification that only one dissolution is permitted per year.

According to the terms of Articles 20 and 21 of the 1958 constitution, ultimate control over policy-making, at least in the domestic field, seemed to have been assigned to the prime minister and Council of Ministers. The constitutional amendment of October 1962, which provided for the direct election of the president, to replace the previous arrangement of indirect election by a 'college' of members of parliament and department and municipal councillors, radically changed the executive power balance, enhancing the president's authority, since he or she was the sole nationally elected figure in the Republic. As a consequence, between 1958 and 1986 the president was seen as the 'legitimate' leader of the incumbent governing coalition. He or she was served by an extensive and influential 'Elysée office' and was able to assert dominance over the broad outlines of both domestic and external policy, the prime minister being assigned to the lowlier role of 'parliamentary manager', government organizer, and detailed policy implementer.

In March 1986, when the opposition coalition managed to secure a National Assembly majority and force President Mitterrand to appoint its leader, Jacques Chirac, as prime minister, this power balance was temporarily reordered. The new prime minister proceeded, between 1986–88, to establish himself, in the domestic sphere at least, as the dominant executive force, leaving to the President a narrower figurehead, or symbolic, role. Fresh presidential and Assembly elections in May and June 1988 brought to an end this party political executive split, but there was a new period of 'cohabitation' between March 1993 and May 1995, with Edouard Balladur as prime minister after the 'right coalition' secured a crushing victory in National Assembly elections.

The cabinet ministers serving the president and prime minister are unusual in that they are drawn from both political and technocratic backgrounds and, as a consequence of the 'incompatibility' clause (Article 23) built into the 1958 constitution, are unable to hold parliamentary seats during their period in government. For this reason, National Assembly candidates are required to designate a running mate (*suppléant*) to assume their positions as deputies if they are appointed as government ministers or Constitutional Council members, or if they are elected to the Senate or Constitutional Council, or if they die. These *suppléants* are expected to stand down if a minister later resigns or is dismissed.

In some respects, the French ministerial cabinet is thus closer to the American 'specialist presidential' than the British parliamentary 'collective executive' model. French ministers do, however, participate in and lead National Assembly debates in their relevant areas, appear before standing committees, and are subject to written and oral questioning by Assembly members. Cabinet ministers also work closely with an unusually skilled and influential civil service, being served, themselves, by small, high-powered advisory 'cabinets'.

The 1958 constitution can be amended by parliament by means of a 60% majority vote in both chambers. Alternatively, under the terms of Article 11, the president is allowed, theoretically at the request of the government or parliament, to call a national referendum on constitutional change, as well as in connection with treaty ratification. Since 1961 there have been eight such referenda. The most recent, which concerned ratification of the Maastricht Treaty on European Union, was held on 20 September 1992. Turnout was 70%, with 51% of voters approving ratification of the Treaty. In August 1995 Article 11 was amended to enable the president to call referenda on a wider range of subjects, including economic and social policy and the public services. As a safeguard, when a referendum is called by the president, parliament is entitled to debate the issue.

Functioning as a judicial 'watchdog', there is a nine-member Constitutional Council (CC), whose task is to ensure that decrees and legislation proposed by the government and parliament conform to the precepts of the constitution and that a correct 'balance' is maintained between the executive and the legislature. Its members, who serve nonrenewable nine-year terms, are chosen, three at a time, at triennial intervals, a third by the president of the Republic, another third by the president of the Senate and a final third by the president of the National Assembly. Roland Dumas, formerly a Socialist Party foreign minister between 1984–86 and 1988–93, became president of the Council in March 1995.

The Conseil d'Etat (CE), staffed by senior civil servants, is an additional, and older, judicial review body, which gives nonbinding advice on the constitutionality of bills introduced and serves as a final court of appeal in disputes between the citizen and the administration. Compared with the American Supreme Court or the German Federal Constitutional Court, both the CC and CE are bodies of restricted authority. Since 1974, however, when it was made possible for groups of 60 senators or Assembly members to send bills direct to the Constitutional Council for binding constitutional vetting, its influence has increased significantly. For example, in January 1994 the CC annulled the Balladur administration's attempted reform of the 1850 Loi Falloux, concerned with state and private education funding.

The constitution may be amended in two ways: by the National Assembly and Senate meeting in joint session as a Congress, with the proposed change receiving at least 60% support; or by the amendment bill being passed in identical form separately by the National Assembly and Senate and then approved by the public in a referendum. The constitutional reforms of August 1995 were secured by the former route, attracting 79% support within the constitutional Congress.

The French Republic also comprises four constituent 'overseas departments', French Guiana, Guadeloupe, Martinique, and Réunion, each of which has its own elected general and regional council; two overseas 'collective territories', Mayotte and St Pierre and Miquelon, which are administered by appointed commissioners assisted by elected general councils; and four 'overseas territories', French Polynesia, the French Southern and Antarctic Territories, New Caledonia, and the Wallis and Futuna Islands, which are governed by appointed high commissioners working with elected territorial assemblies. These territories, whose political structures are described more fully in **Chapter 8**, send members, as has already been noted, to the Republic's parliament.

Political parties

Contemporary French politics are dominated by three major and two minor political parties. On occasions, impelled by the country's pact-inducing two-ballot electoral process, these parties informally group themselves into two broader-based 'left' and 'right' coalitions, which are based around an ideological divide whose roots can be traced back to the French Revolution.

The dominant force on the left is the Socialist Party (Parti Socialiste: PS). The PS, though dating back ideologically to the Radical Republicans of the 19th century, was originally formed as a unified force in 1905 by Jean Jaurès (1859–1914). Later, at the December 1920 Tours congress, it split, the left-wing majority breaking away to form the French Communist Party (Parti Communiste Français: PCF), and leaving behind a moderate socialist rump under the banner Section Française de l'Internationale Ouvrière (SFIO) and led by Léon Blum (1872–1950).

The Socialists remained dwarfed by the PCF until the 1970s, but participated in a number of Third and Fourth Republic coalition governments and built up a solid local government base. The party's fortunes rapidly advanced from 1969, when the SFIO was radically remodelled. It adopted the designation PS and absorbed several smaller left and centre-left groupings, while accepting a new electoral strategy based upon a tactical alliance with the PCF, the 'Union of the Left', which was established in 1972. The motive force behind these changes was François Mitterrand, a shrewd former wartime Resistance leader and postwar centre-left National Assembly member, who eventually brought the PS into power in 1981, establishing in the process the party's clear ascendancy over the outmanoeuvred, fading PCF.

Currently, the PS, led since June 1995 by Lionel Jospin, has a membership of 200,000 and a national support rating of around 20–25%. Much of this support is drawn from blue- and white-collar workers, particularly those in the public sector. For example, a high proportion of its National Assembly members are ex-teachers or lecturers. Regionally, it polls strongest in the industrialized Central-Nord and Paris outer suburbs, as well as in the poor, small farmer areas of the southeast and southwest. The PS also enjoys the backing of the influential 550,000-member Confédération Française Démocratique du Travail (CFDT) labour union.

Within the party there are a number of ideological- and personality-based factions. These include groupings led by Lionel Jospin, on the centre-left, and by former prime ministers, Laurent Fabius and Michel Rocard, on the social democratic right wing. The left-wing former defence minister, Jean-Pierre Chevènement, also headed the 'Socialism and Realism' faction, later known as the Citizens' Movement, until his resignation from the PS in April 1993. When President Mitterrand was in power, a dominant 'Mitterrandiste current' received support from both Jospin and Fabius, thus bridging the divide. Each faction enjoys representation on the party's ruling Executive Committee and National Secretariat through an internal system of proportional representation.

Closely allied to the PS is the Left Radical Movement (Mouvement des Radicaux de Gauche: MRG), a party which was founded in 1973 as a breakaway from the centre-left Radical Party, whose current president is Jean-François Hory.

Further to the left is the PCF, a party which participated in a government coalition with the PS between 1981 and 1984. The PCF, although secure in the support of the powerful 1.5 million-member Confédération Générale du Travail (CGT) labour union and with local government bases in the 'red belt' inner suburbs around Paris, has been a declining electoral force since the mid-1970s, its share of the national vote having been more than halved to around 10%. The party's traditionally close ties with Moscow and fossilized ideological outlook have been prime alienating factors. Led between 1972 and 1994 by Georges Marchais (b. 1920) and since January 1994 by National Secretary Robert Hue (b. 1946), a protégé of Marchais, the PCF's membership has fallen greatly from its late 1980s level of 450,000. The party was organized, until the early 1990s, on hierarchical 'democratic-centralist' lines and controlled from above by a 15–20-member Politburo. In 1987–88 the PCF was weakened by its expulsion of a small modernizing 'renovator' faction led by Pierre Juquin, who subsequently stood as an Independent Communist candidate in the April 1988 presidential election. Another leading reformer, Charles Fiterman, lost his National Assembly seat in the March 1993 general election.

On the right of the political spectrum, French party politics have become unusually fractionalized during recent years. The coalition which monopolized central power between 1958 and 1981 showed increasing signs of strain between 1988 and 1991, but has dominated national and local elections since the early 1990s. The most influential party in the 'right coalition' is the Rally for the Republic (Rassemblement pour la République: RPR), which was formed in December 1976 by Jacques Chirac as a successor to the Union of Democrats for the Republic (UDR). The UDR, which was founded in 1968, is itself a successor to the Union for a New Republic (UNR), established by Charles de Gaulle in 1958. Neo-Gaullist in general policy outlook, the RPR, though showing signs of mellowing, favours a nationalistic approach in foreign policy matters and, domestically, a firm law and order programme. In the economic sphere, however, the contemporary RPR has flirted with a 'new conservative' freer market and deregulationary strategy which differs substantially from the state interventionist and protectionist programme favoured by its UNR and UDR precursors. The RPR claims a membership of 700,000 and currently is supported by around 20% of the electorate. Middle-class business and small shopkeeping groups, Catholic churchgoers, the elderly, and the rural areas of northern, western, and central France constitute core categories and bases of party support. Its chairman is Prime Minister Alain Juppé, who is the standard-bearer for a moderate centrist pro-European strand of Gaullism. An anti-

European left-wing government interventionist RPR faction is led by Philippe Séguin, while Charles Pasqua, the former interior minister, heads an anti-European and anti-immigration right-wing faction.

Challenging the RPR as the principal political force on the right is the Union for French Democracy (Union pour la Démocratie Française; UDF), an organization which was formed by President Valéry Giscard d'Estaing, Prime Minister Raymond Barre, and Jean Lecanuet in February 1978 to bring together the smaller parties of the centre-right into an effective electoral alliance. Today, the 300,000-member UDF still remains an umbrella coalition rather than a formal political party, embracing an extensive range of opinions. In general, however, the policy outlook of UDF members is more liberal in the domestic and social policy spheres and more internationalist and pro-European in the external policy sphere than the RPR.

Within the UDF, which is chaired by former president Giscard d'Estaing, there are four leader-orientated parties: the Republican Party (RP: Parti Républicain), which was founded, under the designation Independent Republicans, in 1962 by Giscard d'Estaing and has been led since June 1995 by François Léotard, the party's President; the Centre of Social Democrats (Centre des Démocrates Sociaux; CDS), formed in 1976 and led by a 'troika' of Pierre Mehaignerie (president), François Bayrou (secretary general), and Philippe Douste-Blazy; the Social Democratic Party (Parti Social-Démocrate: PSD), which was formed in 1973 and is led by Max Lejeune; and the Radical Party (Parti Radical), which dates back to 1901 and was a dominant force during the Third and Fourth Republics and is now led by Yves Galland. In June 1988 the CDS established a new centrist group in the National Assembly, termed the Union of the Centre (Union du Centre: UDC), to which a number of UDF independents, including Raymond Barre, pledged their allegiance.

On the far right of the political spectrum, the National Front (Front National: FN), which was established in 1972 by the demagogic former paratrooper Jean-Marie Le Pen, has risen to national prominence since the early 1980s through its promotion of a crude racist and extremist programme, founded on the twin planks of immigrant repatriation and the restoration of capital punishment. The FN has been excluded, with partial local exceptions, from electoral coalitions with the parties of the 'conventional right'. Despite this, it has managed to secure a steady 10% and greater share of the popular vote in national contests between 1984 and 1995, polling particularly strongly in the Marseilles region.

There are more than 30 other minor national and regional parties currently operating. These include the anti-Maastricht right-wing Movement for France, formed in November 1994 by the former UDF member Philippe de Villiers; the state interventionist 'orthodox Gaullist' Movement of Democrats, which was established in 1974 by Michel Jobert; the far-left Revolutionary Communist League (LCR), which was formed in 1973 and is led by Alain Krivine; the Workers' Struggle Party (Lutte Ouvrière; LO), a Trotskyist party dating from 1968 and led by Arlette Laguiller; the leftist Unified Socialist Party (PSU), founded in 1960; the

fundamentalist-ecologist Greens (Les Verts), which was established in 1984 and is led by Dominique Voynet; and the more pragmatic Génération Ecologie, led by Brice Lalonde.

Since 1988 the financing of French political parties has been subject to regulation, with state subventions being introduced and upper spending limits imposed on parliamentary and presidential campaigns.

Latest elections

In the most recent presidential election, which was held in April–May 1995, Jacques Chirac (RPR) was elected on the second ballot, held on 7 May 1995, securing 52.6% of the popular vote compared to Lionel Jospin's (PS) 47.4%. In the first round of voting, held on 23 April, nine candidates participated. The results were: Jospin (PS), with a 23% vote share; Chirac (RPR), 21%; Edouard Balladur (RPR), 19%; Jean-Marie Le Pen (FN), 15%; Robert Hue (PCF), 9%; Arlette Laguiller (Trotskyist), 5%; Philippe de Villiers (Movement for France), 5%; Dominique Voynet (Greens), 3%; and Jacques Cheminade (New Solidarity Federation), 0.3%. Turnout was 78% in the first round and 80% in the second. Chirac's first-round vote share was the lowest achieved by any successful candidate since direct presidential elections began in 1965. In the second round a record 6% of ballot papers were left blank, so, in fact, Chirac won only 49.5% of the votes cast, making him the first president ever to be elected with less than half the total poll.

National Assembly elections were last held, in two rounds, on 21 and 28 March 1993. The ruling PS polled disastrously, winning just 28% of the second-ballot vote and 54 of the Assembly's 577 seats. The former prime minister, Michel Rocard, and the foreign minister, Roland Dumas, were among PS electoral casualties. The MRG and other PS allies won a further 16 seats, with 3% of the second-ballot vote, while the PCF captured 23 seats, based on a 9% share of the first-ballot poll and 5% of the second ballot. The RPR and UDF, which fought the election in alliance, achieved a crushing victory, winning 460 Assembly seats and 54% of the second-ballot vote. Other minor parties of the 'conventional right' captured 24 seats, with 4% of the vote, but the extremist FN and the environmentalist Les Verts and Génération Ecologie, despite capturing respectively 12%, 4%, and 4% of the first-round vote, won no seats. Five thousand, three hundred and nineteen candidates contested the election, but only 35 female deputies were elected.

In mid-1995 the RPR-UDF 'right coalition' also controlled two-thirds of the seats in the Senate, 20 of the country's 22 regional councils and four-fifths of departmental councils. A complex system of weighted proportional election is used in municipal elections, with half the seats automatically going to the party that secures an absolute majority in the first round of voting or tops the poll in the second-round run-off contest. The remaining seats are then divided proportionately among parties which secure at least 10% of the vote.

Political history

A united French state was first constituted in AD 741 by King Pepin (c. 715–768), founder of the Frankish Carolingian dynasty, whose successor, Charlemagne (747–814),

established a pan-European empire. Authority was thereafter decentralized until the founding of the Paris-centred Capetian dynasty (987–1328), whose branches, the Valois (1328–1589) and Bourbon (1589–1792), ruled France for eight centuries. Under the Bourbon King Louis XIV (1638–1715), who reigned from 1643 to 1715, a centralized absolutist state was established, served by a well organized bureaucracy. This monarchical *ancien régime* was overthrown during the early stages of the French Revolution (1789–99), with a Republic being declared in 1792 and parliamentary democracy established.

Later, following a coup in 1799, this system gave way to the military dictatorship of Napoléon Bonaparte (1769–1821), who was proclaimed Emperor of the French in 1804, inaugurating the 'First Empire' (1804–14). A new pan-European empire was temporarily carved out, before military defeats between 1812 and 1814 forced Napoléon's abdication and the restoration, under Louis XVIII (ruled 1814–24), Charles X (ruled 1824–30), and the 'citizen king' Louis-Philippe (ruled 1830–48), of the Bourbon dynasty.

Attempts to increase the monarch's powers were checked by revolutions in 1830 and 1848, the latter resulting in the Crown's overthrow and the establishment of the Second Republic in 1848. This was brought to an end in 1852 when the Republic's president, Louis Napoléon (1808–73), the nephew of Napoléon Bonaparte, re-established an expansionary system of plebiscitary autocracy, designated the Second Empire. Following his defeat in the Franco-Prussian War (1870–71), Louis Napoléon was ousted and a liberal parliamentary democracy, based on universal manhood suffrage, the Third Republic (1870–1940), was established. This Republic, riven by conflicts between the clerical and militarist right and the radical and socialist left, was characterized by government instability, with more than 100 different administrations during its life. Despite these strains and inner tensions, the Third Republic's political structure survived, remaining intact until the invasion, defeat, and occupation by German forces during the early stages of World War II.

During the war a collaborationist puppet government, the 'Vichy regime', headed by the veteran military leader, Marshal Henri Pétain (1856–1951), was established, with Nazi German backing, but was opposed by the underground *maquis* and UK-based Free French resistance organization, led by General Charles de Gaulle (1890–1970). With Allied support, France was liberated in August 1944 and a 'united front' provisional government, headed by de Gaulle, and including communists, was installed, while a new constitution was being framed. This interim administration was successful in restoring a sense of national unity. It also introduced a far-reaching series of pragmatic social and economic reforms, including the nationalization of strategic enterprises, the extension of the franchise to women, and the creation of a comprehensive social security system.

In January 1946 a new constitution was adopted, proclaiming the establishment of a Fourth Republic and providing for a weak political executive and powerful parliament, the National Assembly, which was to be elected under a generous system of proportional representation. De Gaulle, who had favoured a strong presidentialist system, immediately resigned as interim president and set up, in 1947, a populist political movement of his own, the Rally for French People (RPF), which briefly rose to prominence before fading and being disbanded in 1953.

With numerous small party groupings achieving Assembly representation, political activity in the new Fourth Republic was characterized by intense factional bargaining and renewed executive instability: 26 different governments held power between 1946 and 1958. In these circumstances, effective executive authority passed into the hands of the French civil service, which, by introducing a new system of 'indicative economic planning', engineered rapid economic reconstruction. Decolonization in French Indochina in 1954 and Morocco and Tunisia in 1956, and entry into the European Economic Community (EEC) in 1957, were also achieved.

The Fourth Republic eventually collapsed in 1958 as a result of a political and military crisis over Algerian independence, which threatened to lead to a French army revolt. De Gaulle was called back from retirement in May 1958 to head a government of national unity. He proceeded to oversee the framing of a constitution for the new Fifth Republic which considerably strengthened the executive, in the shape of a president and prime minister. De Gaulle, who became president in January 1959, restored domestic stability and presided over the decolonization of Francophone Africa, including the granting of independence to Algeria in April 1962. Close economic links were maintained, however, with France's former colonies. He also initiated a new independent foreign policy, withdrawing France from the integrated military command structure of the North Atlantic Treaty Organization (NATO) in 1966 and developing an autonomous nuclear deterrent force, the *force de frappe*.

The de Gaulle era was one of rapid economic growth, per-capita GDP almost doubling between 1960 and 1970, and socio-economic change, involving large-scale rural–urban migration and occupational transformation. Politically, however, it was a period characterized by a strong centralization of power and tight media censorship. In March 1967 the public reacted against this paternalism by voting the 'right coalition' a reduced National Assembly majority. A year later, in May 1968, major student and workers' demonstrations, termed the 'May Events', in Paris, which spread to the provinces, paralysed the nation and briefly threatened the government's continued existence. De Gaulle responded by calling fresh National Assembly elections in June 1968 in which, fighting on a law and order platform, his Union of Democrats for the Republic (UDR) secured a landslide victory. Ten months later, however, in April 1969, de Gaulle, was defeated in a referendum over proposals for Senate and local government reform. He resigned the presidency and retired from political affairs at the age of 79.

The man who had been de Gaulle's prime minister between 1962 and 1968, Georges Pompidou (1911–74), was elected as the new president in June 1969 and continued to pursue Gaullist policies until his death in April 1974.

Pompidou's successor as president was Valéry Giscard d'Estaing (b. 1926), leader of the centre-right Independent Republicans. He attempted to set the country on a new, modernist course, introducing liberalizing reforms in the social sphere and establishing a more cooperative and activist role within the European Community (EC). His policies were undermined, however, by the internal wranglings of his ambitious 'right coalition' partner, Jacques Chirac (b. 1932), who served as prime minister between 1974 and 1976, before leaving to set up a new neo-Gaullist party, the Rally for the Republic (RPR). The government was also operating in the context of deteriorating external economic conditions.

Nevertheless, France performed better than many of its European competitors between 1974 and 1981, with the President launching a major nuclear power programme to save on energy imports and a new prime minister, in the person of the former Sorbonne monetarist professor, Raymond Barre (b. 1924), following a new liberal 'freer market' economic strategy. However, with unemployment standing at 1.7 million on polling day, Giscard was defeated in the presidential election of May 1981 by the experienced Socialist Party (PS) leader, François Mitterrand (1916–1996), a former network commander in the French Resistance and an unsuccessful challenger for the presidency in 1965 and 1974.

Mitterrand's victory, which constituted the first presidential success for the 'left coalition' during the Fifth Republic, was immediately succeeded by a landslide victory for the PS and its Communist Party (PCF) and Left Radical Movement (MRG) allies in the elections to the National Assembly which were held in June 1981. The new government, which was headed by the socialist–traditionalist former mayor of Lille, Pierre Mauroy (b. 1928), as prime minister, and included in its ranks four PCF ministers, set about implementing a radical and ambitious policy of social reform and political decentralization, with the aim of fundamentally transforming the character of French society. In the economic sphere, a programme of industrial and financial nationalization and enhanced state investment and formal planning was instituted, while a series of reflationary budgets attempted to curb unemployment. In March 1983, however, financial constraints, during a period of deepening world recession, forced a switch towards a more conservative fiscal strategy of austerity, *le rigueur*. This U-turn in economic policy was completed in July 1984 when Mauroy was replaced as prime minister by the young social democratic technocrat, Laurent Fabius (b. 1946), a move which prompted the resignation from the government of the PCF's four cabinet ministers.

During 1985 and 1986, with a tightening of the fiscal screw, unemployment rose sharply to more than 2.5 million and, as a consequence, racial tensions and workers' unrest increased in urban areas. The extreme right-wing National Front (FN), led by Jean-Marie Le Pen (b. 1928), a former paratrooper and right-wing Poujadist deputy, campaigning for immigrant repatriation and a tougher penal policy, benefited from these conflicts, capturing 10% of the popular vote in the National Assembly elections of March 1986 and, helped by the recent adoption of a new proportional representation system, 35 Assembly seats. In this election, the 'left coalition', now in tatters, lost its Assembly majority, compelling President Mitterrand to appoint the leader of the 'right coalition' and mayor of Paris, Jacques Chirac, as his new prime minister in what was to be a unique experiment in power-sharing, or 'cohabitation'.

Chirac quickly succeeded in establishing himself as the dominant force in this 'shared executive' and proceeded to set about introducing a radical 'new conservative' programme of denationalization, deregulation, and 'desocialization'. In this strategy, utilizing 'guillotine' and decree powers to steamroller measures through, he had initial success. However, during the autumn and winter months of 1986–87, Chirac's educational and economic reforms encountered serious opposition from students and workers, necessitating policy concessions which, combined with growing acrimony within the ranks of the 'right coalition', served fatally to undermine the prime minister's national standing.

As a consequence, Chirac was comfortably defeated by the incumbent Mitterrand in the presidential election of April–May 1988, by a margin of 54% of the national vote against 46%. In National Assembly elections, which were held in June 1988, the PS, despite disarray in the ranks of the 'right coalition', also emerged as the largest single party, capturing 260 of the 577 seats after securing 45% of the second-ballot vote, but failed to secure an overall parliamentary majority.

Interpreting the result as a reflection of the public's desire for government from the 'centre', President Mitterrand appointed Michel Rocard (b. 1930), a popular moderate social democrat, as prime minister at the head of a minority PS government, which included several prominent centre party representatives. The new prime minister pledged himself to implement a progressive programme, aimed at protecting the underprivileged and improving the quality of life, and called upon the opposition parties to work with the PS for 'tolerance, justice, progress and solidarity'. Terming their strategy the 'opening to the centre', the aim of the president and prime minister appeared to be to encourage defections from the ranks of the centre-right Union for French Democracy (UDF) to a new left-of-centre PS-led alliance. This would redress the imbalance between the 'conventional left' vis-à-vis the RPR-led 'conventional right', thus creating an effective social democratic and conservative based two-party system, leaving the extremist PCF and FN isolated and marginalized on the political fringes.

In June 1988 Prime Minister Rocard negotiated the Matignon Accord, designed to resolve a dispute over autonomy between indigenous Kanaks and French settlers in the strife-torn French overseas territory of New Caledonia. This agreement was approved in a referendum held in France in November 1988. Between 1988 and 1990, against the backcloth of a strong economic upturn, attention focused increasingly on the 'quality of life', with the Green Party gaining 11% of the national vote in the European Parliament elections of June 1989. However, the extreme-right National Front continued to do well in municipal elections and, in December 1989, secured a National Assembly by-election victory in Dreux, west of Paris. This persuaded the government to adopt a harsher line against illegal immigration and to announce new programmes for the integration of Muslim immigrants, from Algeria, Tunisia, and other areas with French colonial ties, into mainstream French society.

The Rocard government narrowly survived a censure vote in the National Assembly in November 1990. This followed an outbreak of serious student violence in Paris and earlier antipolice race riot in the Lyon suburbs. A commission set up to look at the problems of immigrant integration reported in 1991 that France's foreign population was 3.7 million (6.8% of the population), the same as in 1982. However, 10 million citizens were of 'recent foreign origin'.

The 1990–91 Gulf crisis, caused by the invasion and annexation in August 1990 of Kuwait by Iraq, which formerly had close ties with France, caused divisions within the PS. Following Iraqi violation of the French ambassador's residence in Kuwait in September 1990, the French government dispatched 5,000 troops to Saudi Arabia to participate in the US-led anti-Iraqi UN coalition. This prompted the resignation, in February 1991, of the left-wing defence minister Jean-Pierre Chevènement. In an effort to provide 'new impetus' to his administration, in May 1991 President Mitterrand replaced Rocard with Edith Cresson (b. 1934), the former minister for European affairs, who became France's first woman prime minister. However, with the economy in recession since 1990 and unemployment climbing (to more than 10%), racial disturbances increasing, farmers protesting against a recently introduced agricultural restructuring programme, and the reputation of the PS being damaged by a succession of financial scandals, opinion polls showed the acerbic Cresson to have become the most unpopular prime minister of the Fifth Republic. The public approval rating of Mitterrand, by now the Fifth Republic's longest-serving president, also slumped, standing at 35% in January 1992.

Not unexpectedly, the PS polled disastrously in regional council elections held in March 1992, capturing a humiliating 18% share of the national vote, finishing only narrowly ahead of the National Front and the ecologist parties, Les Verts and Génération Ecologie. President Mitterrand responded by dismissing Cresson and, in April 1992, appointed his close ally Pierre Bérégovoy (1922–93) as the new prime minister. As finance minister, Bérégovoy had been blamed by Cresson for the nation's economic troubles, having raised interest rates to match German levels in pursuit a 'strong franc' policy, but he was respected by the country's financial community.

The new Bérégovoy administration pledged to cut taxes to stimulate economic recovery and set up new training schemes to help the unemployed. In addition, in an attempt to woo environmentalist voters, a moratorium on nuclear testing was announced. In September 1992 a national referendum was held on approval of the Maastricht Treaty on EC economic and political union. A 'Yes' vote of 51.1% was narrowly secured. In the 21 and 28 March 1993 National Assembly elections the PS faced a united 'right coalition' opposition, with the RPR and UDF having signed a formal election pact as early as April 1991. As a consequence, and with the economy still mired in recession, which had been exacerbated by a slowdown in Germany, the PS was heavily defeated. Along with its allies, it attracted 32% of the national vote but captured just 70 of the 577 National Assembly seats, while the RPR, UDF and other 'conventional right' allies won, with 58% of the vote, 484 seats, and thus a clear majority.

In the aftermath of this electoral debacle, Pierre Bérégovoy, who was greatly affected by media allegations of impropriety over a FFr 1 million interest-free loan, committed suicide by gunshot in May 1993. Jacques Chirac, the recognized leader of the victorious 'right coalition', was unwilling to become prime minister, following his experience of 'cohabitation' between 1986–88. Instead, his patrician RPR colleague, Edouard Balladur (b. 1929), who had been economy and finance minister between 1986–88, was appointed Prime Minister on 29 March 1993, on the tacit understanding that he would not challenge Chirac for the RPR's presidential nomination in 1995.

From March 1993 President Mitterrand, afflicted by prostate cancer and visibly ailing, became an increasingly remote head of state, concentrating on foreign affairs and his ceremonial functions, leaving Balladur's RPR–UDF administration to dominate the domestic scene. With the forceful Charles Pasqua as interior minister, this new government introduced a strict new anti-immigration programme. However, its chief priorities were the reduction of the budget deficit, securing currency stability, and the creation of a more dynamic economy through measures such as further privatization, including the partial sale of state-owned Renault motor vehicles, and a reduction in the level of the minimum wage paid to young workers. Although during 1993 French GDP contracted by 0.9%, the unemployment level edged up, beyond the 3 million mark, to 11.7%, and in July 1993 the EC's Exchange Rate Mechanism (ERM), in which the franc was bound, effectively collapsed, Balladur remained popular and respected as prime minister. During 1994 economic growth resumed. However, following student protests, the government was obliged to shelve its plans to introduce the lower minimum wage and three cabinet ministers resigned after judicial investigations into fraud charges. Still the RPR–UDF polled strongly in local cantonal elections in March 1994, capturing 45% of the first-round vote, but in the June 1994 elections to the European Parliament the two parties, which fielded separate candidate lists, won just 26% of the national vote. The PS polled even more disappointingly, attracting just 14% of the vote. This prompted the resignation of Michel Rocard, who had been PS leader since April 1993. Instead, in this Euro-election, voters turned to two new contrasting parties, 'The Other Europe', an anti-Maastricht party led by a UDF dissident, Philippe de Villiers, and 'Energie Radicale', a pro-European grouping led by Bernard Tapie, a flamboyant business executive and former PS-aligned populist minister who had been charged with fraud in December 1993 and was to be found guilty in 1995. Each of these parties attracted 12% of the popular vote.

On 18 January 1995 Prime Minister Balladur announced publicly his candidacy for the French presidential elections to be held in April–May 1995 to the chagrin of Jacques Chirac, who had declared himself a candidate on 4 November 1994. Balladur presented himself as an 'above-party' candidate 'for all the French people, without distinction, without exclusion' and appeared clear favourite to top the first ballot. The PS had hoped to persuade Jacques Delors (b. 1925), who was set to retire as president of the European Commission, to become its candidate. However, although it seemed likely that Delors might be elected French president, he believed that the PS would be unable to win a parliamentary majority and was unwilling to work with the 'right coalition' in a 'cohabitation' administration. The PS thus chose,

on 2 February 1995, Lionel Jospin (b. 1937), a moderate former PS leader and education minister, as its candidate.

As campaigning moved underway, the aloof Balladur, whose reputation for integrity was besmirched by his implication in a telephone-tapping affair and his admission that he had profited from share dealings, rapidly lost ground to the experienced Chirac. Presenting himself in this, his third, presidential challenge as a more populist 'man of the people', under the slogan '*La France pour tous*', Chirac pledged to raise public sector wages, boost pensions, help farmers, encourage job creation, but also to cut taxes and the budget deficit, and heal social rifts. In the first ballot, held on 23 April 1995, Chirac finished ahead of Balladur, attracting 21% of the vote to the latter's 19%, but, unexpectedly, Jospin, noted for his personal integrity and straightforward approach, finished in first position, with 23% of the vote. The extremist Jean-Marie Le Pen won 15% national support, as a record 37% of the vote went to fringe candidates. The second ballot head-to-head contest between Jospin and Chirac, held on 7 May 1995, resulted in the expected victory for the 'right coalition', but the margin was narrower than anticipated, with Chirac securing 52.6% of the vote.

Chirac was sworn in as president on 17 May 1995, being driven to his inauguration in an old Citroën CX to symbolically mark what he promised would be a 'simple presidency'. He appointed as prime minister the moderate pro-European Alain Juppé (b. 1945), who had been foreign minister since 1993, and included a record 12 women ministers in the 42-member cabinet. A close RPR lieutenant of the new president, Juppé faced the problem of implementing the contradictory economic programme which emerged from Chirac's electoral pledges. However, the new administration had a dynamic, but mixed, start. In June 1995, the new government unveiled an ambitious FFr 60-billion package to promote jobs – the French unemployment rate, at 12.2%, was well above the OECD average of 7.4% – and boost house construction, and help the poor and elderly through increasing the minimum wage and pensions, but also announced that nuclear tests would be resumed in the Pacific. The former measures were well received, but the last drew international condemnation. In the same month, the parties of the conventional right polled less strongly than expected in municipal elections and the extremist National Front captured the mayorships of three important southern towns, Toulon, Marignane, and Orange, and trebled its number of local councillors to 1,075. In August 1995 the constitution was amended significantly to widen the range of issues on which the president could call referenda and to extend parliamentary oversight of the executive through providing for a nine-month annual National Assembly session. In the same month, Alain Madelin, the right-wing finance minister who pressed for rapid cuts in welfare spending and reduction in taxes, was sacked and replaced by the more moderate Jean Arthuis, as Prime Minister Juppé stressed the need for gradual reform 'without haste'. Dogged by accusations that he had used his influence when Paris's financial director to secure accommodation at a reduced cost for his son, the prime minister reshuffled his cabinet in November 1995, eliminating 9 of its 42 posts, in an effort to recover lost momentum.

GERMANY

Federal Republic of Germany (FRG)
Bundesrepublik Deutschland

Capital: Berlin*

*Berlin was chosen as the new official capital of the expanded FRG in 1991, but Bonn will remain the administrative capital, being the site of the federal parliament, until mid-1999

Social and economic data
Area: 357,000 km^2
Population: 80,600,000*
Pop. density per km^2: 226*
Urban population: 86%**
Literacy rate: 99%**
GDP: $1,789, 261 million**; per-capita GDP: $22,500**
Government defence spending (% of GDP): 2.1%**
Currency: Deutschmark (DM)
Economy type: high income
Labour force in agriculture: 8%**

*1994
**1992

Ethnic composition
The population is overwhelmingly, 93%, of Germanic stock, but in the far north there are notable Danish and Slavonic ethnic minorities. Also, in 1990, 5.9 million foreigners, including 1.9 million officially recognized *Gastarbeiter* ('guest workers'), predominantly Turks and South Europeans (Greeks, Italians, and Yugoslavs), resided in the country, constituting 7% of the total population. By 1993 the FRG had received more than 200,000 refugees fleeing the Yugoslav civil war. German is the main language, but there is a small Sorbian-speaking minority in eastern Germany.

Religions
Forty-three per cent of the population is Protestant, belonging to the Lutheran Church, United Evangelical Church, and churches of the Lutheran tradition; 36% is Roman Catholic, the faith being strongest in the south and west; 2%, drawn chiefly from the Turkish community, adheres to Sunni Islam; and 18% is nonreligious. The Protestant community predominates in the eastern *Länder* and during the communist era was identified with the peace, ecological, and dissident movements.

Political features
State type: liberal democratic
Date of state formation: 1871/1949/1990*
Political structure: federal
Executive: parliamentary
Assembly: two-chamber
Party structure: multiparty
Human rights rating: 98%
International affiliations: AG (observer), BDEAC, BOAD, CE, CERN, CSS, EEA, ESA, EU, G-5, G-7, G-10, IAEA, IBRD, IMF, IWC, NACC, NAM (guest), NATO, OECD, OSCE, UN, WEU, WTO

*Germany was first united in 1871; The FRG was established in 1949 to which the *Länder* of eastern Germany acceded in 1990

Local and regional government
Below the *Land* administrations, which are described under the heading **Political system** below, there are elected town and district councils, empowered to levy and collect property taxes.

Head of state
Federal President Roman Herzog, since 1994

Head of government
Chancellor Dr Helmut Kohl, since 1982

Political leaders since 1970
GDR: 1950–71 Walter Ulbricht (SED)*, 1971–89 Erich Honecker (SED)*, 1989 Egon Krenz (SED)*, 1989–90 Hans Modrow (PDS)**, 1990 Lothar de Maiziere (CDU)**

FRG Chancellors: 1969–74 Willy Brandt (SPD), 1974–82 Helmut Schmidt (SPD), 1982–   Dr Helmut Kohl (CDU)

*Communist Party leader
**Prime minister

Political system
With memories of the destructive 1933–45 Nazi autocracy fresh in their minds, the Allied military governors and German provincial leaders in 1948–49 drafted the FRG's constitution with the clear goal of creating a stable parliamentary form of government, diffusing authority, and safeguarding liberties. The document, termed the 'Basic Law', borrowed eclectically from British, American, and neighbouring European constitutional models, while drawing specific lessons from Germany's own flawed constitutional history.

To prevent an excessive centralization of power, a federal system of government was established, built around

The Länder (states) of the Federal Republic of Germany					Table 60
Länder	Area (sq km)	1990 population ('000)	Capital	Länder* government	Bundesrat seats
Eastern Germany					
Berlin	883	3,410**	Berlin	CDU–SPD	4
Brandenburg	29,059	2,641	Potsdam	SPD	4
Mecklenburg–Western Pomerania	23,838	1,964	Schwerin	CDU–SPD	3
Saxony	18,337	4,901	Dresden	CDU	4
Saxony–Anhalt	20,445	2,965	Magdeburg	SPD–Greens/Alliance	4
Thuringia	16,251	2,684	Erfurt	CDU–SPD	4
	(108,813)	(18,565)			(23)
Western Germany					
Baden–Württemberg	35,751	9,618	Stuttgart	CDU–SPD	6
Bavaria	70,553	11,221	Munich	CSU	6
Bremen	404	674	Bremen	SPD–CDU	3
Hamburg	755	1,626	Hamburg	SPD–Statt Party	3
Hesse	21,144	5,660	Wiesbaden	SPD–Greens	4
Lower Saxony	47,439	7,284	Hanover	SPD	6
North–Rhine–Westphalia	34,068	17,104	Düsseldorf	SPD–Greens	6
Rhineland–Palatinate	19,848	3,702	Mainz	SPD–FDP	4
Saarland	2,569	1,065	Saarbrucken	SPD	3
Schleswig–Holstein	15,728	2,595	Kiel	SPD	4
	(248,259)	(60,549)			(45)
All Germany	357,072	79,114	Berlin	CDU–CSU–FDP	68

*In July 1995
**East Berlin, 1.28 million; West Berlin, 2.13 million.

originally ten *Länder*, or states, and 16 since unification in 1990, as shown in Table 60 above, each with its own constitution and elected single-chamber assembly (*Landtag* or *Bürgerschaft*), from which a government is drawn, headed by a minister-president. Bavaria is the exception, having two chambers. These *Länder* have original powers in the spheres of education, police, local government, culture, and environmental protection and are responsible for the administration of federal legislation through their own civil services. They have substantial local taxation authority and are assigned shares of federal income tax and value-added tax (VAT) revenues, being responsible for half of total government spending in the FRG. There are plans to merge the *Länder* of Berlin and Brandenburg, from 1999, into one state, subject to approval in a referendum in May 1996.

At the centre, the May 1949 constitution, amended for unification in October 1990, established, through a deliberate system of checks and balances, a firmly rooted parliamentary democracy, built around a two-chamber legislature comprising a directly elected lower house, the Bundestag (Federal Diet or Assembly) of at least 656 members, currently 672, and an indirectly elected 68-member upper house, the Bundesrat (Federal Council).

Bundestag members are elected by universal adult suffrage for a four-year term through a complicated form of 'personalized proportional representation', termed the additional member system (AMS). Under this system electors are given two votes, one, the *Erststimme*, for a local single-member district constituency seat, the result being decided by a simple plurality, and the other vote, the *Zweitstimme*, for a *Land* (state) party list. Half the assembly is filled by 'constituency members' and half by 'list members'. The *Zweitstimme* votes are decisive in determining proportionate party representation. They are totalled so as to establish percentage levels of party support at the state level and to work out proportionate seat allocations. To achieve such proportionality, list seats are added, where necessary, to those already gained by the parties locally from the *Erststimme* constituency contests. In this allotment process, 'balancing' *Zweitstimme* seats are drawn in rank order from the topmost names appearing on the relevant party's state list. To qualify for shares of these state list seats, political parties must, however, have won at least 5% of the national vote or, alternatively, three direct *Erststimme* seats. In the special case of the December 1990 first all-German general election, the '5% rule' was applied separately to eastern and western Germany.

Occasionally, as a result of unusual, regionally concentrated, *Erststimme* support, a party may secure more district *Erststimme* seats than it appears 'entitled' to on a state-wide percentage basis. It is allowed to retain these 'excess' (*Überhangmandate*) seats, the size of the Bundestag being increased accordingly.

Members of the Bundesrat are not directly elected. Instead, individual *Land* governments send nominated party delegations, consisting of between three to six members, dependent upon population size. For this reason, the Bundesrat is never dissolved, its composition only changing as *Land* governments rise and fall. The delegations sent to the current administrative capital, Bonn, which comprise senior *Land* ministers, automatically led by the minister-president, are required to cast their votes *en bloc*.

The Bundestag is the more dominant of the two chambers in the federal assembly, electing, from the ranks of the majority party or coalition, a chancellor (Bundeskanzler: prime minister) and a 16–20-member cabinet to constitute the executive government of the Federal Republic. Once elected, a chancellor can only be removed by Bundestag members through a 'constructive vote of no confidence', in which a majority of members vote positively in favour of an alternative executive leader. This constitutional device has been employed successfully on only one occasion, in September 1982, and brought into office the present chancellor.

The chancellor, who is served by a large, 400-member, private office, is a potentially powerful leader. However, the coalition character of postwar FRG politics, with the consequent apportionment of cabinet posts on a negotiated party basis, has meant that a number of leading ministers, for example Foreign Affairs Minister Hans-Dietrich Genscher, who continuously held his post between 1974 and 1992, have been able to establish a significant degree of independence. More generally, German cabinet ministers, who are not required to be Bundestag deputies, although most are, are frequently technocrats who specialize in their department's affairs, serving lengthy terms, in contrast to the generalist ministers of most other West European states.

Work in both the Bundestag and Bundesrat is effected through a vigorous system of all-party functional committees. The Bundestag takes the lead in this legislative process. However, although the Bundesrat has few initiating rights, it enjoys considerable veto powers. Thus, all legislation relating to *Länder* responsibilities must receive its approval, more than 60% of Bundestag laws falling into this category. In addition, constitutional amendments, of which there have been more than 30 since 1949, require a two-thirds Bundesrat, and Bundestag, majority. Finally, on other matters, the Bundesrat is allowed to suggest amendments to Bundestag legislation, send disputed items to a joint Bundestag–Bundesrat 'conciliation committee' and can temporarily block items of which it disapproves until a countervailing 50% or 66% Bundestag vote is passed. In the legislative period running up to the October 1994 general election, the Bundesrat, which was dominated by the opposition Social Democratic Party (SPD) and Greens, initially rejected 16% of the 504 laws approved by the Bundestag. Three of these laws were subsequently rejected, following mediation.

For the purpose of electing a federal president (Bundespräsident) as head of state, members of the Bundestag join together every five years with an equal number of representatives elected by *Land* parliaments in a special Federal Convention (Bundesversammlung). The president is, however, primarily a titular and ceremonial figure, possessing few effective powers.

Adherence to the 1949/1990 constitution is ensured by a special independent Federal Constitutional Court, based at Karlsruhe, which is staffed by 16 judges. They are selected half by the Bundestag and half by the Bundesrat, following nominations by balanced all-party committees, and serve terms of up to 12 years. The Court functions as a guarantor of civil liberties and adjudicator in federal–*Land* disputes. Similar constitutional courts function at the *Land* level.

Political parties

FRG politics have been dominated since 1949 by two major parties, the Christian Democratic Union (CDU: Christlich Demokratische Union Deutschlands) and Social Democratic Party (Sozialdemokratische Partei Deutschlands: SPD), and one minor party, the Free Democratic Party (FDP: Freie Demokratische Partei). A fourth party, the Greens (die Grünen), has emerged as a notable challenging force since the early 1980s, while the Bavarian-based Christian Social Union (Christlich Soziale Union: CSU) has worked in close, though sometimes uneasy, partnership with the CDU at the federal level. In the eastern *Länder*, the Party of Democratic Socialism (PDS: Partei des Demokratischen Sozialismus) is a significant force, being the reform-socialist heir to the formerly dominant communist Socialist Unity Party of Germany (Sozialistische Einheitspartei Deutschlands: SED).

With the exception of the November 1972 Bundestag election, the conservative CDU has consistently gained most support at national level, forming the principal party of government between 1949–69 and since 1982. However, the SPD has been the dominant force during recent years at the *Länder* level, controlling the majority of state assemblies, either on its own or in partnership with the Greens and even, on occasions, with the FDP and, in a 'grand coalition', with the CDU. As a consequence, the SPD currently controls the federal Bundesrat.

The CDU was originally established at the state level in the autumn of 1945 as a loose amalgamation of independent Catholic and Protestant zonal parties who had resisted National Socialism (Nazism) during the interwar years and whose members shared a commitment to private enterprise, state welfare provision, and an antipathy to communism. During the 1950s, the CDU's support base, which had traditionally been concentrated in the rural, Catholic *Länder* of southern and western Germany and in rural, Protestant Schleswig-Holstein and Lower Saxony, broadened, as it absorbed further minor regional, centrist, and conservative parties. Ideologically, it became identified with the 'social market economy' approach to economic management, which became a key element behind the postwar West German 'economic miracle'. The success of this strategy drew to the party new blue-collar support, establishing it as a broadly based, 'catch-all', centre-right force. In its approach to external relations, the CDU gave firm and early support to membership of the European Community (EC) and the North Atlantic Treaty Organization (NAT0).

In 1994 the CDU, led by Chancellor Kohl, claimed a membership of 650,000. Since unification it has received an infusion of more than 100,000 members from the eastern *Länder*, predominantly Protestant, of a Calvinist disposition. Its sister party in Bavaria, the CSU, which was established in 1946, has a membership of 190,000. The CSU is a noticeably more conservative body and was led between 1961 and 1988 by the forthright Dr Franz-Josef Strauss. It has been headed since 1988 by Theo Waigel (b. 1939), the federal finance minister.

The CDU, constituting, as its name suggests, a 'Union' of *Land* groupings, is notoriously decentralized in structure. Financially, it draws an unusually high proportion, almost 30%, of its annual income in the form of donations, chiefly from business.

The dominant party on the left of the political spectrum is the SPD. Formed in 1875, during the Bismarckian era, it began as a Marxist body, drawing initial support from urban industrial workers. With a membership in excess of 1 million, it became the major political party in Germany during the liberal Weimar Republic (1919–33), forming governments between 1919 and 1920 and between 1928 and 1930. Following the defection of ultra-leftist groupings, its policy stance moderated but it was forced into exile during the Nazi era and subsequently electorally weakened by the country's partition in 1945.

During the 1950s the SPD, with a national support rating of only 30%, found itself in perpetual opposition at the federal level, but held power at the state level in the industrialized western *Länder* of Bremen, Hamburg, Hesse, and North Rhine–Westphalia. However, at its 1959 Bad Godesberg conference, a fundamental revision of policy strategy was effected, bringing to an end the party's earlier opposition to membership of the EEC/EC and NATO, disavowing its traditional Marxist connections, class orientation, and anticlericalism and proclaiming its acceptance of the country's postwar 'social market economy' strategy. The adoption of this moderate, new, left-of-centre Godesberg Programme of Principles, coupled with the party's innovative espousal of East–West détente (*Ostpolitik*), and the dynamic new generation leadership provided by Willy Brandt and Helmut Schmidt, proved successful in significantly broadening the SPD's support base. This enabled it, in alliance with the FDP, to become the party of federal government between 1969 and 1982.

Since 1982, as a result of mounting internal divisions over domestic and foreign policy which shifted its centre of gravity leftwards and encouraged the FDP to switch allegiance to the CDU, the SPD has been forced back into opposition at the federal level. The party remains, however, a significant force, having, in 1994, a membership of 860,000 and enjoying informal labour union support. Unification in 1990 brought to the party an additional 30,000 members from the eastern Länder. Its organizational structure is the most effective in the FRG, being unusually centralized, with control from above being effected by an elected National Executive Committee and inner 13-member Presidium, chaired since November 1995 by Oskar Lafontaine. Its organization is also among the most progressive, with, following rules passed at the SPD congress of August 1988, at least 40% of the party's posts, and a similar proportion of its Bundestag seats, being required to be filled by women by 1998.

The FDP, a centrist liberal grouping, although very small compared to the CDU and SPD in terms of national support, averaging 8% of the national vote in elections since 1949, has functioned as a critical 'hinge party'. Helped by the AMS electoral system, with the 'ticket-splitting' which this makes possible, the FDP has been in a position to regularly hold the balance of power in the Bundestag and has formed the junior partner in federal coalition governments in all but seven years, 1957–61 and 1966–69, since 1949. As a reward for its assembly support, the FDP has received 20% of cabinet portfolios in these administrations, including such key ministries as foreign affairs, economic affairs, and justice. In addition, it has secured the election of two of its leaders, Dr Theodor Heuss (1884–1963), between 1949 and 1959, and Walter Scheel (b. 1919), between 1974 and 1979, to the prestigious post of federal president and another, Martin Bangemann (b. 1934), to the EC Commission in 1988.

The FDP, although its antecedents go back to previous Second Reich (1871–1918) and Weimar Republic centrist groupings, was originally formed by Heuss in December 1948, by absorbing smaller liberal parties. During the 1950s its support came chiefly from marginal farming communities, the self-employed, and small-town conservatives. However, after Scheel became party chair in 1968, it became more progressive in its outlook, winning new support from white-collar groups. Today, there is still tension between its conservative-liberal wing, of which its leader until 1993, Count Otto Graf Lambsdorff (b. 1927), was a prominent member and which espouses a free market economic approach, and a more socially and environmentally conscious progressivist faction with a strong regional base in Baden-Württemberg, in the southwest and the northern city states of Hamburg and Bremen. In 1991 party membership stood at 200,000, two-thirds of whom were new recruits from the eastern *Länder*, after the eastern League of Free Democrats (BFD) was absorbed in 1990. However, between 1992–95 the FDP polled disastrously in a series of state elections, falling below the 5% qualification level in all but one contest, Hesse in February 1995, and only secured representation in the Bundestag in the October 1994 federal election as a result of CDU supporters casting *Zweitstimme* votes for this coalition partner. This led former leader Lambsdorff to describe the party as being in 'existential danger'. In June 1995, with membership down to just 84,000, Wolfgang Gerhardt, from Hesse, replaced Klaus Kinkel as the FDP's chair.

The FRG's fourth significant party, the Greens, originated as a loose coalition of locally based environmental action groups which began operations during the later 1970s and had growing successes in a number of Land constituency contests. In January 1980 they were established as an umbrella organization which embraced these groupings and began to develop a unique 'postindustrial' or 'new politics' policy programme, which included opposition to nuclear weapons and the NATO alliance, environmentalism, feminism, and utopian eco-socialism. Having secured representation in a number of *Landtage* and *Bürgerschäfte* between 1980–83, the Greens succeeded in surmounting the 5% national support hurdle and captured seats in the Bundestag at both the 1983 and 1987 general elections.

Outside the assembly chambers, they played an even more prominent role at the head of a burgeoning 'peace movement' during the early and mid-1980s. By 1987 they claimed a national membership of 42,000. However, the party had become progressively divided into antagonistic radical ('Fundi'), moderate ('Realo'), and neutral ('Neutralo') factions, fomenting a series of anarchic feuds. The party has a highly decentralized organizational structure which has exacerbated such infighting. More impressively, the Greens, since their inception, have pioneered and operated a unique collective form of national and parliamentary leadership, with, until 1991, personnel being regularly rotated. Women are assured of equal representation at all executive levels. The Greens suffered a dip in support during 1989–91 as attention focused on the prospect of, and economic and social consequences of, reunification. As a result, their national support fell to below 4% in the October 1990 general election. However, in the 1994 general election, having merged with the eastern Germany-based Alliance '90, the Greens attracted, at 7.3%, a higher level of national support than the FDP and polled even more strongly in *Land* elections in 1995, notably in industrialized North Rhine–Westphalia, where they attracted 10% support. Led in Bonn by the pragmatic 'Realo' Joschka Fischer (b. 1948), the Greens now share power in coalition governments with the SPD in three *Länder*, including North Rhine–Westphalia, and may supplant the FDP as the 'third force' 'swing party' in the 1998 federal election.

In the eastern *Länder*, the PDS, the reformed and liberalized successor of the communist SED, which dominated East German politics between 1945 and 1989, has established itself as a significant force. The SED itself originated as the German Communist Party (KPD), which was formed in 1918, but was merged, in 1946, under Soviet pressure, with East Germany's SPD to form the SED. Currently, the reform-socialist PDS is led in parliament by the engaging Dr Gregor Gysi (b. 1948), a Jewish lawyer from Berlin, with Lothar Bisky as party chair, and has a membership of 123,000. It attracts nearly 20% support in the eastern *Länder*, but barely 1% of the vote in the western *Länder*. Sixty per cent of its members and 30% of its supporters are aged over 60.

Numerous minor parties also operate both nationally and regionally in the FRG. At the national level are the far-right 15,000-member German National Party (Nationaldemokratische Partei Deutschlands: NPD), which dates from 1964; the right-wing nationalist Republicans (die Republikaner); and the neo-Nazi German People's Union (DVU). The NDP rose briefly to prominence between 1966 and 1968 and, led by Martin Mussgnug, now claims a membership of 15,000. The Republicans, an anti-immigrant extremist party formed in 1983 by a former Nazi Waffen-SS officer, Franz Schönhuber, has polled strongly in local elections since the late 1980s, as has the DVU, a body set up in Munich in 1987 by Gerhard Frey, the wealthy publisher of the neo-Nazi *National Zeitung* newspaper. In 1993 the Republicans gained temporary representation in the Bundestag when Rudolf

Krause, a right-wing CDU deputy, defected to the party. Schönhuber was ousted as leader of the Republicans and replaced by Rolf Schlierer (b. 1955) in December 1994, after the former had attempted to negotiate an alliance with the DVU. Other smaller neo-fascist groups have sprung up in the eastern *Länder*.

At the Land level, small regionalist parties, such as the South Schleswig Electoral Union (Sudschleswigscher Wahlerverband: SSW), established in 1948 to represent the Danish-speaking minority of northern Schleswig-Holstein, the Statt-Partei ('Instead of a Party'), established in Hamburg in September 1993, and the Work for Bremen (AFB) party, established in May 1995, have secured *Landtag* representation.

Under the terms of Article 21 of the 'Basic Law', political parties have been assigned a special role, described as 'forming the political will of the people'. As a result, under the terms of the Party Law of 1967, which was amended in 1981, public financial support has been provided to assist their operations. Currently, parties which secure in excess of 0.5% of the federal vote are given an official subsidy of DM5 per vote received. Similar, though lower, subsidies are paid by *Land* governments for state contests and by the central government for European Parliament elections. These subsidies constitute a third of annual party revenues.

In return for this support, the parties are subject to regulation concerning internal financial and electoral matters, and the Federal Constitutional Court reserves the right to ban groupings which are deemed to be antidemocratic, and thus unconstitutional. This sanction was employed in 1952 and 1956, when the quasi-fascist Socialist Reich Party and ultra-leftist Communist Party of Germany (Kommunistische Partei Deutschlands: KPD) were outlawed. Since 1989 ten out of some 70 neo-Nazi groups have been banned, including the National Gathering (Nationale Sammlung) and Free German Workers' Party.

Latest elections

The most recent Bundestag elections, which were held on 16 October 1994, resulted in victory for the incumbent CDU–CSU–FDP government coalition, but with a much reduced majority of ten seats, compared to the record majority of 134 which had been achieved in the October 1990 first all-German general election. The CDU, led by Chancellor Kohl, did not, as usual, contest Bavaria, and the CSU, led by Theo Waigel, fought only Bavarian seats.

The CDU attracted 34% and the CSU 7% of the all-German vote, winning 244 and 50 seats respectively. This was the CDU–CSU's lowest combined share of the national vote since 1949 and represented a 2.3% loss of support since 1990. The FDP, helped by *Zweitstimme* votes cast by CDU supporters, surmounted the 5% of the vote representation threshold, attracting 6.9% of the vote and capturing 47 seats. However, the party's vote share was 4.1% down on 1990. The opposition SPD, led since June 1993 by Rudolf Scharping, the minister-president of the Rhineland–Palatinate, advanced by 3.1% to secure a 36.4% share of the all-German vote and capture 252 seats, making it the largest single party in the new Bundestag. The Greens, who had failed to achieve Bundestag representation in the western *Länder* in 1990, advanced by 3.4% to win 7.3% of the national vote and 49 seats. The PDS attracted only 4.4% of the all-German vote, against 2.4% in 1990, but polled strongly in the six eastern *Länder*, where the party's support averaged 18%. By virtue of winning four directly elected *Erststimme* seats in east Berlin, the PDS qualified for party list seats, capturing 30 seats in all. Thirty-five other parties contested this general election, but failed to secure representation. These included the far-right Republicans, who received 1.9% national support. The electoral turnout was 79% and 3,923 candidates contested this poll. There were 16 *Überhangmandaten* ('overhang' or 'excess seats') caused by a party having directly elected in a given *Land* more deputies than it was, on a proportional representation basis, entitled to. The size of the Bundestag was thus increased from 656 deputies to 672.

The last indirect presidential election was held on 23 May 1994 and was won, on the third round of voting by the Bundesversammlung electoral college, by the CDU's nominee, Roman Herzog, who defeated the SPD's Johannes Rau by a margin of 696 votes against 605.

Political history

Formerly a confederation of 39 principalities within the Holy Roman Empire (First Reich), a united German Empire was forged in 1871, after two failed liberal democratic revolutions in 1830 and 1848, by Prussia's astute prime minister, the 'Iron Chancellor' Otto von Bismarck (1815–98), with the Hohenzollern King Wilhelm I (1797–1888) as German emperor (kaiser). A democracy of types did emerge after 1871, with a bicameral parliament (Reichstag) and universal male suffrage, but it was the kaiser and chancellor, as head of the traditional landed and military elite and buttressed by a nationalist and statist ideology, who wielded real power. During this imperial Second Reich (1871–1919) Germany advanced economically, emerging as an important industrial power, and carved out an extensive overseas empire. Military defeat in World War I brought the abdication of the kaiser and the creation of the parliamentary Weimar Republic in 1919. However, this experiment in liberal democracy lasted only 14 years, being overthrown by the fascist Nazi Third Reich dictatorship which was established from 1933 by Adolf Hitler (1889–1945), a believer in the notion of the existence of an Aryan German 'master race'. The Weimar Republic was encumbered by tremendous economic problems – brought on by postwar territorial losses, crippling reparation charges, and the onset of a world economic depression – and a flawed constitution, which created a confused 'dual executive' with power shared by an elected president and a chancellor (prime minister) dependent for support on a lower house which was elected by a generous form of proportional representation which promoted party fission. Between 1919 and 1933, 15 different chancellors held office and in the final years of the Weimar era power shifted increasingly towards the conservative president, Paul von Hindenburg (1847–1934).

In the Reichstag election of November 1932 Hitler's National Socialist German Workers (Nazi) party secured 33% of the popular vote and in January 1933 von Hindenburg appointed Hitler as chancellor. An Enabling Act was passed in March 1933, granting Hitler dictatorial powers and, on the death of von Hindenburg in August 1934, the posts of president and chancellor were fused under Hitler's new designation *Führer* ('leader'). Freedom of speech and assembly was abolished; the 1919 Treaty of Versailles and reparations agreements were repudiated; the Rhineland was remilitarized in 1936 and Austria and the Czech Sudetenland annexed in 1938–39; and a long series of persecutions began, climaxing in the murder of millions of Jews, gypsies, and political opponents. Although Hitler's interventionist and autarchic economic policies enjoyed a substantial measure of success at home, his decision to declare war on Poland on 1 September 1939, resulting in World War II, proved to be self-destructive. From the winter of 1942 German forces, which had controlled much of continental Europe, met with increasing external resistance, as the Soviet Red Army turned the tide at Volgograd (Stalingrad).

The Third Reich finally collapsed in May 1945, following the suicide of Hitler, as the allies advanced upon Berlin, and the large German Empire was thereafter dismembered. The eastern, Prussian, half was divided between Poland, the USSR, and the newly created Soviet satellite state, the German Democratic Republic (GDR). Out of the larger western portion, comprising the British, American, and French occupation zones, a new Federal Republic of Germany (FRG) was formed in May 1949. During the period of allied military control, 1945–49, a policy of demilitarization, decentralization, and democratization was instituted and a new, intended to be provisional, constitution framed. This constitution included the goal of eventual German reunification. Between 1948 and 1949, West Berlin was subjected to blockade by the Soviet Union, but survived to form a constituent Land in the FRG, following an airlift operation by the Allied powers.

Politics in the FRG during its first decade were dominated by the Christian Democratic Union (CDU), led by the popular Dr Konrad Adenauer (1876–1967), a former lord mayor of Cologne who had been imprisoned by the Nazis between 1934 and 1944 for opposition to the regime and served as chancellor between 1949 and 1963. Adenauer and his economics minister, Dr Ludwig Erhard (1897–1977), who was later chancellor between 1963–66, established a successful new approach to economic management termed the 'social market economy' (*soziale Marktwirtschaft*), which involved the state's encouragement of free-market productive forces, combined with strategic interventions so as to reconcile interest-group differences, guide the market in a socially responsible direction, and secure adequate welfare provision.

This new 'liberal-corporatist' managerial approach, combined with the injection of aid under the Marshall Plan and the enterprise of the nation's labour force, more than 2 million of whom were refugees from the partitioned East (GDR), contributed towards a phase of rapid economic reconstruction and growth during the 1950s and 1960s, an era now termed the 'miracle years'. During this period, West Germany, as the FRG was then popularly known, was also reintegrated into the international community. It regained its full sovereignty in 1954, entered the North Atlantic Treaty Organization (NATO) in 1955, emerging as a loyal supporter of the United States, and, under Adenauer's committed lead, joined the new European Economic Community (EEC) in 1957. Close rel-ations were also developed with France, enabling the Saarland to be amicably returned to Germany in January 1957.

In August 1961, East Germany's construction of a fortified wall around West Berlin, to prevent refugees from leaving the GDR, created a political crisis which vaulted West Berlin's mayor, Willy Brandt (1913–92), to international prominence. Domestically, Brandt played a pivotal role in shifting the Social Democratic Party (SPD) away from its traditional Marxist affiliation towards a more moderate position, following the party's 1959 Bad Godesberg conference. Support for the SPD steadily increased after this policy switch and the party joined the CDU in a 'grand coalition' led by the CDU's Dr Kurt Kiesinger (1904–88), between 1966 and 1969, and then secured power itself, with the support of the Free Democratic Party (FDP), under the leadership of Brandt in 1969.

As Chancellor, Brandt, working closely with the SPD's defence expert, Egon Bahr, introduced the new foreign policy of *Ostpolitik*, which sought reconciliation with Eastern Europe as a means of improving social contacts between the two Germanies. Treaties in 1970 normalized relations with the Soviet Union and Poland and recognized the Oder–Neisse border line, while, in September 1972, a 'Basic Treaty' was effected with East Germany, which acknowledged the GDR's borders and separate existence, enabling both countries to join the United Nations in 1973.

Willy Brandt resigned as chancellor in May 1974, following a revelation that his personal assistant, Günther Guillaume, had been an East German spy. Brandt's replacement as chancellor, the former finance minister, Helmut Schmidt (b. 1918), adhered to *Ostpolitik* and emerged as a leading advocate of European cooperation, while at home he introduced a series of important social reforms.

In the federal election of October 1976, the SPD–FDP coalition only narrowly defeated the CDU–CSU. Four years later, however, it secured a comfortable victory after the controversial Dr Franz-Josef Strauss (1915–88) had forced his way to the head of the CDU–CSU ticket. Soon after this election triumph, divisions emerged between the left wing of the SPD and the liberal-conservative wing of the FDP on defence policy, particularly over the proposed stationing by the end of 1983 of new short- and medium-range Cruise and Pershing-II American nuclear missiles in West Germany. There were also differences on economic strategy, during a period of gathering world recession. Chancellor Schmidt fought to maintain a moderate centrist course and to hold together his party's factions, but the FDP eventually withdrew from the federal coalition in September 1982 and joined forces with the CDU, led by Dr Helmut Kohl (b. 1930), to unseat the chancellor in a 'constructive vote of no confidence'. Helmut Schmidt immediately retired from politics and the SPD, led by the efficient but colourless Hans-Jöchen Vogel (b. 1926), was heavily defeated in the Bundestag elections of March 1983. In this contest, the SPD significantly lost votes on the left to the ascendant environmentalist Green Party, which, capturing 5.6% of the national vote, became the first new party since 1957 to gain representation in the Bundestag.

The new Kohl administration, with the FDP's Hans-Dietrich Genscher (b. 1927) remaining as foreign affairs minister, adhered closely to the external policy of the previous chancellorship. At home, however, a freer market economy approach was pursued. With unemployment rising to a level of 2.5 million in 1984, problems of social unrest emerged, while violent demonstrations greeted the stationing of American nuclear missiles on German soil during 1983–84. Internally, the Kohl administration was also rocked by scandals over illegal party funding by business donors, the 'Flick Affair', which briefly touched the chancellor himself. However, a strong recovery in the German economy from 1985 enabled the CDU–CSU–FDP coalition to secure re-election in the federal election of January 1987.

In this contest, both the minority parties, the FDP and the Greens, polled strongly. In contrast, the opposition SPD, led this time by Johannes Rau (b. 1931), the popular Schmidtite minister-president of the large state of North Rhine–Westphalia, secured its lowest share of the national vote since 1961. This defeat opened divisions within the party over future tactical strategies, with a number of influential figures advocating an alliance with the Greens. By the summer of 1989, however, with the fortunes of the Greens in decline, as a result of internal conflicts and changing global strategic conditions, and with popular support for the SPD showing signs of returning, the party, now led once again by Hans-Jöchen Vogel, recommitted itself to a centre-left course. At the *Land* level, the SPD, helped by local factors, secured a string of electoral victories. However, a disturbing feature of many of the elections held during 1989 was the rising level of support for far-right fascist parties, notably the Republicans and the German People's Union (DVU). This was a result of a sudden influx of both ethnic and non-ethnic German immigrants and asylum seekers, totalling 1.2 million during 1988–89, drawn predominantly from Eastern Europe, where previously firmly entrenched communist regimes were fast collapsing.

One such regime was the neighbouring GDR. Formed out of the Soviet zone of occupation, during the years immediately after 1945 a socialist regime on the Soviet Stalinist model had been established rapidly, involving the creation of a *de facto* one-party political system, the nationalization of industries and financial institutions, and agricultural collectivization. Popular opposition to this 'Sovietization' surfaced in mass demonstrations and a general strike in June 1953, at a time of food shortages. These were forcibly suppressed by Soviet troops and the ruling communist party (SED) was purged. In March 1954 the GDR secured full sovereignty from the USSR. Eight years later, in August 1961, the Berlin Wall was constructed to stem the growing movement of refugees to the FRG. During the 1960s economic reforms, known as the 'New Economic Mechanism', gave a boost to the East German growth rate, improving living conditions and easing social tensions. Minor reforms continued under the pragmatic Erich Honecker (1912–94), who replaced the Stalinist Walter Ulbricht (1893–1973) as SED leader in 1971 and supported the East–West détente process. However, as the 1980s progressed the SED regime became increasingly sclerotic and resisted the calls for more radical structural reform that began to be made by Mikhail Gorbachev, who became Communist Party leader in the Soviet Union in 1985.

Between May and November 1989, within the space of six months, the SED regime suddenly and unexpectedly collapsed. During much of this period, Honecker was personally incapacitated by serious illness and in his absence there was policy drift. The trigger for the regime's downfall was the decision by the reform-communist government in Hungary to open its borders to the West. This led to an exodus of tens of thousands of 'Ossis' (East Germans) to the FRG from August 1989, destabilizing the faltering GDR economy. At the same time, a grassroots Protestant church-led prodemocracy movement began to gather strength. Centred originally in Leipzig and around the intelligentsia-dominated Neue Forum (New Forum) dissident grouping, it became a mass movement, spreading to East Berlin and Dresden, with the visit to the GDR of Gorbachev on 6–7 October 1989.

Initially, these large demonstrations were broken up firmly by the GDR's security forces. However, from 9 October 1989 the will of the authorities faltered and, on 18 October 1989, Honecker and other 'old guard' colleagues resigned from their leadership positions. Egon Krenz (b. 1937), the former chief of the security forces (Stasi), took over as the new SED leader and head of state, but proved unable to stabilize a fast deteriorating situation. He legalized the formation of opposition parties and on 9 November 1989 opened the Berlin Wall, allowing free movement to the FRG. However, revelations of long-standing corruption within the SED's ruling elite discredited both Krenz and the communist party. On 6 December 1989 Krenz resigned as head of state and two days later, at an extraordinary congress, the SED was thoroughly purged and relaunched as a new reform-socialist force, the Party of Democratic Socialism (PDS). Meanwhile Honecker was placed under house arrest awaiting trial on charges of treason, corruption, and abuse of power and in January 1990 the Stasi headquarters in East Berlin were stormed by a seething crowd.

Dr Hans Modrow (b. 1928), the respected reform-communist mayor of Dresden, directed the GDR's affairs as prime minister, heading an all-party coalition 'government of national responsibility' until a multiparty general election was held in March 1990. However, the East German economy continued to deteriorate, with 1,500 people leaving each day for the western *Länder*, following the 1989 exodus of 344,000, and countrywide work stoppages increasing. Surprisingly, the March 1990 GDR general election was won by the East German CDU-dominated three-party Alliance for Germany, which secured a 48% share of the vote, to the East German SPD's 22% and the PDS's 16%. The Alliance, led by Lothar de Maiziere (b. 1940), a Protestant lay official and lawyer, was committed to securing rapid reunification with the FRG and immediately entered into negotiations with the Bonn government. With the crucial backing of the USSR and United States, whose agreement as wartime occupying powers in Berlin was required, this goal was achieved on 3 October 1990, with the official capital being designated as Berlin. The new FRG remained within NATO and, in return for the German promise of substantial payments, the USSR/Russia agreed to withdraw all Warsaw Pact troops from the eastern *Länder* by the end of 1994. This agreement was honoured, the last Russian troops leaving Berlin in August 1994. Political unification was preceded, from 1 July 1990, by German Economic and Monetary Union (GEMU), at a generous Ostmark–Deutschmark currency conversion rate of 1:1, and the establishment, in March 1990, of a trust body, the Treuhandanstalt, to oversee the privatization of 8,000 state-owned industrial enterprises. Reunification was achieved by the GDR acceding to the FRG and its existing political institutions, although new *Land* constitutions were subsequently framed and approved in referenda by the eastern states between 1990–94. This resulted in the addition of six *Länder*, with a combined population of 17 million. State elections were held on 14 October 1990 in these new *Länder*, which had replaced 14 regions (*Bezirke*), and right-of-centre parties polled strongly. Two months later, on 2 December 1990, the first all-German general election since 1932 was held. Popularly acclaimed as the 'Unification Chancellor', having set out a ten-point programme for reunification as early as December 1989, Helmut Kohl and his CDU–CSU–FDP governing coalition secured a clear victory, winning 55% of the all-German vote. However, the new coalition government was to contain just three east German politicians. The SPD, led by the charismatic Saarland minister-president Oskar Lafontaine (b. 1943) and stressing the likely high future economic costs of the unification process, lost support in this general election, as did the Greens, who polled below the 5% electoral hurdle in the western *Länder*.

As predicted by the SPD, Chancellor Kohl's 'honeymoon period' was to be short-lived. As 1991–92 progressed tremendous problems arose in securing the smooth economic and social integration of the relatively backward eastern *Länder*, whose average income per head was less than half that enjoyed in western Germany and many of whose industries were overmanned, technologically outdated, and had been rendered 'market-less' as a result of the collapse of the Comecon trading bloc. Hundreds of thousands of 'Ossis' became unemployed as economic restructuring caused consecutive 15% and 20% declines in eastern German GDP in 1991 and 1992, with a third of the workforce either unemployed or on short-time, and more than 90% of 'Ossis' said they now felt like second-class citizens. This fuelled anti-Kohl demonstrations in Leipzig and Dresden in March 1991 and, later, neo-Nazi-directed racist violence. Foreign asylum seekers' hostels were specifically targetted, notably in Rostock in August 1992. The popular standing of Chancellor Kohl also plummetted in the western *Länder* during 1991–92. This was the consequence of the chancellor's backtracking on a campaign pledge not to raise taxes to pay for the East's integration and of successive hikes in German interest rates, as inflation began to climb to around 4% and the budget deficit increased, and as the western German economy moved itself from boom conditions into recession, with the unemployment rate rising to more than 7%. The gathering international recession, itself partly caused by rising German interest rates, which badly damaged the European Exchange Rate Mechanism (ERM), exacerbated the situation. Defeat in Kohl's home *Land* of Rhineland–Palatinate in April 1991 meant that the CDU lost, to the SPD, the majority it had held in the Bundesrat upper house since October 1990.

Support for the CDU also slumped in the Hesse communal elections of March 1993, in which the extremist Republicans attracted 8% of the vote. Pressure mounted for the government to impose tighter restrictions on asylum-seeking immigrants. However, in general, despite the eastern German economy at last beginning to grow by 6%, against a 2%

decline in the western *Länder,* 1993 was a year of *Verdrossenheit* ('disillusionment and dissatisfaction') with politics. Nevertheless, the 'solidarity pact' on the future funding of unification negotiated in March 1993 by Kohl with the SPD's leader since May 1991, Bjorn Engholm (b. 1939), and state minister-presidents helped stabilize the situation, providing for a higher share of VAT receipts to go directly to *Länder,* thus reducing the extent of financial transfers required from western to eastern *Länder* after 1995, and imposing a 7.5% income tax surcharge to meet the resulting shortfall in federal revenue.

During 1994 there were a succession of state, European Parliament, and presidential elections, culminating in the holding of a general election on 16 October 1994 at a time when the all-German economy was beginning to revive. The SPD polled strongly in the Saxony Anhalt state election in eastern Germany, held in June 1994, but lost ground, along with the FDP, in the Euro-elections of the same month. Roman Herzog (b. 1934), a former president of the Federal Constitutional Court and the CDU nominee of Chancellor Kohl, was elected in May 1994 by the two chambers of parliament to become the new state president, replacing the widely respected Richard von Weizsacker (b. 1920), who had served a maximum two terms. However, the October 1994 general election saw the Bundestag majority of the ruling CDU–CSU–FDP coalition reduced substantially from 134 seats to just 10 seats. The coalition's share of the all-German vote fell to 48%. The FDP polled particularly weakly, attracting less than 7% of the vote, while the CDU–CSU's combined vote share, at 41%, was their lowest ever in a federal election. The opposition SPD, led since June 1993 by Rudolf Scharping (b. 1948) and pledging to reduce unemployment and housing shortages and to impose a 10% 'solidarity surcharge' on high-income earners, captured 36% of the vote, up 3% on 1990, while the Greens re-entered parliament after winning 7% national support.

A largely unchanged new cabinet, headed by Chancellor Kohl, was sworn in on 17 November 1994 and was pledged to implement a right-of-centre programme of continued privatization, tight control over public spending, fighting increasing levels of crime, and encouraging both a deepening and an expansion eastwards of the European Union. However, the political future of an important stabilizing element within the coalition, the liberal FDP, appeared in doubt from 1995 after it failed to surmount the 5% representation hurdle in a succession of state elections, prompting its leader, Klaus Kinkel (b. 1936), the foreign minister, to resign in May 1995. The FDP seemed set to be supplanted as the crucial 'third force' and federal 'swing party' by the unpredictable Greens, whose support in state elections now averaged 10%. In June 1995 Germany broke with a 50-year-old taboo when the Bundestag approved the deployment of 1,500 soldiers and medical staff and fighter bombers in the Balkans war zone. Made possible by a 1994 Constitutional Court ruling allowing such armed missions outside the NATO region provided that they were for humanitarian reasons, this decision marked Germany's first tentative move towards a global military role. In November 1995 the left-wing prime minister of Saarland, Oskar Lafontaine, dramatically won the SPD leadership from Rudolf Scharping.

ICELAND

Republic of Iceland

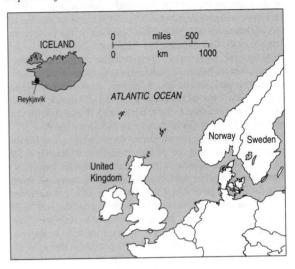

Capital: Reykjavik

Social and economic data
Area: 102,850 km^2
Population: 300,000*
Pop. density per km^2: 2.5*
Urban population: 91%**
Literacy rate: 99%**
GDP: $5,200 million**; per-capita GDP: $20,516**
Government defence spending (% of GDP): 0.0%**
Currency: krona
Economy type: high income
Labour force in agriculture: 10%**

*1994
**1992

Ethnic composition
Most of the population is descended from Norwegians and Celts. Icelandic is the official language.

Religions
The Evangelical Lutheran Church of Iceland is the national church, to which about 93% of the population adheres, but there is complete religious freedom. There are also about 1,800 Roman Catholics.

Political features
State type: liberal democratic
Date of state formation: 1944
Political structure: unitary
Executive: parliamentary
Assembly: one-chamber
Party structure: multiparty
Human rights rating: N/A
International affiliations: CE, EEA, EFTA, IAEA, IBRD, IMF, NACC, NATO, NC, OECD, OSCE, UN, WEU (associate), WTO

Local and regional government

There are seven administrative districts, ranging in population from about 10,000 to about 140,000.

Head of state

President Vigdís Finnbogadóttir, since 1970

Head of government

Prime Minister Davíd Oddsson, since 1991

Political leaders since 1970

1970–71 Johann Hafstein (IP–SDP coalition), 1971–74 Olafur Johannesson (PP–PA coalition), 1974–78 Geir Hallgrimsson (IP–PP coalition), 1978–79 Olafur Johannesson (PP–PA–SDP coalition), 1979–80 Benedikt Grondal (SDP), 1980–83 Gunnar Thoroddsen (IP–PA–PP coalition), 1983–87 Steingrímur Hermannsson (PP–IP coalition), 1987–91 Thorsteinn Pálsson (IP–PP–SDP coalition), 1991– Davíd Oddsson (IP–SDP coalition)

Political system

The constitution dates from independence in 1944. It provides for a president, as head of state, who is elected for four years by universal adult suffrage, and an assembly, called the Althing. It has 60 members, also elected by universal adult suffrage, through a party list system of proportional representation, for a four-year term.

The president appoints the prime minister and cabinet on the basis of parliamentary support and they are collectively responsible to the Althing.

Political parties

There are some seven parties and the electoral system tends to encourage a spread of assembly representation and, hence, coalitions of parties. The main parties are the Independence Party (IP), the Progressive Party (PP), the People's Alliance (PA), the Social Democratic Party (SDP), the Awakening of the Nations (AN) party, and the Women's Alliance (WA).

The IP was formed in 1929 by an amalgamation of the Conservative and Liberal parties. It has a right-of-centre orientation.

The PP dates from 1916 and is a rural-based centrist party.

The PA was founded in 1956 by a union of SDP dissidents and the Socialist Unity Party. It has a socialist orientation.

The SDP was formed in 1916 as the political arm of Iceland's labour movement. It has a moderate left-of-centre orientation.

The AN was formed in January 1995 as a left-wing breakaway from the SDP.

The WA is also a comparatively new party, having been formed in 1983. It is concerned with the promotion of women's and children's interests.

Latest elections

The results of the April 1995 general election were as illustrated in the following table.

Political history

Iceland became independent in 1944, when the Convention which linked it to Denmark was terminated. In 1949 it joined the North Atlantic Treaty Organization (NATO) and the

	% votes	Seats
IP	37.1	25
PP	23.3	15
SDP	11.4	7
PA	14.3	9
WA	4.9	3
AN	7.2	4
Other parties	1.8	0

Council of Europe and in 1953 the Nordic Council. Since independence it has always been governed by coalitions of the leading parties, sometimes right-wing left-wing groupings, but mostly moderate.

Externally, most of Iceland's problems have been connected with the excessive exploitation of the fishing grounds around its coasts, while domestically governments have been faced with the recurring problem of inflation. It became a member of the European Free Trade Association (EFTA) in 1970, but remains opposed to membership of the European Union (EU) since it perceives the EU's fishing quotas policy as inimical to the nation's interest.

In May 1985 the Althing unanimously declared the country a 'nuclear free zone', banning the entry of all nuclear weapons. The 1987 elections ended control of the Althing by the coalition of the Independence and Progressive parties, giving more influence to the minor parties, including the Women's Alliance which doubled its seat tally. In the 1991 general election the Independence Party strengthened its position, in votes and seats, and a centre-right coalition was formed, led by Davíd Oddsson (b. 1948). A new coalition was formed with the PP after April 1995.

IRELAND

Republic of Ireland
Eire

Capital: Dublin

Social and economic data

Area: 70,283 km^2
Population: 3,500,000*
Pop. density per km^2: 50
Urban population: 58%**
Literacy rate: 99%**
GDP $43,000 million**; per-capita GDP: $12,104**
*Government defence spending (% of GDP): 1.1***
Currency: punt
Economy type: high income
Labour force in agriculture: 14%**

*1994
**1992

Ethnic composition

Most of the population has Celtic origins. Although Irish (Gaeltacht) is the official language, English is most widely

used and Irish is spoken only in restricted areas, mainly in the West. Official documents are printed in both languages.

Religions
Almost all the population is Christian, about 95% Roman Catholic.

Political features
State type: liberal democratic
Date of state formation: 1937
Political structure: unitary
Executive: parliamentary
Assembly: two-chamber
Party structure: multiparty
Human rights rating: 94%
International affiliations: CE, EEA, ESA, EU, IAEA, IBRD, IMF, IWC, OECD, OSCE, UN, WEU (observer), WTO

Local and regional government
The country is divided into four provinces containing 26 counties. The counties and towns have elected councils.

Head of state
President Mary Robinson, since 1990

Head of government
Prime Minister John Bruton, since 1994

Political leaders since 1970
1966–73 Jack Lynch (Fianna Fáil), 1973–77 Liam Cosgrave (Fine Gael–Labour coalition), 1977–79 Jack Lynch (Fianna Fáil), 1979–81 Charles Haughey (Fianna Fáil), 1981–82 Garret FitzGerald (Fine Gael– Labour coalition), 1982 Charles Haughey (Fianna Fáil), 1982–87 Garret FitzGerald (Fine Gael–Labour coalition), 1987–89 Charles Haughey (Fianna Fáil), 1989–92 Charles Haughey (Fianna Fáil–Progressive Democrats coalition), 1992 Albert Reynolds (Fianna Fáil–Progressive Democrats coalition), 1993–94

Albert Reynolds (Fianna Fáil–Labour coalition), 1994– John Bruton (Fine Gael–Labour coalition)

Political system
The 1937 constitution provides for a president, elected by universal adult suffrage for a seven-year term, and a two-chamber National Parliament, consisting of a Senate (Seanad éireann) and a House of Representatives (Dáil éireann), serving a five-year term. The Senate has 60 members, 11 nominated by the prime minister and 49 elected by panels representative of most aspects of Irish life. The Dáil consists of 166 members elected by universal adult suffrage, through the single transferable vote system of proportional representation. The president appoints a prime minister (Taoiseach) who is nominated by the Dáil. He or she chooses the cabinet and all are collectively responsible to the Dáil, which is subject to dissolution by the president if the government loses its confidence within the five-year term.

Political parties
The system of proportional representation encourages the formation of several parties, of which there are some 14, the four most significant being Fianna Fáil, Fine Gael, the Labour Party, and the Progressive Democrats.

The term Fianna Fáil literally means Soldiers of Destiny. The party was formed in 1926 by the charismatic leader Éamon de Valera, and was originally a wing of Sinn Féin (The Workers' Party). It was always a party of radical republicanism, calling for the complete independence of Ireland. It now has a moderate centre-right orientation and favours the peaceful reunification of the island.

Fine Gael means Irish Tribe, or United Ireland Party, and is descended from the Society of the Irish. It was originally founded in 1922 to support the first government established within the new Irish Free State, and was reformed in 1933. It has a moderate centre-left orientation.

The Labour Party dates from 1912, when it was part of Ireland's Trade Union Congress. In 1930 it was decided to separate the industrial and political functions of the movement and the Labour Party became a separate organization. It has a moderate left-of-centre orientation.

The Progressive Democrats Party was formed as recently as 1985 and represents a new departure in Irish politics, being more radical than the other established parties. It seeks a peaceful solution to the problems in Northern Ireland, the encouragement of private enterprise, the abolition of the Seanad, and a clear distinction between church and state.

Latest elections
The results of the November 1992 Dáil elections were as follows:

	% votes	Seats
Fianna Fáil	39.11	68
Fine Gael	24.47	45
Labour Party	19.31	33
Progressive Democrats	4.68	10
Other parties	12.42	10

The results of the 1993 Seanad elections were as follows:

	Seats
Fianna Fáil	19
Fine Gael	17
Labour Party	5
Progressive Democrats	2
Others	17

In the November 1990 presidential elections Mary Robinson (b. 1944), supported by the Labour Party and the Workers' Party, won in the second round with 51.9% of the votes, defeating the Fianna Fáil candidate, Brian Lenihan, and the Fine Gael candidate, Austin Currie.

Political history
Ireland was joined to Great Britain by the Act of Union of 1801 but by the 1880s there was a strong movement for home rule. This was conceded in 1914 but its implementation was delayed by World War I, resulting in fierce riots in Dublin in 1916, the Easter Rebellion. Guerrilla activities continued after the war, through what was called the Irish Republican Army (IRA), which was formed by Michael Collins (1890–1922) in 1919. In 1921 a treaty gave southern Ireland dominion status within the British Commonwealth, while the six northern counties of Ulster remained part of the United Kingdom, but with limited self-government.

The Irish Free State, as southern Ireland was formally called in 1922, was accepted by IRA leader Michael Collins but not by many of his colleagues, who transferred their allegiance to Éamon de Valera (1882–1975), leader of the Fianna Fáil party. He, too, eventually acknowledged the partition in 1937, when a new constitution was proclaimed in Dublin, giving the country the name of Eire and establishing it as a sovereign state. The IRA continued its fight for an independent, unified Ireland through a campaign of violence, mainly in Northern Ireland but also on the British mainland and, to a lesser extent, in the Irish republic. Eire remained part of the Commonwealth until 1949, when it left, declaring itself the Republic of Ireland, while Northern Ireland remained a constituent part of the United Kingdom.

Despite the sympathy of governments in Dublin for reunification, all have condemned the violence of the IRA and have dealt strongly with it within Ireland itself. In 1973 Ireland's traditional party, Fianna Fáil, which had held office for more than 40 years, was defeated and Liam Cosgrave (b. 1920) formed a coalition of the Fine Gael and Labour parties. In 1977 Fianna Fáil returned to power, with Jack Lynch (b. 1917) as prime minister. Meanwhile, the IRA violence intensified, with the murder of Earl Mountbatten of Burma in Ireland, in 1979, and the massacre of 18 British soldiers in Northern Ireland.

Lynch resigned later the same year and was succeeded by Charles Haughey (b. 1925), now leader of Fianna Fáil. His aim was a united Ireland, with a large measure of independence for the six northern counties. He called an early general election, in 1981, but failed to win a majority, allowing Dr Garret FitzGerald (b. 1926), leader of the Fine Gael party, to form another coalition with Labour. The following year, however, he was defeated on his budget proposals and resigned. Charles Haughey returned to office, with a minority government, but he too was forced to resign later the same year, resulting in the return of FitzGerald.

Various ideas were then explored in an effort to resolve the Irish problem, culminating in the signing of the Anglo-Irish Agreement in 1985, providing for regular consultation and the exchange of information on political, legal, security, and cross-border matters. The Agreement also said that no change in the status of Northern Ireland would be made without the consent of a majority of the people. The Agreement was strongly criticized by the leaders of Ulster's two main Protestant Unionist parties.

At the start of 1987 Garret FitzGerald's coalition came to the end of its life and a general election was called. It was won by Fianna Fáil and Charles Haughey returned to power. His relations with the British government proved to be more successful than many people had predicted and the Anglo-Irish Agreement continued to be honoured by the new administration. Meanwhile, the young former finance and fustice minister, Alan Dukes, had succeeded FitzGerald as leader of Fine Gael.

In 1989 Haughey, in an attempt to secure an overall majority in the Dáil, called a general election. Again he failed and was forced to form a coalition with the Progressive Democrats. His standing in the country, and within his own party, deteriorated and in February 1992 he lost the leadership to his former finance minister, Albert Reynolds (b. 1935). It was hoped that Reynolds' calm but firm approach would strengthen Ireland domestically and internationally.

At first these hopes seemed to have been realized and in June 1992 the Irish people voted emphatically to ratify the Maastricht Treaty on closer European union. However, as the year progressed, Reynolds' touch seemed to have deserted him and in November, after losing a confidence vote, he sought a personal mandate through a successful general election result. He did not, however, obtain his clear victory and was obliged to enter a coalition with the Labour Party, with its leader, Dick Spring (b. 1950), as his deputy.

Growing in confidence, in October 1993 Reynolds unveiled a six-year national development plan to achieve 'the transformation of Ireland' and in the following month furthered the Northern Ireland peace process by agreeing a 'joint declaration' with the United Kingdom's prime minister, John Major, aimed at securing a just and lasting settlement.

1994 started on a high note but fell away when, in November, after a deep disagreement with Dick Spring over a judicial appointment, Prime Minister Reynolds lost Labour's support and was forced to resign. After some manoeuvring, the Fine Gael leader, John Bruton (b. 1947), who had replaced Alan Dukes in November 1990, agreed a new coalition with Labour. Reynolds relinquished the Fianna Fáil leadership and was succeeded by his former finance minister, Bertie Ahern.

ITALY

Republic of Italy
Repubblica Italiana

Capital: Rome

Social and economic data
Area: 301,225 km^2
Population: 57,800,000*
Pop. density per km^2: 192*
Urban population: 69%**
Literacy rate: 97%**
GDP: $1,187,000 million**; per-capita GDP: $20,513**
Government defence spending (% of GDP): 2.0%**
Currency: lira
Economy type: high income
Labour force in agriculture: 10%**

*1994
**1992

Ethnic composition
The population is mostly Italian but there are minorities of German origin in the Dolomites and Slovenes around Trieste. Italian is the national language.

Religions
About 90% of the population is Roman Catholic. This was the state religion between 1929 and 1984.

Political features
State type: liberal democratic
Date of state formation: 1861
Political structure: unitary
Executive: parliamentary
Assembly: two-chamber
Party structure: multiparty

Human rights rating: 90%
International affiliations: AG (observer), ALADI (observer), CE, CERN, CSCE, EEA, ESA, EU, G-7, G-10, IAEA, IBRD, IMF, NACC, NATO, OECD, UN, WEU, WTO

Local and regional government
The country is divided into 20 regions, five of which, Sicily Sardinia, Trentino-Alto Adige, Friuli-Venezia Giulia, and Valle d'Aosta, have a special status and enjoy a greater measure of autonomy, because of their geographical, cultural, or linguistic differences. Each region has a popularly elected council. Since the mid-1970s increasing powers have been devolved from the centre to the regions and today more than 30% of the national budget is under regional control.

Head of state
President Oscar Luigi Scalfaro, since 1992

Head of government
Prime Minister Lamberto Dini, since 1995

Political leaders since 1970
1970 Mariano Rumor (DC-led coalition), 1970–72 Emilio Colombo (DC-led coalition), 1972–73 Giulio Andreotti (DC-led coalition), 1973–74 Mariano Rumor (DC-led coalition), 1974–76 Aldo Moro (DC-led coalition), 1976 Aldo Moro (DC), 1976–79 Giulio Andreotti (DC), 1979–80 Francesco Cossiga (DC-led coalition), 1980–81 Arnaldo Forlani (DC-led coalition), 1981–83 Giovanni Spadolini (PRI-led coalition), 1983 Amitore Fanfani (DC-led coalition), 1983–87 Bettino Craxi (PSI-led coalition), 1987 Amitore Fanfani (DC-led coalition), 1987–88 Giovanni Goria (DC-led coalition), 1988–89 Ciriaco De Mita (DC-led coalition), 1989–92 Giulio Andreotti (DC-led coalition), 1992–93 Giuliano Amato (PSI-led coalition), 1993–94 Carlo Azeglio Ciampi (DC-led coalition), 1994–95 Silvio Berlusconi (Freedom Alliance), 1995– Lamberto Dini (technocrat administration)

Political system
The 1948 constitution provides for a two-chamber assembly, consisting of a 315-member Senate and a 630-member Chamber of Deputies, both serving five-year terms. The 315 elected members of the Senate are regionally representative and there are also seven life senators. The voting age is set at 25 years for Senate elections, but at 18 years for the lower house. All members of the Chamber were formerly elected through a party list system of proportional representation, but in 1993 the electoral system underwent major reform. Now three-quarters of the members are elected by simple majority voting, the remaining quarter by the party list system. Candidates need at least 4% of the national vote to be successful. Polling is now confined to a single day, instead of being spread over two rounds. The two chambers have equal powers.

    The president is a constitutional head of state and is elected for a seven-year term by an electoral college consisting of both assembly chambers and 58 regional representatives. The president appoints the prime minister and cabinet, which is called the Council of Ministers, and they are all collectively responsible to the assembly.

In October 1988 the Chamber of Deputies voted to abolish the practice of secret voting in the chamber, except on civil rights issues or matters affecting non-Italian groups.

As noted in Chapter 6, there is frequent use of referenda in the political system.

Political parties

In anticipation of the 1994 general election there was a major realignment of political parties, some existing ones reforming and new ones being created. Three major blocs emerged: the right-wing Freedom Alliance; the centrist Pact for Italy; and the left-wing Progressive Alliance.

The Freedom Alliance included the Christian Democratic Centre (CCD), Forza Italia (Go Italy!), the National Alliance (AN), the Northern League (LN), the Panella List, and the Union of the Democratic Centre (UDC).

The Pact for Italy comprised the Italian Popular Party (PPI), and the Pact for Italy (Patto per l'Italia, or Patto Segni).

The Progressive Alliance consisted of the Communist Refoundation (RC), the Democratic Alliance (AD), the Democratic Party of the Left (PDS), the Greens (Verdi), the Italian Socialist Party (PSI), and The Network (La Rete).

The CCD is the right wing of the Christian Democratic Party (DC) which was formed in 1943 as the successor to the pre-Fascist Popular Party. It is a Christian centrist party and strongly anticommunist.

Forza Italia was created in 1994 as a political vehicle for the media magnate, Silvio Berlusconi, owner of three television channels, several newspapers, and the AC Milan football team. He took the slogan of the AC Milan's supporters, 'Come on Italy!' as the party's name.

The AN was formerly part of the Italian Social Movement (MSI), a neo-Fascist party founded in 1946.

The LN, or Lombard League, was formed in 1979 and named after the 12th-century federation of northern cities that rebelled against the Emperor Frederick Barbarossa. It opposes the granting of subsidies by the economically rich north to the underdeveloped south and promotes the cause of federalism and regionalism. A conservative-populist body, it is led by Umberto Bossi (b. 1941).

The Panella List is a radical grouping consisting of the followers of the libertarian politician Marco Pannella.

The UDC developed from the Italian Liberal Party (PLI) which was founded in 1848 by Count Camilio di Cavour, who played such a key role in the unification of Italy. The PLI dominated the nation's politics in its early years but it moved steadily to the right.

The PPI is a revival of the pre-Fascist Popular Party, founded in 1919, which in 1943 was replaced by the Christian Democratic Party (DC). It has a Catholic centrist orientation.

The Pact for Italy was founded in 1994 by a former DC member, Mario Segni. It is strongly reformist.

The RC is the survivor of the Italian Communist Party, still adhering to Marxist principles.

The AD is an alliance of some members of the Socialist and Republican parties, the PSI and the PRI, particularly those who promoted the 1993 referendum on constitutional change.

The PDS was originally the Italian Communist Party, formed in 1921. It changed its name to the Democratic Party of the Left (PDS) in 1991. It has a moderate left-wing orientation.

Verdi was founded in 1987 as a branch of the European Green movement.

The PSI was established in 1892 as Italy's first mass party. In its present form it contains the remnants of the old party left after the creation of the AD.

La Rete was formed in 1991 as a strongly anti-Mafia party.

Latest elections

The 1994 general election results were as follows:

Senate		
	% votes	Seats
Freedom Alliance	42.0	156
Progressive Alliance	33.0	122
Pact for Italy	17.0	31
Others	8.0	6

Chamber of Deputies		
	% votes	Seats
Freedom Alliance	42.9	366
Progressive Alliance	34.4	213
Pact for Italy	15.7	46
Others	7.0	5

Political history

Italy became a unified kingdom in 1861 and soon afterwards set about acquiring a colonial empire by a mixture of purchase and seizure. The Fascist period, between 1922 and 1943, was notable for an extensive programme of public works but the liaison with Nazi Germany drew it into World War II and eventual defeat. In 1946, after a referendum, the monarchy was abolished and Italy became a republic, adopting a new constitution in 1948.

The postwar period has seen rapid changes of government and the striking of many deals between the political parties. Until 1963 the Christian Democrats were dominant but this was followed by a succession of coalition governments, most with Christian Democratic involvement. In 1976 the Communists became a significant force, winning more than a third of the votes for the Chamber of Deputies. With this show of support, they pressed for what they called the 'historic compromise', a broad-based government with representatives from the Christian Democratic, Socialist, and Communist parties, which would, in effect, be an alliance between Communism and Roman Catholicism. This was rejected, however, by the Christian Democrats.

Apart from a brief period in 1977–78, the other parties successfully excluded the Communists from power-sharing, forcing them to become part of the opposition. In 1980 the Socialists returned to share power with the Christian Democrats and Republicans and they continued in a number of subsequent coalitions of mixed composition. Then, in 1983, the leader of the Socialist Party, Bettino Craxi (b. 1934), became the first Socialist prime minister in the republic's history, leading a coalition of Christian Democrats, Socialists, Republicans, Social Democrats, and Liberals. Despite criticisms of Craxi's strong-willed style of leadership, the coalition parties could find no acceptable alternative so continued to give him support. The Craxi government saw an improvement in the state of the Italian economy, although the north–south divide in productivity and prosperity persisted.

In August 1986 an agreement was reached that Craxi would hand over power to the DC leader, Ciriaco De Mita (b. 1928), in March 1987, allowing the coalition to stay in office until the general election in June 1988. However, when Craxi did resign the Socialists withdrew their support from the Christian Democrats, precipitating a constitutional crisis. Amitore Fanfani, of the Christian Democrats, headed a caretaker government for a time then Giovanni Goria (b. 1943) formed another unstable coalition, leaving Italian politics in a state of continuing uncertainty. Goria held office for eight months, twice threatening to resign, then in March 1988 he submitted his resignation on a nuclear power issue and it was accepted by the president. Ciriaco De Mita, leader of the Christian Democrats, then took up the challenge, forming a five-party coalition, including the Socialists, led by Craxi.

In February 1989 De Mita was replaced as DC leader by Arnaldo Forlani, but continued as prime minister. In May 1989, however, he resigned and, after much manoeuvring, the veteran politician, Giulio Andreotti, was recalled to form yet another coalition. In 1991 Andreotti formed another government, the 50th since the end of World War II, and remained in office until the April 1992 general election.

The result was inconclusive and threw the political system into disarray. President Cossiga resigned and it was a month before a permanent replacement could be found, in the shape of the veteran politician, Oscar Luigi Scalfaro (b. 1918). After weeks of bargaining, Giuliano Amato of the Socialist Party managed to form Italy's 51st postwar government, a broad coalition of parties. The uncertainty of the political situation had its effect on the economy and in September 1992 the lira was devalued and Italy withdrew from the European Exchange Rate Mechanism (ERM).

Amid allegations of corruption, Bettino Craxi resigned as Socialist Party leader and was replaced by Giorgio Benvenuto. Under the leadership of the brave, crusading Milan magistrate, Antonio Di Pietro, a wide-ranging Tangentopoli ('kickback city') probe was instigated from 1992. It revealed the long-suspected depth and systematic nature of political corruption. Clearly implicated in bribes-for-contracts deals and payoffs from the Mafia, leading politicians and business executives were arrested almost daily during 1993, with even Giulio Andreotti implicated. This led to the formation of a 'government of technocrats' headed by Carlo Azeglio Ciampi, a governor of the Bank of Italy. Meanwhile Craxi had been absolved from prosecution for corruption and Benvenuto had resigned the Socialist Party leadership and had been succeeded by Ottaviano del Turro.

Disillusionment with the instability in Italian politics stimulated a demand for the reform of the voting system and in a referendum in April 1993 there was an overwhelming vote for change. There were also votes to end the state financing of parties and abolish a number of state ministries.

In January 1994 Prime Minister Ciampi resigned to make way for a general election and, in anticipation of this, there was a fundamental realignment of the political parties, resulting in the formation of three main groupings, to the right, in the centre, and to the left of the political spectrum. A new political force emerged in the shape of the media tycoon, Silvio Berlusconi (b. 1936), who launched Forza Italia as the spearhead of the right-wing Freedom Alliance. Berlusconi used his television channels and newspapers, and his own popularity as owner of the AC Milan football team, to promote his political ambitions and in the March 1994 elections the Freedom Alliance, led by Forza Italia, secured a surprise landslide victory. The formerly dominant Christian Democrats, who had disbanded and reformed themselves as the Popular Party within the centrist Pact for Italy, were so badly tarnished by the corruption scandals that they finished in a distant third position. After considerable manoeuvring, Berlusconi formed a right-wing coalition with Forza Italia, the profederalist Northern League (LN) and the neofascist National Alliance (AN) as the main partners.

Berlusconi's honeymoon as the nation's leader was short-lived. In July 1994 he was accused of fraud, through his many business interests, and his younger brother Paolo was placed under house arrest. Opposition to his free-market economic policies provoked industrial resistance, including a one-day strike. In December 1994, rather than risk losing a confidence vote in parliament, Berlusconi resigned and was replaced by ex-banker Lamberto Dini, who had been an independent member of the Freedom Alliance government.

Dini led a cabinet of nonelected technocrats, receiving support from the Democratic Party of the Left (PDS), the Popular Party (the successor to the DC), and the LN, with fierce opposition being provided by Forza Italia and the AN.

The Dini administration sought to reform the state pensions system to reduce the budget deficit. With the support of the Reconstructed Communists, in October 1995, it survived a 'no confidence' vote called by Forza Italia, whose leader Berlusconi was set to stand trial in January 1996 on company tax evasion and bribery charges.

LIECHTENSTEIN

Principality of Liechtenstein
Fürstentum Liechtenstein

Capital: Vaduz

Social and economic data
Area: 160 km^2
Population: 29,000*
Pop. density per km^2: 181*
Urban population: 87%**
Literacy rate: 99%**
GDP: $1,025 million**; per-capita GDP: $35,500**
Government defence spending (% of GDP): 0%**
Currency: Swiss franc

Economy type: high income
Labour force in agriculture: 3%**

*1994
**1992

Ethnic composition
The indigenous population is of German-speaking Aleman-nic origin, while a third are foreign-born resident workers.

Religions
Roman Catholicism is the main religion.

Political features
State type: liberal democratic
Date of state formation: 1342
Political structure: unitary
Executive: parliamentary
Assembly: one-chamber
Party structure: multiparty
Human rights rating: N/A
International affiliations: CE, EFTA, IAEA, OSCE, UN, WTO

Local and regional government
The Principality is divided into two districts, Oberland (Upper Country) and Unterland (Lower Country), which, in turn, comprise 11 communes.

Head of state
Prince Hans Adam von und zu Liechtenstein II, since 1984

Head of government
Prime Minister Mario Frick, since 1993

Political leaders since 1970
1978–93 Hans Brunhart (VU), 1993 Markus Büchel (FBP), 1993– Mario Frick (VU)

Political system
The October 1921 constitution established a hereditary prin-cipality, with a single-chamber parliament, the Landtag or Diet. The prince is the formal and constitutional head of state. He may dissolve parliament (Landtag) at any time and his approval is required for all legislation before it may become law. The Landtag has 25 members, elected for a four-year term through a system of proportional representa-tion, based on the use of two district-level constituencies and the rule that parties which secure less than 8% of the votes cast fail to qualify for the distribution of seats.

Until 1984 only men were entitled to vote. Women, who constitute 67% of the electorate, were then given suffrage, which now extends to all adults aged 20 and over.

A group of five people, a prime minister and four council-lors, are elected by the Landtag to form the principality's government (Collegial Board) for the duration of parliament.

Political parties
There are four political parties, the two most dominant being the Patriotic Union (VU) and the Progressive Citizens' Party (FBP). The VU was founded in 1918 and remodelled in 1938. It has a firm support base in the mountainous south of the principality. The FBP is a northern-based party. Both par-ties share a similar conservative ideological outlook.

Latest elections
In the October 1993 Landtag elections the VU won 13 seats, the FBP 11, and the Free List one seat.

Political history
Liechtenstein was founded as a sovereign state in 1342 and has remained within its present boundaries since 1432. It did not, however, adopt its current name until 1719, when it was purchased by the present ruling family and formed part of the Holy Roman Empire until 1806. Between 1815 and 1866 the state was a member of the German Confederation, before leaving to become a fully independent Principality.

However, because of its small size and the decision to abolish its armed forces in 1868, Liechtenstein has found it convenient, while remaining neutral in external disputes, to associate itself with larger neighbouring nations in inter-national matters. For example, from 1923 it shared a customs union with Switzerland, which also represented it inter-nationally. Previously Austria undertook its diplomatic rep-resentation. In 1991 it became a full member of the European Free Trade Area (EFTA) and in 1992 a member of the United Nations. It has been a member of the Council of Europe since 1978.

Liechtenstein is one of the world's richest countries, with an income per head comparable to that of Switzerland and Japan and twice as great as that of the United Kingdom. High technology precision engineering, international bank-ing, aided by its favourable tax structure and legal system, and tourism constitute the three pillars of this successful economy.

After 42 years as the main government party, the FBP was defeated by the VU in 1970 but returned to power four years later. After a close election result in 1978 the VU returned to government and remained in office until 1993. There were two general elections in that year. In the first, in February, the FBP won most seats but not an overall majority and the leading FBP candidate, Markus Büchel, formed an FBP–VU coalition. Büchel was defeated on a vote of confidence moved by his own party in September, and another election was called. This time the VU secured a narrow majority and its leading candidate, Mario Frick, formed a new administration.

Prince Franz Josef II, who succeeded to the throne in 1938, and was *de facto* ruler for four and a half decades, handed over executive powers to his son and heir, Prince Hans Adam (b. 1945), in August 1984. He later died in 1989.

LUXEMBOURG

Grand Duchy of Luxembourg
Grand-Duché de Luxembourg

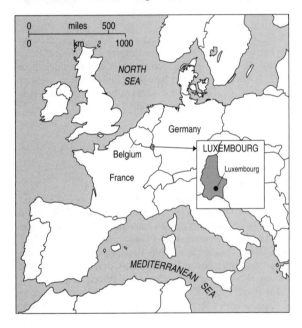

Capital: Luxembourg

Social and economic data
Area: 2,590 km²
Population: 400,000*
Pop. density per km²: 154*
Urban population: 85%**
Literacy rate: 100%**
GDP: $12,600 million**; per-capita GDP: $32,500**
Government defence spending (% of GDP): 1.0%**
Currency: Luxembourg franc
Economy type: high income
Labour force in agriculture: 3%**

*1994
**1992

Ethnic composition
Most of the population are descended from the Moselle Franks. Letzeburgish, a German–Moselle–Frankish dialect

is the official language. French is used in government communications and German is the language of commerce and the media.

Religions
Ninety-five per cent of the population is Roman Catholic. There are also about 4,000 Evangelicals.

Political features
State type: liberal democratic
Date of state formation: 1848
Political structure: unitary
Executive: parliamentary
Assembly: one-chamber
Party structure: multiparty
Human rights rating: N/A
International affiliations: BENELUX, BLEU, CE, EEA, EU, IAEA, IBRD, IMF, NACC, NATO, OECD, OSCE, UN, WEU, WTO

Local and regional government
The country is divided into three districts, which are further subdivided into 13 cantons. The cantons are administered by the central government and at a lower level are municipalities, with elected councils and appointed mayors.

Head of state
Grand Duke Jean I, since 1964

Head of government
Prime Minister Jean-Claude Junker, since 1995

Political leaders since 1970
1969–74 Pierre Werner (PCS–PD coalition), 1974–79 Gaston Thorn (POSL–PD coalition), 1979–84 Pierre Werner (PCS–PD coalition), 1984–95 Jacques Santer (PCS–POSL coalition), 1995– Jean-Claude Junker (PCS–POSL coalition)

Political system
Luxembourg is a hereditary and constitutional monarchy. The constitution dates from 1868 but has been revised in 1919 and 1956. It provides for a single-chamber assembly, the Chamber of Deputies, with 60 members, elected by universal adult suffrage through a party list system of proportional representation, for a five-year term. There is also an advisory body called the Council of State whose 21 members are appointed by the grand duke for life. Any decision of the Council of State can be overruled by the Chamber. The grand duke also appoints a prime minister and Council of Ministers who are collectively responsible to the Chamber.

Political parties
There are some seven political parties, the most significant being the Christian Social Party (PCS), the Luxembourg Socialist Workers' Party (POSL), and the Democratic Party 'Liberals' (PD).

The PCS was founded in 1914 as the Party of the Right. It took its present name in 1944. It has often been seen as the 'natural' party of government, having been a member of most coalitions. It stands for political stability and planned economic expansion, and is a strong European Union supporter. It has a moderate centre-right orientation.

The POSL was formed in 1902 as the working class party, with strong links with the union movement. It has a moderate socialist orientation.

The PD dates from 1945 and was partly based on the anti-German resistance movement. Its predecessor was the prewar Liberal Party and PD members are now popularly described as the 'Liberals'. The party has a centrist orientation.

Latest elections
The results in the June 1994 general election were as follows:

	Seats
PCS	21
POSL	17
PD	12
Greens	5
Other parties	5

Political history
Originally part of the Holy Roman Empire, Luxembourg became a Duchy in 1354. It was made a Grand Duchy in 1815 but, like Belgium, under Netherlands rule. Belgium secured its independence in 1839, taking part of Luxembourg with it. The Grand Duchy achieved full independence in 1848.

Although a small country, Luxembourg occupies an important pivotal position in Western Europe, being a founder member of many international organizations, including the European Coal and Steel Community (ECSC), the European Atomic Energy Commission (EURATOM), and the European Community (EC) itself. It formed an economic union with Belgium and the Netherlands in 1948 (Benelux), which was the forerunner of wider European cooperation. Today, Luxembourg constitutes one of the European Union's three centres of administration.

Grand Duchess Charlotte, who had been the country's ruler for 45 years, abdicated in 1964 and was succeeded by her son Prince Jean (b. 1925). She died, at a considerable age, in 1985.

The proportional representation voting system has resulted in a series of coalition governments. The Christian Social Party headed most coalitions between 1945 and 1974 when its dominance was challenged by the Socialists. It regained pre-eminence in 1979 and is a leading member of the current administration.

In January 1995 Jacques Santer (b. 1937), who had been prime minister since 1984, was appointed president of the Commission of the European Union. He was succeeded by Jean-Claude Junker, leading a reformed PCS–POSL coalition government.

MALTA

Republic of Malta
Repubblika Ta'Malta

Capital: Valletta

Social and economic data
Area: 316 km²
Population: 400,000*
Pop. density per km²: 1,266*
Urban population: 88%**
Literacy rate: 81%**
GDP: $2,800 million**; per-capita GDP: $7,900**
Government defence spending (% of GDP): 0.8%**
Currency: Maltese lira
Economy type: high income
Labour force in agriculture: 5%**

*1994
**1992

Ethnic composition
The population is essentially European, supposedly originating from Carthage. Both Maltese, which is a Semitic language, and English are spoken.

Religions
Roman Catholicism is the state religion and it is practised by about 98% of the population.

Political features
State type: liberal democratic
Date of state formation: 1964
Political structure: unitary
Executive: parliamentary
Assembly: one-chamber
Party structure: two-party
Human rights rating: N/A
International affiliations: ACP (observer), CE, CSCE,CW, IBRD, IMF, NAM, UN, WTO

Local and regional government
There is no local government as such, the whole country being administered as a single unit from the capital, Valletta.

Head of state
President Ugo Mifsud Bonnici, since 1994

Head of government
Prime Minister Dr Edward Fenech-Adami, since 1987

Political leaders since 1970
1962–71 Giorgio Borg Olivier (PN), 1971–84 Dom Mintoff (MLP), 1984–87 Karmenu Mifsud Bonnici (MLP), 1987– Edward Fenech-Adami (PN)

Political system
The 1974 constitution provides for a single-chamber assembly, the House of Representatives, with 65 members elected by universal adult suffrage, through a system of proportional representation, using the single transferable vote, for a five-year term. The president is the formal head of state and is elected by the House, again for a five-year term. He or she appoints a prime minister and cabinet, drawn from and collectively responsible to the House, which is subject to dissolution within its five-year term.

The constitution was amended in 1987 providing for a change in assembly representation. Under the amendment any party which wins more than 50% of the total vote in a general election will automatically be given a majority in the House of Representatives, regardless of the number of seats it actually wins.

Political parties
There are five political parties but two have dominated Malta's politics since independence. They are the Malta Labour Party (MLP) and the Nationalist Party (PN).

The MLP was officially founded in 1921 and first came to power in 1955. It has a moderate left-of-centre orientation and argues strongly for Malta's neutrality and nonalignment and opposes membership of the European Union.

The origins of the PN go back to 1880 but it became a recognizable party in the 1920s. It has a Christian right-of-centre orientation and believes in European cooperation.

Latest elections
In the February 1992 general election the PN won 34 seats with a 51.8% share of the vote. The MLP won 31 seats with a 46.5% vote. The turnout was 96%.

Political history
Malta became a British Crown Colony in 1815 and, subsequently, a vital naval base. Its importance was recognized by the unique distinction of the award of the George Cross decoration by the British monarch in 1942. From 1945 onwards the island enjoyed growing self-government and in 1955 Dom Mintoff (b. 1916), leader of the Malta Labour Party (MLP), became prime minister.

A referendum held in 1956 approved a proposal by the MLP for integration with the United Kingdom but this was strongly opposed by the conservative Nationalist Party (PN), led by Dr Giorgio Borg Olivier. Eventually, in 1958, the British proposals were rejected by Mintoff, who resigned, causing a constitutional crisis. By 1961 both parties were in favour of independence and, after Borg Olivier became prime minister in 1962, independence talks began. Malta became a fully independent state within the Commonwealth,

and under the British Crown, in 1964, having signed a ten-year defence and economic aid treaty.

In 1971 Mintoff and the MLP were returned to power with a policy of international neutrality and nonalignment. He declared the 1964 treaty invalid and began to negotiate a new arrangement for leasing the Maltese NATO base and obtaining the maximum economic benefit from it for his country. Eventually, in 1972, a seven-year agreement was signed and Malta became a republic in 1974. In 1979 the British closed its naval base, necessitating diversification of the island's economy.

In the 1976 general election the MLP was returned with a reduced majority. It also won a narrow majority in the House of Representatives in 1981, even though the Nationalists had a bigger share of the popular vote. As a result, Nationalist MPs refused to take up their seats for over a year. Relations between the two parties were also damaged by allegations of progovernment bias in the broadcasting service. At the end of 1984 Mintoff announced his retirement and Karmenu Mifsud Bonnici succeeded him as MLP leader and prime minister.

In the 1987 general election the PN won a narrow votes victory and, as a result of the constitutional change, a narrow assembly majority. Its leader since 1977, Dr Fenech-Adami (b. 1934), became prime minister. In 1992 the PN marginally increased its majority and retained power. Karmenu Mifsud Bonnici stepped down as MLP leader and was succeeded by Alfred Sant. In 1994 Victor Tabone completed his five-year term as president and was succeeded by Ugo Mifsud Bonnici, a former PN leader.

Since taking office, Prime Minister Fenech-Adami has taken a more pro-European and pro-American stance than some of his predecessors and in 1993 Malta received a positive response to its 1990 application for EU membership, being advised that only aspects of the island's economy and legal system might create difficulties.

MONACO

Principality of Monaco
Principanté de Monaco

Capital: Monaco-Ville

Social and economic data
Area: 2 km^2
Population: 28,000*
Pop. density per km^2: 14,000*
Urban population: 100%**
Literacy rate: 100%**
GDP: $615 million**; per-capita GDP: $22,000**
Government defence spending (% of GDP): 0%**
Currency: French franc
Economy type: high income
Labour force in agriculture: 0%**

*1994
**1992

Ethnic composition
Nineteen per cent of the population is Monegasque and 58% French. French is the official language but Monegasque (a

mixture of French Provençal and Italian Ligurian), Italian, and English are also spoken.

Religions
The chief religion is Roman Catholicism.

Political features
State type: liberal democratic
Date of state formation: 1297
Political structure: unitary
Executive: parliamentary
Assembly: one-chamber
Party structure: non-party
Human rights rating: 99%
International affiliations: IAEA, IWC, OSCE, UN

Local and regional government
There is no local or regional government.

Head of state
Prince Rainier III, since 1949

Head of government
Minister of State Paul Dijoud, since 1994

Political leaders since 1970
1986–94 Jean Aussell, 1994–   Paul Dijoud

Political system
The 1911 constitution was modified in 1917 and then largely rewritten in 1962. It preserves Monaco as a hereditary principality but an earlier concept of attributing the prince with a divine right to rule has been deleted. Legislative power is shared between the Prince and a single-chamber National Council (Conseil National), with 18 members elected by universal adult suffrage for a five-year term. Voting is restricted to Monagesque citizens aged 21 and over, and a two-ballot majoritarian system is employed. Executive power is formally vested in the prince, Rainier III (b. 1923) since 1949, but, in practice, exercised by a four-member Council of Government, headed by a minister of state, who is a French civil servant chosen by the prince.

Political parties
There are no political parties as such but in recent years National Council elections have been contested by lists of candidates, the two significant ones being the Liste Campora, led by Jean-Louis Campora, and the Liste Medecin, led by Jean-Louis Medecin. Both are moderate centrist groupings.

Latest elections
In the January 1993 National Council elections the Liste Campora won 15 seats, the Liste Medecin, two, and the other seat was won by an independent.

Political history
Once part of the Holy Roman Empire, Monaco became a Genoese possession during the 12th century, later coming under the rule of the Grimaldi dynasty in 1297. The principality, after alternate periods under Spanish, French, and Sardinian control, became an independent state, under the protection of France, in 1861 and that close relationship has continued. Agreements between the two countries, made in 1918–19, state that Monaco will be incorporated into France if the reigning prince dies without leaving a male heir. France is closely involved in the government of Monaco, providing a civil servant, of the prince's choosing, to head its Council of Government, as well as providing its interior minister. During World War II, the principality was occupied by the Italians (1941–43) and Germans (1943-45). The small state has developed into a prosperous centre for tourism, which attracts 1.5 million visitors a year. Banking is also an important business and there are light industries, most notably cosmetics and micro-electronics. Monaco is also attractive as a 'shelter' for tax exiles. It became a full member of the United Nations in 1993.

NETHERLANDS

Kingdom of the Netherlands
Koninkrijk der Nederlanden

Capital: Amsterdam (seat of government: The Hague)

Social and economic data
Area: 37,938 km^2
Population: 15,300,000*
Pop. density per km^2: 403*
Urban population: 89%**
Literacy rate: 99%**
GDP: $312,000 million**; per-capita GDP: $20,593**
Government defence spending (% of GDP): 2.2%**
Currency: guilder
Economy type: high income
Labour force in agriculture: 5%**

*1994
**1992

Ethnic composition
Most of the population is primarily of Germanic stock, with some Gallo-Celtic mixtures. There is also a sizeable

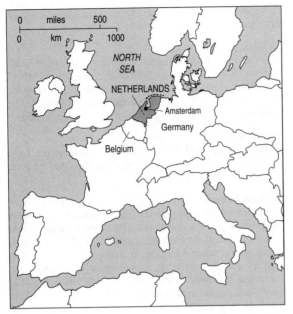

minority of Indonesians and Surinamese, from the former East Indies colonies. The official and widely used language is Dutch.

Religions
About 38% of the population is Roman Catholic, about 30% is Protestant, distributed among 11 different denominations, and there are also other Christian and Jewish religious communities.

Political features
State type: liberal democratic
Date of state formation: 1648
Political structure: unitary
Executive: parliamentary
Assembly: two-chamber
Party structure: multiparty
Human rights rating: 98%
International affiliations: AG (observer), BENELUX, CE, CERN, EEA, ESA, EU, G-10, IBRD, IMF, IWC, NACC, NAM (guest), NATO, OECD, OSCE, UN, WEU, WTO

Local and regional government
The Netherlands has a well developed system of regional and local government. The country is divided into 12 provinces, each with an appointed sovereign's commissioner, who presides over a Provincial Council, elected in a similar fashion to the Second Chamber of the national assembly, and a Provincial Executive. There are also about 770 municipalities, with elected councils and executives, presided over by appointed burgomasters.

Head of state
Queen Beatrix Wilhemina Armgard, since 1980

Head of government
Prime Minister Wim Kok, since 1994

Political leaders since 1970
1967–71 Petrus J S de Jong (VVD-led coalition), 1971–73 Barend Biesheuvel (ARP-led coalition), 1973–77 Joop den Uyl (PvdA-led coalition), 1977–83 Andries van Agt (CDA-led coalition), 1983–94 Ruud (Rudolph) Lubbers (CDA-led coalition), 1994– Wim Kok (PvdA-led coalition)

Political system
The Netherlands is a constitutional and hereditary monarchy. Its first constitution dates back to 1814 and, after many revisions, a new version, preserving much of what had preceded it, came into force in February 1983. It provides for a two-chamber assembly, called the States-General, consisting of a First Chamber of 75 and a Second Chamber of 150. Members of the First Chamber are indirectly elected by representatives of 12 Provincial Councils for a six-year term, half retiring every three years, and members of the Second Chamber are elected by universal adult suffrage, through a party list system of proportional representation, for a four-year term.

The queen appoints a prime minister as head of government, and a cabinet, or Council of Ministers, chosen by the prime minister. Athough they are not permitted to be members of the assembly, they may attend its meetings and take part in debates and they are all collectively responsible to it.

Legislation is introduced in the Second Chamber but must be approved by both before it becomes law. The Second Chamber has the right to amend bills but the First Chamber can only approve or reject. There is also a Council of State, which is the government's oldest advisory body and acts like a collective elder statesperson. Its members are intended to represent a broad cross-section of the country's life, and include former politicians, scholars, judges and business executives, all appointed for life. The queen is its formal president but its day-to-day operation is in the hands of an appointed vice president.

Political parties
The proportional representation system of elections to the Second Chamber encourages a multiplicity of political parties. Religion, as well politics, often plays a large part in the formation of the various groups. Of the current 19 parties, the most significant are the Christian Democratic Appeal (CDA), the Labour Party (PvdA), the People's Party for Freedom and Democracy (VVD), the Democrats '66 (D'66), the Political Reformed Party (SGP), the Evangelical Political Federation (RPF), the Reformed Political Association (GPV), the Green Left, and the General League of the Elderly (AOV).

The CDA was formed in 1980 by federating the Anti-Revolutionary Party (ARP), the Christian Historical Union (CHU) and the Catholic People's Party (CDA). It has a Christian right-of-centre orientation.

The PvdA was created in 1946 by the union of the Socialist Democratic Workers' Party with other left-wing progressive groups. It is now a moderate left-of-centre party.

The VVD dates from 1948 and is largely the present-day equivalent of the prewar Liberal State Party and the Liberal Democratic Party. It is a free-enterprise centrist party which strongly supports state welfare policies and industrial democracy.

D'66, as its name implies, was founded in 1966 on a platform calling for constitutional reform. It is now a centrist party with a strong advocacy of environmental issues.

The SGP is a Calvinist party dating from 1918, when the Anti-Revolutionary Party split. It has a centrist orientation.

The RPF is another Calvinist party which was formed in 1975. It has a more radical stance than the SGP.

The GPV is a third Calvinist party, dating from 1948. It is largely supported by the more fundamentalist members of the Church.

The Green Left is a left-of-centre ecological grouping.

The AOV is one of two newly formed parties promoting the needs and aspirations of pensioners.

Latest elections

The results of the 1991 First Chamber elections were as follows:

	Seats
CDA	27
PvdA	16
VVD	12
D'66	12
Green Left	4
SGP	2
RPF	1
GPV	1

The results of the May 1994 Second Chamber elections were as follows:

	% votes	Seats
PvdA	24.0	37
CDA	22.2	34
VVD	19.9	31
D'66	15.5	24
SGP/RPF/GPV	4.8	7
AOV	3.6	6
Green Left	3.5	5
Other parties	6.5	6

Political history

Holland, Belgium, and Flanders, then known as the Low Countries, were ruled by the Dukes of Burgundy in the 15th century and then by Spain from the 16th. The Dutch rebelled against the tyranny of Philip II (1527–98) of Spain, and particularly his attempts to stamp out Protestantism. They temporarily won their freedom in 1579, only to have it taken away again, until eventually, in 1648, the independence of the Dutch Republic was recognized. Between 1795 and 1813 the country was overrun by the French, and then the Congress of Vienna joined the north as the Kingdom of the United Netherlands, under William I, in 1814. The southern

part broke away, in 1830, to form the separate kingdom of Belgium.

Until 1945 the Netherlands had always followed a path of strict neutrality but its occupation by the Germans between 1940 and 1945 persuaded it to adopt a policy of mutual cooperation with its neighbours. It became a member of the Western European Union (WEU), the North Atlantic Treaty Organization (NATO), the Benelux Customs Union, the European Coal and Steel Community (ECSC), the European Atomic Energy Community (EURATOM), and the European Community (EC) itself and, as a 'good European', it has been in the forefront of subsequent EC developments. For example, it was during its presidency in 1991 that the Maastricht Treaty, which converted the Community into a Union, was formulated. It was ratified by a clear parliamentary majority in 1992.

Meanwhile, in 1980 Queen Juliana (b. 1909), who had reigned since 1948, abdicated in favour of her eldest daughter, Beatrix (b. 1938).

All governments since 1945 have been coalitions of one kind or another, differences between the parties being concerned mainly with economic policies, apart from a major debate in 1981 about the siting of US cruise missiles on Dutch soil. The 1988 general election resulted in yet another coalition, with the CDA and the PvdA sharing 106 of the 150 seats in the Second Chamber. In May 1989 Prime Minister Ruud Lubbers (b. 1939) resigned following opposition to his proposals for tighter pollution laws, but, after the September general election, he was persuaded to return to lead yet another coalition.

The May 1994 general election was again inconclusive and, after months of negotiation, the Labour Party leader Wim Kok (b. 1938) formed the country's first 'left–right' coalition of the PvdA, VVD, and D'66.

NORWAY

Kingdom of Norway
Kongeriket Norge

Capital: Oslo

Social and economic data
Area: 324,219 km^2
Population: 4,300,000*
Pop. density per km^2: 13*
Urban population: 76%**
Literacy rate: 99%**
GDP: $104,000 million**; per-capita GDP: $24,000**
Government defence spending (% of GDP): 3.1%**
Currency: Norwegian krone
Economy type: high income
Labour force in agriculture: 7%**

*1994
**1992

Ethnic composition

The majority of the population is of Nordic descent and there is a Lapp minority of about 20,000 in the far north of the country.

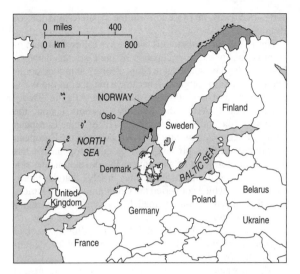

Religions
About 92% of the population belongs to the Church of Norway which is the established Evangelical Lutheran Church. There are also about 21,000 Roman Catholics.

Political features
State type: liberal democratic
Date of state formation: 1905
Political structure: unitary
Executive: parliamentary
Assembly: one-chamber
Party structure: multiparty
Human rights rating: 97%
International affiliations: CBSS, CE, CERN, EEA, EFTA, ESA, IAEA, IBRD, IMF, IWC, NACC, NAM (guest), NATO, NC, OECD, OSCE, UN, WEU (associate), WTO

Local and regional government
The country is divided into 19 counties (*fylker*), ranging in population from under 80,000 to nearly 450,000. The administrative head of each county is appointed by the central government and below the county level are municipalities. There are elected county and municipal councils. The political system in the Norwegian dependency of Svalbard is described in *Chapter 8*.

Head of state
King Harald V, since 1991

Head of government
Gro Harlem Brundtland, since 1990

Political leaders since 1970
1965–71 Per Borten (SP coalition), 1971–72 Trygve Bratteli (DNA), 1972–73 Lars Korvald (CPP coalition), 1973–76 Trygve Bratteli (DNA), 1976–81 Odvar Nordli (DNA coalition), 1981 Gro Harlem Brundtland (DNA coalition), 1981–83 Kare Willoch (Conservative Party), 1983–86 Kare Willoch (Conservative coalition), 1986–89 Gro Harlem Brundtland (DNA coalition), 1989–90 Jan Syse (Conservative coalition), 1990– Gro Harlem Brundtland (DNA coalition)

Political system
Norway is a constitutional hereditary monarchy and its constitution dates from 1814. The king is the formal head of state and the assembly consists of a single-chamber parliament, the Storting. The Storting has 165 members, elected for a four-year term by universal adult suffrage through a party list system of proportional representation. Once elected, it divides itself into two parts, a quarter of the members being chosen to form an upper house, the Lagting, and the remainder a lower house, the Odelsting.

All legislation must be first introduced in the Odelsting and then passed to the Lagting for approval, amendment, or rejection. A bill must be passed by both houses before it can become law, unless it has been passed twice by the Odelsting and rejected twice by the Lagting. In this case it will be considered by the combined Storting who may then pass it by a two-thirds majority. Once a bill has had parliamentary approval it must receive the royal assent.

The king appoints a prime minister and State Council on the basis of support in the Storting, to which they are all responsible.

Political parties
There are currently some 14 political parties, the six most significant being the Norwegian Labour Party (DNA), the Conservative Party (the 'Right'), the Christian People's Party (KrF), the Centre Party (Sp), the Progress Party (FrP), and the Socialist Left Party (SV).

The DNA was founded in 1887 as a democratic socialist party. It has a moderate left-of-centre orientation and has favoured membership of the European Union.

The Conservative Party was founded in 1884 to oppose the Liberal Party, which at the time was pressing for a transfer of more power from the monarchy to parliament. Its orientation is now progressive right-of-centre.

The KrF was formed in 1933 by a group of religious temperance Liberal Party dissidents. Since that time it has grown and widened its appeal. It has a centre-left orientation.

The Sp originally started in 1920 as the Agrarian League. It soon changed its name to the Farmers' Party and adopted its present title in 1959. It now has a left-of-centre nonsocialist orientation, with particular concern for rural interests.

The FrP is a right-wing populist grouping.

Latest elections
The results of the September 1993 general election were as follows:

	% votes	Seats
DNA	37.0	67
Sp	16.8	32
Conservatives	16.9	28
KrF	7.9	13
FrP	6.3	10
SV	7.9	13
Others	7.2	2

Political history
Norway was linked to Sweden until 1905 when it chose its own monarch, Prince Charles of Denmark, who took the title

of King Haakon VII (1872–1957). He ruled for 52 years until his death. He was succeeded by his son Olav V (1903–91) and his grandson Harald V (b. 1937), who is the reigning monarch.

The experience of German occupation between 1940 and 1945 persuaded the Norwegians to abandon their traditional neutral stance and join the North Atlantic Treaty Organization (NATO) in 1949, the Nordic Council in 1952, and the European Free Trade Area (EFTA) in 1960. Norway was accepted into membership of the European Community in 1972 but a referendum held that year rejected the proposal and the application was withdrawn.

The country has enjoyed a generally stable political history, with the proportional representaton system of voting often producing coalition governments. Its exploitation of the oil and gas resources of the North Sea have given it a per-capita income higher than most of its European neighbours, including France, Germany, and the United Kingdom. In 1988 Prime Minister Gro Harlem Brundtland (b. 1939), leader of the dominant Labour Party since 1981, was awarded the Third World Foundation annual prize for leadership in environmental and development issues.

In October 1989 Mrs Brundtland lost a vote of confidence and resigned. Her successor, Jan Syse, leading a Conservative–Liberal coalition, found himself in similar difficulties and a year later Mrs Brundtland returned, heading a minority Labour government.

In November 1992 it was announced that Norway would apply for readmission to the European Community but this was eventually abandoned after a referendum held in November 1994 came out against membership.

Norwegian politicians have been diplomatically active in recent years, co-chairing peace negotiations in former Yugoslavia and playing a significant role in the Middle East peace process.

PORTUGAL

Republic of Portugal
República Portuguesa

Capital: Lisbon

Social and economic data
Area: 92,080 km²
Population: 9,900,000*
Pop. density per km²: 107*
Urban population: 36%**
Literacy rate: 85%**
GDP: $73,000 million**; per-capita GDP: $7,451**
Government defence spending (% of GDP): 2.8%**
Currency: escudo
Economy type: high income
Labour force in agriculture: 19%**

*1994
**1992

Ethnic composition
Carthage and Rome were early influences on the ethnic composition of Portugal which is one of the oldest European

countries. Most of the present-day population is descended from the Caucasoid peoples who inhabited the whole of the Iberian peninsula in classical and pre-classical times. There are a number of minorities from Portugal's overseas possessions and former possessions. Portuguese is the national language.

Religions
About 90% of the population is Roman Catholic but there is freedom of worship for all faiths.

Political features
State type: liberal democratic
Date of state formation: 1128
Political structure: unitary
Executive: dual
Assembly: one-chamber
Party structure: multiparty
Human rights rating: 92%
International affiliations: ALADI (observer), CE, CERN, EEA, EU, IAEA, IBRD, IMF, Lusophone, NACC, NAM (guest), NATO, OECD, OSCE, UN, WEU, WTO

Local and regional government
There are two Autonomous Regions, in the Azores and Madeira, to which significant powers have been devolved. Each has a minister responsible for it in the mainland government and a chairman of a regional government, appointed by the minister. Local government on the mainland and in the Autonomous Regions is based on municipalities and parishes with elected councils. The overseas dependency of Macao (see *Chapter 8*) reverts to Chinese rule in 1999.

Head of state
President Dr Mário Alberto Nobre Lopes Soares, since 1986

Head of government
Prime Minister António Guterres since 1995

Political leaders since 1970

1968–74 Marcello Caetano (military), 1974–75 António Ribeiro de Spínola (military), 1975–76 Francisco da Costa Gomes, 1976–78 Mário Lopez Soares (PS), 1978–79 Carlos Mota Pinto (PS–CDS coalition), 1979–80 Francisco Sa Carneiro (AD coalition), 1980–83 Francisco Pinto Balsemão (PSD coalition), 1983–85 Mário Lopez Soares (PSD coalition), 1985–95 Aníbal Cavaco Silva (PSD), 1995– Antonio Guterres

Political system

The 1976 constitution, revised in 1982, provides for a president, elected by universal adult suffrage for a five-year term, and a single-chamber 230-member Assembly, elected through a party list system of proportional representation, and serving a four-year term. The president is limited to two successive terms. Four of the Assembly members represent Portuguese overseas territory.

The president appoints a prime minister and the latter's chosen Council of Ministers (cabinet), who are all responsible to the Assembly, which is subject to dissolution during its four-year term. There is also a Council of State, chaired by the President, which acts as a supreme national advisory body.

The relationship between the president and prime minister has been rather different from that of a constitutional head of state to a political head of government and, at times, has displayed aspects of the dual executive of the Fifth Republic of France. The president has often been an active politician rather than a formal symbol, and this has sometimes led to clashes between the two. Presidents have also been largely drawn from the armed forces and have had to work with civilian prime ministers. The current president is not only the first civilian to hold the post since the 1920s, but also a former prime minister himself.

Political parties

There are currently some 19 political parties, the three most significant being the Social Democratic Party (PSD), the Socialist Party (PS), and the People's party (PP). An electoral alliance, the United Democratic Coalition (UDC), of left-wing and ecological parties, was formed specifically to fight the 1986, 1991 and 1995 elections.

The PSD was quickly organized immediately after the coup of 1974 by former liberal members of the old National Assembly. It has a moderate centre-right orientation.

Originally the PS was founded in 1875 as Portugal's first socialist party. In its present form it dates from 1973. It is an internationalist party which takes a progressive, socialist stance and is led by António Guterres.

The PP was formed in 1974 as the Democratic Social Centre Party (CDS) by officials of the Caetano government soon after it had been removed from office. It is now a right-wing force which opposes European integration.

Latest elections

In the 1991 presidential election Mário Soares was re-elected with 70.43% of the vote. His closest rival, Basilia Horta, obtained 14.07%.

The results of the October 1995 Assembly elections, with a turnout of 67%, were as follows:

	% votes	Seats
PS	43.9	112
PSD	34.0	88
PP	9.1	15
CDU	8.6	15
Other parties	4.4	0

Political history

After being a monarchy for nearly 800 years, Portugal became a republic in 1910. The country remained economically backward and riddled with corruption until the start of the virtual dictatorship of Dr António de Oliveira Salazar (1889–1970) in 1928. Social conditions were greatly improved at the cost of a loss of personal liberties.

Salazar was succeeded as prime minister in 1968 by Dr Marcello Caetano who was unsuccessful at liberalizing the political system or dealing with the costly wars in Portugal's colonies of Angola and Mozambique. Criticisms of his administration led to a military coup in April 1974 to 'save the nation from government'. A Junta of National Salvation was set up, headed by General António Ribeiro de Spínola. He became president a month later, with a military colleague replacing the civilian prime minister. The new president promised liberal reforms, but, after disagreements within the Junta, Spínola resigned in September and was replaced by General Francisco da Costa Gomes. In 1975 there was a swing to the left among the military and President Gomes narrowly avoided a communist coup by collaborating with the leader of the moderate Socialist Party, Mário Soares (b. 1924).

In April 1976 a new constitution, designed to return the country gradually to civilian rule, was adopted, and the Supreme Revolutionary Council, which had been set up to head the new military regime, was renamed the Council of the Revolution and demoted to the role of a consultative body, under the chair of the president. Then Portugal's first free Assembly elections in 50 years were held. The Socialist Party won 36% of the vote and Soares formed a minority government. In June the army chief, General António Ramalho Eanes (b. 1935), won the presidency, with the support of centre and left-of-centre parties. After surviving precariously for over two years, Soares resigned in July 1978.

A period of political instability followed, with five prime ministers in two and a half years until, in December 1980, President Eanes invited Dr Francisco Balsemão, a cofounder of the Social Democratic Party (PSD), to form a centre-party coalition. Dr Balsemão survived many challenges to his leadership, which included his temporary resignation following a vote of no confidence, and then, in August 1982, he won a major victory when the Assembly approved his draft of a new constitution which would reduce the powers of the president, abolish the Council of the Revolution, and move the country to a fully civilian government. In December 1982, however, Balsemão resigned, but was recalled as a caretaker prime minister until a successor as PSD leader could be agreed.

In the April 1983 general election the Socialist Party (PS) won 101 of the Assembly's 230 seats and, after lengthy negotiations, Soares entered a coalition with the PSD, whose leader was now former Finance Minister Professor Aníbal Cavaco Silva (b. 1939). In June 1985 the PS–PSD coalition broke up and a premature general election was called. The result was, again, inconclusive and the new PSD leader eventually managed to form a minority government. In the 1986 presidential election Mário Soares, the PS leader, won a surprising victory to become Portugal's first civilian president for 60 years. He promised a more open style of presidency which would work more cooperatively with the prime minister.

After a three-week political crisis, in which the left-wing opposition to Cavaco Silva's coalition forced a vote of confidence, President Soares dissolved the Assembly and called a general election, Cavaco Silva being asked to continue as caretaker prime minister. The result was an overwhelming victory for the PSD, strengthening Cavaco Silva's position at the expense of the left-of-centre Democratic Renewal Party (PRD) and communists, and enabling Portugal's first majority government to be formed.

Portugal entered the European Community in 1986 and in the 1991 elections President Soares was re-elected and the PSD continued in office, with a slightly reduced majority.

Cavaco Silva stepped down as PSD leader for the October 1995 general election and was succeeded by the former defence minister, Fernando Nogueira. The election was won by the centre-left PS, led by António Guterres. The new PS minority administration pledged itself to continue the PSD's drive for closer integration of the European Union, including monetary union, and to increase spending on education.

SAN MARINO

Most Serene Republic of San Marino
Serenissima Repubblica di San Marino

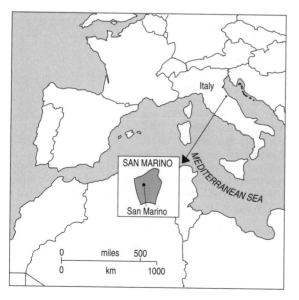

Capital: San Marino

Social and economic data
Area: 61 km²
Population: 23,000*
Pop. density per km²: 377*
Urban population: 90%**
Literacy rate: 96%**
GDP: $200 million**; per-capita GDP: $9,091**
Government defence spending (% of GDP): 0%**
Currency: Italian lira
Economy type: high income
Labour force in agriculture: 3%**

*1994
**1992

Ethnic composition
The population is predominantly Italian.

Religions
The chief religion is Roman Catholicism.

Political features
State type: liberal democratic
Date of state formation: c. AD 301
Political structure: unitary
Executive: parliamentary
Assembly: one-chamber
Party structure: multiparty
Human rights rating: N/A
International affiliations: CE, NAM (guest), OSCE, UN

Local and regional government
The country is divided into nine 'Castles', or districts, which correspond to the original nine parishes of the republic. Each 'Castle' is governed by a castle captain and an Auxiliary Council, who serve, respectively, two- and five-year terms.

Heads of state and heads of government
Two captains regent, elected for a six-month period

Political system
Because of its small size, San Marino is able to operate a uniquely intimate form of direct democracy, echoing some of the features of the ancient Greek city states. It does not have a formal constitution, though a basic set of 'governing principles' was framed in 1600, and the system of government is derived from its early origins. For the whole country there is a single-chamber Great and General Council composed of 60 members, elected by universal adult suffrage for a five-year term, through a system of proportional representation. The Council elects two of its members, one representing the capital and one the country, to serve a six-month term as captains regent and together they share the duties of head of state and head of government. They preside over a cabinet of ten, elected by the Council for a five-year term, called the Congress of State.

To encourage expatriate voting, the state pays 75% of the return fare of any Sammarinese living abroad to return home to vote.

Political parties

There are a number of political parties, the three most significant being the San Marino Christian Democrat Party (PDCS), the Socialist Party (PS), and the Progressive Democratic Party (PDP).

The PDCS was formed in 1948 and has a Christian right-of-centre orientation.

The PS is an amalgamation of two left-of-centre parties, the Socialist Party (PSS), formed in 1975, and the Socialist Unity Party (PSU).

The PDP is the reformed Communist Party, which was founded in 1941. It has a moderate left-wing orientation.

Latest elections

The results of the May 1993 general election were as follows:

	Votes	Seats
PDCs	9,010	26
PS	5,167	14
PDP	4,046	11
Others	3,555	9

Political history

San Marino was founded by a Christian saint, St Marinus, at the start of the 4th century AD as a refuge against religious persecution. It survived as a city-state after the unification of Italy in the late 19th century, thus being able to claim the distinction of being the world's oldest republic. It has a treaty of friendship with Italy, dating originally from 1862, but which was renewed in 1939 and 1971, and its multiparty system mirrors that of the larger country that surrounds it. A Communist–Socialist administration was in power between 1945 and 1957, when it was ousted in a bloodless 'revolution'. For the past 40 years it has been governed by a series of left-wing and centre-left coalitions. The current one comprising and Christian Democrats and Socialists dates from March 1992. The state relies heavily on earnings derived from tourism, more than 3 million visitors passing through its borders annually, but also, in recent decades, it has developed a number of light industries, most notably cement, leather, and textile production.

San Marino became a full member of the United Nations in 1992.

SPAIN

Kingdom of Spain
Reino de España

Capital: Madrid

Social and economic data
Area: 504,880 km^2
Population: 39,200,000*
Pop. density per km^2: 78*

Urban population: 79%**
Literacy rate: 95%**
GDP: $548,000 million**; per-capita GDP: $14,022**
Government defence spending (% of GDP): 1.5%**
Currency: peseta
Economy type: high income
Labour force in agriculture: 13%**

*1994
**1992

Ethnic composition
The present-day population can mostly trace its origins back to Moorish, Roman, and Carthaginian ancestry. The main language is Castilian Spanish. Catalan is spoken in the north-east, Basque in the north, and Galician in the north-west.

Religions
The majority of people are Roman Catholics. There are also about 300,000 Muslims and about 12,000 Jews.

Political features
State type: liberal democratic
Date of state formation: 1492
Political structure: unitary
Executive: parliamentary
Assembly: two-chamber
Party structure: multiparty
Human rights rating: 87%
International affiliations: AG (observer), ALADI (observer), CE, CERN, CSCE, EEA, ESA, EU, IAEA, IBRD, IMF, IWC, NACC, NAM (guest), NATO, OECD, UN, WEU, WTO

Local and regional government
The country is divided into 50 provinces and although not a federal state, Spain has developed a system of regional self-government, whereby each of the provinces has its own Council (Diputación Provincial) and civil governor. The

devolution process was extended in 1979 when 17 Autonomous Communities, or regions, were approved, each with an assembly, elected through a party list system of proportional representation for a four-year term, and a president of government, elected by the assembly. The powers of the autonomous Communities are specified in the constitution. The 17 Communities are Andalucía, Aragón, Asturias, the Balearic Islands, the Basque country, the Canary Isles, Cantabria, Castilla y León, Castilla–La Mancha, Cataluña, Extremadura, Galicia, Madrid, Murcia, Navarra, La Rioja, and Valencia.

Head of state
King Juan Carlos I, since 1975

Head of government
Prime Minister Felipe González Márquez, since 1982

Political leaders since 1970
1939–1974 Francisco Franco y Bahamonde (National Movement), 1974–76 Carlos Arias Navarro (National Movement), 1976–81 Adolfo Suárez González (UCD), 1981–82 Leopoldo Calvo Sotelo (UCD), 1982– Felipe González Márquez (PSOE)

Political system
The 1978 constitution creates a constitutional monarchy, with a hereditary king as formal head of state. He appoints a prime minister, called a president of Government, and a Council of Ministers, all of whom are responsible to the National Assembly (Las Cortes Generales). The Cortes consists of two chambers, the Congress of Deputies with 350 members, and the Senate with 257. Deputies are elected by universal adult suffrage through a party list system of proportional representation, and 208 of the senators are directly elected to represent the whole country and 49 to represent the regions. All serve a term of four years.

Political parties
Until 1975 only one political party was permitted, the Falange, later to be known as the National Movement, but now some 21 national parties currently operate, the two most significant being the Socialist Workers' Party (PSOE) and the Popular Party (PP). There are also some 35 regionally based parties.

The PSOE can be traced back to 1879 and the Socialist Workers' Party, which merged with the Popular Socialist Party in 1978 and adopted its present name. It now has about 215,000 members and a democratic socialist orientation.

The PP was formed in 1976 as the Popular Alliance (AP), shortly after General Franco's death. It has a right-of-centre orientation and is led by José Maria Aznar (b. 1953).

Also significant, with seats in the Cortes, are the United Left (IU), a left-wing coalition which includes the Communist Party, the (Catalan) Convergence and Union (CIU), and the Basque Nationalist Party (PNV).

Latest elections
The results of the June 1993 general election were as follows:

	Senate seats	Congress of % votes	Deputies seats
PSOE	117	38.68	159
PP	107	34.82	141
Other parties	27	26.5	50*

IU, 18; CIU, 17; PNV, 5; others, 10

Political history
Prior to the declaration of a republic in 1931, Spain had been a kingdom since the 1570s. It was a major international power in the 17th and 18th centuries but was weakened by political disunity in the 19th century. The creation of a republic did little to heal the regional rifts, particularly in Catalonia and the Basque area. At the same time, a political swing to the left by the republican government, coupled with criticisms and physical attacks on the church, antagonized the military. In 1936 a group of army commanders in Spanish Morocco revolted and the Spanish Civil War began. Spain soon became a battleground for virtually every ideology in Europe, as well as a test-bed for the weaponry of the rising Fascist and Nazi dictatorships. With their help, the insurgents, led by General Francisco Franco (1892–1975), won and in 1939 established a neofascist regime of strong, personal rule.

During World War II Spain remained neutral, though sympathetic towards Nazi Germany. In 1947 Franco, known as the 'Caudillo' (ruler), allowed the revival of an assembly with limited powers, but which was not directly elected. He also announced that after his death the monarchy would be restored and named the grandson of the last monarch, Prince Juan Carlos de Bourbon (b. 1938), as his successor. Franco died in 1975 and King Juan Carlos succeeded him as head of state. There followed a slow but steady progress to democratic government, with a new liberal constitution being endorsed by referendum in December 1978. It confirmed Spain as a constitutional monarchy, allowed political parties to operate freely and guaranteed self-government to the provinces and regions. Adolfo Suárez, leader of the Democratic Centre Party (UCD), became the first prime minister under the new constitution.

As Spain adjusted itself to constitutional government after 36 years of military rule, it faced two main internal problems – the demands for independence by extremists in the northern, Basque region and the possibility of right-wing elements in the army seizing power and reverting to a Franco-style government. It therefore embarked upon policies which were aimed to satisfy the calls for regional recognition and to firmly establish Spain within the international community. They included a devolution of power to the regions, entry into the North Atlantic Treaty Organization (NATO), and later membership of the European Community (EC).

By 1981, however, the government was showing signs of strain and Suárez suddenly resigned, to be succeeded by his deputy, Calvo Sotelo, who was immediately confronted with an attempted army coup in Madrid led by Lieutenant Colonel

Antonio Tejero. At the same time the military commander of Valencia, Lieutenant General Milans del Bosch, declared a state of emergency there and sent tanks on to the streets. Both uprisings failed and the two officers were tried and imprisoned. Sotelo's decision to take Spain into NATO in 1982 was widely criticized and, after defections from the party, he was forced to call a general election in October 1982.

The result was a sweeping victory for the Socialist Workers' Party (PSOE), led by Felipe González (b. 1942). With the Basque separatist organization, ETA, stepping up its campaign for independence by widespread terrorist activity, the government committed itself to strong anti-terrorist measures while, at the same time, promising a greater degree of devolution for the Basques. ETA's activities increased in intensity, however, spreading in 1985 to the Mediterranean holiday resorts and threatening Spain's lucrative tourist industry. Eventually a truce was agreed but this collapsed in 1989. The truce was revived in 1992 but was again short-lived. The threat of new violence remained but there were signs that ETA was losing support within the Basque community.

The PSOE had fought the election on a policy of taking Spain out of NATO and carrying out an extensive programme of nationalization. Once in office, however, González showed himself to be a supreme pragmatist. His nationalization programme was much more selective than had been expected and he left the decision whether or not to remain in NATO to a referendum to be held in the spring of 1986. In January 1986 Spain became a full member of the European Community and in March the referendum showed popular support for remaining in NATO. The PSOE won a clear majority in the July general election of that year, despite being faced with an electoral alliance by some of the main opposition parties. González was therefore returned for another term as prime minister. Tough policies to tackle the country's economic problems resulted in a wave of industrial strikes in 1987 and other expressions of dissatisfaction with the government. By 1988, however, there were clear signs that the government's prescriptions were working and the economy had become one of the fastest growing in Europe.

In November 1992 the Maastricht Treaty on greater European unity was formally ratified, but events were moving against the government. In April 1993, amid allegations of fraud within the PSOE, González said he would seek a general election to renew his mandate. Despite gains by the PP in the June 1993 election, the PSOE survived for a fourth term in office. In July 1993 González was able to form a minority government, which received support from the minor Catalan and Basque parties. Meanwhile the economy had moved into recession and unemployment had risen to over 20%, the highest in the European Union. The González administration responded by launching a major programme of privatization. Early in 1995 renewed allegations of fraud, leading to the resignation of ministers, put pressure on the PSOE and its leader and in September 1995 the Catalan nationalist coalition, led by Jordi Pujol, the Catalan regional president, announced that it was withdrawing its crucial support from the minority government. This resulted in the draft budget being rejected in October 1995.

SWEDEN

Kingdom of Sweden
Konungariket Sverige

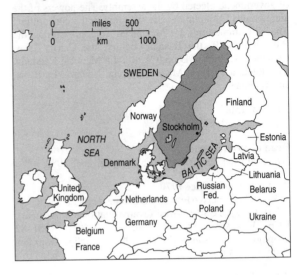

Capital: Stockholm

Social and economic data
Area: 449,700 km^2
Population: 8,700,000*
Pop. density per km^2: 19*
Urban population: 84%**
Literacy rate: 99%**
GDP: $200,000 million**; per-capita GDP: $23,000**
Government defence spending (% of GDP): 2.3%**
Currency: Swedish krona
Economy type: high income
Labour force in agriculture: 4%**

*1994
**1992

Ethnic composition
The population consists almost entirely of Teutonic stock, with small minorities of Lapps, Finns, and Germans. Swedish is the official language but minorities speak Finnish and Lapp.

Religions
The Evangelical Lutheran Church (Church of Sweden) is the established church and about 92% of the population belongs to it. There are other Protestant denominations, about 120,000 Roman Catholics, and about 16,000 Jews.

Political features
State type: liberal democratic
Date of state formation: 1523
Political structure: unitary
Executive: parliamentary
Assembly: one-chamber
Party structure: multiparty
Human rights rating: 98%

International affiliations: AG (observer), CBSS, CE, CERN, EEA, ESA, EU, G-10, IAEA, IBRD, IMF, IWC, NAM (guest), NC, OECD, OSCE, PFP, UN, WTO

Local and regional government
There is a strongly devolved system of local government, with 24 counties (*lan*) and 279 municipalities, all with representative institutions. It is estimated that at least 40% of public administration is conducted at a subnational level.

Head of state
King Carl XVI Gustav, since 1973

Head of government
Prime Minister Ingvar Carlsson, since 1994

Political leaders since 1970
1969–75 Olof Palme (SAP), 1975–78 Thorbjörn Fälldin (Centre Party coalition), 1978–79 Ola Ullsten (Liberal coalition), 1979–81 Thorbjörn Fälldin (Centre–Moderate–Liberal coalition), 1981–82 Thorbjörn Fälldin (Centre Party), 1982–86 Olof Palme (SAP), 1986–91 Ingvar Carlsson (SAP), 1991–94 Carl Bildt (Moderate), 1994– Ingvar Carlsson (SAP)

Political system
Sweden is a constitutional hereditary monarchy with the king as formal head of state and a popularly elected government. The constitution dates from 1809 and has since been amended several times. It is based on four fundamental laws, the Instrument of Government Act, the Act of Succession, the Freedom of the Press Act, and the Riksdag (Parliament) Act. It provides for a single-chamber assembly, the Riksdag of 349 members, elected by universal adult suffrage through a party list system of proportional representation for a three-year term. The prime minister is nominated by the Speaker of the Riksdag and then confirmed by a vote of the whole House. The prime minister chooses a cabinet and all are then responsible to the Riksdag. The king now has a purely formal role, the normal duties of a constitutional monarch, such as dissolving the Riksdag and deciding who should be asked to form an administration, being undertaken by the speaker of the Riksdag.

Political parties
There are currently some nine active political parties, the most significant being the Social Democratic Labour Party (SAP), the Moderate Party (M), the Liberal Party (Fp), the Centre Party (C), the Christian Democratic Community Party (KdS), the Left Party (Vp), and the Ecology Party (MpG).

The SAP was founded in 1889 and is Sweden's largest political party, with over 1 million members. It has a moderate left-of-centre orientation.

The Moderate Party was formed in 1904 as the Conservative Party. It changed its name in 1969. It has a right-of-centre stance.

The Liberal Party dates from 1902 and used to be the main opposition to the Conservatives. It has a centre-left orientation.

The Centre Party was founded in 1910 as the Agrarian Party, mainly to represent farming interests. It changed its

name in 1958 in an attempt to widen the basis of its support. As its name implies, it has a centrist orientation.

The KdS was formed in 1964 to promote Christian values in political life. It takes a Christian, centrist stance.

The Vp dates originally from 1917 when it was the Left Social Democratic Party of Sweden. In 1921 it was renamed the Communist Party and later, in 1967, it adopted its present name. It has a European, Marxist orientation.

The MpG is part of the European Green movement.

Latest elections
The results of the 1994 Riksdag elections were as follows:

	% votes	Seats
SAP	45.25	161
M	22.37	80
C	7.65	27
Fp	7.19	26
Vp	6.17	22
MpG	5.02	18
KdS	4.06	15
Others	2.29	0

Political history
Sweden has been a constitutional monarchy since the beginning of the 19th century. It was united with Norway until 1905, when King Oscar II (reigned 1872–1907) gave up the Norwegian throne. The country has a long tradition of neutrality, a record of great political stability, a highly developed social welfare system, and a flair for innovative and open popular government. For example, the ombudsman system, which provides the ordinary citizen with redress against the abuse of administrative power, is a Swedish invention and Sweden was one of the first countries in the world to adopt a system of open government.

Between 1951 and 1968 the Social Democratic Labour Party (SAP) was in power, sometimes alone and sometimes as the senior partner in a coalition. In 1968 the Social Democrats formed their first majority government since the mid-1940s and in 1969 the leadership of the party changed hands, Olof Palme (1927–86) becoming prime minister. In the general election two years later Palme lost his overall majority but continued at the head of a minority government. During the next six years he carried out two major reforms of the constitution, reducing the chambers in the assembly from two to one in 1971, and in 1975 removing the last vestiges of the monarch's constitutional powers.

The 1976 general election was fought on the issue of the level of taxation needed to fund the welfare system and Palme was defeated, Thorbjörn Fälldin, leader of the Centre Party, forming a centre-right coalition government. The Fälldin administration fell in 1978 on the issue of its wish to follow a non-nuclear energy policy and was replaced by a minority Liberal government, led by Ola Ullsten. Fälldin returned in 1979, heading another coalition, and in a referendum held in the following year there was a narrow majority in favour of continuing with a limited nuclear energy programme. Fälldin remained in power, with some cabinet reshuffling, until 1982, when the Social Democrats, with Olof Palme, returned with a minority government.

Palme was faced with deteriorating relations with the USSR, arising from suspected violations of Swedish territorial waters, but the situation had improved substantially by 1985. After the general election in that year, Palme was able to continue with Communist support and then, in February 1986, Sweden and the world were shocked by the news of his murder by an unknown assailant in the centre of Stockholm, as he and his wife were returning home on foot from a visit to a cinema. The deputy prime minister, Ingvar Carlsson (b. 1934), took over as prime minister and leader of the SAP, continuing the broad policy line of his predecessor. In the 1988 general election the SAP government of Carlsson was re-elected but in the September 1991 general election he was defeated and the Moderate Party leader, Carl Bildt (b. 1949), formed a 'bourgeois coalition' comprising the Moderate Party, Liberal Party, Centre Party, and KdS. This set out to dismantle some aspects of Sweden's vaunted 'social democratic' welfare system. As the economy deteriorated during 1992, with the unemployment rate climbing to 14%, Bildt's conservative coalition, in an unprecedented fashion, agreed to work with the Social Democrats to solve the country's problems.

In the 1994 general election the SAP increased its vote share and seat holding and returned to power, Ingvar Carlsson preferring to lead a minority government and rejecting the offer of a centre-left coalition. In November 1994 the Swedish people, in a referendum, voted in favour of European Union membership. This was achieved in January 1995. In August 1995 it was announced that Carlsson would step down as prime minister in 1996 once his party had chosen a replacement. The favourite to succeed him was the deputy prime minister, Mona Sahlin, until in November 1995 Sahlin faced a criminal investigation into an alleged misuse of a government credit card.

In the country's first ever elections to the European Parliament in September 1995 the turnout at 40% was well below half the normal level for assembly elections. The Social Democrats attracted only 29% of the support, while nearly a third of the electorate voted for anti-EU Green and Left party candidates.

SWITZERLAND

The Swiss Confederation
Schweizerische Eidgenossenschaft
Confédération Suisse
Confederazione Suizzera

Capital: Bern

Social and economic data
Area: 41,290 km²
Population: 6,900,000*
Pop. density per km²: 168*
Urban population: 63%**
Literacy rate: 99%**

GDP: $249,000 million**; per-capita GDP: $36,231**
Government defence spending (% of GDP): 1.5%**
Currency: Swiss franc
Economy type: high income
Labour force in agriculture: 6%**

*1994
**1992

Ethnic composition
The great majority of people are of Alpine stock. There is also a strong Nordic element. There are three official languages: German, spoken by about 70%, French by 20%, and Italian by 10%.

Religions
About 47% of the population is Roman Catholic and about 44% Protestant.

Political features
State type: liberal democratic
Date of state formation: 1648
Political structure: federal
Executive: limited presidential
Assembly: two-chamber
Party structure: multiparty
Human rights rating: 96%
International affiliations: AG (observer), CE, CERN, EFTA, ESA, G-10, IMF, IWC, NAM (guest), OECD, OSCE

Local and regional government
Switzerland is a federation of 20 cantons and six half-cantons, a canton (derived from Old French) being the name for a political division. The federal government is allocated specific powers by the constitution and the residue is left with the cantons, each having its own constitution, assembly and government. At a level below the cantons are more than 3,000 communes, whose populations range from fewer than

20 to 350,000, in the case of Zürich. Direct democracy is encouraged through communal assemblies and referenda.

Head of state and head of government
President Kaspar Villiger (1995); Jean-Paul Delamuraz (1996)

Political leaders since 1970
The federal president is appointed by the Federal Assembly to serve a one-year term, from January to December.

Political system
The constitution dates from 1874 and provides for a two-chamber Federal Assembly, consisting of a National Council (Nationalrat) and a Council of States (Standerat). The National Council has 200 members, elected by universal adult suffrage through a party list system of proportional representation for a four-year term. The Council of States has 46 members, each canton electing two representatives and each half-canton one. Members of the Council of States are elected for three or four years, depending on the constitutions of the individual cantons. The federal government is in the hands of a Federal Council (Bundesrat), consisting of seven members elected for a four-year term by the Assembly, and each heading a particular federal department. The Federal Assembly also appoints one member to act as federal head of state and head of government for a year, the term of office beginning on 1 January. As related in *Chapter 6*, Switzerland is noted for its frequent resort to referenda and citizens' initiatives.

Political parties
There are currently some 22 nationally based political parties, the most significant being the Radical Democratic Party of Switzerland (FDP/PRD), the Swiss Social Democratic Party (SP/PS), the Christian Democratic Party of Switzerland (CVP/PDC), the Swiss People's Party (SVP/UDC), the Swiss Liberal Party (LPS/PLS), and the Green Party (GPS/PES). The alternative acronyms in brackets are derived from the German or French spelling of each name.

The FDP/PRD led the movement which resulted in the creation of the Federative State and constitution of 1848 and has been an important force in Swiss politics ever since. It has a radical centre-left orientation.

The SP/PS was founded in 1888 as a Marxist party. Since then its outlook has been modified so that it now has a moderate left-of-centre stance.

The CVP/PDC was formed in 1912 as the Conservative People's Party. It changed its name in 1957. It is a Christian moderate centrist party.

The SVP/UDC dates from 1919 when it began more as a broad-based interest group than a political party. At one time it had the name of the Farmers', Artisans' and Bourgeois Party. It now has a centrist orientation.

The LPS/PLS began in the early 19th century as the Swiss Liberal-Democratic Union. It changed its name in 1977. It is a federalist centre-left party.

The GPS/PES is a product of the growth of ecological interest groups and parties which has been evident throughout Europe during recent decades.

Latest elections
The results of the October 1995 National Council elections were as follows:

	% votes	Seats
FDP/PRD	20.2	45
SP/PS	21.8	54
CVP/PDC	17.0	34
SVP/UDC	14.9	29
GPS/PES	5.0	9
LPS/PLS	2.7	7
Other parties	18.4	2

The October 1995 National Council elections proved to be no challenge to the four-party centre-right coalition, which includes the pro-European, urban-based Social Democrats, and the anti-EU, rural based Swiss People's Party, which has governed the country since 1959.

Political history
Switzerland has for centuries been recognized as the leading neutral country of the world and, as such, has been the base for many international organizations and the host of many international peace conferences. Although it was once the home of the League of Nations, it has not, as yet, itself become a member of the United Nations. A referendum held in 1986 rejected the advice of the government and came out overwhelmingly against membership. Entry into the European Union and European Economic Area has also been opposed. Its domestic politics have been characterized by coalition governments and a stability which has enabled it to become one of the richest per-capita countries in the world.

Switzerland has tended to be a male-orientated nation and women were not allowed to vote in federal elections until 1971. The first female cabinet minister was not appointed until 1984. She resigned in 1988 and another woman was not appointed until 1993.

UNITED KINGDOM (UK)

United Kingdom of Great Britain and Northern Ireland

Capital: London

Social and economic data
Area: 244,100 km^2
Population: 57,800,000*
Pop. density per km^2: 238*
Urban population: 89%**
Literacy rate: 99%**
GDP: $1,024,000 million**; per-capita GDP: $17,760**
Government defence spending (% of GDP): 3.6%**
Currency: pound sterling
Economy type: high income
Labour force in agriculture: 2%**

*1994
**1992

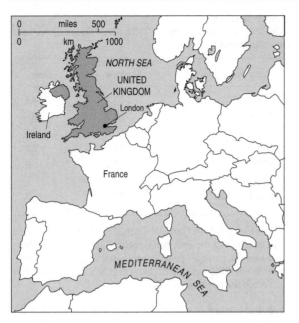

Ethnic composition

The people of the United Kingdom consist of 81.5% English, 9.6% Scots, 2.4% Irish, 1.9% Welsh, and 2% West Indians, Asians, and Africans. English is the predominant language, with Welsh spoken by about a fifth of the Welsh population. Gaelic is a smaller minority tongue.

Religions

There are two established religions, the (Anglican) Church of England and the (Presbyterian) Church of Scotland. Nominally 55% of the population is Anglican, but only 5% is practising and regularly attends church. There are also substantial numbers of Roman Catholics (9%), Jews, Muslims (2%), and Hindus, many of whom are devout adherents to their sects.

Political features

State type: liberal democratic
Date of state formation: 1707/1921*
Political structure: unitary
Executive: parliamentary
Assembly: two-chamber
Party structure: multiparty
Human rights rating: 93%
International affiliations: AG (observer), CE, CERN, CW, EEA, ESA, EU, G-5, G-7, G-10, IAEA, IBRD, IMF, IWC, NACC, NATO, OECD, OSCE, SPC, UN, WEU, WTO

*Great Britain 1707; United Kingdom 1921.

Local and regional government

The United Kingdom consists of four countries within a unitary system: England, with about 83% of the total population, Scotland, with about 9%, Wales, with about 5%, and Northern Ireland, with about 3%.

The government minister responsible for the internal affairs of England is the home secretary, who is based in London. The minister for Scotland's internal affairs is the secretary of state for Scotland, who is based partly in London and partly in Edinburgh. There are more than 6,000 civil servants working in the Scottish Office in Edinburgh. The minister responsible for the internal affairs of Wales is the secretary of state for Wales, who is based partly in London and partly in Cardiff, where the Welsh Office employs about 1,000 civil servants. The minister responsible for Northern Ireland's internal affairs is the secretary of state for Northern Ireland, who is based partly in London and partly in Belfast. From 1922 until 1972 Northern Ireland had its own elected parliament, but the violence and discord there persuaded the United Kingdom government in London to dissolve it in 1972 and to govern the province directly through the secretary of state. A return to parliamentary responsibility within Northern Ireland has been promised when a political solution to the province's discord has been agreed. All four responsible ministers are members of the United Kingdom cabinet.

Geographically within the British Isles, and enjoying the protection of the United Kingdom government, but politically not strictly a part of the United Kingdom, are the Channel Islands of Jersey, Guernsey, Sark and their dependencies, and the Isle of Man; see *Chapter 8*. The Channel Islands have their own assembly and government and are not bound by legislation of the UK Parliament. The Isle of Man enjoys a broadly similar independence.

For administrative purposes, England and Wales are divided into 47 counties, 369 districts, and, within the districts, several thousand parishes. Greater London is divided into 28 boroughs, plus the City of London. Counties and districts and the London boroughs have elected councils and parishes have either elected councils or meetings. A major review of the structure was completed in 1995 and a modified arrangement was promised by the government.

Scotland is divided into nine regions, within which are 53 districts, three islands or groups, and, roughly equivalent to the parishes in England and Wales, over 1,300 communities. The regions, districts, islands, and communities all have elected councils.

Northern Ireland is divided into six counties within which are districts, with elected councils, broadly similar to those in England and Wales.

Head of state

Queen Elizabeth II, since 1952

Head of government

Prime Minister John Major since 1990

Political leaders since 1970

1970–74 Edward George Heath (Conservative), 1974–76 James Harold Wilson (Labour), 1976–79 Leonard James Callaghan (Labour), 1979–90 Margaret Hilda Thatcher (Conservative), 1990–   John Major (Conservative)

Political system

The United Kingdom is a classic example of a constitutional monarchy based on a system of parliamentary government. There is no written constitution, the main features being contained in individual pieces of legislation and certain practices followed by successive governments which are regarded as constitutional conventions. Cabinet government, which is at the heart of the system, is founded on convention, and the relationship between the monarch, as head of state, and the prime minister, as head of government, is similarly based. In theory this makes the unwritten constitution extremely flexible. In practice, however, it is as rigid as if it were written, and more rigid than many that have been formally set down. The features that provide this rigidity, as well as ensuring political stability, are the fact that Parliament is sovereign, in that it is free to make and unmake any laws that it chooses, and the concept of the rule of law, which says that all governments are subject to the laws which Parliament makes, as interpreted by the courts. The queen is one part of the trinity of Parliament, the other parts being the two legislative and debating chambers, the House of Lords and the House of Commons. Since becoming a member of the European Union (EU) the supremacy of the UK Parliament has been challenged by the superior laws of the EU and it has become clear that, as long as it continues in membership, domestic legislation can in certain circumstances be overridden by that of the EU as a whole.

The House of Lords has three main kinds of members: those who are there by accident of birth, the hereditary peers; those who are there because of some office they hold; and those who are appointed to serve for life, the life peers. There are nearly 800 hereditary peers and peeresses and they include 5 royal dukes, 26 nonroyal dukes, 29 marquesses, 157 earls, 103 viscounts, and 474 barons. Among those sitting because of the position they hold are two archbishops and 24 bishops of the Church of England and nine senior judges, known as the law lords. The rest, numbering over 400, are the appointed life peers, who now include about 65 women, or peeresses.

The House of Commons has 651 members, elected by universal adult suffrage, by a simple plurality voting system, from single-member geographical constituencies, each constituency containing on average about 65,000 electors. Although the House of Lords is termed the Upper House, its powers, in relation to those of the Commons, have been steadily reduced so that now it has no control over financial legislation and merely a delaying power of a year over other bills. Before an act of Parliament becomes law it must pass through a five-stage process in each chamber – first reading, second reading, committee stage, report stage, and third reading – and then receive the formal royal assent. Bills, other than financial ones, can be introduced in either House, but most begin in the Commons.

The monarch appoints the prime minister on the basis of support in the House of Commons and he or she, in turn, chooses and presides over a cabinet. The simple voting system favours two-party politics and both chambers of Parliament are physically designed to accommodate two parties, the government, sitting on one side of the presiding speaker, and the opposition on the other. No matter how many parties are represented in Parliament only one, that with the second largest number of seats in the Commons, is recognized as the official opposition, and its leader is paid a salary out of public funds and provided with appropriate office facilities within the Palace of Westminister, as the Houses of Parliament are called.

Political parties

There are currently some 21 active political parties but this number is subject to variation, particularly when elections are taking place. Parties are not required to register and the only restriction on their operations is the requirement that parliamentary candidates make a deposit of £500, which will be forfeited if less than 5% of the total votes cast in the constituency are obtained. There are also restrictions on the amount that can be spent by candidates during an election campaign.

Despite the number of parties in existence, the simple plurality voting system, combined with a number of social, economic, and demographic factors, has invariably resulted in two-party politics, the two major groups being the Conservative and Unionist Party and the Labour Party. There is one other national party currently represented in the House of Commons: the Liberal Democrats.

Contesting only in Scottish constituencies is the Scottish Nationalist Party (SNP), and only in Welsh constituencies the Welsh Nationalist Party (Plaid Cymru). There are also four Northern Ireland parties represented at Westminster: the Official Ulster Unionist Party (OUUP), the Democratic Unionist Party (DUP), the Social Democratic Labour Party (SDLP), the Ulster People's Unionist Party (UPUP). Sinn Féin was represented till 1992.

The Conservative Party dates from the Tories of the 17th century who supported the Duke of York's claim to the English throne against the Whigs. They were regarded as 'conservators' because of their belief in traditional values and came to be called the Conservatives in the early 1830s. The title Unionist was added to indicate their support for the union of Ireland and England. In its present form, the party was established in 1870. It has a right-of-centre orientation.

The Labour Party was founded in 1900 following a meeting of trade unionists and representatives of a number of socialist organizations. Prior to this there had been an Independent Labour Party and, later, a Labour Representation Committee. It has both individual members and affiliated members, through membership of trade unions or other affiliated bodies. The party has a moderate left-of-centre orientation.

The Liberal Democrats were formed in 1988 by a merger of the Liberal Party and a majority of members of the Social Democratic Party (SDP). The Liberals can trace their origins back to the Whigs of the 17th century, when they were the main opponents of the Tories. They changed their name to the Liberal Party in the 1850s. The SDP was formed in 1981 by four leading dissidents from the Labour Party. The party has a centre-left orientation.

The rump of the SDP consists of the minority of members of the party formed in 1981 who chose not to merge with the Liberal Party. It no longer operates as a national party.

The SNP was formed in 1934 with the aim of securing the recognition of an independent Scotland, with its own elected assembly. The degree of independence currently sought is a matter of debate within the party.

Plaid Cymru was formed in 1925 with aims for Wales similar to those of the SNP for Scotland. The two parties have cooperated from time to time in pursuit of their common purposes.

The OUUP was formed in 1905 and for a long time supported the policies of the Conservative Party. However, since the signing of the Anglo-Irish Agreement in 1985, and subsequent developments in the search for a lasting peace in Northern Ireland, differences have arisen between them. The OUUP is the largest single party in the province.

The DUP was formed in 1971 by dissident Ulster Unionists who adopted a less moderate and more right-wing stance than the OUUP, and bitterly opposed the Anglo-Irish Agreement.

The SDLP was formed in 1970 and has strong links with the Labour Party, which has never contested seats in Northern Ireland. The party has a moderate left-of-centre orientation and was a strong supporter of the Anglo-Irish Agreement and the reconciliation of all views and opinions in Northern Ireland.

Sinn Féin was formed in 1970 and is the political wing of the Irish Republican Army (IRA). It has a strongly pro-United Ireland stance but has demonstrated its wish to secure a united Ireland through peaceful political channels.

The UPUP was formed in 1980 from the former Ulster Progressive Unionist Party, its main aim being to promote devolution in the Province.

Latest elections

The results of the April 1992 general election were as follows:

	% share of vote	House of Commons seats
Conservatives	41.9	336
Labour	34.4	271
Liberal Democrats	17.9	20
SNP	1.9	3
Plaid Cymru	0.5	4
*Northern Ireland Parties	2.0	17

*OUP, 9 seats; DUP, 3 seats; SDLP, 4 seats; UPUP, 1 seat

Political history

England has been a monarchy since the 10th century, apart from the brief period of the Commonwealth between 1649 and 1660, and Wales a united principality since the 11th century. The two nations were united in 1535. Scotland has been a kingdom since the 9th century and joined England and Wales, to form the state of Great Britain, in 1707. Northern Ireland was originally joined to Great Britain, as part of the single nation of Ireland, in 1801. In 1921 Southern Ireland broke away to become the Irish Free State, and eventually the Republic of Ireland, while six of the nine northern counties of Ulster remained in the United Kingdom of Great Britain and Northern Ireland.

By exploration, commercial enterprise, and force of arms, on land and sea, a great empire was created, particularly during the 18th and 19th centuries, which covered a quarter of the world's surface and included a quarter of its population. In 1945 the United Kingdom was still at the hub of this empire and, although two world wars had gravely weakened it, many of its citizens, and some of its politicians, still saw it as a world power. The reality of its position soon became apparent in 1945 when the newly elected Labour government, led by Clement Attlee (1883–1967), confronted the problems of rebuilding the damaged economy. This renewal was greatly helped, as in other West European countries, by support from the United States in the shape of the Marshall Plan.

The period of Labour government, from 1945 to 1951, saw the carrying through of an ambitious programme of public ownership and investment and the laying of the foundations of a national health service and welfare state which became the envy of the world. During the same period a civilized dismemberment of the British Empire, restyled the British Commonwealth, was started. It was a process which was to continue through to the 1980s.

In 1951 the Conservative Party returned to power under Sir Winston Churchill (1874–1965) and, although there were changes in emphasis in domestic and foreign policies, the essential features of the welfare state and the public sector were retained. Both administrations, Labour and Conservative, however, missed an opportunity to seize the leadership of Europe so that by the mid-1950s the framework for the European Community had been created, with the United Kingdom an onlooker rather than a participant. In 1955 Sir Winston Churchill, now in his 81st year, handed over to his heir apparent, the distinguished foreign secretary, Sir Anthony Eden (1897–1977).

In little more than a year Eden found himself confronted by what he perceived to be a threat as great as that from Germany in the 1930s, but now it was from the President of Egypt, Gamal Nasser, who had taken possession of the Suez Canal. Eden's perception of the threat posed by Nasser was not shared by everyone, not even within the Conservative Party. The invasion of Egypt, in conjunction with France and Israel, brought widespread criticism and was abandoned in the face of pressure from the United States and the United Nations. Eden resigned, on the grounds of ill health, and the Conservatives chose Harold Macmillan (1894–1986) as their new leader and prime minister.

Macmillan skillfully and quickly repaired the damage caused within the party, and internationally, by his predecessor's ill-judged adventure and, with a booming economy and rising living standards, had by the early 1960s won himself the reputation of 'Super Mac'. Internationally, he acquired a reputation for wise statemanship, establishing a close working relationship with his United States contemporary, President Dwight Eisenhower and then the relatively youthful John F Kennedy. He also did much to cement the unique voluntary partnership of nations which the Commonwealth had become. He was, nevertheless, sufficiently realistic to see that the United Kingdom's long-term economic and political future lay in Europe. The Conservatives won the 1959 general election with an increased majority and in 1961 the first serious, if belated, attempt was made to join the European Community, only to have it blocked by the French president, Charles de Gaulle.

Despite rising living stadards, the UK's economic performance was not as successful as that of many of its competitors, particularly Germany and Japan. It was against this background that Macmillan unexpectedly resigned in 1963, on the grounds of ill health, and was succeeded by the Foreign Secretary Lord Home (1903–1995), who immediately renounced his title to become Sir Alec Douglas-Home.

In the general election in the following year the Labour Party was returned with a slender majority and its leader, Harold Wilson (1916–95), became prime minister. The election had been fought on the issue of the relative decline of the economy and the need to regenerate it. Wilson's immediate prescription was institutional change. He created a new Department of Economic Affairs (DEA), to challenge the short-term conservatism of the Treasury, and brought in a leading trade unionist to head a new Department of Technology. In an early general election in 1966 Wilson increased his Commons majority appreciably but his promises of fundamental changes in economic planning, industrial investment, and improved work practices were not fulfilled. The DEA was disbanded in 1969 and in the same year an ambitious plan for the reform of industrial relations was also dropped in the face of trade union opposition.

In 1970 the Conservatives returned to power under Edward Heath (b. 1916), who was as much committed to economic and industrial reform as his Labour predecessor. He, too, saw institutional change as one way of achieving the results he wanted and created two new central 'super-departments', Trade and Industry and Environment, and a high-powered 'think-tank' to advise the government on long-term strategy, the Central Policy Review Staff (CPRS). He chose to change the climate of industrial relations through legislation, introducing a long and complicated Industrial Relations Bill. He also saw entry into the European Community as the 'cold shower of competition' which industry needed and membership was successfully negotiated in 1972. Heath's 'counter revolution', as he saw it, was frustrated by economic events. Powerful trade unions thwarted his industrial relations reforms and the European 'cold shower', combined with the sharp rise in oil prices in 1973, forced a drastic U-turn in economic policy. Instead of 'lame ducks' being forced to seek their own salvations, he found it necessary to take ailing industrial companies, such as Rolls Royce, into public ownership. The introduction of a statutory incomes policy precipitated a national miners' strike in the winter of 1973–74 and Heath decided to challenge the unions by holding an early general election in 1974.

The result was a 'hung' Parliament, with Labour winning the biggest number of seats but no single party having an overall majority. Heath tried briefly to form a coalition with the Liberals and, when this failed, resigned. Harold Wilson returned to the premiership, heading a minority government, but in another general election later the same year won enough additional seats to give him a working majority. He had taken over a damaged economy and a nation puzzled and divided by the events of the previous years. He turned to Labour's natural ally and founder, the trade union movement, for support and jointly they agreed a 'social contract'. The government pledged itself to redress the imbalance between management and unions which had resulted from the Heath industrial relations legislation and the unions promised to cooperate in a voluntary industrial and incomes policy. Wilson was, at the same time, faced with opposition from within his party and in March 1976, apparently tired and disillusioned, he decided to retire in mid-term, arguing that it was a move he had always planned.

He was succeeded by James Callaghan (b. 1912), his senior by some four years. Callaghan was now leading an increasingly divided party and a government with a dwindling parliamentary majority. Meanwhile, there had been changes in the other two parties, Edward Heath being unexpectedly ousted by the relatively inexperienced Margaret Thatcher (b. 1925), and the Liberal Party leader, Jeremy Thorpe (b. 1929), resigning after an unsavoury personal scandal and being succeeded by the young Scottish MP, David Steel (b. 1938). Callaghan and his strong cabinet team decided to continue along the path of solid consensual economic recovery, built around the 'social contract' incomes policy and then, in 1976, their plans were upset by an unexpected financial crisis arising from a drop in confidence in the overseas exchange markets, a rapidly falling pound, and a drain on the country's foreign reserves. After a soul-searching debate within the cabinet, it was decided to seek help from the International Monetary Fund (IMF) and submit to its stringent economic policies. Within weeks the crisis was over and within months the economy was showing clear signs of improvement. Whether or not the storm could have been weathered without IMF help was a matter debated for some time afterwards. Then in 1977, to shore up his slender parliamentary majority, Callaghan entered into an agreement with the new leader of the Liberal Party, David Steel, the 'Lib–Lab Pact'. This lasted for some 18 months, resulting in Labour pursuing moderate nonconfrontational policies in consultation with the Liberals, who, in turn, voted with the government. During this period the economy improved dramatically and by the summer of 1978 it seemed certain that Callaghan would call a general election with every chance of winning it. Without apparently consulting his cabinet colleagues, he decided to continue until at least the spring of 1979 but in the winter events turned destructively against him. The Lib–Lab Pact had effectively finished by the autumn and soon afterwards the social contract with the unions began to disintegrate. The government was faced with widespread and damaging strikes in the public sector, with essential services badly affected. Callaghan's pre-election period became the 'winter of discontent'. At the end of March 1979 he lost a vote of confidence in the House of Commons and was forced into a general election.

The Conservatives returned to power under the United Kingdom's first woman prime minister, Margaret Thatcher. She had inherited a cabinet containing a majority of Heath politicians and it was nearly two years before she made any major changes. She had also inherited a number of inflationary public sector pay awards which were a residue of the winter of discontent. The honouring of these, plus a budget from the chancellor, Sir Geoffrey Howe (b. 1926), which doubled the rate of value-added tax (VAT), resulted in a sharp rise in the price level and interest rates. As the Conservatives had come into power pledged to reduce inflation, this became the government's main, if not sole, economic target and, in pursuing it, by mainly monetarist policies, the level of unemployment rose from 1.3 million to 2 million in the first year. Mrs Thatcher had had a narrow experience in government, being a cabinet minister in only one department, but it was in foreign affairs where she was least equipped. She relied strongly, therefore, on the foreign secretary, Lord Carrington (b. 1919) and it was under his influence that the independence of Zimbabwe (Rhodesia) was achieved bloodlessly in 1980.

Meanwhile, important changes were taking place in the other parties. Callaghan resigned the leadership of the Labour Party in 1980 and was replaced by the left-winger Michael Foot (b. 1913), and early in 1981 three Labour shadow cabinet members, David Owen (b. 1938), Shirley Williams (b. 1930), and William Rodgers (b. 1928), with the former deputy leader, Roy Jenkins (b. 1920), broke away to form a new centre-left group, the Social Democratic Party (SDP). The new party made an early and spectacular impression, winning a series of by-elections within months of its creation.

Unemployment continued to rise, passing the 3 million mark in January 1982, and the Conservatives, and their leader in particular, were receiving low ratings in the public opinion polls. A fortuitous and unforeseen event rescued them, the Argentine invasion of the Falkland Islands. Margaret Thatcher's determined decision to launch an invasion to recover the islands, in the face of apparently appalling odds, finally confirmed her as the resolute conviction politician she claimed to be. The general election of 1983 was fought with the euphoria of the Falklands victory still in the air and the Labour Party, under its new leader, divided and unconvincing. The Conservatives had a landslide victory, winning more Commons seats than any party since 1945, and yet with appreciably less than half the popular vote.

Mrs Thatcher was now able to firmly establish her position, making changes which meant that more than half her original cabinet had been replaced. The next three years were, however, marked by a sequence of potentially damaging events: rising unemployment; a dispute at the government's main intelligence gathering station, GCHQ; a bitter and protracted miners' strike; increasing violence in Northern Ireland; an attempted assassination of leading members of the Conservative Party during their annual conference; riots in inner city areas; embarrassing prosecutions under the Official Secrets Act; and the resignations of two prominent cabinet ministers. Meanwhile, the violence in Northern Ireland continued and, in 1985, in an effort to secure some improvement, an agreement was signed with the Irish government, providing for greater cooperation in security matters, including the exchange of intelligence. The Anglo-Irish Agreement was strongly opposed by Unionist parties in the province. On the positive side, the inflation rate continued to fall and by the winter of 1986–87 the economy was buoyant enough to enable the Chancellor to allow a pre-election spending and credit boom.

Meanwhile, there had been leadership changes in two of the other parties. Michael Foot was replaced by his young Welsh protégé, Neil Kinnock (b. 1942), and Roy Jenkins was smoothly replaced by David Owen as SDP leader. Despite the unemployment figures and criticisms of Margaret

Thatcher's increasingly authoritarian style of government, the Conservatives won the June election with virtually the same share of the popular vote as they had secured four years earlier, but with a slightly reduced parliamentary majority. Although the Labour Party had run what was generally considered to have been a very good campaign, its share of the popular vote showed only a marginal improvement and its seat tally only a modest gain. The Liberal–SDP Alliance had experienced a poor election, its vote share dropping and its seat count remaining virtually static.

The main political parties reacted differently in the aftermath of the 1987 general election. Margaret Thatcher regarded the result as a vindication of her earlier policies and strengthened her control of the party and her government, at the same time pressing ahead with an expansive privatization programme. Her stated aim was to obliterate all traces of socialism from the British political scene. The Labour Party, stung by the jibes of its opponents that it was 'unelectable', embarked upon a massive reassessment of its policies and structure. The Liberal leader, David Steel, disillusioned with the election result and tired of being the dog wagged by the tail of the SDP leader, David Owen, made an immediate call for a full merger of the two parties. This was eventually agreed, amid considerable acrimony and some confusion, and in 1988 the new party of the Social and Liberal Democrats, or the Liberal Democrats, as they became, was born, with a new leader, the youngish Member for Yeovil, Paddy Ashdown (b. 1941). Not all of the SDP members chose to join the new grouping. Three MPs, led by David Owen, and a few thousand followers, stayed together and retained the SDP label, but this group eventually lost its leader and its role as a political party and in 1990 it was formally wound up.

Divisions within the Conservative Party, particularly over European policy, forced a leadership election in November 1990, Mrs Thatcher being challenged by her former cabinet colleague Michael Heseltine (b. 1933). After an inconclusive first ballot Mrs Thatcher withdrew and John Major (b. 1943), the chancellor of the Exchequer, was elected party leader and prime minister.

Throughout 1991 the economy deteriorated and Major postponed asking for a dissolution of Parliament until April 1992. Contrary to many expectations and opinion poll predictions, the Conservatives won the election, with an overall majority of 21 seats. The Labour Party leader announced his intention to resign and, in July 1992, he was succeeded by the Scottish MP, John Smith (1938–94).

During the remainder of 1992 divisions within the Conservative Party, centred on Europe and the Maastricht Treaty on closer union, resurfaced while the state of the economy worsened. In September the pound was devalued and the United Kingdom withdrew from the Exchange Rate Mechanism (ERM). The standing of the prime minister, and his Chancellor, had fallen to an all-time low. During 1993 the government's problems increased and its popularity continued to wane, the Conservatives faring badly in local and parliamentary by-elections.

In May 1994 the nation was stunned by the sudden death of the Labour Party leader, John Smith, resulting in an almost unprecedented display of cross-party sadness and concern. His successor, the young articulate lawyer, Tony

Blair (b. 1953), proved to be an even greater threat to the government's likelihood of regaining its popularity rating. As the leader of a 'New Labour', as he described it, Blair sought to recast the image and policy stance of his party so as to attract the wider middle-class electorate as well as traditional supporters and, despite some opposition from diehard elements, he was largely successful.

The one redeeming feature of the government's policies was its success in securing a cessation of terrorist activity in Northern Ireland with the prospect of substantive talks between representatives of the divided communities during 1995, leading eventually to a lasting peace in the province.

Even this success had been won at the expense of the possibility of losing the guaranteed support of Unionist MPs in Parliament. At the same time, the debate about Britain's future relationship with its partners in the European Union continued, causing rifts not only in the parliamentary party but within the government itself.

Allegations by the opposition of sleaze within the Conservative ranks prompted Prime Minister John Major to establish a committee on standards in public life. The report of this committee, under Lord Nolan, and that of the inquiry into arms sales to Iraq, chaired by Lord Justice Scott, were seen by some observers as potential time bombs, threatening to explode before the next general election, which would have to be held by the spring of 1997 at the very latest. Following the publication of the Nolan report, MPs decided on a free vote in November 1995 to require Members to declare all outside earnings resulting from their positions in parliament, and to ban all paid lobbying.

VATICAN CITY STATE

Temporal State of the Bishop of Rome
Stato della Città del Vaticano

Capital: Vatican City, Rome

Social and economic data
Area: 0.4 km²
Population: 700*
Pop. density per km²: 1,750*
Literacy rate: N/A
GDP: N/A; per-capita GDP: N/A
Government spending on defence (% of GDP): N/A
Economy type: high income
Labour force in agriculture: N/A

*1994

Religions
Roman Catholicism is the sole religion.

Political features
State type: theocracy
Date of state formation: 1377/1929
Political structure: unitary
Executive: absolute (theocratic)
Assembly: none
Party structure: none
Human rights rating: N/A

Head of state
His Holiness Pope John Paul II, since 1978

Head of government
Cardinal Angelo Sodano, since 1990

Political system
The Vatican City State came into being through the Lateran Treaty of February 1929, under which the king of Italy recognized the sovereignty of the pope over the city of the Vatican. The pope, the supreme pontiff of the Universal Church, is elected for life by 120 members of the Sacred College of Cardinals. He appoints a Pontifical Commission (PC), headed by a president, to administer the State's affairs on his behalf and under his direction. The PC comprises seven cardinals, each appointed for a five-year period, served by lay staff headed by a Special Delegate. Routine Vatican administration has been entrusted since 1984 to the secretary of state.

In the Vatican, the central administration of the Roman Catholic Church throughout the world is also conducted by 11 Congregations, each under the direction of a cardinal, three secretariats, and numerous committees, councils, and commissions.

Political history
The Vatican City State is a direct successor to early papal states which had ruled much of the central Italian peninsula during the millennium between the era of Charlemagne and the unification of Italy in 1870–71. The Vatican Palace in Rome had served as the papal residence since 1377 and remained so during the period between 1871 and 1929 when the Vatican was formally absorbed within the new Italian state. Under the terms of the 1929 Lateran Agreement, signed by Benito Mussolini (1883–1945) and Pope Pius XI (1857–1939), full sovereign jurisdiction over the Vatican City State was restored to the Holy See, which is the formal title of the bishopric of Rome. The new state was declared a neutral and inviolable territory.

This treaty was reaffirmed in the Italian constitution of 1947. Under the terms of a Concordat, also agreed in 1929, Roman Catholicism became the state religion in Italy, enjoying special legal privileges. This status was also reaffirmed in 1947. However, a new Concordat was signed in February 1984, and subsequently ratified in June 1985, under which Catholicism ceased to be the Italian state religion.

The present (266th) pope, John Paul II (b. 1920), formerly Cardinal Karol Wojtyla, took up his office in October 1978. Born in Poland and having previously served as as archbishop of Kraków in Poland, he is the first non-Italian pope since 1522. In May 1981 and May 1982 he survived two assassination attempts and has since established himself as a vigorous and influential leader. As head of a church claiming more than 750 million adherents worldwide, 26% of whom live in Europe, 53% in the Americas, and the remaining 21% in Africa, Asia, and Oceania, Pope John Paul II has travelled extensively, drawing large audiences wherever he visits.

Oceania

The region we have called Oceania occupies a total land area of nearly 9 million square kilometres, equivalent to around 7% of the world total, but, as its name implies, the total land–sea coverage is considerably greater. It extends from 47 degrees south, at the foot of New Zealand, to 21 degrees north, at the top of the Philippines. The southern part enjoys a cool temperate climate while the central and northern areas are subtropical or tropical. Above all, it is a region of water and islands. Some of the islands are small and uninhabited, others are large, and the biggest of all, Australia, is twice the size of India and large enough to be regarded as a continent. The number of islands defies comprehension – in the Philippines alone, for example, there are more than 7,000.

Within the region are 15 sovereign states, three of which (Belau, the Federated States of Micronesia, or FSM, and the Marshall Islands) were formerly United Nations (UN) Trust Territories until the early 1990s. The largest in areal size is Australia and the largest in population, the Philippines. Oceania is very much a region of contrasts. For example, Australia has a population density of two people per square kilometre, while tiny Nauru has 476. Many countries are still undeveloped, or only partly developed, while others have well established secondary and tertiary industries and sophisticated infrastructures. Six of the 15 nations within Oceania have low per-capita GDPs, whereas those of Australia, Nauru, and New Zealand are high. Overall, the region comprises less than 2% of both the world's population and GDP, with average GDP in the region standing at $4,255 in c. 1992.

Until comparatively recently much of the region was one of the most isolated and inaccessible parts of the world. The nearest neighbour to Nauru, for example, is Kiribati, over 300 kilometres away. Before World War II the journey from Europe to Australia was, for most people, a matter of weeks, rather than days. Now it can be accomplished, by scheduled airlines, in hours. The same can be said of most other parts of the region. The earlier isolation, which led to the region being used as a nuclear testing ground for the United States (on Bikini atoll), Britain (on Christmas Island), and France (on Mururoa atoll), is now being removed, not just for a wealthy minority, but for an increasing number of people of comparatively modest incomes. All this has meant not only that Europeans and Americans are wanting – and getting – to know more about the region but that the inhabitants of Oceania are becoming less inward-looking themselves.

Despite many other differences, most of the 15 states in the region share certain common cultural and political features. Christianity, which was introduced, along with initially debilitating Western diseases, by European missionaries to the Pacific island states, is the predominant religion. The constituent states generally display high levels of representative government. As Table 61 shows, 12 are established liberal democracies, two we have defined as emergent democracies, and only one, Tonga, does not have a pluralist political system. Eight have parliamentary executives, on the British model, and six have limited presidential executives, on the lines of that in the United States. Tonga, with its virtually unique system of hereditary paternalistic monarchs, is, again, the exception to the rule. Even their voting methods show a high degree of uniformity, 10 of the 15 employing the simple plurality system.

This comparative uniformity in political processes can be largely explained by the historical backgrounds of the 15 nations. Eleven of them were, at one time or another, under British control and are still active members of the Commonwealth. The 'non-British' exceptions are the Philippines, which was a United States possession for nearly 50 years until it achieved full independence in 1946, and the three ex-UN Trust Territories, which were under American tutelage from the end of World War II until they secured independence under the terms of 'Compacts of Free Association' with the United States. The links between the United Kingdom and the other Commonwealth countries in the region, and those between the Philippines and the three former UN Trust Territories and the United States, are still strong, although the former are not nearly as strong as they were in earlier decades. Britain's membership of the European Union has done much to force countries such as Australia and New Zealand to realign their attitudes and establish closer links with their neighbours and with the dominant economic force lying on the region's periphery, Japan. Nine of the states of the region have no independent armed forces of their own, being reliant on external 'great powers' for their ultimate defence.

The United States, in the 19th century and the early part of the 20th century, was described as the 'New World'. Today that epithet could, more appropriately, be applied to parts of Oceania, and particularly Australia and New Zealand. Australia is no longer regarded as a cultural backwater, but rather a leader in the arts of literature, drama, music, and filmmaking. Although much of its interior will probably remain undeveloped for many years to come, the potential for development is undoubtedly there. Many of the smaller Oceanic countries will be handicapped by geographical factors and a lack of natural resources which has meant that their economies are heavily reliant on foreign aid. But, as they work together more in joint endeavours and develop new activities, notably tourism, they too have the capacities to improve their circumstances. However, a major threat to the very existence of several of the region's small low-lying island states is the likely rise in the sea level if 'global warming' continues.

A final point should be made. Oceania, in the form we have defined it, is a somewhat artificial entity and its proximity to the fast growing economies in parts of neighbouring Asia should not be forgotten. If we include in our calculations the 'Pacific Rim' states of Japan, which during World War II ruled nearly a thousand Pacific islands, China, Taiwan, the Koreas, Thailand, Malaysia, and Hong Kong, then we are looking at a highly dynamic and potentially very important part of the world.

Recommended reading

Dommen, EC and Hein, P L (eds) *States, Micro-states and Islands*, Croom Helm, 1985

Dorney, S *Papua New Guinea: People, Politics and History since 1975*, Random House (Australia), 1990

Jaensch, D *The Politics of Australia*, Macmillan (Australia), 1992

Linder, S B *The Pacific Century*, Stanford University Press, 1986

Winchester, *The Pacific*, Hutchinson, 1994

AUSTRALIA

Commonwealth of Australia

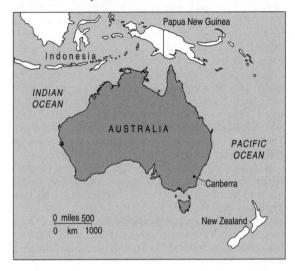

Capital: Canberra

Social and economic data
Area: 7,686,850 km²
Population: 17,800,000*
Pop. density per km²: 2*
Urban population: 85%**
Literacy rate: 99%**
GDP: $299,000 million**; per-capita GDP: $17,065**

Oceania: social, economic, and political data

Country	Area (sq km)	c. 1992–94 Population (m)	c. 1992–94 Pop. density per sq km	c. 1992 Adult literacy rate (%)	World ranking	Income type	c. 1991 Human rights ranking (%)
Australia	7,686,850	17.800	2	99	8	high	91
Belau	508	0.016	31	n/a		middle	n/a
Fiji	18,376	0.700	38	79	109	middle	n/a
Kiribati	861	0.075	87	90	80	low	n/a
Marshall Islands	180	0.049	272	95	59	middle	n/a
Micronesia	700	0.102	146	95	59	middle	n/a
Nauru	21	0.010	476	99	8	high	n/a
New Zealand	267,844	3.500	13	99	8	high	98
Papua New Guinea	462,840	4.100	9	52	146	low	70
Philippines	300,000	66.500	222	94	66	low	72
Solomon Islands	27,556	0.380	14	60	131	low	n/a
Tonga	748	0.101	135	99	8	middle	n/a
Tuvalu	26	0.009	346	95	59	low	n/a
Vanuatu	12,190	0.160	13	66	123	middle	n/a
Western Samoa	2,831	0.163	58	98	34	low	n/a
Total/average/range	8,781,531	93.665	11	52–99			70–98

Key:		AV	alternative vote	PR	proportional representation
A	appointed	E	elected	SB	second ballot
AMS	additional member systerm	F	federal	SP	simple plurality

Government defence spending (% of GDP): 2.4%**
Currency: Australian dollar
Economy type: high income
Labour force in agriculture: 5%**

*1994
**1992

Ethnic composition
About 99% of the population is of European descent – British, Maltese, Italian, Greek, Dutch, and Polish, in that order. The remaining 1% is Aborigine or Asian. English is the official language.

Religions
About 30% of the population is practising Anglican and 25% Roman Catholic.

Political features
State type: liberal democratic
Date of state formation: 1901
Political structure: federal
Executive: parliamentary
Assembly: two-chamber
Party structure: two-party
Human rights rating: 91%
International affiliations: AG (observer), ANZUS, APEC, CP, CW, IAEA, IBRD, IMF, IWC, NAM (guest), OECD, SPC, SPF, UN, WTO

Local and regional government
Australia is a federal nation, consisting of the six states of New South Wales, Victoria, Queensland, Western Australia, South Australia, and Tasmania; and the Northern Territory and Australian Capital Territory.

The states are modern-day equivalents of the 19th-century colonies which were federated to become a single nation. State identification therefore remains a strong feature of Australian life. This aspect is accentuated by the size of the country and the distribution of the population. Most communities are in coastal areas, and particularly the east and south coasts, and around the major cities of Sydney, Melbourne, Brisbane, Perth, Adelaide; and the capital, Canberra.

The federal system is modelled on that of the United States, with each state having its own governor, representing the queen, and its own executive, legislative, and judicial system, but the detailed arrangements for each state vary.

New South Wales has a two-chamber assembly consisting of a Legislative Council of 45 members, directly elected for the duration of three federal parliaments, with a third retiring every four years, and a Legislative Assembly of 99 members, directly elected for a four-year term.

Victoria has a similar arrangement, with 44 members in the Legislative Council, elected for six years, half retiring every three years, and a Legislative Assembly of 88, elected for four years.

The Queensland assembly has a single chamber of 82 members, directly elected for a three-year term.

South Australia has a two-chamber assembly consisting of a Legislative Council of 22 members, elected by proportional representation for a six-year term, half retiring every three years, and a House of Assembly of 47 members, directly elected for three years.

Western Australia also has a Legislative Council and a Legislative Assembly. The Council has 34 members elected

Table 61

World ranking	Date of state formation	State structure	State type	Executive type	Number of assembly chambers	Party structure	Lower house electoral system
20	1901	F	Lib-dem	Parliamentary	2	two	PR-AV
	1994	U	Lib-dem	Lim-pres	2	none	SP
	1970	U	Em-dem	Parliamentary	2	multi	SP
	1979	U	Lib-dem	Lim-pres	1	two	SB
	1990	U	Lib-dem	Lim-pres	1	two	SP
	1986	F	Lib-dem	Lim-pres	1	none	SP
	1968	U	Lib-dem	Lim-pres	1	none	SP
4	1853	U	Lib-dem	Parliamentary	1	multi	PR-AMS
47	1975	U	Lib-dem	Parliamentary	1	multi	SP
43	1946	U	Em-dem	Lim-pres	2	multi	SP
	1978	U	Lib-dem	Parliamentary	1	multi	SP
	1831/1970	U	Absolutist	Absolutist	1	trans	mixed-E/A
	1978	U	Lib-dem	Parliamentary	1	none	SP
	1980	U	Lib-dem	Parliamentary	1	multi	PR
	1962	U	Lib-dem	Parliamentary	1	multi	SP

U	unitary	Lim-pres	Limited presidential
Lib-dem	Liberal democratic	Trans	Transitional
Em-dem	Emergent democratic		

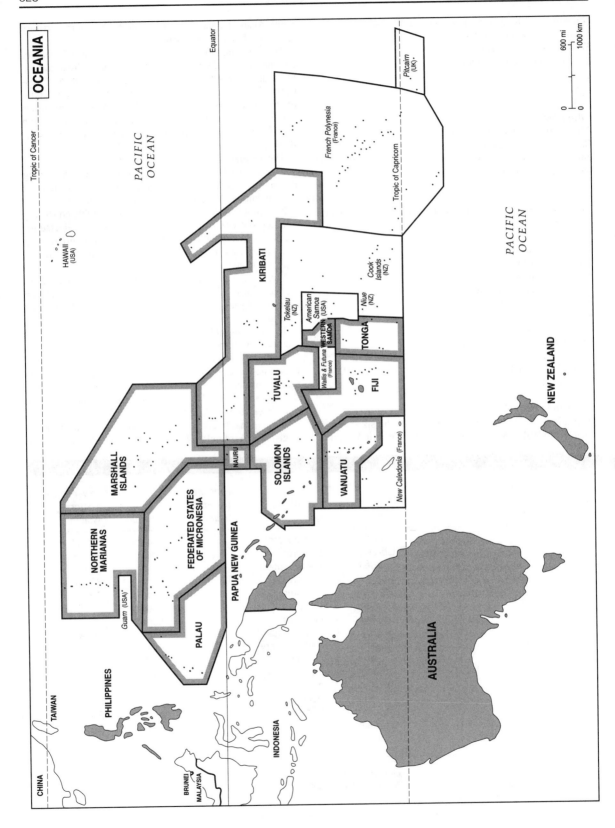

OCEANIA

PACIFIC OCEAN

PACIFIC OCEAN

Equator

Tropic of Cancer

Tropic of Capricorn

600 mi

1000 km

Pitcairn (UK)

French Polynesia (France)

HAWAII (USA)

KIRIBATI

Cook Islands (NZ)

Tokelau (NZ)

American Samoa (USA)

Niue (NZ)

WESTERN SAMOA

TONGA

TUVALU

Wallis & Futuna (France)

FIJI

NAURU

SOLOMON ISLANDS

VANUATU

New Caledonia (France)

MARSHALL ISLANDS

FEDERATED STATES OF MICRONESIA

PAPUA NEW GUINEA

NORTHERN MARIANAS

Guam (USA)

PALAU

NEW ZEALAND

PHILIPPINES

TAIWAN

CHINA

BRUNEI

MALAYSIA

INDONESIA

AUSTRALIA

for six years, half retiring every three years, and the Assembly has 57 members elected for three years.

Tasmania has a two-chamber arrangement, with 19 members in the Legislative Council elected for six years, retiring in rotation, and 35 members in the House of Assembly, elected for four years.

The Northern Territory has a single-chamber assembly, the Legislative Assembly, with 25 members elected for a four-year term, and the Australian Capital Territory, in Canberra, has an elected House of Assembly of 18 members, with essentially an advisory function on matters affecting the Territory itself.

Head of state
Queen Elizabeth II, represented by Governor General William (Bill) Hayden since 1989

Head of government
Prime Minister Paul Keating, since 1991

Political leaders since 1970
1968–71 John Gorton (Liberal Party), 1971–72 William McMahon (Liberal–Country Party coalition), 1972–75 Gough Whitlam (ALP), 1975–83 Malcolm Fraser (Liberal–Country Party coalition), 1983–91 Bob Hawke (ALP), 1991–   Paul Keating (ALP)

Political system
Australia is an independent sovereign nation within the Commonwealth, retaining the British monarch as head of state, and a governor general as her representative. The constitution was adopted in 1900 and came into effect on 1 January 1901. As in the United Kingdom, there is a parliamentary executive, in the shape of the prime minister and cabinet, drawn from the federal assembly and answerable to it.

The federal assembly consists of two chambers: an elected Senate of 76 (12 for each of the six states, two for the Australian Capital Territory, and two for the Northern Territory) and a House of Representatives of 147, elected by universal adult suffrage. Senators serve for six years and members of the House of Representatives for three years. Voting is compulsory and the majoritarian system of the alternative vote is used for elections to both chambers.

In March 1986 the United Kingdom Parliament removed the last relics of British legislative control over Australia.

Political parties
There are some ten political parties, the most significant being the Australian Labor Party (ALP), the Liberal Party of Australia, and the National Party of Australia. Although now all national organizations, there are still clear local divergencies and parts of the country where each party is particularly strong or weak.

The ALP was founded in 1891 and is Australia's oldest party. It is moderately left of centre, supporting the democratic socialization of industry, production, distribution, and exchange.

The Liberal Party of Australia dates from 1944, although its origins go back towards the beginning of this century when free traders and protectionists fused together and were later joined by breakaway groups from the ALP. In its modern form it is largely the achievement of the notable Australian politician, Sir Robert Menzies. It advocates free enterprise, social justice, and individual initiative and liberty.

The National Party of Australia was formed in 1916 as the Country Party to represent the interests of farmers. Its orientation is centrist, with an emphasis on the needs of people outside the metropolitan areas.

Latest elections
After the March 1993 general election the seat holdings in the two chambers were as follows:

	Senate	House of Representatives
ALP	30	80
Liberals	30	49
National Party	6	16
Others	10	2

Political history
Although Australia was visited by Europeans as early as the 17th century, the main immigration came towards the end of the 18th century when Captain James Cook (1728–79) claimed New South Wales as a British colony. Exploration of the interior began in the next century when there was rapid expansion, aided by gold discoveries. With this growth other colonies were developed. A depression in the 1890s prompted the growth of trade unionism and the foundation of the Australian Labor Party. By the end of the century the movement towards a federation and self-government had developed sufficiently for the establishment of the Commonwealth of Australia in 1901, with Canberra to be created as the federal capital.

Since 1945 Australia has strengthened its ties with India and other Southeast Asian countries and this realignment was accelerated following Britain's entry into the European Community in 1973. The links with its original founder are now more emotional and historic than economic or political.

Politically, the immediate postwar years were dominated by the Liberal Party which, under Robert Menzies (1894–1978), held power for 17 years. He retired in 1966 and was succeeded by Harold Holt (1908–67). Holt died in a swimming accident the following year and in 1968 John Gorton (b. 1911) took over the premiership. In 1971 he lost a vote of confidence in the House and resigned, to be succeeded by William McMahon (b. 1908), heading a Liberal–Country Party coalition.

Then, at the end of 1972, the Liberal hegemony was broken and the Australian Labor Party, led by Gough Whitlam (b. 1916), took office. A general election in 1974 gave the Labor Party a fresh mandate to govern although its majority in the House was reduced and it had lost control of the Senate. In 1975 the Senate blocked the government's financial legislation and, with Whitlam unwilling to resign, the governor general, Sir John Kerr (1914–90), took the unprecedented step of dismissing him and his cabinet and inviting Malcolm Fraser (b. 1930) to form a Liberal–Country party coalition caretaker administration. The wisdom of the governor general's action was widely questioned and eventually, in 1977, he himself resigned.

In the 1977 general election the coalition was returned with a reduced majority and this became even smaller in 1980. In the 1983 general election the coalition was eventually defeated and the Australian Labor Party, under Bob Hawke (b. 1929), again took office. Hawke immediately honoured an election pledge and called together leaders of employers and unions to agree a prices and incomes policy and to deal with the problem of growing unemployment. He called a general election in December 1984, 15 months earlier than necessary, and was returned with a reduced majority.

After taking office, Hawke developed a distinctive foreign policy for Australia, placing even greater emphasis than his predecessors on links with Southeast Asia and, in 1986, boldly imposing trading sanctions against South Africa as a means of influencing its dismantling of the system of apartheid.

In 1988 it was surprisingly announced that Bill Hayden (b. 1933), the foreign minister in Bob Hawke's administration, was to be Australia's next governor general, in February 1989, and, in accepting the post, Hayden announced that he would not also accept the customary knighthood.

In the 1990 general election the Liberal Party improved its position in the House and, with a decline in its fortunes and a deteriorating economy, in 1991 the ALP chose a new leader, the former finance minister, Paul Keating (b. 1954). Bob Hawke immediately announced his withdrawal from active politics. The ALP won an unprecedented fifth term in the March 1993 House of Representatives elections, Keating describing the result as the 'sweetest victory ever'.

Within two years the leadership of the Liberal Party changed hands twice, John Hewson resigning as leader of the opposition in May 1994 and his successor, Alexander Downer, being replaced by John Howard in January 1995.

During his time as prime minister, Paul Keating progressively distanced Australia from its British roots, ending the acceptance of royal honours in October 1992 and removing the oath of allegiance to the Crown two months later. Republican status was seen as the ultimate goal.

BELAU (PALAU)

Republic of Belau

Capital: Koror (on Koror island)

Social and economic data
Area: 508 km²
Population: 15,500*
Pop. density per km²: 31*
Urban population: N/A
Literacy rate: N/A
GDP: N/A*
Government defence spending (% of GDP): 0%**
Currency: US dollar

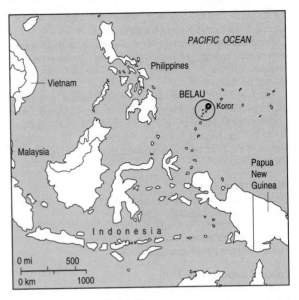

Economy type: middle income
Labour force in agriculture: N/A

*1992
**The United States is responsible for Belau's defence

Ethnic composition
The population is predominantly Micronesian, with English and Palauan being spoken.

Religions
The main religion is Christianity, chiefly Roman Catholicism.

Political features
State type: liberal democratic
Date of state formation: 1994
Political structure: unitary
Executive: limited presidential
Assembly: two-chamber
Party structure: none
Human rights rating: N/A
International affiliations: SPC, UN

Local and regional government
Each of the Republic's 16 states has its own elected legislature and governor, and, below, there are elected magistrates and municipal councils.

Head of state and head of government
President Kuniwo Nakamura, since 1992

Political leaders since 1970
1984–85 Haruo Remeliik (independent), 1985–88 Lazarus Salii (independent), 1988 Thomas Remengesau (independent), 1988–92 Ngiratkel Etpison (independent), 1992– Kuniwo Nakamura (independent)

Political system
Under the terms of the January 1981 constitution, as amended in 1992, Belau has a democratic representative

form of government, which blends elements of the indigenous system of hereditary female chiefs with American democracy. Executive authority is held by a president, who is directly elected for a four-year term and heads an eight-member cabinet, which includes the vice president. There is also a presidential advisory body, composed of the paramount chiefs of the 16 constituent states. The legislature, or Belau National Congress (Olbiil era Kelulau), is a two-chamber body, comprising a 14-member Senate, or upper house, and a 16-member House of Delegates, or lower chamber. Senators are elected from demographically based constituencies, four being returned from northern Belau, nine from Koror, and one from the southern islands. Delegates are elected from each of the 16 states which comprise the Republic: Kayangel, Ngerchelong, Ngaraard, Ngardmau, Ngaremlengui, Ngiwal, Melekeok, Ngchesar, Ngatpang, Aimeliik, Airai, Koror, Peleliu, Angaur, Sonsorol, and Tobi. Each state has its own elected legislature and governor.

Political parties
During the later 1980s two political coalitions were formed, the Ta Belau Party and the Coalition for Open, Honest and Just Government, to respectively support and oppose the Compact of Free Association. These are not formally organized political parties.

Latest elections
The most recent legislature and presidential elections were held on 4 November 1992. The presidential run-off election was won narrowly by Kuniwo Nakamura, who secured 50.7% of the national vote, defeating Johnson Toribiong, who attracted 49.3% support.

Political history
Belau comprises more than 350 (mostly uninhabited) islands, islets and atolls in the West Micronesia Caroline Islands group, lying in a 650-kilometre-long chain in the West Pacific Ocean, 960 kilometres east of the Philippines and 7,150 kilometres southwest of Hawaii. Fifty-eight per cent of the population lives in the capital, Koror.

Belau has a similar history to the Federated States of Micronesia with which it forms part of the Caroline Islands group. A Republic was proclaimed in January 1981 when, following its approval in a referendum held in July 1979, a locally drafted constitution came into effect. Later, in August 1982, a 'Compact of Free Association' was signed with the United States, providing for Belau's independence, though the United States remained responsible for the Republic's defence and security.

This Compact was approved by 60% of those who voted in a referendum held in February 1983. However, fewer than the required 75% supported the proposal to amend the Republic's constitution so as to allow the transit, storage, or disposal of nuclear, chemical, or biological weapons, which, otherwise, was outlawed by one of its clauses. The United States government viewed this constitutional change as essential if it was to fulfil its defence obligations and thus refused to endorse the Compact. A new Compact was framed in 1986, in which the United States, anxious to make use of Belau's ports as a possible naval alternative to its Philippines bases, agreed to provide, over a 15-year period, $421 million

in economic assistance to the islands. However, after the failures of plebiscites held in February 1986, October 1986, and June 1987 to secure the necessary 75% majority support to change the constitution, the Compact was unratified.

Following pressure from pronuclear supporters of the Compact, an effort was made to break this impasse, in a new referendum held in August 1987. This proposed changing the plebiscitary majority required for amending the constitution from 75% to only 51%. Support for this proposed change was achieved, the required majority for both the Compact and constitutional nuclear clause change being obtained in an ensuing referendum. However, in April 1988, the Supreme Court of Belau ruled these changes unconstitutional. Five months later, in August 1988, the Republic's president, Lazarus Salii, was found dead with a gunshot wound to his head. Initial reports suggested that, like Belau's first president, Haruo Remeliik in June 1985, he had been assassinated by political opponents. Later evidence suggested, however, that the president had committed suicide because of both policy failures and pending corruption charges.

A further referendum in 1990 failed to resolve the Compact issue. This left Belau as the only surviving part of the Trust Territory of the Pacific Islands which had not either formally achieved 'independence' or become a US Commonwealth Territory and prompted the United States to declare in May 1991 that if Belau did not soon adopt the Compact it should consider commencing independence negotiations. However, in November 1992 the requirement for the approval of constitutional amendments was reduced, by referendum, to a simple majority. This margin was achieved comfortably in November 1993 when, in an eighth referendum, 68% of voters approved a constitutional amendment designed to pave the way for implementation of the Compact with the United States. Full independence was achieved on 1 October 1994, after all legal challenges by the Compact's opponents had been dismissed, and in November 1994 Belau became a member of the United Nations.

FIJI

Capital: Suva on Viti Levu

Social and economic data
Area: 18,376 km^2
Population: 700,000*
Pop. density per km^2: 38*
Urban population: 37%**
Literacy rate: 79%**
GDP: $1,200**; per-capita GDP: $1,650**
Government defence spending (% of GDP): 1.7%**
Currency: Fiji dollar
Economy type: middle income
Labour force in agriculture: 44%**

*1994
**1992

Ethnic composition
Fiji is one of the few countries in the world where the native population is in a minority. Fijians, who are ethnically a mix-

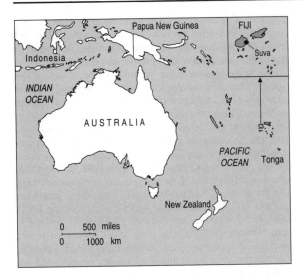

system of government retains much of its British origins, with a two-chamber parliament, comprising a Senate and a House of Representatives, and a parliamentary executive, consisting of a prime minister and cabinet, drawn from and responsible to the House of Representatives.

In 1990, however, the interim government established after the military coup amended the constitution so as effectively to guarantee a majority in both chambers of the assembly for the Melanese population.

The Senate has 22 appointed members, eight on the advice of the Great Council of Fijian Chiefs, seven on the advice of the prime minister, six on the advice of the leader of the opposition, and one on the advice of the Council of Rotuma Island, which is a dependency of Fiji. It has a life of six years.

The House of Representatives has 70 members, elected for five years through a simple plurality voting system. Thirty-seven seats are reserved for indigenous Fijians, 27 for Indians, five for other races, and one for a representative of Rotuma.

ture of Melanesians and Polynesians, comprise only 48% of the population, while about 51% are Asians who were brought to the country from India as indentured labourers during the period of British colonial rule. Fijian and Hindi are the official languages but English is widely spoken.

Religions

Most ethnic Fijians are Christians, mainly Protestant, while the Asian majority are Hindus, Muslims, or Sikhs.

Political features

State type: emergent democratic
Date of state formation: 1970
Political structure: unitary
Executive: parliamentary
Assembly: two-chamber
Party structure: multiparty
Human rights rating: N/A
International affiliations: ACP, CP, CW, IBRD, IMF, SPC, SPF, UN, WTO

Local and regional government

For administrative purposes, the country consists of four divisions.

Head of state

President Ratu Sir Kamisese Mara, since 1994

Head of government

Prime Minister Major General Sitiveni Rabuka, since 1992

Political leaders since 1970

1970–87 Kamisese Kapaiwai Tuimacilai Mara (AP), 1987 Lieutenant Sitiveni Rabuka (military), 1987–92 Kamisese Kapaiwai Tuimacilai Mara (AP), 1992– Major General Sitiveni Rabuka (FPP)

Political system

Fiji was a constitutional monarchy within the Commonwealth, with the British monarch as the formal head of state, until a military coup in 1987 established a republic. The

Political parties

There are some six political parties, the most significant being the Fijian Political Party (FPP), the National Federation Party (NFP), the Fijian Labour Party (FLP), and the General Voters' Party (GVP).

The FPP was formed in 1990 as the political vehicle for Sitiveni Rabuka. It has a right-of-centre orientation.

The NFP was formed in 1960 by the merging of the multi-racial, but chiefly Indian, Federation Party and the National Democratic Party. Its orientation is moderate left-of-centre.

The FLP dates from 1985. It is a left-of-centre party, drawing most of its support from the Indian community.

The GVP was founded as an ally of the FPP and has a similar orientation.

Latest elections

In the February 1994 general election the FPP won 31 of the 37 Melanese seats in the House of Representatives and, of the 27 Indian seats, the NFP won 20 and the FLP 7. The remaining seats went to the GVP and independents.

Political history

A British possession since 1874, Fiji achieved full independence within the Commonwealth in 1970. Before independence there had been racial tensions between Indians, descended from workers who had been brought to Fiji in the late 19th century, and Fijians, so the constitution incorporated an electoral device which would help to ensure racial balance in the House of Representatives. The leader of the Alliance Party (AP), Ratu Sir Kamisese Mara, became prime minister at the time of independence and held office until there was a brief military coup in 1987.

The AP was traditionally supported by ethnic Fijians and the National Federation Party (NFP) by Indians. The main divisions between the two centred on land ownership, with the Fijians owning more than 80% of the land and defending their traditional rights, and the Indians claiming greater security of land tenure. The Fijian Labour Party (FLP) was formed in 1985 and in the April 1987 general election gained power in association with the NFP. This provoked an unsuccessful coup the following month, led by Lieutenant Colonel Sitiveni Rabuka (b. 1948). In September 1987 a second coup succeeded and Rabuka announced that he had abrogated the constitution and assumed the role of head of state. After some indecision and confusion Fiji was declared a republic, the British queen ceasing to be head of state and the country automatically leaving the Commonwealth.

In December 1987 a civilian government was restored, with Mara resuming as prime minister, and Rabuka retaining control of the security forces as minister for home affairs. The former governor general, Sir Penaja Ganilau, resumed his role as head of state, now in the position of Fiji's first president.

Rabuka prepared for the future by forming the Fijian Political Party (FPP) as the vehicle for his political ambitions, and in the 1992 general election his party won 30 seats, allowing him to form a coalition government with the General Voters' Party (GVP).

In November 1993 the government's budget was rejected by parliament so Prime Minister Rabuka announced that there would be a general election in early 1994. President Ganilau died in December 1993 and was succeeded by his deputy, Ratu Sir Kamisese Mara.

In the February 1994 general election the FPP, supported by the GVP and two independents, secured a parliamentary majority and Rabuka began a second term as prime minister.

KIRIBATI

Republic of Kiribati

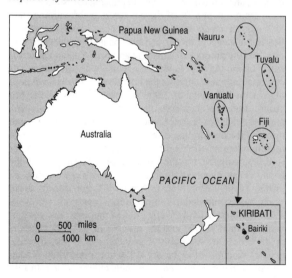

Capital: Bairiki (on Tarawa Atoll)

Social and economic data
Area: 861 km²
Population: 75,000*
Pop. density per km²: 87*
Urban population: 36%*
Literacy rate: 90%*
GDP: $54 million*; per-capita GDP: $720*

Government defence spending (% of GDP): 0%**
Currency: Australian dollar
Economy type: low income
Labour force in agriculture: N/A

*1992
**Kiribati has no armed forces

Ethnic composition
The population is predominantly Micronesian, with a Polynesian minority also to be found, as well as a few Europeans and Chinese. I-Kiribati (Gilbertise) is the local language, with English being used for official business.

Religions
The islands adhere both to the Protestant, chiefly Congregational, and Roman Catholic faiths in almost equal proportions. Traditional beliefs and practices also survive.

Political features
State type: liberal democratic
Date of state formation: 1979
Political structure: unitary
Executive: limited presidential
Assembly: one-chamber
Party structure: two-party*
Human rights rating: N/A
International affiliations: ACP, ADB, CW, ESCAP**, IBRD**, ICAO**, IDA**, IFC**, IMF**, ITU**, SPC, SPEC, SPF, UNESCO**, UPU**, WHO**

*though many deputies are elected as independents
**UN bodies of which Kiribati is a member, although it is not formally a member of the UN

Local and regional government
The islands are divided into seven administrative districts: Banaba, Northern Gilbert Islands, Central Gilbert Islands, Southern Gilbert Islands, Southeastern Gilbert Islands, Line Islands, and the Phoenix Group, with a district officer in charge of each. In addition, elected councils function on each inhabited island, enjoying considerable autonomy.

Head of state and head of government
President Teburoro Tito, since 1994

Political leaders since 1970
1974–78 Naboua Ratieta (independent), 1978–91 Ieremia T Tabai (independent), 1991–94 Teatao Teannaki (NPP), 1994 Council of State, 1994– Teburoro Tito (MTM)

Political system
Kiribati is an independent republic within the Commonwealth, with a constitution which dates from independence in June 1979. It provides for a president, known as the Beretitenti, and a 41-member single-chamber assembly, the Maneaba ni Maungatabu. The president combines the roles of head of state and head of government, and is elected by universal adult suffrage for a four-year term. After each general election the Maneaba nominates from among its members three or four candidates for president, who then stand in a national contest.

The Maneaba itself comprises 39 popularly elected members, one nominated representative of the inhabitants of the island of Banaba, and, if he is not an elected member, an Attorney General who serves in an *ex officio* capacity. All members serve a four-year term, and the assembly is subject to dissolution during that period.

The president governs with the help of a vice president (Kauoman-ni-Beretitenti) and a cabinet composed of up to eight additional ministers, chosen from and responsible to the Maneaba. At present, the president holds the portfolios of foreign affairs and international trade. A Council of State, composed of the speaker of the Maneaba, the chief justice, and the chairperson of the Public Service Commission, carries out the functions of the president and Maneaba during the period between dissolution and the holding of fresh elections.

Political parties

Traditionally, all candidates for the Maneaba have fought as independents, but in recent years an embryonic party system has emerged. In 1985 an opposition party, the Christian Democratic Party, was formed by Maneaba members opposed to the policy strategy of President Tabai. Led by Teburoro Tito, it is now known as the Maneaban Te Mauri (MTM) party and has been the dominant force in parliament since July 1994. The formerly dominant grouping, the National Progressive Party (NPP), though not constituting a formal political party, had effectively ruled Kiribati since independence.

Latest elections

The most recent Maneaba elections were held on 21–22 and 28–29 July 1994. As usual, contests were fought in multi-member constituencies, with a second run-off ballot among the three leading candidates in constituencies where no candidate obtained the requisite 50% of the votes cast. In this election, 260 candidates contested the 39 elected seats. The NPP's representation fell from 19 to just seven seats, with half of the former cabinet being defeated. The MTM, with 13 seats, emerged as the biggest party and provided all seven of the candidates who secured direct election on the first ballot. Nineteen independents were returned.

The presidential election was held on 30 September 1994 and was contested by four candidates, all from the MTM. The victor, Teburoro Tito, secured 51% of the 21,188 votes cast, 7,000 more than his nearest rival, Tewareka Tentoa, who became vice president.

Political history

Kiribati comprises three groups of 33 low-lying coral atolls plus Banaba, a raised volcanic atoll in the west. The whole group is situated in the southwest Pacific Ocean and scattered over an area of 5 million square kilometres. In the centre, lying on the equator, are the 16 Gilbert Islands; to the east are the eight uninhabited Phoenix Islands; and to the north lie eight of the 11 Line Islands, the remaining three being uninhabited dependencies of the United States. Thirty-three per cent of the population lives on Tarawa Atoll, principally at the port and town of Bairiki, in the Gilbert group.

Kiribati was visited by the Spanish in 1606, before being officially 'discovered' by the British navy during the late 18th century. Designated the Gilbert Islands, in 1892 they were joined with the Ellice Islands, now called Tuvalu, to the south, to form a British protectorate. They became a formal colony in 1916, under the designation Gilbert and Ellice Islands Colony (GEIC). A resident commissioner was based at Tarawa Atoll, although supreme authority rested with the Western Pacific High Commission (WPHC), which had its headquarters in Fiji. The colony was extended to embrace Ocean Island, Christmas Island, or Kiritmati, three of the Line Islands, and the eight Phoenix Islands, then uninhabited, between 1916 and 1937.

The GEIC was invaded and occupied by the Japanese in 1942, during World War II, but, following fierce fighting on Tarawa Atoll, which caused great and lasting damage, they were removed by United States naval forces in 1943 and British control was restored. During the 1960s, as a means of preparing the islands for self-government, a succession of legislative and executive bodies was established, culminating in the creation of a House of Assembly in May 1974. This comprised 28 elected members and three official members. Naboua Ratieta was elected from among these members as the GEIC's first chief minister, and chose a four- to six-member ministerial cabinet.

In October 1975, following a referendum, the Polynesian-peopled Ellice Islands, fearing domination in an independent GEIC from the Micronesian Gilbert Islands majority, broke away to form the separate territory of Tuvalu. This reduced the size of the Gilbert Islands' House of Assembly by eight elected members. During the mid-1970s, a separatist movement also developed among the people of Ocean Island, or Banaba, an atoll which was rich in phosphate resources, producing more than 80% of the country's export earnings and 50% of government tax revenue. Opencast phosphate mining was in the hands of the British Phosphate Commission, who exported the produce to Australia and New Zealand as fertilizer. The mining had, however, adversely affected Banaba's environment, necessitating the resettlement of the local population on Rabi Island, 2,600 kilometres away in the Fiji group. Banaba's leaders, the Rabi Council of Leaders, pressed for large-scale compensation for this damage and opposed the distribution of revenue derived from phosphate mining over the whole Gilbert Islands territory. They, therefore, campaigned for the constitutional separation of the island. They eventually accepted a British government *ex gratia* compensation offer in April 1981, but, during recent years, have continued to campaign for separation.

The Gilbert Islands were granted internal self-government in January 1977 and the number of elective members in the House of Assembly was increased to 36. After the general election of February 1978 the opposition leader, Ieremia Tabai, was chosen as the new chief minister. In July 1979 the islands were finally granted full independence as a republic within the Commonwealth under the designation Kiribati. The House of Assembly was also now renamed the Maneaba ni Maungatabu and Chief Minister Tabai became the country's first president. He was re-elected after parliamentary and presidential elections in March and May 1982. Within seven months of the elections, however, as a result of the Maneaba's rejection of proposals to raise civil servants' salaries, the assembly had to be dissolved and fresh parliamentary and presidential elections were held in January and February 1983. President Tabai was again returned to office.

During 1985 opposition to the Tabai government began to mount when a controversial fishing agreement was negotiated with a Soviet state-owned company, Sovrybflot. The move prompted the formation of the country's first political party, the Christian Democratic Party, by the opposition leader, Dr Harry Tong, and 15 members of the Maneaba. The 12-month fishing agreement, which expired in October 1986, was not, however, renewed, the Soviet company claiming that the fees charged by the government had been too high. Following this, Tabai was elected for a fourth term as president in May 1987.

Having served the maximum mandate permitted by the constitution, Tabai was succeeded as executive president in July 1991 by the former vice president, Teatao Teannaki. Charged by opposition deputies with the misuse of public funds, Teannaki's government was brought down in May 1994 after a vote of no confidence was carried. A three-member Council of State held power pending fresh elections. These parliamentary and presidential elections, which were held in July and September 1994, resulted in victory for candidates of the former opposition, the Maneaban Te Mauri (MTM), ending 15 years of rule by the National Progressive Party (NPP). Teburoro Tito was sworn in as president on 1 October 1994.

Despite the 1985–86 Soviet fishing incident, Kiribati has generally pursued a moderate pro-Western foreign policy. In September 1979 a treaty of friendship was signed with the United States, under which the United States relinquished its claims to the Line and Phoenix Islands, including Canton and Enderbury. This was followed in October 1986 by the signing of a five-year agreement by the South Pacific Forum (SPF), of which body Kiribati is an influential member, to grant American tuna boats the right to fish within the 'exclusive economic zones' of the Forum's member states. In return, America paid Kiribati US$5.7 million in 1992. In the same year a new agreement was signed with South Korea, allowing its fishing vessels to operate within Kiribati waters for an annual fee of US$2 million. A significant factor behind this pro-Western policy approach has been Kiribati's heavy dependency on foreign development aid, particularly since the closure of the Banaba phosphate works in 1979. Nevertheless, the new administration of President Tito has pledged to reduce the country's dependence on foreign aid.

Kiribati is faced with problems of a high rate of population growth (2% per annum), which has led to recent resettlement on outlying atolls, the depletion of its important tuna fish stock as a result of the use of drift nets by Asian fleets, and the threat that rising sea levels brought about by the 'greenhouse effect' could well submerge a country where none of the land is more than 2 metres above sea level.

MARSHALL ISLANDS

Republic of the Marshall Islands (RMI)

Capital: Dalap-Uliga-Darrit Municipality (on Majuro Atoll)

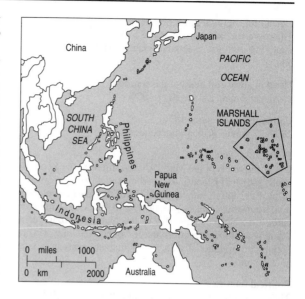

Social and economic data
Area: 180 km^2
Population: 49,000*
Pop. density per km^2: 272*
Urban population: N/A
Literacy rate: 95%*
GDP: $75 million*; per-capita GDP: $1,530*
Government defence spending (% of GDP): 0%**
Currency: US dollar
Economy type: middle income
Labour force in agriculture: N/A

*1992
**The United States is responsible for the Marshall Islands' defence

Ethnic composition
Ninety-seven per cent of the population is Marshallese, of predominantly Micronesian ethnic stock. English (official) and Marshallese are spoken.

Religions
The main religion is Christianity, including Roman Catholicism and various Protestant churches, notably the Assembly of God, Jehovah's Witnesses, Seventh-Day Adventists, and the Church of Jesus Christ of Latter-Day Saints.

Political features
State type: liberal democratic
Date of state formation: 1990
Political structure: unitary
Executive: limited presidential*
Assembly: one-chamber
Party structure: two-party**
Human rights rating: N/A
International affiliations: AsDB, ESCAP, IBRD, IMF, SPC, SPEC, SPF, UN

*but with parliamentary features
**although only one formal party exists

Local and regional government

There is a rudimentary system of local government on each inhabited atoll, with elected magistrates and municipal councils.

Head of state and head of government

President Amata Kabua, since 1979

Political leaders since 1970

1979–   Amata Kabua (independent)

Political system

Under the terms of the May 1979 constitution, the Republic of the Marshall Islands has a parliamentary form of government. Legislative authority rests with the 33-member Nitijela, from whose ranks a president, who heads an 11-member cabinet, is elected. The term of the Nitijela is four years. There is a 12-member consultative Council of Chiefs (Iroij), comprising traditional leaders, for matters relating to land and custom.

Political parties

There is no organized party system, but in June 1991 the Ralik Ratak Democratic Party (RRDP) was founded by Tony DeBrum, a former foreign minister and protégé of President Kabua, to oppose the group which Kabua led.

Latest elections

The most recent Nitijela elections were held in November 1995, producing a pro-Kabua legislature which re-elected him, for the fourth time, as president.

Political history

The Marshall Islands comprise two parallel groups of island chains, the Ratak (Sunrise) and Ralik (Sunset), comprising 34 atolls and 870 reefs in the west Pacific Ocean region of northeast Micronesia, 3,200 kilometres southwest of Hawaii and 2,100 kilometres southeast of Guam. Thirty-seven per cent of the population lives on Majuro Atoll.

The islands were visited by the Spanish navigator Miguel de Saavedra in 1529 and remained under Spanish influence until being annexed and colonized by Germany in 1885. At the start of World War I, in 1914, the Japanese occupied the islands, afterwards administering them under the terms of a League of Nation mandate between 1920 and 1944, when they were removed by US forces.

After the war the islands were placed under United States administration as part of the United Nations (UN) Trust Territory of the Pacific Islands. Part of the area was used for testing US atomic and hydrogen bombs, necessitating abandonment of Bikini and Enewetak atolls, while a large missile range was built at Kwajalein. In moves towards autonomy set in train by the US Carter administration, the Marshall Islands District adopted its own constitution in May 1979 and in October 1982 a 'Compact of Free Association' was signed by the United States. Under the terms of this Compact, the islands secured full independence, but the United States remained responsible for their defence and was allowed to retain its military bases for at least 15 years. In return, it pledged to provide annual aid of $30 million. It was also required to set up a $150-million trust fund to compensate for claims made against the US government in connec-

tion with contamination caused by the nuclear tests of the 1940s and 1950s. There was also a 'rent' payment for land still used for missile tracking.

The Compact was approved in a plebiscite on the islands in September 1983 and, following endorsement by the UN Trusteeship Council, came into effect in October 1986. The UN trusteeship was terminated in December 1990 and the islands became a full member of the United Nations on 17 September 1991. Amata Kabua, who became president in 1979, was re-elected in 1983, 1987, 1991 and 1995. He has sought to promote the development of tourism, on Majuro, and a tuna-fishing industry in an economy which is heavily dependent on US aid. In February 1994 a US court ruled that Amata Kabua had legal title to the position of paramount chief of the Marshall Islands, a post that had been claimed by his uncle, Kabua Kabua.

MICRONESIA, THE FEDERATED STATES OF (FSM)

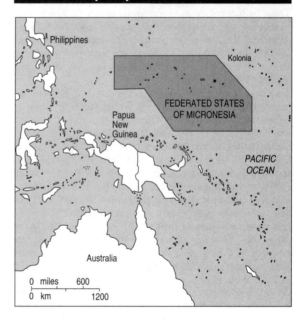

Capital: Kolonia (on Pohnpei)

Social and economic data

Area: 700 km²
Population: 102,000*
Pop. density per km²: 146*
Urban population: N/A
Literacy rate: 95%*
GDP: $160 million*; per-capita GDP: $1,570*
Government defence spending (% of GDP): 0%**
Currency: US dollar
Economy type: middle income
Labour force in agriculture: N/A

*1992
**The United States is responsible for the FSM's defence.

Ethnic composition

The main ethnic groups are Trukese (41%) and Pohnpeian (26%), both Micronesian. English is the official language.

Religions

The main religion is Christianity, predominantly Roman Catholicism, but with Protestant churches also represented, including the Assembly of God, Jehovah's Witnesses, and Seventh-Day Adventists.

Political features

State type: liberal democratic
Date of state formation: 1986
Political structure: federal
Executive: limited presidential*
Assembly: one-chamber
Party structure: none
Human rights rating: N/A
International affiliations: AsDB, ESCAP, IBRD, IMF, SPC, SPEC, SPF, UN

*but with parliamentary features

Local and regional government

Below the state legislatures there are elected magistrates and municipal councils.

Head of state and head of government

President Bailey Olter, since 1991

Political leaders since 1970

1987–91 John Haglegam (independent), 1991– Bailey Olter (independent)

Political system

Under the terms of the May 1979 constitution, each of the constituent states of the FSM has its own assembly, elected for a four-year term, governor, and constitution. In Chuuk the legislature is bicameral, comprising a ten-member Senate and 28-member House of Representatives, while in Kosrae, Pohnpei, and Yap the legislatures are unicameral, comprising 14 members, 27 members, and 10 members respectively. Four of the representatives of the Yap assembly are elected from its outer islands of Ulithi and Woleal. There is also a federal assembly, termed the National Congress of the FSM. This contains 14 members, termed senators. Each state elects one 'Senator at Large' to serve a four-year term, while the remaining ten members serve two-year terms and are elected from constituencies designed to reflect the relative populations of the states. An executive president and vice president are elected by the Congress after each general election from among the four 'Senators at Large' on a rotational basis, with by-elections being held to fill the places vacated. The president works with a cabinet of around five members.

Political parties

There are no organized political parties.

Latest elections

The most recent elections to the Congress of the FSM were held in March 1995, with Bailey Olter, the former vice president, being unanimously re-elected president by the chamber in May 1995. His predecessor, John Haglegam, failed to secure re-election as a 'Senator at Large' in the May 1991 general election.

Political history

The FSM comprises four states, Yap, Chuuk (formerly Truk), Pohnpei (formerly Ponape), and Kosrae, which form, together with Belau, the archipelago of the Caroline Islands, situated in south-central Micronesia in the west Pacific Ocean, 800 kilometres east of the Philippines. There are more than 600 islands in the archipelago, 40 of which are of some size and inhabited. Fifty per cent of the population lives in Chuuk state, 31% in Pohnpei, 12% in Yap, and 7% in Kosrae.

The islands have a similar history to the Marshall Islands, although they did not come under German control until 1898, when they were purchased, under the designation of the Caroline Islands, from Spain. After World War II they were placed, by the United Nations, under United States administration and, until 1979, were governed by a local administrator appointed by the US president. In May 1979, however, a constitution was adopted, establishing the 'Federated States of Micronesia'. In October 1982, a 'Compact of Free Association' was signed with the United States, under which the FSM became independent, though the United States remained responsible for their defence and security. This Compact was approved in a plebiscite held in June 1983 and came into effect in October 1986, following its endorsement by the United Nations Trusteeship Council. This established the FSM as a 'sovereign, self-governing state'. In December 1990 the Trust status was terminated and in September 1991 the FSM became a full member of the United Nations. Currently, nearly nine-tenths of FSM budget outlays are funded from US economic aid, but attempts are being made to develop tourism and tuna processing. The economic and defence provisions of the November 1986 Compact with the United States are renewable after 15 years.

NAURU

Republic of Nauru

Capital: Yaren*

**de facto*, although there is no official capital

Social and economic data

Area: 21 km^2
Population: 10,000*
Pop. density per km^2: 476*
Urban population: N/A
Literacy rate: 99%*
GDP: $90 million*; per-capita GDP: $9,000*
Government defence spending (% of GDP): 0%**
Currency: Australian dollar
Economy type: high income
Labour force in agriculture: N/A

*1992

**Nauru has no armed forces, Australia being responsible for the country's defence

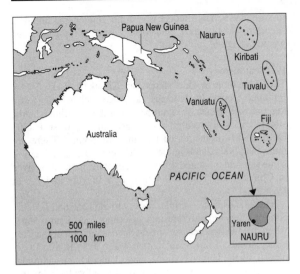

Ethnic composition

Fifty-eight per cent of the population are indigenous Nauruans of mixed Polynesian, Micronesian, and Melanesian descent, 26% are Tuvaluans/Kiribatians, 8% are Chinese, and 8% are a mixture of Australians and New Zealanders. Nauruan is the national language, with English also being widely understood.

Religions

Fifty-eight per cent of the population are Protestants, belonging to the Nauruan Protestant Church, 24% Roman Catholics, and 8% (the Chinese community) Confucians and Taoists.

Political features

State type: liberal democratic
Date of state formation: 1968
Political structure: unitary
Executive: limited presidential*
Assembly: one-chamber
Party structure: none
Human rights rating: N/A
International affiliations: CW (special status), ESCAP**, ICAO**, ITU**, SPC, SPEC, SPF, UPU**, WHO**

*but with parliamentary features
**UN bodies to which Nauru belongs, although it is not formally a member of the UN

Local and regional government

The country is divided into 14 districts which are grouped, for electoral purposes, into eight divisions. Elected local councils function at the district level.

Head of state and head of government

President Lagumot Harris, since 1995

Political leaders since 1970

1968–76 Hammer DeRoburt (independent), 1976–78 Bernard Dowiyogo (NP), 1978 Hammer DeRoburt (independent), 1978 Lagumot Harris (NP), 1978–86 Hammer DeRoburt (independent), 1986 Kennan Adeang (independent), 1986 Hammer DeRoburt (independent), 1986 Kennan Adeang (independent), 1987–89 Hammer DeRoburt (independent), 1989 Kenas Aroi (independent), 1989–95 Bernard Dowiyogo (independent) 1995– Lagumot Harris (independent)

Political system

The constitution dates from independence in January 1968. It provides for a single-chamber Parliament of 18 members, elected by universal adult suffrage for a three-year term, and a president who is both head of state and head of government. Voting in parliamentary elections is compulsory for those over 20 years of age. The president and cabinet are elected by Parliament, from among its members, and are responsible to it. Although the president has broad powers, Parliament is, nevertheless, empowered to pass bills without his or her formal assent. The size of the country allows for a very intimate style of government, with the president, combining several portfolios, including external affairs and island development and industry, in a cabinet of only six.

Political parties

Traditionally, members of Parliament have been elected as independents, but have grouped themselves into majority and minority pro- and anti-government factions. In February 1987, however, a formal political party, the Democratic Party of Nauru (DPN), was formed by the opposition leader, Kennan Adeang. It is a loose grouping, comprising around eight parliamentary members. The party declares its principal aim to be the curtailment of presidential powers and the promotion of democracy. It is effectively a successor to the Nauru Party (NP), which, formed by Lagumot Harris and Bernard Dowiyogo in December 1976, no longer functions.

Latest elections

The most recent parliamentary elections were held November 1995. All members were elected as independents. Parliament elected Lagumot Harris as president. A record 67 candidates contested.

Political history

Nauru is a small isolated island, composed of phosphatic rock, in the west central Pacific Ocean, lying 42 kilometres south of the equator and 4,000 kilometres northeast of Sydney, Australia. The population lives in small, scattered, coastal settlements. There is no urban centre as such and the island, being low-lying, is in danger of being submerged if the 'greenhouse effect' results in a substantial rise in the sea level.

The island was discovered in 1798 by the British whaler, Captain John Fearn, and was called 'Pleasant Island'. Between the 1830s and 1880s it became a haven for white runaway convicts and deserters, before being placed under German rule in 1888, when the western Pacific was partitioned into British and German 'zones of influence'. The Germans discovered and intensively exploited the island's high grade phosphate reserves. After Germany's defeat in World War I, however, Nauru was placed under a joint British, Australian, and New Zealand mandate by the League of Nations, and was then administered on the other trustees' behalf by Australia.

During World War II, Nauru was invaded and occupied by the Japanese between 1942 and 1945 and was devastated. Two-thirds of the population were deported to Chuuk (Truk) Atoll, 1,600 kilometres to the northwest, situated today in the Federated States of Micronesia, and all the mining facilities were destroyed. It was reoccupied by Australian forces in 1945 and the Nauruans were repatriated from Chuuk. After the war Nauru was designated a United Nations (UN) Trust Territory, subject to the continuing administration of the former mandatory powers. As part of a process of preparation for self-government, and in response to local community pressure, a local governing council was established in 1951 and an elected assembly in January 1966. Two years later, in January 1968, full independence was achieved. Nauru became a republic and was designated a 'special member' of the Commonwealth, which meant that, because of its small size, it did not have direct representation at meetings of heads of government.

Hammer DeRoburt (1923–92), who had held the position of head chief of Nauru since 1956, was elected the country's first president in May 1968 and was re-elected in May 1971 and December 1973. Criticisms of his personal style of government led to his replacement in December 1976 by Bernard Dowiyogo, leader of the Nauru Party grouping. However, mounting assembly opposition to Dowiyogo by DeRoburt supporters forced his resignation in April 1978 and the recall of DeRoburt. President DeRoburt was duly re-elected in December 1978, December 1980, and in May and December 1983. Parliamentary opposition to the government's annual budget forced DeRoburt's resignation in September 1986 and his replacement as president by the opposition leader, Kennan Adeang. Within a fortnight, however, following a successful 'no-confidence' motion, Adeang was ousted. DeRobert returned as President, but briefly lost power again to Adeang following the general election of December 1986. Fresh elections in January 1987 gave DeRoburt an effective majority and prompted the defeated Adeang to form the Democratic Party of Nauru as a formal opposition grouping.

In 1989 a vote of no confidence forced DeRoburt's resignation. He was initially replaced by Kenas Aroi, a former finance minister. However, Aroi soon resigned because of ill health and, after the general election of December 1989, Parliament elected Bernard Dowiyogo as the new president by ten votes to DeRoburt's six. This was DeRoburt's final challenge for the presidency. He died in July 1992 and was given a state funeral. Dowiyogo was re-elected president in November 1992, defeating his challenger, Buraro Detudamo, by ten votes to seven. He was replaced as premier by Lagumot Harris in November 1995.

Nauru achieved economic independence in 1970 when the company called the British Phosphate Commissioners, which had been in charge of the phosphate industry during the period of Australian rule, was nationalized and renamed the Nauru Phosphate Corporation. However, with the island's phosphate reserves set to run out between 1995 and 2010, recent attempts have been made to reinvest the substantial profits, which hitherto enabled the people to enjoy a high standard of living and welfare provision, in new shipping, aviation, and offshore banking ventures. In addition, in August 1993 the Australian government agreed to pay Nauru US$73 million in compensation for damage inflicted by phosphate mining during the pre-independence period which has left 80% of Nauru agriculturally barren.

In its external relations, Nauru has sought to pursue an independent course, remaining outside the United Nations, although links with Australia, Britain, and New Zealand remain close. It is a member of the South Pacific Forum (SPF), which has negotiated fisheries management treaties with Western and Southeast Asian nations with the aim of reducing excessive exploitation of tuna stocks and securing large foreign currency payments for fishing licences.

NEW ZEALAND

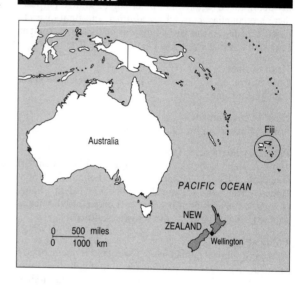

Capital: Wellington

Social and economic data
Area: 267,844 km^2
Population: 3,500,000*
Pop. density per km^2: 13*
Urban population: 84%**
Literacy rate: 99%**
GDP: $41,000 million**; per-capita GDP: $12,060**
Government defence spending (% of GDP): 1.5%**
Currency: New Zealand dollar
Economy type: high income
Labour force in agriculture: 10%**

*1994
**1992

Ethnic composition
About 87% of the population is of European origin, mostly British, about 9% Maori, and about 2% Pacific Islander. English is the official language and Maori is also spoken.

Religions
There are about 895,000 Anglicans, 495,000 Roman Catholics, 170,000 members of other Christian denominations, and 30,000 Maoris.

Political features

State type: liberal democratic
Date of state formation: 1853/1947
Political structure: unitary
Executive: parliamentary
Assembly: one-chamber
Party structure: multiparty
Human rights rating: 98%
International affiliations: ANZUS (membership suspended), APEC, CP, CW, IAEA, IBRD, IMF, IWC, NAM (guest), OECD, SPC, SPF, UN, WTO

Local and regional government

For planning and civil defence purposes, the country is divided into 22 regions. For other administrative purposes there are counties, boroughs, and urban and rural districts, based broadly on the British system of local government. Each unit has an elected council.

Head of state

Queen Elizabeth II, represented by Governor General Dame Cath Tizzard since 1990

Head of government

Prime Minister Jim Bolger, since 1990

Political leaders since 1970

1969–72 Keith Holyoake (National), 1972–74 Norman Kirk (Labour), 1974–75 Wallace Rowling (Labour), 1975–84 Robert Muldoon (National), 1984–89 David Lange (Labour), 1989–90 Geoffrey Palmer (Labour), 1990 Michael Moore (Labour) 1990–   Jim Bolger (National)

Political system

As a constitutional monarchy, New Zealand's system of government displays many features found in that of the United Kingdom, including the absence of a written constitution. As in Britain, the constitution is the progressive product of legislation, much of it passed by the Parliament in London. The governor general represents the British monarch as formal head of state and appoints the prime minister who chooses a cabinet, all of whom are drawn from and collectively responsible to the single-chamber assembly, the House of Representatives. This has 99 members, including four Maoris, elected by universal adult suffrage from single-member constituencies by a simple plurality voting system. It has a maximum life of three years and is subject to dissolution within that period.

In November 1993 it was agreed, following a national referendum, that from 1996 the size of the House would be increased to 120 and voting would be by the semi-proportional representation additional member system, half the members being directly elected and half drawn from party lists.

Political parties

Of some six active political parties, two have dominated the political scene for most of the time since New Zealand has been an independent state. They are the Labour Party and the New Zealand National Party, but in recent years there has been a significant realignment and three other parties have been formed in an effort to break the two-party system. They are the Alliance Party, the New Zealand First Party (NZFP), and the United New Zealand Party (UNZ).

The Labour Party was formed in 1916. It has a moderate left-of-centre orientation and advocates democratic socialist policies. It is led by Helen Clark.

The New Zealand National Party was founded in 1936 as an anti-Labour party during the period of economic depression. It has a centre-right free-enterprise orientation.

The Alliance Party is an alliance of five left-of-centre parties formed in 1993 by the former Labour Party president, Jim Anderton. It is led now by Sandra Lee.

The NZFP was also formed in 1993 by Winston Peters, a former member of Jim Bolger's cabinet. It has a centrist orientation.

The UNZ was formed in 1995 as a centrist breakaway from the Labour Party and National Party.

Latest elections

The results of the 1993 general election were as follows:

	% votes	Seats
National Party	35.2	50
Labour Party	34.7	45
Alliance Party	18.7	2
NZFP	9.0	2
Others	2.4	0

Political history

New Zealand was a dependency of the colony of New South Wales, Australia, until 1841, when it became a separate British colony. It was made a Dominion in the British Empire in 1907 and then granted full independence by the Statute of Westminster of 1931. Independence was formally accepted by the New Zealand parliament in 1947.

It has been in the forefront of democratic government, being, for example, the first country in the world to give women the right to vote, in 1893. It also has a record of great political stability, with the centrist New Zealand National Party holding office from the 1930s until it was eventually replaced by a Labour Party administration, led by Norman Kirk (1923–74), in 1972. During this period of stability, New Zealand built up a social security system which became the envy of the world.

The economy was thriving at the time Kirk took office but there were clouds on the horizon, including the danger of growing inflation. This was aggravated by the 1973–74 energy crisis which resulted in a balance of payments deficit. Meanwhile, the Labour government was following a more independent foreign policy line, to some extent influenced by Britain's decision to join the European Community, with its possible effects on New Zealand's future exports. It began a phased withdrawal from some of the country's military commitments in Southeast Asia and established diplomatic relations with China. Norman Kirk died in August 1974 and was succeeded by the finance minister, Wallace Rowling (b. 1927).

The state of the economy worsened and in the 1975 general election the National Party, led by Robert Muldoon

(1921–92), was returned to power with a clear working majority. However, the economy failed to revive and in the 1978 general election Muldoon's majority was greatly reduced. In 1984 he introduced controversial labour legislation which was widely opposed by the trade unions. To renew his mandate, he called an early election and was swept out of office by the Labour Party, now led by David Lange (b. 1942).

The Labour Party had fought the election on a non-nuclear defence policy, which Lange immediately put into effect, forbidding any vessels carrying nuclear weapons or powered by nuclear energy to enter New Zealand's ports. This put a great strain on relations with the United States. In 1985 the trawler *Rainbow Warrior*, the flagship of the environmentalist pressure group Greenpeace which was monitoring nuclear tests in French Polynesia, was mined, with loss of life, by French secret service agents in Auckland harbour. The French Prime Minister eventually admitted responsibility and New Zealand subsequently demanded compensation.

In 1984 Sir Robert Muldoon, as he now was, was defeated in elections for the leadership of the National Party by James McLay but he, in turn, was replaced in 1986 by Jim Bolger (b. 1935). Sir Robert died in 1992, at the age of 70. In August 1987 Lange was re-elected with a majority of 17 but his 'free-enterprise' economic policies created tensions within the Labour Party, resulting in the creation of a small breakaway party, the New Labour Party (NLP), in 1989. In the same year Lange resigned and was replaced by his deputy, Geoffrey Palmer (b. 1942). The National Party won a decisive victory in the 1990 general election and its leader, Jim Bolger, became prime minister.

During 1993, in anticipation of the next general election, there were substantial party realignments, the New Zealand First Party (NZFP) being formed by dissident National Party members and the Alliance Party founded on the basis of the coming together of left-of-centre politicians disenchanted with the Labour Party.

Although Bolger's hard-nosed economic policies had proved unpopular, the National Party won a narrow victory in the November 1993 general election and Bolger continued in office. Voters also approved, in a national referendum, a change in the future from the first-past-the-post to an additional member system (AMS) form of proportional representation, on the German model. In September 1994 one of Prime Minister Bolger's junior ministers, Ross Meurant, resigned to form a new Right of Centre Party (ROC), initially threatening the government's position. Eventually Bolger managed to continue by entering a working relationship with the ROC.

During 1995 there were further party changes, Jim Anderton resigning the leadership of the five-party Alliance and a new Labour Party breakaway grouping being formed, the United New Zealand Party (UNZ).

New Zealand's relations with France, which had been soured by the sinking of the *Rainbow Warrior* in 1985, deteriorated further in 1995 when the French government announced its intention to resume nuclear tests in the Pacific. The New Zealand government said it would test the legality of the French decision in the international courts.

PAPUA NEW GUINEA

The Independent State of Papua New Guinea

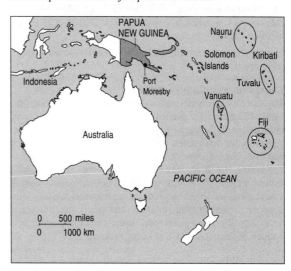

Capital: Port Moresby

Social and economic data
Area: 462,840 km²
Population: 4,100,000*
Pop. density per km²: 9*
Urban population: 16%**
Literacy rate: 52%**
GDP: $3,800 million**; per-capita GDP: $975**
Government defence spending (% of GDP): 1.7%**
Currency: kina
Economy type: low income
Labour force in agriculture: 66%**

*1994
**1992

Ethnic composition
The population is mainly Melanesian, particularly in the coastal areas. Further inland, on New Guinea and on the larger islands, Papuans predominate. On the outer archipelagos and islands mixed Micronesian-Melanesians are to be found. A small Chinese minority, numbering 3,000, also exists. The official language is pidgin English, but about 750 indigenous languages are spoken locally among what is an intensely regionalized population.

Religions
More than half the population is nominally Christian, of whom 60% are Roman Catholic and 40% belong to the Evangelical Lutheran Church. The rest mainly follow traditional magico-ritual pantheistic beliefs and practices.

Political features
State type: liberal democratic
Date of state formation: 1975
Political structure: unitary*
Executive: parliamentary

Assembly: one-chamber
Party structure: multiparty
Human rights rating: 70%
International affiliations: ACP, AsDB, APEC, ASEAN
(observer), CW, CP, ESCAP, INRD, IMF, NAM, SG, SPC,
SPEC, SPF, UN

*although considerable authority has been devolved to the
provinces

Local and regional government
The country is divided into 19 provinces, plus a National
Capital District. As part of a decentralization programme
launched in 1978, directly elected provincial assemblies and
governments have been established in the provinces and
National Capital District and enjoy a substantial measure of
autonomy. However, legislation was passed controversially
in June 1995 to abolish the provincial government system. It
established, instead, non-elected provincial bodies composed of national parliamentarians and local councillors, and
headed by appointed governors. Within the provinces there is
a range of district, town, and village councils.

Head of state
Queen Elizabeth II, represented by Governor General Wiwa
Korowi since 1991

Head of government
Prime Minister Sir Julius Chan, since 1994

Political leaders since 1970
1972–80 Michael Somare (PP), 1980–82 Sir Julius Chan
(PPP), 1982–85 Michael Somare (PP), 1985–88 Paias
Wingti (PDM), 1988–92 Rabbie Namaliu (PP), 1992–94
Paias Wingti (PDM), 1994–   Sir Julius Chan (PPP)

Political system
Papua New Guinea is a constitutional monarchy within the
Commonwealth with the British Crown represented by a resident governor general as formal head of state. The constitution dates from independence in September 1975 and
provides for a parliamentary system of government, broadly
based on the Westminster model. There is a single-chamber
assembly, the National Parliament, which consists of 109
members elected by universal adult suffrage for a five-year
term through a simple plurality voting system. Eighty-nine
members represent 'open', or local, single-member constituencies, 20 provincial constituencies, and there is provision in the constitution, though, as yet, unfulfilled, for a
further three members to be nominated and appointed on a
two-thirds majority vote of parliament. Each elector has two
votes, one of which is cast for the local and one for the
provincial seat. The National Parliament is subject to dissolution within its term.

The governor general formally appoints a prime minister
and National Executive Council (NEC), or cabinet, whose 28
members, the maximum number permitted under the constitution, are drawn from and responsible to the National Parliament. The government needs parliament's approval for its
legislative proposals and may be removed by a vote of no
confidence, without fresh elections necessarily being
required. Under the terms of a recently adopted convention,

a no-confidence vote may not be called until at least 18
months after a government's formation. Currently, the prime
minister is also minister for foreign affairs and trade.

The governor general, who must be a 'mature' and
'respected' citizen of Papua New Guinea, is appointed by the
British monarch on the recommendation of the prime minister. He or she serves a six-year term and is elegible for reap-
pointment once only, requiring a two-thirds parliamentary
majority to secure a second term. The principal role of governor general, as a result of the shifting coalition character of
politics in faction-ridden Papua New Guinea, is as 'govern-
ment-maker'. To amend the constitution, a two-thirds majority of the National Parliament members is required twice in
succession, within a period of six weeks.

Political parties
Political parties in Papua New Guinea are weak organizations, dominated by personalities, patronage and regional
differences. They lack the formal policy-making and membership structures of the West European kind. Their assembly members are frequently persuaded to 'cross the floor' and
temporarily join other groupings in the National Parliament.
Ideological differences between them are limited.

Of the ten parties which currently function the most
important six, in terms of parliamentary representation, are
the Papua New Guinea Party (Pangu Pati: PP), the People's
Democratic Movement (PDM), the National Party (NP), the
Melanesian Alliance (MA), the People's Action Party (PAP),
and the People's Progress Party (PPP).

The PP, currently led by the deputy prime minister, Chris
Haiveta, is the country's oldest and most influential party,
having been founded in June 1967 to campaign for internal
self-government and eventual independence and for the
adoption of pidgin as the official language. It has a strong
urban base in north New Guinea and the coast, and is the best
organized party in the country, with more than 75 local
branches. Its former leader, Michael Somare (b. 1936), governed the country for eight of the first ten years after independence. However, the formation of the PDM in 1985, by
15 of its former parliamentary representatives, including
Paias Wingti (b. 1951), undermined the PP, siphoning away
crucial support. Despite this, under the leadership of Rabbie
Namaliu, it succeeded in returning to power as the governing
party between 1988 and 1992.

The NP is a highlands-based party. It was formed in May
1978, under the designation the People's United Front (PUF),
by Iambakey Okuk, a former member of the once influential
United Party (UP). The UP was formed in 1969 initially to
oppose independence and has fought since for maintaining
close links with Australia. The NP is a generally conservative
grouping and, following the death of Sir Iambakey Okuk in
November 1986, has been led by Michael Mel.

The MA had its origins in a secessionist movement which,
in September 1975, declared the ethnically distinct, eastern,
copper-producing island of Bougainville the 'Independent
Republic of the North Solomons'. A year later this movement, after securing the granting of greater autonomy for the
region, accepted the island's position within Papua New
Guinea. It subsequently transformed itself into a political
party, originally called the Bougainville Pressure Group, and

contested seats in the 1977 general election. It later adopted the designation Alliance for Progress and Regional Development (APRD), but is commonly known as the MA. Led since its inception by Father John Momis, the party is regarded as a left-of-centre socialist body, demanding 'liberation from foreign domination' and favouring greater local participation in economic decision-taking. The MA draws the bulk of its support from Bougainville dock and copper industry workers and white-collar professionals.

The PAP was formed to fight the 1987 election. It is led by Akoka Doi.

The PPP is a much older party, dating back to 1970. A conservative non-highlands based grouping, it has long been led by Sir Julius Chan, the current prime minister. The party enjoys strong support in the islands north of New Guinea – New Ireland, New Britain, and the North Solomons.

In May 1995 a new political party, the Movement for Greater Autonomy, was founded by the premiers of several northern provinces who opposed the government's plans to abolish the provincial government system.

Latest elections

In the most recent National Parliament elections, held between 13–27 June 1992, the results were as follows:

Party	Seats
Pangu Pati (PP)	22
People's Democratic Movement (PDM)	15
People's Action Party (PAP)	13
People's Progress Party (PPP)	10
Melanesian Alliance (MA)	9
League for National Advancement (LNA)	5
National Party (NP)	2
Melanesian United Front	1
Independents	31

Many of the 'independents' were expected to later align with one of the established parties. The election in one constituency was postponed because of the death of a candidate.

As usual, because of the remoteness and ruggedness of much of the country, the election process extended over two weeks. In addition, illiterate voters were allowed to cast 'whispering votes', quietly intimating their choices in the ear of the presiding election officer who then proceeded to mark the ballot paper accordingly. The election campaign was dominated by allegations of government corruption and a record 59 incumbents lost their seats, including 15 ministers. At the opening session of the new parliament on 17 July 1992, Paias Wingti narrowly defeated Rabbie Namaliu for the premiership and, on 30 August 1994, following Wingti's forced resignation, Sir Julius Chan was elected the new prime minister.

Political history

Papua New Guinea is an extensive island grouping in the southwest Pacific Ocean, 160 kilometres northeast of Australia. It comprises the eastern half of the large island of New Guinea; the volcanic Bismarck (Mussau, New Britain, New Hanover, and New Ireland) and Louisiade archipelagos; the Trobriand and D'Entrecasteaux Islands; and an assortment of smaller groups. The country shares a 777-kilometre-long border with Indonesia (Irian Jaya) to the west and is skirted by the Solomon Islands in the east.

New Guinea had been inhabited by indigenous Melanesians for more than 9,000 years before it was first visited by a European, the Portuguese navigator Jorge de Menezes, in 1526. Dutch merchants later made regular trips to the island during the 17th century, before the Dutch East India Company established control over the western portion of the island, incorporating it into the Netherlands East Indies in 1828. More than half a century later, under the terms of the Anglo-Dutch Agreement of 1885, Britain took possession of the southern portion of New Guinea and adjacent islands, while Germany assumed control of the northeast, which included New Britain, New Ireland, and Bougainville.

In 1901 Britain transferred its rights to Australia, which proceeded to rename the territories Papua in 1906. Then, in 1914, during World War I, Australia invaded and established control over German New Guinea. From the merged territories, Papua New Guinea was formed. It was designated, first, a Mandate Territory by the League of Nations between 1921 and 1946 and then, from 1947, a Trust Territory by the United Nations (UN), and placed under Australian guardianship. The two territories were administered jointly by Australia, but formally retained their separate status.

During World War II, parts of Papua New Guinea were invaded and occupied by the Japanese between 1942 and 1945. The territory was reunited, however, after the war and Australia, under the terms of its UN agreement, began to prepare it for self-government. In November 1951 a Legislative Council was established and then, in June 1964, an elected House of Assembly. The state was formally named Papua New Guinea in July 1971 and secured internal self-government in December 1973. Finally, in September 1975, full independence within the Commonwealth was achieved, with the House of Assembly redesignated the National Parliament.

The first prime minister after independence was Michael Somare, leader of the nationalist Pangu Pati (PP). He had been chief minister in the interim government since 1972. Despite allegations of governmental inefficiency and discrimination against the Highland provinces, Somare remained in office until 1980. At first he headed a PP and People's Progress Party (PPP) coalition and then, from October 1978, a PP and United Party (UP) alliance. However, Somare, following a corruption scandal, was eventually defeated on a confidence vote in the National Parliament in March 1980 and a new government was formed by the PPP leader and former deputy prime minister, Sir Julius Chan.

In the general election of June 1982 the PP won 47 National Parliament seats, compared with 39 in 1977, and the UP 10, compared with 38, enabling Somare to return to power the following August, leading a coalition with the UP and nine independents. In March 1985, however, the deputy prime minister, Paias Wingti, resigned from the PP and, forming a tactical alliance with PPP leader Chan, proceeded to challenge Somare for the premiership. Somare quickly responded by forming a new coalition with the National Party (NP) and Melanesian Alliance (MA) and successfully fought off, by 68 votes to 19, a no-confidence challenge in parliament. Fourteen dissident members, who had been expelled from the PP by Somare, immediately set up a new opposition party, the People's Democratic Movement (PDM), under the leadership of Wingti.

Later, in August 1985, Iambakey Okuk's NP departed from the government coalition. This, coupled with mounting opposition to Somare's tax-raising budget strategy, fatally weakened the government and in November 1985 Somare was eventually defeated by 58 votes to 51 in a no-confidence motion. Wingti took over as prime minister, at the head of a five-party coalition comprising the PDM, PPP, NP, UP, and MA, with Chan as deputy prime minister, and set about instituting a new programme of public spending economies as a means of tackling the economic crisis. At the general election of June–July 1987 Wingti's PDM secured 18 seats, losing two, and formed the core of a new coalition government which incorporated the People's Action Party (PAP), whose leader, Ted Diro, was brought into the cabinet as 'minister without portfolio'. In November 1987, however, following charges of misappropriation of election funds, Diro was forced to resign.

Faced with a no-confidence motion in April 1988, Wingti, requiring the PAP's support, brought Diro back into the National Executive Council. This controversial move created a constitutional crisis, precipitating shifts in coalition alliances. Three months later, in July 1988, Wingti was defeated, by 58 votes to 50, on a no-confidence motion. He was replaced as prime minister by the former foreign minister Rabbie Namaliu, who had been elected leader of the PP in succession to Michael Somare in May 1988. Namaliu established a new six-party coalition government which comprised the PP, MA, PAP, Papua Party, NP, and the recently formed League for National Advancement (LNA), with Michael Somare serving as foreign minister.

The new government was faced by a deteriorating internal law and order situation. In Port Moresby soldiers rioted in February 1989 over inadequate pay increases and in June 1989 a state of emergency had to be imposed on Bougainville island because of the growing strength of the Bougainville Revolutionary Army (BRA) separatist movement, which, led by Francis Ona, had forced the closure of the island's important Panguna copper mine a month earlier. This mine had provided 20% of the government's revenue and 44% of export earnings. In March 1990 government forces were evacuated from the island under a cease-fire agreement after the conflict had escalated, claiming several hundred lives. An economic blockade was then imposed on BRA-controlled Bougainville, prompting Ona to make a unilateral declaration of independence. This embargo was lifted after the Honiara Accord was signed in January 1991 by the BRA and Namaliu government, but was soon reimposed when the agreement broke down. Refusing to countenance the grant of independence, a military solution was sought to the conflict.

In the 1992 general election support for the PP declined and the largest gains were made by the PAP and the PPP. Following this result the National Parliament narrowly restored Wingti as prime minister, leading a PDM, PPP, and a League for National Advancement (LNA) coalition. The new administration instituted a drive against political corruption and crime, which had both increased during recent years, introduced a conservative new internal security law, and proposed significant reform of the regional and local government structure. However, in August 1994 Wingti was replaced as prime minister by Sir Julius Chan (PPP), formerly deputy prime minister and foreign minister. This followed a Supreme Court ruling that a snap re-election in September 1993, contrived by Wingti in order to prolong the government's period of immunity from a vote of no confidence for a further 18 months, was invalid. Chan's government swiftly negotiated a cease-fire in the six-year secessionist guerrilla war on Bougainville. The terms of the agreement included the holding of peace talks with the BRA, a lifting of the blockade on the island, and the deployment of a multinational peacekeeping force. However, the guerrilla war resumed after a breakdown in the peace talks. A decision in June 1995 to abolish the system of provincial government led to a split in the cabinet and the dismissal of five dissenting ministers.

In its external relations, despite continuing border demarcation disputes, Papua New Guinea has maintained close diplomatic ties with Australia since independence, receiving, in return, substantial economic aid. The country, as a result of its relative size, has also been able to establish itself as the leader of the group of small island states in the South Pacific which have achieved independence during recent decades. It is a founder member of the South Pacific Forum (SPF) and, together with Vanuatu and the Solomon Islands, a leader of the 'Spearhead Group' (SG), which was set up in March 1988 with the aim of perserving Melanesian cultural traditions and securing independence for the French Overseas Territory of New Caledonia. Relations with Papua New Guinea's western neighbour, Indonesia, have traditionally been strained as a result of the latter's maltreatment of Melanesians in Irian Jaya, the western part of New Guinea. In 1963 Indonesia foiled an independence bid by Irian Jaya and, in more recent years, has been involved in fighting guerrillas of the Free Papua Movement (OPM) and with importing Javanese settlers into the territory, the so-called 'transmigration programme'. These actions have prompted the flight of more than 10,000 Melanesian refugees into Papua New Guinea. Despite these tensions, a Treaty of Mutual Respect, Friendship and Cooperation was signed by the two countries in October 1986, providing for the settlement of disputes by peaceful means.

During the 1980s Papua New Guinea experienced mounting economic difficulties as a result of both rapid population growth, 2.6% per annum, and falling world prices for its copra, coffee, and cocoa exports. However, the discovery of substantial gold and oil reserves has made the country's economic prospects more promising.

THE PHILIPPINES

Republic of the Philippines
Republika ng Pilipinas

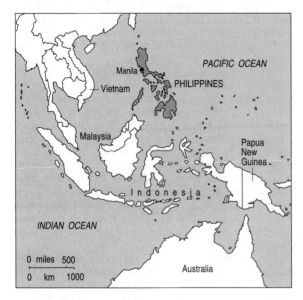

Capital: Manila

Social and economic data
Area: 300,000 km^2
Population: 66,500,000*
Pop. density per km^2: 222*
Urban population: 44%**
Literacy rate: 94%**
GDP: $52,462 million**; per-capita GDP: $800**
Government defence spending (% of GDP): 2.2%**
Currency: Philippine peso
Economy type: low income
Labour force in agriculture: 44%**

*1994
**1992

Ethnic composition
The Philippines is a pluralistic society, comprising more than 50 ethnic communities. However, a sense of national unity imbues these communities, with 95% of the population designated 'Filipinos', an Indo-Polynesian ethnic grouping. The official language is Pilipino, based on Tagalog, with 72 local dialects and languages also being spoken.

Religions
Eighty-four per cent of the population adheres to the Roman Catholic faith, 4% to Islam, 4% to the Aglipayan or Independent Philippine Christian Church, and 4% to the Protestant Church.

Political features
State type: emergent democratic
Date of state formation: 1946
Political structure: unitary

Executive: limited presidential
Assembly: two-chamber
Party structure: multiparty
Human rights rating: 72%
International affiliations: AsDB, APEC, ASEAN, CP, ESCAP, G-24, G-77, IBRD, ICFTU, IMF, LORCS, NAM, OIC (observer), WTO

Local and regional government
The country is divided into 12 regions, 75 provinces headed by governors, 1,550 cities and municipalities governed by mayors, and 41,818 neighbourhoods. Local government is by citizens' assemblies (*barangays*), with autonomy granted to any region if it is endorsed by referendum. Since January 1988 governors and mayors have been popularly elected, as have advisory councils. An active decentralization programme is underway, with, in November 1989, Muslim Mindanao, comprising four provinces, with an area of 13,122 square kilometres and a population of 1.83 million, being granted autonomy.

Head of state and head of government
President Fidel Ramos, since 1992

Political leaders since 1970
1965–86 Ferdinand Marcos (Nationalist Party/New Society Movement), 1986–92 Corazon Aquino (People's Power Movement), 1992– Fidel Ramos (Lakas–NUCD)

Political system
The present constitution which, following approval by a national referendum, became effective in February 1987, replaced the earlier one of 1973 which had been amended in 1984. It provides for a United States-style limited presidential system in which the executive works in tandem with an influential two-chamber legislature, Congress.

The upper chamber of Congress, the Senate, comprises 24 members who are directly elected by universal adult suffrage, initially for a special five-year term, but thereafter for a six-year term. Senators must be at least 35 years of age and may serve no more than two consecutive terms. They are elected in national-level contests, with the top 24 candidates being returned.

The lower chamber, the House of Representatives, comprises a maximum of 250 members, 204 of whom are directly elected at the district level, and 46 may be appointed by the president from 'lists of nominees proposed by indigenous, but nonreligious, minority groups, such as the urban poor, peasantry, women and youth'. Representatives must be at least 25 years of age and are restricted to a maximum of three consecutive three-year terms.

As in the United States, the Congress is a powerful legislative institution, enjoying substantial autonomy vis-à-vis the executive. Bills originate within Congress, the approval of both chambers being required for their passage. Joint 'conference sessions' are convened to iron out differences when they arise. The Senate has special authority over foreign affairs, two-thirds approval from it being required for the ratification of all international treaties and agreements.

Executive authority resides with the president, who serves as head of state, chief executive of the republic and commander in chief of the armed forces. The president, together with a vice president, who automatically assumes the presidency for the remainder of the unexpired term in the case of the president's death or resignation, is popularly elected in a direct national contest for a nonrenewable six-year term. The office holder must be at least 40 years of age, a native-born literate citizen, and must have resided in the country for at least ten years prior to the election. The president appoints an executive cabinet of around 25–35 members to take charge of departmental administration. He or she also appoints ambassadors, military officers, and government department chiefs. These appointments are subject, however, to the approval by majority vote of the Commission on Appointments (COA), a 25-member body consisting of 12 senators and 12 representatives, elected from the political parties represented in each chamber on the basis of proportional representation. The COA is chaired, *ex officio*, by the president of the Senate.

The president and his or her cabinet cannot directly introduce legislation into Congress. They are expected, however, to set the 'policy agenda' and ensure that suitable legislation is introduced by their party supporters within Congress. To become law, all bills that have been approved by Congress must also be signed by the president before they can become law. The president can veto such measures, but this veto can be overridden by a two-thirds majority in Congress. Finally, in an emergency, the president may proclaim martial law or suspend the writ of *habeas corpus* for a period of up to 60 days. However, these actions may be revoked by Congress by majority vote.

The 1987 constitution is a determinedly liberal and democratic document, building in substantial checks and balances between the legislative and executive branches of government in an effort to prevent the recrudescence of authoritarian executive rule that was the feature of the 1972–86 period. A substantially independent judiciary, headed by a 15-member Supreme Court, whose members are appointed for four-year terms by the president, with the approval of the COA, and four Constitutional Commissions – for Appointments, Audit, Civil Service, and Elections – also operate as a means of checking abuses of privileges. In addition, the 1987 constitution includes a special 'Bill of Rights' which guarantees civil liberties, including 'freedom of speech, of the press and of petition to the Government'; access to official information; the right to form trade unions and to assemble in public gatherings'; the right of *habeas corpus*; and the prohibition of 'the intimidation, detention, torture or secret confinement of apprehended persons'.

Proposals to amend the constitution may initially be made either by a vote of three-quarters of the members of Congress; or by a Constitutional Convention, convened by a vote of two-thirds of the members of Congress; or through a public petition signed by at least 12% of the country's registered voters. Proposed amendments are then submitted to the people in a national plebiscite and, to become valid, must secure a majority of the votes cast.

Political parties

Political parties were banned between 1972 and 1978 but permitted in the 1984 elections, since when, inspired by the events of 1986–87, a new 'party system', based on broad government and opposition groupings, has begun to develop. In general, however, political parties in the Philippines, compared with those of Western Europe, are weak affairs, and based primarily on personalities and local patronage ties. Internally they are highly factionalized and formal organizational structures remain inchoate. Instead, fluid opportunistic and ephemeral tactical alliances are effected between 'vote controlling' bosses at the local level.

Currently the most important political grouping is the Laban ng Demokratikong Pilipino (LDP: Democratic Filipino Struggle Party), a centrist liberal-democratic coalition which was formed to support Corazon Aquino in 1987 and is led by her brother, José Cojuangco Jr. It includes the Partido Demokratiko Pilipino–Lakas ng Bayan (PDP–Laban; estd. 1983), led by Ramón Mitra. Formerly a member of the LDP–DFSP, Fidel Ramos, the current president, after failing to secure its presidential nomination, left it in November 1991 to establish his own Lakas ng EDSA–National Union of Christian Democrats (NUCD). Another traditional ally of the LDP–DFSP, but not allied with Ramos, is the Liberal Party. First established in 1988, it split in 1988 and is now led by Jovito Salonga.

The two main conservative opposition parties are the Nationalist (Nacionalista) Party and the New Society Movement. The Nationalist Party, first founded in 1907, is a right-wing grouping which was resurrected in 1987 by Corazon Aquino's opponents, Salvador Laurel and Juan Ponce Enrile. The party split into contending factions during 1991–92 as its three leading figures, Laurel, Enrile, and Eduardo Cojuangco, the estranged cousin of Corazon Aquino, vied for its presidential nomination. Conjuangco's faction became known as the Nationalist People's Coalition and has supported the Ramos administration in a 'rainbow coalition' with the Liberal Party and LDP defectors since June 1992. The New Society Movement (NSM: Kilusan Bagong Lipunan), founded in 1978, is a conservative pro-Marcos family force, led by Imelda Marcos, who returned to the Philippines in November 1991, despite facing law suits for alleged embezzlement during her late husband's years in power, and was elected to the House of Representatives in May 1995. Another important opposition party is the People's Reform Party (PRP), which was set up in 1991 to support the presidential candidacy of Miriam Defensor Santiago.

Also opposed to the government, and officially banned until September 1992, is the National Democratic Front, an umbrella alliance of 14 left-wing groups, the two most important of which are the Communist Party of the Philippines (CPP: estd. 1968) and the New People's Army (NPA). The NPA is the Maoist CPP's 25,000-member guerrilla wing. It was founded in 1969 and currently exercises *de facto* control over a sixth of the country's villages. Its leader, Romulo Kintanar, was arrested in August 1991 but released in August 1992 as a conciliatory gesture by the new Ramos administration.

Latest elections

The most recent presidential election, held on 11 May 1992, was contested by seven candidates. It took more than a month for the official results to be collated, but the final shares of the national vote were as below:

	% votes
Fidel Ramos (Lakas–NUCD)	23.6%
Miriam Defensor Santiago (PRP)	19.7%
Eduardo Cojuangco	18.2%
(Nationalist People's Coalition)	
Ramón Mitra (LDP)	14.6%
Imelda Marcos (New Society Movement)	10.3%
Jovito Salonga (Liberal Party)	10.2%
Salvador Laurel (Nationalist Party)	3.4%

Miriam Santiago, a former judge who enjoyed strong support in the Manila region, briefly undertook a hunger strike in protest against alleged, but unproven, ballot-rigging during what, by Philippines standards, was a comparatively peaceful and orderly campaign. More than 100 died in pre-election violence, but this was well down on the 158 killings recorded in the 1986 presidential campaign and the death toll of 90% during the 1971 local elections.

The concurrent vice-presidential election was won by Joseph Estrada, a former film star who was leader of the Partido ng Masang Pilipino (PMP), with a 33% share of the national vote.

The most recent congressional elections were held on 8 May 1995 for 204 House seats and 12 Senate seats, half of the total number. President Ramos's ruling coalition, dominated by the Lakas (Christian Democratic) party and Laban (Liberal Democratic) party, secured a landslide victory, capturing 90% of the House seats and nine of the 12 Senate seats, those elected including Gloria Macapagal-Arroyo and Ramón Magsaysay, both children of former presidents, and 180 House seats. The pro-Ramos coalition also won 80% of the provincial governorships and mayoral positions contested. Three prominent members of the opposition were elected: Gregorio 'Gringo' Honasan, the former army colonel who had led coups against former President Aquino, to the Senate; Miriam Defensor-Santiago, also to the Senate; and Imelda Marcos to a House seat. However, Imelda Marcos's son, Ferdinand 'Bong Bong' Marcos Jr failed in his challenge for a Senate seat. More than 80 people were killed in election campaign related violence, with voting having to be delayed on Mindanao island until 27 May.

Political history
The Philippines consist of an archipelago of more than 7,100 islands and islets, of which around 700 are inhabited, extending 1,851 kilometres between the southeast and the northwest. Eleven islands, Luzon, Mindanao, Samar, Negros, Palawan, Panay, Mindoro, Leyte, Cebu, Bohol, and Masbate, account for 93% of the land area and population, the two most important, Luzon and Mindanao, contributing two-thirds. More than half the country's total area is forested.

The islands of the Philippines were subject to successive waves of Malay, Indonesian, and Chinese settlement before being 'discovered' by Ferdinand Magellan (c. 1480–1521) and subsequently conquered by Spanish forces in 1565. Roman Catholicism was introduced during the reign of Philip II (1527–98), after whom the islands were named, replacing the Muslim religion which had been spread by Arab traders and missionaries. Under Spanish rule a sugar, tobacco, rubber, and coffee based plantation economy was established, with rigid socio-economic stratification developing between the darker skinned, Malay-origin, peasantry (indios) and the fairer skinned, estate-owning, 'mixed blood' (mestizo) elite, of Spanish and Chinese origin. A series of armed nationalist revolts broke out during the 19th century and continued after the islands were ceded by Spain to the United States in December 1898, after the war the two countries fought over Cuba. This resulted in the concession of increasing degrees of internal self-government to the Philippines, in 1916 and 1935.

During World War II the Philippines were occupied by the Japanese, between 1942 and 1945, before becoming a fully independent republic in July 1946. A succession of Presidents drawn from the islands' wealthy estate-owning elite followed between 1946 and 1965: Manual Roxas (1946–48), Elpidio Quirino (1948–53), Ramón Magsaysay (1953–57), Carlos García (1957–61), and Diosdado Macapagal (1961–65). They did little to improve the lot of the ordinary peasant. A partial exception, between 1953 and 1957 was the honest humble-born Ramón Magsaysay. During Magsaysay's presidency, the Philippines enjoyed a period of extended economic growth which temporarily established the country as the richest per capita, after Japan, in Asia. The internal menace posed by the communist Hukbalahap guerrillas, an insurgency grouping which had originally been formed to fight the Japanese but which had continued its operations after independence, was suppressed through a skilful combination of force and incentives. However, following Magsaysay's death in an air crash in 1957, the country rapidly retrogressed under the corrupt and lacklustre stewardships of García and Macapagal.

In the presidential election of November 1965, Diosdado Macapagal, leader of the Liberal Party, was eventually defeated by Ferdinand Marcos (1917–89), the dynamic young leader of the Nationalist Party. Marcos, promising a new start, initiated a programme of rapid economic development, based on import-substituting industrialization and infrastructural investment. He was re-elected in 1969, but during his second term encountered growing opposition from new communist insurgents, the New People's Army (NPA), in Luzon in the north, and from Muslim separatists, the Moro National Liberation Front (MNLF), in Mindanao province in the south. In September 1972, 14 months before his second, and constitutionally his last, term had been completed, and with the economy deteriorating rapidly and the communist insurgency growing in strength, Marcos declared martial law, suspended the constitution, and began to rule by decree. The birth of a 'New Society' was proclaimed.

The following year, President Marcos announced a return to democratic government. A new constitution, providing for a single-chamber National Assembly (Batasang Pambansa), a constitutional President and an executive prime minister, elected by the Assembly, was formally promulgated. However, Marcos proposed that, for the time being, he should remain in office and continue to rule by decree. Referenda in July 1973, February 1975, and October 1976 approved these actions, allowing him to retain power. Criticisms of Marcos's authoritarian and corrupt leadership were, however, growing and in November 1977 the main opposition leader, Benigno Aquino, was sentenced to death, for alleged subversion, by a military tribunal.

In April 1978 martial law was relaxed and elections for an interim National Assembly held, resulting in an overwhelming victory for Marcos and his supporters' party, the New Society Movement, a party which had been specially formed for the election by former Nationalist Party members. Soon afterwards Aquino, who was a sick man, was temporarily released from prison to travel to the United States for medical attention. In January 1981, martial law was lifted completely and hundreds of political prisoners released. Marcos then won approval, by referendum, for a partial return to democratic government, with himself as president for a new six-year term, working with a prime minister and Executive Council. Political and economic conditions deteriorated, however, as the NPA guerrilla insurgency escalated. With GDP growth now negative, unemployment climbed to over 30% and, following the sudden rise in the international oil price between 1979 and 1982, national indebtedness, and debt-serving problems increased sharply.

In August 1983 the opposition leader, Benigno Aquino ,returned from the United States and was immediately shot dead on his arrival at Manila airport. A commission of inquiry reported 11 months later that Aquino had been killed by the military guard escorting him as part of a broader conspiracy. This act had momentous repercussions for the Marcos regime, serving to unite a previously disunited opposition. National Assembly elections were held in May 1984, amid violence and widespread claims of corruption, and although they resulted in success for the government party, which captured 68% of the 183 elective seats, they also registered significant gains for the opposition. Then, early in 1986, the main anti-Marcos movement, the United Nationalist Democratic Organization (UNIDO), chose Aquino's widow, Corazon Aquino (b. 1933), despite her political inexperience, to contest new elections for the presidency which Marcos had been persuaded to hold, as a means of maintaining American economic and diplomatic support.

The presidential campaign of December 1985–February 1986 proved violent, resulting in more than 150 deaths, and widespread electoral fraud was witnessed by international observers. On 16 February 1986, following polling a week earlier, the National Assembly declared Marcos the winner by 54% to 46%. This result, however, was immediately disputed by an independent electoral watchdog, the National Citizens' Movement for Free Elections (Namfrel). Corazon Aquino began a nonviolent protest, termed 'People's Power', which gathered massive popular support, particularly from the Roman Catholic Church. President Marcos also came under strong international pressure, particularly from his former ally, the United States, to stand down. On 22 February 1986 the army, led by Chief of Staff Lieutenant General Fidel Ramos (b. 1928) and Defence Minister Juan Enrile, declared its support for Corazon Aquino and on 25 February 1986

Marcos, given guarantees of safe passage, left, with his wife Imelda, for exile in Hawaii.

On assuming the presidency, Corazon Aquino immediately dissolved the pro-Marcos National Assembly and announced plans for the framing of a new 'freedom constitution'. She proceeded to govern in a conciliatory fashion, working with an emergency coalition cabinet team, comprising a broad cross-section of radical, liberal, and conservative opposition politicians and senior military figures. Five hundred political prisoners were freed and an amnesty granted to the NPA's commmunist guerrillas, in an effort to bring an end to the 17-year-old insurgency. She also introduced a major rural employment economic programme. The new administration was faced, however, during the summer and autumn months of 1986, with a series of attempted coups by pro-Marcos supporters, as well as internal opposition from Defence Secretary Enrile, resulting in his dismissal in November 1986.

In February 1987 a new constitution was overwhelmingly approved by 76% of the voters in a national plebiscite. This gave Aquino a mandate to rule as president until 30 June 1992 and paved the way for elections to the new two-chamber Congress in May 1987.

The congressional elections resulted in a huge majority for the supporters of President Aquino. In August 1987, however, the government was rocked by another attempted military coup, the most serious thus far, led by Colonel Gregorio Honasan, an army officer linked closely with Enrile, in which 53 people were killed in intense fighting in Manila and Cebu. Facing accusations of 'policy drift', President Aquino responded by making a major cabinet reshuffle in September 1987. This involved the replacement of Vice President Laurel as foreign affairs secretary by Senator Raúl Manglapus, and the sacking of Finance Secretary Jaime Ongpin and the president's 'leftist' executive secretary, Joker Arroyo. These changes signalled a shift to the right for the Aquino administration, which, concerned to maintain internal order and prevent further coup attempts by the disaffected military, proceeded to approve a series of tough measures to deal with the NPA insurgency and a more conservative economic and social programme. Included in the latter was an important, though diluted, land reform act, which was passed by Congress in June 1988 and which included favourable compensation terms for substantial estate holders. A regional referendum, proposing the merging of 13 southern provinces which had been at the centre of a 20-year-old Muslim separatist struggle, was rejected in nine of the provinces, resulting in autonomy, as Muslim Mindanao, for just four provinces.

During her presidency Corazon Aquino enjoyed firm backing from the United States. The Philippines received $1.5 billion of economic and military aid between 1985 and 1989 and in December 1989 American air support was provided to help foil a further coup attempt planned by Honasan and the right-wing Young Officers Union (YOU). However, despite Aquino's advocacy of renewal of the US leases to the important Subic Bay naval and Clark Field air bases, the Philippines Senate voted, in September 1991, to reject renewal. A US pull-out duly occurred, with the bases, in any case, having been badly damaged by a major eruption of the long-dormant Mount Pinatubo volcano in June 1991, killing 343 people and rendering 200,000 homeless.

Corazon Aquino stepped down as president at the end of June 1992, being replaced by her chosen heir, Fidel Ramos, who won the May 1992 direct presidential election and formed a cabinet which included six members from the Aquino administration. With seven candidates contesting, including Imelda Marcos, whose husband had died in exile in Hawaii in September 1989, Ramos, a liberal Protestant and former general, was able to secure just 24% of the national vote. This left him with a much weaker popular mandate than had been enjoyed by Aquino. The new president was forced to work with a Senate in which he lacked majority support. In the House of Representatives, Ramos put together what became known as a 'rainbow coalition', comprising members of the Liberal Party, the Nationalist People's Coalition, and 55 'Laban' defectors from the LDP. During his first two years in power the economy, hit by power shortages and fiscal constraints, stagnated. However, from 1994 an economic upturn commenced, with annual GDP growth more than 5% in 1984 and 1985. Internal order also improved as a result of a series of imaginative initiatives by Ramos, including the formation in August 1992 of a National Unification Commission (NUC) to consult with rebel groups, the legalization of the formerly proscribed CPP, the conditional release of communist leaders and rebel soldiers, and the disarming of the private armies maintained by provincial landlords and politicians. During 1993 and 1994 peace talks were held with both the communist NPA and the Muslim-secessionist MNLF and Moro Islamic Liberation Front (MILF) and a number of temporary cease-fires were negotiated. President Ramos's promising early record secured endorsement in the mid-term congressional elections of May 1995 when the ruling pro-Ramos coalition parties won around 80% of House and Senate seats and governorships contested.

SOLOMON ISLANDS

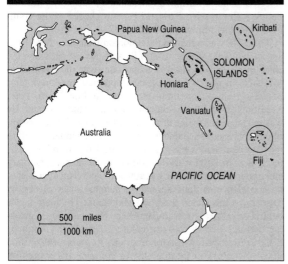

Capital: Honiara

Social and economic data
Area: 27,556 km^2
Population: 380,000*

Pop. density per km^2: 14*
Urban population: 8%**
Literacy rate: 60%
GDP: \$240 million*; per-capita GDP: \$630**
Government defence spending (% of GDP): 0%***
Currency: Solomon Islands dollar
Economy type: low income
Labour force in agriculture: 30%**

*1994
**1992
***The Solomon Islands have no defence forces

Ethnic composition
Ninety-three per cent of the population is Melanesian, 4% Polynesian, 1.5% Micronesian, 0.7% European, and 0.2% Chinese. The official language is English, although many local languages are also spoken.

Religions
Ninety-five per cent of the population is Christian: 34% adhering to the Church of Melanesia (Anglican), 19% to the Roman Catholic Church, 17% to the South Seas Evangelical Church, 11% to the United Church, and 10% to the Seventh-Day Adventist Church. Traditional ancestor worship also prevails.

Political features
State type: liberal democratic
Date of state formation: 1978
Political structure: unitary
Executive: parliamentary
Assembly: one-chamber
Party structure: multiparty
Human rights rating: N/A
International affiliations: ACP, AsDB, CW, ESCAP, G-77, IBRD, IMF, IWC, SG, SPC, SPEC, SPF, UN, WFTU

Local and regional government
The country is divided into four districts, within which there are nine elected local government councils. Seven of them have provincial assemblies, Western, Guadalcanal, Central, Malaita, Santa Isabel, Eastern, and San Cristobal, and one, Honiara, has a town council.

Head of state
Queen Elizabeth II, represented by Governor General Moses Puibangara Pitakaka since 1994

Head of government
Prime Minister Solomon Mamaloni, since 1994

Political leaders since 1970
1974–76 Solomon Mamaloni (PPP), 1976–81 Peter Kenilorea (SIUPA), 1981–84 Solomon Mamaloni (PAP), 1984–86 Sir Peter Kenilorea (SIUPA), 1986–89 Ezekiel Alebua (SIUPA), 1989–93 Solomon Mamaloni (PAP/independent), 1993–94 Francis Billy Hilly (independent/NCP), 1994– Solomon Mamaloni (GNUR)

Political system
The most recent constitution dates from independence in July 1978. This established the state as a constitutional

monarchy within the Commonwealth, in which a resident governor general represents the British Crown as head of state. The governor general, who must be a Solomon Islands citizen, is appointed for a renewable five-year term on the recommendation of the assembly. This is called the National Parliament and is a single-chamber body of 47 members elected by universal adult suffrage, on a simple plurality basis, in single-member constituencies. The parliamentary system adheres closely to the Westminster model, with the governor general formally appointing a prime minister who is elected by MPs and a cabinet of about 19 members, on the prime minister's recommendation, drawn from and collectively responsible to the assembly, which is subject to dissolution within its four-year term.

Political parties

Political parties in the Solomon Islands are loose, personality-, regional- and patronage-based groupings, rather than disciplined and ideologically united units. Currently parties are aligned in two opposing blocks: the National Coalition Partners (NCP) and the Group for National Unity and Reconciliation (GNUR).

The NCP was formed after the May 1993 general election to force the GNUR leader, Solomon Mamaloni, from power. It is a loose coalition comprising independents and six parties: the Labour Party (LP; estd. 1988), led by Joses Tuhanuku; the National Action Party of the Solomon Islands (NAPSI; estd. 1993), led by Francis Saemala; the federalist People's Alliance Party (PAP), led by David Kausimae; the centralist Solomon Islands United Party (SIUPA/UP; estd. 1973), led by the former prime minister, Ezekiel Alebua; the rural-interest orientated Nationalist Front for Progress (NFP; estd. 1985), led by Andrew Nori; and the Christian Fellowship Group (CFG). The SIUPA/UP, a conservative party, originated as an outgrowth of the Civil Servants Association, and was the dominant force in Solomon Islands politics for much of the period between 1976 and 1989. A faction, led by Andrew Nori, split from the SIUPA in October 1985, and, known as the NFP, established itself as an 'open forum' for those wishing to discuss land disputes. The PAP, which was the governing party, though in coalitions, between 1976–81 and 1984–86, is a centre-left force. It was formed in 1973 under the designation People's Progressive Party (PPP), before uniting with the Rural Alliance Party, which was established in 1977, to form the PAP in 1979. The PAP favours greater decentralization of power and the strengthening of regional Melanesian alliances.

Opposed to the NCP is the GNUR, a party formed in 1993 by the then prime minister, Solomon Mamaloni, leader of the PAP until 1990, to contest the general election. It became the governing party in November 1994.

Latest elections

In the most recent elections, held on 26 May 1993, the GNUR clearly emerged as the largest single-party grouping, winning 21 seats. However, the six parties which subsequently formed the NCP gained a slim parliamentary majority overall. The seats won by individual parties within the NCP were: PAP, 7; NAPSI, 5; LP, 4; CFG, 3; UP, 2; and NFP, 1. Independents won four seats. A record 280 candidates contested the elections.

Political history

The Solomon Islands are an archipelago of several hundred small islands, situated in the south Pacific Ocean, scattered between Papua New Guinea in the northwest and Vanuatu in the southeast. The six principal islands are Choiseul, Guadalcanal, Malaita, New Georgia, San Cristobal, and Santa Isabel. The bulk of the population resides in dispersed settlements along the coasts and is involved in subsistence agriculture or work on copra and palm oil plantations.

The islands, which at the time were inhabited by Melanesians, were 'discovered' by the Spanish navigator Alvaro de Mendaña in 1568, but were not visited again by Europeans until the later 18th century. The Northern Solomon Islands became a German protectorate in 1885 and the Southern Solomon Islands a British protectorate in 1893. Five years later Germany ceded its possessions to Britain and, in 1900, a unified British Solomon Islands Protectorate (BSIP) was formed. This was placed under the jurisdiction of the Western Pacific High Commission (WPHC), whose headquarters were in Fiji. A resident commissioner was placed in charge of day-to-day administration. During World War II, the islands were invaded by Japan in 1942, but recaptured by the United States a year later.

After the war the islands remained under British control, the WPHC moving its headquarters to Honiara. Elected island councils began to be established and, under a constitution adopted in October 1960, legislative and executive councils were established. These were amalgamated into a single elected Governing Council, based on a ministerial system, under the terms of the March 1970 constitution, as amended in 1973. In April 1974, following the adoption of a new constitution, the islands became substantially self-governing, a 24-member Legislative Assembly being established, from whose members a chief minister, who enjoyed the right to appoint a cabinet, or Council of Ministers, was selected. Solomon Mamaloni, leader of the newly formed People's Progressive Party (PPP), was chosen as the country's first chief minister in August 1974.

The BSIP was renamed the Solomon Islands in June 1975 and in January 1976 became fully self-governing, when the chief minister was allowed to preside over the Council of Ministers in place of the British-appointed governor. After new Legislative Assembly elections, in June 1976, Peter Kenilorea (b. 1943) was chosen as the new chief minister. He was redesignated prime minister, and the Legislative Assembly the National Parliament, when full independence within the Commonwealth was granted in July 1978. Kenilorea was re-elected in August 1980, following fresh parliamentary elections, but the following year was defeated on a motion of no confidence in the National Parliament and replaced by former chief minister, Solomon Mamaloni. The main factor behind Kenilorea's downfall had been his resistance to growing pressure, which was particularly strong in the commercially developed Western District, to decentralize and devolve powers to the regions. In contrast, his successor, Mamaloni, warmly supported the idea and one of his first actions as prime minister was to create five ministerial posts specifically for provincial affairs.

By the time of the October 1984 general election, support for Sir Peter Kenilorea, as he had become, had risen and he was put back into office, at the head of a coalition government. He immediately abolished the five provincial ministries, restoring the balance between central and regional power. Support for the governing party soon began to wane, however. Kenilorea narrowly survived no-confidence votes in Parliament in September 1985 and July 1986 and was forced to reconstitute his coalition when the Solomons Ano Sagufenua (SAS) Party withdrew its support. Following allegations that he had secretly accepted US$47,000 of French aid to repair cyclone damage to his home village in Malaita province, and faced with a fresh no-confidence motion, Kenilorea eventually resigned as prime minister in December 1986. He was replaced, following three secret ballots in Parliament, by the deputy prime minister and fellow Solomon Islands United Party (SIUPA) member, Ezekiel Alebua. Kenilorea continued, however, to hold ministerial office, serving, first, as natural resources minister and then, from February 1988, as joint foreign minister and deputy prime minister, while Alebua continued to adhere to the existing policy course. However, at the general election of February 1989 support for the SIUPA slumped, its seat tally being halved, and the PAP, led by Mamaloni, re-emerged as the dominant political party. In March 1989 Mamaloni became head of a new PAP government which was determined to reduce the influence of 'foreign aid personnel' and which promised to reform the constitution so as to establish a republic.

In October 1990, encountering mounting criticism at a time of financial crisis, Mamaloni gave up the leadership of the PAP, but despite protests, carried on as prime minister. He headed a government of 'national unity' which included, as foreign affairs minister, Sir Peter Kenilorea. Mamaloni's actions created splits both within the PAP and the opposition. He held on to power until June 1993 when, following a general election, a coalition of opposition legislators ensured that Francis Billy Hilly became the new prime minister. However, the new administration was weakened by the resignation of several ministers in November 1993, and in October 1994, having lost his parliamentary majority, Hilly was dismissed as premier by Governor General Moses Pitakaka. Solomon Mamaloni, as leader of the GNUR, the largest grouping within Parliament, returned as prime minister on 7 November 1994, defeating Sir Baddeley Devesi, a former governor general, by 29 parliamentary votes to 18.

Since the 1960s the broad strategy of successive governments has been to diversify the Solomons' economic base, reducing dependence on copra exports, by encouraging tuna, timber, palm kernel, and cocoa exports. This has been successfully achieved. Nevertheless, the country was adversely affected by the decline in world commodity prices during the early 1980s, resulting in a decline in GDP and a sharp rise in inflation and a widening balance of payments deficit. The current rapid rate of population growth, around 3.8% per annum, has not helped matters. As a consequence, the country remains dependent on economic aid for 15% of its GDP.

In its external relations the Solomon Islands, under the SIUPA administrations, pursued a moderate, pro-Western course. This contrasted with the more radical approach of the PAP between 1981 and 1984, when relations with the United States were strained by the government's refusal to allow nuclear-powered warships within the Solomons' territorial waters and by the seizure of an American fishing boat in June 1984, for violating its claimed 200-mile sea limit. In March 1988 the Solomon Islands, as part of a new, broader 'Pacific strategy', joined Vanuatu and Papua New Guinea to form the 'Spearhead Group' (SG), with the aim of preserving Melanesian cultural traditions.

TONGA

The Kingdom of Tonga
Pule'anga Fakatu'i 'o Tonga

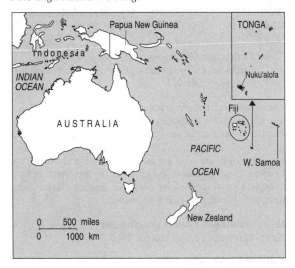

Capital: Nuku'alofa

Social and economic data
Area: 748 km²
Population: 101,000*
Pop. density per km²: 135*
Urban population: 21%*
Literacy rate: 99%*
GDP: $136 million*; per-capita GDP: $1,350*
Government defence spending (% of GDP): 0%**
Currency: Pa'anga or Tongan dollar, which is pegged to the Australian dollar
Economy type: middle income
Labour force in agriculture: 44%*

*1992
**Tonga has no army, but has a national police force

Ethnic composition
Ninety-eight per cent of the population is of Tongan ethnic stock, a Polynesian group with a small mixture of Melanesian. The remainder is European and part-European. Tongan (Tongatabu) is the official language, with English and Polynesian subdialects also being widely spoken.

Religions
The population is almost entirely Christian. Forty-seven per cent and 9% respectively adhere to the Methodist Free Wesleyan Church of Tonga and Church of Tonga, 15% to Roman

Catholicism, and 14% to the Church of Jesus Christ of Latter-Day Saints (Mormon).

Political features

State type: absolutist
Date of state formation: 1970
Political structure: unitary
Executive: absolute
Assembly: one-chamber
Party structure: in transition*
Human rights rating: N/A
International affiliations: ACP, AsDB, CW, ESCAP**, FAO**, G-77, IBRD**, ICAO**, ICFTU, IDA**, IFAD**, IFC**, IMF**, ITU**, LORCS, SPC, SPEC, SPF, UNCTAD**, UNESCO**, UNIDO**, UPU**, WFTU, WHO**

*Tonga's first formal party was established in 1994
**UN bodies which Tonga belongs to, although it is not formally a member of the UN

Local and regional government

For administrative purposes, the country is divided into three districts – Vava'u, Ha'apai, and Tongatapu – corresponding to its three island groups. The first two districts are administered by governors who are *ex officio* members of the Privy Council. For Tongatapu, the king acts as governor. Below, there is a small network of town and district officials who have been popularly elected since 1965.

Head of state and head of government

King Taufa'ahau Tupou IV, since 1965

Political leaders since 1970

1965–   King Taufa'ahau Tupou IV

Political system

Tonga is an independent hereditary monarchy within the Commonwealth. Its constitution dates from 1875, having been most recently revised in 1970, and provides for a king who is both head of state and head of government. He appoints and presides over a Privy Council, which also serves as a cabinet, and consists of himself and 11 ministers appointed for life. The cabinet is led by the prime minister and includes, as *ex officio* members, the governors of Ha'apai and Vava'u. Between 1965 and 1991 Prince Fatafehi Tu'ipelehake, the king's younger brother, was prime minister. He was replaced in August 1991 by the king's cousin, Baron Vaea. There is a single-chamber Legislative Assembly of 30 members, who include the king, the Privy Council, 9 hereditary nobles, elected by the 33 hereditary nobles of Tonga, and 9 representatives of the people, elected by universal adult suffrage. The Assembly has a life of three years and meets at least once a year, usually for a session which lasts between two to four months. Legislation, in the form of ordinances, passed by the executive is subject to review by the Assembly.

Political parties

Traditionally there have been no official political parties in Tonga, 'People's Representatives' being elected as independents. However, within the Legislative Assembly informal pro- and anti-government groupings do form from time to time. In 1992 the Pro-Democracy, or People's Democratic, Movement opposition group was unofficially founded and in August 1994 the People's Party, led by the commoner Akilisi Pohiva and supported by four other commoner MPs, became the country's first formal political party.

Latest elections

In the most recent Legislative Assembly elections, held in February 1993, the nine 'People's Representatives', or commoners, who were elected included supporters of democratization.

Political history

Tonga is an island chain in the southwest Pacific Ocean, 2,250 kilometres northeast of New Zealand and 640 kilometres east of Fiji, between 18 and 22 degrees south of the equator. It comprises 133 inhabited and 36 uninhabited volcanic and coral islands divided into three main groups, Vava'u in the north, Ha'apai in the centre, and Tongatapu-Eua in the south. Sixty-eight per cent of the population resides on the main island of Tongatapu, on which the capital of Nuku'alofa is situated.

The first European visitor to Tonga was the Dutch explorer, Abel Tasman (1603–59) in 1643. More than a century later, in 1773, the islands were charted by Captain James Cook (1728–79) and dubbed the 'Friendly Islands'. The contemporary Tongan dynasty was founded in 1831 by Prince Taufa'ahau Tupou, who took the name King George Tupou I when he ascended the throne. He consolidated the kingdom by conquest, encouraged the spread of Christianity, and, in 1875, granted a constitution. In 1900 his great-grandson, King George Tupou II, signed a Treaty of Friendship and Protection under which Tonga formally became a British protectorate. Tonga retained its independence and substantial internal autonomy, but handed over control of its foreign policy and defence to the United Kingdom. This position was broadly reaffirmed in revised treaties which were signed in 1958 and 1967, under which Tonga was granted increased control over its internal affairs.

Queen Salote Tupou III (1900–65), who had ascended the throne in 1918, died in December 1965 and was succeeded by her son Prince Tupouto'a Tungi (b. 1918), who had been prime minister since 1949. He assumed the title King Taufa'ahau Tupou IV and appointed his brother, Prince Fatafehi Tu'ipelehake as the new prime minister. Full independence, within the Commonwealth, was finally achieved in June 1970, giving the nation control over its foreign affairs. The country's foreign policy approach since independence has, however, changed little, the country remaining the strongest supporter of the Western powers in the Pacific region, particularly close links being maintained with Britain, Australia, and New Zealand. Tonga remains dependent on foreign development aid for more than a fifth of its current GDP and is still heavily reliant on its traditional cash crop exports of coconuts, vanilla, and pumpkins, and despite recent lucrative growth in the tourist and fishing industries, unemployment remains high, inducing substantial emigration. In recent years, popular demands for constitutional reforms have grown. In February 1990 three prodemocracy candidates were elected to the

Legislative Assembly and in 1992 an unofficial political party, the People's Democratic Movement, was founded to campaign for democratization. Led by Akilisi Pohiva, a magazine editor and reform-minded legislator, and supported by Fr Seluini 'Akau'ola, a Catholic priest, it won six of the nine commoner seats contested in the February 1993 general election and became known as the People's Party in August 1994. The king has firmly resisted reform of the Legislative Assembly so as to provide for an elected majority. However, Crown Prince Tupouto'a, the foreign affairs and defence minister, has expressed support for the establishment of political parties and a formalized political structure.

TUVALU

South West Pacific State of Tuvalu

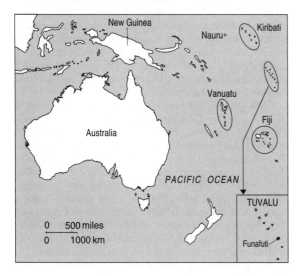

Capital: Fongafale (on Funafuti Atoll)

Social and economic data
Area: 26 km²
Population: 9,000*
Pop. density per km²: 346*
Urban population: 30%*
Literacy rate: 95%*
GDP: $5 million*; per-capita GDP: $560*
Government defence spending (% of GDP): 0%**
Currency: Tuvalu dollar, which is pegged to the Australian dollar
Economy type: low income
Labour force in agriculture: N/A

*1992
**Tuvalu has no army

Ethnic composition
The population is almost entirely of Polynesian stock, maintaining close ties with the Samoans and Tokelauans to the south and east. Tuvaluan and English are the principal languages.

Religions
Ninety-eight per cent of the population adheres to the Protestant Church of Tuvalu (Ekalesia Tuvalu) which was established in 1861. It is a Congregationalist body derived from the London Missionary Society. In 1991 Parliament approved legislation to establish the Church of Tuvalu as the State Church and prohibit new religions from the islands.

Political features
State type: liberal democratic
Date of state formation: 1978
Political structure: unitary
Executive: parliamentary
Assembly: one-chamber
Party structure: no parties
Human rights rating: N/A
International affiliations: ACP, CW (special status), ESCAP*, SPC, SPEC, SPF, UNESCO*, UPU*, WHO*

*UN bodies which Tuvalu belongs to, although it is not formally a member of the UN

Local and regional government
For local government, each of the nine inhabited atolls has its own six-member island council, headed by a president. The councils meet in large council halls (*maneabas*), which are also used to sleep as many as 1,000 people during the annual communal feasts, which last for several weeks.

Head of state
Queen Elizabeth II, represented by Governor General Tulaga Manuella since 1994

Head of government
Prime Minister Kamuta Laatasi, since 1993

Political leaders since 1970
1975–81 Toaripi Lauti (independent), 1981–89 Dr Tomasi Puapua (independent), 1989–93 Bikenibeu Paeniu (independent), 1993– Kamuta Laatasi (independent)

Political system
The constitution dates from October 1978 when Tuvalu became an independent state within the Commonwealth, accepting the British monarch as head of state, represented by a resident governor general. The system of government contains elements of the British, Westminster, model, with a single-chamber Parliament of 12 members and a prime minister and cabinet, of four additional ministers, elected by and responsible to it. The governor general must be a citizen of Tuvalu and is appointed on the recommendation of the prime minister for a four-year term. The prime minister also currently holds the portfolios of foreign affairs and economic planning. Members of Parliament are elected by universal adult suffrage through a simple plurality voting system for a four-year term. The Parliament is subject to dissolution during its term. Four atolls, Nanumea, Niutao, Vaitupu, and Funafuti, each send two representatives to Parliament, with Niulakita being regarded, for electoral purposes, as part of Niutao. The remaining four atolls return one member each.

Political parties

There are no political parties. Members are elected to Parliament as independents, but alliances are subsequently established within the legislature based on clan loyalties and family connections.

Latest elections

The most recent parliamentary elections were held in November 1993, 12 independents being returned, with an average of three candidates contesting each seat.

Political history

Tuvalu is a small island grouping in the southwest Pacific Ocean, 1,050 kilometres north of Fiji and 4,020 kilometres northeast of Sydney, Australia. It comprises the low-lying coral atolls of Funafuti, on which 34% of the population resides, Vaitupu, with 15%, Nanumea, 11%, Niutao, 11%, Nukufetau, 8%, Nanumanga, 7%, Nui, 7%, Nukulailai, 4%, and Niulakita, 1%, and extends 560 kilometres from north to south.

The islands were invaded and occupied by Samoans during the 16th century. In the mid-19th century, between 1850 and 1875, European slave traders visited Tuvalu and captured the indigenous Melanesians for forced labour in the guano mines and on the coffee plantations of South America. As a result of both these activities and the importation of European diseases, the islands' population fell markedly from an estimated 20,000 to barely 3,000.

In 1877, when the British established the Western Pacific High Commission (WPHC), with its headquarters on Fiji, Tuvalu, which at this time was known as the Ellice, or Lagoon, Islands, was placed under its charge. Fifteen years later, in 1892, the islands were officially declared a British Protectorate and were linked, for administrative purposes, with the larger, Micronesian-peopled, Gilbert Islands, known today as Kiribati. From 1916 the protectorate was ruled formally as a colony under the designation Gilbert and Ellice Islands Colony (GEIC), a resident commissioner being based on Tarawa Atoll in the Gilbert group.

During World War II the GEIC was invaded and occupied by Japan in 1942. A year later, the Japanese were removed by American naval forces and British control was reestablished. After the war a succession of advisory and legislative councils were set up, paving the way for self-government. This culminated, in May 1974, in the establishment of a House of Assembly, comprising 28 elected members, eight from the Ellice Islands, and three official members. The assembly elected a chief minister and between four to six cabinet ministers, one of whom had to be from the Ellice Islands. The British seemed, at this time, to be preparing the way for granting independence to the GEIC as a constituent whole. This, however, was strongly opposed by the Ellice Islanders, who feared domination by the Micronesians of the Gilbert Islands. They therefore pressed for separate status and in a referendum held on the Ellice Islands in August–September 1974 they voted overwhelmingly, by a 90% majority, for this option. Thus, in October 1975, reverting to their traditional name of Tuvalu, meaning 'eight standing together', the Ellice Islands became a separate British dependency. The eight Ellice Islands representatives of the former GEIC House of Assembly constituted themselves as a new Tuvalu House of Assembly and elected Toaripi Lauti as their first chief minister.

In the House of Assembly elections of August 1977, the number of elective seats was increased to 12 and a year later, in October 1978, following the framing in London of a constitution, Tuvalu became fully independent as a 'special member' of the Commonwealth. This meant that, because of its small size, it did not participate in heads of government meetings. Lauti became the country's prime minister and the House of Assembly was redesignated Parliament.

In the first post-independence parliamentary elections, of September 1981, Lauti, who had been involved in an alleged investment scandal, was replaced as prime minister, following a 7–5 parliamentary vote against him. His successor was Dr Tomasi Puapua (b. 1938), who was re-elected in July 1985. During 1986 constitutional changes designed to reduce the authority of the governor general, and in particular his or her right to reject the advice of the incumbent government, were mooted. However, in February 1986, in a national poll held to decide whether Tuvalu should remain a constitutional monarchy or become a republic, only one atoll supported republican status.

The September 1989 general election saw the replacement of Dr Puapua by Bikenibeu Paeniu. However, the general election of September 1993 resulted in a Parliament split evenly between supporters of Paeniu and ex-premier, Puapua. Governor General Toaripi Lauti was thus forced to dissolve Parliament and call fresh elections in November 1993. With the support of Dr Puapua, the new legislature elected on 10 December 1993, as prime minister, Kamuta Laatasi, who defeated Paeniu by seven votes to five. In July 1994 Prime Minister Laatasi controversially forced Governor General Toomu Sione, who was only seven months into his four-year term, to resign on the grounds that his appointment, by Paeniu, had been politically motivated. Tulaga Manuella became the new governor general.

As a result of its scanty resource base, with much of the soil too poor to make cultivation feasible, economic development has been slow in Tuvalu. Rapid population growth, currently at 3.4% per annum, and the closure of the phosphate mines in neighbouring Kirabati in 1979, where many Tuvaluans worked, have made matters worse, depressing living standards in recent years. As a consequence, the country has become highly dependent on overseas development aid, more than a quarter of its GDP being derived from this source.

In its conduct of foreign relations, close links have been maintained with Britain and the United States. Tuvalu has, however, been a strong opponent of the French nuclear weapons testing programme based at Mururoa Atoll, in French Polynesia, and has urged Western governments to take action to combat the 'greenhouse effect' which threatens the country's very existence if sea levels continue to rise. In 1995 Tuvalu removed the Union Jack from its national flag. This move, influenced by the reduced amount of economic aid supplied by Britain, was seen as the first step towards the removal of the British queen as head of state and the declaration of a republic.

VANUATU

The Republic of Vanuatu
La République de Vanuatu

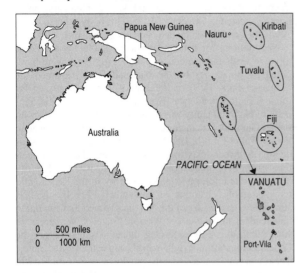

Capital: Port-Vila

Social and economic data
Area: 12,190 km^2
Population: 160,000*
Pop. density per km^2: 13*
Urban population: 27%**
Literacy rate: 66%**
GDP: $188 million**; per-capita GDP: $1,210**
Government defence spending (% of GDP): N/A***
Currency: vatu
Economy type: middle income
Labour force in agriculture: 60%**

*1993
**1992
***Vanuatu has only a small, 300-member paramilitary force

Ethnic composition
Ninety-five per cent of the population is Melanesian, 3% European or mixed European, and 2% Vietnamese, Chinese or from other Pacific islands. Bislama (ni-Vanuatu pidgin English) is the official language, with English and French also being widely understood.

Religions
Thirty-three per cent of the population belongs to the Presbyterian Church of Vanuatu, 13% to the Church of the Province of Melanesia, 13% to the Roman Catholic Church, and 10% to other Christian churches, including the Apostolic, Churches of Christ, Assemblies of God, and Seventh-Day Adventists. Nine per cent adheres to animist beliefs.

Political features
State type: liberal democratic
Date of state formation: 1980

Political structure: unitary
Executive: parliamentary
Assembly: one-chamber
Party structure: multiparty
Human rights rating: N/A
International affiliations: ACP, AsDB, CW, ESCAP, G-77, IBRD, ICFTU, IMF, NAM, SG, SPC, SPEC, SPF, UN, WFTU

Local and regional government
The country is divided into four administrative regions, with headquarters at Lenakel (Tanna), Vila, Lamap (Malakula), and Espíritu Santo. Considerable power has been constitutionally devolved to six regional councils, which, in 1994, replaced 11 local government councils.

Head of state
President Jean-Marie Leye, since 1994

Head of government
Prime Minister Serge Vohor, since 1995

Political leaders since 1970
1978–80 Father Gerard Leymang (independent), 1980–91 Father Walter Lini (VP), 1991 Donald Kalpokas (VP), 1991–95 Maxime Carlot Korman (UMP) 1995 Serge Vohor (Unity Front)

Political system
Vanuatu is an independent republic within the Commonwealth. The constitution dates from independence in July 1980. It provides for a president, who functions as a ceremonial head of state and is elected for a five-year term in a secret ballot by a 55-member electoral college consisting of Parliament and the presidents of the country's regional councils. A two-thirds majority is required in this election. Parliament consists of a single chamber of 49 members, elected by universal adult suffrage, through a system which embraces an element of proportional representation, for a four-year term. A prime minister is elected from among the members of Parliament, who then appoints and presides over a 9–11-member Council of Ministers. In the spring of 1995 the prime minister, Maxime Carlot Korman, also held the public service, foreign affairs and tourism, immigration, language services, and media services ministerial portfolios. There is a National Council of Chiefs, comprising custom chiefs elected by District Councils of Chiefs, which is empowered to make recommendations to Parliament on subjects connected with the preservation and promotion of traditional culture and languages.

Political parties
The Vanuaaku Parti (VP: 'Party of Our Land') was formed in 1972 as the New Hebrides National Party (NHNP). Led by Donald Kalpokas, it promotes a unique 'Melanesian socialist' programme, founded on nonalignment overseas and, domestically, the transfer of lands held by non-natives to the indigenes. The VP was the ruling party from 1980, but its national support, drawn predominantly from English-speaking Melanesian Protestant groups, declined significantly in the general elections of 1979 and 1983 and it was defeated in 1991. Its former leader, Father Walter Lini, founded the

National United Party (NUP) in 1991, but the NUP subsequently split into two opposed factions. In May 1994 the NUP's congress expelled 16 members, including Deputy Prime Minister John Sethy Regenvanu, who defied party instructions to withdraw support from the Maxime Carlot Korman government. These expelled members immediately formed the new People's Democratic Party.

The ruling party since 1991 has been a Francophone umbrella grouping, the Union of Moderate Parties (UMP), led by Maxime Carlot Korman. The UMP was associated with the 1980 Espíritu Santo rebellion and enjoys strong Roman Catholic support.

The other main parties are the Melanesian Progressive Party (MPP), founded in 1988 by VP dissidents, notably Barak Sope; the Tan Union, representing rural interests; the Fren Melanesian Party (FMP), a splinter group formed when the UMP superseded the New Hebrides Federal Party in 1982; and the Na-Griamel (NG) Movement, led by Franky Stephens, the son of Jimmy Stevens, leader of the 1980 Espíritu Santo revolt, who died in 1994. The NG has provided support to the Carlot Korman government.

Latest elections
In the most recent parliamentary elections, held in November 1995, the VP dominated Unity Front won 20 seats, the UMP 17, the NUP 9 and the FMP, NG and an independent one a piece.

The most recent presidential election was held on 2 March 1994 and was won by Jean-Marie Leye (UMP), who secured 41 of the electoral college's 55 votes.

Political history
The Republic of Vanuatu, formerly known as the New Hebrides, is an irregular Y-shaped chain of 13 volcanic islands and 70 islets in the southwest Pacific Ocean lying between Fiji and New Caledonia. Sixty per cent of the population resides on the four main islands of Efate, Espíritu Santo, Malakula, and Tanna. The bulk of the inland portions of the islands are densely forested, settlements being concentrated on the coastal fringes.

The islands were first visited by the Portuguese navigator Pedro Fernandez de Queiras in 1606, before being charted and named the New Hebrides by the British explorer James Cook (1728–79) in 1774. During the 19th century they were disputed by both Britain and France until 1887, when a joint naval commission was placed in charge of their administration. From 1906, the New Hebrides (Nouvelles-Hébrides) were placed under a joint Anglo-French condominium, with each power being responsible for its own citizens, governing in its own language, and having its own forces and institutions. British and French missionaries, planters, and traders subsequently settled in the country, which escaped occupation by Japan during World War II.

After the war an indigenous political grouping, Na-Griamel (NG) began to develop, and was formally established in 1963. It campaigned against the acquisition of native land by Europeans, more than a third of the country's land being owned by foreigners by the 1960s. Later, in 1972, the New Hebrides National Party (NHNP) was formed, enjoying the support of Protestant missions and British interests. It was opposed by the Union of New Hebrides Communities (UNHC), a body which had been established by pro-French groups. Discussions began in London in 1974 about eventual independence and they resulted in the creation of a 42-member Representative Assembly, 29 members being directly elected in November 1975. This body superseded an Advisory Council which had been operating since 1957.

Negotiations for establishing a timetable for a gradual move towards independence, planned for 1980, were hampered by objections by the National Party, renamed the Vanuaaku Party (VP) in January 1977, which pressed for immediate independence. Eventually, however, a Government of National Unity was formed in December 1978, with Father Gerard Leymang as chief minister and the VP leader, Father Walter Lini (b. 1942), a former Anglican priest, as his deputy. A further delay was caused in 1980 when French settlers and pro-NG plantation workers on the island of Espíritu Santo revolted, after a sweeping victory in the Representative Assembly elections of November 1979 by the VP. Jimmy Stevens, leader of the NG, proclaimed Espíritu Santo independent under the designation 'State of Vemarana' in June 1980, allegedly receiving financial support from the Phoenix Foundation, a right-wing group in the United States. The revolt was, controversially, put down by British, French, and Papua New Guinean troops after several days of fighting and Stevens was imprisoned for 11 years.

Agreement was finally reached about independence in July 1980, with the new sovereign state remaining within the Commonwealth and its name being changed to the Republic of Vanuatu. The first president was the former deputy chief minister George Kalkoa, who adopted the name Sokomanu, or 'leader of thousands', and the first prime minister was Father Lini. In the November 1983 general election the VP was re-elected, with a slightly reduced majority, and Father Lini continued as prime minister.

Lini proceeded to pursue a controversial left-of-centre nonaligned foreign policy, which included support for the Kanak National Liberation Front (KNLF) which was fighting for independence in French-ruled New Caledonia, and the possible establishment of diplomatic relations with the USSR and Libya. This soured relations with France and provoked mounting parliamentary opposition, the government's actions being viewed as likely to discourage both inward foreign investment and the expansion of the tourist industry, with consequential adverse effects on the country's economic development. During 1986 three antigovernment opposition parties, the National Democratic Party (NDP), the New People's Party (NPP), and the Vanuatu Labour Party (VLP), were formed. However, in the general election of November 1987, the VP retained its assembly majority and Lini, despite ailing health, was re-elected prime minister.

Nevertheless, opposition to Lini's domestic and external policies continued to grow during 1988. In response, in July 1988 the prime minister expelled from Parliament his intra-party rival Barak Sope, together with four supporters, as well as 18 opposition MPs who had boycotted Parliament in protest. Five months later, in December 1988, Lini was dismissed as prime minister and Parliament dissolved by President Ati George Sokomanu, who appointed his nephew, Sope, head of an interim administration. Within days, however, following a Supreme Court ruling that these actions had been unconstitutional, security forces loyal to the former prime minister arrested both the president and Sope, reinstating Lini in power. Fred Timakata, formerly the minister of health, was elected the new president in January 1989, with, two months later, Sokomanu, Sope, and Carlot each being initially sentenced to between five and six years' imprisonment for their seditious actions in December 1988. The Court of Appeal quashed these sentences in April 1989.

Despite suffering a heart attack, Lini clung to office, still dismissing colleagues who disagreed with him, until, in August 1991, as opposition within the VP mounted, he lost the leadership of the party and was then dismissed as prime minister. He was replaced by the VP's general secretary, Donald Kalpokas. The general election of December 1991 produced an inconclusive result, but eventually the UMP leader, Maxime Carlot Korman, formed a coalition with the Anglophone NUP, which had been set up in 1991 by ex-premier Walter Lini. In August 1993 the NUP split between a pro-government faction, led by the deputy prime minister, John Sethy Regenvanu, and including three other colleagues, and an opposition faction, led by Lini. The six-member Lini faction left the governing coalition whose popularity declined as a combination of the damage inflicted in March 1993 by 'Cyclone Prema' and falling copra prices produced hardship during 1992–93, while Regenvanu and 15 colleagues were expelled from the NUP and formed the new government-aligned People's Democratic Party in May 1994. Na-Griamel switched allegiance to the government in 1995. The November 1995 general election brought victory for the Unity Front and Serge Vohor became prime minister.

Externally, Vanuatu's relations with France reached a low point in October 1987, when the French ambassador was expelled from the country for providing 'substantial financial assistance' to opposition parties. However, diplomatic relations were restored in October 1992 by the new Francophone administration of Maxime Carlot Korman. Relations with the United States improved after Vanuatu's signing of a five-year fishing agreement in October 1986, under which American trawlers were granted licences to fish for tuna within the country's 'exclusive fishing zone'. The general thrust of Vanuatu's foreign policy since independence has, however, been to promote greater cooperation between the small states of the Pacific region. As part of this strategy, Vanuatu joined Papua New Guinea and the Solomon Islands in forming, in March 1988, the 'Spearhead Group' (SG), whose aim is to preserve Melanesian cultural traditions and campaign for New Caledonia's independence.

WESTERN SAMOA

The Independent State of Western Samoa
Samoa i Sisifo

Capital: Apia

Social and economic data
Area: 2,831 km²
Population: 163,000*

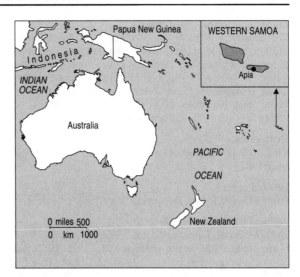

Pop. density per km²: 58*
Urban population: 27%**
Literacy rate: 98%**
GDP: $153 million**; per-capita GDP: $945**
Government defence spending (% of GDP): 0%***
Currency: tala, or Western Samoa dollar
Economy type: low income
Labour force in agriculture: 60%**

*1993
**1992
***Western Samoa, which has no army, relies on New Zealand for its defence

Ethnic composition
Ninety per cent of the population is of Samoan, or Polynesian, ethnic stock and 10% Euronesian, or mixed European and Polynesian. Samoan, a Polynesian dialect, and English are the official languages.

Religions
Ninety-nine per cent of the population is Christian. Forty-five per cent belongs to the Congregational Christian Church in Samoa, which was established in 1830 as the London Missionary Society; 22% is Roman Catholic; 19% belongs to the Methodist Church in Samoa, which was founded in 1828; 8% follows the Church of Jesus Christ of Latter-Day Saints (Mormons), established in 1888; and 4% belongs to the Seventh-Day Adventist Church, which was founded in 1895.

Political features
State type: liberal democratic
Date of state formation: 1962
Political structure: unitary
Executive: parliamentary
Assembly: one-chamber
Party structure: multiparty
Human rights rating: N/A
International affiliations: ACP, AsDB, CW, ESCAP, G-77, IBRD, ICFTU, IMF, LORCS, SPC, SPEC, SPF, UN

Local and regional government

The country is divided into 24 districts for development and law and order administration. However, the real units of local government are the villages (*nu'u*) and subvillages (*pitonu'u*), where extended family (*aiga*) heads (*matai*) gather in assemblies (*fonos*), each headed by a chief (*ali'i*). These local assemblies direct the use and distribution of family land and assets and supervise welfare provision.

Head of state

King (O le Ao O le Malo) Susuga Malietoa Tanumafili II, since 1962

Head of government

Prime Minister Tofilau Eti Alesana, since 1988

Political leaders since 1970

1970–73 Tupua Tamasese Lealofi (independent), 1973–75 Fiame Mata'afa Mulinu'u (independent), 1975–76 Tupua Tamasese Lealofi (independent), 1976–82 Tupuola Taisi Efi (independent), 1982 Va'ai Kolone (HRPP), 1982 Tupuola Taisi Efi (independent), 1982–85 Tofilau Eti Alesana (HRPP), 1985–88 Va'ai Kolone (VKG), 1988 Tupuola Taisi Efi (CDP), 1988– Tofilau Eti Alesana (HRPP)

Political system

Western Samoa is an independent state within the Commonwealth. The constitution dates from independence in January 1962 and provides for a parliamentary system of government, with a constitutional head of state (O le Ao O le Malo), a single-chamber Legislative Assembly (Fono), and a prime minister and cabinet drawn from and responsibile to the Assembly. The head of state is normally elected by the Assembly for a five-year term from among the holders of the country's four paramount titles. However, the present holder of the office has been elected for life.

The Assembly has 49 members. Forty-seven of these are Samoans, who, until 1991, were elected by holders of Matai titles, or elected clan chiefs. There were about 16,000 of such chiefs, but the system was undermined by the purchasing of Matai titles by those seeking election. Thus, following a referendum held in October 1990, a switch to universal suffrage was made for these seats. The remaining two members are elected by people, mainly Europeans, who appear on the individual voters' rolls. The Assembly has traditionally had a life of three years, but it was extended to five years in 1993. Only members of the Matai are eligible to stand for election.

The head of state appoints the prime minister and a cabinet of up to eight further Fono members, on the basis of Assembly support. The current prime minister, Tofilau Eti Alesana, holds three additional ministerial portfolios: foreign affairs, broadcasting, and police and prisons. Cabinet decisions are subject to review by an Executive Council, which is composed of the head of state and cabinet. A stress on consensus and the blending of both traditional and modern representative forms, in a conservative manner, the 'Samoan Way' (*fa'a Samoa*), permeates and distinguishes the political system.

Political parties

Prior to 1979 there were no formal political parties, all candidates for election standing as independents. Then, in February 1979, the Human Rights Protection Party (HRPP) was formed by opposition Fono deputies, led by Va'ai Kolone, a former chairperson of the Public Accounts Committee. The party opposed the rapid economic development plans of the Tupuola Taisi Efi government and emerged, under the leadership of Tofilau Eti Alesana, as the dominant party between 1982 and 1985. In 1985 it was weakened by the breakaway of a faction supporting former leader, Va'ai Kolone. This breakaway group later became, through the union of the Va'ai Kolone Group (VKG) and the Christian Democratic Party (CDP; estd. 1985), led by Tupuola Taisi Efi, the Samoan National Development Party (SNDP).

In February 1993 the Samoa Democratic Party (SDP) was formed by Le Tagaloa Pita.

Latest elections

In the most recent Fono elections, held on 5 April 1991, the HRPP captured 26 seats, the SNDP, 18, and independents, 3. In post-election political manoeuvring, the HRPP secured a four further seats and the SNDP lost two. These were the first elections held under universal adult suffrage, with an estimated 80,000 voters becoming newly enfranchised. In May 1991 petitions were filed at the Supreme Court against 11 deputies who were accused of illegal electoral practices.

Political history

Western Samoa is a volcanic island grouping in the southwest Pacific Ocean, 2,575 kilometres northeast of Auckland, New Zealand, and between 13 and 15 degrees south of the equator. It comprises two large inhabited islands, Upolu and Savaii, which are 18 kilometres apart, two much smaller inhabited islands, Apolima and Manono, and four tiny uninhabited islands, Fanuatapu, Nuutele, Nuula, and Nuusafee. The inland portions of the inhabited islands are mountainous, covered with extinct volcanoes, and agriculturally barren. The bulk of the population therefore lives in scattered coastal villages, with 72% of the total on Upolu island.

The islands of Samoa were first discovered by Dutch and French traders during the 1720s, but had been previously inhabited by Polynesians for more than 2,000 years. During the early 19th century, Christian missionaries began to settle here and from that time Germany, Britain, and the United States vied with each other for their control, intriguing with local paramount chiefs in a series of mid-century civil wars. Eventually, in 1899, a treaty was signed between the three Western powers, recognizing American paramountcy over the islands east of 171 degrees longitude west, which were to be called American Samoa, and German supremacy over the other islands, named Western Samoa. Britain was given control of Tonga and the Solomon Islands as part of this agreement. German control lasted, however, barely a decade. On the outbreak of World War I in 1914, New Zealand took over Western Samoa and thereafter administered the islands, first as a League of Nations Mandated Territory, between 1919 and 1945, and then, from 1946, as a United Nations (UN) Trust Territory.

During the interwar years, New Zealand rule was challenged by a nationalist organization, the Mau, which resorted to civil disobedience. After World War II, as part of its trusteeship agreement, New Zealand began to promote self-government, introducing a cabinet form of government in 1959 and a provisional constitution in October 1960. This paved the way for Western Samoa's achievement of full independence, within the Commonwealth, on 1 January 1962, after the holding of a UN-sponsored plebiscite. Initially, the office of head of state in the newly independent country was held jointly by two traditional rulers. However, on the death of one of them, in April 1963, the other, Malietoa Tanumafili II, became the sole head, for life, serving as a constitutional monarch. Effective executive power was held by the prime minister, who, at the time of independence, was Fiame Mata'afa Mulinu'u. He had occupied that position since 1959.

Mata'afa lost power to Tupua Tamasese Lealofi in the general election of 1970. He regained it, however, in 1973, after fresh elections, and continued to serve as prime minister until his death in May 1975. Tamasese briefly succeeded him, before being replaced by his cousin Tupuola Taisi Efi, the first prime minister not of royal blood, in the March 1976 general election. Tupuola Efi held power for six years, being re-elected by the Legislative Assembly in March 1979. At the general election of February 1982, however, the opposition groupings, who had combined in 1979 to form the Human Rights Protection Party (HRPP), won a narrow majority and their leader, Va'ai Kolone, became prime minister. Within seven months, however, he was forced to resign, after charges of electoral malpractice, including impersonation of the dead. Tupuola Efi briefly returned to power for three months, but, when his budget proposal was voted down in the Fono in December 1982, resigned to be replaced by the HRPP leader, Tofilau Eti Alesana.

The HRPP won a decisive victory in the February 1985 general election, substantially increasing its Fono majority, by securing 31 of the 47 seats, and Tofilau Eti continued as prime minister. At the end of the year, however, he resigned because of opposition within the Assembly to his budget plan and the defection from the HRPP grouping of supporters of Va'ai Kolone. The head of state refused to call another general election and Va'ai Kolone was appointed as the new prime minister, putting together a coalition of 'independents' and members of the newly formed Christian Democratic Party (CDP), led by former prime minister, Tupuola Taisi Efi. Va'ai held power until the general election of February 1988. This resulted in a disputed 'hung parliament' after which Tupuola Efi was first chosen as prime minister and, then, from April 1988, the HRPP leader, Tofilau Eti.

Voters narrowly accepted government proposals for a switch from indirect elections by Matai chiefs to universal adult suffrage in a referendum held in October 1990 and opposed by the SNDP. A linked proposal to create a second chamber comprising Matai chiefs was rejected. The HRPP won the April 1991 general election and Tofilau Eti continued for what he declared would be his final term as prime minister. Tupua Taisi Efi lost his seat and Fiame Naomi, the daughter of Western Samoa's first prime minister, became the first female cabinet minister.

In 1988 the Christian Democrats had formed an opposition group, the Samoan National Development Party (SNDP), with the former VKG leader, Va'ai Kolone. The life of the Fono was extended by two years in 1993 and its size increased by two seats by the government. This led to opposition protests, particularly by the newly formed Samoa Democracy Party (SDP), but the HRPP won the two new seats, which were contested in 1992.

Western Samoa has maintained close links with New Zealand since independence, entering into a Treaty of Friendship in 1962. Western Samoa has a free-enterprise economic system, encouraging inward foreign investment, but remains predominantly subsistence-based and is highly dependent on remittances sent home by its nationals working overseas and on foreign development aid. In December 1991 the country was struck by the worst cyclone in living memory, 'Cyclone Val'. Considerable damage was inflicted both to the infrastructure and to the main export crop, taro, and a state of emergency was declared. Australia and New Zealand immediately provided substantial assistance.

South America

The region of South America extends from the Panamanian border in the north to Cape Horn in the south, and is bounded to the east by the Atlantic Ocean and to the west by the Pacific. The total land area is nearly 18 million square kilometres, almost five times greater than Northern and Western Europe and only slightly smaller than the North American half-continent of the United States and Canada. Its total population, at 308 million in 1994, is greater than that of the United States and Canada combined but, like them, it has a relatively low population density.

The fact that it is frequently referred to as Latin America, or Spanish America, reveals its colonial origins. Most of the present modern states were settled by Spanish explorers in the heyday of Spain's imperial supremacy, and most achieved independence during the 19th century. The major exception is Brazil, whose origins are Portuguese, rather than Spanish.

All 12 states in the region are liberal, or emergent democracies, some having recently emerged from overt or covert military rule. The South American military have always tended to be near, or just below, the surface of political activity in most states, so that the region is now enjoying its strongest period of democratic government.

Whereas the Caribbean states virtually universally adopted the Westminster style of political system, those of South America have been modelled more on that of the United States. All of them have favoured a limited presidential executive and a quarter are federal states.

Although democratic systems now predominate, the human rights records of some countries in the region are still not good and there is always a danger that representative institutions will be overthrown in some unpredictable coup. Parts of South America are rife with drug trafficking and this had impacted strongly, in some states, on political processes, making apparently fair elections fraudulent. However, pluralist democracy, restored to Brazil in 1985, has proved sufficiently robust to successfully accommodate the peaceful removal of a president, Collor de Mello, for impeachment on charges of embezzlement.

Spanish influence, or Spanishness (*hispanidad*) as it is often called, waned significantly during the years of the Franco regime in Spain but, with the return of the monarchy and the revival of pluralist politics in their 'home country', South Americans are showing a great resurgence of interest in Spain and are forging, or reforging, links with it.

Now that Spain is a member of the European Union (EU), connections with its former South American colonies promise to give it more weight in discussions with other Union members than its previous solitary position might have credited. For the South American states there is an attraction, even in the case of Brazil, in Spain becoming an important power in the region again, particularly as United States influence has been showing signs of a decline. How the administration in Washington would react to such a challenge to its leadership is difficult to judge.

As Spain relinquished most of its South American colonies during the 19th century, France began to fill the cultural gap

South America: social, economic, and political data

Country	Area (sq km)	c. 1992–94 Population (m)	c. 1992–94 Pop. density per sq km	c. 1992 Adult literacy rate (%)	World ranking	Income type	c. 1991 Human rights rating (%)
Argentina	2,766,889.0	32.500	12	95	59	middle	84
Bolivia	1,098,600.0	7.700	7	63	128	low	71
Brazil	8,512,000.0	156.600	18	75	112	middle	69
Chile	756,950.0	13.800	18	94	66	middle	80
Colombia	1,138,994.0	33.400	31	87	89	middle	60
Ecuador	270,670.0	11.300	42	80	105	middle	83
Guyana	215,000.0	0.800	4	92	76	low	n/a
Paraguay	406,750.0	4.600	11	88	84	middle	70
Peru	1,285,220.0	22.900	18	82	99	middle	54
Surinam	163,265.0	0.400	2	65	124	middle	n/a
Uruguay	176,215.0	3.100	18	94	66	middle	90
Venezuela	912,050.0	20.600	22	85	94	middle	75
Total/average/range	17,702,603.0	307.700	17	63–95			54–90

Key:		PR	proportional representation	Lib-dem	Liberal democratic
F	federal	SP	simple plurality	Em-dem	Emergent democratic
PL	party list	U	unitary	Lim-pres	Limited presidential

and Britain the economic one. In the 20th century, of course, the United States has been the rising influence. However, US interference in Latin American domestic affairs has often had a boomerang effect and not realized its original purpose. It has merely succeeded in irritating, or antagonizing, the proudly independent South American states.

Despite their long histories of political independence, and despite the wealth of natural resources in many areas, the economies of the 12 South American countries do not have a particularly good record. Ten fall into the 'middle income' category and two, Bolivia and Guyana, achieve only 'low income' status. The international indebtedness of most of them continues to grow, and some, notably Brazil, have battled with enormously high levels of inflation, but the future is not entirely bleak.

Political changes in Europe will, increasingly, have their impact on South America. The resurgence of Spain has already been noted but it is also interesting to speculate about the future position of Castro's Cuba, in the neighbouring region of Central America and the Caribbean, now that it has been abandoned by its former Soviet patron. Many observers of the political and economic scene saw the 1980s as an era of lost opportunities, during which the countries in the region might have raised their levels of investment and living standards, but failed to do so. There are hopeful prospects, however, for the last years of the 20th century and the North American Free Trade Agreement (NAFTA), which has already expanded beyond Canada, the United States, and Mexico to Chile, might suggest a way forward for the nations of the south.

Recommended reading

Calvert, P (ed.) *Political and Economic Encyclopaedia of South America and the Caribbean*, Longman, 1991

Corradi, J E *The Fitful Republic: Economy, Society and Politics in Argentina*, Westview Press, 1985

Diamond, L, Linz, J and Lipset, S M (eds) *Democracy in Developing Countries*, Vol. 4 *Latin America*, Lynne Rienner, 1989

O'Donnell, G, Schmitter, P C and Whitehead, L (eds) *Transitions from Authoritarian Rule: Prospects for Democracy*, Vol. II *Latin America*, Johns Hopkins University Press, 1986

McDonald, R and Ruhl, J M *Party Politics and Elections in Latin America*, Westview Press, 1989

Masterson, D M *Militarism and Politics in Latin America: Peru from Sanchez Cerro to Sendero Luminoso*, Greenwood Press, 1991

Przeworski, A *Democracy and the Market: Political and Economic Reforms in Eastern Europe and Latin America*, Cambridge University Press, 1991

Stepan, A *Rethinking Military Politics: Brazil and the Southern Cone*, Princeton University Press, 1988

Table 62

World ranking	Date of state formation	State structure	State type	Executive type	Number of assembly chambers	Party structure	Lower house electoral system
28	1816	F	Lib-dem	Lim-pres	2	two	SP
45	1825	U	Lib-dem	Lim-pres	2	multi	SP
49	1822	F	Lib-dem	Lim-pres	2	multi	PR-PL
36	1818	U	Em-dem	Lim-pres	2	multi	SP
60	1830	U	Lib-dem	Lim-pres	2	multi	SP
30	1830	U	Lib-dem	Lim-pres	1	multi	PR-PL
	1966	U	Lib-dem	Lim-pres	1	two	PR-PL
47	1811	U	Em-dem	Lim-pres	2	multi	PR-PL
69	1824	U	Lib-dem	Lim-pres	1	two	PR-PL
	1975	U	Em-dem	Lim-pres	1	multi	SP
21	1825	U	Lib-dem	Lim-pres	2	multi	PR-PL
40	1830	F	Lib-dem	Lim-pres	2	multi	PR-PL

SOUTH AMERICA

NICARAGUA

COSTA
RICA   PANAMA

Aruba
(Neth)

Netherlands
Antilles
(Neth)

BARBADOS

GRENADA

TRINIDAD & TOBAGO

VENEZUELA

COLOMBIA

GUYANA

SURINAM

FRENCH
GUIANA

ATLANTIC
OCEAN

Equator

ECUADOR

PERU

BRAZIL

BOLIVIA

PARAGUAY

Tropic of Capricorn

CHILE

URUGUAY

PACIFIC
OCEAN

ARGENTINA

ATLANTIC
OCEAN

Falkland Islands
(UK)

0   600 mi

0   1000 km

ARGENTINA

Republic of Argentina
República Argentina

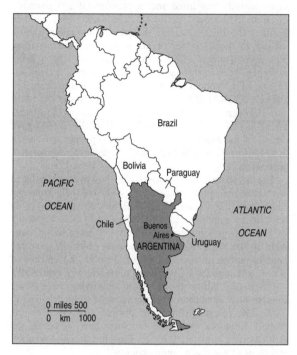

Capital: Buenos Aires

Social and economic data
Area: 2,766,889 km^2
Population: 32,500,000*
Pop. density per km^2: 12*
Urban population: 87%**
GDP: $200,000 million**; per-capita GDP: $6,153**
Government defence spending (% of GDP): 2.4%**
Currency: peso
Economy type: middle income
Labour force in agriculture: 13%**

*1994
**1992

Ethnic composition
About 85% of the population is of European descent, mainly Spanish, and 15% are mestizos, offspring of Spanish-American and American-Indian parents. The almost universally used language is Spanish.

Religions
About 90% of the population adheres to the Roman Catholic faith, which is a quasi-state religion. The constitution, for example, requires the president to be a Roman Catholic.

Political features
State type: liberal democratic
Date of state formation: 1816
Political structure: federal
Executive: limited presidential
Assembly: two-chamber
Party structure: two-party
Human rights rating: 84%
International affiliations: AG (observer), ALADI, BCIE, G-11, G-15, G-24, IAEA, IBRD, IMF, IWC, Mercosur, OAS, RG, SELA, UN, WTO

Local and regional government
Argentina is a federal state comprising the Federal District, 23 provinces, and the National Territory of Tierra del Fuego. Each province has its own elected governor and assembly, responsible for all matters which have not been specifically entrusted to the federal government. Each governor serves a four-year term and is either directly elected by popular vote or through an electoral college. Two-thirds of the provincial assemblies have single chambers and the other third have two. In most provinces the governor appoints the city mayors but the mayor of Buenos Aires, is popularly elected.

Head of state and head of government
President Carlos Saúl Menem, since 1989

Political leaders since 1970
1966–1973 (military), 1973 Héctor Cámpora (Justice–Peronist Party), 1973–74 Juan Perón (Peronist), 1974–76 Isabel Perón (Peronist), 1976–78 General Jorge Videla (military), 1978–81 General Roberto Viola (military), 1981–82 General Leopoldo Galtieri (military), 1982–83 General Reynaldo Bignone (military), 1983–89 Raúl Alfonsín Foulkes (UCR), 1989– Carlos Saúl Menem (PJ)

Political system
The 1994 constitution, which substantially amended the original of 1853, provides for a president, who is head of state and head of government, and a two-chamber legislature, consisting of the Senate and the Chamber of Deputies. The president is elected by universal suffrage for a four-year term, renewable once only. The Senate has 69 members, two nominated by each provincial assembly as general representatives and the remaining third representing minorities. Senators serve a nine-year term, with one-third of the seats renewable every three years. The Chamber of Deputies has 257 members, directly elected by universal suffrage for a four-year term, with half the seats renewable every two years.

Political parties
There are many political parties and groups, the four most significant being the Radical Union Party (UCR), the Justice Party (PJ), the Front for a Country in Solidarity (Frepaso), and the Movement for Dignity and Independence (Modin). The UCR was formed in 1890 and has a moderate centrist orientation. The PJ represents the present-day Peronist movement and was founded in 1945. It is a populist force which operates through two wings. Modin is a right-wing body. Frepaso, a centre-left coalition of socialists, communists and Christian Democrats, was formed in 1994.

Latest elections
In the 1995 presidential election President Menem was re-elected with 49.8% of the vote.

In the concurrent Chamber of Deputies elections the PJ won 137 seats, the UCR 69, and Frepaso 26.

Political history
Colonized by Spain in the 16th century, Argentina achieved independence in 1816. The country experienced a series of internal conflicts, peace only being achieved through strong, often dictatorial, governments. The first relatively free and democratic elections took place in 1916 and were won by the UCR, which had been formed 26 years earlier. In 1930 the first of what were to be a series of military coups ousted the civilian government. Two years later there was a return to civilian rule but a second military coup, in 1945, saw the arrival of Lieutenant General Juan Domingo Perón (1895–1974), who, with his widely popular first wife, Eva (Evita) Duarte Perón (1919–52), created the Peronista Party, favouring policies of extreme nationalism and social improvements. Perón admired Franco's Spanish brand of fascism and set about expanding and strengthening the urban working class, at the expense of the agricultural community. He relied heavily on the military for support.

Evita Perón died in 1952 and, with her death, her husband's popularity faded. Three years later he was forced to resign and a civilian government was restored. Perón went into exile in Spain from where he continued to oversee his party's affairs. Another coup in 1966 brought back military rule and then, in 1973, the success of the Justice (Peronist) Party brought Dr Héctor Cámpora to the presidency, essentially to pave the way for Perón's return. Cámpora resigned after three months and was replaced by Perón, this time with a new wife, María Estela Martínez de Perón, 'Isabelita' (b. 1931), as vice president. A year later Perón died and his widow took over.

Isabelita did not enjoy the same degree of popularity as Evita had done nor was her government successful in managing the economy. It was not surprising, therefore, that two years after her succession she was ousted in yet another military coup, led by Lieutenant General Jorge Videla. The constitution was amended, political and trade union activity banned, and a policy of harsh repression of left-wing elements was pursued, during which it is estimated that between 6,000 and 15,000 people 'disappeared'. Although he had been confirmed in office until 1981, in 1978 General Videla announced his retirement and was succeeded by General Roberto Viola, who promised a speedy return to democratic government. Three years later Viola died of a sudden heart attack and was replaced by the commander in chief of the army, General Leopoldo Galtieri (b. 1926).

During the next two years the state of the economy worsened and Galtieri, following the examples of many political leaders, sought to divert attention from internal problems by creating an external diversion. In April 1982 he ordered the invasion of the Islas Malvinas, or Falkland Islands (see *Chapter 8*), over which Britain's claims to sovereignty had long been disputed. After a short, undeclared, war, during which 755 Argentinians lost their lives, the islands were reoccupied by British forces and, with the defeat, Galtieri's stock fell and he was forced to resign in a bloodless coup. He and other members of the military junta he led were later declared by a military commission of inquiry to be responsible for the Falklands failure and were given prison sentences.

General Reynaldo Bignone took over the government and announced that the 1853 constitution would be revived and democratic elections held. The ban on political and trade union activity was lifted and in presidential and assembly elections in October 1983 the UCR, led by Dr Raúl Alfonsín Foulkes (b. 1927), secured the presidency and a narrow victory in the Chamber of Deputies. The new president announced a radical reform of the armed forces, leading to the retirement of more than half of the senior officers, and the setting up of a National Commission on the Disappearance of Persons (CONADEP) to investigate the events of the 'dirty war' between 1976 and 1983, when thousands of 'disappearances' had taken place. A report by CONADEP in 1984 gave details of the deaths of more than 8,000 people and named 1,300 army officers who had been involved in the campaign of repression.

The Alfonsín administration was, however, soon faced with economic problems, forcing it to seek help from the International Monetary Fund (IMF) and the adoption of an austerity programme, described by Alfonsín as an 'economy of war'. The government's popularity fell and a swing to the right in the September 1987 assembly elections gave the smaller parties in the Chamber of Deputies the balance of power, although the UCR remained the largest single block.

Externally, Alfonsín set about improving Argentina's international reputation by undertaking a six-nation tour in 1986. The re-establishment of normal relations with the United Kingdom continued to elude him, however, the British prime minister, Margaret Thatcher showing no obvious signs of wanting a rapprochement.

Alfonsín was limited by the constitution to one term as president and in elections for his successor, in May 1989, the PJ candidate, Carlos Saúl Menem (b. 1935), was victorious. Although Menem had spoken belligerently about regaining the Falklands during the election campaign, soon after his assumption of the presidency there were signs of improving relations between Argentina and Britain, and this improvement developed quietly rather than dramatically, consular ties eventually being restored. Domestically, Menem embarked on an extensive privatization programme, often in the face of left-wing opposition. He also succeeded in bringing down the level of inflation from 200% a month in 1989 to 11% per annum in 1994 and in 1991 Argentina joined Brazil, Uruguay, and Paraguay to form Mercosur, the 'Common Market of the Southern Cone'.

In 1993 the PJ won a comfortable majority in the Chamber of Deputies and in 1994 the constitution was amended to allow the president to seek another term of office. Despite undergoing a heart operation in October 1993, Menem fought the 1995 presidential election and won convincingly. The PJ also secured a majority in the Chamber of Deputies.

BOLIVIA

Republic of Bolivia
República de Bolivia

Capital: Sucre (legal capital and seat of the judiciary); La Paz (seat of government)

Social and economic data
Area: 1,098,600 km^2
Population: 7,700,000*
Pop. density per km^2: 7*
Urban population: 52%**
Literacy rate: 63%**
GDP: $5,270 million**; per-capita GDP: $684**
Government defence spending (% of GDP): 1.9%**
Currency: boliviano
Economy type: low income
Labour force in agriculture: 46%**

*1994
**1992

Ethnic composition
The population comprises 30% Quechua Indians, 25% Aymara Indians, 25–30% of mixed race, and 5–15% of European descent. The official languages are Spanish, Quechua, and Aymara.

Religions
The great majority of people, over 5 million, follow the Roman Catholic faith, although religious freedom is guaranteed for everyone.

Political features
State type: liberal democratic
Date of state formation: 1825
Political structure: unitary
Executive: limited presidential
Assembly: two-chamber
Party structure: multiparty
Human rights rating: 71%
International affiliations: AG, ALADI, AP, G-11, IAEA, IBRD, IMF, NAM, OAS, RG, SELA, UN, WTO

Local and regional government
Bolivia is divided into nine departments, ranging in population from under 43,000 to nearly 2 million. Each department is governed by a prefect, appointed by the president.

Head of state and head of government
President Gonzalo Sanchez de Lozada, since 1993

Political leaders since 1970
1970–71 General Juan Torres Gonzáles (military), 1971–80 Colonel Hugo Banzer Suárez (military), 1980–81 General Luis García (military), 1981–82 General Celso Torrelio Villa (military), 1982 General Guido Vildoso (military), 1982–85 Hernan Siles Zuazo (MNR), 1985–89 Victor Paz Estenssoro (MNR–Izquierda), 1989–93 Jaime Paz Zamora (MIR), 1993– Gonzalo Sanchez de Lozada (MNR)

Political system
Bolivia became an independent republic in 1825 after nearly 300 years of Spanish rule. It adopted its first constitution in 1826 and since then a number of variations have been produced, the present one being based on that of 1947. After years of abrogation, it was revived, after a *coup d'état*, in 1964. It provides for a two-chamber National Congress consisting of a 27-member Senate and a 130-member Chamber of Deputies, both elected for four years by universal adult suffrage, through a simple plurality voting procedure. The president is also directly elected for a four-year term and combines the roles of head of state and head of government. The president chooses and appoints the cabinet. If no candidate obtains a clear majority in the presidential election, the president is chosen by Congress.

Political parties
There is a large number of political parties, the most significant being the National Revolutionary Movement (MNR), the Nationalist Democratic Action Party (ADN), the Movement of the Revolutionary Left (MIR), and the Solidarity and Civic Union (UCS).

The MNR was founded in 1942 by Victor Paz Estenssoro. Its orientation is right-of-centre. The ADN is a right-wing grouping, formed in 1979 and led by Hugo Banzer. The MIR is a left-wing party formed in 1971. The UCS is a more recent, populist, free-market party.

Latest elections
The June 1993 presidential election was won by the MNR candidate, Gonzalo Sanchez. As neither he nor any of his rivals had won an absolute majority, the final choice was passed to the National Congress, but, before its decision was taken, his nearest rival, Hugo Banzer, once a military dictator, withdrew his candidacy, leaving the field clear for Sanchez.

The results of the concurrent congressional elections were as shown in the table on the following page.

Political history
Bolivia became a Spanish colony in 1538 and took its name from Simón Bolívar (1783–1830), the legendary figure who liberated it in 1825. Since then it has had a very chequered political history, experiencing more than 60 revolutions, 70 presidents, and 11 constitutions. Distracted by its internal

	Senate seats	Chamber of Deputies seats
MNR	17	52
Patriotic Accord*	8	35
UCS	1	20
Others	1	23

*ADN–MIR coalition

problems, Bolivia lost large tracts of land to its three neighbours, Chile in 1884, Brazil in 1903, and Paraguay in 1938.

In 1951 Dr Victor Paz Estenssoro (b. 1907), who had founded the MNR in 1942, returned from exile in Argentina to fight the presidential election. He failed to get an absolute majority and the sitting president transferred power to an army junta. However, a popular uprising, supported by the MNR and a section of the army, demanded the return of Paz, who assumed the presidency the following year and immediately embarked on a programme of social reform.

Paz lost the 1956 election to an MNR colleague who was to become a bitter rival, Hernán Siles Zuazo, but was returned to power in 1960. In 1964, following strikes and civil disorder, a coup led by the vice president, General René Barrientos, overthrew the Paz government and a military junta was installed. Two years later Barrientos fought for and won the presidency. He met great opposition from left-wing groups and in 1967 a guerrilla uprising, led by Dr Ernesto ('Che') Guevara (1928–67) was only put down with US help. In 1969 President Barrientos was killed in an air crash and replaced by the vice president. He, in turn, was replaced by General Alfredo Ovando, who, after a military power struggle, was ousted by General Juan Torres, who was also to be removed in 1971 by a fellow officer, Colonel Hugo Banzer.

Banzer announced a return to constitutional government but another attempted coup in 1974 prompted him to postpone elections, ban all trade union and political activity, and proclaim that there would be military government until at least 1980. Succumbing to mounting pressure for a return to a more democratic form of government, Banzer agreed to elections in 1978. There were allegations of widespread electoral fraud, prompting, in the same year, two more military coups. Elections were eventually held in 1979 and the two ex-presidents who had been rivals before, in 1956, Dr Siles and Dr Paz, received virtually identical votes. An interim administration was installed, pending fresh elections. An election in 1980 proved equally inconclusive and was followed by the 189th military coup in Bolivia's 154 years of independence.

General Luis García was installed as president but forced to resign the following year after allegations of involvement in drug trafficking. He was replaced by General Celso Torrelio who promised to fight corruption and return the country to democratic government within three years. In 1982 a inly civilian cabinet was appointed but rumours of an ending coup resulted in Torrelio's resignation. A military led by the hardliner General Guido Vildoso, was d. Because of the worsening economic situation, the junta decided to ask Congress to elect a president and Dr Siles, who had won most votes in the close elections of 1979 and 1980, was chosen to head a coalition cabinet. Economic aid from the United States and Europe, which had been cut off in 1980, resumed but the economy continued to deteriorate. There was widespread opposition to the government's austerity measures and, in an attempt to secure national unity, President Siles even embarked on a five-day hunger strike.

A general strike and another abortive army coup followed in 1985, prompting President Siles to resign. Again, the election was inconclusive, with no candidate winning an absolute majority. The veteran MNR leader, Dr Paz, at the age of 77, was chosen by Congress as the new president. Despite strict austerity measures, including a wage freeze, to attempt to curb inflation, which had reached 23,000% in 1985, Bolivia's economy worsened.

In the 1989 presidential election there was no conclusive result, the eventual new president, Jaime Paz Zamora (MIR), being determined by the National Congress in August 1989. After negotiations, he formed a coalition government with the ADN and Christian Democrats.

The 1993 presidential election was decided in a similar fashion, Gonzalo Sanchez de Lozada (b. 1930), representing the MNR, eventually being elected. In the concurrent National Congress elections the MNR won most seats but not an overall majority. A government was eventually formed with the support of the UCS and the small centrist Free Bolivia Movement (MBL). By 1994 the annual inflation rate had been brought down to single figures and the Sanchez administration was encouraging foreign inward investment in the country's state-owned industry.

BRAZIL

The Federative Republic of Brazil
A República Federativa do Brasil

Capital: Brasília

Social and economic data
Area: 8,512,000 km^2
Population: 156,600,000*
Pop. density per km^2: 18*
Urban population: 77%**
Literacy rate: 75%**
GDP: $424,000 million**; per-capita GDP: $ 2,708**
Government defence spending (% of GDP): 1%**
Currency: real
Economy type: middle income
Labour force in agriculture: 29%**

*1994
**1992

Ethnic composition
There is a wide range of ethnic groups including about 55% of European origin, mainly Portuguese, Italian, and German, about 38% of mixed parentage, and about 6% of Black African origin, as well as American Indians and Japanese.

The official and almost universally used language is Portuguese. English and Spanish are also spoken.

Religions
Nearly 90% of the population is Roman Catholic, the rest being Protestant or Spiritualist.

Political features
State type: liberal democratic
Date of state formation: 1822
Political structure: federal
Executive: limited presidential
Assembly: two-chamber
Party structure: multiparty
Human rights rating: 69%
International affiliations: AG (obsercer), ALADI, AP, G-11, G-15, G-24, IAEA, IBRD, IMF, IWC, Lusophone, Mercosur, NAM (observer), OAS, RG, SELA, UN, WTO

Local and regional government
Brazil is divided into five geographical regions, central-west, northeast, north, southeast, and south. The regions are subdivided into 26 states and a federal district (Brasília). The populations of the states range from about 300,000 to over 25 million, the federal district has a population of nearly 1.2 million, and the populations of the territories vary from just over 1,000 to nearly 80,000. Each state has a constitution modelled on that of the federal constitution, with an elected single-chamber assembly and governor. The governor of the federal district is appointed by and directly responsible to the president.

The powers and duties of the federal government are set out in the constitution and include responsiblility for external affairs, defence, and nationwide services, such as communi-cations, education, agriculture, and maritime and labour law. The residue of powers and duties is left with the states.

Below state level there are municipalities with elected councils and mayors.

Head of state and head of government
President Fernando Henrique Cardoso, since 1995

Political leaders since 1970
1969–74 General Emilio Garrastazu Medici (military), 1974–78 General Ernesto Geisel (military), 1978–85 General João Baptista de Figueiredo (military), 1985 Tancredo Neves (PFL), 1985–89 José Sarney Costa (PDS), 1989–92 Fernando Collor de Mello (PRN), 1992–94 Itamar Franco (PRN), 1995– Fernando Henrique Cardoso (PSDB)

Political system
The 1988 constitution provides for a federal system, based broadly on the US model, with a two-chamber National Congress consisting of a Senate of 81 members and a Chamber of Deputies of variable size. The number of deputies is determined by the population of each state and each territory is represented by one deputy. The Chamber of Deputies had 517 members in 1994. Senators are elected on the basis of one per state for an eight-year term, at four-year intervals for one-third and two-thirds of the seats alternatively. Deputies are elected for a four-year term. Elections to both chambers are by universal adult suffrage through a party list system of voting. Voting is compulsory for people between the ages of 18 and 69 and optional for people younger than 18 or older than 69.

The constitution also provides for a president to be elected by universal adult suffrage for a five-year term, not subject to renewal, governing through a cabinet of his or her own choosing. In May 1994 the constitution was amended to reduce the presidential term to four years.

The 1988 constitution which replaced that of 1969, which had been amended several times, transferred considerable power from the president to Congress, placing the executive somewhere between a limited presidential and a parliamentary one. In a national referendum held in 1993 there was a vote in favour of the current presidential system and against a parliamentary system or restoration of the monarchy.

Other novel features of the constitution include the extension of the franchise to 16-year-olds and an unusual legal device, the *habeas data*, which gives people the right of access to personal files held by the National Intelligence Agency.

Political parties
Historically, Brazilian political parties were built on the power of landowners who were also the local political bosses. As the country experienced its succession of military and civilian rulers, in the period after 1945, so the parties adapted to the changing political scene, regularly regrouping. In 1965 all political parties were banned except for two which were given official recognition, one as the government party and one as the opposition. The practice of operating controlled parties was ended in 1979 and for a period other parties were permitted to operate under strictly controlled conditions. In 1985 all restrictions were removed and the free formation of parties was allowed.

Among twenty now operating, the most significant are the National Reconstruction Party (PRN), the Social Democratic Party (PSDB), the Brazilian Democratic Movement Party (PMDB), the Liberal Front Party (PFL), the Democratic Labour Party (PDT), the Workers' Party (PT) and the Brazilian Progressive Party (PPB).

The PRN was formed in 1989 to promote the candidacy of Fernando Collor de Mello for the presidency. It has a right-of-centre orientation.

The PSDB was formed in 1988 by dissidents from six other parties. It has a generally moderate centrist stance and is led by President Cardoso.

The PMDB was formed in 1980 as a direct descendant of an older party, the Brazilian Democratic Movement (MBD) which, between 1965 and 1979, was the official opposition party. It retained most of the moderate elements of the old MBD and in 1982 merged with the Popular Party (PP). Its orientation is centre-left and it is led by Luiz Henrique.

In 1984 some Social Democratic Party (PDS) members joined with others from the PMDB to fight the 1985 presidential election and formed the moderate centre-right PFL, led now by Antonio Magalhaes.

The PDT is another moderate left-of-centre grouping and was formed in 1980.

The PT was the first independent labour party and also dates from 1980. Its orientation is left-of-centre and it is led by Luis Inácio 'Lula' da Silva.

The PPB, formed in September 1995 through the merger of three progressive parties, is the third largest bloc in Congress.

Latest elections

The October 1994 presidential election was won by the PSDB candidate, Fernando Henrique Cardoso, who, with 54.3% of the vote, secured victory in the first round. His chief challenger was the PT's Lula da Silva.

The results of the concurrent congressional elections were as follows:

	Senate seats	Chamber of Deputies seats
PSDB–PFL coalition	33	175
PMDB	23	105
Leftish coalition, including the PT	13	77
Others	12	160

Political history

Brazil became a Portuguese colony from 1500 and in 1808 the king of Portugal, in the face of a French invasion of his country, moved the capital from Lisbon to Salvador in Brazil. He returned to Lisbon in 1821 leaving his son, Crown ￼nce Pedro (1798–1834), as regent. In 1822 Pedro declared ｚil an independent kingdom and assumed the title ￼ror Pedro I. He was succeeded by his son, Pedro II ￼-91), who persuaded large numbers of Portuguese to ￼e, resulting in a rapid development of the centre of

the country, largely on the basis of slavery. In 1888 slavery was abolished, in 1889 a republic was established, and in 1891 a constitution for a federal state was adopted.

The 1920s saw great social unrest and the world economic crisis of 1930 produced a major revolt which brought Dr Getúlio Vargas (1883–1954) to the presidency. He continued in office and, in the role of a benevolent dictator, influenced by the Italian leader, Benito Mussolini, set up a profascist state known as 'Esatado Novo', until ousted by the army in 1945. General Eurico Dutra was elected president and a new constitution was adopted. In 1950 Vargas returned to power but in 1954, faced with the threat of impeachment, he committed suicide. He was succeeded by Dr Juscelino Kubitschek. Six years later the capital was moved from Rio de Janeiro to Brasília.

In 1961 Dr Janio Quadros won the presidency but resigned after seven months, to be succeeded by the vice president, João Goulart, who was suspected by the army of having left-wing leanings. They forced an amendment to the constitution, restricting presidential powers and creating the office of prime minister. However, a referendum in 1963 brought back a fully presidential system, with Goulart choosing his own cabinet.

Dissatisfaction with the civilian administration resulted in a bloodless coup in 1964, which brought General Humberto Castelo Branco to power. He immediately banned all political parties, then gave recognition to two artificially created groups on which he felt he could rely, the pro-government National Renewal Alliance (ARENA) and an opposition party, the Brazilian Democratic Movement (MBD). This heralded a 21-year period of military rule (1964–85) during which the Brazilian economy expanded rapidly, but social and political rights were severely restricted.

In 1967 Branco named Marshal Artur da Costa e Silva as his successor and a new constitution was adopted. In 1969, however, da Costa resigned because of ill health and a new military junta took over. In 1974 General Ernesto Geisel was chosen as president, under the terms of the constitution, by an electoral college and he continued in office until succeeded by General João Baptista de Figueiredo in 1978. The following year legislation was passed to allow a return to a multiparty operation, but under strictly contolled conditions. President Figueiredo continued in office until 1985, the last few years of his presidency witnessing a deterioration in the state of the economy with strikes and mass rallies calling for the return of full democratic government.

In 1985 restrictions on political activity were removed and Tancredo Neves became the first civilian president for 21 years, amid a nationwide wave of optimism. He died within months of assuming office and was succeeded by the vice president, José Sarney Costa (b. 1930). The constitution was amended to provide for the election of the president by direct universal suffrage and a new constitution, creating a near-parliamentary executive, was adopted in October 1988.

In December 1989 Fernando Collor de Mello (b. 1949), governor of the state of Alagoas, emerged from comparative obscurity to be elected president at the age of 40. However, within a year of his taking office, disenchantment with his economic policies grew and in September 1992, following allegations of past corruption, he was removed from office, prior to his impeachment. He was replaced by the vice president, Itamar Franco (b. 1931).

Franco's popularity declined as inflation continued to soar, and he was also criticized for indiscreet behaviour during the 1994 Rio carnival. In a surprisingly successful attempt to control inflation, in July 1994 a new currency was introduced, the real, at parity with the US dollar.

In November 1994 the PSDB candidate, Fernando Cardoso, was elected president and his PSDB–PFL coalition won most seats, but not an overall majority, in the concurrent congressional elections. In the following month former President Collor was acquitted on charges of corruption because of insufficient evidence.

CHILE

The Republic of Chile
República de Chile

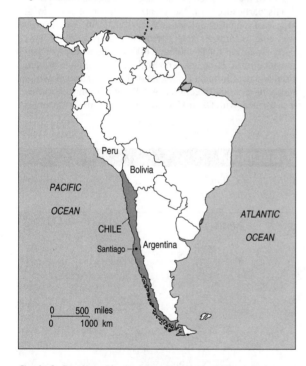

Capital: Santiago (the legislature meets at Valparaíso)

Social and economic data
Area: 756,950 km^2
Population: 13,800,000*
Pop. density per km^2: 18*
Urban population: 85%**
Literacy rate: 94%**
GDP: $37,000 million**; per-capita GDP: $2,681**
Currency: Chilean peso
Economy type: middle income
Labour force in agriculture: 19%**

*1994
**1992

Ethnic composition
The population is fairly homogeneous, consisting of about 65% mestizos (offspring of Spanish American and American Indian parents) and 30% European, the remainder being mainly Indian. Class is a more divisive factor than race. The official language is Spanish.

Religions
Roman Catholicism was the established religion until 1925 and it remains the dominant faith, being practised by about 80% of the population. Among the religious minorities are about 30,000 Jews.

Political features
State type: emergent democratic
Date of state formation: 1818
Political structure: unitary
Executive: limited presidential
Assembly: two-chamber
Party structure: multiparty
Human rights rating: 80%
International affiliations: ALADI, APEC, G-11, G-15, IAEA, IBRD, IMF, IWC, NAM, OAS, RG, SELA, UN, WTO

Local and regional government
The country is divided into 13 regions which are further subdivided into 51 provinces.

Head of state and head of government
President Eduardo Frei Ruiz-Tagle, since 1994

Political leaders since 1970
1970–73 Salvador Allende (Unidad Popular), 1973–90 General Augusto Pinochet (military), 1990–94 Patricio Aylwin (PDC), 1994– Eduardo Frei (PDC)

Political system
After a coup in 1973 Chile was ruled by a military junta until a new constitution came into effect in July 1989, following approval in a referendum. It provides for a president, who is head of state and head of government, and a two-chamber assembly of a Senate and Chamber of Deputies. The president is elected by universal suffrage for a four-year term and appoints a cabinet of ministers, headed by a prime minister. The Senate has 47 members, 38 popularly elected and nine appointed by the outgoing government and the Supreme Court. They serve an eight-year term. The Chamber of Deputies has 120 members, popularly elected for a four-year term.

Political parties
Of over 30 parties, the most significant are the Christian Democrat Party (PDC), the Socialist Party of Chile (PS), the Radical Party (PR), the Party for Democracy (PPD), the Party of National Renewal (RN), the Independent Democratic Union (UDI), and the Union of the Centre-Centre (UCC).

The Coalition of Parties for Democracy (CPD) was formed in 1988 to oppose the Pinochet regime and includes the PDC, PS, PR, PPD, and other left-of-centre groupings.

The PDC was formed in 1957. It has within it left-wing and centrist factions, but is predominantly a centre-right force. The PS was formed in 1933. It has a left-wing orientation. The PR dates from 1863 and has a left-of-centre orientation. The PPD is a left-of-centre party within the CPD. The RN was founded in 1987 and is a right-wing party. The UDI is another right-wing party, formed in 1989. The UCC is another right-wing grouping.

Latest elections

In the December 1993 presidential election the PDC candidate, Eduardo Frei, was a clear winner, with 58% of the vote.

In the concurrent 1993 congressional elections the CPD lost one of its Senate seats and was left with 21. In the Chamber of Deputies, although it won a majority of seats, it failed to secure the two-thirds majority it had hoped for. Seat holdings were as follows:

	Senate	Chamber of Deputies
PDC	13	37
RN	11	31
PS	5	26
UDI	3	15
PPD	2	
UCC	1	
PR	1	6
Others	2	5

Political history

The first European to sight Chile was Ferdinand Magellan (c. 1480–1521), in 1520, at which time the country was under Inca rule. It became part of the Spanish Empire 21 years later. It won its independence from Spain in 1818 and soon became a dominant power in western Latin America. Through most of the 20th century, however, there have been struggles between left- and right-wing political factions.

Between 1964 and 1970 the Christian Democrats, under Eduardo Frei (b. 1943), were in power, followed by a left-wing coalition led by Dr Salvador Allende (1908–73), who was the world's first democratically elected Marxist head of state. He promised to create social justice by constitutional means and embarked upon an extensive nationalization programme, which included the US-owned copper mines. Allende was seen by the CIA in Washington as a pro-Cuban communist and opposition to him within Chile was encouraged. The culmination of this movement to overthrow him was an attack on the presidential palace in 1973 by the army, led by General Augusto Pinochet (b. 1915). The government was ousted and Allende killed, the new regime claiming he ʼommitted suicide. Pinochet became president and any ʼponents were imprisoned, after torturing, or just made to ʼappear'.

ʼ1976 Pinochet established what he called an 'authoriʼdemocracy', all political parties being banned, despite ʼdemnation, and in 1978 he secured an endorsement ʼlicies through a referendum. In 1980 a new constituʼnnounced, as a 'transition to democracy' by 1989,

but reports of imprisonments and tortures continued to be received by the world outside.

Opposition to the Pinochet regime grew, with widespread demands for a return to democratic government, and when in 1986 Pinochet, at the age of 71, announced that he was considering serving another eight-year term opposition groups decided to work together to oppose him in the 1988 plebiscite to ratify him as the sole nominee for the presidency. The result of the plebiscite, answering the question whether or not Pinochet should continue for another term, was a 'No' vote of 55% and a 'Yes' vote of 43%. The general said he would honour the result but declined to step down before the end of his current term of office.

Eventually, in June 1989 the general agreed to constitutional changes which would permit fully pluralist politics, the amendments to be put forward for approval in a national plebiscite. The result was an overwhelming vote for change and in December 1989 Patricio Aylwin Azocár (b. 1915), leader of the Christian Democrats, was elected president.

His party also won the greatest number of seats in the House of Deputies but not an overall majority. However, he was able to form a stable government, founded on a multi-party Coalition for Democracy (CPD). The December 1993 presidential election was won by the CPD nominee, Eduardo Frei, and his Christian Democrat party was also successful in the congressional elections. A CPD coalition government was formed, with Dante Cordova as prime minister from July 1995.

COLOMBIA

Republic of Colombia
República de Colombia

Capital: Bogotá

Social and economic data
Area: 1,138,994 km^2

Population: 33,400,000*
Pop. density per km²: 31*
Urban population: 69%**
Literacy rate: 87%*
GDP: $41,000 million**; per-capita GDP: $1,227**
Government defence spending (% of GDP): 1%**
Currency: Colombian peso
Economy type: middle income
Labour force in agriculture: 28%

*1994
**1992

Ethnic composition
Although the main ethnic groups are of mixed Spanish, Indian, and African blood, Colombia is one of the most Spanish of all South American countries and Spanish customs and values predominate. Spanish is the national language.

Religions
About 95% of the population is Roman Catholic and Roman Catholicism is sufficiently strong to be regarded as the quasi-state religion.

Political features
State type: liberal democratic
Date of state formation: 1830
Political structure: unitary
Executive: limited presidential
Assembly: two-chamber
Party structure: multiparty
Human rights rating: 60%
International affiliations: ACS, AG, ALADI, AP, G-3, G-11, G-24, IAEA, IBRD, IMF, NAM, OAS, RG, SELA, UN, WTO

Local and regional government
Although it does not have a federal system of government, the country is divided into 23 departments, four intendencies, and five commissaries, enjoying considerable autonomy. Below these levels are municipalities. Each department has a governor appointed by the president and there are regional elected assemblies.

Head of state and head of government
President Ernesto Samper Pizano, since 1994

Political leaders since 1970
1970–74 Misael Pastrana Borrero (PSC), 1974–78 Alfonso López Michelsen (PL), 1978–82 Julio Cesar Turbay Ayala (PL), 1982–86 Belisario Betancur Cuartas (PSC), 1986–90 Virgilio Barco Vargas (PL), 1990–94 Cesar Gaviria Trujillo (PL), 1994–   Ernesto Samper (PL)

Political system
The July 1991 constitution, which, with 397 articles, is one of the longest in the world, provides for a president who is head of state and head of government and a two-chamber Congress, consisting of a 102-member Senate and a 163-member House of Representatives.

The president is directly elected by universal suffrage for a four-year nonrenewable term. Members of Congress are elected in the same way for the same term length. Of the 163 members of the House of Representatives there must be two from each of the 23 national departments. The president appoints a cabinet over which he or she presides.

Political parties
There are some twenty political parties, the most significant being the Liberal Party (PL), the Conservative Party (PSC), the April 19th Movement (ADM–19), and the National Salvation Movement (MSN). The PL and the PSC have dominated the political scene for most of the 20th century but this dominance is being increasingly challenged.

Although there are strong democratic traditions, politics in Colombia have long been stained by violence between the two ruling parties and from left-wing opposition groups and the drug barons, based in Colombia's second city, Medellín, and in Cali.

The Liberal Party was founded in 1815. It is divided into two factions, the official group and the independent group, who call themselves New Liberalism. The party has a centrist orientation.

The Conservative Party was formed in 1849. It too has a history of internal factionalism but this is not as clearly defined as in the Liberal Party. Its political stance is right-of-centre.

The ADM–19 was a left-wing guerrilla group which reformed itself into a legitimate party in 1991.

The MSN is a right-of-centre coalition which has come together in recent years.

Latest elections
In the 1994 presidential elections, which were postponed from March to May–June, the PL candidate, Ernesto Samper Pizano, won 50.4% of the vote in the second-round run-off, his PSC rival, Andrés Pastrana Arango, obtaining 48.6%.

In the March 1994 congressional elections the results were as follows:

	Senate seats	House of Representatives seats
PL	52	89
PSC	21	56
Other parties	29	18*

*ADM–19 15 seats

Political history
Colombia became a Spanish colony in the 16th century and obtained its independence in 1819, as part of a union with Ecuador, Panama, and Venezuela. In 1903 it became entirely independent. Since then two main political parties, the Conservatives and the Liberals, have dominated Colombian politics. Between 1860 and 1884 the Liberals were in power,

between 1884 and 1930 it was the Conservatives, between 1930 and 1946 the Liberals, and between 1946 and 1953 the Conservatives. In 1948 the left-wing mayor of the capital city, Bogotá, was assassinated and there followed a decade of near civil war, 'La Violencia', during which it is thought that well over a quarter of a million people died. The legacy of this war was the continuation of left-wing guerrilla activity through to the 1980s.

In 1957, in an effort to halt the violence, the Conservatives and Liberals agreed to form a National Front, with the presidency alternating between them. In 1970, the National Front was challenged by the National Popular Alliance (ANAPO), with a special appeal to the working classes, but the Conservative–Liberal cooperation continued and when in 1978 the Liberals won majorities in both chambers of Congress and the presidency they kept the National Front accord.

In 1982 the Liberals retained their majorities in Congress but Dr Belisario Bentacur won the presidency for the Conservatives. He sought a truce with the left-wing guerrillas by granting them an amnesty and freeing political prisoners. He also embarked upon a radical programme of public works expenditure. His plans suffered a major blow in 1984 when his minister of justice, who had been using harsh measures to curb drug dealing, was assassinated. Betancur's reaction was to strengthen his anti-drug campaign.

In the May 1986 elections the presidency changed hands again, going to the Liberal Virgilio Barco Vargas by a record margin. In 1990 the presidency was again won by the Liberals.

The new young president, Cesar Gaviria, embarked on further constitutional reform and an effort of reconciliation with the guerrilla groups who were opposing him. In 1991, as a new constitution came into effect, most, including the April 19th Movement (ADM–19), abandoned their struggle and converted themselves into political parties. However, the Colombian Revolutionary Armed Forces (Farc) and the National Liberation Army remained active, sabotaging oil pipelines.

The Liberals dominated the first elections under the new constitution, winning the presidency and a majority in both congressional chambers. Meanwhile, the war against the drug barons continued, Pablo Escobar (1949–93), leader of the Medellín ring, being killed in December 1993 while attempting to avoid arrest after escaping from prison in 1992. However, another drugs cartel, based in Cali, remained a serious threat.

In the March 1994 elections the Liberals retained their control of Congress, but with a reduced majority, and the party's candidate, Ernesto Samper (b. 1951), won the presidency.

In 1995 President Samper decreed a state of emergency to fight the rising wave of violence and guerrilla activities and in the summer of 1995 six of the top seven Cali drugs cartel leaders were arrested and imprisoned. However, there were current allegations that the 1994 Samper presidential campaign had received at least $6 million in 'dirty money' the Cali cartel. This led to mounting calls for the presiresign and investigations by a committee of Con-

ECUADOR

Republic of Ecuador
República del Ecuador

Capital: Quito

Social and economic data
Area: 270,670 km²
Population: 11,300,000*
Pop. density per km²: 42*
Urban population: 58%**
Literacy rate: 80%**
GDP: $12,681 million**; per-capita GDP: $1,123**
Currency: sucre
Economy type: middle income
Labour force in agriculture: 38%**

*1994
**1992

Ethnic composition
The population is about 55% mestizo (offspring of Spanish American and American Indian parents), 25% Indian, 10% Spanish, and 10% African. The official language is Spanish but Quecha and other indigenous languages are spoken.

Religions
About 90% of the population is Roman Catholic. There are also other Christian and Jewish minorities.

Political features
State type: liberal democratic
Date of state formation: 1830
Political structure: unitary
Executive: limited presidential

Assembly: one-chamber
Party structure: multiparty
Human rights rating: 83%
International affiliations: AG, ALADI, AP, G-11, IAEA, IBRD, IMF, IWC, NAM, OAS, RG, SELA, UN

Local and regional government

Ecuador is not a fully federal state, but has a devolved system of 21 provinces, including the Galápagos Islands, each administered by an appointed governor.

Head of state and head of government

President Sixto Durán Ballén, since 1992

Political leaders since 1970

1968–72 José María Velasco (PLR), 1972–76 General Guillermo Rodríguez Lara (military), 1976–79 General Alfredo Poveda Burbano (military), 1979–81 Jaime Roldos Aguilera (Coalition of Popular Forces: CFP), 1981–84 Osvaldo Hurtado Larrea (CFP), 1984–88 León Febres Cordero (PSC), 1988–92 Rodrigo Borja Cevallos (ID), 1992– Sixto Durán Ballén (PUR)

Political system

The 1979 constitution provides for a president, elected by universal adult suffrage for a nonrenewable four-year term, and a single-chamber National Congress, the Chamber of Representatives, with 77 members. Sixty-five are elected on a provincial basis every two years and 12 are elected nationally every four years. Voting in presidential elections is by the majoritarian system of second ballot and for the Congress by the party list system of proportional representation.

Political parties

There are some 18 political parties, the most significant being the Democratic Left (ID), the Republican Unity Party (PUR), the Social Christian Party (PSC), the Conservative Party (PC), and the Ecuadorean Roldosist Party (PRE).

The ID was formed in 1970 as a result of a split in the Liberal Party (PLR: estd. 1895). It has a moderate socialist orientation. The PUR is a coalition of conservative parties which came together in recent years. The PSC is a right-wing party formed in 1951 and led by León Febres Cordero. The PC is Ecuador's oldest party, having been established in 1855, and has a right-wing orientation. The PRE is a populist party formed in 1982.

Latest elections

In the May 1992 elections for the National Congress seats were won as follows:

	National Congress Seats
PSC	21
PRE	13
PUR	12
ID	7
PC	6
Others	18

The May and July 1992 presidential elections were won by Sixto Durán Ballén, the 70-year-old PUR candidate, with 57.9% of the votes in the second ballot. His rival, Jaime Nebot Saadi (PSC), had 42.1% of the votes.

Political history

Under Spanish rule from the 16th century, Ecuador became part of Gran Colombia in 1822 and then a fully independent state in 1830. From independence onwards the political pendulum has swung from the Conservatives to the Liberals, from civilian to military rule, and from democratic to dictatorial government. By 1948 some stability was evident and eight years of Liberal government ensued.

In 1956 Dr Camilo Ponce became the first Conservative president for 60 years. Four years later a Liberal, Dr José María Velasco, who had been president in 1933–35, 1944–47 and 1952–56, was re-elected. He was deposed in a 1961 coup by the vice president, who, in the following year, was himself dismissed and replaced by a military junta. In 1968 Velasco returned from exile and took up the presidency again. Another coup in 1972 put the military back in power until, in 1979, when it seemed as if Ecuador had returned permanently to its pre-1948 political pattern, a new, democratic constitution was adopted.

The 1979 constitution has survived, even though a deteriorating economy has resulted in strikes, demonstrations, and, in 1982, a state of emergency. In the 1984 elections no party or coalition of parties won a clear majority in the National Congress, and León Febres Cordero won the presidency for the PSC, on a promise of 'bread, roofs and jobs'. With no immediate support in Congress, his policies seemed likely to be blocked but in 1985 he won a majority there when five opposition members decided to change allegiance and support him. At the end of his term of office, Cordero was succeeded by one of the leaders of the left-wing Progressive Democratic Front coalition, Rodrigo Borja. However, President Borja's austerity measures failed to find public favour.

In July 1992 Sixto Durán Ballén (b. 1922), representing the conservative coalition led by the Republican Unity Party (PUR), won the presidency and in the Congress the PSC emerged as the largest party, followed by the PRE and PUR. Lacking an overall majority in Congress, Duran called for a 'national consensus' and formed a coalition which included PSC members and others from the business sector. A privatization programme was launched and Ecuador, which had been a significant oil producer since the 1970s, withdrew from OPEC in November 1992 to enable it to increase its output levels. In February 1995 a long-running border dispute with Peru was finally resolved. In September 1995, the Duran Ballen administration was rocked by Parliament's dismissal of three key ministers, including the vice president and finance minister, who were accused of masterminding the country's biggest corruption scandal.

GUYANA

The Cooperative Republic of Guyana

Capital: Georgetown

Social and economic data
Area: 215,000 km^2

Population: 800,000*
Pop. density per km²: 4*
Urban population: 34%**
Literacy rate: 92%**
GDP: $343 million**; per-capita GDP: $428**
Government defence spending (% of GDP): 1.3%**
Currency: Guyana dollar
Economy type: low income
Labour force in agriculture: 20%*

*1994
**1992

Ethnic composition
About 51% of the population are East Indians, descended from settlers from the subcontinent of India, and about 43% are Afro-Indian. There are also small American-Indian, Chinese, and European minorities. Racial tensions led to violence in 1964 and 1978. English is the official language but Hindi, Urdu, and Amerindian dialects are also spoken.

Religions
There are about 430,000 Hindus, 125,000 Anglicans, 120,000 Muslims, and 94,000 Roman Catholics.

Political features
State type: liberal democratic
Date of state formation: 1966
Political structure: unitary
Executive: limited presidential
Assembly: one-chamber
Party structure: two-party
Human rights rating: N/A
International affiliations: ACP, ACS, AP, CARICOM, CW, IBRD, IMF, NAM, OAS, SELA, UN, WTO

Local and regional government
The country is divided into ten regions, each with an elected Regional Democratic Council, which is represented on the National Assembly by one member. Day-to-day administration is by an appointed commissioner.

Head of state (executive)
President Cheddi Jagan, since 1992

Head of government
Prime Minister Sam Hinds, since 1992

Political leaders since 1970
1964–85 Forbes Burnham (PNC), 1985–92 Desmond Hoyte (PNC), 1992–   Cheddi Jagan (PPP)

Political system
Guyana is a sovereign republic within the Commonwealth. The 1980 constitution provides for a single-chamber National Assembly of 65 members, 53 elected by universal suffrage, through a party list system of proportional representation, and 12 elected by the regions. They serve a five-year term. The executive president is the nominee of the party winning most votes in the National Assembly elections and serves for the life of the Assembly. The president appoints a cabinet which is collectively responsible to the Assembly. The political system therefore represents an adaptation of a parliamentary to a limited presidential executive.

Political parties
Although there are some 14 active parties and a proportional representation system of voting is used, a two-party system effectively operates, the main parties being the People's National Congress (PNC) and the People's Progressive Party (PPP).

The PNC was formed in 1955 by dissidents from the PPP. Its supporters are mainly Indian descendants. It has a centrist orientation.

The PPP dates from 1950. It is a left-wing reformed-Marxist party and draws its support mainly from Afro-Indians.

Latest elections
In the October 1992 general election the PPP won 28 of the 53 directly elected seats, with 52.3% of the popular vote. The PNC won 23 seats, with a vote of 43.6%.

Political history
Guyana was originally a Dutch colony which was seized by Britain in 1814. It became a colony of the British Empire, as British Guiana, with large numbers of Indian and Chinese labourers imported to work on sugar plantations. It achieved full independence, within the Commonwealth, in 1966.

The move from colonial to republican status was gradual and not entirely smooth. In 1953 a constitution, providing for free elections to an assembly, was introduced and the left-wing People's Progressive Party (PPP), led by Dr Cheddi Jagan (b. 1918), won the popular vote. Within months, however, the United Kingdom government suspended the constitution and put in its own interim administration, claiming that the PPP threatened to become a communist dictatorship.

In 1957 a breakaway group from the PPP founded a new party, the People's National Congress (PNC), which was socialist, rather than Marxist–Leninist. A revised constitution was introduced at the end of 1956 and fresh elections were held in 1957. The PPP won again and Jagan became chief minister. Internal self-government was granted in 1961 and, with the PPP again the successful party, Jagan became prime minister.

A system of proportional representation, based on party lists, was introduced in 1963 and in the 1964 elections, under the new voting procedures, the PPP, although winning most votes, did not have an overall majority so a PPP–PNC coalition was formed, with the PNC leader, Forbes Burnham (1923–85), as prime minister. This coalition took the country through to full independence in 1966.

The PNC won the 1968 election and in 1970 legislation was passed to make Guyana a 'Cooperative Socialist Republic' within the Commonwealth. The PNC was again successful in the 1973 general election, but the PPP, dissatisfied with the results, claiming that there had been ballot-rigging, decided to boycott the Assembly. Then, in 1976, it partly relented, offering the government its 'critical support'. Discussions began about framing a new constitution and in 1980, after a referendum, a new version was adopted. It turned a parliamentary executive into a limited presidential one, making the president both head of state and head of government.

The 1981 elections, which were declared fraudulent by the opposition parties, made Burnham the new executive president. The following years of his administration were marked by a deteriorating economy and cool relations with the United States, whose invasion of Grenada he condemned. He died in August 1985 and was succeeded by Desmond Hoyte (b. 1929).

Hoyte faced problems with the economy, which led the government to promote inward investment. This had a measure of success, with GDP growing by 7% per annum during 1992 and 1993. Hoyte was also confronted with criticisms of unnecessary delays in producing accurate electoral lists. This resulted in a delay in the holding of a general election, which was due in December 1991. When the election was eventually held, in October 1992, the PPP, led by the veteran politician, Cheddi Jagan, won a clear victory and the contest was generally considered to have been the fairest since independence. In 1993 a programme of privatization was approved by parliament.

PARAGUAY

The Republic of Paraguay
La República del Paraguay

Capital: Asunción

Social and economic data
Area: 406,750 km²
Population: 4,600,000*
Pop. density per km²: 11*
Urban population: 49%**
Literacy rate: 88%*
GDP: $6,446 million**; per-capita GDP: $1,401**
Government defence spending (% of GDP): 1.9%**
Currency: guaraní
Economy type: middle income
Labour force in agriculture: 49%**

*1994
**1992

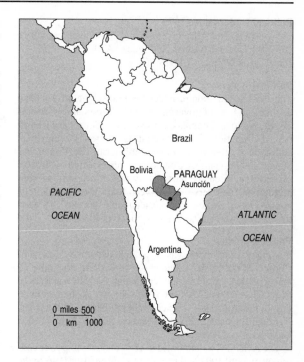

Ethnic composition
Paraguay is unusual in that, instead of the Spanish colonizers assimilating the indigenous population, the reverse has happened, so that now less than 5% of the population can be said to be clearly Spanish or Indian. The overwhelming majority are, therefore, mixed-race mestizos. Spanish is the official language but the majority of people speak Guarani, an indigenous Indian language.

Religions
Roman Catholicism is the established religion and 90% of the population practises it, but religious freedom for all is guaranteed in the constitution. There are also Anglican and Baptist minorities.

Political features
State type: emergent democratic
Date of state formation: 1811
Political structure: unitary
Executive: limited presidential
Assembly: two-chamber
Party structure: multiparty
Human rights rating: 70%
International affiliations: AG (observer), ALADI, IAEA, IBRD, IMF, Mercosur, OAS, RG, SELA, UN, WTO

Local and regional government
The country is divided into 19 departments, each administered by a governor appointed by the president. The departments are further subdivided into municipalities, each with a small elected board. The largest municipalities have appointed mayors.

Head of state and head of government
President Juan Carlos Wasmosy, since 1993

Political leaders since 1970
1954–89 General Alfredo Stroessner Mattiauda (military),
1989–93 General Andrés Rodríguez (ANR–PC), 1993–
Juan Carlos Wasmosy (ANR–PC)

Political system
The 1992 constitution provides for a president, who is head
of state and head of government, and a two-chamber assembly, the National Congress, consisting of a Senate and Chamber of Deputies. The president is elected by universal
suffrage for a five-year nonrenewable term. The 45-member
Senate and 80-member Chamber are also elected by universal suffrage, through a party list system of proportional representation, and serve a five-year term. The president is
assisted by an elected vice president and appoints and leads
the cabinet, which is called the Council of Ministers.

Political parties
For many years there was a 'model' two-party system of
Conservatives versus Liberals but now there are some 11
active parties, the most significant being the National Repub-
lican Association (ANR–PC), also known as the Colorado
Party; the Authentic Radical Liberal Party (PLRA); the
National Encounter (EN); the Radical Liberal Party (PLR);
and the Liberal Party (PL).

The ANR–PC was founded in 1887 and was in power continuously until 1904 and returned to power from 1946 to the
present day. It has traditionally received the support of the
military and contains two factions, the militants and the traditionalists. Its overall orientation is right of centre.

The PLRA is the major surviving part of the old Liberal
Party which was originally formed in 1887. It has a centre-
left orientation.

The Liberal Party also exists in its own right (PL) and in
another form, the PLR. Both have centrist orientations.

The EN is a coalition formed by supporters of the former
president, General Stroessner. It has a right-of-centre orientation.

Latest elections
The first fully democratic presidential election, in May 1993,
was won by the ANR–PC candidate, Juan Carlos Wasmosy,
with 40.9% of the vote, his nearest rival, the PLRA candidate
Domingo Laino, obtaining 32.1%, and the EN nominee,
Guillermo Caballero Vargas, securing 23.1%.

The results of the concurrent congressional elections were
as follows:

	Senate seats	Chamber of Deputies seats
ANR-PC	20	40
PLRA	17	32
EN	8	8

Political history
Paraguay was first colonized by Spain in 1537 and soon
became a major settlement, the Jesuits arriving to convert the
Indians in 1609. It achieved full independence in 1811, but,
under the dictator General José Francia, became isolated
between 1814 and 1840. As a landlocked country, it needed
access to the sea and this involved in a violent and damaging war with Brazil, Argentina, and Uruguay between 1865
and 1870, which resulted in the loss of half its people and
much territory. The two main political parties, Conservative
and Liberal, were both founded in the late 1880s. There then
followed a period of political instability until the Liberal
leader, Edvard Schaerer, came to the presidency in 1912 and
formed an administration which gained foreign confidence
and attracted foreign investment. This relative stability continued, even though many of the presidencies were short-
lived, until the Chaco Wars erupted with Bolivia between
1929 and 1935. Paraguay was the victor but, again, the cost
was great on both sides.

After 1940 Paraguay was mostly under the control of military governments led by strong autocratic leaders. General
Morinigo was president from 1940 to 1947 and General
Alfredo Stroessner (b. 1912), the commander in chief from
1951, became president in a coup in 1954. He was re-elected
in 1958, 1963, 1968, 1973, 1978, 1983, and 1988. During the
1977–81 US presidency of Jimmy Carter the repressive
Stroessner regime came under strong criticism for its violation of human rights and this resulted in some tempering of
the general's ruthless rule. Criticism by the succeeding right-
wing 1981–89 US administration of President Ronald
Reagan was less noticeable. Stroessner maintained his
supremacy by ensuring that the armed forces and business
community shared in the spoils of office and by preventing
any opposition groups from coalescing into a credible challenge.

From 1984 onwards there was increased speculation about
the eventual succession to the presidency. There was a division of opinion within his own party, the militant faction
favouring Stroessner seeking an eighth term, with his son,
Gustavo, then succeeding him, and the traditionalists believing that he should retire in 1988. The general, however,
decided to stay on and in February 1988 was re-elected for
yet another term. Early in 1989, however, he was overthrown
and forced into exile in Brazil by General Andrés Rodríguez,
who replaced him. He promised early elections, which he
and the Colorado Party won in 1989.

A new constitution was adopted in 1992 and under its
terms the country's first genuinely free elections were held in
May 1993. The presidency was won by the Colorado candidate, Juan Carlos Wasmosy (b. 1939), and his party also
secured most seats in Congress, but not an overall majority.
Without that majority, the new president tried to a agree a
'governability pact' with the main opposition parties, but
they were reluctant to support him without a promise of
greater constitutional reform. Eventually a cabinet was
appointed, criticized by the opposition as being too reactionary.

PERU

Republic of Peru
República del Perú

Capital: Lima

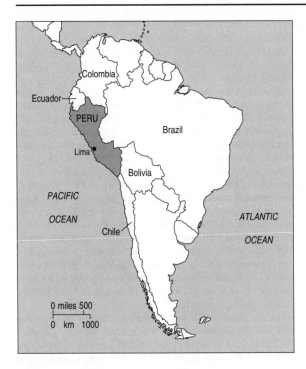

Social and economic data
Area: 1,285,220 km^2
Population: 22,900,000*
Pop. density per km^2: 18*
Urban population: 71%**
Literacy rate: 82%**
GDP: $34,100 million**; per-capita GDP: $1,490**
Government defence spending (% of GDP): 1.4**
Currency: new sol
Economy type: middle income
Labour force in agriculture: 35%**

*1994
**1992

Ethnic composition
About 45% of the population is South American Indian, about 37% mestizo (offspring of Spanish American and American Indian parents), 15% European, and 3% African. The three official languauges are Spanish, Quecha, and Aymara.

Religions
Roman Catholicism is the official religion and about 90% of the population practises it, but all beliefs are tolerated.

Political features
State type: liberal democratic
Date of state formation: 1824
Political structure: unitary
Executive: limited presidential
Assembly: one-chamber
Party structure: two-party
Human rights rating: 54%
International affiliations: AG (observer), ALADI, AP, G-11, IAEA, IBRD, IMF, IWC, NAM, OAS, RG, SELA, UN, WTO

Local and regional government
The country is divided into 11 regions, the constitutional province of Callao, and 24 departments. Each department is administered by an appointed prefect. Within the departments are provinces and districts administered by sub-prefects and governors respectively.

Head of state (executive)
President Alberto Keinya Fujimori, since 1990

Head of government
Prime Minister Dante Cordova, since 1995

Political leaders since 1970
1968–75 General Juan Velasco Alvarado (military), 1975–78 Francisco Morales Bermúdez (military), 1978–80 Victor Raúl Haya de la Torre (APRA), 1980–85 Fernando Belaúnde Terry (AP), 1985–90 Alan García Pérez (APRA), 1990– Alberto Keinya Fujimori (Cambio '90)

Political system
The 1993 constitution provides for an executive president, who is head of state, and a single-chamber 120-member National Congress. The president is elected by universal adult suffrage for a five-year term, renewable once only. The National Congress is also elected by universal suffrage, from a national party list, for the same term length. The president appoints a prime minister and a Council of Ministers.

Political parties
In the 1980s two groups dominated Peruvian politics, the American Popular Revolutionary Alliance (APRA) and an alliance of six left-wing parties called the Unified Left (IU). This dominance was challenged and disturbed in the 1990s and now, of some 30 groupings, the most significant, in addition to APRA and the IU, are Change '90 (Cambio '90), the New Majority (Nueva Mayoría: NM), the Popular Christian Party (PPC), and the Union for Peru (UPP).

APRA was founded in 1924 in Mexico by Victor Raúl Haya de la Torre, who had been exiled from Peru by the military regime. It was originally formed to fight imperialism throughout South America but Peru was the only country in which it became established. Haya de la Torre returned in 1930 and APRA became the first popular party to challenge the Peruvian establishment and its rivalry with the military leadership has been a constant feature since the 1930s. It has a moderate left-wing orientation.

The IU was formed in 1980 as an alliance of ten left-wing groups combining to fight the subsequent elections.

Cambio '90 was formed by a group of independent politicians to fight the 1990 presidential election. It has a right of centre orientation and supports Alberto Fujimori.

The NM has a similar background and orientation but dates from 1992, when it joined Cambio '90 for the 1992 congressional elections.

The PPC was formed in 1966 by dissidents from the Christian Democratic Party (PDC), which was founded ten years earlier. It has a right-of-centre orientation.

The UPP is a new centrist grouping which supported the candidacy of the former United Nations Secretary General, Javier Pérez de Cuéllar, for the presidency.

Latest elections
Alberto Fujimori was re-elected in April 1995, securing 64.4% of the popular vote. His nearest rival, Javier Pérez de Cuéllar, obtained 21.8%.

In the 1995 congressional elections the results were as follows:

	Seats won
Cambio '90/Nueva mayoria	67
UPP	17
APRA	8
Other parties	28

Political history
From the 12th century Peru was the centre of the South American Indian Inca empire, which extended during the 15th century from Quito in Ecuador to beyond Santiago in southern Chile. Its capital was at Cuzco in the Andes. The relatively advanced Inca civilization was destroyed by Spanish conquistadores, led by Francisco Pizzaro (c. 1475–1541) in 1532–33, seizing and murdering the Inca king, Atahualpa (c. 1502–33). Thereafter, Spain had a firm grip on Peru and the people had to fight long and hard to obtain their independence. They were eventually victorious in 1824.

There was progress between 1844–62 under the rule of General Ramón Castilla, but the country lost some territory to Chile after a war between 1879–83, fought in alliance with Bolivia. At the start of the 20th century civilian governments held power, but from the mid-1920s right-wing dictatorships dominated. Amazonian territory was secured from Ecuador after victory in a brief war (1941) and in 1945 free elections returned. Although APRA was the largest party in Congress it was constantly thwarted by smaller conservative groups, anxious to protect their business interests. In 1948 a group of army officers, led by General Manuel Odría, ousted the elected government, banned APRA, and installed a military junta. Odría became president in 1950 and remained in power until 1956. In the meantime APRA had become a more moderate party and the ban on it had been lifted.

In 1963 military rule ended and Fernando Belaúnde Terry (b. 1913), the joint candidate of the Popular Action (AP) and Christian Democrat (PDC) parties, won the presidency, while APRA took the largest share of the Chamber of Deputies seats. Following economic problems and industrial unrest, Belaúnde was deposed in a bloodless coup in 1968 and the army returned to power with an all-military Council of Ministers, led by General Velasco. This instituted a populist programme of land reform. Another bloodless coup in 1975 brought in General Morales Bermúdez who judged that the time for a return to constitutional government had come.

Fernando Belaúnde was re-elected in May 1980 and embarked upon a programme of agrarian and industrial reform but at the end of his presidency, in 1985, the country was in a state of economic and social crisis. Peru's fragile democracy somehow survived and Belaúnde became the first civilian president to hand over power to another constitutionally elected civilian, the young Social Democrat, Alan García Pérez (b. 1949).

García promised to end internal terrorism, which was being spearheaded by the extreme left-wing Sendero Luminoso ('Shining Path') guerrilla movement, which also exploited the illegal cocaine drugs trade, and to halt the decline in the economy. He declared his support for the Sandinista government in Nicaragua and criticized US policy throughout Latin America. He then embarked on a programme of cleansing the army and police of the 'old guard'. By February 1986 about 1,400 had elected to retire. After trying to expand the economy, while controlling inflation with price and exchange controls, he announced his intention of nationalizing the banks and insurance companies. Meeting considerable opposition from the business community, the decision was postponed. By the middle of 1988 the economy had still not revived and García came under widespread pressure to seek help from the IMF, as inflation reached the rate of 400% per month in 1990.

In the April 1990 presidential election a late entrant, a Catholic Japanese-born immigrant, Alberto Fujimori (b. 1938), sponsored by a group of independents, Cambio '90 (Change '90), defeated the Democratic Front candidate, the novelist Mario Vargas Llosa (b. 1937), a former communist who had moved to the centre-right.

With the economy showing little sign of improvement, despite the launching of a privatization programme, public unrest with the government grew and in April 1992 Fujimori decided to ally himself with the military, to avoid a potential coup. He suspended the constitution, detained opposition leaders, and temporarily ruled by decree. Accused of becoming a dictator, he said he would return the country to fully democratic government in 1993. In August of that year the Congress agreed to allow Fujimori an additional term, in 1995, and in December 1993, following approval in an October referendum, a new constitution was adopted.

In February 1994 Alfonso Bustamente, who had been appointed prime minister under the new constitution and had enjoyed considerable success in managing the economy, resigned following a disagreement with the president over his handling of a human rights issue. He was replaced by the foreign minister, Efrain Goldenberg Schreiber. In August 1994 President Fujimori revealed that he was removing his wife, Susana Higuchi, as first lady because of her political disloyalty. In the following month she announced that she had formed a new party, Harmony 21st Century, and that she would fight the next presidential election under its banner. However, her application to register as a candidate was rejected by the National Election Board (JNE) because she had not obtained the necessary minimum of 100,000 valid supporters. Meanwhile, there were sporadic outbreaks of violence by the Maoist Shining Path and Tupac Amaru Revolutionary Movement (MRTA) guerrillas. However, these were not seen as serious threats by the president. In 1992, Abimael Guzman Renoso, leader of the Shining Path, was captured and during 1994 more than 6,000 of the organization's guerrillas surrendered to the authorities.

With the economic situation improving rapidly, GDP growing by 12% in 1994, and inflation under control, Fujimori was challenged in the 1995 presidential election by the former UN secretary general, Javier Pérez de Cuéllar (b. 1920), whom he easily defeated, as well as his supporting party grouping. The New Majority alliance was successful in the concurrent congressional elections. In June 1995 President Fujimori controversially promulgated an amnesty for people who had previously been convicted of human rights crimes. His critics accused him of trying to win favour with the military, some of whom would benefit from the amnesty. In July 1995 Dante Cordova, the former education minister, was made prime minister.

SURINAM

Republic of Surinam
Republiek Suriname

Capital: Paramaribo

Social and economic data
Area: 163,265 km²
Population: 400,000*
Pop. density per km²: 2*
Urban population: 43%**
Literacy rate: 65%**
GDP: $541 million**; per-capita GDP: $1,210**
Government defence spending (% of GDP): 3.1%**
Currency: Surinam guilder
Economy type: middle income
Labour force in agriculture: 20%**

*1994
**1992

Ethnic composition
There is a very wide ethnic composition, including Creoles, East Indians, Indonesians, Africans, Amerindians, Europeans, and Chinese. Most people speak the native Creole language, Sranang Tongo, known as Negro English or taki-taki. Chinese, English, French, and Spanish are also spoken.

Religions
About 45% of the population is Christian, 28% Hindu, and 20% Muslim.

Political features
State type: emergent democratic
Date of state formation: 1975
Political structure: unitary
Executive: limited presidential
Assembly: one-chamber
Party structure: multiparty
Human rights rating: N/A
International affiliations: ACP, ACS, AP, CARICOM, IBRD, IMF, NAM, OAS, SELA, UN, WTO

Local and regional government
The country is divided into nine administrative districts, each controlled by a district commissioner. There is little or no representative local government.

Head of state and head of government
President Ronald Venetiaan, since 1991

Political leaders since 1970
1969–73 Jules Sedney (VHP), 1973–80 Henck Arron (NPS), 1980–82 Henk Chin A Sen (PNR), 1982–88 Lieutenant Colonel Desi Bouterse (military/NDP), 1988–90 Ramsewak Shankar (FDD), 1990–91 Johan Kraag (NPS), 1991– Ronald Venetiaan (NF)

Political system
The constitution was suspended in 1980 and in 1982 an interim president took office as head of state, with ultimate power held by the army, through its commander in chief who was also chair of the Supreme Council, the country's controlling group. A nominated 31-member National Assembly was established in January 1985, consisting of 14 military, 11 trade union, and 6 business nominees, and given 27 months in which to prepare a new constitution. This was approved in September 1987.

The 1987 constitution provides for a National Assembly of 51 members, elected by universal adult suffrage through a simple plurality voting system for a five-year term. Once elected, the assembly then elects a president, who is both head of state and head of government, to serve a similar term. It describes the army as the 'vanguard of the people'.

Political parties
There are some 15 political parties, the main groupings being the New Front (NF), the National Democratic Party (NDP), and the Democratic Alternative 1991 (DA '91).

The NF, formerly called the Front for Democracy and Development (FDD), is a coalition of four parties: the Party for National Unity and Solidarity (KTPI); the Surinam National Party (NPS); the Progressive Reform Party (VHP); and the Surinam Labour Party (SPA). It was originally formed in 1987 to fight the election, and then recast in 1991.

The KTPI dates from 1947 and draws its support mainly from the Indonesian population.

The NPS began in 1946 and has largely Creole support. The VHP is a predominantly Indian party, and the SPA is a multiracial grouping. The NF has a left-of-centre orientation.

The NDP was formed in 1987 by Desi Bouterse, mainly to legitimize his regime. It is based on Standvaste, a mass movement which resulted from the coup of 1982. It has a left-wing and military orientation.

The DA '91 is an alliance of three left-of-centre parties, formed to fight the 1991 elections.

Latest elections
In the May 1991 National Assembly elections the NF won 30 of the 51 seats, the NDP, 12, and the DA '91, 9.

Because the NF did not have two-thirds of the seats required to elect the president, there was a delay of four months, while bargaining took place, before the new president, Ronald Venetiaan, assumed office. Venetiaan was formally elected president in September 1991 by an 817-member United People's Assembly, which was specially convened by the National Assembly.

Political history
Britain was the first European power to establish a settlement in Surinam, in 1651. In 1667 the Dutch took over, only to be removed by the British in 1799. The colony was finally restored to the Netherlands in 1819. As Dutch Guiana, it became in 1954 an equal member of the Kingdom of the Netherlands, with internal self-government. Full independence was achieved in 1975, with Dr Johan Ferrier as president and Henck Arron, leader of the mainly Creole Surinam National Party (NPS), as prime minister.

In 1980 Arron's government was overthrown in an army coup but President Ferrier refused to recognize the military regime and appointed Dr Henk Chin A Sen, of the Nationalist Republican Party (PNR), to head a civilian administration. Five months later the army staged another coup and President Ferrier was replaced by Dr Chin A Sen. The new president announced details of a draft constitution which would reduce the role of the military, whereupon the army, led by Lieutenant Colonel Desi Bouterse, dismissed Dr Chin A Sen and set up a Revolutionary People's Front.

There followed months of confusion in which a state of siege and then martial law were imposed. Between February 1980 and January 1983 there were no fewer than six attempted coups by different army groups. Because of the chaotic conditions aid from the Netherlands and the United States was stopped and Bouterse was forced to look elsewhere for assistance, making agreements with Libya and Cuba. The partnership between the army, the trade unions, and business, which had operated since 1981, eventually broke up in 1985 and Bouterse turned to the traditional parties which had operated prior to the 1980 coup.

The ban on political activity was lifted in anticipation of the adoption of a new constitution based on civilian rule. Leaders of the Creole, Indian, and Indonesian parties were invited to take seats on a Supreme Council, with Wym Udenhout, a former colleague of Bouterse, as interim prime minister. In September 1987 a new constitution was approved

and elections to the National Assembly were held in November. The combined opposition parties, which had formed an alliance under the umbrella name Front for Democracy and Development (FDD), won an overwhelming victory and then elected Ramsewak Shankar as the new president. In December 1990 the military, under the direction of Commander in Chief Lieutenant Colonel Bouterse, persuaded Shankar to 'resign' and Johan Kraag, of the minority NPS, took over as interim president.

For the May 1991 general election the FDD was reformed into a coalition, the New Front (NF), which contained the Party for National Unity and Solidarity (KTPI), the Surinam National Party (NPS), the Surinam Labour Party (SPA), and the Progressive Reform Party (VHP). Eventually, the newly elected Congress chose Ronald Venetiaan, a former education minister, as president. In 1992 a peace agreement was reached between government troops and guerrillas who had destabilized the state and in November 1992 Lieutenant Colonel Bouterse, instrumental in the coups of 1980 and 1990 which had led to a suspension of vital economic aid from the Netherlands, was replaced as commander in chief of the armed forces by a candidate proposed by the civilian government.

URUGUAY

The Eastern Republic of Uruguay
La República Oriental del Uruguay

Capital: Montevideo

Social and economic data
Area: 176,215 km^2
Population: 3,100,000*

Pop. density per km²: 18*
Urban population: 89%**
Literacy rate: 94%**
GDP: $8,100 million**; per-capita GDP: $2,612**
Government defence spending (% of GDP): 1.8%**
Currency: new Uruguayan peso
Economy type: middle income
Labour force in agriculture: 15%**

*1994
**1992

Ethnic composition

The great majority of the population is of European descent, about 54% Spanish, and about 22% Italian. There are minorities from other European countries. Spanish is the national language.

Religions

All religions are tolerated but most of the population (58%) is Roman Catholic.

Political features

State type: liberal democratic
Date of state formation: 1825
Political structure: unitary
Executive: limited presidential
Assembly: two-chamber
Party structure: multiparty
Human rights rating: 90%
International affiliations: AG (observer), ALADI, G-11, IAEA, IBRD, IMF, Mercosur, NAM (observer), OAS, RG, SELA, UN, WTO

Local and regional government

The country is divided into 19 departments or regions, ranging in population from less than 24,000 to nearly 1.3 million. Each department is administered by an appointed *intendente*. Cities have elected councils and mayors.

Head of state and head of government

President Julio María Sanguinetti, since 1995

Political leaders since 1970

1967–72 Jorge Pacheco Areco (PN), 1972–76 Juan María Bordaberry Arocena (PC), 1976–81 General Aparicio Méndez Manfredini (military), 1981–85 General Grigorio Alvárez Armellino (military) 1985–90 Julio María Sanguinetti (PC coalition), 1990–95 Luis Alberto Lacalle Herrera (PN coalition), 1995– Julio María Sanguinetti (PC coalition)

Political system

The 1966 constitution provides for a president, who is head of state and head of government, elected by universal adult suffrage for a five-year term, and a two-chamber assembly, consisting of a Senate and a Federal Chamber of Deputies. The Senate has up to 30 members and the Chamber of Deputies 99, all elected by universal adult suffrage through a modified party list system of proportional representation, which ensures that there are at least two deputies representing each of the republic's 19 departments. Both chambers serve a five-year term. The president is assisted by a vice president and presides over a Council of Ministers.

Political parties

There are over 20 active political groupings, the most significant being the Colorado Party (PC), the National (Blanco) Party (PN), the New Space (NE), and Progressive Encounter (EP).

The PC was formed in 1836, following a successful revolt against the oppressive government of Fructuoso Rivera. It took the name of Colorado, or red, from the colour of the headbands of the revolutionaries who fought in the civil war. It now has a progressive centre-left orientation.

PN supporters had white headbands, hence the name Blanco. It, too, began in 1836 in similar circumstances to the birth of the PC, but on the opposite side in the civil war. The PN has a traditionalist right-of-centre orientation.

The NE was formed in 1989 by Amplio Front (FA) dissidents. It, also, has a moderate social-democratic stance.

The EP is an alliance of left-wing parties.

Latest elections

The PC candidate, Julio María Sanguinetti, was narrowly elected president in November 1994, with his presidency taking effect from March 1995.

The results of the concurrent assembly elections were as follows:

	Senate seats	Chamber of Deputies seats
PC	11	32
PN	10	31
EP	9	31
NE	–	5

Political history

Uruguay was under Portuguese rule in the 17th century and under Spanish control for the next 100 years. It achieved full independence in 1825. The period that followed saw a series of local disturbances, leading to a civil war in 1836. After that the country enjoyed relative peace so that Uruguay gained a reputation for being not only the smallest but the most politically stable of all South American republics. Under the presidencies of José Battle (between 1903–7 and 1911–15), a successful ranching economy and the rudiments of a welfare state were established. However, during the 1930s depression there was a reversion to a military dictatorship.

Between 1951 and 1966 there was a collective leadership called 'collegiate government' and then a new constitution was adopted and the Blanco candidate, Jorge Pacheco Areco, was elected as a single president. His presidency was marked by high inflation, labour unrest, and growing guerrilla activity by left-wing sugar workers, the Tupamaros.

In 1972 Pacheco was replaced by the Colorado candidate, Juan María Bordaberry Arocena. Within a year the Tupamaros had been crushed and all other left-wing groups banned. Bordaberry now headed a repressive regime, under which the normal democratic institutions had been destroyed. When, in 1976, he refused any movement towards constitutional government, he was deposed by the army and Dr Aparicio Méndez Manfredini was made president.

Despite promises to return to democratic government, the severe repression continued and political opponents were imprisoned. In 1981 the deteriorating economy made the army anxious to return to constitutional government and a retired general, Gregorio Alvárez Armellino, was appointed to serve as president for an interim period until full constitutional government was restored. Discussions between the army and the main political parties failed to reach agreement on the form of constitution to be adopted and civil unrest, in the shape of strikes and demonstrations, grew. By 1984 antigovernment activity had reached a crisis point and eventually all the main political leaders signed an agreement for a Programme of National Accord.

The 1966 constitution, with some modifications, was restored and in 1985 a general election was held. The Colorado Party won a narrow majority and its leader, Dr Julio María Sanguinetti (b. 1936), became president. The army stepped down and by 1986 President Sanguinetti was presiding over a government of National Accord in which all the main parties were represented.

The November 1989 presidential and assembly elections produced a PN president, Luis Alberto Lacalle Herrera (b. 1941), and a PN–PC coalition government and the earlier signs that Uruguay was returning to the form of government which, historically, had made it a model democracy, were confirmed. The Lacalle administration concentrated on fighting inflation and promoting the development of a more competitive private sector. The economy began to grow strongly from 1992, with inflation down to 50% per annum. However, the government's planned privatization initiative had to be halted when, in December 1992, 78% of the public voted against the measure in a national referendum. In March 1995 the PC candidate, the former president, Julio María Sanguinetti, returned to office. Earlier, in November 1994, his party won a plurality of seats in assembly elections which were characterized by the strong showing of the recently formed left-of-centre Progressive Encounter (EP), which ended the two-party dominance of the PN and PC. The new president said he would appoint a broad-based cabinet, to ensure 'governability'.

VENEZUELA

The Republic of Venezuela
La República de Venezuela

Capital: Caracas

Social and economic data
Area: 912,050 km²
Population: 20,600,000*
Pop. density per km²: 22*
Urban population: 91%**
Literacy rate: 85%*
GDP: $51,000 million*; per-capita GDP: $2,560**
Government defence spending (% of GDP): 2.4%**
Currency: bolívar

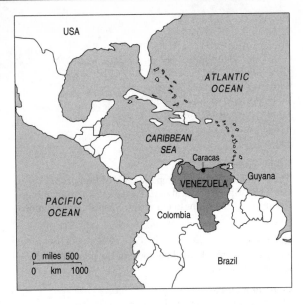

Economy type: middle income
Labour force in agriculture: 12%**

*1994
**1992

Ethnic composition
About 67% of the population are mestizos (offspring of Spanish-American and American-Indian parents), 21% Europeans, 10% Africans, and 2% Indians. Spanish is the official language.

Religions
Roman Catholicism is the state religion and the great majority of the population (92%) practise it. There is, however, complete freedom of worship for all denominations.

Political features
State type: liberal democratic
Date of state formation: 1830
Political structure: federal
Executive: limited presidential
Assembly: two-chamber
Party structure: multiparty
Human rights rating: 75%
International affiliations: ACS, AG, ALADI, AP, BCIE, CARICOM (observer), G-3, G-11, G-15, G-24, IAEA, IBRD, IMF, IWC, NAM, OAS, OPEC, RG, SELA, UN, WTO

Local and regional government
Venezuela is a federal nation of 20 states, two federal territories, 72 federal dependencies, and one federal district, based on the capital, Caracas. It is, however, a comparatively weak system because each state is heavily dependent on the federal government for finance. State governments are headed by governors appointed by the president and have elected assemblies. For administrative purposes, they are further subdivided into electorates and then municipalities.

Head of state and head of government
President Rafael Caldera Rodríguez, since 1994

Political leaders since 1970
1969–74 Dr Rafael Caldera Rodríguez (COPEI), 1974–79 Carlos Andrés Pérez Rodríguez (AD), 1979–84 Luis Herrera (COPEI), 1984–89 Jaime Lusinchi (AD), 1989–93 Carlos Andrés Pérez Rodríguez (AD), 1993 Octavio Lepage (interim), 1993–94 Ramón José Velásquez (AD–COPEI interim), 1994–   Dr Rafael Caldera Rodríguez (CN)

Political system
The 1961 constitution contains features similar to those of the United States and provides for a president, who is head of state and head of government, and a two-chamber National Congress, consisting of a Senate and a Chamber of Deputies. The president is elected by universal adult suffrage for a five-year term and may not serve two consecutive terms. The Senate has 43 members elected by universal adult suffrage, on the basis of two representatives for each state and two for the Federal District, plus all living ex-presidents, *ex officio*. The Chamber has 205 deputies, elected by universal adult suffrage, through a party list system of proportional representation. Both chambers serve five-year terms. The president appoints and presides over a Council of Ministers (cabinet).

Political parties
There are more than 20 political parties, the most significant being the Democratic Action Party (AD), the Christian Social Party (COPEI), the National Convergence (CN), the Movement towards Socialism (MAS), and the Radical Cause (LCR).

The AD was formed in 1936 as the National Democratic Party and adopted its present name in 1941. It has a moderate left-of-centre orientation.

COPEI was founded in 1946 by the leader of the Catholic Student Movement. It adopts a Christian centre-right stance.

The centre-right CN is a wide-ranging spectrum of 17 parties, formed in 1993, and including some former COPEI members.

The MAS dates from 1971 and was formed by members of the Communist Party who broke away after the Soviet invasion of Czechoslovakia. It has a left-of-centre orientation.

The LCR is another nontraditional party, with a left-wing orientation.

Latest elections
In the December 1993 presidential election Rafael Caldera Rodríguez, the CN candidate, was successful, with 30.5% of the votes, the remainder being split between the AD, COPEI, and the LCR.

In the December 1993 assembly elections the results were as follows in the above table.

Political history
Venezuela was first colonized by Spain in the 16th century and from then until independence was achieved, in 1830, there were repeated rebellions against Spanish rule. In the 19th century the independence movement was led by Francisco Miranda (1752–1816) and Símon Bolívar (1783–1830).

	Senate seats	Chamber of Deputies seats
AD	16	56
COPEI	14	54
CN/MAS	10	52
LCR	9	40
Others	–	3

The latter established, in 1823, the state of Gran Colombia, which included the area of present-day Colombia, Ecuador, and Venezuela, driving out the Spanish royalist forces. Venezuela became an independent republic when Gran Colombia was dissolved in 1830. Between 1870 and 1889 the caudillo (military leader), Antonio Guzmán Blanco (1829–99), ruled as a benevolent dictator, modernizing the infrastructure and developing agriculture and education.

From 1909 to 1935 the country suffered under the harsh dictatorship of General Juan Vicente Gómez (1864–1935), who developed Venezuela's rich oil resources, making it the world's largest exporter of petroleum, but passed little of the wealth on to the ordinary inhabitants. The first free elections were held in 1947 but were soon followed by another period of repression, this time under General Marcos Pérez Jiménez. Venezuela had to wait until 1959 before the democratically elected government of Rómulo Betancourt came to power.

A new constitution was adopted in 1961 and three years later Betancourt became the first president to complete his full term of office. He was succeeded in 1964 by Dr Raúl Leoni and then, in 1969, Dr Rafael Caldera Rodríguez (b. 1916) was elected as Venezuela's first Christian Social Party (COPEI) president. He did much to bring economic and political stability, although underground abductions and assassinations still occurred. In 1974 Carlos Andrés Pérez Rodríguez (b. 1922) of the Democratic Action Party (AD) came to the presidency and the movement towards greater stability continued. In 1979 Dr Luis Herrera, leader of the Christian Social Party (COPEI), was elected, but without a working majority in Congress so he was dependent on the other parties for legislative support.

Against a background of growing economic problems, the 1983 general election was contested by 20 parties and 13 presidential candidates. It was a bitterly fought campaign and resulted in the election of Dr Jaime Lusinchi (b. 1924) as president and a win for the AD in Congress. President Lusinchi's austere economic policies were unpopular and throughout 1985 he worked hard to try to conclude a social pact between the government, trade unions, and business. He also reached an agreement with the government's creditor bankers for a rescheduling of Venezuela's large public debt. In the 1988 presidential election Lusinchi was decisively defeated by his AD rival, the former president, Carlos Andrés Pérez Rodríguez, who embarked upon the strict austerity programme in return for IMF loans, resulting in protest riots in Caracas.

The public unrest continued in 1992 and the government had to deal with an attempted coup by a group of army officers. As his unpopularity grew, the president promised constitutional reforms but in May 1993 he was accused by the

Senate of corruption and the embezzlement of government funds, and this charge was endorsed by the Supreme Court. Pérez was suspended from office and the chairperson of the Senate, Octavio Lepage, was made interim president. The following month the Congress elected Senator Ramón José Velásquez to serve the remaining eight months of Pérez's presidency, and he was given special powers to introduce economic and financial measures by decree. In August 1993 Pérez was permanently suspended and made ineligible for public office again.

In the December 1993 presidential election the voters turned their backs on the two traditional parties and elected as the new president the veteran COPEI politician and former head of state, Dr Rafael Caldera Rodríguez, who now headed the National Convergence (CN) coalition which had campaigned against government corruption and had promised to suspend a planned privatization initiative. The concurrent congressional elections resulted in a sharing of the Senate and Chamber of Deputies seats by all the main political parties.

3

Towards One World

CHAPTER 8

The Relics of Empire – Colonies, Dependencies, and Semi-Sovereign States

8.1 The building of the colonial empires: 1492–1919

Nine-tenths of the contemporary sovereign states outside Western Europe have, at one time or another during the two centuries before 1945, been subject to external rule by the 'great' colonial powers of Europe, the United States, or Japan. The notable exceptions have been Japan itself, China, apart from Manchuria and the coastal 'treaty port' enclaves, Afghanistan, until 1979–89, Iran, Saudi Arabia, (North) Yemen, Liberia, since 1847, Thailand, Bhutan, and Nepal. 'Informal' external influence was, however, strong in many of these states, Nepal and Bhutan, for example, being bound by strict treaty obligations to Britain until 1947.

The process of modern colonization occurred in a series of distinct phases. It began in the late 15th and early 16th centuries, with the conquest of Southern and Central America, including the Caribbean, by Spain and Portugal, the indigenous Amerindian civilization being destroyed and replaced by a new mixed, white-creole-black, plantation and mining economy. This was followed, during the 7th century, by the Netherlands' assertion of supremacy over the East Indies' 'spice islands', and the creation of British and French settlements in coastal North America.

The majority of the early colonies on the mainland of the Americas were, following revolts by the settlers, to secure their independence during the late 18th and early 19th centuries, as Table 63 shows. Elsewhere in the world, however, European interests multiplied, an extensive new chain of dependencies being established across South and Southeast Asia, Australasia, Africa, and the Caribbean during what was the dominant era of imperial expansion, between the 1770s and the 1920s. The lead in this second phase of colonialism was taken by Britain and France. Also involved in the process were the rising nations of central, eastern, and southern Europe, notably Germany, tsarist Russia, and Italy, the ambitious small kingdom of Belgium, the old imperial states of the Netherlands, Spain, and Portugal, and the emergent world powers of the United States and Japan.

Imperial expansion during this 'mature' phase usually took the form of the imposition of a ruling body, or person,

Wave of colonial expansion			Table 63

The initial wave of colonial expansion – the Americas, 1496–1903 (22 states)

Country	Date of colonization	Original colonizing power	Date of independence
Argentina	1516	Spain	1816
Bolivia	1530s	Spain	1825
Brazil	1532	Portugal	1822
Canada	1604	France & UK	1851–67*
Chile	1541	Spain	1818
Colombia	1538	Spain	1821/30**
Costa Rica	1563	Spain	1821
Cuba	1511	Spain	1899
Dominican Republic	1496	Spain	1844
Ecuador	1532	Spain	1821/30**
El Salvador	1525	Spain	1821/38†
Guatemala	1524	Spain	1839
Haiti	1697	France	1804
Honduras	1523	Spain	1821/38†
Mexico	1521	Spain	1821
Nicaragua	1552	Spain	1838
Panama	1513	Spain	1821/1903††
Paraguay	1537	Spain	1811
Peru	1533	Spain	1824
United States of America	1607	United Kingdom	1776
Uruguay	1624	Spain	1825
Venezuela	1567	Spain	1821/30**

* Canada was not fully freed from the supremacy of Acts of the UK Parliament until 1931, while Newfoundland remained under British administration until 1949
** These states formed part of a federation between 1821 and 1830
† Part of a federation of Central American States until 1838
†† Part of Colombia until 1903

on indigenous peoples, or even indirect control, rather than the emigration and settlement of white colonists. The exceptions were the settler colonies of Australia and New Zealand, upland parts of southern and eastern Africa, and the tea and rubber planter belts of Southeast Asia. The expansion was at its maximum, in areal terms, at the time of the Versailles Settlement of 1919, when nearly all of Africa, South and Southeast Asia, Oceania, and the Caribbean, as well as much of West Asia and the Middle East, had been politically incorporated into the imperial nexus.

8.2 The decolonization process: 1920–95

During the interwar years, the first halting steps towards decolonization were taken, beginning in the Middle East, where, in 1922, Britain, prompted by the outbreak of serious nationalist riots, transferred full sovereignty in Egypt. It continued to maintain, however, a strategic military presence to protect its Suez Canal interests. Then, in 1932 and 1944 respectively, Britain and France, which had been administering the territories under League of Nations mandates since 1920, conceded independence to Iraq and Lebanon. During the same period the 'white settler' Dominions of Canada and South Africa, which had experienced a substantial measure of self-government from as early as the mid-19th century, became effectively fully independent with the passage of the Statute of Westminster, in 1931. Australia and New Zealand, the other two overseas Dominions, delayed accepting the terms of this legislation until 1942 and 1947 respectively. These cases were, however, the exceptions. Elsewhere, the 1920s and 1930s were a period of imperial consolidation, and even some further expansion by countries such as fascist Italy, militarist Japan, and, finally, remotivated to imperial ambitions, Nazi Germany.

Matters changed dramatically after World War II, the process of decolonization now gaining an unstoppable momentum. The initial factor behind this sea change was the strain imposed on ruler–colony relations by the war itself. For example, in the case of India, where a powerful nationalist movement had already won significant political concessions during the interwar period, the British government was forced, in 1940, to offer the carrot of Dominion Status as a means of securing civilian cooperation in the war effort. By the end of the war, however, the popular desire for full independence had become irresistible, with the result that full sovereignty, on a partitioned basis, was transferred in August 1947. The adjacent South Asian countries of Ceylon (Sri Lanka) and Burma (Myanmar) soon followed suit and were granted independence in 1948. The loss of the Indian subcontinent, the linchpin of the British imperial system, was to have far-reaching consequences, undermining its whole economic and strategic rationale.

Further to the east, in Southeast Asia, the French and Dutch colonies in 'Indochina' and the 'East Indies' had been even more seriously affected by the events of World War II. Between 1942 and 1945 both had been occupied by Japan, which had sponsored new puppet nationalist governments. The reimposition of European colonial rule proved highly unpopular and was fiercely resisted. Full autonomy was thus granted to the Dutch 'East Indies', now Indonesia, in 1949 and substantial semi-autonomy, within the 'French Union', to France's possessions in Indochina: Vietnam, Cambodia, and Laos. They achieved full independence some five years later after a prolonged military struggle.

During the later 1940s and mid-1950s, the British- and French-administered states of North Africa and the Middle East were also granted independence: Syria in 1946; Israel, formerly Palestine, in 1948; Libya in 1951; and Sudan, Morocco, and Tunisia, all in 1956. In addition, the 'informal colony' of Oman regained full sovereignty in foreign and defence affairs, in 1951, and Eritrea was handed over to Ethiopian control in 1952. It was not, however, until the Suez and Algerian crises of 1956 and 1958 that the pace of decolonization decisively quickened. Both events had profound repercussions on the internal political dynamics of the two leading imperial nations, and on their global outlooks, resulting in the accession to power of the realistic decolonizers, Harold Macmillan (1894–1986; prime minister 1957–63), in the United Kingdom, and General Charles de Gaulle (1890–1970; president 1959–69), in France. These crises also transformed public opinion, adding a new moral imperative to a decolonization process which had now gained an irresistible momentum.

The first indication of this changed perspective was the granting of full independence to the British West African colony of Ghana, known as the Gold Coast, in March 1957, by the handing over of power to the popular radical socialist, Kwame Nkrumah (1909–72). Ushering in, what the British prime minister, Harold Macmillan, termed, a 'wind of change' across black Africa: 33 African states secured independence during the next 10 years. In one year alone, 1960, 17 new African states were proclaimed. Independence was also granted during this hectic decolonization phase, between 1957 and 1968, to nine small island states in the Caribbean, Oceania, and East Asia, as Tables 64 and 65 show.

By the early 1970s, Britain and France, playing the leading roles in the decolonization process, as can be seen in Table 64, had divested themselves of their principal mainland-based colonial possessions. They were now left mainly in control of small island dependencies in the Caribbean and Oceania, as well as treaty protectorates in the Gulf region. These were slowly 'set free', at an average rate of two per annum, during the 1970s and early 1980s.

Ironically, the last substantial European overseas empire was maintained during this period by Portugal, the pioneer of European imperial expansion. Comprising Guinea-Bissau in West Africa, Angola in southwestern Africa, Mozambique in southeastern Africa, and the offshore islands of Cape Verde and São Tomé e Príncipe, this empire covered more than 2,000 square kilometres and had been under Portuguese rule for almost 500 years. With its still untapped mineral wealth and energy reserves, it remained, moreover, of considerable economic value to the colonial power, attracting extensive white settlement during the 1960s. Portuguese rule and immigration were, however, becoming increasingly unpopular with the indigenous population, fuelling a powerful guerrilla resistance movement, which was supplied with modern

The changing pace of decolonization between 1920 and 1995 — Table 64

The distribution of former colonial powers in relation to the countries 'freed' during this period

Number of countries 'freed' per year*

Period	Under British control	Under French control	Under Dutch control	Under Belgian control	Under Portuguese control	Under US control	Under Russian /USSR control	Under control of other states	Total
1920–45	5	1	–	–	–	–	–	1	7
1946–50	6	1	1	–	–	2	–	2	12
1951–55	2.7	3.3	–	–	–	–	–	–	6
1956–60	7.5	16.5	–	1	–	–	–	–	25
1961–65	13	1	–	2	–	–	1	–	17
1966–70	9	–	–	–	–	–	–	2	11
1971–75	5	1	1	–	5	–	–	2	14
1976–80	7.5	1.5	–	–	–	–	–	–	9
1981–85	4	–	–	–	–	–	–	–	4
1986–90	–	–	–	–	–	–	1	1	2
1991–95	–	–	–	–	–	3	14	–	17
1920–95	59.7	25.3	2	3	5	5	15	9	124
% share of total	48.1	20.4	1.6	2.4	4.0	4.0	12.1	7.3	100

* Where control was shared between two or more colonial powers, the number of 'freed' countries is shown proportionately

Regional distribution of 'freed' countries, 1920–95

Period	Central & Southern Africa	Middle East & North Africa	Asia	Central America & the Caribbean	South America	North America	Oceania	Western Europe	Central, Eastern, & Southern Europe	Total
1920–45	2	3	–	–	–	1	1	–	–	7
1946–50	–	3	8	–	–	–	1	–	–	12
1951–55	1	2	3	–	–	–	–	–	–	6
1956–60	20	2	2	–	–	–	–	1	–	25
1961–65	10	2	1	2	–	–	1	1	–	17
1966–70	5	1	–	1	1	–	3	–	–	11
1971–75	6	4	–	2	1	–	1	–	–	14
1976–80	1	1	–	3	–	–	4	–	–	9
1981–85	–	–	1	3	–	–	–	–	–	4
1986–90	1	–	1	–	–	–	–	–	–	2
1991–95	–	–	5	–	–	–	3	–	9	17
1920–95	46	18	21	11	2	1	14	2	9	124
% share of total	37.1	14.5	16.9	8.9	1.6	0.8	11.3	1.6	7.3	100

arms by the Soviet Union's Cuban and East German proxies. This eventually had calamitous repercussions for the Lisbon regime, provoking a left-wing coup by disaffected army units which succeeded in bringing down the conservative dictatorship of Marcello Caetano (1906–80), in April 1974. In the immediate wake of this power change Portugal's African dependencies pressed for independence. Unable and unwilling to resist, the new Lisbon regime hastily acceded to the requests, and within the space of 14 months, between October 1974 and November 1975, the empire was dissolved.

This left, during the 1980s, only one major land-based European overseas empire that dated back to the pre-1945 period, the one established by tsarist Russia in Central Asia between 1846–95. It was an empire inherited by the 'anti-colonial' Soviet Union, but which it had firmly consolidated and incorporated within its federal structure. After the war the Soviet Union also established an informal hegemony

The decolonization process, 1922–95   *Table 65*

Year of decolonization or transfer of sovereignty	State	Last colonizing power	Date of establishment of control
1922	Egypt	Britain	1882
1931	Canada*	Britain (France 1604–1763)	1713–63
1932	Iraq	Britain (M)	1920
1934	South Africa*	Britain (Netherlands 1652–1795)	1795–1824
1941	Ethiopia	Italy (MO)	1936
1942	Australia*	Britain	1788
1944	Lebanon	France (M)	1920
1946	Jordan	Britain (M)	1920
1946	Mongolia	China	1689
1946	Philippines	United States (Spain 1565–1898)	1689
1946	Syria	France (M)	1920
1947	India & Pakistan (incl E Pakistan, later Bangladesh)	Britain	late 18th–early 19th c
1947	New Zealand*	Britain	1840
1948	Myanmar (Burma)	Britain (Japan 1942–45)	1824–86
1948	Israel (formerly W Palestine)	Britain (M)	1920
1948	North Korea	Soviet Union (OZ) (Japan 1910–45)	1945
1948	South Korea	United States (OZ) (Japan 1910–45)	1945
1948	Sri Lanka (Ceylon)	Britain	1798
1949	Indonesia	Netherlands (Japan 1942–45)	1595
1951	Libya	70% Britain & 30% France (Italy 1912–42)	1942
1951	Oman	Britain (MP)	1891
1952	Eritrea	Britain (Italy until 1941)	1941
1954	Cambodia (Kampuchea)	France (Japan 1941–45)	1863
1954	Laos	France (Japan 1940–45)	1893
1954	Vietnam	France (Japan 1940–45)	1867–83
1956	Morocco	France	1912
1956	Sudan	Britain	1899
1956	Tunisia	France	1881
1957	Ghana	Britain	1901
1957	Malaysia	Britain (Portugal 1511–1641 Netherlands 1641–1795)	1795–1888
1957	Singapore	Britain	1819
1958	Guinea	France	1898
1960	Benin	France	1892
1960	Burkina Faso (Upper Volta)	France	1896
1960	Cameroon	80% France & 20% Britain (M) (Germany 1884–1916)	1919
1960	Central Africa Republic	France	1901
1960	Chad	France	1900
1960	Congo	France	1910
1960	Cyprus	Britain	1914
1960	Gabon	France	1890
1960	Côte d'Ivoire	France	1893
1960	Madagascar	France	1885
1960	Mali	France	1881–99
1960	Mauritania	France	1904–12
1960	Niger	France	1901
1960	Nigeria	Britain	1861–99
1960	Senegal	France	1659–1840
1960	Somalia	Britain (Italy 1908–41)	1884–86

continued

The decolonization process, 1922–95 (continued)   Table 65

Year of decolonization or transfer of sovereignty	State	Last colonizing power	Date of establishment of control
1960	Togo	66% France & 34% Britain (M) (Germany 1884–1914)	1914
1960	Zaire	Belgium	1885–1908
1961	Kuwait	Britain (MP)	1899
1961	Sierra Leone	Britain	1808
1961	Tanzania	Britain (M) (Germany 1885–1914)	1914
1962	Algeria	France	1830
1962	Burundi	Belgium (M) (Germany 1895–1916)	1916
1962	Jamaica	Britain (Spain 1509–1655)	1655
1962	Rwanda	Belgium (M) (Germany 1894–1916)	1916
1962	Trinidad & Tobago	Britain (Spain 1552–1797)	1797–1820
1962	Uganda	Britain	1888
1962	Western Samoa	New Zealand (M) (Germany 1900–14)	1914
1963	Kenya	Britain (Portugal 1498–1699)	1888–95
1964	Malawi	Britain	1887–92
1964	Malta	Britain	1814
1964	Zambia	Britain	1891–1923
1965	Gambia	Britain	1816
1965	Maldives	Britain	1887
1965	Rhodesia (later Zimbabwe: UDI)	Britain	1897–1923
1966	Barbados	Britain	1624
1966	Botswana	Britain	1885
1966	Guyana	Britain (Netherlands 1616–1796)	1796–1814
1966	Lesotho	Britain	1868
1967	South Yemen	Britain	1839
1968	Equatorial Guinea	Spain (Portugal 1494–1778, Spain 1778–81, Britain 1781–1843)	1858
1968	Mauritius	Britain (Netherlands 1598–1710, France 1715–1810)	1810
1968	Nauru	Australia (M) (Germany 1888–1914, Japan 1942–45)	1914
1968	Swaziland	Britain (South Africa 1894–1902)	1881
1970	Fiji	Britain	1874
1970	Tonga	Britain	1900
1971	Bahrain	Britain (MP)	1861
1971	Qatar	Britain (MP) (also temp 1868–72)	1916
1971	United Arab Emirates	Britain (MP)	1892
1973	Bahamas	Britain	1629
1974	Grenada	Britain (France 1674–1762)	1762
1974	Guinea–Bissau	Portugal	late 15th c
1975	Angola	Portugal	1491
1975	Cape Verde	Portugal	late 15th c
1975	Comoros	France	1912
1975	Mozambique	Portugal	1505
1975	Papua New Guinea	Australia (50% German 1885–1914, 50% Britain 1885–1901)	1901
1975	São Tomé e Príncipe	Portugal	1471
1975	Spanish Sahara (W Sahara)	Spain	1912
1975	Surinam	Netherlands (Britain 1651–67, 1779–1802, & 1804–16)	1816
1976	Seychelles	Britain (France 1768–1814)	1814

continued

The decolonization process, 1922–95 (continued) *Table 65*

Year of decolonization or transfer of sovereignty	State	Last colonizing power	Date of establishment of control
1977	Djibouti	France	1859
1978	Dominica	Britain (France 1778–83)	1763
1978	Solomon Islands	Britain (50% Germany 1885–1900)	1885
1978	Tuvalu	Britain	1875
1979	Kiribati	Britain	1892
1979	St Lucia	Britain (France 1651–1803)	1803
1979	St Vincent & the Grenadines	Britain (France 1779–83)	1783
1980	Vanuatu	Britain & France (JT)	1887
1981	Antigua & Barbuda	Britain	1632
1981	Belize	Britain	17th c–1862
1983	St Kitts–Nevis	Britain	1623
1984	Brunei	Britain	1888
1989	Afghanistan	Russia (USSR) (MO)	1979
1990	Namibia	South Africa (Britain 1884–1915, Germany 1884–1915)	1915
1991	Armenia	Russia (USSR) (Turkey 1639–1918, West Armenia; Persia 1639–1828, East Armenia; Independent 1918–20)	1828
1991	Azerbaijan	Russia (USSR) (Independent 1918–20)	1805
1991	Belarus	Russia (USSR) (Independent 1918–19, Germany 1941–44)	1795
1991	Estonia	Russia (USSR) (Independent 1919–40, Russia 1940–41, Germany 1941–44)	1721
1991	Georgia	Russia (USSR) (Independent 1918–21)	1801
1991	Kazakhstan	Russia (USSR)	early 18th c
1991	Kyrgyzstan	Russia (USSR)	1876
1991	Latvia	Russia (USSR) (Russia 1918–19, 1939–41, Independent 1919–39, Germany 1941–44)	late 18th c
1991	Lithuania	Russia (USSR) (Germany 1915–18, 1941–44, Russia 1918–19, 1939–41, Independent 1919–39)	1795
1991	Marshall Islands	United States (TT) (Spain 1529–1885, Germany 1885–1914, Japan 1914–45)	1945
1991	Micronesia, Federated States of	United States (TT) (Spain 16th c–1898, Germany 1898–1914, Japan 1914–45)	1945
1991	Moldova	Russia (USSR)	1812
1991	Tajikistan	Russia (USSR)	late 19th c
1991	Turkmenistan	Russia (USSR)	1870s
1991	Ukraine	Russia (USSR) (Independent 1917–20, Germany 1941–44)	1654
1991	Uzbekistan	Russia (USSR)	1876
1994	Belau (Palau)	United States (TT)	1945

* The white–settler colonies of Australia, Canada, New Zealand, and South Africa achieved de-facto independence from British control at earlier dates than those shown. The separate Australian states, for example, enjoyed a substantial measure of autonomy as early as 1855–68; the Canadian colonies between 1851 and 1867; and New Zealand and Cape Colony in South Africa as early as 1853. These powers were extended in 1907 when Dominion status was conferred. Not until the dates shown, however, following the passage of the Statute of Westminster, 1931, were these territories fully freed from the supremacy of Acts of the United Kingdom parliament.

Key:

JT	Joint condominium	M	League of Nations 'mandate' territory
MO	Military occupation	OZ	Occupied zone
MP	Independent and fully internally self-governing, but dependent on British military protection, much in the same way as Bhutan and Nepal	TT	UN Trust Territory
		UDI	Unilateral declaration of independence

over its East European neighbours, although the economic relationship by no means corresponded to a classic imperial one in terms of the nature of the goods interchanged, the USSR exporting mineral and energy products westwards and importing manufactured items. In addition, Afghanistan was invaded by the Soviet Red Army in 1979 and a puppet regime installed. Two other major communist powers, China, in the case of Tibet, and Vietnam, in relation to Laos and Cambodia, also maintained both formal and quasi-formal imperial control over neighbouring regions.

These communist informal and formal empires disintegrated dramatically between 1989 and 1991 as a result of economic problems at the centre, the consequence both of overly rigid central-planning systems and of the crippling defence burden, and of the growth in nationalist sentiment in the colonized territories. The latter was particularly evident in the Soviet 'satellite states' of Central and Eastern Europe and the voicing of this sentiment was made possible by the glasnost ('political openness') initiative instituted by the reformist Mikhail Gorbachev (b. 1931), who became the Communist Party leader in the Soviet Union in 1985. Abandoning the existing imperialist 'Brezhnev doctrine', which had held that the Soviet Union would always intervene militarily to ensure that 'correct' socialism was upheld within its 'sphere of influence', Gorbachev sanctioned the withdrawal of the Red Army from Afghanistan in 1989 and permitted the overthrow of entrenched communist regimes in Bulgaria, Czechoslovakia, East Germany, Hungary, Poland, and Romania during 1989–90. Also during 1989, Vietnam, partly responding to Soviet prompting and partly influenced by its own economic considerations, withdrew all its forces stationed in Cambodia and Laos.

Gorbachev fought harder to preserve communist and Russian control over the formally colonized 14 republics that formed constituent parts of the Soviet Union. However, the dynamics of his glasnost and perestroika ('economic restructuring') reform programme were such that the unbottling of previously suppressed nationalist sentiment, particularly in the Baltic republics, Georgia, west Ukraine, and parts of Soviet Central Asia, proved to be corrosive of the entire Union. In September 1991, following the failure of an anti-Gorbachev coup in Moscow by nationalist–communist hardliners, the independence of the three Baltic republics of Estonia, Latvia, and Lithuania was reluctantly recognized by Moscow. Three months later, the USSR was itself dissolved.

8.3 Remaining colonial possessions and dependencies in the world today

There currently exist, on the broadest count, 42 regularly inhabited colonies or dependencies, controlled by 11 colonial powers. These territories and the controlling nations are set out, in an aggregated form, in Tables 66, 67, and 68. They total fewer than 16 million people, a number that corresponds to less than 0.3% of the global population. This compares with the situation in 1945 when almost a third of the world's population lived in colonies or dependencies or with early 1960, when the proportion stood at 5%.

Included in these figures are the occupied territory of Western Sahara, the Chinese 'Autonomous Region' of Xizang (Tibet), and the French 'internal' 'Collective Territory' of Corsica. These areas do not always feature in textbook dependency categories. They have, however, been included in this chapter so as to provide more detailed treatments of their political structures and histories. Taken together, they embrace 2.6 million people, a figure that is equivalent to 17% of the colonies/dependencies total.

In the remaining colonial territories and dependencies, there are fewer than 13 million people. Almost three-quarters of this total is accounted for by the two British and United States dependencies of Hong Kong and Puerto Rico, with, as Table 68 shows, the majority of the other 'colonial relics'

Contemporary colonies, dependencies, and external territories				Table 66
Controlling state	Number of inhabited colonies, dependencies, & external territories	Area ('000 sq km)	Population (million) (c. 1992)	% share of total colonial population
Australia	3	0.18	0.004	0.0
China	1	1221.60	2.196	14.2
Denmark	2	2177.00	0.103	0.7
France	10*	128.27	2.236	14.4
Morocco	1	252.12	0.200	1.3
Netherlands	2	0.99	0.264	1.7
New Zealand	3	0.51	0.023	0.1
Norway	1	62.92	0.004	0.0
Portugal	1	0.02	0.487	3.1
United Kingdom	13	15.56	6.063	39.1
United States	5	10.54	3.928	25.3
Total	42	3869.71	15.508	100.0

*Including Corsica

Distribution of contemporary colonies | **Table 67**

Regional distribution of contemporary colonies, dependencies, and external territories*

	Oceania	Central America & Caribbean	North America	South America	Asia	Middle East & North Africa	Central & Western Europe	Southern Africa
Number	13	12	2*	2	3	1	6**	3
Area (sq km '000)	25.52	14.28	2175.84	102.17	1222.69	252.12	73.78	3.30
Population (m)	0.628	4.912	0.062	0.120	8.483	0.200	0.418	0.685
% share of total colonial population	4.0	31.7	0.4	0.8	54.7	1.3	2.7	4.4

* Includes Greenland in the Arctic
** Includes Svalbard in the Arctic

Distribution of contemporary colonies by population size | **Table 68**

Distribution of contemporary colonies, dependencies, and external territories by population size

	Below 10,000	> 10,000– 50,000	> 50,000– 100,000	> 100,000– 500,000	> 500,000– 1 m	1 m–6 m	Total
Number of colonies, dependencies, & external territories	11	10	5	12	1	3	42

---

being relatively tiny communities, with populations below 100,000. The territories still held by six of the colonial powers, Australia, Denmark, New Zealand, the Netherlands, Norway, and Portugal, are particularly small. Only two of them, controlled by the Netherlands and Portugal, are the residue of earlier, and greater, empires. Instead, there are three powers, the United Kingdom, the United States, and France, which dominate any record of contemporary colonial holdings, the territories still under their control embracing, respectively, 39%, 25%, and 14% of the total colonial/dependency population. The territories they administer are spread across the world. There is, however, a notable numerical concentration in Oceania and the Caribbean, many of the dependencies being island communities, too small to have an independent political and economic viability. In a few cases, most notably in some of the French Oceania dependencies, colonial control has been maintained against the wishes of a significant proportion of the indigenous population. In general, however, in the bulk of the other, still dependent, territories no discernible independence movement is visible and, colony–colonizer cultural and economic ties remain strong.

8.4 Profiles of existing colonies and dependencies

In the pages that now follow we shall try to sketch a profile of each of the countries which still remain within the category of colony or dependency, following a similar approach to that taken in Part 2: in other words, on the bases of their political structures and recent histories.

8.4.1 Australia's dependencies

Australia's dependencies are called External Territories, of which, as Table 69 shows, there are seven. Five of them are within the Oceania region, two of which are uninhabited. The other two, both uninhabited, are within Antarctica. Details of the political structures and histories of the inhabited regions are given below.

CHRISTMAS ISLAND

Location
Oceania. In the Indian Ocean 360 km south of Java and 1,400 km north-west of Australia.

Social and economic data
Area: 135 km^2
Population: 1,275*
Pop. density per km^2: 9*
Economy type: high income (c. $15,000 per capita)
Currency: Australian dollar

*1991

Ethnic composition
Around 58% of the population are ethnic Chinese, 25% Malay, and 12% 'European'. English is the official language.

Religions

Fifty-five per cent of the population, chiefly the Chinese community, are Buddhists.

Political system

The island, which became an Australian Territory in October 1958, is governed by an administrator appointed by the governor general of Australia and responsible to the minister for territories. For municipal government, a Christmas Island Shire Council was established in 1992.

Political history

Discovered on Christmas Day in 1643 by Captain W Mynars, the island, then uninhabited, was annexed by Britain in 1888, and administered as part of the Straits Settlement Crown Colony, together with Singapore, Malacca, Penang, and the Cocos Islands. During World War II it was occupied by Japan. In 1958, following the grant of independence to Singapore, under whose direct responsibility it had been placed since 1900, Britain transferred its sovereignty to Australia. Since then it has been ruled as part of the Northern Territory. The island's economy has traditionally been dependent on the recovery of phosphates, for which Chinese workers were imported. In 1987 the phosphate mine was closed because of industrial unrest, but it was reopened by private operators in 1990. Efforts are also now being made to develop the island for tourism. A nine-member advisory Island Assembly was formed in 1985, with annual elections by proportional representation. It was dissolved in 1987, but a new Shire Council was established in 1992. In an unofficial referendum, held on 7 May 1994 and organized by the Christmas Islands Workers' Union, the option of secession from Australia was rejected, but 85% of those participating called for greater autonomy.

COCOS (KEELING) ISLANDS

Location

Oceania. In the Indian Ocean, southwest of Christmas Island and 3,685 km west of Darwin.

Social and economic data

Area: 14 km^2
Population: 647*
Pop. density per km^2: 46*
Economy type: middle income (c. $3,000 per capita)
Currency: Australian dollar

*1991

Ethnic composition

The principal island, Home Island, is peopled by local Cocos Malays, who form 58% of the islands' total population, while the other major island, West Island, is settled chiefly by Europeans.

Religions

Around 57% of the population, comprising chiefly the ethnic Malay community, are Muslims, and 22% are Christians.

Political system

The Australian government is represented on the islands by an administrator, appointed by the governor general of Australia and responsible to the minister of territories. Most local government functions are, however, undertaken by a Cocos Islands Council, which was established in July 1979 and whose authority was expanded in 1984. Following the islands' vote in April 1984 to become fully integrated with Australia, the islanders now enjoy the rights and privileges of ordinary Australian citizens, including voting rights in Australian Parliament elections.

Political history

The Cocos Islands, a group of low-lying coral atolls thickly covered with coconut palms, were discovered in 1609 by Captain William Keeling of the East India Company. They were originally settled by Malays brought to the islands by Alexander Hare and John Clunies-Ross, in 1826–27. They were annexed to the British Crown in 1857 and incorporated in the Settlement of Singapore from 1903, although their economic interests, which were mainly the extraction of copra from coconuts, had been granted to the Clunies-Ross family in 1886. In November 1955 administration was transferred to

Australia's external territories			Table 69
Territory	Date of first coming under Australian administration	Area (sq km)	Population (c. 1991)
The Ashmore & Cartier Islands	1931	5	uninhabited
The Australian Antarctic Territory	1936	6,112	uninhabited
Christmas Island	1958	135	1,275
Cocos (Keeling) Islands	1955	14	647
Coral Sea Islands	1969	22*	uninhabited
Heard Island & McDonald Islands	1947	412	uninhabited
Norfolk Island	1913	35	2,285
Total	–	6,735	4,207

* This figure is the area of land only. The islands cover one million sq km of ocean

Australia and in 1978 the Australian government bought out the Clunies-Ross family's interests and established a Cocos Malay cooperative to manage the copra plantation. In April 1984 the islands' residents voted to become part of Australia.

NORFOLK ISLAND

Capital: Kingston

Location
Oceania, in the Western Pacific 1,488 km northeast of Sydney, off eastern Australia, and almost midway between Australia and New Zealand.

Social and economic data
Area: 35 km^2
Population: 2,285*
Pop. density per km ^{2}: 65*
Economy type: middle-high income (c. $6,000–7,000 per capita)
Currency: Australian dollar

*1991

Ethnic composition
The population comprises descendants of those who migrated from Pitcairn in the mid-19th century, and who speak Tahitian, and more recent 'mainlander' immigrants from Australia, New Zealand, and Britain, who speak English.

Religions
The inhabitants are predominantly, 71%, Christians, belonging to the Church of England (38%), the Uniting Church (16%), and the Roman Catholic Church (11%).

Political system
The Australian government is represented on the island by an administrator, appointed by the governor general of Australia and responsible to the minister for territories. Since the passage of the Norfolk Island Act in 1979, there has been a progression towards a form of responsible legislative and executive self-government, founded on an elected nine-member Legislative Assembly, from which is drawn a five-member ministerial Executive Council, headed by a president of the Legislative Assembly, a position analogous to that of a chief minister. In 1985 the powers of the Assembly and Council were extended to cover such matters as civil defence and public works and services. Legislative Assemby elections are held every three years and are determined by an unusual 'cumulative method of voting', in which electors are allowed to cast as many votes as there are vacancies, subject to the proviso that they may not give more than four votes to any one candidate. In the May 1992 general election, 18 candidates contested the nine seats.

Political history
The island, which was then uninhabited, was first visited by Captain James Cook (1728–79) in 1774 and originally served as a British penal settlement, between 1788 and 1814 and 1826 and 1855. After 1856 there was an influx of people from over-populated Pitcairn Island, some of them descendents of those who had settled there after the 'Mutiny of the

Bounty', in 1789. In 1913 Norfolk Island became an Australian 'external territory', forming part of the New South Wales colony. Since 1979 it has been substantially self-governing and its economy has become increasingly reliant on tourism. In December 1991 the island's population overwhelmingly rejected an Australian government proposal that it be included in the Australian federal electorate.

8.4.2 China's dependency

China's one dependency is Xizang, or Tibet. It is one of the country's five Autonomous Regions. Details of its political structure and history are given below.

XIZANG (TIBET)

Capital: Lhasa

Location
Asia, in a mountainous region in southwest China, bordered to the south by Bhutan, India, and Nepal, to the west by India, to the east by Sichuan province, China, and to the north by Xinjiang autonomous region, China. The country is one of immense strategic importance to China, being the site of between 50,000–100,000 troops, as well having a major nuclear missile base at Nagchuka.

Social and economic data
Area: 1,221,600 km^2
Population: 2,196,000*
Pop. density per km ^{2}: 2*
Economy type: low income
Currency: Chinese renminbi or yuan

*1992

Ethnic composition
Predominantly Tibetan, with a growing Han Chinese immigrant minority.

Religions
The Tibetans adhere to Tibetan (yellow sect) Buddhism, in the form of Lamaism. There are, however, barely 1,000 lamas, or Buddhist monks/priests today, compared with 110,000, in 6,000 monasteries and temples, prior to 1959.

Political system
Xizang constitutes one of the five Autonomous Regions of the People's Republic of China (PRC) and has its own People's Government and Local People's Congress. The controlling force in Tibet is the Communist Party of China (CPC), headed by a local party first secretary. As an Autonomous Region, Xizang is allowed to conduct its government's affairs in its own language and uphold local customs and culture. It enjoys, however, little real political autonomy, being required to adhere to decisions made in Beijing (Peking) by the leadership of the ruling CPC.

Political history
Xizang was an independent kingdom from the 5th century AD, with the Dalai Lama, popularly viewed as a reincarn-

ation of the Compassionate Buddha, emerging as its spiritual and temporal ruler, or 'god king', from 750 AD onwards. The country was conquered and ruled by the Mongols between 1279 and 1368 and came under nominal Chinese sovereignty between about 1700 and 1912. However, independence was regained, under the Dalai Lama's leadership, after a revolt in 1912. China's rule over Xizang was nominally re-established in 1950 and Tenzin Gyatso (b. 1935), who had been designated in 1937 by the monks of Lhasa as the 14th Dalai Lama, was forced to flee to Chumbi in south Xizang and the Buddhist monks, who constituted a quarter of the population, were forced out of their monasteries. The Dalai Lama negotiated an autonomy agreement with the Chinese authorities in 1951, enabling him to return as nominal spiritual and temporal head of state, but the Chinese People's Liberation Army (PLA) had effective control over the country.

In 1959, a Tibetan uprising spread from bordering regions to Lhasa and was supported by the Xizang local government. The rebellion was, however, brutally suppressed by the PLA. As a result, the Dalai Lama and 9,000, subsequently mounting to 100,000, Tibetans were forced into permanent exile in Dharamsala, in India, where an alternative, democratically-based government was formed. The Chinese proceeded to dissolve the Xizang local government, abolish serfdom, collectivize agriculture, and suppress Lamaism.

In 1965 Xizang became an Autonomous Region of China. Industrialization, based on the production of textiles, chemicals, and agricultural machinery, was encouraged and 200,000 Han Chinese settled in the country. Chinese rule continued to be resented, however, and the economy languished, thousands dying from famine. From 1979 the new leadership in Beijing, dominated by Deng Xiaoping (b. 1904), adopted a more liberal and pragmatic policy towards Xizang. Traditional agriculture, livestock, and trading practices were restored, under the 1980 slogan 'relax, relax and relax again', a number of older political leaders and rebels were rehabilitated or pardoned, and the promotion of local Tibetan cadres was encouraged. In addition, a more tolerant attitude towards Lamaism was adopted, with temples damaged during the 1965–68 Cultural Revolution being repaired, and attempts were made to persuade the Dalai Lama to return from exile. However, the violent pro-independence demonstrations by Buddhist monks, which erupted in Lhasa in September and October 1987, in March and December 1988, and in March 1989, which were forcibly suppressed by Chinese troops, at the cost of hundreds of lives, exhibited the continuing strength of nationalist feeling. Since 1989 security in the Autonomous Region has been subject to stricter control from Beijing, with human rights abuses being routinely recorded by Western monitors. In 1989 the Dalai Lama was awarded the Nobel Peace Prize for his commitment to the nonviolent liberation of his homeland. In May 1995, a six-year-old boy was designated the new reincarnation of the Panchem Lama, second ranking in the country's spiritual hierarchy, by the Dalai Lama.

8.4.3 Denmark's dependencies

Denmark has two dependencies, described as Outlying Territories. Their political structures and histories follow.

Danish outlying territories			Table 70
Territory	Date of first coming under Danish administration	Area (sq km)	Population (c. 1992)
Faroe Islands	1380	1,399	47,310
Greenland	985*	2,175,600**	55,385
Total	–	2,176,999	102,695

* Formally in 1917
** 80% covered by ice-cap

FAROE ISLANDS

Capital: Torshavn

Location
Western Europe. A group of 21 volcanic islands, 18 of which are inhabited, in the North Atlantic between Iceland and the Shetland Isles, some 320 km to the southeast. They are situated 1,000 km away from Denmark. The largest islands are Stromo and Ostero.

Social and economic data
Area: 1,399 km^2
Population: 47,310*
Pop. density per km ^{2}: 34*
Economy type: high income (c. $12,000 per capita)
Currency: Danish krone
*1992

Ethnic composition
The inhabitants are predominantly ethnic Faroese. Five per cent of the workforce are immigrants. The main language is Faroese, but Danish is a compulsory school subject.

Religions
The population is predominantly Christian, in the form of the Evangelical Lutheran Protestant Church of Denmark.

Local governmnent
Power has been decentralized to 50 local authorities.

Head of government
Prime Minister Edmund Joensen, since 1994

Political system
An elected assembly (Logting) of 32 members has operated since 1852. Twenty-seven of its seats are filled by direct election under universal adult suffrage (minimum voting age 18 years) on the basis of proportional representation in seven multimember constituencies. There are a further five supplementary seats, which are dependent upon the numbers of people voting. The parliamentary term is four years. A six-member cabinet (Landsstyri), headed by a chairperson, or prime minister (Logmadur), is responsible to the chamber. This assembly has, since 1948, been devolved full authority for internal affairs, but the Danish government, which is represented on the islands by a High Commissioner, has respon-

sibility for foreign affairs and regulates education, social welfare, civil, criminal, and church affairs, and currency matters. The islands elect two representatives to the Danish parliament (Folketing), having been represented there since 1851.

Political parties

Eight political parties currently operate in the Faroes. They are the Social Democratic Party (SDP: Javnaoarflokkurin), the Union Party (UP), the Republican Party (RP), the Faroese People's Party (FPP: Folkaflokkurin), the Home Rule Party (HRP), the Christian People's Party–Progressive and Fishing Industry Party (CPP–PFIP), the allied Centre Party (CP), and the Workers' Front (WF; estd. 1994) of trade unionists.

The left-of-centre SDP was established in 1928, and has a membership of about 1,000. It has frequently participated in coalition governments, with the UP, RP, FPP, and HRP, since 1958 and is social democratic in outlook. The UP was founded in 1906. It is a conservative party which stands for close links with the Danish Crown and dominated the Logting before 1958. The RP dates from 1948. It favours secession from Denmark and the establishment of a fully independent republic. It has participated in government coalitions, with the HRP, CPP–PFIP, SDP, and FPP, since the early 1960s. The FPP was established in 1940 and is a liberal-conservative, right-of-centre party, in favour of free enterprise and greater economic autonomy. It has also participated in government coalitions, with the RP, SDP, HRP, and CPP–PFIP, since the early 1960s. The HRP was formed in 1906 and now has a membership of about 1,700. It is a centrist party, originally formed to press for greater legislative devolution. It was a regular member of government coalitions between 1948–70. The CPP–PFIP is a minor centre-left party, formed in 1954, which favours increased internal self-government.

Latest elections

The most recent Logting elections were held on 7 July 1994 and resulted in the SDP capturing five seats, half its November 1990 tally; the opposition UP, eight; the FPP, six; the RP, four; the WF, three; the HRP, two; the CPP–PFIP, two; and the CP, two.

Political history

The islands were settled by the Norse during the 8th–9th centuries and became part of the Kingdom of Norway in the 11th century. They passed to Denmark in 1380, when Queen Margrethe I (1353–1412) inherited Norway. However, the Faroes were not finally separated administratively from Danish-ruled Norway until 1709, when a Danish royal trade monopoly was established. During World War II, following the German invasion of Denmark, they were temporarily occupied by British troops. Home rule was granted in 1948. Fishing is the principal industry, employing a quarter of the labour force, and is the chief export earner, although stocks are now declining as a consequence of overfishing. Danish subsidies account for a sixth of GDP and provide nearly 30% of government revenue. Although Denmark joined the European Community in 1973, the Faroes remained outside.

Following the November 1984 general election a four-party centre-left coalition government, consisting of the SDP,

HRP, RP, and CPP–PFIP, and headed by the SDP's leader Atli Dam, was formed. The Social Democratic coalition lost its majority, however, in the general election of November 1988, when there was a swing to the right, with the FPP emerging as the new dominant force. The FPP's leader, Jogvan Sundstein, became the new Logmadur (prime minister), heading a centre-right coalition, including the HRP, RP, and CPP–PFIP and pledging to support the fishing industry, while pursuing an economic austerity programme in an effort to tackle a mounting level of governmnent debt. There was a new early general election in November 1990, after the FPP's coalition partners withdrew their support. The SDP re-emerged as the largest single party, with ten Logting seats to the FPP's seven, and a 'grand coalition' was formed by the SDP and FPP, headed by Atli Dam. Led by Marita Petersen, the SDP lost support in the July 1994 general election, winning just five seats, and the opposition right-of-centre UP emerged as the largest single party. In September 1994 a broad-based coalition was formed embracing the UP, SDP, HRP, and new WF, with Edmund Joensen, leader of the UP, the new prime minister. During the early 1990s the Faroes' economy, crippled by a huge trade deficit and public-spending deficit, went into severe recession, with the unemployment rate climbing to 25% and nearly a tenth of islanders emigrating.

GREENLAND

Kalaallitt Nunaat

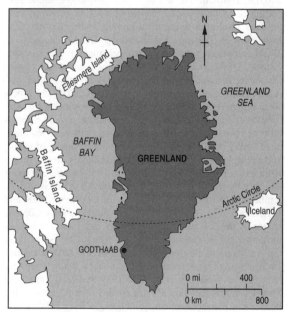

Capital: Godthaab (Nuuk)

Location

Arctic. Greenland is the second largest island in the world, after Australia. It is situated in the North Atlantic and Arctic Oceans, northeast of Canada. The interior is covered by an ice-sheet, with only 16% ice-free and 5% habitable by humans.

Social and economic data

Area: 2,175,600 km^2
Population: 55,385*
Pop. density per km ^{2}: 0.2**
Economy type: high income (c. $10,000 per capita)
Currency: Danish krone

*1992
**Based on ice-free area

Ethnic composition

The population is predominantly Inuit (Eskimo), with Danish admixtures. Greenlandic, an Inuit (Eskimo) language, and Danish are the official languages.

Religions

Chiefly Shamanism and Evangelical Lutheran Christianity.

Local government

There are 19 settlement councils responsible for local affairs.

Head of government

Prime Minister Lars Emil Johansen, since 1991

Political system

In 1979 a new parliament (Landsting) was set up to replace the existing Greenland Provincial Council. It consists of 31 members, elected for four-year terms by universal adult suffrage (minimum age 18 years) on the basis of proportional representation. A seven-member government (Landsstyre) is drawn from the Landsting, being based on the strength of the parties, and is headed by a prime minister. Denmark is represented on the island by a high commissioner and has control over foreign affairs, defence, monetary policy, and constitutional matters. Greenland also sends two representatives to the Danish Folketing and used to elect one Euro-MP.

Political parties

There are five political parties: the Forward (Siumut) Party; the Feeling of Community/Solidarity (Atassut) Party; the Eskimo/Inuit Brotherhood (Inuit Ataqatigiit: IA); the Centre Party (Akulliit Partiiat, or CP); and the Polar Party (Issitruppartii: IP).

The Siumut is the most important of the five, regularly drawing support from nearly 40% of the electorate. Although originating as a movement in 1971, it was formally established as a party in 1977 and has a current membership of 5,000. It is a centre-left body which spearheaded the movement for self-rule and opposed Greenland's European Community entry terms. Drawing its support from the fishing and hunting community, the Siumut, led by a Lutheran pastor, Jonathan Motzfeldt, formed Greenland's first home-rule government in 1979. The Atassut, a centre-right conservative grouping which dominated the pre-autonomy Council, is the second most important party, normally able to attract around 30% of the vote. The IA is a socialist party which was founded in 1978 and advocates full independence for Greenland. The CP is a liberal party, formed in 1991, which supports the open-sea fishing industry. The right-of-centre IP, formed in 1987, favours a reduced state role in the economy, including privatization of the state's trawler fleet.

Latest elections

The most recent general election was held on 5 March 1995. Siumut attracted 39% of the territory's vote and captured 12 Landsting seats, while its coalition partner, the IA, won 20% of the vote and six seats. Atassut, with 30% of the vote, won ten seats.

Political history

The island was settled by seal-hunting eskimos from North America c. 2,500 BC and colonized by the Danish king, Erik the Red, in 985 AD. The southwest of the island was colonized by Danes between the 12th and 15th centuries, but these colonies were later abandoned. New settlements were founded in the 17th century and a Danish colony was set up in 1721. Danish sovereignty extended over the whole island in 1917. An agreement for the joint defence of Greenland, within the North Atlantic Treaty Organization (NATO), was signed with the United States in 1951 and an American air base and, later, a radar station, were established at Thule in the far north. In 1953 the island became fully part of Denmark, returning two members to the Danish parliament (Folketing). Following a referendum supported by 70% of voters, it was granted home-rule in 1979.

On 1 February 1985, after a referendum held in February 1982 had resulted in a 53% majority in favour of withdrawal, Greenland left the European Community, which it had joined, with Denmark, in 1973. There had been an overwhelming, 71% to 29%, vote against entering in October 1972. Following the May 1987 general election a new Siumut – IA coalition was formed, with Jonathan Motzfeldt, prime minister since 1979, remaining in office. The coalition broke down in June 1988 and Siumut found a new governing partner in the Atassut party. However, after the March 1991 general election the Siumut–IA coalition was reformed, and Siumut's new leader, Lars Emil Johansen, became prime minister. The Siumut–IA was re-elected in March 1995. Fishing, especially cod, is the principal industry, but a very high proportion of the island's GDP, and nearly half of the government's annual revenue, is derived from annual subsidies from Denmark.

8.4.4 France's dependencies

The French dependencies consist of four Overseas Departments, two Overseas Collective Territories, four Overseas Territories, and one Internal Collective Territory, as listed in Table 71.

FRENCH OVERSEAS DEPARTMENTS

Départements d'Outre-Mer

Overseas Departments, which form integral parts of the French Republic, have an administrative structure similar to that of the Departments of metropolitan France, although the former have their own Courts of Appeal. Prior to the decentralization reforms of 1982, each Overseas Department was administered by a central government-appointed prefect, assisted by a directly elected General Council and an indirectly elected Regional Council. After the reforms the prefect was renamed Commissaire de la République (government

French overseas departments, territories, and collective territories				Table 71
Name	Date of first coming under French administration	Area (sq km)	Population (c. 1991)	French National Assembly (NA) & Senate (S) seats
Overseas departments				
French Guiana	1817	90,000	118,000	2NA,1S
Guadeloupe	1613	1,780	400,000	4NA,2S
Martinique	1635	1,100	400,000	4NA,2S
Reunion	1642	2,512	602,000	5NA,3S
Overseas collective territories				
Mayotte	1843	376	76,000	1NA,1S
St Pierre and Miquelon	c17/1816	242	6,392	1NA,1S
Overseas territories				
French Polynesia	1842	4,200	200,000	2NA,1S
French Southern & Antarctic Territories	–	7,567*	210**	–
New Caledonia	1853	19,103	170,000	2NA,1S
Wallis & Futuna Islands	1842	274	13,700	1NA,1S
Total	–	127,154	1,986,302	22NA,13S
Internal collective territory				
Corsica	1768	8,680	250,000	–

*Excludes 500,000 sq km of the uninhabited mainland of Antarctica
**Scientific mission workers

commissioner), his or her formal executive power being transferred to the General Council, while the powers of the Regional Council, which was now directly elected, were considerably increased in the social, economic, and cultural spheres. An earlier plan to merge the two councils into one was blocked by a decision of the French Constitutional Council in December 1982. French Overseas Departments also send representatives to the French national parliament and participate in French presidential elections.

FRENCH GUIANA

La Guyane Française

Capital: Cayenne

Location
South America. French Guiana lies between Surinam, to the west, and Brazil, to the east and south, on the north coast of South America.

Social and economic data
Area: 90,000 km^2
Population: 118,000*
Pop. density per km ^{2}: 1.3*
Literacy rate: 83%
Economy type: middle income
Currency: French franc

*1991

Ethnic composition
The population is a mixture of Creoles, Europeans, Amerindians, and Africans. French is the official language, but a creole patois is also spoken.

Religions
Seventy-eight per cent of the population is Roman Catholic.

Local government
The country is divided into two districts of Cayenne and Saint Laurent du Maroni.

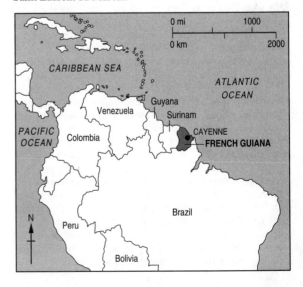

Political system

French Guiana is administered by an appointed French government commissioner (Commissaire de la République), who is assisted by a two-chamber body comprising the 19-member General Council (Conseil Général) and the 31-member Regional Council (Conseil de Région). Both are directly elected for six-year terms and exercise a number of local powers. Additionally, the inhabitants elect two members to the French National Assembly and send, through indirect elections, one representative to the Senate. The Department is also represented at the European Parliament in Strasbourg.

Political parties

The principal political parties are the two conservative groups, the Rally for the Republic (RPR) and Guyanese Union of Liberal Forces (UFLG); the Guiana Socialist Party (PSG); the leftist Guyanese Democratic Action Party (Action Démocratique Guyanaise: ADG); the Guyanese Democratic Force (Forces Démocratiques Guyanaises: FDG); and the separatist Guyanese Popular National Party (Parti National Populaire Guyanais: PNPG). The FDG was set up in 1989 by Georges Othily, who had been expelled from the PSG in June 1989 for working too closely with opposition parties. The PNPG was established in 1985, before which it was known as the Union of Guyanese Workers (UTG).

Latest elections

The most recent elections to the General and Regional Councils were held on 22 March 1992 and were won by the PSG, which captured 10 General Council and 16 Regional Council seats, with a 40% share of the vote. The PSG leader, Elie Castor, remained president of the General Council and the party's secretary-general, Antoine Karam, was elected president of the Regional Council, defeating Georges Othily, the former president, whose new FDG won 10 Regional Council seats. In the March 1993 elections to the French Assembly, the RPR retained its seat, while the other was won by a dissident independent socialist, Christiane Taubira-Delanon, taking advantage of divisions within the PSG.

Political history

First settled by France in 1604, the area was, successively, under Dutch, English, and Portuguese rule during the 17th and 18th centuries before French control was re-established and recognized in 1817. It was used as a penal colony during the 19th century, including the notorious Devil's Island, and remained economically undeveloped, possessing few natural resources except timber. In 1946 French Guiana became an Overseas Department of the French Republic, making it subject to the same laws and system of government as France's mainland departments. Such departmental status was opposed during the 1970s by left-wing groups, led by the Guiana Socialist Party (PSG), who demanded greater internal autonomy and called for increased priority to be given to economic development. In response, the French government introduced an indirectly elected Regional Council in 1974, which became directly elected and was given increased authority in 1983. In addition, France provided substantial amounts of economic aid. After five years of growth, the economy began to slow down from 1991 and unemployment began to rise, leading to a general strike in October 1992.

The PSG has been the dominant force in the Regional Council since the latter's inception. Georges Othily, who was then PSG leader, was re-elected president of the Council following the elections of March 1986. He was later expelled from the party in June 1989, but, nevertheless, took the Department's one seat in the French Senate in September 1989. The PSG, led by Antoine Karam, held on to power after the March 1992 elections. However, facing accusations that its domination of French Guiana had become corrupt, its majority was greatly reduced and the FDG, a new party formed by Othily, polled strongly.

GUADELOUPE

Capital: Basse-Terre

Location

Central America. Guadeloupe consists of a group of islands in the central Lesser Antilles, of the eastern Caribbean, lying between Dominica, to the south, and Antigua and Montserrat, to the northwest. The two principal islands are Basse-Terre and Grande-Terre, on which 43% and 48%, respectively, of the total population live.

Social and economic data

Area: 1,780 km^2
Population: 400,000*
Pop. density per km^2: 225*
Literacy rate: 90%
Economy type: middle income
Currency: French franc
*1993

Ethnic composition

Ninety per cent of the population are blacks or mulattos, 5% Caucasians, and 4% East Indians. French, spoken in a creole dialect, is the main and official language. English is the main language on St Martin island.

Religions

Ninety-five per cent of the population is Roman Catholic.

Local government

The islands are divided into three *arrondissements* (districts), which are subdivided into 34 communes.

Political system

The country is administered by an appointed French government commissioner (Commissaire de la République), who is assisted by a two-chamber body comprising the 42-member General Council (Conseil Général) and the 41-member Regional Council (Conseil de Région). Both are elected for a period of up to six years and exercise a number of local powers. The Regional Council is responsible for economic and social planning and the General Council for internal executive power. In addition, Guadeloupe elects four members to the French National Assembly and sends two, indirectly elected, representatives to the Senate. The Department is also represented at the European Parliament in Strasbourg.

Political parties

The principal political parties are the two conservative groups, Rally for the Republic (RPR) and Union for French Democracy (UDF); the left-of-centre Guadeloupe Socialist Party (Fédération Guadeloupéenne du Parti Socialiste: FGPS) and Socialist Party-Dissidents (FRUI-G); the Guadeloupe Communist Party (PCG), which was established in 1944, and the Guadeloupean Progressive Democratic Party (PPDG), which was formed in 1991 by a breakaway group of PCG militants; and the Popular Union for the Liberation of Guadeloupe (UPLG), a pro-independence force formed in 1978.

Latest elections

The most recent elections to the Regional Council were held on 31 January 1993, after earlier elections, held in March 1992, were annulled as a consequence of irregularities. They were won by the Guadeloupe Objective, a centre-right electoral alliance of the RPR and UDF, which captured 22 of the 41 seats. The FGPS and PPDG each won four seats, the FRUI-G and UPLG three apiece, and the PCG, two. Lucette Michaux-Chévery, of the RPR, who had become president of the Regional Council in March 1992 with FRUI-G support, retained the position and was also re-elected to the French National Assembly in March 1993. Dominique Larifla, leader of the FRUI-G and a French National Assembly deputy, was re-elected president of the General Council in the March 1992 elections. The PPDG, FGPS, and 'various right' (divers droit) won the Department's other three French National Assembly seats in March 1993.

Political history

Discovered by Christopher Columbus (1451–1506) in 1493, the islands of Guadeloupe were occupied by France in 1635. They became renowned for sugar production and remained under French rule for the next three centuries, apart from brief British occupations in the 18th and early 19th centuries. The country became an Overseas Department of the French Republic in 1946. During the 1960s opposition to the monopoly of economic power by white (Creole) settlers and to the restrictions imposed by the status of being a Department, led to a movement for greater internal autonomy, spearheaded by the Guadeloupe Communist Party (PCG). In response to these demands, an indirectly elected Regional Council was established in 1974. This body became directly elected, with increased powers, from February 1983. A small extremist minority, led by the Popular Movement for an Independent Guadeloupe (Mouvement Populaire pour une Guadeloupe Indépendante: MPGI) and the outlawed Caribbean Revolutionary Alliance (Alliance Révolutionnaire Caraïbe: ARC), a left-wing extremist group, continued to seek full independence during the 1980s. The ARC, which is now disbanded, resorted to terrorist bombing outrages. However, despite a deterioration in economic conditions from the 1970s, caused by the steady decline of the sugar industry, which sent the unemployment rate to above 25%, electoral support for pro-independence parties remained below 5%. There was, however, a gradual shift in support away from the parties of the right and centre towards those of the pro-autonomy 'conventional left', the Guadeloupe Socialist Party (FGPS) and PCG.

This persuaded the formerly pro-independence UPLG to moderate its stance and to declare, in March 1990, that it would henceforth participate in elections and seek associated status for Guadeloupe.

The FGPS, with support from the PCG, won control of the General Council and Regional Council following the elections of March 1985 and 1986, with the party's leader, Dominique Larifla, becoming president of the General Council. Larifla, by now a dissident member of the FGPS, remained president of the General Council after the March 1992 elections, but the RPR captured the presidency of the Regional Council, with the support of FGPS dissidents.

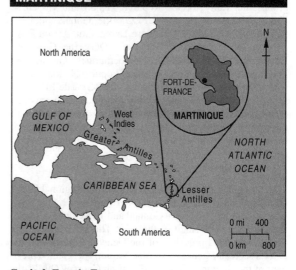

MARTINIQUE

Capital: Fort-de-France

Location

Central America and the Caribbean. Martinique is one of the Windward Islands in the eastern Caribbean, situated between Dominica, to the north, and St Lucia, to the south.

Social and economic data

Area: 1,100 km²
Population: 400,000*
Pop. density per km²: 364*
Literacy rate: 93%
Economy type: middle income
Currency: French franc
*1993

Ethnic composition

Ninety per cent of the population are of African and African-Caucasian-Indian descent. French is the official language, with a creole patois widely spoken.

Religions

Ninety per cent of the population is Roman Catholic.

Local government

The island is divided into three *arrondissements* (districts), which are subdivided into 34 communes.

Political system
Martinique is administered by an appointed French government commissioner (Commissaire de la République), assisted by a two-chamber body comprising the 45-member General Council (Conseil Général) and the 41-member Regional Council (Conseil de Région). Both are elected for a term of up to six years and exercise a number of local powers. In addition, Martinique elects four members to the French National Assembly and sends, through indirect election, two representatives to the French Senate. The Department is also represented at the European Parliament in Strasbourg.

Political parties
The principal political parties are the two conservative groups, the Rally for the Republic (RPR) and Union for French Democracy (UDF); the left-of-centre Progressive Party of Martinique (Parti Progessiste Martiniquais: PPM), which was established in 1957, and the Martinique Socialist Federation (Fédération Socialiste de la Martinique: FSM), which is a local branch of the mainland Socialist party; the Martinique Communist Party (PCM), which was formed in 1920 and was affiliated to the French Communist Party until 1957; and the secessionist Martinique Independence Movement (Mouvement Indépendentiste Martiniquais: MIM), also known as Patriotes Martiniquais.

Latest elections
In the most recent Regional Council election, held in March 1992, the RPR and UDF formed an electoral alliance, the Union for France, which attracted 26% of the vote and won 16 of the 41 seats. The MIM and PPM, each with 16% of the vote, captured nine seats apiece; the PCM, four; and the FSM, three. The RPR–UDF also secured control of the General Council. In the March 1993 French National Assembly elections, the RPR–UDF won three seats and the PPM one.

Political history
Martinique was discovered by Spanish navigators in 1493 and became a French colony in 1635. Famed for its sugar production and as the birthplace of the Empress Josephine (1763–1814), the island became an Overseas Department of the French Republic in 1946. Despite the country's close cultural integration with France, a nationalist movement emerged during the 1950s and 1960s, spearheaded by the Progressive Party of Martinique (PPM) and the Martinique Communist Party (PCM), which opposed the concentration of economic power in the hands of white settler families (békés). In response to this movement, consultative General and Regional Councils were created in 1960 and 1974 respectively. The Regional Council became directly elected and was granted additional powers, including greater control over taxation, local police, and economic affairs, in 1983, as part of the metropolitan Socialist government's decentralization initiative. The PPM and PCM continue to seek greater autonomy, but only a small, though growing, minority of the population, less than 5%, support a campaign for full independence from France.

This extreme policy has been championed by the Martinique Independence Movement (MIM) and the outlawed, and now disbanded, Caribbean Revolutionary Alliance (ARC) terrorist organization. The island's economy has been in a depressed condition during recent years, the sugar industry continuing to decline, and growth in new export lines, for example bananas, has been adversely affected by the European Union's new competitive regime for exports to its single market. More than a quarter of the labour force are currently unemployed and emigration to France and French Guiana is now at a level of 15,000 per annum.

Following the March 1986 elections, the parties of the left (PPM, FSM and PCM) retained control of the Regional Council, with 21 seats, after forming a 'Union of the Left' and the PPM's leader, Aimé Césaire, was re-elected Council president. The centre-right RPR–UDF, although a minority, controlled the administration of the General Council after the elections of March 1985. However, the PPM captured the Council's presidency in March 1992 and Emile Capgras, of the PCM, concurrently became president of the Regional Council.

RÉUNION

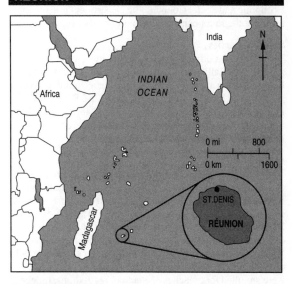

Capital: Saint-Denis

Location
Central and Southern Africa. Réunion, formerly Bourbon, island lies in the Indian Ocean 800 km east of Madagascar. Thirty-five per cent of its area is under forest, and both active and dormant volcanoes are to be found in the interior.

Social and economic data
Area: 2,512 km^2
Population: 602,000*
Pop. density per km ^{2}: 240*
Literacy rate: 79%
Economy type: middle income
Currency: French franc

*1991

Ethnic composition
The population comprises a mixture of people of European, African, Indian, and Chinese descent. There are also more

than 3,000 French troops based on the island, which serves as the headquarters of French military forces in the Indian Ocean. The official language is French.

Religions
Ninety per cent of the population is Roman Catholic.

Local government
The island is divided into four *arrondissements* (districts), which are subdivided into 24 communes and 36 cantons.

Political system
The island is administered by an appointed French government commissioner (Commissaire de la République), assisted by a two-chamber body consisting of the 44-member General Council (Conseil Général) and the 45-member Regional Council (Conseil de Région). Both are directly elected for six-year terms and exercise a number of local powers. In addition, Réunion elects five members to the French National Assembly, and sends, through indirect election, three representatives to the French Senate and one to the Economic and Social Council. The Department is also represented at the European Parliament in Strasbourg.

Political parties
The principal political parties are the three right-of-centre groups, the Rally for the Republic (RPR), the Union for French Democracy (UDF), and France-Réunion-Avenir (FRA), which was established in 1986; the Réunion Communist Party (PCR), which was founded in 1959; and the Socialist Party (PS). The pro-autonomy Movement for an Independent Réunion (MIR) was formed in 1981.

Latest elections
The most recent General Council elections were held on 20 and 27 March 1994 and resulted in the PS winning control from the RPR and Christophe Payet, from the PS, being elected Council president in April 1994. The left-of-centre PS and PCR draw the bulk of their support from poor Creole (Afro-Asian) urban and rural workers who seek improved labour conditions. Regional Council elections were last held on 20 June 1993 after earlier elections held in March 1992 were annulled for breaches of electoral regulations. Independent candidates representing Tele Free-DOM, an unauthorized television service, won a plurality of seats and the presidency of the Council. In the March 1993 elections to the French National Assembly the UDF won two seats and the RPR, PS, and PCR one apiece.

Political history
Discovered by the Portuguese in 1513, Réunion was annexed by France in 1642, serving initially as a penal colony and then, from 1665, as a post of the French East India Company. During the 18th century the island was developed into a major coffee exporter, this crop being replaced by sugarcane during the 19th century. Réunion was designated an Overseas Department of the French Republic in 1946 and was given the additional status of a region in 1974. Despite calls on the part of the Organization of African Unity (OAU) for the island's 'liberation' there is majority support on Réunion for continued French control. The left-wing parties, however, favour enhanced autonomy. Réunion's economy, which

remains heavily dependent on the sugar industry, has been depressed during recent years. As a consequence, despite growth in the tourist sector, the unemployment rate has risen to 35%, forcing the island to draw increasingly on the mainland for development grants. Discontent with the island's social and economic conditions provoked riots in February and March 1991 when the broadcasting transmitters of the unauthorized television service, Tele Free-DOM, were seized by the French authorities. The director of Tele Free-DOM, Dr Camille Sudre, was subsequently elected president of the Regional Council in March 1992, with PCR support, after independent candidates representing Tele Free-DOM polled strongly. In March 1994 Eric Boyer of the RPR, the president of the General Council and a senator, was sentenced to two years' imprisonment for corruption.

FRENCH OVERSEAS COLLECTIVE TERRITORIES

Collectivités Territoriales

The status of a Collective Territory (CT) is intermediate between that of an Overseas Department and an Overseas Territory. CTs constitute integral parts of the French Republic. They are administered by an appointed government commissioner (Commissaire de la République), who works with an elected General Council, and they send representatives to the French parliament and participate in French presidential elections.

MAYOTTE (MAHORE)

Capital: Dzaoudzi

Location
Central and Southern Africa. Mayotte consists of a volcanic island group that forms part of the Comoro archipelago, between Madagascar and the African mainland. The two main islands are Grande Terre and La Petite Terre.

Social and economic data
Area: 376 km^2
Population: 76,000*
Pop. density per km^2: 202*
Economy type: low income
Currency: French franc

*1991

Principal languages
French (official) and Mahorian, a Swahili dialect.

Religions
Ninety-eight per cent of the population adheres to Islam.

Local government
Mayotte is divided into 17 communes.

Political system
The islands are administered by an appointed French government commissioner (Commissaire de la République), who works with the assistance of an elected 17-member General Council (Conseil Général). In addition, Mayotte

elects one member to the French National Assembly and one representative to the French Senate.

Political parties

Four political parties operate on the islands, including branches of the mainland Union for French Democracy (UDF) and Rally for the Republic (RPR). The RPR branch is termed the Mayotte Federation of the Rally for the Republic (FMRPR). The dominant political party on the islands is the Mayotte People's Movement (Mouvement Populaire Mahorais: MPM). The MPM led the movement for Mayotte's exclusion from the independent Republic of the Comoros and has since campaigned for full departmental status within France. Its leader, Younoussa Bamana, is president of the General Council. The Party for the Democratic Rally of Mayotte (PRDM), formed in 1978, seeks unification with the Federal Islamic Republic of the Comoros.

Latest elections

The most recent elections to the General Council were held on 20 and 27 March 1994 and resulted in the MPM retaining control of the Council. The March 1993 election to the French National Assembly was won by the Martinique-born Henry Jean-Baptiste, of the UDF–Centre of Social Democrats.

Political history

The most populous of the Comoros group of islands in the Indian Ocean, Mayotte, together with its sister islands, was a French colony from 1843, and attached to Madagascar from 1914. Later, in 1947, the Comoros Islands were designated a French Overseas Territory, and granted internal autonomy within the French Republic in 1961. It was agreed, in 1973, that eventual independence would be secured in 1979. However, when the Comoran parliament declared unilateral independence in July 1975, Mayotte refused to join the new state, preferring to remain formally linked to France. The French government granted Mayotte special status as a Collective Territory of the French Republic in December 1976, a decision which was reaffirmed by the French National Assembly in December 1979 and October 1984. They rejected, however, the Mayotte People's Movement's demands for full departmental status, because of the island's economic backwardness. The Comoran government continues to claim sovereignty over Mayotte and is supported in this view by the United Nations General Assembly and the Organization of African Unity (OAU), officially representing Mayotte in the UN. The island is heavily dependent on French economic aid. A referendum to determine the future of the island has been postponed indefinitely. Immigration from the Comoros in recent years has caused tension in Mayotte.

ST PIERRE AND MIQUELON (SPM)

Iles Saint-Pierre-et-Miquelon

Capital: Saint-Pierre

Location

North America. It consists of a small group of eight rocky islands lying 25 km south of Newfoundland, in the North Atlantic Ocean. Ninety per cent of the population lives on Saint-Pierre Island.

Social and economic data

Area: 242 km^2
Population: 6,392*
Pop. density per km^2: 26*
Literacy rate: 99%
Economy type: high income
Currency: French franc

*1990

Principal language

French

Religions

Ninety-seven per cent of the population is Roman Catholic.

Political system

The islands are administered by an appointed French government commissioner (Commissaire de la République), who is assisted by a 19-member General Council (Conseil Général), which is elected for a six-year term. Fifteen of the General Council's members are elected from St Pierre and four from Miquelon. In addition, the islands elect one member to the French National Assembly and one representative to the French Senate and one to the Economic and Social Council.

Political parties

The dominant political party is the left-of-centre Socialist Party (PS), which controls the General Council and provides its president, Marc Plantagenest. The right-of-centre Union for French Democracy (UDF), Rally for the Republic (RPR), and Centre of Social Democrats (CDS) also operate.

Political history

The islands, which were first visited and settled by Breton and Basque fishermen during the 16th and 17th centuries, constitute the remnants of the once extensive French empire in North America. They were formally designated French territory in 1816 and gained departmental status in the French Republic in July 1976. This move, tying the local economy into the remote institutions of metropolitan France and the European Community, disrupted economic relations with neighbouring Canada and was opposed by local politicians and trade unionists. In 1978 and 1980 there were general strikes in protest and in the March 1982 General Council election, Socialist candidates, campaigning for a change in the islands' status, swept the board. This persuaded the French government to grant them special status as a Collective Territory, in June 1985. The islands continue to serve as the centre for the French Atlantic cod fishing, although this industry has been in steady decline since the mid-1970s, seriously depressing the local economy. During recent years, a dispute has developed between the French and Canadian governments over cod quotas and territorial limits, France claiming a 13,000-square-nautical-mile 'exclusive economic zone' in the waters around St Pierre and Miquelon. This conflict, which was heightened by recent offshore gas and petroleum exploration, was resolved, to Canada's advantage, by the International Court of Justice, which set the 'exclusive economic zone' at only 2,537 square nautical miles.

FRENCH OVERSEAS TERRITORIES

Territoires d'Outre-Mer

Overseas territories, which form integral parts of the French Republic, are administered by an appointed high commissioner or chief administrator, who works with an elected Territorial Assembly or Congress. They send representatives to the French parliament and participate in French presidential elections.

FRENCH POLYNESIA

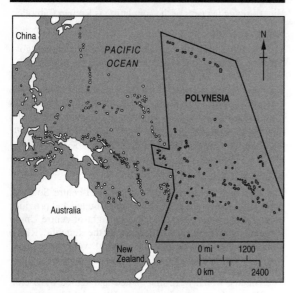

Capital: Papeete, on the island of Tahiti

Location
Oceania. French Polynesia comprises five scattered volcanic and coral island groups in the southeastern Pacific Ocean, between the Cook Islands, to the west, and Kiribati to the northeast. The largest island, on which 75% of the population lives, is Tahiti.

Social and economic data
Area: 4,200 km^2
Population: 200,000*
Pop. density per km ^{2}: 48*
Literacy rate: 95%
Economy type: high income
Currency: Pacific franc
*1993

Ethnic composition
Seventy per cent of the population is Polynesian, 18% Chinese, and 12% European. French is the official language, but Polynesian languages are spoken by the indigenous population.

Religions
About 55% of the population is Protestant and 35% Roman Catholic.

Local government
Under the terms of constitutional changes adopted in 1990, five consultative Archipelago Councils have been established, comprising territorial and municipal elected representatives.

Political system
Under the terms of the 1984 constitution, as amended in 1990, an appointed French high commissioner controls defence, foreign policy, justice, and monetary affairs, while a 41-member Territorial Assembly (Assemblée Territoriale), which is directly elected for a five-year term, appoints, from its own ranks, a president and ten-member Council of Ministers (COM). The COM has considerable autonomy in internal policy matters. French Polynesia also elects two members to the French National Assembly and one each to the French Senate and Economic and Social Council. The territory is also represented at the European Parliament in Strasbourg.

Political parties
The five principal political parties are the right-of-centre Rally for the Republic/Popular Union Party (RPR/Tahoeraa Huiraatira), the Pupu Here Ai'a Te Nunaa (PHA), the Ia Mana Te Nunaa, the New Land Party (Ai'a Api), and the Polynesian Liberation Front (Front de Libération de la Polynésie: FLP).

The RPR/Tahoeraa Huiraatira was established in 1958, and is led by Gaston Flosse. It supports the maintenance of close links with France, though with enhanced internal autonomy. The party split in 1987 after Flosse was forced to resign as president of the COM, following corruption charges, and Alexandre Leontieff formed the breakaway Te Tiaraama. The PHA is a pro-autonomy party which was founded in 1965. It is led by the mayor of Papeete, Jean Juventin. The Ia Mana Te Nunaa was formed in 1976 and advocates 'socialist independence'. The New Land Party dates from 1982, being formed after a split in the United Front Party (Te E'a Api). The FLP campaigns for independence and is led by Oscar Temaru.

Latest elections
The most recent Territorial Assembly elections were held on 17 March 1991 and resulted in the RPR winning a plurality of seats, 18 out of 41; while the PHA- and Te Tiaraama-dominated Polynesian Union won 14 seats; the New Land Party, five; and the FLP, four. Gaston Flosse returned as president of the COM, a position he had filled during 1986–87, forming an initial coalition with the New Land Party and then, from September 1991, with the PHA. The territory's two French National Assembly seats were won in March 1993 by Gaston Flosse and Jean Juventin from the ruling RPR–PHA coalition.

Political history
The islands of French Polynesia were visited by Spanish and Portuguese explorers in the late 16th century and by the French and British in the 1760s. Tahiti became a French protectorate in 1842, the remaining islands being annexed between 1880 and 1900. In 1957 French Polynesia was made an Overseas Territory of the French Republic, ruled by an appointed governor and an advisory Territorial Assembly.

During the mid-1970s, a separatist movement, spearheaded by Francis Sanford, leader of the United Front Party (Te E'a Api), gained strength. France responded by devolving greater authority to the Territorial Assembly and its Council of Ministers under new constitutions of 1977, 1984, and 1990.

Mururoa Atoll, in the Tuamotu Archipelago, has been a controversial nuclear test site since 1966. However, despite the adverse environmental aspects, its use has brought an influx of French military personnel into the territory, 5,400 being stationed in French Polynesia in 1993, and provided economic opportunities in the service and construction industries. Between 1992 and 1995 the French government of President François Mitterrand (b. 1916) suspended its nuclear testing programme, while compensating French Polynesia for the associated financial losses. However, in June 1995 the new French president, Jacques Chirac (b. 1932), announced that testing would resume at Mururoa Atoll from September 1995. This led to antinuclear and anticolonial riots in Papeete in September 1995.

As the Territory achieves an increasing degree of independence from metropolitan France, it has begun to develop closer ties with leading states in Asia and the Pacific, notably Australia, New Zealand, South Korea, Japan, and Taiwan.

Income tax was imposed in French Polynesia for the first time in 1994, as a means of funding infrastructural improvements, but the immediate consequence was widespread disorder, forcing 100 police officers to be flown in from France in October 1994.

NEW CALEDONIA

Nouvelle Calédonie

Capital: Nouméa

Location
Oceania. New Caledonia comprises the large, mountainous island of Grande Terre, or New Caledonia, the adjacent Loyalty Islands and, 400 km to the northwest, the uninhabited Chesterfield Islands. They are situated in the South Pacific Ocean, 1,500 km east of Queensland, Australia. Forty-one per cent of the population lives in the capital, Nouméa, on Grande Terre.

Social and economic data
Area: 19,103 km^2
Population: 170,000*
Pop. density per km^2: 9*
Literacy rate: 91%
Economy type: high income
Currency: Pacific franc

*1991

Ethnic composition
Forty-three per cent of the population is Melanesian, 37% European settlers, termed Caldoches, 8% Wallisian, 4% Polynesian, 4% Indonesian, and 2% Vietnamese. France maintains a force of 4,800 military personnel in New Caledonia. The official language is French, but the indigenous Kanak community also speaks Melanesian languages.

Religions
About 60% of the population is Roman Catholic.

Local government
The territory is divided into three provinces and subdivided into 32 communes, administered by locally elected councils and mayors. There are also eight Regional Consultative Custom Councils, for the maintenance of Kanak traditions.

Political system
Following the 'Fabius plan' of April 1985, New Caledonia has enjoyed a considerable degree of autonomy. A high commissioner represents the French government's interests in the islands and retains control over defence, foreign policy, finance, external trade, secondary education, and justice. New Caledonia is divided into three provinces, North, South, and the Loyalty Islands, each of which has the status of a self-governing territorial unit and has its own directly elected assembly of 32, 15, and seven members respectively, each headed by a president. Assembly terms are up to six years. The three assemblies together constitute the Territorial Congress (Congrès Territorial), which sits under the French High Commissioner. The Territorial Congress is responsible for the budget, fiscal affairs, primary education, and infrastructure, while the provincial assemblies are responsible for cultural affairs, land reform, and local economic development. The Territory also elects two deputies to the French National Assembly, one Senator and one Economic and Social Councillor, and is represented in the European Parliament at Strasbourg.

Political parties
There are five principal political parties in New Caledonia. Two of them, the extreme right-wing National Front (FN) and the right-of-centre Rally for Caledonia within the Republic (Rassemblement pour la Calédonie dans la République: RPCR), led by Jacques Lafleur, are settler-orientated bodies which favour retaining French control over the islands. One, the Calédonie Demain, is a right-wing breakaway from the RPCR and FN. Three, the Melanesian-orientated Kanak Socialist National Liberation Front (Front de Libération Nationale Kanake Socialiste: FLNKS), a six-party alliance created in 1984, including the Caledonian Union (UC) and the Kanak Liberation Party (Palika), and led by Paul Neaoutyine, and the Loyalty Islands-based Kanak Socialist Liberation Party (Libération Kanake Socialiste: LKS), and its offshoot, the Anti Neo-colonial Front, press for full independence. The LKS withdrew from the Matignon Accord in April 1991.

Latest elections
The most recent legislature elections were held on 9 July 1995 and resulted in the FLNKS retaining control of the North and Loyalty Islands provincial assemblies and the RPCR the South assembly. For the Territory as a whole, the RPCR lost its overall majority, capturing 22 of the 54 Territorial Congress seats. The Caledonie For All party, a non-racial group formed just before the election, won seven seats. The territory's two French National Assembly seats were both won by the RPCR in March 1993.

Political history

Discovered by James Cook (1728–79) in 1774, New Caledonia was annexed by France in 1853, and was initially used, between 1871 and 1898, as a penal settlement. It became an Overseas Territory of the French Republic in 1946. Friction developed between the urban-based French settlers (*Caldoches*) and the local Melanesians (*Kanaks*) during the 1970s. Many of the Caldoches had been attracted to the Territory during the 1960s nickel boom, New Caledonia being the world's third largest nickel producer. The Kanaks, however, constituted a majority in rural areas. In response to Kanak demands for self-government, the authority of the locally elected Territorial Assembly, which had been established in 1956, was increased in December 1976. Direct 'Commissioner rule' had to be imposed in 1979 when pro-independence parties gained control of the Assembly's Council of Government and in September 1981 tensions were heightened, following the assassination of Pierre Declercq, leader of the separatist movement. Further cultural and political reforms were suggested by France's socialist Mitterrand administration after 1981, including proposals, in January 1985, for independence 'in association with' France, subject to a referendum. The holding of a national referendum, planned for July 1985, was violently opposed, however, by the Kanak Socialist National Liberation Front (FLNKS), forcing the declaration of a state of emergency.

The poll was shelved and a new 'Fabius plan' of regional devolution adopted instead. Regional councils were elected in September 1985 and a referendum on independence was held in September 1987. In this poll, 98% of those who voted gave approval to New Caledonia remaining part of the French Republic. Turnout was only 59%, however, with the bulk of the Melanesian community adhering to the advice of the FLNKS and boycotting the poll. Soon after the referendum, Bernard Pons, the minister for overseas departments and territories in France's conservative (RPR) Chirac administration, submitted an administrative reorganization plan to New Caledonia's Territorial Assembly. This settler-biased scheme was accepted by Rally for Caledonia within the Republic (RPCR) Assembly members, but was strongly criticised by the FLNKS. This prompted a renewed outbreak of Kanak violence by militant factions during the run-up to the French presidential and new regional elections, in April–May 1988.

The return of the Socialists to power in Paris in June 1988 was swiftly followed by a fresh initiative by Michel Rocard (b. 1930), the new French prime minister. After a fortnight of negotiations in Paris, a compromise settlement was agreed by the FLNKS and RPCR leaders, Jean-Marie Tjibao and Jacques Lafleur, in late June. The outcome was a decision to delay the holding of another referendum on independence until 1998, and, instead, to establish, in June 1989, a new system of local government based on the division of the territory into three self-governing provinces: one in the south for white settlers, and two, in the north and outer islands, for Kanaks. This scheme, which was planned to bring to an end a year of direct administration from Paris, was approved in a national referendum held throughout the French Republic in November 1988. It was accompanied by a generous, new economic development programme, targeted at poor Kanak

rural areas. However, its long-term success in securing communal peace remains to be proven. External pressure for decolonization has increased during recent years, particularly since the United Nations General Assembly decision, in December 1986, to reinscribe New Caledonia on the UN list of non-self-governing territories. Internal Kanak disquiet with the June 1988 Matignon Accord surfaced in May 1989 with the assassination of Tjibaou by a separatist extremist. High levels of youth unemployment among the Melanesian community were a factor behind riots in Nouméa in the spring of 1992. Provincial elections held in July 1995 produced once again pro-independence Kanak majorities in the North province and Loyalty Islands, while the South province remained dominated by white, pro-French settlers.

WALLIS AND FUTUNA ISLANDS (WFI)

Capital: Mata-Utu, on Wallis Island

Location

Oceania. The Territory comprises two groups of islands, the Wallis and the Futuna and Alofi. They are situated in the south-central Pacific Ocean to the northeast of Fiji and west of Western Samoa. Sixty-five per cent of the population lives on Wallis Island.

Social and economic data

Area: 274 km^2
Population: 13,700*
Pop. density per km^2: 50*
Economy type: low income
Currency: Pacific franc

*1990

Ethnic composition

The population is predominantly Polynesian. French and Wallisian (Uvean), a Polynesian language, are spoken.

Religions

Almost entirely Roman Catholic.

Political system

The islands are administered by an appointed French chief administrator, who is assisted by a 20-member Territorial Assembly (Assemblée Territoriale), which is directly elected for five-year terms on a common roll and elects its own president. The Territory elects one member to the French National Assembly and one representative to the Senate. The three traditional kingdoms, one on Wallis and two, Sigave and Alo, on Futuna, from which the territory was formed retain a number of limited powers. The three kings, along with three appointed members of the Territorial Assembly, form a six-member Council of the Territory which advises the chief administrator.

Political parties

The two dominant political parties are the right-of-centre Rally for the Republic (RPR) and the Taumu'a Lelei (Bright Future). Also of importance are the centre-right Union for French Democracy (UDF) and its affiliate, the Lua kae tahi party. The Futuna-based Local Popular Union (Union Populaire Locale: UPL), formed in April 1985 by the Territorial Assembly's then president, Falakiko Gata, a former member of the RPR, places emphasis on local issues.

Latest elections
The most recent Territorial Assembly elections, held on 22 March 1992, were won by the Taumu'a Lelei party, which captured 11 of the 20 seats. The remaining nine seats were won by the RPR, which had controlled the Assembly since 1964. Among the 13 new members elected were the legislature's first two women deputies. The centre-left Movement of Left Radicals (MRG) holds the Territory's one French National Assembly seat after the elections of March 1993.

Political history
The Futuna island group was discovered by Dutch explorers in 1616 and the Wallis islands by the British in 1767. They were later settled by French missionaries in the early 19th century, becoming a French dependency in 1842 and protectorate in 1888. Following a local referendum in December 1959, the WFI was designated an Overseas Territory of the French Republic in July 1961. In contrast to the French Pacific territories of French Polynesia and New Caledonia, there is no secessionist movement at present on the islands. However, there have been calls by the kings of Futuna for two separate, Wallis and Futuna, Overseas Territories to be created. Lacking natural resources, the WFI exports little and is heavily dependent on economic aid from France and remittances sent home by the 14,000 nationals employed in New Caledonia and Vanuatu.

FRENCH 'INTERNAL' COLLECTIVE TERRITORY

This category is a special one, since Corsica is so close to France that it is not usually thought of as an 'overseas' dependency. Prior to the decentralization reforms of 1982, it constituted the 22nd region of metropolitan France. It was then, however, elevated to the status of a Collective Territory and given a parliament with substantive powers, thus distinguishing it from the other 21 regions of metropolitan France.

CORSICA

Corse

Capital: Ajaccio

Location
Western Europe. Corsica is an island in the Mediterranean Sea, west of Italy and north of Sardinia.

Social and economic data
Area: 8,680 km²
Population: 250,000*
Pop. density per km²: 29*
Economy type: high income
Currency: French franc

*1990

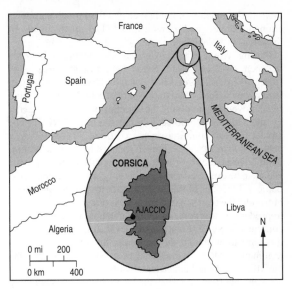

Ethnic composition
More than half the population are native Corsicans.

Religions
Predominantly Roman Catholic.

Local government
The island is divided into two departments (Haute-Corse and Corse-du-Sud), five *arrondissements* (districts), 52 cantons, and 360 communes.

Political system
Corsica forms an integral part of the French Republic. Since 1982, however, it has been given the special status of a Collective Territory, with its own directly elected, 51-member parliament. This has the power to scrutinize bills passed by the French National Assembly and propose amendments applicable to the island. The 'Joxe plan' autonomy bill approved by the French National Assembly in 1992 gives the island still greater autonomy in the education, training, transport, and tourism sectors.

Political parties
The principal political parties are the moderate Radical Party, based principally in the north (Haute-Corse); the Bonapartist Party, based in Ajaccio; the conservative Gaullist Party, based in the far south (Corse-du-Sud); the Communist Party; the Socialist Party (PS); the Union for the Corsican People, a moderate autonomist movement; and the Corsican Movement for Autodetermination (MCA), the political wing of the banned Corsican National Liberation Front (FNLC), a separatist, extremist organization. Political activity is clan-based and intensely localized.

Political history
The island, which had earlier been ruled by the Phocaeans of Ionia, the Etruscans, the Carthaginians, the Romans, the Vandals, and the Arabs, came under Genoa's control during the 14th century, before being sold to France in 1768. Under French rule it remained underdeveloped, but its people made

their mark in metropolitan France and the French empire as eminent soldiers and administrators. The most notable of these was Napoleon Bonaparte.

During World War II, Corsica was occupied by Italy between 1942 and 1943. Since 1962 French *pieds noirs* (refugees from Algeria) settled on the island, largely as vineyard owners. Their relative prosperity fuelled a radical separatist movement, involving the bombing of 'colonial targets', by the Corsican National Liberation Front (FNLC). The annual level of bombings increased from 200 in 1975 to a peak of 800 in 1982. The French socialist Mitterrand administration responded by granting considerable autonomy to the island, to be exercised through a directly elected regional parliament. Elections to this body were held in 1982 and 1984, but, under the proportional representation system used, failed to produce a clear party or coalition majority. Terrorism has continued since 1982 at a reduced level, although only 5% of the population support the Corsican Movement for Autodetermination (MCA) or the FNLC extremists. In January 1987 the MCA itself was banned and dissolved by the French government, but from mid-1989 the FLNC resumed its bombing and assassination campaign, targeting banks and other financial institutions. During 1994–95 the FNLC split into two antagonistic wings. This resulted in a fratricidal war and a new level of violence, with drug-running and crime syndicates involved.

8.4.5 Morocco's dependency

Western Sahara, which Morocco has controlled in one way or another since the early 1950s, is in strict legality an occupied territory, rather than a colony or dependency, and its future has yet to be finally determined. Details of its political structure and history are given below.

WESTERN SAHARA

Capital: La'youn

Location
Middle East and North Africa. It is situated in northwest Africa, between Morocco, to the north, and Mauritania, to the south, with the Atlantic Ocean to the west. The bulk of the territory is desert.

Social and economic data
Area: 252,120 km^2
Population: 200,000*
Pop. density per km^2: 0.8*
Currency: Morrocan dirham

*1992

Ethnic composition
The territory is peopled predominantly by nomads. The main language is Arabic (Moroccan and Hassaniya).

Religions
The principal religion is Sunni Islam.

Local government
For administrative purposes, the territory is divided into the provinces of La'youn, Oued Eddahab, Es-Semara, and Boujdour.

Political system and parties
Since 1976, as a result of the territory's disputed status, Western Sahara has had two competing governments, both of which claim legitimacy. The Moroccan-controlled area is divided into the four provinces noted above and administered by Moroccan officials. The nationalist Polisario Front (PF), which was set up in 1973, also, however, claims to rule this territory and has its own Saharan Arab Democratic Republic (SADR), 'government in exile', headed by a president, Mohammed Abdelazziz, and prime minister, Bouchraya Bayoune. It also includes a seven-member Executive Council, a 25-member Political Bureau and a 101-member, elected legislative, Saharawi National Assembly. At its refugee camps in south-western Algeria, there is also a rudimentary form of local government, based on people's councils. The PF is a socialist organization, campaigning for the establishment of a fully independent and non-aligned Arab–Islamic state.

Political history
The 1,000-km-long Saharan coastal region between French-dominated Morocco and Mauritania was designated a Spanish 'sphere of influence' in 1884, being situated opposite the Spanish-ruled Canary Islands. However, Morocco had long laid claim to this border region and when it secured independence from France, in 1956, re-activated its claim by invading Spanish Sahara, only to be repulsed by Spanish troops. From 1965, after the discovery of rich phosphate resources at Bu Craa, in the heart of the territory, Moroccan interest was rekindled, but in a peaceful manner. Meanwhile, within Spanish Sahara, nationalist sentiment began to awaken and in 1973 the Yema'a, a council of local elders and elected officials, pressed for self-determination. A more radical nationalist group, the Polisario Front (Frente Popular de Liberación de Sakiet el Hamra y Río de Oro), was also formed, in May 1973, to fight for independence.

These calls were rejected by neighbouring Morocco and Mauritania, who soon after the death of the Spanish ruler, General Franco, had moved in to divide the territory between themselves. This partition was finally effected during 1975–76, when Spain withdrew completely. Morocco secured two-thirds of the land area, including the phosphate mines, and Mauritania the rest. The Polisario nationalist forces, however, refused to accept this division and, declaring the establishment of their own Saharan Arab Democratic Republic (SADR: República Arabe Saharaui Democrática), proceeded to wage a guerrilla war against both Morocco and Mauritania, benefiting from indirect support provided by Algeria and Libya.

Polisario was successful in its struggle with Mauritania and forced its recognition of the SADR in August 1979. The SADR was also accepted, in February 1982, as a full member of the Organization of African Unity (OAU). However, Morocco, by establishing an 'electronic defensive wall', which was a 2,500-km-long sand barrier, 2.75 metres high, on which modern electronic surveillance devices were put, and by the receipt of support from the United States, remained impregnable. It kept control of the key towns and phosphate mines of Western Sahara, while conceding most of the surrounding, largely unpopulated, desert interior to Polisario. It also occupied much of the Mauritania-conceded area in the south.

With an army of more than 100,000 stationed in the territory and faced with a Polisario force of barely 8,000, the Moroccans gradually began to gain the upper hand, during the mid-1980s, and progressively extended their defensive wall outwards. They were boosted by Libya's decision to end its support for Polisario, in 1984, and by a gradual calming of Algeria's socialist revolutionary ardour, culminating, in May 1988, in the formal re-establishment of Algerian–Moroccan diplomatic relations. Three months later, in August 1988, a United Nations-sponsored settlement of the 'Western Saharan dispute' was effected in Geneva, when representatives from Morocco and the Polisario Front accepted a plan to hold a referendum, based on 1974 voting rolls, in Western Sahara, to decide the territory's political future. As part of this agreement, a UN special representative was to be appointed to serve as a temporary pro-consul to run the civil administration and ensure order and political neutrality during the run-up to the planned referendum. A cease-fire was agreed between Morocco and Polisario in 1991. However, the referendum failed to be held, as anticipated, in 1992 and, although the Polisario Front and Moroccan government held direct talks for the first time in July 1993, problems over voter identification were so great that doubts were expressed as to whether the referendum would ever be held. In July 1995 the United States warned both sides that it would withdraw its support for the UN operation if a referendum was not held soon.

8.4.6 Netherlands' dependencies

The two dependencies of the Netherlands represent the residue of what was once a considerable colonial empire, dating back to the 17th century, which had been built up on the basis of trade and exploration. Details of the political structures and histories of these remaining overseas possessions are given below.

ARUBA

Capital: Oranjestad

Location
Central America and the Caribbean. Aruba is the westernmost island of the Lesser Antilles group, situated in the southeastern Caribbean, 30 km north of Venezuela.

Social and economic data
Area: 193 km^2
Population: 70,145*
Pop. density per km^2: 363*
Economy type: middle-high income (c. $6,000–7,000 per capita)
Currency: Aruban guilder (or florin)

*1992

Principal languages
Dutch (official), Papiamento (a local form of creole), spoken by the majority of the population, Spanish, and English.

Religions
Eighty per cent of the population is Roman Catholic.

Political system
There is a 21-member single chamber assembly, termed the Island Council (Staten), elected by universal adult suffrage for a four-year term and subject to dissolution during that time. Executive authority for internal affairs is wielded by an eight-member Council of Ministers, headed by a prime minister and responsible to the Staten. Dutch interests are overseen by a crown-appointed governor, who serves as commander-in-chief of the island's armed forces and has executive authority in external matters.

Political parties
There are three principal political parties: the People's Electoral Movement (MEP); the Aruba People's Party (AVP); and the Aruban Liberal Organization (OLA). The MEP was established in 1971, has a current membership of 1,200 and is led by Nelson Oduber, who was prime minister 1989–94. It is a secular, cross-race, social democratic party which dominated the Staten until 1985. The AVP was formed in 1942 and is led by the popular Henny Eman. Like the MEP, it campaigned for separation from Curaçao during the 1970s, but boycotted the MEP-induced referendum on the subject, in 1977. With minority party support, it gained a majority in the Staten following the elections of November 1985 and Eman became the island's first prime minister. Among the minor parties, the Aruban Patriotic Party (PPA), which was formed in 1949, and opposes full independence, and National Democratic Action (ADN), formed in 1985, are the most influential.

Latest elections
In the most recent Staten elections, held, following the collapse of a MEP–PPA–ADN coalition government, on 29 July 1994, the AVP won ten seats, the MEP, nine, and the OLA, two seats. An AVP–OLA coalition government was formed, headed from August 1994 by Henny Eman.

Political history
The island was colonized by Holland in 1636 and became a member of the Netherlands Antilles autonomous federation in 1954. The economy developed significantly from the 1930s, following the establishment of a large oil refinery at St Nicolaas in 1929. This created growing resentment at the island's political dominance by adjacent Curaçao and the redistributive drain of wealth to other poorer islands in the federation. During the 1970s the People's Electoral Movement (MEP) exploited this sentiment by campaigning for Aruba's secession from the federation. A referendum on the issue was forced in March 1977, 82% of the electorate voting for withdrawal and independence. Formal separation from the federation was finally achieved on 1 January 1986, following the report of a commission on the subject. The Netherlands remains responsible for the defence and external

relations of the island. Full independence was planned for 1996, but in March 1994 the island shelved the idea and opted instead for special status. The island's economy in recent years has been in a depressed condition, following the closure of the oil refinery in March 1985, but an economic recovery began in 1988, based on tourism. During recent years, Aruba has improved its relations with the other Netherlands Antilles, entering into a cooperative economic union from 1987, and with neighbouring Caribbean and Latin American states, including Venezuela, which has traditionally claimed the Dutch Leeward Islands, including Aruba.

THE NETHERLANDS ANTILLES

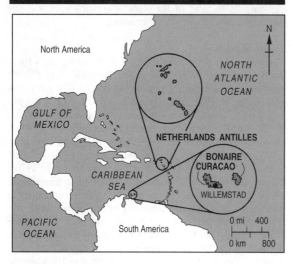

Capital: Willemstad, on Curaçao

Location
Central America and the Caribbean. The Netherlands Antilles consists of two island groups, 800 km apart, in the southeastern Caribbean. The main group is the 'Leeward Islands', which includes Curaçao, Bonaire, and, formerly, Aruba. It is 60 km north of Venezuela. The other group is the 'Windward Islands' and consists of the three small volcanic islands of St Eustatius, Saba, and St Maarten situated to the north east.

Social and economic data
Area: 800 km^2
Population: 194,000*
Pop. density per km^2: 243*
Literacy rate: 92%
Economy type: high income (c. $7,500 per capita)
Currency: Netherlands Antilles guilder (or florin)
*1992

Ethnic composition
Eighty-five per cent of the population is of mixed African descent. Dutch (official on the Leeward Islands), Papiamento (a local form of creole), Spanish, and English (official on the Windward Islands) are the main languages.

Religions
Roman Catholicism is the predominant religion, especially on the Leeward Islands and Saba. Protestantism is strong on St Eustatius and St Maarten in the Windward Islands.

Local government
Each of the five island territories has its own Island Council, Executive Council, and lieutenant governor to manage local affairs in what is, effectively, a federal system.

Political system
A crown-appointed governor serves as head of state and oversees Dutch interests, having control of the islands' defence and external affairs. The governor is assisted by an Advisory Council. Executive authority for internal affairs rests with a six-member Council of Ministers, responsible to an elected assembly, the Staten. This is composed of 22 members elected by universal adult suffrage for a four-year term and subject to dissolution within this period. Each island group forms an electoral district for election purposes, Curaçao returning 14 members, Bonaire and St Maarten three each, and Saba and St Eustatius one member each. A proportional representation system is used in the cases of the multimember districts.

Political parties
The principal political party is the Curaçao-based Partido Antia Restruktura (PAR), formed in 1993 by Miguel Pourier. It is a 'social-Christian' body, as is the Curaçao-based National People's Party (PNP), founded in 1948 and led by Maria Liberia-Peters, the prime minister between 1984–85 and 1988–93. The third significant party is the socialist New Antilles Movement (MAN), formed in 1979 and led by Dominico (Don) Martina, who was prime minister between 1979–84 and 1985–88. Other significant parties are the liberal-socialist Democratic Party (DP), which was established in 1944. It is divided between Curaçao, Bonaire, and St Maarten branches. Another party is the Bonaire Patriotic Union (UPB).

Latest elections
In the most recent Staten elections, held on 25 February 1994, the PAR attracted 39% of the vote and captured eight of the 22 seats. The PNP won 18% of the vote and three seats; the MAN 13% of the vote and two seats; the DP 14% of the vote and five seats; the St Maarten Patriotic alliance two seats; and the BPU and Windward Islands People's Movement one seat apiece.

Political history
Originally claimed by Spain, the Netherlands Antilles were colonized by Holland during the 1630s, Curaçao developing into a prosperous entrepôt for the Caribbean trade. Sovereignty was periodically contested by France and Britain during the 18th century, before the islands were finally confirmed as Dutch territories in 1816. The abolition of slavery in 1863 ushered in a period of economic depression which was only ended during the 1920s by the establishment of petroleum refineries on Aruba and Curaçao islands. In 1954 the island group was granted full autonomy over domestic affairs, while remaining within the Kingdom of the Netherlands.

During the 1960s and 1970s internal politics were characterized by intense inter-island rivalries, most notably between Curaçao and Aruba, and policy-making was paralysed by the coalition nature of the governments returned. Arguments over revenue sharing and rights to prospective offshore oil reserves eventually led to the withdrawal of Aruba from the Netherlands Antilles federation in 1986. In recent years, the economy, which is heavily dependent on the refining of oil imported from Venezuela, for export to the United States, and 'offshore' financial services, has been in a depressed condition, forcing unpopular budgetary retrenchment. There have also been charges of government corruption. The 'metropolitan' Dutch government envisages the Netherlands Antilles eventually adopting a commonwealth structure, with the 'Antilles of Five' forming themselves into two parts: Curaçao and Bonaire; and St Maarten, Saba, and St Eustatius. However, in a November 1993 referendum, electors in Curaçao rejected the government plan for separate status and voted overwhelmingly for continuance of the current Antillean federation.

8.4.7 New Zealand's dependencies

New Zealand's four dependencies were acquired 'second hand', all having been British possessions but, after it had achieved full independence, being more sensibly administered by New Zealand than by the 'mother country'. Their political structures and histories are set out below.

New Zealand's territories			Table 72
New Zealand's overseas (associated) territories			
Territory	Date of first coming under New Zealand administration	Area (sq km)	Population (c. 1992)
Cook Islands	1901	237	19,000
Niue	1901	259	2,321
Ross Dependency	1923	414	Uninhabited
Tokelau	1925	12	1,700
Total	-	922	23,021

COOK ISLANDS

Capital: Avarua, on Rarotonga Island

Location
Oceania. The islands are situated in the South Pacific Ocean, 2,600 km northeast of Auckland, New Zealand. There are six large and nine small volcanic and coral islands in the Cook group, scattered widely across almost 2 million square kilometres of the South Pacific. The highest-lying and most important island is Rarotonga, which is in the southern island group.

Social and economic data
Area: 237 km^2
Population: 19,000*
Pop. density per km^2: 80*
Literacy rate: 92%
Economy type: middle income (c. $2,000 per capita)
Currency: New Zealand dollar

*1991

Ethnic composition
Eighty-one per cent of the population is Polynesian; 8% mixed Polynesian and European; 8% mixed Polynesian and other races; and 2% European. English is the official language, but Cook Islands' Maori is also spoken.

Religions
Seventy per cent of the population belongs to the Cook Islands (Congregational) Christian Church and 16% is Roman Catholic.

Local government
Each of the main islands, except Rarotonga, has an elected mayor and appointed government representative. Rarotonga is divided into three tribal districts (*vaka*).

Political system
There is a 25-member Legislative Assembly, which is elected for a five-year term by universal adult suffrage. Ten deputies represent the main island of Rarotonga, 14 represent constituencies on the other 14 islands, and one represents Cook Islanders resident in New Zealand. The Assembly selects from its ranks a prime minister, who oversees a cabinet of his or her choosing and also holds a wide range of functional portfolios. Hereditary island chiefs are represented in a second assembly chamber, the House of Ariki. This body, however, has no legislative powers. An appointed high commissioner represents the British Crown as the islands' formal head of state, and the New Zealand government has a representative on Rarotonga.

Political parties
There are three principal political parties: the Cook Islands Party (CIP), which was formed in 1965 and, under the leadership of Sir Albert Henry, held power continuously between 1965 and 1978; the Democratic Party (DP), established in 1971, and the dominant party between 1978–89; and the Alliance Party (AP), formed in 1992.

Latest elections
In the most recent general election, held on 24 March 1994, the CIP, led by Prime Minister Sir Geoffrey Henry, a cousin of Sir Albert Henry, increased its majority, capturing 20 of the 25 available seats, based on a 45% share of the vote. The DP, with 15% of the vote, won three seats, and the AP, with 21% of the vote, two seats. Turnout was 86%.

Political history
The islands, which were first visited by Captain James Cook (1728–79) in 1773, and subsequently named after him, were annexed by Britain in 1888, but were later transferred to New Zealand, in 1901. In 1965 they became internally self-governing in 'free association' and with common citizenship

with New Zealand, which retains responsibility for defence and foreign affairs. Their chief importance lies in their coconut, pineapple, and citrus fruit production, fruit processing constituting the main industry, and as a growing tourist centre. However, the islands have a huge trade deficit and rely on substantial aid to sustain their living standards. Three-quarters of this aid is supplied by New Zealand and currently amounts to $12 million, or $630 per year for each inhabitant. In late 1991 cyclones Val and Wasa struck the islands, causing damage estimated at $2 million. In March 1994 the islanders voted in a referendum to reject the adoption of a Maori name for the islands. The Cook Islands are a member of the South Pacific Forum and favour the establishment of a South Pacific 'nuclear-free zone'.

NIUE

Capital: Alofi

Location
Oceania. Niue is a coral island situated in the South Pacific Ocean west of the Cook Islands and 2,140 km northeast of New Zealand. The population lives in small coastal villages, with a concentration in Alofi.

Social and economic data
Area: 259 km^2
Population: 2,321*
Pop. density per km ^{2}: 9*
Literacy rate: 94%
Economy type: low-middle income (c. $1,500–2,000 per capita)
Currency: New Zealand dollar
*1994

Ethnic composition
The inhabitants are predominantly Polynesian and mixed Polynesian. English is the official language, but Niuean is also spoken. Some 10,000 Niueans live in New Zealand.

Religions
Three-quarters of the population belong to the Ekalesia Niue, a Protestant organization.

Political system
There is an elected 20-member Legislative Assembly, comprising 14 village representatives and six members elected on a common roll. Government is in the hands of a cabinet of four, headed by a prime minister, and drawn from the Assembly's ranks. The New Zealand government has an official representative on the island, stationed at Alofi.

Political parties
Until recently, candidates for election to the Assembly have stood as independents. To contest the general election of March 1987, however, the island's first political party, the Niue People's Action Party (NPAP), was founded by Young Viviani. It has been highly critical of the government's record of economic management. Viviani briefly became prime minister during 1992–93.

Latest elections
The most recent Assembly elections were held on 27 February 1993, with a record 24 candidates contesting the six common-roll seats. Following the contest, in March 1993 Frank Lui, a former labour minister, became prime minister.

Political history
The island, when visited by Captain James Cook (1728–79) in 1774, was already inhabited. Its indigenous population, who were at first hostile to Europeans, were converted to Christianity by missionaries during the 19th century and, following petitioning by the islanders, a British protectorate was established in 1900. In the following year Niue was annexed by New Zealand. Full internal self-government, in 'free association' with New Zealand, was granted in October 1974, with New Zealand retaining reponsibility for the island's defence and external affairs. The economy is founded upon passion fruit, copra, and handicraft exports, but, despite this, is heavily dependent on foreign aid and support from New Zealand. In 1991 the New Zealand government announced it was reducing its aid allocation by 10% in an effort to compel the Niue government to reduce the public sector labour force and spend more on development. In December 1992 the island was rocked by the death of Sir Robert Rex, who had dominated politics in Niue, being its prime minister since the early 1950s. Niue is a member of the South Pacific Forum.

TOKELAU

Capital: Nukunonu

Location
Oceania. Tokelau consists of three coral atolls, Atafu, Fakaofo, and Nukunonu, situated in the South Pacific Ocean, 480 km north of Western Samoa and 3,500 km north-northeast of New Zealand.

Social and economic data
Area: 12 km^2
Population: 1,700*
Pop. density per km ^{2}: 142*
Literacy rate: 97%
Economy type: low income (c. $1,000 per capita)
Currency: New Zealand dollar
*1990

Ethnic composition
The population is wholly Polynesian, enjoying close family and cultural links with Western Samoa. English is the second language. Around 2,300 inhabitants have migrated to New Zealand, sending home earnings for their families.

Religions
The majority of people belong to the Roman Catholic or Congregational Church.

Political system
The islands are governed directly by a resident administrator of the New Zealand Ministry of Foreign Affairs. In practice, much of the executive work is delegated to an official secre-

tary, based at Tokelau. At the local level, however, the islands are substantially self-governing. On each atoll there is a Council of Elders (COE: or Taupulega), comprising the heads of family groups plus two members elected triennially by universal adult suffrage. One is the Faipule, or commissioner, who presides over the Council and represents the atoll in its dealings with the New Zealand administration, and the other is the Pulenuku, who is responsible for village affairs. Twice a year, 15 delegates from each atoll COE convene in a General Fono, or meeting, chaired by the islands' three Faipule.

Political history
The islands were made a British protectorate in 1877 and formed part of the Gilbert and Ellice Islands colony, together with Kiribati and Tuvalu, from 1916. In 1925 they were transferred to New Zealand, becoming formally part of New Zealand in 1949. Copra is the principal revenue-earning product and the sale of licences to foreign fleets to fish in its exclusive economic zone is another important source of income, but 80% of the island's annual budget expenditure is paid for from a subsidy provided by New Zealand.

8.4.8 Norway's dependencies

Norway has five dependencies, all situated in the Arctic or Antarctic regions, and most of them uninhabited. The one inhabited possession, Svalbard, was finally secured by an international treaty after its sovereignty had been contested by other European powers.

SVALBARD

Capital: Long Year City (Longyearbyen) on Spitsbergen

Location
Arctic. Svalbard is an archipelago composed of nine main islands, the most important being Spitsbergen. It is situated in the Arctic Ocean, 650 km north of Norway.

Social and economic data
Area: 62,924 km^2
Population: 3,700*
Pop. density per km^2: 0.06*
*1994

Ethnic composition
Sixty-two per cent of the population is Russian and 36% Norwegian.

Political system
The island is administered by a Norwegian governor (*Sysselmann*) resident at Longyearbyen.

Political history
The island group was discovered by the Dutch seafarer Willem Barents (c. 1550–1597) in 1596 and briefly served as a centre for whale hunting during the 17th century, with its sovereignty being contested by Denmark–Norway, Britain, and the Netherlands. Interest in the islands was reawakened during the early 20th century with the discovery of coal deposits. In 1920 Norway's sovereignty claims were upheld in an international agreement, the Svalbard Treaty, formally ratified in 1925. In return, Norway agreed to allow free scientific and economic access to other nations. Norway and Russia currently maintain permanent mining settlements on the islands, while Poland has a small research station.

8.4.9 Portugal's dependencies

Portugal was once one of the world's leading colonial powers, and one of the last to concede sovereignty to the local communities. It now has only one possession and that will pass to Chinese control at the end of the century.

MACAO

Macau

Capital: Macao

Location
Asia. The territory consists of the coastal peninsula of Macao and the two small islands of Taipa and Coloane, situated on the Zhujiang or Pearl River delta in southeast China, 64 km west of Hong Kong.

Social and economic data
Area: 17 km^2
Population: 487,000*
Pop. density per km^2: 28,647*
Literacy rate: 79%

Norwegian dependencies			Table 73
Dependency	Date of first coming under Norwegian administration	Area (sq km)	Population (1994)
Bouvet Island	1928	60	uninhabited
Jan Mayen Island	1929	380	uninhabited
Peter I Island	1931	180	uninhabited
Queen Maud Island	1939	(Antarctic Territory)	uninhabited
Svalbard	1920	62,924	3,700
Total	–	63,544	3,700

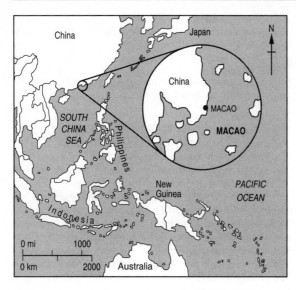

Economy type: middle-upper income (c. $6,000–7,000 per capita)

Currency: pataca

*1992

Ethnic composition
Ninety-nine per cent of the population is Chinese, speaking Cantonese, which is the joint official language, alongside Portuguese.

Religions
The people are predominantly (45%) Buddhists, with 15% adhering to Roman Catholicism.

Political system
Designated a Special Territory of Portugal, executive power is held by a governor, appointed by the president of Portugal, who is assisted by a cabinet of seven Portuguese-appointed under-secretaries. Foreign affairs are controlled by the president of Portugal. The governor works in consultation with a local Legislative Assembly which comprises 23 members, eight of whom are elected directly by universal adult suffrage, eight elected indirectly by business associations, and seven appointed by the governor. The members serve four-year terms and elect a president from among themselves. The governor also presides over a Superior Council of Security, which includes three Legislative Assembly members, and a Consultative Council, five of whose members are indirectly elected by local administrative bodies and interest groups.

Political parties
There are no formal political parties in Macao. However, three civil associations are represented in the Legislative Assembly: the Electoral Union (UNE), the Pro-Macao, and the Flower of Friendship and Development of Macao (FADEM).

Latest elections
The most recent Legislative Assembly elections, held in September 1992, saw 50 candidates contest the eight directly elected seats. Pro-Beijing candidates won four of the seats. Turnout was 59% of the registered electorate, corresponding to 14% of the population.

Political history
Macao was first established as a Portuguese missionary and trading post in 1537, before being leased by China in 1557. Later, in 1849, it was annexed by Portugal and formally recognized as a colony by the Chinese government under the terms of an 1887 treaty. The colony's commercial importance steadily diminished during the later 19th and early 20th centuries, as Macao harbour silted up and trade was diverted to the British entrepôt of Hong Kong and other Treaty Ports. It was forced, instead, to concentrate on the local 'country' trade, as well as on gambling and tourism.

In 1951 Macao became more closely integrated with mainland Portugal, and was designated a Portuguese Overseas Province. This entitled it to send an elected representative to the Lisbon parliament. However, after the Portuguese revolution of 1974, the colony, redesignated a 'Special Territory', was granted greater autonomy, based upon the adoption, in February 1976, of an 'organic statute' which established the present political structure.

In June 1986, the Portuguese and Chinese governments began negotiations over the question of the return of Macao's sovereignty, under similar 'one country, two systems' terms as had been agreed in 1984 by Britain and China for Hong Kong. These negotiations were successfully concluded in March 1987, when the 'Macao Pact' was signed. Under the terms of this concord, Portugal has agreed to formally hand over sovereignty to the People's Republic on 20 December 1999. In return, the People's Republic has undertaken to maintain the capitalist economic and social system of the port enclave for at least 50 years thereafter. Under Chinese rule, Macao will be redesignated a 'special administrative region' (SAR) and will have its own assembly which, with a similar basis of representation to the current Legislative Assembly, will contain 'a majority of elected members'. To overseee the transfer of power, a Sino–Portuguese Joint Liaison Committee has been established. In July 1991 the Draft Basic Law of the Macao SAR was published. It provides for the future chief executive of the SAR to be selected by a 300-member electoral college.

8.4.10 United Kingdom's dependencies

The British Empire began when the first successful English colony was founded at Jamestown, Virginia, in 1607. At its peak, at the end of the 19th century, it covered a quarter of the world's land surface and included a quarter of its peoples. It had spread over every continent to every race. Now most of the greatest empire history has ever recorded consists of separate, independently sovereign, states, banded together, as much by sentiment and history as other ties, within the Commonwealth. This global body is described, with other world and regional groupings, in **Chapter 9**. What is left of the British Empire today consists of a number of states which still enjoy the protection of the British Crown. Their political structures and histories are given below.

UNITED KINGDOM CROWN DEPENDENCIES

These islands, although lying offshore, do not form integral parts of the United Kingdom. Instead they are designated as Crown Dependencies, enjoying effective self-government in internal affairs.

THE CHANNEL ISLANDS

Capitals:
St Helier, on Jersey, and St Peter Port, on Guernsey

Location
Western Europe. The Channel Islands comprise the islands of Guernsey, Jersey, Alderney, Sark, Herm, Jethou, Brechou, and Lihou, and lie in the English Channel off the northwest coast of France. Fifty-eight per cent of the population lives on Jersey and 40% on Guernsey.

Social and economic data
Area: 196 km^2
Population: 146,000*
Pop. density per km^2: 743*
Literacy rate: 100%
Economy type: high income (c. $12,000 per capita)
*1991

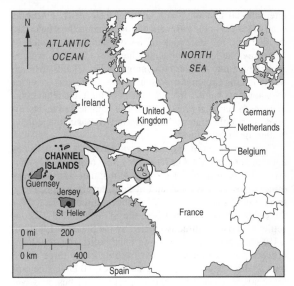

Religions
Christianity, mainly Church of England and Roman Catholic.

Political system
The Channel Islands are internally self-governing. However, the United Kingdom is responsible for their defence and

Name	Date of first coming under British administration	Area (sq km)	Population (c. 1992)
United Kingdom crown dependencies and British dependent territories			**Table 74**
UK crown dependencies			
Channel Islands	1066	196	14,600
Isle of Man	1765	572	69,800
British dependent territories			
Anguilla	1650	96	8,960
Bermuda	1612	53	58,000
British Antarctic Territory	1908	1,710,000	uninhabited*
British Indian Ocean Territory	1965	60	uninhabited*
British Virgin Islands	1666	153	16,644
Cayman Islands	1670	259	27,200
Falkland Islands	1765/1833	12,173	2,120
Gibraltar	1704	6	32,000
Hong Kong	1841/1860	1,071	5,800,000
Montserrat	1632	102	12,500
Pitcairn Islands	1790	36	55
St Helena & Dependencies	1659	411	7,100
South Georgia & the South Sandwich Islands**	1775	3,903	uninhabited*
Turks & Caicos Islands	1765	430	14,000
Total	-	1,729,521	6,062,979

* With the periodic exception of scientific or military personnel
** Dependencies of the Falkland Islands between 1908 and 1985, with the Falklands' governor continuing to serve as their administrative commissioner

international relations, with Queen Elizabeth II serving as head of state. For the purposes of government, the islands are divided into the Bailiwick of Jersey and the Bailiwick of Guernsey, the latter embracing Guernsey island, as well as Alderney, Sark, and the remaining smaller islands. In each Bailiwick the Crown is represented by a lieutenant governor who appoints bailiffs from the ranks of the local legal community, to serve as presidents of the representative assemblies, termed the States of Deliberation (SD), and the judicial bodies, or Royal Courts.

Government on the islands is conducted by Committees appointed by the SD. On Jersey, the SD comprises 12 senators, who are elected for six-year terms, half retiring every three years. At the local and at-large levels, respectively, there are 12 constables and 29 deputies, directly elected for three-year terms. On Guernsey, the SD consists of 12 conseillers, who are indirectly elected by the States of Election, a 108-member body comprising local political and judicial officers, for six-year terms, half retiring every three years, plus 33 directly elected people's deputies, 10 Douzaine representatives, elected by their respective parishes, and two Alderney representatives. In Alderney, the SD is a 12-member body, directly elected for a three-year term. Finally, in Sark, the assembly, called the Chief Pleas, consists of 12 popularly elected members plus 40 tenants nominated by the feudal suzerain of the island, the seigneur.

Political parties
Members sit in the SDs usually as independents, although the Jersey Democratic Movement has occasionally held a number of seats.

Political history
The islands were granted to the Duke of Normandy in the 10th century, being attached to the Crown of England in 1066. They are the only part of Normandy to have remained under British rule since 1204 and were the only British possession to have been occupied by Germany during World War II. The islands enjoy tax sovereignty and, with imports exempt from British value-added tax, and local income tax levels low, they have developed into 'tax haven' finance centres in recent decades.

THE ISLE OF MAN

Capital: Douglas

Location
Western Europe. The Isle of Man lies in the Irish Sea, equidistant from Scotland, to the northeast, England, to the east, and Northern Ireland, to the west.

Social and economic data
Area: 572 km^2
Population: 69,800*
Pop. density per km^2: 122*
Literacy rate: 100%
Economy type: middle income (c. $6,000 per capita)

*1991

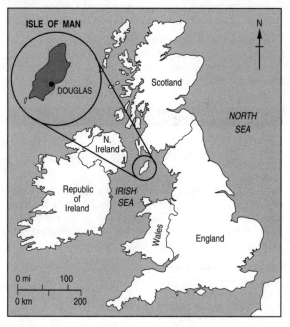

Religions
Christianity, especially the Church of England.

Political system
Queen Elizabeth II is head of state, under the designation 'Lord of Man', and has ultimate responsibility for the island's good government, being represented on the island by an appointed lieutenant governor. The Isle of Man is dependent on the United Kingdom for its defence and external relations. In internal matters, however, it is substantially self-governing, having its own legislative assembly, the Court of Tynwald, and legal and administrative systems, as well as control over direct taxation. The Court of Tynwald, which traces its roots back to Scandinavian times, is a two-chamber body, comprising the Legislative Council, or Upper House, and the House of Keys, or Lower House. The Legislative Council consists of the lieutenant governor, a president, the lord bishop of Sodor and Man, the attorney general and seven members elected by the House of Keys. The House of Keys consists of 24 members who are directly elected by universal adult suffrage for five-year terms. Both chambers sit together as one body in the legislature, but vote separately.

Political parties
Most members sit as independents, although a number of political parties, most notably the Manx Labour Party and the Sons of Man (Mec Vannin) nationalist party, have won seats from time to time.

Political history
The Isle of Man was ruled successively by the Welsh, during the 6th to 9th centuries, the Vikings/Norwegians, from the 9th century to 1266, and the Scots, between 1266 and 1765, before being purchased by the British government, in 1765. Because of its independent fiscal policies, the island has, like the Channel Islands, become something of a tax haven in recent years.

BRITISH DEPENDENT TERRITORIES

These are overseas territories enjoying a colonial status, with varying degrees of internal autonomy.

ANGUILLA

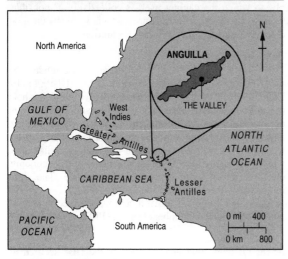

Capital: The Valley

Location
Central America and the Caribbean. Anguilla is an island in the Eastern Caribbean, the most northerly of the Leeward Islands, and situated 112 km northwest of St Christopher and Nevis, and 8 km north of St Maarten.

Social and economic data
Area: 96 km^2
Population: 8,960*
Pop. density per km ^{2}: 93*
Economy type: middle income (c. $3,500 per capita)
Currency: East Caribbean dollar

*1992

Language
English is the official language.

Religions
Christianity, especially Anglican and Methodist, with a Roman Catholic minority.

Political system
Under the terms of the 1982 constitution, as amended in 1990, the British Crown is represented on Anguilla by an appointed governor who is responsible for external affairs, defence, the judiciary, the 'offshore' banking sector, and internal security, and presides over meetings of the Executive Council and House of Assembly. The Executive Council, or cabinet, comprises a chief minister, with whom the governor works closely, and three other ministers drawn from the House of Assembly, as well as two *ex officio* members, the attorney general and the permanent secretary for finance. The House of Assembly consists of seven members

directly elected for five-year terms, as well as two nominated and two *ex officio* representatives.

Political parties
Three political parties currently operate: the Anguilla National Alliance (ANA), which was known as the People's Progressive Party (PPP) prior to 1980 and dominated politics until 1994, with Sir Emile Gumbs as chief minister 1984–94; the Anguilla Democratic Party (ADP), which was known as the Anguilla People's Party (APP) prior to the resignation of Ronald Webster as party leader in 1984; and the Anguilla United Party (AUP), which, originally formed in 1979, was revived in 1984 by Webster and is now led by Chief Minister Hubert Hughes.

Latest elections
In the March 1994 general election each of the three parties won two seats, with the other being won by an independent, and an AUP–ADP coalition government was formed, headed by Hubert Hughes.

Political history
Anguilla was first colonized by English settlers from overcrowded St Christopher (St Kitts) in 1650. It became more closely tied with St Christopher in 1825 and was later formally incorporated in the colony of St Kitts-Nevis-Anguilla (SNA). In February 1967 this colony, together with others in the Eastern Caribbean, became an internally self-governing state in association with the United Kingdom, Britain retaining responsiblity for its defence and external affairs.

However, in May 1967, under the leadership of Ronald Webster, a local business executive and leader of the People's Progressive Party (PPP), Anguilla, alleging domination by its larger associated islands, revolted, refusing to accept rule from St Christopher. After attempts to reach a compromise had failed and Anguilla had voted to cut all ties with the UK and declare independence, British troops were sent there, in March 1969. A crown-appointed British commissioner was installed and a truce signed. Subsequently, in July 1971, Anguilla was designated a dependency of Britain and two months later all troops were withdrawn.

A new constitution was framed in 1976, providing for a government of elected representatives, and in December 1980 the island was formally separated from the SNA. Ronald Webster served as the island's chief minister between 1976 and 1977 and between 1980 and 1984, but, after being replaced as the party's leader in February 1977 by Emile Gumbs, left the PPP to form the Anguilla United Party (AUP), and the Anguilla People's Party (APP), in 1979 and 1981 respectively. In the March 1984 general election, however, Webster's APP was heavily defeated, its leader losing his seat. Gumbs, who had earlier served as chief minister between 1977 and 1980, returned to office, as leader of the Anguilla National Alliance (ANA), the successor party to the PPP. He proceeded to implement a policy programme geared towards revitalizing the economy, unemployment standing at 40% in 1984, by encouraging tourism and foreign inward investment. By 1990 tourism contributed 29% of GDP and the unemployment rate had fallen to 1%. Gumbs, who was later knighted, remained as chief minister until his retirement from politics in February 1994.

BERMUDA

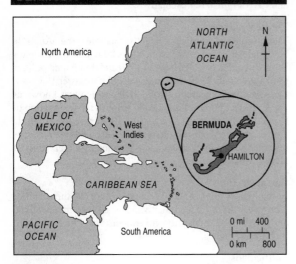

Capital: Hamilton, on Main Island, or Great Bermuda

Location

Central America and the Caribbean. Bermuda is an archipelago consisting of 138 low-lying coral islands and islets stretching 35 km east and west and 22 km north and south, and lying in the Atlantic Ocean 917 km off the coast of South Carolina, United States. Twenty of the islands are inhabited.

Social and economic data

Area: 53 km^2
Population: 58,000*
Pop. density per km ^{2}: 1,094*
Literacy rate: 98%
Economy type: high income (c. $23,000 per capita)
Currency: Bermuda dollar (equivalent to US dollar)

*1993

Ethnic composition

Two-thirds of the population are black, the remainder being of British or Portuguese stock. English is the official language, but some Portuguese is also spoken.

Religions

Christianity, with 42% of the people Anglicans and 16% Roman Catholics.

Local government

The country is divided into nine parishes, with St George and Hamilton constituting two municipalities.

Political system

Bermuda is internally self-governing. However, Britain remains, under the terms of the 1968 constitution, as amended in 1973 and 1979, responsible for the islands' external affairs, defence, and internal security, including the police, with British interests being represented by a crown-appointed governor. The islands' assembly has two chambers: the 11-member Senate and the 40-member House of Assembly. Three of the Senate's members are appointed by the governor, five by the prime minister and three by the leader of the

opposition. The members of the House of Assembly are all directly elected by universal adult suffrage for five-year terms, standing in 20 two-member constituencies. The minimum voting age is 21 years. From the majority grouping in the House of Assembly, the governor appoints a prime minister to preside over a 12-member cabinet of his or her own choosing. At least six cabinet ministers must be drawn from the assembly, to which the cabinet itself is collectively responsible. There is also a Governor's Council which is used by the governor and ministers for consultative purposes.

Political parties

Three political parties currently operate in Bermuda. The most important is the United Bermuda Party (UBP), led by David Saul, the prime minister since August 1995. It has held power continuously since 1968. It is liberal-conservative in outlook and supports multiracialism and free enterprise. The main opposition party is the Progressive Labour Party (PLP), led by Frederick Wade. This is a moderate-socialist force which advocates the 'Bermudianization' of the economy, electoral reform, and eventual independence. The third minor party, the National Liberal Party (NLP), is a centrist grouping led by Gilbert Darrell, and was formed in August 1985 by breakaway members from the PLP.

Latest elections

At the October 1993 general election the UBP secured its eighth successive election victory, capturing 22 seats in the House of Assembly, with 10 black and 12 white MPs. However, its share of the popular vote fell sharply, while the PLP, drawing in support from younger voters, won the other 18 seats and had one of its deputies elected speaker of the House of Assembly.

Political history

The islands were discovered by and named after the Spanish mariner, Juan de Bermudez, in 1515. They were later colonized by British settlers in 1612, forming part of the Virginia Company's charter, before being transferred to the British Crown, in 1684. During the 17th century the economy was based on tobacco growing, whaling, and ship building. Bermuda also served as a penal settlement, until 1862, and a naval station, before developing into an Atlantic trading entrepôt during the 19th century. The islands were granted a new constitution, conceding internal autonomy and establishing a new ministerial system.

Popular politics were to be characterized, however, by intense rivalry between the moderate, though predominantly white, United Bermuda Party (UBP) and the more radical, black-led, pro-independence Progressive Labour Party (PLP). The general election of May 1968, which was won by the UBP, was accompanied by serious race riots. This was followed by a wave of murders in 1972–73, including that of the governor, Sir Richard Sharples. Further race riots broke out in December 1977, after two blacks were hanged for complicity in the 1972–73 incidents. This forced the despatch of British troops to restore order. To investigate the causes of this racial tension, a Royal Commission was set up, in February 1978. This later recommended, in its report of August 1978, a redrawing of constituency boundaries to improve the PLP's prospects of capturing seats. However, despite implementation of this recommendation, the UBP continued to win Assembly majorities in the elections of December 1980, February 1983, October 1985, February 1989, and October 1993.

The 1978 Royal Commission also recommended early independence for Bermuda, but the majority of the population oppose this. This was evidenced by a referendum held in August 1995 when, with a turnout of 57%, only 26% voted in favour of independence. Sir John Swan, the prime minister since 1982, and seven of his black colleagues in the UBP had advocated independence, while the party's remaining 14 members, including all its white deputies, had opposed it. The opposition PLP, which favoured independence in principle, urged its predominantly black supporters to abstain, arguing that electoral reform must come first. Defeat in the plebiscite brought Swan's resignation as premier and seemed likely to be followed by defeat for the divided UBP in the 1997 general election.

The country currently has one of the highest per-capita GDPs in the world, having developed, in recent decades, with the British guarantee of security, into a major centre for tourism and financial services, as well as as an offshore 'tax shelter' for more than 6,000 international companies. The United States has an air base on the islands at Kindley Field, held on a 99-year lease. A sharp drop in tourist arrivals in 1991 provoked the government into passing a bill classifying the hotel business as an 'essential industry' since it employs a third of the workforce and contributes 35% of GDP.

THE BRITISH VIRGIN ISLANDS

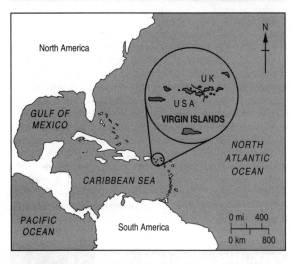

Capital: Road Town, on Tortola island

Location
Central America and the Caribbean. The British Virgin Islands consist of 60 mountainous islands and islets situated at the north end of the Leeward Islands, or Lesser Antilles, chain, 90 km east of Puerto Rico and adjoining the US Virgin Islands. Sixteen of the islands are inhabited, 83% of the population living on Tortola island and 13% on Virgin Gorda.

Social and economic data
Area: 153 km^2
Population: 16,644*
Pop. density per km^2: 109*
Literacy rate: 98%
Economy type: high income (ca. $10,000 per capita)
Currency: US dollar

*1991

Ethnic composition
The population is predominantly of Negro or mixed Negro and European descent. English is the official language.

Religions
Christianity, especially Protestant, with a Roman Catholic minority.

Political system
Under the terms of the 1977 constitution, the British Crown is represented on the Virgin Islands by an appointed governor who has sole responsibility for external affairs, defence, judicial, and internal security matters. The governor also serves as chairperson of a six-member Executive Council, or cabinet, and possesses reserve legislative powers. There is also a Legislative Council, which comprises nine members directly elected from single-member constituencies, an appointed speaker and one *ex officio* member, the attorney general. From the majority grouping in the Legislative Council is drawn a chief minister and three other ministers who work with the governor and attorney general in the Executive Council. The minimum voting age has been 18 years since 1979. In April 1994 the British government accepted a proposal from the constitutional commission to enlarge the Legislative Council to 13 seats, with the four additional members representing the whole territory in a single constituency.

Political parties
Three political parties currently function on the islands: the Virgin Islands Party (VIP), led by Chief Minister H Lavity Stoutt; the United Party (UP), led by Cyril B Romney; and the Independent People's Movement (IPM), which was formed in 1989. Stoutt had previously served as chief minister during the later 1960s and between 1979 and 1983, returning to power at the general election of September 1986. In the November 1990 election the VIP was re-elected, winning six seats, while the IPM won one seat and an independent candidate two.

Political history
Tortola was originally settled by the Dutch in 1648. It was colonized by British planters in 1666 and formally annexed by Britain in 1672. A form of constitutional government was granted in 1774 and in 1834 slavery was abolished. From 1872 the islands formed part of the British federal colony of the Leeward Islands, before later becoming a separate Crown Colony, in July 1956. They received their own appointed administrator, known as governor from 1971, in 1960 and a constitution was promulgated in 1967 which provided for a ministerial system. This was superseded by a new constitution in June 1977 which extended the degree of internal self-government.

Politics have been characterized since 1967 by the alternation in power of the Virgin Islands Party (VIP), led by H Lavity Stoutt, and a coalition of United Party (UP) and independent deputies. Cyril Romney, an independent councillor, served as chief minister from November 1983, but lost power to Stoutt in September 1986, after his reputation had been damaged by his alleged connection with a company which was under investigation by the British police and US Drug Enforcement Administration. Since the mid-1970s, the islands' economy has developed rapidly, principally as a result of a boom in tourism, the number of annual visitors having tripled to more than 320,000. The tourist industry now contributes nearly 50% of GDP and one-third of employment. Following the passage of the Business Companies Act by the Legislative Council in 1984, which simplified procedures for company registrations, the Virgins have also attracted much foreign 'offshore capital', more than 30,000 international companies being registered by 1990, utilizing the islands as a 'tax shelter'. The business sector contributes a quarter of GDP.

CAYMAN ISLANDS

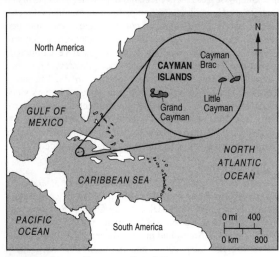

Capital: George Town, on Grand Cayman

Location
Central America and the Caribbean. The Cayman Islands consist of the islands of Grand Cayman, Cayman Brac, and Little Cayman, and lie in the Western Caribbean, 290 km northwest of Jamaica and 240 km south of Cuba. Ninety-three per cent of the population lives on Grand Cayman and 6% on Cayman Brac.

Social and economic data
Area: 259 km^2
Population: 27,200*
Pop. density per km^2: 105*
Literacy rate: 97%
Economy type: high income (c. $26,000 per capita)
Currency: Cayman Islands dollar
*1992

Ethnic composition
Sixty per cent of the population are of mixed descent. English is the official language.

Religions
Christianity is the chief religion, predominantly of the Anglican and Baptist churches, with a Roman Catholic minority.

Political system
Under the terms of the 1959 constitution, as revised in 1972 and 1992, the British Crown is represented on the Caymans by an appointed governor who has sole responsiblity for external affairs, defence, judicial, public service, and internal security matters. The governor also serves as chairman of the Executive Council, or cabinet, which comprises three appointed *ex officio* members and five elected representatives drawn from the Legislative Council. The latter five serve as ministers. The Legislative Assembly consists of three official representatives and 15 members elected by universal adult suffrage from six electoral districts for a four-year term.

Political parties
Party politics collapsed in the 1960s and, until 1991 and the formation of the Progressive Democratic Party (PDP), candidates contested elections both as independents and in loose 'teams', the most important of which has been the 'National Team'. All candidates favour the Caymans' continued dependent status and liberal–conservative economic strategy.

Latest elections
In the November 1992 general election the 'National Team' grouping, which includes the nucleus of the PDP, won 12 of the 15 Legislative Assembly seats.

Political history
The Caymans were first visited by Christopher Columbus (1451–1506) in 1503, but were never settled by the Spanish. They were subsequently ceded, with Jamaica, to Britain under the terms of the 1670 Treaty of Madrid. Grand Cayman island was later colonized by British military deserters from Jamaica, from where it was administered. The islands of Cayman Brac and Little Cayman were permanently settled only from 1833, and until 1877 were not administratively connected with Grand Cayman. On Jamaica's independence in 1962, the islands were made a separate British Crown Colony and have subsequently grown into an important centre for tourism, currently attracting almost half a million visitors annually, as well as for oil transhipment and as an offshore 'tax shelter' for foreign businesses and banking companies.

FALKLAND ISLANDS (MALVINAS)

Capital: Port Stanley, on East Falkland Island

Location
South America. The Falkland Islands consist of two large islands, East and West Falkland, and around 200 smaller islands, all situated in the South Atlantic Ocean, 770 km northeast of Cape Horn. Seventy per cent of the population live in the capital.

Social and economic data
Area: 12,173 km^2
Population: 2,120*
Pop. density per km^2: 0.2*
Economy type: high income (c. $8,500 per capita)
Currency: Falkland Islands pound (equivalent to pound sterling)

*1991

Ethnic composition
Most of the population are of British descent. In addition to the population total shown above, there were 1,500 British troops stationed on the island in 1994. English is the official language.

Religions
Christianity, based on the Anglican, Roman Catholic, and United Free Churches.

Political system
Under the terms of the October 1985 constitution, the Falkland Islands are administered by a crown-appointed governor, who works with an advisory Executive Council composed of two, non-voting, *ex officio* members, a chief executive, and a financial secretary, and three representatives elected by the Legislative Council. The Falkland Islands' Legislative Council comprises eight directly elected members and the two non-voting *ex officio* representatives.

Political parties
Members of the Legislative Council are elected as independents, although one political party was formed in 1988: the Desire the Right Party (DRP). The DRP favours a limited rapprochement with Argentina.

Political history
The Falklands were first visited by the English navigator John Davis (c. 1550–1605) in 1592 and in the late 17th cen-

tury were named after Lord Falkland, treasurer of the British Navy. East Falkland was colonized by French settlers from St Malo in 1764 and given the name Iles Malouines, and West Falkland by British settlers in 1765. From 1767, however, the Spanish, who took over the French settlement, gradually gained the upper hand, ejecting the British in 1774. British sovereignty was never ceded, however. During the early 19th century, Spanish influence waned, its garrison being withdrawn in 1811, and, following a brief period of occupation, between 1826 and 1831, by the Republic of Buenos Aires, Britain reasserted her possession in 1833. Formal annexation of the Falkland Islands and their dependencies took place in 1908 and 1917, a modest, sheep-raising, settler economy being established.

Argentina, however, never relinquished its claim over the islands ('Islas Malvinas') and in 1966, at the instigation of the United Nations, negotiations to resolve the continuing dispute were started. During the early 1970s, relations thawed. Britain's Heath administration (1970–74) signed a communications agreement which effectively gave Argentina control over air access to the islands. Following this, the Buenos Aires government extended the Port Stanley airstrip, enabling tourists to visit the Falklands and islanders to make use of Argentinian schools and hospitals. The British government appeared anxious to foster closer socio-economic links between the Falklands and the Argentinian mainland, but consistently refused, in intergovernment talks, to countenance any transfer of sovereignty against the wishes of the inhabitants, who consistently favoured maintaining their British connection.

After the accession to power, in 1976, in Buenos Aires, of a nationalist-minded military junta, led by Lieutenant General Jorge Videla, Anglo–Argentinian relations deteriorated. In December 1977, a military invasion was threatened and, in response, the British Callaghan administration (1976–79) despatched a hunter-killer submarine to the islands. Two years later, the new Conservative Thatcher administration (1979–90) recommended negotiations with the Argentinian government. However, the two compromise options suggested to resolve the dispute, condominium, or joint sovereignty and rule, or 'lease-back', the transfer of formal sovereignty to Argentina, who would, in turn, lease back the islands' administration to Britain, were overwhelmingly rejected when put before the islands' Council. A third, Argentinian-sponsored, option, designated 'most pampered region' status, which would involve the transfer of sovereignty in return for Argentinian guarantees to retain the existing democratic form of government and local legal and education systems, was also rejected. Two years later, on 2 April 1982, soon after the accession to power in Buenos Aires of another military leader, the intransigent General Leopoldo Galtieri (b. 1926), Port Stanley was invaded by Argentinian troops. The British government immediately responded by despatching a naval 'task force' and a fierce conflict ensued in which 255 British, 755 Argentinian, and three Falklander lives were lost, before, on 14 June 1982, the 12,000 Argentinian troops on the islands surrendered and British control was restored.

After this war, the British government instituted a new 'Fortress Falklands' policy, based on establishing a large permanent garrison on the islands to deter future Argentinian aggression. A 278-km-wide protection and fishing zone was declared, licences being sold to foreign trawler companies seeking to fish within it. New development schemes were also promoted by the islands' newly established Falklands Islands Development Agency, resulting in a boom in the islands' once moribund economy. Despite UN calls for a re-opening of negotiations to find a peaceful solution to the 'Falklands issue' and the accession to power of a new democratic administration in Argentina, the British government has declined to enter into talks and the islanders' right to self-determinantion was guaranteed in the Falklands' 1985 constitution. Full diplomatic relations between the United Kingdom and Argentina were restored in February 1990 and in September 1991 the two governments signed agreements substantially reducing military restrictions in the South Atlantic.

GIBRALTAR

Capital: Gibraltar

Location
Western Europe. Gibraltar consists of a narrow peninsula connected to the southwest tip of Spain by an isthmus.

Social and economic data
Area: 6 km²
Population: 32,000*
Pop. density per km²: 5,333*
Literacy rate: 99%
Economy type: middle-upper income
(c. $6,000–7,000 per capita)
Currency: Gibraltar pound

*1992

Ethnic composition
Seventy per cent of the population are Gibraltarians and 20% British. More than a thousand Moroccan labourers also work

on 'The Rock'. English is the official language, but most of the population are bilingual in English and Spanish.

Religions
Three-quarters of the population are Roman Catholics, 8% members of the Church of England, 10% are Muslims, and 3% Jewish.

Political system
Under the terms of the 1969 constitution, British interests in Gibraltar have been represented by a crown-appointed governor, who is advised by the Gibraltar Council, a body which comprises four *ex officio* and five elected members of the House of Assembly. The United Kingdom is responsible for the territory's defence and external affairs, as well as matters of internal security. Since 1969, full control over the remainder of internal affairs has been vested in the elected House of Assembly and a Council of Ministers, or cabinet, drawn from the majority grouping within the Assembly.

The House of Assembly consists of a speaker appointed by the governor, two *ex officio* representatives, the attorney general and the financial and development secretary, and 15 members who are popularly elected for four-year terms. The electoral system is unique, allowing each elector to vote for a maximum of eight candidates. The Council of Ministers, which constitutes the territory's 'internal executive', has seven ministers and a chief minister drawn from the House.

Political parties
Four political parties currently function. The two most important are the moderate-socialist Gibraltar Socialist Labour Party (GSLP), which was established in 1976 and is led by its founder, José (Joe) Bossano, and the centre-left Gibraltar Social Democrats (GSD), formed in 1989. The GSLP, a strongly nationalist body, seeks to achieve full independence for 'The Rock' within the European Union, while the opposition GSD supports the participation of Gibraltar in Anglo-Spanish negotiations. The Gibraltar National Party (GNP), formed in 1991, advocates self-determination for Gibraltar. The centre-right Gibraltar Labour Party–Association for the Advancement of Civil Rights (GLP–AACR), formed in 1942 and led by Adolfo Canepa, dominated political affairs in Gibraltar prior to 1988, with its former leader, Sir Joshua Hasan, serving continuously as chief minister between 1964 and 1969 and between 1972 and 1987 and Canepa as chief minister in 1987–88. However, opposition to the December 1987 Anglo-Spanish transport accord, which sanctioned joint civilian use of Gibraltar's airport, caused a split in the GLP–AACR and, since its electoral defeat in March 1988, the GLP–AACR has been inactive.

Latest elections
In the general election of 16 January 1992 the GSLP secured eight seats in the House of Assembly and the GSD seven, based on 73% and 20% shares of the popular vote. The GNP won 5% of the votes but no seats.

Political history
Gibraltar has long served as a strategic promontory, commanding the western entrance to the Mediterranean and boasting excellent port facilities. Occupied by Arabs from

711 AD, it passed to the Moorish kingdom of Granada during the 15th century and subsequently fell under Spanish control. During the War of the Spanish Succession (1701–14), it was captured by an Anglo-Dutch force in 1704 and was formally ceded to Britain by Spain under the terms of the Treaty of Utrecht (1713). It was designated a Crown Colony in 1830 and, following World War II, during which it served as a strategic base for Allied naval forces, a Legislative Council was established in 1950. In 1963 the Franco government in Spain began to campaign for the territory's return to Spain, exerting diplomatic pressure through the United Nations and economic pressure, culminating in the closure of the frontier with Spain and the withdrawal of the Spanish labour force. In accordance with a UN resolution which called for the interests of the people of Gibraltar to be taken into account, the British government held a referendum on the sovereignty question in September 1967 in which an overwhelming (95%) majority voted to retain the link with the United Kingdom. A new constitution was thus framed and adopted in 1969 in which full internal self-government was conceded, but in which the UK government undertook never to enter into arrangements to transfer the territory's sovereignty to another state against their freely and democratically expressed wishes.

Spain remained intransigent, continuing to claim Gibraltar's sovereignty and keeping the border closed until General Franco's death in November 1975. Thereafter Anglo-Spanish relations slowly thawed, beginning with the restoration of Gibraltar–Spain telephone links in December 1977 and culminating in the re-opening of the border in February 1985: a year before Spain's entry into the European Community. In March 1991 the British government withdrew the majority of its army personnel from Gibraltar because Spain's commitment to the EC and NATO had made the need for substantial defences unnecessary. At the same time, it reassured Gibraltarians that no change in sovereignty would be contemplated without their agreement.

José Bossano, leader of the Gibraltar Socialist Labour Party (GSLP), became chief minister in March 1988 and has sought to achieve self-determination within the European Union. However, this has been rejected by Spain, which continues to claim sovereignty and has been concerned at the apparent lack of action by the Gibraltar authorities to stop money laundering and drug smuggling occurring in its territory.

HONG KONG

Xianggang
British Crown Colony of Hong Kong

Capital: Hong Kong

Location
Asia. Hong Kong lies off the south coast of China, 145 km southeast of Guangzhou or Canton, and comprises the island of Hong Kong, Stonecutter's Island, the Kowloon Peninsula, and the New Territories, which are part of the Chinese mainland.

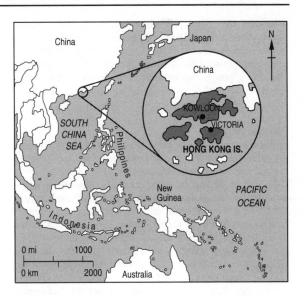

Social and economic data
Area: 1,071 km[2]
Population: 5,800,000*
Pop. density per km [2]: 5,415*
Literacy rate: 90%
Economy type: high income (c. $17,000 per capita)
Currency: Hong Kong dollar

*1994

Ethnic composition
Fifty-seven per cent of the population are Hong Kong Chinese and 40% refugees from the Chinese mainland. English and Cantonese are the official languages.

Religions
Predominantly Buddhist, mixed with Confucianism and Daoism, with a 9% Christian minority.

Local government
Hong Kong is divided into the three regions of Hong Kong Island, Kowloon, and New Territories, with 18 districts below, each having its own advisory local board or committee. The first fully democratic local board elections were held in September 1994.

Political system
Hong Kong is administered by a crown-appointed governor who presides over an unelected Executive Council, or cabinet. This is composed of four *ex officio* and ten nominated, unofficial representatives and one appointed, official member. The governor also chairs a 60-member Legislative Council (Legco), comprising, from 1995, 20 members elected by geographical constituency, 30 members indirectly elected to represent professional and other 'functional constituencies', and 10 indirectly elected by an 'election committee'. The Executive Council serves as a consultative body for administrative matters, while the Legislative Council, which has two sub-committees, scrutinizes all government expenditure proposals and advises the governor on the enactment of the territory's laws. An Urban Council (Urbco),

composed, from 1995, of 32 elected members, is responsible for the urban areas of Hong Kong Island and Kowloon. There is also a 27-member elected Regional Council. Voting has been limited traditionally to 200,000–300,000 professional and skilled people, but by 1995, with the minimum voting age reduced from 21 to 18 years, the number of registered electors was 2.45 million.

Political parties

Political parties are now being developed in Hong Kong as the political system is democratized. Notable recently formed parties include the pro-reform Democratic Party (DP), led by Martin Lee, and its allies, the largest single group in the Legco with 28 seats after the September 1995 elections; and the Association for Democracy and People's Livelihood (ADPL). The four leading pro-China parties are the Liberal Party, the Liberal Democratic Foundation (LDF), the Hong Kong Progressive Alliance (HKPA), and the Democratic Alliance for the Betterment of Hong Kong (DAB), which includes communist members. The Chinese Communist Party and Kuomintang (Chinese Nationalist Party; Taiwan-based) also have organizations in Hong Kong.

Political history

Hong Kong Island was occupied by Britain in 1841 and ceded by the Chinese government under the terms of the 1842 Treaty of Nanking. The Kowloon Peninsula and Stone-cutter's Island were acquired under the Peking (Beijing) Convention of 1860 and the New Territories secured on a 99-year lease signed in June 1898. The colony, which developed into a major entrepôt for Sino–British trade during the late 19th and early 20th centuries, was occupied by Japanese forces between December 1941 and August 1945. The restored British administration promised, after 1946, to introduce a greater degree of self-government. These plans were shelved, however, after the 1949 communist revolution in mainland China.

During the 1950s almost 1 million Chinese, predominantly Cantonese, refugees fled to Hong Kong. This immigration continued during the 1960s and 1970s, raising the colony's population from 1 million in 1946 to 5 million in 1980 and forcing the imposition of strict border controls. Hong Kong's economy expanded rapidly during the corresponding period, the colony developing into one of the major commercial, financial, and industrial centres in Asia.

As the date for the termination of the New Territories' lease approached, negotiations on Hong Kong's future were opened between the British and Chinese governments during the early 1980s. These culminated in a unique agreement signed in Beijing, in December 1984, by which the British government agreed to transfer full sovereignty of the islands and New Territories to China in July 1997 in return for a Chinese assurance that Hong Kong's social and economic freedoms and capitalist lifestyle would be preserved for at least 50 years. Under this 'one country, two systems' agreement, Hong Kong would, in 1997, become a special administrative region within China, with its own laws, currency, budget, and tax system and retain its free port status and authority to negotiate separate international trade agreements. The existing, only partly directly elected, Legislative Council (Legco)

will be replaced by a similar, still partially elected legislature, headed by a chief executive. The chief executive will replace the governor and will be selected by an appointed 600-member electoral college and subject to removal by the Chinese government.

In preparation for its future withdrawal from the colony, the British government introduced indirect elections, to select a portion of the new Legislative Council, in 1984 and direct elections for seats on lower-tier local councils, in 1985. A Sino–British joint liaison group was also established to monitor the functioning of the new agreement and a 58-member Basic Law Drafting Committee, which included 23 representatives from Hong Kong, was formed in Beijing, in June 1985, to draft a new constitution. The first draft of this Basic Law was published in April 1988 and a 176-member Basic Law Consultative Committee established to collect public comments on its provisions. Events in mainland China in June 1989 raised considerable doubts among the population about the value of the People's Republic's 'one country, two systems' assurances, and increased pressure on the British authorities to accelerate the pre-1997 internal democratization process.

In 1992 the former UK Conservative Party chairperson, Chris Patten (b. 1944), was appointed governor. He swiftly put forward proposals for enhanced democratization. This raised objections from Beijing, claiming that the 1984 agreement was being breached. In June 1994 the Legco approved a political reform which substantially widened the franchise and the elective element within the Legco and other councils. However, the Chinese government made it clear that it rejected these reforms and that the Legco and other councils would be disbanded upon China's resumption of sovereignty in July 1997 and that a new, initially appointed, Special Administrative Region Legislative Council would be established. In 1994–95 democratic elections were held to the District Boards, Urban, Regional, and Legislative Councils, with the pro-democracy Democracy Party polling strongly. In July 1995 Governor Patten survived a no-confidence motion tabled in the Legco by Democratic Party deputies. In the September 1995 Legco elections pro-Beijing parties fared badly, with the Democratic Party and its allies capturing most seats.

MONTSERRAT

Capital: Plymouth

Location

Central America and the Caribbean. Montserrat is a volcanic island lying 43 km southwest of Antigua in the Leeward Islands group of the Lesser Antilles in the Eastern Caribbean. Thirty per cent of the population lives in the capital.

Social and economic data

Area: 102 km^2
Population: 12,500*
Pop. density per km ^{2}: 123*
Literacy rate: 97%
Economy type: middle income (c. $4,000 per capita)
Currency: East Caribbean dollar

*1990

Ethnic composition
The population is predominantly of mixed African and European descent. English is the official language.

Religions
Christianity, especially Anglican, with a Roman Catholic minority.

Political system
Under the terms of the 1960 constitution, as amended in 1977 and 1989, the British Crown is represented on the island by an appointed governor who is responsible for defence, foreign affairs, and internal security. The governor also serves as president of a seven-member Executive Council, or cabinet, which also includes a chief minister, three other ministers drawn from among the elected members of the legislature, and the attorney general and financial secretary, both *ex officio*. The legislature, or Legislative Council, is a 12-member body consisting of two official members, three nominated, including a speaker, and seven members directly elected for four years. The Executive Council's chief minister and ministers are chosen from the Legislative Council. The 1989 constitutional amendment provided for the island's right to self-determination.

Political parties
There are four political parties currently operating. The most important is the National Progressive Party (NPP), formed in 1991 by a former civil servant, Reuben Meade. The other three are the People's Liberation Movement (PLM), led by John A Osborne, who served as chief minister between 1978 and 1991; the National Development Party (NDP); and the Progressive Democratic Party (PDP). All the parties support the island's present dependent status, although the PLM is pledged to securing eventual independence when it becomes 'economically viable'. In the meantime, it campaigns for greater development expenditure to improve the island's agricultural potential, as well as its educational and physical infrastructure.

Latest elections
In the October 1991 general election the NPP won four of the seven elective seats and the PLM and NDP one apiece. The PDP failed to secure representation.

Political history
Montserrat was first visited in 1493 by Christopher Columbus (1451–1506), who named the island after the Abbey of Montserrat, near Barcelona. In 1632 it was colonized by English settlers, who had moved from the overcrowded Caribbean island of St Christopher (St Kitts), and Irish political prisoners sent by Oliver Cromwell (1599–1658). They proceeded to establish a plantation economy based on slave labour. However, the island was not formally made a British Crown Colony until 1871. Between 1871 and 1956 Montserrat was administered as a division of the federal colony of the Leeward Islands. When the federation was dissolved, it became a separate colony, opting not to join the West Indies Associated States, which was established in 1967. Since 1960 the island has had its own administrator, who was redesignated governor in 1971, and constitutional system.

The dominant political party from 1978 to 1991 was the People's Liberation Movement (PLM), a moderate, nationalist body, led by John Osborne. The party supported the development of agriculture, cotton and peppers being important export crops, light manufacturing, 'offshore' finance, and the tourist industry, which currently contributes 25% of Montserrat's GDP. However, in September 1989 Hurricane Hugo caused widespread damage to the island. The PLM, with the reputation of its leader, Osborne, tarnished by charges of corruption on which he was later acquitted, was defeated in the October 1991 general election by the newly formed National Progressive Party (NPP), led by Reuben Meade. In August 1995 more than half the island was evacuated in fear of a full eruption of the Chances Peak volcano.

PITCAIRN ISLANDS

Capital: Adamstown, on Pitcairn Island

Location
Oceania. The Pitcairn Islands consist of volcanic Pitcairn Island and the uninhabited atolls of Ducie, Henderson, and Oeno, all situated in the southeastern Pacific Ocean, east of French Polynesia.

Social and economic data
Area: 35.5 km^2
Population: 55*
Pop. density per km^2: 1.6*
Economy type: high income (c. $8,000 per capita)
Currency: Pitcairn dollar (equivalent to the New Zealand dollar)

*1994

Languages
Pitcairnese English

Religions
Seventh Day Adventist Church

Political system
As a Crown Colony, Pitcairn is administered by the British high commissioner in New Zealand. Under the terms of the Local Government Ordinance of 1964, the High Commissioner governs in consultation with an Island Council, presided over by the island magistrate, who is elected for a three-year term. The Island Council consists of the island secretary, an *ex officio* representative, as well as five appointed and four elected members.

Political history
Pitcairn Island was discovered by the British navigator Philip Carteret (d. 1796) in 1767 and was settled in 1790 by nine mutineers from HMS *Bounty*, in 1790. It was annexed as a British colony in 1838, but by 1856 the population had outgrown the island's resources, forcing 194 inhabitants to move to Norfolk Island, off the east coast of Australia. Forty-three Pitcairn islanders later returned home, in 1864 and since then the island has remained permanently settled. In 1898 Pitcairn was brought within the jurisdiction of the high commissioner for the Western Pacific. It was later transferred

to the Governor of Fiji, in 1952, but since Fiji's independence, in 1970, it has been governed by the British high commissioner in New Zealand. Despite the high costs involved in administering the island, Britain announced in 1993 that it would not abandon its responsibilities to the island since independence was not a viable option and no other state wanted to take over the administration.

ST HELENA AND DEPENDENCIES

Capital: Jamestown

Location
Central and Southern Africa. St Helena and its dependencies constitute a volcanic island grouping situated in the South Atlantic Ocean. St Helena lies 1,930 km off the southwest coast of Africa. The dependency of Ascension island is 1,131 km northwest of St Helena, while the dependency of Tristan da Cunha island lies 2,100 km to the northeast.

Social and economic data
Area: 411 km^2
Population: 7,100*
Pop. density per km ^{2}: 17*
Literacy rate: 97%
Economy type: middle income (c. $1,800 per capita)
Currency: St Helena pound

*1992

Religions
Christianity, principally Anglican, with a Roman Catholic minority.

Political system
Under the terms of its 1989 constitution, St Helena is administered by a crown-appointed governor, who works with a Legislative Council and an Executive Council. The Legislative Council comprises the speaker and the chief secretary, the financial secretary and the attorney general, as *ex officio* members, and 12 elected members. The Executive Council, or cabinet, presided over by the governor, also includes the three *ex officio* members noted above and five of the elected members of the Legislative Council. The task of the Legislative Council is to oversee the work of government departments.

The dependencies of Ascension and Tristan da Cunha are governed by appointed administrators. Tristan da Cunha also has an advisory Council, consisting of eight elected and three nominated members.

Political parties
Two political parties nominally exist. These are the St Helena Labour Party, which was established in 1975, and the St Helena Progressive Party, formed in 1973, which favours the retention of close economic links with Britain; both have been inactive since 1976.

Political history
The island of St Helena was discovered by the Portuguese navigator Joao da Nova Castella in 1502 and subsequently became a port of call for ships en route to the East Indies. It

was annexed and occupied by the British East India Company in 1659 and, before being brought under direct crown rule in 1834, gained fame as the place of Napoleon's exile between 1815 and 1821.

Ascension Island was discovered in 1501, but remained uninhabited until occupied by Britain in 1815. It was made a dependency of St Helena in 1922 and today serves as an important commercial and military communications centre. During the Falklands War, of 1982, it also served as a crucial staging post for the naval 'task force' which had been sent to the South Atlantic.

Tristan da Cunha, which has been occupied since 1816, is currently the site of a small crayfish processing plant operated by a subsidiary of the South Atlantic Islands Development Corporation.

TURKS AND CAICOS ISLANDS

Capital: Cockburn Town, on Grand Turk island

Location
Central America and the Caribbean. The Turks and Caicos Islands consist of 30 islands, which form the southeastern archipelago of the Bahamas chain in the West Atlantic Ocean, 144 km north of the Dominican Republic and Haiti, and 920 km southeast of Miami. Forty-two per cent of the population lives on Grand Turk, 19% on South Caicos, 17% on North Caicos, 13% on Providenciales, and 5% on Middle Caicos island.

Social and economic data
Area: 430 km^2
Population: 14,000*
Pop. density per km ^{2}: 33*
Literacy rate: 98%
Economy type: middle income (c. $5,000 per capita)
Currency: US dollar

*1993

Ethnic composition
The population is predominantly of African descent. English is the official language.

Religions
Christianity, chiefly Baptist and Anglican.

Political system
Under the terms of the 1976 constitution, later amended in March 1988, executive power is exercised by a crown-appointed governor, who is responsible for defence, external affairs, internal security, and official appointments. The governor presides over an eight-member Executive Council, or cabinet, comprising three *ex officio* representatives and five chosen, including a chief minister, by the governor from among the elected members of the Legislative Council. The Legislative Council consists of seven appointed members and 13 representatives directly elected for four-year terms.

Political parties
Four political parties currently function, the most important two of which are the People's Democratic Movement

(PDM), which was formed in 1976 and is led by Derek Taylor, and the Progressive National Party (PNP). Both parties are strong supporters of a free enterprise economy and favour continued development of the islands' tourist and financial services industries. There are five electoral districts on the islands and thus a number of multimember constituencies.

Latest elections
In the January 1995 Legislative Council election, the PDM won eight of the 13 contested seats, the formerly dominant PNP four seats, and one went to the independent former chief minister, Norman Saunders.

Political history
The Turks and Caicos Islands were first linked administratively to the Bahamas in 1765, before being made dependencies of Jamaica, in 1874. They subsequently became a unit territory within the Federation of the West Indies in 1959 and, on Jamaica's independence in 1962, were made a Crown Colony. Under this new arrangement, the islands were first administered from the Bahamas, but in 1972 received their own governor.

The first elections under the new 1976 constitution were won by the People's Democratic Movement (PDM), a political party which was, initially, strongly committed to achieving independence. In 1980 Britain agreed to accede to this on the condition that the PDM again won a Legislative Council majority in the general election of November 1980. It failed to achieve this, however, being handicapped by the death of its leader and founder, J A G S McCartney, in an accident in June 1980. Instead, the Progressive National Party (PNP), which favoured continued dependent status, secured a Legislative Council majority in both this and the subsequent May 1984 general election. As a consequence, the question of independence faded from the political agenda.

Instead, the islands' politics became dominated by a series of high-level scandals. These began in March 1985, when the chief minister and PNP leader, Norman Saunders, together with two senior colleagues, was forced to resign, after charges of drug smuggling into the United States. All three were later convicted and imprisoned. A year later, in July 1986, Saunders' replacement as chief minister, Nathaniel Francis (PNP), was also compelled to step down, after the publication of a report by a commission of inquiry found him, and two ministerial colleagues, guilty of unconstitutional behaviour and administrative malpractice. The government was immediately dissolved by the governor and a special five-member Advisory Council set up to take over the work of the Executive Council while the islands' political future was reviewed by a special constitutional commission. The recommendations subsequently made by this commission were accepted by the UK government, in March 1987, and formed the basis for an amended constitution, which came into force after the general election of March 1988 and which strengthened the reserve powers of the governor. This election was won by the PDM, with Oswald Skippings becoming chief minister. Power alternated again at the April 1991 election, won by the PNP-led by Washington Missick, and in January 1995 the PDM won.

8.4.11 United States' dependencies

The dependencies of the United States have been acquired in a variety of ways. Guam and Puerto Rico were ceded, as part of the spoils of victory after a war; the American Virgin Islands were purchased; others had been held as Trust Territories, on behalf of the United Nations; and many, particularly in the Pacific, form part of what the United States sees as its defensive shield. In total, including three military bases, there are eight territories in the anti-imperialist United States' 'mini-empire'.

United States external territories			Table 75
Territory	Date of first coming under United States administration	Area (sq km)	Population (c. 1991)
External territories			
American Samoa	1899/1922	195	40,400
Guam	1899	549	133,000
US Virgin Islands	1917	355	111,000
Commonwealth territories			
Northern Mariana Islands	1947	471	43,300
Puerto Rico	1898	8,959	3,600,000
Military bases			
Johnston Atoll	1898	2	330
Midway Islands	1867	5	50
Wake Islands	1898	8	300
Total	–	10,544	3,928,380

FORMAL DEPENDENCIES
('UNINCORPORATED/EXTERNAL TERRITORIES')

AMERICAN SAMOA

Capital: Pago Pago, on Tutuila

Location
Oceania. American Samoa consists of five main volcanic islands and two coral atolls situated in the central South Pacific Ocean, 3,550 km north-northeast of New Zealand. Ninety-three per cent of the population lives on the western-most island of Tutuila.

Social and economic data
Area: 195 km²
Population: 40,400*
Pop. density per km ²: 207*
Economy type: middle income (c. $6,000 per capita)
Currency: US dollar

*1991

Ethnic composition
The indigenous population is of Polynesian origin. English and Samoan, a Polynesian language, are spoken.

Religions
Fifty per cent of the population adheres to the Christian Congregational Church and 20% is Roman Catholic.

Local government
The islands are divided, for administrative purposes, into 15 counties, which are grouped into Eastern, Western, and Manu'a districts.

Political system
Under the terms of the 1967 constitution, executive power is exercised by a governor, who is directly elected for a four-year term, and is limited to two terms. The governor has the authority to appoint heads of government departments, subject to the approval of the assembly, and can veto legislation. The assembly, termed the Fono, is a two-chamber body, comprising an 18-member Senate, elected, according to Samoan custom, from among local male chiefs (*matai*) for four-year terms, and a 20-member House of Representatives, whose members are popularly elected every two years. Swain's Island, with a population of only 27, also sends one non-voting member to the House. The Fono meets twice a year, in January and July, for a maximum of 45 days a year. American Samoa has, since 1981, also sent a non-voting delegate to the US House of Representatives, who is elected every two years. Changes to the 1967 constitution have been drafted by a constitutional convention and await ratification by the US Congress. These include increasing the size of the Senate and House of Representatives.

Political parties
Most candidates are elected as independents, though some stand as Democrats and Republicans, identifying with the mainland US parties. The governor, A P Lutali, was elected in November 1992.

Latest elections
The most recent elections, held on 8 November 1994, concurrently with US congressional elections, saw the election of a Democrat as the territory's representative in the US House of Representatives and the defeat of one-third of those seeking re-election to American Samoa's lower house.

Political history
The islands of American Samoa were first visited by Europeans in the early 18th century and the London Missionary Society established a base there in 1830. They were ruled by local chiefs grouped together to form the independent Kingdom of Samoa. In 1878 the United States was given permission by the Kingdom to establish a naval base at Pago Pago and, from 1899, when the Treaty of Berlin, signed by America, Britain and Germany, recognized US rights in the area, it gradually gained dominance over the region. In 1900 and 1904 the chiefs of the western and eastern islands, respectively, accepted US sovereignty and later, in 1922, after residual German claims had been removed, the islands were officially designated an 'unincorporated territory' of the United States.

American Samoa was, initially, between 1900–51, placed under the administration of the US Department of the Navy and, thereafter, of the Department of the Interior, power being devolved to a resident governor. The governor was, for a long time, an American appointee, working, since 1948, with an advisory two-chamber assembly. Under the terms of the 1960 constitution, which was amended in 1967, the authority of this assembly was increased and in November 1977 direct elections for the governorship were introduced. Peter Coleman became the first governor, between 1978 and 1984. The Samoan economy, which is heavily dependent on the tuna industry, is closely tied to the American economy. Many Samoans have emigrated to the United States in search of work during recent years and the country receives substantial economic aid from the mainland. In September 1988, its delegate to the US House of Representatives, Fofo Sunia, was forced to resign his seat after being convicted of fraud over the use of his official expense account, and sentenced to five months' imprisonment. In December 1991 the islands were hit by Cyclone Val, which damaged 60% of dwellings and destroyed 95% of the subsistence crops.

GUAM

Capital: Agana

Location
Oceania. Guam is the largest and southernmost of the Mariana Islands, being situated in the West Pacific Ocean, 5,920 km west of Hawaii and 2,400 km east of Manila.

Social and economic data
Area: 549 km²
Population: 133,000*
Pop. density per km²: 242*
Literacy rate: 96%

Economy type: middle income (c. $5,500 per capita)
Currency: US dollar

*1990

Ethnic composition
Forty-two per cent of the population are Chamorros, a mixture of Micronesian, Filipino, and Spanish, 24% Caucasians, and 21% Filipinos. Fifteen thousand US military personnel and their dependants also live on Guam. The official language is English, but Japanese and Chamorro, the local language, are also spoken.

Religions
Roman Catholicism is practised by about 90% of the population.

Political system
Under the terms of the 1950 Guam 'Organic Act', or constitution, executive power is wielded by a governor, who is directly elected every four years. Legislative authority lies with a 21-member Legislature, whose members (senators) are elected biennially. It is empowered to pass laws regulating local affairs. A member, who may vote in committees but not on the floor, is elected to the the US House of Representatives every two years. However, residents of Guam, although classed as citizens of the United States, cannot vote in US presidential elections.

Political parties
Two political parties operate on the island, the Republican Party and the Democratic Party, both of which are mainland party affiliates.

Latest elections
In the November 1994 elections the Democrats won 13 seats to the Republicans' eight, and Carl Gutierrez, a Democrat, was elected Governor, with 55% of the vote.

Political history
Guam was 'discovered' by Ferdinand Magellan (c. 1480–1521) in 1521 and claimed by Spain in 1565. The native Micronesian population, which was estimated to be 100,000 in 1521, declined rapidly during the later 16th and throughout the 17th and early 18th centuries, reaching a low of less than 5,000 in 1741, as a result of Spanish aggression and exposure to imported diseases. It later revived, however, through intermarriage with Spaniards and Filipinos. Spain ceded Guam to the United States after the Spanish-American war of 1898 and the country became an 'unincorporated territory' of the United States.

During World War II, the island fell under Japanese control, between December 1941 and July 1944. When American rule was re-established greater authority was progressively devolved to local inhabitants and its administration was transferred, in 1950, from the US Department of the Navy to the Department of the Interior. In 1970, the island's governor was directly elected for the first time and in September 1976 support for the maintenance of close ties with the United States was reaffirmed in a referendum. In November 1987, a referendum came out in support of the island negotiating a new relationship with the United States

and discussions began in 1989 for a bill which would combine elements of free association with US citizenship and confer the status of commonwealth on the territory.

With a fine deep-water port at Apra, Guam has become one of the most important American naval and airforce bases in the Pacific. Currently, there are 7,300 US troops stationed on the island, and a third of its surface is covered by military installations. Guam is also a commercial and financial entrepôt and growing tourist centre, particularly for the Japanese. Its economy has, however, been in a depressed condition since the early 1970s. In August 1992 Typhoon Wake struck the island, causing damage estimated at $250 million and leaving 5,000 people homeless, and in August 1993 a powerful earthquake caused almost equal damage.

UNITED STATES VIRGIN ISLANDS

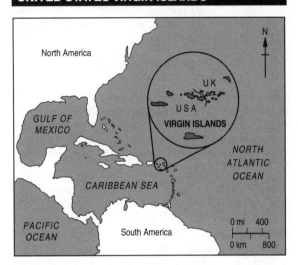

Capital: Charlotte Amalie, on St Thomas

Location
Central America and the Caribbean. The US Virgin Islands consist of more than 50 islands in the south and west of the Virgin Islands group, situated in the Caribbean Sea, 64 km east of Puerto Rico. The two principal islands, accounting for 50% and 47% of the total population respectively, are St Croix and St Thomas. The island of St John is also inhabited.

Social and economic data
Area: 355 km^2
Population: 111,000*
Pop. density per km ^{2}: 313*
Literacy rate: 90%
Economy type: high income (ca. $12,000 per capita)
Currency: US dollar

*1991

Ethnic composition
Twenty to twenty-five per cent of the population are native-born, 35–40% come from other Caribbean islands, 10% from the US mainland, and 5% from Europe. Four-fifths of the

population are black. English is the official language, but Spanish and Creole are widely spoken.

Religions
The population is predominantly Protestant, with a 28% Roman Catholic minority.

Local government
The governor is represented on each of the three inhabited islands by an appointed administrator.

Political system
The islands have been granted a measure of self-government under the constitution of 1936, as amended in 1954, 1970, and 1973. Executive power is wielded by a directly elected governor, who serves a four-year term. The governor appoints, on the advice of the assembly, the heads of government departments and is required to approve any legislation. The assembly, termed the Senate, is a single-chamber body, comprising 15 members, popularly elected for two-year terms, who represent two legislative districts. Since 1968 the US Virgin Islands have elected a non-voting delegate to the US House of Representatives. The islands' citizens are debarred, however, from voting in US presidential elections.

Political parties
The principal political parties are the Democratic Party of the Virgin Islands, the Republican Party, both of which are mainland affiliates, and the Independent Citizens Movement, a breakaway group from the Democratic Party. The Democrats are the dominant party.

Latest elections
In the last gubernatorial elections, held in November 1994, Roy L Schneider was elected governor.

Political history
Originally discovered by Christopher Columbus (1451–1506) in 1493, the islands passed, successively, into English, French, and Dutch control, before the Danish West Indies Company colonized St Thomas and St John islands in 1671. To these, the Danes added St Croix, which they had acquired from France in 1733, and established sugar plantations. Following a decline in the sugar trade, the United States, recognizing the islands' strategic importance in relation to the Panama Canal, took them over in 1917, purchasing them for US $25 million.

They became an 'unincorporated territory' of the United States and were originally placed under the administrative control of the US Department of the Navy, before being transferred to the Department of the Interior in 1931. The islanders were granted American citizenship in 1927 and have enjoyed increasing degrees of self-government since the 'Organic Law', which granted universal suffrage to all adults who could read and write English, was adopted in 1936. Popular election of the governor, who had previously been appointed by the US president, commenced in 1970. However, proposals for increased autonomy were rejected in referenda held in March 1979 and November 1981. In a referendum held in October 1991, 90% of electors voted for continued or enhanced territorial status and rejected the alternative options of independence or integration with the United States. However, the low turnout of just 27% invalidated the result of this plebiscite.

The islands have developed as a major centre for tourism and have attracted, in growing numbers, white 'tax shelter' immigrants. St Croix is also an important centre for petroleum refining.

COMMONWEALTH TERRITORIES

THE NORTHERN MARIANA ISLANDS

Commonwealth of the Northern Mariana Islands (CNMI)

Capital: Garapan, on Saipan

Location
Oceania. The territory consists of 16 islands and atolls in northern Micronesia in the West Pacific Ocean, 5,280 km west of Hawaii and 2,800 km east of the Philippines. Eighty-eight per cent of the population lives on the island of Saipan, 7% on Rota, and 5% on Tinian.

Social and economic data
Area: 471 km^2
Population: 43,300*
Pop. density per km^2: 92*
Economy type: high income (ca. $15,000 per capita)
Currency: US dollar

*1990

Ethnic composition
Predominantly Micronesian. English is the official language, but Chamorro, Carolinian, and Japanese are also spoken.

Religions
The population is predominantly Roman Catholic.

Political system
Under the terms of the October 1977 constitution, the Northern Marianas Islands are internally self-governing as a US 'Commonwealth Territory'. Executive power is exercised by a directly elected governor and legislative authority by a bicameral assembly composed of a nine-member Senate and an 18-member House of Representatives, elected biennially. The islands' inhabitants enjoy US citizenship. A non-voting representative is sent by the territory to the US Congress, being elected every four years.

Political parties
The principal political parties are the Democratic Party, led by Governor Froilan C Tenorio, and the Republican Party, mirroring the US two-party system.

Latest elections
In the most recent gubernatorial elections, held in November 1993, the Democrats won control of the office of governor, ending 12 years of Republican dominance. However, the Republicans maintained substantial majorities in the Senate and House, after the November 1995 elections, and provided the territory's non-voting representative in the US Congress. Turnout was 79% in these elections.

Political history

The islands of the Northern Marianas group were discovered by European explorers during the 1520s. They fell successively under Spanish (1565–1898), German (1899–1914), Japanese (1914–21 and 1941–44), and League of Nations (1921–41) control, before being liberated by US marines in 1944–45 and becoming, along with Palau (now Belau), the Federated States of Micronesia (FSM) and the Marshall Islands, part of the United States' United Nations Trust Territory of the Pacific Islands, in 1947. Under the terms of this trusteeship agreement, the United States was given administrative control of the islands, but was charged with preparing them for eventual independnece. Unlike the other UN Trust Territories, which chose to seek semi-independence under the terms of 'Compacts of Free Association' with the United States, in January 1978, following a referendum in June 1975, the Northern Marianas became a 'Commonwealth Territory' of the United States. As such they enjoyed considerable powers of internal self-government. In November 1986, the American administration conferred full US citizenship on the residents of the islands and this was recognized internationally, when the UN Trusteeship terminated in December 1990. Substantial economic aid has been provided by the US government during recent years. In return, the United States has acquired control of much land on Tinian island for military purposes.

PUERTO RICO

Commonwealth of Puerto Rico (COPR)
Estado Libre Asociado de Puerto Rico

Capital: San Juan

Location
Central America and the Caribbean. Puerto Rico is the easternmost island of the Greater Antilles, situated between the Dominican Republic to the west and the US Virgin Islands to the east, and 1,600 km southeast of Miami.

Social and economic data
Area: 8,959 km^2
Population: 3,600,000*
Pop. density per km ^{2}: 402*
Literacy rate: 89%
Economy type: high income (c. $7,000 per capita)
Currency: US dollar

*1994

Ethnic composition
The population is predominantly of European (Hispanic) descent. Spanish and English are the official languages.

Religions
Roman Catholicism is practised by about 85% of the population.

Local government
The island is divided into 78 'municipal districts', which include surrounding rural areas, each of which is governed by a mayor and municipal assembly, elected for a four-year term.

Political system
Under the constitution, called the 'Public Law', of 1952, Puerto Rico is a self-governing 'Commonwealth', voluntarily associated with the United States. Both states share a common currency and market, while the United States is responsible for the COPR's defence. However, Puerto Rico's position differs from that of a full member state in that its inhabitants, while officially designated US citizens and able to vote in national party primary elections, may not vote in presidential elections and are represented in the US Congress only by a resident commissioner, who, elected quadrennially, participates in House of Representatives' debates, but may only vote in committee. In addition, most US federal taxes, social security being an exception, are not levied in Puerto Rico.

Executive power is exercised by a governor, who is directly elected for a four-year term and works with a cabinet of 15 secretaries. Legislative authority is held by a two-chamber Legislative Assembly, which is composed of a 27-member Senate and a 53-member House of Representatives, sitting each year between January and May. Assembly members are elected every four years, in November, at the same time as the US president, in accordance with an electoral procedure designed to ensure minority party representation. Sixteen senators are returned, two from each of the eight senatorial districts, and 40 representatives are elected in single-member constituencies, by a simple plurality voting system. The remaining places in each chamber are 'at large' seats, reserved for minority party legislators. The legislative process is similar to that in the United States, the governor's approval being required for the enactment of bills. A veto can, however, be overridden by a two-thirds majority vote.

Political parties
The principal political parties in Puerto Rico are the liberal, pro-Commonwealth, 660,000-member, Popular Democratic Party (PPD), which was established in 1939; the 225,000-member New Progressive Party (PNP), formed in 1967 and led by Governor Pedro J Rossello, which favours federation as a constituent state within the United States; and the 60,000-member Puerto Rican Independence Party (PIP), dating from 1946 and with a social democratic, pro-separatist orientation. The PPD and PNP are the dominant forces, each regularly securing about 45% of the popular vote in what is essentially a two-party system.

Latest elections
The most recent gubernatorial and legislative elections, held in November 1992, were won by the PNP.

Political history
Discovered by Christopher Columbus (1451–1506) in 1493, when known by the Arawak Indian name of Boriquen, Puerto Rico was annexed by Spain in 1509. The Spanish exploited gold and sugar resources during the succeeding centuries, during which period the indigenous Carib and Arawak Indians, newly exposed to European diseases, were virtually wiped out, and replaced by a new mixed-race population. Following the Spanish-American war of 1898, Puerto Rico was ceded to the United States, under the terms of the Treaty of Paris, in December 1898. It was declared an

'unincorporated territory' of the United States, administered by a US-appointed governor, working with an elected local assembly.

In March 1917, under the terms of the Jones–Shafroth Act, the island's inhabitants were granted US citizenship and in 1947 direct elections for the post of governor were introduced. In July 1952, following approval of a draft constitution in a referendum held a year earlier, the territory was given special status as a 'Commonwealth', 'freely associated' with the United States, enjoying extensive powers of self-government.

During the 1950s and 1960s, Puerto Rican politics were dominated by the Popular Democratic Party (PPD), who were strong supporters of the country's 'Commonwealth' status. A split occurred within the party's ranks, however, in 1967, leading to the formation of the New Progressive Party (PNP), following a referendum in which 60.5% of voters supported continued 'Commonwealth' status. Some 38.9% favoured full incorporation within the United States as a constituent state and 0.6% favoured independence. The PNP, led by Carlos Romero Barcelo, held the governorship between 1977 and 1984 and pressed for Puerto Rico's inclusion as a state of the United States. This served to fan terrorist outrages by separatist extremists grouped in the Armed Forces for National Liberation (FALN) organization. Barcelo was, however, defeated by the PDP's Hernandez Colon in the November 1984 governorship contest. Hernandez Colon was re-elected in 1988, but did not contest the 1992 gubernatorial election, which was won by Pedro Rossello of the PNP, with 49.9% of the popular vote. A new, nonbinding referendum on the island's constitutional future was held in November 1993 and, despite Rossello's advocacy of the statehood option, produced another majority in favour of maintaining the current 'Commonwealth' status.

Since the launching of the programme 'Operation Bootstrap' in 1948, there has been considerable industrial development on the island, most notably in the textiles and electrical equipment 'light industrial' sector. However, the pace of economic development slowed down from the mid-1970s. As a consequence, the current unemployment rate is around 17%, and two-thirds of Puerto Rico's population live below the official US poverty line. In such circumstances, there has been considerable outmigration to the United States during recent years, more than 2 million Puerto Ricans now living on the American mainland.

Recommended reading

Fieldhouse, D K *The Colonial Empires: A Comparative Study from the Eighteenth Century*, 2nd edn., Macmillan, 1982

Holland, R F *European Decolonization, 1918–1981: An Introductory Survey*, Macmillan, 1985

Kennedy, K *The Rise and Fall of the Great Powers: Economic Change and Military Conflict from 1500 to 2000*, Fontana, 1988

Taylor, P J *Political Geography: World Economy, Nation-State and Locality*, Longman, 1985, Chap. 3

CHAPTER 9

The World Grows Smaller: International Cooperation

9.1 Competition or cooperation?

Ever since the birth of the nation-state, its history has been one of competition rather than cooperation. Nations have vied with each other in trade. One state has tried to impose its own religion on another. Empires have been created by strong countries dominating the weak. Where cooperation has occurred it has nearly always been on the basis of national self-interest and rarely in any altruistic, international sense.

International alliances have often been between major powers which have temporarily joined forces, in military terms, to attack, or defend themselves against, another opposing alliance. During the 19th and early 20th centuries the political maps of the world were drawn and redrawn as a result of treaties and agreements reached by victors in international disputes, the provisions of which were then imposed on the vanquished.

The two most significant examples of such international decision-taking in the present century are the treaties signed at the end of the two World Wars, in 1918 and 1945. The terms of the Treaty of Versailles, of 1919, sowed the seeds of World War II, 21 years later, but its lessons were partially learnt by the statespeople who had the responsibility of trying to secure lasting world peace after 1945.

Since 1945 there has been a virtually unending succession of regional conflicts but a global war has so far been avoided and there are encouraging prospects of greater, rather than less, international cooperation. A number of factors have contributed to this new sense of urgency and optimism in international affairs.

First, improvements in the ease and speed of communication have made the world shrink in physical terms.

Second, the complexities of production and distribution have resulted in international cooperation on a scale hitherto unknown, resulting in the growth of multinational, rather than national, corporations.

Third, there has been a growing realization that the economies of the major nation-states cannot be seen as discrete, separate entities, but are so intermeshed that the success or failure of one has its impact on the others.

Fourth, there has been a recognition in the years since 1945 that it is in the interests of the advanced world to assist the economic and social progress of the underdeveloped world by financial and technical means.

Fifth, the possibility of a nuclear holocaust has persuaded the major powers to step back from the brink of another global war.

The sixth, and ultimately the most significant factor in the long term, is the increasing recognition of the fragility of the world's ecology, in other words, the 'green factor'.

Seventh, and last, have been the recent encouraging moves towards more pluralistic and democratic political systems in many states, including, of course, the major changes resulting from the demise of the Soviet Union in 1991 and the repercussions of these changes in other parts of the world.

There are encouraging signs, therefore, that in the years ahead, running into the 21st century, international cooperation, rather than competition, is likely to be the prevalent force. It would be unwise, however, to be overoptimistic. Political attitudes can quickly change and a regime favouring positive cooperation can easily be replaced by one based on negative self-interest. Nevertheless, there is already a widespread, and sometimes complex, array of global and regional schemes of cooperation already in being, some more successful than others, and those which have already proved their worth might well provide the foundation for yet greater future collaboration.

9.2 Global cooperation: the United Nations Organization

The United Nations (UN) originated from a conference held at Dumbarton Oaks, Washington, DC, between World War II allies, the Soviet Union, the United Kingdom, and the United States, at the end of September and the beginning of October, 1944. The name 'United Nations' was devised by Franklin Roosevelt and was first used in the Declaration by United Nations, on 1 January 1942, when representatives of 26 nations pledged their governments to continue fighting the Axis powers of Germany, Italy, and Japan. Its forerunner was the League of Nations which had been established after World War I but had failed to fulfil its early promise and had eventually been abandoned by the United States.

United Nations membership | Table 76

Country	Year of admission	1994 contribution to UN budget (%)	Country	Year of admission	1994 contribution to UN budget (%)
Afghanistan	1946	0.01	Equatorial Guinea	1968	0.01
Albania	1955	0.01	Eritrea	1993	0.01
Algeria	1962	0.16	Estonia	1991	0.05
Andorra	1993	0.01	Ethiopia*	1945	0.01
Angola	1976	0.01	Fiji	1970	0.01
Antigua & Barbuda	1981	0.01	Finland	1955	0.61
Argentina*	1945	0.48	France*	1945	6.32
Armenia	1992	0.08	Gabon	1960	0.01
Australia*	1945	1.46	Gambia	1965	0.01
Austria	1955	0.85	Georgia	1992	0.16
Azerbaijan	1992	0.16	Germany**	1973/1990	8.94
Bahamas	1973	0.02	Ghana	1957	0.01
Bahrain	1971	0.02	Greece*	1945	0.37
Bangladesh	1974	0.01	Grenada	1974	0.01
Barbados	1966	0.01	Guatemala*	1945	0.02
Belarus*	1945	0.37	Guinea	1958	0.01
Belau	1994	0.01	Guinea-Bissau	1974	0.01
Belgium*	1945	0.99	Guyana	1966	0.01
Belize	1981	0.01	Haiti*	1945	0.01
Benin	1960	0.01	Honduras*	1945	0.01
Bhutan	1971	0.01	Hungary	1955	0.15
Bolivia*	1945	0.01	Iceland	1946	0.03
Bosnia-Herzegovina	1992	0.02	India*	1945	0.31
Botswana	1966	0.01	Indonesia	1950	0.14
Brazil*	1945	1.62	Iran*	1945	0.60
Brunei	1984	0.02	Iraq*	1945	0.14
Bulgaria	1955	0.10	Ireland	1955	0.20
Burkina Faso	1960	0.01	Israel	1949	0.26
Burundi	1962	0.01	Italy	1955	4.79
Cambodia	1955	0.01	Jamaica	1962	0.01
Cameroon	1960	0.01	Japan	1956	13.95
Canada*	1945	3.07	Jordan	1955	0.01
Cape Verde	1975	0.01	Kazakhstan	1992	0.26
Central African Republic	1960	0.01	Kenya	1963	0.01
Chad	1960	0.01	Korea, North	1991	0.04
Chile*	1945	0.08	Korea, South	1991	0.89
China***	1945	0.72	Kuwait	1963	0.20
Colombia*	1945	0.11	Kyrgyzstan	1992	0.04
Comoros	1975	0.01	Laos	1955	0.01
Congo	1960	0.01	Latvia	1991	0.10
Costa Rica*	1945	0.01	Lebanon*	1945	0.01
Côte d'Ivoire	1945	0.01	Lesotho	1966	0.01
Croatia	1992	0.10	Liberia*	1945	0.01
Cuba*	1945	0.07	Libya	1955	0.21
Cyprus	1960	0.03	Liechtenstein	1990	0.01
Czech Republic	1993	0.32	Lithuania	1991	0.11
Denmark*	1945	0.70	Luxembourg*	1945	0.07
Djibouti	1977	0.01	Macedonia	1993	0.01
Dominica	1978	0.01	Madagascar	1960	0.01
Dominican Republic*	1945	0.01	Malawi	1964	0.01
Ecuador*	1945	0.02	Malaysia	1957	0.14
Egypt*	1945	0.07	Maldives	1965	0.01
El Salvador*	1945	0.01	Mali	1960	0.01

continued

United Nations membership (continued)					Table 76
Country	Year of admission	1994 contribution to UN budget (%)	Country	Year of admission	1994 Contribution to UN budget (%)
Malta	1964	0.01	Senegal	1960	0.01
Marshall Islands	1991	0.01	Seychelles	1976	0.01
Mauritania	1961	0.01	Sierra Leone	1961	0.01
Mauritius	1968	0.01	Singapore	1965	0.14
Mexico*	1945	0.78	Slovakia	1993	0.10
Micronesia	1991	0.01	Slovenia	1992	0.07
Moldova	1992	0.15	Solomon Isles	1978	0.01
Monaco	1993	0.01	Somalia	1960	0.01
Mongolia	1961	0.01	South Africa*	1945	0.34
Morocco	1956	0.03	Spain	1955	2.24
Mozambique	1975	0.01	Sri Lanka	1955	0.01
Myanmar (Burma)	1948	0.01	Sudan	1956	0.01
Namibia	1990	0.01	Surinam	1975	0.01
Nepal	1955	0.01	Swaziland	1968	0.01
Netherlands*	1945	1.58	Sweden	1946	1.22
New Zealand*	1945	0.24	Syria*	1945	0.05
Nicaragua*	1945	0.01	Tajikistan	1992	0.03
Niger	1960	0.01	Tanzania	1961	0.01
Nigeria	1960	0.16	Thailand	1946	0.13
Norway*	1945	0.55	Togo	1960	0.01
Oman	1971	0.04	Trinidad & Tobago	1962	0.04
Pakistan	1947	0.06	Tunisia	1956	0.03
Panama*	1945	0.01	Turkey*	1945	0.34
Papua New Guinea	1975	0.01	Turkmenistan	1992	0.04
Paraguay*	1945	0.01	Uganda	1962	0.01
Peru*	1945	0.06	Ukraine*	1945	1.48
Philippines*	1945	0.06	United Arab Emirates	1971	0.19
Poland*	1945	0.38	United Kingdom*	1945	5.27
Portugal	1955	0.24	United States of America*	1945	25.00
Qatar	1971	0.04	Uruguay*	1945	0.04
Romania	1955	0.15	Uzbekistan	1992	0.19
Russian Federation†	1945	5.68	Vanuatu	1981	0.01
Rwanda	1962	0.01	Venezuela*	1945	0.40
St Kitts–Nevis	1983	0.01	Vietnam	1977	0.01
St Lucia	1979	0.01	Yemen**	1947	0.01
St Vincent & Grenadines	1980	0.01	Yugoslavia††	1945	0.11
Samoa	1976	0.01	Zaire	1960	0.01
San Marino	1992	0.01	Zambia	1964	0.01
São Tomé e Príncipe	1975	0.01	Zimbabwe	1980	0.01
Saudi Arabia*	1945	0.80			

* founder members
** represented by two countries until unification 1990
*** represented by the republic of China (Taiwan) to 1971 and by the People's Republic thereafter
† became a separate member upon the demise of the USSR which was a founder member 1945
†† founder member but suspended from membership 1993

The sovereign countries that are not UN members are Kiribati, Nauru, Switzerland, Taiwan, Tonga, Tuvalu, and Vatican City.

The Dumbarton Oaks conference produced a set of proposals which were put before a conference held in San Francisco on 25–26 June 1945 and, after certain amendments had been agreed, a Charter was signed by 50 of the 51 founder members, on 26 June 1945. Poland, although a founder member, did not sign it at the time but at a later date. The United Nations officially came into being on 24 October 1945, which is now celebrated annually as United Nations Day. Membership is open to all peace-loving nations and currently stands at 185. The names of member states and the dates of their admission are shown in Table 76 above.

The major declared aims of the United Nations are to maintain international peace and security and to develop international cooperation in economic, social, cultural, and humanitarian problems, and, in pursuit of these aims, it has erected an impressive institutional structure of councils, commissions, committees, and agencies, as well as the International Court of Justice. Some institutions, such as the International Court, are developments of earlier bodies from the days of the League of Nations and before. Others are new creations.

Under the terms of Article 2(7) of its Charter, the United Nations is precluded from interfering in the domestic affairs of states. However, Chapter VI permits its involvement in mediation and peacekeeping activities, with the consent of the parties, and Chapter VII, the use of force and imposition of mandatory sanctions. Between 1988 and 1995 the UN launched 23 new peacekeeping operations, compared to just 13 between 1945 and 1987.

9.2.1 Principal UN institutions

The principal UN institutions are the General Assembly, the Security Council, the Economic and Social Council, the International Court of Justice, and the Secretariat. The permanent headquarters of the UN are in the United Nations Plaza, Lower Manhattan, New York City, and meetings of its main organizations are usually held there, but they can be, and sometimes are, arranged elsewhere. The International Court of Justice is based in The Hague, in the Netherlands, and several other UN bodies have their headquarters in Geneva, Switzerland.

General Assembly

The General Assembly is the UN parliament of which all nations are members, each having one vote. It meets once a year at the UN headquarters in New York in a session beginning on the third Tuesday in September, running through to the end of the year, or into the following year if business demands it. It can be summoned to meet at any time in an emergency session and there have been over 25 such special sessions convened to date, covering such topics as peace-keeping in Lebanon, the Suez crisis, Afghanistan, Namibia, Bosnia-Herzegovina, and the economic situation in Africa. Below the main Assembly is a network of committees.

General-Assembly decisions are made by simple majority voting but on certain important matters, such as the condemnation of an act by one of its members, a two-thirds majority is needed. If the Assembly feels that the Security Council is not fulfilling its chief responsibility of maintaining international peace satisfactorily it may take it upon itself to consider a special case, such as an act of aggression, or some other breach of the peace, and recommend action to be taken.

Security Council

The Security Council has a membership of 15. There are five permanent members, China, France, the Russian Federation, the United Kingdom, and the United States, and the other ten are elected for two-year terms by a two-thirds vote of the General Assembly. Retiring members are not eligible for immediate re-election. Any UN member may be invited to participate in its discussions if they bear on its interests, but only the permanent or elected members are permitted to vote.

It has been argued in recent years that the Council's permanent membership should be updated to include former 'Axis' states, such as Japan and Germany, which, more than half a century after World War II, can justifiably claim to be leading members of the world community.

In pursuit of its responsibility for maintaining peace and security, the Council may call on armed forces, and other assistance, from member states. It has at its disposal a Military Staff Committee composed of the chiefs of staff of the countries of the permanent members. The presidency of the Security Council is held for a month at a time by a representative of a member state, in English language alphabetical order. The Council has two standing committees: a Committee of Experts and a Committee on the Admission of New Members.

Economic and Social Council

The Economic and Social Council is responsible for economic, social, cultural, educational, health, and related matters. It has 54 members, again elected by a two-thirds majority vote of the General Assembly. The Council has a large number of functional and regional commissions and committees working for it as well as hundreds of nongovernmental agencies which have been granted consultative status.

International Court of Justice

The International Court of Justice is composed of independent judges, elected by the Security Council and the General Assembly, sitting separately, and chosen because of their competence in international law, irrespective of their nationalities. There are 15 judges, no two of whom can be nationals of the same state. Candidates for election are nominated by national groups and, once elected, serve for nine years, and may be immediately re-elected. Only states, not individuals, may be parties to cases before the Court.

The Court is based at The Hague, in the Netherlands, but may sit elsewhere if it chooses. It sits permanently, except for customary judicial vacations. Its official languages are English and French and it reaches its decisions by a majority of votes of the judges present. The president and vice-president are elected by the Court itself and serve three-year terms. If the votes of judges are equal, the president has a casting vote. Judgements are final, and there is no appeal.

Secretariat

The United Nations Secretariat consists of the secretary-general, who is its chief administrator, under and assistant secretaries-general and a large international staff. The secretary-general is appointed by the General Assembly for a five-year term, which can be renewed. The present occupant, Boutros Boutros-Ghali (b. 1922), of Egypt, took up his appointment in January 1992. The first holder of the post was Trygve Lie (1896–1968), of Norway (1946–53), and subsequent holders were Dag Hammarskjöld (1905–61), of Sweden (1953–61), U Thant (1909–74), of Myanmar (1961–71), Kurt Waldheim (b. 1918), of Austria (1972–81), and Javier Pérez de Cuéllar (b. 1920), of Peru (1981–1992).

Being UN secretary-general is clearly an important, and prestigious, job, but experience shows that its significance depends very much on what a particular holder makes of it.

Trygve Lie and Dag Hammarskjöld, who was killed in an air crash while on UN business, became well known, even to ordinary people, as did U Thant, to a lesser degree. Hammarskjöld was awarded the Nobel Peace Prize for his efforts. Kurt Waldheim, on the other hand, made a less marked impression. Javier Pérez de Cuéllar became a popular, and even famous, international figure and did much to revive the standing of the UN, which had fallen to a low ebb during the 1970s. In 1991 a 28-nation UN military coalition, led by the United States, liberated Kuwait from Iraqi occupation, following the 'Operation Desert Storm' Gulf War. This provided an example of a new assertiveness for the UN in defence of the post-Cold War 'New World Order'.

The present holder of the post, Boutros Boutros-Ghali, has served during one of the organization's most troublesome and testing periods. His successes have included the securing of peace accords in Angola and Mozambique and between Israel and the Palestine Liberation Organization (PLO) and the overseeing of multiparty elections in Cambodia and a return to democracy in Haiti. However, a lasting political settlement in divided Afghanistan and Cyprus has so far eluded him and the civil wars in Somalia, Rwanda, and the former Yugoslavia have stretched the UN's credibility almost to breaking point. In addition, UN finances have become strained by the cost of its 16,000 employed staff and 9,000 consultants and the burden of its peacekeeping missions. In 1995 more than 70,000 troops were deployed at an annual cost of nearly $4 billion in peacekeeping operations in 15 countries and disputed territories, namely: Angola, Cyprus, El Salvador, Georgia, India and Pakistan, Iraq and Kuwait, Israel's borders, the Lebanon, Liberia, Mozambique, Rwanda, Somalia, Western Sahara, and in Croatia and Bosnia-Herzegovina, where more than 55,000 troops have been deployed.

9.2.2 UN specialized agencies

Working directly within the United Nations organizational structure are a number of specialized agencies, funded by the UN through contributions from the 185 member states. The scale of these contributions, which are based broadly on the principle of the 'ability to pay', are shown in Table 76. However, in 1994 the General Assembly vote had been withdrawn from 13 member states as a consequence of repeated failure to pay their agreed fees, while the United States and Russia were, respectively, $780 million and $500 million in arrears. The specialized agencies operate mainly from the headquarters in New York or from Geneva, in Switzerland.

International Atomic Energy Agency (IAEA)
The IAEA was established in 1957 to accelerate and enlarge the contribution of atomic energy to peace, health, and prosperity throughout the world and to prevent its diversion from peaceful purposes to military ends. It has negotiated safeguard agreements with over 160 individual states. The Agency is based in Vienna, Austria, and has 123 members.

International Labour Organization (ILO)
The ILO predates the United Nations itself, having been originally created in 1919 by the League of Nations. It is an intergovernmental agency with a tripartite membership of government, employer, and worker representatives. It seeks to improve labour conditions, raise living standards, and promote productive employment through international cooperation. It became part of the UN in 1946 and in 1969 was awarded the Nobel Peace Prize. It conducts research into industrial relations and publishes conventions and recommendations. If a member state ratifies a convention it automatically agrees to bring its national law into line with it. Recommendations are not binding but all member states have a duty to consider them.

The ILO consists of the International Labour Conference, which is its supreme deliberative body and meets annually in Geneva, and the International Labour Office, which is also in Geneva. In 1960 it established the International Institute for Labour Studies and, in 1965, a training institution in Turin, Italy, particularly concerned with the needs of developing countries. Indeed, much of the ILO's work in recent years has been orientated towards the less developed parts of the world. It has 171 members.

Food and Agriculture Organization (FAO)
A conference in May 1943 at Hot Springs, Virginia, in the United States, provided the stimulus for the setting up of the FAO in October 1945. Its aims are to raise levels of nutrition and standards of living, to improve the production and distribution of food and agricultural products, to improve the living standards of rural populations, and, by accomplishing all these things, to eliminate hunger. Like many other UN agencies, the FAO tends to concentrate its efforts on the less developed parts of the world. It provides guidance on food production and can sponsor relief in emergency situations. It operates from Rome and has 157 members.

United Nations Educational, Scientific and Cultural Organization (UNESCO)
UNESCO came into being in 1946 as a result of a conference held in London, in November 1945, under the auspices of the UK and French governments. Its main purpose is to promote peace by encouraging international collaboration in education, science, and culture. It attempts to do this through teacher-training programmes, the promotion of research, and the dissemination of information. Its headquarters are in Paris and it has 181 members.

World Health Organization (WHO)
The World Health Organization was founded in April 1948. Its main purpose is to assist all peoples in attaining the highest possible levels of health. It does this by research, teaching, and guidance through recommended standards of behaviour. For example, it has, in recent years, sponsored greater international cooperation in the prevention and treatment of AIDS and related infections. It has also made recommendations on the quality control of drugs. Its headquarters are in Geneva and it has regional offices in the Congo, Egypt, Denmark, the Philippines, India, and the United States. It has 189 members.

International Monetary Fund (IMF)
The inspiration for the IMF was the International Monetary Conference held at Bretton Woods, New Hampshire, in the

United States, in July 1944, under the chairmanship of the US secretary to the treasury, Henry Morgenthau. Conference delegates, including the British delegation led by the celebrated economist Lord Keynes, agreed to the creation of a Fund which would promote international monetary cooperation, establish a multilateral system of payments, and help remedy any serious disequilibrium in a country's balance of payments by allowing it to draw on the resources of the Fund while it took measures to correct the imbalance. The IMF was established on 27 December 1945, as an independent organization, and began operating on 1 March 1947. It became associated with the UN, on the basis of mutual cooperation, on 15 November 1947.

IMF members subscribe to the Fund on a quota basis, determined by their ability to pay at the time of membership. The Fund itself can also borrow to supplement its resources. Most of the assistance given by the IMF is, naturally, to less developed countries but occasionally it is asked to provide temporary help to economically advanced nations. The United Kingdom, for example, had recourse to the Fund in 1976. When it is asked to assist, the IMF's representatives invariably impose conditions to ensure that the problem to be dealt with is only a temporary phenomenon. The headquarters of the IMF are in Washington, DC, and it also has offices in Paris and Geneva. Its membership totals 179.

International Bank for Reconstruction and Development (IBRD)
The IBRD is often popularly known as the 'World Bank'. Like the IMF, it too was conceived at the Bretton Woods Conference. Its purpose is to provide funds and technical assistance to help the economies of the poorer nations of the world. It obtains its own funds from capital paid in by member countries, from loans, from repayments, from income from investments, and from fees paid for the technical services it provides. Its headquarters are in Washington, DC, where it also has a staff college, called the Economic Development Institute. One hundred and seventy-eight states are members.

International Development Association (IDA)
The IDA is an agency of the World Bank, concentrating on providing financial and technical help to the poorest nations. It came into existence in 1960 and now has 155 members.

International Finance Corporation (IFC)
The IFC is affiliated to the World Bank and was established in 1956. It makes investments in companies, to assist their development, or provides loans. It is particularly active in helping new ventures or providing finance for established companies which wish to expand or diversify. It has 161 members.

International Civil Aviation Organization (ICAO)
The idea for creating the ICAO came from a conference on international aviation held in Chicago at the end of 1944. The Organization was formally set up on 4 April 1947. Its objectives are to establish technical standards for safety and efficiency in air navigation, to develop regional plans for ground facilities and services for civil aviation, and generally to provide advice to airline operators. Its headquarters are in Montreal, Canada.

Universal Postal Union (UPU)
The UPU was established as long ago as 1875 when the Universal Postal Convention was adopted at a Congress in Berne, Switzerland. It was originally called the General Postal Union and changed its name in 1878. Currently, 158 countries are members. Its aim is to improve the standards of postal services and promote international cooperation. Its headquarters are in Berne.

International Telecommunication Union (ITU)
The aims of the ITU are to maintain and extend international cooperation in improving telecommunications of all kinds by promoting the development of technical skills and services and harmonizing national activities. It originated in 1932 when, at a conference in Madrid, it was decided to merge the Telegraph Convention of 1865 and the Radiotelegraph Convention of 1906 into a single convention and functioning organization. The ITU's headquarters are in Geneva.

World Meteorological Organization (WMO)
The Directors of the International Meteorological Organization, which had been set up in 1873, met in Washington, DC, in 1947 and adopted a convention establishing the WMO. Its main aim is to facilitate worldwide cooperation in the creation and maintenance of a network of stations for making meteorological observations and to ensure the rapid exchange of information. The headquarters of the WMO are in Geneva.

International Maritime Organization (IMO)
Known until 1982 as the Intergovernmental Maritime Consultative Organization (IMCO), the IMO was established as a specialized agency of the UN in 1948. It began to operate effectively in 1959. Its aim is to promote cooperation between governments on technical matters affecting merchant shipping, with the objective of improving safety at sea. It formulates and publishes conventions and regulations and has its headquarters in London. The UN Convention on the Law of the Sea came into force in 1994.

World Trade Organization (WTO)
The World Trade Organization (WTO) came into operation on 1 January 1995 as the successor to the General Agreement on Tariffs and Trade (GATT). The GATT was negotiated in 1947 as a multilateral treaty, laying down a common code of conduct in international trade and providing a forum for discussion of trade problems, with the objective of reducing trade barriers. Part of its purpose was to help less developed countries, through its 'most-favoured-nation' (MFN) treatment, which gave protection to 'infant economies'.

The WTO resulted from the Final Act of the Uruguay Round of the GATT which was formally approved in April 1994. This Final Act was the culmination of over seven years of negotiations, which had started at Punta del Este, Uruguay, in September 1986. The new organization is now a permanent trade-monitoring body, with a status commensurate with that of the International Monetary Fund (IMF) and the World Bank and has been given a wider remit than its predecessor.

The WTO will have a ministerial conference, attended by representatives of all its members, at least once every two years and a General Council will keep a continuing oversight of its affairs. The members of the GATT have, automatically, become members of the WTO, and, with the accession of Liechtenstein, Grenada, Paraguay, Guinea-Bissau, the United Arab Emirates, St Christopher and Nevis, Qatar, Angola, Honduras, Slovenia, and Guinea during 1994, the total membership rose to 125. Membership entails acceptance of the results of the Uruguay Round, without exception. Like the GATT, it has its headquarters in Geneva.

World Intellectual Property Organization (WIPO)

WIPO was established in 1967 as the successor to the United International Bureau for the Protection of Intellectual Property. It became a UN specialized agency in 1974. Its primary purpose is to protect intellectual property, which, in general, means patents and trademarks, throughout the world. It is based in Geneva.

International Fund for Agricultural Development (IFAD)

IFAD is the result of a recommendation of a World Food Conference which was held in 1974. The Fund began operating in 1977 with the prime objective of mobilizing funds for agricultural and rural development. IFAD has its headquarters in Rome and has 157 members.

9.2.3 UN Development Programme (UNDP)

The UN Development Programme was established in 1965 to promote higher standards of living in the poorer nations and to try to remedy the economic imbalance between industrialized and developing countries, to be achieved mainly by the economically advanced countries providing financial and technical help and by adopting economic and commercial policies favouring the less advanced nations.

The UNDP is headed by an administrator who is responsible to a Governing Council of its 48 member states. It has its headquarters in New York and operates through a number of regional commissions which are described later in this chapter.

9.3 Global cooperation: the Commonwealth

The Commonwealth is the modern successor to the British Empire. It is formally described as a free association of sovereign independent states. It has no charter, treaty, or constitution, the association being based on a desire for cooperation, consultation, and mutual assistance. The current membership is shown in Table 77. It comprises 53 sovereign countries situated in seven of the world's nine regions and with a combined population of 1.6 billion, or nearly 30% of the global total. In addition, the more than 20 dependencies of Australia, New Zealand, and the United Kingdom, covered in *Chapter 8*, are regarded as 'Commonwealth countries'.

It has been described as the world's most unusual 'club' and is a singularly British institution, still echoing the United Kingdom's imperial past. In recent years, however, the influence of the 'mother country' has shown signs of weakening and there are indications that the leadership might be taken up by states such as India, Canada, or Australia. Nevertheless, it is inconceivable that the Commonwealth could survive in anything like its present form without Britain's active participation.

As the successor to the British Empire, the Commonwealth was effectively established in 1931, when the Statute of Westminster gave full autonomy to the white-settler dominions of Australia, Canada, New Zealand, and South Africa. The Commonwealth was initially based on allegiance to a common Crown. However, in 1949, India chose to become a republic and from that date the modern Commonwealth was born, based now on the concept of the British Monarch being a symbol, rather than a legal entity, and, as such, the 'Head of the Commonwealth'. At the moment 17 of the 53 members accept the British queen as their head of state, 31 are republics, and five have their own local monarchs.

Politically, 31, or 58%, of the sovereign states in the Commonwealth were liberal democracies in 1995, 11 were emergent democracies, three each had absolutist, military and authoritarian nationalist regimes, and two had nationalistic socialist regimes.

Heads of government of Commonwealth countries meet every two years to discuss international affairs and areas of cooperation. Finance ministers meet annually and other ministers as and when the need arises. The Commonwealth is not a mutual defence organization and most member countries are committed to regional treaties.

The Commonwealth is frequently criticized because it has little real power to influence world affairs. Its supporters would argue that its strength lies in its voluntary nature and that, should the need arise, its potentially immense resources could be put to considerable use. Britain's role as the originator of the Commonwealth would be crucial in this respect but as it is increasingly committed to its role in Europe its place within the wider organization is put into some doubt.

The Commonwealth is serviced by a Secretariat which is based in Marlborough House, Pall Mall, London, and headed by the secretary-general, Chief E Chukwuemeka Anyaoku, of Nigeria. The Secretariat's staff come from a wide range of member countries which also pay its operating costs.

Perhaps as an indication of its international standing, there have been, somewhat surprisingly, a number of recent enquiries about possible membership from countries which historically have not been associated with Britain or its empire. In 1995 Cameroon and Mozambique were the first members to be admitted which had not been fully under British rule.

9.4 Global cooperation: the Non-Aligned Movement

The Non-Aligned Movement is an informal grouping of developing countries who meet triennially in an international conference to promote the interests of the poorer South. The

The Commonwealth (53 states)   Table 77

Region/state	Year of independence	Date joined	Regime type	Head of state
Asia (8)				
Bangladesh	1971	1972	Em-dem	president
Brunei	1984	1984	Absolutist	local monarch
India	1947	1947	Lib-dem	president
Malaysia	1957	1957	Lib-dem	local monarch
The Maldives	1965	1982	Auth-nat	president
Pakistan	1947	1947/1989	Em-dem	president
Singapore	1965	1965	Lib-dem	president
Sri Lanka	1948	1948	Lib-dem	president
Central America & the Caribbean (11)				
Antigua & Barbuda	1981	1981	Lib-dem	British monarch
Bahamas	1973	1973	Lib-dem	British monarch
Barbados	1966	1966	Lib-dem	British monarch
Belize	1981	1982	Lib-dem	British monarch
Dominica	1978	1978	Lib-dem	president
Grenada	1974	1974	Lib-dem	British monarch
Jamaica	1962	1962	Lib-dem	British monarch
St Kitts–Nevis	1983	1983	Lib-dem	British monarch
St Lucia	1979	1979	Lib-dem	British monarch
St Vincent & the Grenadines	1979	1979	Lib-dem	British monarch
Trinidad & Tobago	1962	1962	Lib-dem	president
Central & Southern Africa (19)				
Botswana	1966	1966	Lib-dem	president
Cameroon	1960	1995	Em-dem	president
The Gambia	1965	1965	Military	military
Ghana	1957	1957	Em-dem	president
Kenya	1963	1963	Auth-nat	president
Lesotho	1966	1966	Em-dem	local monarch
Malawi	1964	1964	Em-dem	president
Mauritius	1968	1968	Lib-dem	British monarch
Mozambique	1975	1995	Em-dem	president
Namibia	1990	1990	Em-dem	president
Nigeria*	1960	1960	Military	military
The Seychelles	1976	1976	Em-dem	president
Sierra Leone	1961	1961	Military	military
South Africa	1931	1931/1994	Em-dem	president
Swaziland	1968	1968	Absolutist	local monarch
Tanzania	1961	1961	Nat-soc	president
Uganda	1962	1962	Auth-nat	president**
Zambia	1964	1980	Em-dem	president
Zimbabwe	1980	1980	Nat-soc	president
North America (1)				
Canada	1931	1931	Lib-dem	British monarch

continued

The Commonwealth (53 states) (continued)				Table 77
Region/state	Year of independence	Date joined	Regime type	Head of state
Northern & Western Europe (3)				
Cyprus	1960	1961	Lib-dem	president
Malta	1964	1964	Lib-dem	president
United Kingdom	-	1931	Lib-dem	British monarch
Oceania (10)				
Australia	1931	1931	Lib-dem	British monarch
Kiribati	1979	1979	Lib-dem	president
Nauru	1968	1968	Lib-dem	president
New Zealand	1931	1931	Lib-dem	British monarch
Papua New Guinea	1975	1975	Lib-dem	British monarch
Solomon Islands	1978	1978	Lib-dem	British monarch
Tonga	1970	1970	Absolutist	local monarch
Tuvalu	1978	1978	Lib-dem	British monarch
Vanuatu	1980	1980	Lib-dem	president
Western Samoa	1962	1962	Lib-dem	president
South America (1)				
Guyana	1966	1966	Lib-dem	president

Note: Fiji was a Commonwealth member, with the British queen as head of state, until a republic was established in 1987. Ireland withdrew from the Commonwealth and Pakistan and South Africa withdrew in 1961 and 1972, but later rejoined in 1989 and 1994 respectively.
* Nigeria's membership was suspended in November 1995 because of its human rights record
** Uganda also has a local tribal monarch, the King of Buganda, who was reinstated in 1993

Key:
Em-dem	Emergent democratic	Auth-nat	Authoritarian nationalist
Lib-dem	Liberal democratic	Nat-soc	Nationalistic socialist

origins of the movement can be traced back to the conference of Afro-Asian nations that was held in Bandung, Indonesia, in 1955, proclaiming anti-colonialism and neutrality between East and West power blocs during the Cold War era. Its founding fathers were the Indian prime minister, Jawaharlal Nehru (1889–1964), Ghana's prime minister, Kwame Nkrumah (1909–1972), Egypt's president, Gamal Abdel Nasser (1918–1970), Indonesia's president Achmed Sukarno (1901–1970), and Yugoslavia's president, Tito (1892–1980), with the first official conference being held in Belgrade, Yugoslavia, 1961.

With the end of the Cold War, the chief issues promoted by the movement have been international action against poverty, environmental destruction, nuclear testing, and drug-trafficking. The most recent, the eleventh conference held in October 1995 at Cartagena, Columbia, was attended by delegates and heads of states from 113 developing countries, including Nelson Mandela (b. 1918), the South African president, Fidel Castro (b. 1927), the Cuban president, and Yasser Arafat (b. 1929), the leader of the Palestine Liberation Organization (PLO). Its members hold more than half the world's population and, including in its ranks Saudi Arabia

and Kuwait, 85% of oil resources, but only 7% of global GDP.

9.5 Global cooperation: Conference on Security and Cooperation in Europe/ Organization for Security and Cooperation in Europe (CSCE/OSCE)

The Helsinki Final Act was signed by 35 countries, including the then Soviet Union and the United States, at the end of a Conference on Security and Cooperation in Europe (CSCE) in 1975 during the era of East–West détente. The Act registered agreement on cooperation in a number of areas, such as security, economics, science, techology, and human rights. The competences of the CSCE were extended by the 1990 Charter of Paris for a New Europe, which was generally regarded as marking an end to the 'Cold War' between the Eastern European bloc and the West. In particular, it was agreed that fact-finding teams could be sent to investigate alleged human rights abuses in any member country. In December 1994 members agreed to change the CSCE's title to the Organization for Security and Cooperation in Europe (OSCE), to denote its permanent status.

In addition to its original aims, the OSCE seeks to strengthen pluraliist democracy and the settling of disputes between member states by peaceful means. Its membership now includes all internationally recognized countries in Europe plus Canada and the United States: a total of 53, although Yugoslavia's membership was suspended in 1992. A Council of Foreign Ministers acts as its central decision-taking forum and a Committee of Senior Officials (CSO) implements these decisions. It has a Secretariat based in Prague and a Conflict Prevention Centre and a Forum for Security and Cooperation, based in Vienna.

9.6 Global cooperation: Organization of the Islamic Conference (OIC)

The OIC was established in May 1971 following a conference of Muslim heads of state in Rabat, Morocco, in 1969, and meetings of Islamic foreign ministers in Jeddah and Karachi, in 1970. The main aim of the Organization is to promote Islamic solidarity and its members include 52 countries in the Middle East and North, Central and Southern Africa, and Asia, plus the Palestine Liberation Organization (PLO). The OIC has its headquarters and secretariat in Jeddah, Saudi Arabia.

9.7 Global cooperation: the Antarctic Treaty

The Antarctic Treaty was signed in 1959 by 13 countries which conduct scientific research in Antarctica. The membership has risen to 39, including 10 consultative members. The main objective of the Treaty is to promote peaceful international scientific cooperation in the region.

9.8 Interregional cooperation

There are several examples of mutual cooperation between countries which cut across the regions we have defined for the purposes of this book. Some are sponsored by the United Nations, some by the European Community, some are the products of Commonwealth membership, some have been inspired by the United States, on the basis of enlightened self-interest, and some are examples of self-help by states in different, but physically adjacent, regions.

9.8.1 UN interregional groups

Within the United Nations organization there are four Commissions intended to promote cooperation between under- or less-developed countries in various parts of the world.

Economic Commission for Africa (ECA)

ECA was founded by the UN in 1958. The total current membership consists of 50 states, representing virtually the whole of North, Central and Southern Africa. The purpose of the Commission is to promote and facilitate concerted action for the economic and social development of Africa, and it seeks to achieve this through research and the coordination of national policies.

Some examples of ECA's work are the establishment of the African Development Bank, in 1964, the creation of the Association of African Central Banks, in 1969, and the setting up of the Centre for Mineral Resources Development at Dar es Salaam, Tanzania, in 1976. It is a regular publisher of largely statistical material, and operates from Addis Ababa, in Ethiopia.

Economic and Social Commission for Asia and the Pacific (ESCAP)

ESCAP was founded in 1947 as the Economic Commission for Asia and the Far East and changed its name in 1974. It currently has 35 full members and 10 associate members. Most of the full members are states in Asia or Oceania but other countries with interests in the regions, such as the United States, the United Kingdom, the Russian Federation, France, and the Netherlands also enjoy full membership. The associate members are the smaller countries of Asia and Oceania.

ESCAP performs a broadly similar role in Asia and Oceania to that of ECA in Africa. It, too, has had success in setting up a number of ventures and organizations, such as the Asian and Pacific Centre for Development Administration, the Asian Clearing Union, and the Asian Development Bank. ESCAP has its headquarters in Bangkok, Thailand.

Economic Commission for Europe (ECE)

ECE was also founded in 1947 and includes all Western and Eastern European countries except Switzerland, which participates in a consultative capacity. The United States is also a consultant. The Commission's role is similar to that of the other UN interregional commissions. It is based in Geneva.

Economic Commission for Latin America (ECLA)

ECLA was founded in 1948 with the object of raising the level of economic activity in Latin America, which, in the Commission's terms, includes what we have defined as Central America and the Caribbean and South America. It currently has 33 members. They include, in addition to the countries of the regions, Canada, France, the Netherlands, the United Kingdom, and the United States. Its headquarters are in Santiago, Chile.

Economic Commission for Western Asia (ECWA)

ECWA was founded in 1973 and operates from the UN building in Amman, Jordan. It was set up to provide a better service for countries previously catered for by the UN Economic and Social Office in Beirut. Its objectives are broadly similar to those of ECLA. The use of the term 'Western Asia' in its title is a little misleading since its 14 members, which include 13 countries plus the Palestine Liberation Organization (PLO), are all situated in the Middle East or North or Central Africa.

9.8.2 Commonwealth-inspired interregional cooperation

Colombo Plan for Cooperative Economic Development in South and Southeast Asia (CP)

The purpose of the Colombo Plan is to facilitate and coordinate economic and social development in the countries of South and Southeast Asia. It was set up in 1951 within the framework of the Commonwealth, on the initiative of the Commonwealth foreign ministers. Since that date it has lost much of its original Commonwealth character and most of its current members are not in the Commonwealth. They now total 26 and include, as well as the original Commonwealth states in the region, Afghanistan, Cambodia, Canada, Indonesia, Iran, Japan, South Korea, Laos, the Philippines, Thailand, the United Kingdom, and the United States. The Plan's headquarters are in Colombo, Sri Lanka.

9.8.3 Northern and Western European-inspired interregional cooperation

The Lomé Convention

The Lomé Convention takes its name from Lomé, the capital of Togo, in Africa, where, in 1975 the members of the European Community (EC) agreed to assist the less developed countries of Africa, the Caribbean, and the Pacific by establishing a 'special relationship' with them so that they would not suffer unduly from the tariff policies of the EC. The countries concerned include virtually all those in Central and Southern Africa, most of those in the Caribbean, and the smaller states of Oceania. Under the terms of the Convention the EC guarantees the 69 states who benefit from it virtually unrestricted access for their agricultural products to Western European markets. The 69 ACP (Asia–Caribbean–Pacific) countries, as they are called, may, for their part, operate varying degrees of protection of their own economies. Aid to the ACP nations is also provided from the European Development Fund. The original Convention was renewed in 1981, 1985 and 1990.

Organization for Economic Cooperation and Development (OECD)

The OECD is the expanded successor Organization for European Economic Cooperation (OEEC) which was set up in 1948, at the instigation of the United States, to promote economic recovery in postwar Europe. The new body was established in 1961 and now has 26 members, including members of the EU and EFTA, plus Australia, Canada, the Czech Republic, Japan, Mexico, New Zealand, Turkey, and the United States. In its expanded form its objective is to promote freer trade and to stimulate Western aid to undeveloped countries. An inner core of the seven most developed states, Canada, France, Germany, Italy, Japan, the United Kingdom, and the United States, forms the 'Group of Seven'. Since 1975 the heads of governments of these countries have met for informal annual summits on major economic, monetary and political problems. The presidents of the EU Commission and Russia have observer status at these meetings.

European Bank for Reconstruction and Development (EBRD)

The EBRD was founded in 1990 to assist the economic reconstruction of Central and Eastern Europe by financing industrial and economic expansion, using loan guarantees, equity investment, and underwriting, to promote the transition to free-market economies. The Bank was originally proposed by French President François Mitterrand (b. 1916) and his former adviser, Jacques Attali, became its first president. Its members include Albania, Armenia, Australia, Austria, Azerbaijan, Belarus, Belgium, Bulgaria, Canada, Croatia, Cyprus, the Czech Republic, Denmark, Egypt, Estonia, Finland, France, Georgia, Germany, Greece, Hungary, Iceland, Ireland, Israel, Italy, Japan, Kazakhstan, South Korea, Kyrgyzstan, Latvia, Liechtenstein, Lithuania, Luxembourg, Macedonia, Malta, Mexico, Moldova, Morocco, the Netherlands, New Zealand, Norway, Poland, Portugal, Romania, Russia, Slovakia, Slovenia, Spain, Sweden, Switzerland, Tajikistan, Turkey, Turkmenistan, the Ukraine, the United Kingdom, the United States, Uzbekistan, the Commission of the European Union, and the European Investment Bank. Its headquarters are in London.

9.8.4 Central, Eastern, and Southern European-inspired interregional cooperation

Central European Initiative (CEI)

This body, founded in August 1990 as the Pentagonale Group, adopted the designation CEI in 1992. Its objectives are improved relations between the states of Central Europe and with neighbouring West European countries, with the aim of eventual membership of the European Union. The ten members are Austria, Bosnia-Herzegovina, Croatia, the Czech Republic, Hungary, Italy, Macedonia, Poland, Slovakia, and Slovenia.

Commonwealth of Independent States (CIS)

The CIS was formed following the demise of the Soviet Union in December 1991 and was intended to replace it, but a number of former Soviet republics refused to join, preferring full independence. Eventually, its membership settled on Armenia, Azerbaijan, Belarus, Georgia (from 1994), Kazakhstan, Kyrgyzstan, Moldova, the Russian Federation, Tajikistan, Turkmenistan, Ukraine, and Uzbekistan. It has a Council of Heads of State and a Council of Heads of Government, and the post of chairperson is rotated. Its administrative headquarters are at Minsk, Belarus, but with no firm political foundation and its members frequently divided on policy, its future is uncertain. However, in 1994 the CIS successfully negotiated cease-fires in Abkhazia, situated in Georgia, and the Nagorno-Karabakh dispute between Armenia and Azerbaijan, stationing peacekeeping forces in these regions, as well as in Tajikistan. An early objective of the CIS, the creation of a 'single economic space' has been largely abandoned, although, in 1994, the three Central Asian states of Kazakhstan, Kyrgyzstan, and Uzbekistan created their own social, economic, and military union.

Council of Baltic Sea States (COBSS)

This interregional grouping, founded in March 1992, comprises ten states from Northern and Western Europe and Central and Eastern Europe situated in the Baltic region: Denmark, Estonia, Finland, Germany, Latvia, Lithuania, Norway, Poland, Russia, and Sweden.

Danube Commission

The Danube Commission is based on a convention controlling navigation on the River Danube, which was signed in Belgrade in 1948. The convention confirmed that navigation from Ulm, in Germany, to the Black Sea was open and free to people, shipping, and merchandise of all states. The Commission, which ensures the convention's enforcement, is composed of representatives of all the seven states through which the Danube flows. The Commission comprises Austria, Bulgaria, Germany, Hungary, Romania, Russia, Slovakia, Ukraine, and Yugoslavia (suspended). Its headquarters are in Budapest, Hungary.

9.8.5 Middle East-inspired interregional cooperation

Organization of Petroleum Exporting Countries (OPEC)

OPEC was formed in Baghdad, Iraq, in 1960 with five founder members: Iran, Iraq, Kuwait, Saudi Arabia, and Venezuela. Its membership later expanded to include, in addition to the founder members, Algeria, Gabon, Indonesia, Libya, Nigeria, Qatar, and the United Arab Emirates. Its primary object is to coordinate the production and pricing policies of the major oil producers so as to guarantee stable prices and stable incomes, based on what the Organization would claim to be a fair return on capital invested. Despite its existence, oil prices on world markets have often been as much affected by changing economic conditions as by OPEC policies. It has, however, since coming into existence, done much to eliminate the worst examples of the exploitation of primary producing countries by the industrialized nations. The headquarters of OPEC are in Vienna, Austria.

9.8.6 Central and Southern African-inspired interregional cooperation

African Development Bank (ADB)

The ADB was founded in 1963 to promote and finance economic development across the continent. Its members include 51 African and 25 non-African countries. Its headquarters are at Abidjan, the Ivory Coast.

Organization of African Unity (OAU)

The OAU was founded in Addis Ababa in 1963, on the initiative of Emperor Haile Selassie of Ethiopia. Its main aims are to further African unity and solidarity; to coordinate political, economic, cultural, health, scientific, and defence policies; and to eliminate colonialism in Africa. There are 53 countries in membership, representing virtually the whole of Central and Southern Africa, plus Algeria, Egypt and Tunisia, in North Africa, and the Middle East. The Organiz-

ation is headed by an Assembly of Heads of State and Government which meets annually and a Council of Ministers which meets twice a year. It also has a Secretariat based in Addis Ababa. The elected post of OAU chairman is a highly prestigious position in Africa. South Africa joined in 1994.

9.8.7 United States-inspired interregional cooperation

As a leading industrial and military power, and as part of a strategy of mutual defence and economic development, the United States has promoted or sponsored a number of interregional groups with European and North, Central and South American countries. Military groups are described later, in paragraph 9.10.

Organization of American States (OAS)

The OAS was founded in 1948 by a charter signed at Bogotá, Colombia, by representatives of 35 states in North, Central, and South America, and the Caribbean, including the United States. Its declared purpose is: 'To achieve an order of peace and justice, promoting solidarity among the American states; to defend their sovereignty, their territorial integrity and their independence; to establish new objectives and standards for the promotion of the economic, social and cultural development of the peoples of the Hemisphere, and to speed the process of economic integration.'

The origins of the OAS go back as far as 1826 when the First Congress of American States was convened by the Venezuelan revolutionary leader, Simón Bolívar. Since those early days the Organization has become more formally institutionalized, with a General Assembly, a Permanent Council, consisting of one representative from each of the member states, and numerous other councils, commissions and committees. Although its objectives are clearly, and impressively, stated in its charter, and although its structure appears to be democratically representative of all the signatories, the OAS has become increasingly dominated by the United States, so that, in pursuit of the Monroe Doctrine, enunciated in 1823, which effectively warned off European powers from America's 'back yard', what is regarded as 'good' for the American continent is mostly what is seen as good in the eyes of the United States, and this is an attitude often resented by many of the OAS members. The headquarters of the OAS are in Washington, DC.

Inter-American Development Bank (IADB)

The IADB was founded in 1959, at the instigation of the OAS, to finance economic and social development, particularly in the less wealthy regions of the Americas. Its membership is wider than that of the OAS and includes Austria, Belgium, Canada, Denmark, Finland, France, Germany, Israel, Italy, Japan, the Netherlands, Spain, Sweden, Switzerland, and the United Kingdom, as well as the states of Central and Southern America, the Caribbean, and the United States. Its headquarters are in Washington, DC.

North American Free Trade Agreement (NAFTA)

The North American Free Trade Agreement was signed by the United States, Canada, and Mexico in August 1992 and ratified by the US Congress in November 1993. The first trade pact of its kind to link two highly-industrialized countries to a developing one, it created a free market of 375 million people, with a total GDP of US$6,800 billion, equivalent to 30% of global GDP. It was preceded, in 1989, by a bilateral agreement between Canada and the United States to form a free-trade zone aimed to rival the European Union. From January 1994 tariffs and restrictions on trade in manufactured goods and agricultural produce will be progressively eliminated over a 10 to 15 year period and investment into low-wage Mexico by Canada and the United States progressively increased. Although the Agreement was initially viewed with caution by the Canadian government and opposed by US labour unions, it was welcomed by the European Union, provided it operated within agreed WTO rules. In December 1994 it was agreed to admit Chile into the Agreement.

9.8.8 Latin American-inspired interregional cooperation

In an effort to avoid overdependence on the United States, and to come out of the shadow of living in its 'back yard', some Latin American states have sought to pursue a more independent economic policy line.

Association of Caribbean States (ACS)
The Association of Caribbean States resulted from an agreement signed in Colombia in July 1994 by countries in the Caribbean basin to adopt a common approach to regional political policies and markets and to foster economic cooperation and eventual integration. Its 25 members include the states of the Caribbean and Central America and the South American states of Colombia, Surinam, and Venezuela. Associate membership has been accepted by 12 dependent territories in the region. Seen as a reaction to the creation of the North American Free Trade Agreement (NAFTA) between the United States, Canada, and Mexico, observers doubt its viability in view of its much smaller potential market of 200 million.

Group of Rio
The Group of Rio was founded in 1987 from the Contadora Group, an alliance between Colombia, Mexico, Panama, and Venezuela to establish a general peace treaty for Latin America, as a 'permanent mechanism for joint political action'. To create the Group, the original Contadora members were joined by Argentina, Bolivia, Brazil, Chile, Ecuador, Paraguay, Peru, and Uruguay. The venues for its meetings rotate among member states.

Group of Three
The Group of Three is a free-trade bloc formed in 1994 by Colombia, Mexico, and Venezuela.

Latin American Economic System (*Sistema Económico Latinoamericana*) (LAES/SELA)
LAES was founded by treaty in 1975 as the successor to the Latin American Economic Coordination Commission. The aim was to have a purely Latin American organization, with neither of the developed nations of North America involved. Its purpose is to create and promote multinational enterprises in the region, to provide markets, and to stimulate technological and scientific cooperation. Its membership has widened and now includes Argentina, Barbados, Bolivia, Brazil, Chile, Colombia, Costa Rica, Cuba, the Dominican Republic, Ecuador, El Salvador, Grenada, Guatemala, Guyana, Haiti, Honduras, Jamaica, Mexico, Nicaragua, Panama, Paraguay, Peru, Spain, Surinam, Trinidad and Tobago, Uruguay, and Venezuela. Its headquarters are in Caracas, Venezuela.

Latin American Integration Association (*Asociación Latino-Americana de Integración* (ALADI)
ALADI was formed in 1980 to replace the Latin American Free Trade Association (LAFTA). LAFTA encouraged trade by across-the-board tariff cuts while ALADI takes into account the different stages of economic development that individual countries have reached and so applies tariff reductions preferentially. The ultimate aim of the Association is to create a fully fledged common market. It has 11 member countries, all of them, except Mexico, in South America. ALADI is based in Montevideo, Uruguay.

9.8.9 Asian-inspired interregional cooperation

Association of Southeast Asian Nations (ASEAN)
ASEAN is an association of traditionally noncommunist states in Southeast Asia which was formed in 1967 by the signing of the Bangkok Declaration. The declared aims of the Association are to foster economic and social progress and cultural development and to promote peace in the region. Its members include Brunei, Indonesia, Malaysia, the Philippines, Singapore, and Thailand, and its headquarters are in Jakarta, Indonesia. Russia and Vietnam have attended recent ASEAN meetings as observers. In 1992 ASEAN leaders reached agreement on a mutual tariff reduction scheme and the eventual goal of establishing an ASEAN Free Trade Area (AFTA) by the year 2008. There is an ASEAN Regional Forum on security, which consists of the ASEAN states, the United States, Japan, Canada, Australia, South Korea, New Zealand, the European Union, China, Laos, Papua New Guinea, Russia, and Vietnam. In July 1995 reform communist Vietnam was admitted to ASEAN as the organization's seventh member.

Asia–Pacific Economic Cooperation (APEC)
APEC was formed in 1989, on the initiative of the Australian prime minister, Bob Hawke, to promote multilateral trade in the Asia–Pacific region. Its members include Australia, Brunei, Canada, Chile, China, Hong Kong, Indonesia, Japan, South Korea, Malaysia, Mexico, New Zealand, Papua New Guinea, the Philippines, Singapore, Taiwan, Thailand, and the United States. Together they account for more than half of the world's GDP. Operating within APEC, but excluding Australia and the United States, is the East Asian Economic Caucus (EAEC), which is dominated by members of ASEAN.

9.8.10 Oceania-inspired interregional cooperation

Rarotonga Treaty

The Rarotonga Treaty was signed in 1987 by Australia, Fiji, Indonesia, New Zealand, and the then Soviet Union, formally declaring the South Pacific a nuclear-free zone.

9.9 Intraregional cooperation

There are many examples of cooperation within our defined regions. Some are primarily political and cultural, such as the Arab League, many are essentially economic and at least one, the Palestine Liberation Organization (PLO), is intended to be an instrument for creating a new, independent state. To try to include every intraregional group currently operating would be a virtually impossible task but those which are described below are seen as the most significant as well as being representative of their respective regions.

9.9.1 Northern and Western Europe

World War II had a profound and lasting effect on the countries of Northern and Western Europe, whether they were the 'victors' or the 'vanquished'. Above all else, it convinced the leading politicians of the countries which had experienced the war at first hand, France, Belgium, Luxembourg, the Netherlands, Germany, and Italy, that they should take steps to set up institutions which would make another war in Europe virtually impossible. The first practical step towards this end, in 1951, was the establishment of the European Coal and Steel Community (ECSC), in the belief that if the leading nations shared coal and steelmaking facilities, which were seen as the basic raw materials of war, future conflicts would be avoided. The ECSC was followed, in 1955, by the European Investment Fund and then, two years later, in 1957, by the momentous signing in Rome of the treaties which established the European Economic Community (EEC) and the European Atomic Energy Community (Euratom). The preamble to the treaty setting up the EEC declared its objectives as: the establishment of the foundations of an even closer union among European peoples; the improvement of their working and living conditions; the progressive abolition of restrictions on trade between them; and the development of the prosperity of overseas countries. In 1986 the Single European Act provided for the establishment of a single market in 1992, entailing the free movement of goods, services, capital, and people between member states. The 1991 Maastricht Treaty on European Union agreed a series of objectives that include the eventual establishment of a single currency and a more assertive role on the international scene.

The founder members of the EEC were France, Germany, Italy, the Netherlands, Belgium, and Luxembourg. The United Kingdom, Ireland, and Denmark were admitted into membership in 1973, Greece in 1981, Spain and Portugal in 1986, and Austria, Finland, and Sweden in 1995. Applications for membership have also been made by Turkey, Cyprus, and Malta, while the recently democratized states of Central Europe, including the Czech Republic, Hungary, Poland, Slovakia, Bulgaria, and Romania, which are 'associate members', and Slovenia aspire to full membership. Following the ratification in November 1993 of the Maastricht Treaty, the European Community became the European Union (EU). The EU's 15 member countries have a combined population of more than 360 million, far greater than that of the United States, and a GDP of $6,700 billion, equivalent to almost 30% of global GDP.

Other forms of Northern and Western European cooperation are important but all are overshadowed by the sheer size, economic and political importance, and enormous potential of the Union.

European Union (EU)

The main EU institutions are the Commission, the Council of Ministers, the Committee of the Regions, the Committee of Permanent Representatives (COREPER), the Economic and Social Committee, the Court of Justice, and the European Parliament. An additional institution, the European Monetary Institute, was established in 1994 as a precursor to a European Central Bank.

The **European Commission** is at the heart of the Union's decision-taking process. It consists of 20 members: two each from France, Germany, Italy, Spain, and the United Kingdom, and one each from Austria, Belgium, Denmark, Finland, Greece, Ireland, Luxembourg, the Netherlands, Portugal, and Sweden. The members are nominated by each state for a four-year, renewable, term of office. One member is chosen as president for a five-year, renewable, term. The post of president, occupied from January 1995 by Jacques Santer (b. 1937), is a mixture of head of government and head of the European civil service, and a highly respected appointment.

Although the commissioners are drawn proportionately from member states, each takes an oath on appointment not to promote national interests. They head a comparatively large bureaucracy, with 20 directorates-general, each responsible for a particular department. Critics often complain about the size of the EU permanent machine but it is not unduly large in relation to the scope of its activities and its workload.

The **Council of Ministers of the European Union** is the supreme decision-taking body and consists of one minister from each of the 15 member countries. The actual representatives vary according to the subject matter under discussion. If it is economic policy it will be the finance ministers, if it is agricultural policy, the agriculture ministers. It is the foreign ministers, however, who tend to be the most active. The presidency of the Council changes hands at six-monthly intervals, each member state taking its turn.

The **Committee of the Regions** debates and advises on the Union's regional policy. It comprises 222 representatives: 24 each from France, Germany, Italy, and the United Kingdom; 21 from Spain; 12 each from Austria, Belgium, Greece, the Netherlands, Portugal, and Sweden; nine each from Denmark, Finland, and Ireland; and six from Luxembourg.

The **Committee of Permanent Representatives (COREPER)** is a subsidiary body of officials, often called 'ambassadors', who act on behalf of the Council. Its members are senior civil servants who have been temporarily released by member states to work for the Union.

The **Economic and Social Committee** is a consultative body consisting of representatives from member countries and covering a wide range of interests. For example, they may include employers, members of labour unions, professional people, farmers, and so on. The Committee advises the Council of Ministers and the Commission.

The **European Court of Justice** consists of judges and officials appointed by the member states. Its task is to ensure that the Union treaties are fairly observed and that regulations and directives are followed. The Court can make rulings but it has no powers of its own to enforce them. This is the responsibility of the individual member states in their own national courts.

Membership of the **European Parliament** is determined by the populations of member states. The total number of seats is 626, of which Germany has 99, France, Italy, and the United Kingdom 87 each, Spain 64, the Netherlands 31, Belgium, Greece, and Portugal 25 each, Sweden 22, Austria, 21, Denmark and Finland 16 each, Ireland 15 and Luxembourg 6. Members are elected for five-year terms in large Euro-constituencies. Voting is by a system of proportional representation in all countries except the United Kingdom (excluding Northern Ireland). The party composition of the European Parliament, following the June 1994 elections, is shown in Table 78.

More than three-quarters of the deputies for the Socialist party group were supplied by five states: the United Kingdom (62), Germany (40), France (29), Spain (22), and Italy (19). Seventy-nine per cent of the deputies for the right-of-centre European People's Party were drawn similarly from these states, namely: Germany (47), Italy (40), France (29), Spain (28), and the United Kingdom (18).

European parliament 1994	Table 78
Party composition of the European parliament 1994	
Ideological and European Party Groupings	
Left	*280 seats*
Left Unity (extremist)	28 seats
Socialists	221 seats
Rainbow Party	8 seats
Greens	23 seats
Right	*223 seats*
European Right (extremist)	12 seats
European People's Party	204 seats
European Democratic Alliance	7 seats
Centre	*62 seats*
Liberal and Democratic Reformists	28 seats
Independents	34 seats
Total	*565 seats*

EU operational methods. Policy is made and carried out within the Union in the following way. The Commission makes a particular proposal which will have first been worked on by one of the 20 directorates. The proposal is sent to the Council of Ministers who will initially pass it to COREPER for further examination. At the same time it will be passed to the European Parliament for consideration. The Parliament's role, although still mainly consultative, has been enhanced since the Maastricht Treaty. It has the right to reject the Union budget, to be consulted on the appointment of Commissioners and can dismiss the Commission if it has good grounds for doing so.

After examination by COREPER, with the addition of any views of the European Parliament, the proposal is formally considered by the Council of Ministers who decide whether or not action should be taken. Voting in the Council is weighted in favour of the larger member states, but votes are taken only rarely. Either there is a unanimous decision or, if one or more of the ministers argue that the policy would be against national interests, the proposal is likely to be shelved. Once the Council has agreed a policy proposal it is passed back to the Commission for implementation.

A policy decision can take one of two forms. It can be a regulation or a directive. Both are legally binding but a regulation applies to all member states whereas a directive only relates to one or more specific countries.

Decision-taking within the Union is only partially democratic and only marginally accountable to the electorates of the member states but, as the European Parliament becomes more firmly established, on broad European party lines, its influence, and eventually its powers, will undoubtedly grow.

Although a single European market, with all internal barriers to trade removed, has been created, the broader objective of agreeing common economic and foreign policies, eventually leading, as pro-Europeans would hope, to political union, is a much longer-term aim and some heads of government would clearly like to postpone its implementation indefinitely, or even summarily abandon it.

The Commission, the Council of Ministers, and COREPER are based in Brussels, the European Parliament meets in Luxembourg and Strasbourg, France, and the European Court of Justice sits in Luxembourg.

Council of Europe

The Council of Europe was established in Strasbourg in 1949 to secure 'a greater measure of unity between the European countries', by the discussion of common interests and problems and the discovery of new methods and areas of cooperation. Its membership is wider than that of the European Union, including Albania, Andorra, Bulgaria, Cyprus, the Czech Republic, Estonia, Hungary, Iceland, Liechtenstein, Lithuania, Malta, Moldova, Norway, Poland, Romania, San Marino, Slovakia, Slovenia, Switzerland, and Turkey, as well as the 15 European Union members. It has a Consultative Assembly which meets annually and a Standing Committee to represent it when it is not in session.

The Council has been particularly active, and effective, in the field of human rights. Under the European Convention of Human Rights of 1950, it established the European Commission of Human Rights, also based in Strasbourg, to investigate complaints by states or individuals. The findings of the Commission are then considered by the European Court of Human Rights, in Strasbourg, which was formed in 1959. Many European states have recognized the jurisdiction of the Court by making its decisions binding nationally, and this has resulted in ordinary citizens who feel aggrieved by judgements in their own national courts, taking their cases, over the heads of governments, to Strasbourg.

Benelux

A customs union, to encourage trade between the three countries, was established by Belgium, the Netherlands, and Luxembourg in 1948 and was called Benelux. It was later overtaken by the creation of the European Economic Community (EEC), and the other bodies which now form part of the European Union (EU), but in 1960, by the Benelux Treaty, the economic union of the three states was formalized. This made them, in economic terms, a single unit, while retaining their political independence and their obligations to the European Union. The organization has a Committee of Ministers, comprising at least three ministers from each state, which meets every two months, and a Council of Economic Union which is an umbrella body with the task of coordinating the work of the many Benelux committees. The head of the permanent Secretariat, which is based in Brussels, is always Dutch and is assisted by two deputies from the other member states.

European Free Trade Association (EFTA)

EFTA was originally established in 1960 as a free trade alternative to the European Economic Community (EEC). Its original members included Austria, Denmark, Norway, Portugal, Sweden, Switzerland, and the United Kingdom. Finland became an associate member in 1961 and Iceland a full member in 1970. It soon became clear that EFTA could never supplant the EEC and several members began to apply for entry into the Community. Denmark and the United Kingdom left in 1972, Portugal in 1985 and Austria, Finland, and Sweden in 1994. EFTA now comprises Iceland, Liechtenstein, Norway, and Switzerland. It is essentially an economic association whereby import duties between the member countries have been abolished. It has its headquarters in Geneva.

In 1973 the EC signed agreements with EFTA members, setting up a combined free-trade area, and a further pact was signed in 1991 to create a European Economic Area (EEA) from 1994, giving EFTA greater access to the EU market. The EEA covers 18 nations, comprising the EU 15 plus Iceland, Liechtenstein, and Norway, but not Switzerland, with a population exceeding 365 million.

Despite their reduced numbers, the remaining EFTA members agreed, in December 1994, to keep it, and the EEA, in existence.

Nordic Council

The Nordic Council was founded in 1953 by Denmark, Iceland, Norway and Sweden as a consultative body to increase cooperation between them. They were joined in 1956 by Finland. Council members are elected by the parliaments of the member states: 16 each from Denmark, Finland, Norway, and Sweden and five from Iceland. The Council does not have permanent headquarters.

European Space Agency (ESA)

ESA is an organization to promote space research and technology for peaceful purposes. It was originally founded in 1973 and reorganized in 1980. Its members include Austria, Belgium, Denmark, France, Germany, Ireland, Italy, the Netherlands, Norway, Spain, Sweden, Switzerland, and the United Kingdom. ESA has developed a number of scientific and communication satellites, as well as the Ariane rocket.

European Organization for Nuclear Research (*Conseil Européen pour la Recherche Nucléaire*, renamed *Organisation Européenne pour la Recherche Nucléaire*; still known as CERN)

CERN was established in 1954 as a cooperative venture for research into nuclear energy for peaceful purposes. Its members include 19 major European countries who provide teams of scientists to work together at laboratories at Meyrin, near Geneva.

9.9.2 Central and Eastern Europe

Baltic Council

Originally in operation between 1934–40, this body was revived in May 1990 by the three Baltic republics of Estonia, Latvia, and Lithuania, which were part of the Soviet Union until 1991. During 1990–91 the Council was used to coordinate the independence strategies of the three republics. It now promotes economic cooperation, with the aim of establishing a Baltic Common Market.

Black Sea Economic Cooperation Zone

This grouping was founded in 1992 to promote trade and economic cooperation and control pollution of the Black Sea. The nine member states are Armenia, Azerbaijan, Bulgaria, Georgia, Moldova, Romania, Russia, Turkey, and the Ukraine.

Visegrad Group

In October 1991, recently democratized Czechoslovakia, Hungary and Poland signed the Visegrad cooperation treaty. This was extended in December 1992 by a Central European Free Trade Agreement (CEFTA). With the division of Czechoslovakia into the Czech and Slovak sovereign republics, the 'Visegrad Three' became the 'Visegrad Four' and in 1995 close ties were also developed with Slovenia.

9.9.3 Middle East and North Africa

Cooperation within the Middle East and North Africa is generally founded on a strong, and proud, sense of a common identity among Arabs, even though the region contains many races and religions. Israel has been excluded from virtually all the cooperative groups and associations and this has, undoubtedly, contributed to its sense of isolation and suspicions about neighbouring states. Future harmony in the region depends greatly on whether the degree of mutual trust which has been established between Egypt and Israel can be extended to the wider Arab world.

League of Arab States (*Al Jamia al Arabiyyah*) or Arab League

The Arab League was founded in 1945 largely on the initiative of Egypt. It now has 22 members, comprising all the states of the Middle East and North Africa except Israel, plus the Comoros. Its declared purpose is 'to strengthen the close ties linking sovereign Arab States and to coordinate their policies and activities and direct them to the common good of the Arab countries'. It also acts as a mediator in disputes between Arab nations. The main body in the League is the Council which includes representatives of all the member states and usually meets twice a year, in March and September. Attached to it are 16 specialist, functional committees. There are a large number of agencies and bureaux operating with the League. The headquarters, with the secretariat, used to be in Cairo but when Egypt signed a peace treaty, in 1979, with Israel it was suspended from membership and the headquarters moved to Tunis. Egypt has since been readmitted.

Arab Common Market

The Arab Common Market, providing for the abolition of customs duties on agricultural products, and reductions on other items, came into effect in 1965. Membership was open to all Arab League states but only Egypt, Iraq, Jordan, and Syria have signed the treaty which set it up.

Arab Monetary Fund (AMF)

The AMF was established in 1976 by 20 Arab states plus the PLO to provide a mechanism for promoting greater stability in exchange rates and to coordinate Arab economic and monetary policies. The Fund's headquarters are in Abu Dhabi, in the United Arab Emirates. It operates mainly by regulating petrodollars within the Arab community to make it less dependent on the West for the handling of its surplus funds.

Organization of Arab Petroleum Exporting Countries (OAPEC)

OAPEC was established in 1968 to safeguard the interests of its members and to encourage cooperation in economic activity within the petroleum industry. It currently has ten members: Algeria, Bahrain, Egypt, Iraq, Kuwait, Libya, Qatar, Saudi Arabia, Syria, and the United Arab Emirates. Its headquarters are in Kuwait.

Palestine Liberation Organization (PLO)

The PLO was founded in 1964 with the objective of bringing about an independent state of Palestine. It contains a number of factions, the most important being *al-Fatah*, which is led by Yasser Arafat (b. 1929). To achieve its main aim it has pursued a mixed policy of diplomacy and guerrilla activity. Although it has long been recognized in the Arab world as a legitimate political body, its reputation among Western nations has not been good, some political leaders referring to it as a terrorist organization. However, in 1988, when Jordan announced its decision to relinquish its responsibility for the Israeli-occupied West Bank, and Arafat later publicly accepted the right of Israel to exist as an independent state, world opinion changed and the PLO became an organization which could be regarded as the legitimate representative of the Palestinians and, therefore, could provide the nucleus of an independent Palestine state.

Palestine National Authority (PNA)

The Palestine National Authority was appointed in 1994 to take over from Israel the management of Palestinian affairs in Gaza–Jericho, following the peace agreement between the PLO and Israel and the subsequent Israeli withdrawal. The PNA has jurisdiction over the whole of the formerly occupied areas, except for Israeli settlers and nationals. Israel retains responsibility for external defence and foreign affairs. The PNA held its first meeting in Gaza on 26 June 1994 and on 5 July 1994 the PLO leader, Yasser Arafat, formally swore in its members. It is intended to be an interim body, to be replaced by a more democratic, permanent one at a later date. On 5 December 1994 Israel extended the PNA's remit to include the administration of health and the collection of taxes but, in the same month, the Israeli parliament, the Knesset, passed legislation that would allow Israel to close PNA offices which had been set up outside the self-rule areas, notably Orient House, in East Jerusalem. The occupants of Orient House said they would continue their political activities despite the new legislation.

Cooperative Council for the Arab States of the Gulf (CCASG)

The CCASG was established in 1981 as an exclusively Arab organization for promoting peace in the Persian Gulf area. Its declared purpose is 'to bring about integration, coordination and cooperation in economic, social, defence and political affairs among Arab Gulf states'. Its members include Bahrain, Kuwait, Oman, Qatar, Saudi Arabia, and the United Arab Emirates and its headquarters are at Riyadh, Saudi Arabia.

9.9.4 Central and Southern Africa

Cooperation in economic and social matters in Central and Southern Africa has been fragmentary and sometimes duplicated. Because of this, it has been less effective than in some other regions of the world. This lack of cohesion has arisen partly because of the sheer size of the continent and the poor communications within it, particularly between the east and west coasts, and partly because of tribal and language differences.

Cooperation is, therefore, frequently subregional and often influenced by the colonial histories of particular countries. Thus those states which used to form part of the French empire cooperate more naturally with other French-speaking countries whereas former British colonies tend to link with countries where English is the principal language.

Southern African Development Community (SADC)

The SADC was formed at its first conference in Arusha, Tanzania, in July 1979, when representatives of Angola, Botswana, Lesotho, Malawi, Mozambique, Swaziland, Tanzania, Zambia, and Zimbabwe agreed to work more closely together to reduce their economic dependence on South Africa. Since then an organization has been formed with its headquarters in Gabarone, Botswana. Annual meetings of heads of state and heads of government are held and SADC ministers meet at least twice a year to formulate plans. The main areas that the organization has targeted as needing particular attention are transport and communications, energy and mining, and industrial production, and a number of sector units have been set up to implement proposals. Member states have agreed to share the scarce water that flows over their land. With the ending of apartheid in South Africa from 1991 and the establishment there of an all-race multiparty democracy in 1994, the SADC aims have changed and it is now a 12-member body, with Mauritius (from 1995), Namibia and South Africa becoming new members. In August 1995 SADC leaders agreed to seek to create a Southern African economic community, with free trade by the year 2000, free movement of people and, eventually, a single currency. The combined population of the SADC was 133 million in 1994 and the GDP $150 billion. However, South Africa dominates, with 31% of the population and 78% of the GDP. Currently, only 10% of Southern Africa's trade takes place within the region.

Organisation Commune Africaine et Mauricienne (OCAM)
OCAM was founded in 1965 as the *Organisation Commune Africaine et Malgache*. This was itself a successor to the *Union Africaine et Malgache de Coopération Economique*, which had operated between 1961 and 1965. In 1970 the name of *Organisation Commune Africaine, Malgache et Mauricienne* was adopted but when Madagascar withdrew from the Organization in 1975 the present name was adopted. The full membership now includes Benin, Burkina Faso, the Central African Republic, Côte d'Ivoire, Niger, Rwanda, Senegal, and Togo. The declared purpose of OCAM is to strengthen the solidarity and close ties between member states and to raise living standards and coordinate economic policies. Through the Organization, members share an airline, a merchant fleet and a common postal and communications system. The headquarters of OCAM are at Bangui in the Central African Republic.

Council of the Entente (CE) (*Conseil de l'Entente*)
The CE was set up in 1959 by four states, Benin, Burkina Faso, Côte d'Ivoire and Niger, to strengthen economic links and promote industrial development. Togo joined in 1966 when a Mutual Aid and Loan Guarantee Fund was established. The headquarters of the Council are in Abidjan, Côte d'Ivoire.

Economic Community of West African States (ECOWAS) (*Communauté Economique des Etats de l'Afrique de l'Ouest*)
ECOWAS was established in 1975, by the Treaty of Lagos, to promote economic cooperation and development. Its members include Benin, Burkina Faso, Cape Verde, Gambia, Ghana, Guinea, Guinea-Bissau, Côte d'Ivoire, Liberia, Mali, Mauritania, Niger, Nigeria, Senegal, Sierra Leone, and Togo. Its headquarters are in Lagos, Nigeria.

Preferential Trade Area for Eastern and Southern African States (PTA)
The PTA was established in 1981 with the objective of increasing economic and commercial cooperation between member states, harmonizing tariffs and reducing trade barriers, with the eventual aim of creating a common market. The current members include Burundi, the Comoros, Djibouti,

Ethiopia, Kenya, Lesotho, Malawi, Mauritius, Rwanda, Somalia, Swaziland, Tanzania, Uganda, Zambia, and Zimbabwe. The headquarters of the PTA are in Lusaka, Zambia.

9.9.5 Central America and the Caribbean

Caribbean Community and Common Market (CARICOM)
CARICOM was founded in 1973 as a successor to the Caribbean Free Trade Association, as a vehicle for increasing economic cooperation and reducing trade barriers in the area. Its members include Antigua and Barbuda, Barbados, Belize, Dominica, Grenada, Guyana, Jamaica, Montserrat, St Christopher and Nevis, St Lucia, St Vincent and the Grenadines, and Trinidad and Tobago. The headquarters of CARICOM are at Georgetown, Guyana. In 1994 CARICOM sponsored the formation of the Association of Caribbean States (ACS) trade group.

Central American Common Market (CACM)
The CACM is roughly the mainland equivalent of CARICOM. It was founded in 1961 with similar objectives and its members include Costa Rica, Guatemala, El Salvador, Honduras, and Nicaragua. Its headquarters are in Guatemala City.

Organization of Central American States (ODECA)
ODECA was founded in 1951 for the purpose of strengthening unity in Central America and fostering economic, political and social cooperation, with a view to avoiding overdependence on the United States and its dominance in the Organization of American States (OAS). ODECA's membership includes Costa Rica, El Salvador, Guatemala, Honduras and Nicaragua. Its headquarters are in San Salvador.

9.9.6 South America

The Amazon Pact
The Amazon Pact is a treaty signed in 1978 by Bolivia, Brazil, Colombia, Ecuador, Guyana, Peru, Surinam, and Venezuela to protect and control the development of the Amazon River.

Andean Group (AG)
The Andean Group, also known as the Andean Sub-Regional Group, or the Andean Common Market, was established under the Cartegena Agreement of 1969 to promote the balanced and harmonious development of member countries through economic integration. The members include Bolivia, Colombia, Ecuador, Peru, and Venezuela, with Mexico as a working partner since 1972. Chile was originally a member but left in 1976. The Group aims to harmonize policies on tariffs, the protection of intellectual property, such as patents and trademarks, and industrial and commercial development. Its institutions include a parliament and an executive commission and its headquarters are in Lima, Peru. In 1992 an Andean Pact was established to create a freetrade area.

URUPABOL
URUPABOL is a tripartite commission which was formed in 1981 by Bolivia, Paraguay and Uruguay to foster economic and commercial cooperation.

Mercosur (Southern Common Market)
Mercosur was founded in March 1991 by the Asunción Treaty signed by Argentina, Brazil, Paraguay, and Uruguay, to create a common market for the four member states. It was formally inaugurated on 1 January 1995. With a population of more than 197 million, it constitutes the fourth largest free trade bloc after the North American Free Trade Area (NAFTA), 375 million people, the European Union (EU), 360 million, and the Association of Southeast Asian Nations (ASEAN), 340 million.

From 1 January 1995 tariffs among member states were removed for about 90% of traded goods and common tariffs, averaging 14%, were imposed on about 80% of goods imported from outside the market. On 23 January 1995 foreign ministers of the countries in the Andean Pact, Bolivia, Colombia, Ecuador, Peru, and Venezuela, agreed to seek a free-trade agreement with MERCOSUR.

9.9.7 Asia

South Asian Association for Regional Cooperation (SAARC)
The forum was established in 1985 to foster cooperation between the seven South Asian states of Bangladesh, Bhutan, India, Maldives, Nepal, Pakistan, and Sri Lanka. An annual summit is held and in 1993 a South Asian Preferential Tariff Agreement was unveiled, with the goal of lowering or abolishing tariffs on intraregional trade.

9.9.8 Oceania

South Pacific Commission (SPC)
The SPC was established by an agreement signed in Canberra, Australia, in 1947, with the objective of encouraging economic and social cooperation in the region. Its members include most of the states in Oceania, including the dependencies, plus France, the United Kingdom, and the United States, which are involved because of their past and present interests in the region. The headquarters are in Nouméa, New Caledonia.

South Pacific Forum (SPF)
The SPF was created in 1971, as an offshoot of the SPC, to provide an opportunity for member states to meet annually to discuss common interests and develop common policies. The first meeting of the Forum's heads of government was held in New Zealand in 1971. The membership includes Australia, the Cook Islands, Fiji, Kiribati, the Marshall Islands, Micronesia, Nauru, New Zealand, Niue, Papua New Guinea, the Solomon Islands, Tonga, Tuvalu, Vanuatu, and Western Samoa. In 1985 the Forum adopted a treaty for creating a nuclear-free zone in the Pacific.

South Pacific Bureau for Economic Cooperation (SPEC)
SPEC was founded in 1973, following a meeting of the South Pacific Forum (SPF), as a practical scheme for stimulating economic cooperation and the development of trade. The headquarters of SPEC are in Suva, Fiji.

Spearhead Group of Melanesian Countries
This body was formed in 1988 by Vanuatu, Papua New Guinea, and the Solomon Islands to promote increased political and economic cooperation among the small Melanesian-peopled states of the Pacific Region. Annual leadership summits are held, with observers from Fiji and New Caledonia also attending.

9.10 Military cooperation

The examples of global, interregional, and intraregional cooperation described above are generally positive and peaceful in character. However, a number of military pacts and organizations have been established to provide what states and regions see as vital defences against possible aggression. There are now hopeful signs that nations, and groups of nations, are beginning to talk more openly with each other, across the barriers that military organizations inevitably create.

ANZUS
This three-member defence alliance, comprising Australia, New Zealand, and the United States, was established in 1951 to coordinate defence policy and preserve peace in the Pacific region. The member states undertake joint military and naval exercises and share defence and technical intelligence.

North Atlantic Treaty Organization (NATO)
NATO was established under the North Atlantic Treaty of 1949, which was signed by Belgium, Canada, Denmark, France, Iceland, Italy, Luxembourg, the Netherlands, Norway, Portugal, the United Kingdom, and the United States. It is a mutual defence treaty by which it was agreed that 'an armed attack against one or more in Europe or North America shall be considered an attack against all'. Greece and Turkey joined the Organization in 1952, Germany was admitted in 1955 and Spain in 1982. France withdrew from the Organization, but not the alliance, in 1966. Greece withdrew politically, but not militarily, in 1974, and its re-entry was opposed by Turkey in 1980.

NATO's supreme body is the Council of Foreign Ministers of all the participating nations and its Secretariat is based in Brussels, where there is also a Military Committee composed of the chiefs-of-staff of the member countries. The military headquarters, Supreme Headquarters Allied Powers, Europe (SHAPE), are at Chièvres, near Mons, in Belgium. The two Supreme Allied Commanders, Europe and Atlantic, are US military officers and the Allied Commander, Channel, is a British Admiral. In 1960 it was agreed to form a permanent, multinational unit, called the Allied Mobile Force (AMF), to move immediately to any NATO country which appeared to be under threat. This mobile unit is based in Heidelberg, in Germany.

NATO was originally formed to oppose a threat from the Soviet Union and its Warsaw Pact satellites and, although it has remained the keystone of Western defence for more than 40 years, relations between its members have not always been harmonious. The main areas of contention have been the degree of US dominance, the presence of nuclear weapons on European soil and the respective levels of contribution by signatories to the Organization's upkeep.

The changed climate created by the demise of the Soviet Union in December 1991 added another dimension to NATO's role and in January 1994 a 'Partnership for Peace' programme was launched. It invited former members of the Warsaw Pact, which was NATO's opposing organization in the 'Cold War' era, and ex-Soviet republics to take part in a wide range of military cooperation agreements, without the implication of imminent NATO membership. Partners train alongside NATO and open up their defence plans to NATO scrutiny and advice. Romania was the first to join, followed by Albania, Azerbaijan, Estonia, Finland, Latvia, Lithuania, Poland, Sweden, Armenia, Austria, Bulgaria, Belarus, Hungary, Malta, the Russian Federation, Slovenia, Macedonia, Moldova, the Ukraine, Uzbekistan, and Slovakia.

During the civil war in parts of the former Yugoslavia the United Nations Security Council made use of NATO's air resources to defend and support its own ground and naval units. In December 1995 Javier Solana became NATO secretary-general, as 60,000 NATO troops were deployed in Bosnia-Herzegovina to replace a UN mission.

Western European Union (WEU)

The WEU is based on the Brussels Treaty of 1948 and was established in 1955 as a forum for the discussion of defence issues by West European governments. Its members include Belgium, France, Germany, Greece, Italy, Luxembourg, the Netherlands, and the United Kingdom, and, since 1989, Portugal and Spain. There is an Assembly which meets twice yearly in Paris, and sometimes in The Hague, and a Council, consisting of the foreign ministers of the member states, which normally meets quarterly. The Union is pledged, under its charter, to work closely with NATO. It has a permanent Secretariat based in London, but there has been pressure from the British government to locate both the Assembly and the Secretariat in Brussels. Other EU members, who are not also in the WEU, are sometimes invited to attend Assembly meetings as observers and in May 1994 Bulgaria, the Czech Republic, Estonia, Hungary, Latvia, Lithuania, Poland, Romania, and Slovakia became associate partners.

Recommended reading

Bennett, A L *International Organisations: Principles and Issues*, Prentice-Hall, 1988

Berridge, G R *International Politics: States, Power and Conflict since 1945*, 2nd edn., Harvester Wheatsheaf, 1992

Brogan, P *World Conflicts: Why and Where they are Happening*, 2nd edn., Bloomsbury, 1992

Chan, S *The Commonwealth in World Politics: A Study of International Action 1965–1985*, Lester Crook Academic, 1988

Commonwealth Yearbook (annual), HMSO

Dinan, D *Ever Closer Union*, Macmillan, 1994

Faringdon, H *Strategic Geography: NATO, the Warsaw Pact and the Superpowers*, 2nd edn., Routledge, 1989

Hocking, B and Smith, M *World Politics: An Introduction to International Relations*, Harvester Wheatsheaf, 1990

Jacobs, F, Corbett, R and Shackleton, M *The European Parliament*, Longman, 1992

Kaplan, L S *NATO and the United States: The Enduring Alliance*, Twayne, 1988

Kennedy, P *Preparing for the Twenty-First Century*, Harper Collins, 1993

Nicoll, W and Salmon, T *Understanding the New European Community*, Harvester Wheatsheaf, 1993

Osmanczyk, E J *Encyclopaedia of the United Nations and International Agreements*, 2nd edn., Taylor & Francis, 1990

Parsons, A *From Cold War to Hot Peace: UN Interventions 1947–1994*, Michael Joseph, 1994

Pinder, J *European Community: The Building of a Union*, Oxford University Press, 1991

Reynolds, P A *An Introduction to International Relations*, Longman, 1994

Righter, R *Utopia Lost: The United Nations and World Order*, The Twentieth Century Fund, 1995

Roberts, A and Kingsbury, B (eds.) *United Nations, Divided World: The UN's Role in International Relations*, 2nd edn., Clarendon Press, 1993

Segal, G *The World Affairs Companion: The Essential One Volume Guide to Global Issues*, 2nd edn., Simon & Schuster, 1991

Appendices

Postwar political leaders in the world's leading states   Appendix A

China: leaders of the Communist Party

Term	Name
1935–76	Mao Zedong
1976–81	Hua Guofeng
1981–87	Hu Yaobang
1987–89	Zhao Ziyang
1989–	Jiang Zemin

France: presidents and prime ministers during the Fifth Republic

Term	Name	Party
Presidents		
1959–69	Gen. Charles de Gaulle	Gaullist
1969–74	Georges Pompidou	Gaullist
1974–81	Valery Giscard d'Estaing	Republican/Union for French Democracy
1981–95	François Mitterrand	Socialist
1995–	Jacques Chirac	Neo-Gaullist RPR
Prime ministers		
1959–62	Michel Debre	Gaullist
1962–68	Georges Pompidou	Gaullist
1968–69	Maurice Couve de Murville	Gaullist
1969–72	Jacques Chaban Delmas	Gaullist
1972–74	Pierre Messmer	Gaullist
1974–76	Jacques Chirac	Gaullist
1976–81	Raymond Barre	Union for French Democracy
1981–84	Pierre Mauroy	Socialist
1984–86	Laurent Fabius	Socialist
1986–88	Jacques Chirac	Neo-Gaullist RPR
1988–91	Michel Rocard	Socialist
1991–92	Edith Cresson	Socialist
1992–93	Pierre Beregovoy	Socialist
1993–95	Edouard Balladur	Neo-Gaullist RPR
1995–	Alain Juppé	Neo-Gaullist RPR

Federal Republic of Germany: chancellors

Term	Name	Party
1949–63	Konrad Adenauer	Christian Democrat
1963–66	Ludwig Erhard	Christian Democrat
1966–69	Kurt Kiesinger	Christian Democrat
1969–74	Willy Brandt	Social Democrat
1974–82	Helmut Schmidt	Social Democrat
1982–	Helmut Kohl	Christian Democrat

India: prime ministers

Term	Name	Party
1949–64	Jawaharlal Nehru	Congress
1964–66	Lal Bahadur Shastri	Congress
1966–77	Indira Gandhi	Congress (I)
1977–79	Morarji Desai	Janata/coalition
1979–80	Charan Singh	Janata/Lok Dal/coalition
1980–84	Indira Gandhi	Congress (I)
1984–89	Rajiv Gandhi	Congress (I)
1989–90	Viswanath Pratap Singh	Janata Dal/coalition
1990–91	Chandra Shekhar	Janata Dal (Socialist)/coalition
1991–	PV Narasimha Rao	Congress

Japan: prime ministers

Term	Name	Party
1945–46	Kijuro Shidehara	coalition
1946–47	Shigeru Yoshida	Liberal
1947–48	Tetsu Katayama	coalition
1948–48	Hitoshi Ashida	Democratic
1948–54	Shigeru Yoshida	Liberal
1954–56	Ichiro Hatoyama	Liberal/Liberal Democrat
1956–57	Tanzan Ishibashi	Liberal Democrat
1957–60	Nobusuke Kishi	Liberal Democrat
1960–64	Hayato Ikeda	Liberal Democrat
1964–72	Eisaku Sato	Liberal Democrat
1972–74	Kakuei Tanaka	Liberal Democrat
1974–76	Takeo Miki	Liberal Democrat
1976–78	Takeo Fukuda	Liberal Democrat
1978–80	Masayoshi Ohira	Liberal Democrat
1980–82	Zenko Suzuki	Liberal Democrat
1982–87	Yasuhiro Nakasone	Liberal Democrat
1987–89	Noboru Takeshita	Liberal Democrat
1989–89	Sosuke Uno	Liberal Democrat
1989–91	Toshiki Kaifu	Liberal Democrat
1991–93	Kiichi Miyazawa	Liberal Democrat
1993–94	Morihiro Hosokawa	Japan New/coalition
1994–94	Tsutomu Hata	Shinseito/coalition
1994–	Tomiichi Muroyama	Social Democrat/coalition

continued

Postwar political leaders in the world's leading states (continued)   Appendix A

Soviet Union/Russia: leaders of the Communist party*/Russian president**

Term	Name
1922–53	Joseph Stalin*
1953–64	Nikita Khrushchev*
1964–82	Leonid Brezhnev*
1982–84	Yuri Andropov*
1984–85	Konstantin Chernenko*
1985–91	Mikhail Gorbachev *
1990–	Boris Yeltsin**

United Kingdom: prime ministers

Term	Name	Party
1945–51	Clement Attlee	Labour
1951–55	Winston Churchill	Conservative
1955–57	Anthony Eden	Conservative
1957–63	Harold Macmillan	Conservative
1963–64	Alec Douglas-Home	Conservative
1964–70	Harold Wilson	Labour
1970–74	Edward Heath	Conservative
1974–76	Harold Wilson	Labour
1976–79	James Callaghan	Labour
1979–90	Margaret Thatcher	Conservative
1990–	John Major	Conservative

United States: presidents

Term	Name	Party
1945–53	Harry S Truman	Democrat
1953–61	Dwight D Eisenhower	Republican
1961–63	John F Kennedy	Democrat
1963–69	Lyndon B Johnson	Democrat
1969–74	Richard Nixon	Republican
1974–77	Gerald Ford	Republican
1977–81	Jimmy Carter	Democrat
1981–89	Ronald Reagan	Republican
1989–93	George Bush	Republican
1993–	Bill Clinton	Democrat

Glossary of Abbreviations and Acronyms

ACP	African, Caribbean and Pacific signatories to the Lomé Convention
ACS	Association of Caribbean States
ADB	African Development Bank
AFESD	Arab Fund for Social and Economic Development
AfDB	African Development Bank
AG	Andean Group
AL	Arab League
ALADI	Latin American Integration Association
AMF	Arab Monetary Fund
AMU	Arab Maghreb Union
ANZUS	Australian, New Zealand, United States Security Treaty
AP	Amazon Pact
APEC	Asia–Pacific Economic Cooperation
AsDB	Asian Development Bank
ASEAN	Association of Southeast Asian Nations
AT	Antarctic Treaty
BADEA	Arab African Economic Development Bank
BC	Baltic Commission
BCIE	Central American Economic Integration Bank
BDEAC	Central African States Development Bank
Benelux	Benelux Economic Union
BIS	Bank for International Settlements
BLEU	Belgo–Luxembourg Economic Union
BOAD	West African Development Bank
CACM	Central American Common Market
CARICOM	Caribbean Community and Common Market
CBSS	Council of the Baltic Sea States
CCASG	Cooperative Council for the Arab States of the Gulf
CDB	Caribbean Development Bank
CE	Council of Europe
CEAO	West African Economic Community
CEEAC	Economic Community of Central African States
CEI	Central European Initiative
CEPGL	Economic Community of the Great Lakes Countries
CERN	European Council for Nuclear Research
CILSS	Permanent Inter–State Committee on Drought Control in the Sahel

CIS	Commonwealth of Independent States
CP	Colombo Plan
CSCE	Conference on Security and Cooperation in Europe (renamed OSCE)
CW	Commonwealth
DDS	Damascus Declaration States
EADB	East African Development Bank
EBRD	European Bank for Reconstruction and Development
EC	European Community
ECA	Economic Commission for Africa
ECE	Economic Commission for Europe
ECLAC	Economic Commission for Latin America and the Caribbean
ECO	Economic Cooperation Organization
ECOWAS	Economic Community of West African States
ECWA	Economic Commission for Western Asia
EEA	European Economic Area
EFTA	European Free Trade Association
ESA	European Space Agency
ESCAP	Economic and Social Commission for Asia and the Pacific
ESCWA	Economic and Social Commission for Western Asia
EU	European Union
FAO	Food and Agriculture Organization
FLS	Front Line States
FZ	Franc Zone
GATT	General Agreement on Tariffs and Trade
G-3	Group of Three
G-5	Group of Five
G-7	Group of Seven
G-11	Group of Eleven (Cartegena Group)
G-15	Group of Fifteen
G-24	Group of Twenty-four
G-77	Group of Seventy-seven
GCC	Gulf Cooperation Council
GDP	Gross domestic product
Geplacea	Group of Latin American and Caribbean Sugar Exporting Countries
IADB	Inter-American Development Bank
IAEA	International Atomic Energy Agency

IBRD	International Bank for Reconstruction and Development (World Bank)	**OECS**	Organization of Eastern Caribbean States
ICAO	International Civil Aviation Organization	**OIC**	Organization of the Islamic Conference
ICC	International Chamber of Commerce	**OMVG**	Gambia River Development Organization
ICFTU	International Confederation of Free Trade Unions	**OMVS**	Senegal River Development Organization
IDA	International Development Association	**OPEC**	Organization of Petroleum Exporting Countries
IDB	Inter-American Development Bank	**OSCE**	Organization for Security and Cooperation in Europe
IEA	International Energy Authority		
IFAD	International Fund for Agricultural Development	**PFP**	Partnership for Peace
		PLO	Palestine Liberation Organization
IFC	International Finance Corporation	**PNA**	Palestine National Authority
IGADD	Inter-Governmental Authority on Drought and Development	**PTA**	Preferential Trade Area for Eastern and Southern African States
ILO	International Labour Organization	**RG**	Rio Group
IMF	International Monetary Fund	**SAARC**	South Asian Association for Regional Cooperation
IMO	International Maritime Organization	**SADC**	Southern African Development Community
IOC	Indian Ocean Commission	**SELA**	Latin American Economic System
IsDB	Islamic Development Bank	**SG**	Spearhead Group
ITU	International Telecommunication Union	**SPC**	South Pacific Commission
IWC	International Whaling Commission	**SPEC**	South Pacific Bureau for Economic Cooperation
KBO	Kagera Basin Organization		
LCBC	Lake Chad Basin Commission	**SPF**	South Pacific Forum
LORCS	League of Red Cross and Red Crescent Societies	**UDEAC**	Central African Customs and Economic Union
Mercosur	Southern Common Market	**UN**	United Nations
MRU	Mano River Union	**UNCTAD**	United Nations Conference on Trade and Development
NACC	North Atlantic Cooperation Council		
NAFTA	North American Free Trade Agreement	**UNESCO**	United Nations Educational, Scientific and Cultural Organization
NAM	Non-Aligned Movement		
NATO	North Atlantic Treaty Organization	**UNIDO**	United Nations Industrial Development Organization
NC	Nordic Council		
NEA	Nuclear Energy Authority	**UPU**	Universal Postal Union
NIB	Nordic Development Bank	**VG**	Visegrad Group
OAPEC	Organization of Arab Petroleum Exporting Countries	**WCC**	World Council of Churches
		WEU	Western European Union
OAS	Organization of American States	**WFTU**	World Federation of Trade Unions
OAU	Organization of African Unity	**WHO**	World Health Organization
ODECA	Organization of Central American States	**WIPO**	World Intellectual Property Organization
OECD	Organization for Economic Cooperation and Development	**WMO**	World Meteorological Organization
		WTO	World Trade Organization

Data Sources

Annual Register (annual), Longman

Bogdanor, V (ed.) *The Blackwell Encyclopedia of Political Institutions*, Basil Blackwell, 1987

Central Intelligence Agency – The World Factbook, CIA, 1994

Day, A J and Degenhardt, H W *Political Parties of the World: A Keesing's Reference Publication*, 3rd edn., Longman, 1988

Day, A J and Munro, D *A World Record of Major Conflict Areas*, Edward Arnold, 1990

Day, A J *et al.* (eds) *Border and Territorial Disputes*, 3rd edn., Longman, 1992

Delury, G E (ed.) *World Encyclopedia of Political Systems*, Vols I–III, 2nd edn., Longman, 1987

The Economist (weekly), London

World Atlas of Elections, The Economist Publications, 1987

Pocket World in Figures, The Economist Publications, 1995

Europa Publications:
   Africa South of the Sahara Yearbook (annual)
   Europa Yearbook (annual)
   Far East and Australasia Yearbook (annual)
   Middle East and North Africa Yearbook (annual)

Evans, G and Newnham, J *The Dictionary of World Politics: A Reference Guide to Concepts, Ideas and Institutions*, Harvester Wheatsheaf, 1992

Facts on File, the Index of World Events, (weekly) Facts on File, 1940–

The Financial Times (daily), London

Gorvin, I (ed.) *Elections since 1945: A Worldwide Reference Companion*, Longman, 1989

The Guardian (daily), London

The Guiness European Data Book: Facts, Figures, Issues, Guinness, 1994

The Guinness World Fact Book, Guinness, 1994

Humana, C (ed.) *World Human Rights Guide*, Oxford University Press, 1992

The Hutchinson Encyclopedia, 10th edn., Helicon, 1994

The Hutchinson Guide to the World, 2nd edn., Helicon, 1993

The Independent (daily), London

Keesing's Record of World Events (monthly), Longman, 1931–

Kidron, M and Segal, R *The New State of the World Atlas*, revised 1st edn., Pan Books, 1987

Kidron, M and Smith, D *The New State of War and Peace: An International Atlas*, Grafton, 1991

Kurian, G T *Encyclopedia of the Third World*, Vols I–III, 4th edn., Facts on File, 1992

Kurian, G T *The New Book of World Rankings*, 3rd edn., Facts on File, 1991

Kurian, G T *Atlas of the Third World*, 2nd edn., Facts on File, 1992

Lawson, E (ed.) *Encyclopaedia of Human Rights*, Taylor and Francis, 1991

Mackie, T T and Rose, R *International Almanac of Electoral History*, 3rd edn., Macmillan, 1991

Minority Rights Group Reports, MRG, London

Newsweek (weekly)

The Observer (weekly), London

Ransley, J (ed.) *Chambers Dictionary of Political Biography*, Chambers, 1991

South (monthly), South Publications

Statesman's Yearbook (annual), Macmillan, 1864–

Sunday Times (weekly), London

Time Magazine (weekly)

The Times (daily), London

The Times Guide to the Nations of the World: History, Politics, Geography, Statistics, Maps and Flags, Times Books, 1994

United Nations *Statistical Yearbook* (annual)

The World Almanac and Book of Facts (annual)

World Tables 1994, World Bank, 1994

Index

Please note

Names

In certain states in Asia, for example China and the Koreas, the family name (surname) precedes the personal name, for example Deng Xiaoping. In Latin American countries the family name usually appears in the middle, as in Ernesto Samper Pizano, shown in this index as Samper Pizano, Ernesto.

Country entries

The term 'country entry' indicates a full political, economic and social profile of the respective state.

P